Heritage of

Western Civilization

Edited and with Introductions by

JOHN LOUIS BEATTY
University of California at Riverside

OLIVER A. JOHNSON
University of California at Riverside

HERITAGE

Englewood Cliffs, N.J.

PRENTICE-HALL, INC.

of **WESTERN CIVILIZATION** *Select Readings*

© 1958, *by* PRENTICE-HALL, INC.
Englewood Cliffs, New Jersey

Library of Congress Catalog Card Number: 58–8552

Printed in the United States of America

38689

Third printing............January, 1959

Woodcuts by Ellen Raskin

Typographical design by Walter Behnke

$\mathscr{P}$*reface*

ooks, generally, are the result of their author's reaction to a specific situation or problem. Either he feels some discontent with the level of knowledge about a subject or he has a special message to convey or a new story to relate; or else his experience indicates a present inadequacy that he believes his volume will remedy. The original reason for the preparation of this book was the last. The inadequacy we felt arose from the difficulties encountered in attempting to teach beginning college students something of their own heritage by using the available collections of readings drawn from the history of Western civilization.

The fault in most of these collections stems either from the lack of a clearly defined editorial rationale or from a rationale that has been too narrowly defined. In addition, most of them suffer from a serious pedagogical flaw—the almost inescapable urge on the part of the editors to be as broadly inclusive as possible, to include parts of the work of as many people of major importance (as well as many of minor importance) as can be jammed between the covers of a book. It is hoped by this means to introduce the student to virtually all the names he should be expected to remember as he pursues his course of study.

This seems to be a laudable educational aim, but it tends to fall between two stools. On the one hand, such a book provides many names and little by which to remember those names. On the other hand, it forces the editors to use such short selections that the quality of the work of the author and the intent of his writing tend to be lost, again leaving the student with little or nothing.

We have sought to avoid these pitfalls by permitting normal course structure to determine the general outlines of our book. Believing that the most a student could be expected to assimilate with understanding each week would be about two selections, especially if these were of sufficient length really to acquaint him with the personality, the mind, and the work of the author, and assuming the normal academic year to be about thirty weeks long, we arrived at the approximate total number of selections to include, hoping always that the result would be pedagogically sound and intellectually rewarding. To suggest, however, that we have reduced the entire heritage of the West to a set of about sixty readings would be flagrant arrogance on our part. And certainly the decisions concerning inclusion or exclusion have been in many cases painful. Why Polybius and not Livy or Cicero? Why Luther and not Calvin? Why *Unam Sanctam* without *De Rerum Novarum?* These questions (and many others) can be answered only on the level of thoughtful, careful, and painful editorial fiat. In any event, we are convinced that the materials included here will provide the beginning student with a significant introduction to and sampling of his civilization's past. If these two goals are met, this book will have served him well.

The plan of the work is relatively simple. We have arrayed the readings in rough chronological sequence, but have altered that order in a few cases where it did not seem most fitting. Thus, Cellini precedes Erasmus, and the *Old Testament* follows Juvenal. The sixty or so readings have been divided into seven sections—Greece, Rome, the Middle Ages, Renaissance and Reformation, Early Modern Europe, the Nineteenth Century, and the Contemporary World. Each section begins with a general introduction to the period that aims at providing a broad framework into which the selections may be fitted. Each of these selections is introduced individually as well.

There is no single theme or central thread running through the book, such as the growth of freedom, the evolution of democracy, or the relationship of man to God. As a matter of fact, we have deliberately avoided organizing the book around a central theme. This decision arose out of the conviction that such an organization would inevitably result in a distorted picture of the past. Instead, we have presented selections that we believe throw light on *many* of the major issues and attitudes of Western civilization. Our hope is that the student himself will detect the relevance of a variety of themes to his own experience.

Our obligations to those who assisted us in this work are real, many, and varied. It is impossible to single out particular persons for special citation. Our colleagues at the University of California at Riverside, other colleagues at various colleges and universities throughout the country, and the librarians of at least eight libraries have all been most generous of their time and effort. Naturally, not all their advice and counsel has been accepted, but even a rejected criticism forces re-examination and further thought, and so is helpful. Our greatest debt, of course, is that owed the authors of the works here included and the translators of those works. Without them there would be no book of readings.

J. L. B.
O. A. J.

Contents

GREECE

Herodotus	THE HISTORY OF HERODOTUS, 6
Thucydides	HISTORY OF THE PELOPONNESIAN WAR, 16
Sophocles	ANTIGONE, 29
The Last Days of Socrates	APOLOGY, 49
	CRITO, 60
	PHAEDO, 68
Plato	THE REPUBLIC, 71
Aristotle	THE NICOMACHEAN ETHICS, 78
	THE POLITICS, 88

ROME

Polybius	THE HISTORIES, 104
Lucretius	DE RERUM NATURA, 116
Plutarch	LIFE OF CAESAR, 130
Epictetus	THE ENCHIRIDION, 144
Juvenal	SATIRE III, 157

THE MIDDLE AGES

The Old Testament GENESIS, 169
EXODUS, 172
THE FIRST BOOK OF THE KINGS, 175
ISAIAH, 177
EZEKIEL, 179
THE BOOK OF JOB, 180

The New Testament ST. MATTHEW, 185
THE ACTS OF THE APOSTLES, 189
THE EPISTLE OF PAUL THE APOSTLE TO THE ROMANS, 194

St. Augustine THE CONFESSIONS, 197
THE ENCHIRIDION, 202

St. Benedict THE RULE OF ST. BENEDICT, 209

Einhard LIFE OF THE EMPEROR CHARLES, 215

Manorialism RIGHTS AND RANKS OF PEOPLE, 231
SURVEYS OF CERTAIN MANORS BELONGING
TO THE ABBEY OF PETERBOROUGH, 235

Aucassin and Nicolete THE SONG-STORY OF AUCASSIN AND NICOLETE, 237

Magna Carta 253

St. Francis of Assisi THE LITTLE FLOWERS OF ST. FRANCIS, 261

Papal Political Documents THE SECOND LETTER OF GREGORY VII TO HERMANN,
BISHOP OF METZ, 270
THE BULL *Unam Sanctam* OF BONIFACE VIII, 277

St. Thomas Aquinas SUMMA CONTRA GENTILES, 280
SUMMA THEOLOGICA, 286

Sir John Froissart CHRONICLES, 294

RENAISSANCE AND REFORMATION

Pico della Mirandola ON THE DIGNITY OF MAN, 303
Niccolò Machiavelli THE PRINCE, 307
Benvenuto Cellini THE LIFE OF BENVENUTO CELLINI, 318

Desiderius Erasmus   IN PRAISE OF FOLLY, 331

Martin Luther   AN OPEN LETTER TO THE CHRISTIAN NOBILITY
      OF THE GERMAN NATION CONCERNING THE
      REFORM OF THE CHRISTIAN ESTATE, 345

The Counter Reformation   THE CANONS AND DECREES OF THE COUNCIL OF TRENT, 355
      SPIRITUAL EXERCISES OF ST. IGNATIUS OF LOYOLA, 362

EARLY MODERN EUROPE

Francis Bacon   NOVUM ORGANUM, 370

René Descartes   DISCOURSE ON METHOD, 380

Thomas Hobbes   LEVIATHAN, 393

Bishop Bossuet   POLITICS DRAWN FROM THE VERY WORDS OF
      HOLY SCRIPTURE, 403

Jean-Baptiste Colbert   MEMOIRS ON THE FINANCIAL AFFAIRS OF FRANCE
      TO SERVE AS A HISTORY, 411
      LOUIS XIV TO THE MUNICIPAL MAGISTRATES AND
      INHABITANTS OF MARSEILLES, 413
      PROPOSAL AND USEFUL ADVICE CONCERNING THE
      COMMERCE OF HOLLAND, 414

Isaac Newton   OPTICS, 416
      THE MATHEMATICAL PRINCIPLES OF NATURAL
      PHILOSOPHY, 418

John Locke   OF CIVIL GOVERNMENT, 421
      AN ESSAY CONCERNING HUMAN UNDERSTANDING, 432

Voltaire   PHILOSOPHICAL DICTIONARY, 438
      CANDIDE: OR, THE OPTIMIST, 443

Adam Smith   AN INQUIRY INTO THE NATURE AND CAUSES OF
      THE WEALTH OF NATIONS, 459

Jean Jacques Rousseau   THE SOCIAL CONTRACT, 474

General Cahiers   CAHIER OF THE CLERGY OF DOURDAN, 485
      CAHIER OF THE NOBLES OF DOURDAN, 489
      CAHIER OF THE THIRD ESTATE OF DOURDAN, 494
      THE AUGUST 4TH DECREES, 498

THE NINETEENTH CENTURY

Edmund Burke   REFLECTIONS ON THE REVOLUTION IN FRANCE, 506

Romanticism in Literature   PROMETHEUS, 518
TINTERN ABBEY, 519

Thomas Malthus   AN ESSAY ON THE PRINCIPLE OF POPULATION, 521

*Georg Wilhelm Friedrich
Hegel*   THE PHILOSOPHY OF RIGHT, 530

The Sadler Report   534

*Karl Marx and Friedrich
Engels*   MANIFESTO OF THE COMMUNIST PARTY, 545

John Stuart Mill   ON LIBERTY, 560

Charles Darwin   THE ORIGIN OF SPECIES, 573
THE DESCENT OF MAN, 585

William Graham Sumner   THE CHALLENGE OF FACTS, 587

Friedrich Nietzsche   THE WILL TO POWER, 604

Theodore Roosevelt   EXPANSION AND PEACE, 614

Sidney Webb   SOCIALISM: TRUE AND FALSE, 619

THE CONTEMPORARY WORLD

Sigmund Freud   AN OUTLINE OF PSYCHOANALYSIS, 632

Vladimir Ilyich Lenin   WHAT IS TO BE DONE? 637
STATE AND REVOLUTION, 640

Fascism   MEIN KAMPF, 649
THE DOCTRINE OF FASCISM, 651

John Dewey   LIBERALISM AND SOCIAL ACTION, 663

George Orwell   NINETEEN EIGHTY-FOUR, 679

Alfred North Whitehead   SCIENCE AND THE MODERN WORLD, 694

Heritage of
Western Civilization

GREECE

THE NAVAL ENGAGEMENT fought between the Greeks and Persians off the island of Salamis in 480 B.C. must be ranked as one of the truly decisive battles of Western history. For at Salamis the Greeks, following up their victory at Marathon ten years earlier, succeeded in halting the imperial march of Xerxes to the west and hence in gaining a century and a half of security from foreign conquest. This relatively brief respite was brought to a close by the armies of Philip of Macedon and his son, Alexander the Great, in the latter part of the fourth century. But while it lasted, the Greeks perfected a civilization whose achievements still stand as objects of admiration and inspiration for Western man.

The center of classical Greek civilization was the *polis* or city-state. Ancient Greece was divided into hundreds of *poleis*, each a tiny unit politically independent and culturally unique. Athens, for example, one of the largest of the *poleis*, had a total population of just over three hundred thousand and an area roughly equal to that of Rhode Island. The forms of government varied widely from *polis* to *polis*, and even within the same *polis* at different times.

By far the most important form—at least so far as later Western history is concerned—was the Athenian democracy, particularly as it appeared in the Age of Pericles during the fifth century B.C. Although the Athenians shared with us the belief that democratic government means rule by the people, their democracy differed from ours in one important respect: We, because of the very size and complexity of the nation in which we live, must exercise our sovereignty through representatives, but in Athens the people could rule directly. Every adult male citizen was a member of the Assembly, the sole legislative body of the city-state. From the ranks of the Assembly a Council of Five Hundred was chosen annually to supervise the administrative affairs of the *polis*. From the Council, in turn, an executive committee of fifty was chosen to conduct the day-to-day business of administration for a term lasting one-tenth of a year. One member of this committee was then chosen as chairman for each twenty-four-hour period. Since all these selections were made by lot, any citizen of the *polis* might be called on to serve as the chief administrative officer of Athens for a day.

But for the average Greek the *polis* was more than just the political unit within which he happened to live. It was also the center of his social, intellectual, aesthetic, and religious life. Aristotle, in the beginning of his work on political theory, the *Politics*, takes a typically Greek attitude toward the *polis* in the statement which is usually translated, "Man is a political animal," but which in the original Greek reads, "Man is by nature an animal intended to live in a *polis*." Here Aristotle is implying that only within the *polis* can one live a truly human life. The philosopher Socrates expresses a similar feeling toward the *polis*. Though unjustly condemned to death by an Athenian court, he rejected a chance to escape from prison, insisting that, because he owed his very being to his *polis*, he must accept whatever Athens decreed for him, even execution.

Many scholars have been convinced that Athens in the fifth century B.C. represents the high point of Western civilization. In the words of the contemporary historian, H. D. F. Kitto, Athens "was clearly the most civilized society that has yet existed." Whether or not we accept this evaluation, it is true that today, over two thousand years later, the world still finds the accomplishments of the Athenians—in art and architecture, poetry, drama, history, political theory, science, mathematics, philosophy, and religion—a source of instruction and enjoyment.

One of the finest appreciations of Athens' achievements was made by a great Athenian leader—Pericles. The occasion was a funeral oration that he delivered in 431 B.C. just outside the city walls, in honor of the Athenian soldiers who had fallen in the first year of the Peloponnesian War. For Pericles, the highest honor that could be paid to the dead was to say that they "were worthy of Athens." By Athens he referred not just to the city in which they had lived, but to the way of life that they, as Athenians, had shared. The Athenians, Pericles told his audience, are "lovers of the beautiful." The truth of Pericles' claim was self-evident, for anyone listening to him could have verified it simply by turning his head and gazing back at the city itself. Had he done so he would have found the view dominated by the Acropolis, rising high above the plain and crowned with temples. In the center stood the Parthenon, which had been completed less than a decade before Pericles delivered his oration. Dedicated to Athena, goddess of wisdom and protectress of Athens, the Parthenon embodied an ideal of beauty based on architectural symmetry or balance.

The ideal of balance so completely realized in the Parthenon was pursued in all forms of Greek art. And, outside the aesthetic realm, it was an ideal that pervaded Greek civilization. Just as the Greek experienced pleasure in a well-proportioned building, so he delighted in a well-balanced personality and tried in his own life to follow the path of moderation. The life of moderation is summed up in Aristotle's famous doctrine of the Golden Mean, perhaps the most closely reasoned defense ever made of a civilization and its way of life. Behind the Greek ideal of moderation and balance stands their belief that the universe is a rational order, operating according to fixed laws. The orderliness of the universe, the Greeks argued, is good, hence order anywhere must be good, and disorder must be evil. When the Greeks translated this belief into aesthetic and moral terms, they found their ideal of beauty in the ordered symmetry of the Parthenon, and their conception of the good life in the moderation of the Golden Mean.

Because they were convinced that men are beings capable of reasoning, the Greeks concluded that we can comprehend the world in which we live. This faith—that man can understand the Universe—along with the conclusions they reached in their own attempts to do so, is probably the greatest single contribution that the Greeks made to Western civilization. The Greek faith in reason permeated their entire intellectual and cultural life. To take the most obvious example, it made possible their phenomenal achievements in science. Earlier civilizations, in the Near East and Egypt, had developed advanced technologies, but the Greeks were the first theoretical scientists in Western history. What set them apart from their predecessors was their ability to generalize, to see an object or an event not simply in its individuality but as an instance of a universal rule or pattern. They were led to seek the general laws governing natural events—in other words, to become theoretical scientists—by their conviction that man can, by the use of his own reasoning powers, discover the rational pattern of the Universe.

This tendency to generalize shows itself over and over again in Greek thought. Thucydides, in the introduction to his *History of the Peloponnesian War*, states that he is interested not just in recounting the events of the war but in revealing the general pattern of war. The Greek tragedians attempted to trace out the patterns in which universal moral law revealed itself in the lives of men. This emphasis on universal law in Greek tragedy led the twentieth-century philosopher, A. N. Whitehead, to conclude that the tragic poets must be considered the originators of scientific thought. Greek generalization reached its highest expression in Plato's Form of the Good, one of the most difficult concepts in Western thought. For Plato's belief that the Form of the Good is the heart of Reality is really a philosophical formulation of the Greek faith in the ultimate unity, rationality, and goodness of the Universe.

And yet the Greeks failed to generalize in one crucial area, that of practical politics. It was this failure that led to their downfall. Loyalty to their own *polis* and jealousy of all the others prevented the Greeks from ever uniting to form a single nation. The unwillingness of the Greeks to cooperate in a common cause nearly led to disaster as early as the Persian Wars, for, as Herodotus makes clear, the Athenian naval commander at the battle of Salamis had to deceive his Peloponnesian allies to keep them from fleeing the enemy. The political disunity of the Greeks reached its climax a half-century later, in the Peloponnesian War between Athens and Sparta. This war (431-404 B.C.) marked the turning point in the history of Greece. Though the Greeks produced much of value, particularly in science and philosophy in later years, the great period of Greek civilization was ended by this long and costly struggle. The resources of the Greek *poleis*, of defeated Athens in particular, were dissipated, and in the fourth century the proud city-states fell easy prey to the invading Macedonians from the north. Thus ended one of the most brilliant episodes in the history of Western man.

Herodotus

History is the art of telling the most complicated and fascinating story ever told —the story of man and his past. Since history is essentially story-telling, the person who tells the story best, who is the ablest *raconteur*, is obviously the best historian. This does not mean that history is simply imaginative literature, however, for the records and the factual foundation of the past are the very warp and woof of the story. Thus the story-teller must respect those qualities that are the essence of good historical writing: accuracy in assembling and presenting facts, right reason in analyzing the facts, and sobriety and judgment in interpreting the facts. But even the possession of these qualities will not insure that an author will write good history, for story-telling is above all else an act of communication, and an author who fails to communicate fails to tell the story. History is written to be read, and the best historian is the one who tells his tale with wit and imagination, using every literary device at his command to carry the reader along on the stream of his narrative.

The first historian to measure up to these demanding standards was Herodotus (484-*c.*424 B.C.), a citizen of the Greek city-state of Halicarnassus in Asia Minor. In the latter part of the fifth century B.C. Herodotus undertook to record the history of the wars between the city-states of Greece and the great Persian Empire. His purpose, he tells us, was to preserve the memory of the great events that had occurred during the wars and of the heroic deeds that had been performed on both sides. And so he skilfully unfolded his tale in nine books, each named for one of the nine muses of Greek mythology. Herodotus was the first writer to go beyond the simple ticking-off of events in chronological sequence. He analyzed motives and searched for relationships between events, trying to generalize and to work out a broad pattern into which individual happenings could be fitted. For this reason he is often called "the father of history."

Occasionally, Herodotus is criticized for being naive or over-credulous, or even because he knew no language other than Greek. No matter how valid these criticisms may be, Herodotus did try to verify his accounts through logic and documentation, accepting or rejecting what was told him according to the lights of reason and credibility.

The following two selections are from the first and eighth books of the *History of the Persian Wars*. The first is the general introduction from Book I, entitled Clio (after the muse of History); and the second—from Book VIII, entitled Urania (after the muse of Astronomy)—is a vivid account of the Battle of Salamis, fought between the Greek and Persian navies in 480 B.C.

THE HISTORY OF HERODOTUS

THE FIRST BOOK, ENTITLED "CLIO"

These are the researches of Herodotus of Halicarnassus, which he publishes, in the hope of thereby preserving from decay the remembrance of what men have done, and of preventing the great and wonderful actions of the Greeks and the Barbarians from losing their due meed of glory; and withal to put on record what were their grounds of feud.

. . .

THE EIGHTH BOOK, ENTITLED "URANIA"

[The Greeks are facing a combined land-sea invasion by the Persians under Xerxes. The selection begins with a council of war attended by the naval leaders of the Greek poleis and their allies, who are attempting to decide how best to repel the invaders. Ed.]

49. When the captains from these various nations were come together at Salamis, a council of war was summoned; and Eurybiades proposed that any one who liked to advise, should say which place seemed to him the fittest, amongst those still in the possession of the Greeks, to be the scene of a naval combat. Attica, he said, was not to be thought of now; but he desired their counsel as to the remainder. The speakers mostly advised, that the fleet should sail away to the Isthmus, and there give battle in defence of the Peloponnese; and they urged as a reason for this, that if they were worsted in a sea-fight at Salamis, they would be shut up in an island, where they could get no help; but if they were beaten near the Isthmus, they could escape to their homes.

THE HISTORY OF HERODOTUS, trans. G. Rawlinson (London, 1858): I, 153; IV, 305-313, 315-319, 323-343.

50. As the captains from the Peloponnese were thus advising, there came an Athenian to the camp, who brought word that the barbarians had entered Attica, and were ravaging and burning everything. For the division of the army under Xerxes was just arrived at Athens from its march through Bœotia, where it had burnt Thespiæ and Platæa—both which cities were forsaken by their inhabitants, who had fled to the Peloponnese—and now it was laying waste all the possessions of the Athenians. Thespiæ and Platæa had been burnt by the Persians, because they knew from the Thebans that neither of those cities had espoused their side.

51. Since the passage of the Hellespont and the commencement of the march upon Greece, a space of four months had gone by; one while the army made the crossing, and delayed about the region of the Hellespont; and three while they proceeded thence to Attica, which they entered in the archonship of Calliades. They found the city forsaken; a few people only remained in the temple, either keepers of the treasures, or men of the poorer sort. These persons having fortified the citadel with planks and boards, held out against the enemy. It was in some measure their poverty which had prevented them from seeking shelter in Salamis; but there was likewise another reason which in part induced them to remain. They imagined themselves to have discovered the true meaning of the oracle uttered by the Pythoness, which promised that "the wooden wall should never be taken"—the wooden wall, they thought, did not mean the ships, but the place where they had taken refuge.

52. The Persians encamped upon the hill over against the citadel, which is called Mars' hill by the Athenians, and began the

siege of the place, attacking the Greeks with arrows whereto pieces of lighted tow were attached, which they shot at the barricade. And now those who were within the citadel found themselves in a most woeful case, for their wooden rampart betrayed them; still, however, they continued to resist. It was in vain that the Pisistratidæ came to them and offered terms of surrender—they stoutly refused all parley, and among their other modes of defence, rolled down huge masses of stone upon the barbarians as they were mounting up to the gates: so that Xerxes was for a long time very greatly perplexed, and could not contrive any way to take them.

53. At last, however, in the midst of these many difficulties, the barbarians made discovery of an access. For verily the oracle had spoken truth; and it was fated that the whole mainland of Attica should fall beneath the sway of the Persians. Right in front of the citadel, but behind the gates and the common ascent —where no watch was kept, and no one would have thought it possible that any foot of man could climb—a few soldiers mounted from the sanctuary of Aglaurus, Cecrops' daughter, notwithstanding the steepness of the precipice. As soon as the Athenians saw them upon the summit, some threw themselves headlong from the wall, and so perished; while others fled for refuge to the inner part of the temple. The Persians rushed to the gates and opened them, after which they massacred the suppliants. When all were slain, they plundered the temple, and fired every part of the citadel.

. . . .

56. Meanwhile, at Salamis, the Greeks no sooner heard what had befallen the Athenian citadel, than they fell into such alarm that some of the captains did not even wait for the council to come to a vote, but embarked hastily on board their vessels, and hoisted sail as though they would take to flight immediately. The rest, who stayed at the council board, came to a vote that the fleet should give battle at the Isthmus. Night now drew on, and the captains, dispersing from the meeting, proceeded on board their respective ships.

57. Themistocles, as he entered his own vessel, was met by Mnesiphilus, an Athenian, who asked him what the council had resolved to do. On learning that the resolve was to stand away for the Isthmus, and there give battle on behalf of the Peloponnese, Mnesiphilus, exclaimed:—

If these men shall sail away from Salamis, thou wilt have no fight at all for the one fatherland; for they will all scatter themselves to their own homes; and neither Eurybiades nor any one else will be able to hinder them, or to stop the breaking up of the armament. Thus will Greece be brought to ruin through evil counsels. But haste thee now; and, if there be any possible way, seek to unsettle these resolves— mayhap thou mightest persuade Eurybiades to change his mind, and continue here.

58. The suggestion greatly pleased Themistocles; and without answering a word, he went straight to the vessel of Eurybiades. Arrived there, he let him know that he wanted to speak with him on a matter touching the public service. So Eurybiades bade him come on board, and say whatever he wished. Then Themistocles, seating himself at his side, went over all the arguments which he had heard from Mnesiphilus, pretending as if they were his own, and added to them many new ones besides; until at last he persuaded Eurybiades, by his importunity, to quit his ship and again collect the captains to council.

59. As soon as they were come, and before Eurybiades had opened to them his purpose in assembling them together, Themistocles, as men are wont to do when they are very anxious, spoke much to divers of them; whereupon the Corinthian captain, Adeimantus, the son of Ocytus, observed—"Themistocles, at the games

they who start too soon are scourged."
"True," rejoined the other in his excuse,
"but they who wait too late are not
crowned."

60. Thus he gave the Corinthian at this
time a mild answer; and towards Eurybiades himself he did not use any of those arguments which he had urged before, or say
aught of the allies betaking themselves to
flight if once they broke up from Salamis;
it would have been ungraceful for him,
when the confederates were present, to
make accusation against any; but he had
recourse to quite a new sort of reasoning,
and addressed him as follows:—

With thee it rests, O! Eurybiades, to save
Greece, if thou wilt only hearken unto me, and
give the enemy battle here, rather than yield
to the advice of those among us, who would
have the fleet withdrawn to the Isthmus. Hear
now, I beseech thee, and judge between the
two courses. At the Isthmus thou wilt fight in
an open sea, which is greatly to our disadvantage, since our ships are heavier and fewer in
number than the enemy's; and further, thou
wilt in any case lose Salamis, Megara, and
Egina, even if all the rest goes well with us.
The land and sea force of the Persians will advance together; and thy retreat will but draw
them towards the Peloponnese, and so bring
all Greece into peril. If, on the other hand,
thou doest as I advise, these are the advantages
which thou wilt so secure: in the first place, as
we shall fight in a narrow sea with few ships
against many, if the war follows the common
course, we shall gain a great victory: for to
fight in a narrow space is favourable to us—in
an open sea, to them. Again, Salamis will in
this case be preserved, where we have placed
our wives and children. Nay, that very point
by which ye set most store, is secured as much
by the other; for whether we fight here or at
the Isthmus, we shall equally give battle in
defence of the Peloponnese. Assuredly ye will
not do wisely to draw the Persians upon that
region. For if things turn out as I anticipate,
and we beat them by sea, then we shall have
kept your Isthmus free from the barbarians,
and they will have advanced no further than
Attica, but from thence have fled back in disorder; and we shall, moreover, have saved
Megara, Egina, and Salamis itself, where an

oracle has said that we are to overcome our
enemies. When men counsel reasonably, reasonable success ensues; but when in their counsels they reject reason, God does not choose
to follow the wanderings of human fancies.

61. When Themistocles had thus spoken,
Adeimantus the Corinthian again attacked
him, and bade him be silent, since he was a
man without a city; at the same time, he
called on Eurybiades not to put the question at the instance of one who had no
country, and urged that Themistocles
should show of what state he was envoy,
before he gave his voice with the rest. This
reproach he made, because the city of
Athens had been taken, and was in the
hands of the barbarians. Hereupon Themistocles spake many bitter things against
Adeimantus and the Corinthians generally;
and for proof that he had a country, reminded the captains, that with two hundred ships at his command all fully manned
for battle, he had both city and territory
as good as theirs; since there was no Grecian state which could resist his men if
they were to make a descent.

62. After this declaration, he turned to
Eurybiades, and addressing him with greater warmth and earnestness—"If thou wilt
stay here," he said, "and behave like a
brave man, all will be well—if not, thou
will bring Greece to ruin. For the whole
fortune of the war depends on our ships.
Be thou persuaded by my words. If not,
we will take our families on board, and
go, just as we are, to Siris in Italy, which
is ours from of old, and which the prophecies declare we are to colonise some day or
other. You then, when you have lost allies
like us, will hereafter call to mind what I
have now said."

63. At these words of Themistocles, Eurybiades changed his determination; principally, as I believe, because he feared
that if he withdrew the fleet to the Isthmus, the Athenians would sail away, and
knew that without the Athenians, the rest

of their ships could be no match for the fleet of the enemy. He therefore decided to remain, and give battle at Salamis.

64. And now, the different chiefs, notwithstanding their skirmish of words, on learning the decision of Eurybiades, at once made ready for the fight. Morning broke, and, just as the sun rose, the shock of an earthquake was felt both on shore and at sea; whereupon the Greeks resolved to approach the gods with prayer, and likewise to send and invite the Æacids to their aid. And this they did, with as much speed as they had resolved on it. Prayers were offered to all the gods; and Telamon and Ajax were invoked at once from Salamis, while a ship was sent to Egina to fetch Æacus himself, and the other Æacids.

• • •

66. The men belonging to the fleet of Xerxes, after they had seen the Spartan dead at Thermopylae, and crossed the channel from Trachis to Histiaea, waited there by the space of three days, and then sailing down through the Euripus, in three more came to Phalêrum. In my judgment, the Persian forces both by land and sea when they invaded Attica, were not less numerous than they had been on their arrival at Sêpias and Thermopylae. For against the Persian loss in the storm and at Thermopylae, and again in the sea-fights off Artemisium, I set the various nations which had since joined the king—as the Malians, the Dorians, the Locrians, and the Bœotians—each serving in full force in his army except the last, who did not number in their ranks either the Thespians or the Plataeans; and together with these, the Carystians, the Andrians, the Tenians, and the other people of the islands, who all fought on this side except the five states already mentioned. For as the Persians penetrated further into Greece, they were joined continually by fresh nations.

67. Reinforced by the contingents of all these various states, except Paros, the bar-

barians reached Athens. As for the Parians, they tarried at Cythnus, waiting to see how the war would go. The rest of the sea forces came safe to Phalêrum; where they were visited by Xerxes, who had conceived a desire to go aboard and learn the wishes of the fleet. So he came and sate in a seat of honour; and the sovereigns of the nations, and the captains of the ships, were sent for to appear before him, and as they arrived took their seats according to the rank assigned them by the king. In the first seat sate the king of Sidon; after him, the king of Tyre; then the rest in their order. When the whole had taken their places, one after another, and were set down in orderly array, Xerxes, to try them, sent Mardonius and questioned each, whether a sea-fight should be risked or no.

68. Mardonius accordingly went round the entire assemblage, beginning with the Sidonian monarch, and asked this question; to which all gave the same answer, advising to engage the Greeks, except only Artemisia, who spake as follows:—

Say to the king, Mardonius, that these are my words to him: I was not the least brave of those who fought at Euboea, nor were my achievements there among the meanest; it is my right, therefore, O my lord, to tell thee plainly, what I think to be most for thy advantage now. This then is my advice. Spare thy ships, and do not risk a battle; for these people are as much superior to thy people in seamanship, as men to women. What so great need is there for thee to incur hazard at sea? Art thou not master of Athens, for which thou didst undertake thy expedition? Is not Greece subject to thee? Not a soul now resists thy advance. They who once resisted, were handled even as they deserved. Now learn how I expect that affairs will go with thy adversaries. If thou art not over-hasty to engage with them by sea, but wilt keep thy fleet near the land, then whether thou abidest as thou art, or marchest forward towards the Peloponnese, thou wilt easily accomplish all for which thou art come hither. The Greeks cannot hold out against thee very long; thou wilt soon part them asunder, and scatter them to their several homes. In the island where they lie, I hear they have no food in store; nor is it likely, if thy land force begins its march towards the Peloponnese, that they will remain quietly where they are—at least such as come from that region. Of a surety *they* will not greatly trouble themselves to give battle on behalf of the Athenians. On the other hand, if thou art hasty to fight, I tremble lest the defeat of thy sea force bring harm likewise to thy land army. This, too, thou shouldst remember, O king; good masters are apt to have bad servants, and bad masters good ones. Now, as thou art the best of men, thy servants must needs be a sorry set. These Egyptians, Cyprians, Cilicians, and Pamphylians, who are counted in the number of thy subject-allies, of how little service are they to thee!

69. As Artemisia spake, they who wished her well were greatly troubled concerning her words, thinking that she would suffer some hurt at the king's hands, because she exhorted him not to risk a battle; they, on the other hand, who disliked and envied her, favoured as she was by the king above all the rest of the allies, rejoiced at her declaration, expecting that her life would be the forfeit. But Xerxes, when the words of the several speakers were reported to him, was pleased beyond all others with the reply of Artemisia; and whereas, even before this, he had always esteemed her much, he now praised her more than ever. Nevertheless, he gave orders that the advice of the greater number should be followed; for he thought that at Euboea the fleet had not done its best, because he himself was not there to see—whereas this time he resolved that he would be an eye-witness of the combat.

70. Orders were now given to stand out to sea; and the ships proceeded towards Salamis, and took up the stations to which they were directed, without let or hindrance from the enemy. The day, however, was too far spent for them to begin the battle, since night already approached: so they prepared to engage upon the morrow. The Greeks, meanwhile, were in great dis-

tress and alarm, more especially those of the Peloponnese; who were troubled that they had been kept at Salamis to fight on behalf of the Athenian territory; and feared that, if they should suffer defeat, they would be pent up and besieged in an island, while their own country was left unprotected.

. . .

74. . . . At first they conversed together in low tones, each man with his fellow, secretly, and marvelled at the folly shown by Eurybiades; but presently the smothered feeling broke out, and another assembly was held; whereat the old subjects provoked much talk from the speakers, one side maintaining that it was best to sail to the Peloponnese and risk battle for that, instead of abiding at Salamis and fighting for a land already taken by the enemy; while the other, which consisted of the Athenians, Eginetans, and Megarians, was urgent to remain and have the battle fought where they were.

75. Then Themistocles, when he saw that the Peloponnesians would carry the vote against him, went out secretly from the council, and instructing a certain man what he should say, sent him on board a merchant ship to the fleet of the Medes. The man's name was Sicinnus; he was one of Themistocles' household slaves, and acted as tutor to his sons; in after times, when the Thespians were admitting persons to citizenship, Themistocles made him a Thespian, and a rich man to boot. The ship brought Sicinnus to the Persian fleet, and there he delivered his message to the leaders in these words:—

The Athenian commander has sent me to you privily, without the knowledge of the other Greeks. He is a well-wisher to the king's cause, and would rather success should attend on you than on his countrymen; wherefore he bids me tell you, that fear has seized the Greeks and they are meditating a hasty flight. Now then it is open to you to achieve the best work that ever ye wrought, if only ye will hinder their escaping. They no longer agree among themselves, so that they will not now make any resistance—nay, 'tis likely ye may see a fight already begun between such as favour and such as oppose your cause.

The Messenger, when he had thus expressed himself, departed and was seen no more.

76. Then the captains, believing all that the messenger had said, proceeded to land a large body of Persian troops on the islet of Psyttaleia, which lies between Salamis and the mainland; after which, about the hour of midnight, they advanced their western wing towards Salamis, so as to inclose the Greeks. At the same time the force stationed about Ceos and Cynosura moved forward, and filled the whole strait as far as Munychia with their ships. This advance was made to prevent the Greeks from escaping by flight, and to block them up in Salamis, where it was thought that vengeance might be taken upon them for the battles fought near Artemisium. The Persian troops were landed on the islet of Psyttaleia, because, as soon as the battle began, the men and wrecks were likely to be drifted thither, as the isle lay in the very path of the coming fight,—and they would thus be able to save their own men and destroy those of the enemy. All these movements were made in silence, that the Greeks might have no knowledge of them; and they occupied the whole night, so that the men had no time to get their sleep.

77. I cannot say that there is no truth in prophecies, or feel inclined to call in question those which speak with clearness, when I think of the following:—

When they shall bridge with their ships to the sacred strand of Diana Girt with the golden falchion, and eke to marine Cynosura, Mad hope swelling their hearts at the downfall of beautiful Athens—Then shall godlike Right extinguish haughty Presumption, Insult's furious offspring, who thinketh to overthrow all things. Brass with brass shall mingle, and Mars with blood shall empurple Ocean's waves.

Then—then shall the day of Grecia's freedom Come from Victory fair, and Saturn's son all-seeing.

When I look to this, and perceive how clearly Bacis spoke, I neither venture myself to say anything against prophecies, nor do I approve of others impugning them.

78. Meanwhile, among the captains at Salamis, the strife of words grew fierce. As yet they did not know that they were encompassed, but imagined that the barbarians remained in the same places where they had seen them the day before.

79. In the midst of their contention, Aristides, the son of Lysimachus, who had crossed from Egina, arrived in Salamis. He was an Athenian, and had been ostracised by the commonalty, yet I believe, from what I have heard concerning his character, that there was not in all Athens a man so worthy or so just as he. He now came to the council, and standing outside, called for Themistocles. Now Themistocles was not his friend, but his most determined enemy. However, under the pressure of the great dangers impending, Aristides forgot their feud, and called Themistocles out of the council, since he wished to confer with him. He had heard before his arrival of the impatience of the Peloponnesians to withdraw the fleet to the Isthmus. As soon therefore as Themistocles came forth, Aristides addressed him in these words:—

Our rivalry at all times, and especially at the present season, ought to be a struggle, which of us shall most advantage our country. Let me then say to thee, that so far as regards the departure of the Peloponnesians from this place, much talk and little will be found precisely alike. I have seen with my own eyes that which I now report; that, however much the Corinthians or Eurybiades himself may wish it, they cannot now retreat; for we are enclosed on every side by the enemy. Go in to them, and make this known.

80. "Thy advice is excellent," answered the other, "and thy tidings are also good.

That which I earnestly desired to happen, thine eyes have beheld accomplished. Know that what the Medes have now done was at my instance; for it was necessary, as our men would not fight here at their own free will, to make them fight whether they would or no. But come now, as thou hast brought the good news, go in and tell it. For if I speak to them, they will think it a feigned tale, and will not believe that the barbarians have inclosed us around. Therefore do thou go to them, and inform them how matters stand. If they believe thee, 'twill be for the best; but if otherwise, it will not harm. For it is impossible that they should now flee away, if we are indeed shut in on all sides, as thou sayest."

81. Then Aristides entered the assembly, and spoke to the captains: he had come, he told them, from Egina, and had but barely escaped the blockading vessels— the Greek fleet was entirely inclosed by the ships of Xerxes—and he advised them to get themselves in readiness to resist the foe. Having said so much, he withdrew. And now another contest arose, for the greater part of the captains would not believe the tidings.

82. But while they still doubted, a Tenian trireme, commanded by Paneatius the son of Sôsimenes, deserted from the Persians and joined the Greeks, bringing full intelligence. For this reason the Tenians were inscribed upon the tripod at Delphi among those who overthrew the barbarians. With this ship, which deserted to their side at Salamis, and the Lemnian vessel which came over before at Artemisium, the Greek fleet was brought to the full number of 380 ships; otherwise it fell short by two of that amount.

83. The Greeks now, not doubting what the Tenians told them, made ready for the coming fight. At dawn of day, all the men-at-arms were assembled together, and speeches were made to them, of which the best was that of Themistocles; who

throughout contrasted what was noble with what was base, and bade them, in all that came within the range of man's nature and constitution, *always* to make choice of the nobler part. Having thus wound up his discourse, he told them to go at once on board their ships, which they accordingly did; and about this time the trireme, that had been sent to Egina for the Æacidae, returned; whereupon the Greeks put to sea with all their fleet.

84. The fleet had scarce left the land when they were attacked by the barbarians. At once most of the Greeks began to back water, and were about touching the shore, when Ameinias of Pallené, one of the Athenian captains, darted forth in front of the line, and charged a ship of the enemy. The two vessels became entangled, and could not separate, whereupon the rest of the fleet came up to help Ameinias, and engaged with the Persians. Such is the account which the Athenians give of the way in which the battle began; but the Eginetans maintain that the vessel which had been to Egina for the Æacidae, was the one that brought on the fight. It is also reported, that a phantom in the form of a woman appeared to the Greeks, and, in a voice that was heard from end to end of the fleet, cheered them on to the fight; first, however, rebuking them, and saying—"Strange men, how long are ye going to back water?"

85. Against the Athenians, who held the western extremity of the line towards Eleusis, were placed the Phoenicians; against the Lacedaemonians, whose station was eastward towards the Piraeus, the Ionians. Of these last a few only followed the advice of Themistocles, to fight backwardly; the greater number did far otherwise. I could mention here the names of many trierarchs who took vessels from the Greeks, but I shall pass over all excepting Theomêstor the son of Androdamas, and Phylacus the son of Histiaeus, both Samians. I

show this preference to them, inasmuch as for this service Theomêstor was made tyrant of Samos by the Persians, while Phylacus was enrolled among the king's benefactors, and presented with a large estate in land. In the Persian tongue the king's benefactors are called Orosangs.

86. Far the greater number of the Persian ships engaged in this battle were disabled—either by the Athenians or by the Eginetans. For as the Greeks fought in order and kept their line, while the barbarians were in confusion and had no plan in anything that they did, the issue of the battle could scarce be other than it was. Yet the Persians fought far more bravely here than at Euboea, and indeed surpassed themselves; each did his utmost through fear of Xerxes, for each thought that the king's eye was upon himself.

87. What part the several nations, whether Greek or barbarian, took in the combat, I am not able to say for certain; Artemisia, however, I know, distinguished herself in such a way as raised her even higher than she stood before in the esteem of the king. For after confusion had spread throughout the whole of the king's fleet, and her ship was closely pursued by an Athenian trireme, she, having no way to fly, since in front of her were a number of friendly vessels, and she was nearest of all the Persians to the enemy, resolved on a measure which in fact proved her safety. Pressed by the Athenian pursuer, she bore straight against one of the ships of her own party, a Calyndian, which had Damasithymus, the Calyndian king, himself on board. I cannot say whether she had had any quarrel with the man while the fleet was at the Hellespont, or not—neither can I decide whether she of set purpose attacked his vessel, or whether it merely chanced that the Calyndian ship came in her way—but certain it is that she bore down upon his vessel and sank it, and that thereby she had the good fortune to procure her-

self a double advantage. For the commander of the Athenian trireme, when he saw her bear down on one of the enemy's fleet, thought immediately that her vessel was a Greek, or else had deserted from the Persians, and was now fighting on the Greek side; he therefore gave up the chase, and turned away to attack others.

88. Thus in the first place she saved her life by the action, and was enabled to get clear off from the battle; while further, it fell out that in the very act of doing the king an injury she raised herself to a greater height than ever in his esteem. For as Xerxes beheld the fight, he remarked (it is said) the destruction of the vessel, whereupon the bystanders observed to him —"Seest thou, master, how well Artemisia fights, and how she has just sunk a ship of the enemy?" Then Xerxes asked if it were really Artemisia's doing; and they answered, "Certainly; for they knew her ensign:" while all made sure that the sunken vessel belonged to the opposite side. Everything, it is said, conspired to prosper the queen—it was especially fortunate for her, that not one of those on board the Calyndian ship survived to become her accuser. Xerxes, they say, in reply to the remarks made to him, observed—"My men have behaved like women, and my women like men!"

89. There fell in this combat Ariabignes, one of the chief commanders of the fleet, who was son of Darius and brother of Xerxes, and with him perished a vast number of men of high repute, Persians, Medes, and allies. Of the Greeks there died only a few; for as they were able to swim, all those that were not slain outright by the enemy escaped from the sinking vessels and swam across to Salamis. But on the side of the Barbarians more perished by drowning than in any other way, since they did not know how to swim. The great destruction took place when the ships which had been first engaged began to fly; for they who were stationed in the rear,

anxious to display their valour before the eyes of the king, made every effort to force their way to the front, and thus became entangled with such of their own vessels as were retreating.

90. In this confusion the following event occurred: certain Phoenicians belonging to the ships which had thus perished made their appearance before the king, and laid the blame of their loss on the Ionians, declaring that they were traitors, and had willfully destroyed the vessels. But the upshot of this complaint was, that the Ionian captains escaped the death which threatened them, while their Phoenician accusers received death as their reward. For it happened that, exactly as they spoke, a Samothracian vessel bore down on an Athenian and sank it, but was attacked and crippled immediately by one of the Eginetan squadron. Now the Samothracians were expert with the javelin, and aimed their weapons so well, that they cleared the deck of the vessel which had disabled their own, after which they sprang on board, and took it. This saved the Ionians. Xerxes, when he saw the exploit, turned fiercely on the Phoenicians—(he was ready, in his extreme vexation, to find fault with any one)—and ordered their heads to be cut off, to prevent them, he said, from casting the blame of their own misconduct upon braver men. During the whole time of the battle Xerxes sate at the base of the hill called Ægaleôs, over against Salamis; and whenever he saw any of his own captains perform any worthy exploit he inquired concerning him; and the man's name was taken down by his scribes, together with the names of his father and his city. Ariarammes too, a Persian, who was a friend of the Ionians, and present at the time whereof I speak, had a share in bringing about the punishment of the Phoenicians.

91. When the rout of the Barbarians began, and they sought to make their escape to Phalêrun, the Eginetans, awaiting them in the channel, performed exploits worthy to be recorded. Through the whole of the confused struggle the Athenians employed themselves in destroying such ships as either made resistance or fled to shore, while the Eginetans dealt with those which endeavoured to escape down the straits; so that the Persian vessels were no sooner clear of the Athenians than straightway they fell into the hands of the Eginetan squadron.

92. It chanced here that there was a meeting between the ship of Themistocles, which was hasting in pursuit of the enemy, and that of Polycritus, son of Crius the Eginetan, which had just charged a Sidonian trireme. The Sidonian vessel was the same that captured the Eginetan guardship off Sciathus, which had Pytheas, the son of Ischenous, on board—that Pytheas, I mean, who fell covered with wounds, and whom the Sidonians kept on board their ship, from admiration of his gallantry. This man afterwards returned in safety to Egina, for when the Sidonian vessel with its Persian crew fell into the hands of the Greeks, he was still found on board. Polycritus no sooner saw the Athenian trireme than knowing at once whose vessel it was, as he observed that it bore the ensign of the admiral, he shouted to Themistocles jeeringly, and asked him, in a tone of reproach, if the Eginetans did not show themselves rare friends to the Medes. At the same time, while he thus reproached Themistocles, Polycritus bore straight down on the Sidonian. Such of the barbarian vessels as escaped from the battle fled to Phalêrum, and there sheltered themselves under the protection of the land army.

93. The Greeks who gained the greatest glory of all in the seafight of Salamis were the Eginetans, and after them the Athenians. The individuals of most distinction were Polycritus the Eginetan, and two Athenians, Eumenes of Anayrus, and

Aminias of Pallené; the latter of whom had pressed Artemisia so hard. And assuredly, if he had known that the vessel carried Artemisia on board, he would never have given over the chase till he had either succeeded in taking her, or else been taken himself. For the Athenian captains had received special orders touching the queen, and moreover a reward of ten thousand drachmas had been proclaimed for any one who should make her prisoner; since there was great indignation felt that a woman should appear in arms against Athens. However, as I said before, she escaped; and so did some others whose ships survived the engagement; and these were all now assembled at the port of Phalêrum.

94. The Athenians say that Adeimantus, the Corinthian commander, at the moment when the two fleets joined battle, was seized with fear, and being beyond measure alarmed, spread his sails, and hasted to fly away; on which the other Corinthians, seeing their leader's ship in full flight, sailed off likewise. They had reached in their flight that part of the coast of Salamis where stands the temple of Minerva Sciras, when they met a light bark, a very strange apparition: it was never discovered that any one had sent it to them, and till it appeared they were altogether ignorant how the battle was going. That there was something beyond nature in the matter they judged from this—that when the men in the bark drew near to their ships they addressed them, saying—"Adeimantus, while thou playest the traitor's part, by withdrawing all these ships, and flying away from the fight, the Greeks whom thou hast deserted are defeating their foes as completely as they ever wished in their prayers." Adeimantus, however, would not believe what the men said; whereupon they told him, "he might take them with

him as hostages, and put them to death if he did not find the Greeks winning." Then Adeimantus put about, both he and those who were with him; and they rejoined the fleet when the victory was already gained. Such is the tale which the Athenians tell concerning them of Corinth; these latter however do not allow its truth. On the contrary, they declare that they were among those who distinguished themselves most in the fight. And the rest of Greece bears witness in their favour.

95. In the midst of the confusion Aristides, the son of Lysimachus, the Athenian, of whom I lately spoke as a man of the greatest excellence, performed the following service. He took a number of the Athenian heavy-armed troops, who had previously been stationed along the shore of Salamis, and landing with them on the islet of Psyttaleia, slew all the Persians by whom it was occupied.

96. As soon as the sea-fight was ended, the Greeks drew together to Salamis all the wrecks that were to be found in that quarter, and prepared themselves for another engagement, supposing that the king would renew the fight with the vessels which still remained to him. Many of the wrecks had been carried away by a westerly wind to the coast of Attica, where they were thrown upon the strip of shore called Côlias. Thus not only were the prophecies of Bacis and Musæus concerning this battle fulfilled completely, but likewise, by the place to which the wrecks were drifted, the prediction of Lysistratus, an Athenian soothsayer, uttered many years before these events, and quite forgotten at the time by all the Greeks, was fully accomplished. The words were:—

Then shall the sight of the oars fill Colian dames with amazement.

. . . .

Thucydides

Thucydides (*c.*471–*c.* 396 B.C.) was the greatest of classical historians and might even be ranked as the greatest historian in Western civilization. Although not the equal of Herodotus as a relater of fascinating stories, he has a style of presentation that carries the reader along easily and gracefully. Thucydides' primary concern was to present the true history of the Peloponnesian War between Athens and Sparta, a war in which he himself was an active participant. As a general in the Athenian army he failed to prevent a Spartan force from capturing an important military stronghold, and was banished from Athens for twenty years. Much of this time he spent traveling in enemy territory and observing the course of the struggle.

In his search for truth, Thucydides imposed on himself certain critical techniques and methods. He ruthlessly discarded any story that could not be verified by documentary evidence or eye-witness accounts, or that failed to stand the test of logical analysis. As a result, the *History of the Peloponnesian War* is an extraordinarily trustworthy source of knowledge about fifth-century Greece. There is one qualification, however: Thucydides often put speeches into the mouths of historical personages. Thus, the Melian Dialogue and Pericles' Funeral Oration reproduced here appear as direct quotations, although they were actually written by Thucydides himself. Thucydides was careful to emphasize that this was simply a dramatic technique, however, and that he was trying only to convey the accurate meaning or general sense of what was said and not the full text of the speech as it was delivered.

Thucydides' contributions to the art of history include a meticulous use of source materials, an emphasis on rational and natural explanations of history and a denial of supernatural explanations, an understanding of military and naval strategy, and an awareness of the economic basis of military strength. Even his reason for writing the *History* is noteworthy. Herodotus had written, as he himself says, to preserve the memory of great events. But Thucydides wrote to instruct, to teach others the causes of events and the motivations behind men's actions, so that future generations might be able, by studying the record that he made available, to avoid the mistakes of the Greeks and the terrible consequences to which those mistakes had ultimately led.

HISTORY OF THE PELOPONNESIAN WAR

Book I

1. Thucydides, an Athenian, wrote the history of the war in which the Peloponnesians and the Athenians fought against one another. He began to write when they first took up arms, believing that it would be great and memorable above any previous war.[1] For he argued that both states were then at the full height

THUCYDIDES, trans. B. Jowett, 2nd ed. (Oxford, 1900): I, 1, 14-16, 125-135, 241-244; II, 167-177.

[1] [*Thucydides is here referring to himself in the third person. Ed.*]

of their military power, and he saw the rest of the Hellenes either siding or intending to side with one or other of them. No movement ever stirred Hellas more deeply than this; it was shared by many of the Barbarians, and might be said even to affect the world at large. . . .

.   .   .

[*Thucydides continues with a short sketch of the history of Greece. He concludes that, contrary to legend, the previous wars in which Greeks had been involved were mostly on a very small scale. Ed.*]

.   .   .

20. Such are the results of my inquiry into the early state of Hellas. They will not readily be believed upon a bare recital of all the proofs of them. Men do not discriminate, and are too ready to receive ancient traditions about their own as well as about other countries. For example, most Athenians think that Hipparchus was actually tyrant when he was slain by Harmodius and Aristogeiton; they are not aware that Hippias was the eldest of the sons of Peisistratus, and succeeded him, and that Hipparchus and Thessalus were only his brothers. At the last moment, Harmodius and Aristogeiton suddenly suspected that Hippias had been forewarned by some of their accomplices. They therefore abstained from attacking him, but, wishing to do something before they were seized, and not to risk their lives in vain, they slew Hipparchus, with whom they fell in near the temple called Leocorium as he was marshalling the Panathenaic procession. There are many other matters, not obscured by time, but contemporary, about which the other Hellenes are equally mistaken. For example, they imagine that the kings of Lacedaemon in their council have not one but two votes each, and that in the army of the Lacedaemonians there is a division called the Pitanate division; whereas they never had anything of the sort. So little trouble do men take in the search after truth; so readily do they accept whatever comes first to hand.

21. Yet any one who upon the grounds which I have given arrives at some such conclusion as my own about those ancient times, would not be far wrong. He must not be misled by the exaggerated fancies of the poets, or by the tales of chroniclers who seek to please the ear rather than to speak the truth. Their accounts cannot be tested by him; and most of the facts in the lapse of ages have passed into the regions of romance. At such a distance of time he must make up his mind to be satisfied with conclusions resting upon the clearest evidence which can be had. And, though men will always judge any war in which they are actually fighting to be the greatest at the time, but, after it is over, revert to their admiration of some other which has preceded, still the Peloponnesian, if estimated by the actual facts, will certainly prove to have been the greatest ever known.

22. As to the speeches which were made either before or during the war, it was hard for me, and for others who reported them to me, to recollect the exact words. I have therefore put into the mouth of each speaker the sentiments proper to the occasion, expressed as I thought he would be likely to express them, while at the same time I endeavored, as nearly as I could, to give the general purport of what was actually said. Of the events of the war I have not ventured to speak from any chance information, nor according to any notion of my own; I have described nothing but what I either saw myself, or learned from others of whom I made the most careful and particular inquiry. The task was a laborious one, because eye-witnesses of the same occurrences gave different accounts of them, as they remembered or were interested in the actions of one side or the other. And very likely the strictly historical character of my narrative

may be disappointing to the ear. But if he who desires to have before his eyes a true picture of the events which have happened, and of the like events which may be expected to happen hereafter in the order of human things, shall pronounce what I have written to be useful, then I shall be satisfied. My history is an everlasting possession, not a prize composition which is heard and forgotten.

.   .   .

Book II

.   .   .

34. During the same winter,[2] in accordance with an old national custom, the funeral of those who first fell in this war was celebrated by the Athenians at the public charge. The ceremony is as follows: Three days before the celebration they erect a tent in which the bones of the dead are laid out, and every one brings to his own dead any offering which he pleases. At the time of the funeral the bones are placed in chests of cypress wood, which are conveyed on hearses; there is one chest for each tribe. They also carry a single empty litter decked with a pall for all whose bodies are missing, and cannot be recovered after the battle. The procession is accompanied by any one who chooses, whether citizen or stranger, and the female relatives of the deceased are present at the place of interment and make lamentation. The public sepulchre is situated in the most beautiful spot outside the walls; there they always bury those who fall in war; only after the battle of Marathon the dead, in recognition of their pre-eminent valor, were interred on the field. When the remains have been laid in the earth, some man of known ability and high reputation, chosen by the city, delivers a suitable oration over them; after which the people depart. Such is the manner of inter-

---

[2] [*After the first year of the Peloponnesian War, 431* B.C. *Ed.*]

ment; and the ceremony was repeated from time to time throughout the war. Over those who were the first buried Pericles was chosen to speak. At the fitting moment he advanced from the sepulchre to a lofty stage, which had been erected in order that he might be heard as far as possible by the multitude, and spoke as follows:—

FUNERAL SPEECH

35. "Most of those who have spoken here before me have commended the lawgiver who added this oration to our other funeral customs; it seemed to them a worthy thing that such an honor should be given at their burial to the dead who have fallen on the field of battle. But I should have preferred that, when men's deeds have been brave, they should be honored in deed only, and with such an honor as this public funeral, which you are now witnessing. Then the reputation of many would not have been imperilled on the eloquence or want of eloquence of one, and their virtues believed or not as he spoke well or ill. For it is difficult to say neither too little nor too much; and even moderation is apt not to give the impression of truthfulness. The friend of the dead who knows the facts is likely to think that the words of the speaker fall short of his knowledge and of his wishes; another who is not so well informed, when he hears of anything which surpasses his own powers, will be envious and will suspect exaggeration. Mankind are tolerant of the praises of others so long as each hearer thinks that he can do as well or nearly as well himself, but, when the speaker rises above him, jealousy is aroused and he begins to be incredulous. However, since our ancestors have set the seal of their approval upon the practice, I must obey, and to the utmost of my power shall endeavor to satisfy the wishes and beliefs of all who hear me.

36. "I will speak first of our ancestors,

for it is right and becoming that now, when we are lamenting the dead, a tribute should be paid to their memory. There has never been a time when they did not inhabit this land, which by their valor they have handed down from generation to generation, and we have received from them a free state. But if they were worthy of praise, still more were our fathers, who added to their inheritance, and after many a struggle transmitted to us their sons this great empire. And we ourselves assembled here to-day, who are still most of us in the vigor of life, have chiefly done the work of improvement, and have richly endowed our city with all things, so that she is sufficient for herself both in peace and war. Of the military exploits by which our various possessions were acquired, or of the energy with which we or our fathers drove back the tide of war, Hellenic or Barbarian, I will not speak; for the tale would be long and is familiar to you. But before I praise the dead, I should like to point out by what principles of action we rose to power, and under what institutions and through what manner of life our empire became great. For I conceive that such thoughts are not unsuited to the occasion, and that this numerous assembly of citizens and strangers may profitably listen to them.

37. "Our form of government does not enter into rivalry with the institutions of others. We do not copy our neighbors, but are an example to them. It is true that we are called a democracy, for the administration is in the hands of the many and not of the few. But while the law secures equal justice to all alike in their private disputes, the claim of excellence is also recognized; and when a citizen is in any way distinguished, he is preferred to the public service, not as a matter of privilege, but as the reward of merit. Neither is poverty a bar, but a man may benefit his country whatever be the obscurity of his condition. There is no exclusiveness in our public life, and in our private intercourse we are not suspicious of one another, nor angry with our neighbor if he does what he likes; we do not put on sour looks at him which, though harmless, are not pleasant. While we are thus unconstrained in our private intercourse, a spirit of reverence pervades our public acts; we are prevented from doing wrong by respect for authority and for the laws, having an especial regard to those which are ordained for the protection of the injured as well as to those unwritten laws which bring upon the transgressor of them the reprobation of the general sentiment.

38. "And we have not forgotten to provide for our weary spirits many relaxations from toil; we have regular games and sacrifices throughout the year; at home the style of our life is refined; and the delight which we daily feel in all these things helps to banish melancholy. Because of the greatness of our city the fruits of the whole earth flow in upon us; so that we enjoy the goods of other countries as freely as of our own.

39. "Then, again, our military training is in many respects superior to that of our adversaries. Our city is thrown open to the world, and we never expel a foreigner or prevent him from seeing or learning anything of which the secret if revealed to an enemy might profit him. We rely not upon management or trickery, but upon our own hearts and hands. And in the matter of education, whereas they from early youth are always undergoing laborious exercises which are to make them brave, we live at ease, and yet are equally ready to face the perils which they face. And here is the proof. The Lacedaemonians come into Attica not by themselves, but with their whole confederacy following; we go alone into a neighbor's country; and although our opponents are fighting for their homes and we on a foreign soil, we have seldom any difficulty in overcoming

them. Our enemies have never yet felt our united strength; the care of a navy divides our attention, and on land we are obliged to send our own citizens everywhere. But they, if they meet and defeat a part of our army, are as proud as if they had routed us all, and when defeated they pretend to have been vanquished by us all.

40. "If then we prefer to meet danger with a light heart but without laborious training, and with a courage which is gained by habit and not enforced by law, are we not greatly the gainers? Since we do not anticipate the pain, although, when the hour comes, we can be as brave as those who never allow themselves to rest; and thus too our city is equally admirable in peace and in war. For we are lovers of the beautiful, yet simple in our tastes, and we cultivate the mind without loss of manliness. Wealth we employ, not for talk and ostentation, but when there is a real use for it. To avow poverty with us is no disgrace: the true disgrace is in doing nothing to avoid it. An Athenian citizen does not neglect the state because he takes care of his own household; and even those of us who are engaged in business have a very fair idea of politics. We alone regard a man who takes no interest in public affairs, not as a harmless, but as a useless character; and if few of us are originators, we are all sound judges of a policy. The great impediment to action is, in our opinion, not discussion, but the want of that knowledge which is gained by discussion preparatory to action. For we have a peculiar power of thinking before we act and of acting too, whereas other men are courageous from ignorance but hesitate upon reflection. And they are surely to be esteemed the bravest spirits who, having the clearest sense both of the pains and pleasures of life, do not on that account shrink from danger. In doing good, again, we are unlike others; we make our friends

by conferring, not by receiving favors. Now he who confers a favor is the firmer friend, because he would fain by kindness keep alive the memory of an obligation; but the recipient is colder in his feelings, because he knows that in requiting another's generosity he will not be winning gratitude, but only paying a debt. We alone do good to our neighbors not upon a calculation of interest, but in the confidence of freedom and in a frank and fearless spirit.

41. "To sum up: I say that Athens is the school of Hellas, and that the individual Athenian in his own person seems to have the power of adapting himself to the most varied forms of action with the utmost versatility and grace. This is no passing and idle word, but truth and fact; and the assertion is verified by the position to which these qualities have raised the state. For in the hour of trial Athens alone among her contemporaries is superior to the report of her. No enemy who comes against her is indignant at the reverses which he sustains at the hands of such a city; no subject complains that his masters are unworthy of him. And we shall assuredly not be without witnesses; there are mighty monuments of our power which will make us the wonder of this and of succeeding ages; we shall not need the praises of Homer or of any other panegyrist whose poetry may please for the moment, although his representation of the facts will not bear the light of day. For we have compelled every land and every sea to open a path for our valor, and have everywhere planted eternal memorials of our friendship and of our enmity. Such is the city for whose sake these men nobly fought and died; they could not bear the thought that she might be taken from them; and every one of us who survive should gladly toil on her behalf.

42. "I have dwelt upon the greatness

of Athens because I want to show you that we are contending for a higher prize than those who enjoy none of these privileges, and to establish by manifest proof the merit of these men whom I am now commemorating. Their loftiest praise has been already spoken. For in magnifying the city I have magnified them, and men like them whose virtues made her glorious. And of how few Hellenes can it be said as of them, that their deeds when weighed in the balance have been found equal to their fame! Methinks that a death such as theirs has been gives the true measure of a man's worth; it may be the first revelation of his virtues, but is at any rate their final seal. For even those who come short in other ways may justly plead the valor with which they have fought for their country; they have blotted out the evil with the good, and have benefited the state more by their public services than they have injured her by their private actions. None of these men were enervated by wealth or hesitated to resign the pleasures of life; none of them put off the evil day in the hope, natural to poverty, that a man, though poor, may one day become rich. But, deeming that the punishment of their enemies was sweeter than any of these things, and that they could fall in no nobler cause, they determined at the hazard of their lives to be honorably avenged, and to leave the rest. They resigned to hope their unknown chance of happiness; but in the face of death they resolved to rely upon themselves alone. And when the moment came they were minded to resist and suffer, rather than to fly and save their lives; they ran away from the word of dishonor, but on the battle-field their feet stood fast, and in an instant, at the height of their fortune, they passed away from the scene, not of their fear, but of their glory.

43. "Such was the end of these men; they were worthy of Athens, and the living need not desire to have a more heroic spirit, although they may pray for a less fatal issue. The value of such a spirit is not to be expressed in words. Any one can discourse to you forever about the advantages of a brave defence which you know already. But instead of listening to him I would have you day by day fix your eyes upon the greatness of Athens, until you become filled with the love of her; and when you are impressed by the spectacle of her glory, reflect that this empire has been acquired by men who knew their duty and had the courage to do it, who in the hour of conflict had the fear of dishonor always present to them, and who, if ever they failed in an enterprise, would not allow their virtues to be lost to their country, but freely gave their lives to her as the fairest offering which they could present at her feast. The sacrifice which they collectively made was individually repaid to them; for they received again each one for himself a praise which grows not old, and the noblest of all sepulchres—I speak not of that in which their remains are laid, but of that in which their glory survives, and is proclaimed always and on every fitting occasion both in word and deed. For the whole earth is the sepulchre of famous men; not only are they commemorated by columns and inscriptions in their own country, but in foreign lands there dwells also an unwritten memorial of them, graven not on stone but in the hearts of men. Make them your examples, and, esteeming courage to be freedom and freedom to be happiness, do not weigh too nicely the perils of war. The unfortunate who has no hope of a change for the better has less reason to throw away his life than the prosperous who, if he survive, is always liable to a change for the worse, and to whom any accidental fall makes the most serious difference. To a man of spirit,

cowardice and disaster coming together are far more bitter than death, striking him unperceived at a time when he is full of courage and animated by the general hope.

44. "Wherefore I do not now commiserate the parents of the dead who stand here; I would rather comfort them. You know that your life has been passed amid manifold vicissitudes; and that they may be deemed fortunate who have gained most honor, whether an honorable death like theirs, or an honorable sorrow like you, and whose days have been so ordered that the term of their happiness is likewise the term of their life. I know how hard it is to make you feel this, when the good fortune of others will too often remind you of the gladness which once lightened your hearts. And sorrow is felt at the want of those blessings, not which a man never knew, but which were a part of his life before they were taken from him. Some of you are of an age at which they may hope to have other children, and they ought to bear their sorrow better; not only will the children who may hereafter be born make them forget their own lost ones, but the city will be doubly a gainer. She will not be left desolate, and she will be safer. For a man's counsel cannot have equal weight or worth, when he alone has no children to risk in the general danger. To those of you who have passed their prime, I say; 'Congratulate yourselves that you have been happy during the greater part of your days; remember that your life of sorrow will not last long, and be comforted by the glory of those who are gone. For the love of honor alone is ever young, and not riches, as some say, but honor is the delight of men when they are old and useless.'

45. "To you who are the sons and brothers of the departed, I see that the struggle to emulate them will be an arduous one. For all men praise the dead, and, however

pre-eminent your virtue may be, hardly will you be thought, I do not say to equal, but even to approach them. The living have their rivals and detractors, but when a man is out of the way, the honor and good-will which he receives is unalloyed. And, if I am to speak of womanly virtues to those of you who will henceforth be widows, let me sum them up in one short admonition: To a woman not to show more weakness than is natural to her sex is a great glory, and not to be talked about for good or for evil among men.

46. "I have paid the required tribute, in obedience to the law, making use of such fitting words as I had. The tribute of deeds has been paid in part; for the dead have been honorably interred, and it remains only that their children should be maintained at the public charge until they are grown up; this is the solid prize with which, as with a garland, Athens crowns her sons living and dead, after a struggle like theirs. For where the rewards of virtue are greatest, there the noblest citizens are enlisted in the service of the state. And now, when you have duly lamented, every one his own dead, you may depart."

.   .   .

Book III

.   .   .

82. For not long afterwards[3] nearly the whole Hellenic world was in commotion; in every city the chiefs of the democracy and of the oligarchy were struggling, the one to bring in the Athenians, the other the Lacedaemonians. Now, in time of peace, men would have had no excuse for introducing either, and no desire to do so, but when they were at war and both sides could easily obtain allies to the hurt of their enemies and the advantage of themselves, the dissatisfied party were only too ready to invoke foreign aid.

[3] [*In 427* B.C., *or four years after Pericles' Funeral Oration. Ed.*]

And revolution brought upon the cities of Hellas many terrible calamities, such as have been and always will be while human nature remains the same, but which are more or less aggravated and differ in character with every new combination of circumstances. In peace and prosperity both states and individuals are actuated by high motives, because they do not fall under the dominion of imperious necessities; but war which takes away the comfortable provision of daily life is a hard master, and tends to assimilate men's characters to their conditions.

When troubles had once begun in the cities, those who followed carried the revolutionary spirit further and further, and determined to outdo the report of all who had preceded them by the ingenuity of their enterprises and the atrocity of their revenges. The meaning of words had no longer the same relation to things, but was changed by them as they thought proper. Reckless daring was held to be loyal courage; prudent delay was the excuse of a coward; moderation was the disguise of unmanly weakness; to know everything was to do nothing. Frantic energy was the true quality of man. A conspirator who wanted to be safe was a recreant in disguise. The lover of violence was always trusted, and his opponent suspected. He who succeeded in a plot was deemed knowing, but a still greater master in craft was he who detected one. On the other hand, he who plotted from the first to have nothing to do with plots was a breaker up of parties and a poltroon who was afraid of the enemy. In a word, he who could outstrip another in a bad action was applauded, and so was he who encouraged to evil one who had no idea of it. The tie of party was stronger than the tie of blood, because a partisan was more ready to dare without asking why. (For party associations are not based upon any established law, nor do they seek the public good;

they are formed in defiance of the laws and from self-interest.) The seal of good faith was not divine law, but fellowship in crime. If an enemy when he was in the ascendant offered fair words, the opposite party received them, not in a generous spirit, but by a jealous watchfulness of his actions. Revenge was dearer than self-preservation. Any agreements sworn to by either party, when they could do nothing else, were binding as long as both were powerless. But he who on a favorable opportunity first took courage and struck at his enemy when he saw him off his guard, had greater pleasure in a perfidious than he would have had in an open act of revenge; he congratulated himself that he had taken the safer course, and also that he had over-reached his enemy and gained the prize of superior ability. In general, the dishonest more easily gain credit for cleverness than the simple for goodness; men take a pride in the one, but are ashamed of the other.

The cause of all these evils was the love of power originating in avarice and ambition, and the party-spirit which is engendered by them when men were fairly embarked in a contest. For the leaders on either side used specious names, the one party professing to uphold the constitutional equality of the many, the other the wisdom of an aristocracy, while they made the public interests, to which in name they were devoted, in reality their prize. Striving in every way to overcome each other, they committed the most monstrous crimes; yet even these were surpassed by the magnitude of their revenges which they pursued to the very utmost, neither party observing any definite limits either of justice or public expediency, but both alike making the caprice of the moment their law. Either by the help of an unrighteous sentence, or grasping power with the strong hand, they were eager to satiate the impatience of party-spirit. Neither faction cared for religion; but any fair pretence which succeeded in effecting some odious purpose was greatly lauded. And the citizens who were of neither party fell a prey to both; either they were disliked because they held aloof, or men were jealous of their surviving.

83. Thus revolution gave birth to every form of wickedness in Hellas. The simplicity which is so large an element in a noble nature was laughed to scorn and disappeared. An attitude of perfidious antagonism everywhere prevailed; for there was no word binding enough, nor oath terrible enough to reconcile enemies. Each man was strong only in the conviction that nothing was secure; he must look to his own safety, and could not afford to trust others. Inferior intellects generally succeeded best. For, aware of their own deficiencies, and fearing the capacity of their opponents, for whom they were no match in powers of speech, and whose subtle wits were likely to anticipate them in contriving evil, they struck boldly and at once. But the cleverer sort, presuming in their arrogance that they would be aware in time, and disdaining to act when they could think, were taken off their guard and easily destroyed.

· · ·

Book V

· · ·

84. In the ensuing summer, Alcibiades sailed to Argos with twenty ships, and seized any of the Argives who were still suspected to be of the Lacedaemonian faction, three hundred in number; and the Athenians deposited them in the subject islands near at hand. The Athenians next made an expedition against the island of Melos[4] with thirty ships of their own, six Chian, and two Lesbian, twelve hundred hoplites and three hundred arch-

4 [*In 416 B.C. Ed.*]

ers besides twenty mounted archers of their own, and about fifteen hundred hoplites furnished by their allies in the islands. The Melians are colonists of the Lacedaemonians who would not submit to Athens like the other islanders. At first they were neutral and took no part. But when the Athenians tried to coerce them by ravaging their lands they were driven into open hostilities. The generals, Cleomedes the son of Lycomedes and Tisias the son of Tisimachus, encamped with the Athenian forces on the island. But before they did the country any harm they sent envoys to negotiate with the Melians. Instead of bringing these envoys before the people, the Melians desired them to explain their errand to the magistrates and to the chief men. They spoke as follows:—

85. "Since we are not allowed to speak to the people, lest, forsooth, they should be deceived by seductive and unanswerable arguments which they would hear set forth in a single uninterrupted oration (for we are perfectly aware that this is what you mean in bringing us before a select few), you who are sitting here may as well make assurance yet surer. Let us have no set speeches at all, but do you reply to each several statement of which you disapprove, and criticise it at once. Say first of all how you like this mode of proceeding."

86. The Melian representatives answered: —"The quiet interchange of explanations is a reasonable thing, and we do not object to that. But your warlike movements, which are present not only to our fears but to our eyes, seem to belie your words. We see that, although you may reason with us, you mean to be our judges; and that at the end of the discussion if the justice of our cause prevail and we therefore refuse to yield, we may expect war; if we are convinced by you, slavery."

87. ATH: Nay, but if you are only going to argue from fancies about the future, or

if you meet us with any other purpose than that of looking your circumstances in the face and saving your city, we have done; but if this is your intention we will proceed.

88. MEL: It is an excusable and natural thing that men in our position should have much to say and should indulge in many fancies. But we admit that this conference has met to consider the question of our preservation; and therefore let the argument proceed in the manner which you propose.

89. ATH: Well, then, we Athenians will use no fine words; we will not go out of our way to prove at length that we have a right to rule, because we overthrew the Persians; or that we attack you now because we are suffering any injury at your hands. We should not convince you if we did; nor must you expect to convince us by arguing that, although a colony of the Lacedaemonians, you have taken no part in their expeditions, or that you have never done us any wrong. But you and we should say what we really think, and aim only at what is possible, for we both alike know that into the discussion of human affairs the question of justice only enters where the pressure of necessity is equal, and that the powerful exact what they can, and the weak grant what they must.

90. MEL: Well, then, since you set aside justice and invite us to speak of expediency, in our judgment it is certainly expedient that you should respect a principle which is for the common good; and that to every man when in peril a reasonable claim should be accounted a claim of right, and any plea which he is disposed to urge, even if failing of the point a little, should help his cause. Your interest in this principle is quite as great as ours, inasmuch as you, if you fall, will incur the heaviest vengeance, and will be the most terrible example to mankind.

91. ATH: The fall of our empire, if it should fall, is not an event to which we look forward with dismay; for ruling states such as Lacedaemon are not cruel to their vanquished enemies. And we are fighting not so much against the Lacedaemonians as against our own subjects who may some day rise up and overcome their former masters. But this is a danger which you may leave to us. And we will now endeavor to show that we have come in the interests of our empire, and that in what we are about to say we are only seeking the preservation of your city. For we want to make you ours with the least trouble to ourselves, and it is for the interests of us both that you should not be destroyed.

92. MEL: It may be your interest to be our masters, but how can it be ours to be your slaves?

93. ATH: To you the gain will be that by submission you will avert the worst; and we shall be all the richer for your preservation.

94. MEL: But must we be your enemies? Will you not receive us as friends if we are neutral and remain at peace with you?

95. ATH: No, your enmity is not half so mischievous to us as your friendship; for the one is in the eyes of our subjects an argument of our power, the other of our weakness.

96. MEL: But are your subjects really unable to distinguish between states in which you have no concern, and those which are chiefly your own colonies, and in some cases have revolted and been subdued by you?

97. ATH: Why, they do not doubt that both of them have a good deal to say for themselves on the score of justice, but they think that states like yours are left free because they are able to defend themselves, and that we do not attack them because we dare not. So that your subjection will give us an increase of security, as well as an extension of empire. For we are masters of the sea, and you who are is-

landers, and insignificant islanders too, must not be allowed to escape us.

98. MEL: But do you not recognize another danger? For once more, since you drive us from the plea of justice and press upon us your doctrine of expediency, we must show you what is for our interest, and, if it be for yours also, may hope to convince you:—Will you not be making enemies of all who are now neutrals? When they see how you are treating us they will expect you some day to turn against them; and if so, are you not strengthening the enemies whom you already have, and bringing upon you others who, if they could help, would never dream of being your enemies at all?

99. ATH: We do not consider our really dangerous enemies to be any of the peoples inhabiting the mainland who, secure in their freedom, may defer indefinitely any measures of precaution which they take against us, but islanders who, like you, happen to be under no control, and all who may be already irritated by the necessity of submission to our empire—these are our real enemies, for they are the most reckless and most likely to bring themselves as well as us into a danger which they cannot but foresee.

100. MEL: Surely then, if you and your subjects will brave all this risk, you to preserve your empire and they to be quit of it, how base and cowardly it would be in us, who retain our freedom, not to do and suffer anything rather than be your slaves.

101. ATH: Not so, if you calmly reflect: for you are not fighting against equals to whom you cannot yield without disgrace, but you are taking counsel whether or no you shall resist an overwhelming force. The question is not one of honor but of prudence.

102. MEL: But we know that the fortune of war is sometimes impartial, and not always on the side of numbers. If we yield now all is over; but if we fight there

is yet a hope that we may stand upright.

103. ATH: Hope is a good comforter in the hour of danger, and when men have something else to depend upon, although hurtful, she is not ruinous. But when her spendthrift nature has induced them to stake their all, they see her as she is in the moment of their fall, and not till then. While the knowledge of her might enable them to be ware of her, she never fails. You are weak and a single turn of the scale might be your ruin. Do not you be thus deluded; avoid the error of which so many are guilty, who, although they might still be saved if they would take the natural means, when visible grounds of confidence forsake them, have recourse to the invisible to prophecies and oracles and the like, which ruin men by the hopes which they inspire in them.

104. MEL: We know only too well how hard the struggle must be against your power, and against fortune, if she does not mean to be impartial. Nevertheless we do not despair of fortune; for we hope to stand as high as you in the favor of heaven, because we are righteous, and you against whom we contend are unrighteous; and we are satisfied that our deficiency in power will be compensated by the aid of our allies the Lacedaemonians; they cannot refuse to help us, if only because we are their kinsmen, and for the sake of their own honor. And therefore our confidence is not so utterly blind as you suppose.

105. ATH: As for the Gods, we expect to have quite as much of their favor as you: for are we not doing or claiming anything which goes beyond common opinion about divine or men's desires about human things. For of the Gods we believe, and of men we know, that by a law of their nature wherever they can rule they will. This law was not made by us, and we are not the first who have acted upon it; we did but inherit it, and shall bequeath it to all

time, and we know that you and all mankind, if you were as strong as we are, would do as we do. So much for the Gods; we have told you why we expect to stand as high in their good opinion as you. And then as to the Lacedaemonians—when you imagine that out of very shame they will assist you, we admire the simplicity of your idea, but we do not envy you the folly of it. The Lacedaemonians are exceedingly virtuous among themselves, and according to their national standard of morality. But in respect of their dealings with others, although many things might be said, a word is enough to describe them —of all men whom we know they are the most notorious for identifying what is pleasant with what is honorable, and what is expedient with what is just. But how inconsistent is such a character with your present blind hope of deliverance!

106. MEL: That is the very reason why we trust them; they will look to their interest, and therefore will not be willing to betray the Melians, who are their own colonists, lest they should be distrusted by their friends in Hellas and play into the hands of their enemies.

107. ATH: But do you not see that the path of expediency is safe, whereas justice and honor involve danger in practice, and such dangers the Lacedaemonians seldom care to face?

108. MEL: On the other hand we think that whatever perils there may be, they will be ready to face them for our sakes, and will consider danger less dangerous where we are concerned. For if they need our aid we are close at hand, and they can better trust our loyal feeling because we are their kinsmen.

109. ATH: Yes, but what encourages men who are invited to join in a conflict is clearly not the good-will of those who summon them to their side, but a decided superiority in real power. To this no men look more keenly than the Lacedaemoni-

ans; so little confidence have they in their own resources that they only attack their neighbors when they have numerous allies, and therefore they are not likely to find their way by themselves to an island, when we are masters of the sea.

110. MEL: But they may send their allies: the Cretan sea is a large place; and the masters of the sea will have more difficulty in overtaking vessels which want to escape than the pursued in escaping. If the attempt should fail they may invade Attica itself, and find their way to allies of yours whom Brasidas did not reach; and then you will have to fight, not for the conquest of a land in which you have no concern, but nearer home, for the preservation of your confederacy and of your own territory.

111. ATH: Help may come from Lacedaemon to you as it has come to others, and should you ever have actual experience of it, then you will know that never once have the Athenians retired from a siege through fear of a foe elsewhere. You told us that the safety of your city would be your first care, but we remark that, in this long discussion, not a word has been uttered by you which would give a reasonable man expectation of deliverance. Your strongest grounds are hopes deferred, and what power you have is not to be compared with that which is already arrayed against you. Unless after we have withdrawn you mean to come, as even now you may, to a wiser conclusion, you are showing a great want of sense. For surely you cannot dream of flying to that false sense of honor which has been the ruin of so many when danger and dishonor were staring them in the face. Many men with their eyes still open to the consequences have found the word 'honor' too much for them, and have suffered a mere name to lure them on, until it has drawn down upon them real and irretrievable calamities; through their own folly they have

incurred a worse dishonor than fortune would have inflicted upon them. If you are wise you will not run this risk; you ought to see that there can be no disgrace in yielding to a great city which invites you to become her ally on reasonable terms, keeping your own land, and merely paying tribute; and that you will certainly gain no honor if, having to choose between two alternatives, safety and war, you obstinately prefer the worse. To maintain our rights against equals, to be politic with superiors, and to be moderate towards inferiors is the path of safety. Reflect once more when we have withdrawn, and say to yourselves over and over again that you are deliberating about your one and only country, which may be saved or may be destroyed by a single decision.

112. The Athenians left the conference: the Melians, after consulting among themselves, resolved to persevere in their refusal, and made answer as follows:—"Men of Athens, our resolution is unchanged; and we will not in a moment surrender that liberty which our city, founded seven hundred years ago, still enjoys; we will trust to the good-fortune which by the favor of the Gods has hitherto preserved us, and for human help to the Lacedaemonians, and endeavor to save ourselves. We are ready however to be your friends, and the enemies neither of you nor of the Lacedaemonians, and we ask you to leave our country when you have made such a peace as may appear to be in the interest of both parties."

113. Such was the answer of the Melians; the Athenians, as they quitted the conference, spoke as follows:—"Well, we must say, judging from the decision at which you have arrived, that you are the only men who deem the future to be more certain than the present, and regard things unseen as already realized in your fond anticipation, and that the more you cast yourselves upon the Lacedaemonians and fortune, and hope, and trust them, the more complete will be your ruin."

114. The Athenian envoys returned to the army; and the generals, when they found that the Melians would not yield, immediately commenced hostilities. They surrounded the town of Melos with a wall, dividing the work among the several contingents. They then left troops of their own and of the allies to keep guard both by land and by sea, and retired with the greater part of their army; the remainder carried on the blockade.

. . .

116 . . . The place was now closely invested, and there was treachery among the citizens themselves. So the Melians were induced to surrender at discretion. The Athenians thereupon put to death all who were of military age, and made slaves of the women and children. They then colonised the island, sending thither 500 settlers of their own.

Sophocles

The life of Sophocles, the tragic poet, spanned the fifth century. Born in 496, he was just old enough to remember the battle of Marathon, and in 480 he led a chorus of Athenian youths in the ceremonial celebration of the naval victory at Salamis. He reached the height of his creative powers in the Age of Pericles. His *Antigone* was produced in 441, three years before the completion of the Parthenon, and his *King Oedipus* was produced around 430, the year before the death of Pericles. Sophocles died in 406 at the age of ninety, two years before the Athenian defeat in the Peloponnesian War.

To understand the tragic drama *Antigone*, we must realize that, according to Greek religion, the body of the deceased had to be buried before the soul could enter Hades. Thus Antigone had a sacred duty to bury her brother, a duty that she believed took precedence over all others, even obedience to the decrees of the state. The tragedy, therefore, can be interpreted as a clash between divine law, championed by Antigone, and human or political law, championed by Creon. Such an interpretation, though, does not exhaust the meaning of the play. Viewed as a dramatic portrayal of human character, the tragedy that destroys both Antigone and Creon becomes the inevitable result of a clash between two strong-willed individuals, each dedicated to an ideal in itself good but neither willing to make any compromise between his ideal and that held by the other.

ANTIGONE

CHARACTERS:

ISMENE
ANTIGONE } *daughters of* OEDIPUS

CREON, *King of Thebes*

HAEMON, *son of* CREON

TEIRESIAS, *a blind prophet*

SENTRY

MESSENGER

EURYDICE, *wife of* CREON

CHORUS *of Theban elders*

King's Attendants

Queen's Attendants

BOY *leading* TEIRESIAS

SOLDIERS

SCENE: BEFORE THE PALACE AT THEBES.

[*Enter* ISMENE *from the central door of the Palace.* ANTIGONE *follows, anxious and urgent; she closes the door carefully, and comes to join her sister.*

ANTIGONE: Ismene, my sister, mine own dear sister, knowest thou what ill there is, of all bequeathed by Oedipus, that Zeus

THE ANTIGONE, trans. R. C. Jebb, 2nd ed. (Cambridge, 1891).

fulfils not for us twain while we live? Nothing painful is there, nothing fraught with ruin, no shame, no dishonour, that I have not seen in thy woes and mine. And now what new edict is this of which they tell, that our Captain hath just published to all Thebes? Knowest thou aught? Hast thou heard? Or is it hidden from thee that our friends are threatened with the doom of our foes?

ISMENE: No word of friends, Antigone, gladsome or painful, hath come to me, since we two sisters were bereft of brothers twain, killed in one day by a twofold blow; and since in this last night the Argive host hath fled, I know no more, whether my fortune be brighter, or more grievous.

ANTIGONE: I knew it well, and therefore sought to bring thee beyond the gates of the court, that thou mightest hear alone.

ISMENE: What is it? 'Tis plain that thou art brooding on some dark tidings.

ANTIGONE: What, hath not Creon destined our brothers, the one to honoured burial, the other to unburied shame? Eteocles, they say, with due observance of right and custom, he hath laid in the earth, for his honour among the dead below. But the hapless corpse of Polyneices—as rumour saith, it hath been published to the town that none shall entomb him or mourn, but leave unwept, unsepulchred, a welcome store for the birds, as they espy him, to feast on at will.

Such, 'tis said, is the edict that the good Creon hath set forth for thee and for me,— yes, for *me*,—and is coming hither to proclaim it clearly to those who know it not; nor counts the matter light, but, whoso disobeys in aught, his doom is death by stoning before all the folk. Thou knowest it now; and thou wilt soon show whether thou art nobly bred, or the base daughter of a noble line.

ISMENE: Poor sister,—and if things stand thus, what could I help to do or undo?

ANTIGONE: Consider if thou wilt share the toil and the deed.

ISMENE: In what venture? What can be thy meaning?

ANTIGONE: Wilt thou aid this hand to lift the dead?

ISMENE: Thou wouldst bury him—when 'tis forbidden to Thebes?

ANTIGONE: I will do my part,—and thine, if thou wilt not,—to a brother. False to him will I never be found.

ISMENE: Ah, over-bold! when Creon hath forbidden?

ANTIGONE: Nay, he hath no right to keep me from mine own.

ISMENE: Ah me! think, sister, how our father perished, amid hate and scorn, when sins bared by his own search had moved him to strike both eyes with self-blinding hand; then the mother wife, two names in one, with twisted noose did despite unto her life; and last, our two brothers in one day, —each shedding, hapless one, a kinsman's blood,—wrought out with mutual hands their common doom. And now *we* in turn —we two left all alone—think how we shall perish, more miserably than all the rest,

if, in defiance of the law, we brave a king's decree or his powers. Nay, we must remember, first, that we were born women, as who should not strive with men; next, that we are ruled of the stronger, so that we must obey in these things, and in things yet sorer. I, therefore, asking the Spirits Infernal to pardon, seeing that force is put on me herein, will hearken to our rulers; for 'tis witless to be over-busy.

ANTIGONE: I will not urge thee,—no, nor, if thou yet shouldst have the mind, wouldst thou be welcome as a worker with *me*. Nay, be what thou wilt; but I will bury him: well for me to die in doing that. I shall rest, a loved one with him whom I have loved, sinless in my crime; for I owe a longer allegiance to the dead than to the living: in that world I shall abide for ever. But if *thou* wilt, be guilty of dishonouring laws which the gods have stablished in honour.

ISMENE: I do them no dishonour; but to defy the State—I have no strength for that.

ANTIGONE: Such be thy plea:—I, then, will go to heap the earth above the brother whom I love.

ISMENE: Alas, unhappy one! How I fear for thee!

ANTIGONE: Fear not for me: guide thine own fate aright.

ISMENE: At least, then, disclose this plan to none, but hide it closely,—and so, too, will I.

ANTIGONE: Oh, denounce it! Thou wilt be far more hateful for thy silence, if thou proclaim not these things to all.

ISMENE: Thou hast a hot heart for chilling deeds.

ANTIGONE: I know that I please where I am most bound to please.

ISMENE: Aye, if thou canst; but thou wouldst what thou canst not.

ANTIGONE: Why, then, when my strength fails, I shall have done.

ISMENE: A hopeless quest should not be made at all.

ANTIGONE: If thus thou speakest, thou wilt have hatred from me, and wilt justly be subject to the lasting hatred of the dead. But leave me, and the folly that is mine alone, to suffer this dreadful thing; for I shall not suffer aught so dreadful as an ignoble death.

ISMENE: Go, then, if thou must; and of this be sure,—that, though thine errand is foolish, to thy dear ones thou art truly dear.

[*Exit* ANTIGONE *on the spectators' left.* ISMENE *retires into the Palace by one of the two side-doors.*

CHORUS: Beam of the sun, fairest light that ever dawned on Thebe of the seven gates, thou hast shone forth at last, eye of golden day, arisen above Dirce's streams! The warrior of the white shield, who came from Argos in his panoply, hath been stirred by thee to headlong flight, in swifter career; who set forth against our land by reason of the vexed claims of Polyneices; and, like shrill-screaming eagle, he flew over into our land, in snow-white pinion sheathed, with an armed throng, and with plumage of helms.

He paused above our dwellings; he ravened around our sevenfold portals with spears athirst for blood; but he went hence, or ever his jaws were glutted with our gore, or the Fire-god's pine-fed flame had seized our crown of towers. So fierce was the noise of battle raised behind him, a thing too hard for him to conquer, as he wrestled with his dragon foe.

For Zeus utterly abhors the boasts of a proud tongue; and when he beheld them coming on in a great stream, in the haughty pride of clanging gold, he smote with brandished fire one who was now hasting to shout victory at his goal upon our ramparts.

Swung down, he fell on the earth with a crash, torch in hand, he who so lately, in the frenzy of the mad onset, was raging against us with the blasts of his tempestuous hate. But those threats fared not as he hoped; and to other foes the mighty War-god dispensed their several dooms, dealing havoc around, a mighty helper at our need.

For seven captains at seven gates, matched against seven, left the tribute of their panoplies to Zeus who turns the battle; save those two of cruel fate, who, born of one sire and one mother, set against each other their twain conquering spears, and are sharers in a common death.

But since Victory of glorious name hath come to us, with joy responsive to the joy of Thebe whose chariots are many, let us enjoy forgetfulness after the late wars, and visit all the temples of the gods with night-long dance and song; and may Bacchus be our leader, whose dancing shakes the land of Thebe.

But lo, the king of the land comes yonder, Creon, son of Menoeceus, our new ruler by the new fortunes that the gods have given; what counsel is he pondering, that he hath proposed this special conference of elders, summoned by his general mandate?

[*Enter* CREON, *from the central doors of the Palace, in the garb of king; with two Attendants.*

CREON: Sirs, the vessel of our State, after being tossed on wild waves, hath once more been safely steadied by the gods: and ye, out of all the folk, have been called apart by my summons, because I knew, first of all, how true and constant was your reverence for the royal power of Laius; how again, when Oedipus was ruler of our land, and when he had perished, your steadfast loyalty still upheld their children. Since, then, his sons have fallen in one day by a twofold doom,—each smitten by the other, each stained with a brother's blood,—I now possess the throne and all its powers, by nearness of kinship to the dead.

No man can be fully known, in soul and spirit and mind, until he hath been seen versed in rule and law-giving. For if any, being supreme guide of the State, cleaves not to the best counsels, but, through some fear, keeps his lips locked, I hold, and have ever held, him most base; and if any makes a friend of more account than his fatherland, that man hath no place in my regard. For I—be Zeus my witness, who sees all things always—would not be silent if I saw ruin, instead of safety, coming to the citizens; nor would I ever deem the country's foe a friend to myself; remembering this, that our country is the ship that bears us safe, and that only while she prospers in our voyage can we make true friends.

Such are the rules by which I guard this city's greatness. And in accord with them is the edict which I have now published to the folk touching the sons of Oedipus;—that Eteocles, who hath fallen fighting for our city, in all renown of arms, shall be entombed, and crowned with every rite that follows the noblest dead to their rest. But for his brother, Polyneices,—who came back from exile, and sought to consume utterly with fire the city of his fathers and the shrines of his fathers' gods,—sought to taste of kindred blood, and to lead the remnant into slavery;—touching this man, it hath been proclaimed to our people that none shall grace him with sepulture or lament, but leave him unburied, a corpse for birds and dogs to eat, a ghastly sight of shame.

Such the spirit of my dealing; and never, by deed of mine, shall the wicked stand in honour before the just; but whoso hath good will to Thebes, he shall be honoured of me, in his life and in his death.

CHORUS: Such is thy pleasure, Creon, son of Menoeceus, touching this city's foe, and its friend; and thou hast power, I ween, to take what order thou wilt, both for the dead, and for all us who live.

CREON: See, then, that ye be guardians of the mandate.

CHORUS: Lay the burden of this task on some younger man.

CREON: Nay, watchers of the corpse have been found.

CHORUS: What, then, is this further charge that thou wouldst give?

CREON: That ye side not with the breakers of these commands.

CHORUS: No man is so foolish that he is enamoured of death.

CREON: In sooth, that is the meed; yet lucre hath oft ruined men through their hopes.

[*Enter* GUARD.

My liege, I will not say that I come breathless from speed, or that I have plied a nimble foot; for often did my thoughts make me pause, and wheel round in my path, to return. My mind was holding large discourse with me; 'Fool, why goest thou to thy certain doom?' 'Wretch, tarrying again? And if Creon hears this from another, must not thou smart for it?' So debating, I went on my way with lagging steps, and thus a short road was made long. At last, however, it carried the day that I should come hither—to thee; and, though my tale be nought, yet will I tell it; for I come with a good grip on one hope,—that I can suffer nothing but what is my fate.

CREON: And what is it that disquiets thee thus?

GUARD: I wish to tell thee first about myself—I did not do the deed—I did not see the doer—it were not right that I should come to any harm.

CREON: Thou hast a shrewd eye for thy mark; well dost thou fence thyself round against the blame:—clearly thou hast some strange thing to tell.

GUARD: Aye, truly; dread news makes one pause long.

CREON: Then tell it, wilt thou, and so get thee gone?

GUARD: Well, this is it.—The corpse—some one hath just given it burial, and gone away,—after sprinkling thirsty dust on the flesh, with such other rites as piety enjoins.

CREON: What sayest thou? What living man hath dared this deed?

GUARD: I know not; no stroke of pickaxe was seen there, no earth thrown up by mattock; the ground was hard and dry, unbroken, without track of wheels; the doer was one who had left no trace. And when the first day-watchman showed it to us, sore wonder fell on all. The dead man was veiled from us; not shut within a tomb, but lightly strewn with dust, as by the hand of one who shunned a curse. And no sign met the eye as though any beast of prey or any dog had come nigh to him, or torn him.

Then evil words flew fast and loud among us, guard accusing guard; and it would e'en have come to blows at last, nor was there any to hinder. Every man was the culprit, and no one was convicted, but all disclaimed knowledge of the deed. And we were ready to take red-hot iron in our hands;—to walk through fire;—to make oath by the gods that we had not done the deed,—that we were not privy to the planning or the doing.

At last, when all our searching was fruitless, one spake, who made us all bend our faces on the earth in fear; for we saw not how we could gainsay him, or escape mischance if we obeyed. His counsel was that this deed must be reported to thee, and not hidden. And this seemed best; and the lot doomed my hapless self to win this prize. So here I stand,—as unwelcome as unwilling, well I wot; for no man delights in the bearer of bad news.

CHORUS: O King, my thoughts have long been whispering, can this deed, perchance, be e'en the work of gods?

CREON: Cease, ere thy words fill me utterly with wrath, lest thou be found at once an old man and foolish. For thou sayest what is not to be borne, in saying that the gods have care for this corpse. Was it for high reward of trusty service that they sought to hide his nakedness, who came to burn their pillared shrines and sacred treasures, to burn their land, and scatter its laws to the winds? Or dost thou behold the gods honouring the wicked? It cannot be. No! From the first there were certain in the town that muttered against me, chafing at this edict, wagging their heads in secret; and kept not their necks duly under the yoke, like men contented with my sway.

'Tis by them, well I know, that these have been beguiled and bribed to do this deed. Nothing so evil as money ever grew to be current among men. This lays cities low, this drives men from their homes, this trains and warps honest souls till they set themselves to works of shame; this still teaches folk to practise villainies, and to know every godless deed.

But all the men who wrought this thing for hire have made it sure that, soon or late, they shall pay the price. Now, as Zeus still hath my reverence, know this—I tell it thee on my oath:—If ye find not the very author of this burial, and produce him before mine eyes, death alone shall not be enough for you, till first, hung up alive, ye have revealed this outrage,—that henceforth ye may thieve with better knowledge whence lucre should be won, and learn that it is not well to love gain from every source. For thou wilt find that ill-gotten pelf brings more men to ruin than to weal.

GUARD: May I speak? Or shall I just turn and go?

CREON: Knowest thou not that even now thy voice offends?

GUARD: Is thy smart in the ears, or in the soul?

CREON: And why wouldst thou define the seat of my pain?

GUARD: The doer vexes thy mind, but I, thine ears.

CREON: Ah, thou art a born babbler, 'tis well seen.

GUARD: May be, but never the doer of this deed.

CREON: Yea, and more,—the seller of thy life for silver.

GUARD: Alas! 'Tis sad, truly, that he who judges should misjudge.

CREON: Let thy fancy play with 'judgment' as it will;—but, if ye show me not the doers of these things, ye shall avow that dastardly gains work sorrows.   [*Exit.*

GUARD: Well, may he be found! so 'twere best. But, be he caught or be he not—fortune must settle that—truly thou wilt not see me here again. Saved, even now, beyond hope and thought, I owe the gods great thanks.   [*Exit.*

CHORUS: Wonders are many, and none is more wonderful than man; the power that crosses the white sea, driven by the stormy south-wind, making a path under surges that threaten to engulf him; and Earth, the eldest of the gods, the immortal, the unwearied, doth he wear, turning the soil with the offspring of horses, as the ploughs go to and fro from year to year.

And the light-hearted race of birds, and the tribes of savage beasts, and the sea-brood of the deep, he snares in the meshes of his woven toils, he leads captive, man excellent in wit. And he masters by his arts the beast whose lair is in the wilds, who roams the hills; he tames the horse of shaggy mane, he puts the yoke upon its neck, he tames the tireless mountain bull.

And speech, and wind-swift thought, and all the moods that mould a state, hath he taught himself; and how to flee the arrows of the frost, when 'tis hard lodging under the clear sky, and the arrows of the rushing rain; yea, he hath resource for all; without resource he meets nothing that must come: only against Death shall he call for aid in vain; but from baffling maladies he hath devised escapes.

Cunning beyond fancy's dream is the fertile skill which brings him, now to evil, now to good. When he honours the laws of the land, and that justice which he hath sworn by the gods to uphold, proudly stands his city: no city hath he who, for his rashness, dwells with sin. Never may he

share my hearth, never think my thoughts, who doth these things!

[*Enter the* GUARD, *on the spectators' left, leading in* ANTIGONE.

What portent from the gods is this?—my soul is amazed. I know her—how can I deny that yon maiden is Antigone?

O hapless, and child of hapless sire,—of Oedipus! What means this? Thou brought a prisoner?—thou, disloyal to the King's laws, and taken in folly?

GUARD: Here she is, the doer of the deed:—we caught this girl burying him:—but where is Creon?

CHORUS: Lo, he comes forth again from the house, at our need.

CREON: What is it? What hath chanced, that makes my coming timely?

GUARD: O King, against nothing should men pledge their word; for the after-thought belies the first intent. I could have vowed that I should not soon be here again,—scared by thy threats, with which I had just been lashed: but,—since the joy that surprises and transcends our hopes is like in fulness to no other pleasure,—I have come, though 'tis in breach of my sworn oath, bringing this maid; who was taken showing grace to the dead. This time there was no casting of lots; no, this luck hath fallen to me, and to none else. And now, Sire, take her thyself, question her, examine her, as thou wilt; but I have a right to free and final quittance of this trouble.

CREON: And thy prisoner here—how and whence hast thou taken her?

GUARD: She was burying the man; thou knowest all.

CREON: Dost thou mean what thou sayest? Dost thou speak aright?

GUARD: I saw her burying the corpse that thou hadst forbidden to bury. Is that plain and clear?

CREON: And how was she seen? how taken in the act?

GUARD: It befell on this wise. When we

had come to the place,—with those dread menaces of thine upon us,—we swept away all the dust that covered the corpse, and bared the dank body well; and then sat us down on the brow of the hill, to windward, heedful that the smell from him should not strike us; every man was wide awake, and kept his neighbour alert with torrents of threats, if any one should be careless of this task.

So went it, until the sun's bright orb stood in mid heaven, and the heat began to burn: and then suddenly a whirlwind lifted from the earth a storm of dust, a trouble in the sky, and filled the plain, marring all the leafage of its woods; and the wide air was choked therewith: we closed our eyes, and bore the plague from the gods.

And when, after a long while, this storm had passed, the maid was seen; and she cried aloud with the sharp cry of a bird in its bitterness,—even as when, within the empty nest, it sees the bed stripped of its nestlings. So she also, when she saw the corpse bare, lifted up a voice of wailing, and called down curses on the doers of that deed. And straightway she brought thirsty dust in her hands; and from a shapely ewer of bronze, held high, with thrice-poured drink-offering she crowned the dead.

We rushed forward when we saw it, and at once closed upon our quarry, who was in no wise dismayed. Then we taxed her with her past and present doings; and she stood not on denial of aught,—at once to my joy and to my pain. To have escaped from ills one's self is a great joy; but 'tis painful to bring friends to ill. Howbeit, all such things are of less account to me than mine own safety.

CREON: Thou—thou whose face is bent to earth—dost thou avow, or disavow, this deed?

ANTIGONE: I avow it; I make no denial.

CREON: [*To* GUARD] Thou canst betake thee whither thou wilt, free and clear of a grave charge.   [*Exit* GUARD.

[*To* ANTIGONE] Now, tell me thou—not in many words, but briefly—knewest thou that an edict had forbidden this?

ANTIGONE: I knew it: Could I help it? It was public.

CREON: And thou didst indeed dare to transgress that law?

ANTIGONE: Yes; for it was not Zeus that had published me that edict; not such are the laws set among men by the Justice who dwells with the gods below; nor deemed I that thy decrees were of such force, that a mortal could override the unwritten and unfailing statutes of heaven. For their life is not of to-day or yesterday, but from all time, and no man knows when they were first put forth.

Not through dread of any human pride could I answer to the gods for breaking *these*. Die I must,—I knew that well (how should I not?)—even without thy edicts. But if I am to die before my time, I count that a gain: for when any one lives, as I do, compassed about with evils, can such an one find aught but gain in death?

So for me to meet this doom is trifling grief; but if I had suffered my mother's son to lie in death an unburied corpse, that would have grieved me; for this, I am not grieved. And if my present deeds are foolish in thy sight, it may be that a foolish judge arraigns my folly.

CHORUS: The maid shows herself passionate child of passionate sire, and knows not how to bend before troubles.

CREON: Yet I would have thee know that o'er-stubborn spirits are most often humbled; 'tis the stiffest iron, baked to hardness in the fire, that thou shalt oftenest see snapped and shivered; and I have known horses that show temper brought to order by a little curb; there is no room for pride, when thou art thy neighbour's slave.—This girl was already versed in insolence when she transgressed the laws that had been set forth; and, that done, lo, a second insult,

—to vaunt of this, and exult in her deed.

Now verily I am no man, she is the man, if this victory shall rest with her, and bring no penalty. No! be she sister's child, or nearer to me in blood than any that worships Zeus at the altar of our house,—she and her kinsfolk shall not avoid a doom most dire; for indeed I charge that other with a like share in the plotting of this burial.

And summon her—for I saw her e'en now within,—raving and not mistress of her wits. So oft, before the deed, the mind stands self-convicted in its treason, when folks are plotting mischief in the dark. But verily this, too, is hateful,—when one who hath been caught in wickedness then seeks to make the crime a glory.

ANTIGONE: Wouldst thou do more than take and slay me?

CREON: No more, indeed; having that, I have all.

ANTIGONE: Why then dost thou delay? In thy discourse there is nought that pleases me,—never may there be!—and so my words must needs be unpleasing to thee. And yet, for glory—whence could I have won a nobler, than by giving burial to mine own brother? All here would own that they thought it well, were not their lips sealed by fear. But royalty, blest in so much besides, hath the power to do and say what it will.

CREON: Thou differest from all these Thebans in that view.

ANTIGONE: These also share it; but they curb their tongues for thee.

CREON: And art thou not ashamed to act apart from them?

ANTIGONE: No; there is nothing shameful in piety to a brother.

CREON: Was it not a brother, too, that died in the opposite cause?

ANTIGONE: Brother by the same mother and the same sire.

CREON: Why, then, dost thou render a grace that is impious in his sight?

ANTIGONE: The dead man will not say that he so deems it.

CREON: Yea, if thou makest him but equal in honour with the wicked.

ANTIGONE: It was his brother, not his slave, that perished.

CREON: Wasting this land; while *he* fell as its champion.

ANTIGONE: Nevertheless, Hades desires these rites.

CREON: But the good desires not a like portion with the evil.

ANTIGONE: Who knows but this seems blameless in the world below?

CREON: A foe is never a friend—not even in death.

ANTIGONE: 'Tis not my nature to join in hating, but in loving.

CREON: Pass, then, to the world of the dead, and, if thou must needs love, love them. While I live, no woman shall rule me.

[*Enter* ISMENE *from the house, led in by two Attendants.*

CHORUS: Lo, yonder Ismene comes forth, shedding such tears as fond sisters weep; a cloud upon her brow casts its shadow over her darkly-flushing face, and breaks in rain on her fair cheek.

CREON: And thou, who, lurking like a viper in my house, wast secretly draining my life-blood, while I knew not that I was nurturing two pests, to rise against my throne—come, tell me now, wilt thou also confess thy part in this burial, or wilt thou forswear all knowledge of it?

ISMENE: I have done the deed,—if she allows my claim—and share the burden of the charge.

ANTIGONE: Nay, justice will not suffer thee to do that: thou didst not consent to the deed, nor did I give thee part in it.

ISMENE: But, now that ills beset thee, I am not ashamed to sail the sea of trouble at thy side.

ANTIGONE: Whose was the deed, Hades

and the dead are witnesses: a friend in words is not the friend that I love.

ISMENE: Nay, sister, reject me not, but let me die with thee, and duly honour the dead.

ANTIGONE: Share not thou my death, nor claim deeds to which thou hast not put thy hand: my death will suffice.

ISMENE: And what life is dear to me, bereft of thee?

ANTIGONE: Ask Creon; all thy care is for him.

ISMENE: Why vex me thus, when it avails thee nought?

ANTIGONE: Indeed, if I mock, 'tis with pain that I mock thee.

ISMENE: Tell me,—how can I serve thee, even now?

ANTIGONE: Save thyself: I grudge not thy escape.

ISMENE: Ah, woe is me! And shall I have no share in thy fate?

ANTIGONE: Thy choice was to live; mine, to die.

ISMENE: At least thy choice was not made without my protest.

ANTIGONE: One world approved thy wisdom; another, mine.

ISMENE: Howbeit, the offence is the same for both of us.

ANTIGONE: Be of good cheer; thou livest; but my life hath long been given to death, that so I might serve the dead.

CREON: Lo, one of these maidens hath newly shown herself foolish, as the other hath been since her life began.

ISMENE: Yea, O King, such reason as nature may have given abides not with the unfortunate, but goes astray.

CREON: Thine did, when thou chosest vile deeds with the vile.

ISMENE: What life could I endure, without her presence?

CREON: Nay, speak not of her 'presence'; she lives no more.

ISMENE: But wilt thou slay the betrothed of thine own son?

CREON: Nay, there are other fields for him to plough.

ISMENE: But there can never be such love as bound him to her.

CREON: I like not an evil wife for my son.

ANTIGONE: Haemon, beloved! How thy father wrongs thee!

CREON: Enough, enough of thee and of thy marriage!

CHORUS: Wilt thou indeed rob thy son of this maiden?

CREON: 'Tis Death that shall stay these bridals for me.

CHORUS: 'Tis determined, it seems, that she shall die.

CREON: Determined, yes, for thee and for me. —[*To the two Attendants*] No more delay—servants, take them within! Henceforth they must be women, and not range at large; for verily even the bold seek to fly, when they see Death now closing on their life.

[*Exeunt Attendants, guarding* ANTIGONE *and* ISMENE.—CREON *remains.*

CHORUS: Blest are they whose days have not tasted of evil. For when a house hath once been shaken from heaven, there the curse fails nevermore, passing from life to life of the race; even as, when the surge is driven over the darkness of the deep by the fierce breath of Thracian sea-winds, it rolls up the black sand from the depths, and there is a sullen roar from windvexed headlands that front the blows of the storm.

I see that from olden time the sorrows in the house of the Labdacidae are heaped upon the sorrows of the dead; and generation is not freed by generation, but some god strikes them down, and the race hath no deliverance.

For now that hope of which the light had been spread above the last root of the house of Oedipus—that hope, in turn, is brought low—by the blood-stained dust due to the gods infernal, and by folly in speech, and frenzy at the heart.

Thy power, O Zeus, what human trespass can limit? That power which neither Sleep, the all-ensnaring, nor the untiring months of the gods can master; but thou, a ruler to whom time brings not old age, dwellest in the dazzling splendour of Olympus.

And through the future, near and far, as through the past, shall this law hold good: Nothing that is vast enters into the life of mortals without a curse.

For that hope whose wanderings are so wide is to many men a comfort, but to many a false lure of giddy desires; and the disappointment comes on one who knoweth nought till he burn his foot against the hot fire.

For with wisdom hath some one given forth the famous saying, that evil seems good, soon or late, to him whose mind the god draws to mischief; and but for the briefest space doth he fare free of woe.

But lo, Haemon, the last of thy sons;—comes he grieving for the doom of his promised bride, Antigone, and bitter for the baffled hope of his marriage?

[*Enter* HAEMON.

CREON: We shall know soon, better than seers could tell us.—My son, hearing the fixed doom of thy betrothed, art thou come in rage against thy father? Or have I thy good will, act how I may?

HAEMON: Father, I am thine; and thou, in thy wisdom, tracest for me rules which I shall follow. No marriage shall be deemed by me a greater gain than thy good guidance.

CREON: Yea, this, my son, should be thy heart's fixed law,—in all things to obey thy father's will. 'Tis for this that men pray to see dutiful children grow up around them in their homes,—that such may requite their father's foe with evil, and honour, as their father doth, his friend. But he who begets unprofitable children—what shall we say that he hath sown, but troubles for himself, and much triumph for his foes? Then do not thou, my son, at pleasure's beck, dethrone thy reason for a woman's sake; knowing that this is a joy that soon grows cold in clasping arms,—an evil woman to share thy bed and thy home. For what wound could strike deeper than a false friend? Nay, with loathing, and as if she were thine enemy, let this girl go to find a husband in the house of Hades. For since I have taken her, alone of all the city, in open disobedience, I will not make myself a liar to my people—I will slay her.

So let her appeal as she will to the majesty of kindred blood. If I am to nurture mine own kindred in naughtiness, needs must I bear with it in aliens. He who does his duty in his own household will be found righteous in the State also. But if any one transgresses, and does violence to the laws, or thinks to dictate to his rulers, such an one can win no praise from me. No, whomsoever the city may appoint, that man must be obeyed, in little things and great, in just things and unjust; and I should feel sure that one who thus obeys would be a good ruler no less than a good subject, and in the storm of spears would stand his ground where he was set, loyal and dauntless at his comrade's side.

But disobedience is the worst of evils. This it is that ruins cities; this makes homes desolate; by this, the ranks of allies are broken into headlong rout: but, of the lives whose course is fair, the greater part owes safety to obedience. Therefore we must support the cause of order, and in no wise suffer a woman to worst us. Better to fall from power, if we must, by a man's hand; then we should not be called weaker than a woman.

CHORUS: To us, unless our years have stolen our wit thou seemest to say wisely what thou sayest.

HAEMON: Father, the gods implant reason in men, the highest of all things that we call our own. Not mine the skill—far from me be the quest!—to say wherein thou speakest not aright; and yet another man, too, might have some useful thought. At least, it is my natural office to watch, on thy behalf, all that men say, or do, or find to blame. For the dread of thy frown forbids the citizen to speak such words as would offend thine ear; but I can hear these murmurs in the dark, these moanings of the city for this maiden; 'no woman,' they say, 'ever merited her doom less,—none ever was to die so shamefully for deeds so glorious as hers; who, when her own brother had fallen in bloody strife, would not leave him unburied, to be devoured by carrion dogs, or by any bird:—deserves not *she* the meed of golden honour?'

Such is the darkling rumour that spreads in secret. For me, my father, no treasure is so precious as thy welfare. What, indeed, is a nobler ornament for children than a prospering sire's fair fame, or for sire than son's? Wear not, then, one mood only in thyself; think not that thy word, and thine alone, must be right. For if any man thinks that he alone is wise,—that in speech, or in mind, he hath no peer,—such a soul, when laid open, is ever found empty.

No, though a man be wise, 'tis no shame for him to learn many things, and to bend in season. Seest thou, beside the wintry torrent's course, how the trees that yield to it save every twig, while the stiff-necked perish root and branch? And even thus he who keeps the sheet of his sail taut, and never slackens it, upsets his boat, and finishes his voyage with keel uppermost.

Nay, forgo thy wrath; permit thyself to change. For if I, a younger man, may offer my thought, it were far best, I ween, that men should be all-wise by nature; but, otherwise—and oft the scale inclines not so —'tis good also to learn from those who speak aright.

CHORUS: Sire, 'tis meet that thou should-est profit by his words, if he speaks aught in season, and thou, Haemon, by thy father's; for on both parts there hath been wise speech.

CREON: Men of my age—are we indeed to be schooled, then, by men of his?

HAEMON: In nothing that is not right; but if I am young, thou shouldest look to my merits, not to my years.

CREON: Is it a merit to honour the unruly?

HAEMON: I could wish no one to show respect for evil-doers.

CREON: Then is not she tainted with that malady?

HAEMON: Our Theban folk, with one voice, denies it.

CREON: Shall Thebes prescribe to me how I must rule?

HAEMON: See, there thou hast spoken like a youth indeed.

CREON: Am I to rule this land by other judgment than mine own?

HAEMON: That is no city, which belongs to one man.

CREON: Is not the city held to be the ruler's?

HAEMON: Thou wouldst make a good monarch of a desert.

CREON: This boy, it seems, is the woman's champion.

HAEMON: If thou art a woman; indeed, my care is for thee.

CREON: Shameless, at open feud with thy father!

HAEMON: Nay, I see thee offending against justice.

CREON: Do I offend, when I respect mine own prerogatives?

HAEMON: Thou dost not respect them, thou tramplest on the gods' honours.

CREON: O dastard nature, yielding place to a woman!

HAEMON: Thou wilt never find me yield to baseness.

CREON: All thy words, at least, plead for that girl.

HAEMON: And for thee, and for me, and for the gods below.

CREON: Thou canst never marry her, on this side the grave.

HAEMON: Then she must die, and in death destroy another.

CREON: How! doth thy boldness run to open threats?

HAEMON: What threat is it, to combat vain resolves?

CREON: Thou shalt rue thy witless teaching of wisdom.

HAEMON: Wert thou not my father, I would have called thee unwise.

CREON: Thou woman's slave, use not wheedling speech with me.

HAEMON: Thou wouldest speak, and then hear no reply?

CREON: Sayest thou so? Now, by the heaven above us—be sure of it—thou shalt smart for taunting me in this opprobrious strain. Bring forth that hated thing, that she may die forthwith in his presence—before his eyes—at her bridegroom's side!

HAEMON: No, not at my side—never think it—shall she perish; nor shalt thou ever set eyes more upon my face:—rave, then, with such friends as can endure thee. [*Exit* HAEMON.

CHORUS: The man is gone, O King, in angry haste; a youthful mind, when stung, is fierce.

CREON: Let him do, or dream, more than man—good speed to him!—But he shall not save these two girls from their doom.

CHORUS: Dost thou indeed purpose to slay both?

CREON: Not her whose hands are pure: thou sayest well.

CHORUS: And by what doom mean'st thou to slay the other?

CREON: I will take her where the path is loneliest, and hide her, living, in a rocky vault, with so much food set forth as piety prescribes, that the city may avoid a public stain. And there, praying to Hades, the only god whom she worships, perchance she will

obtain release from death; or else will learn, at last, though late, that it is lost labour to revere the dead. [*Exit* CREON.

CHORUS: Love, unconquered in the fight, Love, who makest havoc of wealth, who keepest thy vigil on the soft cheek of a maiden; thou roamest over the sea, and among the homes of dwellers in the wilds; no immortal can escape thee, nor any among men whose life is for a day; and he to whom thou hast come is mad.

The just themselves have their minds warped by thee to wrong, for their ruin: 'tis thou that hast stirred up this present strife of kinsmen; victorious is the love-kindling light from the eyes of the fair bride; it is a power enthroned in sway beside the eternal laws; for there the goddess Aphrodite is working her unconquerable will.

But now I also am carried beyond the bounds of loyalty, and can no more keep back the streaming tears, when I see Antigone thus passing to the bridal chamber where all are laid to rest.

ANTIGONE: See me, citizens of my fatherland, setting forth on my last way, looking my last on the sunlight that is for me no more; no, Hades who gives sleep to all leads me living to Acheron's shore; who have had no portion in the chant that brings the bride, nor hath any song been mine for the crowning of bridals; whom the lord of the Dark Lake shall wed.

CHORUS: Glorious, therefore, and with praise, thou departest to that deep place of the dead: wasting sickness hath not smitten thee; thou hast not found the wages of the sword; no, mistress of thine own fate, and still alive, thou shalt pass to Hades, as no other of mortal kind hath passed.

ANTIGONE: I have heard in other days how dread a doom befell our Phrygian guest, the daughter of Tantalus, on the Sipylian heights; how, like clinging ivy, the growth of stone subdued her; and the rains fail not, as men tell, from her wasting form, nor fails the snow; while beneath her weeping lids the tears bedew her bosom; and most like to hers is the fate that brings me to my rest.

CHORUS: Yet she was a goddess, thou knowest, and born of gods; we are mortals, and of mortal race. But 'tis great renown for a woman who hath perished that she should have shared the doom of the godlike, in her life, and afterward in death.

ANTIGONE: Ah, I am mocked! In the name of our fathers' gods, can ye not wait till I am gone,—must ye taunt me to my face, O my city, and ye, her wealthy sons? Ah, fount of Dirce, and thou holy ground of Thebe whose chariots are many; ye, at least, will bear me witness, in what sort, unwept of friends, and by what laws I pass to the rock-closed prison of my strange tomb, ah me unhappy! who have no home on the earth or in the shades, no home with the living or with the dead.

CHORUS: Thou hast rushed forward to the utmost verge of daring; and against that throne where Justice sits on high thou hast fallen, my daughter, with a grievous fall. But in this ordeal thou art paying, haply, for thy father's sin.

ANTIGONE: Thou hast touched on my bitterest thought,—awaking the ever-new lament for my sire and for all the doom given to us, the famed house of Labdacus. Alas for the horrors of the mother's bed! alas for the wretched mother's slumber at the side of her own son,—and my sire! From what manner of parents did I take my miserable being! And to them I go thus, accursed, unwed, to share their home. Alas, my brother, ill-starred in thy marriage, in thy death thou hast undone my life!

CHORUS: Reverent action claims a certain praise for reverence; but an offence against power cannot be brooked by him who hath power in his keeping. Thy self-willed temper hath wrought thy ruin.

ANTIGONE: Unwept, unfriended, without marriage-song, I am led forth in my sorrow on this journey that can be delayed no more. No longer, hapless one, may I behold yon day-star's sacred eye; but for my fate no tear is shed, no friend makes moan.

CREON: Know ye not that songs and wailings before death would never cease, if it profited to utter them? Away with her— away! And when ye have enclosed her, according to my word, in her vaulted grave, leave her alone, forlorn—whether she wishes to die, or to live a buried life in such a home. Our hands are clean as touching this maiden. But this is certain—she shall be deprived of her sojourn in the light.

ANTIGONE: Tomb, bridal-chamber, eternal prison in the caverned rock, whither I go to find mine own, those many who have perished, and whom Persephone hath received among the dead! Last of all shall I pass thither, and far most miserably of all, before the term of my life is spent. But I cherish good hope that my coming will be welcome to my father, and pleasant to thee, my mother, and welcome, brother, to thee; for, when ye died, with mine own hands I washed and dressed you, and poured drink-offerings at your graves; and now, Polyneices, 'tis for tending thy corpse that I win such recompense as this.

And yet I honoured thee, as the wise will deem, rightly. Never, had I been a mother of children, or if a husband had been mouldering in death, would I have taken this task upon me in the city's despite. What law, ye ask, is my warrant for that word? The husband lost, another might have been found, and child from another, to replace the first-born; but, father and mother hidden with Hades, no brother's life could ever bloom for me again. Such was the law whereby I held thee first in honour; but Creon deemed me guilty of error therein, and of outrage, ah brother mine! And now he leads me thus, a captive in his hands; no bridal bed, no bridal song hath been mine, no joy of marriage, no portion in the nurture of children; but thus, forlorn of friends, unhappy one, I go living to the vaults of death.

And what law of heaven have I transgressed? Why, hapless one, should I look to the gods any more,—what ally should I invoke,—when by piety I have earned the name of impious? Nay, then, if these things are pleasing to the gods, when I have suffered my doom, I shall come to know my sin; but if the sin is with my judges, I could wish them no fuller measure of evil than they, on their part, mete wrongfully to me.

CHORUS: Still the same tempest of the soul vexes this maiden with the same fierce gusts.

CREON: Then for this shall her guards have cause to rue their slowness.

ANTIGONE: Ah me! that word hath come very near to death.

CREON: I can cheer thee with no hope that this doom is not thus to be fulfilled.

ANTIGONE: O city of my fathers in the land of Thebe! O ye gods, eldest of our race!—they lead me hence—now, now—they tarry not! Behold me, princes of Thebes, the last daughter of the house of your kings,—see what I suffer, and from whom, because I feared to cast away the fear of Heaven!

[ANTIGONE *is led away by the* GUARDS.

CHORUS: Even thus endured Danae in her beauty to change the light of day for brass-bound walls; and in that chamber, secret as the grave, she was held close prisoner; yet was she of a proud lineage, O my daughter, and charged with the keeping of the seed of Zeus, that fell in the golden rain.

But dreadful is the mysterious power of fate; there is no deliverance from it by wealth or by war, by fenced city, or dark, sea-beaten ships.

And bonds tamed the son of Dryas, swift to wrath, that king of the Edonians; so paid he for his frenzied taunts, when, by the will of Dionysus, he was pent in a rocky prison. There the fierce exuberance of his madness slowly passed away. That man learned to know the god, whom in his frenzy he had provoked with mockeries; for he had sought to quell the god-possessed women, and the Bacchanalian fire; and he angered the Muses that love the flute.

And by the waters of the Dark Rocks, the waters of the twofold sea, are the shores of Bosporus, and Thracian Salmydessus; where Ares, neighbour to the city, saw the accurst, blinding wound dealt to the two sons of Phineus by his fierce wife,—the wound that brought darkness to those vengeance-craving orbs, smitten with her bloody hands, smitten with her shuttle for a dagger.

Pining in their misery, they bewailed their cruel doom, those sons of a mother hapless in her marriage; but she traced her descent from the ancient line of the Erechtheidae; and in far-distant caves she was nursed amid her father's storms, that child of Boreas, swift as a steed over the steep hills, a daughter of gods; yet upon her also the grey Fates bore hard, my daughter.

[*Enter* TEIRESIAS, *led by a* BOY, *on the spectators' right.*

TEIRESIAS: Princes of Thebes, we have come with linked steps, both served by the eyes of one; for thus, by a guide's help, the blind must walk.

CREON: And what, aged Teiresias, are thy tidings?

TEIRESIAS: I will tell thee; and do thou hearken to the seer.

CREON: Indeed, it has not been my wont to slight thy counsel.

TEIRESIAS: Therefore didst thou steer our city's course aright.

CREON: I have felt, and can attest, thy benefits.

TEIRESIAS: Mark that now, once more, thou standest on fate's fine edge.

CREON: What means this? How I shudder at thy message!

TEIRESIAS: Thou wilt learn, when thou hearest the warnings of mine art. As I took my place on mine old seat of augury, where all birds have been wont to gather within my ken, I heard a strange voice among them; they were screaming with dire, feverish rage, that drowned their language in a jargon; and I knew that they were rending each other with their talons, murderously; the whirr of wings told no doubtful tale.

Forthwith, in fear, I essayed burnt-sacrifice on a duly kindled altar; but from my offerings the Fire-god showed no flame; a dank moisture, oozing from the thigh-flesh, trickled forth upon the embers, and smoked, and sputtered; the gall was scattered to the air; and the streaming thighs lay bared of the fat that had been wrapped round them.

Such was the failure of the rites by which I vainly asked a sign, as from this boy I learned; for he is my guide, as I am guide to others. And 'tis thy counsel that hath brought this sickness on our state. For the altars of our city and of our hearths have been tainted, one and all, by birds and dogs, with carrion from the hapless corpse, the son of Oedipus: and therefore the gods no more accept prayer and sacrifice at our hands, or the flame of meat-offering; nor doth any bird give a clear sign by its shrill cry, for they have tasted the fatness of a slain man's blood.

Think, then, on these things, my son. All men are liable to err; but when an error hath been made, that man is no longer witless or unblest who heals the ill into which he hath fallen, and remains not stubborn. Self-will, we know, incurs the charge of folly. Nay, allow the claim of the dead; stab not the fallen; what prowess is it to slay the slain anew? I have sought thy good, and for thy good I speak: and never is it sweeter to learn from a good counsellor than when he counsels for thine own gain.

CREON: Old man, ye all shoot your shafts at me, as archers at the butts;—ye must needs practice on me with seer-craft also; —aye, the seer-tribe hath long trafficked in me, and made me their merchandise. Gain your gains, drive your trade, if ye list, in the silver-gold of Sardis and the gold of India; but ye shall not hide that man in the grave, —no, though the eagles of Zeus should bear the carrion morsels to their Master's throne—no, not for dread of that defilement will I suffer his burial:—for well I know that no mortal can defile the gods. —But, aged Teiresias, the wisest fall with a shameful fall, when they clothe shameful thoughts in fair words, for lucre's sake.

TEIRESIAS: Alas! Doth any man know, doth any consider . . .

CREON: Whereof? What general truth dost thou announce?

TEIRESIAS: How precious, above all wealth, is good counsel.

CREON: As folly, I think, is the worst mischief.

TEIRESIAS: Yet thou art tainted with that distemper.

CREON: I would not answer the seer with a taunt.

TEIRESIAS: But thou dost, in saying that I prophesy falsely.

CREON: Well, the prophet-tribe was ever fond of money.

TEIRESIAS: And the race bred of tyrants loves base gain.

CREON: Knowest thou that thy speech is spoken of thy king?

TEIRESIAS: I know it; for through me thou hast saved Thebes.

CREON: Thou art a wise seer; but thou lovest evil deeds.

TEIRESIAS: Thou wilt rouse me to utter the dread secret in my soul.

CREON: Out with it!—Only speak it not for gain.

TEIRESIAS: Indeed, methinks, I shall not, —as touching thee.

CREON: Know that thou shalt not trade on my resolve.

TEIRESIAS: Then know thou—aye, know it well—that thou shalt not live through many more courses of the sun's swift chariot, ere one begotten of thine own loins shall have been given by thee, a corpse for corpses; because thou hast thrust children of the sunlight to the shades, and ruthlessly lodged a living soul in the grave; but keepest in this world one who belongs to the gods infernal, a corpse unburied, unhonoured, all unhallowed. In such thou hast no part, nor have the gods above, but this is a violence done to them by thee. Therefore the avenging destroyers lie in wait for thee, the Furies of Hades and of the gods, that thou mayest be taken in these same ills.

And mark well if I speak these things as a hireling. A time not long to be delayed shall awaken the wailing of men and of women in thy house. And a tumult of hatred against thee stirs all the cities whose mangled sons had the burial-rite from dogs, or from wild beasts, or from some winged bird that bore a polluting breath to each city that contains the hearths of the dead.

Such arrows for thy heart—since thou provokest me—have I launched at thee, archer-like, in my anger,—sure arrows, of which thou shalt not escape the smart. —Boy, lead me home, that he may spend his rage on younger men, and learn to keep a tongue more temperate, and to bear within his breast a better mind than now he bears.

[*Exit* TEIRESIAS.

CHORUS: The man hath gone, O King, with dread prophecies. And, since the hair on his head, once dark, hath been white, I know that he hath never been a false prophet to our city.

CREON: I, too, know it well, and am troubled in soul. 'Tis dire to yield; but, by resistance, to smite my pride with ruin—this, too, is a dire choice.

CHORUS: Son of Menoeceus, it behoves thee to take wise counsel.

CREON: What should I do, then? Speak, and I will obey.

CHORUS: Go thou, and free the maiden from her rocky chamber, and make a tomb for the unburied dead.

CREON: And this is thy counsel? Thou wouldst have me yield?

CHORUS: Yea, King, and with all speed; for swift harms from the gods cut short the folly of men.

CREON: Ah me, 'tis hard, but I resign my cherished resolve,—I obey. We must not wage a vain war with destiny.

CHORUS: Go, thou, and do these things; leave them not to others.

CREON: Even as I am I'll go:—on, on, my servants, each and all of you,—take axes in your hands, and hasten to the ground that ye see yonder! Since our judgment hath taken this turn, I will be present to unloose her, as I myself bound her. My heart misgives me, 'tis best to keep the established laws, even to life's end.

CHORUS: O thou of many names, glory of the Cadmeian bride, offspring of loud-thundering Zeus! thou who watchest over famed Italia, and reignest, where all guests are welcomed, in the sheltered plain of Eleusinian Deo! O Bacchus, dweller in Thebe, mother-city of Bacchants, by the softly-gliding stream of Ismenus, on the soil where the fierce dragon's teeth were sown!

Thou hast been seen where torch-flames glare through smoke, above the crests of the twin peaks, where move the Corycian nymphs, thy votaries, hard by Castalia's stream.

Thou comest from the ivy-mantled slopes of Nysa's hills, and from the shore green with many-clustered vines, while thy name is lifted up on strains of more than mortal power, as thou visitest the ways of Thebe:

Thebe, of all cities, thou holdest first in honour, thou, and thy mother whom the lightning smote; and now, when all our people is captive to a violent plague, come thou with healing feet over the Parnassian height, or over the moaning strait!

Oh thou with whom the stars rejoice as they move, the stars whose breath is fire; O master of the voices of the night; son begotten of Zeus; appear, O king, with thine attendant Thyiads, who in night-long frenzy dance before thee, the giver of good gifts, Iacchus!

[*Enter* MESSENGER, *on the spectators' left hand.*]

MESSENGER: Dwellers by the house of Cadmus and of Amphion, there is no estate of mortal life that I would ever praise or blame as settled. Fortune raises and Fortune humbles the lucky or unlucky from day to day, and no one can prophesy to men concerning those things which are established. For Creon was blest once, as I count bliss; he had saved this land of Cadmus from its foes; he was clothed with sole dominion in the land; he reigned, the glorious sire of princely children. And now all hath been lost. For when a man hath forfeited his pleasures, I count him not as living,—I hold him but a breathing corpse. Heap up riches in thy house, if thou wilt; live in kingly state; yet, if there be no gladness therewith, I would not give the shadow of a vapour for all the rest, compared with joy.

CHORUS: And what is this new grief that thou hast to tell for our princes?

MESSENGER: Death; and the living are guilty for the dead.

CHORUS: And who is the slayer? Who the stricken? Speak.

MESSENGER: Haemon hath perished; his blood hath been shed by no stranger.

CHORUS: By his father's hand, or by his own?

MESSENGER: By his own, in wrath with his sire for the murder.

CHORUS: O prophet, how true, then, hast thou proved thy word!

MESSENGER: These things stand thus; ye must consider of the rest.

CHORUS: Lo, I see the hapless Eurydice, Creon's wife, approaching; she comes from the house by chance, haply,—or because she knows the tidings of her son.

[*Enter* EURYDICE.]

EURYDICE: People of Thebes, I heard your words as I was going forth, to salute the goddess Pallas with my prayers. Even as I was loosing the fastenings of the gate, to open it, the message of a household woe smote on mine ear: I sank back, terror-stricken, into the arms of my handmaids, and my senses fled. But say again what the tidings were; I shall hear them as one who is no stranger to sorrow.

MESSENGER: Dear lady, I will witness of what I saw, and will leave no word of the truth untold. Why, indeed, should I soothe thee with words in which I must presently be found false? Truth is ever best.—I attended thy lord as his guide to the furthest part of the plain, where the body of Polyneices, torn by dogs, still lay unpitied. We prayed the goddess of the roads, and Pluto, in mercy to restrain their wrath; we washed the dead with holy washing; and with freshly-plucked boughs we solemnly burned such relics as there were. We raised a high mound of his native earth; and then we turned away to enter the maiden's nuptial chamber with rocky couch, the caverned mansion of the bride of Death. And, from afar off, one of us heard a voice of loud wailing at that bride's unhallowed bower; and came to tell our master Creon.

And as the King drew nearer, doubtful sounds of a bitter cry floated around him; he groaned, and said in accents of anguish, 'Wretched that I am, can my foreboding be true? Am I going on the wofullest way that ever I went? My son's voice greets me. —Go, my servants,—haste ye nearer, and when ye have reached the tomb, pass through the gap, where the stones have been wrenched away, to the cell's very mouth,— and look, and see if 'tis Haemon's voice that

I know, or if mine ear is cheated by the gods.'

This search, at our despairing master's word, we went to make; and in the furthest part of the tomb we descried *her* hanging by the neck, slung by a threadwrought halter of fine linen; while *he* was embracing her with arms thrown around her waist,—bewailing the loss of his bride who is with the dead, and his father's deeds, and his own ill-starred love.

But his father, when he saw him, cried aloud with a dread cry, and went in, and called to him with a voice of wailing:—'Unhappy, what a deed hast thou done! What thought hath come to thee? What manner of mischance hath marred thy reason? Come forth, my child! I pray thee—I implore!' But the boy glared at him with fierce eyes, spat in his face, and, without a word of answer, drew his cross-hilted sword:—as his father rushed forth in flight, he missed his aim;—then, hapless one, wroth with himself, he straightway leaned with all his weight against his sword, and drove it, half its length, into his side; and, while sense lingered, he clasped the maiden to his faint embrace, and, as he gasped, sent forth on her pale cheek the swift stream of the oozing blood.

Corpse enfolding corpse he lies; he hath won his nuptial rites, poor youth, not here, yet in the halls of Death; and he hath witnessed to mankind that, of all curses which cleave to man, ill counsel is the sovereign curse.   [EURYDICE *retires into the house.*

CHORUS: What wouldst thou augur from this? The lady hath turned back, and is gone, without a word, good or evil.

MESSENGER: I, too, am startled; yet I nourish the hope that, at these sore tidings of her son, she cannot deign to give her sorrow public vent, but in the privacy of the house will set her handmaids to mourn the household grief. For she is not untaught of discretion, that she should err.

CHORUS: I know not; but to me, at least, a strained silence seems to portend peril, no less than vain abundance of lament.

MESSENGER: Well, I will enter the house, and learn whether indeed she is not hiding some repressed purpose in the depths of a passionate heart. Yea, thou sayest well: excess of silence, too, may have a perilous meaning.   [*Exit* MESSENGER.

[*Enter* CREON, *on the spectators' left, with* ATTENDANTS, *carrying the shrouded body of* HAEMON *on a bier.*

CHORUS: Lo, yonder the King himself draws near, bearing that which tells too clear a tale,—the work of no stranger's madness,—if we may say it,—but of his own misdeeds.

CREON: Woe for the sins of a darkened soul, stubborn sins, fraught with death! Ah, ye behold us, the sire who hath slain, the son who hath perished! Woe is me, for the wretched blindness of my counsels! Alas, my son, thou hast died in thy youth, by a timeless doom, woe is me!—thy spirit hath fled,—not by thy folly, but by mine own!

CHORUS: Ah me, how all too late thou seemest to see the right!

CREON: Ah me, I have learned the bitter lesson! But then, methinks, oh then, some god smote me from above with crushing weight, and hurled me into ways of cruelty, woe is me,—over-throwing and trampling on my joy! Woe, woe, for the troublous toils of men!

[*Enter* MESSENGER *from the house.*

MESSENGER: Sire, thou hast come, methinks, as one whose hands are not empty, but who hath store laid up besides; thou bearest yonder burden with thee; and thou art soon to look upon the woes within thy house.

CREON: And what worse ill is yet to follow upon ills?

MESSENGER: Thy queen hath died, true

mother of yon corpse—ah, hapless lady!—by blows newly dealt.

CREON: Oh Hades, all-receiving, whom no sacrifice can appease! Hast thou, then, no mercy for me? O thou herald of evil, bitter tidings, what word dost thou utter? Alas, I was already as dead, and thou hast smitten me anew! What sayest thou, my son? What is this new message that thou bringest—woe, woe is me!—of a wife's doom,—of slaughter heaped on slaughter?

CHORUS: Thou canst behold: 'tis no longer hidden within.

[*The doors of the Palace are opened, and the corpse of* EURYDICE *is disclosed.*

CREON: Ah me,—yonder I behold a new, a second woe! What destiny, ah what, can yet await me? I have but now raised my son in my arms,—and there, again, I see a corpse before me! Alas, alas, unhappy mother! Alas, my child!

MESSENGER: There, at the altar, self-stabbed with a keen knife, she suffered her darkening eyes to close, when she had wailed for the noble fate of Megareus who died before, and then for his fate who lies there,—and when, with her last breath, she had invoked evil fortunes upon thee, the slayer of thy sons.

CREON: Woe, woe! I thrill with dread. Is there none to strike me to the heart with two-edged sword?—O miserable that I am, and steeped in miserable anguish!

MESSENGER: Yea, both this son's doom, and that other's, were laid to thy charge by her whose corpse thou seest.

CREON: And what was the manner of the violent deed by which she passed away?

MESSENGER: Her own hand struck her to the heart, when she had learned her son's sorely lamented fate.

CREON: Ah me, this guilt can never be fixed on any other of mortal kind, for my acquittal! I, even I, was thy slayer, wretched that I am—I own the truth. Lead me away, O my servants, lead me hence with all speed, whose life is but as death!

CHORUS: Thy counsels are good, if there can be good with ills; briefest is best, when trouble is in our path.

CREON: Oh, let it come, let it appear, that fairest of fates, for me, that brings my last day,—aye, best fate of all! Oh, let it come, that I may never look upon to-morrow's light!

CHORUS: These things are in the future; present tasks claim our care: the ordering of the future rests where it should rest.

CREON: All my desires, at least, were summed in that prayer.

CHORUS: Pray thou no more; for mortals have no escape from destined woe.

CREON: Lead me away, I pray you; a rash, foolish man; who have slain thee, ah my son, unwittingly, and thee, too, my wife—unhappy that I am! I know not which way I should bend my gaze, or where I should seek support; for all is amiss with that which is in my hands,—and yonder, again, a crushing fate hath leapt upon my head.

[*As* CREON *is being conducted into the house, the coryphaeus speaks the closing verses.*

CHORUS: Wisdom is the supreme part of happiness; and reverence towards the gods must be inviolate. Great words of prideful men are ever punished with great blows, and, in old age, teach the chastened to be wise.

The Last Days
of Socrates

Although Socrates (c.470-399 B.C.) was an influential philosopher and teacher, he wrote nothing. Therefore we must rely on secondary accounts for information about his life and beliefs. Such accounts, particularly the writings of his most famous disciple, Plato, make it possible to reconstruct the broad outlines of his career. Socrates was born in Athens, the son of a stone-cutter. Instead of learning his father's trade, he began early in life to frequent the Athenian market-place, where he listened to the intellectuals of the city argue questions of politics, art, morality, and philosophy.

Before long, he had acquired a reputation as a man of wisdom and had gathered about himself a group of young disciples, who were intrigued by the unusual manner in which he taught. Unlike the *sophists* ("wise men"), the professional teachers of the day who were willing to teach anyone anything for a suitable fee, Socrates professed to be completely ignorant. Instead of attempting to teach, he wandered about Athens seeking wisdom by asking questions of everyone he met, including the city's leading politicians, military leaders, artists, and philosophers. As might be expected, under Socrates' questioning many of the self-styled sages of Athens proved to be without wisdom. Although Socrates' unflinching quest for wisdom and truth won him many loyal followers, it inevitably aroused the enmity of those whose ignorance he unmasked. Through their influence in Athens, his enemies succeeded in having him brought to trial and condemned to death. But they were unable to silence him, for his words live on in the Dialogues of Plato.

Although he professed to have no wisdom of his own, Socrates did have a positive philosophy. The basic premise of his philosophy was the doctrine that *virtue is knowledge*, or that the good life is the life of wisdom. To gain knowledge and, hence, virtue, he believed, education is necessary. But knowledge is not something that can be poured into an individual from the outside. Rather, it is something that lies deep within each man and needs only to be drawn out. Socrates' method for bringing this inborn knowledge to the surface was to ask a series of questions, a technique that is known as the *dialectic method*.

The selections that follow are an account of the last days of Socrates written by Plato some time after the events described. Socrates had been haled into court by a group of accusers, a sort of "un-Athenian activities committee," who charged him with being an atheist and a corrupter of youth. In Plato's *Apology*, Socrates is represented as replying to the charges with a general defense of his way of life. In the *Crito*, Plato pictures Socrates waiting in prison for his execution and arguing with a friend (who has arranged for his escape) about whether he would be justified in running away, even though he has been unjustly convicted. The extract from the *Phaedo* records Socrates' death. These selections give us a fresh and living portrait of Socrates the man, a fairly comprehensive account of his philosophy, and a glimpse of the social and legal structure of the Athens of his day.

APOLOGY

How you have felt, O men of Athens, at hearing the speeches of my accusers, I cannot tell; but I know that their persuasive words almost made me forget who I was:—such was the effect of them; and yet they have hardly spoken a word of truth. But many as their falsehoods were, there was one of them which quite amazed me;—I mean when they told you to be upon your guard, and not to let yourselves be deceived by the force of my eloquence. They ought to have been ashamed of saying this, because they were sure to be detected as soon as I opened my lips and displayed my deficiency: they certainly did appear to be most shameless in saying this, unless by the force of eloquence they mean the force of truth; for then I do indeed admit that I am eloquent. But in how different a way from theirs! Well, as I was saying, they have hardly uttered a word, or not more than a word, of truth; but you shall hear from me the whole truth: not, however, delivered after their manner, in a set oration duly ornamented with words and phrases. No, indeed! but I shall use the words and arguments which occur to me at the moment; for I am certain that this is right, and that at my time of life I ought not to be appearing before you, O men of Athens, in the character of a juvenile orator—let no one expect this of me. And I must beg of you to grant me one favor, which is this —If you hear me using the same words in my defence which I have been in the habit of using, and which most of you may have heard in the agora, and at the tables of the money-changers, or anywhere else, I would ask you not to be surprised at this, and not to interrupt me. For I am more

THE DIALOGUES OF PLATO, trans. B. Jowett (New York, 1871), I, 315-321, 326-333, 336-339.

than seventy years of age, and this is the first time that I have ever appeared in a court of law, and I am quite a stranger to the ways of the place; and therefore I would have you regard me as if I were really a stranger, whom you would excuse if he spoke in his native tongue, and after the fashion of his country;—that I think is not an unfair request. Never mind the manner, which may or may not be good; but think only of the justice of my cause, and give heed to that: let the judge decide justly and the speaker speak truly.

And first, I have to reply to the older charges and to my first accusers, and then I will go on to the later ones. For I have had many accusers, who accused me of old, and their false charges have continued during many years; and I am more afraid of them than of Anytus and his associates, who are dangerous, too, in their own way. But far more dangerous are these, who began when you were children, and took possession of your minds with their falsehoods, telling of one Socrates, a wise man, who speculated about the heaven above, and searched into the earth beneath, and made the worse appear the better cause. These are the accusers whom I dread; for they are the circulators of this rumor, and their hearers are too apt to fancy that speculators of this sort do not believe in the gods. And they are many, and their charges against me are of ancient date, and they made them in days when you were impressible—in childhood, or perhaps in youth—and the cause when heard went by default, for there was none to answer. And hardest of all, their names I do not know and can not tell; unless in the chance case of a comic poet. But the main body of these slanderers who from envy and malice have wrought upon you—and there are some of them who are convinced themselves, and impart their convictions to others—all these, I say, are most difficult to deal with; for I can not have them up here, and examine them, and therefore I must simply fight with shadows in my own defence, and examine when there is no one who answers. I will ask you then to assume with me, as I was saying, that my opponents are of two kinds; one recent, the other ancient: and I hope that you will see the propriety of my answering the latter first, for these accusations you heard long before the others, and much oftener.

Well, then, I will make my defence, and I will endeavor in the short time which is allowed to do away with this evil opinion of me which you have held for such a long time; and I hope that I may succeed, if this be well for you and me, and that my words may find favor with you. But I know that to accomplish this is not easy—I quite see the nature of the task. Let the event be as God wills: in obedience to the law I make my defence.

I will begin at the beginning, and ask what the accusation is which has given rise to this slander of me, and which has encouraged Meletus to proceed against me. What do the slanderers say? They shall be my prosecutors, and I will sum up their words in an affidavit. "Socrates is an evil-doer, and a curious person, who searches into things under the earth and in heaven, and he makes the worse appear the better cause; and he teaches the aforesaid doctrines to others." That is the nature of the accusation, and that is what you have seen yourselves in the comedy of Aristophanes, who has introduced a man whom he calls Socrates, going about and saying that he can walk in the air, and talking a deal of nonsense concerning matters of which I do not pretend to know either much or little—not that I mean to say anything disparaging of any one who is a student of natural philosophy. I should be very sorry

if Meletus could lay that to my charge. But the simple truth is, O Athenians, that I have nothing to do with these studies. Very many of those here present are witnesses to the truth of this, and to them I appeal. Speak then, you who have heard me, and tell your neighbors whether any of you have ever known me hold forth in few words or in many upon matters of this sort. . . . You hear their answer. And from what they say of this you will be able to judge of the truth of the rest.

As little foundation is there for the report that I am a teacher, and take money; that is no more true than the other. Although, if a man is able to teach, I honor him for being paid. There is Gorgias of Leontium, and Prodicus of Ceos, and Hippias of Elis, who go the round of the cities, and are able to persuade the young men to leave their own citizens, by whom they might be taught for nothing, and come to them, whom they not only pay, but are thankful if they may be allowed to pay them. There is actually a Parian philosopher residing in Athens, of whom I have heard; and I came to hear of him in this way:—I met a man who has spent a world of money on the sophists, Callias, the son of Hipponicus, and knowing that he had sons, I asked him: "Callias," I said, "if your two sons were foals or calves, there would be no difficulty in finding some one to put over them; we should hire a trainer of horses, or a farmer probably who would improve and perfect them in their own proper virtue and excellence; but as they are human beings, whom are you thinking of placing over them? Is there any one who understands human and political virtue? You must have thought about this as you have sons; is there any one?" "There is," he said. "Who is he?" said I; "and of what country? and what does he charge?" "Evenus the Parian," he replied; "he is the man, and his charge is five minae." Happy is Evenus, I said to myself, if he really has this wisdom, and teaches at such a modest charge. Had I the same, I should have been very proud and conceited; but the truth is that I have no knowledge of the kind, O Athenians.

I dare say that some one will ask the question, "Why is this, Socrates, and what is the origin of these accusations of you: for there must have been something strange which you have been doing? All this great fame and talk about you would never have arisen if you had been like other men: tell us, then, why this is, as we should be sorry to judge hastily of you." Now I regard this as a fair challenge, and I will endeavor to explain to you the origin of this name of "wise," and of this evil fame. Please to attend then. And although some of you may think that I am joking, I declare that I will tell you the entire truth. Men of Athens, this reputation of mine has come of a certain sort of wisdom which I possess. If you ask me what kind of wisdom, I reply, such wisdom as is attainable by man, for to that extent I am inclined to believe that I am wise; whereas the persons of whom I was speaking have a super-human wisdom, which I may fail to describe, because I have it not myself; and he who says that I have, speaks falsely, and is taking away my character. And here, O men of Athens, I must beg you not to interrupt me, even if I seem to say something extravagant. For the word which I will speak is not mine. I will refer you to a wisdom who is worthy of credit, and will tell you about my wisdom—whether I have any, and of what sort—and that witness shall be the God of Delphi. You must have known Chaerephon; he was early a friend of mine, and also a friend of yours, for he shared in the exile of the people, and returned with you. Well, Chaerephon, as you know, was very impetuous in all his doings, and he went to Delphi and boldly asked the oracle to tell him whether—as I was saying, I must beg

you not to interrupt—he asked the oracle to tell him whether there was any one wiser than I was, and the Pythian prophetess answered, that there was no man wiser. Chaerephon is dead himself; but his brother, who is in court, will confirm the truth of this story.

Why do I mention this? Because I am going to explain to you why I have such an evil name. When I heard the answer, I said to myself, What can the god mean? and what is the interpretation of this riddle? for I know that I have no wisdom, small or great. What then can he mean when he says that I am the wisest of men? And yet he is a god, and can not lie; that would be against his nature. After long consideration, I at last thought of a method of trying the question. I reflected that if I could only find a man wiser than myself, then I might go to the god with a refutation in my hand. I should say to him, "Here is a man who is wiser than I am; but you said that I was the wisest." Accordingly I went to one who had the reputation of wisdom, and observed him—his name I need not mention; he was a politician whom I selected for examination—and the result was as follows: When I began to talk with him, I could not help thinking that he was not really wise, although he was thought wise by many, and wiser still by himself; and I went and tried to explain to him that he thought himself wise, but was not really wise; and the consequence was that he hated me, and his enmity was shared by several who were present and heard me. So I left him, saying to myself, as I went away: Well, although I do not suppose that either of us knows anything really beautiful and good, I am better off than he is,—for he knows nothing, and thinks that he knows. I neither know nor think that I know. In this latter particular, then, I seem to have slightly the advantage of him. Then I went to another who had still higher philosophical pretensions, and my conclusion was exactly the same. I made another enemy of him, and of many others besides him.

After this I went to one man after another, being not unconscious of the enmity which I provoked, and I lamented and feared this: but necessity was laid upon me,—the word of God, I thought, ought to be considered first. And I said to myself, Go I must to all who appear to know, and find out the meaning of the oracle. And I swear to you, Athenians, by the dog I swear!—for I must tell you the truth—the result of my mission was just this: I found that the men most in repute were all but the most foolish; and that some inferior men were really wiser and better. I will tell you the tale of my wanderings and of the "Herculean" labors, as I may call them, which I endured only to find at last the oracle irrefutable. When I left the politicians, I went to the poets; tragic, dithyrambic, and all sorts. And there, I said to myself, you will be detected; now you will find out that you are more ignorant than they are. Accordingly, I took them some of the most elaborate passages in their own writings, and asked what was the meaning of them—thinking that they would teach me something. Will you believe me? I am almost ashamed to speak of this, but still I must say that there is hardly a person present who would not have talked better about their poetry than they did themselves. That showed me in an instant that not by wisdom do poets write poetry, but by a sort of genius and inspiration; they are like diviners or soothsayers who also say many fine things, but do not understand the meaning of them. And the poets appeared to me to be much in the same case; and I further observed that upon the strength of their poetry they believed themselves to be the wisest of men in other things in which they were not wise. So I departed, conceiving myself to be superior to them

for the same reason that I was superior to the politicians.

At last I went to the artisans, for I was conscious that I knew nothing at all, as I may say, and I was sure that they knew many fine things; and in this I was not mistaken for they did know many things of which I was ignorant, and in this they certainly were wiser than I was. But I observed that even the good artisans fell into the same error as the poets:—because they were good workmen they thought that they also knew all sorts of high matters, and this defect in them overshadowed their wisdom—therefore I asked myself on behalf of the oracle, whether I would like to be as I was, neither having their knowledge nor their ignorance, or like them in both; and I made answer to myself and the oracle that I was better off as I was.

This investigation has led to my having enemies of the worst and most dangerous kind, and has given occasion also to many calumnies. And I am called wise, for my hearers always imagine that I myself possess the wisdom which I find wanting in others: but the truth is, O men of Athens, that God only is wise; and in this oracle he means to say that the wisdom of men is little or nothing; he is not speaking of Socrates, he is only using my name as an illustration, as if he said, He, O men, is the wisest who, like Socrates, knows that his wisdom is in truth worth nothing. And so I go my way, obedient to the god, and make inquisition into the wisdom of any one, whether citizen or stranger, who appears to be wise; and if he is not wise, then in vindication of the oracle I show him that he is not wise; and this occupation quite absorbs me, and I have no time to give either to any public matter of interest or to any concern of my own, but I am in utter poverty by reason of my devotion to the god.

There is another thing:—young men of the richer classes, who have not much to

do, come about me of their own accord; they like to hear the pretenders examined, and they often imitate me, and examine others themselves; there are plenty of persons, as they soon enough discover, who think that they know something, but really know little or nothing; and then those who are examined by them instead of being angry with themselves are angry with me: This confounded Socrates, they say; this villainous misleader of youth!— and then if somebody asks them, Why, what evil does he practice or teach? they do not know, and can not tell; but in order that they may not appear to be at a loss, they repeat the ready-made charges which are used against all philosophers about teaching things up in the clouds and under the earth, and having no gods, and making the worse appear the better cause; for they do not like to confess that their pretence of knowledge has been detected—which is the truth; and as they are numerous and ambitious and energetic, and are all in battle array and have persuasive tongues, they have filled your ears with their loud and inveterate calumnies. And this is the reason why my three accusers, Meletus and Anytus and Lycon, have set upon me; Meletus, who has a quarrel with me on behalf of the poets; Anytus, on behalf of the craftsmen; Lycon, on behalf of the rhetoricians: and as I said at the beginning, I can not expect to get rid of this mass of calumny all in a moment. And this, O men of Athens, is the truth and the whole truth; I have concealed nothing, I have dissembled nothing. And yet, I know that this plainness of speech makes them hate me, and what is their hatred but a proof that I am speaking the truth?—this is the occasion and reason of their slander of me, as you will find out either in this or in any future inquiry.
[*Socrates then cross-examines and discredits his chief accuser. Ed.*]

Some one will say: And are you not ashamed, Socrates, of a course of life which is likely to bring you to an untimely end? To him I may fairly answer: There you are mistaken: a man who is good for anything ought not to calculate the chance of living or dying; he ought only to consider whether in doing anything he is doing right or wrong—acting the part of a good man or of a bad. Whereas, according to your view, the heroes who fell at Troy were not good for much, and the son of Thetis above all, who altogether despised danger in comparison with disgrace; and when his goddess mother said to him, in his eagerness to slay Hector, that if he avenged his companion Patroclus, and slew Hector, he would die himself—"Fate," as she said, "waits upon you next after Hector;" he, hearing this, utterly despised danger and death, and instead of fearing them, feared rather to live in dishonor, and not to avenge his friend. "Let me die next," he replies, "and be avenged of my enemy, rather than abide here by the beaked ships, a scorn and a burden of the earth." Had Achilles any thought of death and danger? For wherever a man's place is, whether the place which he has chosen or that in which he has been placed by a commander, there he ought to remain in the hour of danger; he should not think of death or of anything, but of disgrace. And this, O men of Athens, is a true saying.

Strange, indeed, would be my conduct, O men of Athens, if I who, when I was ordered by the generals whom you chose to command me at Potidaea and Amphipolis and Delium, had not remained where they placed me, like any other man, facing death; if, I say, now, when, as I conceive and imagine, God orders me to fulfil the philosopher's mission of searching into myself and other men, I were to desert my post through fear of death, or any other fear; that would indeed be strange, and I might justly be arraigned in court for denying the existence of the gods, if I disobeyed the oracle because I was afraid of death: then I should be fancying that I was wise when I was not wise. For this fear of death is indeed the pretence of wisdom, and not real wisdom, being the appearance of knowing the unknown; since no one knows whether death, which they in their fear apprehend to be the greatest evil, may not be the greatest good. Is there not here conceit of knowledge, which is a disgraceful sort of ignorance? And this is the point in which, as I think, I am superior to men in general, and in which I might perhaps fancy myself wiser than other men,—that whereas I know but little of the world below, I do not suppose that I know; but I do know that injustice and disobedience to a better, whether God or man, is evil and dishonorable, and I will never fear or avoid a possible good rather than a certain evil. And therefore if you let me go now, and reject the counsels of Anytus, who said that if I were not put to death I ought not to have been prosecuted, and that if I escape now, your sons will all be utterly ruined by listening to my words—if you say to me, Socrates, this time we will not mind Anytus, and will let you off, but upon one condition, that you are not to inquire and speculate in this way any more, and that if you are caught doing this again you shall die:—if this was the condition on which you let me go, I should reply: Men of Athens, I honor and love you; but I shall obey God rather than you, and while I have life and strength I shall never cease from the practice and teaching of philosophy, exhorting any one whom I meet after my manner, and convincing him, saying: O my friend, why do you, who are a citizen of the great and mighty and wise city of Athens, care so much about laying up the greatest amount of money and honor and reputation, and

so little about wisdom and truth and the greatest improvement of the soul, which you never regard or heed at all? Are you not ashamed of this? And if the person with whom I am arguing, says: Yes, but I do care; I do not depart or let him go at once; I interrogate and examine and cross-examine him, and if I think that he has no virtue, but only says that he has, I reproach him with undervaluing the greater, and overvaluing the less. And this I should say to every one whom I meet, young and old, citizen and alien, but especially to the citizens, inasmuch, as they are my brethren. For this is the command of God, as I would have you know; and I believe that to this day no greater good has ever happened in the state than my service to the God. For I do nothing but go about persuading you all, old and young alike, not to take thought for your persons or your properties, but first and chiefly to care about the greatest improvement of the soul. I tell you that virtue is not given by money, but that from virtue come money and every other good of man, public as well as private. This is my teaching, and if this is the doctrine which corrupts the youth, my influence is ruinous indeed. But if any one says that this is not my teaching, he is speaking an untruth. Wherefore, O men of Athens, I say to you, do as Anytus bids or not as Anytus bids, and either acquit me or not; but whatever you do, know that I shall never alter my ways, not even if I have to die many times.

Men of Athens, do not interrupt, but hear me; there was an agreement between us that you should hear me out. And I think that what I am going to say will do you good: for I have something more to say, at which you may be inclined to cry out; but I beg that you will not do this. I would have you know, that if you kill such a one as I am, you will injure yourselves more than you will injure me. Meletus and Anytus will not injure me: they can not; for it is not in the nature of things that a bad man should injure a better than himself. I do not deny that he may, perhaps, kill him, or drive him into exile, or deprive him of civil rights; and he may imagine, and others may imagine, that he is doing him a great injury: but in that I do not agree with him; for the evil of doing as Anytus is doing—of unjustly taking away another man's life—is greater far. And now, Athenians, I am not going to argue for my own sake, as you may think, but for yours, that you may not sin against the God, or lightly reject his boon by condemning me. For if you kill me you will not easily find another like me, who, if I may use such a ludicrous figure of speech, am a sort of gadfly, given to the state by the God; and the state is like a great and noble steed who is tardy in his motions owing to his very size, and requires to be stirred into life. I am that gadfly which God has given the state, and all day long and in all places am always fastening upon you, arousing and persuading and reproaching you. And as you will not easily find another like me, I would advise you to spare me. I dare say that you may feel irritated at being suddenly awakened when you are caught napping; and you may think that if you were to strike me dead as Anytus advises, which you easily might, then you would sleep on for the remainder of your lives, unless God in his care of you gives you another gadfly. And that I am given to you by God is proved by this:—that if I had been like other men, I should not have neglected all my own concerns or patiently seen the neglect of them during all these years, and have been doing yours, coming to you individually like a father or elder brother, exhorting you to regard virtue; this, I say, would not be like human nature. And had I gained anything, or if my exhortations had been paid, there would have been some sense in that; but now, as you will perceive, not even the

impudence of my accusers dares to say that I have ever exacted or sought pay of any one; they have no witness of that. And I have a witness of the truth of what I say; my poverty is a sufficient witness.

Some one may wonder why I go about in private giving advice and busying myself with the concerns of others, but do not venture to come forward in public and advise the state. I will tell you the reason of this. You have often heard me speak of an oracle or sign which comes to me, and is the divinity which Meletus ridicules in the indictment. This sign I have had ever since I was a child. The sign is a voice which comes to me and always forbids me to do something which I am going to do, but never commands me to do anything, and this is what stands in the way of my being a politician. And rightly, as I think. For I am certain, O men of Athens, that if I had engaged in politics, I should have perished long ago, and done no good either to you or to myself. And don't be offended at my telling you the truth: for the truth is, that no man who goes to war with you or any other multitude, honestly struggling against the commission of unrighteousness and wrong in the state, will save his life; he who will really fight for the right, if he would live even for a little while, must have a private station and not a public one.

I can give you as proofs of this, not words only, but deeds, which you value more than words. Let me tell you a passage of my own life which will prove to you that I should never have yielded to injustice from any fear of death, and that if I had not yielded I should have died at once. I will tell you a story—tasteless perhaps and commonplace, but nevertheless true. The only office of state which I ever held, O men of Athens, was that of senator: the tribe Antiochis, which is my tribe, had the presidency at the trial of the generals who had not taken up the bodies of the slain after the battle of Arginusae; and you proposed to try them all together, which was illegal, as you all thought afterwards; but at the time I was the only one of the Prytanes who was opposed to the illegality, and I gave my vote against you; and when the orators threatened to impeach and arrest me, and have me taken away, and you called and shouted, I made up my mind that I would run the risk, having law and justice with me, rather than take part in your injustice because I feared imprisonment and death. This happened in the days of the democracy. But when the oligarchy of the Thirty was in power, they sent for me and four others into the rotunda, and bade us bring Leon the Salaminian from Salamis, as they wanted to execute him. This was a specimen of the sort of commands which they were always giving with the view of implicating as many as possible in their crimes; and then I showed, not in word only but in deed, that, if I may be allowed to use such an expression, I cared not a straw for death, and that my only fear was the fear of doing an unrighteous or unholy thing. For the strong arm of that oppressive power did not frighten me into doing wrong; and when we came out of the rotunda the other four went to Salamis and fetched Leon, but I went quietly home. For which I might have lost my life, had not the power of the Thirty shortly afterwards come to an end. And to this many will witness.

Now do you really imagine that I could have survived all these years, if I had led a public life, supposing that like a good man I had always supported the right and had made justice, as I ought, the first thing? No indeed, men of Athens, neither I nor any other. But I have been always the same in all my actions, public as well as private, and never have I yielded any base compliance to those who are slanderously termed my disciples, or to any other. For the truth is that I have no regular disciples: but if anyone likes to come and hear me while I am pursuing my mission, whether he be young or old, he may freely come. Nor do I converse with those who pay only, and not with those who do not pay; but any one, whether he be rich or poor, may ask and answer me and listen to my words; and whether he turns out to be a bad man or a good one, that can not be justly laid to my charge, as I never taught him anything. And if any one says that he has ever learned or heard anything from me in private which all the world has not heard, I should like you to know that he is speaking an untruth.

But I shall be asked, Why do people delight in continually conversing with you? I have told you already, Athenians, the whole truth about this: they like to hear the cross-examination of the pretenders to wisdom; there is amusement in this. And this is a duty which the God has imposed upon me, as I am assured by oracles, visions, and in every sort of way in which the will of divine power was ever signified to any one. This is true, O Athenians; or, if not true, would be soon refuted. For if I am really corrupting the youth, and have corrupted some of them already, those of them who have grown up and have become sensible that I gave them bad advice in the days of their youth should come forward as accusers and take their revenge; and if they do not like to come themselves, some of their relatives, fathers, brothers, or other kinsmen, should say what evil their families suffered at my hands. Now is their time. Many of them I see in the court. There is Crito, who is of the same age and of the same deme with myself, and there is Critobulus his son, whom I also see. Then again there is Lysanias of Sphettus, who is the father of Aeschines—he is present; and also there is Antiphon of Cephisus, who is the father of Epigenes; and there are the brothers of several who have associated with me. There is Nicostratus the son of Theosdotides, and the brother of Theodotus (now Theodotus himself is dead, and therefore he, at any rate, will not seek to stop him); and there is Paralus the son of Demodocus, who had a brother Theages; and Adeimantus the son of Ariston, whose brother Plato is present; and Aeantodorus, who is the brother of Apollodorus, whom I also see. I might mention a great many others, any of whom Meletus should have produced as witnesses in the course of his speech; and let him still produce them, if he has forgotten—I will make way for him. And let him say, if he has any testimony of the sort which he can produce. Nay, Athenians, the very opposite is the truth. For all these are ready to witness on behalf of the corruptor, of the destroyer of their kindred, as Meletus and Anytus call me: not the corrupted youth only—there might have been a motive for that—but their uncorrupted elder relatives. Why should they too support me with their testimony? Why, indeed, except for the sake of truth and justice, and because they know that I am speaking the truth, and that Meletus is lying.

Well, Athenians, this and the like of this is nearly all the defence which I have to offer. Yet a word more. Perhaps there may be some one who is offended at me, when he calls to mind how he himself on a similar, or even a less serious occasion, had recourse to prayers and supplications with many tears, and how he produced his children in court, which was a moving spectacle, together with a posse of his relations and friends; whereas I, who am probably in danger of my life, will do none of these things. Perhaps this may come into his mind, and he may be set against me, and vote in anger because he is displeased at this. Now if there be such a person among you, which I am far from affirming, I may fairly reply to him: My friend, I am a man, and like other men, a creature of flesh and blood, and not of wood or stone, as Homer says; and I have a family, yes, and sons, O Athenians, three in number, one of whom is growing up, and the two others are still young; and yet I will not bring any of them hither in order to petition you for an acquittal. And why not? Not from any self-will or disregard of you. Whether I am or am not afraid of death is another question, of which I will not now speak. But my reason simply is, that I feel such conduct to be discreditable to myself, and you, and the whole state. One who has reached my years, and who has a name for wisdom, whether deserved or not, ought not to demean himself. At any rate, the world has decided that Socrates is in some way superior to other men. And if those among you who are said to be superior in wisdom and courage, and any other virtue, demean themselves in this way, how shameful is their conduct! I have seen men of reputation, when they have been condemned, behaving in the strangest manner: they seemed to fancy that they were going to suffer something dreadful if they died, and that they could be immortal if you only allowed them to live; and I think that they were a dishonor to the state, and that any stranger coming in would say of them that the most eminent men of Athens, to whom the Athenians themselves give honor and command, are no better than women. And I say that these things ought not to be done by those of us who are of reputation; and if they are done, you ought not to permit them; you ought rather to show that you are more inclined to condemn, not the man who is quiet, but the man who gets up a doleful scene, and makes the city ridiculous.

But, setting aside the question of dishonor, there seems to be something wrong in petitioning a judge, and thus procuring an acquittal instead of informing and convincing him. For his duty is, not to make a present of justice, but to give judgment; and he has sworn that he will judge according to the laws and not according to his own good pleasure; and neither he nor we should get into the habit of perjuring ourselves—there can be no piety in that. Do not then require me to do what I consider dishonorable and impious and wrong, especially now, when I am being tried for impiety on the indictment of Meletus. For if, O men of Athens, by force of persuasion and entreaty, I could overpower your oaths, then I should be teaching you to believe that there are no gods, and convict myself, in my own defence, of not believing in them. But that is not the case; for I do believe that there are gods, and in a far higher sense than that in which any of my accusers believe in them. And to you and to God I commit my cause, to be determined by you as is best for you and me.

[*He is found guilty by 281 votes to 220, and is condemned to death. Ed.*]

. . . .

Not much time will be gained, O Athenians, in return for the evil name which you will get from the detractors of the city, who will say that you killed Socrates, a wise man; for they will call me wise even although I am not wise when they want to reproach you. If you had waited a little while, your desire would have been fulfilled in the course of nature. For I am far advanced in years, as you may perceive, and not far from death. I am speaking now only to those of you who have condemned me to death. And I have another thing to say to them: You think that I was convicted through deficiency of words—I mean, that if I had thought fit to leave nothing undone, nothing unsaid, I might have gained an acquittal. Not so; the deficiency which led to my conviction was not of words—certainly not. But I had not the boldness or impudence or inclination

to address you as you would have liked me to address you, weeping and wailing and lamenting, and saying and doing many things which you have been accustomed to hear from others, and which, as I say, are unworthy of me. But I thought that I ought not to do anything common or mean in the hour of danger: nor do I now repent of the manner of my defence, and I would rather die having spoken after my manner, than speak in your manner and live. For neither in war nor yet at law ought any man to use every way of escaping death. For often in battle there is no doubt that if a man will throw away his arms, and fall on his knees before his pursuers, he may escape death; and in other dangers there are other ways of escaping death, if a man is willing to say and do anything. The difficulty, my friends, is not in avoiding death, but in avoiding unrighteousness; for that runs faster than death. I am old and move slowly, and the slower runner has overtaken me, and my accusers are keen and quick, and the faster runner who is unrighteousness, has overtaken them. And now I depart hence condemned by you to suffer the penalty of death, and they too go their ways condemned by the truth to suffer the penalty of villainy and wrong; and I must abide by my award—let them abide by theirs. I suppose that these things may be regarded as fated—and I think that they are well.

And now, O men who have condemned me, I would fain prophesy to you; for I am about to die, and that is the hour in which men are gifted with prophetic power. And I prophesy to you who are my murderers, that immediately after my death punishment far heavier than you have inflicted on me will surely await you. Me you have killed because you wanted to escape the accuser, and not to give an account of your lives. But that will not be as you suppose: far otherwise. For

I say that there will be more accusers of you than there are now; accusers whom hitherto I have restrained: and as they are younger they will be more severe with you, and you will be more offended at them. For if you think that by killing men you can avoid the accuser censuring your lives, you are mistaken; that is not a way of escape which is either possible or honorable; the easiest and the noblest way is not to be crushing others, but to be improving yourselves. This is the prophecy which I utter before my departure to the judges who have condemned me.

Friends, who would have acquitted me, I would like also to talk with you about this thing which has happened, while the magistrates are busy, and before I go to the place at which I must die. Stay then awhile, for we may as well talk with one another while there is time. You are my friends, and I should like to show you the meaning of this event which has happened to me. O my judges—for you I may truly call judges—I should like to tell you of a wonderful circumstance. Hitherto the familiar oracle within me has constantly been in the habit of opposing me even about trifles, if I was going to make a slip or error about anything; and now as you see there has come upon me that which may be thought, and is generally believed to be, the last and worst evil. But the oracle made no sign of opposition, either as I was leaving my house and going out in the morning, or when I was going up into this court, or while I was speaking, at anything which I was going to say; and yet I have often been stopped in the middle of a speech, but now in nothing I either said or did touching this matter has the oracle opposed me. What do I take to be the explanation of this? I will tell you. I regard this as a proof that what has happened to me is a good, and that those of us who think that death is an evil are in error. This is a great proof to me of what I am saying, for the customary sign would surely have opposed me had I been going to evil and not to good.

Let us reflect in another way, and we shall see that there is great reason to hope that death is a good, for one of two things: —either death is a state of nothingness and utter unconsciousness, or, as men say, there is a change and migration of the soul from this world to another. Now if you suppose that there is no consciousness, but a sleep like the sleep of him who is undisturbed even by the sight of dreams, death will be an unspeakable gain. For if a person were to select the night in which his sleep was undisturbed even by dreams, and were to compare with this the other days and nights of his life, and then were to tell us how many days and nights he had passed in the course of his life better and more pleasantly than this one, I think that any man, I will not say a private man, but even the great king will not find many such days or nights, when compared with the others. Now if death is like this, I say that to die is gain; for eternity is then only a single night. But if death is the journey to another place, and there, as men say, all the dead are, what good, O my friends and judges, can be greater than this? If indeed when the pilgrim arrives in the world below, he is delivered from the professors of justice in this world, and finds the true judges who are said to give judgment there, Minos and Rhadamanthus and Aeacus and Triptolemus, and other sons of God who were righteous in their own life, that pilgrimage will be worth making. What would not a man give if he might converse with Orpheus and Musaeus and Hesiod and Homer? Nay, if this be true, let me die again and again. I, too, shall have a wonderful interest in a place where I can converse with Palamedes, and Ajax the son of Telamon, and other heroes of old, who have suffered death through an unjust judgment; and there will be no small pleasure, as I think, in comparing my own sufferings with theirs. Above all, I shall be able to continue my search into true and false knowledge; as in this world, so also in that; I shall find out who is wise, and who pretends to be wise, and is not. What would not a man give, O judges, to be able to examine the leader of the great Trojan expedition; or Odysseus or Sisyphus, or numberless others, men and women too! What infinite delight would there be in conversing with them and asking them questions! For in that world they do not put a man to death for this; certainly not. For besides being happier in that world than in this, they will be immortal, if what is said is true.

Wherefore, O judges, be of good cheer about death, and know this of a truth—that no evil can happen to a good man, either in life or after death. He and his are not neglected by the gods; nor has my own approaching end happened by mere chance. But I see clearly that to die and be released was better for me; and therefore the oracle gave no sign. For which reason, also, I am not angry with my accusers or my condemners; they have done me no harm, although neither of them meant to do me any good; and for this I may gently blame them.

Still I have a favor to ask of them. When my sons are grown up, I would ask you, O my friends, to punish them; and I would have you trouble them, as I have troubled you, if they seem to care about riches, or anything, more than about virtue; or if they pretend to be something when they are really nothing,—then reprove them, as I have reproved you, for not caring about that for which they ought to care, and thinking that they are something when they are really nothing. And if you do this, I and my sons will have received justice at your hands.

The hour of departure has arrived, and we go our ways—I to die, and you to live. Which is better God only knows.

CRITO

SCENE: THE PRISON OF SOCRATES

SOCRATES. Why have you come at this hour, Crito? it must be quite early?

CRITO. Yes, certainly.

SOC. What is the exact time?

CR. The dawn is breaking.

SOC. I wonder that the keeper of the prison would let you in.

CR. He knows me, because I often come, Socrates; moreover, I have done him a kindness.

SOC. And are you only just come?

CR. No, I came some time ago.

THE DIALOGUES OF PLATO, trans. B. Jowett (New York, 1871), I, 347-359.

SOC. Then why did you sit and say nothing, instead of awakening me at once?

CR. Why, indeed, Socrates, I myself would rather not have all this sleeplessness and sorrow. But I have been wondering at your peaceful slumbers, and that was the reason why I did not awaken you, because I wanted you to be out of pain. I have always thought you happy in the calmness of your temperament; but never did I see the like of the easy, cheerful way in which you bear this calamity.

SOC. Why, Crito, when a man has reached my age he ought not to be repining at the prospect of death.

CR. And yet other old men find themselves in similar misfortunes, and age does not prevent them from repining.

soc. That may be. But you have not told me why you come at this early hour.

cr. I come to bring you a message which is sad and painful; not, as I believe, to yourself, but to all of us who are your friends, and saddest of all to me.

soc. What! I suppose that the ship has come from Delos, on the arrival of which I am to die?

cr. No, the ship has not actually arrived, but she will probably be here to-day, as persons who have come from Sunium tell me that they left her there; and therefore to-morrow, Socrates, will be the last day of your life.

soc. Very well, Crito; if such is the will of God, I am willing; but my belief is that there will be a delay of a day.

cr. Why do you say this?

soc. I will tell you. I am to die on the day after the arrival of the ship?

cr. Yes; that is what the authorities say.

soc. But I do not think that the ship will be here until to-morrow; this I gather from a vision which I had last night, or rather only just now, when you fortunately allowed me to sleep.

cr. And what was the nature of the vision?

soc. There came to me the likeness of a woman, fair and comely, clothed in white raiment, who called to me and said: O Socrates,

> "The third day hence to Phthia shalt thou go."

cr. What a singular dream, Socrates!

soc. There can be no doubt about the meaning, Crito, I think.

cr. Yes; the meaning is only too clear. But, Oh! my beloved Socrates, let me entreat you once more to take my advice and escape. For if you die I shall not only lose a friend who can never be replaced, but there is another evil: people who do not know you and me will believe that I might have saved you if I had been willing to give money, but that I did not care. Now, can there be a worse disgrace than this—that I should be thought to value money more than the life of a friend? For the many will not be persuaded that I wanted you to escape, and that you refused.

soc. But why, my dear Crito, should we care about the opinion of the many? Good men, and they are the only persons who are worth considering, will think of these things truly as they happened.

cr. But do you see, Socrates, that the opinion of the many must be regarded, as is evident in your own case, because they can do the very greatest evil to any one who has lost their good opinion.

soc. I only wish, Crito, that they could; for then they could also do the greatest good, and that would be well. But the truth is, that they can do neither good nor evil: they can not make a man wise or make him foolish; and whatever they do is the result of chance.

cr. Well, I will not dispute about that; but please to tell me, Socrates, whether you are not acting out of regard to me and your other friends: are you not afraid that if you escape hence we may get into trouble with the informers for having stolen you away, and lose either the whole or a great part of our property; or that even a worse evil may happen to us? Now, if this is your fear, be at ease; for in order to save you we ought surely to run this, or even a greater risk; be persuaded, then, and do as I say.

soc. Yes, Crito, that is one fear which you mention, but by no means the only one.

cr. Fear not. There are persons who at no great cost are willing to save you and bring you out of prison; and as for the informers, you may observe that they are far from being exorbitant in their demands; a little money will satisfy them. My means, which, as I am sure, are ample, are at your service, and if you have a scruple about spending all mine, here are strangers who will give you the use of theirs; and one of them, Simmias the Theban, has brought a sum of money for this very purpose; and Cebes and many others are willing to spend their money too. I say therefore, do not on that account hesitate about making your escape, and do not say, as you did in the court, that you will have a difficulty in knowing what to do with yourself if you escape. For men will love you in other places to which you may go, and not in Athens only; there are friends of mine in Thessaly, if you like to go to them, who will value and protect you, and no Thessalian will give you any trouble. Nor can I think that you are justified, Socrates, in betraying your own life when you might be saved; this is playing into the hands of your enemies and destroyers; and moreover I should say that you were betraying your children; for you might bring them up and educate them; instead of which you go away and leave them, and they will have to take their chance; and if they do not meet with the usual fate of orphans, there will be small thanks to you. No man should bring children into the world who is unwilling to persevere to the end in their nurture and education. But you are choosing the easier part, as I think, not the better and manlier, which would rather have become one who professes virtue in all his actions, like yourself. And indeed, I am ashamed not only of you, but of us who are your friends, when I reflect that this entire business of yours will be attributed to our want of courage. The trial need never have come on, or might have been brought to another issue; and the end of all, which is the crowning absurdity, will seem to have been permitted by us, through cowardice and baseness, who might have saved you, as you might have saved yourself, if we had been good for anything (for there was no difficulty in escaping); and we did not see how disgraceful, Socrates, and also miserable all this will be to us as well as to you. Make your mind up then, or rather have your mind already made up, for the time of deliberation is over, and there is only one thing to be done, which must be done, if at all, this very night, and which any delay will render all but impossible; I beseech you therefore, Socrates, to be persuaded by me, and to do as I say.

soc. Dear Crito, your zeal is invaluable, if a right one; but if wrong, the greater the zeal the greater the evil; and therefore we ought to consider whether these things shall be done or not. For I am and always have been one of those natures who must be guided by reason, whatever the reason may be which upon reflection appears to me to be the best; and now that this fortune has come upon me, I can not put away the reasons which I have before given; the principles which I have hitherto honored and revered I still honor, and unless we can find other and better principles on the instant, I am certain not to agree with you; no, not even if the power of the multitude could inflict many more imprisonments, confiscations, deaths, frightening us like children with hobgoblin terrors. But what will be the fairest way of considering the question? Shall I return to your old argument about the opinions of men? some of which are to be regarded, and others, as we were saying, are not to be regarded. Now were we right in maintaining this before I was condemned? And has the argument which was once good now proved to be talk for the sake of talking;—in fact an amusement only, and altogether vanity? That is what I want to consider with your help, Crito:—whether, under my present circumstances, the argument appears to be in any way different or not; and is to be allowed by me or disallowed. That argument, which, as I believe, is maintained by many who assume to be authorities, was to the effect, as I was saying, that the opinions of some men are to be regarded, and of other men not to be regarded. Now you, Crito, are a disinterested person who are not going to die tomorrow—at least, there is no human probability of this, and you are therefore not liable to be deceived by the circumstances in which you are placed. Tell me then, whether I am right in saying that some opinions, and the opinions of some men only, are to be valued, and other opinions, and the opinions of other men, are not to be valued. I ask you whether I was right in maintaining this?

CR. Certainly.

SOC. The good are to be regarded, and not the bad?

CR. Yes.

SOC. And the opinions of the wise are good, and the opinions of the unwise are evil?

CR. Certainly.

SOC. And what was said about another matter? Was the disciple in gymnastics supposed to attend to the praise and blame and opinion of every man, or of one man only —his physician or trainer, whoever that was?

CR. Of one man only.

SOC. And he ought to fear the censure and welcome the praise of that one only, and not of the many?

CR. That is clear.

SOC. And he ought to live and train, and eat and drink in the way which seems good to his single master who has understanding, rather than according to the opinion of all other men put together?

CR. True.

SOC. And if he disobeys and disregards the opinion and approval of the one, and regards the opinion of the many who have no understanding, will he not suffer evil?

CR. Certainly he will.

SOC. And what will the evil be, whither tending and what affecting, in the disobedient person?

CR. Clearly, affecting the body; that is what is destroyed by the evil.

SOC. Very good; and is not this true, Crito, of other things which we need not separately enumerate? In the matter of just and unjust, fair and foul, good and evil, which are the subjects of our present consultation, ought we to follow the opinion of the many and to fear them; or the opinion of the one man who has understanding, and whom we ought to fear and reverence more than all the rest of the world: and whom deserting we shall destroy and injure that principle in us which may be assumed to be improved by justice and deteriorated by injustice;—is there not such a principle?

CR. Certainly there is, Socrates.

SOC. Take a parallel instance:—if, acting under the advice of men who have no understanding, we destroy that which is improvable by health and deteriorated by disease—when that has been destroyed, I say, would life be worth having? And that is— the body?

CR. Yes.

SOC. Could we live, having an evil and corrupted body?

CR. Certainly not.

SOC. And will life be worth having, if that higher part of man be depraved, which is improved by justice and deteriorated by injustice? Do we suppose that principle, whatever it may be in man, which has to do with justice and injustice, to be inferior to the body?

CR. Certainly not.

SOC. More honored, then?

CR. Far more honored.

SOC. Then, my friend, we must not regard what the many say of us: but what he, the one man who has understanding of just and unjust, will say, and what the truth will say. And therefore you begin in error when you suggest that we should regard the opinion of the many about just and unjust, good and evil, honorable and dishonorable. —Well, some one will say, "but the many can kill us."

CR. Yes, Socrates; that will clearly be the answer.

SOC. That is true: but still I find with surprise that the old argument is, as I conceive, unshaken as ever. And I should like to know whether I may say the same of another proposition—that not life, but a good life, is to be chiefly valued?

CR. Yes, that also remains.

SOC. And a good life is equivalent to a just and honorable one—that holds also?

CR. Yes, that holds.

SOC. From these premisses I proceed to argue the question whether I ought or ought not to try and escape without the consent of the Athenians: and if I am clearly right in escaping, then I will make the attempt; but if not, I will abstain. The other considerations which you mention, of money and loss of character and the duty of educating children, are, as I fear, only the doctrines of the multitude, who would be as ready to call people to life, if they were able, as they are to put them to death—and with as little reason. But now, since the argument has thus far prevailed, the only question which remains to be considered is, whether we shall do rightly either in escaping or in suffering others to aid in our escape and paying them in money and thanks, or whether we shall not do rightly: and if the latter, then death or any other calamity which may ensue on my remaining here must not be allowed to enter into the calculation.

CR. I think that you are right, Socrates; how then shall we proceed?

SOC. Let us consider the matter together, and do you either refute me if you can, and I will be convinced; or else cease, my dear friend, from repeating to me that I ought to escape against the wishes of the Athenians: for I am extremely desirous to be persuaded by you, but not against my own better judgment. And now please to consider my first position, and do your best to answer me.

CR. I will do my best.

SOC. Are we to say that we are never intentionally to do wrong, or that in one way we ought and in another way we ought not to do wrong, or is doing wrong always evil and dishonorable, as I was just now saying, and as has been already acknowledged by us? Are all our former admissions which were made within a few days to be thrown away? And have we, at our age, been earnestly discoursing with one another all our life long only to discover that we are no better than children? Or are we to rest assured, in spite of the opinion of the many, and in spite of consequences whether better or worse, of the truth of what was then said, that injustice is always an evil and dishonor to him who acts unjustly? Shall we affirm that?

CR. Yes.

SOC. Then we must do no wrong?

CR. Certainly not.

SOC. Nor when injured injure in return, as the many imagine; for we must injure no one at all?

CR. Clearly not.

SOC. Again, Crito, may we do evil?

CR. Surely not, Socrates.

SOC. And what of doing evil in return for evil which is the morality of the many—is that just or not?

CR. Not just.

SOC. For doing evil to another is the same as injuring him?

CR. Very true.

SOC. Then we ought not to retaliate or render evil for evil to any one, whatever evil we may have suffered from him. But I would have you consider, Crito, whether you really mean what you are saying. For this opinion has never been held, and never will be held, by any considerable number of persons; and those who are agreed and those who are not agreed upon this point have no common ground, and can only despise one another when they see how widely they differ. Tell me, then, whether you agree with and assent to my first principle, that neither injury nor retaliation nor warding off evil by evil is ever right. And shall that be the premiss of our argument? Or do you decline and dissent from this? For this has been of old and is still my opinion; but, if you are of another, let me hear what you have to say. If, however, you remain of the same mind as formerly, I will proceed to the next step.

CR. You may proceed, for I have not changed my mind.

SOC. Then I will proceed to the next step, which may be put in the form of a question:—Ought a man to do what he admits to be right, or ought he to betray the right?

CR. He ought to do what he thinks right.

SOC. But if this is true, what is the application? In leaving the prison against the will of the Athenians, do I wrong any? or rather do I not wrong those whom I ought least to wrong? Do I not desert the principles which were acknowledged by us to be just? What do you say?

CR. I can not tell, Socrates; for I do not know.

SOC. Then consider the matter in this way: —Imagine that I am about to play truant (you may call the proceeding by any name which you like), and the laws and the government come and interrogate me: "Tell us, Socrates," they say; "what are you about? Are you going by an act of yours to overturn us—the laws and the whole state, as far as in you lies? Do you imagine that a state can subsist and not be overthrown, in which the decisions of law have no power, but are set aside and overthrown by individuals?" What will be our answer, Crito, to these and the like words? Any one, and especially a clever rhetorician, will have a good deal to urge about the evil of setting aside the law which requires a sentence to be carried out; and we might reply, "Yes; but the state has injured us and given an unjust sentence." Suppose I say that?

CR. Very good, Socrates.

SOC. "And was that our agreement with you?" the law would say; "or were you to abide by the sentence of the state?" And if I were to express astonishment at their saying this, the law would probably add: "Answer, Socrates, instead of opening your eyes: you are in the habit of asking and answering questions. Tell us what complaint you have to make against us which justifies you in attempting to destroy us and the state? In the first place did we not bring you into existence? Your father married your mother by our aid and begat you. Say whether you have any objection to urge against those of us who regulate marriage?" None, I should reply. "Or against those of us who regulate the system of nurture and education of children in which you were trained? Were not the laws, who have the charge of this, right in commanding your father to train you in music and gymnastic?" Right, I should reply. "Well then, since you were brought into the world and nurtured and educated by us, can you deny in the first place that you are our child and slave, as your fathers were before you? And if this is true you are not on equal terms with us; nor can you think that you have a right to do to us what we are doing to you. Would you have any right to strike or revile or do any other evil to a father or to your master, if you had one, when you have been struck or reviled by him, or received some other evil at his hands?—you would not say this? And because we think right to destroy you, do you think that you have any right to destroy us in return, and your country as far as in you lies? And will you, O professor of true virtue, say that you are justified in this? Has a philosopher like you failed to discover that our country is more to be valued and higher and holier far than mother or father or any ancestor, and more to be regarded in the eyes of the gods and of men of understanding? also to be soothed, and gently and reverently entreated when angry, even more than a father, and if not persuaded, obeyed? And when we are punished by her, whether with imprisonment or stripes, the punishment is to be endured in silence; and if she lead us to wounds or death in battle, thither we follow as is right; neither may any one yield or retreat or leave his rank, but whether in battle or in a court of law, or in any other place, he must do what his city and his country order him; or he must change their view of what is just: and if he may do no violence to his father or mother, much less may he do violence to his country." What answer shall we make to this, Crito? Do the laws speak truly, or do they not?

CR. I think that they do.

SOC. Then the laws will say: "Consider, Socrates, if this is true, that in your present attempt you are going to do us wrong. For, after having brought you into the world, and nurtured and educated you, and given you and every other citizen a share in every good that we had to give, we further proclaim and give the right to every Athenian, that if he does not like us when he has come of age and has seen the ways of the city, and made our acquaintance, he may go where he pleases and take his goods with him; and none of us laws will forbid him or interfere with him. Any of you who does not like us and the city, and who wants to go to a colony or to any other city, may go where he likes, and take his goods with him. But he who has experience of the manner in which we order justice and administer the state, and still remains, has entered into an implied contract that he will do as we command him. And he who disobeys us is, as we maintain, thrice wrong; first, because in disobeying us he is disobeying his parents; secondly, because we are the authors of his education; thirdly, because he has made an agreement with us that he will duly obey our commands; and he neither obeys them nor convinces us that our commands are wrong; and we do not rudely impose them, but give him the alternative of obeying or convincing us;—that is what we offer, and he does neither. These are the sort of accusations to which, as we were saying, you, Socrates, will be exposed if you accomplish your intentions; you, above all other Athenians." Suppose I ask, why is this? they will justly retort upon me that I above all other men have acknowledged the agreement. "There is clear proof," they will say, "Socrates, that we and the city were not displeasing to you. Of all Athenians you have been the most constant resident in the city, which, as you never leave, you may be supposed to love. For you never went out of the city either to see the games, except once when you went to the Isthmus, or to any other place unless when you were on military service; nor did you travel as other men do. Nor had you any curiosity to know other states or their laws: your affections did not go beyond us and our state; we were your special favorites, and you acquiesced in our government of you; and this is the state in which you begat your children, which is a proof of your satisfaction. Moreover, you might, if you had liked, have fixed the penalty at banishment in the course of the trial—the state which refuses to let you go now would have let you go then. But you pretended that you preferred death to exile, and that you were not grieved at death. And now you have forgotten these fine sentiments, and pay no respect to us the laws, of whom you are the destroyer; and are doing what only a miserable slave would do, running away and turning your back upon the compacts and agreements which you made as a citizen. And first of all answer this very question: Are we right in saying that you agreed to be governed according to us in deed, and not in word only? Is that true or not?" How shall we answer that, Crito? Must we not agree?

CR. There is no help, Socrates.

SOC. Then will they not say: "You, Socrates, are breaking the covenants and agreements which you made with us at your leisure, not in any haste or under any compulsion or deception, but having had seventy years to think of them, during which time you were at liberty to leave the city, if we were not to your mind, or if our covenants appeared to you to be unfair. You had your choice, and might have gone either to Lacedaemon or Crete, which you often praise for their good government, or to some other Hellenic or foreign state. Whereas you, above all other Athenians, seemed to be so fond of the state, or, in other words, of us her laws (for who would like a state that has no laws), that you never stirred out of her; the halt, the blind, the maimed were not more stationary in her than you were. And now you run away and forsake your agreements. Not so, Socrates, if you will take our advice; do not make yourself ridiculous by escaping out of the city.

"For just consider, if you transgress and err in this sort of way, what good will you do either to yourself or to your friends? That your friends will be driven into exile and deprived of citizenship, or will lose their property, is tolerably certain; and you yourself, if you fly to one of the neighboring cities, as, for example, Thebes or Megara, both of which are well governed cities, will come to them as an enemy, Socrates, and their government will be against you, and all patriotic citizens will cast an evil eye upon you as a subverter of the laws, and you will confirm in the minds of the judges the justice of their own condemnation of you. For he who is a corrupter of the laws is more than likely to be corrupter of the young and foolish portion of mankind. Will you then flee from well-ordered cities and virtuous men? and is existence worth having on these terms? Or will you go to them without shame, and talk to them, Socrates? And what will you say to them? What you say here about virtue and justice and institutions and laws being the best things among men? Would that be decent of you? Surely not. But if you go away from well-governed states to Crito's friends in Thessaly, where there is a great disorder and license, they will be charmed to have the tale of your escape from prison, set off with ludicrous particulars of the manner in which you were wrapped in a goatskin or some other disguise, and metamorphosed as the fashion of runaways is—that is very likely; but will there be no one to remind you that in your old age you violated the most sacred laws from a miserable desire of a little more life. Perhaps not, if you keep them in a good temper; but if they are out of temper you will hear many degrading things; you will live, but how?—as the flatterer of all men, and the servant of all men; and doing what? —eating and drinking in Thessaly, having gone abroad in order that you may get a dinner. And where will be your fine sentiments about justice and virtue then? Say that you wish to live for the sake of your children, that you may bring them up and educate them—will you take them into Thessaly and deprive them of Athenian citizenship? Is that the benefit which you would confer upon them? Or are you under the impression that they will be better cared for and educated here if you are still alive, although absent from them; for that your friends will take care of them? Do you fancy that if you are an inhabitant of Thessaly they will take care of them, and if you are an inhabitant of the other world they will not take care of them? Nay; but if they who call themselves friends are truly friends, they surely will.

"Listen, then, Socrates, to us who have

brought you up. Think not of life and children first, and of justice afterwards, but of justice first, that you may be justified before the princes of the world below. For neither will you nor any that belong to you be happier or holier or juster in this life, or happier in another, if you do as Crito bids. Now you depart in innocence, a sufferer and not a doer of evil; a victim, not of the laws, but of men. But if you go forth, returning evil for evil, and injury for injury, breaking the covenants and agreements which you have made with us, and wronging those whom you ought least to wrong, that is to say, yourself, your friends, your country, and us, we shall be angry with you while you live, and our brethren, the laws in the world below, will receive you as an enemy; for they will know that you have done your best to destroy us. Listen, then, to us and not to Crito."

This is the voice which I seem to hear murmuring in my ears, like the sound of the flute in the ears of the mystic; that voice, I say is humming in my ears, and prevents me from hearing any other. And I know that anything more which you may say will be vain. Yet speak, if you have anything to say.

CR. I have nothing to say, Socrates.
SOC. Then let me follow the intimations of the will of God.

PHAEDO

SCENE: THE PRISON OF SOCRATES

. . .

When he had done speaking, Crito said: And have you any commands for us, Socrates—anything to say about your children, or any other matter in which we can serve you?

Nothing particular, he said: only, as I have always told you, I would have you look to yourselves; that is a service which you may always be doing to me and mine as well as to yourselves. And you need not make professions; for if you take no thought for yourselves, and walk not according to the precepts which I have given you, not now for the first time, the warmth of your professions will be of no avail.

We will do our best, said Crito. But in what way would you have us bury you?

In any way that you like; only you must get hold of me, and take care that I do not walk away from you. Then he turned to us, and added with a smile:—I can not make Crito believe that I am the same Socrates who has been talking and conducting the argument; he fancies that I am the other Socrates whom he will soon see, a dead body—and he asks, How shall he bury me? And though I have spoken many words in the endeavor to show that when I have drunk the poison I shall leave you and go to the joys of the blessed,—these words of mine, with which I comforted you and myself, have had, as I perceive, no effect upon Crito. And therefore I want you to be surety for me now, as he was surety for me at the trial: but let the promise be of another sort; for he was my surety to the judges that I would remain, but you must be my surety to him that I shall not remain, but go away and depart; and then he will suffer less at my death, and not be grieved when he sees my body being burned or buried. I would not have him sorrow at my hard lot, or say at the

THE DIALOGUES OF PLATO, trans. B. Jowett (New York, 1871), I, 444-447.

burial, Thus we lay out Socrates, or, Thus, we follow him to the grave or bury him; for false words are not only evil in themselves, but they infect the soul with evil. Be of good cheer, then, my dear Crito, and say that you are burying my body only, and do with that as is usual, and as you think best.

When he had spoken these words, he arose and went into the bath-chamber with Crito, who bid us wait; and we waited, talking and thinking of the subject of discourse, and also of the greatness of our sorrow; he was like a father of whom we were being bereaved, and we were about to pass the rest of our lives as orphans. When he had taken the bath his children were brought to him—(he had two young sons and an elder one); and the women of his family also came, and he talked to them and gave them a few directions in the presence of Crito; and he then dismissed them and returned to us.

Now the hour of sunset was near, for a good deal of time had passed while he was within. When he came out, he sat down with us again after his bath, but not much was said. Soon the jailer, who was the servant of the eleven, entered and stood by him, saying:—To you, Socrates, whom I know to be the noblest and gentlest and best of all who ever came to this place, I will not impute the angry feelings of other men, who rage and swear at me, when, in obedience to the authorities, I bid them drink the poison—indeed, I am sure that you will not be angry with me; for others, as you are aware, and not I, are the guilty cause. And so fare you well, and try to bear lightly what must needs be; you know my errand. Then bursting into tears he turned away and went out.

Socrates looked at him and said: I return your good wishes, and will do as you bid. Then turning to us, he said, How charming the man is: since I have been in prison he has always been coming to see me, and at times he would talk to me, and was as good as could be to me, and now see how generously he sorrows for me. But we must do as he says, Crito; let the cup be brought, if the poison is prepared: if not, let the attendant prepare some.

Yet, said Crito, the sun is still upon the hill-tops, and many a one has taken the draught late, and after the announcement has been made to him, he has eaten and drunk, and indulged in sensual delights; do not hasten then, there is still time.

Socrates said: Yes, Crito, and they of whom you speak are right in doing thus, for they think that they will gain by the delay; but I am right in not doing thus, for I do not think that I should gain anything by drinking the poison a little later; I should be sparing and saving a life which is already gone; I could only laugh at myself for this. Please then to do as I say, and not to refuse me.

Crito, when he heard this, made a sign to the servant; and the servant went in, and remained for some time, and then returned with the jailer carrying the cup of poison. Socrates said: You, my good friend, who are experienced in these matters, shall give me directions how I am to proceed. The man answered: You have only to walk about until your legs are heavy, and then to lie down, and the poison will act. At the same time he handed the cup to Socrates, who in the easiest and gentlest manner, without the least fear or change of color or feature, looking at the man with all his eyes, Echecrates, as his manner was, took the cup and said: What do you say about making a libation out of this cup to any god? May I, or not? The man answered: We only prepare, Socrates, just so much as we deem enough. I understand, he said: yet I may and must pray to the gods to prosper my journey from this to that other world—may this then, which is my prayer, be granted to me. Then holding the cup to his lips, quite readily and cheerfully he drank off the poison. And hitherto most of us had been able to control our sorrow; but now when we saw him drinking, and saw too that he had finished the draught, we could no longer forbear, and in spite of myself my own tears were flowing fast; so that I covered my face and wept over myself, for certainly I was not weeping over him, but at the thought of my own calamity in having lost such a companion. Nor was I the first, for Crito, when he found himself unable to restrain his tears, had got up and moved away, and I followed; and at that moment, Apollodorus, who had been weeping all the time, broke out into a loud cry which made cowards of us all. Socrates alone retained his calmness: What is this strange outcry? he said. I sent away the women mainly in order that they might not offend in this way, for I have heard that a man should die in peace. Be quiet then, and have patience. When we heard that, we were ashamed, and refrained our tears; and he walked about until, as he said, his legs began to fail, and then he lay on his back, according to the directions, and the man who gave him the poison now and then looked at his feet and legs; and after a while he pressed his foot hard, and asked him if he could feel; and he said, No; and then his leg, and so upwards and upwards, and showed us that he was cold and stiff. And he felt then himself and said: When the poison reaches the heart, that will be the end. He was beginning to grow cold about the groin, when he uncovered his face, for he had covered himself up, and said (they were his last words)—he said: Crito, I owe a cock to Asclepius; will you remember to pay the debt? The debt shall be paid, said Crito; is there anything else? There was no answer to this question; but in a minute or two a movement was heard, and the attendants uncovered him; his eyes were set, and Crito closed his eyes and mouth.

Such was the end, Echecrates, of our friend, whom I may truly call the wisest, and justest, and best of all men whom I have ever known.

Plato

Among the host of handsome and brilliant young men who dogged the footsteps of Socrates about Athens, one youth stood out from the rest, both physically and intellectually. His real name was Aristocles, but he soon acquired the nickname Plato ("the broad-shouldered one"). The son of a wealthy and noble family—on his mother's side he was descended from the great lawgiver, Solon—Plato (427-347 B.C.) was preparing for a career in politics when the trial and execution of Socrates changed the course of his life. He abandoned his political career and turned to philosophy, opening a school on the outskirts of Athens dedicated to the Socratic search for wisdom. Plato's school, known as the Academy, was the first university in the history of the West. It continued in operation for over nine hundred years, from 387 B.C. until it was closed by an edict of Justinian in A.D. 529.

Unlike Socrates, Plato was a writer as well as a teacher. His writings are in the form of dialogues, with Socrates as the principal speaker. In the selection that follows, the "Allegory of the Cave" (perhaps the most famous passage in all his writings), Plato describes symbolically the predicament in which man finds himself and proposes a way of salvation. In addition, the Allegory presents, in brief form, most of Plato's major philosophical theories: his belief that the world revealed by our senses is not the real world but only a poor copy of it, and that the real world can be apprehended only intellectually; his idea that knowledge cannot be transferred from teacher to student, but rather that education consists of directing the student's mind toward what is real and important and allowing him to apprehend it for himself; his faith that the universe ultimately is good; his conviction that enlightened men have an obligation to the rest of society, and that a good society must be one in which truly wise men are the rulers. Woven into these themes is a defense of the life of Socrates and a condemnation of Athenian society for having executed him.

The Allegory is from Book VII of Plato's best-known work, *The Republic*, which represents a conversation between Socrates and some friends on the nature of justice, and which includes Plato's plan for an ideal state ruled by philosophers. The influence of *The Republic* can be detected in almost all subsequent writing on political theory in Western history.

THE REPUBLIC

[The Allegory of the Cave]

. . .

Now then, I [*Socrates*] proceeded to say, go on to compare our natural condition, so far as education and ignorance are concerned, to a state of things like the following. Imagine a number of men living in an underground, cavernous chamber, with an entrance open to the light, extending along the entire length of the cavern, in which they have been confined from their childhood, with their legs and necks so shackled, that they are obliged to sit still and look straight forwards, because their chains render it impossible for them to turn their heads round: and imagine a bright fire burning some way off, above and behind them, and an elevated roadway passing between the fire and the prisoners, with a low wall built along it, like the screens which conjurors put up in front of their audience, and above which they exhibit their wonders.

I have it, he replied.

Also figure to yourself a number of persons walking behind this wall, and carrying with them statues of men, and images of other animals, wrought in wood and stone and all kinds of materials, together with various other articles, which overtop the wall; and, as you might expect, let some of the passers-by be talking, and others silent.

You are describing a strange scene, and strange prisoners.

They resemble us, I replied. For let me ask you, in the first place, whether persons so confined could have seen anything of

THE REPUBLIC OF PLATO, trans. J. L. Davies and D. J. Vaughan. 3d ed. (London, 1866), pp. 235-243.

themselves or of each other, beyond the shadows thrown by the fire upon the part of the cavern facing them?

Certainly not, if you suppose them to have been compelled all their lifetime to keep their heads unmoved.

And is not their knowledge of the things carried past them equally limited?

Unquestionably it is.

And if they were able to converse with one another, do you not think that they would be in the habit of giving names to the objects which they saw before them?

Doubtless they would.

Again; if their prison-house returned an echo from the part facing them, whenever one of the passers-by opened his lips, to what, let me ask you, could they refer the voice, if not to the shadow which was passing?

Unquestionably they would refer it to that.

Then surely such persons would hold the shadows of those manufactured articles to be the only realities.

Without a doubt they would.

Now consider what would happen if the course of nature brought them a release from their fetters, and a remedy for their foolishness, in the following manner. Let us suppose that one of them has been released, and compelled suddenly to stand up, and turn his neck round and walk with open eyes towards the light; and let us suppose that he goes through all these actions with pain, and that the dazzling splendour renders him incapable of discerning those objects of which he used formerly to see the shadows. What answer should you expect him to make, if some one were to tell him that in those days he was watching foolish phantoms, but that now he is somewhat nearer to reality, and is turned towards things more real, and sees more correctly; above all, if he were to point out to him the several objects that are passing by, and question

him, and compel him to answer what they are? Should you not expect him to be puzzled, and to regard his old visions as truer than the objects now forced upon his notice?

Yes, much truer.

And if he were further compelled to gaze at the light itself, would not his eyes, think you, be distressed, and would he not shrink and turn away to the things which he could see distinctly, and consider them to be really clearer than the things pointed out to him?

Just so.

And if some one were to drag him violently up the rough and steep ascent from the cavern, and refuse to let him go till he had drawn him out into the light of the sun, would he not, think you, be vexed and indignant at such treatment, and on reaching the light, would he not find his eyes so dazzled by the glare as to be incapable of making out so much as one of the objects that are now called true?

Yes, he would find it so at first.

Hence, I suppose, habit will be necessary to enable him to perceive objects in that upper world. At first he will be most successful in distinguishing shadows; then he will discern the reflections of men and other things in water, and afterwards the realities; and after this he will raise his eyes to encounter the light of the moon and stars, finding it less difficult to study the heavenly bodies and the heaven itself by night, than the sun and the sun's light by day.

Doubtless.

Last of all, I imagine, he will be able to observe and contemplate the nature of the sun, not as it *appears* in water or on alien ground, but as it *is* in itself in its own territory.

Of course.

His next step will be to draw the conclusion, that the sun is the author of the seasons and the years, and the guardian of all things in the visible world, and in a manner the cause of all those things which he and his companions used to see.

Obviously, this will be his next step.

What then? When he recalls to mind his first habitation, and the wisdom of the place, and his old fellow-prisoners, do you not think he will congratulate himself on the change, and pity them?

Assuredly he will.

And if it was their practice in those days to receive honour and commendations one from another, and to give prizes to him who had the keenest eye for a passing object, and who remembered best all that used to precede and follow and accompany it, and from these data divined most ably what was going to come next, do you fancy that he will covet these prizes, and envy those who receive honour and exercise authority among them? Do you not rather imagine that he will feel what Homer describes, and wish extremely

> 'to drudge on the lands of a master,
> Under a portionless wight,'

and be ready to go through anything, rather than entertain those opinions, and live in that fashion?

For my own part, he replied, I am quite of that opinion. I believe he would consent to go through anything rather than live in that way.

And now consider what would happen if such a man were to descend again and seat himself on his old seat? Coming so suddenly out of the sun, would he not find his eyes blinded with the gloom of the place?

Certainly, he would.

And if he were forced to deliver his opinion again, touching the shadows aforesaid, and to enter the lists against those who had always been prisoners, while his sight continued dim, and his eyes unsteady,—and if this process of initiation lasted a considerable time,—would he not be made a laughingstock, and would it not be said of him, that he had gone up only to come back again with his eyesight destroyed, and that it was not worth while even to attempt the ascent? And if any one endeavoured to set them free and carry them to the light, would they not go so far as to put him to death, if they could only manage to get him into their power.

Yes, that they would.

Now this imaginary case, my dear Glaucon, you must apply in all its parts to our former statements, by comparing the region which the eye reveals, to the prison-house, and the light of the fire therein to the power of the sun: and if, by the upward ascent and the contemplation of the upper world, you understand the mounting of the soul into the intellectual region, you will hit the tendency of my own surmises, since you desire to be told what they are; though, indeed, God only knows whether they are correct. But, be that as it may, the view which I take of the subject is to the following effect. In the world of knowledge, the essential Form of Good is the limit of our inquiries, and can barely be perceived; but, when perceived, we cannot help concluding that it is in every case the source of all that is bright and beautiful,—in the visible world giving birth to light and its master, and in the intellectual world dispensing, immediately and with full authority, truth and reason;—and that whosoever would act wisely, either in private or in public, must set this Form of Good before his eyes.

To the best of my power, said he, I quite agree with you.

That being the case, I continued, pray agree with me on another point, and do not be surprised, that those who have climbed so high are unwilling to take a part in the affairs of men, because their souls are ever loath to desert that upper region. For how could it be otherwise, if the preceding simile is indeed a correct representation of their case?

True, it could scarcely be otherwise.

Well: do you think it a marvellous thing, that a person, who has just quitted the contemplation of divine objects for the study of human infirmities, should betray awkwardness, and appear very ridiculous, when with his sight still dazed, and before he has become sufficiently habituated to the darkness that reigns around, he finds himself compelled to contend in the courts of law, or elsewhere, about the shadows of justice, or images which throw the shadows, and to enter the lists in questions involving the arbitrary suppositions entertained by those who have never yet had a glimpse of the essential features of justice?

No, it is anything but marvellous.

Right: for a sensible man will recollect that the eyes may be confused in two distinct ways and from two distinct causes,— that is to say, by sudden transitions either from light to darkness, or from darkness to light. And, believing the same idea to be applicable to the soul, whenever such a person sees a case in which the mind is perplexed and unable to distinguish objects, he will not laugh irrationally, but he will examine whether it has just quitted a brighter life, and has been blinded by the novelty of darkness, or whether it has come from the depths of ignorance into a more brilliant life, and has been dazzled by the unusual splendour; and not till then will he congratulate the one upon its life and condition, and compassionate the other; and if he chooses to laugh at it, such laughter will be less ridiculous than that which is raised at the expense of the soul that has descended from the light of a higher region.

You speak with great judgment.

Hence, if this be true, we cannot avoid adopting the belief, that the real nature of education is at variance with the account given of it by certain of its professors, who pretend, I believe, to infuse into the mind a knowledge of which it was destitute, just as sight might be instilled into blinded eyes.

True; such are their pretensions.

Whereas, our present argument shows us that there is a faculty residing in the soul of each person, and an instrument enabling each of us to learn; and that, just as we might suppose it to be impossible to turn the eye round from darkness to light without turning the whole body, so must this faculty, or this instrument, be wheeled round, in company with the entire soul, from the perishing world, until it be enabled to endure the contemplation of the real world and the brightest part thereof, which, according to us, is the Form of Good. Am I not right?

You are.

Hence, I continued, this very process of revolution must give rise to an art, teaching in what way the change will most easily and most effectually be brought about. Its object will not be to generate in the person the power of seeing. On the contrary, it assumes that he possesses it, though he is turned in a wrong direction, and does not look towards the right quarter; and its aim is to remedy this defect.

So it would appear.

Hence, while, on the one hand, the other so-called virtues of the soul seem to resemble those of the body, inasmuch as they really do not preexist in the soul, but are formed in it in the course of time by habit, and exercise; the virtue of wisdom, on the other hand, does most certainly appertain, as it would appear, to a more divine substance, which never loses its energy, but by change of position becomes useful and serviceable, or else remains useless and injurious. For you must, ere this, have noticed how keen-sighted are the puny souls of those who have the reputation of being clever but vicious, and how sharply they see through the things to which they are directed, thus proving that their powers of vision are by no means feeble, though they have been compelled to become the servants of wickedness, so that the more sharply they see, the more numerous are the evils which they work.

Yes, indeed it is the case.

But, I proceeded, if from earliest childhood these characters had been shorn and stripped of those leaden, earth-born weights, which grow and cling to the pleasures of eating and gluttonous enjoyments of a similar nature, and keep the eye of the soul turned upon the things below;—if, I repeat, they had been released from these snares, and turned round to look at objects that are true, then these very same souls of these very same men would have had as keen an eye for such pursuits as they actually have for those in which they are now engaged.

Yes, probably it would be so.

Once more: is it not also probable, or rather is it not a necessary corollary to our previous remarks, that neither those who are uneducated and ignorant of truth, nor those who are suffered to linger over their education all their life, can ever be competent overseers of a state,—the former, because they have no single mark in life, which they are to constitute the end and aim of all their conduct both in private and in public; the latter, because they will not act without compulsion, fancying that, while yet alive, they have been translated to the islands of the blest.

That is true.

It is, therefore, our task, I continued, to constrain the noblest characters in our colony to arrive at that science which we formerly pronounced the highest, and to set eyes upon the good, and to mount that ascent we spoke of; and, when they have mounted and looked long enough, we must take care to refuse them that liberty which is at present permitted them.

Pray what is that?

The liberty of staying where they are, and refusing to descend again to those prisoners, or partake of their toils and honours, be they mean or be they exalted.

Then are we to do them a wrong, and make them live a life that is worse than the one within their reach?

You have again forgotten, my friend, that law does not ask itself how some one class in a state is to live extraordinarily well. On the contrary, it tries to bring about this result in the entire state; for which purpose it links the citizens together by persuasion and by constraint, makes them share with one another the benefit which each individual can contribute to the common weal, and does actually create men of this exalted character in the state, not with the intention of letting them go each on his own way, but with the intention of turning them to account in its plans for the consolidation of the state.

True, he replied; I had forgotten.

Therefore reflect, Glaucon, that far from wronging the future philosophers of our state, we shall only be treating them with strict justice, if we put them under the additional obligation of watching over their fellow citizens, and taking care of them. We shall say: It is with good reason that your compeers elsewhere refuse to share in the labours of their respective states. For they take root in a city spontaneously, in defiance of the prevailing constitution; and it is but fair that a self-sown plant, which is indebted to no one for support, should have no inclination to pay to anybody wages for attendance. But in your case, it is we that have begotten you for the state as well as for yourselves, to be like leaders and kings of a hive,—better and more perfectly trained than the rest, and more capable of playing a part in both modes of life. You must therefore descend by turns, and associate with the rest of the

community, and you must habituate yourselves to the contemplation of these obscure objects. For, when habituated, you
will see a thousand times better than the
residents, and you will recognize what
each image is, and what is its original, because you have seen the realities of which
beautiful and just and good things are copies. And in this way you and we shall find
that the life of the state is a substance, and
not a phantom like the life of our present states, which are mostly composed of
men who fight among themselves for shadows, and are at feud for the administration
of affairs, which they regard as a great
boon. Whereas I conceive the truth stands
thus: That city in which the destined rulers are least eager to rule, will inevitably
be governed in the best and least factious
manner, and a contrary result will ensue if
the rulers are of a contrary disposition.

You are perfectly right.

And do you imagine that our pupils,
when addressed in this way, will disobey
our commands, and refuse to toil with us
in the state by turns, while they spend
most of their time together in that bright
region?

Impossible, he replied: for certainly it is
a just command and those who are to obey
it are just men. No; doubtless each of them
will enter upon his administration as an
unavoidable duty,—conduct the reverse of
that pursued by the present rulers in each
state.

True, my friend; the case stands thus. If
you can invent for the destined rulers a
life better than ruling, you may possibly
realize a well-governed city: for only in
such a city will the rulers be those who
are really rich, not in gold, but in a
wise and virtuous life, which is the wealth
essential to a happy man. But if beggars,
and persons who hunger after private advantages, take the reins of the state, with
the idea that they are privileged to snatch
advantage from their power, all goes
wrong. For the post of magistrate is thus
made an object of strife; and civil and intestine conflicts of this nature, ruin not
only the contending parties, but also the
rest of the state.

That is most true.

And can you mention any life which
contemns state-offices, except the life of
true philosophy?

No indeed, I cannot.

Well, but the task of government must
be undertaken by persons not enamoured
of it: otherwise, their rivals will dispute
their claim.

Unquestionably it must.

Then what other persons will you compel to enter upon the duties of guardians
of the state, if you discard those who understand most profoundly the means of attaining the highest excellence in the administration of a country, and who also
possess honours of a different stamp, and a
nobler life than that of a statesman?

I shall not discard them, he replied; I
shall address myself only to them.

Aristotle

Aristotle (384-322 B.C.) was a native of Macedonia. At the age of eighteen he journeyed to Athens and enrolled as a student in the Academy. There he remained for twenty years, until the death of Plato. He then moved to Asia Minor to become political adviser to the ruler of a small kingdom. While there he married the king's niece. It is said that he spent his honeymoon gathering sea shells for use in scientific studies. From Asia Minor he was called back to his native Macedonia to serve as tutor to Alexander the Great, who was then a boy of twelve. When Alexander set out to conquer the world, Aristotle returned to Athens and established a school of his own, the Lyceum, as a rival to the Academy. For the next eleven years he divided his time among teaching, public lecturing, and writing. His philosophical system is known as the *peripatetic* (or "walking") philosophy, a title derived from his habit of pacing back and forth as he lectured.

At the death of Alexander in 323, Aristotle, because of his former association with the conqueror, found himself unpopular in Athens. Fearing the anger of the mob and remembering the fate of Socrates, he fled the city, not wishing, as he put it, "to give the Athenians a second chance of sinning against philosophy." He died in exile the following year.

Aristotle was a remarkably productive writer. His extant works include major treatises on physics, astronomy, zoology, biology, botany, psychology, logic, ethics, metaphysics, political theory, constitutional history, rhetoric, and the theory of art. His influence on the intellectual history of the West has been at least equal to that of Plato. Wherever his works have been studied there has been intellectual ferment, activity, and development. Partly as a result of Aristotle's influence, the Moslems of the Near East enjoyed an intellectual golden age while Europe was still deep in the Dark Ages. The rediscovery of Aristotle by Europeans, through their contact with the Moslems, contributed directly to the cultural awakening in Europe that culminated in the high Middle Ages of the thirteenth century. Since the rise of modern science the philosophy of Aristotle has come under increasingly sharp attack; nevertheless, many of his main concepts and theories remain alive and vigorous in our own century.

The following selections are from two of Aristotle's major works, *The Nicomachean Ethics* and *The Politics*. The *Ethics*, with its emphasis on reason, moderation, and harmony, reflects, perhaps better than any other extant writing, the highest ideals of the Greek way of life. And Aristotle's views, in *The Politics*, on the social nature of man, the purpose of government, and the most desirable kind of society, have formed the basis, along with Plato's *Republic*, for almost all subsequent political theory in the West.

THE NICOMACHEAN ETHICS

Book I

In every art and in every way to knowledge there is some 'good' which we seek to attain. The objects which determine human choice and action are those from which we expect to gain some 'good.' Hence some have properly defined the *Summum Bonum* as 'the good at which *all* things aim.' This is a universal law: not only things which are moved by conscious thought, aim, by that motion, at some good, but also things which are moved by the laws of nature are led towards the realization of some good end, or purpose, though it be unconsciously, like an arrow shot at a mark. There is thus an 'end' in every form of moral action or of physical movement.

. . .

Since every process of thought and every movement of the will has some purpose at which it aims, what is that purpose at which we say that the Science of Life aims? All actions being directed, as has been shown, to the realization of some purpose, what is that purpose towards which the Science of Society is directed, and what is that culmination of all good things attainable by action, which is 'the end' of the Science of Society?

So far as this is a question of *words*, there is but one single name applied to this ultimate end by the mass of mankind; and so far the masses are in perfect accord with the *élite*:—all men call this end *happiness*, and suppose that 'being happy' is exactly equivalent to 'living well and faring well.'

But as for what happiness really is,—upon that point men are at issue, and philosophers do not give the same account of it as mankind in general. The masses proclaim happiness to be one of those goods which are palpable and conspicuous, and which are commonly thought to be dear to men, such as pleasure or wealth or honour, different men preferring different objects, but all of the same character. Ofttimes even the same person will give a fluctuating account of it, now calling it one thing, now another (*e.g.*, in sickness, health; in poverty, riches); and generally, men apply the name of happiness to some particular thing for which they have a desire at the moment. Again, those who are enamoured of philosophy are eager to learn subjects of which they are conscious of being ignorant; and hence admire and envy those who utter grand truths transcending their own horizon. Others, again, consider that beyond the multitude of particular goods, there is some other good, subsisting by itself, which constitutes happiness, and which is in truth the *cause* to all other things of their goodness.

To examine, however, all the opinions held about happiness is surely a futile task. Sufficient is it for our purpose if we examine the opinions which are most in vogue and approved by men generally or which seem to rest upon some ground of reason.

. . . Men entertain divergent opinions upon the nature of happiness. In fact, every man defines happiness in such a way as to reflect the tenor and inclinations of his own life. Hence the masses (whose passions are unbridled) maintain that pleasure is happiness, and for that reason the life they love is the life of enjoyment.

Indeed, if we look at the world as a whole, there are three general types of lives: the life devoted to pleasure, the life of social interests, and the life of contemplation.

The first life, that of pleasure, has in it nothing that is sacred. Those who follow

THE MORAL PHILOSOPHY OF ARISTOTLE, trans. W. M. Hatch. Completed after his death by others (London, 1879), pp. 12, 19, 23-24, 33-34, 36-38, 59-64, 72, 74-76, 90-94, 96-100.

such a life are thoroughly slave-like, and live the life of mere animals. In fact their life seems only worthy of consideration from the fact that there are many men in high positions who make it their choice, and cultivate tastes like those of a Sardanapalus.

The second life is one which the better kind of men prefer. Those who follow a line of noble conduct think that honour is their true end, honour being pretty generally the 'end' of that social life to which I am referring, and the aim sought for by all. But it is evident that this is not the ultimate end of man: on the contrary, it must itself also be added to the list of those things which *seem* only to be good, and which have no existence beyond appearance. For that which is in very truth the good of man, and in virtue of which he is happy, must needs be something depending upon his own self. Honour, on the contrary, does not depend upon the person upon whom it is conferred, but rather on the person who confers it. Happiness, therefore, does not consist in honour: if a man is to be happy, his 'good' must be a thing peculiarly his own, and difficult to be wrested from him.

Moreover, the reason why men pursue honour, is that they may have an assurance about themselves that they are virtuous; hence they seek to be honoured by men of sound judgment by whom they are personally known, and to be honoured on the ground of their moral worth. It is clear, therefore, that the reason why men pursue honour is that they may have the reputation of being good and worthy men, and that on the score of their virtue; and thus it is evident that honour is not pursued for its own sake, but on account of the virtue implied in it. Hence honour itself will not be our ultimate end, but rather virtue.

Yet even virtue fails of being the *perfect* good, and therefore happiness which is our perfect good cannot consist in virtue. That virtue *is* imperfect, is evident. It is possible for a man to have a habit of virtue, though he be slumbering or in some other way inactive all life through, or though he be evil-entreated, or unfortunate, or fallen into great calamities, and, in consequence thereof, have his virtue marred and incomplete. If a man's life is thus situated, no one would call him happy:—much less would one assure it as a fact that 'happiness is the habit of virtue,' and name it accordingly.

Let these considerations suffice for discussing the claims of the life of self-indulgence and the life of social interests. I have in fact treated the subject sufficiently in my Public Lectures. As for the life of meditation, I shall have to examine into that by-and-by. For the present I have a different object in view.

There is, however, still one other life, that of the money-maker; but this has practically been already considered in the lives above described. The man who pursues pleasure, equally with the man who pursues honour, wishes to amass riches. Hence I said that there are *three* types of lives which are specially prominent, the life of the money-maker being included in our previous survey.

Such a life is, in fact, an unnatural existence for a man. So far from pursuing that 'good' which is the 'perfect good' of man, it does not even profess to pursue it. Hence there are not many by whom it is embraced. Few there are who make it their choice to have money as the end of all their endeavours and interests in life. It is also evident that not even does the money-maker himself seek wealth as the 'chief good.' Wealth is sought only for the sake of its uses, and with a view to an ulterior purpose, for the sake, that is, of pleasure or honour. But the 'chief good' must needs be good *for its own sake*.

.   .   .

But we must endeavour to render it still more evident what the real nature of this 'end' is. Hitherto we have not made any definite statement about it, but have still to examine its real character. The discussion has been traversing a circle and has made no actual progress, but has come round to the very point which was premised in the Introduction that the 'end' of all human action will be the Summum Bonum and the highest interest of man.

Since then the ends of action are various, and some of them are not chosen by us for their own sake, but for the sake of different ends, namely, the ends of the Sciences which are Sovereign Sciences, as we have already shown, being simply 'instrumental ends' in view of those higher ends—just as wealth which is the end of the money-maker's life is useful also to the statesman for the furthering of his special end; or as the flute which is the 'end' of the flute-maker is useful also to the flute player for his playing; and as in the same way all instruments are serviceable with a view to further uses; since, I say, there are certain kinds of ends which are not 'goods' *per se*, all ends cannot be final or perfect ends. Yet the good for the sake of which we perform all our actions, ought to be a thing final and perfect; hence it cannot be any one of the ends of this kind, namely, imperfect ends. Nay, if there be many perfect ends, the Summum Bonum will be the most perfect of all; and if there be only one perfect end, then that one perfect end will be the good sought for in all human endeavour.

Now we say that an end which is sought for *per se* and for its own sake is more perfect than one sought for the sake of something beyond. Again, since there are certain goods sought for as well for their own sakes as also for other objects, (*e.g.*, health and the power of thought,) among such ends that is the more perfect which is sought for its own sake alone, and never for the sake of aught else. Such a good is not more perfect simply through combination with other goods, but without qualification in and by itself it is a perfect good.

Such attributes as these of finality and perfection are thought to be characteristic of happiness in the very highest degree. We make our choice of happiness invariably for its own sake. Honour and pleasure and sound sense and all virtue are also things which we make choice of for their own sake (since we should still make our choice of them, though no result accrued therefrom); yet at the same time we also make choice of them for the sake of happiness, actuated by the impression that through their means we may be happy. On the other hand no one makes choice of happiness for the sake of pleasure and such things, nor in fact for any motive beyond itself. Consequently happiness will be the good sought for in all the transactions and endeavours of men.

·   ·   ·

Now, to describe happiness as 'the good which is sought by the Science of Life,' and as 'that which is best for man,' is evidently a truism. It is required that we should explain the nature of happiness with greater perspicuity. This desire may be satisfied if we can discover the work which is distinctive of man, in so far as he is *man*. Just as the 'good' of every craftsman depends upon his work, the good of a piper depending upon his piping, of a statuary on his statues, the same principle holding good of every work and of every action, precisely so the special good of man depends upon his own peculiar work—if there be any work peculiar and characteristic of man *as man*. But is it possible that, though there are certain works and actions proper to the carpenter and the shoemaker, there is no work proper to *man*, but that he is so constituted as to be a thing without a purpose? Is it not rather the truth that just as there is seen to be a special function for the eye, for the hand, and for the foot, and in fact for each one of our physical members, so also, beyond the functions of the parts, one might find a function for *man* as a moral unity?

What, then, is this special function of

man? Mere life, of course, is common also to plants: what we are seeking is the characteristic function of men. We may, therefore, dismiss the consideration of mere life. But following after this life of growth and increase, or the life of plants, there comes the life of sensation, a life more nearly approaching to the life of reason; and we must here examine into its claims. Yet this life of sensation is shared in common by other organizations, by the horse and the ox, and animals generally; hence neither is this the *special* work of man of which we are in quest.

There is only one alternative, that the special work of man should be a 'life manifested in action within the sphere of Reason.' This, again, is found to bear a twofold aspect. Under one aspect it is irrational in itself, though obedient and submissive to reason. Under another aspect it contains reason, and consciously exercises it. The element which contains reason, and consciously exercises it, is the faculty of arranging and coordinating; whereas the element which is irrational is ordered and arranged by the other. Hence the rational element is more distinctive than the other, the special activity of man—since this rational life is a real activity, whereas the other element is called 'passive' or 'receptive' only.

The special work of man, therefore, is 'an energy of the soul in conformity with perfect Reason' when the soul is exercising thought; or not devoid of Reason when it is moved in respect of its passive conditions acting in association with Reason.

Since, then, the energy of man is an energy in accordance with Reason—though it be exercised well and nobly, its excellence does not prevent its being still a human energy. The functions of the lute-player, and of the skilful lute-player, are not distinct in kind, it being the part of the lute-player to play the lute, and of the good lute-player to play artistically; but the functions of playing and of skilful playing are not distinct in kind, any more than a horse is distinct in kind, any more than a horse is distinct from a good horse. If this be true, and we regard the work of man as a kind of life, and life as an activity of the soul, and actions in accordance with Reason, it will be the special function of a good man to develop his faculties nobly in accordance with Reason. But a thing is ever done well and exquisitely when it is in accord with the ideal which is special and peculiar to it. The activity of man, therefore, will be well and exquisitely developed when it is in accord with the ideal which is special and peculiar to it: and this ideal is Virtue. Hence the ideal special to man is 'an activity of the soul *in accordance with Virtue*;' and if there are many Virtues, his ideal activity will be in accordance with the best and most perfect among them.

Here, then, has been discovered what is the 'perfection of man.' As has been shown 'the good' or 'perfection' of a thing is its 'end.' There has thus been discovered also 'the end' of human actions and of human endeavours; and it has been shown that the end of human actions is identical with happiness. Our task, therefore, has been fulfilled, and happiness has been discovered.

But it is also necessary that if the work of man is to have free range for being perfected, there should be an unbroken harmony of external conditions in which it may be exercised. It is not the solitary swallow nor the one bright day which produces summer; so neither does one single day nor a brief spell of sunshine make a man's whole career blessed and happy.

.   .   .

Now since happiness is 'a conscious exercise of the human faculties in harmony with perfect virtue' we must further consider the nature of virtue: the examination of it will render more distinct our theory of happiness. This is clearly a subject which all genuine statesmen must consider, from the desire which they must feel to render the citizens virtuous and obedient to the laws, as the legislators of the Cretans and Lacedemonians and others like-minded in the ancient States have done.

Hence it is evident that an 'Inquiry concerning virtue' will be consequent upon the scope originally laid down for our Treatise; *i.e.*, 'the end of the Science of civil life.'

We must, therefore, examine the nature of virtue—the virtue of course which is proper to man, since the happiness or perfection of which we went in search at starting was a perfection of *man*.

Now since the special excellence of man is not an excellence of the body but of the mind or soul (indeed we define happiness as an activity of the *soul*), and since the excellence into which the statesman inquires is a *human* excellence, it is evident that he ought to know how the economy of the soul is constituted. In the same way it is essential that one who is to treat successfully an eye-disease should have a knowledge of the whole body. But even more than the physician, it is right that the statesman should understand the phenomena of the soul in proportion as statesmanship is more excellent and of higher worth than is the art of healing. Yet all physicians of repute labour earnestly to gain a knowledge of the body, so that it is only reasonable that statesmen also should understand the condition of the soul; yet we need not carry our speculations further than may suffice to elucidate the theory of virtue.

To elaborate a scientific theory of soul, and to exhibit its wider issues, would be beyond the scope of our purpose. I have already treated of psychology, not only in various compilations but also *viva voce* with those whom I have met in discussion; and I will here adopt some of the conclusions at which we have arrived.

I premise then that there are two divisions of the soul, one rational, the other irrational. But as for the question whether these parts are separable and distinct from one another, as the parts of the body are,

and as other things are which can be broken up into their component elements, or whether they are in fact one and only logically distinct (like the concave and convex in the circumference of a circle, which are in reality one and in their nature inseparable though differing in definition, that of the concave being one thing, that of the convex another)—this is a question which tends in no way to the elucidation of the problem before us.

We will now proceed to speak of the irrational part of the soul. In this division there is one element which is vegetative— I am alluding to the power of nutrition and of growth which is common to all plants and animals. This power indeed is found in all things capable of growth and even in embryos, and it is this self-same power which is found in creatures who are full grown (for it would be absurd to suppose it to be any other).

In this faculty, however, it is impossible to detect the excellence of *man* in the proper sense of the term: its excellence is shared by all organized life. Indeed this power of increase and of growth is of a nature to operate even when men are asleep, and more so then than at any other time; but the special excellence of man is of a very different character from that. The good man is never so little distinguishable from the bad man as when asleep; and for this reason men say that 'for half their days the happy are in no wise different from the wretched,' that is, during the period of sleep. There is good reason in the proverb, sleep being inaction both to the good and to the vicious soul. Only one may say so much—that the slumbers of the good are purer and better than those of the bad; since the physical inclinations of the daytime penetrate in a sense even to sleep; and hence 'the visions of the night' assume a healthier form to the good than to common mortals.

But enough of these speculations: sufficient to have shown that the nutritive part of the soul is devoid of that *human* excellence with which our business lies.

But there is another power or tendency in the soul not in every respect irrational (as the one first mentioned was) but in a way participating in reason, and even entering into conflict with it. On this account we sometimes praise the reason of the strong-minded man, and sometimes that of the weak-minded man, since both hold out against a force opposed to them—in the one case as long as is right, and in the other case at any rate up to a certain point. Hence there is evidently another power within them which contends and struggles against reason. In simple truth, just as paralytic parts of the body, when men strive to move them to the right, swing contrariwise back to the left, so is it also in regard to the soul. The impulses in men of weak character bear them back in a direction contrary to the suggestions of reason. But in the case of bodies we see the part that is strained back; whereas in the soul there is nothing that we can see. Still though this moral struggle is not seen with the eyes, it is a real fact, and we must take it into our consideration that there is a power within the soul besides reason, opposed to it, and in conflict with it. To describe the mode in which this conflict takes place is immaterial to the purpose which we have in hand.

Yet this element also has unmistakably a share of reason, as we have shown, in so far as it is obedient to reason. This irrational element (I mean the impulsive or appetitive part of the soul) is guided and governed by the reason of the strong-minded man: even more easily controlled and influenced is it by the reason of the temperate and brave man in whose character every element is in perfect accord with reason.

Accordingly it is evident that the irrational part of the soul is twofold. In one respect it is absolutely irrational, as the principle of vegetation, of growth and of nutrition. In the other aspect it participates in reason up to a certain point, as the principle of impulse and desire—a principle which participates in reason in so far as it is submissive and obedient thereto. That this irrational part is to a certain extent governed by reason is a fact rendered evident by the counsels and exhortations and reproaches which are addressed to it; and by means of which many of our irrational inclinations are brought to order.

But a man is said to 'share in reason' in a double sense, just as he is said to 'have reason.' We speak of a man 'admitting the reasons' of his father or friends—*i.e.*, betaking himself to them and following the advice which they give. We speak also of a man 'admitting the reasons' of mathematical demonstrations—*i.e.*, comprehending their meaning and having knowledge or scientific perception of them. In an exactly similar way a man is said to '*share* in reason' in a double sense. In one respect he is said to 'share in reason' absolutely and in his own right just like the purely intellectual part of the soul. In another sense a man is said to share in reason on account of his being submissive to reason, in the way in which one is submissive to his father.

Corresponding with this division of the soul is the classification of virtue into distinct forms. We say that certain virtues which belong to the rational part of the soul are intellectual virtues, and that certain others which belong to the impulsive or appetitive part of the soul are moral virtues. The intellectual virtues are such as philosophy, insight, and prudence; and the moral virtues such as liberality and temperance. When we speak of a man's nature, we do not say that he is philosophic or that he has comprehension, but that he is, for instance, gentle and temperate; though we praise the student of philosophy in respect of the excellence of his mental habit, which is in fact a virtue. For whatever states of mind are praiseworthy we call virtues.

Book II

Now since virtue is a perfection of the soul, and one element in the soul is rational and another element impulsive, it necessarily follows that virtue also is of a two-fold character: as the excellence of our intellectual nature it takes the form of Philosophy and Thought; and as the excellence of our emotional nature, it is called *Moral* Virtue.

To a certain extent *intellectual* excellence has its origin in Nature. It receives its earliest impulse from nature—man being by nature a receptive being, and capable of assimilating knowledge; and it gains a certain degree of increase from the natural disposition in certain cases. Yet, for the most part, and among men generally, it owes its earliest rise and its after development to instruction, and hence requires experience and length of years to mature it.

The causes which produce *moral* excellence are different from this. Moral excellence is a result brought about by the constant practice of moral acts. All that Nature contributes to moral excellence is the capacity she gives us for growing to be virtuous; and all that instruction contributes is the knowledge that it is our duty to be virtuous. But as for being virtuous in fact, and in our own personal behaviour, nothing but constant practice of virtuous actions can secure *that* to us. . . .

Consequently it is clear that there is not one of the moral virtues which is formed in us by nature. Had we been good spontaneously by force of nature, we could never have been impelled in an opposite direction by force of habit. But as an actual fact, we *are* so impelled; and hence it is clear that no single moral excellence is formed within us by nature. Nothing that is impelled in a certain way by a law of nature changes and assumes an opposite tendency under the influence of habit. No one, for example, will ever accustom a stone to gravitate upwards, though he throw it into the air ten thousand times; nor could we habituate fire to tend downwards. In fact, whenever a thing has a certain tendency from nature, it can never be made to change that tendency by force of habit.

It is not, therefore, through a law of nature nor yet in violation of any such law, that the virtues grow up within us. What we receive from nature is the *capacity* for virtue: we are so constituted by nature as to admit of the virtues being impressed upon us, though we only acquire those virtues in fact and are made perfect therein, by habit.

Again, in the case of our *natural* faculties, we first have them perfectly matured, and afterwards simply put them to their uses. We found ourselves, for instance, with the faculties of sight and hearing fully developed, and so employed them for their uses. It was not from having repeatedly seen and heard that we gained our senses of sight and hearing: on the contrary, it was from being in possession of these senses that we exercised them.

On the other hand, we only gain our *moral* faculties by having first put ourselves to the test of action (as we must do also to acquire artistic skill). What we have to learn in order to perform, we learn by the very process of performing. Men become builders by building houses, and harpists by practising upon the harp. In a precisely similar manner, men grow to be righteous by performing right actions, and self controlled by performing acts of self control, and brave by performing acts of bravery.

.   .   .

For these reasons it is a matter of great consequence, as determining the character of our habits or moral tendencies, whether the practices to which we become habituated from youth upwards be good or evil; nay, rather, the entire difference in the character of our moral tendencies is owing to this early habituation.

.   .   .

But we must not merely describe virtue as 'a habit;' we must add the further qualification what *kind* of habit it is, *i.e.*, that it is a *virtuous* habit, while vice is a vicious habit.

Now thus much may be at once assumed respecting virtue—that like all excellence, it adorns the object which possesses it, and causes it to be in a right state, and brings the work which is effected by means thereof to an excellent effect. The excellence of the eye, for instance, perfects the eye and makes it a good eye and renders its function, *i.e.*, seeing, effectual: it is through the excellence of the eye that we see well. Similarly also the excellence of the horse distinguishes the horse itself and makes it a good horse and renders its operation effectual: it is through such excellence that it is able to bear its rider easily, and to gallop, and to stand the shock of the foe.

Since this principle is of universal application, the excellence proper to man will show the same characteristics, and will be 'a habit of mind in virtue whereof a man proves himself a good man, and is enabled to accomplish the proper work of his life successfully and nobly.'

How such a state can be brought about, was explained a few pages back. We showed that the man who was resolutely determined to live in the practice of virtue ever aimed at 'a mean state' in regard to those impulses which lead to the forming of emotions, and further habituated himself to such a line of moderation.

This principle of moderation will be made yet more clear by the considerations which I will now proceed to give, from the careful examination, that is, of the distinctive and special characteristics of virtue or excellence as such.

Let us, then, regard the matter in the following aspect. In everything which is contin-

uous, for instance a line, a superficies, a body, a speech, a period of time—in fact, in everything which is capable of being divided into parts, one may take a part which is greater or less or equal. In the case, for example, of extended space: if ten feet be too much and two feet too little, the 'equal' will be that which contains six feet, and that is called also 'the mean,' because it exceeds two feet in the same proportion as it is exceeded by ten feet. The case is similar also in regard to 'discrete' quantity. If 20 be too much and 10 too little, 15 will be a fair equality, because 15 exceeds 10 the less in the same proportion as it falls short of 20 the greater. An 'equal' of this kind is called 'a mean,' and an arrangement of ratios of this kind is arithmetical proportion. In the case of discrete quantity it is not invariably necessary to find the arithmetical proportion (since we cannot carry on our division to infinity); but in the case of continuous quantity we may do so (since that is capable of being divided into infinite parts).

We do not, therefore, always determine this mean in the same manner. At one time we judge of it by the standard of the thing itself, at another time by a standard that is relative to ourselves. In respect of the thing itself the mean between 10 and 2 is 6, 6 exceeding and being exceeded to the same extent. But a mean is relative to ourselves when the middle and the excess and the defect is taken from our own point of view. For instance, if it be too much for anyone to eat 10 pounds, and 2 pounds be too little for him, it does not follow that 6 pounds is the quantity which keeps the mean and is suitable to our constitution: it is possible that either more or less may be needed to satisfy. In respect therefore of the thing itself, 6 pounds are the 'mean' between 10 and 2, and what is equal; but in reference to our own needs perhaps 7, perhaps 5, pounds, that is to say, whatever number of pounds is suitable to the constitution. A dinner of 6 pounds will be too little for a Milo, [*a famous wrestler*] as being in a thorough state of training, and his trainer will provide him with a more ample allowance; whereas such a quantity would be excessive for a man who is just commencing systematic training.

The same principle applies to running and wrestling: we judge of the 'mean' from the stand-point of those who are being trained for competition. Indeed, anyone who presides over the regulation of any profession seeks the mean, avoiding the excess or defect; but the mean which he pursues is one relative to ourselves and to our own circumstances, and not the mean which is absolute.

Thus it is that every science finishes off with true grace its proper functions; and accordingly we are wont to say in reference to works of art when beautifully executed that it is impossible to add a single line or to take away a single touch, indicating thereby that a perfect work avoids equally excess and defect, under the idea that extravagance or defect spoils the beauty of a work, whilst a chastened simplicity preserves it.

But since virtue is more delicately exact and more important than any art (just as also nature is), it will itself also have regard to this principle of the 'mean' or relative fitness.

The virtue of which I am now speaking, is not intellectual but moral virtue (the circumstances being different in regard to intellectual virtue), moral virtue being concerned with emotions and actions which are capable of being more numerous and stronger, or on the other hand, less, than what is fitting; and hence what is 'due,' *i.e.*, what is 'equal,' is also found therein. It is possible to be afraid or to be confident, to indulge in passion, to be roused to anger or to pity, and generally to have the sensations of pleasure or pain in excess or in defect, and in either issue, improperly. To experience these feelings invariably at the proper time and in the proper manner, under proper circumstances and against proper persons and with proper motives . . . this is the moral ideal, and the true Best, and that in which virtue consists.

.   .   .

Virtue is, therefore, 'a permanent state of mind, formed with the concurrence of the will and based upon an ideal of what is best in actual life—an ideal fixed by Reason according as the moral sense of the good man would determine its application.' This ideal is 'a mean state' between two vices, one tending to excess and the other to defect: it goes beyond the one and falls short of the other—since one of these faults goes beyond what is right and the other falls short of it, whereas virtue seeks only what is fitting, *i.e.*, 'the mean,' and makes that mean its choice.

.   .   .

But we must not merely say in a general way that 'virtue is a mean state,' and that 'vice consists in extremes,' but we must further explain in detail what particular virtue is a mean between what particular extremes. In discussions bearing upon conduct, while general propositions are more comprehensive, and are applicable to the larger number of instances, specific truths are the more real and trustworthy, inasmuch as they fit on closely to actions for the very reason that actions always take place under specific circumstances, and with the exigencies of specific circumstances true principles of course harmonize.

We will therefore take such cases as we require from the Diagram which I have unfolded before you. As has been explained, virtue lies midway between an excess and defect in every single phase of the moral life (excepting only such as are inherently vicious *per se*).

In reference to fear or confidence—these being emotions of the soul, the perfect frame of mind is Courage, while the extremes are cowardice as a defect, and recklessness as an excess. From the point of view of fear there is no special name for the excess, though there is from the point of view of confidence. (There are indeed many such phases of mind which have no special name.) Moreover, there is no special name for the excess of confidence, though there is a special idea—that of cowardice—drawn from the excess of fear. Hence, of the extremes the one derives its name from fear, the other from confidence.

In reference to pleasures and pains, both the extremes and the mean states are for the most part without any distinctive name, especially in regard to *pains*. But in reference to such pleasures as are purely bodily there is a mean state, 'temperance,' and an excess, 'dissoluteness.' The defect has no special name, inasmuch as there are few who entirely refrain themselves from every form of gratification: it may, however, be classed as 'insensateness.'

In reference to the feeling which we experience in giving or receiving money the true disposition is liberality, while the perversions of the mean are prodigality as an excess, and niggardliness as a defect. Yet in certain conditions the reverse is true, that prodigality is a defect, and niggardliness an excess. In *giving* money, prodigality is an excess, and illiberality a defect, whereas in *receiving* money illiberality is an excess, and prodigality a defect.

There is yet another form of the perfect state with corresponding extremes in reference to the giving and receiving of money; and that is magnificence, differing from liberality in that it lavishes vast sums, whereas liberality has only small sums to lavish. The excess of this virtue is want of taste and vulgarity and its defect meanness. These extremes again differ from the extremes of liberality: the points of difference shall be explained later on.

In regard to the emotions involved in honour and dishonour, the perfect state is mag-

nanimity, the excess 'vain-glory,' as it is called, and the defect, littleness of soul.

Corresponding to the differences which we said existed in the dispositions that relate to money, liberality and magnificence, the former being concerned with small sums, the latter with great sums, there is similarly in regard to honour a certain disposition which differs from high-mindedness in being concerned with small interests, while high-mindedness is concerned with great interests.

Now it is possible for a man to strive after honour as is fitting, or to a degree beyond what is right, or even less than is fitting. The man who is extravagant in his desires is an ambitious man, and his mental state ambitiousness. The man who lacks a proper ambition is an unambitious man (but his mental state has no distinctive name). The perfect attitude in such matters is also nameless, but it differs from magnanimity upon the point which has been mentioned.

Inasmuch as the virtuous character (*i.e.*, the man who holds the true mean) has no special name of his own, he is called after the extremes, since he partakes of the character of both: at one time we call him ambitious, at another time unambitious, and at one time we praise the ambitious man, at another the unambitious man. The grounds upon which we do so will be explained in the sequel.

Let us now proceed to enumerate the states of mind which still remain, seeking in each case for 'the mean' and for the extremes.

In the matter of anger, the mean state is good temper, the ideal character being called the good-tempered man. The two extremes have no special name, though the excess may be named passionateness, and the man who shows the excess, the passionate man; and deficiency of anger may be called impassivity, and the man who shows it, the impassive man.

There are further three other 'mean states,' which to a certain extent enter into one another, though they present also characteristic differences. In the actions we perform, and in the words we utter in our intercourse with our fellow men, part of what we say and do is said and done for the sake of amusement, part for the sake of that general gratification which we find in life.

Hence there are of necessity three 'mean states' in respect thereto. In what is said or done with a view to truth, the mean state is truthfulness; and in reference to pleasure, the state which has reference to relaxation or amusement is politeness, and that which is concerned with pleasantness generally is friendliness.

These three states all enter into one another, because they are all concerned with intercourse in word and deed, but they are different the one from the other because the relations with which they are concerned are different. Their extremes have no special name, but we must find terms for them for the sake of perspicuity, and in order that our readers may readily follow the course of the argument.

1. Let the extremes of truth, then, be named as follows:—assertion tending towards exaggeration, boastfulness, and the corresponding character, the boastful man; while if the assertion tends towards suppression, it is reservation, and the corresponding character, the reserved man.

2. In regard to politeness, the excess is buffoonery, and the man who shows the excess the buffoon; while the state which falls short of politeness is boorishness, and the man who has such a deficiency, a boor.

3. In regard to friendship, the man who is excessive therein, and that with no selfish aim, may be called the courtier; but if his motive be his own profit or advantage, then he is a flatterer. If, again, he falls short of friendliness, and is in every respect ungracious, then he is a man who is quarrelsome and cross-grained.

THE POLITICS

Book I

Every state is a community of some kind, and every community is established with a view to some good; for mankind always act in order to obtain that which they think good. But, if all communities aim at some good, the state or political community, which is the highest of all, and which embraces all the rest, aims, and in a greater degree than any other, at the highest good.

Now there is an erroneous opinion that a statesman, king, householder, and master are the same, and that they differ, not in kind, but only in the number of their subjects. For example, the ruler over a few is called a master; over more, the manager of a household; over a still larger number, a statesman or king, as if there were no difference between a great household and a small state. The distinction which is made between the king and the statesman is as follows: When the government is personal, the ruler is a king; when, according to the principles of the political science, the citizens rule and are ruled in turn, then he is called a statesman.

But all this is a mistake; for governments differ in kind, as will be evident to any one who considers the matter according to the method which has hitherto guided us. As

THE POLITICS OF ARISTOTLE, trans. B. Jowett (Oxford, 1885), I, 1-5, 77-87, 89-92, 126-129.

in other departments of science, so in politics, the compound should always be resolved into the simple elements or least parts of the whole. We must therefore look at the elements of which the state is composed, in order that we may see in what they differ from one another, and whether any scientific distinction can be drawn between the different kinds of rule.

He who thus considers things in their first growth and origin, whether a state or anything else, will obtain the clearest view of them. In the first place there must be a union of those who cannot exist without each other; for example, of male and female, that the race may continue; and this is a union which is formed, not of deliberate purpose, but because, in common with other animals and with plants, mankind have a natural desire to leave behind them an image of themselves. And there must be a union of natural ruler and subject, that both may be preserved. For he who can foresee with his mind is by nature intended to be lord and master, and he who can work with his body is a subject, and by nature a slave; hence master and slave have the same interest. Nature, however, has distinguished between the female and the slave. For she is not niggardly, like the smith who fashions the Delphian knife for many uses; she makes each thing for a single use, and every instrument is best made when intended for one and not for many uses. But among barbarians no distinction is made between women and slaves, because there is no natural ruler among them; they are a community of slaves, male and female. Wherefore the poets say, —'It is meet that Hellenes should rule over barbarians;' as if they thought that the barbarian and the slave were by nature one.

Out of these two relationships between man and woman, master and slave, the family first arises, and Hesiod is right when he says,—'First house and wife and an ox for the plough,' for the ox is the poor man's slave. The family is the association estab-lished by nature for the supply of men's every day wants, and the members of it are called by Charondas 'companions of the cupboard' and by Epimenides the Cretan, 'companions of the manger.' But when several families are united, and the association aims at something more than the supply of daily needs, then comes into existence the village. And the most natural form of the village appears to be that of a colony from the family, composed of the children and grandchildren, who are said to be 'suckled with the same milk.' And this is the reason why Hellenic states were originally governed by kings; because the Hellenes were under royal rule before they came together, as the barbarians still are. Every family is ruled by the eldest, and therefore in the colonies of the family the kingly form of government prevailed because they were of the same blood. As Homer says [of the Cyclopes]:—'Each one gives law to his children and to his wives.' For they lived dispersedly, as was the manner in ancient times. Wherefore men say that the Gods have a king, because they themselves either are or were in ancient times under the rule of a king. For they imagine, not only the forms of the Gods, but their ways of life to be like their own.

When several villages are united in a single community, perfect and large enough to be nearly or quite self-sufficing, the state comes into existence, originating in the bare needs of life, and continuing in existence for the sake of a good life. And therefore, if the earlier forms of society are natural, so is the state, for it is the end of them, and the [completed] nature is the end. For what each thing is when fully developed, we call its nature, whether we are speaking of a man, a horse, or a family. Besides, the final cause and end of a thing is the best, and to be self-sufficing is the end and the best.

Hence it is evident that the state is a creation of nature, and that man is by nature a political animal. And he who by nature and not by mere accident is without a state, is either above humanity, or below it; he is the

'Tribeless, lawless, hearthless one,'

whom Homer denounces—the outcast who is a lover of war; he may be compared to a bird which flies alone.

Now the reason why man is more of a political animal than bees or any other gregarious animals is evident. Nature, as we often say, makes nothing in vain, and man is the only animal whom she has endowed with the gift of speech. And whereas mere sound is but an indication of pleasure or pain, and is therefore found in other animals (for their nature attains to the perception of pleasure and pain and the intimation of them to one another, and no further), the power of speech is intended to set forth the expedient and inexpedient, and likewise the just and the unjust. And it is a characteristic of man that he alone has any sense of good and evil, of just and unjust, and the association of living beings who have this sense makes a family and a state.

Thus the state is by nature clearly prior to the family and to the individual, since the whole is of necessity prior to the part; for example, if the whole body be destroyed, there will be no foot or hand, except in an equivocal sense, as we might speak of a stone hand; for when destroyed, the hand will be no better. But things are defined by their working and power; and we ought not to say that they are the same when they are no longer the same, but only that they have the same name. The proof that the state is a creation of nature and prior to the individual is that the individual, when isolated, is not self-sufficing; and therefore he is like a part in relation to the whole. But he who is unable to live in society, or who has no need because he is sufficient for himself, must be either a beast or a god: he is no part of a state. A social instinct is implanted in all men by nature, and yet

he who first founded the state was the greatest of benefactors. For man, when perfected, is the best of animals, but, when separated from law and justice, he is the worst of all; since armed injustice is the more dangerous, and he is equipped at birth with the arms of intelligence and with moral qualities which he may use for the worst ends. Wherefore, if he have not virtue, he is the most unholy and the most savage of animals, and the most full of lust and gluttony. But justice is the bond of men in states, and the administration of justice, which is the determination of what is just, is the principle of order in political society.

.   .   .

Book III

.   .   .

We have next to consider whether there is only one form of government or many, and if many, what they are, and how many, and what are the differences between them.

A constitution is the arrangement of magistracies in a state, especially of the highest of all. The government is everywhere sovereign in the state, and the constitution is in fact the government. For example, in democracies the people are supreme, but in oligarchies, the few; and, therefore, we say that these two forms of government are different: and so in other cases.

First, let us consider what is the purpose of a state, and how many forms of government there are by which human society is regulated. We have already said, in the former part of this treatise, when drawing a distinction between household-management and the rule of a master, that man is by nature a political animal. And therefore, men, even when they do not require one another's help, desire to live together all the same, and are in fact brought together by their common interests in proportion as they severally attain to any measure of well-being. This is certainly the chief end, both of individuals and of states. And also for the sake of mere life (in which there is possibly some noble element) mankind meet together and maintain the political community, so long as the evils of existence do not greatly overbalance the good. And we all see that men cling to life even in the midst of misfortune, seeming to find in it a natural sweetness and happiness.

There is no difficulty in distinguishing the various kinds of authority; they have been often defined already in popular works. The rule of a master, although the slave by nature and the master by nature have in reality the same interests, is nevertheless exercised primarily with a view to the interest of the master, but accidentally considers the slave, since, if the slave perish, the rule of the master perishes with him. On the other hand, the government of a wife and children and of a household, which we have called household-management, is exercised in the first instance for the good of the governed or for the common good of both parties, but essentially for the good of the governed, as we see to be the case in medicine, gymnastic, and the arts in general, which are only accidentally concerned with the good of the artists themselves. (For there is no reason why the trainer may not sometimes practise gymnastics, and the pilot is always one of the crew.) The trainer or the pilot considers the good of those committed to his care. But, when he is one of the persons taken care of, he accidentally participates in the advantage, for the pilot is also a sailor, and the trainer becomes one of those in training. And so in politics: when the state is framed upon the principle of equality and likeness, the citizens think that they ought to hold office by turns. In the order of nature every one would take his turn of service; and then again, somebody else would look after his interest, just as he, while in office, had looked after theirs. [That was originally the way.] But now-a-days, for the sake of the advantage which is to be gained from the public revenues and from office, men want to be always in office. One might imagine that the rulers, being sickly, were only kept in health while they continued in office; in that case we may be sure that they would be hunting after places. The conclusion is evident: that governments, which have a regard to the common interest, are constituted in accordance with strict principles of justice, and are therefore true forms; but those which regard only the interest of the rulers are all defective and perverted forms, for they are despotic, whereas a state is a community of freemen.

Having determined these points, we have next to consider how many forms of government there are, and what they are; and in the first place what are the true forms, for when they are determined the perversions of them will at once be apparent. The words constitution and government have the same meaning, and the government, which is the supreme authority in states, must be in the hands of one, or of a few, or of many. The true forms of government, therefore, are those in which the one, or the few, or the many, govern with a view to the common interest; but governments which rule with a view to the private interest, whether of the one, or of the few, or of the many, are perversions. For citizens, if they are truly citizens, ought to participate in the advantages of a state. Of forms of government in which one rules, we call that which regards the common interests, kingship or royalty; that in which more than one, but not many, rule, aristocracy (the rule of the best); and it is so called, either because the rulers are the best men, or because they have at heart the best interests of the state and of the citizens. But when the citizens at large administer the state for the common interest, the government is called by the generic name,—a constitution. And there is a reason for this use of language. One man or a few may excel in virtue; but of virtue there are many kinds: and as the number increases it becomes more difficult for them to attain perfection in every kind, though they may in military virtue, for this is found in the masses. Hence, in a constitutional government the fighting-men have the supreme power, and those who possess arms are the citizens.

Of the above-mentioned forms, the perversions are as follows:—of royalty, tyranny; of aristocracy, oligarchy; of constitutional government, democracy. For tyranny is a kind of monarchy which has in view the interest of the monarch only; oligarchy has in view the interest of the wealthy; democracy, of the needy: none of them the common good of all.

But there are difficulties about these forms of government, and it will therefore be necessary to state a little more at length the nature of each of them. For he who would make a philosophical study of the various sciences, and does not regard practice only, ought not to overlook or omit anything, but to set forth the truth in every particular. Tyranny, as I was saying, is monarchy exercising the rule of a master over political society; oligarchy is when men of property have the government in their hands; democracy, the opposite, when the indigent, and not the men of property, are the rulers. And here arises the first of our difficulties, and it relates to the definition just given. For democracy is said to be the government of the many. But what if the many are men of property and have the power in their hands? In like manner oligarchy is said to be the government of the few; but what if the poor are fewer than the rich, and have the power in their hands because they are stronger? In these cases the distinction which we have drawn between these different forms of government would no longer hold good.

Suppose, once more, that we add wealth to the few and poverty to the many, and name the governments accordingly—an oligarchy is said to be that in which the few and the wealthy, and a democracy that in which the many and the poor are the rulers —there will still be a difficulty. For, if the only forms of government are the ones already mentioned, how shall we describe those other governments also just mentioned by us, in which the rich are the more numerous and the poor are the fewer, and both govern in their respective states?

The argument seems to show that, whether in oligarchies or in democracies, the number of the governing body, whether the greater number, as in a democracy, or the smaller number, as in an oligarchy, is an accident due to the fact that the rich everywhere are few, and the poor numerous. But if so, there is a misapprehension of the causes of the difference between them. For the real difference between democracy and oligarchy is poverty and wealth. Wherever men rule by reason of their wealth, whether they be few or many, that is an oligarchy, and where the poor rule, that is a democracy. But as a fact the rich are few and the poor many: for few are well-to-do, whereas freedom is enjoyed by all, and wealth and freedom are the grounds on which the oligarchical and democratical parties respectively claim power in the state.

Let us begin by considering the common definitions of oligarchy and democracy, and what is justice oligarchical and democratical. For all men cling to justice of some kind, but their conceptions are imperfect and they do not express the whole idea. For example, justice is thought by them to be, and is, equality, not, however, for all, but only for equals. And inequality is thought to be, and is, justice; neither is this for all, but only for unequals. When the persons are omitted, then men judge erroneously. The reason is that they are passing judgment on themselves, and most people are bad judges in their own case. And whereas justice implies a relation to persons as well as to things, and a just distribution, as I have already said in the Ethics, embraces alike persons and things, they acknowledge the equality of the things, but dispute about the merit of the persons, chiefly for the reason which I have just given,—because they are bad judges in their own affairs; and secondly, because both the parties to the argument are speaking of a limited and partial justice, but imagine themselves to be speaking of absolute justice. For those who are unequal in one respect, for example wealth, consider themselves to be unequal in all; and any who are equal in one respect, for example freedom, consider themselves to be equal in all. But they leave out the capital point. For if men met and associated out of regard to wealth only, their share in the state would be proportioned to their property, and the oligarchical doctrine would then seem to carry the day. It would not be just that he who paid one mina should have the same share of a hundred minae, whether of the principal or of the profits, as he who paid the remaining ninety-nine. But a state exists for the sake of a good life, and not for the sake of life only: if life only were the object, slaves and brute animals might form a state, but they cannot, for they have no share in happiness or in a life of free choice. Nor does a state exist for the sake of alliance and security from injustice, nor yet for the sake of exchange and mutual intercourse; for then the Tyrrhenians and the Carthaginians, and all who have commercial treaties with one another, would be the citizens of one state. True, they have agreements about imports, and engagements that they will do no wrong to one another, and written articles of alliance. But there are no magistracies common to the contracting parties who will enforce their engagements; different states have each their own magistracies. Nor does one state take care that the citizens of the other are such as they ought to be, nor see that those who come under the terms of the treaty do no wrong or wickedness at all, but only that they do no injustice to one another. Whereas, those who care for good government take into consideration [the larger question of] virtue and vice in states. Whence it may be further inferred that virtue must be the serious care of a state which truly deserves the name: for [without this ethical end] the community becomes a mere alliance which differs only in place from alliances of which the members live apart; and law is only a convention, 'a surety to one another of justice,' as the sophist Lycophron says, and has no real power to make the citizens good and just.

This is obvious; for suppose distinct places, such as Corinth and Megara, to be united by a wall, still they would not be one city, not even if the citizens had the right to intermarry, which is one of the rights peculiarly characteristic of states. Again, if men dwelt at a distance from one another, but not so far off as to have no intercourse, and there were laws among them that they should not wrong each other in their exchanges, neither would this be a state. Let us suppose that one man is a carpenter, another a husbandman, another a shoemaker, and so on, and that their number is ten thousand: nevertheless, if they have nothing in common but exchange, alliance, and the like, that would not constitute a state. Why is this? Surely not because they are at a distance from one another: for even supposing that such a community were to meet in one place, and that each man had a house of his own, which was in a manner his state, and that they made alliance with one another, but only against evil-doers; still an accurate thinker would not deem this to be a state, if their intercourse with one another was of the same character after as before their union. It is clear then that a state is not a mere society, having a common place, established for the prevention of crime and for the sake of exchange. These are conditions without which a state cannot exist; but all of them together do not constitute a state, which is a community of well-being in families and aggregations of families, for the sake of a perfect and self-sufficing life.

Such a community can only be established among those who live in the same place and intermarry. Hence arise in cities family connexions, brotherhoods, common sacrifices, amusements which draw men together. They are created by friendship, for friendship is the motive of society. The end is the good life, and these are the means towards it. And the state is the union of families and villages having for an end a perfect and self-sufficing life, by which we mean a happy and honourable life.

Our conclusion, then, is that political society exists for the sake of noble actions, and not of mere companionship. And they who contribute most to such a society have a greater share in it than those who have the same or a greater freedom or nobility of birth but are inferior to them in political virtue; or than those who exceed them in wealth but are surpassed by them in virtue.

From what has been said it will be clearly seen that all the partisans of different forms of government speak of a part of justice only.

There is also a doubt as to what is to be the supreme power in the state:—is it the multitude? Or the wealthy? Or the good? Or the one best man? Or a tyrant? Any of these alternatives seems to involve disagreeable consequences. If the poor, for example, because they are more in number, divide among themselves the property of the rich, —is not this unjust? No, by heaven (will be the reply), for the lawful authority [i.e., the people] willed it. But if this is not injustice, pray what is? Again, when [in the first division] all has been taken, and the majority divide anew the property of the minority, is it not evident, if this goes on, that they will ruin the state? Yet surely, virtue is not the ruin of those who possess her, nor is justice destructive of a state; and therefore this law of confiscation clearly cannot be just. If it were, all the acts of a tyrant must of necessity be just; for he only coerces other men by superior power, just as the multitude co-erce the rich. But is it just then that the few and the wealthy should be the rulers? And what if they, in like manner, rob and plunder the people,—is this just? If so, the other case [i.e., the case of the majority plundering the minority] will likewise be just. But there can be no doubt that all these things are wrong and unjust.

Then ought the good to rule and have supreme power? But in that case everybody else, being excluded from power, will be dishonoured. For the offices of a state are posts of honour; and if one set of men always hold them, the rest must be deprived of them. Then will it be well that the one best man should rule? Nay, that is still more oligarchical, for the number of those who are dishonoured is thereby increased. Some one may say that it is bad for a man, subject as he is to all the accidents of human passion, to have the supreme power, rather than the law. But what if the law itself be democratical or oligarchical, how will that help us out of our difficulties? Not at all; the same consequences will follow.

Most of these questions may be reserved for another occasion. The principle that the multitude ought to be supreme rather than the few best is capable of a satisfactory explanation, and, though not free from difficulty, yet seems to contain an element of truth. For the many, of whom each individual is but an ordinary person, when they meet together may very likely be better than the few good, if regarded not individually but collectively, just as a feast to which many contribute is better than a dinner provided out of a single purse. For each individual among the many has a share of virtue and prudence, and when they meet together they become in a manner one man, who has many feet, and hands, and senses; that is a figure of their mind and disposition. Hence the many are better judges than a single man of music and poetry; for some understand one part, and some another, and among them, they understand the whole. There is a similar combination of qualities in good men, who differ from any individual of the many, as the beautiful are said to differ from those who are not beautiful, and works of art from realities, because in them the scattered elements are combined, although, if taken separately, the eye of one person or some other feature in another person would be fairer than in the picture. Whether this principle can apply to every democracy, and to all bodies of men, is not clear. Or rather, by heaven, in some cases it is impossible of application; for the argument would equally hold about brutes; and wherein, it will be asked, do some men differ from brutes? But there may be bodies of men about whom our statement is nevertheless true. And if so, the difficulty which has been already raised, and also another which is akin to it—*viz.* what power should be assigned to the mass of freemen and citizens, who are not rich and have no personal merit—are both solved. There is still a danger in allowing them to share the great offices of state, for their folly will lead them into error, and their dishonesty into crime. But there is a danger also in not letting them share, for a state in which many poor men are excluded from office will necessarily be full of enemies. The only way of escape is to assign to them some deliberative and judicial functions. For this reason Solon and certain other legislators give them the power of electing to offices, and of calling the magistrates to account, but they do not allow them to hold office singly. When they meet together their perceptions are quite good enough, and combined with the better class they are useful to the state (just as impure food when mixed with what is pure sometimes makes the entire mass more wholesome than a small quantity of the pure would be), but each individual, left to himself, forms an imperfect judgment.

. . . .

In all sciences and arts the end is a good, and especially and above all in the highest of all—this is the political science of which the good is justice, in other words, the common interest. All men think justice to be a sort of equality; and to a certain extent they agree in the philosophical distinctions which have been laid down by us about Ethics. For they admit that justice is a thing having relation to persons, and that equals ought to have equality. But there still remains a question; equality or inequality of what? here is a difficulty which the political philosopher has to resolve. For very likely some persons will say that offices of state ought to be unequally distributed according to superior excellence, in whatever respect, of the citizen, although there is no other difference between him and the rest of the community; for that those who differ in any one respect have different rights and claims. But, surely, if this is true, the complexion or height of a man, or any other advantage, will be a reason for his obtaining a greater share of political rights. The error here lies upon the surface, and may be illustrated from the other arts and sciences. When a number of flute-players are equal in their art, there is no reason why those of them who are better born should have better flutes given to them; for they will not play any better on the flute, and the superior instrument should be reserved for him who is the superior artist. If what I am saying is still obscure, it will be made clearer as we proceed. For if there were a superior flute-player who was far inferior in birth and beauty, although either of these may be a greater good than the art of flute-playing, and persons gifted with these qualities may excel the flute-player in a greater ratio than he excels them in his art, still he ought to have the best flutes given to him, unless the advantages of wealth and birth contribute to excellence in flute-playing, which they do not. Moreover upon this principle any good may be compared with any other. For if a given height, then height in general may be measured either against height or against freedom. Thus if A excels in height more than B in virtue, and height in general is more excellent than virtue, all things will be commensurable [which is absurd]; for if a certain magnitude is greater than some other, it is clear that some other will be equal. But since no such comparison can be made, it is evident that there is good reason why in politics men do not ground their claim to office on every sort of inequality any more than in the arts. For if some be slow, and others swift, that is no reason why the one should have little and the others much; it is in gymnastic contests that such excellence is rewarded. Whereas the rival claims of candidates for office can only be based on the possession of elements which enter into the composition of a state [such as wealth, virtue, etc.]. And therefore the noble, or free-born, or rich, may with good reason claim office; for holders of offices must be freemen and tax-payers: a state can be no more composed entirely of poor men than entirely of slaves. But if wealth and freedom are necessary elements, justice and valour are equally so; for without the former a state cannot exist at all, without the latter not well.

If the existence of the state is alone to be considered, then it would seem that all, or some at least, of these claims are just; but, if we take into account a good life, as I have already said, education and virtue have superior claims. As, however, those who are equal in one thing ought not to be equal in all, nor those who are unequal in one thing to be unequal in all, it is certain that all forms of government which rest on either of these principles are perversions. All men have a claim in a certain sense, as I have already admitted, but they have not an absolute claim. The rich claim because they have a greater share in the land, and land is the common element of the state; also they are gen-

erally more trustworthy in contracts. The free claim under the same title as the noble; for they are nearly akin. And the noble are citizens in a truer sense than the ignoble, since good birth is always valued in a man's own home and country. Another reason is, that those who are sprung from better ancestors are likely to be better men, for nobility is excellence of race. Virtue, too, may be truly said to have a claim, for justice has been acknowledged by us to be a social virtue, and it implies all others. Again, the many may urge their claim against the few; for, when taken collectively, and compared with the few, they are stronger and richer and better. But, what if the good, the rich, the noble, and the other classes who make up a state, are all living together in the same city, will there, or will there not, be any doubt who shall rule?—No doubt at all in determining who ought to rule in each of the above-mentioned forms of government. For states are characterized by differences in their governing bodies—one of them has a government of the rich, another of the virtuous, and so on. But a difficulty arises when all these elements coexist. How are we to decide? Suppose the virtuous to be very few in number: may we consider their numbers in relation to their duties, and ask whether they are enough to administer the state, or must they be so many as will make up a state? Objections may be urged against all the aspirants to political power. For those who found their claims on wealth or family have no basis of justice; on this principle, if any one person were richer than all the rest it is clear that he ought to be the ruler of them. In like manner he who is very distinguished by his birth ought to have the superiority over all those who claim on the ground that they are freeborn. In an aristocracy, or government of the best, a like difficulty occurs about virtue; for if one citizen be better than the other members of the government, however good they may be, he too, upon the same principle of justice, should rule over them. And if the people are to be supreme because they are stronger than the few, then if one man, or more than one, but not a majority, is stronger than the many, they ought to rule, and not the many.

All these considerations appear to show that none of the principles on which men claim to rule, and hold all other men in subjection to them, are strictly right. To those who claim to be masters of the state on the ground of their virtue or their wealth, the many might fairly answer that they themselves are often better and richer than the few—I do not say individually, but collectively. And another ingenious objection which is sometimes put forward may be met in a similar manner. Some persons doubt whether the legislator who desires to make the justest laws ought to legislate with a view to the good of the higher classes or of the many, when the case which we have mentioned occurs [*i.e.*, when all the elements coexist]. Now what is just or right is to be interpreted in the sense of 'what is equal;' and that which is right in the sense of being equal is to be considered with reference to the advantage of the state, and the common good of the citizens. And a citizen is one who shares in governing and being governed. He differs under different forms of government, but in the best state he is one who is able and willing to be governed and to govern with a view to the life of virtue.

· · ·

Book IV

· · ·

We have now to enquire what is the best constitution for most states, and the best life for most men, neither assuming a standard of virtue which is above ordinary persons, nor an education which is exceptionally favoured by nature

and circumstances, nor yet an ideal state which is an aspiration only, but having regard to the life in which the majority are able to share, and to the form of government which states in general can attain. As to those aristocracies, as they are called, of which we were just now speaking, they either lie beyond the possibilities of the greater number of states, or they approximate to the so-called constitutional government, and therefore need no separate discussion. And in fact the conclusion at which we arrive respecting all these forms rests upon the same grounds. For if it has been truly said in the Ethics that the happy life is the life according to unimpeded virtue, and that virtue is a mean, then the life which is in a mean, and in a mean attainable by every one, must be the best. And the same principles of virtue and vice are characteristic of cities and of constitutions; for the constitution is in a figure the life of the city.

Now in all states there are three elements; one class is very rich, another very poor, and a third in a mean. It is admitted that moderation and the mean are best, and therefore it will clearly be best to possess the gifts of fortune in moderation; for in that condition of life men are most ready to listen to reason. But he who greatly excels in beauty, strength, birth or wealth, or on the other hand who is very poor, or very weak, or very much disgraced, finds it difficult to follow reason. Of these two the one sort grow into violent and great criminals, the others into rogues and petty rascals. And two sorts of offences correspond to them, the one committed from violence, the other from roguery. The petty rogues are disinclined to hold office, whether military or civil, and their aversion to these two duties is as great an injury to the state as their tendency to crime. Again, those who have too much of the goods of fortune, strength, wealth, friends, and the like, are neither willing nor able to submit to authority. The evil begins at home: for when they are boys by reason of the luxury in which they are brought up, they never learn, even at school, the habit of obedience. On the other hand, the very poor, who are in the opposite extreme, are too degraded. So that the one class cannot obey, and can only rule despotically; the other knows not how to command and must be ruled like slaves. Thus arises a city, not of freemen, but of masters and slaves, the one despising, the other envying; and nothing can be more fatal to friendship and good fellowship in states than this: for good fellowship tends to friendship; when men are at enmity with one another, they would rather not even share the same path. But a city ought to be composed, as far as possible, of equals and similars; and these are generally the middle classes. Wherefore the city which is composed of middle-class citizens is necessarily best governed; they are, as we say, the natural elements of a state. And this is the class of citizens which is most secure in a state, for they do not, like the poor, covet their neighbours' goods; nor do others covet theirs, as the poor covet the goods of the rich; and as they neither plot against others, nor are themselves plotted against, they pass through life safely. Wisely then did Phocylides pray,—

'Many things are best in the mean; I desire to be of a middle condition in my city.'

Thus it is manifest that the best political community is formed by citizens of the middle class, and that those states are likely to be well-administered. in which the middle class is large, and larger if possible than both the other classes, or at any rate than either singly; for the addition of the middle class turns the scale, and prevents either of the extremes from being dominant. Great then is the good fortune of a state in which the citizens have a moderate and sufficient property; for where some possess much, and the others nothing, there may arise an extreme democracy, or a pure oligarchy; or a tyranny may grow out of either extreme,—either out of the most rampant democracy, or out of an oligarchy; but it is not so likely to arise out of a middle and nearly equal condition. I will explain the reason of this hereafter, when I speak of the revolutions of states. The mean condition of states is clearly best, for no other is free from faction; and where the middle class is large, there are least likely to be factions and dissensions. For a similar reason large states are less liable to faction than small ones, because in them the middle class is large; whereas in small states it is easy to divide all the citizens into two classes who are either rich or poor, and to leave nothing in the middle. And democracies are safer and more permanent than oligarchies, because they have a middle class which is more numerous and has a greater share in the government; for when there is no middle class, and the poor greatly exceed in number, troubles arise, and the state soon comes to an end. A proof of the superiority of the middle class is that the best legislators have been of a middle condition; for example, Solon, as his own verses testify; and Lycurgus, for he was not a king; and Charondas, and almost all legislators.

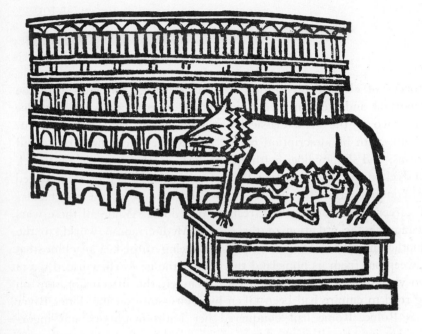

ROME

ONE HISTORIAN of classical civilization has stated flatly, "Far and away the most important and frequent events in ancient history are wars."[1] As we have seen, two of the great classical historians chose war as their theme —Herodotus with his description of the conflict between the Greeks and the Persians, and Thucydides with his analysis of the struggle of Greek against Greek in the Peloponnesian War. The inter-Greek wars were ended only by conquest from the north and the beginnings of the spectacular military career of Alexander the Great of Macedonia. While all these wars were occupying the attention of the eastern Mediterranean world, to the West another mighty military machine was being forged, a machine that was to sweep out from its homeland to conquer the civilized world. By 338 B.C., two years before the accession of Alexander, the first major step on the long road to empire had been taken by a city-state on the Tiber River known as Rome. Rome had conquered her Latin neighbors and incorporated them into the Roman state.

In the succeeding three hundred years, Rome enjoyed the most sustained series of military triumphs the world had ever seen. By 265 B.C., she had extended her rule over most of the Italian peninsula; by about 200 B.C., she had brought most of Spain, the rest of Italy, and Sicily, Corsica, and Sardinia under her dominion; during the next hundred years she conquered southern Gaul, the rest of Spain, parts of North Africa, Macedonia, Greece, and about half of Asia Minor; and by the time of the birth of Jesus, the rest of Asia Minor, Syria, Egypt, most of North Africa, and all of Gaul had been added to the Roman tribute lists. Of course, these remarkable conquests were not carried out without occasional reverses and defeats. Hannibal's invasion and occupation of the Italian peninsula from 218 B.C. to 203 B.C. was the most serious reversal. But, though Hannibal's success pointed to certain Roman weaknesses, it revealed the sources of Roman strength as well.

The long road to empire was engineered and paved by the Roman army. Seldom has there been a finer military machine than the one developed by the Republic of Rome. Quite early, Rome transformed her armed forces from an ill-trained mob into a professional, highly trained,

<hr>

[1] Michael Grant, *Ancient History* (London, 1952), p. 128.

rigorously disciplined body of citizen-soldiers who could be used at great distances from Rome and who served for long periods of time. The weapons of the Roman soldier were superior to those of his opponents, particularly after the adoption of a short cut-and-thrust sword which made him especially effective in close combat. The fundamental unit of the Roman army was the legion, an adaptation of the successful Macedonian phalanx. In its final form, the legion was composed of 3,000 heavily armed infantry men, all of whom were so dedicated to the honor and reputation of the legion that the defeat of the legion or the loss of its eagles constituted an unthinkable disgrace. Reinforcing their devotion to the legion was a deep-seated loyalty to Rome.

Somehow the Romans managed to instill this devotion to Rome even into the peoples they conquered, and Roman citizenship became highly prized and eagerly sought. The leaders of the Roman Republic were wise enough to offer to the allies and former enemies of Rome a limited citizenship, with the possibility of full citizenship later on. Thus all shared the hope of being able to say, "*Civis Romanus sum*"—I am a Roman citizen. What a powerful phrase! The man who could say that was protected by the fear of Roman law and of Roman justice; he shared in the glory that was Rome and the triumphs that were Roman; he contributed to the governance of the world-wide empire, for he could vote in its elections, serve in its courts, and act as an official in its administration.

But if military success was a glory of the Roman Republic, it was also a curse. The creation of a world empire led to the creation of an imperial organization—an organization that the republican city-state of Rome was incapable of maintaining without undergoing violent internal change. The peasant-soldiers began to grumble over being kept away from the land year after year; the military leaders became too accustomed to commanding obedience; the mother-city became too used to triumph and success. All contributed to the final disappearance of the Republic. The citizen's loyalty to his legion and to the Republic was transformed into loyalty to his commander, and the legions became private armies. Plutarch may have admired his Caesar, but only because Caesar sought to restore political order to the chaos that had developed in the last century of the Roman Republic. The disappearance of the small land-owner, the development of a wealthy class, corruption in government administration, and the evolution of a complex bureaucracy to administer the empire were all factors in the disintegration of the old system and the emergence of the Roman Empire.

The concept of empire—and of emperor—took several generations to emerge fully. But it was clearly present when Augustus took the title *princeps* (first citizen), even though he continued the fiction of republican rule after his triumph over both the Senate and the assassins of Julius Caesar. Happily for Rome, Augustus and his successor, Tiberius, were talented and powerful enough to resolve the civil difficulties and to stabilize the administration so that Rome was able to withstand the abuse and corruption of the regimes that followed. Not even madness, frivolity, and palace intrigue could disturb the quiet workings of the Empire—the civil administration functioned smoothly, the army maintained the peace, commerce was active, and industry continued prosperous. The *Pax Romana* lasted two hundred years—years during which the civilized world enjoyed a new freedom from the perennial warfare of the ancient world.

It was during these centuries of peace that Roman civilization achieved the heights of its glory. Its accomplishments in architecture have rarely been matched. Recognizing the arch (which the Greeks had not discovered) as a thing of beauty as well as utility, the Romans were able to bridge wide rivers, to supply the vast city of Rome with water from far-off hills and mountains, and to erect the Colosseum, which seated nearly fifty thousand spectators at the gladiatorial games and contests. The realistic portrait sculpture of the Romans has never been equaled. Perhaps this excellence was a reflection of the practical, hard, peasant virtues of the Roman citizen. But the greatest triumphs of Roman civilization lay not in art, architecture, literature, or speculative thought, but in the realm of the practical and the everyday. Law, military order, and civil administration were the accomplishments that were most truly Roman. And these three most clearly reveal the Roman genius—the desire for order and efficiency and the ability to attain them. This desire, together with the Roman dedication to duty, right, state, and honor, is manifested in the works of Cicero and the teachings of Epictetus.

The Roman world made its greatest contribution to Western civilization almost inadvertently, when an obscure province under Roman rule produced the man Jesus. Although his life and teachings have inspired millions in succeeding ages, Jesus himself would undoubtedly have questioned the organization that grew up to spread his beliefs. The first two centuries after Christ were a time of peace and tranquility, but they were also a time in which the common man felt lost and devoid of spiritual comfort. The Christian faith proffered balm and security for the difficulties of this world and salvation in the next. And as the faith spread, the Roman genius for order and efficiency again manifested itself; for the growing Church, with its increasingly complex activities, modeled its organization on that of the civil administration. Bishops established cathedrals in provincial urban centers, and local churches were set up in the smaller cities and towns. The capstone to this structure was natural, obvious, and logical—the Bishop of Rome was to head the Church just as the emperor led the Empire.

But Rome could not solve the problems of world dominion. The Empire had stabilized the regime created by the Republic, but it had been unable to develop a solution to the basic problems raised by empire. How could a state maintain a great army without being dominated by it? Or, a different problem, how could a city-state maintain a very large army of citizen-soldiers without extending citizenship to them? And if citizenship were extended, how could it instill in these citizens the same dedication and devotion found in the native Roman? Whatever the problems were and whatever solutions to them hindsight might offer, one thing at least remains: the history and glory of Rome lasted over eight hundred years, a long time indeed in the recorded history of man.

Polybius

Any eyewitness account of an event has intrinsic value. But when the witness is a person of intellectual and emotional detachment, his account is likely to be much more rewarding. Substance is added to the narrative, too, when the observer is a man with analytical powers of the first order. Such a man was the Greek historian, Polybius, who continued the great tradition of Herodotus and Thucydides.

Polybius (*c*.205-*c*.123 B.C.) was brilliantly equipped to write the history of his own time, for he had had a literary education and was widely experienced in affairs of state.

He had served both as a *hipparch* (cavalry commander) in the armed forces of his native city-state of Megalopolis and as a diplomat charged with the delicate task of reconciling his fellow Greeks to their somewhat anomalous relationship to the rapidly expanding Roman Republic. When the Romans carried Polybius off to Italy (167 B.C.) as one of a thousand Greek hostages, he took advantage of the opportunity and launched into the writing of his *Histories*. Through the intervention of a friend, he was able to spend most of his sixteen years of exile in Rome, where he could examine original documents

and observe the workings of the Roman government at first hand. His circle of friends included many of the most powerful men of the time. In 150 B.C. he was permitted to return to Greece, where he bent all his efforts toward creating an atmosphere of understanding between the Greeks and the Romans. Polybius died at the age of eighty-two, after falling from a horse.

The following selection reflects his experiences in Rome and the observations he made while he was there. Taken from Book VI of the *Histories*, it is, as Polybius says, "a disquisition on the Roman constitution."

THE HISTORIES

Book VI

PREFACE

1. I am aware that some will be at a loss to account for my interrupting the course of my narrative for the sake of entering upon the following disquisition on the Roman constitution. But I think that I have already in many passages made it fully evident that this particular branch of my work was one of the necessities imposed on me by the nature of my original design; and I pointed this out with special clearness in the preface which explained the scope of my history. I there stated that the feature of my work which was at once the best in itself, and the most instructive to the students of it, was that it would enable them to know and fully realise in what manner, and under what kind of constitution, it came about that nearly the whole world fell under the power of Rome in somewhat less than fifty-three years,— an event certainly without precedent. This being my settled purpose, I could see no more fitting period than the present for making a pause, and examining the truth of the remarks about to be made on this constitution. In private life if you wish to satisfy yourself as to the badness or goodness of particular persons, you would not, if you wish to get a genuine test, examine their conduct at a time of uneventful repose, but in the hour of brilliant success or conspicuous reverse. For the true test of a perfect man is the power of bearing with spirit and dignity violent changes of fortune. An examination of a constitution should be conducted in the same way: and therefore being unable to find in our day a more rapid or more sig-

THE HISTORIES OF POLYBIUS, trans. Evelyn S. Shuck-burgh (London, 1889), I, 458-460, 467-474, 494-507.

nal change than that which has happened to Rome, I reserved my disquisition on its constitution for this place. . . .

What is really educational and beneficial to students of history is the clear view of the causes of events, and the consequent power of choosing the better policy in a particular case. Now in every practical undertaking by a state we must regard as the most powerful agent for success or failure the form of its constitution; for from this as from a fountain-head all conceptions and plans of action not only proceed, but attain their consummation. . . .

3. Of the Greek republics, which have again and again risen to greatness and fallen into insignificance, it is not difficult to speak, whether we recount their past history or venture an opinion on their future. For to report what is already known is an easy task, nor is it hard to guess what is to come from our knowledge of what has been. But in regard to the Romans it is neither an easy matter to describe their present state, owing to the complexity of their constitution; nor to speak with confidence of their future, from our inadequate acquaintance with their peculiar institutions in the past whether affecting their public or their private life. It will require then no ordinary attention and study to get a clear and comprehensive conception of the distinctive features of this constitution.

Now, it is undoubtedly the case that most of those who profess to give us authoritative instruction on this subject distinguish three kinds of constitutions, which they designate *kingship, aristocracy, democracy.* But in my opinion the question may be fairly put to them, whether they name these as being the *only* ones, or as the best. In either case I think they are wrong. For it is plain that we must regard as the *best* constitution that which partakes of all these three elements. And this is no mere assertion, but has been proved by the example of Lycurgus, who was the first to construct a constitution—that of Sparta—on this principle. Nor can we admit that these are the *only* forms: for we have had before now examples of absolute and tyrannical forms of government, which, while differing as widely as possible from kingship, yet appear to have some points of resemblance to it; on which account all absolute rulers falsely assume and use, as far as they can, the title of king. Again there have been many instances of oligarchical governments having in appearance some analogy to aristocracies, which are, if I may say so, as different from them as it is possible to be. The same also holds good about democracy.

. . .

11. . . . I will now endeavour to describe [the constitution] of Rome at the period of their disastrous defeat at Cannae.

I am fully conscious that to those who actually live under this constitution I shall appear to give an inadequate account of it by the omission of certain details. Knowing accurately every portion of it from personal experience, and from having been bred up in its customs and laws from childhood, they will not be struck so much by the accuracy of the description, as annoyed by its omissions; nor will they believe that the historian has purposely omitted unimportant distinctions, but will attribute his silence upon the origin of existing institutions or other important facts to ignorance. What is told they depreciate as insignificant or beside the purpose; what is omitted they desiderate as vital to the question: their object being to appear to know more than the writers. But a good critic should not judge a writer

by what he leaves unsaid, but from what he says: if he detects mis-statement in the latter, he may then feel certain that ignorance accounts for the former; but if what he says is accurate, his omissions ought to be attributed to deliberate judgment and not to ignorance. So much for those whose criticisms are prompted by personal ambition rather than by justice. . . .

Another requisite for obtaining a judicious approval for an historical disquisition, is that it should be germane to the matter in hand; if this is not observed, though its style may be excellent and its matter irreproachable, it will seem out of place, and disgust rather than please. . . .

As for the Roman constitution, it had three elements, each of them possessing sovereign powers: and their respective share of power in the whole state had been regulated with such a scrupulous regard to equality and equilibrium, that no one could say for certain, not even a native, whether the constitution as a whole were an aristocracy or democracy or despotism. And no wonder: for if we confine our observation to the power of the Consuls we should be inclined to regard it as despotic; if on that of the Senate, as aristocratic; and if finally one looks at the power possessed by the people it would seem a clear case of democracy. What the exact powers of these several parts were, and still, with slight modifications, are, I will now state.

12. The Consuls, before leading out the legions, remain in Rome and are supreme masters of the administration. All other magistrates, except the Tribunes, are under them and take their orders. They introduce foreign ambassadors to the Senate; bring matters requiring deliberation before it; and see to the execution of its decrees. If, again, there are any matters of state which require the authorisation of the people, it is their business to see to them, to

summon the popular meetings, to bring the proposals before them, and to carry out the decrees of the majority. In the preparations for war, also, and in a word in the entire administration of a campaign, they have all but absolute power. It is competent to them to impose on the allies such levies as they think good, to appoint the Military Tribunes, to make up the roll for soldiers and select those that are suitable. Besides they have absolute power of inflicting punishment on all who are under their command while on active service: and they have authority to expend as much of the public money as they choose, being accompanied by a quaestor who is entirely at their orders. A survey of these powers would in fact justify our describing the constitution as despotic,—a clear case of royal government. Nor will it affect the truth of my description, if any of the institutions I have described are changed in our time, or in that of our posterity: and the same remarks apply to what follows.

13. The Senate has first of all the control of the treasury, and regulates the receipts and disbursements alike. For the Quaestors cannot issue any public money for the various departments of the state without a decree of the Senate, except for the service of the Consuls. The Senate controls also what is by far the largest and most important expenditure, that, namely, which is made by the censors every *lustrum* for the repair or construction of public buildings; this money cannot be obtained by the censors except by the grant of the Senate. Similarly all crimes committed in Italy requiring a public investigation, such as treason, conspiracy, poisoning, or wilful murder, are in the hands of the Senate. Besides, if any individual or state among the Italian allies requires a controversy to be settled, a penalty to be assessed, help or protection to be afforded, —all this is the province of the Senate. Or

again, outside Italy, if it is necessary to send an embassy to reconcile warring communities, or to remind them of their duty, or sometimes to impose requisitions upon them, or to receive their submission, or finally to proclaim war against them,—this too is the business of the Senate. In like manner the reception to be given foreign ambassadors in Rome, and the answers to be returned to them, are decided by the Senate. With such business the people have nothing to do. Consequently, if one were staying at Rome when the Consuls were not in town, one would imagine the constitution to be a complete aristocracy: and this has been the idea entertained by many Greeks, and by many kings as well, from the fact that nearly all the business they had to do with Rome was settled by the Senate.

14. After this one would naturally be inclined to ask what part is left for the people in the constitution, when the Senate has these various functions, especially the control of the receipts and expenditure of the exchequer; and when the Consuls, again, have absolute power over the details of military preparation, and an absolute authority in the field? There is, however, a part left the people, and it is a most important one. For the people is the sole fountain of honour and of punishment; and it is by these two things and these alone that dynasties and constitutions and, in a word, human society are held together: for where the distinction between them is not sharply drawn both in theory and practice, there no undertaking can be properly administered,—as indeed we might expect when good and bad are held in exactly the same honour. The people then are the only court to decide matters of life and death; and even in cases where the penalty is money, if the sum to be assessed is sufficiently serious, and especially when the accused have held the higher magistracies. And in re-

gard to this arrangement there is one point deserving especial commendation and record. Men who are on trial for their lives at Rome, while sentence is in process of being voted,—if even only one of the tribes whose votes are needed to ratify the sentence has not voted,—have the privilege at Rome of openly departing and condemning themselves to a voluntary exile. Such men are safe at Naples or Praeneste or at Tibur, and at other towns with which this arrangement has been duly ratified on oath.

Again, it is the people who bestow offices on the deserving, which are the most honourable rewards of virtue. It has also the absolute power of passing or repealing laws; and, most important of all, it is the people who deliberate on the question of peace or war. And when provisional terms are made for alliance, suspension of hostilities, or treaties, it is the people who ratify them or the reverse.

These considerations again would lead one to say that the chief power in the state was the people's, and that the constitution was a democracy.

15. Such, then, is the distribution of power between the several parts of the state. I must now show how each of these several parts can, when they choose, oppose or support each other.

The Consul, then, when he has started on an expedition with the powers I have described, is to all appearance absolute in the administration of the business in hand; still he has need of the support both of people and Senate, and, without them, is quite unable to bring the matter to a successful conclusion. For it is plain that he must have supplies sent to his legions from time to time; but without a decree of the Senate they can be supplied neither with corn, nor clothes, nor pay, so that all the plans of a commander must be futile, if the Senate is resolved either to shrink from danger or hamper his plans. And again,

whether a Consul shall bring any undertaking to a conclusion or no depends entirely on the Senate: for it has absolute authority at the end of a year to send another Consul to supersede him, or to continue the existing one in his command. Again, even to the successes of the generals, the Senate has the power to add distinction and glory, and on the other hand to obscure their merits and lower their credit. For these high achievements are brought in tangible form before the eyes of the citizens by what are called "triumphs." But in these triumphs the commanders cannot celebrate with proper pomp, or in some cases celebrate at all, unless the Senate concurs and grants the necessary money. As for the people, the Consuls are pre-eminently obliged to court their favour, however distant from home may be the field of their operations; for it is the people, as I have said before, that ratifies, or refuses to ratify, terms of peace and treaties; but most of all because when laying down their office they have to give an account of their administration before it. Therefore in no case is it safe for the Consuls to neglect either the Senate or the goodwill of the people.

16. As for the Senate, which possesses the immense power I have described, in the first place it is obliged in public affairs to take the multitude into account, and respect the wishes of the people; and it cannot put into execution the penalty for offences against the republic, which are punishable with death, unless the people first ratify its decrees. Similarly even in matters which directly affect the senators, —for instance, in the case of a law depriving senators of certain dignities and offices, or even actually cutting down their property,—even in such cases the people have the sole power of passing or rejecting the law. But most important of all is the fact that, if the Tribunes interpose their veto, the Senate not only are unable to pass a

decree, but cannot even hold a meeting at all, whether formal or informal. Now, the Tribunes are always bound to carry out the decree of the people, and above all things to have regard to their wishes: therefore, for all these reasons the Senate stands in awe of the multitude, and cannot neglect the feelings of the people.

17. In like manner the people on its part is far from being independent of the Senate, and is bound to take its wishes into account both collectively and individually. For contracts, too numerous to count, are given out by the censors in all parts of Italy, for the repairs or construction of public buildings; there is also the collection of revenue from many rivers, harbours, gardens, mines, and land—everything, in a word, that comes under the control of the Roman government: and in all these the people at large are engaged; so that there is scarcely a man, so to speak, who is not interested either as a contractor or as being employed in the works. For some purchase the contracts from the censors for themselves; and others go partners with them; while others again go security for these contractors, or actually pledge their property to the treasury for them. Now over all these transactions the Senate has absolute control. It can grant an extension of time; and in case of unforseen accident can relieve the contractors from a portion of their obligation, or release them from it altogether, if they are absolutely unable to fill it. And there are many details in which the Senate can inflict great hardships, or, on the other hand, grant great indulgences to the contractors: for in every case the appeal is to it. But the most important point of all is that the judges are taken from its members in the majority trials, whether public or private, in which the charges are heavy. Consequently, all citizens are much at its mercy; and being alarmed at the uncertainty as to when they may need its aid, are cautious about resisting or actively opposing its will. And for a similar reason men do not rashly resist the wishes of the Consuls, because one and all may become subject to their absolute authority on a campaign.

18. The result of this power of the several estates for mutual help or harm is a union sufficiently firm for all emergencies, and a constitution than which it is impossible to find a better. For whenever any danger from without compels them to unite and work together, the strength which is developed by the State is so extraordinary, that everything required is unfailingly carried out by the eager rivalry shown by all classes to devote their whole minds to the need of the hour, and to secure that any determination come to should not fail for want of promptitude; while each individual works, privately and publicly alike, for the accomplishment of the business in hand. Accordingly, the peculiar constitution of the State makes it irresistible, and certain of obtaining whatever it determines to attempt. Nay, even when these external alarms are past, and the people are enjoying their good fortune and the fruits of their victories, and, as usually happens, growing corrupted by flattery and idleness, show a tendency to violence and arrogance,—it is in these circumstances, more than ever, that the constitution is seen to possess within itself the power of correcting abuses. For when any one of the three classes becomes puffed up, and manifests an inclination to be contentious and unduly encroaching, the mutual interdependency of all the three, and the possibility of the pretentions of any one being checked and thwarted by the others, must plainly check this tendency: and so the proper equilibrium is maintained by the impulsiveness of the one part being checked by its fear of the other.

.   .   .

THE ROMAN REPUBLIC COMPARED
WITH OTHERS

43. Nearly all historians have recorded as constitutions of eminent excellence those of Lacedaemonia, Crete, Mantinea, and Carthage. Some have also mentioned those of Athens and Thebes. The former I may allow to pass; but I am convinced that little need be said of the Athenian and Theban constitutions: their growth was abnormal, the period of their zenith brief, and the changes they experienced unusually violent. Their glory was a sudden and fortuitous flash, so to speak; and while they still thought themselves prosperous, and likely to remain so, they found themselves involved in circumstances completely the reverse. The Thebans got their reputation for valour among the Greeks, by taking advantage of the senseless policy of the Lacedaemonians, and the hatred of the allies toward them, owing to the valour of one, or at most two, men who were wise enough to appreciate the situation. Since fortune quickly made it evident that it was not the peculiarity of their constitution, but the valour of their leaders, which gave the Thebans their success. For the great power of Thebes notoriously took its rise, attained its zenith, and fell to the ground with the lives of Epaminondas and Pelopidas. We must therefore conclude that it was not its constitution, but its men, that caused the high fortune which it then enjoyed.

44. A somewhat similar remark applies to the Athenian constitution also. For though it perhaps had more frequent interludes of excellence, yet its highest perfection was attained during the brilliant career of Themistocles; and having reached that point it quickly declined, owing to its essential instability. For the Athenian demus is always in the position of a ship without a commander. In such a ship, if fear of the enemy, or the occurrence of a storm induce the crew to be of one mind and to obey the helmsman, everything goes well; but if they recover from this fear, and begin to treat their officers with contempt, and to quarrel with each other because they are no longer all of one mind,—one party wishing to continue the voyage, and the other urging the steersman to bring the ship to anchor; some letting out the sheets, and others hauling them in, and ordering the sails to be furled,—their discord and quarrels make a sorry show to lookers on; and the position of affairs is full of risk to those on board engaged in the same voyage: and the result has often been that, after escaping the dangers of the wildest seas, and the most violent storms, they wreck their ship in harbour and close to shore. And this is what has often happened to the Athenian constitution. For, after repelling, on various occasions, the greatest and most formidable dangers by the valour of its people and their leaders, there have been times when, in periods of secure tranquillity, it has gratuitously and recklessly encountered disaster. Therefore I need say no more about either it, or the Theban constitution: in both of which a mob manages everything on its own unfettered impulse —a mob in the one city distinguished for headlong outburst of fiery temper, in the other trained in long habits of violence and ferocity.

45. Passing to the Cretan polity there are two points which deserve our consideration. The first is how such writers as Ephorus, Xenophon, Callisthenes and Plato—who are the most learned of the ancients—could assert that it was like that of Sparta; and secondly how they came to assert that it was at all admirable. I can agree with neither assertion; and I will explain why I say so. And first as to its dissimilarity with the Spartan constitution. The peculiar merit of the latter is said to be its land laws, by which no one pos-

sesses more than another, but all citizens have an equal share in the public land. The next distinctive feature regards the possession of money: for as it is utterly discredited among them, the jealous competition which arises from inequality of wealth is entirely removed from the city. A third peculiarity of the Lacedaemonian polity is that, of the officials by whose hands and with whose advice the whole government is conducted, the kings hold an hereditary office, while the members of the Gerusia are elected for life.

46. Among the Cretans the exact reverse of all these arrangements obtains. The laws allow them to possess as much land as they can get with no limitation whatever. Money is so highly valued among them, that its possession is not only thought to be necessary but in the highest degree creditable. And in fact greed and avarice are so native to the soil in Crete, that they are the only people in the world among whom no stigma attaches to any sort of gain whatever. Again all their offices are annual and on a democratical footing. I have therefore often felt at a loss to account for these writers speaking of the two constitutions, which are radically different, as though they were closely united and allied. But, besides overlooking these important differences, these writers have gone out of their way to comment at length on the legislation of Lycurgus: "He was the only important legislator," they say, "who saw the important points. For there being two things on which the safety of a commonwealth depends,—courage in the face of the enemy and concord at home,—by abolishing covetousness, he with it removed all motive for civil broil and contest: whence it has been brought about that the Lacedaemonians are the best governed and most united people in Greece." Yet while giving utterance to these sentiments, and though they see that, in contrast to this, the Cretans by

their ingrained avarice are engaged in countless public and private seditions, murders and civil wars, they yet regard these facts as not affecting their contention, but are bold enough to speak of the two constitutions as alike. Ephorus, indeed, putting aside names, employs expressions so precisely the same, when discoursing on the two constitutions, that, unless one noticed the proper names, there would be no means whatever of distinguishing which of the two he was describing.

47. In what the difference between them consists I have already stated. I will now address myself to showing that the Cretan constitution deserves neither praise nor imitation.

In my mind, then, there are two things fundamental to every state, in virtue of which its powers and constitution become desirable or objectionable. These are customs and laws. Of these the desirable are those which make men's private lives holy and pure, and the public character of the state civilised and just. The objectionable are those whose effect is the reverse. As, then, when we see good customs and good laws prevailing among certain people, we confidently assume that, in consequence of them, the men and their civil constitution will be good also, so when we see private life full of covetousness, and public policy of injustice, plainly we have reason for asserting their laws, particular customs, and general constitution to be bad. Now, with few exceptions, you could find no habits prevailing in private life more steeped in treachery than those in Crete, and no public policy more inequitable. Holding, then, the Cretan constitution to be neither like the Spartan, nor worthy of choice or imitation, I reject it from the comparison which I have instituted.

Nor again would it be fair to introduce the Republic of Plato, which is also spoken of in high terms by some philosophers. For just as we refuse admission to the athletic contests to those actors or athletes who have not acquired a recognised position or trained for them, so we ought not to admit this Platonic constitution to the contest for the prize of merit unless it can first point to some genuine and practical achievement. Up to this time the notion of bringing it into comparison with the constitutions of Sparta, Rome, and Carthage would be like putting up a statue to compare with living and breathing men. Even if such a statue were faultless in point of art, the comparison of the lifeless with the living would naturally leave an impression of imperfection and incongruity upon the minds of the spectators.

48. I shall therefore omit these, and proceed with my description of the Laconian constitution. Now it seems to me that for securing unity among the citizens, for safeguarding the Laconian territory, and preserving the liberty of Sparta inviolate, the legislation and provisions of Lycurgus were so excellent, that I am forced to regard his wisdom as something superhuman. For the equality of landed possessions, the simplicity in their food, and the practice of taking it in common, which he established, were well calculated to secure morality in private life and to prevent civil broils in the State; as also their training in the endurance of labours and dangers to make men brave and noble minded: but when both these virtues, courage and high morality, are combined in one soul or in one state, vice will not readily spring from such a soil, nor will such men easily be overcome by their enemies. By constructing his constitution therefore in this spirit, and of these elements, he secured two blessings to the Spartans,—safety for their territory, and a lasting freedom for themselves after he was gone. He appears however to have made no one provision whatever, particular or general, for the acquisition of the territory of their neighbours; or for the assertion of their supremacy; or, in a word, for any policy of aggrandisement at all. What he had still to do was to impose such a necessity, or create such a spirit among the citizens, that, as he had succeeded in making their individual lives independent and simple, the public character of the state should also become independent and moral. But the actual fact is, that, though he made them the most disinterested and sober-minded men in the world, as far as their own ways of life and their national institutions were concerned, he left them in regard to the rest of Greece ambitious, eager for supremacy, and encroaching in the highest degree.

49. For in the first place is it not notorious that they were the first Greeks to cast a covetous eye upon the territory of their neighbours, and that accordingly they waged a war of subjugation on the Messenians? In the next place is it not related in all histories that in their dogged obstinacy they bound themselves with an oath never to desist from the siege of Messene until they had taken it? And lastly it is known to all that in their efforts for supremacy in Greece they submitted to do the bidding of those whom they had once conquered in war. For when the Persians invaded Greece, they conquered them, as champions of the liberty of the Greeks; yet when the invaders had retired and fled, they betrayed the cities of Greece into their hands by the peace of Antalcidas, for the sake of getting money to secure their supremacy over the Greeks. It was then that the defect in their constitution was rendered apparent. For as long as their ambition was confined to governing their immediate neighbours, or even the Peloponnesians only, they were content with the resources and supplies provided by Laconia itself, having all material of war ready to hand, and being able without much expenditure of time to return home or convey provisions with them. But

directly they took in hand to despatch naval expeditions, or to go on campaigns by land outside the Peloponnese, it was evident that neither their iron currency, nor their use of crops for payment in kind, would be able to supply them with what they lacked if they abided by the legislation of Lycurgus; for such undertakings required money universally current, and goods from foreign countries. Thus they were compelled to wait humbly at Persian doors, impose tribute on the islanders, and exact contribution from all the Greeks: knowing that, if they abided by the laws of Lycurgus, it was impossible to advance any claims upon any outside power at all, much less upon the supremacy in Greece.

50. My object, then, in this digression is to make it manifest by actual fact that, for guarding their own country with absolute safety, and for preserving their own freedom, the legislation of Lycurgus was entirely sufficient; and for those who are content with these objects we must concede that there neither exists, nor ever has existed, a constitution and civil order preferable to that of Sparta. But if any one is seeking aggrandisement, and believes that to be a leader and ruler and despot of numerous subjects, and to have all looking and turning to him, is a finer thing than that,—in this point of view we must acknowledge that the Spartan constitution is deficient, and that of Rome superior and better constituted for obtaining power. And this has been proved by actual facts. For when the Lacedaemonians strove to possess themselves of the supremacy in Greece, it was not long before they brought their own freedom itself into danger. Whereas the Romans, after obtaining supreme power of the Italians themselves, soon brought the whole world under their rule,—in which achievement the abundance and availability of their supplies largely contributed to their success.

51. Now the Carthaginian constitution seems to me originally to have been well contrived in these most distinctively important particulars. For they had kings, and the Gerusia had the powers of an aristocracy, and the multitude were supreme in such things as affected them; and on the whole the adjustment of its several parts was very like that of Rome and Sparta. But about the period of its entering on the Hannibalian war the political state of Carthage was on the decline, that of Rome improving. For whereas there is in every body, or polity, or business a natural stage of growth, zenith, and decay; and whereas everything in them is best at the zenith; we may thereby judge of the difference between these two constitutions as they existed at that period. For exactly so far as the strength and prosperity of Carthage preceded that of Rome in point of time, by so much was Carthage then past its prime, while Rome was exactly at its zenith, as far as its political constitution was concerned. In Carthage therefore the influence of the people in the policy of the state had already risen to be supreme, while at Rome the Senate was at the height of its power: and so, as in the one measures were deliberated upon by the many, in the other by the best men, the policy of the Romans in all public undertakings proved the stronger; on which account, though they met with capital disasters, by force of prudent counsels they finally conquered the Carthaginians in the war.

52. If we look however at separate details, for instance at the provisions for carrying on a war, we shall find that whereas for a naval expedition the Carthaginians are the better trained and prepared,—as it is only natural with a people with whom it has been hereditary for many generations to practise this craft, and to follow the seaman's trade above all nations in the world,—yet, in regard to military service

on land, the Romans train themselves to a much higher pitch than the Carthaginians. The former bestow their whole attention upon this department: whereas the Carthaginians wholly neglect their infantry, though they do take some slight interest in the cavalry. The reason of this is that they employ foreign mercenaries, the Romans native and citizen levies. It is in this point that the latter polity is preferable to the former. They have their hopes of freedom ever resting on the courage of mercenary troops: the Romans on the valour of their own citizens and the aid of their allies. The result is that even if the Romans have suffered a defeat at first, they renew the war with undiminished forces, which the Carthaginians cannot do. For, as the Romans are fighting for country and children, it is impossible for them to relax the fury of their struggle; but they persist with obstinate resolution until they have overcome their enemies. What has happened in regard to their navy is an instance in point. In skill the Romans are much behind the Carthaginians, as I have already said; yet the upshot of the whole naval war has been a decided triumph for the Romans, owing to the valour of their men. For although nautical science contributes largely to success in sea-fights, still it is the courage of the marines that turns the scale most decisively in favour of victory. The fact is that Italians as a nation are by nature superior to Phoenicians and Libyans both in physical strength and courage; but still their habits also do much to inspire the youth with enthusiasm for such exploits. One example will be sufficient of the pains taken by the Roman state to turn out men ready to endure anything to win a reputation in their country for valour.

53. Whenever one of their illustrious men dies, in the course of his funeral, the body with all its paraphernalia is carried into the forum to the Rostra, as a raised platform there is called, and sometimes is propped upright upon it so as to be conspicuous, or, more rarely, is laid upon it. Then with all the people standing round, his son, if he has left one of full age and he is there, or, failing him, one of his relations, mounts the Rostra and delivers a speech concerning the virtues of the deceased, and the successful exploits performed by him in his lifetime. By these means the people are reminded of what has been done, and made to see it with their own eyes,—not only such as were engaged in the actual transactions but those also who were not;—and their sympathies are so deeply moved, that the loss appears not to be confined to the actual mourners, but to be a public one affecting the whole people. After the burial and all the usual ceremonies have been performed, they place the likeness of the deceased in the most conspicuous spot in his house, surmounted by a wooden canopy or shrine. This likeness consists of a mask made to represent the deceased with extraordinary fidelity both in shape and colour. These likenesses they display at public sacrifices adorned with much care. And when any illustrious member of the family dies, they carry these masks to the funeral, putting them on men whom they thought as like the originals as possible in height and other personal peculiarities. And these substitutes assume clothes according to the rank of the person represented: if he was a consul or praetor, a toga with purple stripes; if a censor, whole purple; if he had also celebrated a triumph or performed any exploit of that kind, a toga embroidered with gold. These representatives also ride themselves in chariots, while the fasces and axes, and all the other customary insignia of the particular offices, lead the way, according to the dignity of the rank in the state enjoyed by the deceased in his lifetime; and on arriving at the Rostra they all take their seats

on ivory chairs in their order. There could not easily be a more inspiring spectacle than this for a young man of noble ambitions and virtuous aspirations. For can we conceive any one to be unmoved at the sight of all the likenesses collected together of the men who have earned glory, all as it were living and breathing? Or what could be a more glorious spectacle?

54. Besides, the speaker over the body about to be buried, after having finished the panegyric of this particular person, starts upon the others whose representatives are present, beginning with the most ancient, and recounts the successes and achievements of each. By this means the glorious memory of brave men is continually renewed; the fame of those who have performed any noble deed is never allowed to die; and the renown of those who have done good service to their country becomes a matter of common knowledge to the multitude, and part of the heritage of posterity. But the chief benefit of the ceremony is that it inspires young men to shrink from no exertion for the general welfare, in the hope of obtaining the glory which awaits the brave. And what I say is confirmed by this fact. Many Romans have volunteered to decide a whole battle by single combat; not a few have deliberately accepted certain death, some in time of war to secure the safety of the rest, some in time of peace to preserve the safety of the commonwealth. There have also been instances of men in office putting their own sons to death, in defiance of every custom and law, because they rated the interests of their country higher than those of natural ties even with their nearest and dearest. There are many stories of this kind, related of many men in Roman history; but one will be enough for our present purpose; and I will give the name as an instance to prove the truth of my words.

55. The story goes that Horatius Cocles, while fighting with two enemies at the head of the bridge over the Tiber, which is the entrance to the city on the north, seeing a large body of men advancing to support his enemies, and fearing that they would force their way into the city, turned round, and shouted to those behind him to hasten back to the other side and break down the bridge. They obeyed him: and whilst they were breaking the bridge, he remained at his post receiving numerous wounds, and checked the progress of the enemy: his opponents being panic stricken, not so much by his strength as by the audacity with which he held his ground. When the bridge had been broken down, the attack of the enemy was stopped; and Cocles then threw himself into the river with his armour on and deliberately sacrificed his life, because he valued the safety of his country and his own future reputation more highly than his present life, and the years of existence that remained to him. Such is the enthusiasm and emulation for noble deeds that are engendered among the Romans by their customs.

56. Again the Roman customs and principles regarding money transactions are better than those of the Carthaginians. In the view of the latter nothing is disgraceful that makes for gain; with the former nothing is more disgraceful than to receive bribes and to make profit by improper means. For they regard wealth obtained from unlawful transactions to be as much a subject of reproach, as a fair profit from the most unquestioned source is of commendation. A proof of the fact is this. The Carthaginians obtain office by open bribery, but among the Romans the penalty for it is death. With such a radical difference, therefore, between the rewards offered to virtue among the two people, it is natural that the ways adopted for obtaining them should be different also.

But the most important difference for the better which the Roman commonwealth appears to me to display is in their religious beliefs. For I conceive that what in other nations is looked upon as a reproach, I mean a scrupulous fear of the gods, is the very thing which keeps the Roman Commonwealth together. To such an extraordinary height is this carried among them, both in private and public business, that nothing could exceed it. Many people might think this unaccountable; but in my opinion their object is to use it as a check upon the common people. If it were possible to form a state wholly of philosophers, such a custom would perhaps be unnecessary. But seeing that every multitude is fickle, and full of lawless desires, unreasoning anger, and violent passion, the only resource is to keep them in check by mysterious terrors and scenic effects of this sort. Wherefore, to my mind, the ancients, were not acting without purpose or at random, when they brought in among the vulgar those opinions about the gods, and the belief in the punishments in Hades: much rather do I think that men nowadays are acting rashly and foolishly in rejecting them. This is the reason why, apart from anything else, Greek statesmen, if entrusted with a single talent, though protected by ten checking-clerks, as many seals, and twice as many witnesses, yet cannot be induced to keep faith: whereas among the Romans, in their magistracies and embassies, men have the handling of a great amount of money, and yet from pure respect to their oath keep their faith intact. And, again, in other nations it is a rare thing to find a man who keeps his hands out of the public purse, and is entirely pure in such matters: but among the Romans it is a rare thing to detect a man in the act of committing such a crime. . . .

RECAPITULATION AND CONCLUSION

57. That to all things, then, which exist there is ordained decay and change I think requires no further arguments to show: for the inexorable course of nature is sufficient to convince us of it.

But in all polities we observe two sources of decay existing from natural causes, the one external, the other internal and self-produced. The external admits of no certain or fixed definition, but the internal follows a definite order. What kind of polity, then, comes naturally first, and what second, I have already stated in such a way, that those who are capable of taking in the whole drift of my argument can henceforth draw their own conclusions as to the future of the Roman polity. For it is quite clear, in my opinion. When a commonwealth, after warding off many great dangers, has arrived at a high pitch of prosperity and undisputed power, it is evident that, by the lengthened continuance of great wealth within it, the manner of life of its citizens will become more extravagant; and that the rivalry for office, and in other spheres of activity, will become fiercer than it ought to be. And as this state of things goes on more and more, the desire of office and the shame of losing reputation, as well as the ostentation and extravagance of living, will prove the beginning of a deterioration. And of this change the people will be credited with being the authors, when they become convinced that they are being cheated by some from avarice, and are puffed up with flattery by others from love of office. For when that comes about, in their passionate resentment and acting under the dictates of anger, they will refuse to obey any longer, or to be content with having equal powers with their leaders, but will demand to have all or far the greatest themselves. And when that comes to pass the constitution will receive a new name, which sounds better than any other in the world, liberty or democracy; but, in fact, it will become that worst of all governments, mob-rule.

Lucretius

Lucretius (*c*.94-55 B.C.) was a philosopher-poet, and his poem *De Rerum Natura* ("On the Nature of Things") was devoted to an explanation and defense of the philosophical theory of materialism. Lucretius did not originate the materialistic philosophy. Rather, it had been developed over a long period of time by various Greek thinkers, including Leucippus (fifth century B.C.), who originated the theory; by his pupil Democritus (*c*.460-370 B.C.), who developed it into a complete explanation of the universe; and by Epicurus (*c*.341-270 B.C.), who worked out its ethical and theological implications. Unfortunately, the works of the first two of these philosophers have been lost— even though Democritus is reputed to have been almost as prolific a writer as Aristotle. Consequently, knowledge of their views comes to us indirectly, through Epicurus, Lucretius, and others. Ever since materialism was originated by Leucippus, it has remained one of the major philosophical explanations of the world. And its influence has spread from philosophy to science. The basic assumptions of the New-tonian system, for example, represent an application of materialism to the realm of physics. Contemporary behavioristic psychologists have attempted to provide a scientific explanation of mental activities in materialistic terms.

Almost nothing is known of the life of Lucretius beyond the traditional story, which is highly questionable, that he was driven mad by a love-potion, wrote his poetry between fits of insanity, and finally committed suicide. The selection that follows is from the first three books of his *De Rerum Natura*. The first two books are devoted to an exposition of the materialist theory. In the third book, Lucretius discusses the implications of this theory for human life —in particular, its denial of personal immortality. Because the soul is mortal, death means oblivion; therefore it is not to be feared. The wise man, rather than thinking of death, will live life to the fullest.

DE RERUM NATURA

Book 1

Thou Mother of the Aenead race, delight
Of men and gods, bountiful Venus, thou

LUCRETIUS, *De Rerum Natura*, trans. R. C. Trevel-yan (Cambridge: At the University Press, 1937), pp. 1-15, 36-37, 45-48, 57-58, 88, 93-95, 107-108, 118-123, 125-127. Courtesy of Cambridge University Press.

Who under the sky's gliding constellations
Fillest ship-carrying ocean with thy presence
And the corn-bearing lands, since through thy
    power
Each kind of living creature is conceived
Then riseth and beholdeth the sun's light:
Before thee, Goddess, do the winds and clouds
Of heaven take flight, before thee and thy
    coming:

For thee the daedal earth puts forth sweet
flowers:
Beholding thee the smooth deep laughs, the sky
Grows calm and shines with wide-outspreading
light.
For soon as the day's vernal countenance
Has been revealed, and fresh from wintry
bonds
Blows the birth-giving breeze of the West
wind,
First do the birds of air give sign of thee,
Goddess, and thine approach, as through their
hearts
Pierces thine influence. Next the herds, grown
wild,
Bound over the glad pastures and swim
through
The rapid streams, as captured by thy charm
Each one with eager longing follows thee
Withersoever thou wouldst lure them on.
And thus through seas, mountains and rushing
rivers,
Through the birds' leafy homes and the green
plains,
Striking bland love into the hearts of all,
Thou art the cause that following his lust
Each should renew his race after his kind.
Therefore since thou alone art Nature's mis-
tress,
And since without thine aid naught can rise
forth
Into the glorious regions of the light,
Nor aught grow to be gladsome and delectable,
Thee would I win to help me while I write
These verses.

.   .   .

When prostrate upon earth lay human life,
Visibly trampled down and foully crushed
Beneath Religion's cruelty, who meanwhile
Out of the regions of the heavens above
Showed forth her face, lowering on mortal
men
With horrible aspect, first did a man of
Greece[1]
Dare to lift up his mortal eyes against her;
The first was he to stand up and defy her.
Him neither stories of the gods, nor lightnings,
Nor heaven with muttering menaces could
quell,

[1] [*Lucretius is referring to Epicurus. Ed.*]

But all the more did they arouse his soul's
Keen valour, till he longed to be the first
To break through the fast-bolted doors of Na-
ture.
Therefore his fervent energy of mind
Prevailed, and he passed onward, voyaging far
Beyond the flaming ramparts of the world,
Ranging in mind and spirit far and wide
Throughout the unmeasured universe; and
thence
A conqueror he returns to us, bringing back
Knowledge both of what can and what can-
not
Rise into being, teaching us in fine
Upon what principle each thing has its powers
Limited, and its deep-set boundary stone.
Therefore now has Religion been cast down
Beneath men's feet, and trampled on in turn:
Ourselves heaven-high his victory exalts.

Herein this fear assails me, lest perchance
You should suppose I would initiate you
Into a school of reasoning unholy,
And set your feet upon a path of sin:
Whereas in truth too often has this Religion
Given birth to sinful and unholy deeds.
So once at Aulis did those chosen chiefs,
Those foremost heroes of the Danaan host,
Foully defile the Trivian Virgin's altar
With Iphianassa's lifeblood. For so soon
As the fillet wreathed around her maiden locks
Had streamed in equal lengths down either
cheek,
And soon as she was aware of her sire standing
Sorrowful by the altar, and at his side
The priestly ministers hiding the knife,
And the folk shedding tears at sight of her,
Speechless in terror, dropping on her knees,
To the earth she sank down. Nor in that hour
Of anguish might it avail her that she first
Had given the name of father to the king;
For by the hands of men lifted on high
Trembling to the altar she was borne,
Not that, when the due ceremonial rites
Had been accomplished, she might be escorted
By the clear-sounding hymenaeal song,
But that a stainless maiden foully stained,
In the very season of marriage she might fall
A sorrowful victim by a father's stroke,
That so there might be granted to the fleet

A happy and hallowed sailing. To such crimes
Religion has had power to persuade men.

.   .   .

This terror therefore and darkness of the mind
Must needs be scattered not by the sun's beams
And day's bright arrows, but by contemplation
Of Nature's aspect and her inward law.
And this first principle of her design
Shall be our starting point: nothing is ever
Begotten by divine will out of nothing.
In truth the reason fear so dominates
All mortals, is that they behold on earth
And in the sky many things happening,
Yet of these operations by no means
Can they perceive the causes, and so fancy
That they must come to pass by power divine.
Therefore when we have understood that
   nothing
Can be born out of nothing, we shall then
Win juster knowledge of the truth we seek,
Both from what elements each thing can be
   formed,
And in what way all things can come to pass
Without the intervention of the Gods.

For if things came from nothing, every kind
Might be born out of every thing; naught
   then
Would require seed. Thus men might rise from
   ocean,
The scaly race out of the land, while birds
Might suddenly be hatched forth from the sky:
Cattle and other herds and every kind
Of wild beast, bred by no fixed law of birth,
Would inhabit tilth and wilderness alike.
No fruit would remain constant to its tree,
But would change; every tree might bear all
   kinds.
For if there were not for each kind its own
Begetting bodies, how could there be for things
A fixed unvarying mother? But in fact
Since all are formed from fixed seeds, each is
   born
And issues into the borders of the light
From that alone wherein resides its substance
And its first-bodies. And for this cause all
   things
Cannot be generated out of all,
Since in each dwells its own particular power.
Again why do we see in spring the rose,
Corn in the summer's heat, vines bursting forth

When autumn summons them, if not because
When the fixed seeds of things at the right
   time
Have flowed together, there is then revealed
Whatever is thus made, while the due seasons
Are present, and the quickened earth brings
   forth
Safely into the borders of the light
Her tender nurslings? But if they were formed
From nothing, they would suddenly spring up
At unfixed periods and unsuitable times,
Since there would then be no first elements
That could be kept from a begetting union
By the unpropitious season. Then again,
For things to increase they would have no need
Of lapse of time that seeds might flock to-
   gether,
If they could grow from nothing. Suddenly
Small babes would become youths; trees would
   arise
Shooting up in a moment from the ground.
But nothing of the kind, 'tis plain, takes place,
Seeing that all things grow little by little,
As befits, from determined seed, and growing
Preserve their kind: so that you may perceive
That all things become greater and are nour-
   ished
Out of their own substance. Furthermore
Without fixed annual seasons for the rain
Earth could not put her gladdening produce
   forth,
Nor yet, if kept apart from nourishment,
Could living creatures propagate their kind
Or sustain life: so that with greater reason
You may think many things have many atoms
In common, as we see that different words
Have common letters, than that anything
Can come to being without first elements.
Again, why could not Nature have produced
Men of such mighty bulk, that they could
   wade
Through the deep places of the sea, or rend
Huge mountains with their hands, or in one
   life
Overpass many living generations,
If it be not because there has been assigned
A fixed substance for begetting things,
And what can thence arise is thus ordained?
Lastly, since it is evident that tilled grounds
Excell the untilled, and yield to labouring
   hands

A richer harvest, we may thence infer
That in the earth there must be primal atoms,
Which, when we turn her teeming clods with
  coulters,
Labouring the soil, we stimulate to rise.
But if none such existed, you would then
See all things without any toil of ours
Spring up far richer of their own accord.
Therefore we must confess this truth, that
  nothing
Can come from nothing, since seed is required
For each thing, out of which it may be born
And lift itself into the air's soft breezes.

Furthermore Nature dissolves each form back
Into its own first-bodies, nor does she ever
Annihilate things. For if aught could be mortal
In all its parts, then each thing would be
  snatched
From our eyes to destruction in a moment:
For there would be no need of any force
To cause disruption of its parts, and loosen
Their fastenings. But in fact each is composed
Of everlasting seeds; so till some force
Arrive that with a blow can shatter things
To pieces, or can penetrate within
Through their void spaces and so break them
  up,
Nature will not permit the dissolution
Of anything to be seen. Again, if time
Utterly destroys, consuming all the substance
Of whatsoever it removes from sight
As the years lapse, out of what then does
  Venus
Bring back into the light of life the race
Of living creatures each after its kind?
Or, once brought back, whence can the
  daedal earth
Nourish and increase them, giving food to each
After its kind? Whence do its own fountains
And far-drawn rivers from without keep full
The sea? Whence does the aether feed the
  stars?
For infinite past time and lapse of days
Surely must long since have consumed all
  things
Formed of a body that must die. But if
Throughout that period of time long past
Elements have existed out of which
Our world of things is composed and remade,
Assuredly such atoms must be endowed

With an immortal nature: none of them
Therefore can turn to nothing. Then again
The same force and the same cause would
  destroy
All things without distinction, were it not
That an eternal substance held them fast,
A substance interwoven part with part
By bonds more or less close. For without
  doubt
A mere touch would be cause enough for
  death,
Seeing that any least amount of force
Must needs dissolve the texture of such things,
None of which had an everlasting body.
But in fact since the mutual fastenings
Of the atoms are dissimilar, and their substance
Is everlasting, things endure with body
Uninjured, till some force arrive which proves
Strong enough to dissolve the texture of each.
Therefore no single thing ever returns
To nothing, but at their disruption all
Pass back into the particles of matter.
Lastly the rain-showers perish, when the Sky-
  father
Has flung them into the lap of mother Earth.
But then luxuriant crops spring up, and boughs
Are green upon the trees; the trees themselves
Grow, and with fruits are laden: from this
  source
Moreover both our own race and the race
Of beasts are nourished; for this cause we see
Glad towns teeming with children, leafy
  woods
Singing with young birds' voices on all sides;
For this cause cattle about the joyous meadows
Wearied with fatness lay their bodies down,
And from their swollen udders oozing falls
The white milk stream; for this cause a new
  brood
Gambols and frolics over the tender grass
On weak limbs, their young hearts with pure
  milk thrilled.
None therefore of those things that seem to
  perish
Utterly perishes, since Nature forms
One thing out of another, and permits
Nothing to be begotten, unless first
She has been recruited by another's death.

Now listen: since I have proved to you that
  things

Cannot be formed from nothing, and likewise
Proved that they cannot be brought back to
    nothing
When once they have been begotten, lest you
    yet
Should tend in any way to doubt my words,
Because the primal particles of things
Can never be distinguished by the eyes,
Consider now these further instances
Of bodies which you must yourself admit
Are real things, and yet cannot be seen.
First the wind's violent force scourges the sea,
Whelming huge ships and scattering the
    clouds;
And sometimes with impetuous hurricane
Scouring the plains, it strews them with great
    trees,
And ravages with forest-rending blasts
The mountain-tops: with such rude savagery
Does the wind howl and bluster and wreak its
    rage
With menacing uproar. Thus we may be sure
That winds must be invisible substances
That sweep the seas, the lands, the clouds of
    heaven,
Ravaging and dishevelling them all
With sudden hurricane gusts. Onward they
    stream..
Multiplying destruction, just as when
The soft nature of water all at once
With overflooding current rushes forward
Swelled with copious rains by a mighty spate
Of water swooping down from the high hills,
Hurtling together broken forest boughs
And entire trees: nor can the sturdy bridges
Sustain the oncoming water's sudden force:
In such wise turbulent with much rain the
    river
Flings its whole mighty strength against the
    piles:
With a loud crashing roar it deals havoc,
And rolls the huge stones on beneath its waves,
Sweeping before it all that stems its flood.
In this way then must wind-blasts also move;
And when like a strong stream they have
    hurled themselves
Towards any quarter, they thrust things before
    them
And overwhelm them with repeated on-
    slaughts,
Often in writhing eddy seizing them

To bear them away in swiftly circling swirl.
Winds therefore must be invisible substances
Beyond all doubt, since in their works and
    ways
We find that they resemble mighty rivers
Which are of visible substance. Then again
We can perceive the various scents of things,
Yet never see them coming to our nostrils:
Heats too we see not, nor can we observe
Cold with our eyes, nor ever behold sounds:
Yet must all these be of a bodily nature,
Since they are able to act upon our senses.
For naught can touch or be touched except
    body.
Clothes also, hung up on a shore where waves
Are breaking, become moist, and then grow
    dry
If spread out in the sun. Yet in what way
The water's moisture has soaked into them,
Has not been seen, nor again in what way
The heat has driven it out. The moisture
    therefore
Is dispersed into tiny particles,
Which our eyes have no power to see at all.
Furthermore after many revolutions
Of the sun's year, a finger-ring is thinned
Upon the under side by being worn:
Water falling in drops hollows a stone:
The bent ploughshare of iron insensibly
Grows smaller in the fields; and we behold
The paving-stones of roads worn down at
    length
By the footsteps of the people. Then again
The brazen statues near the city gates
Show right hands wearing thinner by the
    touch
Of those who greet them ever as they pass
    by.
Thus we perceive that all such things grow
    less,
For they have been worn down: and yet what
    bodies
Are leaving them each moment, this the grudg-
    ing
Nature of vision has precluded us
From seeing. Finally whatever time
And Nature add to things little by little,
Obliging them to grow by slow degrees,
No effort of our eyesight can behold.
So too whenever things grow old by age
Or through corruption, and wherever rocks

That overhang the sea are gnawed away
By the corroding brine, you cannot discern
What they are losing at any single moment.
Thus Nature operates by unseen bodies.

And yet all things are not on every side
Held packed together by their bodily nature;
For there is also such a thing as void.
To have learnt this will prove in many ways
Most useful to you; for you need not then
Wander in doubt, for ever questioning
About the universe of things, mistrustful
Of my discourse. Space then, intangible, void,
And emptiness exist. If none existed,
Then things would have no power to move at all;
For that which is matter's function, to resist
And hinder, would be present at all times
To all things. Nothing therefore could advance,
Since no one thing would be the first to yield.
But as it is, we see before our eyes
Through seas and lands and through the heights of heaven
That many things in many ways are moving
In divers fashions, which, were there no void,
Would not so much be utterly deprived
Of restless motion, but could never at all
Have been begotten, since on every side
Matter, packed closely, would have been at rest.
Again, however solid things may seem,
Yet that their substance must in truth be porous,
You may perceive from this. In rocks and caves
The liquid moisture of water oozes through,
And the whole place weeps with abundant drops:
Food is distributed through every part
Of an animal's body: trees grow and put forth
Their fruits in season, because nourishment
Through all their stems and branches is dispersed
All over them, upward from their deepest roots:
Sounds pass through walls, and glide into closed rooms;
Stiffening cold penetrates to the bones.
Yet, if there were no void spaces wherethrough
Each particle may find its way, all this

Never would you find happening at all.
Lastly, why do we see some things surpass
Others in weight, though of no larger bulk?
For if there be within a ball of wool
Just as much substance as in a lump of lead,
'Tis natural that both should weigh the same,
Because the function of substance is to press
Everything down, while on the contrary
Void in its nature is always without weight.
So when the one, though just as large, is found
The lighter, this proves clearly that it holds
More void; whereas the heavier of the two
Shows that there is more substance in itself,
And far less empty space. Thus what we are seeking
With such keen reasoning, certainly exists
Mingled in things, which is what we call void.

.   .   .

But since I have shown how these most solid atoms
Are flying to and fro perpetually
Unvanquished through all time, come, let me now
Unfold whether a limit to their sum
Exists or no. Likewise as to the void
Which has been found to exist, or call it room,
Or space, wherein every event goes on,
Let us see clearly whether the whole of this
Be altogether finite, or spreads out
Limitless to immeasurable depths.

Well then, the universe is limited
In no direction, else it needs must have
An utmost border. Now it is clear that nothing
Can have an utmost border, if there be not
Something beyond to bound it, so that a point
Is seen, further than which our sense must fail
To follow the thing. But since we must admit
That nothing can exist outside the sum,
It has no utmost border, and so lacks
Limit and boundary. And it matters not
In which of its regions you may take your stand;
So surely, whatsoever place a man
May occupy, he leaves the universe
On every side as infinite as before.
Moreover, grant that all existing space
Is indeed finite, if a man should run
The whole way to the utmost boundaries

And fling a flying javelin, would you then
Rather suppose that, hurled with vigorous
    force,
It travels onward whither it was aimed
And flies afar? or do you think that something
Might interfere and check its flight? For one
Of these two theories you must grant and
    adopt.
Yet both preclude escape, constraining you
To concede that the universe expands
Without limit. For whether there be something
To check the dart, forbidding it to reach
And occupy the goal that was its aim,
Or whether it speed forward, in either case
The javelin has not started from the limit.
In this way I shall follow you; and wherever
You choose to place the utmost boundaries,
I shall ask, what then happens to the dart.
It will be found that nowhere can a limit
Be fixed; that there will always still be room
Wherein the javelin's flight may be prolonged.

. . .

Book II

. . .

Now listen, and I will set forth by what mo-
    tion
The generating particles of matter
Beget different things, and then in turn
Dissolve what was begotten; by what force
They are compelled to act thus; what velocity
Is given them to traverse the great void:
Do thou fail not to give heed to my words.
For without doubt matter does not cohere
Close-packed together, since we behold each
    thing
To be decreasing, and perceive that all
Are as it were ebbing through lapse of time,
As age withdraws them from our eyes; and
    yet
The sum is seen to remain unimpaired,
Because the particles that quit each form
Lessen the things from which they pass away,
Augment those they have come to; cause the
    first
To grow old, but the second to blossom
    forth—
Nor yet with these do they abide. And so
The sum of things is evermore renewed,
And mortals live by mutual interchange.
Some breeds wax, others wane, and in short
    space

The tribes of living creatures are all changed,
And like runners hand on the torch of life.

If you should think that the primordial atoms
Can stay still, and by staying still give birth
To new motions of things, then far astray
You wander from true reasoning. For since
They are roaming through void space, it must
    needs be
That the primordial atoms all move on
Either by their own weight, or else perchance
By the blow of some other. For whenever,
As often happens in their swift career,
They have met and collided, it results
That at once they recoil in opposite ways:
Nor is this strange; since they are very hard,
Of heavy and solid mass, and from behind
Nothing obstructs them. And that you may
    see
More clearly that all particles of matter
Are darting to and fro continually,
Remember that for the whole universe
There is no bottom, and that primal atoms
Have no place whereon they may sink to rest,
Since I have shown in many words, and
    proved
By sure reason, that space is without end
Or limit, but spreads round on every side
Immeasurably. Now since this is the truth,
Assuredly no rest has been allotted
To primal atoms throughout the deep void,
But rather, driven along in unceasing
And varied motion, some when they collide,
Rebound over great intervals, while others
Are hurled but a short distance from the blow.
And all those particles that congregating
In denser union, collide and rebound ·
Through minute intervals, being entangled
By their own close-locked shapes, these atoms
    form
The strong substance of rocks, and stubborn
    lumps
Of iron, and all other things like these.
Then of the rest a smaller number roam
Through the great void, and leaping far apart
Recoil afar over huge intervals.
These give us thin air and the sun's bright
    splendour.
Many moreover roam through the great void,
Which have been thrown off from the combi-
    nations

That form things, and wherever they have
  entered
Have been unable to adapt their motions.
An image illustrating what I tell you
Is constantly at hand and taking place
Before our very eyes. Do but observe:
Whenever beams make their way in and pour
The sunlight through the dark rooms of a
  house,
You will see many tiny bodies mingling
In many ways within those beams of light
All through the empty space, and as it were
In never-ending conflict waging war,
Combating and contending troop with troop
Without pause, kept in motion by perpetual
Meetings and separations; so that this
May help you to imagine what it means
That the primordial particles of things
Are always tossing about in the great void.
To this degree a small thing may suggest
A picture of great things, and lead the way
To new conceptions. There is another reason
Why you should give attention to those bodies
Which are seen wavering confusedly
In the sun's rays: such waverings indicate
That underneath appearance there must be
Motions of matter secret and unseen.
For many bodies you will here observe
Changing their course, urged by invisible
  blows,
Driven backward and returning whence they
  came,
Now this way and now that, on all sides
  round.
These wandering motions, you must know, are
  caused
In all these bodies by primordial atoms.
For first the primal particles of things
Move of themselves; those bodies next, that
  form
Small combinations, and that, so to speak,
Are nearest to the powers of primal atoms,
Smitten by their invisible blows are stirred
To movement; and thereafter they in turn
Rouse other bodies that are somewhat larger
And so motion ascends from primal atoms,
And issues to our senses step by step.
Thus it is that those bodies also move
Which we can see in the sun's light, and yet
The blows that drive them are not visible.

   .   .   .

Intelligent reasoning easily can explain
Why it is that the fire of the lightning
Has far more power to penetrate than ours
Which is born from pine-torches here on
  earth.
For you may say that the celestial fire
Of lightning is more subtle, being formed
Of such small shapes that it can pass through
  holes
Which our terrestrial fire, sprung from logs
And born of pine-wood, cannot penetrate.
Furthermore light will pass through horn, but
  rain
Is thrown off. Why? unless those particles
Of light are smaller than are those whereof
Water's fostering liquid is composed.
And swiftly as we see wines flow through a
  strainer,
Yet sluggish olive-oil will take its time,
Undoubtedly because it is composed
Of elements either larger or more hooked
And mutually entangled: and thus it is
These particles cannot become so quickly
Detached from one another, and percolate
Each singly through their several openings.

Moreover liquids such as honey and milk,
Held in the mouth, cause pleasure to the
  tongue;
Whereas wormwood and pungent centaury
Have such sour natures that they writhe the
  mouth
With loathsome flavour; thus you may easily
  know
That things which touch the senses pleasantly
Are made of smooth round bodies; while all
  those
Which seem bitter and harsh, are held to-
  gether
By particles more hooked, and for this cause
Are wont to tear their way into our senses,
And as they enter to break through the body.
All things in short whose contact with our
  senses
Is pleasant or unpleasant, differ thus
One from the other because they are composed
Of unlike shapes: so you must never think
That the harsh shuddering of the strident saw
Is made of elements just as smooth as those
Of tuneful melodies that musicians waken
And shape with nimble fingers on the strings;

Nor must you think that atoms of like form
Pass through men's nostrils when foul carcasses
Are burning, and when the stage is freshly
    sprinkled
With saffron of Cilicia, while hard by
The altar is breathing forth Pancheaean
    odours;
Nor fancy that the pleasant colours of things
Which can regale the eyes, are formed of seed
Like that of those which make the pupil smart
And force it to weep tears, or those of aspect
So foul as to seem hideous and loathsome.
For no shape whatsoever, that has power
To gratify the senses, has been formed
Without some smoothness in its elements;
Whereas no harsh and painful shape is found
To be without some roughness in its atoms.
Also some elements are rightly thought
To be neither smooth nor altogether hooked
With barbed points, but seem rather to have
    small
Slightly projecting angles, insomuch
That they can tickle yet not hurt the senses.

· · ·

Book III

Now since I have demonstrated of what kind
Are the first elements of all things, and how
Various are the divers shapes wherein
They are flying onward of their own accord
Driven in eternal motion, and in what way
Out of these can be formed each several thing;
After these themes it would seem best that
    now
The nature of the mind and of the soul
Should be elucidated in my verses,
And fear of Acheron driven headlong forth,
That dread which troubles from its lowest
    depths
The life of man, and overshadowing all
With the blackness of death, will not allow
Any pleasure to be unalloyed and pure.

· · ·

                              The nature
Of mind and soul is bodily. For since
It is seen to propel the limbs, rouse up
The body from sleep, alter the countenance,
Govern and turn the whole man round about,
None of which things we see can come to
    pass
Without touch, nor yet touch without a body,

Must we not then confess that mind and soul
Are of a bodily nature? Furthermore
You perceive that the mind within our body
Is acted upon together with it, and feels
In unison with it. When the shattering force
Of a weapon, thrust within and laying bones
And sinews bare, fails to endamage life,
Yet faintness follows, and a pleasurable
Sinking down to the ground, and on the
    ground
There comes to pass a tumult of the mind,
And now and then a kind of hesitating
Desire to rise. Therefore the mind's nature
Must be material, since it feels distress
When it is wounded by material weapons.

And now, what is the substance of this mind,
And of what elements it is composed,
I will go on to explain to you. First I say
It is extremely subtle, and is formed
Of particles exceedingly minute.
That this is so, if you consider well,
You may be thus convinced. No visible ac-
    tion
Takes place with such rapidity as the mind
Conceives it happening and itself begins it.
Therefore the mind bestirs itself more quickly
Than any of those things which by their na-
    ture
Are clearly visible to our eyes. But that
Which is so very mobile, must consist
Of seeds which are quite round and quite
    minute,
So that they may be stirred and set in motion
By a small impulse. Thus water is moved
And ripples at the least impulse, being formed
Of particles that are small and quick to roll.
The nature of honey on the other hand
Is more stable; it is a sluggish fluid,
And moves more slowly; for its whole mass of
    matter
Coheres more closely, since it is not formed
Of such smooth bodies, nor so fine and round.
A light and gentle breath has force enough
To blow down a high heap of poppy seed
From top to bottom, but on a pile of stones
Or corn-ears it has no effect at all.
Therefore the mobility of bodies
Is in proportion to their littleness
And to their smoothness; while the greater
    weight

And the more roughness bodies may possess,
The stabler will they be. Since then we have found
The mind's nature pre-eminently mobile,
It needs must be composed of particles
Exceedingly minute and smooth and round.
The knowledge of this truth you will find useful
And serviceable in many ways, my friend.
Here likewise is a fact which shows how thin
Must be the texture of which the mind is formed,
And in how small a space it might be enclosed,
Could it be gathered into a single mass:
For soon as the untroubled sleep of death
Has laid hold on a man, and mind and soul
Have passed away, you then can discern nothing,
Which sight or weight can measure, taken away
From the whole body: death leaves all intact,
Except the vital sense and glowing warmth.
It follows that the whole soul must consist
Of very small seeds, and is interwoven
Through sinews, veins and flesh; since, when already
All of it has withdrawn from the whole body,
Yet the external contour of the limbs
Is preserved unimpaired and not one jot
Of weight is lost. Even so, when the flavour
Of wine has vanished, or when the sweet breath
Of unguent has dispersed into the air,
Or its taste has departed from some body,
Nevertheless the thing itself appears
No smaller to the eye, nor does aught seem
Subtracted from its weight; surely because
Many but tiny seeds make up the savours
And scent in the whole body of such things.
Therefore you may be certain of this truth:
The substance of the mind and soul is formed
Of very minute seeds, since, when it flees,
It takes none of the weight away with it.

> · · ·

                    Just as a mere eye,
When torn out by the roots, can discern nothing
Apart from the whole body, so the soul
And mind clearly can do naught by themselves;

Doubtless because, mingled through veins and flesh,
Sinews and bones, their atoms are confined
By the whole body, and cannot freely leap
Asunder, leaving wide spaces between them;
And therefore, being thus pent in, they move
In those sense-giving motions, which outside
The body, forced forth into the winds of air,
They have no power to move in after death,
Since they are not confined in the same way.
For air would be a body and a live thing,
Were the soul able to hold itself together
And keep enclosed within the air those motions
Which it was wont before to carry on
Within the sinews and inside the body.
And therefore I insist that when the whole
Enveloping body has been broken up,
And when the breath of life has been forced forth,
You must admit that both the mind's sensations
And the soul are dissolved, since for both body
And soul the cause of life is their close union.

> · · ·

Death then is nothing to us, nor one jot
Does it concern us, since the nature of mind
Is known to be mortal. And as in times long past
We felt no unhappiness when from every side
Gathering for conflict came the Punic hosts,
And all that was beneath the heights of heaven,
Shaken by the tumult and dismay of war,
Shuddered and quaked, and mortals were in doubt
To whose empire all human power would fall
By land and sea; so when we shall be no more,
When body and soul, out of which we are formed
Into one being, shall have been torn apart,
'Tis plain nothing whatever shall have power
To befall us, who then shall be no more,
Or stir our feeling, no, not if earth with sea
In ruin shall be mingled, and sea with sky.
[Grant even that the powers of mind and soul,
After they have been severed from the body,
Have feeling still, yet that to us is nothing,
Who by the binding marriage tie between
Body and soul are formed into one being.

Nor if Time should collect our scattered atoms
After our death, and bring them back to
    where
They now are placed, and if once more the
    light
Of life were given to us, not even that
Would in the least concern us, once the chain
Of self-awareness had been snapped asunder.
And in fact now we are not concerned at all
About those selves which we have been before,
Nor do they cause us any vexation now.
For when you look back on the whole past
    course
Of infinite time, and think how manifold
Matter's motions must be, then easily
May you believe this too, that these same
    atoms
Of which we now are formed, have often be-
    fore
Been placed in the same order as they are
    now:
Yet this can no remembrance bring us back;
For a break in life has since been interposed,
And all the atomic motions are dispersed
Wandering far astray from the old sensations.]
For if a man be destined to endure
Misery and suffering, he must first exist
In his own person at that very time,
So that evil may befall him. But since death
Precludes this, and forbids him to exist
To whom these ills might happen, we may be
    sure
That after death there is nothing we need
    dread,
That he who exists not cannot become miser-
    able,
And that it makes no difference at all
If he should never have been born before
At any time, when once he has been robbed
By death that dies not of his life that dies.

Therefore when you hear someone crying out
Against his lot, that after death his body
Must either rot away laid in the grave,
Or be consumed by flames or jaws of beasts,
You may be sure that his words ring not
    true,
That in his heart there lurks some secret sting,
Though he himself deny that he believes
Any sense will remain with him in death.
For he grants not, I think, what he professes

To grant, nor yet the ground of his profession,
Nor by the roots does he expel and thrust
Himself from life, but all unwittingly
Assumes that of self something will survive.
For when a living man forbodes that birds
And beasts will rend his body after death,
He is pitying himself; for he can neither
Distinguish his true self from the dead man,
Nor withdraw wholly from the outcast body,
But while in fancy he is standing there,
He imagines that dead man to be himself
And with his own feelings impregnates him.
So he complains because he was born mortal,
Nor sees that there will be in real death
No other self which living can lament
That he has perished, none that will stand by
And feel pain that he lies mangled or burn-
    ing.
For in truth, if after death it be an evil
To be mauled by devouring jaws of beasts,
I cannot see why it should be a pain
Less cruel to be laid out on a pyre
And scorched with hot flames, or to be em-
    balmed
In stifling honey and to grow stiff and cold
Couched on the smooth slab of a chilly stone,
Or to be crushed down under a weight of
    earth.

"Now no more shall thy home nor thy dear
    wife
Receive thee in gladness, nor shall thy sweet
    children
Run forth to meet thee and snatch kisses from
    thee,
And touch thee to the heart with silent joy.
No more canst thou be prosperous in thy do-
    ings,
A bulwark to thy friends. Poor wretch!" men
    cry,
"How wretchedly has one disastrous day
Stript thee of all life's many benefits!"
Yet this thereto they add not: "Nor withal
Does craving for these things beset thee more."
This truth, could men but grasp it once in
    thought
And follow thought with words, would forth-
    with set
Their spirits free from a huge ache and dread.
"Thou, as thou art, sunk in the sleep of death,
Shalt so continue through all time to come,

Delivered from all feverish miseries:
But we who watched thee on thy dreadful
    pyre
Change into ashes, we insatiably
Bewept thee; nor shall any lapse of days
Remove that lifelong sorrow from our hearts."
Of him who spoke thus, well might we in-
    quire,
What grief so exceeding bitter is there here,
If in the end all comes to sleep and rest,
That one should therefore pine with lifelong
    misery.
Why, no one feels the want of self and life
When body and mind alike are sunk in slum-
    ber.
For all we care, such sleep might be eternal:
No craving for ourselves moves us at all.
And yet, when starting up from sleep a man
Collects himself, the atoms of his soul
Throughout his frame have not been wander-
    ing far
From their sense-stirring motions. Therefore
    death
Must needs be thought far less to us than
    sleep,
If less can be than what we see is nothing:
For the dispersion of the turmoiled atoms,
That comes with death, is greater; nor has ever
Anyone yet awakened, upon whom
Has once fallen the chill arrest of life.

This too is oft men's wont, when they lie
    feasting
Wine-cup in hand with garland-shaded brows:
Thus from the heart they speak: "Brief is life's
    joy
For poor frail men. Soon will it be no more,
Nor ever afterwards may it be called back."
As though a foremost evil to be feared
After their death were this, that parching
    thirst
Would burn and scorch them in their misery,
Or craving for aught else would then beset
    them.

Furthermore, if Nature suddenly found voice,
And thus in person upbraided one of us:
"What is it, mortal, can afflict thee so,
That thou to such exceeding bitter grief
Shouldst yield? Why thus bemoan and bewail
    death?

For if the life thou hast lived hitherto
Was pleasant to thee, and not all thy blessings,
As though poured into a perforated jar,
Have flowed through and gone thanklessly to
    waste,
Why not then, like a guest replete with life,
Take thy departure, and with a tranquil mind
Enter, thou fool, upon repose untroubled?
But if all that thou hast enjoyed has perished
Squandered away, and life is a mere grievance,
Why seek to add thereto what in its turn
Must all come to destruction and be lost
Unprofitably? Why both of life and travail
Dost thou not rather make an end at once?
For there is nothing more I can contrive
Or find to please thee. All things are the same
At all times. Though thy body be not yet
Decayed with years, nor have thy worn-out
    limbs
Grown feeble, yet all things remain the same;
Though thou shouldst overlive all generations,
Nay, even more if thou shouldst never die"—
What could we answer, save that Nature's
    claim
Was just, and her indictment a true plea?
But if now someone more advanced in years
Should miserably complain and lament death
Beyond all reason, would she not yet more
    justly
Lift up her voice and chide him with sharp
    speech?
"Hence with thy tears, buffoon. Cease thy
    complaints.
After thou hast enjoyed all life's best gifts
Thou now decayest. But because thou hast
    yearned
Always for what was absent, and despised
That which was present, life has glided from
    thee
Incomplete and unprofitable; so now
Ere thou didst look for it, at thy pillow Death
Has taken his stand, before thou canst depart
Satisfied with existence and replete.
Yet now resign all vanities that so ill
Befit thine age: come then, with a good grace
Rise and make room for others; for thou
    must."
Justly, I think, would she so plead with him,
Justly reproach and chide: for things grown
    old
Yield place and are supplanted evermore

By new, and each thing out of other things
Must be replenished; and to the black pit
Of Tartarus no man ever is consigned.
Matter is needed, that therefrom may grow
Succeeding generations: which yet all,
When they have lived their life, shall follow
    thee.
Thus it is all have perished in past times
No less than thou, and shall hereafter perish.
So one thing out of another shall not cease
For ever to arise; and life is given
To none in fee, to all in usufruct.

. . .

This too thou may'st say sometimes to thy-
    self:
"Even the good king Ancus closed his eyes
To the light of day, who was so many times
Worthier than thou, unconscionable man.
Since then many others, kings and potentates
Who had dominion over mighty nations,
Have perished: and he too, even he, who once
Across the great sea paved a path whereby
His legions might pass over, bidding them
Cross dry-shod the salt deeps, and to show
    scorn
Trampled upon the roaring of the waves
With horses, even he, bereft of light,
Forth from his dying body gasped his soul.
The Scipios's offspring, thunderbolt of war,
Terror of Carthage, gave his bones to the earth
As though he were the meanest household
    slave.
Consider too the inventors of wise thoughts
And arts that charm; consider the companions
Of the Heliconian sisters, among whom
Homer bears the sceptre without a peer;
Yet he now sleeps the same sleep as they all.
Likewise Democritus, when a ripe old age
Had warned him that the memory-stirring mo-
    tions
Were waning in his mind, by his own act
Willingly offered himself up to death.
Even Epicurus died, when his life's light
Had run its course, he who in intellect
Surpassed the race of men, quenching the
    glory
Of all else, as the sun in heaven arising
Quenches the stars. Then wilt thou hesitate
And feel aggrieved to die? thou for whom life
Is well-nigh dead whilst yet thou art alive
And lookest on the light; thou who dost waste

Most of thy time in sleep, and waking snorest,
Nor ceasest to see dreams; who hast a mind
Troubled with empty terror, and ofttimes
Canst not discover what it is that ails thee,
When, poor besotted wretch, from every side
Cares crowd upon thee, and thou goest astray
Drifting in blind perplexity of soul."

If only men—even as they clearly feel
That weighing down their minds there is a
    load
Which with its heavy oppression wears them
    out—
Might learn too what the causes of it are,
And whence comes this great pile of misery
Crushing their breasts, they would not spend
    their lives,
As now so oft we see, none of them knowing
What it may be he wants, and seeking ever
By change of place to lay his burden down.
Oft he who is weary of home, from his great
    mansion
Will go forth, and then suddenly return,
Finding himself no happier abroad.
He posts to his villa galloping his ponies,
As though hurrying with help to a house on
    fire,
Yawns on the very threshold, nay sinks down
Heavily into sleep to seek oblivion,
Or even perhaps starts headlong back to town.
In this way each man flies from his own self;
Yet from that self in fact he has no power
To escape: he clings to it in his own despite,
And loathes it too, because, though he is sick,
He perceives not the cause of his disease:
Which if he could but comprehend aright,
Each would put all things else aside and first
Study to learn the nature of the world,
Since 'tis our state during eternal time,
Not for one hour merely, that is in doubt,
That state wherein mortals will have to pass
The whole time that awaits them after death.

Moreover, what base craving for mere life
Is this, that can so potently compel us
In anxious perils to feel such dismay?
For indeed certain is the end of life
That awaits mortals; nor can death be
    shunned:
Meet it we must. Furthermore in the same

Pursuits and actions do we pass our days
For ever, nor may we by living on
Forge for ourselves any new form of pleasure;
But what we crave, while it is absent, seems
To excel all things else; then, when 'tis ours,
We crave some other thing, gaping wide-
    mouthed,
Always possessed by the same thirst of life.
What fortune future time may bring, we know
    not,
Nor what chance has in store for us, nor yet

What end awaits us. By prolonging life
No least jot may we take from death's
    duration;
Naught may we steal away therefrom, that so
Haply a less long while we may be dead.
Therefore as many ages as you please
Add to your life's account; yet none the less
Will that eternal death be waiting for you;
And not less long will that man be no more,
Whose life has reached its end today, than he
Who has died many months and years ago.

Plutarch

Little is known of the life of Plutarch—there are many legends but few verifiable facts. He was a Greek, born in Boeotia around 40 A.D., and educated in Athens. He spent much of his life in the service of his native city-state, although he seems to have found time for considerable travel, including several brief visits to Rome, where he devoted himself to study. He died, highly honored, in Boeotia around 120 A.D.

It is difficult to consider Plutarch as anything other than a moralist. Although his fame rests firmly on the merits of his major work, *The Parallel Lives,* he was neither a great biographer nor a good historian. In his biographies he does not attempt to provide complete accounts of the lives of his subjects; rather, he carefully selects details and anecdotes to point up the good or bad qualities in the character and the actions of the person. As history, *The Parallel Lives* gives only imperfect accounts of an age, with no attempt to recount events systematically.

Even the organization of the book reveals the moralist at work. The lives are arranged in pairs, with the biography of a prominent Greek followed by the biography of a distinguished Roman. Frequently a pair of parallel lives is accompanied by a chapter in which the two are compared. It is in these comparisons that Plutarch reveals his penchant for drawing moral conclusions.

The following selection is from the life of Julius Caesar. In the *Parallel Lives* this brief biography is preceded, for obvious reasons, by the life of Alexander the Great. This particular translation was made in the seventeenth century by the English poet, John Dryden.

LIFE OF CAESAR

.   .   .

Thus far have we followed Caesar's actions before the wars of Gaul. After this, he seems to begin upon a new life and scene of action. And the period of those wars which he now fought, and those many expeditions in which he subdued Gaul, showed him to be a soldier and general not in the least inferior to any of the greatest and most admired commanders who had ever appeared at the head of armies. For if we compare him with the Fabii, the Metelli, the Scipios, and with those who were his contemporaries, or not long before him, Sulla, Marius, the two Luculli, or even Pompey himself, whose glory, it may be said, went up at that time to heaven for every excellence in war, we shall find Caesar's actions to have surpassed them all. One he may be held to have outdone in consideration of the difficulty of the country in which he fought, another in the extent of territory which he conquered; some, in the number and strength of the enemy whom he defeated; one man, because of the wildness and perfidiousness of the tribes whose good-will he conciliated, another in his humanity and clemency to those he overpowered; others, again, in his gifts and kindnesses to his soldiers; all alike in the number of the battles which he fought and the enemies whom he killed. For he had not pursued the wars in Gaul full ten years when he had taken by storm above eight hundred towns, subdued three hundred states, and of the three millions of men, who made up the gross sum of those with whom at several times he engaged, he had killed one million and taken captive a second.

He was so much master of the good-will and hearty service of his soldiers that those

PLUTARCH'S LIVES, trans. John Dryden (Boston, 1859), IV, 271-274, 278-279, 286-295, 312-328.

who in other expeditions were but ordinary men displayed a courage past defeating or withstanding when they went upon any danger where Caesar's glory was concerned. Such a one was Acilius, who, in the sea-fight before Marseilles, had his right hand struck off with a sword, yet did not quit his buckler out of his left, but struck the enemies in the face with it, till he drove them off and made himself master of the vessel. Such another was Cassius Scaeva, who, in a battle near Dyrrhachium, had one of his eyes shot out with an arrow, his shoulder pierced with one javelin, and his thigh with another; and having received one hundred and thirty darts upon his target, called to the enemy, as though he would surrender himself. But when two of them came up to him, he cut off the shoulder of one with a sword, and by a blow over the face forced the other to retire, and so with the assistance of his friends, who now came up, made his escape.

.   .   .

This love of honour and passion for distinction were inspired into them and cherished in them by Caesar himself, who, by his unsparing distribution of money and honours, showed them that he did not heap up wealth from the wars for his own luxury, or the gratifying of his private pleasures, but that all he received was but a public fund laid by for the reward and encouragement of valour, and that he looked upon all he gave to deserving soldiers as so much increase to his own riches. Added to this also, there was no danger to which he did not willingly expose himself, no labour from which he pleaded exemption. His contempt of danger was not so much wondered at by his soldiers because they knew how much he coveted honour. But his enduring so much hardship, which he did to all appearance beyond his natural strength, very much astonished them. For he was a spare man, had a soft and white skin, was distempered in the head and subject to an epilepsy, which, it is said, first seized him at Corduba. But he did not make the weakness of his constitution a pretext for his ease, but rather used war as the best physic against his indispositions; whilst, by indefatigable journeys, coarse diet, frequent lodging in the field, and continual laborious exercise, he struggled with his diseases and fortified his body against all attacks. He slept generally in his chariots or litters, employing even his rest in pursuit of action. In the day he was thus carried to the forts, garrisons, and camps, one servant sitting with him, who used to write down what he dictated as he went, and a soldier attending behind him with his sword drawn. He drove so rapidly that when he first left Rome he arrived at the river Rhone within eight days. He had been an expert rider from his childhood; for it was usual with him to sit with his hands joined together behind his back, and so to put his horse to its full speed. And in this way he disciplined himself so far as to be able to dictate letters from on horseback, and to give directions to two who took notes at the same time, or, as Oppius says, to more. And it is thought that he was the first who contrived means for communicating with friends by cipher, when either press of business, or the large extent of the city, left him no time for a personal conference about matters that required despatch. How little nice he was in his diet may be seen in the following instance. When at the table of Valerius Leo, who entertained him at supper at Milan, a dish of asparagus was put before him on which his host instead of oil had poured sweet ointment, Caesar partook of it without any disgust, and reprimanded his friends for finding fault with it. "For it was enough," said he, "not to eat what you did not like; but he who reflects on another man's want of breeding shows he wants it as much himself." Another time upon the road he was

driven by a storm into a poor man's cottage, where he found but one room, and that such as would afford but a mean reception to a single person, and therefore told his companions places of honour should be given up to the greater men, and necessary accommodations to the weaker, and accordingly ordered that Oppius, who was in bad health, should lodge within, whilst he and the rest slept under a shed at the door.

.   .   .

He now, after settling everything in Gaul, came back again, and spent the winter by the Po, in order to carry on the designs he had in hand at Rome. All who were candidates for offices used his assistance, and were supplied with money from him to corrupt the people and buy their votes, in return of which, when they were chosen, they did all things to advance his power. But what was more considerable, the most eminent and powerful men in Rome in great numbers came to visit him at Lucca; Pompey, and Crassus, and Appius, the governor of Sardinia, and Nepos, the pro-consul of Spain, so that there were in the place at one time one hundred and twenty lictors and more than two hundred senators. In deliberation here held, it was determined that Pompey and Crassus should be consuls again for the following year; that Caesar should have a fresh supply of money, and that his command should be renewed to him for five years more. It seemed very extravagant to all thinking men that those very persons who had received so much money from Caesar should persuade the senate to grant him more, as if he were in want. Though in truth it was not so much upon persuasion as compulsion that, with sorrow and groans for their own acts, they passed the measure. Cato was not present, for they had sent him seasonably out of the way into Cyprus; but Favonius, who was a zealous imitator of Cato, when he found he could do no good by opposing it, broke out of the house, and loudly declaimed against these proceedings to the people, but none gave him any hearing, some slighting him out of respect to Crassus and Pompey, and the greater part to gratify Caesar, on whom depended their hopes.

.   .   .

Caesar had long ago resolved upon the overthrow of Pompey, as had Pompey, for that matter, upon his. For Crassus, the fear of whom had hitherto kept them in peace, having now been killed in Parthia, if the one of them wished to make himself the greatest man in Rome, he had only to overthrow the other; and if he again wished to prevent his own fall, he had nothing for it but to be beforehand with him whom he feared. Pompey had not been long under any such apprehensions, having till lately despised Caesar as thinking it no difficult matter to put down him whom he himself had advanced. But Caesar had entertained this design from the beginning against his rivals, and had retired, like an expert wrestler, to prepare himself apart for the combat. Making the Gallic wars his exercise-ground, he had at once improved the strength of his soldiery, and had heightened his own glory by his great actions, so that he was looked on as one who might challenge comparison with Pompey. Nor did he let go any of those advantages which were now given him both by Pompey himself and the times, and the ill-government of Rome, where all who were candidates for offices publicly gave money, and without any shame bribed the people, who, having received their pay, did not contend for their benefactors with their bare suffrages, but with bows, swords, and slings. So that after having many times stained the place of election with blood of men killed upon the spot, they left the city at last without a government at all, to be carried about like a ship without a pilot to steer her; while all who had any wisdom could only be thankful if a course of such wild and stormy disorder and madness might end no worse than in a monarchy. Some were so bold as to declare openly that the

government was incurable but by a monarchy, and that they ought to take that remedy from the hands of the gentlest physician, meaning Pompey, who, though in words he pretended to decline it, yet in reality made his utmost efforts to be declared dictator. Cato, perceiving his design, prevailed with the senate to make him sole consul, that with the offer of a more legal sort of monarchy he might be withheld from demanding the dictatorship. They over and above voted him the continuance of his provinces, for he had two, Spain and all Africa, which he governed by his lieutenants, and maintained armies under him, at the yearly charge of a thousand talents out of the public treasury.

Upon this Caesar also sent and petitioned for the consulship and the continuance of his provinces. Pompey at first did not stir in it, but Marcellus and Lentulus opposed it, who had always hated Caesar, and now did everything, whether fit or unfit, which might disgrace and affront him. For they took away the privilege of Roman citizens from the people of New Comun, who were a colony that Caesar had lately planted in Gaul, and Marcellus, who was then consul, ordered one of the senators of that town, then at Rome, to be whipped, and told him he laid that mark upon him to signify he was no citizen of Rome, bidding him, when he went back again, to show it to Caesar. After Marcellus's consulship, Caesar began to lavish gifts upon all the public men out of the riches he had taken from the Gauls; discharged Curio, the tribune, from his great debts; gave Paulus, then consul, fifteen hundred talents, with which he built the noble court of justice adjoining the Forum, to supply the place of that called Fulvian. Pompey, alarmed at these preparations, now openly took steps, both by himself and his friends, to have a successor appointed in Caesar's room, and sent to demand back the soldiers whom he had lent him to carry on the wars in Gaul. Caesar returned them, and made each soldier a present of two hundred and fifty drachmas. The officer who brought them home to Pompey spread amongst the people no very fair or favourable report of Caesar, and flattered Pompey himself with false suggestions that he was wished for by Caesar's army; and though his affairs here were in some embarrassment through the envy of some, and the ill state of the government, yet there the army was at his command, and if they once crossed into Italy would presently declare for him; so weary were they of Caesar's endless expeditions and so suspicious of his designs for a monarchy. Upon this Pompey grew presumptuous, and neglected all warlike preparations, as fearing no danger, and used no other means against him than mere speeches and votes, for which Caesar cared nothing. And one of his captains, it is said, who was sent by him to Rome, standing before the senate house one day, and being told that the senate would not give Caesar a longer time in his government, clapped his hand on the hilt of his sword and said, "But this shall."

Yet the demands which Caesar made had the fairest colours of equity imaginable. For he proposed to lay down his arms, and that Pompey should do the same, and both together should become private men, and each expect a reward of his services from the public. For that those who proposed to disarm him, and at the same time to confirm Pompey in all the power he held, were simply establishing the one in the tyranny which they accused the other of aiming at. When Curio made these proposals to the people in Caesar's name, he was loudly applauded, and some threw garlands towards him, and dismissed him as they do successful wrestlers, crowned with flowers. Antony, being tribune, produced a letter sent from Caesar on this occasion, and read it, though the consuls did what they could to oppose it. But Scipio, Pompey's father-in-law, proposed in the senate that if Caesar did not lay down his arms

within such a time he should be voted an enemy; and the consuls putting it to the question, whether Pompey should dismiss his soldiers, and again, whether Caesar should disband his, very few assented to the first, but almost all to the latter. But Antony proposing again, that both should lay down their commissions, all but a very few agreed to it. Scipio was upon this very violent, and Lentulus, the consul, cried aloud, that they had need of arms, and not of suffrages, against a robber; so that the senators for the present adjourned, and appeared in mourning as a mark of their grief for the dissension.

Afterwards there came other letters from Caesar, which seemed yet more moderate, for he proposed to quit everything else, and only to retain Gaul within the Alps, Illyricum, and two legions, till he should stand a second time for a consul. Cicero, the orator, who was lately returned from Cilicia, endeavoured to reconcile differences, and softened Pompey, who was willing to comply in other things, but not to allow him the soldiers. At last Cicero used his persuasions with Caesar's friends to accept of the provinces and six thousand soldiers only, and so to make up the quarrel. And Pompey was inclined to give way to this, but Lentulus, the consul, would not hearken to it, but drove Antony and Curio out of the senatehouse with insults, by which he afforded Caesar the most plausible pretence that could be, and one which he could readily use to inflame the soldiers, by showing them two persons of such repute and authority who were forced to escape in a hired carriage in the dress of slaves. For so they were glad to disguise themselves when they fled out of Rome.

There were not about him at that time above three hundred horse and five thousand foot; for the rest of his army, which was left behind the Alps, was to be brought after him by officers who had received orders for that purpose. But he thought the first motion towards the design which he had on foot did not require large forces at present, and that what was wanted was to make his first step suddenly, and so as to astound his enemies with the boldness of it; as it would be easier, he thought, to throw them into consternation by doing what they never anticipated than fairly to conquer them, if he had alarmed them by his preparations. And therefore he commanded his captains and other officers to go only with their swords in their hands, without any other arms, and make themselves masters of Ariminum, a large city of Gaul with as little disturbance and bloodshed as possible. He committed the care of these forces to Hortensius, and himself spent the day in public as a standerby and spectator of the gladiators, who exercised before him. A little before night he attended to his person, and then went into the hall, and conversed for some time with those he had invited to supper, till it began to grow dusk, when he rose from table and made his excuses to the company, begging them to stay till he came back, having already given private directions to a few immediate friends that they should follow him, not all the same way, but some one way, some another. He himself got into one of the hired carriages, and drove at first another way, but presently turned towards Ariminum. When he came to the river Rubicon, which parts Gaul within the Alps from the rest of Italy, his thoughts began to work, now he was just entering upon the danger, and he wavered much in his mind when he considered the greatness of the enterprise into which he was throwing himself. He checked his course and ordered a halt, while he revolved with himself, and often changed his opinion one way and the other, without speaking a word. This was when his purposes fluctuated most; presently he also discussed the matter with his friends who were about him (of which number Asinius Pollio was one), computing how many calamities his passing that river would bring upon mankind, and what a relation of it would be

transmitted to posterity. At last, in a sort of passion, casting aside calculation, and abandoning himself to what might come, and using the proverb frequently in their mouths who enter upon dangerous and bold attempts, "The die is cast," with these words he took the river. Once over, he used all expedition possible, and before it was day reached Ariminum and took it. It is said that the night before he passed the river he had an impious dream that he was unnaturally familiar with his own mother.

As soon as Ariminum was taken, wide gates, so to say, were thrown open, to let in war upon every land alike and sea, and with the limits of the province, the boundaries of the laws were transgressed. Nor would one have thought that, as at other times, the mere men and women fled from one town of Italy to another in their consternation, but that the very towns themselves left their sites and fled for succour to each other. The city of Rome was overrun, as it were, with a deluge, by the conflux of people flying in from all the neighbouring places. Magistrates could no longer govern, nor the eloquence of any orator quiet it; it was all but suffering shipwreck by the violence of its own tempestuous agitation. The most vehement contrary passions and impulses were at work everywhere. Nor did those who rejoiced at the prospect of the change altogether conceal their feelings, but when they met, as in so great a city they frequently must, with the alarmed and dejected of the other party, they provoked quarrels by their bold expressions of confidence in the event. Pompey, sufficiently disturbed of himself, was yet more perplexed by the clamours of others; some telling him that he justly suffered for having armed Caesar against himself and the government; others blaming him for permitting Caesar to be insolently used by Lentulus, when he made such ample concessions, and offered such reasonable proposals towards an accommodation. Favonius bade him now stamp upon the ground; for once talking big in the senate, he desired them not to trouble themselves about making any preparations for the war, for that he himself, with one stamp of his foot, would fill all Italy with soldiers. Yet, still Pompey at that time had more forces than Caesar; but he was not permitted to pursue his own thoughts, but, being continually disturbed with false reports and alarms, as if the enemy was close upon him and carrying all before him, he gave way, and let himself be borne down by the general cry. He put forth an edict declaring the city to be in a state of anarchy, and left it with orders that the senate should follow him, and that no one should stay behind who did not prefer tyranny to their country and liberty.

The consuls at once fled, without making even the usual sacrifices; so did most of the senators, carrying off their own goods in as much haste as if they had been robbing their neighbours. Some, who had formerly much favoured Caesar's cause, in the prevailing alarm quitted their own sentiments, and without any prospect of good to themselves, were carried along by the common stream. It was a melancholy thing to see the city tossed in these tumults, like a ship given up by her pilots, and left to run, as chance guides her, upon any rock in her way. Yet, in spite of their sad condition, people still esteemed the place of their exile to be their country for Pompey's sake, and fled from Rome, as if it had been Caesar's camp. Labienus even, who had been one of Caesar's nearest friends, and his lieutenant, and who had fought by him zealously in the Gallic wars, now deserted him and went over to Pompey. Caesar sent all his money and equipage after him, and then sat down before Corfinium, which was garrisoned with thirty cohorts under the command of Domitius. He, in despair of maintaining the defence, requested a physician, whom he had among his attendants, to give him poison; and taking the dose, drank it, in hopes of being despatched by it. But soon after, when he was told that Caesar showed the utmost clemency towards those he took prisoners, he lamented his misfortune, and blamed the hastiness of his resolution. His physician consoled him by informing him that he had taken a sleeping draught, not a poison; upon which, much rejoiced, and rising from his bed, he went presently to Caesar, and gave him the pledge of his hand, yet afterwards again went over to Pompey. The report of these actions at Rome quieted those who were there and some who had fled thence returned.

Caesar took into his army Domitius's soldiers, as he did all those whom he found in any town enlisted for Pompey's service. Being now strong and formidable enough, he advanced against Pompey himself, who did not stay to receive him, but fled to Brundusium, having sent the consuls before with a body of troops to Dryyhachium. Soon after, upon Caesar's approach, he set to sea, as shall be more particularly related in his life. Caesar would have immediately pursued him, but wanted shipping, and therefore went back to Rome, having made himself master of all Italy without bloodshed in the space of sixty days. When he came thither, he found the city more quiet than he expected, and many senators present, to whom he addressed himself with courtesy and deference, desiring them to send to Pompey about any reasonable accommodations towards a peace. But nobody complied with this proposal; whether out of fear of Pompey, whom they had deserted, or that they thought Caesar did not mean what he said, but thought it his interest to talk plausibly. Afterwards, when Metellus, the tribune, would have hindered him from taking money out of the public treasury, and adduced some laws against it, Caesar replied that arms and laws had each their own time; "If what I do displeases you, leave the place; war allows no free talking. When I have laid down my arms, and made peace, come back and make what speeches you please. And this," he added, "I tell you in diminution of my own just right, as indeed you and all others who have appeared against me and are now in my power may be treated as I please." Having said this to Metellus, he went to the doors of the treasury and the keys being not to be found, sent for smiths to force them open. Metellus again making resistance and some encouraging him in it, Caesar, in a louder tone, told him he would put him to death if he gave him any further disturbance. "And this," said he, "you know, young man, is more disagreeable for me to say than to do." These words made Metellus withdraw for fear, and obtained speedy execution henceforth for all orders that Caesar gave for procuring necessaries for the war.

He was now proceeding to Spain, with the determination of first crushing Afranius and Varro, Pompey's lieutenants, and making himself master of the armies and provinces under them, that he might then more securely advance against Pompey, when he had no enemy left behind him. In this expedition his person was often in danger from ambuscades, and his army by want of provisions, yet he did not desist from pursuing the enemy, provoking them to fight, and hemming them with his fortifications, till by main force he made himself master of their camps and their forces. Only the generals got off, and fled to Pompey.

When Caesar came back to Rome, Piso, his father-in-law, advised him to send men to Pompey to treat of a peace; but Isauricus, to ingratiate himself with Caesar, spoke against it. After this, being created dictator by the senate, he called home the exiles, and gave back their rights as citizens to the children of those who had suffered under Sulla; he relieved the debtors by an act remitting some part of the interest on their debts, and passed some other measures of the same sort, but not many. For within eleven days he resigned his dictatorship, and having declared himself consul, with Servilius Isauricus, hastened again to the war.

· · ·

[*After completely defeating Pompey and his enemies, and enforcing his rule in Spain, Egypt, Africa, and elsewhere, Caesar returned to Rome. Ed.*]

He was now chosen a fourth time consul, and went into Spain against Pompey's sons. They were but young, yet had gathered together a very numerous army, and showed they had courage and conduct to command it, so that Caesar was in extreme danger. The great battle was near the town of Munda, in which Caesar, seeing his men hard pressed, and making but a weak resistance, ran through the ranks among the soldiers, and crying out, asked them whether they were not ashamed to deliver him into the hands of boys. At last, with great difficulty, and the best efforts he could make, he forced back the enemy, killing thirty thousand of them, though with the loss of one thousand of his best men. When he came back from the fight, he told his friends that he had often fought for victory, but this was the first time he had ever fought for life. This battle was won on the feast of Bacchus, the very day in which Pompey, four years before, had set out for the war. The younger of Pompey's sons escaped; but Didius, some days after the fight, brought the head of the elder to Caesar. This was the last war he was engaged in. The triumph which he celebrated for this victory displeased the Romans beyond anything, for he had not defeated foreign generals or barbarian kings, but had destroyed the children and family of one of the greatest men of Rome, though unfortunate; and it did not look well to lead a procession in celebration of the calamities of his country, and to rejoice in those things for which no other apology could be made either to gods or men than their being absolutely necessary. Besides that, hitherto he had never sent letters or messengers to announce any victory over his fellow-citizens, but had seemed rather to be ashamed of the action than to expect honour from it.

Nevertheless his countrymen, conceding all to his fortune, and accepting the bit, in the hope that the government of a single person would give them time to breathe after so many civil wars and calamities, made him dictator for life. This was indeed a tyranny avowed, since his power now was not only absolute, but perpetual, too. Cicero made the first proposals to the senate for conferring honours upon him, which might in some sort be said not to exceed the limits of ordinary human moderation. But others, striving which should deserve most, carried them so excessively high, that they made Caesar odious to the most indifferent and moderate sort of men, by the pretensions and extravagance of the titles which they decreed him. His enemies, too, are thought to have had some share in this, as well as his flatterers. It gave them advantage against him, and would be their justification for any attempt they should make upon him; for since the civil wars were ended, he had nothing else that he could be charged with. And they had good reason to decree a temple to Clemency, in token of their thanks for the mild use he made of his victory. For he not only pardoned many of those who fought against him, but, further, to some gave honours and offices; as particularly to Brutus and Cassius, who both of them were praetors. Pompey's images that were thrown down he set up again, upon which Cicero also said that by raising Pompey's statues he had fixed his own. When his friends advised him to have a guard, and several offered their services, he would not hear of it; but said it was better to suffer death once than always to live in fear of it. He looked upon the affections of the people to be the best and surest guard, and entertained them again with public feasting and general distributions of corn; and to gratify his army, he sent out colonies to several places, of which the most remarkable were Carthage and Corinth; which as before they had been ruined at the same time, so now were restored and repeopled together.

As for the men of high rank, he promised to some of them future consulships and praetorships, some he consoled with other offices and honours, and to all held out hopes of favour by the solicitude he showed to rule with the general good-will, insomuch that upon the death of Maximus one day before his consulship was ended, he made Caninius Revilius consul for that day. And when many went to pay the usual compliments and attentions to the new consul, "Let us make haste," said Cicero, "lest the man be gone out of his office before we come."

Caesar was born to do great things, and had a passion after honour, and the many noble exploits he had done did not now serve as an inducement to him to sit still and reap the fruit of his past labours, but were incentives and encouragements to go on, and raised in him ideas of still greater actions, and a desire of new glory, as if the present were all spent. It was in fact a sort of emulous struggle with himself, as it had been with another, how he might outdo his past actions by his future. In pursuit of these thoughts, he resolved to make war upon the Parthians, and when he had subdued them, to pass through Hyrcania; thence to march along by the Caspian Sea to Mount Caucasus, and so on about Pontus, till he came into Scythia; then to overrun all the countries bordering upon Germany, and Germany itself; and so to return through Gaul into Italy, after completing the whole circle of his intended empire, and bounding it on every side by the ocean. While preparations were making for this expedition, he proposed to dig through the isthmus on which Corinth stands; and appointed Anienus to superintend the work. He had also a design of diverting the Tiber, and carrying it by a deep channel directly from Rome to Circeii, and so into the sea near Tarracina, that there might be a safe and easy passage for all merchants who traded to Rome. Besides this, he intended to drain all the marshes by Pomentium and Setia, and gain ground enough from the water to employ many thousands of men in tillage. He proposed further to make great mounds on the shore nearest Rome, to hinder the sea from breaking in upon the land, to clear the coast at Ostia of all the hidden rocks and shoals that made it unsafe for shipping, and to form ports and harbours fit to receive the large number of vessels that would frequent them.

These things were designed without being carried into effect; but his reformation of the calendar in order to rectify the irregularity of time was not only projected with great scientific ingenuity, but was brought to its completion, and proved of very great use. For it was not only in ancient time that the Romans had wanted a certain rule to make the revolutions of their months fall in with the course of the year, so that their festivals and solemn days for sacrifice were removed by little and little, till at last they came to be kept at seasons quite the contrary to what was at first intended, but even at this time the people had no way of computing the solar year; only the priests could say the time, and they, at their pleasure, without giving any notice, slipped in the intercalary month, which they called Mercedonius. Numa was the first who put in this month, but his expedient was but a poor one and quite inadequate to correct all the errors that arose in the returns of the annual cycles, as we have shown in his life. Caesar called in the best philosophers and mathematicians of his time to settle the point, and out of the systems he had before him formed a new and more exact method of correcting the calendar, which the Romans use to this day, and seem to succeed better than any nation in avoiding the errors occasioned by the inequality of the cycles. Yet even this gave offence to those who looked with an evil eye on his position, and felt oppressed by his power. Cicero the orator, when some one in his company chanced to say the next morning Lyra would rise, replied, "Yes, in accord-

ance with the edict," as if even this were a matter of compulsion.

But that which brought upon him the most apparent and mortal hatred was his desire of being king; which gave the common people the first occasion to quarrel with him, and proved the most specious pretence to those who had been his secret enemies all along. Those who would have procured him that title gave it out that it was foretold in the Sibyls' books that the Romans should conquer the Parthians when they fought against them under the conduct of a king, but not before. And one day, as Caesar was coming down from Alba to Rome, some were so bold as to salute him by the name of king; but he, finding the people disrelished it, seemed to resent it himself, and said his name was Caesar, not King. Upon this there was a general silence, and he passed on looking not very well pleased or contented. Another time, when the senate had conferred on him some extravagant honours, he chanced to receive the message as he was sitting on the rostra, where, though the consuls and praetors themselves waited on him, attended by the whole body of the senate, he did not rise, but behaved himself to them as if they had been private men, and told them his honours wanted rather to be retrenched than increased. This treatment offended not only the senate, but the commonalty too, as if they thought the affront upon the senate equally reflected upon the whole republic; so that all who could decently leave him went off, looking much discomposed. Caesar, perceiving the false step he had made, immediately retired home; and laying his throat bare, told his friends that he was ready to offer this to any one who would give the stroke. But afterwards he made the malady from which he suffered the excuse for his sitting, saying that those who are attacked by it lose their presence of mind if they talk much standing; that they presently grow giddy, fall into convulsions, and quite lose their reason. But this was not the reality, for he would willingly have stood up to the senate, had not Cornelius Balbus, one of his friends, or rather flatterers, hindered him. "Will you not remember," said he, "you are Caesar, and claim the honour which is due to your merit?"

He gave a fresh occasion of resentment by his affront to the tribunes. The Lupercalia were then celebrated, a feast at the first institution belonging, as some writers say, to the shepherds, and having some connection with the Arcadian Lycaea. Many young noblemen and magistrates run up and down the city with their upper garments off, striking all they meet with thongs of hide, by way of sport; and many women, even of the highest rank, place themselves in the way, and hold out their hands to the lash, as boys in a school do to the master, out of a belief that it procures an easy labour to those who are with child, and makes those conceive who are barren. Caesar, dressed in a triumphal robe, seated himself in a golden chair at the rostra to view this ceremony. Antony, as consul, was one of those who ran this course, and when he came into the Forum, and the people made way for him, he went up and reached to Caesar a diadem wreathed with laurel. Upon this there was a shout, but only a slight one, made by the few who were planted there for that purpose; but when Caesar refused it, there was universal applause. Upon the second offer, very few, and upon the second refusal, all again applauded. Caesar finding it would not take, rose up, and ordered the crown to be carried into the capitol. Caesar's statues were afterwards found with royal diadems on their heads. Flavius and Marullus, two tribunes of the people, went presently and pulled them off, and having apprehended those who first saluted Caesar as king committed them to prison. The people followed them with acclamations, and called them by the name of Brutus, because Brutus was the first who ended the succession of kings, and transferred the power which before was lodged in one man into the hands of the senate and people. Caesar so far resented this, that he displaced Marullus and Flavius; and in urging his charges against them, at the same time ridiculed the people, by himself giving the men more than once the names of Bruti and Cumaei.

This made the multitude turn their thoughts to Marcus Brutus, who, by his father's side, was thought to be descended from that first Brutus, and by his mother's side from the Servilii, another noble family, being besides nephew and son-in-law to Cato. But the honours and favours he had received from Caesar took off the edge from the desires he might himself have felt for overthrowing the new monarchy. For he had not only been pardoned himself after Pompey's defeat at Pharsalis, and had procured the same grace for many of his friends, but was one in whom Caesar had a particular confidence. He had at that time the most honourable praetorship for the year, and was named for the consulship four years after, being preferred before Cassius, his competitor. Upon the question as to choice, Caesar, it is related, said that Cassius had the fairer pretensions, but that he could not pass by Brutus. Nor would he afterwards listen to some who spoke against Brutus, when the conspiracy against him was already afoot, but laying his hand on his body, said to the informers, "Brutus will wait for this skin of mine," intimating that he was worthy to bear rule on account of his virtue, but would not be base and ungrateful to gain it. Those who desired a change, and looked on him as the only, or at least the most proper, person to effect it, did not venture to speak with him; but in the night-time laid papers about his chair of state, where he used to sit and determine causes with such sentences in them as, "You are asleep, Brutus," "You are no longer Brutus." Cassius, when he perceived his ambition a little raised upon this, was more instant than before to work him yet further, having himself a private grudge against Caesar for most reasons that we have mentioned in the Life of Brutus.

Fate, however, is to all appearance more unavoidable than unexpected. For many strange prodigies and apparitions are said to have been observed shortly before this event. As to the lights in the heavens, the noises heard in the night, and the wild birds which perched in the Forum, these are not perhaps worth taking notice of in so great a case as this. Strabo, the philosopher, tells us that a number of men were seen, looking as if they were heated through with fire, contending with each other; that a quantity of flame issued from the hand of a soldier's servant, so that they who saw it thought he must be burnt, but that after all he had no hurt. As Caesar was sacrificing, the victim's heart was missing, a very bad omen, because no living creature can subsist without a heart. One finds it also related by many that a soothsayer bade him prepare for some great danger on the Ides of March. When this day was come, Caesar, as he went to the senate, met this soothsayer, and said to him by way of raillery, "The Ides of March are come," who answered him calmly, "Yes they are come, but they are not past." The day before his assassination he supped with Marcus Lepidus; and as he was signing some letters according to his custom, as he reclined at table, there arose a question what sort of death was the best. At which he immediately, before any one could speak, said "A sudden one."

After this, as he was in bed with his wife, all the doors and windows of the house flew open together; he was startled at the noise and the light which broke into the room, and sat up in his bed, where by the moonshine he perceived Calpurnia fast asleep, but heard her utter in her dream some indistinct words and inarticulate groans. She fancied at that time she was weeping over Caesar, and holding him butchered in her arms. Others say this was not her dream, but that she dreamed that a pinnacle, which the senate, as Livy relates, had ordered to be raised on Caesar's house by way of ornament and grandeur, was tumbling down, which was the occasion of her tears and ejaculations. When it was day, she begged of Caesar, if it were possible, not to stir out, but to adjourn the senate to another time; and if he slighted her dreams, that she would be pleased to consult his fate by sacrifices and other kinds of divination. Nor was he himself without some suspicion and fears; for he never before discovered any womanish superstition in Calpurnia, whom he now saw in such great alarm. Upon the report which the priests made to him, that they had killed several sacrifices, and still found them inauspicious, he resolved to send Antony to dismiss the senate.

In this juncture, Decimus Brutus, surnamed Albinus, one whom Caesar had such confidence in that he made him his second heir, who nevertheless was engaged in the conspiracy with the other Brutus and Cassius, fearing lest if Caesar should put off the senate to another day the business might get wind, spoke scoffingly and in mockery of the diviners, and blamed Caesar for giving the senate so fair an occasion of saying he had put a slight upon them, for that they were met upon his summons, and were ready to vote unanimously that he should be declared king of all the provinces out of Italy, and might wear a diadem in any other place but Italy, by sea or land. If any one should be sent to tell them they might break up for the present, and meet again when Calpurnia should chance to have better dreams, what would his enemies say? Or who would with any patience hear his friends, if they should presume to defend his government as not arbitrary and tyrannical? But if he was possessed so far as to think this day unfortunate, yet it were more decent to go himself to the senate, and to adjourn it in his own person. Brutus, as he spoke these words, took Caesar by the hand, and conducted him forth. He was not gone far from the door, when a servant of some other person's made towards him, but not being able to come up to him, on account of the crowd of those who pressed about him, he made his way into the house, and committed himself to Calpurnia, begging of her to secure him till Caesar returned, because he had matters of great importance to communicate to him.

Artemidorus, a Cnidian, a teacher of Greek logic, and by that means so far acquainted with Brutus and his friends as to have got into the secret, brought Caesar in a small written memorial the heads of what he had to depose. He had observed that Caesar, as he received any papers, presently gave them to the servants who attended on him; and therefore came as near to him as he could, and said, "Read this, Caesar, alone, and quickly, for it contains matter of great importance which nearly concerns you." Caesar received it, and tried several times to read it, but was still hindered by the crowd of those who came to speak to him. However, he kept it in his hand by itself till he came into the senate. Some say it was another who gave Caesar this note, and that Artemidorus could not get to him, being all along kept off by the crowd.

All these things might happen by chance. But the place which was destined for the scene of this murder, in which the senate met that day, was the same in which Pompey's statue stood, and was one of the edifices which Pompey had raised and dedicated with his theatre to the use of the public, plainly showing that there was something of a supernatural influence which guided the action and ordered it to that particular place. Cassius, just before the act, is said to have looked towards Pompey's statue, and silently implored his assistance, though he had been inclined to the doctrines of Epicurus. But this occasion, and the instant danger, carried him away out of all his reasonings, and filled him for the time with a sort of inspiration. As for Antony, who was firm to Caesar, and a strong man, Brutus Albinus kept him outside the house, and delayed him with a long conversation contrived on purpose. When Caesar entered, the senate stood up to show their respect for him, and of Brutus's confederates, some came about his chair and stood behind it, others met him, pretending to add their petitions to those of Tillius Cimber, in behalf of his brother who was in exile; and they followed him with their joint applications till he came to his seat. When he was sat down, he refused to comply with their requests, and upon their urging him further began to reproach them severely for their importunities, when Tillius, laying hold of his robe with both his hands, pulled it down from his neck, which was the signal for the assault. Casca gave him the first cut in the neck, which was not mortal nor dangerous, as coming from one who at the beginning of such a bold action was probably much disturbed; Caesar immediately turned about, and laid his hand upon the dagger and kept hold of it. And both of them at the same time cried out, he that received the blow, in Latin, "Vile Casca, what does this mean?" and he that gave it, in Greek, to his brother, "Brother, help!" Upon this first onset, those who were not privy to the design were astonished, and their horror and amazement at what they saw were so great that they durst not flee, nor assist Caesar, nor so much as speak a word. But those who came prepared for the business enclosed him on every side, with their naked daggers in their hands. Which way soever he turned he met with blows, and saw their swords levelled at his face and eyes, and was encompassed, like a wild beast in the toils, on every side. For it had been agreed they should each of them make a thrust at him, and flesh themselves with his blood; for which reason Brutus also gave him one stab in the groin. Some say that he fought and resisted all the rest, shifting his body to avoid the blows, and calling out for help, but that when he saw Brutus's sword drawn, he covered his face with his robe and submitted, letting himself fall, whether it were by chance, or that he was pushed in that direction by his murderers, at the foot of the pedestal on which Pompey's statue stood, and which was thus wetted with his blood. So that Pompey himself seemed to have presided, as it were, over the revenge done upon his adversary, who lay here at his feet, and breathed out his soul through his multitude of wounds, for they say he received three-and-twenty. And the conspirators themselves were many of them wounded by each other, whilst they all levelled their blows at the same person.

When Caesar was despatched, Brutus stood forth to give a reason for what they had done, but the senate would not hear him, but flew out of doors in all haste, and filled the people with so much alarm and distraction, that some shut up their houses, others left their counters and shops. All ran one way or the other, some to the place to see the sad spectacle, others back again after they had seen it. Antony and Lepidus, Caesar's most faithful friends, got off privately and hid themselves in some friends' houses. Brutus and his followers, being yet hot from the deed, marched in a body from the senate-house to the capitol with their drawn swords, not like persons who thought of escaping, but with an air of confidence and assurance, and as they went along, called to the people to resume their liberty, and invited the company of any more distinguished people whom they met. And some of these joined the procession and went up along with them, as if they also had been of the conspiracy, and could claim a share in the honour of what had been done. As, for example Caius Octavius and Lentulus Spinther, who suffered afterwards for their vanity, being driven off by Antony and the young Caesar, and lost the honour they desired, as well as their lives, which it cost them, since no one believed they had any share in the action. For neither did those who punished them profess to revenge the fact, but

the ill-will. The day after, Brutus with the rest came down from the capitol and made a speech to the people, who listened without expressing either any pleasure or resentment, but showed by their silence that they pitied Caesar and respected Brutus. The senate passed acts of oblivion for what was past, and took measures to reconcile all parties. They ordered that Caesar should be worshipped as a divinity, and nothing, even of the slightest consequence, should be revoked which he had enacted during his government. At the same time they gave Brutus and his followers the command of provinces, and other considerable posts. So that all the people now thought things were well settled, and brought to the happiest adjustment.

But when Caesar's will was opened, and it was found that he had left a considerable legacy to each one of the Roman citizens, and when his body was seen carried through the marketplace all mangled with wounds, the multitude could no longer contain themselves within the bounds of tranquillity and order, but heaped together a pile of benches, bars, and tables, which they placed the corpse on, and setting fire to it, burnt it on them. Then they took brands from the pile and ran, some to fire the houses of the conspirators, others up and down the city to find out the men and tear them to pieces, but met, however, with none of them, they having taken effectual care to secure themselves.

One Cinna, a friend of Caesar's, chanced the night before to have an odd dream. He fancied that Caesar invited him to supper, and that upon his refusal to go with him, Caesar took him by the hand and forced him, though he hung back. Upon hearing the report that Caesar's body was burning in the market-place, he got up and went thither, out of respect to his memory, though his dream gave him some ill apprehensions, and though he was suffering from a fever. One of the crowd who saw him there asked another who that was, and having learned his name, told it to his next neighbour. It presently passed for a certainty that he was one of Caesar's murderers, as, indeed, there was another Cinna, a conspirator, and they, taking this to be the man, immediately seized him and tore him limb from limb upon the spot.

Brutus and Cassius, frightened at this, within a few days retired out of the city. What they afterwards did and suffered, and how they died, is written in the Life of Brutus. Caesar died in his fifty-sixth year, not having survived Pompey above four years. That empire and power which he had pursued through the whole course of his life with so much hazard, he did at last with much difficulty compass, but reaped no other fruits from it than the empty name and invidious glory. But the great genius which attended him through his life-time even after his death remained as the avenger of his murder, pursuing through every sea and land all those who were concerned with it, and suffering none to escape, but reaching all who in any sort or kind were either actually engaged in the fact, or by their counsels any way promoted it.

The most remarkable of mere human coincidences was that which befell Cassius, who, when he was defeated at Philippi, killed himself with the same dagger which he had made use of against Caesar. The most signal preternatural appearances were the great comet, which shone very bright for seven nights after Caesar's death, and then disappeared, and the dimness of the sun, whose orb continued pale and dull for the whole of that year, never showing its ordinary radiance at its rising, and giving but a weak and feeble heat. The air consequently was damp and gross for want of stronger rays to open and rarify it. The fruits, for that reason, never properly ripened, and began to wither and fall off for want of heat before they were fully formed. But above all, the phantom which appeared to Brutus showed the murder was not pleasing to the gods. The story of it is this.

Brutus, having to pass his army from Abydos to the continent on the other side, laid himself down one night, as he used to do, in his tent, and was not asleep, but thinking of his affairs, and what events he might expect. For he is related to have been the least inclined to sleep of all men who have commanded armies, and to have had the greatest natural capacity for continuing awake, and employing himself without need of rest. He thought he heard a noise at the door of his tent, and looking that way, by the light of his lamp, which was almost out, saw a terrible figure, like that of a man, but of unusual stature and severe countenance. He was somewhat frightened at first, but seeing it neither did nor spoke anything to him, only stood silently by his bedside, he asked who it was. The spectre answered him, "Thy evil genius, Brutus, and thou shalt see me at Philippi." Brutus answered courageously, "Well, I shall see you," and immediately the appearance vanished.

When the time was come, he drew up his army near Philippi against Antony and Caesar [*Augustus*], and in the first battle won the day, routed the enemy, and plundered Caesar's camp. The night before the second battle, the same phantom appeared to him again, but spoke not a word. He presently understood his destiny was at hand, and exposed himself to all the danger of the battle. Yet he did not die in the fight, but seeing his men defeated, got up to the top of a rock, and there presenting his sword to his naked breast, and assisted, as they say, by a friend, who helped him to give the thrust, met his death.

Epictetus

Epictetus (*c.* 50-120 A.D.), like Lucretius before him, taught a philosophy that had been originated by the Greeks. This philosophy was Stoicism, developed by a philosopher of the third century B.C. named Zeno, who felt that he was carrying on the intellectual tradition of Socrates. The name Stoicism derives from Zeno's practice of lecturing in a colonnade in Athens known as the *Stoa Poikile*, or Painted Porch.

The Romans regarded Stoicism as a particularly satisfying philosophy of life and were attracted to it in large numbers. Because many of the Romans who embraced Stoicism occupied high offices in the government, Stoicism has often been called the "official" philosophy of Rome. Included among the famous Roman Stoics were Cicero, the great orator, statesman, and defender of the Republic; Seneca, the tragedian and minister of government under Nero; and the Emperor Marcus Aurelius.

Epictetus himself was born in Asia Minor and was transported to Rome as a slave during the reign of Nero. His Roman masters recognized his abilities and sent him to the best school in the city, where he fell under the influence of Stoicism, the prevailing philosophical doctrine at the time. Like Socrates, Epictetus wrote nothing; the only record we have of his teachings consists of notes taken down by his disciples.

Some scholars believe that in Epictetus' home town in Asia Minor there was a community of the new religious sect called Christians and that Epictetus was influenced by their doctrines. This explanation could account for the similarities between his views and those of the Christian philosophers who followed soon after him. But so could the opposite assumption, that the Christian writers were influenced by Epictetus. Whatever the exact historical relationship between Roman Stoicism and early Christianity, the parallels between many of their doctrines are sometimes quite striking.

The Enchiridion (or Manual), which follows, consists of sayings, admonitions, and general advice on the conduct of life intended by Epictetus for the guidance of his followers.

THE ENCHIRIDION

I

Of things some are in our power, and others are not. In our power are opinion, movement towards a thing, desire, aversion; and in a word, whatever are our own acts: not in our power are the body, property, reputation, offices, and in a word, whatever are not our own acts. And the things in our power are by nature free, not subject to restraint nor hindrance: but the things not in our power are weak, slavish, subject to restraint, in the power of oth-

THE DISCOURSES OF EPICTETUS, trans. G. Long (London, 1877), pp. 379-404.

ers. Remember then that if you think the things which are by nature slavish to be free, and the things which are in the power of others to be your own, you will be hindered, you will lament, you will be disturbed, you will blame both gods and men: but if you think that only which is your own to be your own, and if you think that what is another's as it really is, belongs to another, no man will ever compel you, no man will hinder you, you will never blame any man, you will accuse no man, you will do nothing involuntarily, no man will harm you, you will have no enemy, for you will not suffer any harm.

If then you desire such great things, remember that you must not lay hold of them with a small effort; but you must leave alone some things entirely, and postpone others for the present. But if you wish for these things also, and power and wealth, perhaps you will not gain even these very things because you aim also at those former things: certainly you will fail in those things through which alone happiness and freedom are secured. Straightway then practise saying to every harsh appearance, You are an appearance, and in no manner what you appear to be. Then examine it by the rules which you possess, and by this first and chiefly, whether it relates to the things which are in our power or to things which are not in our power: and if it relates to anything which is not in our power, be ready to say, that it does not concern you.

II

Remember that desire contains in it the profession of obtaining that which you desire; and the profession in aversion is that you will not fall into that which you attempt to avoid: and he who fails in his desire is unfortunate; and he who falls into that which he would avoid, is unhappy. If then you attempt to avoid only the things contrary to nature which are within your power, you will not be involved in any of the things

which you would avoid. But if you attempt to avoid disease or death or poverty, you will be unhappy. Take away then aversion from all things which are not in our power, and transfer it to the things contrary to nature which are in our power. But destroy desire completely for the present. For if you desire anything which is not in our power, you must be unfortunate: but of the things in our power, and which it would be good to desire, nothing yet is before you. But employ only the power of moving towards an object and retiring from it; and these powers indeed only slightly and with exceptions and with remission.

III

In every thing which pleases the soul, or supplies a want, or is loved, remember to add this to the description; what is the nature of each thing, beginning from the smallest? If you love an earthen vessel, say it is an earthen vessel which you love; for when it has been broken, you will not be disturbed. If you are kissing your child or wife, say that it is a human being whom you are kissing, for when the wife or child dies, you will not be disturbed.

IV

When you are going to take in hand any act, remind yourself what kind of an act it is. If you are going to bathe, place before yourself what happens in the bath: some splashing the water, others pushing against one another, others abusing one another, and some stealing: and thus with more safety you will undertake the matter, if you say to yourself, I now intend to bathe, and to maintain my will in a manner conformable to nature. And so you will do in every act: for thus if any hindrance to bathing shall happen, let this thought be ready: it was not this only that I intended, but I intended also to maintain my will in a way conformable to nature; but I shall not maintain it so, if I am vexed at what happens.

V

Men are disturbed not by the things which happen, but by the opinions about the things: for example, death is nothing terrible, for if it were, it would have seemed so to Socrates; for the opinion about death, that it is terrible, is the terrible thing. When then we are impeded or disturbed or grieved, let us never blame others, but ourselves, that is, our opinions. It is the act of an ill-instructed man to blame others for his own bad condition; it is the act of one who has begun to be instructed, to lay the blame on himself; and of one whose instruction is completed, neither to blame another, nor himself.

VI

Be not elated at any advantage, which belongs to another. If a horse when he is elated should say, I am beautiful, one might endure it. But when you are elated, and say, I have a beautiful horse, you must know that you are elated at having a good horse. What then is your own? The use of appearances. Consequently when in the use of appearances you are conformable to nature, then you will be elated, for then you will be elated at something good which is your own.

VII

As on a voyage when the vessel has reached a port, if you go out to get water, it is an amusement by the way to pick up a shell fish or some bulb, but your thoughts ought to be directed to the ship, and you ought to be constantly watching if the captain should call, and then you must throw away all those things, that you may not be bound and pitched into the ship like sheep: so in life also, if there be given to you instead of a little bulb and a shell a wife and child, there will be nothing to prevent you from taking them. But if the captain should call, run to the ship, and leave all those things without regard to them. But if you are old, do not even go far from the ship, lest when you are called you make default.

VIII

Seek not that the things which happen should happen as you wish; but wish the things which happen to be as they are, and you will have a tranquil flow of life.

IX

Disease is an impediment to the body, but not to the will, unless the will itself chooses. Lameness is an impediment to the leg, but not to the will. And add this reflection on the occasion of every thing that happens; for you will find it an impediment to something else, but not to yourself.

X

On the occasion of every accident that befalls you, remember to turn to yourself and inquire what power you have for turning it to use. If you see a fair man or a fair woman, you will find that the power to resist is temperance. If labour be presented to you, you will find that it is endurance. If it be abusive words, you will find it to be patience. And if you have been thus formed to the proper habit, the appearances will not carry you along with them.

XI

Never say about any thing, I have lost it, but say I have restored it. Is your child dead? It has been restored. Is your wife dead? She has been restored. Has your estate been taken from you? Has not then this also been restored? But he who has taken it from me is a bad man. But what is it to you, by whose hands the giver demanded it back? So long as he may allow you, take care of it as a thing which belongs to another, as travellers do with their inn.

XII

If you intend to improve, throw away such thoughts as these: if I neglect my affairs, I shall not have the means of living: unless I chastise my slave, he will be bad. For it is better to die of hunger and so to be released from grief and fear than to live in abundance with perturbation; and it is better for your slave to be bad than for you to be unhappy. Begin then from little things. Is the oil spilled? Is a little wine stolen? Say on the occasion, at such price is sold freedom from perturbation; at such price is sold tranquillity, but nothing is got for nothing. And when you call your slave, consider that it is possible that he does not hear; and if he does hear, that he will do nothing which you wish. But matters are not so well with him, but altogether well with you, that it should be in his power for you to be not disturbed.

XIII

If you would improve, submit to be considered without sense and foolish with respect to externals. Wish to be considered to know nothing: and if you shall seem to some to be a person of importance, distrust yourself. For you should know that it is not easy both to keep your will in a condition conformable to nature and to secure external things: but if a man is careful about the one, it is an absolute necessity that he will neglect the other.

XIV

If you would have your children and your wife and your friends to live for ever, you are silly; for you would have the things which are not in your power to be in your power, and the things which belong to others to be yours. So if you would have your slave to be free from faults, you are a fool; for you would have badness not to be badness, but something else. But if you wish not to fail in your desires, you are able to do that. Practise then this which you are able to do. He is the master of every man who has the power over the things, which another person wishes or does not wish, the power to confer them on him or to take

them away. Whoever then wishes to be free, let him neither wish for any thing nor avoid anything which depends on others: if he does not observe this rule, he must be a slave.

XV

Remember that in life you ought to behave as at a banquet. Suppose that something is carried round and is opposite to you. Stretch out your hand and take a portion with decency. Suppose that it passes by you. Do not detain it. Suppose that it is not yet come to you. Do not send your desire forward to it, but wait till it is opposite to you. Do so with respect to children, so with respect to a wife, so with respect to magisterial offices, so with respect to wealth, and you will be some time a worthy partner of the banquets of the gods. But if you take none of the things which are set before you, and even despise them, then you will be not only a fellow banqueter with the gods, but also a partner with them in power. For by acting thus Diogenes and Heracleitus and those like them were deservedly divine, and were so called.

XVI

When you see a person weeping in sorrow either when a child goes abroad or when he is dead, or when the man has lost his property, take care that the appearance do not hurry you away with it, as if he were suffering in external things. But straightway make a distinction in your own mind, and be in readiness to say, it is not that which has happened that afflicts this man, for it does not afflict another, but it is the opinion about this thing which afflicts the man. So far as words then do not be unwilling to show him sympathy, and even if it happens so, to lament with him. But take care that you do not lament internally also.

XVII

Remember that thou art an actor in a play, of such a kind as the author may choose; if short, of a short one; if long, of a long one: if he wishes you to act the part of a poor man, see that you act the part naturally; if the part of a lame man, of a magistrate, of a private person, do the same. For this is your duty, to act well the part that is given to you; but to select the part, belongs to another.

XVIII

When a raven has croaked inauspiciously, let not the appearance hurry you away with it; but straightway make a distinction in your mind and say, None of these things is signified to me, but either to my poor body, or to my small property, or to my reputation, or to my children or to my wife: but to me all significations are auspicious if I choose. For whatever of these things results, it is in my power to derive benefit from it.

XIX

You can be invincible, if you enter into no contest in which it is not in your power to conquer. Take care then when you observe a man honoured before others or possessed of great power or highly esteemed for any reason, not to suppose him happy, and be not carried away by the appearance. For if the nature of the good is in our power, neither envy nor jealousy will have a place in us. But you yourself will not wish to be a general or senator or consul, but a free man: and there is only one way to this, to despise the things which are not in our power.

XX

Remember that it is not he who reviles you or strikes you, who insults you, but it is your opinion about these things as being insulting. When then a man irritates you, you must know that it is your own opinion which has irritated you. Therefore especially try not to be carried away by the appearance. For if you once gain time and delay, you will more easily master yourself.

XXI

Let death and exile and every other thing which appears dreadful be daily before your eyes; but most of all death: and you will never think of anything mean nor will you desire any thing extravagantly.

XXII

If you desire philosophy, prepare yourself from the beginning to be ridiculed, to expect that many will sneer at you, and say, He has all at once returned to us as a philosopher; and whence does he get this supercilious look for us? Do you not show a supercilious look; but hold on to the things which seem to you best as one appointed by God to this station. And remember that if you abide in the same principles, these men who first ridiculed will afterwards admire you: but if you shall have been overpowered by them, you will bring on yourself double ridicule.

XXIII

If it should ever happen to you to be turned to externals in order to please some person, you must know that you have lost your purpose in life. Be satisfied then in every thing with being a philosopher; and if you wish to seem also to any person to be a philosopher, appear so to yourself, and you will be able to do this.

XXIV

Let not these thoughts afflict you, I shall live unhonoured and be nobody nowhere. For if want of honour is an evil, you cannot be in evil through the means of another any more than you can be involved in any thing base. Is it then your business to obtain the rank of a magistrate, or to be received at a banquet? By no means. How then can this be want of honour? And how will you be nobody nowhere, when you ought to be somebody in those things only which are in your power, in which indeed it is permitted to you to be a man of the greatest worth? But your friends will be without assistance! What do you mean by being without assistance? They will not receive money from you, nor will you make them Roman citizens. Who then told you that these are among the things which are in our power, and not in the power of others? And who can give to another what he has not himself? Acquire money then, your friends say, that we also may have something. If I can acquire money and also keep myself modest, and faithful and magnanimous, point out the way, and I will acquire it. But if you ask me to lose the things which are good and my own, in order that you may gain the things which are not good, see how unfair and silly you are. Besides, which would you rather have, money or a faithful and modest friend? For this end then rather help me to be such a man, and do not ask me to do this by which I shall lose that character. But my country, you say, as far as it depends on me, will be without my help. I ask again, what help do you mean? It will not have porticoes or baths through you. And what does this mean? For it is not furnished with shoes by means of a smith, nor with arms by means of a shoemaker. But it is enough if every man fully discharges the work that is his own: and if you provided it with another citizen faithful and modest, would you not be useful to it? Yes. Then you also cannot be useless to it. What place then, you say, shall I hold in the city? Whatever you can, if you maintain at the same time your fidelity and modesty. But if when you wish to be useful to the state, you shall lose these qualities, what profit could you be to it, if you were made shameless and faithless?

XXV

Has any man been preferred before you at a banquet, or in being saluted, or in being invited to a consultation? If these things are good, you ought to rejoice that he has obtained them: but if bad, be not grieved because you have not obtained them; and remember that you cannot, if you do not the same things in order to obtain what is not in our own power, be considered worthy of the same things. For how can a man obtain an equal share with another when he does not visit a man's doors as that other man does, when he does not attend him when he goes abroad, as the other man does; when he does not praise him as another does? You will be unjust then and insatiable, if you do not part with the price, in return for which those things are sold, and if you wish to obtain them for nothing. Well, what is the price of lettuces? An obolus perhaps. If then a man gives up the obolus, and receives the lettuces, and if you do not give up the obolus and do not obtain the lettuces, do not suppose that you receive less than he who has got the lettuces; for as he has the lettuces, so you have the obolus which you did not give. In the same way then in the other matter also you have not been invited to a man's feast, for you did not give to the host the price at which the supper is sold; but he sells it for praise, he sells it for personal attention. Give then the price, if it is for your interest, for which it is sold. But if you wish both not to give the price and to obtain the things, you are insatiable and silly. Have you nothing then in place of the supper? You have indeed, you have the not flattering of him, whom you did not choose to flatter; you have the not enduring of the man when he enters the room.

XXVI

We may learn the will of nature from the things in which we do not differ from one another: for instance, when your neighbour's slave has broken his cup, or any thing else, we are ready to say forthwith, that it is one of the things which happen. You must know then that when your cup also is broken, you ought to think as you did when your neighbour's cup was broken. Transfer this reflection to greater things also. Is another man's child or wife dead? There is no one who would not say, this is an event incident to man. But when a man's own child or wife is dead, forthwith he calls out, Wo to me, how wretched I am. But we ought to remember how we feel when we hear that it has happened to others.

XXVII

As a mark is not set up for the purpose of missing the aim, so neither does the nature of evil exist in the world.

XXVIII

If any person was intending to put your body in the power of any man whom you fell in with on the way, you would be vexed: but that you put your understanding in the power of any man whom you meet, so that if he should revile you, it is disturbed and troubled, are you not ashamed at this?

XXIX

In every act observe the things which come first, and those which follow it; and so proceed to the act. If you do not, at first you will approach it with alacrity, without having thought of the things which will follow; but afterwards, when certain base things have shewn themselves, you will be ashamed. A man wishes to conquer at the Olympic games. I also wish indeed, for it is a fine thing. But observe both the things which come first, and the things which follow; and then begin the act. You must do every thing according to rule, eat according to strict orders, abstain from delicacies, exercise yourself as you are bid at appointed times, in heat, in cold, you must not drink cold water, nor wine as you choose; in a word, you must deliv-

er yourself up to the exercise master as you do to the physician, and then proceed to the contest. And sometimes you will strain the hand, put the ankle out of joint, swallow much dust, sometimes be flogged, and after all this be defeated. When you have considered all this, if you still choose, go to the contest: if you do not, you will behave like children, who at one time play at wrestlers, another time as flute players, again as gladiators, then as trumpeters, then as tragic actors: so you also will be at one time an athlete, at another a gladiator, then a rhetorician, then a philosopher, but with your whole soul you will be nothing at all; but like an ape you imitate every thing that you see, and one thing after another pleases you. For you have not undertaken any thing with consideration, nor have you surveyed it well; but carelessly and with cold desire. Thus some who have seen a philosopher and having heard one speak, as Euphrates [a contemporary philosopher] speaks,—and who can speak as he does?—they wish to be philosophers themselves also. My man, first of all consider what kind of thing it is: and then examine your own nature, if you are able to sustain the character. Do you wish to be a pentathlete or a wrestler? Look at your arms, your thighs, examine your loins. For different men are formed by nature for different things. Do you think that if you do these things, you can eat in the same manner, drink in the same manner, and in the same manner loathe certain things? You must pass sleepless nights, endure toil, go away from your kinsmen, be despised by a slave, in every thing have the inferior part, in honour, in office, in the courts of justice, in every little matter. Consider these things, if you would exchange for them, freedom from passions, liberty, tranquillity. If not, take care that, like little children, you be not now a philosopher, then a servant of the publicani, then a rhetorician, then a procurator for Caesar. These things are not consistent. You must be one man, either good or bad. You must either cultivate your own ruling faculty, or external things; you must either exercise your skill on internal things or on external things; that is you must either maintain the position of a philosopher or that of a common person.

XXX

Duties are universally measured by relations. Is a man a father? The precept is to take care of him, to yield to him in all things, to submit when he is reproachful, when he inflicts blows. But suppose that he is a bad father. Were you then by nature made akin to a good father? No; but to a father. Does a brother wrong you? Maintain then your own position towards him, and do not examine what he is doing, but what you must do that your will shall be conformable to nature. For another will not damage you, unless you choose: but you will be damaged then when you shall think that you are damaged. In this way then you will discover your duty from the relation of a neighbour, from that of a citizen, from that of a general, if you are accustomed to contemplate the relations.

XXXI

As to piety towards the Gods you must know that this is the chief thing, to have right opinions about them, to think that they exist, and that they administer the All well and justly; and you must fix yourself in this principle, to obey them, and to yield to them in every thing which happens, and voluntarily to follow it as being accomplished by the wisest intelligence. For if you do so, you will never either blame the Gods, nor will you accuse them of neglecting you. And it is not possible for this to be done in any other way than by withdrawing from the things

which are not in our power, and by placing the good and the evil only in those things which are in our power. For if you think that any of the things which are not in our power is good or bad, it is absolutely necessary that, when you do not obtain what you wish, and when you fall into those things which you do not wish, you will find fault and hate those who are the cause of them; for every animal is formed by nature to this, to fly from and to turn from the things which appear harmful and the things which are the cause of the harm, but to follow and admire the things which are useful and the causes of the useful. It is impossible then for a person who thinks that he is harmed to be delighted with that which he thinks to be the cause of the harm, as it is also impossible to be pleased with the harm itself. For this reason also a father is reviled by his son, when he gives no part to his son of the things which are considered to be good: and it was this which made Polynices and Eteocles enemies, the opinion that royal power was a good. It is for this reason that the cultivator of the earth reviles the Gods, for this reason the sailor does, and the merchant, and for this reason those who lose their wives and their children. For where the useful is, there also piety is. Consequently he who takes care to desire as he ought and to avoid as he ought, at the same time also cares after piety. But to make libations and to sacrifice and to offer first fruits according to the custom of our fathers, purely and not meanly nor carelessly nor scantily nor above our ability, is a thing which belongs to all to do.

XXXII

When you have recourse to divination, remember that you do not know how it will turn out, but that you are come to inquire from the diviner. But of what kind it is, you know when you come, if indeed you are a philosopher. For if it is any of the things which are not in our power, it is absolutely necessary that it must be neither good nor bad. Do not then bring to the diviner desire or aversion: if you do, you will approach him with fear. But having determined in your mind that every thing which shall turn out is indifferent, and does not concern you, and whatever it may be, for it will be in your power to use it well, and no man will hinder this, come then with confidence to the Gods as your advisers. And then when any advice shall have been given, remember whom you have taken as advisers, and whom you will have neglected, if you do not obey them. And go to divination, as Socrates said that you ought, about those matters in which all the inquiry has reference to the result, and in which means are not given either by reason nor by any other art for knowing the thing which is the subject of the inquiry. Therefore when we ought to share a friend's danger or that of our country, you must not consult the diviner whether you ought to share it. For even if the diviner shall tell you that the signs of the victims are unlucky, it is plain that this is a token of death or mutilation of part of the body or of exile. But reason prevails that even with these risks we should share the dangers of our friend and of our country. Therefore attend to the greater diviner, the Pythian God, who ejected from the temple him who did not assist his friend when he was being murdered.

XXXIII

Immediately prescribe some character and some form to yourself, which you shall observe both when you are alone and when you meet with men.

And let silence be the general rule, or let only what is necessary be said, and in a few words. And rarely and when the occasion calls we shall say something; but about none of the common subjects, not about gladiators, nor horse races, nor about athletes, nor about eating or drinking, which are the usual subjects; and especially not about men, as blaming them or praising them, or comparing them. If then you are able, bring over by your conversation the conversation of your associates to that which is proper; but if you should happen to be confined to the company of strangers, be silent.

Let not your laughter be much, nor on many occasions, nor excessive.

Refuse altogether to take an oath, if it is possible: if it is not, refuse as far as you are able.

Avoid banquets which are given by strangers and by ignorant persons. But if ever there is occasion to join in them, let your attention be carefully fixed, that you slip not into the manners of the vulgar. For you must know, that if your companion be impure, he also who keeps company with him must become impure, though he should happen to be pure.

Take the things which relate to the body as far as the bare use, as food, drink, clothing, house, and slaves: but exclude every thing which is for show or luxury.

As to pleasure with women, abstain as far as you can before marriage: but if you do indulge in it, do it in the way which is conformable to custom. Do not however be disagreeable to those who indulge in these pleasures, or reprove them; and do not often boast that you do not indulge in them yourself.

If a man has reported to you, that a certain person speaks ill of you, do not make any defence to what has been told you: but reply, The man did not know the rest of my faults, for he would not have mentioned these only.

It is not necessary to go to the theatres often: but if there is ever a proper occasion for going, do not show yourself as being a partisan of any man except yourself, that is, desire only that to be done which is done, and for him only to gain the prize who gains the prize; for in this way you will meet with no hindrance. But abstain entirely from shouts and laughter at any thing or person, or violent emotions. And when you are come away, do not talk much about what has passed on the stage, except about that which may lead to your own improvement. For it is plain, if you do talk much that you admired the spectacle.

Do not go to the hearing of certain persons' recitations nor visit them readily. But if you do attend, observe gravity and sedateness, and also avoid making yourself disagreeable.

When you are going to meet with any person, and particularly one of those who are considered to be in a superior condition, place before yourself what Socrates or Zeno would have done in such circumstances, and you will have no difficulty in making a proper use of the occasion.

When you are going to any of those who are in great power, place before yourself that you will not find the man at home, that you will be excluded, that the door will not be opened to you, that the man will not care about you. And if with all this it is your duty to visit him, bear what happens, and never say to yourself that it was not worth the trouble. For this is silly, and marks the character of a man who is offended by externals.

In company take care not to speak much and excessively about your own acts or dangers: for as it is pleasant to you to make mention of your own dangers, it is not so pleasant to others to hear what has happened to you. Take care also not to provoke laughter; for this is a slippery way towards vulgar habits, and is also adapted to diminish the respect of your neighbours. It is a dangerous habit also to approach obscene talk. When then any thing of this kind happens, if there is a good opportunity, rebuke the man who has proceeded to this talk: but if there is not an opportunity, by your silence at least, and blushing and expression of dissatisfaction by your countenance, show plainly that you are displeased at such talk.

XXXIV

If you have received the impression of any pleasure, guard yourself against being carried away by it; but let the thing wait for you, and allow yourself a certain delay on your own part. Then think of both times, of the time when you will enjoy the pleasure, and of the time after the enjoyment of the pleasure when you will repent and will reproach yourself. And set against these things how you will rejoice if you have abstained from the pleasure, and how you will commend yourself. But if it seem to you seasonable to undertake the thing, take care that the charm of it, and the pleasure, and the attraction of it shall not conquer you: but set on the other side the consideration how much better it is to be conscious that you have gained this victory.

XXXV

When you have decided that a thing ought to be done and are doing it, never avoid being seen doing it, though the many shall form an unfavourable opinion about it. For if it is not right to do it, avoid doing the thing; but if it is right, why are you afraid of those who shall find fault wrongly?

XXXVI

As the proposition it is either day or it is night is of great importance for the disjunctive argument, but for the conjunctive is of no value, so in a symposium to select the larger share is of great value for the body, but for the maintenance of the social feeling is worth nothing. When then you are eating with another, remember to look not only to the value for the body of the things set before you, but also to the value of the behaviour towards the host which ought to be observed.

XXXVII

If you have assumed a character above your strength, you have both acted in this matter in an unbecoming way, and you have neglected that which you might have fulfilled.

XXXVIII

In walking about as you take care not to step on a nail or to sprain your foot, so take care not to damage your own ruling faculty: and if we observe this rule in every act, we shall undertake the act with more security.

XXXIX

The measure of possession is to every man the body, as the foot is of the shoe. If then you stand on this rule, you will maintain the measure: but if you pass beyond it, you must then of necessity be hurried as it were down a precipice. As also in the matter of the shoe, if you go beyond the necessities of the foot, the shoe is gilded, then of a purple colour, then embroidered: for there is no limit to that which has once passed the true measure.

XL

Women forthwith from the age of fourteen are called by the men mistresses. Therefore since they see that there is nothing else that they can obtain, but only the power of lying with men, they begin to decorate themselves, and to place all their hopes in this. It is worth our while then to take care that they may know that they are valued by men for nothing else than appearing decent and modest and discreet.

XLI

It is a mark of a mean capacity to spend much time on the things which concern the body, such as much exercise, much eating, much drinking, much easing of the body, much copulation. But these things should be done as subordinate things: and let all your care be directed to the mind.

XLII

When any person treats you ill or speaks ill of you, remember that he does this or says this because he thinks that it is his duty. It is not possible then for him to follow that which seems right to you, but that which seems right to himself. Accordingly if he is wrong in his opinion, he is the person who is hurt, for he is the person who has been deceived; for if a man shall suppose the true conjunction to be false, it is not the conjunction which is hindered, but the man who has been deceived about it. If you proceed then from these opinions, you will be mild in temper to him who reviles you: for say on each occasion, It seemed so to him.

XLIII

Every thing has two handles, the one by which it may be borne, the other by which it may not. If your brother acts unjustly, do not lay hold of the act by that handle wherein he acts unjustly, for this is the handle which cannot be borne: but lay hold of the other, that he is your brother, that he was nurtured with you, and you will lay hold of the thing by that handle by which it can be borne.

XLIV

These reasonings do not cohere: I am richer than you, therefore I am better than you; I am more eloquent than you, therefore I am better than you. On the contrary these rather cohere, I am richer than you, therefore my possessions are greater than yours: I am more eloquent than you, therefore my speech is superior to yours. But you are neither possession nor speech.

XLV

Does a man bathe quickly? do not say that he bathes badly, but that he bathes quickly. Does a man drink much wine? do not say that he does this badly, but say that he drinks much. For before you shall have determined the opinion, how do you know whether he is acting wrong? Thus it will not happen to you to comprehend some appearances which are capable of being comprehended, but to assent to others.

XLVI

On no occasion call yourself a philosopher, and do not speak much among the uninstructed about theorems: but do that which follows from them. For example at a banquet do not say how a man ought to eat, but eat as you ought to eat. For remember that in this way Socrates also altogether avoided ostentation: persons used to come to him and ask to be recommended by him to philosophers, and he used to take them to philosophers: so easily did he submit to being overlooked. Accordingly if any conversation should arise among uninstructed persons about any theorem, generally be silent; for there is great danger that you will immediately vomit up what you have not digested. And when a man shall say to you, that you know nothing, and you are not vexed, then be sure that you have begun the work of philosophy. For even sheep do not vomit up their grass and show to the shepherds how much they have eaten; but when they have internally digested the pasture, they produce externally wool and milk. Do you also show not your theorems to the uninstructed, but show the acts which come from their digestion.

XLVII

When at a small cost you are supplied with every thing for the body, do not be proud of this; nor, if you drink water, say on every occasion, I drink water. But consider first how much more frugal the poor are than we, and how much more enduring of labour. And if you ever wish to exercise yourself in labour and endurance, do it for yourself, and not for others: do not embrace statues. But if you are ever very thirsty, take a draught of cold water, and spit it out, and tell no man.

XLVIII

The condition and characteristic of an uninstructed person is this: he never expects from himself profit nor harm, but from externals. The condition and characteristic of a philosopher is this: he expects all advantage and all harm from himself. The signs of one who is making progress are these: he censures no man, he praises no man, he blames no man, he accuses no man, he says nothing about himself as if he were somebody or knew something; when he is impeded at all or hindered, he blames himself: if a man praises him, he ridicules the praiser to himself: if a man censures him, he makes no defence: he goes about like weak persons, being careful not to move any of the things which are placed, before they are firmly fixed: he removes all desire from himself, and he transfers aversion to those things only of the things within our power which are contrary to nature: he employs a moderate movement towards every thing: whether he is considered foolish or ignorant, he cares not: and in a word he watches himself as if he were an enemy and lying in ambush.

XLIX

When a man is proud because he can understand and explain the writings of Chrysippus [an early Greek Stoic], say to yourself, If Chrysippus had not written obscurely, this man would have had nothing to be proud of. But what is it that I wish?

To understand Nature and to follow it. I inquire therefore who is the interpreter: and when I have heard that it is Chrysippus, I come to him. But I do not understand what is written, and therefore I seek the interpreter. And so far there is yet nothing to be proud of. But when I shall have found the interpreter, the thing that remains is to use the precepts. This itself is the only thing to be proud of. But if I shall admire the exposition, what else have I been made unless a grammarian instead of a philosopher? except in one thing, that I am explaining Chrysippus instead of Homer. When then any man says to me, Read Chrysippus to me, I rather blush, when I cannot show my acts like to and consistent with his words.

L

Whatever things are proposed to you for the conduct of life abide by them, as if they were laws, as if you would be guilty of impiety if you transgressed any of them. And whatever any man shall say about you, do not attend to it: for this is no affair of yours. How long will you then still defer thinking yourself worthy of the best things, and in no matter transgressing the distinctive reason? Have you accepted the theorems, which it was your duty to agree to, and have you agreed to them? What teacher then do you still expect that you defer to him the correction of yourself? You are no longer a youth, but already a full-grown man. If then you are negligent and slothful, and are continually making procrastination after procrastination, and proposal after proposal, and fixing day after day, after which you will attend to yourself, you will not know that you are not making improvement, but you will continue ignorant both while you live and till you die. Immediately then think it right to live as a full-grown man, and one who is making proficiency, and let every thing which appears to you to be

the best be to you a law which must not be transgressed. And if any thing laborious, or pleasant or glorious or inglorious be presented to you, remember that now is the contest, now are the Olympic games, and they cannot be deferred; and that it depends on one defeat and one giving way that progress is either lost or maintained. Socrates in this way became perfect, in all things improving himself, attending to nothing except to reason. But you, though you are not yet a Socrates, ought to live as one who wishes to be a Socrates.

LI

The first and most necessary place in philosophy is the use of theorems, for instance, that we must not lie: the second part is that of demonstrations, for instance, How is it proved that we ought not to lie: the third is that which is confirmatory of these two and explanatory, for example, How is this a demonstration? For what is demonstration, what is consequence, what is contradiction, what is truth, what is falsehood? The third part is necessary on account of the second, and the second on account of the first; but the most necessary and that on which we ought to rest is the first. But we do the contrary. For we spend our time on the third topic, and all our earnestness is about it: but we entirely neglect the first. Therefore we lie; but the demonstration that we ought not to lie we have ready to hand.

LII

In every thing we should hold these maxims ready to hand:

Lead me, O Zeus, and thou O Destiny,
The way that I am bid by you to go:
To follow I am ready. If I choose not,
I make myself a wretch, and still must follow.

But whoso nobly yields unto necessity,
We hold him wise, and skill'd in things divine.

And the third also: O Crito, if so it pleases the Gods, so let it be; Anytus and Melitus are able indeed to kill me, but they cannot harm me.

Juvenal

The Roman Juvenal was the greatest satiric poet who ever lived, asserts Gilbert Highet in the opening sentence of his book, *Juvenal the Satirist* (Oxford, 1954). And Juvenal's Third Satire is commonly regarded as the most penetrating and the most incisive of all the sixteen satires published by this second-century Roman. In this brief essay Juvenal "describes" his city, with all its filth and corruption, its lavishness and decadence. In the course of his descriptions, Juvenal gives us a portrait of himself—a man who knew how to hate.

Juvenal was a latter-day elder Cato who wanted to resurrect the virtues of self-reliance, independence, maturity, and quiet self-confidence. He sought a return to the virtues of the Republic, which, it may be suspected, he tended to romanticize. Juvenal was probably a preaching Stoic to whom the precepts of Epictetus represented the whole and final truth.

To claim that Juvenal was more than a preaching Stoic—that he actually practiced his preachments—would be to go far beyond the known facts. The speculations about his life are many; the facts are few. He is thought to have been born in Aquinum some sixty miles southeast of Rome around 60 A.D. and to have died about 130. He may have had military experience; he may have been exiled to Egypt; he may have been the son of a freed slave; he may have lived on charity; he may have been wealthy. Such, at least, are some of the speculations that have sprung from diligent and thoughtful probings of his *Satires*, but very little can be claimed with assurance. Perhaps here Juvenal shows his real genius, since, even in this most personally revealing of literary *genres*, he has managed to conceal information concerning himself almost completely.

The following verse translation is by John Dryden, the English poet of the seventeenth century.

SATIRE III

Grieved though I am an ancient friend to
  lose,
I like the solitary seat he chose;

THE SATIRES OF DECIMUS JUNIUS JUVENALIS, trans. John Dryden, in *The British Poets, including Translations* (Chiswick, 1822), XLVI, 142-160.

In quiet Cumae fixing his repose:
Where, far from noisy Rome secure he lives,
And one more citizen to Sibyl gives.
The road to Bajae, and that soft recess
Which all the gods with all their bounty bless.
Though I in Prochyta with greater ease

Could live than in a street of palaces.
What scene so desert, or so full of fright,
As towering houses tumbling in the night,
And Rome on fire beheld by its own blazing
    light?
But worse than all the clattering tiles, and
    worse
Than thousand padders, is the poet's curse:
Rogues that in dogdays cannot rhyme forbear;
But without mercy read, and make you hear.
    Now while my friend, just ready to depart,
Was packing all his goods in one poor cart;
He stopp'd a little at the conduit gate,
Where Numa model'd once the Roman state,
In mighty councils with his nymph retired:
Though now the sacred shades and founts are
    hired
By banish'd Jews, who their whole wealth can
    lay
In a small basket, on a wisp of hay;
Yet such our avarice is, that every tree
Pays for his head; not sleep itself is free:
Nor place, nor persons, now are sacred held,
From their own grove the Muses are expell'd:
Into this lonely vale our steps we bend,
I and my sullen discontented friend:
The marble caves and aqueducts we view;
But how adulterate now, and different from
    the true!
How much more beauteous had the fountain
    been
Embellish'd with her first created green,
Where crystal streams through living turf had
    run,
Contented with an urn of native stone!
    Then thus Umbricius (with an angry frown,
And looking back on this degenerate town),
Since noble arts in Rome have no support,
And ragged virtue not a friend at court,
No profit rises from the' ungrateful stage,
My poverty increasing with my age,
'Tis time to give my just disdain a vent,
And, cursing, leave so base a government.
Where Dedalus his borrow'd wings laid by,
To that obscure retreat I choose to fly:
While yet few furrows on my face are seen,
While I walk upright, and old age is green,
And Lachesis has somewhat left to spin.
Now, now 'tis time to quit this cursed place,
And hide from villains my too honest face:
Here let Arturius live, and such as he;

Such manners will with such a town agree.
Knaves who in full assemblies have the knack
Of turning truth to lies, and white to black;
Can hire large houses, and oppress the poor
By farm'd excise; can cleanse the common
    shore;
And rent the fishery; can bear the dead;
And teach their eyes dissembled tears to shed,
All this for gain; for gain they sell their very
    head.
These fellows (see what fortune's power can
    do)
Were once the minstrels of a country show:
Follow'd the prizes through each paltry town,
By trumpet-cheeks and bloated faces known.
But now grown rich, on drunken holidays,
At their own costs exhibit public plays:
Where, influenced by the rabble's bloody will,
With thumbs bent back they popularly kill.
From thence return'd, their sordid avarice
    rakes
In excrements again, and hires the jakes.
Why hire they not the town, not every thing,
Since such as they have fortune in a string?
Who, for her pleasure, can her fools advance;
And toss them topmost on the wheel of
    chance.
What's Rome to me, what business have I
    there,
I who can neither lie nor falsely swear?
Nor praise my patron's undeserving rhymes,
Nor yet comply with him, nor with his times;
Unskill'd in schemes by planets to foreshow,
Like canting rascals, how the wars will go:
I neither will nor can prognosticate
To the young gaping heir his father's fate:
Nor in the entrails of a toad have pry'd,
Nor carried bawdy presents to a bride:
For want of these town virtues, thus alone,
I go conducted on my way by none:
Like a dead member from the body rent;
Maim'd, and unuseful to the government.
Who now is loved, but he who loves the
    times,
Conscious of close intrigues, and dipp'd in
    crimes;
Labouring with secrets which his bosom burn,
Yet never must to public light return?
They get reward alone who can betray:
For keeping honest counsels none will pay
He who can Verres, when he will, accuse,

The purse of Verres may at pleasure use:
But let not all the gold which Tagus hides,
And pays the sea in tributary tides,
Be bribe sufficient to corrupt the breast;
Or violate with dreams thy peaceful rest.
Great men with jealous eyes the friend be-
hold,
Whose secrecy they purchase with their gold.
  I haste to tell thee (nor shall shame
    oppose)
What confidence our wealthy Romans chose:
And whom I most abhor. To speak my mind,
I hate in Rome a Grecian town to find:
To see the scum of Greece transplanted here,
Received like gods, is what I cannot bear.
Nor Greeks alone, but Syrians here abound,
Obscene Orontes diving under ground,
Conveys his wealth to Tyber's hungry shores,
And fattens Italy with foreign whores:
Hither their crooked harps and customs come:
All find receipt in hospitable Rome.
The barbarous harlots crowd the public place:
Go, fools, and purchase an unclean embrace;
The painted mitre court, and the more painted
  face.
Old Romulus and father Mars, look down;
Your herdsman primitive, your homely clown
Is turn'd a beau, in a loose tawdry gown.
His once unkemm'd and horrid locks behold,
Stilling sweet oil; his neck inchain'd with
  gold:
Aping the foreigners in every dress;
Which, bought at greater cost, becomes him
  less.
Meantime they wisely leave their native land;
From Sycion, Samos, and from Alaband,
And Amydon, to Rome they swarm in shoals:
So sweet and easy is the gain from fools.
Poor refugees at first, they purchase here,
And, soon as denizen'd, they domineer;
Grow to the great, a flattering servile rout;
Work themselves inward, and their patrons
  out:
Quick-witted, brazen-faced, with fluent
  tongues,
Patient of labours, and dissembling wrongs.
Riddle me this, and guess him if you can,
Who bears a nation in a single man?
A cook, a conjurer, a rhetorician,
A painter, pedant, a geometrician,
A dancer on the ropes, and a physician.

All things the hungry Greek exactly knows:
And bid him go to heaven, to heaven he
  goes.
In short, no Scythian, Moor, or Thracian born,
But in that town, which arms and arts adorn,
Shall he be placed above me at the board,
In purple clothed, and lolling like a lord?
Shall he before me sign, whom t'other day
A small craft vessel hither did convey;
Where, stow'd with prunes and rotten figs, he
  lay?
How little is the privilege become
Of being born a citizen of Rome!
The Greeks get all by fulsome flatteries;
A most peculiar stroke they have at lies.
They make a wit of their insipid friend;
His blobber-lip, and beetle-brows commend;
His long crane-neck and narrow shoulders
  praise;
You'd think they were describing Hercules.
A creaking voice for a clear treble goes;
Though harsher than a cock that treads and
  crows.
We can as grossly praise; but, to our grief,
No flattery but from Grecians gains belief.
Besides these qualities, we must agree
They mimic better on the stage than we:
The wife, the whore, the shepherdess they
  play,
In such a free, and such a graceful way,
That we believe a very woman shown,
And fancy something underneath the gown.
But not Antiochus, nor Stratocles,
Our ears and ravish'd eyes can only please;
The nation is composed of such as these.
All Greece is one comedian: laugh, and they
Return it louder than an ass can bray.
Grieve, and they grieve; if you weep silently,
There seems a silent echo in their eye:
They cannot mourn like you, but they can
  cry.
Call for a fire, their winter clothes they take:
Begin but you to shiver, and they shake:
In frost and snow, if you complain of heat,
They rub the' unsweating brow, and swear
  they sweat.
We live not on the square with such as these,
Such are our betters who can better please:
Who day and night are like a looking-glass;
Still ready to reflect their patron's face.
The panegyric hand and lifted eye,

Prepared for some new piece of flattery.
E'en nastiness occasions will afford;
They praise a belching, or well p—g lord.
Besides, there's nothing sacred, nothing free
From bold attempts of their rank lechery.
Through the whole family their labours run;
The daughter is debauch'd, the wife is won:
Nor scapes the bridegroom, or the blooming
    son.
If none they find for their lewd purpose fit,
They with the walls and very floors commit:
They search the secrets of the house, and so
Are worship'd there, and fear'd for what they
    know.
    And now we talk of Grecians, cast a view
On what in schools their men of morals do:
A rigid stoic his own pupil slew;
A friend against a friend of his own cloth
Turn'd evidence, and murder'd on his oath.
What room is left for Romans in a town
Where Grecians rule, and cloaks control the
    gown?
Some Diphilus, or some Protogenes,
Look sharply out, our senators to seize:
Engross them wholly by their native art,
And fear no rivals in their bubble's heart:
One drop of poison in my patron's ear,
One slight suggestion of a senseless fear,
Infused with cunning, serves to ruin me;
Disgraced and banish'd from the family.
In vain forgotten services I boast;
My long dependence in an hour is lost:
Look round the world, what country will
    appear,
Where friends are left with greater ease than
    here?
At Rome (nor think me partial to the poor)
All offices of ours are out of door:
In vain we rise, and to the levees run;
My lord himself is up before, and gone:
The praetor bids his lictors mend their pace,
Lest his colleague outstrip him in the race:
The childish matrons are long since awake;
And, for affronts, the tardy visits take.
    'Tis frequent here to see a freeborn son
On the left hand of a rich hireling run;
Because the wealthy rogue can throw away,
For half a brace of bouts, a tribune's pay:
But you, poor sinner, though you love the vice,
And like the whore, demur upon the price:
And, frighted with the wicked sum, forbear

To lend a hand, and help her from the chair.
    Produce a witness of unblemish'd life,
Holy as Numa or as Numa's wife,
Or him who bid the' unhallow'd flames retire,
And snatch'd the trembling goddess from the
    fire!
The question is not put how far extends
His piety, but what he yearly spends:
Quick to the business; how he lives and eats;
How largely gives; how splendidly he treats:
How many thousand acres feed his sheep,
What are his rents? what servants does he
    keep?
The' account is soon cast up; the judges rate
Our credit in the court by our estate.
Swear by our gods, or those the Greeks adore,
Thou art as sure forsworn, as thou art poor:
The poor must gain their bread by perjury;
And e'en the gods, that other means deny,
In conscience must absolve them when they
    lie.
    Add, that the rich have still a gibe in store;
And will be monstrous witty on the poor:
For the torn surtout and the tatter'd vest,
The wretch and all his wardrobe are a jest:
The greasy gown, sullied with often turning,
Gives a good hint to say, 'The man's in
    mourning:'
Or if the shoe be ripp'd, or patches put,
'He's wounded! see the plaister on his foot.'
Want is the scorn of every wealthy fool;
And wit in rags is turn'd to ridicule.
'Pack hence, and from the cover'd benches
    rise
(The master of the ceremonies cries),
This is no place for you, whose small estate
Is not the value of the settled rate;'
The sons of happy punks, the pander's heir,
Are privileged to sit in triumph there,
To clap the first, and rule the theatre.
Up to the galleries for shame retreat;
For, by the Roscian law, the poor can claim
    no seat.
Who ever brought to his rich daughter's bed
The man that poll'd but twelvepence for his
    head?
Who ever named a poor man for his heir,
Or call'd him to assist the judging chair?
The poor were wise who, by the rich
    oppress'd,
Withdrew, and sought a sacred place of rest.

Once they did well, to free themselves from
  scorn;
But had done better, never to return.
Rarely they rise by virtue's aid, who lie
Plunged in the depth of helpless poverty.
At Rome 'tis worse; where house-rent by the
  year,
And servants' bellies cost so devilish dear;
And tavern bills run high for hungry cheer.
To drink or eat in earthenware we scorn,
Which cheaply country cupboards does adorn:
And coarse blue hoods on holidays are worn.
Some distant parts of Italy are known,
Where none but only dead men wear a
  gown:
On theatres of turf, in homely state
Old plays they act, old feasts they celebrate:
The same rude song returns upon the crowd,
And by tradition is for wit allow'd.
The mimic yearly gives the same delights;
And in the mother's arms the clownish infant
  frights.
Their habits (undistinguish'd by degree)
Are plain alike; the same simplicity,
Both on the stage, and in the pit, you see.
In his white cloak the magistrate appears;
The country bumpkin the same livery wears.
But here, attired beyond our purse we go,
For useless ornament and flaunting show:
We take on trust, in purple robes to shine;
And poor are yet ambitious to be fine.
This is a common vice, though all things here
Are sold, and sold unconscionably dear.
What will you give that Cossus may but view
Your face, and in the crowd distinguish you?
May take your incense like a gracious god,
And answer only with a civil nod?
To please our patrons, in this vicious age,
We make our entrance by the favourite page:
Shave his first down, and when he pulls his
  hair,
The consecrated locks to temples bear:
Pay tributary cracknels, which he sells,
And, with our offerings, help to raise his vails.
  Who fears in country towns a house's fall,
Or to be caught betwixt a riven wall?
But we inhabit a weak city here;
Which buttresses and props but scarcely bear:
And 'tis the village mason's daily calling,
To keep the world's metropolis from falling,

To cleanse the gutters, and the chinks to
  close;
And, for one night, secure his lord's repose.
At Cumae we can sleep quite round the year,
Nor falls, nor fires, nor nightly dangers fear;
While rolling flames from Roman turrets fly,
And the pale citizens for buckets cry.
Thy neighbour has removed his wretched
  store
(Few hands will rid the lumber of the poor);
Thy own third story smokes, while thou,
  supine,
Art drench'd in fumes of undigested wine.
For if the lowest floors already burn,
Cocklofts and garrets soon will take the turn;
Where thy tame pigeons next the tiles were
  bred,
Which, in their nests unsafe, are timely fled.
  Codrus had but one bed, so short to boot,
That his short wife's short legs hung dangling
  out;
His cupboard's head six earthen pitchers
  graced,
Beneath them was his trusty tankard placed;
And, to support this noble plate, there lay
A bending Chiron cast from honest clay.
His few Greek books a rotten chest
  contain'd,
Whose covers much of mouldiness complain'd:
Where mice and rats devour'd poetic bread;
And with heroic verse luxuriously were fed.
'Tis true, poor Codrus nothing had to boast,
And yet poor Codrus all that nothing lost.
Begg'd naked through the streets of wealthy
  Rome;
And found not one to feed, or take him
  home.
  But if the palace of Arturius burn,
The nobles change their clothes, the matrons
  mourn;
The city-praetor will no pleadings hear;
The very name of fire we hate and fear;
And look aghast, as if the Gauls were here.
While yet it burns, the' officious nation flies,
Some to condole, and some to bring supplies:
One sends him marble to rebuild, and one
With naked statues of the Parian stone,
The work of Polyclete, that seem to live;
While other images for altars give;
One books and screens, and Pallas to the
  breast;

Another bags of gold, and he gives best.
Childless Arturius, vastly rich before,
Thus by his losses multiplies his store;
Suspected for accomplice to the fire,
That burn'd his palace but to build it higher.
  But, could you be content to bid adieu
To the dear playhouse, and the players too:
Sweet country seats are purchased everywhere,
With lands and gardens, at less price than
    here
You hire a darksome doghole by the year.
A small convenience decently prepared,
A shallow well that rises in your yard,
That spreads his easy crystal streams around,
And waters all the pretty spot of ground.
There love the fork, thy garden cultivate,
And give thy frugal friends a Pythagorean
   treat;
'Tis somewhat to be lord of some small ground
In which a lizard may, at least, turn round.
   'Tis frequent here, for want of sleep, to
    die;
Which fumes of undigested feasts deny;
And, with imperfect heat, in languid stomachs
   fry.
What house secure from noise the poor can
   keep,
When e'en the rich can scarce afford to
   sleep:
So dear it costs to purchase rest in Rome;
And hence the sources of diseases come.
The drover who his fellow drover meets
In narrow passages of winding streets;
The wagoners, that curse their standing teams,
Would wake e'en drowsy Drusius from his
   dreams.
And yet the wealthy will not brook delay,
But sweep above our heads, and make their
   way:
In lofty litters born, and read and write,
Or sleep at ease: the shutters make it night.
Yet still he reaches first the public place:
The press before him stops the client's pace;
The crowd that follows crush his panting sides,
And trip his heels; he walks not, but he rides.
One elbows him, one justles in the shole:
A rafter breaks his head, or chairman's pole:
Stockin'd with loads of fat town dirt he goes,
And some rogue-soldier, with his hobnail'd
   shoes,

Indents his legs behind in bloody rows.
   See with what smoke our doles we cele-
   brate:
A hundred guests, invited, walk in state:
A hundred hungry slaves, with their Dutch
   kitchens, wait.
Huge pans the wretches on their head must
   bear,
Which scarce gigantic Corbulo could rear:
Yet they must walk upright beneath the load;
Nay, run, and running blow the sparkling
   flames abroad.
Their coats, from botching newly brought, are
   torn.
Unwieldy timber-trees in wagons borne,
Stretch'd at their length, beyond their carriage
   lie;
That nod, and threaten ruin from on high.
For should their axle break, its overthrow
Would crush, and pound to dust, the crowd
   below:
Nor friends their friends, nor sires their sons
   could know;
Nor limbs, nor bones, nor carcass would
   remain;
But a mash'd heap, a hotchpotch of the
   slain.
One vast destruction; not the soul alone,
But bodies like the soul, invisibly are flown.
Meantime, unknowing of their fellows' fate,
The servants wash the platter, scour the plate,
Then blow the fire with puffing cheeks, and
   lay
The rubbers, and the bathing-sheets display:
And oil them first; and each is handy in his
   way.
But he for whom this busy care they take,
Poor ghost, is wandering by the Stygian lake:
Affrighted with the ferryman's grim face;
New to the horrors of that uncouth place;
His passage begs with unregarded prayer:
And wants two farthings to discharge his fare.
   Return we to the dangers of the night:
And first behold our houses' dreadful height;
From whence come broken potsherds tumbling
   down;
And leaky ware from garret windows thrown:
Well may they break our heads, that mark the
   flinty stone:
'Tis want of sense to sup abroad too late;

Unless thou first hast settled thy estate.
As many fates attend thy steps to meet
As there are waking windows in the street,
Bless the good gods, and think thy chance is
   rare
To have a pisspot only for thy share.
The scouring drunkard, if he does not fight
Before his bedtime, takes no rest that night.
Passing the tedious hours in greater pain
Than stern Achilles, when his friend was slain:
'Tis so ridiculous, but so true withal,
A bully cannot sleep without a brawl:
Yet though his youthful blood be fired with
   wine,
He wants not wit the danger to decline:
Is cautious to avoid the coach and six,
And on the lackeys will no quarrel fix.
His train of flambeaux, and embroider'd coat,
May privilege my lord to walk secure on foot:
But me, who must by moonlight homeward
   bend,
Or lighted only with a candle's end,
Poor me he fights, if that be fighting, where
He only cudgels, and I only bear.
He stands, and bids me stand: I must abide;
For he's the stronger, and is drunk beside.
   'Where did you whet your knife to-night
     (he cries),
And shred the leeks that in your stomach rise?
Whose windy beans have stuff'd your guts, and
   where
Have your black thumbs been dipp'd in
   vinegar?
With what companion cobbler have you fed,
On old ox-cheeks, or he goat's tougher head?
What, are you dumb? quick, with your
   answer, quick;
Before my foot salutes you with a kick.
Say, in what nasty cellar under ground,
Or what church-porch, your rogueship may be
   found?
Answer, or answer not, 'tis all the same:

He lays me on, and makes me bear the
   blame.
Before the bar, for beating him, you come;
This is a poor man's liberty in Rome.
You beg his pardon; happy to retreat
With some remaining teeth to chew your meat.
   Nor is this all: for, when retired, you think
To sleep securely; when the candles wink,
When every door with iron chains is barr'd,
And roaring taverns are no longer heard;
The ruffian robbers, by no justice awed,
And unpaid cut-throat soldiers, are abroad.
Those venal souls, who, hardened in each ill,
To save complaints and prosecution, kill:
Chased from their woods and bogs, the padders
   come
To this vast city, as their native home;
To live at ease, and safely skulk in Rome.
   The forge in fetters only is employ'd;
Our iron mines exhausted and destroy'd
In shackles; for these villains scarce allow
Goads for the teams, and ploughshares for the
   plough.
Oh! happy ages of our ancestors,
Beneath the kings and tribunitial powers!
One gaol did all their criminals restrain;
Which now the walls of Rome can scarce
   contain.
   More I could say, more causes I could show
For my departure; but the sun is low:
The wagoner grows weary of my stay:
And whips his horses forwards on their way.
Farewell! and when like me o'erwhelm'd with
   care,
You to your own Aquinum shall repair,
To take a mouthful of sweet country air,
Be mindful of your friend; and send me word
What joys your fountains and cool shades
   afford:
Then to assist your satires I will come,
And add new venom when you write of
   Rome.

THE MIDDLE AGES

WHEN WE LOOK BACK from the twentieth century to the Middle Ages, we are confronted with countless difficulties and contradictions. At times the medieval period seems to have been an age of unrelieved violence and warfare, of treachery, intrigue, and bloodshed. At other times the thousand years from 400 to 1400 A.D. seem to have been an "Age of Faith"—an age in which Western man sought to relate human life on earth both to God and to man's eternal destiny. A third impression is that the Middle Ages were a time when society sought stability and security above all else.

It is difficult to reconcile these three impressions, and perhaps it is futile to try. In a sense, they are all valid—the Middle Ages were bloody, *and* religious, *and* stable. To try to resolve all this diversity into a perfectly understandable whole would be to fall under the criticism of the historian who claimed that "History is a chaos upon which historians impose a pattern."

And yet we can attempt to understand the principles and ideals that were accepted and professed by medieval society. For one segment of the population (roughly one-sixth) the world centered around military life—a life dedicated to concepts of honor, justice, bravery, strength, skill, and loyalty. For another segment (roughly one-tenth) the world centered around a concern for the souls of men. To the friars, the priests, and the clerics, this life was transient and unreal, and only the life hereafter had any real meaning. For the rest of the people who lived during the Middle Ages (certainly the vast majority of the population) life was simply a matter of accepting the four seasons, hard work, the need to cultivate the soil, the dictates of the Church, and the demands of the military caste.

Ideally, every element of the social order had its clearly defined function, which suggests that the Middle Ages at least tried to maintain a stability in which every man could lead his life in peace, although perhaps not in plenty. But since stability is a difficult ideal to realize, let alone to maintain, the corollary was control over all elements that might tend to disturb the established way of life. The Church tried (though not very successfully) to eliminate the constant fighting of the feudal class by decreeing the Truce and Peace of God which forbade warfare at certain times. The feudal structure itself was designed to define the rank and station of all its members. A knight swore oaths of allegiance and fidelity to a lord and "became his man"; he was obliged to support his lord against enemies, to protect the lord's family, and to serve at the lord's court. In return, the lord granted lands to his vassal and guaranteed him military protection and knightly station. The lands granted were called the "fief" or "feodum" (whence feudalism), and they were actually worked by serfs. The fief was composed of one or more estates called "manors" and here, too, a mutual contractual obligation existed between the lord of the manor and the serf. In return for military protection the serf accepted the jurisdiction of the lord's court, contracted to work a fixed number of days for the lord, and agreed to pay fixed rents to the lord, of the type listed in the *Surveys of Certain Manors Belonging to the Abbey of Peterborough*. Legally the serf could not leave the manor without the consent of the lord, but also (and most importantly) the serf could not be put off the land nor could the fixed rents be raised. In short, the serf was guaranteed his living, however poor it might have been.

In the later Middle Ages, after the revival of trade and of town life, the desire to guarantee a livelihood to everyone was reflected in the gild organization, and in the many regulations that were imposed on the manufacture and distribution of goods. By agreement within the gild, techniques were prescribed, monopoly was forbidden both in buying and selling, prices were fixed, and all gildsmen shared the market; no one was permitted to "get ahead" of his fellow gildsmen. The very concept of the "just price" described by Saint Thomas Aquinas was an attempt to show that too high a price cheated the buyer and too low a price cheated the seller. In either case, one was deprived of his goods and his well-being.

But stability remained mostly an ideal that was striven for, rather than an actuality that was attained. The failure of the Middle Ages to achieve real stability sprang from the inevitable conflict between medieval political theory and practice on the one hand and medieval theological outlook and organization on the other. Christianity could not be reconciled with militarism; the two were completely antithetical, despite efforts to develop the notion of the "Christian knight" and the "soldiers of God." An even more important source of conflict between the feudal structure and the Catholic hierarchy, however, was the inescapable logic of the situation itself. In a deeply religious age—or in any age, for that matter—men are moved to demonstrate their faith and to glorify their God by building beautiful churches or by giving gifts to support the faith. In the Middle Ages, most bequests took the form of land given over to the maintenance of church officials and functionaries or to provide the necessities of monasteries and nunneries.

This practice created two major difficulties that made conflict between the Church and the feudal system inevitable. First, the land had originally been granted (but not given outright) to a vassal by his liege lord in exchange for military service; if the land was then bequeathed by the vassal to the Church, who was to provide military service to the liege lord? Could a priest or a bishop hire someone to perform the feudal obligations and still remain a Christian? The second major difficulty arose from the vassal's obligation to swear oaths of allegiance, fidelity, and homage to his liege in order to be "invested" with his fief. Here feudalism ran directly afoul of the Church. A bishop, for instance, had already sworn fidelity to the pope at Rome and could not very well serve two masters—his feudal lord and his ecclesiastical superior.

It was out of these difficulties that the whole investiture controversy arose, a controversy that developed into a struggle for supreme political power between the feudal monarchs and the popes. The monarchs were victorious, although the question has never been clearly resolved for the hierarchy of the Catholic Church. In the late Middle Ages the Church mobilized all its arsenal of spiritual weapons in an attempt to win the controversy—papal letters, encyclicals, bulls, interdict, and excommunication. All was to no avail, however. And the use of these spiritual weapons to gain political ends itself tended to discredit them and to deprive the Church of its moral authority. So in a real sense the Church itself helped to prepare the way for the secular attitudes that were to characterize the Renaissance.

The Old Testament

Although this selection and the one following, from the New Testament, do not fall chronologically within the Middle Ages, they have been placed at the beginning of this section because medieval thought and practice were based on the Bible, in a sense that is true of no other period in Western history.

Rather than attempt to illustrate all the variety of the Old Testament, an impossible task for a short selection, we have chosen two important and closely related themes developed by Old Testament writers: the belief in one God (monotheism), and the concept of God as a moral being standing in a definite moral relationship to man. From *Genesis* comes the story of creation and the fall of man. In the sin of Adam and Eve the problem of right and wrong is first raised, and in the punishment for this sin God reveals himself as the judge over mankind. This episode from *Genesis* was to become significant in Christian thought as the source for the central doctrine of "orig-

inal sin." In the selection from *Exodus* God appears as a lawgiver laying down rules of conduct for his chosen people, Israel. The existence of other gods is not denied: indeed, it is directly implied. God's concern seems to be only that he be first among the gods who were worshipped. In the realm of moral conduct, besides the Ten Commandments, the notion of justice is presented, and an important distinction is made between divine and human justice. The contest between Elijah and the prophets of Baal, taken from *1 Kings*, dramatizes the theme, already mentioned in *Exodus*, of the relationship between other gods and the God of Israel. Now, although the existence of a plurality of gods is not explicitly denied, little doubt is left that, so far as Israel is concerned, there is but one Lord, and he is God. In *Isaiah*, the monotheistic theme is expanded in two significant ways: God is characterized, not simply as one among many gods, but as the *only* God. Nor is his influence limited to Israel; rather, he declares himself to be Lord over all the earth and all peoples. The selection from *Ezekiel* returns to the subject of divine justice, and develops the thesis of personal responsibility for sin. The problem of the moral relationship between God and man receives perhaps its most subtle, and certainly its most dramatic, Old Testament statement in the *Book of Job.* The point at issue is basic and perennial: How can the justice of God be reconciled with the fact that the righteous often suffer while the evil prosper? The answer given and Job's acceptance of it reveal a major difference between Hebraic and Greek religious attitudes— the contrast between Job's submission to the will of God and the constant rebellion of the mythical heroes of Greece against the decrees from Olympus.

The selections have been taken from the King James Version of the Bible. For ease in reading, the form has been altered somewhat, though not significantly.

GENESIS

In the beginning God created the heaven and the earth. And the earth was without form, and void; and darkness was upon the face of the deep. And the Spirit of God moved upon the face of the waters. And God said, "Let there be light": and there was light. And God saw the light, that it was good and God divided the light from the darkness. And God called the light Day, and the darkness he called Night. And the evening and the morning were the first day.

And God said, "Let there be a firmament in the midst of the waters, and let it divide the waters from the waters." And God made the firmament, and divided the waters which were under the firmament from the waters which were above the firmament: and it was so. And God called the firmament Heaven. And the evening and the morning were the second day.

And God said, "Let the waters under the heaven be gathered together unto one place, and let the dry land appear": and it was so. And God called the dry land Earth; and the gathering together of the waters called he Seas: and God saw that it was good. And God said, "Let the earth bring forth grass, the herb yielding seed, and the fruit tree yielding fruit after his kind, whose seed is in itself, upon the earth": and it was so. And the earth brought forth grass, and herb yielding seed after his kind, and the tree yielding fruit, whose seed was in itself, after his kind: and God saw that it was good. And the evening and the morning were the third day.

And God said, "Let there be lights in the firmament of the heaven to divide the day from the night; and let them be for signs, and for seasons, and for days, and years: and let them be for lights in the firmament of the heaven to give light upon the earth": and it was so. And God made two great

CHAPTERS I, 2, 3.

lights; the greater light to rule the day, and the lesser light to rule the night: he made the stars also. And God set them in the firmament of the heaven to give light upon the earth. And to rule over the day and over the night, and to divide the light from the darkness: and God saw that it was good. And the evening and the morning were the fourth day.

And God said, "Let the waters bring forth abundantly the moving creature that hath life, and fowl that may fly above the earth in the open firmament of heaven." And God created great whales, and every living creature that moveth, which the waters brought forth abundantly, after their kind, and every winged fowl after his kind: and God saw that it was good. And God blessed them, saying, "Be fruitful, and multiply, and fill the waters in the seas, and let fowl multiply in the earth." And the evening and the morning were the fifth day.

And God said, "Let the earth bring forth the living creature after his kind, cattle, and creeping thing, and beast of the earth after his kind": and it was so. And God made the beast of the earth after his kind, and cattle after their kind, and every thing that creepeth upon the earth after his kind: and God saw that it was good.

And God said, "Let us make man in our image, after our likeness: and let them have dominion over the fish of the sea, and over the fowl of the air, and over the cattle, and over all the earth, and over every creeping thing that creepeth upon the earth." So God created man in his own image, in the image of God created he him; male and female created he them. And God blessed them, and God said unto them, "Be fruitful, and multiply, and replenish the earth, and subdue it: and have dominion over the fish of the sea, and over the fowl of the air, and over every living thing that moveth upon the earth."

And God said, "Behold, I have given you every herb bearing seed, which is upon the face of all the earth, and every tree, in the which is the fruit of a tree yielding seed; to you it shall be for meat. And to every beast of the earth, and to every fowl of the air, and to every thing that creepeth upon the earth, wherein there is life, I have given every green herb for meat": and it was so. And God saw every thing that he had made, and, behold, it was very good. And the evening and the morning were the sixth day.

Thus the heavens and the earth were finished, and all the host of them. And on the seventh day God ended his work which he had made; and he rested on the seventh day from all his work which he had made. And God blessed the seventh day, and sanctified it: because that in it he had rested from all his work which God created and made.

These are the generations of the heavens and of the earth when they were created, in the day that the LORD God made the earth and the heavens. And every plant of the field before it was in the earth, and every herb of the field before it grew: for the LORD God had not caused it to rain upon the earth, and there was not a man to till the ground. But there went up a mist from the earth, and watered the whole face of the ground. And the LORD God formed man of the dust of the ground, and breathed into his nostrils the breath of life; and man became a living soul.

And the LORD God planted a garden eastward in Eden; and there he put the man whom he had formed. And out of the ground made the LORD God to grow every tree that is pleasant to the sight, and good for food; the tree of life also in the midst of the garden, and the tree of knowledge of good and evil. And a river went out of Eden to water a garden; and from thence it was parted, and became into four heads. The name of the first is

Pison: that is it which compasseth the whole land of Havilah, where there is gold; and the gold of that land is good: there is bdellium and the onyx stone. And the name of the second river is Gihon: the same is it that compasseth the whole land of Ethiopia. And the name of the third river is Hiddekel: that is it which goeth toward the east of Assyria. And the fourth river is Euphrates. And the LORD God took the man, and put him into the garden of Eden to dress it and to keep it. And the LORD God commanded the man, saying, "Of every tree of the garden thou mayest freely eat: But of the tree of the knowledge of good and evil, thou shalt not eat of it: for in the day that thou eatest thereof thou shalt surely die."

And the LORD God said, "It is not good that the man should be alone; I will make an help meet for him." And out of the ground the LORD God formed every beast of the field, and every fowl of the air; and brought them unto Adam to see what he would call them: and whatsoever Adam called every living creature, that was the name thereof. And Adam gave names to all cattle, and to the fowl of the air, and to every beast of the field; but for Adam there was not found an help meet for him. And the LORD God caused a deep sleep to fall upon Adam, and he slept: and he took one of his ribs, and closed up the flesh instead thereof. And the rib, which the LORD God had taken from man, made he a woman, and brought her unto the man. And Adam said, "This is now bone of my bones, and flesh of my flesh: she shall be called Woman, because she was taken out of Man. Therefore shall a man leave his father and his mother, and shall cleave unto his wife: and they shall be one flesh." And they were both naked, the man and his wife, and were not ashamed.

Now the serpent was more subtil than any beast of the field which the LORD God had made. And he said unto the woman, "Yea, hath God said, 'Ye shall not eat of every tree of the garden'?" And the woman said unto the serpent, "We may eat of the fruit of the trees of the garden: But of the fruit of the tree which is in the midst of the garden God hath said, 'Ye shall not eat of it, neither shall ye touch it, lest ye die.'" And the serpent said unto the woman, "Ye shall not surely die: For God doth know that in the day ye eat thereof, then your eyes shall be opened, and ye shall be as gods, knowing good and evil." And when the woman saw that the tree was good for food, and that it was pleasant to the eyes, and a tree to be desired to make one wise, she took of the fruit thereof, and did eat, and gave also unto her husband with her; and he did eat. And the eyes of them both were opened, and they knew that they were naked; and they sewed fig leaves together, and made themselves aprons.

And they heard the voice of the LORD God walking in the garden in the cool of the day: and Adam and his wife hid themselves from the presence of the LORD God amongst the trees of the garden. And the LORD God called unto Adam, and said unto him, "Where art thou"? And he said, "I heard thy voice in the garden, and I was afraid, because I was naked; and I hid myself." And he said, "Who told thee that thou wast naked? Hast thou eaten of the tree, whereof I commanded thee that thou shouldest not eat?" And the man said, "The woman whom thou gavest to be with me, she gave me of the tree, and I did eat." And the LORD God said unto the woman, "What is this that thou hast done"? And the woman said, "The serpent beguiled me, and I did eat." And the LORD God said unto the serpent, "Because thou hast done this, thou art cursed above all cattle, and above every beast of the field; upon thy belly shalt thou go, and dust shalt thou eat all the days of thy life: And I will put enmity between thee and the woman, and between thy seed and her seed; it shall bruise thy head, and thou shalt bruise his heel." Unto the woman he said, "I will greatly multiply thy sorrow and thy conception; in sorrow thou shalt bring forth children; and thy desire shall be to thy husband, and he shall rule over thee." And unto Adam he said, "Because thou hast hearkened unto the voice of thy wife, and hast eaten of the tree, of which I commanded thee, saying, 'Thou shalt not eat of it': cursed is the ground for thy sake; in sorrow shalt thou eat of it all the days of thy life; thorns also and thistles shall it bring forth to thee; and thou shalt eat the herb of the field; in the sweat of thy face shalt thou eat bread, till thou return unto the ground; for out of it wast

thou taken: for dust thou art, and unto dust shalt thou return." And Adam called his wife's name Eve; because she was the mother of all living. Unto Adam also and to his wife did the LORD God make coats of skins, and clothed them.

And the LORD God said, "Behold, the man is become as one of us, to know good and evil: and now, lest he put forth his hand, and take also of the tree of life, and eat, and live for ever": Therefore the LORD God sent him forth from the garden of Eden, to till the ground from whence he was taken. So he drove out the man; and he placed at the east of the garden of Eden Cherubim and a flaming sword which turned every way, to keep the way of the tree of life.

EXODUS

. . .

In the third month, when the children of Israel were gone forth out of the land of Egypt, the same day came they into the wilderness of Sinai. For they were departed from Rephidim, and were come to the desert of Sinai, and had pitched in the wilderness; and there Israel camped before the mount. And Moses went up unto God, and the LORD called unto him out of the mountain, saying, "Thus shalt thou say to the house of Jacob, and tell the children of Israel; 'Ye have seen what I did unto the Egyptians, and how I bare you on eagles' wings, and brought you unto myself. Now therefore, if ye will obey my voice indeed, and keep my covenant, then ye shall be a peculiar treasure unto me above all people: for all

CHAPTERS 19; 20:1-17; 21:1-25.

the earth is mine: And ye be unto me a kingdom of priests, and an holy nation.' These are the words which thou shalt speak unto the children of Israel."

And Moses came and called for the elders of the people, and laid before their faces all these words which the LORD commanded him. And all the people answered together, and said, "All that the LORD hath spoken we will do." And Moses returned the words of the people unto the LORD. And the LORD said unto Moses, "Lo, I come unto thee in a thick cloud, that the people may hear when I speak with thee, and believe thee for ever." And Moses told the words of the people unto the LORD.

And the LORD said unto Moses, "Go unto the people, and sanctify them to day and to morrow, and let them wash their clothes.

And be ready against the third day: for the third day the LORD will come down in the sight of all the people upon mount Sinai. And thou shalt set bounds unto the people round about, saying, 'Take heed to yourselves, that ye go not up into the mount, or touch the border of it: whosoever toucheth the mount shall be surely put to death: There shall not an hand touch it, but he shall surely be stoned, or shot through; whether it be beast or man, it shall not live: when the trumpet soundeth long, they shall come up to the mount.' "

And Moses went down from the mount unto the people, and sanctified the people; and they washed their clothes. And he said unto the people, "Be ready against the third day: come not at your wives."

And it came to pass on the third day in the morning, that there were thunders and lightnings, and a thick cloud upon the mount, and the voice of the trumpet exceeding loud; so that all the people that was in the camp trembled. And Moses brought forth the people out of the camp to meet with God; and they stood at the nether part of the mount. And mount Sinai was altogether on a smoke, because the LORD descended upon it in fire: and the smoke thereof ascended as the smoke of a furnace, and the whole mount quaked greatly. And when the voice of the trumpet sounded long, and waxed louder and louder, Moses spake and God answered him by a voice. And the LORD came down upon the mount Sinai, on the top of the mount: and the LORD called Moses up to the top of the mount; and Moses went up. And the LORD said unto Moses, "Go down, charge the people, lest they break through unto the LORD to gaze, and many of them perish. Let the priests also, which come near to the LORD sanctify themselves, lest the LORD break forth upon them." And Moses said unto the LORD, "The people cannot come up to mount Sinai: for thou chargest us, saying, 'Set bounds about the mount, and sanctify it.' " And the LORD said unto him, "Away, get thee down, and thou shalt come up, thou, and Aaron with thee: but let not the priests and the people break through to come up unto the LORD, lest he break forth upon them." So Moses went down unto the people, and spake unto them.

And God spake all these words, saying, "I am the LORD thy God, which have brought thee out of the land of Egypt, out of the house of bondage. Thou shalt have no other gods before me. Thou shalt not make unto thee any graven image, or any likeness of any thing that is in heaven above, or that is in the earth beneath, or that is in the water under the earth. Thou shalt not bow down thyself to them, nor serve them: for I the LORD thy God am a jealous God, visiting the iniquity of the fathers upon the children unto the third and fourth generation of them that hate me: And shewing mercy unto thousands of them that love me, and keep my commandments. Thou shalt not take the name of the LORD thy God in vain; for the LORD will not hold him guiltless that taketh his name in vain. Remember the sabbath day, to keep it holy. Six days shalt thou labour, and do all thy work: But the seventh day is the sabbath of the LORD thy God; in it thou shalt not do any work, thou, nor thy son, nor thy daughter, thy manservant, nor thy maidservant, nor thy cattle, nor thy stranger that is within thy gates. For in six days the LORD made heaven and earth, the sea, and all that in them is, and rested the seventh day: wherefore the LORD blessed the sabbath day, and hallowed it. Honour thy father and thy mother: that thy days may be long upon the land which the LORD thy God giveth thee. Thou shalt not kill. Thou shalt not commit adultery. Thou shalt not steal. Thou shalt not bear false witness against thy neighbour. Thou shalt not covet thy neighbour's house, thou shalt not covet thy neighbour's wife, nor his manservant, nor his maidservant, nor his ox, nor his ass, nor any thing that is thy neighbour's.

.   .   .

"Now these are the judgments which thou shalt set before them.

"If thou buy an Hebrew servant, six years he shall serve: and in the seventh he shall go out free for nothing. If he came in by himself, he shall go out by himself: if he were married, then his wife shall go out with him. If his master have given him a wife, and she have borne him sons or daughters; the wife and her children shall be her master's, and he shall go out by himself. And if the servant shall plainly say, 'I love my master, my wife, and my children; I will not go out free': Then his master shall bring him unto the judges; he shall also bring him to the door, or unto the door post; and his master shall bore his ear through with an awl; and he shall serve him for ever.

"And if a man sell his daughter to be a maidservant, she shall not go out as the menservants do. If she please not her master, who hath betrothed her to himself, then shall he let her be redeemed: to sell her unto a strange nation he shall have no power, seeing he hath dealt deceitfully with her. And if he have betrothed her unto his son, he shall deal with her after the manner of daughters. If he take him another wife; her food, her raiment, and her duty of marriage, shall he not diminish. And if he do not these three unto her, then shall she go out free without money.

"He that smiteth a man so that he die, shall be surely put to death. And if a man lie not in wait, but God deliver him into his hand; then I will appoint thee a place whither he shall flee. But if a man come presumptuously upon his neighbour to slay him with guile; thou shalt take him from mine altar, that he may die.

"And he that smiteth his father, or his mother, shall be surely put to death.

"And he that stealeth a man, and selleth him, or if he be found in his hand, he shall surely be put to death.

"And he that curseth his father, or his mother, shall surely be put to death.

"And if men strive together, and one smite another with a stone, or with his fist, and he die not, but keepeth his bed: If he rise again, and walk abroad upon his staff, then shall he that smote him be quit: only he shall pay for the loss of his time, and shall cause him to be thoroughly healed.

"And if a man smite his servant, or his maid, with a rod, and he die under his hand; he shall be surely punished. Notwithstanding, if he continue a day or two, he shall not be punished: for he is his money.

"If men strive, and hurt a woman with child, so that her fruit depart from her, and yet no mischief follow: he shall be surely punished, according as the woman's husband will lay upon him; and he shall pay as the judges determine. And if any mischief follow, then thou shalt give life for life. Eye for eye, tooth for tooth, hand for hand, foot for foot. Burning for burning, wound for wound, stripe for stripe."

THE FIRST BOOK OF THE KINGS

. . .

And it came to pass after many days, that the word of the LORD came to Elijah in the third year, saying, "Go, shew thyself unto Ahab; and I will send rain upon the earth." And Elijah went to shew himself unto Ahab. And there was a sore famine in Samaria. And Ahab called Obadiah, which was the governor of his house. (Now Obadiah feared the LORD greatly: For it was so, when Jezebel cut off the prophets of the LORD, that Obadiah took an hundred prophets, and hid them by fifty in a cave, and fed them with bread and water.) And Ahab said unto Obadiah, "Go into the land, unto all fountains of water, and unto all brooks: peradventure we may find grass to save the horses and mules alive, that we lose not all the beasts." So they divided the land between them to pass throughout it: Ahab went one way by himself, and Obadiah went another way by himself.

And as Obadiah was in the way, behold, Elijah met him: and he knew him, and fell on his face, and said, "Art thou that my lord Elijah"? And he answered him, "I am: go, tell thy lord, 'Behold, Elijah is here.'" And he said, "What have I sinned, that thou wouldest deliver thy servant into the hand of Ahab, to slay me? As the LORD thy God liveth, there is no nation or kingdom, whither my lord hath not sent to seek thee: and when they said, 'He is not there'; he took an oath of the kingdom and nation, that they found thee not. And now thou sayest, 'Go, tell thy lord, "Behold, Elijah is here."' And it shall come to pass, as soon as I am gone from thee, that the Spirit of the LORD shall carry thee whither I know not; and so when I come and tell Ahab, and he cannot find thee, he shall

CHAPTER 18:1-45.

slay me: but I thy servant fear the LORD from my youth. Was it not told my lord what I did when Jezebel slew the prophets of the LORD, how I hid an hundred men of the LORD's prophets by fifty in a cave, and fed them with bread and water? And now thou sayest, 'Go, tell thy lord, "Behold, Elijah is here"': and he shall slay me."

And Elijah said, "As the LORD of hosts liveth, before whom I stand, I will surely shew myself unto him to day." So Obadiah went to meet Ahab, and told him: and Ahab went to meet Elijah.

And it came to pass, when Ahab saw Elijah, that Ahab said unto him, "Art thou he that troubleth Israel"? And he answered, "I have not troubled Israel; but thou, and thy father's house, in that ye have forsaken the commandments of the LORD, and thou hast followed Baalim. Now therefore send, and gather to me all Israel unto mount Carmel, and the prophets of Baal four hundred and fifty, and the prophets of the groves four hundred, which eat at Jezebel's table."

So Ahab sent unto all the children of Israel, and gathered the prophets together unto mount Carmel. And Elijah came unto all the people, and said, "How long halt ye between two opinions? if the LORD be God, follow him; but if Baal, then follow him." And the people answered him not a word. Then said Elijah unto the people, "I, even I only, remain a prophet of the LORD; but Baal's prophets are four hundred and fifty men. Let them therefore give us two bullocks; and let them choose one bullock for themselves, and cut it in pieces, and lay it on wood, and put no fire under: and I will dress the other bullock, and lay it on wood, and put no fire under: And call ye on the name of your gods, and I will call on the name of the LORD: and the God that answereth by fire, let him be God." And all the people answered and said, "It is well spoken."

And Elijah said unto the prophets of Baal, "Choose you one bullock for yourselves, and dress it first; for ye are many; and call on the name of your gods, but put no fire under." And they took the bullock which was given them, and they dressed it, and called on the name of Baal from morning even until noon, saying, "O Baal, hear us." But there was no voice, nor any that answered. And they leaped upon the altar which was made. And it came to pass at noon, that Elijah mocked them, and said, "Cry aloud: for he is a god; either he is talking, or he is pursuing, or he is in a journey, or peradventure he sleepeth, and must be awaked." And they cried aloud, and cut themselves after their manner with knives and lancets, till the blood gushed out upon them. And it came to pass, when midday was past, and they prophesied until the time of the offering of the evening sacrifice, that there was neither voice, nor any to answer, nor any that regarded.

And Elijah said unto all the people, "Come near unto me." And all the people came near unto him. And he repaired the altar of the LORD that was broken down. And Elijah took twelve stones, according to the number of the tribes of the sons of Jacob, unto whom the word of the LORD came, saying, "Israel shall be thy name": And with the stones he built an altar in the name of the LORD: and he made a trench about the altar, as great as would contain two measures of seed. And he put the wood in order, and cut the bullock in pieces, and laid him on the wood, and said, "Fill four barrels with water, and pour it on the burnt sacrifice, and on the wood." And he said, "Do it the second time." And they did it the second time. And he said, "Do it

the third time." And they did it the third time. And the water ran round about the altar; and he filled the trench also with water. And it came to pass at the time of the offering of the evening sacrifice, that Elijah the prophet came near, and said, "LORD God of Abraham, Isaac, and of Israel, let it be known this day that thou art God in Israel, and that I am thy servant, and that I have done all these things at thy word. Hear me, O LORD, hear me, that this people may know that thou art the LORD God, and that thou hast turned their heart back again."

Then the fire of the LORD fell, and consumed the burnt sacrifice, and the wood, and the stones, and the dust, and licked up the water that was in the trench. And when all the people saw it, they fell on their faces: and they said, "The LORD, he is the God; the LORD, he is the God." And Elijah said unto them, "Take the prophets of Baal; let not one of them escape." And they took them: and Elijah brought them down to the brook Kishon, and slew them there.

And Elijah said unto Ahab, "Get thee up, eat and drink; for there is a sound of abundance of rain." So Ahab went up to eat and to drink. And Elijah went up to the top of Carmel; and he cast himself down upon the earth, and put his face between his knees. And said to his servant, "Go up now, look toward the sea." And he went up and looked, and said, "There is nothing." And he said, "Go again seven more times." And it came to pass at the seventh time, that he said, "Behold there ariseth a little cloud, out of the sea, like a man's hand." And he said, "Go up, say unto Ahab, 'Prepare thy chariot, and get thee down, that the rain stop thee not.'" And it came to pass in the mean while, that the heaven was black with clouds and wind, and there was a great rain.

ISAIAH

. . .

"Yet now hear, O Jacob my servant; and Israel, whom I have chosen: Thus saith the LORD that made thee, and formed thee from the womb, which will help thee; 'Fear not, O Jacob, my servant; and thou, Jesurun, whom I have chosen. For I will pour water upon him that is thirsty, and floods upon the dry ground: I will pour my spirit upon thy seed, and my blessing upon thine offspring: And they shall spring up as among the grass, as willows by the water courses. One shall say, "I am the LORD'S"; and another shall call himself by the name of Jacob; and another shall subscribe with his hand unto the LORD, and surname himself by the name of Israel.' Thus saith the LORD the King of Israel, and his redeemer the LORD of hosts; 'I am the first, and I am the last; and beside me there is no God. And who, as I, shall call, and shall declare it, and set it in order for me, since I appointed the ancient people? And the things that are coming, and shall come, let them shew unto them. Fear ye not, neither be afraid: have not I told thee from that time, and have declared it? ye are even my witnesses. Is there a God beside me? Yea, there is no God; I know not any.

'They that make a graven image are all of them vanity; and their delectable things shall not profit; and they are their own witnesses; they see not, nor know; that they may be ashamed. Who hath formed a god, or molten a graven image that is profitable for nothing? Behold, all his fellows shall be ashamed: and the workmen, they are of men: let them all be gathered together, let them stand up; yet they shall fear, and they shall be ashamed together. The smith·with the tongs both worketh in the coals, and

CHAPTERS 44:1-19; 45:5-25.

fashioneth it with hammers, and worketh it with the strength of his arms: yea, he is hungry, and his strength faileth: he drinketh no water, and is faint. The carpenter stretcheth out his rule; he marketh it out with a line; he fitteth it with planes, and he marketh it out with the compass, and maketh it after the figure of a man, according to the beauty of a man; that it may remain in the house. He heweth him down cedars, and taketh the cypress and the oak, which he strengtheneth for himself among the trees of the forest: he planteth an ash, and the rain doth nourish it. Then shall it be for a man to burn: for he will take thereof, and warm himself; yea, he kindleth it and baketh bread; yea, he maketh a god, and worshippeth it; he make it a graven image, and falleth down thereto. He burneth part thereof in the fire; with part thereof he eateth flesh; he roasteth roast, and is satisfied: yea, he warmeth himself, and saith "Aha, I am warm, I have seen the fire." And the residue thereof he maketh a god, even his graven image: he falleth down unto it, and worshippeth it, and prayeth unto it, and saith, "Deliver me; for thou are my god." They have not known or understood: for he hath shut their eyes, that they cannot see; and their hearts, that they cannot understand. And none considereth in his heart, neither is there knowledge nor understanding to say, "I have burned part of it in the fire; yea, also I have baked bread upon the coals thereof; I have roasted flesh, and eaten it: and shall I make the residue thereof an abomination? shall I fall down to the stock of a tree?"

. . .

'I am the LORD, and there is none else, there is no God beside me: I girded thee, though thou hast not known me: That they may know from the rising of the sun, and from the west, that there is none beside me. I am the LORD, and there is none else. I form the light, and create darkness: I make peace, and create evil: I the LORD do all these things. Drop down, ye heavens, from above, and let the skies pour down righteousness: let the earth open, and let them bring forth salvation, and let righteousness spring up together: I the LORD have created it. Woe unto him that striveth with his Maker! Let the potsherd strive with the potsherds of the earth. Shall the clay say to him that fashioneth it, "What makest thou"? or thy work, "He hath no hands"? Woe unto him that saith unto his father, "What begettest thou"? or to the woman, "What hast thou brought forth"?'

Thus saith the LORD, the Holy One of Israel, and his Maker, 'Ask me of things to come concerning my sons, and concerning the work of my hands command ye me. I have made the earth, and created man upon it: I, even my hands, have stretched out the heavens, and all their host have I commanded. I have raised him up in righteousness, and I will direct all his ways: he shall build my city, and he shall let go my captives, not for price nor reward,' saith the LORD of hosts.

Thus saith the LORD, 'The labour of Egypt, and merchandise of Ethiopia and of the Sabeans, men of stature, shall come over unto thee, and they shall be thine: they shall come after thee; in chains they shall come over, and they shall fall down unto thee, they shall make supplication unto thee, saying, "Surely God is in thee; and there is none else, there is no God. Verily thou art a God that hidest thyself, O God of Israel, the Saviour." They shall be ashamed, and also confounded, all of them: they shall go to confusion together that are makers of idols. But Israel shall be saved in the LORD with an everlasting salvation: ye shall not be ashamed nor confounded world without end.' For thus saith the LORD that created the heavens; God himself that formed the earth and made it; he hath established it, he created it not in vain, he formed it to be inhabited: 'I am the LORD: and there is none else. I have not spoken in secret, in a dark place of the earth: I said not unto the seed of Jacob, "Seek ye me in vain": I the LORD speak righteousness, I declare things that are right.

'Assemble yourselves and come; draw near together, ye that are escaped of the nations: they have no knowledge that set up the wood of their graven image, and pray unto a god that cannot save. Tell ye, and bring them near; yea, let them take counsel together; who hath declared this from ancient time? Who hath told it from that time? Have not I the LORD? And there is no God else beside me; a just God and a Saviour; there is none beside me. Look unto me, and be ye saved, all the ends of the earth: for I am God, and there is none else. I have sworn by myself, the word is gone out of my mouth in righteousness, and shall not return, that unto me every knee shall bow, every tongue shall swear. "Surely," shall one say, "in the LORD have I righteousness and strength": even to him shall men come; and all that are incensed against him shall be ashamed. In the LORD shall all the seed of Israel be justified, and shall glory.' "

EZEKIEL

. . .

The word of the LORD came unto me again, saying, "What mean ye, that ye use this proverb concerning the land of Israel, saying, 'The fathers have eaten sour grapes, and the children's teeth are set on edge' "?

"As I live," saith the LORD God, "ye shall not have occasion any more to use this proverb in Israel. Behold, all souls are mine; as the soul of the father, so also the soul of the son is mine: the soul that sinneth, it shall die. But if a man be just, and do that which is lawful and right, and hath not eaten upon the mountains, neither hath lifted up his eyes to the idols of the house of Israel, neither hath defiled his neighbour's wife, neither hath come near to a menstruous woman, and hath not oppressed any, but hath restored to the debtor his pledge, hath spoiled none by violence, hath given his bread to the hungry, and hath covered the naked with a garment; he that hath not given forth upon usury, neither hath taken any increase, that hath withdrawn his hand from iniquity, hath executed true judgment between man and man, hath walked in my statutes, and hath kept my judgments, to deal truly; he is just, he shall surely live," saith the Lord GOD.

"If he beget a son that is a robber, a shedder of blood, and that doeth the like to any one of these things, and that doeth not any of those duties, but even hath eaten upon the mountains, and defiled his neighbour's wife, hath oppressed the poor and needy, hath spoiled by violence, hath not restored the pledge, and hath lifted up his eyes to the idols, hath committed abomination, hath given forth upon usury, and hath taken increase: shall he then live? He shall

CHAPTER 18.

not live: he hath done all these abominations; he shall surely die; his blood shall be upon him.

"Now, lo, if he beget a son, that seeth all his father's sins which he hath done, and considereth, and doeth not such like, that hath not eaten upon the mountains, neither hath lifted up his eyes to the idols of the house of Israel, hath not defiled his neighbour's wife, neither hath oppressed any, hath not withholden the pledge, neither hath spoiled by violence, but hath given his bread to the hungry, and hath covered the naked with a garment, that hath taken off his hand from the poor, that hath not received usury nor increase, hath executed my judgments, hath walked in my statutes; he shall not die for the iniquity of his father, he shall surely live. As for his father, because he cruelly oppressed, spoiled his brother by violence, and did that which is not good among his people, lo, even he shall die in his iniquity.

"Yet say ye, 'Why? doth not the son bear the iniquity of the father'? When the son hath done that which is lawful and right, and hath kept all my statutes, and hath done them, he shall surely live. The soul that sinneth, it shall die. The son shall not bear the iniquity of the father, neither shall the father bear the iniquity of the son: the righteousness of the righteous shall be upon him, and the wickedness of the wicked shall be upon him. But if the wicked will turn from all his sins that he hath committed, and keep all my statutes, and do that which is lawful and right he shall surely live, he shall not die. All his transgressions that he hath committed, they shall not be mentioned unto him: in his righteousness that he hath done he shall live.

"Have I any pleasure at all that the

wicked should die"? saith the Lord GOD: "and not that he should return from his ways, and live? But when the righteous turneth away from his righteousness, and committeth iniquity, and doeth according to all the abominations that the wicked man doeth, shall he live? All his righteousness that he hath done shall not be mentioned: in his trespass that he hath trespassed, and in his sin that he hath sinned, in them shall he die.

"Yet ye say, 'The way of the LORD is not equal.' Hear now, O house of Israel; Is not my way equal? Are not your ways unequal? When a righteous man turneth away from his righteousness, and committeth iniquity, and dieth in them; for his iniquity that he hath done shall he die. Again, when the wicked man turneth away from his wickedness that he hath committed, and doeth that which is lawful and right, he shall save his soul alive. Because he considereth, and turneth away from all his transgressions that he hath committed, he shall surely live, he shall not die. Yet saith the house of Israel, 'The way of the Lord is not equal,' O house of Israel, are not my ways equal? Are not your ways unequal? Therefore I will judge you, O house of Israel, every one according to his ways," saith the LORD God. "Repent, and turn yourselves from all your transgressions; so iniquity shall not be your ruin. Cast away from you all your transgressions; whereby ye have transgressed; and make you a new heart and a new spirit: for why will ye die, O house of Israel? For I have no pleasure in the death of him that dieth," saith the LORD God: "wherefore turn yourselves, and live ye."

THE BOOK OF JOB

There was a man in the land of Uz, whose name was Job; and that man was perfect and upright, and one that feared God, and eschewed evil. And there were born unto him seven sons and three daughters. His substance also was seven thousand sheep, and three thousand camels, and five hundred yoke of oxen, and five hundred she asses, and a very great household; so that this man was the greatest of all the men of the east. And his sons went and feasted in their houses, every one his day; and sent and called for their three sisters to eat and to drink with them. And it was so, when the days of their feasting were gone about, that Job sent and sanctified them, and rose up early in the morning, and offered burnt offerings according to the number of them all: for Job said, "It may be that my sons have sinned, and cursed God in their hearts." Thus did Job continually.

Now there was a day when the sons of God came to present themselves before the LORD, and Satan came also among them. And the LORD said unto Satan, "Whence comest thou"? Then Satan answered the LORD, and said, "From going to and fro in the earth, and from walking up and down in it." And the LORD said unto Satan, "Hast thou considered my servant Job, that there is none like him in the earth, a perfect and an upright man, one that feareth God, and escheweth evil"? Then Satan answered the LORD, and said, "Doth Job fear God for nought? Hast not thou made an hedge about him, and about his house, and about all that he hath on every side?

CHAPTERS 1; 2:1-10; 10; 21:7-15; 23:2-12; 38; 40:1-14; 42:1-6, 10-17.

Thou hast blessed the work of his hands, and his substance is increased in the land. But put forth thine hand now, and touch all that he hath and he will curse thee to thy face." And the LORD said unto Satan, "Behold, all that he hath is in thy power; only upon himself put not forth thine hand." So Satan went forth from the presence of the LORD.

And there was a day when his sons and his daughters were eating and drinking wine in their eldest brother's house. And there came a messenger unto Job, and said, "The oxen were plowing, and the asses feeding beside them: And the Sabeans fell upon them, and took them away; yea, they have slain the servants with the edge of the sword; and I only am escaped alone to tell thee." While he was yet speaking, there came also another, and said, "The fire of God is fallen from heaven, and hath burned up the sheep, and the servants, and consumed them; and I only am escaped alone to tell thee." While he was yet speaking, there came also another, and said, "The Chaldeans made out three bands, and fell upon the camels, and have carried them away, yea, and slain the servants with the edge of the sword; and I only am escaped alone to tell thee." While he was yet speaking, there came also another, and said, "Thy sons and thy daughters were eating and drinking wine in their eldest brother's house: And, behold, there came a great wind from the wilderness, and smote the four corners of the house, and it fell upon the young men, and they are dead; and I only am escaped alone to tell thee." Then Job arose, and rent his mantle, and shaved his head, and fell down upon the ground, and worshipped. And said, "Naked came I out of my mother's womb, and naked shall I return thither: the LORD gave, and the LORD hath taken away; blessed be the name of the LORD." In all this Job sinned not, nor charged God foolishly.

Again there was a day when the sons of God came to present themselves before the LORD, and Satan came also among them to present himself before the LORD. And the LORD said unto Satan, "From whence comest thou?" And Satan answered the LORD, and said, "From going to and fro in the earth, and from walking up and down in it." And the LORD said unto Satan, "Hath thou considered my servant Job, that there is none like him in the earth, a perfect and an upright man, one that feareth God, and escheweth evil? And still he holdeth fast his integrity, although thou movedst me against him, to destroy him without cause." And Satan answered the LORD, and said, "Skin for skin, yea, all that a man hath will he give for his life. But put forth thine hand now, and touch his bone and his flesh, and he will curse thee to thy face." And the LORD said unto Satan, "Behold, he is in thine hand; but save his life."

So went Satan forth from the presence of the LORD, and smote Job with sore boils from the sole of his foot unto his crown. And he took him a potsherd to scrape himself withal; and he sat down among the ashes.

Then said his wife unto him, "Dost thou still retain thine integrity? Curse God, and die." But he said unto her, "Thou speakest as one of the foolish women speaketh. What? shall we receive good at the hand of God, and shall we not receive evil"? In all this did not Job sin with his lips.

· · ·

[*And Job spake, and said,*] "My soul is weary of my life; I will leave my complaint upon myself; I will speak in the bitterness of my soul. I will say unto God, 'Do not condemn me; shew me wherefore thou contendest with me. Is it good unto thee that thou shouldest oppress, that thou shouldest despise the work of thine hands, and shine upon the counsel of the wicked? Hast thou eyes of flesh? or seest thou as man seeth? Are thy days as the days of man? Are thy years as man's days, that thou enquirest after mine iniquity, and searchest after my sin? Thou knowest that I am not wicked; and there is none that can deliver out of thine hand. Thine hands have made me and fashioned me together round about; yet thou dost destroy me. Remember, I beseech thee, that thou hast made me as the clay; and wilt thou bring me into dust again? Hast thou not poured me out as milk, and curdled me like cheese? Thou hast clothed me with skin and flesh, and hast fenced me with bones and sinews. Thou hast granted me life and favour, and thy visitation hath preserved my spirit. And these things hast thou hid in thine heart: I know that this is with thee.

'If I sin, then thou markest me, and thou wilt not acquit me from mine iniquity. If I be wicked, woe unto me; and if I be righteous, yet will I not lift up my head. I am full of confusion; therefore see thou mine affliction; for it increaseth. Thou huntest me as a fierce lion: and again thou shewest thyself marvellous upon me. Thou renewest thy witnesses against me, and increasest thine indignation upon me; changes and war are against me. Wherefore then hast thou brought me forth out of the womb? Oh that I had given up the ghost, and no eye had seen me! I should have been as though I had not been; I should have been carried from the womb to the grave. Are not my days few? Cease then, and let me alone, that I may take comfort a little, before I go whence I shall not return, even to the land of darkness and the shadow of death; a land of darkness, as darkness itself; and of the shadow of death, without any order, and where the light is as darkness.'

.   .   .

"Wherefore do the wicked live, become old, yea, are mighty in power? Their seed is established in their sight with them, and their offspring before their eyes. Their houses are safe from fear, neither is the rod of God upon them. Their bull gendereth,

and faileth not; their cow calveth, and casteth not her calf. They send forth their little ones like a flock, and their children dance. They take the timbrel and harp, and rejoice at the sound of the organ. They spend their days in wealth, and in a moment go down to the grave. Therefore they say unto God, 'Depart from us; for we desire not the knowledge of thy ways. What is the Almighty, that we should serve him? And what profit should we have, if we pray unto him?'

.   .   .

"Even to day is my complaint bitter: my stroke is heavier than my groaning. Oh that I knew where I might find him! that I might come even to his seat! I would order my cause before him, and fill my mouth with arguments. I would know the words which he would answer me, and understand what he would say unto me. Will he plead against me with his great power? No; but he would put strength in me. There the righteous might dispute with him; so should I be delivered for ever from my judge. Behold, I go forward, but he is not there; and backward, but I cannot perceive him: On the left hand, where he doth work, but I cannot behold him: he hideth himself on the right hand, that I cannot see him. But he knoweth the way that I take: when he hath tried me, I shall come forth as gold. My foot hath held his steps, his way have I kept, and not declined. Neither have I gone back from the commandment of his lips; I have esteemed the words of his mouth more than my necessary food."

.   .   .

Then the LORD answered Job out of the whirlwind, and said, "Who is this that darkeneth counsel by words without knowledge? Gird up now thy loins like a man; for I will demand of thee, and answer thou me. Where wast thou when I laid the foundations of the earth? Declare, if thou hast understanding. Who hath laid the measures thereof, if thou knowest? Or who hath stretched the line upon it? Whereupon are the foundations thereof fastened? Or who laid the corner stone thereof; when the morning stars sang together, and all the sons of God shouted for joy? Or who shut up the sea with doors, when it brake forth, as if it had issued out of the womb? When I made the cloud the garment thereof, and thick darkness a swaddling band for it, and brake up for it my decreed place, and set bars and doors, and said, 'Hitherto shalt thou come, but no further: and here shall thy proud waves be stayed'? Hast thou commanded the morning since thy days; and caused the dayspring to know his place; that it might take hold of the ends of the earth, that the wicked might be shaken out of it? It is turned as clay to the seal; and they stand as a garment. And from the wicked their light is withholden, and the high arm shall be broken. Hast thou entered into the springs of the sea? Or hast thou walked in the search of the depth? Have the gates of death been opened unto thee? Or hast thou seen the doors of the shadow of death? Hast thou perceived the breadth of the earth? Declare if thou knowest it all.

"Where is the way where light dwelleth? And as for darkness, where is the place thereof, that thou shouldest take it to the bound thereof, and that thou shouldest know the paths to the house thereof? Knowest thou it, because thou wast then born? Or because the number of thy days is great? Hast thou entered into the treasures of the snow? Or hast thou seen the treasures of the hail, which I have reserved against the time of trouble, against the day of battle and war? By what way is the light parted, which scattereth the east wind upon the earth? Who hath divided a watercourse for the overflowing of waters, or a way for the lightning of thunder; to cause it to rain on the earth, where no man is; on the Wilderness, wherein there is no man; to satisfy the desolate and waste ground; and to cause the bud of the tender herb to spring forth? Hath the rain a father? Or who hath begotten the drops of dew? Out of whose womb came the ice? And the hoary frost of heaven, who hath gendered it? The waters are hid as with a stone, and the face of the deep is frozen.

"Canst thou bind the sweet influences of Pleiades, or loose the bands of Orion? Canst thou bring forth Massaroth in his season? Or canst thou guide Arcturus with his sons? Knowest thou the ordinances of heaven? Canst thou set the dominion thereof in the earth? Canst thou lift up thy voice to the clouds, that abundance of waters may cover thee? Canst thou send lightnings, that they may go, and say unto thee, 'Here we are'? Who hath put wisdom in the inward parts? Or who hath given understanding to the heart? Who can number the clouds in wisdom? Or who can stay the bottles of heaven, when the dust groweth into hardness, and the clods cleave fast together? Wilt thou hunt the prey for the lion? Or fill the appetite of the young lions, when they couch in their dens, and abide in the covert to lie in wait? Who provideth for the raven his food? When his young ones cry unto God, they wander for lack of meat."

.   .   .

Moreover the LORD answered Job, and said, "Shall he that contendeth with the Almighty instruct him? He that reproveth God, let him answer it."

Then Job answered the LORD, and said, "Behold, I am vile; what shall I answer thee? I will lay mine hand upon my mouth. Once have I spoken; but I will not answer: yea, twice; but I will proceed no further."

Then answered the LORD unto Job out of the whirlwind, and said, "Gird up thy loins now like a man: I will demand of thee, and declare thou unto me. Wilt thou also disannul my judgment? Wilt thou condemn me, that thou mayest be righteous? Hast thou an arm like God? Or canst thou thunder with a voice like him? Deck thyself now with majesty and excellency; and array thyself with glory and beauty. Cast abroad the rage of thy wrath: and behold every one that is proud, and abase him. Look on every one that is proud, and bring him low; and tread down the wicked in their place. Hide them in the dust together; and bind their faces in secret. Then will I also confess unto thee that thine own right hand can save thee."

. . .

Then Job answered the LORD, and said, "I know that thou canst do every thing, and that no thought can be withholden from thee. Who is he that hideth counsel without knowledge? Therefore have I uttered that I understood not; things too wonderful for me, which I knew not. Hear, I beseech thee, and I will speak: I will demand of thee, and declare thou unto me. I have heard of thee by the hearing of the ear: but now mine eye seeth thee. Wherefore I abhor myself, and repent in dust and ashes."

. . .

And the LORD turned the captivity of Job, when he prayed for his friends: also the LORD gave Job twice as much as he had before. Then came there unto him all his brethren, and all his sisters, and all they that had been of his acquaintance before, and did eat bread with him in his house: and they bemoaned him, and comforted him over all the evil that the LORD had brought upon him: every man also gave him a piece of money, and every one an earring of gold. So the LORD blessed the latter end of Job more than his beginning; for he had fourteen thousand sheep, and six thousand camels, and a thousand yoke of oxen, and a thousand she asses. He had also seven sons and three daughters. And he called the name of the first, Jemima; and the name of the second, Kezia; and the name of the third, Kerenhappuch. And in all the land were no women found so fair as the daughters of Job: and their father gave them inheritance among their brethren. After this lived Job an hundred and forty years, and saw his sons, and his sons's sons, even four generations. So Job died, being old and full of days.

The New Testament

The following selections from the New Testament are a combination of early Christian history and doctrine. From the *Gospel of St. Matthew* comes the Sermon on the Mount, the most complete and one of the most beautiful statements of the religious views of Jesus. *The Acts* is a historical book detailing the activities of the founders of the Christian church in the years immediately following the ascension of Christ, as seen through the eyes of the early church fathers several years later. Of crucial import to Western history is the transformation of Christianity from the exclusive possession of an obscure Jewish sect into a message of salvation open to Gentiles as well as to Jews. This was the first step on Christianity's long road to religious domination of the Western world. The selection from *Romans* contains a statement of Christian doctrine by the Apostle Paul, one of the most influential of all Christian theologians. It was Paul who began the task of developing the teachings of Jesus into an organized and consistent body of theological doctrine.

The cornerstone of Paul's doctrine is the theory of original sin, with its related concepts of predestination, election, and grace. Originated by Paul, elaborated by St. Augustine in the fifth century, and reiterated by the Protestant reformer, John Calvin, in the sixteenth century, the doctrine of original sin is of fundamental importance in the history of Christian theology. Although of lesser significance, the notion of justification by faith, also included in the selection from *Romans*, has had a long history. It is associated particularly with the Protestant theology of Martin Luther.

The New Testament selections have been taken from the King James Version of the Bible, with slight alterations in form.

ST. MATTHEW

And seeing the multitudes, he went up into a mountain: And when he was set, his disciples came unto him: And he opened his mouth, and taught them, saying, "Blessed are the poor in spirit: for theirs is the kingdom of heaven. Blessed are they that mourn: for they shall be comforted. Blessed are the meek: for they shall inherit the earth. Blessed are they which do hunger and thirst after righteousness: for they shall be filled. Blessed are the merciful: for they shall obtain mercy. Blessed are the pure in heart: for they shall see God. Blessed are the peacemakers: for they shall be called the children of God. Blessed are they which are persecuted for righteousness' sake: for theirs is the kingdom of heaven. Blessed are ye, when men shall revile you, and persecute you, and shall say all manner of evil against you falsely, for my sake. Rejoice, and be exceeding glad: for great is your reward in heaven: for so persecuted they the prophets which were before you.

CHAPTERS 5, 6, 7.

"Ye are the salt of the earth: but if the salt have lost his savour, wherewith shall it be salted? It is thenceforth good for nothing, but to be cast out, and to be trodden under foot of men. Ye are the light of the world. A city that is set on an hill cannot be hid. Neither do men light a candle, and put it under a bushel, but on a candlestick; and it giveth light unto all that are in the house. Let your light so shine before men, that they may see your good works, and glorify your Father which is in heaven.

"Think not that I am come to destroy the law, or the prophets: I am not come to destroy, but to fulfil. For verily I say unto you, till heaven and earth pass, one jot or one tittle shall in no wise pass from the law, till all be fulfilled. Whosoever therefore shall break one of these least commandments, and shall teach men so, he shall be called the least in the kingdom of heaven: but whosoever shall do and teach them, the same shall be called great in the kingdom of heaven. For I say unto you, that except your righteousness shall exceed the righteousness of the scribes and Pharisees, ye shall in no case enter into the kingdom of heaven.

"Ye have heard that it was said by them of old time, Thou shalt not kill; and whosoever shall kill shall be in danger of the judgment. But I say unto you, That whosoever is angry with his brother without a cause shall be in danger of the judgment: and whosoever shall say to his brother, Ra-ca, shall be in danger of the council: but whosoever shall say, Thou fool, shall be in danger of hell fire. Therefore if thou bring thy gift to the altar, and there rememberest that thy brother hath ought against thee; leave there thy gift before the altar, and go thy way; first be reconciled to thy brother, and then come and offer thy gift. Agree with thine adversary quickly, whiles thou art in the way with him; lest at any time the adversary deliver thee to the judge, and the judge deliver thee to the officer, and thou be cast into prison. Verily I say unto thee, Thou shalt by no means come out thence, till thou hast paid the uttermost farthing.

"Ye have heard that it was said by them of old time, Thou shalt not commit adultery. But I say unto you, That whosoever looketh on a woman to lust after her hath committed adultery with her already in his heart. And if thy right eye offend thee, pluck it out, and cast it from thee: for it is profitable for thee that one of thy members should perish, and not that thy whole body should be cast into hell. And if thy right hand offend thee, cut it off, and cast it from thee: for it is profitable for thee that one of thy members should perish, and not that thy whole body should be cast into hell. It hath been said, Whosoever shall put away his wife, let him give her a writing of divorcement. But I say unto you, That whosoever shall put away his wife, saving for the cause of fornication, causeth her to commit adultery: and whosoever shall marry her that is divorced committeth adultery.

"Again, ye have heard that it hath been said by them of old time, Thou shalt not forswear thyself, but shalt perform unto the Lord thine oaths. But I say unto you, Swear not at all; neither by heaven; for it is God's throne: nor by the earth; for it is his footstool: neither by Jerusalem; for it is the city of the great King. Neither shalt thou swear by thy head, because thou canst not make one hair white or black. But let your communication be, Yea, yea; Nay, nay: for whatsoever is more than these cometh of evil.

"Ye have heard that it hath been said, An eye for an eye, and a tooth for a tooth. But I say unto you, That ye resist not evil: but whosoever shall smite thee on thy right cheek, turn to him the other also. And if any man will sue thee at the law, and take away thy coat, let him have thy cloke also. And whosoever shall compel thee to go a mile, go with him twain. Give to him that asketh thee, and from him that would borrow of thee turn not thou away.

"Ye have heard that it hath been said, Thou shalt love thy neighbour, and hate thine enemy. But I say unto you, Love your enemies, bless them that curse you, do good to them that hate you, and pray for them which despitefully use you, and persecute you; that ye may be the children of your Father which is in heaven: for he maketh his sun to rise on the evil and on the good, and sendeth rain on the just and on the unjust. For if ye love them which love you, what reward have ye? Do not even the publicans the same? And if ye salute your brethren only, what do ye more than others? Do not even the publicans so? Be ye therefore perfect, even as your Father which is in heaven is perfect.

"Take heed that ye do not your alms before men, to be seen of them: otherwise ye have no reward of your Father which is in heaven. Therefore when thou doest thine alms; do not sound a trumpet before thee, as the hypocrites do in the synagogues and in the streets, that they may have glory of men. Verily I say unto you, They have their reward. But when thou doest alms, let not thy left hand know what thy right hand doeth: that thine alms may be in secret: and thy Father which seeth in secret himself shall reward thee openly.

"And when thou prayest, thou shalt not be as the hypocrites are: for they love to pray standing in the synagogues and in the corners of the streets, that they may be seen of men. Verily I say unto you, They have their reward. But thou, when thou prayest, enter into thy closet, and when thou hast shut thy door, pray to thy Father which is in secret; and thy Father which seeth in secret shall reward thee openly. But when ye pray, use not vain repetitions, as the heathen do: for they think that they shall be heard for their much speaking. Be not ye therefore like unto them: for your father knoweth what things ye have need of, before ye ask him. After this manner therefore pray ye: Our Father which art in heaven, hallowed be thy name. Thy kingdom come. Thy will be done in earth, as it is in heaven. Give us this day our daily bread. And forgive us our debts, as we forgive our debtors. And lead us not into temptation, but deliver us from evil: For thine is the kingdom, and the power, and the glory, for ever. A-men.

"For if ye forgive men their trespasses, your heavenly Father will also forgive you: But if ye forgive not men their trespasses, neither will your father forgive your trespasses.

"Moreover when ye fast, be not, as the hypocrites, of a sad countenance: for they disfigure their faces, that they may appear unto men to fast. Verily I say unto you, They have their reward. But thou, when thou fastest, anoint thine head, and wash thy face; that thou appear not unto men to fast, but unto thy Father which is in secret: and thy Father, which seeth in secret, shall reward thee openly.

"Lay not up for yourselves treasures upon earth, where moth and rust doth corrupt, and where thieves break through and steal. But lay up for yourselves treasures in heaven, where neither moth nor rust doth corrupt, and where thieves do not break through nor steal: For where your treasure is, there will your heart be also. The light of the body is the eye: if therefore thine eye be single thy whole body shall be full of light. But if thine eye be evil, thy whole body shall be full of darkness. If therefore the light that is in thee be darkness, how great is that darkness!

"No man can serve two masters: for either he will hate the one, and love the other; or else he will hold to the one, and despise the other. Ye cannot serve God and mammon. Therefore I say unto you, Take no thought for your life, what ye shall eat, or what ye shall drink; nor yet for your body, what ye shall put on. Is not the life more than meat, and the body than raiment? Behold the fowls of the air: for they sow not, neither do they reap, nor gather into barns; yet your heavenly Father feedeth them. Are ye not much better than they? Which of you by taking thought can add one cubit unto his stature? And why take ye thought for raiment? Consider the lilies of the field, how they grow; they toil not, neither do they spin: And yet I say unto you, That even Solomon in all his glory was not arrayed like one of these. Wherefore, if God so clothe the grass of the field, which to day is, and to morrow is cast into the oven, shall he not much more clothe you, O ye of little faith? Therefore take no thought, saying, What shall we eat? or, What shall we drink? or, Wherewithal shall we be clothed? (For after all these things do the Gentiles seek:) for your heavenly Father knoweth that ye have need of all these things. But seek ye first the kingdom of God, and his righteousness; and all these things shall be added unto you. Take therefore no thought for the morrow: for the morrow shall take thought for the things of itself. Sufficient unto the day is the evil thereof.

"Judge not, that ye be not judged. For with what judgment ye judge, ye shall be judged: and with what measure ye mete, it shall be measured to you again. And why beholdest thou the mote that is in thy brother's eye, but considerest not the beam that is in thine own eye? Or how wilt thou say to thy brother, Let me pull out the mote out of thine eye; and, behold, a beam is in thine own eye? Thou hypocrite, first cast out the beam out of thine own eye; and then shalt thou see clearly to cast out the mote out of thy brother's eye.

"Give not that which is holy unto the dogs, neither cast ye your pearls before swine, lest they trample them under their feet, and turn again and rend you.

"Ask, and it shall be given you; seek, and ye shall find; knock, and it shall be opened unto you: For every one that asketh receiveth; and he that seeketh findeth; and to him that knocketh it shall be opened. Or what man is there of you, whom if his son ask bread, will he give him a stone? Or if he ask a fish, will he give him a serpent? If ye then, being evil know how to give good gifts unto your children, how much more shall your Father which is in heaven give good things to them that ask him? Therefore all things whatsoever ye would that men should do to you, do ye even so to them: for this is the law and the prophets.

"Enter ye in at the strait gate: for wide is the gate, and broad is the way, that leadeth to destruction, and many there be which go in thereat: Because strait is the gate, and narrow is the way, which leadeth unto life, and few there be that find it.

"Beware of false prophets, which come to you in sheep's clothing, but inwardly they are ravening wolves. Ye shall know them by their fruits. Do men gather grapes of thorns, or figs of thistles? Even so every good tree bringeth forth good fruit; but a corrupt tree bringeth forth evil fruit. A good tree cannot bring forth evil fruit, neither can a corrupt tree bring forth good fruit. Every tree that bringeth not forth good fruit is hewn down, and cast into the fire. Wherefore by their fruits ye shall know them.

"Not every one that saith unto me, Lord, Lord, shall enter into the kingdom of heaven; but he that doeth the will of my Father which is in heaven. Many will say to me in that day, Lord, Lord, have we not prophesied in thy name? And in thy name have cast out devils? And in thy name done many wonderful works? And then will I profess unto them, I never knew you; depart from me, ye that work iniquity.

"Therefore whosoever heareth these sayings of mine, and doeth them I will liken him unto a wise man, which built his house upon a rock: And the rain descended, and the floods came, and the winds blew, and beat upon that house and it fell not: for it was founded upon a rock. And every one that heareth these sayings of mine, and doeth them not, shall be likened unto a foolish man, which built his house upon the sand: And the rain descended, and the floods came, and the winds blew, and beat upon that house; and it fell: and great was the fall of it." And it came to pass, when Jesus had ended these sayings, the people were astonished at his doctrine: For he taught them as one having authority, and not as the scribes.

THE ACTS OF THE APOSTLES

The former treatise have I made, O Theophilus, of all that Jesus began both to do and teach, until the day in which he was taken up, after that he through the Holy Ghost had given commandments unto the apostles whom he had chosen. To whom also he shewed himself alive after his passion by many infallible proofs, being seen of them forty days, and speaking of the things pertaining to the kingdom of God: And, being assembled together with them, commanded them that they should not depart from Jerusalem, but wait for the promise of the Father, which, saith he, ye have heard of me. For John truly baptized with water; but ye shall be baptized with the Holy Ghost not many days hence.

When they therefore were come together, they asked of him, saying, "Lord, wilt thou at this time restore again the kingdom to Israel"? And he said unto them, "It is not for you to know the times or the seasons, which the Father hath put in his own power. But ye shall receive power, after that the Holy Ghost is come upon you: and ye shall be witnesses unto me both in Jerusalem, and in all Judaea, and in Samaria, and unto the uttermost part of the earth." And when he had spoken these things, while they beheld, he was taken up; and a cloud received him out of their sight. And while they looked stedfastly toward heaven as he went up, behold, two men stood by them in white apparel; which also said, "Ye men of Galilee, why stand ye gazing up into heaven? This same Jesus, which is taken up from you into heaven, shall so come in like manner as ye have seen him go into heaven." Then returned they unto Jerusalem from the mount called Olivet, which is from Jerusalem a sabbath day's journey.

. . . .

And when the day of Pentecost was fully come, they were all with one accord in one place. And suddenly there came a sound from heaven as of a rushing mighty wind, and it filled all the house where they were sitting. And there appeared unto them cloven tongues like as of fire, and it sat upon each of them. And they were all filled with the Holy Ghost, and began to speak with other tongues, as the Spirit gave them utterance. And there were dwelling at Jerusalem Jews, devout men, out of every nation under heaven. Now when this was noised abroad, the multitude came together, and were confounded, because that every man heard them speak in his own language. And they were all amazed and marvelled, saying one to another, "Behold, are not all these which speak Galilaeans? And how hear we every man in our own tongue, wherein we were born? Parthians, and Medes, and Elamites, and the dwellers in Mesopotamia, and in Judaea, and Cappadocia, in Pontus, and Asia. Phrygia, and Pamphylia, in Egypt, and in the parts of Libya about Cyrene, and strangers of Rome, Jews and proselytes, Cretes and Arabians, we do hear them speak in our tongues the wonderful works of God." And they were all amazed, and were in doubt, saying one to another, "What meaneth this"? Others mocking said, "These men are full of new wine."

But Peter, standing up with the eleven, lifted up his voice, and said unto them, "Ye men of Judaea, and all ye that dwell at Jerusalem, be this known unto you, and hearken to my words: For these are not drunken, as ye suppose, seeing it is but the

CHAPTERS 1:1-12; 2:1-41; 6:7-15; 7:1-2, 51-60; 8:1-3; 9:1-22; 10.

third hour of the day. But this is that which was spoken by the prophet Joel; 'And it shall come to pass in the last days,' saith God, 'I will pour out of my Spirit upon all flesh: and your sons and your daughters shall prophesy, and your young men shall see visions, and your old men shall dream dreams: And on my servants and on my handmaidens I will pour out in those days of my Spirit; and they shall prophesy. And I will shew wonders in heaven above, and signs in the earth beneath; blood, and fire, and vapour of smoke: The sun shall be turned into darkness, and the moon into blood, before that great and notable day of the Lord come. And it shall come to pass, that whosoever shall call on the name of the Lord shall be saved.' Ye men of Israel, hear these words; Jesus of Nazareth, a man approved of God among you by miracles and wonders and signs, which God did by him in the midst of you, as ye yourselves also know: Him, being delivered by the determinate counsel and foreknowledge of God, ye have taken, and by wicked hands have crucified and slain: Whom God hath raised up, having loosed the pains of death: because it was not possible that he should be holden of it. For David speaketh concerning him, 'I foresaw the Lord always before my face, for he is on my right hand, that I should not be moved. Therefore did my heart rejoice, and my tongue was glad; moreover also my flesh shall rest in hope: Because thou wilt not leave my soul in hell, neither wilt thou suffer thine Holy One to see corruption. Thou hast made known to me the ways of life; thou shalt make me full of joy with thy countenance.' Men and brethren, let me freely speak unto you of the patriarch David, that he is both dead and buried, and his sepulchre is with us unto this day. Therefore being a prophet, and knowing that God had sworn with an oath to him, that of the fruit of his loins, according to the flesh, he would raise up Christ to sit on his throne; he see-

ing this before spake of the resurrection of Christ, that his soul was not left in hell, neither his flesh did see corruption. This Jesus hath God raised up, whereof we all are witnesses. Therefore being by the right hand of God exalted, and having received of the Father the promise of the Holy Ghost, he hath shed forth this, which ye now see and hear. For David is not ascended into the heavens: but he saith himself, 'The LORD said unto my Lord, "Sit thou on my right hand, until I make thy foes thy footstool." ' Therefore let all the houses of Israel know assuredly, that God hath made that same Jesus, whom ye have crucified, both Lord and Christ."

Now when they heard this, they were pricked in their heart, and said unto Peter and to the rest of the apostles, "Men and brethren, what shall we do"? Then Peter said unto them, "Repent, and be baptized every one of you in the name of Jesus Christ for the remission of sins, and ye shall receive the gift of the Holy Ghost. For the promise is unto you, and to your children, and to all that are afar off, even as many as the Lord our God shall call." And with many other words did he testify and exhort, saying, "Save yourselves from this untoward generation."

Then they that gladly received his word were baptized; and the same day there were added unto them about three thousand souls.

. . .

And the word of God increased; and the number of the disciples multiplied in Jerusalem greatly; and a great company of the priests were obedient to the faith. And Stephen, full of faith and power, did great wonders and miracles among the people.

Then there arose certain of the synagogue, which is called the synagogue of the Libertines, and Cyrenians, and Alexandrians, and of them of Cilicia and of Asia, disputing with Stephen. And they were not able to resist the wisdom and the spirit by which he spake. Then they suborned men, which said, "We have heard him speak blasphemous words against Moses, and against God." And they stirred up the people, and the elders, and the scribes, and came upon him, and caught him, and brought him to the council, and set up false witnesses, which said, "This man ceaseth not to speak blasphemous words against this holy place, and the law: For we have heard him say that this Jesus of Nazareth shall destroy this place, and shall change the customs which Moses delivered us." And all that sat in the council, looking stedfastly on him, saw his face as it had been the face of an angel.

Then said the high priest, "Are these things so"? And he said, "Men, brethren, and fathers, hearken: [*After defending himself by an appeal to the Old Testament, Stephen concludes*] Ye stiffnecked and uncircumcised in heart and ears, ye do always resist the Holy Ghost: as your fathers did, so do ye. Which of the prophets have not your fathers persecuted? And they have slain them which shewed before of the coming of the Just One; of whom ye have been now the betrayers and murderers: who have received the law by the disposition of angels, and have not kept it."

When they heard these things, they were cut to the heart, and they gnashed on him with their teeth. But he, being full of the Holy Ghost, looked up stedfastly into heaven, and saw the glory of God, and Jesus standing on the right hand of God, and said, "Behold, I see the heavens opened, and the Son of man standing on the right hand of God." Then they cried out with a loud voice, and stopped their ears, and ran upon him with one accord, and cast him out of the city, and stoned him: and the witnesses laid down their clothes at a young man's feet, whose name was Saul. And they stoned Stephen, calling upon God, and saying, "Lord Jesus, receive my spirit." And he kneeled down, and cried with a loud voice, "Lord, lay not this sin to their charge." And when he had said this, he fell asleep.

And Saul was consenting unto his death. And at that time there was a great persecution against the church which was at Jerusalem; and they were all scattered abroad throughout the regions of Judaea and Samaria, except the apostles. And devout men carried Stephen to his burial, and made great lamentation over him. As for Saul, he made havock of the church, entering into every house, and haling men and women committed them to prison.

· · · ·

And Saul, yet breathing out threatenings and slaughter against the disciples of the Lord, went unto the high priest, and desired of him letters to Damascus to the synagogues, that if he found any of this way, whether they were men or women, he might bring them bound unto Jerusalem. And as he journeyed, he came near Damascus: and suddenly there shined round about him a light from heaven. And he fell to the earth, and heard a voice saying unto him, "Saul, Saul, why persecutest thou me"? And he said, "Who art thou, Lord"? And the Lord said, "I am Jesus whom thou persecutest: it is hard for thee to kick against the pricks." And he trembling and astonished said, "Lord, what wilt thou have me to do"? And the Lord said unto him, "Arise, and go into the city, and it shall be told thee what thou must do." And the men which journeyed with him stood speechless, hearing a voice, but seeing no man. And Saul arose from the earth; and when his eyes were opened he saw no man: but they led him by the hand, and brought him into Damascus. And he was three days without sight, and neither did eat nor drink.

And there was a certain disciple at Damascus, named Ananias; and to him said the Lord in a vision, "Ananias." And he said, "Behold, I am here, Lord." And the Lord said unto him, "Arise, and go into the street which is called Straight, and enquire in the house of Judas for one called Saul, of Tarsus: for, behold, he prayeth, and hath seen in a vision, a man named Ananias coming in, and putting his hand on him, that he might receive his sight." Then Ananias answered, "Lord, I have heard by many of this man, how much evil he hath done to thy saints at Jerusalem: And here he hath authority from the chief priests to bind all that call on thy name." But the Lord said unto him, "Go thy way: for he is a chosen vessel unto me, to bear my name before the Gentiles, and kings, and the children of Israel: For I will shew him how great things he must suffer for my name's sake." And Ananias went his way and entered into the house; and putting his hands on him said, "Brother Saul, the Lord, even Jesus, that appeared unto thee in the way as thou camest, hath sent me, that thou mightest receive thy sight, and be filled with the Holy Ghost." And immediately there fell from his eyes as it had been scales: and he received sight forthwith, and arose, and was baptized. And when he had received meat, he was strengthened.

Then was Saul certain days with the disciples which were at Damascus. And straightway he preached Christ in the synagogues, that he is the Son of God. But all that heard him were amazed, and said; "Is not this he that destroyed them which called on this name in Jerusalem, and came hither for that intent, that he might bring them bound unto the chief priests"? But Saul increased the more in strength, and confounded the Jews which dwelt at Damascus, proving that this is very Christ.

.   .   .

There was a certain man in Caesarea called Cornelius, a centurion of the band called the Italian band. A devout man, and one that feared God with all his house, which gave much alms to the people, and prayed to God alway. He saw in a vision

evidently about the ninth hour of the day an angel of God coming in to him, and saying unto him, "Cornelius." And when he looked on him, he was afraid, and said, "What is it, Lord"? And he said unto him, "Thy prayers and thine alms are come up for a memorial before God. And now send men to Joppa, and call for one Simon, whose surname is Peter: He lodgeth with one Simon a tanner, whose house is by the sea side: he shall tell thee what thou oughtest to do." And when the angel which spake unto Cornelius was departed, he called two of his household servants, and a devout soldier of them that waited on him continually; and when he had declared all these things unto them, he sent them to Joppa.

On the morrow, as they went on their journey, and drew nigh unto the city, Peter went up upon the housetop to pray about the sixth hour. And he became very hungry, and would have eaten: but while they made ready, he fell into a trance, and saw heaven opened, and a certain vessel descending unto him, as it had been a great sheet knit at the four corners, and let down to the earth: wherein were all manner of fourfooted beasts of the earth, and wild beasts, and creeping things, and fowls of the air. And there came a voice to him, "Rise, Peter; kill, and eat." But Peter said, "Not so, Lord; for I have never eaten any thing that is common or unclean." And the voice spake unto him again the second time, "What God hath cleansed, that call not thou common." This was done thrice: and the vessel was received up again into heaven. Now while Peter doubted in himself what this vision which he had seen should mean, behold, the men which were sent from Cornelius had made enquiry for Simon's house, and stood before the gate, and called, and asked whether Simon, which was surnamed Peter, were lodged there.

While Peter thought on the vision, the

Spirit said unto him, "Behold, three men seek thee. Arise therefore, and get thee down, and go with them, doubting nothing: for I have sent them." Then Peter went down to the men which were sent unto him from Cornelius; and said, "Behold, I am he whom ye seek: what is the cause wherefore ye are come"? And they said, "Cornelius the centurion, a just man, and one that feareth God, and of good report among all the nation of the Jews, was warned from God by an holy angel to send for thee into his house, and to hear words of thee." Then called he them in, and lodged them. And on the morrow Peter went away with them, and certain brethren from Joppa accompanied him. And the morrow after they entered into Caesarea. And Cornelius waited for them, and had called together his kinsmen and near friends. And as Peter was coming in, Cornelius met him, and fell down at his feet, and worshipped him. But Peter took him up, saying, "Stand up; I myself also am a man." And as he talked with him, he went in, and found many that were come together. And he said unto them, "Ye know how that it is an unlawful thing for a man that is a Jew to keep company, or come unto one of another nation; but God hath shewed me that I should not call any man common or unclean. Therefore came I unto you without gainsaying, as soon as I was sent for: I ask therefore for what intent ye have sent for me"? And Cornelius said, "Four days ago I was fasting until this hour; and at the ninth hour I prayed in my house, and, behold, a man stood before me in bright clothing. And said, 'Cornelius, thy prayer is heard, and thine alms are had in remembrance in the sight of God. Send therefore to Joppa, and call hither Simon, whose surname is Peter; he is lodged in the house of one Simon a tanner by the sea side: who, when he cometh, shall speak unto thee.' Immediately therefore I sent to

thee; and thou hast well done that thou art come. Now therefore are we all here present before God, to hear all things that are commanded thee of God."

Then Peter opened his mouth, and said, "Of a truth I perceive that God is no respector of persons: But in every nation he that feareth him, and worketh righteousness, is accepted with him. The word which God sent unto the children of Israel, preaching peace by Jesus Christ (He is Lord of all:) That word, I say, ye know, which was published throughout all Judaea, and began from Galilee, after the baptism which John preached; how God annointed Jesus of Nazareth with the Holy Ghost and with power: who went about doing good, and healing all that were oppressed of the devil; for God was with him. And we are witnesses of all things which he did both in the land of the Jews, and in Jerusalem; whom they slew and hanged on a tree: Him God raised up the third day, and shewed him openly; not to all the people, but unto witnesses chosen before of God, even to us, who did eat and drink with him after he rose from the dead. And he commanded us to preach unto the people, and to testify that it is he which was ordained of God to be the Judge of quick and dead. To him give all the prophets witness, that through his name whosoever believeth in him shall receive remission of sins."

While Peter yet spake these words, the Holy Ghost fell on all them which heard the word. And they of the circumcision which believed were astonished, as many as came with Peter, because that on the Gentiles also was poured out the gift of the Holy Ghost. For they heard them speak with tongues, and magnify God. Then answered Peter, "Can any man forbid water, that these should not be baptized, which have received the Holy Ghost as well as we"? And he commanded them to be baptized in the name of the Lord.

THE EPISTLE OF PAUL THE APOSTLE
TO THE ROMANS

.   .   .

As it is written, There is none righteous, no, not one: There is none that understandeth, there is none that seeketh after God. They are all gone out of the way, they are together become unprofitable; there is none that doeth good, no, not one. Their throat is an open sepulchre; with their tongues they have used deceit; the poison of asps is under their lips: Whose mouth is full of cursing and bitterness: Their feet are swift to shed blood: Destruction and misery are in their ways: And the way of peace have they not known: There is no fear of God before their eyes.

Now we know that what things soever the law saith, it saith to them who are under the law: that every mouth may be stopped, and all the world may become guilty before God. Therefore by the deeds of the law there shall no flesh be justified in his sight: for by the law is the knowledge of sin. But now the righteousness of God without the law is manifested, being witnessed by the law and the prophets; even the righteousness of God which is by faith of Jesus Christ unto all and upon all them that believe: for there is no difference. For all have sinned, and come short of the glory of God; being justified freely by his grace through the redemption that is in Christ Jesus: Whom God hath set forth to be a propitiation through faith in his blood, to declare his righteousness for the remission of sins that are past, through the forbearance of God; to declare, I say, at this time his righteousness: that he might be just, and the justifier of him which believeth in Jesus. Where is boasting then? It is excluded. By what law? or works?

CHAPTERS 3:10-31; 5; 6; 9: 8-21.

Nay: but by the law of faith. Therefore we conclude that a man is justified by faith without the deeds of the law. Is he the God of the Jews only? Is he not also of the Gentiles? Yes, of the Gentiles also: Seeing it is one God, which shall justify the circumcision by faith, and uncircumcision through faith. Do we then make void the law through faith? God forbid: yea, we establish the law.

.   .   .

Therefore being justified by faith, we have peace with God through our Lord Jesus Christ: By whom also we have access by faith into this grace wherein we stand, and rejoice in hope of the glory of God. And not only so, but we glory in tribulations also: knowing that tribulation worketh patience; and patience, experience; and experience, hope: And hope maketh not ashamed; because the love of God is shed abroad in our hearts by the Holy Ghost which is given unto us. For when we were yet without strength, in due time Christ died for the ungodly. For scarcely for a righteous man will one die: yet peradventure for a good man some would even dare to die. But God commendeth his love toward us, in that, while we were yet sinners, Christ died for us. Much more then, being now justified by his blood, we shall be saved from wrath through him. For if, when we were enemies, we were reconciled to God by the death of his Son, much more, being reconciled, we shall be saved by his life. And not only so, but we also joy in God through our Lord Jesus Christ, by whom we have now received the atonement.

Wherefore, as by one man sin entered into the world, and death by sin; and so death passed upon all men, for that all have sinned. (For until the law sin was in the world: but sin is not imputed when there is no law. Nevertheless death reigned from Adam to Moses, even over them that had not sinned after the similitude of Adam's transgression, who is the figure of him that was to come. But not as the offence, so also is the free gift. For if through the offence of one many be dead, much more the grace of God, and the gift by grace, which is by one man, Jesus Christ, hath abounded unto many. And not as it was by one that sinned, so is the gift: for the judgment was by one to condemnation, but the free gift is of many offences unto justification. For if by one man's offence death reigned by one; much more they which receive abundance of grace and of the gift of righteousness shall reign in life by one, Jesus Christ.) Therefore as by the offence of one judgment came upon all men to condemnation; even so, by the righteousness of one the free gift came upon all men unto justification of life. For as by one man's disobedience many were made sinners, so by the obedience of one shall many be made righteous. Moreover the law entered, that the offence might abound. But where sin abounded, grace did much more abound: That as sin hath reigned unto death, even so might grace reign through righteousness unto eternal life by Jesus Christ our Lord.

What shall we say then? Shall we continue in sin, that grace may abound? God forbid. How shall we, that are dead to sin, live any longer therein? Know ye not, that so many of us as were baptized into Jesus Christ were baptized into his death? Therefore we are buried with him by baptism into death: that like as Christ was raised up from the dead by the glory of the Father, even so we also should walk in newness of life. For if we have been planted together in the likeness of his death, we shall be also in the likeness of his resurrection: Knowing this, that our old man is crucified

with him, that the body of sin might be destroyed, that henceforth we should not serve sin. For he that is dead is freed from sin. Now if we be dead with Christ, we believe that we shall also live with him: Knowing that Christ being raised from the dead dieth no more; death hath no more dominion over him. For in that he died, he died unto sin once: but in that he liveth, he liveth unto God. Likewise reckon ye also yourselves to be dead indeed unto sin, but alive unto God through Jesus Christ our Lord.

Let not sin therefore reign in your mortal body, that ye should obey it in the lusts thereof. Neither yield ye your members as instruments of unrighteousness unto sin: but yield yourselves unto God, as those that are alive from the dead, and your members as instruments of righteousness unto God. For sin shall not have dominion over you: for ye are not under the law, but under grace. What then? Shall we sin, because we are not under the law, but under grace? God forbid. Know ye not, that to whom ye yield yourselves servants to obey, his servants ye are to whom ye obey; whether of sin unto death, or of obedience unto righteousness? But God be thanked, that ye were the servants of sin, but ye have obeyed from the heart that form of doctrine which was delivered you. Being then made free from sin, ye became the servants of righteousness.

I speak after the manner of men because of the infirmity of your flesh: for as ye have yielded your members servants to uncleanness and to iniquity unto iniquity; even so now yield your members servants to righteousness unto holiness. For when ye were the servant of sin, ye were free from righteousness. What fruit had ye then in those things whereof ye are now ashamed? For the end of those things is death. But now being made free from sin, and become servants to God, ye have your fruit unto holiness, and the end everlasting life. For the wages of sin is death; but the gift of God is eternal life through Jesus Christ our Lord.

.   .   .

They which are the children of the flesh, these are not the children of God: but the children of the promise are counted for the seed. For this is the word of promise. At this time will I come, and Sarah shall have a son. And not only this; but when Rebecca also had conceived by one, even by our father Isaac; (for the children being not yet born, neither having done any good or evil, that the purpose of God according to election might stand, not of works, but of him that calleth): it was said unto her, The elder shall serve the younger. As it is written, Jacob have I loved, but Esau have I hated. What shall we say then? Is there unrighteousness with God? God forbid. For he saith to Moses, I will have mercy on whom I will have mercy, and I will have compassion on whom I will have compassion. So then it is not of him that willeth, nor of him that runneth, but of God that sheweth mercy. For the scripture saith unto Pharaoh, Even for this same purpose have I raised thee up, that I might shew my power in thee, and that my name might be declared throughout all the earth. Therefore hath he mercy on whom he will have mercy, and whom he will be hardeneth. Thou wilt say then unto me, Why doth he yet find fault? For who hath resisted his will? Nay but, O man, who art thou that repliest against God? Shall the thing formed say to him that formed it, Why hast thou made me thus? Hath not the potter power over the clay, of the same lump to make one vessel unto honour, and another unto dishonour?

St. Augustine

For three hundred years after the death of Christ, the Christian churches were engaged in a continuing struggle. Confronted by scores of pagan cults in the Mediterranean world and by the persecution of the Roman government, the new religion was unable to establish its supremacy until the fourth century. Early in that century, under the emperors Galerius and Constantine (himself a convert), Christianity was recognized and tolerated, and later in the century, under Theodosius, it was proclaimed as the official religion of the Roman Empire.

But the problems of the churches were far from over, for a host of controversies now arose within the ranks of the Christians themselves. The most critical controversy was over questions of doctrine. Innumerable sects, each preaching its own special version of Christian doctrine and combating the views of the others, were scattered throughout the empire. Clearly, if Christianity was to survive, some order had to be brought out of this theological chaos.

Into this scene of confusion stepped Augustine (354-430). Highly intelligent, firmly devoted to his conception of the truth, and possessed of unusual administrative ability, Augustine was admirably fitted for the task first of developing a theological doctrine for the

Christian religion and then of making that doctrine prevail.

After having been attracted as a youth to various pagan cults, Augustine was converted to Christianity in 386 through the influence of Ambrose, Bishop of Milan. The account of his conversion, a valuable revelation of his personality, is given in the first of the following selections, from his remarkable autobiography, *The Confessions.*

Following his conversion, Augustine devoted most of the rest of his life to formulating and disseminating what he believed to be the true Christian doctrine. The main features of this doctrine are given in the second selection, taken from *The Enchiridion* ("Manual"). The central concept, as with St. Paul, is original sin, but with Augustine the theory becomes systematically articulated. Once he had worked out his doctrine completely, Augustine was in a good position to brand opposing theories as heresies. And he devoted much of his time, thought, and energy, especially in later life, to doctrinal controversies in an effort to purge Christian theology of all heretical elements. He was singularly successful in this endeavor, and orthodox Christianity (even with the later additions made by Thomas Aquinas and others) has remained basically Augustinian.

THE CONFESSIONS

Book Eight

O my God, let me with gratitude remember and confess unto Thee Thy mercies bestowed upon me. Let my bones be steeped in Thy love, and let them say, Who is like unto Thee, O Lord? "Thou hast loosed my bonds, I will offer unto Thee the sacrifice of thanksgiving." And how Thou hast loosed them I will declare; and all who worship Thee when they hear these things shall say: "Blessed be the Lord in heaven and earth, great and wonderful is His name." Thy words had stuck fast into my breast, and I was hedged round about by Thee on every side. Of Thy eternal life I was now certain, although I had seen it "through a glass darkly." Yet I no longer doubted that there was an incorruptible substance, from which was derived all other substance; nor did I now desire to be more certain of Thee, but more stedfast in Thee.

THE CONFESSIONS OF ST. AUGUSTINE, trans. J. G. Pilkington (Edinburgh: T. & T. Clark, 1876), pp. 174, 186-188, 196-198, 200-205. Courtesy of T. & T. Clark.

As for my temporal life, all things were uncertain, and my heart had to be purged from the old leaven. The "Way," the Saviour Himself, was pleasant unto me, but as yet I disliked to pass through its straightness. . . .

. . . My will was the enemy master of, and thence had made a chain for me and bound me. Because of a perverse will was lust made; and lust indulged in became custom; and custom not resisted became necessity. By which links, as it were, joined together (whence I term it a "chain"), did a hard bondage hold me enthralled. But that new will which had begun to develope in me, freely to worship Thee, and to wish to enjoy Thee, O God, the only sure enjoyment, was not able as yet to overcome my former wilfulness, made strong by long indulgence. Thus did my two wills, one old and the other new, one carnal, the other spiritual, contend within me; and by their discord they unstrung my soul.

Thus came I to understand, from my own experience, what I had read, how that "the flesh lusteth against the Spirit, and the Spirit against the flesh." I verily lusted both ways; yet more in that which I approved in myself, than in that which I disapproved in myself. For in this last it was now rather not "I," because in much I rather suffered against my will than did it willingly. And yet it was through me that custom became more combative against me, because I had come willingly whither I willed not. And who, then, can with any justice speak against it, when just punishment follows the sinner? Nor had I now any longer my wonted excuse, that as yet I hesitated to be above the world and serve Thee, because my perception of the truth was uncertain; for now it was certain. But I, still bound to the earth, refused to be Thy soldier; and was as much afraid of being freed from all embarrassments, as we ought to fear to be embarrassed.

Thus with the baggage of the world was I sweetly burdened, as when in slumber; and the thoughts wherein I meditated upon Thee were like unto the efforts of those desiring to awake, who, still overpowered with a heavy drowsiness, are again steeped therein. And as no one desires to sleep always, and in the sober judgment of all waking is better, yet does a man generally defer to shake off drowsiness, when there is a heavy lethargy in all his limbs, and, though displeased, yet even after it is time to rise with pleasure yields to it, so was I assured that it were much better for me to give up myself to Thy charity, than to yield myself to my own cupidity; but the former course satisfied and vanquished me, the latter pleased me and fettered me. Nor had I aught to answer Thee calling to me, "Awake, thou that sleepest, and arise from the dead, and Christ shall give thee light." And to Thee showing me on every side, that what Thou saidst was true, I, convicted by the truth, had nothing at all to reply, but the drawling and drowsy words: "Presently, lo, presently;" "leave me a little while." But "presently, presently," had no present; and my "leave me a little

while" went on for a long while. In vain did I "delight in Thy law after the inner man," when "another law in my members warred against the law of my mind, and brought me into captivity to the law of sin which is in my members." For the law of sin is the violence of custom, whereby the mind is drawn and held, even against its will; deserving to be so held in that it so willingly falls into it. "O wretched man that I am! who shall deliver me from the body of this death" but Thy grace only, through Jesus Christ our Lord?

．　．　．

In the midst, then, of this great strife of my inner dwelling, which I had strongly raised up against my soul in the chamber of my heart, troubled both in mind and countenance, I seized upon Alypius, and exclaimed: "What is wrong with us? What is this? What heardest thou? The unlearned start up and 'take' heaven, and we, with our learning, but wanting heart, see where we wallow in flesh and blood! Because others have preceded us, are we ashamed to follow, and not rather ashamed at not following?" Some such words I gave utterance to, and in my excitement flung myself from him, while he gazed upon me in silent astonishment. For I spoke not in my wonted tone, and my brow, cheeks, eyes, colour, tone of voice, all expressed my emotion more than the words. There was a little garden belonging to our lodging, of which we had the use, as of the whole house; for the master, our landlord, did not live there. Thither had the tempest within my breast hurried me, where no one might impede the fiery struggle in which I was engaged with myself, until it came to the issue that Thou knewest, though I did not. But I was mad that I might be whole, and dying that I might have life, knowing what evil thing I was, but not knowing what good thing I was shortly to become. Into the garden, then, I retired, Alypius following my steps. For his presence was no bar to my solitude; or how could he desert me so troubled? We sat down at as great a distance from the house as we could. I was disquieted in spirit, being most impatient with myself that I entered not into Thy will and covenant, O my God, which all my bones cried out unto me to enter, extolling it to the skies. And we enter not therein by ships, or chariots, or feet, no, nor by going so far as I had come from the house to that place where we were sitting. For not to go only, but to enter there, was naught else but to will to go, but to will it resolutely and thoroughly; not to stagger and sway about this way and that, a changeable and half-wounded will, wrestling, with one part falling as another rose.

Finally, in the very fever of my irresolution, I made many of those motions with my body which men sometimes desire to do, but cannot, if either they have not the limbs, or if their limbs be bound with fetters, weakened by disease, or hindered in any other way. Thus, if I tore my hair, struck my forehead, or if, entwining my fingers, I clasped my knee, this I did because I willed it. But I might have willed and not done it, if the power of motion in my limbs had not responded. So many things, then, I did, when to have the will was not to have the power, and I did not that which both with an unequalled desire I longed more to do, and which shortly when I should will I should have the power to do; because shortly when I should will, I should will thoroughly. For in such things the power was one with the will, and to will was to do, and yet was it not done; and more readily did the body obey the slightest wish of the soul in the moving its limbs at the order of the mind, than the soul obeyed itself to accomplish in the will alone this its great will.

Whence is this monstrous thing? And why is it? Let Thy mercy shine on me, that I may inquire, if so be the hiding-places of man's punishment, and the darkest contritions of the sons of Adam, may perhaps answer me. Whence is this monstrous thing? and

why is it? The mind commands the body, and it obeys forthwith; the mind commands itself, and is resisted. The mind commands the hand to be moved, and such readiness is there that the command is scarce to be distinguished from the obedience. Yet the mind is mind, and the hand is body. The mind commands the mind to will, and yet, though it be itself, it obeyeth not. Whence this monstrous thing? and why is it? I repeat, it commands itself to will, and would not give the command unless it willed; yet is not that done which it commandeth. But it willeth not entirely; therefore it commandeth not entirely. For so far forth it commandeth, as it willeth; and so far forth is the thing commanded not done, as it willeth not. For the will commandeth that there be a will;—not another, but itself. But it doth not command entirely, therefore that is not which it commandeth. For were it entire, it would not even command it to be, because it would already be. It is, therefore, no monstrous thing partly to will, partly to be unwilling, but an infirmity of the mind, that it doth not wholly rise, sustained by truth, pressed down by custom. And so there are two wills, because one of them is not entire; and the one is supplied with what the other needs.

．　．　．

Thus was I sick and tormented, accusing myself far more severely than was my wont, tossing and turning me in my chain till that was utterly broken, whereby I now was but slightly, but still was held. And Thou, O Lord, pressedst upon me in my inward parts by a severe mercy, redoubling the lashes of fear and shame, lest I should again give way, and that same slender remaining tie not being broken off, it should recover strength, and enchain me the faster. For I said mentally, "Lo, Let it be done now, let it be done now." And as I spoke, I all but came to a resolve. I all but did it, yet I did it not. Yet fell I not back to my old condition, but took up my position hard by, and drew breath. And I tried again, and wanted but very little of reaching it, and somewhat less, and then all but touched and grasped it; and yet came not at it, nor touched, nor grasped it, hesitating to die unto death, and to live unto life; and the worse, whereto I had been habituated, prevailed more with me than the better, which I had not tried. And the very moment in which I was to become another man, the nearer it approached me, the greater horror did it strike into me; but it did not strike me back, nor turn me aside, but kept me in suspense.

The very toys of toys, and vanities of vanities, my old mistresses, still enthralled me; they shook my fleshly garment, and whispered softly, "Dost thou part with us? And from that moment shall we no more be with thee for ever? And from that moment shall not this or that be lawful for thee for ever?" And what did they suggest to me in the words "this or that?" What is it that they suggested, O my God? Let Thy mercy avert it from the soul of Thy servant. What impurities did they suggest! What shame! And now I far less than half heard them, not openly showing themselves and contradicting me, but muttering, as it were, behind my back, and furtively plucking me as I was departing, to make me look back upon them. Yet they did delay me, so that I hesitated to burst and shake myself free from them, and to leap over whither I was called,—an unruly habit saying to me, "Dost thou think thou canst live without them?"

But now it said this very faintly; for on that side towards which I had set my face, and whither I trembled to go, did the chaste dignity of Continence appear unto me, cheerful, but not dissolutely gay, honestly alluring me to come and doubt nothing, and extending her holy hands, full of a multiplicity of good examples, to receive and embrace me. There were there so many young men and maidens, a multitude of youth and every age, grave widows and ancient virgins, and Con-

tinence herself in all, not barren, but a fruitful mother of children of joys, by Thee, O Lord, her Husband. And she smiled on me with an encouraging mockery, as if to say, "Canst not thou do what these youths and maidens can? Or can one or other do it of themselves, and not rather in the Lord their God? The Lord their God gave me unto them. Why standest thou in thine own strength, and so standest not? Cast thyself upon Him; fear not, He will not withdraw that thou shouldest fall; cast thyself upon Him without fear, He will receive thee, and heal thee." And I blushed beyond measure, for I still heard the muttering of those toys, and hung in suspense. And she again seemed to say, "Shut up thine ears against those unclean members of thine upon the earth, that they may be mortified. They tell thee of delights, but not as doth the law of the Lord thy God." This controversy in my heart was naught but self against self. But Alypius, sitting close by my side, awaited in silence the result of my unwonted emotion.

But when a profound reflection had, from the secret depths of my soul, drawn together and heaped up all my misery before the sight of my heart, there arose a mighty storm, accompanied by as mighty a shower of tears. Which, that I might pour forth fully, with its natural expressions, I stole away from Alypius; for it suggested itself to me that solitude was fitter for the business of weeping. So I retired to such a distance that even his presence could not be oppressive to me. Thus was it with me at that time, and he perceived it; for something, I believe, I had spoken, wherein the sound of my voice appeared choked with weeping, and in that state had I risen up. He then remained where we had been sitting, most completely astonished. I flung myself down, how, I know not, under a certain fig-tree, giving free course to my tears, and the streams of mine eyes gushed out, an acceptable sacrifice unto Thee. And, not indeed in these words, yet to this effect, spake I much unto Thee,—

"But Thou, O Lord, how long?" "How long, Lord? Wilt Thou be angry for ever? Oh, remember not against us former iniquities;" for I felt that I was enthralled by them. I sent up these sorrowful cries,—"How long, how long? To-morrow, and to-morrow? Why not now? Why is there not this hour an end to my uncleanness?"

I was saying these things and weeping in the most bitter contrition of my heart, when, lo, I heard the voice as of a boy or girl, I know not which, coming from a neighbouring house, chanting, and oft repeating, "Take up and read; take up and read." Immediately my countenance was changed, and I began most earnestly to consider whether it was usual for children in any kind of game to sing such words; nor could I remember ever to have heard the like. So, restraining the torrent of my tears, I rose up, interpreting it no other way than as a command to me from Heaven to open the book, and to read the first chapter I should light upon. For I had heard of Antony, that, accidentally coming in whilst the gospel was being read, he received the admonition as if what was read were addressed to him, "Go and sell that thou hast, and give to the poor, and thou shalt have treasure in heaven; and come and follow me." And by such oracle was he forthwith converted unto Thee. So quickly I returned to the place where Alypius was sitting; for there had I put down the volume of the apostles, when I rose thence. I grasped, opened, and in silence read that paragraph on which my eyes first fell,—"Not in rioting and drunkenness, not in chambering and wantonness, not in strife and envying; but put ye on the Lord Jesus Christ, and make

not provision for the flesh, to fulfil the lusts thereof." No further would I read, nor did I need; for instantly, as the sentence ended,—by a light, as it were, of security infused into my heart,—all the gloom of doubt vanished away.

Closing the book, then, and putting either my finger between, or some other mark, I now with a tranquil countenance made it known to Alypius. And he thus disclosed to me what was wrought in him, which I knew not. He asked to look at what I had read. I showed him; and he looked even further than I had read, and I knew not what followed. This it was, verily, "Him that is weak in the faith, receive ye;" which he applied to himself, and discovered to me. By this admonition was he strengthened; and by a good resolution and purpose, very much in accord with his character (wherein, for the better, he was always far different from me), without any restless delay he joined me. Thence we go in to my mother. We make it known to her,—she rejoiceth. We relate how it came to pass,—she leapeth for joy, and triumpheth, and blesseth Thee, who art "able to do exceeding abundantly above all that we ask or think;" for she perceived Thee to have given her more for me than she used to ask by her pitiful and most doleful groanings. For Thou didst so convert me unto Thyself, that I sought neither a wife, nor any other of this world's hopes,—standing in that rule of faith in which Thou, so many years before, had showed me unto her in a vision. And thou didst turn her grief into a gladness, much more plentiful than she had desired, and much dearer and chaster than she used to crave, by having grandchildren of my body.

THE ENCHIRIDION

. . .

God's judgments upon fallen men and angels. The death of the body is man's peculiar punishment.

. . . Now the evils I have mentioned are common to all who for their wickedness have been justly condemned by God, whether they be men or angels. But there is one form of punishment peculiar to man—the death of the body. God had threatened him with this punishment of death if he should sin, leaving him indeed to the freedom of his own will, but yet commanding his obedience under pain of death; and He placed him amid the happiness of Eden, as it were in a protected nook of life, with the intention that, if he preserved his righteousness, he should thence ascend to a better place.

Through Adam's sin his whole posterity were corrupted, and were born under the penalty of death, which he had incurred.

Thence, after his sin, he was driven into exile, and by his sin the whole race of which he was the root was corrupted in him, and thereby subjected to the penalty of death. And so it happens that all descended from him, and from the woman who had led him into sin, and was condemned at the same time with him,—being the offspring of carnal lust on which the same punishment of disobedience was visited,—were tainted with the original sin, and were by it drawn through divers errors and sufferings into that last and endless punishment which they suffer in common with the fallen angels, their corrupters and masters, and the partakers of their doom. And thus "by one man sin entered into the world, and death by sin; and

THE ENCHIRIDION, in *The Works of Aurelius Augustine*, ed. M. Dods, Vol. IX (Edinburgh: T. & T. Clark, 1892), pp. 194-195, 197-200, 206-207, 219, 242-245, 253-255. Courtesy of T. & T. Clark.

so death passed upon all men, for that all have sinned." By "the world" the apostle, of course, means in this place the whole human race.

The state of misery to which Adam's sin reduced mankind, and the restoration effected through the mercy of God.

Thus, then, matters stood. The whole mass of the human race was under condemnation, was lying steeped and wallowing in misery, and was being tossed from one form of evil to another, and, having joined the faction of the fallen angels, was paying the well-merited penalty of that impious rebellion. For whatever the wicked freely do through blind and unbridled lust, and whatever they suffer against their will in the way of open punishment, this all evidently pertains to the just wrath of God. But the goodness of the Creator never fails either to supply life and vital power to the wicked angels (without which their existence would soon come to an end); or, in the case of mankind, who spring from a condemned and corrupt stock, to impart form and life to their seed, to fashion their members, and through the various seasons of their life, and in the different parts of the earth, to quicken their senses, and bestow upon them the nourishment they need. For He judged it better to bring good out of evil, than not to permit any evil to exist. And if He had determined that in the case of men, as in the case of the fallen angels, there should be no restoration to happiness, would it not have been quite just, that the being who rebelled against God, who in the abuse of his freedom spurned and transgressed the command of his Creator when he could so easily have kept it, who defaced in himself the image of his Creator by stubbornly turning away from His light, who by an evil use of his free-will broke away from his wholesome bondage to the

Creator's laws,—would it not have been just that such a being should have been wholly and to all eternity deserted by God, and left to suffer the everlasting punishment he had so richly earned? Certainly so God would have done, had He been only just and not also merciful, and had He not designed that His unmerited mercy should shine forth the more brightly in contrast with the unworthiness of its objects.

. . .

Men are not saved by good works, nor by the free determination of their own will, but by the grace of God through faith.

But this part of the human race to which God has promised pardon and a share in His eternal kingdom, can they be restored through the merit of their own works? God forbid. For what good work can a lost man perform, except so far as he has been delivered from perdition? Can they do anything by the free determination of their own will? Again I say, God forbid. For it was by the evil use of his free-will that man destroyed both it and himself. For, as a man who kills himself must, of course, be alive when he kills himself, but after he has killed himself ceases to live, and cannot restore himself to life; so, when man by his own free-will sinned, then sin being victorious over him, the freedom of his will was lost. "For of whom a man is overcome, of the same is he brought in bondage." This is the judgment of the Apostle Peter. And as it is certainly true, what kind of liberty, I ask, can the bond-slave possess, except when it pleases him to sin? For he is freely in bondage who does with pleasure the will of his master. Accordingly, he who is the servant of sin is free to sin. And hence he will not be free to do right, until, being freed from sin, he shall begin to be the servant of righteousness. And this is true liberty, for he has pleasure in the righteous deed; and it is at the same time a holy bondage, for he is obedient to the will of God. But whence comes this liberty to do right to the man who is in bondage and sold under sin, except he be redeemed by Him who has said, "If the Son shall make you free, ye shall be free indeed"? And before this redemption is wrought in a man, when he is not yet free to do what is right, how can he talk of the freedom of his will and his good works, except he be inflated by that foolish pride of boasting which the apostle restrains when he says, "By grace are ye saved, through faith."

Faith itself is the gift of God; and good works will not be wanting in those who believe.

And lest men should arrogate to themselves the merit of their own faith at least, not understanding that this too is the gift of God, this same apostle, who says in another place that he had "obtained mercy of the Lord to be faithful," here also adds: "and that not of yourselves; it is the gift of God: not of works, lest any man should boast." And lest it should be thought that good works will be wanting in those who believe, he adds further: "For we are His workmanship, created in Christ Jesus unto good works, which God hath before ordained that we should walk in them." We shall be made truly free, then, when God fashions us, that is, forms and creates us anew, not as men—for He has done that already—but as good men, which His grace is now doing, that we may be a new creation in Christ Jesus, according as it is said: "Create in me a clean heart, O God." For God had already created his heart, so far as the physical structure of the human heart is concerned; but the psalmist prays for the renewal of the life which was still lingering in his heart.

The freedom of the will is also the gift of God, for God worketh in us both to will and to do.

And further, should any one be inclined to boast, not indeed of his works, but of the freedom of his will, as if the first merit belonged to him, this very liberty of good action being given to him as a reward he had earned, let him listen to this same preacher of grace, when he says: "For it is God which worketh in you, both to will and to do of His own good pleasure"; and in another place: "So, then, it is not of him that willeth, nor of him that runneth, but of God that showeth mercy." Now as, undoubtedly, if a man is of the age to use his reason, he cannot believe, hope, love, unless he will to do so, nor obtain the prize of the high calling of God unless he voluntarily run for it; in what sense is it "not of him that willeth, nor of him that runneth, but of God that showeth mercy," except that, as it is written, "The preparation of the heart is from the Lord"? Otherwise, if it is said, "It is not of him that willeth, nor of him that runneth, but of God that showeth mercy," because it is of both, that is, both of the will of man and of the mercy of God, so that we are to understand the saying, "It is not of him that willeth, nor of him that runneth, but of God that showeth mercy," as if it meant the will of man alone is not sufficient, if the mercy of God go not with it,—then it will follow that the mercy of God alone is not sufficient, if the will of man go not with it; and therefore, if we may rightly say, "it is not of man that willeth, but of God that showeth mercy," because the will of man by itself is not enough, why may we not also rightly put it in the converse way: "It is not of God that showeth mercy, but of man that willeth," because the mercy of God by itself does not suffice? Surely, if no Christian will dare to say this, "It is not of God that showeth mercy, but of man that willeth," lest he should openly contradict the apostle, it follows that the true interpretation of the saying, "It is not of him that willeth, nor of him that runneth, but of God that showeth mercy," is that the whole work belongs to God, who both makes the will of man righteous, and thus prepares

it for assistance, and assists it when it is prepared. For the man's righteousness of will precedes many of God's gifts, but not all; and it must itself be included among those which it does not precede. We read in Holy Scripture, both that God's mercy "shall prevent me," and that His mercy "shall follow me." It prevents the unwilling to make him willing; it follows the willing to make his will effectual. Why are we taught to pray for our enemies, who are plainly unwilling to lead a holy life, unless that God may work willingness in them? And why are we ourselves taught to ask that we may receive, unless that He who has created in us the wish, may Himself satisfy the wish? We pray, then, for our enemies, that the mercy of God may prevent them, as it has prevented us: we pray for ourselves that His mercy may follow us.

Men, being by nature the children of wrath, needed a Mediator. In what sense God is said to be angry.

And so the human race was lying under a just condemnation, and all men were the children of wrath. Of which wrath it is written: "All our days are passed away in Thy wrath; we spend our years as a tale that is told." Of which wrath also Job says: "Man that is born of a woman is of few days, and full of trouble." Of which wrath also the Lord Jesus says: "He that believeth on the Son hath everlasting life: and he that believeth not the Son shall not see life; but the wrath of God abideth on him." He does not say it will come, but it "abideth on him." For every man is born with it; wherefore the apostle says: "We were by nature the children of wrath, even as others." Now, as men were lying under this wrath by reason of their original sin, and as this original sin was the more heavy and deadly in proportion to the number and magnitude of the actual sins which were added to it, there was need for a Mediator, that is, for a reconciler, who, by the offering of one sacrifice, of which all the sacrifices of the law and the prophets were types, should take away this wrath. Wherefore the apostle says: "For if, when we were enemies, we were reconciled to God by the death of His Son, much more, being reconciled, we shall be saved by His life." Now when God is said to be angry, we do not attribute to Him such a disturbed feeling as exists in the mind of an angry man; but we call His just displeasure against sin by the name "anger," a word transferred by analogy from human emotions. But our being reconciled to God through a Mediator, and receiving the Holy Spirit, so that we who were enemies are made sons ("For as many as are led by the Spirit of God, they are the sons of God"): this is the grace of God through Jesus Christ our Lord.

·   ·   ·   ·   ·

Christ, who was Himself free from sin, was made sin for us, that we might be reconciled to God.

Begotten and conceived, then, without any indulgence of carnal lust, and therefore bringing with Him no original sin, and by the grace of God joined and united in a wonderful and unspeakable way in one person with the Word, the Only-begotten of the Father, a son by nature, not by grace, and therefore having no sin of His own; nevertheless, on account of the likeness of sinful flesh in which He came, He was called sin, that He might be sacrificed to wash away sin. For, under the Old Covenant, sacrifices for sin were called sins. And He, of whom all these sacrifices were types and shadows, was Himself truly made sin. Hence the apostle, after saying, "We pray you in Christ's stead, be ye reconciled to God," forthwith adds: "for He hath made Him to be sin for us who knew no sin; that we might be made the righteousness of God in Him." He does not say, as some incorrect copies read, "He who knew no sin did sin for us," as if Christ had Himself sinned for our sakes; but he says, "Him who knew no sin," that is, Christ, God, to whom we are to be reconciled, "hath made to be sin for us," that is, hath made Him a sacrifice for our sins, by which we might be reconciled to God. He, then, being made sin, just as we are made righteousness (our righteousness being not our own, but God's, not in ourselves, but in Him); He being made sin, not His own, but ours, not in Himself, but in us, showed, by the likeness of sinful flesh in which He was crucified, that though sin was not in Him, yet that in a certain sense He died to sin, by dying in the flesh which was the likeness of sin; and that although He himself had never lived the old life of sin, yet by His resurrection He typified our new life springing up out of the old death in sin.

·   ·   ·   ·   ·

By the sacrifice of Christ all things are restored, and peace is made between earth and heaven.

And, of course, the holy angels, taught by God, in the eternal contemplation of whose truth their happiness consists, know how great a number of the human race are to supplement their ranks, and fill up the full tale of their citizenship. Wherefore the apostle says, that "all things are gathered together in one in Christ, both which are in heaven and which are on earth." The things which are in heaven are gathered together when what was lost therefrom in the fall of the angels is restored from among men; and the things which are on earth are gathered together, when those who are predestined to eternal life are redeemed from their old corruption. And thus, through that single sacrifice in which the Mediator was offered up, the one sacrifice of which the many victims under the law were types, heavenly things are brought into peace with earthly things, and earthly things with heavenly. Wherefore, as the same apostle says: "For it pleased the Father that in Him should all fulness dwell: and, having made peace through the blood of His cross, by Him to reconcile all things to Himself:

by Him, I say, whether they be things in earth or things in heaven."

.   .   .

Predestination to eternal life is wholly of God's free grace.

And, moreover, who will be so foolish and blasphemous as to say that God cannot change the evil wills of men, whichever, whenever, and wheresoever He chooses, and direct them to what is good? But when He does this, He does it of mercy; when He does it not, it is of justice that He does it not; for "He hath mercy on whom He will have mercy, and whom He will He hardeneth." And when the apostle said this, he was illustrating the grace of God, in connection with which he had just spoken of the twins in the womb of Rebecca, "who being not yet born, neither having done any good or evil, that the purpose of God according to election might stand, not of works, but of Him that calleth, it was said unto her, The elder shall serve the younger." And in reference to this matter he quotes another prophetic testimony: "Jacob have I loved, but Esau have I hated." But perceiving how what he had said might affect those who could not penetrate by their understanding the depth of this grace: "What shall we say then?" he says: "Is there unrighteousness with God? God forbid." For it seems unjust that, in the absence of any merit or demerit from good or evil works, God should love the one and hate the other. Now, if the apostle had wished us to understand that there were future good works of the one, and evil works of the other, which of course God foreknew, he would never have said, "not of works," but, "of future works," and in that way would have solved the difficulty, or rather there would then have been no difficulty to solve. As it is, however, after answering, "God forbid;" that is, God forbid that there should be unrighteousness with God; he goes on to prove that there is no unrighteousness in God's doing this, and says: "For He saith

to Moses, I will have mercy on whom I will have mercy, and I will have compassion on whom I will have compassion." Now, who but a fool would think that God was unrighteous, either in inflicting penal justice on those who had earned it, or in extending mercy to the unworthy? Then he draws his conclusion: "So then it is not of him that willeth, nor of him that runneth, but of God that showeth mercy." Thus both the twins were born children of wrath, not on account of any works of their own, but because they were bound in the fetters of that original condemnation which came through Adam. But He who said, "I will have mercy on whom I will have mercy," loved Jacob of His undeserved grace, and hated Esau of His deserved judgment. And as this judgment was due to both, the former learnt from the case of the latter that the fact of the same punishment not falling upon himself gave him no room to glory in any merit of his own, but only in the riches of the divine grace; because "it is not of him that willeth, nor of him that runneth, but of God that showeth mercy." And indeed the whole face, and, if I may use the expression, every lineament of the countenance of Scripture conveys by a very profound analogy this wholesome warning to every one who looks carefully into it, that he who glories should glory in the Lord.

As God's mercy is free, so His judgments are just, and cannot be gainsaid.

Now after commending the mercy of God, saying, "So it is not of him that willeth, nor of him that runneth, but of God that showeth mercy," that he might commend His Justice also (for the man who does not obtain mercy finds, not iniquity, but justice, there being no iniquity with God), he immediately adds: "For the scripture saith unto Pharaoh, Even for this same purpose have I raised thee up, that I might show my power in thee, and that my name might be declared throughout all the earth." And then he draws a conclusion that applies to both, that is, both to His mercy and His justice: "Therefore hath He mercy on whom He will have mercy, and whom He will He hardeneth." "He hath mercy" of His great goodness, "He hardeneth" without any injustice; so that neither can he that is pardoned glory in any merit of his own, nor he that is condemned complain of anything but his own demerit. For it is grace alone that separates the redeemed from the lost, all having been involved in one common perdition through their common origin. Now if any one, on hearing this, should say, "Why doth He yet find fault? for who hath resisted His will?" as if a man ought not to be blamed for being bad, because God hath mercy on whom He will have mercy, and whom He will He hardeneth, God forbid that we should be ashamed to answer as we see the apostle answered: "Nay, but, O man, who are thou that repliest against God? Shall the thing formed say to Him that formed it, Why hast Thou made me thus? Hath not the potter power over the clay, of the same lump to make one vessel unto honour, and another unto dishonour?" Now some foolish people think that in this place the apostle had no answer to give; and for want of a reason to render, rebuked the presumption of his interrogator. But there is great weight in this saying: "Nay, but, O man, who art thou?" and in such a matter as this it suggests to a man in a single word the limits of his capacity, and at the same time does in reality convey an important reason. For if a man does not understand these matters, who is he that he should reply against God? And if he does understand them, he finds no further room for reply. For then he perceives that the whole human race was condemned in its rebellious head by a divine judgment so just, that if not a single member of the race had been redeemed, no one could justly have questioned the justice of God; and that it was right that those who are redeemed should be redeemed in such a way as to show,

by the greater number who are unredeemed and left in their just condemnation, what the whole race deserved, and whither the deserved judgment of God would lead even the redeemed, did not His undeserved mercy interpose, so that every mouth might be stopped of those who wish to glory in their own merits, and that he that glorieth might glory in the Lord.

.   .   .

There is no ground in Scripture for the opinion of those who deny the eternity of future punishments.

It is in vain, then, that some, indeed very many, make moan over the eternal punishment, and perpetual, unintermitted torments of the lost, and say they do not believe it shall be so; not, indeed, that they directly oppose themselves to Holy Scripture, but, at the suggestion of their own feelings, they soften down everything that seems hard, and give a milder turn to statements which they think are rather designed to terrify than to be received as literally true. For "Hath God," they say, "forgotten to be gracious? hath He in anger shut up His tender mercies?" Now, they read this in one of the holy psalms. But without doubt we are to understand it as spoken of those who are elsewhere called "vessels of mercy," because even they are freed from misery not on account of any merit of their own, but solely through the pity of God. Or, if the men we speak of insist that this passage applies to all mankind, there is no reason why they should therefore suppose that there will be an end to the punishment of those of whom it is said, "These shall go away into everlasting punishment;" for this shall end in the same manner and at the same time as the happiness of those of whom it is said, "but the righteous unto life eternal." But let them suppose, if the thought gives them pleasure, that the pains of the damned are, at certain intervals, in some degree assuaged.

For even in this case the wrath of God, that is, their condemnation (for it is this, and not any disturbed feeling in the mind of God that is called His wrath), abideth upon them; that is, His wrath, though it still remains, does not shut up His tender mercies; though His tender mercies are exhibited, not in putting an end to their eternal punishment, but in mitigating, or in granting them a respite from, their torments; for the psalm does not say, "to put an end to His anger," or, "when His anger is passed by," but "in His anger." Now, if this anger stood alone, or if it existed in the smallest conceivable degree, yet to be lost out of the kingdom of God, to be an exile from the city of God, to be alienated from the life of God, to have no share in that great goodness which God hath laid up for them that fear Him, and hath wrought out for them that trust in Him, would be a punishment so great, that, supposing it to be eternal, no torments that we know of, continued through as many ages as man's imagination can conceive, could be compared with it.

The death of the wicked shall be eternal in the same sense as the life of the saints.

This perpetual death of the wicked, then, that is, their alienation from the life of God, shall abide for ever, and shall be common to them all, whatever men, prompted by their human affections, may conjecture as to a variety of punishments, or as to a mitigation or intermission of their woes; just as the eternal life of the saints shall abide for ever, and shall be common to them all, whatever grades of rank and honour there may be among those who shine with an harmonious effulgence.

St. Benedict

Monasticism, both as an idea and as a way of life, grew out of the fundamental Christian position that the perfect life on this earth was a life spent in preparing the soul for the life everlasting. To some men, a quiet life spent in meditation and in the contemplation of the glories of God and the depravities of man seemed most effective in achieving this most important of all conceivable goals. Persons imbued with the desire for solitude and for freedom from the distractions of this fleshly world either became solitary seekers or else gathered together into communities dedicated to the service of the spirit and the humiliation of the flesh. Within these communities—the monasteries and nunneries of the Middle Ages—variant practices grew up and conflicting ideas developed about the proper functions of the well-run monastery. Even more important, too many people were dedicating their life to God without understanding the difficulties and adjustments demanded by such a dedication. All these difficulties, particularly the last, tended to reduce the vitality of the monastic ideal—and, in this context, the perfect Christian ideal.

In the early sixth century, in an attempt to remedy this situation, a former Roman nobleman, Benedict of Nursia (*c.* 480-543), devised his famous rule of conduct for the monastery of Mount Cassino (which he had founded). Benedict set down the ways in which monks should behave and the manners they should cultivate. He made humility and obedience the cardinal virtues for the monk. In addition, Benedict recognized that taking the monastic vows was a serious matter, and he required that anyone who desired to join a regular religious community must serve a year's novitiate before taking the final, irrevocable vows.

Probably one of the reasons for the widespread acceptance of the Rule of Saint Benedict was its flexibility and reasonableness. Harshness, excesses of devotion, and absolute austerity found no place in Benedict's thought, but simplicity, dedication, and human well-being did.

THE RULE OF SAINT BENEDICT

Chapter 4

THE TOOLS OF GOOD WORKS

In the first place, to love the Lord God with all one's heart, all one's soul, and all one's strength.

Then, one's neighbour as oneself.

Then not to kill.

Not to commit adultery.

Not to steal.

Not to covet.

Not to bear false witness.

To honour all men.

Not to do to another what one would not have done to oneself.

To deny oneself, in order to follow Christ.

To chastise the body.

Not to seek soft living.

To love fasting.

To relieve the poor.

To clothe the naked.

To visit the sick.

To bury the dead.

To help the afflicted.

To console the sorrowing.

To avoid worldly conduct.

To prefer nothing to the love of Christ.

SAINT BENEDICT, *The Rule of Saint Benedict*, trans. Justin McCann (Westminster, Maryland: The Newman Press, 1952), pp. 27-49, 85-87, 115. Courtesy of The Newman Press.

Not to yield to anger.

Not to nurse a grudge.

Not to hold guile in one's heart.

Not to make a feigned peace.

Not to forsake charity.

Not to swear, lest perchance one forswear oneself.

To utter truth from heart and mouth.

Not to render evil for evil.

To do no wrong to anyone, and to bear patiently wrongs done to oneself.

To love one's enemies.

Not to render cursing for cursing, but rather blessing.

To bear persecution for justice' sake.

Not to be proud.

Not a wine-bibber.

Not a glutton.

Not somnolent.

Not slothful.

Not a grumbler.

Not a detractor.

To put one's hope in God.

To attribute to God, and not to self, whatever good one sees in oneself.

But to recognize always that the evil is one's own doing, and to impute it to oneself.

To fear the Day of Judgement.

To dread hell.

To desire eternal life with all spiritual longing.

To keep death daily before one's eyes.

To keep constant guard over the actions of one's life.

To know for certain that God sees one everywhere.

When evil thoughts come into one's heart, to dash them at once on the rock of Christ and to manifest them to one's spiritual father.

To keep one's mouth from evil and depraved talk.

Not to love much speaking.

Not to speak vain words or such as move to laughter.

Not to love much or violent laughter.

To listen gladly to holy reading.

To apply oneself frequently to prayer.

Daily in one's prayer, with tears and sighs, to confess one's past sins to God.

To amend those sins for the future.

Not to fulfil the desires of the flesh.

To hate one's own will.

To obey in all things the commands of the abbot, even though he himself (which God forbid) should act otherwise: remembering the Lord's precept: *What they say, do ye; but what they do, do ye not.*

Not to wish to be called holy before one is holy; but first to be holy, that one may more truly be called so.

To fulfil God's commandments daily in one's deeds.

To love chastity.

To hate no man.

Not to be jealous.

Not to give way to envy.

Not to love contention.

To shun vainglory.

To reverence the old.

To love the young.

To pray for one's enemies in the love of Christ.

To make peace with one's adversary before sundown.

And never to despair of God's mercy.

Behold these are the tools of the spiritual craft. If we employ them unceasingly day and night, and on the Day of Judgement render account of them, then we shall receive from the Lord in return that reward which he himself has promised: *Eye hath not seen nor ear heard, what God hath prepared for those that love him.* Now the workshop, wherein we shall diligently execute all these tasks, is the enclosure of the monastery and stability in the community.

Chapter 5

OF OBEDIENCE

The first degree of humility is obedience without delay. This becometh those who hold nothing dearer to them than Christ. Because of the holy service which they have professed, the fear of hell, and the glory of life everlasting, as soon as anything has been ordered by the superior, they receive it as a divine command and cannot suffer any delay in executing it. Of these doth the Lord say: *He hath listened to me and hath obeyed me.* And again he saith to teachers: *He who listens to you, listens to me.*

Such as these, therefore, immediately abandoning their own affairs and forsaking their own will, dropping the work they were engaged on and leaving it unfinished, with swift obedience follow up with their deeds the voice of him who commands them. And almost in the same moment of time that the master's order is issued, is the disciple's work completed, in the swiftness of the fear of the Lord; the two things being rapidly accomplished together by those who are impelled by the desire of attaining life everlasting. Therefore they choose the narrow way, according to the Lord's words: *Narrow is the way which leadeth unto life;* so that not living by their own will, and obeying their own desires and passions, but walking by another's judgement and orders, they dwell in monasteries, and desire to have an abbot over them. Assuredly such as these imitate that saying of the Lord wherein he saith: *I came not to do my own will, but the will of him who sent me.*

But this obedience itself will then be acceptable to God and pleasing to men, if what is commanded be not done timorously, or tardily, or tepidly, nor with murmuring or the raising of objections. For the obedience which is given to superiors is given to God, since he himself said: *He who listens to you, listens to me.* And disciples should give their obedience with a good will, because *God loveth a cheerful giver.* For if the disciple obey with an ill will, and murmur not only in words but even in his heart, then even though he fulfil the command, his work will not be acceptable to God, who sees that his heart is murmuring. For work such as this he will gain no reward; nay, rather, he will incur the punishment due to murmurers, unless he amend and make reparation.

Chapter 6

OF SILENCE

Let us do as saith the prophet: *I said, I will take heed unto my ways, that I offend not with my tongue. I have set a guard to my mouth. I was dumb and was humbled, and kept silence even from good words.* Here the prophet teaches us that if we should at times, for the love of silence, refrain from good talk, we should with more reason still, for fear of sin's punishment, eschew all evil talk. Therefore, on account of the great value of silence, let leave to speak be seldom granted to observant disciples, even though it be for good, holy, and edifying conversations; for it is written:

In much speaking thou shalt not escape sin, and elsewhere: *Death and life are in the power of the tongue.* For it becometh the master to speak and to teach; but it befits the disciple to be silent and to listen.

And therefore, if there be anything to be asked from the superior, let it be sought with all humility and respectful submission. But as for buffoonery and talk that is vain and stirs laughter, we condemn such things everywhere with a perpetual ban, and forbid the disciple to open his mouth for such conversation.

Chapter 7

OF HUMILITY

Holy Scripture crieth out to us, brethren, saying: *Everyone that exalteth himself shall be humbled, and he that humbleth himself shall be exalted.* When it so speaks, it teaches us that all exaltation is a kind of pride; which the prophet shows that he shunned in the words: *Lord, my heart is not exalted nor mine eyes lifted up; neither have I dwelt on high things, nor on marvels that are beyond my reach.* And why? *If I was not humbly minded but exalted my soul with pride; as a child that is weaned from his mother so wilt thou requite my soul.*

Wherefore, brethren, if we wish to attain to the summit of humility and desire to arrive speedily at that heavenly exaltation to which we ascend by the humility of the present life, then must we set up a ladder of our ascending actions like unto that which Jacob saw in his vision, whereon angels appeared to him, descending and ascending. By that descent and ascent we must surely understand nothing else than this, that we descend by self-exaltation and ascend by humility. And the ladder erected is our life in this world, which for the humble of heart is raised up by the Lord unto heaven. Now the sides of this ladder are our body and soul, into which sides our divine vocation has fitted various degrees of humility and discipline which we have to climb.

The first degree of humility, then, is that a man keep the fear of God before his eyes, altogether shunning forgetfulness. Let him ever remember all the commandments of God, and how hell will burn for their sins those that despise him; and let him constantly turn over in his heart the eternal life which is prepared for those that fear him. And guarding himself always from sins and vices, whether of thought, word, hand, foot, or self-will, and checking also the desires of the flesh, let him consider that God is always beholding him from heaven, that his actions are everywhere visible to the eye of the Godhead, and are constantly being reported to God by the angels. The prophet teaches us this when he represents God as always present in our thoughts: *God searcheth the heart and the reins;* and again: *The Lord knoweth the thoughts of men;* and again he saith: *Thou hast understood my thoughts from afar;* and: *The thought of man shall praise thee.* In order then that he may be careful regarding his wrongful thoughts, let the good brother say constantly in his heart: *Then shall I be spotless before him, if I shall have kept myself from my iniquity.*

We are, indeed, forbidden to do our own will by Scripture, which saith to us: *Turn away from thine own will.* Moreover, we ask God in prayer that his will be done in us.

And rightly are we taught not to do our own will, since we dread that sentence of Scripture: *There are ways which to men seem right, but the ends thereof lead to the depths of hell;* and since we fear also what is said of the careless: *They are corrupt and have become abominable in their pleasures.* And in regard to the desires of the flesh, let us believe that God is always present to us, since the prophet says to the Lord: *All my desire is before thee.*

We must be on our guard, then, against evil desires, for death lies close by the gate of delight; whence Scripture gives this command: *Go not after thy lusts.* So if *the eyes of the Lord behold the good and the evil,* and the Lord is ever *looking down from heaven upon the children of men, to see if there be one soul that reflects and seeks God;* and if our deeds are daily, day and night, reported to the Lord by the angels assigned to us: then, brethren, must we constantly beware, as the prophet says in the psalm, lest God some day behold us falling into evil ways and turned unprofitable, and spare us for this present time, because he is merciful and awaits our amendment, but should say to us in the future: *These things didst thou do, and I was silent.*

The second degree of humility is that a man love not his own will, nor delight in fulfilling his own desires, but carry out indeed the saying of the Lord: *I came not to do my own will, but the will of him who sent me.* It is written also: *Self-will hath its punishment, but necessity winneth a crown.*

The third degree of humility is that a man for the love of God subject himself to his superior in all obedience, imitating the Lord, of whom the apostle says: *He was made obedient even unto death.*

The fourth degree of humility is that, meeting in this obedience with difficulties and contradictions and even injustice, he should with a quiet mind hold fast to patience, and enduring neither tire nor run away; for the Scripture saith: *He that shall persevere to the end shall be saved;* and again: *Let thy heart take courage, and wait thou for the Lord.* And showing how the true disciple ought to endure all things, however contrary, for the Lord, it saith in the person of sufferers: *For thy sake we face death at every moment. We are reckoned no better than sheep marked down for slaughter.* Then, confident in their hope of the divine reward, they go on with joy to declare: *But in all these things we over-*

come, through him that hath loved us. And again in another place the Scripture saith: *Thou, O God, hast put us to the proof: thou hast tested us as men test silver in the fire. Thou hast led us into a snare: thou hast bowed our backs with trouble.* And to show that we ought to be under a superior, it goeth on to say: *Thou hast set men over our heads.* Moreover, in adversities and injuries they patiently fulfil the Lord's commands: when struck on one cheek they offer the other, when robbed of their tunic they surrender also their cloak, when forced to go a mile they go two, with the apostle Paul they bear with false brethren, and they bless those that curse them.

The fifth degree of humility is that he humbly confess and conceal not from his abbot any evil thoughts that enter his heart, and any secret sins that he has committed. To this does Scripture exhort us saying: *Make known thy way unto the Lord and hope in him.* And again: *Confess to the Lord, for he is good, and his mercy endureth for ever.* And further: *I have made known my sin to thee, and my faults I have not concealed. I said: I will be my own accuser and confess my faults to the Lord, and with that thou didst remit the guilt of my sin.*

The sixth degree of humility is that a monk be content with the meanest and worst of everything, and esteem himself, in regard to the work that is given him, as a bad and unworthy workman, saying to himself with the prophet: *I am brought to nothing; I am all ignorance; I am become as a dumb beast before thee; yet am I ever close to thee.*

The seventh degree of humility is that he should not only in his speech declare himself lower and of less account than all others, but should in his own inmost heart believe it, humbling himself and saying with the prophet: *But I am a worm and no man, a byword to all men and the laughing-stock of the people. I have been lifted up only to be humbled and confounded;* and again: *It is good for me that thou hast humbled me, that I may learn thy commandments.*

The eighth degree of humility is that a monk do nothing except what is commended by the common rule of the monastery and the example of his superiors.

The ninth degree of humility is that a monk restrain his tongue and keep silence, not speaking until he is questioned. For Scripture showeth that *in much talking thou canst not avoid sin;* and that *the talkative man shall not prosper on the earth.*

The tenth degree of humility is that he be not ready and prompt to laughter, for it is written: *The fool lifteth up his voice in laughter.*

The eleventh degree of humility is that a monk, when he speaks, do so gently and without laughter, humbly and seriously, in few and sensible words, and without clamour. It is written: *A wise man is known by the fewness of his words.*

The twelfth degree of humility is that a monk should not only be humble of heart, but should also in his behaviour always manifest his humility to those who look upon him. That is to say, that whether he is at the Work of God, in the oratory, in the monastery, in the garden, on the road, in the fields, or anywhere else, and whether sitting, walking, or standing, he should always have his head bowed and his eyes downcast, pondering always the guilt of his sins, and considering that he is about to be brought before the dread judgement seat of God. Let him constantly say in his heart what was said with downcast eyes by the publican in the Gospel: *Lord, I a sinner am not worthy to raise mine eyes to heaven;* and again with the prophet: *I am bowed down and humbled on every side.*

Then, when all these degrees of humility have been climbed, the monk will presently come to that perfect love of God which casts out all fear; whereby he will begin to observe without labour, as though naturally and by habit, all those precepts which formerly he did not observe without fear; no longer for fear of hell, but for love of Christ and through good habit and delight in virtue. And this will the Lord deign to show forth by the power of his Spirit in his workman now cleansed from vice and from sin.

.   .   .

Chapter 33

WHETHER MONKS SHOULD HAVE ANYTHING OF THEIR OWN

This vice especially ought to be utterly rooted out of the monastery. Let no one presume to give or receive anything without the abbot's leave, or to have anything as his own, anything whatever, whether book or tablets or pen or whatever it may be; for monks should not have even their bodies and wills at their disposal. But let them look to the father of the monastery for all that they require, and let it be unlawful to have anything which the abbot has not given or allowed. And, as the Scripture saith, *let all things be common to all, nor let anyone say that anything is his own* or claim it for himself. But if anyone shall be found to indulge in this most wicked vice, let him be admonished once and a second time; if he do not amend, let him undergo punishment.

.   .   .

Chapter 49

OF THE OBSERVANCE OF LENT

The life of a monk ought at all times to be lenten in its character; but since few have the strength for that, we therefore urge that in these days of Lent the brethren should lead lives of great purity, and should also in this sacred season expiate the negligences of other times. This will be worthily done if we refrain from all sin and apply ourselves to prayer with tears, to reading, to compunction of heart, and to abstinence. In these days, therefore, let us add something beyond the wonted measure of our service, such as private prayers and abstinence in food and drink. Let each one, over and above the measure prescribed for him, offer God something of his own free will in the joy of the Holy Spirit. That is to say, let him stint himself of food, drink, sleep, talk, and jesting, and look forward with the joy of spiritual longing to the holy feast of Easter. Let each one, however, tell his abbot what he is offering, and let it be done with his consent and blessing; because what is done without the permission of the spiritual father shall be ascribed to presumption and vainglory and not reckoned meritorious. Everything, therefore, is to be done with the approval of the abbot.

Einhard

Rarely can we complain that a biography is too short, that it tantalizes the reader without satisfying his desire to learn more. But this complaint is valid in the case of Einhard's *Life of the Emperor Charles*. This brief work, which is one of our major sources of information about ninth-century Europe and about Charlemagne and his court, is reproduced here in its entirety.

Einhard (who is occasionally called Eginhard) was remarkably well qualified for the task he set himself. Born of a wealthy landholding family in 770 in the eastern part of Charlemagne's territories, he was destined for a career in the Church. At an early age he received his formal education at the monastery of Fulda (in central Germany), which had been heavily endowed by his family, and about 790 he became a member of the court of Charlemagne. Thus began the long association between the emperor and the monk.

Charlemagne loved his circle of intimates—a circle composed of many of the most highly educated and stimulating minds of the times, including the English theologian and teacher, Alcuin of York. It was Einhard's presence in this company that enabled him to observe Charlemagne at short range and to develop the first-hand knowledge of his subject that gives the biography its authenticity. Einhard survived Charlemagne by about twenty-nine years, occupying himself with church-building, acquiring holy relics, taking part in public affairs, and writing. The death of his wife and the political disintegration that set in after Charlemagne's death led Einhard finally to withdraw from public life. He died in 844.

LIFE OF THE EMPEROR CHARLES

PREFACE

Since I have taken upon myself to narrate the public and private life, and no small part of the deeds of my lord and foster-father, the most excellent and most justly renowned King Charles, I have condensed the matter into as brief a form as possible. I have been careful not to omit any facts that could come to my knowledge, but at the same time not to offend by a prolix style those minds that despise everything modern, if one can possibly avoid offending by a new work men who seem to despise also the masterpieces of antiquity, the works of most learned and luminous writers. Very many of them, I have no doubt, are men devoted to a life of literary leisure, who feel that the affairs of the present generation ought not to be passed by, and who do not consider everything done to-day as unworthy of mention and deserving to be given over to silence and oblivion, but are nevertheless seduced by lust of immortality to celebrate the glorious deeds of other times by some sort of composition rather than to deprive posterity of the mention of their own names by not writing at all.

Be this as it may, I see no reason why I should refrain from entering upon a task of this kind, since no man can write with more accuracy than I of events that took place about me, and of facts concerning which I had personal knowledge, ocular demonstration, as the saying goes, and I have no means of ascertaining whether or not any one else has the subject in hand.

In any event, I would rather commit my story to writing, and hand it down to posterity in partnership with others, so to speak, than to suffer the most glorious life of this most excellent king, the greatest of all the princes of his day, and his illustrious deeds, hard for men of later times to imitate, to be wrapt in the darkness of oblivion.

But there are still other reasons, neither

EINHARD, *Life of Charlemagne*, trans. S. E. Turner (New York, 1880).

unwarrantable nor insufficient, in my opinion, that urge me to write on this subject, namely, the care that King Charles bestowed upon me in my childhood, and my constant friendship with himself and his children after I began to take up my abode at court. In this way he strongly endeared me to himself, and made me greatly his debtor as well in death as in life; so that were I unmindful of the benefits conferred upon me to keep silence concerning the most glorious and illustrious deeds of a man who claims so much at my hands, and suffer his life to lack due eulogy and written memorial, as if he had never lived, I should deservedly appear ungrateful, and be so considered, albeit my powers are feeble, scanty, next to nothing indeed, and not at all adapted to write and set forth a life that would tax the eloquence of a Tully.

I submit the book. It contains the history of a very great and distinguished man; but there is nothing in it to wonder at besides his deeds, except the fact that I, who am a barbarian, and very little versed in the Roman language, seem to suppose myself capable of writing gracefully and respectably in Latin, and to carry my presumption so far as to disdain the sentiment that Cicero is said in the first book of the "Tusculan Disputations" to have expressed when speaking of the Latin authors. His words are: "It is an outrageous abuse both of time and literature for a man to commit his thoughts to writing without having the ability either to arrange them or elucidate them, or attract readers by some charm of style." This dictum of the famous orator might have deterred me from writing if I had not made up my mind that it was better to risk the opinions of the world, and put my little talents for composition to the test, than to slight the memory of so great a man for the sake of sparing myself.

I. The Merovingian family, from which the Franks used to choose their kings, is commonly said to have lasted until the time of Childeric, who was deposed, shaved, and thrust into the cloister by command of the Roman Pontiff Stephen. But although, to all outward appearance, it ended with him, it had long since been devoid of vital strength and conspicuous only from bearing the empty epithet Royal; the real power and authority in the kingdom lay in the hands of the chief officer of the court, the so-called Mayor of the Palace, and he was at the head of affairs. There was nothing left the King to do but to be content with his name of King, his flowing hair, and long beard; to sit on his throne and play the ruler; to give ear to the ambassadors that came from all quarters, and to dismiss them, as if on his own responsibility, in words that were, in fact, suggested to him, or even imposed upon him. He had nothing that he could call his own beyond this vain title of King, and the precarious support allowed by the Mayor of the Palace in his discretion, except a single country-seat, that brought him but a very small income. There was a dwelling-house upon this, and a small number of servants attached to it, sufficient to perform the necessary offices. When he had to go abroad, he used to ride in a cart, drawn by a yoke of oxen, driven, peasant-fashion by a ploughman; he rode in this way to the palace and to the general assembly of the people, that met once a year for the welfare of the kingdom, and he returned home in like manner. The Mayor of the Palace took charge of the government, and of everything that had to be planned or executed at home or abroad.

II. At the time of Childeric's deposition, Pepin, the father of King Charles, held this office of Mayor of the Palace, one might almost say, by hereditary right; for Pepin's father, Charles, had received it at the hands of his father, Pepin, and filled it with distinction. It was this Charles that crushed the tyrants who claimed to rule the whole Frank land as their own, and that utterly routed the Saracens, when they attempted the conquest of Gaul, in two great battles—one in Aquitania, near the town of Poitiers, and the other on the River Berre, near Narbonne—and compelled them to return to Spain. This honour was usually conferred by the people only upon men eminent from their illustrious birth and ample wealth. For some years, ostensibly under King Childeric, Pepin, the father of King Charles, shared the duties inherited from his father and grandfather most amicably with his brother, Carloman. The latter, then, for reasons unknown, renounced the heavy cares of an earthly crown and retired to Rome. Here he exchanged his worldly garb for a cowl, and built a monastery on Mt. Oreste, near the Church of St. Sylvester, where he enjoyed for several years the seclusion that he desired, in company with certain others who had the same object in view. But so many distinguished Franks made the pilgrimage to Rome to fulfil their vows, and insisted upon paying their respects to him, as their former lord, on the way, that the repose which he so much loved was broken by these frequent visits, and he was driven to change his abode. Accordingly, when he found that his plans were frustrated by his many visitors, he abandoned the mountain, and withdrew to the Monastery of St. Benedict, on Monte Cassino, in the province of Samnium, and passed the rest of his days there in the exercises of religion.

III. Pepin, however, was raised, by decree of the Roman Pontiff, from the rank of Mayor of the Palace to that of King, and ruled alone over the Franks for fifteen years or more. He died of dropsy, in Paris, at the close of the Aquitanian war, which he had waged with William, Duke of Aquitania, for nine successive years, and left two sons, Charles and Carloman, upon whom, by the grace of God, the succession devolved.

The Franks, in a general assembly of the people, made them both kings, on condition that they should divide the whole kingdom equally between them, Charles to take and rule the part that had belonged to their fa-

ther, Pepin, and Carloman the part which their uncle, Carloman, had governed. The conditions were accepted, and each entered into possession of the share of the kingdom that fell to him by this arrangement; but peace was only maintained between them with the greatest difficulty, because many of Carloman's party kept trying to disturb their good understanding, and there were some even who plotted to involve them in a war with each other. The event, however, showed the danger to have been rather imaginary than real, for at Carloman's death his widow fled to Italy with her sons and her principal adherents, and without reason, despite her husband's brother, put herself and her children under the protection of Desiderius, King of the Lombards. Carolman had succumbed to disease after ruling two years in common with his brother, and at his death Charles was unanimously elected King of the Franks.

IV. It would be folly, I think, to write a word concerning Charles's birth and infancy, or even his boyhood, for nothing has ever been written on the subject, and there is no one alive now who can give information of it. Accordingly, I have determined to pass that by as unknown, and to proceed at once to treat of his character, his deeds, and such other facts of his life as are worth telling and setting forth, and shall first give an account of his deeds at home and abroad, then of his character and pursuits, and lastly of his administration and death, omitting nothing worth knowing or necessary to know.

V. His first undertaking in a military way was the Aquitanian war, begun by his father, but not brought to a close; and because he thought that it could be readily carried through, he took it up while his brother was yet alive, calling upon him to render aid. The campaign once opened, he conducted it with the greatest vigour, notwithstanding his brother withheld the assistance that he had promised, and did not desist or shrink from his self-imposed task until, by his patience and firmness, he had completely gained his ends. He compelled Hunold, who had attempted to seize Aquitania after Warifar's death, and renew the war then almost concluded, to abandon Aquitania and flee to Gascony. Even here he gave him no rest, but crossed the River Garonne, built the Castle of Fronsac, and sent ambassadors to Lupus, Duke of Gascony, to demand the surrender of the fugitive, threatening to take him by force unless he were promptly given up to him. Thereupon Lupus chose the wiser course, and not only gave Hunold up, but submitted himself, with the province which he ruled, to the King.

VI. After bringing this war to an end and settling matters in Aquitania (his associate in authority had meantime departed this life), he was induced, by the prayers and entreaties of Hadrian, Bishop of the city of Rome, to wage war on the Lombards. His father before him had undertaken this task at the request of Pope Stephen, but under great difficulties; for certain leading Franks, of whom he usually took counsel, had so vehemently opposed his design as to declare openly that they would leave the King and go home. Nevertheless, the war against the Lombard king, Astolf, had been taken up and very quickly concluded. Now, although Charles seems to have had similar, or rather just the same grounds for declaring war that his father had, the war itself differed from the preceding one alike in its difficulties and its issue. Pepin, to be sure, after besieging King Astolf a few days in Pavia, had compelled him to give hostages, to restore to the Romans the cities and castles that he had taken, and to make oath that he would not attempt to seize them again: but Charles did not cease, after declaring war, until he had exhausted King Desiderius by a long siege, and forced him to surrender at discretion; driven his son Adalgis, the last hope of the Lombards, not only from his kingdom, but from all Italy; restored to the Romans all that they had lost; subdued Hurodgaus,

Duke of Friuli, who was plotting revolution; reduced all Italy to his power, and set his son Pepin as king over it.

At this point I should describe Charles's difficult passage over the Alps into Italy, and the hardships that the Franks endured in climbing the trackless mountain-ridges, the heaven-aspiring cliffs and ragged peaks, if it were not my purpose in this work to record the manner of his life rather than the incidents of the wars that he waged. Suffice it to say that this war ended with the subjection of Italy, the banishment of King Desiderius for life, the expulsion of his son Adalgis from Italy, and the restoration of the conquests of the Lombard kings to Hadrian, the head of the Roman Church.

VII. At the conclusion of this struggle, the Saxon war, that seems to have been only laid aside for the time, was taken up again. No war ever undertaken by the Frank nation was carried on with such persistence and bitterness, or cost so much labour, because the Saxons, like almost all the tribes of Germany, were a fierce people, given to the worship of devils, and hostile to our religion, and did not consider it dishonourable to transgress and violate all law, human and divine. Then there were peculiar circumstances that tended to cause a breach of peace every day. Except in a few places, where large forests or mountain-ridges intervened and made the bounds certain, the line between ourselves and the Saxons passed almost in its whole extent through an open country, so that there was no end to the murders, thefts, and arsons on both sides. In this way the Franks became so embittered that they at last resolved to make reprisals no longer, but to come to open war with the Saxons. Accordingly war was begun against them, and was waged for thirty-three successive years with great fury; more, however, to the disadvantage of the Saxons than of the Franks. It could doubtless have been brought to an end sooner, had it not been for the faithlessness of the Saxons. It is hard to say how often they were conquered, and, humbly submitting to the King, promised to do what was enjoined upon them, gave without hesitation the required hostages, and received the officers sent them from the King. They were sometimes so much weakened and reduced that they promised to renounce the worship of devils, and to adopt Christianity; but they were no less ready to violate these terms than prompt to accept them, so that it is impossible to tell which came easier to them to do; scarcely a year passed from the beginning of the war without such changes on their part. But the King did not suffer his high purpose and steadfastness—firm alike in good and evil fortune—to be wearied by any fickleness on their part, or to be turned from the task that he had undertaken; on the contrary, he never allowed their faithless behaviour to go unpunished, but either took the field against them in person, or sent his counts with an army to wreak vengeance and exact righteous satisfaction. At last, after conquering and subduing all who had offered resistance, he took ten thousand of those that lived on the banks of the Elbe, and settled them, with their wives and children, in many different bodies here and there in Gaul and Germany. The war that had lasted so many years was at length ended by their acceding to the terms offered by the King; which were renunciation of their national religious customs and the worship of devils, acceptance of the sacraments of the Christian faith and religion, and union with the Franks to form one people.

VIII. Charles himself fought but two pitched battles in this war, although it was long protracted—one on Mount Osning, at the place called Detmold, and again on the bank of the river Hase, both in the space of little more than a month. The enemy were so routed and overthrown in these two battles that they never afterwards ventured to take the offensive or to resist the attacks of the King, unless they were protected by a strong position. A great many of the Frank as well as of the Saxon nobility, men occupying the highest posts of honour, perished in this war, which only came to an end after the lapse of thirty-two years. So many and grievous were the wars that were declared against the Franks in the meantime, and skilfully conducted by the King, that one may reasonably question whether his fortitude or his good fortune is to be more admired. The Saxon war began two years before the Italian war; but although it went on without interruption, business elsewhere was not neglected, nor was there any shrinking from other equally arduous contests. The King, who excelled all the princes of his time in wisdom and greatness of soul, did not suffer difficulty to deter him or danger to daunt him from anything that had to be taken up or carried through, for he had trained himself to bear and endure whatever came, without yielding in adversity, or trusting to the deceitful favours of fortune in prosperity.

IX. In the midst of this vigorous and almost uninterrupted struggle with the Saxons, he covered the frontier by garrisons at the proper points, and marched over the Pyrenees into Spain at the head of all the forces that he could muster. All the towns and castles that he attacked surrendered, and up to the time of his homeward march he sustained no loss whatever; but on his return through the Pyrenees he had cause to rue the treachery of the Gascons. That region is well adapted for ambuscades by reason of the thick forests that cover it; and as the army was advancing in the long line of march necessitated by the narrowness of the road, the Gascons, who lay in ambush on the top of a very high mountain, attacked the rear of the baggage-train and the rear-guard in charge of it, and hurled them down to the very bottom of the valley. In the struggle that ensued, they cut them off to a man; they then plundered the baggage, and dispersed with all speed in every direction under cover of approaching night. The lightness of their armour and the nature of the battleground stood the Gascons in good stead on this occasion, whereas the Franks fought at a disadvantage in every respect, because of the weight of their armour and the unevenness of the ground. Eggihard, the King's steward; Anselm, Count Palatine; and Roland, Governor of the March of Brittany, with very many others, fell in this engagement. This ill turn could not be avenged for the nonce, because the enemy scattered so widely after carrying out their plan that not the least clew could be had to their whereabouts.

X. Charles also subdued the Bretons, who live on the sea-coast, in the extreme western part of Gaul. When they refused to obey him, he sent an army against them, and compelled them to give hostages, and to promise to do his bidding. He afterwards entered Italy in person with his army, and passed through Rome to Capua, a city in Campania, where he pitched his camp and threatened the Beneventans with hostilities unless they should submit themselves to him. Their duke, Aragis, escaped the danger by sending his two sons, Rumold and Grimold, with a great sum of money to meet the King, begging him to accept them as hostages, and promising for himself and his people compliance with all the King's commands, on the single condition that his personal attendance should not be required. The King took the welfare of the people into account rather than the stubborn disposition of the Duke, accepted the proffered hostages, and released him from the obligation to appear before him in consideration of his handsome gift. He retained the younger son only as hostage, and sent the elder back to his father, and returned to Rome, leaving commissioners with Aragis to exact the oath of allegiance, and administer it to the Beneventans. He stayed in Rome several days in order to pay his devotions at the holy places, and then came back to Gaul.

XI. At this time, on a sudden, the Bavarian war broke out, but came to a speedy end.

It was due to the arrogance and folly of Duke Tassilo. His wife, a daughter of King Desiderius, was desirous of avenging her father's banishment through the agency of her husband, and accordingly induced him to make a treaty with the Huns, the neighbours of the Bavarians on the east, and not only to leave the King's commands unfulfilled, but to challenge him to war. Charles's high spirit could not brook Tassilo's insubordination, for it seemed to him to pass all bounds; accordingly he straightway summoned his troops from all sides for a campaign against Bavaria, and appeared in person with a great army on the river Lech, which forms the boundary between the Bavarians and the Alemanni. After pitching his camp upon its banks, he determined to put the Duke's disposition to the test by an embassy before entering the province. Tassilo did not think that it was for his own or his people's good to persist, so he surrendered himself to the King, gave the hostages demanded, among them his own son Theodo, and promised by oath not to give ear to any one who should attempt to turn him from his allegiance; so this war, which bade fair to be very grievous, came very quickly to an end. Tassilo, however, was afterwards summoned to the King's presence, and not suffered to depart, and the government of the province that he had had in charge was no longer intrusted to a duke, but to counts.

XII. After these uprisings had been thus quelled, war was declared against the Slaves who are commonly known among us as Wilzi, but properly, that is to say in their own tongue, are called Welatabians. The Saxons served in this campaign as auxiliaries among the tribes that followed the King's standard at his summons, but their obedience lacked sincerity and devotion. War was declared because the Slaves kept harassing the Abodrite, old allies of the Franks, by continual raids, in spite of all commands to the contrary. A gulf of unknown length, but nowhere more than a hundred miles wide, and in many parts narrower, stretches off towards the east from the Western Ocean. Many tribes have settlements on its shores; and Danes and Swedes, whom we call Northmen, on the northern shore and all the adjacent islands; but the southern shore is inhabited by the Slaves and Aisti, and various other tribes. The Welatabians, against whom the King now made war, were the chief of these; but in a single campaign, which he conducted in person, he so crushed and subdued them that they did not think it advisable thereafter to refuse obedience to his commands.

XIII. The war against the Avars, or Huns, followed, and, except the Saxon war, was the greatest that he waged; he took it up with more spirit than any of his other wars, and made far greater preparations for it. He conducted one campaign in person in Pannonia, of which the Huns then had possession. He intrusted all subsequent operations to his son, Pepin, and the governors of the provinces, to counts even, and lieutenants. Although they most vigorously prosecuted the war, it only came to a conclusion after a seven years' struggle. The utter depopulation of Pannonia, and the site of the Khan's palace, now a desert, where not a trace of human habitation is visible, bear witness how many battles were fought in those years, and how much blood was shed. The entire body of the Hun nobility perished in this contest, and all its glory with it. All the money and treasure that had been years amassing was seized, and no war in which the Franks ever engaged within the memory of man brought them such riches and such booty. Up to that time the Huns had passed for a poor people, but so much gold and silver was found in the Khan's palace, and so much valuable spoil taken in battle, that one may well think that the Franks took justly from the Huns what the Huns had formerly taken unjustly from other nations. Only two of the chief men of the Franks fell in this war—Eric, Duke of Friuli, who was killed in Tarsatch, a town on the coast of Liburnia, by the treachery of the inhabitants; and Gerold, Governor of Bavaria, who met his death in Pannonia, slain, with two men that were accompanying him, by an unknown hand while he was marshalling his forces for battle against the Huns, and riding up and down the line encouraging his men. This war was otherwise almost a bloodless one so far as the Franks were concerned, and ended most satisfactorily, although by reason of its magnitude it was long protracted.

XIV. The Saxon war next came to an end as successful as the struggle had been long. The Bohemian and Linonian wars that next broke out could not last long; both were quickly carried through under the leadership of the younger Charles. The last of these wars was the one declared against the Northmen called Danes. They began their career as pirates, but afterwards took to laying waste the coasts of Gaul and Germany with their large fleet. Their King, Godfred, was so puffed with vain aspirations that he counted on gaining empire over all Germany, and looked upon Saxony and Frisia as his provinces. He had already subdued his neighbours the Abodriti, and made them tributary, and boasted that he would shortly appear with a great army before Aix-la-Chapelle, where the King held his court. Some faith was put in his words, empty as they sound, and it is supposed that he would have attempted something of the sort if he had not been prevented by a premature death. He was murdered by one of his own bodyguard, and so ended at once his life and the war that he had begun.

XV. Such are the wars, most skilfully planned and successfully fought, which this most powerful king waged during the forty-seven years of his reign. He so largely increased the Frank kingdom, which was already great and strong when he received it at his father's hands, that more than double its former territory was added to it. The authority of the Franks was formerly confined to that part of Gaul included between the Rhine and the Loire, the Ocean and the Balearic Sea; to that part of Germany which is inhabited by the so-called Eastern Franks, and is bounded by Saxony and the Danube, the Rhine and the Saale—this stream separates the Thuringians from the Sorabians; and to the country of the Alemanni and Bavarians. By the wars above mentioned he first made tributary Aquitania, Gascony, and the whole of the region of the Pyrenees as far as the River Ebro, which rises in the land of the Navarrese, flows through the most fertile districts of Spain, and empties into the Balearic Sea, beneath the walls of the city of Tortosa. He next reduced and made tributary all Italy from Aosta to Lower Calabria, where the boundary-line runs between the Beneventans and the Greeks, a territory more than a thousand miles long; then Saxony, which constitutes no small part of Germany, and is reckoned to be twice as wide as the country inhabited by the Franks, while about equal to it in length; in addition, both Pannonias, Dacia beyond the Danube, and Istria, Liburnia, and Dalmatia, except the cities on the coast, which he left to the Greek Emperor for friendship's sake, and because of the treaty that he had made with him. In fine, he vanquished and made tributary all the wild and barbarous tribes dwelling in Germany between the Rhine and the Vistula, the Ocean and the Danube, all of which speak very much the same language, but differ widely from one another in customs and dress. The chief among them are the Welatabians, the Sorabians, the Abodriti, and the Bohemians, and he had to make war upon these; but the rest, by far the larger number, submitted to him of their own accord.

XVI. He added to the glory of his reign by gaining the good-will of several kings and nations; so close, indeed, was the alliance that he contracted with Alphonso, King of Galicia and Asturias, that the latter, when sending letters or ambassadors to Charles, invariably styled himself his man. His munificence won the kings of the Scots also to pay such deference to his wishes that they never gave him any other title than lord, or themselves than subjects and slaves: there are letters from them extant in which these feelings in this regard are expressed. His relations with Aaron, King of the Persians, who ruled over almost the whole of the East, India excepted, were so friendly that this prince preferred his favour to that of all the kings and potentates of the earth, and considered that to him alone marks of honour and munificence were due. Accordingly, when the ambassadors sent by Charles to visit the most holy sepulchre and place of resurrection of our Lord and Saviour presented themselves before him with gifts, and made known their master's wishes, he not only granted what was asked, but gave possession of that holy and blessed spot. When they returned, he despatched his ambassadors with them, and sent magnificent gifts, besides stuffs, perfumes, and other rich products of the Eastern lands. A few years before this, Charles had asked him for an elephant, and he sent the only one that he had. The Emperors of Constantinople, Nicephorus, Michael, and Leo, made advances to Charles, and sought friendship and alliance with him by several embassies; and even when the Greeks suspected him of designing to wrest the empire from them, because of his assumption of the title of Emperor, they made a close alliance with him, that he might have no cause of offence. In fact, the power of the Franks was always viewed by the Greeks and Romans with a jealous eye, whence the Greek proverb "Have the Frank for your friend, but not for your neighbor."

XVII. This King, who showed himself so great in extending his empire and subduing foreign nations, and was constantly occupied with plans to that end, undertook also very many works calculated to adorn and benefit his kingdom, and brought several of them to completion. Among these, the most deserving of mention are the basilica of the Holy Mother of God at Aix-la-Chapelle, built in the most admirable manner, and a bridge over the Rhine at Mayence, half a mile long, the breadth of the river at this point. The bridge was destroyed by fire the year before Charles died, but, owing to his death so soon after, could not be repaired, although he had intended to rebuild it in stone. He began two places of beautiful workmanship—one near his manor called Ingelheim, not far from Mayence; the other at Nimeguen, on the Waal, the stream that washes the south side of the island of the Batavians. But, above all, sacred edifices were the object of his care throughout his whole kingdom; and whenever he found them falling to ruin from age, he commanded the priests and fathers who had charge of them to repair them, and made sure by commissioners that his instructions were obeyed. He also fitted out a fleet for the war with the Northmen; the vessels required for this purpose were built on the rivers that flow from Gaul and Germany into the Northern Ocean. Moreover, since the Northmen continually overran and laid waste the Gallic and German coasts, he caused watch and ward to be kept in all the harbours, and at the mouths of rivers large enough to admit the entrance of vessels, to prevent the enemy from disembarking; and in the South, in Narbonensis and Septimania, and along the whole coast of Italy as far as Rome, he took the same precautions against the Moors, who had recently begun their piratical practices. Hence, Italy suffered no great harm in his time at the hands of the Moors, nor Gaul and Germany from the Northmen, save that the Moors got possession of the Etruscan town of Civita Vecchia by treachery, and sacked it, and the Northmen harried some of the islands in Frisia off the German Coast.

XVIII. Thus did Charles defend and increase as well as beautify his kingdom, as is well known; and here let me express my admiration of his great qualities and his extraordinary constancy alike in good and evil fortune. I will now forthwith proceed to give the details of his private and family life.

After his father's death, while sharing the kingdom with his brother, he bore his unfriendliness and jealousy most patiently, and, to the wonder of all, could not be provoked to be angry with him. Later he married a daughter of Desiderius, King of the Lombards, at the instance of his mother; but he repudiated her at the end of a year for some reason unknown, and married Hildegard, a woman of high birth, of Suabian origin. He had three sons by her—Charles, Pepin, and Lewis—and as many daughters—Hruodrud, Bertha, and Gisela. He had three other daughters besides these—Theoderada, Hiltrud, and Ruodhaid—two by his third wife, Fastrada, a woman of East Frankish (that is to say, of German) origin, and the third by a concubine, whose name for the moment escapes me. At the death of Fastrada, he married Liutgard, an Alemannic woman, who bore him no children. After her death he had three concubines—Gersuinda, a Saxon, by whom he had Adaltrud; Regina, who was the mother of Drogo and Hugh; and Ethelind, by whom he had Theodoric. Charles's mother, Berthrada, passed her old age with him in great honour; he entertained the greatest veneration for her; and there was never any disagreement between them except when he divorced the daughter of King Desiderius, whom he had married to please her. She died soon after Hildegard, after living to see three grandsons and as many granddaughters in her son's house, and he buried her with great pomp in the Basilica of St. Denis, where his father lay. He had an only sister, Gisela, who had consecrated herself to a religious life from girlhood, and he cherished as much affection for her as for his mother. She also died a few years before him in the nunnery where she had passed her life.

XIX. The plan that he adopted for his children's education was, first of all, to have both boys and girls instructed in the liberal arts, to which he also turned his own attention. As soon as their years admitted, in accordance with the custom of the Franks, the boys had to learn horsemanship, and to practise war and the chase, and the girls to familiarize themselves with cloth-making, and to handle distaff and spindle, that they might not grow indolent through idleness, and he fostered in them every virtuous sentiment. He only lost three of all his children before his death, two sons and one daughter, Charles, who was the eldest, Pepin, whom he had made King of Italy, and Hruodrud, his oldest daughter, whom he had betrothed to Constantine, Emperor of the Greeks. Pepin left one son, named Bernard, and five daughters, Adelaide, Atula, Guntrada, Berthaid, and Theoderada. The King gave a striking proof of his fatherly affection at the time of Pepin's death: he appointed the grandson to succeed Pepin, and had the granddaughters brought up with his own daughters. When his sons and his daughter died, he was not so calm as might have been expected from his remarkably strong mind, for his affections were no less strong, and moved him to tears. Again, when he was told of the death of Hadrian, the Roman Pontiff, whom he had loved most of all his friends, he wept as much as if he had lost a brother, or a very dear son. He was by nature most ready to contract friendships, and not only made friends easily, but clung to them persistently, and cherished most fondly those with whom he had formed such ties. He was so careful of the training of his sons and daughters that he never took his meals without them when he was at home, and never made a journey without them; his sons would ride at his side, and his daughters follow him, while a number of his body-guard, detailed for their protection, brought up the rear. Strange to say, although they were very handsome women, and he loved them very dearly, he was never willing to marry any of them to a man of

their own nation or to a foreigner, but kept them all at home until his death, saying that he could not dispense with their society. Hence, though otherwise happy, he experienced the malignity of fortune as far as they were concerned; yet he concealed his knowledge of the rumours current in regard to them, and of the suspicions entertained of their honour.

XX. By one of his concubines he had a son, handsome in face, but hunchbacked, named Pepin, whom I omitted to mention in the list of his children. When Charles was at war with the Huns, and was wintering in Bavaria, this Pepin shammed sickness, and plotted against his father in company with some of the leading Franks, who seduced him with vain promises of the royal authority. When his deceit was discovered, and the conspirators were punished, his head was shaved, and he was suffered, in accordance with his wishes, to devote himself to a religious life in the monastery of Prum. A formidable conspiracy against Charles had previously been set on foot in Germany, but all the traitors were banished, some of them without mutilation, others after their eyes had been put out. Three of them only lost their lives; they drew their swords and resisted arrest, and, after killing several men, were cut down, because they could not be otherwise overpowered. It is supposed that the cruelty of Queen Fastrada was the primary cause of these plots, and they were both due to Charles's apparent acquiescence in his wife's cruel conduct, and deviation from the usual kindness and gentleness of his disposition. All the rest of his life he was regarded by every one with the utmost love and affection, so much so that not the least accusation of unjust rigour was ever made against him.

XXI. He liked foreigners, and was at great pains to take them under his protection. There were often so many of them, both in the palace and the kingdom, that they might reasonably have been considered a nuisance; but he, with his broad humanity, was very little disturbed by such annoyances, because he felt himself compensated for these great inconveniences by the praises of his generosity and the reward of high renown.

XXII. Charles was large and strong, and of lofty stature, though not disproportionately tall (his height is well known to have been seven times the length of his foot); the upper part of his head was round, his eyes very large and animated, nose a little long, hair fair, and face laughing and merry. Thus his appearance was always stately and dignified, whether he was standing or sitting; although his neck was thick and somewhat short, and his belly rather prominent; but the symmetry of the rest of his body concealed these defects. His gait was firm, his whole carriage manly, and his voice clear, but not so strong as his size led one to expect. His health was excellent, except during the four years preceding his death, when he was subject to frequent fevers; at the last he even limped a little with one foot. Even in those years he consulted rather his own inclinations than the advice of physicians, who were almost hateful to him, because they wanted him to give up roasts, to which he was accustomed, and to eat boiled meat instead. In accordance with the national custom, he took frequent exercise on horseback and in the chase, accomplishments in which scarcely any people in the world can equal the Franks. He enjoyed the exhalations from natural warm springs, and often practised swimming, in which he was such an adept that none could surpass him; and hence it was that he built his palace at Aix-la-Chapelle, and lived there constantly during his latter years until his death. He used not only to invite his sons to his bath, but his nobles and friends, and now and then a troop of his retinue or bodyguard, so that a hundred or more persons sometimes bathed with him.

XXIII. He used to wear the national, that is to say, the Frank, dress—next his skin a linen shirt and linen breeches, and above these a tunic fringed with silk; while hose fastened by bands covered his lower limbs, and shoes his feet, and he protected his shoulders and chest in winter by a closefitting coat of otter or marten skins. Over all he flung a blue cloak, and he always had a sword girt about him, usually one with a gold or silver hilt and belt; he sometimes carried a jewelled sword, but only on great feast-days or at the reception of ambassadors from foreign nations. He despised foreign costumes, however handsome, and never allowed himself to be robed in them, except twice in Rome, when he donned the Roman tunic, chlamys, and shoes; the first time at the request of Pope Hadrian, the second to gratify Leo, Hadrian's successor. On great feast-days he made use of embroidered clothes, and shoes bedecked with precious stones; his cloak was fastened by a golden buckle, and he appeared crowned with a diadem of gold and gems, but on other days his dress varied little from the common dress of the people.

XXIV. Charles was temperate in eating, and particularly so in drinking, for he abominated drunkenness in anybody, much more in himself and those of his household; but he could not easily abstain from food, and often complained that fasts injured his health. He very rarely gave entertainments, only on great feast-days, and then to large numbers of people. His meals ordinarily consisted of four courses, not counting the roast, which his huntsmen used to bring in on the spit; he was more fond of this than of any other dish. While at table, he listened to reading or music. The subjects of the readings were the stories and deeds of olden time: he was fond, too, of St. Augustine's books, and especially of the one entitled "The City of God." He was so moderate in the use of wine and all sorts of drink that he rarely allowed himself more than three cups in the course of a meal. In summer, after the midday meal, he would eat some fruit, drain a single cup, put off his clothes and shoes, just as he did for the night, and rest for two or three hours. He was in the habit of awaking and rising from bed four or five times during the night. While he was dressing and putting on his shoes, he not only gave audience to his friends, but if the Count of the Palace told him of any suit in which his judgment was necessary, he had the parties brought before him forthwith, took cognizance of the case, and gave his decision, just as if he were sitting on the judgment-seat. This was not the only business that he transacted at this time, but he performed any duty of the day whatever, whether he had to attend to the matter himself, or to give commands concerning it to his officers.

XXV. Charles had the gift of ready and fluent speech, and could express whatever he had to say with the utmost clearness. He was not satisfied with command of his native language merely, but gave attention to the study of foreign ones, and in particular was such a master of Latin that he could speak it as well as his native tongue; but he could understand Greek better than he could speak it. He was so eloquent, indeed, that he might have passed for a teacher of eloquence. He most zealously cultivated the liberal arts, held those who taught them in great esteem, and conferred great honours upon them. He took lessons in grammar of the deacon Peter of Pisa, at that time an aged man. Another deacon, Albin of Britain, surnamed Alcuin, a man of Saxon extraction, who was the greatest scholar of the day, was his teacher in other branches of learning. The King spent much time and labour with him studying rhetoric, dialectics, and especially astronomy; he learned to reckon, and used to investigate the motions of the heavenly bodies most curiously, with an intelligent scrutiny. He also tried to write, and used to keep tablets and blanks in bed under his pillow, that at lei-

sure hours he might accustom his hand to form the letters; however, as he did not begin his efforts in due season, but late in life, they met with ill success.

XXVI. He cherished with the greatest fervour and devotion the principles of the Christian religion, which had been instilled into him from infancy. Hence it was that he built the beautiful basilica at Aix-la-Chapelle, which he adorned with gold and silver and lamps, and with rails and doors of solid brass. He had the columns and marbles for this structure brought from Rome and Ravenna, for he could not find such as were suitable elsewhere. He was a constant worshipper at this church as long as his health permitted, going morning and evening, even after nightfall, besides attending mass; and he took care that all the services there conducted should be administered with the utmost possible propriety, very often warning the sextons not to let any improper or unclean thing be brought into the building, or remain in it. He provided it with a great number of sacred vessels of gold and silver, and with such a quantity of clerical robes that not even the doorkeepers, who fill the humblest office in the church, were obliged to wear their every-day clothes when in the exercise of their duties. He was at great pains to improve the church reading and psalmody, for he was well skilled in both, although he neither read in public nor sang, except in a low tone and with others.

XXVII. He was very forward in succouring the poor, and in that gratuitous generosity which the Greeks call alms, so much so that he not only made a point of giving in his own country and his own kingdom, but when he discovered that there were Christians living in poverty in Syria, Egypt, and Africa, at Jerusalem, Alexandria, and Carthage, he had compassion on their wants, and used to send money over the seas to them. The reason that he zealously strove to make friends with the kings beyond seas was that he might get help and relief to the Christians living under their rule. He cherished the Church of St. Peter the Apostle at Rome above all other holy and sacred places, and heaped its treasury with a vast wealth of gold, silver, and precious stones. He sent great and countless gifts to the popes; and throughout his whole reign the wish that he had nearest at heart was to re-establish the ancient authority of the city of Rome under his care and by his influence, and to defend and protect the Church of St. Peter, and to beautify and enrich it out of his own store above all other churches. Although he held it in such veneration, he only repaired to Rome to pay his vows and make his supplications four times during the whole forty-seven years that he reigned.

XXVIII. When he made his last journey thither, he had also other ends in view. The Romans had inflicted many injuries upon the Pontiff Leo, tearing out his eyes and cutting out his tongue, so that he had been compelled to call upon the King for help. Charles accordingly went to Rome, to set in order the affairs of the Church, which were in great confusion, and passed the whole winter there. It was then that he received the titles of Emperor and Augustus, to which he at first had such an aversion that he declared that he would not have set foot in the Church the day that they were conferred, although it was a great feast-day, if he could have forseen the design of the Pope. He bore very patiently with the jealousy which the Roman emperors showed upon his assuming these titles, for they took this step very ill; and by dint of frequent embassies and letters, in which he addressed them as brothers, he made their haughtiness yield to his magnanimity, a quality in which he was unquestionably much their superior.

XXIX. It was after he had received the imperial name that, finding the laws of his people very defective (the Franks have two sets of laws, very different in many particulars), he determined to add what was wanting, to reconcile the discrepancies, and to correct what was vicious and wrongly cited in them. However, he went no further in this matter than to supplement the laws by a few capitularies, and those imperfect ones; but he caused the unwritten laws of all the tribes that came under his rule to be compiled and reduced to writing. He also had the old rude songs that celebrate the deeds and wars of the ancient kings written out for transmission to posterity. He began a grammar of his native language. He gave the months names in his own tongue, in place of the Latin and barbarous names by which they were formerly known among the Franks. He likewise designated the winds by twelve appropriate names; there were hardly more than four distinctive ones in use before. He called January Wintarmanoth; February, Hornung; March, Lentzinmanoth; April, Ostarmanoth; May, Winnemanoth; June, Brachmanoth; July, Heuvimanoth; August, Aranmanoth; September, Wituman-oth; October, Windumemanoth; November, Herbistmanoth; December, Heilagman-oth. He styled the winds as follows: Subsolanus, Ostroniwint; Eurus, Ostsundroni; Duroauster, Sundostroni; Auster, Sundroni; Austro-Africus, Sundwestroni; Africus, Westsundroni; Zephyrus, Westroni; Caurus, Westnordroni; Circius, Nordwestroni; Septentrio, Nordroni; Aquilo, Nordostroni; Vulturnus, Ostnordroni.

XXX. Towards the close of his life, when he was broken by ill-health and old age, he summoned Lewis, King of Aquitania, his only surviving son by Hildegard, and gathered together all the chief men of the whole kingdom of the Franks in a solemn assembly. He appointed Lewis, with their unanimous consent, to rule with himself over the whole kingdom, and constituted him heir to the imperial name; then, placing the diadem upon his son's head, he bade him be proclaimed Emperor and Augustus. This step was hailed by all present with great favour, for it really seemed as if God had prompted him to it for the kingdom's good; it increased the King's dignity, and struck no little terror into foreign nations. After sending his son back to Aquitania, although weak from age he set out to hunt, as usual, near his palace at Aix-la-Chapelle, and passed the rest of the autumn in the chase, returning thither about the first of November. While wintering there, he was seized, in the month of January, with a high fever, and took to his bed. As soon as he was taken sick, he prescribed for himself abstinence from food, as he always used to do in case of fever, thinking that the disease could be driven off, or at least mitigated, by fasting. Besides the fever, he suffered from a pain in the side, which the Greeks call pleurisy; but he still persisted in fasting, and in keeping up his strength only by draughts taken at very long intervals. He died January twenty-eighth, the seventh day from the time that he took to his bed, at nine o'clock in the morning, after partaking of the holy communion, in the 72nd year of his age and the 47th of his reign.

XXXI. His body was washed and cared for in the usual manner, and was then carried to the church, and interred amid the greatest lamentations of all the people. There was some question at first where to lay him, because in his lifetime he had given no directions as to his burial; but at length all agreed that he could nowhere be more honourably entombed than in the very basilica that he had built in the town at his own expense, for love of God and our Lord Jesus Christ, and in honour of the Holy and Eternal Virgin, His Mother. He was buried there the same day that he died, and a gilded arch was erected above his tomb with his image and an inscription. The words of the inscription were as follows: "In this tomb lies the body of Charles, the Great and Orthodox Emperor, who gloriously extended the kingdom of the Franks, and reigned prosperously for forty-seven years. He died

at the age of seventy, in the year of our Lord 814, the 7th Indiction, on the 28th day of January."

XXXII. Very many omens had portended his approaching end, a fact that he had recognized as well as others. Eclipses both of the sun and moon were very frequent during the last three years of his life, and a black spot was visible on the sun for the space of seven days. The gallery between the basilica and the palace, which he had built at great pains and labour, fell in sudden ruin to the ground on the day of the Ascension of our Lord. The wooden bridge over the Rhine at Mayence, which he had caused to be constructed with admirable skill, at the cost of ten years' hard work, so that it seemed as if it might last forever, was so completely consumed in three hours by an accidental fire that not a single splinter of it was left, except what was under water. Moreover, one day in his last campaign into Saxony against Godfred, King of the Danes, Charles himself saw a ball of fire fall suddenly from the heavens with a great light, just as he was leaving camp before sunrise to set out on the march. It rushed across the clear sky from right to left, and everybody was wondering what was the meaning of the sign, when the horse which he was riding gave a sudden plunge, head foremost, and fell, and threw him to the ground so heavily that his cloak-buckle was broken and his sword-belt shattered; and after his servants had hastened to him and relieved him of his arms, he could not rise without their assistance. He happened to have a javelin in his hand when he was thrown, and this was struck from his grasp with such force that it was found lying at a distance of twenty feet or more from the spot. Again, the palace at Aix-la-Chapelle frequently trembled, the roofs of whatever buildings he tarried in kept up a continual crackling noise, the basilica in which he was afterwards buried was struck by lightning, and the gilded ball that adorned the pinnacle of the roof was shattered by the thunder-bolt and hurled upon the bishop's house adjoining. In this same basilica, on the margin of the cornice that ran around the interior, between the upper and lower tiers of arches, a legend was inscribed in red letters, stating who was the builder of the temple, the last words of which were *Karolus Princeps*. The year that he died it was remarked by some, a few months before his decease, that the letters of the word *Princeps* were so effaced as to be no longer decipherable. But Charles despised, or affected to despise, all these omens, as having no reference whatever to him.

XXXIII. It had been his intention to make a will, that he might give some share in the inheritance to his daughters and the children of his concubines; but it was begun too late and could not be finished. Three years before his death, however, he made a division of his treasures, money, clothes, and other movable goods in the presence of his friends and servants, and called them to witness it, that their voices might insure the ratification of the disposition thus made. He had a summary drawn up of his wishes regarding this distribution of his property, the terms and text of which are as follows:

"In the name of the Lord God, the Almighty Father, Son, and Holy Ghost. This is the inventory and division dictated by the most glorious and most pious Lord Charles, Emperor Augustus, in the 811th year of the Incarnation of our Lord Jesus Christ, in the 43rd year of his reign in France and 37th in Italy, the 11th of his empire, and the 4th Indiction, which considerations of piety and prudence have determined him, and the favour of God enabled him, to make of his treasures and money ascertained this day to be in his treasure-chamber. In this division he is especially desirous to provide not only that the largess of alms which Christians usually make of their possessions shall be made for himself in due course and order

out of his wealth, but also that his heirs shall be free from all doubt, and know clearly what belongs to them, and be able to share their property by suitable partition without litigation or strife. With this intention and to this end he has first divided all his substance and movable goods ascertained to be in his treasure-chamber on the day aforesaid in gold, silver, precious stones, and royal ornaments into three lots, and has subdivided and set off two of the said lots into twenty-one parts, keeping the third entire. The first two lots have been thus subdivided into twenty-one parts because there are in his kingdom twenty-one recognized metropolitan cities, and in order that each archbishopric may receive by way of alms, at the hands of his heirs and friends, one of the said parts, and that the archbishop who shall then administer its affairs shall take the part given to it, and share the same with his suffragans in such manner that one third shall go to the Church, and the remaining two thirds be divided among the suffragans. The twenty-one parts into which the first two lots are to be distributed, according to the number of recognized metropolitan cities, have been set apart one from another, and each has been put aside by itself in a box labelled with the name of the city for which it is destined. The names of the cities to which this alms or largess is to be sent are as follows: Rome, Ravenna, Milan, Friuli, Grado, Cologne, Mayence, Salzburg, Treves, Sens, Besancon, Lyons, Rouen, Rheims, Arles, Vienne, Moutiers-en-Tarantaise, Embrun, Bordeaux, Tours, and Bourges. The third lot, which he wishes to be kept entire, is to be bestowed as follows: While the first two lots are to be divided into the parts aforesaid, and set aside under seal, the third lot shall be employed for the owner's daily needs, as property which he shall be under no obligation to part with in order to the fulfilment of any vow, and this as long as he shall be in the flesh, or consider it necessary for his use. But upon his death, or voluntary renunciation of the affairs of this world, this said lot shall be divided into four parts, and one thereof shall be added to the afore-said twenty-one parts; the second shall be assigned to his sons and daughters, and to the sons and daughters of his sons, to be distributed among them in just and equal partition; the third, in accordance with the custom common among Christians, shall be devoted to the poor; and the fourth shall go to the support of the men-servants and maid-servants on duty in the palace. It is his wish that to this said third lot of the whole amount, which consists, as well as the rest, of gold and silver, shall be added all the vessels and utensils of brass, iron, and other metals, together with the arms, clothing, and other movable goods, costly and cheap, adapted to divers uses, as hangings, coverlets, carpets, woolen stuffs, leathern articles, pack-saddles, and whatsoever shall be found in his treasure-chamber and wardrobe at that time, in order that thus the parts of the said lot may be augmented, and the alms distributed reach more persons. He ordains that his chapel—that is to say, its church property, as well that which he has provided and collected as that which came to him by inheritance from his father—shall remain entire, and not be dissevered by any partition whatever. If, however, any vessels, books, or other articles be found therein which are certainly known not to have been given by him to the said chapel, whoever wants them shall have them on paying their value at a fair estimation. He likewise commands that the books which he has collected in his library in great numbers shall be sold for fair prices to such as want them, and the money received therefrom given to the poor. It is well known that among his other property and treasures are three silver tables, and one very large and massive golden one. He directs and commands that the square silver table, upon which there is a representation of the city of Constantinople, shall be sent to the Basilica of St. Peter the Apostle at Rome, with the other gifts destined therefor; that the round one, adorned with a delineation of the city of Rome, shall be given to the Episcopal Church at Ravenna; that the third, which far surpasses the other two in weight and in beauty of workmanship, and is made in three circles, showing the plan of the whole universe, drawn with skill and delicacy, shall go, together with the golden table, fourthly above mentioned, to increase that lot which is to be devoted to his heirs and to alms.

This deed, and the dispositions thereof, he has made and appointed in the presence of the bishops, abbots, and counts able to be present, whose names are hereto subscribed: Bishops—Hildebald, Ricolf, Arno, Wolfar, Bernoin, Laidrad, John, Theodulf, Jesse, Heito, Waltgaud. Abbots—Fredugis, Adalung, Angilbert, Irmino. Counts—Walacho, Meginher, Otulf, Stephen, Unruoch, Burchard, Meginhard, Hatto, Rihwin, Edo, Ercangar, Gerold, Bero, Hildiger, Rocculf."

Charles's son Lewis, who by the grace of God succeeded him, after examining this summary, took pains to fulfil all its conditions most religiously as soon as possible after his father's death.

Manorialism

The preceding selections have given us some idea of the life of the clerics and the nobles during the Middle Ages. But we can have no genuine understanding of a society without knowing something about the ways in which the vast majority of the people made their living and about the obligations they had toward the political groups that dominated them. For example, our understanding of the ancient world would be vastly enriched if we had reliable accounts of the slave society of Athens or the small landholders of Sparta, or if we knew more of the causes of the Spartacus revolt under the Roman Republic, or if we had detailed information on the organization of the *latifundia* in the days of the Empire. Happily, our information about the daily life of everyman during the Middle Ages is somewhat more abundant, though still far from plentiful.

Generally, the social and economic historian gleans his facts from hundreds of wills, deeds, transaction records, court cases, and the like. And from these minuscule and fragmentary records he draws his generalizations. But we must remember that the people who lived during the Middle Ages were not quantitatively and economically oriented, as we in the modern world are. Consequently, we dare not put too much faith in their recorded statistics—the medieval chronicler might, for example, refer to an army of 60,000 men, but the modern historian would be unwise to accept this figure at face value. Chances are the chronicler picked the number at random to dramatize the notion of a "very large" army. Moreover, general statements and observations on economic matters during the Middle Ages are quite rare, reflecting perhaps a lack of interest in that realm of human activity.

The two documents presented here describe the duties, obligations, and rights of the tillers of the soil. The first, *The Rights and Ranks of People*, is an Anglo-Saxon account dating probably from the early eleventh century. The second, *Surveys of Certain Manors Belonging to the Abbey of Peterborough*, is an Anglo-Norman document of the early twelfth century. These two accounts give us a reasonably accurate picture of the social, economic, political, and religious status of the common working people in medieval society.

RIGHTS AND RANKS OF PEOPLE

Thegn's Law. The law of the thegn is that he be entitled to his book-right,[1] and

RIGHTS AND RANKS OF PEOPLE, trans. S. I. Tucker, in *English Historical Documents 1042-1189*, eds. D. C. Douglas and G. W. Greenaway (London: Eyre & Spottiswoode, 1953), pp. 813-816. Courtesy of Miss S. I. Tucker and Oxford University Press, Inc. The footnotes are the translator's.

[1] Land protected by charter.

that he shall contribute three things in respect of his land: armed service, and the repairing of fortresses and work on bridges.[2] Also in respect of many estates, further service arises on the king's order such as service connected with the deer fence at the king's residence, and equipping a guard

[2] The ancient *trinoda necessitas*.

ship, and guarding the coast, and guarding the lord, and military watch, almsgiving and church dues and many other various things.

Geneat's Right.[3]   Geneat-right is various according to what is fixed in respect of the estate: in some he must pay rent and contribute a pasturage swine a year, ride and perform carrying service and furnish means of carriage, work and entertain his lord, reap and mow, cut deer hedges and keep up places from which deer may be shot, build and fence the lord's house, bring strangers to the village, pay church dues and alms money, act as guard to his lord, take care of the horses, and carry messages far and near wheresoever he is directed.

Cottar's-Right.[4]   The cottar's right is according to the custom of the estate: in some he must work for his lord each Monday throughout the year, or 3 days each week at harvest-time. . . . He does not make land payment.[5] He should have 5 acres: more if it be the custom on the estate; and it is too little if it ever be less; because his work must be frequent. Let him give his hearth-penny[6] on Ascension Day even as each freeman ought to do. Let him also perform services on his lord's demesne-land[7] if he is ordered, by keeping watch on the sea-coast and working at the king's deer fence and such things according to his condition. Let him pay his church dues at Martinmas.

Boor's-Right.   The boor's[8] duties are various, in some places heavy and in others light. On some estates the custom is that he must perform week-work for 2 days in each week of the year[9] as he is directed, and 3 days from the Feast of the Purification to Easter. If he perform carrying service he need not work while his horse is out. At Michaelmas he must pay 10 pence for *gafol*,[10] and at Martinmas 23 sesters of barley, and 2 hens, and at Easter a young sheep or 2 pence. And he must lie from Martinmas to Easter at his lord's fold as often as it falls to his lot; and from the time when ploughing is first done until Martinmas he must each week plough 1 acre, and himself present the seed in the lord's barn. Also [he must plough] 3 acres as boon-work,[11] and 2 for pasturage. If he needs more grass, let him earn it as he may be permitted. Let him plough 3 acres as his tribute land[12] and sow it from his own barn, and pay his hearth-penny.[13] And every pair of boors must maintain 1 hunting dog, and each boor must give 6 loaves to the herdsman of the lord's swine when he drives his herd to the mast-pasture. On the same land to which the customs apply a farmer ought to be given for his occupation of the land 2 oxen, 1 cow, 6 sheep and 7 acres sown on his rood of land. After[14] that year let him perform all the dues that fall to him, and let him be given tools for his work and utensils for his house. When death befalls him let the lord take charge of what he leaves.

[3] *Geneat:* the original meaning of the word is courtier or companion. By the middle of the eleventh century some kind of service was implied. *Geneat* is translated in the Latin version as *Villanus*, but his position does not correspond with that occupied by the typical villein of later surveys. Here he appears as primarily a riding servant, acting perhaps as a bailiff on a large estate. He was a man of some standing. His agricultural work is limited and is confined to boon-works at harvest-time, etc.

[4] The cottar's holding of approximately 5 acres was to be characteristic of the later manorial economy. Sometimes these men were later described as *lundinarii*, "Monday-men."

[5] *landgafol.*

[6] Peter's Pence.

[7] "Inland."

[8] *Gebur.* Compare his service with those of the later villein.

[9] One of the chief characteristics of villein tenure: so many days' work each week for the benefit of the lord.

[10] Perhaps "rent" or "tribute" would be a suitable translation.

[11] Special services at special times of the year.

[12] Probably the lord's land scattered in the strips of the open fields to be cultivated by the peasantry for the lord's benefit.

[13] By contrast to the above a characteristic of freedom.

[14] Or "during."

The estate-law is fixed on each estate: at some places, as I have said, it is heavier, at some places, also, lighter, because not all customs about estates are alike. On some estates a boor must pay tribute in honey, on some in food, on some in ale. Let him who has the shire[15] always know what are the ancient arrangements about the estate and what is the custom of the district.

About the bee-keeper. A bee-keeper if he hold a swarm which is subject to payment must pay what is appointed on that estate. Amongst us it is appointed that he should give 5 sesters of honey as tax: in some estates a greater tax is due. Also at certain times he must be ready for many sorts of work at his lord's pleasure besides boon-work and the cutting of corn when ordered and the mowing of meadows. And if he will be provided with land he must be provided with a horse so as to give it to supply his lord with a beast of burden or to go with his horse himself, whichever he is directed. And many things must a man of such condition do: I cannot recount them all now. When death befalls him let his lord take charge of what he leaves unless there should be anything free.

A swine-herd at pay[16] ought to pay for his animals that are to be slaughtered according to the amount fixed on the estate. On many estates it is fixed that he pay every year 15 swine for killing, 10 old and 5 young. Let him have himself whatever he raises beyond that. On many estates a more severe due is incumbent on the swine-herd. Let each swine-herd take care that after the slaughter of his swine he prepare them properly and singe them: then he will be well entitled to the perquisites. Also he must be—as I said before about the bee-keeper— always ready for every sort of work, and provided with a horse at the lord's need.

A slave swine-herd and a slave bee-keeper after death are liable to one and the same law.

A herdsman slave belonging to his lord who keeps the demesne herd ought to have a young pig kept in a sty, and his perquisites when he has prepared the bacon, and also the dues that belong to a slave.

About men's provisioning. Every slave ought to have as provisions 12 pounds of good corn and 2 carcasses of sheep and 1 good cow for food [17] and the right of cutting wood according to the custom of the estate.

About women's provisioning. For a female slave 8 pounds of corn for food, 1 sheep or 3 pence for winter food, 1 sester of beans for lenten food, whey in summer or 1 penny.

All slaves belonging to the estate ought to have food at Christmas and Easter, a strip of land for ploughing and a "harvest-handful" besides their dues.

About retainers. A retainer[18] ought to have the use of 2 acres, 1 sown and 1 not sown. Let him sow the latter himself. And he is entitled to his food and shoes and gloves.

About the sower. A sower ought to have a seedlip full of every kind of seed when he has properly sown every seed throughout the space of a year.

About the ox-herd. The ox-herd must pasture 2 oxen or more with the lord's herd on the common pasture with the cognizance of the overseer. Let him earn thereby shoes and gloves for himself. And his cow for food must go with the lord's oxen.

About the cow-herd. A cow-herd ought to have an old cow's milk for a week after she has newly calved, and the beestings of a young cow for a fortnight. His cow for food is to go with the lord's cow [?oxen].

About the shepherd. A shepherd's due is

---

[15] Possibly the sheriff, but not necessarily so. The steward of a great lord might be so described.

[16] *gafolswane.*

[17] Note that it is only the food of the slave that is indicated. His obligations are probably regarded as unlimited subject only to the custom of the estate.

[18] Clearly a privileged person on the estate.

that he should have 12 nights' dung at Christmas, and 1 lamb from the year's young ones, 1 bell-wether's fleece, and the milk of his flock for a week after the equinox, and a bowl-full of whey or buttermilk all summer.

About the goat-herd.   A goat-herd ought to have the milk of his herd after Martinmas, and before that his portion of whey, and 1 kid a year old, if he looks after his herd properly.

About the cheese-maker.   100 cheeses pertain to the cheese-maker, and it behoves her to make butter for the lord's table out of the whey pressed out from the cheese; and let her have all the buttermilk except the shepherd's portion.[19]

About the keeper of the granary.   The granary-keeper ought to have the corn spilt at the barn door at harvest-time if his overseer grant it to him, and if he deserves it.

About the beadle.   The beadle ought to be more free from work because of his office, since he is bound to be always ready. Also he ought to have some bit of land for his labour.

About the woodward.   Every tree blown down by the wind ought to go to the woodward.

It[20] is proper that the hayward should be rewarded for his labour in those parts which lie near the pasture; because if he has neglected his work he can expect . . . (if) he has been granted such a piece of land it must be nearest the pasture by custom; because, if out of laziness he neglects his lord's land his own will not be protected if it is provided in this way. If he makes properly secure what he has to guard he will be well entitled to his reward.

The customs of estates are various, as I have said before. Nor do we apply these regulations we have described to all districts. But we declare what the custom is where it is known to us. If we learn better, we will eagerly delight in what we learn and maintain it according to the custom of the district in which we then live.

Wherefore one must delight among the people to learn laws if one does not oneself wish to lose honor on the estate.

There are many common rights: in some districts are due winter provisions, Easter provisions, a harvest feast for reaping the corn, a drinking feast for ploughing, reward for haymaking, food for making the rick, at wood-carrying a log from each load, at corn-carrying food on completion of the rick, and many things which I cannot recount.

This, however, is a memorandum of people's provisions. And all these I have enumerated before.

---

[19] This entry presents certain difficulties. The process of butter-making here described seems impossible. The cheese-maker is definitely a woman.

[20] This entry is defective and obscure. The meaning seems to be that the land of the hayward should be so situated as to suffer first from straying beasts if he has neglected his duties.

SURVEYS OF CERTAIN MANORS BELONGING TO THE ABBEY OF PETERBOROUGH (1125-1128)

This is the description of the manors of the abbey of Peterborough as Walter the archdeacon received them and possessed them in the hand of the king.

In Kettering are 10 hides[1] for the king's geld. And of these 10 hides 40 villeins hold 40 virgates.[1] And these men plough in the spring from each virgate 4 acres for the work of the lord. And besides this they provide ploughs for the work of the lord four times in the winter, and three times in the spring and once in the summer. And these men have 22 ploughs with which they work. And all these men work for the lord 3 days in each week. And besides this they render each year from each virgate by custom 2 shillings and 3 halfpence. And all the men render 50 hens and 640 eggs. And besides this, Ailric holds 13 acres with 2 acres of meadow, and pays for them 16 pence. And there is a mill with a miller and it pays 20 shillings. And 8 cottars each of whom has 5 acres and they work (for the lord) 1 day each week, and twice a year they make malt. And each one of them gives 1 penny for a he-goat (if he has one) and 1 halfpenny for a nanny-goat. And there is a shepherd and a swine-herd who holds 8 acres. And in the court of the demesne there are 4 ploughs with 32 oxen, and 12 cows with 10 calves, 2 beasts for food, 3 draught horses, 300 sheep, 50 pigs, and 16 shillings' worth of the surplus hay from the meadow. The church of Kettering belongs to the altar of the abbey of Peterborough. And for the love of St.

SURVEYS OF CERTAIN MANORS BELONGING TO THE ABBEY OF PETERBOROUGH, in *English Historical Documents 1042-1189*, eds. D. C. Douglas and G. W. Greenaway (London: Eyre & Spottiswoode, 1953), pp. 829-830. Courtesy of Eyre & Spottiswoode (Publishers) Ltd. and Oxford University Press, Inc.

[1] [*A measure of land. Ed.*]

Peter it renders 4 rams and 2 cows or 5 shillings. . . .

In Pilsgate there are 3 hides for the king's geld. And 3 villeins hold 1 hide and 1 virgate. And these have 2 ploughs with which they plough for the lord 8 acres for the winter sowing and 8 acres for the spring sowing; and they work 3 days each week for the lord. And there is 1 bordar and 2 ox-herds holding land by service. And there is 1 shepherd. And there are 44 sokemen. And all these together with the villeins pay 44 shillings a year. And all these sokemen have 8 ploughs and with them they plough for the lord three times a year. And each one of them reaps in August half an acre of the lord's corn, and they give boonwork twice in August. And each one harrows 1 day in spring. And there is a mill which pays 4 shillings. And in the court of the demesne there is 1 plough with 8 oxen, and 1 boar and 2 calves and 1 horse for harrowing and 2 foals. And 180 sheep and 20 pigs. On the Feast of St. Peter [is paid] 6 sheep or 1 cow and 5 ells of cloth.

In Thorpe Achurch are 2 hides and 1 virgate for the king's geld. And there are 12 full villeins and each one of them holds 11 acres and works (for the lord) 3 days each week. And 6 half-villeins who perform the same in proportion to their holdings. And all of these make a customary payment of 10 shillings. And besides this they pay for love of St. Peter 5 'multones,' and 10 ells of cloth, and 10 baskets and 200 loaves. And all these men plough 16½ acres for the lord's work. And there are 6 bordars who pay 7 shillings. And all these pay each year 22 skepfuls of oats in return for dead wood and 22 loaves and 64 hens and 160 eggs. And one sokeman is there who performs service with a horse. And William, son of Ansered, holds a fourth part of 3 yardlands by knight-service. And William, son of Odard the cook, holds a fourth part of 3 yardlands by service in the abbot's kitchen. And the men of this William perform work for the court, that is to say, they provide their ploughs for the lord twice a year. And on the land of this William there are 4 full villeins who reap half an acre in August. And Godric holds a fourth part of 3 yardlands, and for that he and his horse do the abbot's service, providing their own food. And this Godric has 3 villeins and each one of them reaps half an acre for the abbot in August, and with their ploughs they perform two boon-works. In the court of the demesne there are 2 ploughs with 16 oxen, and 3 cows and 8 beasts for food and 1 draught horse and 8 pigs.

In Collingham there are 4 carucates and 1 bovate less a fifth part of 1 bovate for the king's geld. And there are 20 villeins who hold 1½ carucates. Each one of these works for the lord throughout the year 1 day in each week. And in August he performs 3 boon-works. And all these men bring 60 cartloads of wood to the lord's court, and they also dig and provide 20 cartloads of turves, or 20 cartloads of thatch. And they must harrow throughout the winter. And each year they pay 4 pounds of rent. And there are 50 sokemen who hold 2½ carucates of land. And each one of these must work by custom each year for 6 days at the deer hedge. And in August each shall work 3 days. And all these have 14 ploughs and with them they shall work for the lord four times in Lent. And they plough 48 acres, and harrow, and reap in August. And the aforesaid sokemen pay 12 pounds each year. And in the court of the demesne are 2 ploughs with 16 oxen, and 4 cows and calves and 1 beast for food and 160 sheep and 12 pigs. . . .

Aucassin and Nicolete

We do not know who wrote the song-story, *Aucassin and Nicolete,* nor can we date it accurately. A single copy has survived from the thirteenth century, and some scholars believe that it may have been composed a hundred years earlier. Actually, these matters are of little importance, except to the specialist. Whether twelfth or thirteenth century can remain forever a mystery so long as the tale itself survives.

Aucassin and Nicolete is a romance, typical of the romances told and sung by the wandering troubadours of the Middle Ages. It is not, however, the love story of two adolescents, for Aucassin is too much the fearless and skillful knight in armor, and Nicolete is no mewling, love-sick princess. Both are mature and capable people who know their own emotions and desires and who seek to satisfy them. When Nicolete's lover is imprisoned, she competently undertakes to free him; and when Aucassin is forced to fight, he bravely rushes into combat.

The story is reproduced here in its entirety.

THE SONG-STORY OF AUCASSIN AND NICOLETE

'TIS OF AUCASSIN AND NICOLETE

> Who would list to the good lay
> Gladness of the captive grey?
> 'Tis how two young lovers met,
> Aucassin and Nicolete,
> Of the pains the lover bore
> And the sorrows he outwore,
> For the goodness and the grace,
> Of his love, so fair of face.
>
> Sweet the song, the story sweet,
> There is no man hearkens it,
> No man living 'neath the sun,
> So outwearied, so foredone,
> Sick and woful, worn and sad,
> But is healed, but is glad
>   'Tis so sweet.

SO SAY THEY, SPEAK THEY, TELL THEY
THE TALE:

How the Count Bougars de Valence made war on Count Garin de Biaucaire, war so great, and so marvellous, and so mortal that never a day dawned but alway he was there, by the gates and walls, and barriers of the town with a hundred knights, and ten thousand men at arms, horsemen and footmen: so burned he the Count's land, and spoiled his country, and slew his men. Now the Count Garin de Biaucaire was old and frail, and his good days were gone over. No heir had he, neither son nor daughter, save one young man only; such an one as I shall tell you. Aucassin was the name of the damoiseau: fair was he, goodly, and great, and featly fashioned of his body, and limbs. His hair was yellow, in little curls, his eyes blue and laughing, his face beautiful and shapely, his nose high and well set, and so richly seen was he in all things good, that in him was none evil at all. But so suddenly overtaken was he of Love, who is a great master, that he would not, of his will, be

AUCASSIN AND NICOLETE, trans. A. Long (Portland, Me., 1895).

dubbed knight, nor take arms, nor follow tourneys, nor do whatsoever him beseemed. Therefore his father and mother said to him:

"Son, go take thine arms, mount thy horse, and hold thy land, and help thy men, for if they see thee among them, more stoutly will they keep in battle their lives, and lands, and thine, and mine."

"Father," said Aucassin, "I marvel that you will be speaking. Never may God give me aught of my desire if I be made knight, or mount my horse, or face stour and battle wherein knights smite and are smitten again, unless thou give me Nicolete, my true love, that I love so well."

"Son," said the father, "this may not be. Let Nicolete go, a slave girl she is, out of a strange land, and the captain of this town bought her of the Saracens, and carried her hither, and hath reared her and let christen the maid, and took her for his daughter in God, and one day will find a young man for her, to win her bread honourably. Herein hast thou nought to make or mend, but if a wife thou wilt have, I will give thee the daughter of a King, or a Count. There is no man so rich in France, but if thou desire his daughter, thou shalt have her."

"Faith! my father," said Aucassin, "tell me where is the place so high in all the world that Nicolete, my sweet lady and love, would not grace it well? If she were Empress of Constantinople or of Germany, or Queen of France or England, it were little enough for her; so gentle is she and courteous, and debonaire, and compact of all good qualities."

Here singeth one:

> Aucassin was of Biaucaire
> Of a goodly castle there,
> But from Nicolete the fair

None might win his heart away
Though his father, many a day,
And his mother said him nay,
"Ha! fond child, what wouldest thou?
Nicolete is glad enow!
Was from Carthage cast away,
Paynims sold her on a day!
Wouldst thou win a lady fair
Choose a maid of high degree
Such a one is meet for thee."
"Nay of these I have no care,
Nicolete is debonaire,
Her body sweet and the face of her
Take my heart as in a snare,
Loyal love is but her share
    That is so sweet."

THEN SPEAK THEY, SAY THEY, TELL
THEY THE TALE:

When the Count Garin de Biaucaire knew that he would avail not to withdraw Aucassin his son from the love of Nicolete, he went to the Captain of the city, who was his man, and spake to him saying:

"Sir Count; away with Nicolete thy daughter in God; cursed be the land whence she was brought into this country, for by reason of her do I lose Aucassin, that will neither be dubbed knight, nor do aught of the things that fall to him to be done. And wit ye well," he said, "that if I might have her at my will, I would burn her in a fire, and yourself might well be sore adread."

"Sir," said the Captain, "this is grievous to me that he comes and goes and hath speech with her. I had bought the maiden at mine own charges, and nourished her, and baptized, and made her my daughter in God. Yea, I would have given her to a young man that should win her bread honourably. With this had Aucassin thy son nought to make or mend. But, sith it is thy will and thy pleasure, I will send her into that land and that country where never will he see her with his eyes."

"Have a heed to thyself," said the Count Garin, "thence might great evil come on thee."

So parted they each from other. Now the Captain was a right rich man: so had he a rich palace with a garden in face of it; in an upper chamber thereof he let place Nicolete, with one old woman to keep her company, and in that chamber put bread and meat and wine and such things as were needful. Then he let seal the door, that none might come in or go forth, save that there was one window, over against the garden, and strait enough, where through came to them a little air.

Here singeth one:

Nicolete as ye heard tell
Prisoned is within a cell
That is painted wondrously
With colours of a far countrie,
And the window of marble wrought,
There the maiden stood in thought,
With straight brows and yellow hair
Never saw ye fairer fair!
On the wood she gazed below,
And she saw the roses blow,
Heard the birds sing loud and low,
Therefore spoke she wofully:
"Ah me, wherefore do I lie
Here in prison wrongfully:
Aucassin, my love, my knight,
Am I not thy heart's delight,
Thou that lovest me aright!
'Tis for thee that I must dwell
In the vaulted chamber cell,
Hard beset and all alone!
By our Lady Mary's Son
Here no longer will I wonn,
    If I may flee!

THEN SPEAK THEY, SAY THEY, TELL
THEY THE TALE:

Nicolete was in prison, as ye have heard soothly, in the chamber. And the noise and bruit of it went through all the country and all the land, how that Nicolete was lost. Some said she had fled the country, and some that the Count Garin de Biaucaire had let slay her. Whosoever had joy thereof, Aucassin had none, so he went to the Captain of the town and spoke to him, saying:

"Sir Captain, what hast thou made of Nicolete, my sweet lady and love, the thing that best I love in all the world? Hast thou carried her off or ravished her away from me? Know well that if I die of it, the price shall be demanded of thee, and that will be well done, for it shall be even as if thou hadst slain me with thy two hands, for thou hast taken from me the thing that in this world I loved the best."

"Fair Sir," said the Captain, "let these things be. Nicolete is a captive that I did bring from a strange country. Yea, I bought her at my own charges of the Saracens, and I bred her up and baptized her, and made her my daughter in God. And I have cherished her, and one of these days I would have given her to a young man, to win her bread honourably. With this hast thou naught to make, but do thou take the daughter of a King or a Count. Nay more, what wouldst thou deem thee to have gained, hadst thou made her thy leman, and taken her to thy bed? Plentiful lack of comfort hadst thou got thereby, for in Hell would thy soul have lain while the world endures, and into Paradise wouldst thou have entered never."

"In Paradise what have I to win? Therein I seek not to enter, but only to have Nicolete, my sweet lady that I love so well. For into Paradise go none but such folk as I shall tell thee now: Thither go these same old priests, and halt old men and maimed, who all day and night cower continually before the altars, and in the crypts; and such folk as wear old amices and old clouted frocks, and naked folk and shoeless, and covered with sores, perishing of hunger and thirst, and of cold, and of little ease. These be they that go into Paradise, with them have I naught to make. But into Hell would I fain go; for into Hell fare the goodly clerks, and goodly knights that fall in tourneys and great wars, and stout men at arms, and all men noble. With these would I liefly go. And thither pass the sweet ladies and courteous that have two lovers, or three, and their lords also thereto. Thither goes the gold, and the silver, and cloth of vair, and cloth of gris, and harpers, and makers,

and the prince of this world. With these I would gladly go, let me but have with me, Nicolete, my sweetest lady."

"Certes," quoth the Captain, "in vain wilt thou speak thereof, for never shalt thou see her; and if thou hadst word with her, and thy father knew it, he would let burn in a fire both her and me, and thyself might well be sore adread."

"That is even what irketh me," quoth Aucassin. So he went from the Captain sorrowing.

Here singeth one:

Aucassin did so depart
Much in dole and heavy at heart
For his love so bright and dear,
None might bring him any cheer,
None might give good words to hear,
To the palace doth he fare
Climbeth up the palace-stair,
Passeth to a chamber there,
Thus great sorrow doth he bear,
For his lady and love so fair.
"Nicolete how fair art thou,
Sweet thy foot-fall, sweet thine eyes,
Sweet the mirth of thy replies,
Sweet thy laughter, sweet thy face,
Sweet thy lips and sweet thy brow,
And the touch of thine embrace,
All for thee I sorrow now,
Captive in an evil place,
Whence I ne'er may go my ways
     Sister, sweet friend!"

SO SAY THEY, SPEAK THEY, TELL
THEY THE TALE:

While Aucassin was in the chamber sorrowing for Nicolete his love, even then the Count Bougars de Valence, that had his war to wage, forgat it no whit, but had called up his horsemen and his footmen, so made he for the castle to storm it. And the cry of battle arose, and the din, and knights and men at arms busked them, and ran to walls and gates to hold the keep. And the townsfolk mounted to the battlements, and cast down bolts and pikes. Then while the assault was great, and even at its height, the Count Garin de Biaucaire came into the chamber where Aucassin was making lament, sorrowing for Nicolete, his sweet lady that he loved so well.

"Ha! son," quoth he, "how caitiff art thou, and cowardly, that canst see men assail thy goodliest castle and strongest. Know thou that if thou lose it, thou losest all. Son, go to, take arms, and mount thy horse, and defend thy land, and help thy men, and fare into the stour. Thou needst not smite nor be smitten. If they do but see thee among them, better will they guard their substance, and their lives, and thy land and mine. And thou art so great, and hardy of thy hands, that well mightst thou do this thing, and to do it is thy devoir."

"Father," said Aucassin, "what is this thou sayest now? God grant me never aught of my desire, if I be dubbed knight, or mount steed, or go into the stour where knights do smite and are smitten, if thou givest me not Nicolete, my sweet lady, whom I love so well."

"Son," quoth his father, "this may never be: rather would I be quite disinherited and lose all that is mine, than that thou shouldst have her to thy wife, or to love *par amours.*"

So he turned him about. But when Aucassin saw him going he called to him again, saying,

"Father, go to now, I will make with thee fair covenant."

"What covenant, fair son?"

"I will take up arms, and go into the stour, on this covenant, that, if God bring me back sound and safe, thou wilt let me see Nicolete my sweet lady, even so long that I may have of her two words or three, and one kiss."

"That will I grant," said his father.
At this was Aucassin glad.

Here one singeth:

Of the kiss heard Aucassin
That returning he shall win,
None so glad would he have been
Of a myriad marks of gold
Of a hundred thousand fold.

Called for raiment brave of steel,
Then they clad him, head to heel,
Twyfold hauberk doth he don,
Firmly braced the helmet on.
Girt the sword with hilt of gold,
Horse doth mount, and lance doth wield,
Looks to stirrups and to shield,
Wondrous brave he rode to field.
Dreaming of his lady dear
Setteth spurs to the destrere,
Rideth forward without fear,
Through the gate and forth away
        To the fray.

SO SPEAK THEY, SAY THEY, TELL THEY THE TALE:

Aucassin was armed and mounted as ye have heard tell. God! how goodly sat the shield on his shoulder, the helm on his head, and the baldric on his left haunch! And the damoiseau was tall, fair, featly fashioned, and hardy of his hands, and the horse whereon he rode swift and keen, and straight had he spurred him forth of the gate. Now believe ye not that his mind was on kine, nor cattle of the booty, nor thought he how he might strike a knight, nor be stricken again: nor no such thing. Nay, no memory had Aucassin of aught of these; rather he so dreamed of Nicolete, his sweet lady, that he dropped his reins, forgetting all there was to do, and his horse that had felt the spur, bore him into the press and hurled among the foe, and they laid hands on him all about, and took him captive, and seized away his spear and shield, and straightway they led him off a prisoner, and were even now discoursing of what death he should die.

And when Aucassin heard them,
"Ha! God," said he, "sweet Saviour. Be these my deadly enemies that have taken me, and will soon cut off my head? And once my head is off, no more shall I speak with Nicolete, my sweet lady, that I love so well. Natheless have I here a good sword, and sit a good horse unwearied. If now I keep not my head for her sake, God help her never, if she love me more!"

The damoiseau was tall and strong, and the horse whereon he sat was right eager. And he laid hand to sword, and fell a-smiting to right and left, and smote through helm and *nasal*, and arm and clenched hand, making a murder about him, like a wild boar when hounds fall on him in the forest, even till he struck down ten knights, and seven he hurt, and straightway he hurled out of the press, and rode back again at full speed, sword in hand. The Count Bougars de Valence heard say they were about hanging Aucassin, his enemy, so he came into that place, and Aucassin was ware of him, and gat his sword into his hand, and lashed at his helm with such a stroke that he drave it down on his head, and he being stunned, fell grovelling. And Aucassin laid hands on him, and caught him by the *nasal* of his helmet, and gave him to his father.

"Father," quoth Aucassin, "lo here is your mortal foe, who hath so warred on you with all malengin. Full twenty years did this war endure, and might not be ended by man."

"Fair son," said his father, "thy feats of youth shouldst thou do, and not seek after folly."

"Father," saith Aucassin, "sermon me no sermons, but fulfil my covenant."

"Ha! what covenant, fair son?"

"What, father, hast thou forgotten it? By mine own head, whosoever forgets, will I not forget it, so much it hath me at heart. Didst thou not covenant with me when I took up arms, and went into the stour, that if God brought me back safe and sound, thou wouldst let me see Nicolete, my sweet lady, even so long that I may have of her two words or three, and one kiss? So didst thou covenant, and my mind is that thou keep thy word."

"I!" quoth the father, "God forsake me when I keep this covenant! Nay, if she were here, I would let burn her in the fire, and thyself shouldst be sore adread."

"Is this thy last word?" quoth Aucassin.

"So help me God," quoth his father, "yea!"

"Certes," quoth Aucassin, "This is a sorry thing meseems, when a man of thine age lies!"

"Count of Valence," quoth Aucassin, "I took thee?"

"In sooth, Sir, didst thou," saith the Count.

"Give me thy hand," saith Aucassin.

"Sir, with good will."

So he set his hand in the other's.

"Now givest thou me thy word," said Aucassin, "that never whilst thou art living man wilt thou avail to do my father dishonour, or harm him in body, or in goods, but do it thou wilt?"

"Sir, in God's name," saith he, "mock me not, but put me to my ransom; ye cannot ask of me gold nor silver, horses nor palfreys, *vair* nor *gris*, hawks nor hounds, but I will give you them."

"What?" quoth Aucassin. "Ha, knowest thou not it was I that took thee?"

"Yea sir," quoth the Count Bougars.

"God help me never, but I will make thy head fly from thy shoulders, if thou makest not troth," said Aucassin.

"In God's name," said he, "I make what promise thou wilt."

So they did the oath, and Aucassin let mount him on a horse, and took another and so led him back till he was all in safety.

Here one singeth:

When the Count Garin doth know
That his child would ne'er forego
Love of her that loved him so,
Nicolete, the bright of brow,
In a dungeon deep below
Childe Aucassin did he throw.
Even there the Childe must dwell
In a dun-walled marble cell.
There he waileth in his woe
Crying thus as ye shall know.

"Nicolete, thou lily white,
My sweet lady, bright of brow,
Sweeter than the grape art thou,
Sweeter than sack posset good

In a cup of maple wood!
Was it not but yesterday
That a palmer came this way,
Out of Limousin came he,
And at ease he might not be,
For a passion him possessed
That upon his bed he lay,
Lay, and tossed, and knew not rest,
In his pain discomforted.
But thou camest by the bed,
Where he tossed amid his pain,
Holding high thy sweeping train,
And thy kirtle of ermine,
And thy smock of linen fine,
Then these fair white limbs of thine,
Did he look on, and it fell
That the palmer straight was well,
Straight was hale—and comforted,
And he rose up from his bed,
And went back to his own place,
Sound and strong and full of face!
My sweet lady, lily white,
Sweet thy footfall, sweet thine eyes,
And the mirth of thy replies,
Sweet thy laughter, sweet thy face,
Sweet thy lips and sweet thy brow,
And the touch of thine embrace.
Who but doth in thee delight?
I for love of thee am bound
In this dungeon underground,
All for loving thee must lie
Here where loud on thee I cry,
Here for loving thee must die
　　　For thee, my love."

THEN SAY THEY, SPEAK THEY, TELL
THEY THE TALE:

Aucassin was cast into prison as ye have heard tell, and Nicolete, of her part, was in the chamber. Now it was summer time, the month of May, when days are warm, and long, and clear, and the night still and serene. Nicolete lay one night on her bed, and saw the moon shine clear through a window, yea, and heard the nightingale sing in the garden, so she minded her of Aucassin her lover whom she loved so well. Then fell she to thoughts of Count Garin de Biaucaire, that hated her to the death; therefore deemed she that there she would no longer abide, for that, if she were told of, and the Count knew whereat she lay, an ill death would he make her die. Now she knew that the old woman slept who held her company. Then she arose, and clad her in a mantle of silk she had by her, very goodly, and took napkins, and sheets of the bed, and knotted one to the other, and made therewith a cord as long as she might, so knitted it to a pillar in the window, and let herself slip down into the garden, then caught up her raiment in both hands, behind and before, and kilted up her kirtle, because of the dew that she saw lying deep on the grass, and so went her way down through the garden.

Her locks were yellow and curled, her eyes blue and smiling, her face featly fashioned, the nose high and fairly set, the lips more red than cherry or rose in time of summer, her teeth white and small; her breasts so firm that they bore up the folds of her bodice as they had been two apples; so slim was she in the waist that your two hands might have clipped her, and the daisy flowers that brake beneath her as she went tiptoe, and that bent above her instep, seemed black against her feet, so white was the maiden. She came to the postern gate, and unbarred it, and went out through the streets of Biaucaire, keeping always on the shadowy side, for the moon was shining right clear, and so wondered she till she came to the tower where her lover lay. The tower was flanked with buttresses, and she cowered under one of them, wrapped in her mantle. Then thrust she her head through a crevice of the tower that was old and worn, and so heard she Aucassin wailing within, and making dole and lament for the sweet lady he loved so well. And when she had listened to him she began to say:

Here one singeth:

Nicolete the bright of brow
On a pillar leanest thou,
All Aucassin's wail doth hear
For his love that is so dear,
Then thou spakest, shrill and clear,
"Gentle knight withouten fear
Little good befalleth thee,

Little help of sigh or tear,
Ne'er shalt thou have joy of me.
Never shalt thou win me; still
Am I held in evil will
Of thy father and thy kin,
Therefore must I cross the sea,
And another land must win."
Then she cut her curls of gold,
Cast them in the dungeon hold,
Aucassin doth clasp them there,
Kissed the curls that were so fair,
Them doth in his bosom bear,
Then he wept, even as of old,
    All for his love!

THEN SAY THEY, SPEAK THEY, TELL
THEY THE TALE:

When Aucassin heard Nicolete say that she would pass into a far country, he was all in wrath.

"Fair sweet friend," quoth he, "thou shalt not go, for then wouldst thou be my death. And the first man that saw thee and had the might withal, would take thee straightway into his bed to be his leman. And once thou camest into a man's bed, and that bed not mine, wit ye well that I would not tarry till I had found a knife to pierce my heart and slay myself. Nay, verily, wait so long I would not: but would hurl myself on it so soon as I could find a wall, or a black stone, thereon would I dash my head so mightily, that the eyes would start, and my brain burst. Rather would I die even such a death, than know thou hadst lain in a man's bed, and that bed not mine."

"Aucassin," she said, "I trow thou lovest me not as much as thou sayest, but I love thee more than thou lovest me."

"Ah, fair sweet friend," said Aucassin, "it may not be that thou shouldst love me even as I love thee. Woman may not love man as man loves woman, for a woman's love lies in the glance of her eyes, and the bud of her breast, and her foot's tip-toe, but the love of a man is in his heart planted, whence it can never issue forth and pass away."

Now while Aucassin and Nicolete held this parley together, the town's guards came down a street, with swords drawn beneath their cloaks, for the Count Garin had charged them that if they could take her they should slay her. But the sentinel that was on the tower saw them coming, and heard them speaking of Nicolete as they went, and threatening to slay her.

"God!" quoth he, "this were great pity to slay so fair a maid! Right great charity it were if I could say aught to her, and they perceive it not, and she should be on her guard against them, for if they slay her, then were Aucassin, my damoiseau, dead, and that were great pity."

Here one singeth:

Valiant was the sentinel,
Courteous, kind, and practised well,
So a song did sing and tell
Of the peril that befell.
"Maiden fair that lingerest here,
Gentle maid of merry cheer,
Hair of gold, and eyes as clear
As the water in a mere,
Thou, meseems, hast spoken word
To thy lover and thy lord,
That would die for thee, his dear;
Now beware the ill accord,
Of the cloaked men of the sword,
These have sworn and keep their word,
They will put thee to the sword
    Save thou take heed!"

THEN SPEAK THEY, SAY THEY, TELL
THEY THE TALE:

"Ha!" quoth Nicolete, "be the soul of thy father and the soul of thy mother in the rest of Paradise, so fairly and so courteously hast thou spoken me! Please God, I will be right ware of them, God keep me out of their hands."

So she shrank under her mantle into the shadow of the pillar till they had passed by, and then took she farewell of Aucassin, and so fared till she came between wall and fosse, and so looked down, and saw that the fosse was deep and steep, whereat she was sore adread.

"Ah God," saith she, "sweet Saviour! If I let myself fall hence, I shall break my neck, and if here I abide, to-morrow they will take me and burn me in a fire. Yet liefer would I perish here than that to-morrow the folk should stare on me for a gazing-stock."

Then she crossed herself, and so let herself slip into the fosse, and when she had come to the bottom, her fair feet, and fair hands that had not custom thereof, were bruised and frayed, and the blood springing from a dozen places, yet felt she no pain nor hurt, by reason of the great dread wherein she went. But if she were in cumber to win there, in worse was she to win out. But she deemed that there to abide was of none avail, and she found a pike sharpened, that they of the city had thrown out to keep the hold. Therewith made she one stepping place after another, till, with much travail, she climbed the wall. Now the forest lay within two crossbow shots, and the forest was of thirty leagues this way and that. Therein also were wild beasts, and beasts serpentine, and she feared that if she entered there they would slay her. But anon she deemed that if men found her there they would hale her back into the town to burn her.

Here one singeth:

Nicolete, the fair of face,
Climbed upon the coping stone,
There made she lament and moan
Calling on our Lord alone
For his mercy and his grace.
"Father, king of Majesty,
Listen, for I nothing know
Where to flee or whither go.
If within the wood I fare,
Lo, the wolves will slay me there,
Boars and lions terrible,
Many in the wild wood dwell,
But if I abide the day,
Surely worse will come of it,
Surely will the fire be lit
That shall burn my body away,
Jesus, Lord of Majesty,
Better seemeth it to me,
That within the wood I fare,
Though the wolves devour me there

Than within the town to go,
Ne'er be it so!"

THEN SPEAK THEY, SAY THEY, TELL THEY THE TALE:

Nicolete made great moan, as ye have heard; then commended she herself to God, and anon fared till she came unto the forest. But to go deep in it she dared not, by reason of the wild beasts, and beasts serpentine. Anon crept she into a little thicket, where sleep came upon her, and she slept till prime next day, when the shepherds issued forth from the town and drove their bestial between wood and water. Anon came they all into one place by a fair fountain which was on the fringe of the forest, thereby spread they a mantle, and thereon set bread. So while they were eating, Nicolete wakened, with the sound of the singing birds, and the shepherds, and she went unto them saying, "Fair boys, our Lord keep you!"

"God bless thee," quoth he that had more words to his tongue than the rest.

"Fair boys," quoth she, "know ye Aucassin, the son of Count Garin de Biaucaire?"

"Yea, well we know him."

"So may God help you, fair boys," quoth she, "tell him there is a beast in this forest, and bid him come chase it, and if he can take it, he would not give one limb thereof for a hundred marks of gold, nay, nor for five hundred, nor for any ransom."

Then looked they on her, and saw her so fair that they were all astonied.

"Will I tell him thereof?" quoth he that had more words to his tongue than the rest; "foul fall him who speaks of the thing or tells him the tidings. These are but visions ye tell of, for there is no beast so great in this forest, stag, nor lion, nor boar, that one of his limbs is worth more than two deniers, or three at the most, and ye speak of such great ransom. Foul fall him that believes your word, and him that telleth Aucassin. Ye be a Fairy, and we have none liking for your company, nay, hold on your road."

"Nay, fair boys," quoth she, "nay, ye will do my bidding. For this beast is so mighty of medicine that thereby will Aucassin be healed of his torment. And lo! I have five sols in my purse, take them, and tell him: for within three days must he come hunting it hither, and if within three days he find it not, never will he be healed of his torment."

"My faith," quoth he, "the money will we take, and if he come hither we will tell him, but seek him we will not."

"In God's name," quoth she; and so took farewell of the shepherds, and went her way.

Here singeth one:

Nicolete the bright of brow
From the shepherds doth she pass
All below the blossomed bough,
Where an ancient way there was,
Overgrown and choked with grass,
Till she found the cross-roads where
Seven paths do all way fare,
Then she deemeth she will try,
Should her lover pass thereby,
If he love her loyally.
So she gathered white lilies,
Oak-leaf, that in green wood is,
Leaves of many a branch I wis,
Therewith built a lodge of green,
Goodlier was never seen,
Swore by God who may not lie,
"If my love the lodge should spy,
He will rest awhile thereby
If he love me loyally."
Thus his faith she deemed to try,
"Or I love him not, not I,
     Nor he loves me!"

THEN SPEAK THEY, SAY THEY, TELL
THEY THE TALE:

Nicolete built her lodge of boughs, as ye have heard, right fair and feteously, and wove it well, within and without, of flowers and leaves. So lay she hard by the lodge in a deep coppice to know what Aucassin will do. And the cry and the bruit went abroad through all the country and all the land, that Nicolete was lost. Some told that she had fled, and some that the Count Garin had let slay her. Whosoever had joy thereof, no joy had Aucassin. And the Count Garin, his father, had taken him out of prison, and had sent for the knights of that land, and the ladies, and let make a right great feast, for the comforting of Aucassin his son. Now at the high time of the feast, was Aucassin leaning from a gallery, all woful and discomforted. Whatsoever men might devise of mirth, Aucassin had no joy thereof, nor no desire, for he saw not her that he loved. Then a knight looked on him, and came to him, and said:

"Aucassin, of that sickness of thine have I been sick, and good counsel will I give thee, if thou wilt hearken to me—"

"Sir," said Aucassin, "gramercy, good counsel would I fain hear."

"Mount thy horse," quoth he, "and go take thy pastime in yonder forest, there wilt thou see the good flowers and grass, and hear the sweet birds sing. Perchance thou shalt hear some word, whereby thou shalt be the better."

"Sir," quoth Aucassin, "gramercy, that will I do."

He passed out of the hall, and went down the stairs, and came to the stable where his horse was. He let saddle and bridle him, and mounted, and rode forth from the castle, and wandered till he came to the forest, so rode till he came to the fountain and found the shepherds at point of noon. And they had a mantle stretched on the grass, and were eating bread, and making joy.

Here one singeth:

There were gathered shepherds all,
Martin, Esmeric, and Hal,
Aubrey, Robin, great and small.
Saith the one, "Good fellows all,
God keep Aucassin the fair,
And the maid with yellow hair,
Bright of brow and eyes of vair.
She that gave us gold to ware.
Cakes therewith to buy ye know,
Goodly knives and sheaths also.

Flutes to play, and pipes to blow,
May God him heal!"

HERE SPEAK THEY, SAY THEY, TELL
THEY THE TALE:

When Aucassin heard the shepherds, anon he bethought him of Nicolete, his sweet lady he loved so well, and he deemed that she had passed thereby; then set he spurs to his horse, and so came to the shepherds.

"Fair boys, God be with you."

"God bless you," quoth he that had more words to his tongue than the rest.

"Fair boys," quoth Aucassin, "say the song again that anon ye sang."

"Say it we will not," quoth he that had more words to his tongue than the rest, "foul fall him who will sing it again for you, fair sir!"

"Fair boys," quoth Aucassin, "know ye me not?"

"Yea, we know well that you are Aucassin, our damoiseau, natheless we be not your men, but the Count's."

"Fair boys, yet sing it again, I pray you."

"Hearken! by the Holy Heart," quoth he, "wherefore should I sing for you, if it likes me not? Lo, there is no such rich man in this country, saving the body of Garin the Count, that dare drive forth my oxen, or my cows, or my sheep, if he finds them in his fields, or his corn, lest he lose his eyes for it, and wherefore should I sing for you, if it likes me not?"

"God be your aid, fair boys, sing it ye will, and take ye these ten sols I have here in a purse."

"Sir, the money will we take, but never a note will I sing, for I have given my oath, but I will tell thee a plain tale, if thou wilt."

"By God," saith Aucassin, "I love a plain tale better than naught."

"Sir, we were in this place, a little time agone, between prime and tierce, and were eating our bread by this fountain, even as now we do, and a maid came past, the fairest thing in the world, whereby we deemed that she should be a fay, and all the wood shone round about her. Anon she gave us of that she had, whereby we made covenant with her, that if ye came hither we would bid you hunt in this forest, wherein is such a beast that, an ye might take him, ye would not give one limb of him for five hundred marks of silver, nor for no ransom; for this beast is so mighty of medicine, that, an ye could take him, ye should be healed of your torment, and within three days must ye take him, and if ye take him not then, never will ye look on him. So chase ye the beast, an ye will, or an ye will let be, for my promise have I kept with her."

"Fair boys," quoth Aucassin, "ye have said enough. God grant me to find this quarry."

Here one singeth:
Aucassin when he had heard,
Sore within his heart was stirred,
Left the shepherds on that word,
Far into the forest spurred
Rode into the wood; and fleet
Fled his horse through paths of it,
Three words spake he of his sweet,
"Nicolete the fair, the dear,
'Tis for thee I follow here
Track of boar, nor slot of deer,
But thy sweet body and eyes so clear,
All thy mirth and merry cheer,
That my very heart have slain,
So please God to me maintain
I shall see my love again,
  Sweet sister, friend!"

THEN SPEAK THEY, SAY THEY, TELL
THEY THE TALE:

Aucassin fared through the forest from path to path after Nicolete, and his horse bare him furiously. Think ye not that the thorns him spared, nor the briars, nay, not so, but tare his raiment, that scarce a knot might be tied with the soundest part thereof, and the blood sprang from his arms, and flanks, and legs, in forty places, or thirty, so that behind the Childe men might follow on the track of his blood in the grass. But so much he went in thoughts of Nicolete, his lady sweet, that he felt no pain nor torment, and all the day hurled through the forest in this fashion nor heard no word of her. And when he saw Vespers draw nigh, he began to weep for that he found her not. All down an old road, and grassgrown he fared, when anon, looking along the way before him, he saw such an one as I shall tell you. Tall was he, and great of growth, laidly and marvellous to look upon: his head huge, and black as charcoal, and more than the breadth of a hand between his two eyes, and great cheeks, and a big nose and broad, big nostrils and ugly, and thick lips redder than a collop, and great teeth yellow and ugly, and he was shod with hosen and shoon of bull's hide, bound with cords of bark over the knee, all about him a great cloak twy-fold, and he leaned on a grievous cudgel, and Aucassin came unto him, and was afraid when he beheld him.

"Fair brother, God aid thee."

"God bless you," quoth he.

"As God he helpeth thee, what makest thou here?"

"What is that to thee?"

"Nay, naught, naught," saith Aucassin, "I ask but out of courtesy."

"But for whom weepest thou," quoth he, "and makest such heavy lament? Certes, were I as rich a man as thou, the whole world should not make me weep."

"Ha! know ye me?" saith Aucassin.

"Yea, I know well that ye be Aucassin, the son of the Count, and if ye tell me why ye weep, then will I tell you what I make here."

"Certes," quoth Aucassin, "I will tell you right gladly. Hither came I this morning to hunt in this forest; and with me a white hound, the fairest in the world; him have I lost, and for him I weep."

"By the Heart our Lord bare in his breast," quoth he, "are ye weeping for a stinking hound? Foul fall him that holds thee high henceforth! for there is no such rich man in the land, but if thy father asked it of him, he would give thee ten, or fifteen, or twenty, and be the gladder for it. But I have cause to weep and make dole."

"Wherefore so, brother?"

"Sir, I will tell thee. I was hireling to a rich villain, and drove his plough; four oxen had he. But three days since came on me great misadventure, whereby I lost the best of mine oxen, Roger, the best of my team. Him go I seeking, and have neither eaten nor drunken these three days, nor may I go to the town, lest they cast me into prison, seeing that I have not wherewithal to pay. Out of all the wealth of the world have I no more than ye see on my body. A poor mother bare me, that had no more but one wretched bed; this have they taken from under her, and she lies in the very straw. This ails me more than mine own case, for wealth comes and goes; if now I have lost, another tide will I gain, and will pay for mine ox whenas I may; never for that will I weep. But you weep for a stinking hound. Foul fall whoso thinks well of thee!"

"Certes thou art a good comforter, brother, blessed be thou! And of what price was thine ox?"

"Sir, they ask me twenty sols for him, whereof I cannot abate one doit."

"Nay, then," quoth Aucassin, "take these twenty sols I have in my purse, and pay for thine ox."

"Sir," saith he, "gramercy. And God give thee to find that thou seekest."

So they parted each from other, and Aucassin rode on: the night was fair and still, and so long he went that he came to the lodge of boughs, that Nicolete had builded and woven within and without, over and under, with flowers, and it was the fairest lodge that might be seen. When Aucassin was ware of it, he stopped suddenly, and the light of the moon fell therein.

"God!" quoth Aucassin, "here was Nicolete, my sweet lady, and this lodge builded she with her fair hands. For the sweetness of it, and for love of her, will I alight, and rest here this night long."

He drew forth his foot from the stirrup to alight, and the steed was great and tall. He dreamed so much on Nicolete his right sweet lady, that he slipped on a stone, and drave his shoulder out of his place. Then knew he that he was hurt sore, natheless he bore him with what force he might, and fastened with the other hand the mare's son to a thorn. Then turned he on his side, and crept backwise into the lodge of boughs. And he looked through a gap in the lodge and saw the stars in heaven, and one that was brighter than the rest; so began he to say:

Here one singeth:

"Star, that I from far behold,
Star, the Moon calls to her fold,
Nicolete with thee doth dwell,
My sweet love with locks of gold,
God would have her dwell afar,
Dwell with him for evening star,
Would to God whate'er befell,
Would that with her I might dwell.
I would clip her close and strait,
Nay, were I of much estate,
Some king's son desirable,
Worthy she to be my mate,
Me to kiss and clip me well,
　　　　Sister, sweet friend!"

SO SPEAK THEY, SAY THEY, TELL THEY THE TALE:

When Nicolete heard Aucassin, right so came she unto him, for she was not far away. She passed within the lodge, and threw her arms about his neck, and clipped and kissed him.

"Fair sweet friend, welcome be thou."

"And thou, fair sweet love, be thou welcome."

So either kissed and clipped the other, and fair joy was them between.

"Ha! sweet love," quoth Aucassin, "but now was I sore hurt, and my shoulder wried, but I take no force of it, nor have no hurt therefrom since I have thee."

Right so felt she his shoulder and found it was wried from its place. And she so handled it with her white hands, and so wrought in her surgery, that by God's will who loveth lovers, it went back into its place. Then took she flowers, and fresh grass, and leaves green, and bound these herbs on the hurt with a strip of her smock, and he was all healed.

"Aucassin," saith she, "fair sweet love, take counsel what thou wilt do. If thy father let search this forest to-morrow, and men find me here, they will slay me, come to thee what will."

"Certes, fair sweet love, therefore should I sorrow heavily, but, an if I may, never shall they take thee."

Anon gat he on his horse, and his lady before him, kissing and clipping her, and so rode they at adventure.

Here one singeth:

Aucassin the frank, the fair,
Aucassin of the yellow hair,
Gentle knight, and true lover,
From the forest doth he fare,
Holds his love before him there,
Kissing cheek, and chin, and eyes,
But she spake in sober wise,
"Aucassin, true love and fair,
To what land do we repair?"
Sweet my love, I take no care,
Thou art with me everywhere!
So they pass the woods and downs,
Pass the villages and towns,
Hills and dales and open land,
Came at dawn to the sea sand,
Lighted down upon the strand,
　　　　Beside the sea.

THEN SAY THEY, SPEAK THEY, TELL THEY THE TALE:

Aucassin lighted down and his love, as ye have heard sing. He held his horse by the bridle, and his lady by the hands; so went they along the sea shore, and on the sea they saw a ship, and he called unto the sailors, and they came to him. Then held he such speech with them, that he and his lady were brought aboard that ship, and when they were on the high sea, behold a mighty wind and tyrannous arose, marvellous and great, and drave them from land to land, till they came unto a strange country, and won the haven of the castle of Torelore. Then asked they what this land might be, and men told them that it was the country of the King of Torelore. Then he asked what manner of man was he, and was there war afoot, and men said,

"Yea, and mighty!"

Therewith took he farewell of the merchants, and they commended him to God. Anon Aucassin mounted his horse, with his sword girt, and his lady before him, and rode at adventure till he was come to the castle. Then asked he where the King was, and they said that he was in childbed.

"Then where is his wife?"

And they told him she was with the host, and had led with her all the force of that country.

Now when Aucassin heard that saying, he made great marvel, and came into the castle, and lighted down, he and his lady, and his lady held his horse. Right so went he up into the castle, with his sword girt, and fared hither and thither till he came to the chamber where the King was lying.

Here one singeth:

Aucassin the courteous knight
To the chamber went forthright,
To the bed with linen dight
Even where the King was laid.
There he stood by him and said:
"Fool, what mak'st thou here abed?"
Quoth the King: "I am brought to bed
Of a fair son, and anon
When my month is over and gone,
And my healing fairly done,
To the Minister will I fare
And will do my churching there,
As my father did repair.
Then will sally forth to war,
Then will drive my foes afar
     From my countrie!"

THEN SPEAK THEY, SAY THEY, TELL
THEY THE TALE:

When Aucassin heard the King speak on this wise, he took all the sheets that covered him, and threw them all abroad about the chamber. Then saw he behind him a cudgel, and caught it into his hand, and turned, and took the King, and beat him till he was well-nigh dead.

"Ha! fair sir," quoth the King, "what would you with me? Art thou beside thyself, that beatest me in mine own house?"

"By God's heart," quoth Aucassin, "thou ill son of an ill wench, I will slay thee if thou swear not that never shall any man in all thy land lie in of child henceforth for ever."

So he did that oath, and when he had done it,

"Sir," said Aucassin, "bring me now where thy wife is with the host."

"Sir, with good will," quoth the King.

He mounted his horse, and Aucassin gat on his own, and Nicolete abode in the Queen's chamber. Anon rode Aucassin and the King even till they came to that place where the Queen was, and lo! men were warring with baked apples, and with eggs, and with fresh cheeses, and Aucassin began to look on them, and made great marvel.

Here one singeth:

Aucassin his horse doth stay,
From the saddle watched the fray,
All the stour and fierce array;
Right fresh cheeses carried they,
Apples baked, and mushrooms grey,
Whoso splasheth most the ford
He is master called and lord.
Aucassin doth gaze awhile,
Then began to laugh and smile
     And made game.

THEN SPEAK THEY, SAY THEY, TELL
THEY THE TALE:

When Aucassin beheld these marvels, he came to the King, and said, "Sir, be these thine enemies?"

"Yea, Sir," quoth the King.

"And will ye that I should avenge you of them?"

"Yea," quoth he, "with all my heart."

Then Aucassin put hand to sword, and hurled among them, and began to smite to the right hand and the left, and slew many of them. And when the King saw that he slew them, he caught at his bridle and said,

"Ha! fair sir, slay them not in such wise."

"How," quoth Aucassin, "will ye not that I should avenge you of them?"

"Sir," quoth the King, "overmuch already hast thou avenged me. It is nowise our custom to slay each other."

Anon turned they and fled. Then the King and Aucassin betook them again to the castle of Torelore, and the folk of that land counselled the King to put Aucassin forth, and keep Nicolete for his son's wife, for that she seemed a lady high of lineage. And Nicolete heard them, and had no joy of it, so began to say:

Here singeth one:

Thus she spake the bright of brow:
"Lord of Torelore and king,
Thy folk deem me a light thing,
When my love doth me embrace,
Fair he finds me, in good case,
Then am I in such derray,
Neither harp, nor lyre, nor lay,
Dance nor game, nor rebeck play
    Were so sweet."

THEN SPEAK THEY, SAY THEY, TELL
THEY THE TALE:

Aucassin dwelt in the castle of Torelore, in great ease and great delight, for that he had with him Nicolete his sweet love, whom he loved so well. Now while he was in such pleasure and such delight, came a troop of Saracens by sea, and laid siege to the castle and took it by main strength. Anon took they the substance that was therein and carried off the men and maidens captives. They seized Nicolete and Aucassin, and bound Aucassin hand and foot, and cast him into one ship, and Nicolete into another. Then rose there a mighty wind over sea, and scattered the ships. Now that ship wherein was Aucassin, went wandering on the sea, till it came to the castle of Biaucaire, and the folk of the country ran together to wreck her, and there found they Aucassin, and they knew him again. So when they of Biaucaire saw their damoiseau, they made great joy of him, for Aucassin had dwelt full three years in the castle of Torelore, and his father and mother were dead. So the people took him to the castle of Biaucaire, and there were they all his men. And he held the land in peace.

Here singeth one:

Lo ye, Aucassin hath gone
To Biaucaire that is his own,
Dwelleth there in joy and ease
And the kingdom is at peace.
Swears he by the Majesty
Of our Lord that is most high,
Rather would he they should die
All his kin and parentry,
So that Nicolete were nigh,
"Ah sweet love, and fair of brow,
I know not where to seek thee now,
God made never that countrie,
Not by land, and not by sea,
Where I would not search for thee,
    If that might be!"

THEN SPEAK THEY, SAY THEY, TELL
THEY THE TALE:

Now leave we Aucassin, and speak we of Nicolete. The ship wherein she was cast pertained to the King of Carthage, and he was her father, and she had twelve brothers, all princes or kings. When they beheld Nicolete, how fair she was, they did her great worship, and made much joy of her, and many times asked her who she was, for surely seemed she a lady of noble line and high parentry. But she might not tell them of her lineage, for she was but a child when men stole her away. So sailed they till they won the City of Carthage, and when Nicolete saw the walls of the castle, and the countryside, she knew that there had she been nourished and thence stolen away, being but a child. Yet was she not so young a child but that well she knew she had been daughter of the King of Carthage; and of her nurture in that city.

Here singeth one:

Nicolete the good and true
To the land has come anew.
Sees the palaces and walls,
And the houses and the halls!
Then she spake and said, "Alas!
That of birth so great I was,
Cousin of the Admiral
And the very child of him
Carthage counts King of Paynim,
Wild folk hold me here withal;
Nay Aucassin, love of thee
Gentle knight, and true, and free,
Burns and wastes the heart of me,
Ah God grant it of his grace,
That thou hold me, and embrace
That thou kiss me on the face
    Love and lord!"

THEN SPEAK THEY, SAY THEY, TELL THEY THE TALE:

When the King of Carthage heard Nicolete speak in this wise, he cast his arms about her neck.

"Fair sweet love," saith he, "tell me who thou art, and be not adread of me."

"Sir," said she, "I am daughter to the King of Carthage, and was taken, being then a little child, it is now fifteen years gone."

When all they of the court heard her speak thus, they knew well that she spake sooth: so made they great joy of her, and led her to the castle in great honour, as the King's daughter. And they would have given her to her lord a King of Paynim, but she had no mind to marry. There dwelt she three days or four. And she considered by what means she might seek for Aucassin. Then she got her a viol, and learned to play on it, till they would have married her on a day to a great King of Paynim, and she stole forth by night, and came to the seaport, and dwelt with a poor woman thereby. Then took she a certain herb, and therewith smeared her head and her face, till she was all brown and stained. And she let make coat, and mantle, and smock, and hose, and attired herself as if she had been a harper. So took she the viol and went to a mariner, and so wrought on him that he took her aboard his vessel. Then hoisted they sail, and fared on the high seas even till they came to the land of Provence. And Nicolete went forth and took the viol, and went playing through all that country, even till she came to the castle of Biaucaire, where Aucassin lay.

Here singeth one:

At Biaucaire below the tower
Sat Aucassin, on an hour,
Heard the bird, and watched the flower,
With his barons him beside,
Then came on him in that tide,
The sweet influence of love
And the memory thereof;
Thought of Nicolete the fair,
And the dainty face of her
He had loved so many years,
Then was he in dule and tears!
Even then came Nicolete
On the stair a foot she set,
And she drew the viol bow
Through the strings and chanted so;
"Listen, lords and knights, to me,
Lords of high and low degree,
To my story list will ye
All of Aucassin and her
That was Nicolete the fair?
And their love was long to tell
Deep woods through he sought her well,
Paynims took them on a day
In Torelore and bound they lay.
Of Aucassin nought know we,
But fair Nicolete the free
Now in Carthage doth she dwell,
There her father loves her well,
Who is king of that countrie.
Her a husband hath he found,
Paynim lord that serves Mahound!
Ne'er with him the maid will go,
For she loves a damoiseau,
Aucassin, that ye may know,
Swears to God that never mo
With a lover will she go
Save with him she loveth so
    In long desire."

When Aucassin heard Nicolete speak in this wise, he was right joyful, and drew her on one side, and spoke, saying:

"Sweet fair friend, know ye nothing of this Nicolete, of whom ye have thus sung?"

"Yea, Sir, I know her for the noblest creature, and the most gentle, and the best that ever was born on ground. She is daughter to the King of Carthage that took her there where Aucassin was taken, and brought her into the city of Carthage, till he knew that verily she was his own daughter, whereon he made right great mirth. Anon wished he to give her for her lord one of the greatest kings of all Spain, but she would rather let herself be hanged or burned, than take any lord, how great soever."

"Ha! fair sweet friend," quoth the Count Aucassin, "if thou wilt go into that land again, and bid her come and speak to me, I will give thee of my substance, more than thou wouldst dare to ask or take. And know ye, that for the sake of her, I have no will to take a wife, howsoever high her lineage. So wait I for her, and never will I have a wife, but her only. And if I knew where to find her, no need would I have to seek her."

"Sir," quoth she, "if ye promise me that, I will go in quest of her for your sake, and for hers, that I love much."

So he sware to her, and anon let give her twenty livres, and she departed from him, and he wept for the sweetness of Nicolete. And when she saw him weeping, she said:

"Sir, trouble not thyself so much withal. For in a little while shall I have brought her into this city, and ye shall see her."

When Aucassin heard that, he was right glad thereof. And she departed from him, and went into the city to the house of the Captain's wife, for the Captain her father in God was dead. So she dwelt there, and told all her tale; and the Captain's wife knew her, and knew well that she was Nicolete that she herself had nourished. Then she let wash and bathe her, and there rested she eight full days. Then took she an herb that was named Eyebright and anointed herself therewith, and was as fair as ever she had been all the days of her life. Then she clothed herself in rich robes of silk whereof the lady had great store, and then sat herself in the chamber on a silken coverlet, and called the lady and bade her go and bring Aucassin her love, and she did even so. And when she came to the Palace she found Aucassin weeping, and making lament for Nicolete his love, for that she delayed so long. And the lady spake unto him and said:

"Aucassin, sorrow no more, but come thou on with me, and I will shew thee the thing in the world that thou lovest best; even Nicolete thy dear love, who from far lands hath come to seek of thee." And Aucassin was right glad.

Here singeth one:

When Aucassin heareth now
That his lady bright of brow
Dwelleth in his own countrie,
Never man was glad as he.
To her castle doth he hie
With the lady speedily,
Passeth to the chamber high,
Findeth Nicolete thereby.
Of her true love found again
Never maid was half so fain.
Straight she leaped upon her feet:
When his love he saw at last,
Arms about her did he cast,
Kissed her often, kissed her sweet
Kissed her lips and brows and eyes.
Thus all night do they devise,
Even till the morning white.
Then Aucassin wedded her,
Made her lady of Biaucaire,
Many years abode they there,
Many years in shade or sun,
In great gladness and delight.
Ne'er hath Aucassin regret
Nor his lady Nicolete.
Now my story all is done,
　　　Said and sung!

Magna Carta

It is conventional to cite Magna Carta as one of the great charters of liberty in the Anglo-Saxon legal heritage. And yet, if we examine the document with due regard for the time and place of its signing, we may find that the fictions which have grown up around it have obscured its real significance. For example, when English parliamentarians during the Civil War of the seventeenth century sought precedents for their invasion of royal prerogatives, they cited the famous Chapter 39 of the Great Charter. In this section the Crown was to guarantee that "no freeman shall be taken or imprisoned . . . except by the lawful judgment of his peers or by the law of the land." Superficially, this passage may be taken as a guarantee of trial by jury and freedom from arbitrary arrest, and a statement of the subservience of all (including the king) to the law of the land. Thus Magna Carta becomes a milestone on the high road to democracy.

This fiction is certainly attractive, but it remains only a fiction. In 1215 Magna Carta was imposed upon King John by a group of Anglo-Norman barons who insisted that John live within the framework of the feudal contract; the Charter was a solemn agreement— of debatable legal validity, however, since it was extracted from the king by force— that both king and baron would respect their mutual duties and obligations, as defined in the feudal ceremonies of homage, fealty, and investiture.

Here, of course, lies the real significance of Magna Carta. This document presents us with a clear expression of feudal institutions and ideas, and from it we can derive an accurate picture of the most highly developed feudal society of Western Europe. The feudalism that the Normans under William the Conqueror brought to England in 1066 reached its clearest expression when it was laid over the indigenous Anglo-Saxon society. The Great Charter is presented here in its entirety.

MAGNA CARTA

John, by the grace of God, king of England, lord of Ireland, duke of Normandy and Aquitaine, count of Anjou, to the archbishops, bishops, abbots, earls, barons, justiciars, foresters, sheriffs, reeves, servants, and all bailiffs and his faithful people greeting. Know that by the suggestion of God and for the good of our soul and those of all our predecessors and of our heirs, to the honor of God and the exaltation of holy church, and the improvement of our kingdom, by the advice of our venerable fathers Stephen, archbishop of Canterbury, primate of all England and Cardinal of the Holy Roman Church, Henry, archbishop of Dublin, William of London, Peter of Winchester, Joscelyn of Bath and

MAGNA CARTA, in *Select Documents of English Constitutional History*, eds. G. B. Adams and H. M. Stephens (New York, 1901), pp. 42-52.

Glastonbury, Hugh of Lincoln, Walter of Worcester, William of Coventry, and Benedict of Rochester, bishops; of Master Pandulf, subdeacon and member of the household of the lord Pope, of Brother Aymeric, master of the Knights of the Temple in England; and of the noblemen William Marshall, earl of Pembroke, William, earl of Salisbury, William, earl Warren, William, earl of Arendel, Alan of Galloway, constable of Scotland, Warren Fitz-Gerald, Peter Fitz-Herbert, Hubert de Burgh, seneschal of Poitou, Hugh de Nevil, Matthew Fitz-Herbert, Thomas Bassett, Alan Bassett, Philip d'Albini, Robert de Ropesle, John Marshall, John Fitz-Hugh, and others of our faithful.

1. In the first place we have granted to God, and by this our present charter confirmed, for us and our heirs forever, that the English church shall be free, and shall hold its rights entire and its liberties uninjured; and we will that it thus be observed; which is shown by this, that the freedom of elections, which is considered to be most important and especially necessary to the English church, we, of our pure and spontaneous will, granted, and by our charter confirmed, before the contest between us and our barons had arisen; and obtained a confirmation of it by the lord Pope Innocent III.; which we will observe and which we will shall be observed in good faith by our heirs forever.

We have granted moreover to all free men of our kingdom for us and our heirs forever all the liberties written below, to be had and holden by themselves and their heirs from us and our heirs.

2. If any of our earls or barons, or others holding from us in chief by military service shall have died, and when he has died his heir shall be of full age and owe relief, he shall have his inheritance by the ancient relief; that is to say, the heir or heirs of an earl for the whole barony of an earl a hundred pounds; the heir or heirs of

a baron for a whole barony a hundred pounds; the heir or heirs of a knight, for a whole knight's fee, a hundred shillings at most; and who owes less let him give less according to the ancient custom of fiefs.

3. If moreover the heir of any one of such shall be under age, and shall be in wardship, when he comes of age he shall have his inheritance without relief and without a fine.

4. The custodian of the land of such a minor heir shall not take from the land of the heir any except reasonable products, reasonable customary payments, and reasonable services, and this without destruction or waste of men or of property; and if we shall have committed the custody of the land of any such a one to the sheriff or to any other who is to be responsible to us for its proceeds, and that man shall have caused destruction or waste from his custody we will recover damages from him, and the land shall be committed to two legal and discreet men of that fief, who shall be responsible for its proceeds to us or to him to whom we have assigned them; and if we shall have given or sold to any one the custody of any such land, and he has caused destruction or waste there, he shall lose that custody, and it shall be handed over to two legal and discreet men of that fief who shall be in like manner responsible to us as is said above.

5. The custodian moreover, so long as he shall have the custody of the land, must keep up the houses, parks, warrens, fish ponds, mills, and other things pertaining to the land, from the proceeds of the land itself; and he must return to the heir, when he has come to full age, all his land, furnished with ploughs and implements of husbandry according as the time of wainage requires and as the proceeds of the land are able reasonably to sustain.

6. Heirs shall be married without disparity, so nevertheless that before the marriage is contracted, it shall be announced to

the relatives by blood of the heir himself.

7. A widow, after the death of her husband, shall have her marriage portion and her inheritance immediately and without obstruction, nor shall she give anything for her dowry or for her marriage portion, or for her inheritance which inheritance her husband and she held on the day of the death of her husband; and she may remain in the house of her husband for forty days after his death, within which time her dowry shall be assigned to her.

8. No widow shall be compelled to marry so long as she prefers to live without a husband, provided she gives security that she will not marry without our consent, if she holds from us, or without the consent of her lord from whom she holds, if she holds from another.

9. Neither we nor our bailiffs will seize any land or rent, for any debt, so long as the chattels of the debtor are sufficient for the payment of the debt; nor shall the pledges of a debtor be distrained so long as the principal debtor himself has enough for the payment of the debt; and if the principal debtor fails in the payment of the debt, not having the wherewithal to pay it, the pledges shall be responsible for the debt; and if they wish, they shall have the lands and the rents of the debtor until they shall have been satisfied for the debt which they have before paid for him, unless the principal debtor shall have shown himself to be quit in that respect towards those pledges.

10. If any one has taken anything from the Jews, by way of a loan, more or less, and dies before that debt is paid, the debt shall not draw interest so long as the heir is under age, from whomsoever he holds; and if that debt falls into our hands, we will take nothing except the chattel contained in the agreement.

11. And if any one dies leaving a debt owing to the Jews, his wife shall have her dowry, and shall pay nothing of that debt;

and if there remain minor children of the dead man, necessaries shall be provided for them corresponding to the holding of the dead man; and from the remainder shall be paid the debt, saving the service of the lords. In the same way debts are to be treated which are owed to others than the Jews.

12. No scutage or aid shall be imposed in our kingdom except by the common council of our kingdom, except for the ransoming of our body, for the making of our oldest son a knight, and for once marrying our oldest daughter, and for these purposes it shall be only a reasonable aid; in the same way it shall be done concerning the aids of the city of London.

13. And the city of London shall have all its ancient liberties and free customs, as well by land as by water. Moreover, we will and grant that all other cities and boroughs and villages and ports shall have all their liberties and free customs.

14. And for holding a common council of the kingdom concerning the assessment of an aid otherwise than in the three cases mentioned above, or concerning the assessment of a scutage we shall cause to be summoned the archbishops, bishops, abbots, earls, and greater barons by our letters individually; and besides we shall cause to be summoned generally, by our sheriffs and bailiffs all those who hold from us in chief, for a certain day, that is at the end of forty days at least, and for a certain place; and in all the letters of that summons, we will express the cause of the summons, and when the summons has thus been given the business shall proceed on the appointed day, on the advice of those who shall be present, even if not all of those who were summoned have come.

15. We will not grant to any one, moreover, that he shall take an aid from his free men, except for ransoming his body, for making his oldest son a knight, and for once marrying his oldest daughter; and for

these purposes only a reasonable aid shall be taken.

16. No one shall be compelled to perform any greater service for a knight's fee, or for any other free tenement than is owed from it.

17. The common pleas shall not follow our court, but shall be held in some certain place.

18. The recognition of *novel disseisin, mort d'ancestor,* and *darrein presentment* shall be held only in their own counties and in this manner: we, or if we are outside of the kingdom our principal justiciar, will send two justiciars through each county four times a year, who with four knights of each county, elected by the county, shall hold in the county, and on the day and in the place of the county court, the aforesaid assizes of the county.

19. And if the aforesaid assizes cannot be held within the day of the county court, a sufficient number of knights and free-holders shall remain from those who were present at the county court on that day to give the judgments, according as the business is more or less.

20. A free man shall not be fined for a small offence, except in proportion to the measure of the offence; and for a great offence he shall be fined in proportion to the magnitude of the offence, saving his freehold; and a merchant in the same way, saving his merchandise; and the villain shall be fined in the same way, saving his wainage, if he shall be at our mercy; and none of the above fines shall be imposed except by the oaths of honest men of the neighborhood.

21. Earls and barons shall only be fined by their peers, and only in proportion to their offence.

22. A clergyman shall be fined, like those before mentioned, only in proportion to his lay holding, and not according to the extent of his ecclesiastical benefice.

23. No vill or man shall be compelled to make bridges over the rivers except those which ought to do it of old and rightfully.

24. No sheriff, constable, coroners, or other bailiffs of ours shall hold pleas of our crown.

25. All counties, hundreds, wapentakes, and trithings shall be at the ancient rents and without any increase, excepting our demesne manors.

26. If any person holding a lay fief from us shall die, and our sheriff or bailiff shall show our letters-patent of our summons concerning a debt which the deceased owed to us, it shall be lawful for our sheriff or bailiff to attach and levy on the chattels of the deceased found on his lay fief, to the value of that debt, in the view of legal men, so nevertheless that nothing be removed thence until the clear debt to us shall be paid; and the remainder shall be left to the executors for the fulfilment of the will of the deceased; and if nothing is owed to us by him, all the chattels shall go to the deceased, saving to his wife and children their reasonable shares.

27. If any free man dies intestate, his chattels shall be distributed by the hands of his near relatives and friends, under the oversight of the church, saving to each one the debts which the deceased owed to him.

28. No constable or other bailiff of ours shall take any one's grain or other chattels, without immediately paying for them in money, unless he is able to obtain a postponement at the goodwill of the seller.

29. No constable shall require any knight to give money in place of his ward of a castle if he is willing to furnish that ward in his own person or through another honest man, if he himself is not able to do it for a reasonable cause; and if we shall lead or send him into the army he shall be free from ward in proportion to the amount of time during which he has been in the army through us.

30. No sheriff or bailiff of ours or any one else shall take horses or wagons of any free

man for carrying purposes except on the permission of that free man.

31. Neither we nor our bailiffs will take the wood of another man for castles, or for anything else which we are doing, except by the permission of him to whom the wood belongs.

32. We will not hold the lands of those convicted of a felony for more than a year and a day, after which the lands shall be returned to the lords of the fiefs.

33. All the fish-weirs in the Thames and the Medway, and throughout all England shall be done away with, except those on the coast.

34. The writ which is called *praecipe* shall not be given for the future to any one concerning any tenement by which a free man can lose his court.

35. There shall be one measure of wine throughout our whole kingdom, and one measure of ale, and one measure of grain, that is the London quarter, and one width of dyed cloth and of russets and of halbergets, that is two ells within the selvages; of weights, moreover it shall be as of measures.

36. Nothing shall henceforth be given or taken for a writ of inquisition concerning life or limbs, but it shall be given freely and not denied.

37. If any one holds from us by fee farm or by socage or by burgage, and from another he holds land by military service, we will not have the guardianship of the heir or of his land which is of the fief of another, on account of that fee farm, or socage, or burgage; nor will we have the custody of that fee farm, or socage, or burgage, unless that fee farm itself owes military service. We will not have the guardianship of the heir or of the land of any one, which he holds from another by military service on account of any petty serjeanty which he holds from us by the service of paying to us knives or arrows, or things of that kind.

38. No bailiff for the future shall put any one to his law on his simple affirmation, without credible witnesses brought for this purpose.

39. No free man shall be taken or imprisoned or dispossessed, or outlawed, or banished, or in any way destroyed, nor will we go upon him, nor send upon him, except by the legal judgment of his peers or by the law of the land.

40. To no one will we sell, to no one will we deny, or delay right or justice.

41. All merchants shall be safe and secure in going out from England and coming into England and in remaining and going through England, as well by land as by water, for buying and selling, free from all evil tolls, by the ancient and rightful customs, except in time of war, and if they are of a land at war with us; and if such are found in our land at the beginning of war, they shall be attached without injury to their bodies or goods, until it shall be known from us or from our principal justiciar in what way the merchants of our land are treated who shall be then found in the country which is at war with us; and if ours are safe there, the others shall be safe in our land.

42. It is allowed henceforth to any one to go out from our kingdom, and to return, safely and securely, by land and by water, saving their fidelity to us, except in time of war for some short time, for the common good of the kingdom; excepting persons imprisoned and outlawed according to the law of the realm, and people of a land at war with us, and merchants, of whom it shall be done as is before said.

43. If any one holds from any escheat, as from the honor of Wallingford, or Nottingham, or Boulogne, or Lancaster, or from other escheats which are in our hands and are baronies, and he dies, his heir shall not give any other relief, nor do to us any other service than he would do to the baron, if that barony was in the hands of the baron;

and we will hold it in the same way as the baron held it.

44. Men who dwell outside the forest shall not henceforth come before our justiciars of the forest, on common summons, unless they are in a plea of, or pledges for any person or persons who are arrested on account of the forest.

45. We will not make justiciars, constables, sheriffs or bailiffs except of such as know the law of the realm and are well inclined to observe it.

46. All barons who have founded abbeys for which they have charters of kings of England, or ancient tenure, shall have their custody when they have become vacant, as they ought to have.

47. All forests which have been afforested in our time shall be disafforested immediately; and so it shall be concerning river banks which in our time have been fenced in.

48. All the bad customs concerning forests and warrens and concerning foresters and warreners, sheriffs and their servants, river banks and their guardians shall be inquired into immediately in each county by twelve sworn knights of the same county, who shall be elected by the honest men of the same county, and within forty days after the inquisition has been made, they shall be entirely destroyed by them, never to be restored, provided that we be first informed of it, or our justiciar, if we are not in England.

49. We will give back immediately all hostages and charters which have been liberated to us by Englishmen as security for peace or for faithful service.

50. We will remove absolutely from their bailiwicks the relatives of Gerard de Athyes, so that for the future they shall have no bailiwick in England; Engelard de Cygony, Andrew, Peter and Gyon de Chancelles, Gyon de Cygony, Geoffrey de Martin and his brothers, Philip Mark and his brothers, and Geoffrey his nephew and their whole retinue.

51. And immediately after the reëstablishment of peace we will remove from the kingdom all foreign-born soldiers, crossbow men, serjeants, and mercenaries who have come with horses and arms for the injury of the realm.

52. If any one shall have been dispossessed or removed by us without legal judgment of his peers, from his lands, castles, franchises, or his right we will restore them to him immediately; and if contention arises about this, then it shall be done according to the judgment of the twenty-five barons, of whom mention is made below concerning the security of the peace. Concerning all those things, however, from which any one has been removed or of which he has been deprived without legal judgment of his peers by King Henry our father, or by King Richard our brother, which we have in our hand, or which others hold, and which it is our duty to guarantee, we shall have respite till the usual term of crusaders; excepting those things about which the suit has been begun or the inquisition made by our writ before our assumption of the cross; when, however, we shall return from our journey or if by chance we desist from the journey, we will immediately show full justice in regard to them.

53. We shall, moreover, have the same respite and in the same manner about showing justice in regard to the forests which are to be disafforested or to remain forests, which Henry our father or Richard our brother made into forests; and concerning the custody of lands which are in the fief of another, custody of which we have until now had on account of a fief which any one has held from us by military service; and concerning the abbeys which have been founded in fiefs of others than ourselves, in which the lord of the fee has as-

serted for himself a right; and when we return or if we should desist from our journey we will immediately show full justice to those complaining in regard to them.

54. No one shall be seised nor imprisoned on the appeal of a woman concerning the death of any one except her husband.

55. All fines which have been imposed unjustly and against the law of the land, and all penalties imposed unjustly and against the law of the land are altogether excused, or will be on the judgment of the twenty-five barons of whom mention is made below in connection with the security of the peace, or on the judgment of the majority of them, along with the aforesaid Stephen, archbishop of Canterbury, if he is able to be present, and others whom he may wish to call for this purpose along with him. And if he should not be able to be present, nevertheless the business shall go on without him, provided that if any one or more of the aforesaid twenty-five barons are in a similar suit they should be removed as far as this particular judgment goes, and others who shall be chosen and put upon oath, by the remainder of the twenty-five shall be substituted for them for this purpose.

56. If we have dispossessed or removed any Welshmen from their lands, or franchises, or other things, without legal judgment of their peers, in England, or in Wales, they shall be immediately returned to them; and if a dispute shall have arisen over this, then it shall be settled in the borderland by judgment of their peers, concerning holdings of England according to the law of England, concerning holdings of Wales according to the law of Wales, and concerning holdings of the borderland according to the law of the borderland. The Welsh shall do the same to us and ours.

57. Concerning all those things, however, from which any one of the Welsh shall have been removed or dispossessed without

legal judgment of his peers, by King Henry our father, or King Richard our brother, which we hold in our hands, or which others hold, and we are bound to warrant to them, we shall have respite till the usual period of crusaders, those being excepted about which suit was begun or inquisition made by our command before our assumption of the cross. When, however, we shall return or if by chance we shall desist from our journey, we will show full justice to them immediately, according to the laws of the Welsh and the aforesaid parts.

58. We will give back the son of Lewellyn immediately, and all the hostages from Wales and the charters which had been liberated to us as a security for peace.

59. We will act toward Alexander, king of the Scots, concerning the return of his sisters and his hostages, and concerning his franchises and his right, according to the manner in which we shall act toward our other barons of England, unless it ought to be otherwise by the charters which we hold from William his father, formerly king of the Scots, and this shall be by the judgment of his peers in our court.

60. Moreover, all those customs and franchises mentioned above which we have conceded in our kingdom, and which are to be fulfilled, as far as pertains to us, in respect to our men; all men of our kingdom as well clergy as laymen, shall observe as far as pertains to them, in respect to their men.

61. Since, moreover, for the sake of God, and for the improvement of our kingdom, and for the better quieting of the hostility sprung up lately between us and our barons, we have made all these concessions; wishing them to enjoy these in a complete and firm stability forever, we make and concede to them the security described below; that is to say, that they shall elect twenty-five barons of the kingdom, whom they will, who ought with all their power

to observe, hold, and cause to be observed, the peace and liberties which we have conceded to them, and by this our present charter confirmed to them; in this manner, that if we or our justiciar, or our bailiffs, or any one of our servants shall have done wrong in any way toward any one, or shall have transgressed any of the articles of peace or security; and the wrong shall have been shown to four barons of the aforesaid twenty-five barons, let those four barons come to us or to our justiciar, if we are out of the kingdom, laying before us the transgression, and let them ask that we cause that transgression to be corrected without delay. And if we shall not have corrected the transgression or, if we shall be out of the kingdom if our justiciar shall not have corrected it within a period of forty days, counting from the time in which it has been shown to us or to our justiciar, if we are out of the kingdom; the aforesaid four barons shall refer the matter to the remainder of the twenty-five barons, and let these twenty-five barons with the whole community of the country distress and injure us in every way they can; that is to say by the seizure of our castles, lands, possessions, and in such other ways as they can until it shall have been corrected according to their judgment, saving our person and that of our queen, and those of our children; and when the correction has been made, let them devote themselves to us as they did before. And let whoever in the country wishes take an oath that in all the above-mentioned measures he will obey the orders of the aforesaid twenty-five barons, and that he will injure us as far as he is able with them, and we give permission to swear publicly and freely to each one who wishes to swear, and no one will we ever forbid to swear. All those, moreover, in the country who of themselves and their own will are unwilling to take an oath to the twenty-five barons as to distressing and injuring us along with them, we will compel to take the oath by our mandate, as before said. And if any one of the twenty-five barons shall have died or departed from the land or shall in any other way be prevented from taking the above-mentioned action, let the remainder of the aforesaid twenty-five barons choose another in his place, according to their judgment, who shall take an oath in the same way as the others. In all those things, moreover, which are committed to those five and twenty barons to carry out, if perhaps the twenty-five are present, and some disagreement arises among them about something, or if any of them when they have been summoned are not willing or are not able to be present, let that be considered valid and firm which the greater part of those who are present arrange or command, just as if the whole twenty-five had agreed in this; and let the aforesaid twenty-five swear that they will observe faithfully all the things which are said above, and with all their ability cause them to be observed. And we will obtain nothing from any one, either by ourselves or by another by which any of these concessions and liberties shall be revoked or diminished; and if any such thing shall have been obtained, let it be invalid and void, and we will never use it by ourselves or by another.

62. And all ill-will, grudges, and anger sprung up between us and our men, clergy and laymen, from the time of the dispute, we have fully renounced and pardoned to all. Moreover, all transgressions committed on account of this dispute, from Easter in the sixteenth year of our reign till the restoration of peace, we have fully remitted to all, clergy and laymen, and as far as pertains to us, fully pardoned. And moreover we have caused to be made for them testimonial letters-patent of lord Stephen, archbishop of Canterbury, lord Henry, archbishop of Dublin, and of the aforesaid bishops and of Master Pandulf, in respect to

that security and the concessions named above.

63. Wherefore we will and firmly command that the Church of England shall be free, and that the men in our kingdom shall have and hold all the aforesaid liberties, rights and concessions, well and peacefully, freely and quietly, fully and completely, for themselves and their heirs, from us and our heirs, in all things and places,

forever, as before said. It has been sworn, moreover, as well on our part as on the part of the barons, that all these things spoken of above shall be observed in good faith and without any evil intent. Witness the above named and many others. Given by our hand in the meadow which is called Runnymede, between Windsor and Staines, on the fifteenth day of June, in the seventeenth year of our reign.

St. Francis of Assisi

The life of St. Francis of Assisi (*c*.1182-1226) presents an aspect of medieval Christianity that contrasts sharply with those displayed in the great cathedrals, with their wealth and splendor, or in the universities, with their learning and subtle disputation. For Francis centered the Christian life on poverty, innocence, and simple devotion. These ideals, plus that of service to mankind, were the foundations on which he established the

Franciscan order of friars in 1209. The Franciscan friars ("brothers"), unlike the Benedictine and other monks who remained cloistered in their monasteries, were to go out into the world among the common people to preach and to teach, accepting for their services only enough alms to keep themselves clothed and fed.

Francis himself was a mystic —one of those rare individuals who feel that they have come face to face with God and have

communed with him. The selection that follows details the events leading up to St. Francis's greatest mystical experience, the miracle of the stigmata, and concludes with a description of this occurrence.

Although the author of the work from which this selection was taken is unknown, it is believed that he was a member of the Franciscan order who, judging from the style of his written Italian, probably came from Florence.

THE LITTLE FLOWERS OF ST. FRANCIS

When St. Francis was forty-three years of age, in the year one thou-

THE LITTLE FLOWERS OF ST. FRANCIS, trans. T. Okey. *Everyman's Library Edition*, E. P. Dutton & Co., Inc. Reprinted by permission of the publishers.

sand two hundred and twenty-four, he was inspired by God to set forth from the vale of Spoleto and journey into Romagna, with Friar Leo his companion; and as they went they passed by the foot of the burg of

Montefeltro, wherein a great banquet and a great procession were made by reason of the knighting of one of those counts of Montefeltro. And St. Francis, hearing of this solemn festival and that many noblemen of divers countries were assembled together there, said to Friar Leo, "Let us go up thither to this festival, for with God's help we shall gather some good spiritual fruit." Now among the other nobles that were come to that festival from the country round about was a certain rich and mighty nobleman of Tuscany, called Roland of Chiusi di Casentino, who, because of the wondrous things he had heard of the holiness and of the miracles of St. Francis, held him in great devotion, and had a very great desire to behold him and to hear him preach. And St. Francis came up to that burg and entered within, and went to the market-place, where all the host of those nobles was gathered together, and in fervour of spirit climbed on to a low wall and began to preach, taking for the text of his sermon these words in the vulgar tongue—

A joy to me is every pain,
For I await a greater gain.

And upon this text he preached so devoutly and so profoundly by inspiration of the Holy Spirit, proving it by divers pains and martyrdoms of the holy apostles and the holy martyrs, and by the hard penances of the holy confessors, and the many tribulations and temptations of the holy virgins and other saints, that all the people stood with eyes and minds lifted up towards him, and hearkened as if an angel of God were speaking. And among them was the said Roland, who, touched to the heart by God through the wondrous preaching of St. Francis, was minded to confer and take counsel with him, after the sermon, touching the state of his soul. Wherefore, the sermon ended, he drew St. Francis aside and said to him, "O father, fain would I take counsel with thee touching the sal-

vation of my soul." St. Francis answered, "It pleaseth me well; but go this morning, honour thy friends that have bidden thee to this feast, and dine with them, and after thou hast dined, we will speak together as long as it shall please thee." Roland therefore went away to dine, and after he had dined, returned to St. Francis and thus conferred and discoursed with him fully, touching the state of his soul. And at last this Roland said to St. Francis, "I have a mountain in Tuscany most proper for devout contemplation that is called the mount of La Verna, and is very solitary and meet for those that desire to do penance in a place far away from the world, or to lead a solitary life; and if it so please thee, fain would I give it to thee and to thy companions for the salvation of my soul." St. Francis, hearing this bounteous offer of a thing he so much desired, rejoiced with exceeding great joy, and praising and giving thanks, first to God and then to Roland, spake to him thus, "Roland, when you are returned to your house I will send some of my companions to you, and you will show this mountain to them; and if it seem to them a proper place for prayer and penance, from this time forth I accept your charitable offer." This said, St. Francis departed, and when he had made an end of his journey he returned to St. Mary of the Angels; and Roland likewise, when he had celebrated the end of that festival, returned to his castle that was called Chiusi, and was distant a mile from La Verna. And St. Francis, being returned to St. Mary of the Angels, sent forth two of his companions to the said Roland, who, when they were come to him, received them with the greatest joy and charity. And being fain to show them the mount of La Verna, he sent with them full fifty men-at-arms to be their defence against the wild beasts; and these friars, thus escorted, ascended to the top of the mountain and sought diligently about, and at the last they came to a part of the mountain that was meet for a holy place and most proper for contemplation, in which place was an open plain: this spot they chose for the habitation of them and of St. Francis, and there, with the help of the men-at-arms that were in their escort, they made some little cells of the branches of trees. And thus in the name of God they accepted and took possession of the mount of La Verna, and of the friary on that mountain, and departed and returned to St. Francis. And when they were come to St. Francis they related to him how and in what manner they had taken a place on the mount of La Verna most meet for prayer and contemplation. Hearing these tidings, St. Francis rejoiced greatly, and praising and giving thanks to God, spake to these friars with a glad countenance, and said, "My sons, we are drawing nigh to our lent of St. Michael the Archangel, and I steadfastly believe that it is God's will we should keep this fast on the mount of La Verna, that by divine providence hath been prepared for us, in order that we may merit from Christ the joy of consecrating that blessed mount to the honour and glory of God and of His Mother, the glorious Virgin Mary, and the holy angels." This said, St. Francis took with him Friar Masseo of Marignano d'Assisi, that was a man of great wisdom and great eloquence; and Friar Angelo Tancredi of Rieti, that was a very noble gentleman, and in the world had been a knight; and Friar Leo, that was a man of great simplicity and purity, and therefore much beloved of St. Francis. And St. Francis with these three friars set himself to pray, and commended himself and the aforesaid companions to the prayers of the friars that were left behind; and then set forth, in the name of Jesus Christ crucified, with those three to go to the mount of La Verna. And as St. Francis went forth, he called one of those three companions, and he was Friar Masseo, and spake to him thus, "Thou,

Friar Masseo, shalt be our warden and our superior on this journey, I say, while we go and remain together; and thus we will observe our Rule, for whether we say the office, or discourse of God, or keep silence, we will take no thought for the morrow, neither what we shall eat, nor what we shall drink, nor where we shall sleep; but when the hour of rest cometh we will beg a little bread, and then will stay our steps and rest ourselves in the place that God shall prepare for us." Then did these three companions bow their heads, and making the sign of the cross, journeyed on; and the first evening they came to a friary and there lodged. The second evening, by reason of the bad weather and of being so weary they were not able to come to a friary, nor to any burg, nor to any hamlet, and night falling after the bad weather, they took refuge in a deserted and ruined church and there lay down to rest. And while his companions were sleeping, St. Francis betook himself to prayer, and lo, at the first watch of the night there came a great host of fiercest devils with a great noise and tumult and began to do him mighty battle and annoy: for one plucked him here, another there; one pulled him down, another up; one threatened him with one thing, and one rebuked for another; and thus in divers ways they strove to disturb his prayers; but they could not, for God was with him. And when St. Francis had endured these assaults of the devils a long space, he began to cry with a loud voice, "O ye damned spirits, naught can ye avail except in so far as the hand of God suffereth you: therefore in the name of the omnipotent God I say unto you, do ye unto my body whatsoever is permitted you by God, for I suffer all willingly, since no greater enemy have I than my body; therefore, if ye avenge me of mine enemy, ye do me too great a service." Then the devils seized him and with great violence and fury began to drag him about the church and to wreak on him more grievous hurt and annoy than before. Whereat St. Francis began to cry aloud and say, "My Lord Jesus Christ, I thank Thee for the great love and charity Thou hast shown toward me; for 'tis a token of great love when the Lord well punisheth His servant for all his faults in this world, in order that he be not punished in the next. And I am prepared to endure joyfully every pain and every adversity that Thou, my God, art willing to send for my sins." Then the devils, confounded and vanquished by his constancy and patience, departed, and St. Francis came forth from the church in fervour of spirit and entered into a wood that was nigh and betook him to prayer, and with prayers and with tears, and with smitings of the breast, sought Jesus Christ, the beloved spouse of his soul.

And at last, finding Him in the secret places of his soul, now he spake with Him reverently as his Lord; now he gave answer to Him as his Judge; again he besought Him as a father, and yet again he reasoned with Him as a friend. On that night, and in that wood, his companions, after they awoke, stood hearkening and considering what he was doing, and they beheld and heard him with tears and cries devoutly entreat God's mercy for sinners. Then was he heard and seen to bewail, with a loud voice, the Passion of Christ, even as if he beheld it with corporeal eyes. And in that selfsame night they saw him praying with his arms held in the form of a cross, and lifted up from the ground and suspended for a great space, and surrounded by a bright and shining cloud. And thus he passed all that night in these holy exercises, without sleep; and in the morning his companions, knowing that St. Francis, by reason of the fatigues of that night passed without sleep, was very feeble in body, and would have ill borne to go afoot, went to a poor peasant of that country-side, and, for love of God, craved the loan of his ass for St. Francis,

their father, that could not go afoot. This man, hearing the name of Friar Francis, asked of them, "Are ye of those friars of that friar of Assisi whereof so much good is told?" The friars answered, "Yea," and that verily it was for him they craved the sumpter beast. Then this honest fellow saddled the ass with great devotion and solicitude, and led him to St. Francis, and with great reverence bade him mount thereon; and so they went their way, the peasant with them, behind his ass. And after they had journeyed on a while, the peasant said to St. Francis, "Tell me, art thou that Friar Francis of Assisi?" And St. Francis answered, "Yea." "Now strive, then," said the peasant, "to be as good as thou art held to be by all folk, for many have great faith in thee; therefore I admonish thee that thou betray not the hopes men cherish of thee." St. Francis, hearing these words, disdained not to be admonished by a peasant, nor said within himself, "What beast is this that doth admonish me?" as many proud fellows that wear the cowl would say nowadays, but straightway flung himself off the ass and alighted on the ground and knelt down before him, and kissed his feet, and humbly thanked him for that he had deigned to admonish him thus charitably. Then the peasant, together with the companions of St. Francis, raised him up from the ground, with great devotion, and set him again on the ass and journeyed on. And when they had climbed about halfway up the mountain, a great thirst came upon this peasant, for the heat was very great, and toilsome the ascent; whereat he began to cry behind St. Francis, saying, "Ah me! I die of thirst, for if I have not water to drink I shall forthwith choke." Wherefore St. Francis got down from the ass and fell to prayer, and so long he knelt, with hands lifted up to heaven, until he knew by revelation that his prayer was heard of God. Then said St. Francis to the peasant, "Haste; hie thee quickly to that rock, there shalt thou find running water that Jesus Christ in this hour hath, in His mercy, made to issue from that rock." Now runs he to the place that St. Francis had shown to him, and there finds a fair spring which St. Francis, by virtue of his prayers, had made to gush forth from that hard rock; and he drank thereof abundantly, and was comforted. And well it appeareth that that spring was made to flow by God miraculously, at the prayers of St. Francis, for neither before nor after was ever a spring of water seen in that place, nor running water near that place for a great distance. This done, St. Francis, with his companions, and with the peasant, gave thanks to God for the miracle He had shown them, and then journeyed on. And when they were come nigh to the foot of the very rock of La Verna, it pleased St. Francis to rest a while under the oak tree that stood by the way, and there standeth to this day; and resting beneath it, St. Francis began to consider the lay of the place and of the country round about. And lo, while he was thus pondering there came a great multitude of birds from divers parts that, with singing and fluttering of their wings, showed forth great joy and gladness, and surrounded St. Francis, in such wise that some settled on his head, some on his shoulders, and some on his arms, some on his bosom, and some around his feet. His companions and the peasant, beholding this, marvelled greatly, and St. Francis rejoiced in spirit, and spake thus, "I do believe, dearest brothers, that it is pleasing to our Lord Jesus Christ that we abide on this solitary mountain, since our sisters and brothers, the birds, show forth such great joy at our coming." These words said, they rose up and journeyed on; and at last they came to the place that his companions had taken at first.

.   .   .

Then St. Francis made his companions sit down, and instructed them touching the manner of the life that they, and whoso would desire to live like religious, in hermitages, should lead. And among other things, he laid upon them the single-minded observance of holy poverty, saying, "Heed not overmuch Roland's charitable offer, lest ye in any way offend our lady, madonna holy Poverty. Be ye sure that the more we despise poverty, the more the world will despise us, and the greater need we shall suffer; but if we embrace holy poverty, full straitly the world will follow after us and feed us abundantly. God hath called us to this holy Rule of life for the salvation of the world, and hath made this covenant between us and the world, that we give good example to the world and the world provides for our needs. Let us persevere, then, in holy poverty, because that is the way of perfection, and the earnest and pledge of everlasting riches." And after many fair and devout words, and admonitions of this sort, he made an end, saying, "This is the manner of life that I lay on myself and on you; and for that I see me drawing nigh unto death, I purpose to withdraw to a solitary place and make my peace with God, and weep for my sins before Him; and let Friar Leo, when it shall seem good to him, bring me a little bread and water, and on no account to suffer any lay folk to come to me: do ye answer them for me." These words said, he gave them his blessing, and went to the cell under the beech tree, and his companions remained in their habitation with the steadfast purpose to obey the commands of St. Francis. A few days thereafter, as St. Francis was standing beside the said cell, considering the form of the mountain, and marvelling at the exceeding great clefts and caverns in the mighty rocks, he betook himself to prayer; and then it was revealed to him by God that these clefts, so marvellous, had been miraculously made at the hour of the Passion of Christ, when, according to the gospel, the rocks were rent asunder. And this, God willed, should manifestly appear on the mount of La Verna, because there the Passion of our Lord Jesus Christ was to be renewed, through love and pity, in the soul of St. Francis, and in his body by the imprinting of the sacred, hallowed stigmas. No sooner had St. Francis received that revelation than he forthwith locked himself in his cell, and retired wholly into himself, and made him ready for the mystery of this revelation, and from that hour St. Francis, through his unceasing prayers, began to taste more often of the sweetness of divine contemplation; wherefore many times was he so rapt in God that he was seen of his companions to be lifted up bodily from the ground and ravished out of himself.

·   ·   ·

Through this gift of God's grace within him, St. Francis was not only rapt in God by ecstatic contemplation, but many times was likewise comforted by visits of angels. Wherefore, as St. Francis one day was meditating on his death, and on the state of his Order after his death, and saying, "Lord God, what will become of Thy poor little household, that Thou of Thy goodness hast committed to me, a sinner? Who shall comfort them? Who shall correct them? Who shall pray to Thee for them?" And while he was uttering such words, the angel sent of God appeared to him, and comforted him with these words, "I say unto thee, in God's name, that the profession of thy Order shall not fail until the Judgment Day; and none shall be so great a sinner, but that if he love thy Order in his heart, the same shall find mercy in God's sight; and none that evilly persecuteth thy Order shall have length of life. Moreover, no wicked member of thy Order shall long continue therein, except he amend his life. Therefore be not cast down if thou seest some that are not good friars in thy Order, and that observe not the Rule as they ought; think not that for this thy Order shall perish; for ever shall there be of

them—and they shall be many and many— that will observe perfectly the life of the gospel of Christ, and the purity of the Rule; and such as these shall go straightway to life everlasting after the death of the body, without passing through any purgatory. And some shall observe the Rule, but not perfectly; and they, ere they go to paradise, shall pass through purgatory, but the time of their purgation shall be committed to thee by God. But touching those that observe not the Rule at all—have no care of them, saith God, because He careth not." These words said, the angel departed, and St. Francis remained comforted and consoled. As the feast of the Assumption of Our Lady was now drawing nigh, St. Francis seeketh the opportunity of a more solitary and more secret place, wherein he may keep the fast of St. Michael the Archangel, that beginneth with the said feast of the Assumption. Wherefore he calls Friar Leo, and speaks to him thus, "Go and stand at the doorway of the oratory of the friary, and when I call thee do thou return to me." Friar Leo goes and stands at the doorway, and St. Francis withdrew a space and called loudly. Hearing himself called, Friar Leo returns to him, and St. Francis saith, "Son, let us seek a more secret place, whence thou canst not hear me when I call." And, in their search, they caught sight of a secret place on that side of the mountain that looketh to the south, and only too meet for his purpose; but they could not get there, because in front thereof was a horrible and fearful and very great chasm in the rock; wherefore, with great labour, they laid some logs across this chasm, after the manner of a bridge, and passed over. Then St. Francis sent for the other friars, and tells them how that he purposed to keep the lent of St. Michael in that solitary place, and therefore prays them to make a little cell there, so that no call of his might be heard by them. And the little cell of St. Francis being made, he saith to them, "Go ye to your dwelling, and leave me here alone, for with God's help I purpose to keep the fast here, with mind undistraught or unperturbed: therefore let none of you come to me, nor suffer any worldly folk to come to me. But thou only, Friar Leo, shalt come to me, once a day, with a little bread and water, and once again, by night, at the hour of matins: then shalt thou come to me in silence, and when thou art at the foot of the bridge thou shalt say to me, *Domine labia mea aperies,* and if I answer 'Come,' pass thou on to the cell, and we will say matins together; but if I answer not, return thou straightway." And St. Francis said this because sometimes he was so rapt in God that he neither heard nor perceived aught with his bodily senses. This said, St. Francis gave them his blessing, and they returned to the friary. And the feast of the Assumption being come, St. Francis began the holy fast with great abstinence and severity, mortifying his body and comforting his spirit with fervent prayers, watchings, and scourgings; and ever waxing from virtue to virtue in these prayers, he made ready his soul to receive the divine mysteries and divine splendours, and his body to endure the cruel assaults of the devils, wherewith he was ofttimes smitten corporeally; and among other times, on a day during that fast, as St. Francis issued from his cell in fervour of spirit, and went to pray hard by in a hollow cave in the rock, at a great height from the ground and looking on a horrible and fearful abyss, suddenly the devil cometh in a terrible form, with tempest and mighty ruin, and smiteth him to thrust him down the abyss. Whereat St. Francis, having no whither to flee, and being unable to suffer the cruel aspect of the devil, anon turned with hands and face and all his body close to the rock, commending himself to God, and groping about with his hands, if haply he might find aught to cling to. But, as it pleased God, who never let-

teth His servants be tempted beyond what they can endure, straightway the rock, whereto he clung, was hollowed out by a miracle to the form of his body, and received him into itself, in such wise that the said rock was imprinted with the form of the face and the hands of St. Francis, as if he had pressed his hands and face against melted wax; and thus, with God's help, he escaped from the devil. . . .

St. Francis then, as hath been told, persevered in that fast, and albeit he endured many assaults of the devil, none the less did he receive many consolations from God, not only by visits of angels, but likewise of wild birds; for all the time of that lent, a falcon that had built her nest hard by his cell awoke him every night, a little before matins, by her singing and by beating her wings against his cell, and she departed not until he had risen up to say matins. And when St. Francis was more weary at one time than another, or more sick, or more feeble, this falcon, after the manner of a discreet and compassionate person, sang later. And so St. Francis had great pleasure of this clock; for the great solicitude of this falcon drove all sloth away from him and urged him to prayer, and beyond this, she ofttimes by day dwelt familiarly with him. Finally . . . St. Francis, being much weakened in body, in part by his great abstinence, and in part by the assaults of the devil, and being fain to comfort his body with the spiritual food of the soul, began to meditate on the ineffable glory and joy of the blessed in the life eternal; and he began to beseech God to grant him the grace of some foretaste of that joy. And while he remained thus meditating, anon an angel appeared to him with exceeding great splendour, that held a viol in his left hand and a bow in his right; and as St. Francis stood all dazed at this vision, the angel drew his bow once upwards across the viol; and straightway St. Francis heard such sweet melody that it ravished his soul and lifted him beyond all bodily sense, so that, as he afterwards related to his companions, he doubted lest his soul had wholly parted from his body, by reason of the unbearable sweetness, if the angel had drawn the bow downwards again.

.   .   .

And from that time forth St. Francis began to taste and feel more bounteously the sweetness of divine contemplation and of divine visitations. Among which, he had one, immediate and preparatory to the imprinting of the divine stigmas, in this form. The day that goeth before the feast of the Most Holy Cross in the month of September, as St. Francis was praying in secret in his cell, the angel of God appeared to him and spake thus to him in God's name, "I am come to comfort and admonish thee that thou humbly prepare thee and make thee ready, with all patience, to receive that which God willeth to give thee and to work in thee." St. Francis answered, "I am ready to endure patiently all things that my Lord would do with me." This said, the angel departed. The day following, to wit, the day of the Most Holy Cross, St. Francis, on the morn before daybreak, knelt down betimes in prayer before the door of his cell; and turning his face eastwards, prayed in this wise, "O my Lord Jesus Christ, two graces do I pray Thee to grant unto me ere I die: the first, that while I live I may feel in my body and in my soul, so far as is possible, that sorrow, sweet Lord, that Thou didst suffer in the hour of Thy bitterest Passion; the second is, that I may feel in my heart, so far as may be possible, that exceeding love wherewith, O Son of God, Thou wast enkindled to endure willingly for us sinners agony so great." And remaining a long time thus praying, he knew that God would hear him; and that, so far as might be possible to a mere creature, thus far would it be vouchsafed to him to suffer the aforesaid things. St. Francis, having this promise, began to contemplate most de-

voutly the Passion of Christ and His infinite love; and the fervour of devotion waxed so within him that through love and through compassion he was wholly changed into Jesus. And being thus inflamed by this contemplation, he beheld, that same morning, a seraph with six resplendent and flaming wings come down from heaven; which seraph, with swift flight, drew nigh to St. Francis so that he could discern him, and he knew clearly that he had the form of a man crucified; and thus were his wings disposed: two wings were extended over his head; two were spread out in flight; and the other two covered the whole of the body. St. Francis, beholding this, was sore afeard, and yet was he filled with sweetness and sorrow mingled with wonder. Joy had he, exceeding great, at the gracious aspect of Christ that appeared to him thus familiarly and looked on him so graciously; but, on the other hand, seeing him nailed upon the cross, he suffered unspeakable grief and compassion. Thereafter, he marvelled greatly at so stupendous and unwonted a vision, well knowing that the infirmity of the Passion doth not accord with the immortality of the seraphic spirit. And being in this wonderment, it was revealed by the seraph who appeared to him, that that vision had been shown to him in such form, by divine providence, in order that he might understand he was to be changed into the express similitude of the crucified Christ in this wondrous vision, not by bodily martyrdom but by spiritual fire. Then the whole mount of La Verna seemed to flame forth with dazzling splendour, that shone and illumined all the mountains and the valleys round about, as were the sun shining on the earth. Wherefore when the shepherds that were watching in that country saw the mountain aflame and so much brightness round about they were sore afraid, according as they afterwards told the friars, and affirmed that that flame had endured over the mount of La Verna for the space of an hour and more. Likewise, certain muleteers that were going to Romagna, arose up at the brightness of this light which shone through the windows of the inns of that country, and thinking the sun had risen, saddled and loaded their beasts. And as they went their way, they saw the said light wane and the real sun rise. Now Christ appeared in that same seraphic vision, and revealed to St. Francis certain secret and high things that St. Francis would never, during his life, disclose to any man; but, after his death, he revealed them, according as is set forth hereafter. And the words were these, "Knowest thou," said Christ, "what I have done to thee? I have given thee the stigmas that are the marks of my Passion, in order that thou be My standard-bearer. And even as I, on the day of my death, descended into limbo and delivered all the souls I found there by virtue of these My stigmas, so do I grant to thee that every year, on the day of thy death, thou mayst go to purgatory and deliver all the souls thou shalt find there of thy three orders—Minors, Sisters, and Penitents—and others likewise that shall have had great devotion to thee, and thou shalt lead them up to the glory of paradise in order that thou be conformed to Me in thy

death, even as thou art in thy life." This wondrous vision having vanished, after a great space, this secret converse left in the heart of St. Francis a burning flame of divine love, exceeding great, and in his flesh, a marvellous image and imprint of the Passion of Christ. For the marks of the nails began anon to be seen on the hands and on the feet of St. Francis, in the same manner as he had then seen them in the body of Jesus Christ crucified that had appeared to him in the form of a seraph: and thus his hands and feet seemed nailed through the middle with nails, the heads whereof were in the palms of his hands and in the soles of his feet, outside the flesh; and the points came out through the backs of the hands and the feet, so far, that they were bent back and clinched in such wise that one might easily have put a finger of the hand through the bent and clinched ends outside the flesh, even as through a ring: and the heads of the nails were round and black. In like fashion, the image of a lance-wound, unhealed, inflamed, and bleeding, was seen in his right side, whence thereafter blood came out many times from the holy breast of St. Francis and stained his tunic and his nether garments with blood.

Papal Political Documents

Throughout the Middle Ages, the Church and the temporal rulers of Europe carried on a running battle for political supremacy. For a time, the Church seemed assured of victory. It reached the height of its power during the pontificate of Innocent III (1198-1216), who succeeded in forcing King John to surrender England to him, to be held by John in the future as a fief from the papacy. The final victory, however, went to the secular powers, who gradually effected a separation between political authority and spiritual authority, reserving the former for themselves and permitting the Church to exercise the latter.

The documents that follow reflect the Church's position at two different phases during this long struggle. The first document is concerned with a dispute between the Holy Roman Emperor, Henry IV, and Pope Gregory VII, a dispute that resulted in Henry's famous winter pilgrimage to Canossa to seek absolution from the pope. The document is actually a letter, written in 1081, from Gregory to the Bishop of Metz, who had sought papal aid in combating the emperor. It is important because it contains Gregory's view of the position of the Church relative to the state, as well as the main arguments on which that position rested.

The second document, the papal bull *Unam Sanctam*, was written over two hundred years later (1302), during a controversy between Pope Boniface VIII and King Philip the Fair of France. Philip replied to the bull, which flatly asserts the political supremacy of the Church, by having the pope seized. Although Boniface was soon released, he died almost immediately afterward. Philip again took the initiative and managed to convert the papacy into an adjunct of the French throne. This episode marked the turning point in the political fortunes of the Church, for the popes were never able to regain the ascendancy over the secular monarchs that the papacy had enjoyed under Pope Innocent III.

THE SECOND LETTER OF GREGORY VII TO HERMANN, BISHOP OF METZ, MARCH 15, 1081

Gregory, Bishop, servant of the servants of God, to Our well-beloved brother in Christ, Hermann, Bishop of Metz, health and the Apostolic Benediction.

We know your desire to employ yourself, and to confront dangers, in the defence of truth, and We see in your good-will, the action of Divine Providence. The ineffable grace of God and His marvellous bounty, never permit His chosen ones to lapse into complete error, nor do they allow them to be altogether conquered and enslaved by sin. After the salutary trials of persecution, and the anxieties which they have experienced, the elect come forth stronger than

THE SECOND LETTER OF GREGORY VII TO HERMANN, BISHOP OF METZ, MARCH 15, 1081, in A. H. Mathew, *The Life and Times of Hildebrand* (London, 1910), pp. 292-305. [*Gregory's given name was Hildebrand. Ed.*]

before. Fear makes cowards shamelessly rival one another in flight; in like manner, those inspired by manly courage, strive to be in the front rank and to obtain the palm of valour and bravery. If We address this language to your charity, it is because you too wish to be in the front rank in the Christian army; that is, amongst those who, you know well, are closest to, and most worthy of, the God who gives the Victory.

You ask Us to come to your aid by Our writings and to refute the insanity of those, who maintain with their guilty tongues, that the Holy Apostolic See had not the right to excommunicate King Henry, that despiser of the Christian law, that destroyer of Churches, and of the Empire, that abettor and accomplice of heretics, and that it had not power to absolve from the oath of fidelity, which had been sworn to him. It does not seem very necessary for Us to do this, for this power is established by many authentic texts of Holy Scripture. We cannot indeed believe, that those who, for their own damnation, and with unblushing impudence oppose and fight against truth can, in their ignorance or madness, have had the audacity to use these texts as their justification. There would not, however, be anything astonishing in that, for it is the custom of the wicked to seek protection for their vices, and to defend their accomplices; it matters little to them if they ruin themselves by their lies.

To quote one proof from among many. Who does not know that saying of Our Lord and Saviour Jesus Christ, in the Gospel, *Thou art Peter, and upon this rock I will build My church; and the gates of hell shall not prevail against it. I will give to you the keys of the Kingdom of Heaven, and whatsoever you shall bind on earth, shall be bound also in heaven, and whatsoever you shall loose upon earth, shall be loosed also in heaven.*[1] Are kings an exception? Do they not form part of the flock confided to St. Peter by the Son of God? Then, We ask, who will dare to claim that he has nothing to do with the power of St. Peter, that the universal power of binding and loosing given to St. Peter, has no reference to him? No one would act in this manner, but that unhappy man, who, unwilling to bear the yoke of the Lord, would submit to that of the devil and renounce his right to belong to the fold of Christ. By this proud denial of the power divinely granted to St. Peter, he would obtain liberty, a sad liberty indeed, for the more he denied the power, the more heavily would his eternal damnation weigh upon him, on the day of judgment.

As the Holy Fathers accepted, with the greatest respect, this institution ordained by the divine will; this fundamental basis of the constitution of the Church, this

[1] St. Matt. XVI. 18, 19.

privilege, granted by a decree from heaven to blessed Peter, prince of the Apostles; they have always given to the Holy Roman Church, in their general councils, as well as in their decrees, the title of Universal Mother. Just as they have acknowledged her authority in matters of faith and in the teaching of holy religion, so they have also bowed down before her judgments. They have been unanimous in thinking and declaring that the most important questions, the most weighty matters, the declarations of all the Churches, were within her jurisdiction, because she is the Mother and head of all the Churches. They also declared, that it was no more allowable to appeal from her decisions than to modify or reject them. Thus, Pope Gelasius, speaking in the name of a divine authority, and writing to the Emperor Anastasius to show him what his attitude should be towards the head of the holy Apostolic See, expresses himself in these terms: *If, in general, all the faithful ought to be submissive to the priests, when the latter are the faithful interpreters of God, with much more reason ought the Pontiff of the Holy See to be obeyed, placed as he is by God, above all priests, and honoured by the Church with humble and continual submission. Human wisdom, however perfect it may be, cannot rise to such heights of knowledge, as he who enjoys the privilege of being raised above all by Christ Himself, and whom the Church considers and has always held to be her Primate.* In a similar manner, Pope Julius, writing to the Bishops of the East concerning the power of the Apostolic See, speaks as follows: *My brethren, since you were speaking to the Holy Roman and Apostolic Church, you ought to have expressed yourselves, not with irony, but with respect, as our Lord Jesus Christ Himself spoke to His Church, when He said to her, 'Thou art Peter, and upon this rock I will build My church; and the gates of hell shall not prevail against her; I will give to thee the keys of the Kingdom of Heaven.'* By a unique privilege she can indeed open and close, to whom she will, the gate of the heavenly kingdom. Is not he who has such power, he who can open or shut Heaven itself competent to judge of the things of earth! The contrary cannot be maintained. Do you remember the words of St. Paul: *Know you not that we shall judge angels? how much more the things of this world?* The blessed Pope Gregory, writing to a certain senator abbot, asserts that kings, who allow themselves to violate the decrees of the Apostolic See, ought to be deprived of their dignities. *If,* he writes, *any king, priest, judge or any secular, knowing the present decree, dares to offend against it, let him lose his power and dignity, and let him declare himself guilty before God of the iniquity he has committed. If he does not restore what he has unjustly stolen, and do penance in proportion to his fault, let him be deprived of the most holy Body and Blood of our Lord and Redeemer Jesus Christ; and may the vengeance of the eternal judgment fall upon him.*

If blessed Gregory, who was the meekest of the doctors, decreed that kings, who violated the statutes, which he gave to a hospital, should not only be deposed, but excommunicated and damned for ever, who would dare to reproach us for having deposed and excommunicated Henry, the despiser of the apostolic judgments, the fierce enemy of Mother Church, the infamous despoiler and merciless scourge of the whole kingdom, and of the churches? Who, but one, who is still more unworthy than he, would dare to cast reproach upon us? We read in a letter of the blessed Peter, concerning the ordination of Clement: *If any one is a friend to those to whom he (Clement) does not speak, through that very fact, he belongs to those who wish to destroy the Church of God; in the body he seems to be with us; but his spirit and his*

heart are against us. Such an enemy is to be dreaded more than one whose enmity is open, and apparent to all; for the former works evil under cover of false friendship and causes disunion and destruction in the Church. Remark this well, dearly beloved, the blessed Peter judges him, whose conduct is condemned by the Pope, in so severe a manner, that he even goes so far as to condemn those, who are bound to him by friendship, and even those who hold converse with him.

It is, therefore, impossible for a dignity which owes its origin to men of the world, and even to those ignorant of God, not to be in subjection to that dignity, which the Providence of the all-powerful God instituted, to bring honour to Him, and which, in His mercy, He has granted to the whole world. If the Son of this all-powerful God is undoubtedly God and Man, He is also the High Priest, the chief of all priests, and He is now seated at the right hand of the Father, where He intercedes for us without ceasing. The Son of God despised the earthly kingdoms, of which the sons of this world are so proud; it was of His own accord that He chose and embraced the priesthood of the Cross. Every one knows that the first kings and the first dukes, were men ignorant of God, who, influenced by blind cupidity, and intolerable presumption, aided, moreover, by the Demon-prince of this world, strove by the help of robbery, lies and homicide, and almost every vice, to have dominion over their equals, that is, over other men. When these kings and dukes sought afterwards to draw the priests of the Lord into their ways, to whom can one more fitly compare them than to him who is the head of all the sons of pride, to him who tried to tempt the Sovereign of Pontiffs Himself, the Chief of Priests, the Son of the Most High, by showing Him all the kingdoms of the world and saying to Him, *I will give you all this if you fall down at my feet and adore me.*

Who can doubt that the priests of Christ are the fathers and masters of kings; that they are the princes of all the faithful? Is it not an act of utter madness, when the son tries to rule the father, the disciple the master; when he wishes to reduce him to submission by imposing on him iniquitous conditions, though he knows well that this father and master has the power of binding and loosing on earth, as well as in heaven? The blessed Gregory reminds us of this in a letter to the Emperor Maurice. The Emperor Constantine the Great, chief of almost all the kings and princes of the world, thoroughly understood the power of the priesthood. At the Nicean Council, he wished to be placed below the bishops; nor did he try, in any way, to maintain his opinions against theirs; on the contrary, he styled them *Gods*, and protested that it was for him to follow their opinions, and not for them to yield to him. In the letter of Pope Gelasius to the Emperor Anastasius, already quoted, in order that the Emperor might not be offended by the truths he had just heard, the Pope adds: *Oh, Emperor Augustus! two powers govern the world, the sacred authority of the pontiffs and the power of kings; but the authority of priests is the superior one, because before the judgment-seat of God the priest will be held responsible for the conduct of the king.* And a little farther on: *You see by this, that they are not to submit to your wishes; you, on the contrary, are to bow to their decisions.*

Supported by such facts, and by such authority, several Pontiffs have excommunicated kings and emperors. The blessed Pope Innocent excommunicated the Emperor Arcadius, for having allowed St. John Chrysostom to be driven from his See. The Roman Pontiff Zachary made the king of the Franks descend from his throne, not so much on account of the evil deeds he may have committed, as because he was not doing any service in the high position he held. He released the Franks from their oath of fidelity which they had taken to their king, and he put in his place Pepin, the father of the Emperor Charlemagne. The Church acts in the same way when, by right of her apostolic authority, she deposes bishops from their episcopal sees, and releases the soldiers of Christ from the oath of fidelity sworn to them. The blessed Ambrose, who was a saint, but was never Pope, excommunicated and kept out of the Church the Emperor Theodosius the Great, for a crime, which did not appear very serious to other priests. He proved in his writings that the sacerdotal dignity is as much above the royal dignity as gold is superior to lead. Thus, he writes, concerning the very principle of the pastoral office: *There is nothing, my brethren, worthy of being compared to the honour and greatness of the episcopal office; to liken it, for example, to the splendour of the royal State, to the diadem of princes, is like comparing the brightness of gold to the dull lustre of lead. Do we not indeed see kings and princes throwing themselves at the feet of priests, kissing their hands and imploring a share in their prayers?* A little farther on, he says: *You understand, my brethren, that, if I have written to you at such length, it is solely to impress upon you that nothing in this world can equal the excellence of the priesthood and the grandeur of the episcopacy.*

Your fraternity must remember that, no layman receives power equal to that granted to the exorcist, since the latter is made a *spiritual emperor*, for the purpose of casting out demons. Kings and princes, who neither live in accordance with their religion, nor perform their actions from the fear of God, place themselves in the power of the devils, and are held by them in the trammels of bondage. If truly God-fearing priests desire to rule, it is because, inflamed by Divine Love, they desire to promote the honour of God and the salvation of souls. Princes, such as those mentioned above, seek power only in order to gratify their passions, and to give free course to their indomitable pride.

The blessed Augustine says of them, in the first book *Of Christian Doctrine: Whoever aspires to rule those who are naturally his equals, that is, other men, gives proof of intolerable pride.* Since, as has been said, exorcists have received from God power over the demons, much more have they power over those who are enslaved by the demons, and are members of the demon. If the power of exorcists is so great, that of priests is much greater.

Moreover, on his death-bed, every Christian king who wishes to escape hell, to pass from darkness to light, to appear at the judgment-seat of God, after having received absolution for his faults, humbly implores the ministry of the priest. But who is there, I do not say, priest, but even layman, who has ever begged the help of an earthly king, when at the point of death, and filled with anxiety for the salvation of his soul? What king or emperor can, by right of his office, give holy baptism to a Christian, deliver him from the power of the devil, give him entrance among the children of God, or anoint him with the holy chrism? Who, among them, can consecrate the Body and Blood of the Lord, in other words, perform that greatest act of the Christian religion? Has the power of binding and absolving in heaven and on earth been given to any one of them? In all these things, the superiority of the sacerdotal dignity is evident. If not one among them has the power to ordain a cleric of Holy Church, still less have they the right of deposing him for any fault. In ecclesiastical orders, the authority which deposes, ought to be superior to that which ordains. Bishops can consecrate other bishops, but they cannot depose them without the authority of the Apostolic See. Very little discernment is therefore necessary to understand the su-

periority of the priesthood over the royal state. If, in all that concerns their sins, kings are amenable to priests, much more must they be so, to the Roman Pontiff.

On closer examination, the title of king is much better suited to good Christians than to bad princes. The former seek the glory of God, and know how to govern themselves; the latter, preoccupied with their own interests, and not with the interests of God, are enemies to themselves and tyrants to others. The former are part of the Body of Jesus Christ; the latter of the body of the devil. The first-mentioned govern themselves, that they may reign eternally with the Supreme Emperor: the power of the second is exercised in such a way, that they will be lost for ever, with the prince of darkness, the king of all the sons of pride.

It is not surprising if bad bishops make common cause with an impious king; they receive their honours from that king, in an unlawful way, hence they both love and dread him at the same time. By their consent to perform simoniacal ordinations, they, as it were, sell God at a low price. The elect are indissolubly united to their head; the reprobate, in like manner clings tenaciously round him who is the author of evil, especially when the matter at stake is to resist the good. To argue with them is of little avail, rather weep over their sad fate, that the all-powerful God may deliver them from the snares of Satan, and that He may in the end open their eyes to the truth.

So much for kings and emperors, who, intoxicated by earthly glory, reign, not for God, but for themselves. Now, the duty of our office is, to exhort each one according to his position and dignity. We must, therefore, with the help of God, speak of humility to emperors, kings, and other princes, in order that they may resist the waves of pride, which impel them, like the motions of the sea. Earthly glory and worldly cares rapidly develop pride, especially in those who rule; carried along in its current, they cast aside humility; and filled with desires of their own glory, they long for dominion over their fellow-men. It is most important for emperors and kings to learn to practise humility, when their minds aspire to great things, and when they wish to shine with resplendent glory in the eyes of the world. Let them seek motives of fear in all that has hitherto been to them a subject of joy. See what danger is involved in the royal or imperial dignity, how liable it is to fill the heart with uneasiness! Very few of those invested with royal greatness attain to salvation; and those who, by the help of God, are not lost eternally, by virtue of a judgment of the Holy Spirit, are not glorified in Holy Church, as are such numbers of the poor. From the beginning of the world down to our own times, it is impossible to name seven emperors or kings, whose lives have been such models of religious perfection, so filled with miracle, as the lives of innumerable persons who were nothing in the eyes of the world. We believe, however, that through the mercy of the omnipotent God, several of them have been able to save their souls. What emperor or king could be compared, we do not say to the Apostles and Martyrs, but to blessed Martin, or Antony, or Benedict, in regard to the gift of miracles? What emperor or king ever restored the dead to life, cured lepers or gave sight to the blind? We have the Emperor Constantine, of pious memory, the Emperors Theodosius, Honorius, Charles and Louis, who loved justice, spread the Christian religion, and defended the Church: the Church praises and venerates them, yet she does not say that they had, to a striking extent, the gift of miracles. What altars or basilicas are there dedicated to a king or an emperor; has the Church ever allowed Mass to be celebrated in honour of any one of them? Kings and princes, so proud of being above

other men, in this life, ought to fear all the more, lest they should be condemned to eternal fire in the life hereafter. Thus it is written: *The mighty shall be mightily tormented.* They will have to render an account of each subject under their sway. If it is no small labour for any ordinary mortal, filled with the spirit of religion, to save one single soul, that is, his own; how great is not the responsibility of princes who have the charge of thousands of souls! Holy Church punishes severely the sinner who has committed homicide; what then will happen to those who have caused death to thousands of persons for the sake of the glory of this world? It sometimes happens that, after having been the cause of death to many, they utter with their lips a *mea culpa;* but in the depths of their hearts, they rejoice at the extension of their glory and power. They are very far from wishing that they had left their great deeds undone; the fact of having sent their fellow-creatures to Tartarus, fills them with no compunction. Their repentance is worthless in the sight of God, it is not inspired by true contrition of heart, as they do not wish to give up what they have acquired by conquest, and at the cost of so much human blood. They have reason to fear; they ought often to recall to their minds what we have already said, that a very small number of saints is to be found amongst the multitude of kings who have succeeded one another, on the different thrones of the earth, since the beginning of the world. On the other hand, in one single line of Pontiffs, as for instance, the Roman Pontiffs from the time of St. Peter, more than a hundred are distinguished for eminent sanctity. What reason is there for this, unless, as has been already said, it is that kings of the earth and princes, fascinated by a vain desire of glory, subordinate their spiritual interests to the temporal interests of themselves and their kingdoms. Truly godly pontiffs, on the contrary, allow no earthly matters to come between them and the cause of God. The first-mentioned are remorseless in avenging personal affronts; but, when the offence is committed against God, they seem to lack energy to punish the offenders: the second easily forget the wrongs done to themselves, but with difficulty pardon the injuries done to God. The former, engrossed in the things of this world, set little value on spiritual things; the latter, having their thoughts constantly directed towards heaven, feel nothing but contempt for all that is of this earth.

All Christians, therefore, who desire to reign with Christ, must be cautioned against seeking power from motives of earthly ambition; they must not lose sight of the warnings given by the holy and blessed Pope Gregory in the Pastoral: *the line of action to be followed is,* he says, *not to accept power, unless we are forced to do so; unless moreover, we possess the virtues necessary to exercise that power; in case these virtues are wanting, we must not yield, and assume authority, even if we are subjected to violence.* He, who is filled with the fear of God, will take his seat on the Apostolic See with feelings of the keenest anguish, and then only under the utmost compulsion. The merits of blessed Peter, however, will give renewed strength to him who has legitimately obtained his power. What must be the terror and anxiety of one who occupies an earthly throne for the first time, a throne on which even the good and humble lose their virtues, as is proved by the example of Saul and David! In support of the remark, which we have just made, concerning the Apostolic See, the decrees of Pope Symmachus—in accordance with experience—contain the following expressions: *Blessed Peter has transmitted to his successors an inexhaustible dowry of merits, together with an inheritance of innocence;* and later he says: *Who could doubt of the sanctity of him,*

who is invested with such a high dignity? To supply his want of personal merit, he has the merits of his predecessors. To remain worthily on such a height, he requires the bright light that beams from his own life, or that which St. Peter procures for him.

Those who are called spontaneously, and after mature deliberation, to royalty or empire, by Holy Church, ought therefore to answer this call with humility. They should embrace this dignity, not to acquire transitory glory, but to save souls. Let them reflect well on these words of blessed Gregory in the same pastoral: *He who disdains to be like other men, becomes like a rebellious angel. Saul, when raised to sovereign power, instead of continuing to gain merit by his humility, let himself be ruled by pride. His humility was the cause of his elevation to that power of which his pride deprived him.* God Himself gives testimony of this when He says: *When thou wast a little one in thine own eyes, wast thou not made the head of the tribes of Israel?* And, farther on, he says: *Strange contradiction, when he was little in his own eyes he was great in the sight of God; and on the contrary, when he thought himself great, his acts were worthless before God.* Let them engrave on their hearts the words of our Lord in the Gospel: *I seek not My own glory,* and that other saying of His, *Whosoever shall be first among you shall be the servant of all.* Let them always place God's honour before their own; let them practise justice by being faithful in respecting the rights of every one; let them not frequent the assemblies of the wicked; let them, on the contrary, adhere with fidelity to the advice of godly men. They ought never to seek to rule the Church and make a slave of her; instead of acting thus, they must duly honour the priests of the Lord, who are the eyes of the Church, and see in them masters and fathers. If we are obliged to honour our fathers and mothers according to the flesh, much more are we obliged to honour our parents according to the Spirit. If he who curses his own father or mother is to be punished by death, how severely ought not he to be punished who curses his spiritual parents? Under the impulse of their carnal love, princes must not try to place any son of theirs at the head of the flock for which Christ shed His blood; if they know of some one more fitted and more useful than that son, by their inordinate love for that son they might inflict on the Church a grievous wrong. It is a clear proof that we do not love God and our neighbours as Christians ought to love them, if we are unwilling to do all we can to assist our Holy Mother, the Church, in such an important matter. Without the love of God and one's neighbours—that is, without charity—all the good which is done is absolutely worthless for salvation. Those, on the contrary, who act with humility, and give proof of a constant love of God and their neighbours, may hope in the mercy of Him who said, *Learn of Me, because I am meek and humble of heart.* Imitating Him in His humility, they will reject this ephemeral royalty, which is nothing but slavery, exchanging it for another sovereignty, one of true liberty, to last for all eternity.

Reasons such as these may help kings and princes to fortify themselves against pride and vainglory. We have thought it right to lay them briefly before your fraternity, and those who speak through the mouthpiece of the Church, to enable you to pay a courageous and persevering homage to truth—that truth now almost abandoned and left to the defence of but a few brave champions. You remember what blessed Gregory says in the 'Seventh Book of his Morals,' in explaining the verse, *They that fear the hoar frost, the snow shall fall upon them.* Here are his words: *The fear of the adversities of this world causes some to run the risk of eternal misfortune.*

In the name of the Omnipotent God, and through the authority of blessed Peter, prince of apostles, We grant you, brother Hermann, permission to fulfil the Episcopal duties in all the bishoprics of the kingdom of Lorraine in which the Bishops have been excommunicated, for having held intercourse with Henry, formerly called king. This permission will hold good so long as these Bishops remain excommunicated—that is, until they have been absolved, either by Us or by Our lawful successor.

THE BULL UNAM SANCTAM OF BONIFACE VIII

That there is one Holy Catholic and Apostolic Church we are im-

THE BULL UNAM SANCTAM OF BONIFACE VIII in *Translations and Reprints from the Original Sources of European History,* Vol. III, No. 6 (Philadelphia: The Department of History of the University of Pennsylvania, 1912), pp. 20-23. Courtesy of the Department of History of the University of Pennsylvania.

pelled by our faith to believe and to hold —this we do firmly believe and openly confess—and outside of this there is neither salvation or remission of sins, as the bridegroom proclaims in Canticles, "My dove, my undefiled is but one; she is the only one of her mother; she is the choice one of her that bare her." The Church represents one mystic body and of this body Christ is the head; of Christ, indeed, God is the head. In it is one Lord, and one faith, and one baptism. In the time of the flood, there was one ark of Noah, prefiguring the one Church, finished in one cubit, having one Noah as steersman and commander. Outside of this, all things upon the face of the earth were, as we read, destroyed. This Church we venerate and this alone, the Lord saying through his prophets, "Deliver my soul, O God, from the sword; my darling from the power of the dog." He prays thus for the soul, that is for Himself, as head, and also for the body which He calls one, namely, the Church on account of the unity of the bridegroom, of the faith, of the sacraments, and of the charity of the Church. It is that seamless coat of the Lord, which was not rent, but fell by lot. Therefore, in this one and only Church, there is one body and one head,—not two heads as if it were a monster—namely, Christ and Christ's Vicar, Peter and Peter's successor, for the Lord said to Peter himself, "Feed my sheep:" *my* sheep, he said, using a general term and not designating these or those sheep, so that we must believe that all the sheep were committed to him. If, then, the Greeks, or others, shall say that they were not entrusted to Peter and his successors, they must perforce admit that they are not of Christ's sheep, as the Lord says in John, "there is one fold, and one shepherd."

In this Church and in its power are two swords, to wit, a spiritual and a temporal, and this we are taught by the words of the Gospel, for when the Apostles said, "Behold, here are two swords" (in the Church, namely, since the Apostles were speaking), the Lord did not reply that it was too many, but enough. And surely he who claims that the temporal sword is not in the power of Peter has but ill understood the word of our Lord when he said, "Put up thy sword in its scabbard." Both,

therefore, the spiritual and the material swords, are in the power of the Church, the latter indeed to be used for the Church, the former by the Church, the one by the priest, the other by the hand of kings and soldiers, but by the will and sufferance of the priest. It is fitting, moreover, that one sword should be under the other, and the temporal authority subject to the spiritual power. For when the Apostle said, "there is no power but of God and the powers that are of God are ordained," they would not be ordained unless one sword were under the other, and one, as inferior, was brought back by the other to the highest place. For, according to the Holy Dionysius, the law of divinity is to lead the lowest through the intermediate to the highest. Therefore, according to the law of the universe, things are not reduced to order directly, and upon the same footing, but the lowest through the intermediate, and the inferior through the superior. It behooves us, therefore, the more freely to confess that the spiritual power excels in dignity and nobility any form whatsoever of earthly power, as spiritual interests exceed the temporal in importance. All this we see fairly from the giving of tithes, from the benediction and sanctification, from the recognition of this power and the control of these same things. For the truth bearing witness, it is for the spiritual power to establish the earthly power and judge it, if it be not good. Thus, in the case of the Church and the power of the Church, the prophecy of Jeremiah is fulfilled: "See, I have this day set thee over the nations and over the kingdoms"—and so forth. Therefore, if the earthly power shall err, it shall be judged by the spiritual power; if the lesser spiritual power err, it shall be judged by the higher. But if the supreme power err, it can be judged by God alone and not by man, the apostles bearing witness saying, the spiritual man judges all things but he himself is judged by no one. Hence this power, although given to man and exercised by man, is not human, but rather a divine power, given by the divine lips to Peter, and founded on a rock for Him and his successors in Him whom he confessed, the Lord saying to Peter himself, "Whatsoever thou shalt bind," etc. Whoever, therefore, shall resist this power, ordained by God, resists the ordination of God, unless there should be two beginnings, as the Manichaean imagines. But this we judge to be false and heretical,

since, by the testimony of Moses, not in the *beginnings*, but in the *beginning*, God created the heaven and the earth. We, moreover, proclaim, declare and pronounce that it is altogether necessary to salvation for every human being to be subject to the Roman Pontiff.

Given at the Lateran the twelfth day before the Kalends of December, in our eighth year, as a perpetual memorial of this matter.

St. Thomas Aquinas

ST. Thomas Aquinas (1225-1274), the leading philosopher and theologian of medieval scholasticism, was one of the greatest synthesizers the West has ever produced. The task he undertook was to reconcile the philosophy of Aristotle, rediscovered by European scholars through their contacts with the Moslems in Spain and elsewhere, with Christian theology. During a relatively short lifetime, he succeeded in combining these two quite disparate elements into a single comprehensive system of thought capable in principle of explaining everything in the universe that man could know. Questions have been raised about the logical consistency of the Thomistic synthesis, but, whether fully successful or not, it still stands

as a landmark in the intellectual career of Western man.

Beyond their general historical importance, the writings of Thomas have a special significance in the history of Catholicism. Although Thomas was opposed during his lifetime by various religious leaders because of his heavy reliance on the pagan Aristotle, and although his writings were even condemned at several theological centers in the years immediately after his death, within a century his system was generally accepted as the basis for orthodox Catholic philosophy. The authoritativeness of the Thomistic doctrine was formally recognized by the Church in 1879 in the encyclical *Aeterni Patris* of Pope Leo XIII, which ordered all Catholic schools to teach

Thomas's position as the true philosophy. Leo's order was reiterated in 1923 by Pius X, who wrote: "The following canon of the Church's code should be held as a sacred command: In the study of rational philosophy and theology and in the instruction of students the professor should follow entirely the method, doctrine and principles of the Angelic Doctor [Thomas], and hold them religiously."

The two selections that follow reveal something of the breadth of Thomas's interests, as well as the depth of his scholarship and the subtlety of his thought. The second selection, in addition, throws light on the position in which the Church found itself at a time when economic institutions and practices were being fundamentally transformed. The first selection makes clear the sharp contrast between Thomas, who sought whenever possible to justify his beliefs rationally, and St. Francis, whose faith was simple and direct. Nevertheless, Thomas and Francis (as medieval Christians) shared one vital conviction—that there are truths which human reason cannot fathom, truths, therefore, which must be accepted on faith through divine revelation.

SUMMA CONTRA GENTILES

Chapter III

IN WHAT WAY IT IS POSSIBLE TO MAKE KNOWN THE DIVINE TRUTH

Since, however, not every truth is to be made known in the same way, *and it is the part of an educated man to seek for conviction in each subject, only so far as the nature of the subject allows,* as the Philosopher most rightly observes as quoted by Boethius, it is necessary to show first of all in what way it is possible to make known the aforesaid truth.

Now in those things which we hold about God there is truth in two ways. For certain things that are true about God wholly surpass the capability of human reason, for instance that God is three and one: while there are certain things to which even natural reason can attain, for instance that God is, that God is one, and others like these, which even the philosophers proved demonstratively of God, being guided by the light of natural reason.

That certain divine truths wholly surpass the capability of human reason, is most clearly evident. For since the principle of all the knowledge which the reason acquires about a thing, is the understanding of that thing's essence, because according to the Philosopher's teaching the principle of a demonstration is *what a thing is*, it

follows that our knowledge about a thing will be in proportion to our understanding of its essence. Wherefore, if the human intellect comprehends the essence of a particular thing, for instance a stone or a triangle, no truth about that thing will surpass the capability of human reason. But this does not happen to us in relation to God, because the human intellect is incapable by its natural power of attaining to the comprehension of His essence: since our intellect's knowledge, according to the mode of the present life, originates from the senses: so that things which are not objects of sense cannot be comprehended by the human intellect, except in so far as knowledge of them is gathered from sensibles. Now sensibles cannot lead our intellect to see in them what God is, because they are effects unequal to the power of their cause. And yet our intellect is led by sensibles to the divine knowledge so as to know about God that He is, and other such truths, which need to be ascribed to the first principle. Accordingly some divine truths are attainable by human reason, while others altogether surpass the power of human reason.

Again. The same is easy to see from the degrees of intellects. For if one of two men perceives a thing with his intellect with greater subtlety, the one whose intellect is of a higher degree understands many things which the other is altogether unable to grasp; as instanced in a yokel who is utterly incapable of grasping the subtleties

THE "SUMMA CONTRA GENTILES" of St. Thomas Aquinas, trans. Fathers of the English Dominican Province (London: Burns Oates & Washbourne Ltd., 1924), I, 4-15. Courtesy of Benziger Brothers, Inc.

of philosophy. Now the angelic intellect surpasses the human intellect more than the intellect of the cleverest philosopher surpasses that of the most uncultured. For an angel knows God through a more excellent effect than does man, for as much as the angel's essence, through which he is led to know God by natural knowledge, is more excellent than sensible things, even than the soul itself, by which the human intellect mounts to the knowledge of God. And the divine intellect surpasses the angelic intellect much more than the angelic surpasses the human. For the divine intellect by its capacity equals the divine essence, wherefore God perfectly understands of Himself what He is, and He knows all things that can be understood about Him: whereas the angel knows not what God is by his natural knowledge, because the angel's essence, by which he is led to the knowledge of God, is an effect unequal to the power of its cause. Consequently an angel is unable by his natural knowledge to grasp all that God understands about Himself: nor again is human reason capable of grasping all that an angel understands by his natural power. Accordingly just as a man would show himself to be a most insane fool if he declared the assertions of a philosopher to be false because he was unable to understand them, so, and much more, a man would be exceedingly foolish, were he to suspect of falsehood the things revealed by God through the ministry of His angels, because they cannot be the object of reason's investigations.

Furthermore. The same is made abundantly clear by the deficiency which every day we experience in our knowledge of things. For we are ignorant of many of the properties of sensible things, and in many cases we are unable to discover the nature of those properties which we perceive by our senses. Much less therefore is human reason capable of investigating all the truths about that most sublime essence.

With this the saying of the Philosopher is in accord where he says that *our intellect in relation to those primary things which are most evident in nature is like the eye of a bat in relation to the sun.*

To this truth Holy Writ also bears witness. For it is written (Job xi. 7): *Peradventure thou wilt comprehend the steps of God and wilt find out the Almighty perfectly?* and (xxxvi. 26): *Behold God is great, exceeding our knowledge,* and (I Cor. xiii. 9): *We know in part.*

Therefore all that is said about God, though it cannot be investigated by reason, must not be forthwith rejected as false, as the Manicheans and many unbelievers have thought.

Chapter IV

THAT THE TRUTH ABOUT DIVINE THINGS WHICH IS ATTAINABLE BY REASON IS FITTINGLY PROPOSED TO MAN AS AN OBJECT OF BELIEF

While then the truth of the intelligible things of God is twofold, one to which the inquiry of reason can attain, the other which surpasses the whole range of human reason, both are fittingly proposed by God to man as an object of belief. We must first show this with regard to that truth which is attainable by the inquiry of reason, lest it appears to some, that since it can be attained by reason, it was useless to make it an object of faith by supernatural inspiration. Now three disadvantages would result if this truth were left solely to the inquiry of reason. One is that few men would have knowledge of God: because very many are hindered from gathering the fruit of diligent inquiry, which is the discovery of truth, for three reasons. Some indeed on account of an indisposition of temperament, by reason of which many are naturally indisposed to knowledge: so that no efforts of theirs would enable them to reach to the attainment of the highest degree of human knowledge, which consists in knowing God. Some are hindered by the needs of household affairs. For there must needs be among men some that devote themselves to the conduct of temporal affairs, who would be unable to devote so much time to the leisure of contemplative research as to reach the summit of human inquiry, namely the knowledge of God. And some are hindered by laziness. For in order to acquire the knowledge of God in those things which reason is able to investigate, it is necessary to have a previous knowledge of many things: since almost the entire consideration of philosophy is directed to the knowledge of God: for which reason metaphysics, which is about divine things, is the last of the parts of philosophy to be studied. Wherefore it is not possible to arrive at the inquiry about the aforesaid truth except after a most laborious study: and few are willing to take upon themselves this labour for the love of a knowledge, the natural desire for which has nevertheless been instilled into the mind of man by God.

The second disadvantage is that those who would arrive at the discovery of the aforesaid truth would scarcely succeed in doing so after a long time. First, because this truth is so profound, that it is only after long practice that the human intellect is enabled to grasp it by means of reason. Secondly, because many things are required beforehand, as stated above. Thirdly, because at the time of youth, the mind, when tossed about by the various movements of the passions, is not fit for the knowledge of so sublime a truth, whereas *calm gives prudence and knowledge,* as stated in 7 *Phys.* Hence mankind would remain in the deepest darkness of ignorance, if the path of reason were the only available way to the knowledge of God: because the knowledge of God which especially makes men perfect and good, would be ac-

quired only by the few, and by these only after a long time.

The third disadvantage is that much falsehood is mingled with the investigations of human reason, on account of the weakness of our intellect in forming its judgments, and by reason of the admixture of phantasms. Consequently many would remain in doubt about those things even which are most truly demonstrated, through ignoring the force of the demonstration: especially when they perceive that different things are taught by the various men who are called wise. Moreover among the many demonstrated truths, there is sometimes a mixture of falsehood that is not demonstrated, but assumed for some probable or sophistical reason which at times is mistaken for a demonstration. Therefore it was necessary that definite certainty and pure truth about divine things should be offered to man by the way of faith.

Accordingly the divine clemency has made this salutary commandment, that even some things which reason is able to investigate must be held by faith: so that all may share in the knowledge of God easily, and without doubt or error.

Hence it is written (Eph. iv. 17, 18): That *henceforward you walk not as also the Gentiles walk in the vanity of their mind, having their understanding darkened:* and (Isa. liv. 13): *All thy children shall be taught of the Lord.*

Chapter V

THAT THOSE THINGS WHICH CANNOT BE
INVESTIGATED BY REASON ARE FITTINGLY
PROPOSED TO MAN AS AN OBJECT OF FAITH

It may appear to some that those things which cannot be investigated by reason ought not to be proposed to man as an object of faith: because divine wisdom provides for each thing according to the mode of its nature. We must therefore prove that it is necessary also for those things which surpass reason to be proposed by God to man as an object of faith.

For no man tends to do a thing by his desire and endeavour unless it be previously known to him. Wherefore since man is directed by divine providence to a higher good than human frailty can attain in the present life, as we shall show in the sequel, it was necessary for his mind to be bidden to something higher than those things to which our reason can reach in the present life, so that he might learn to aspire, and by his endeavours to tend to something surpassing the whole state of the present life. And this is especially competent to the Christian religion, which alone promises goods spiritual and eternal: for which reason it proposes many things surpassing the thought of man: whereas the old law which contained promises of temporal things, proposed few things that are above human inquiry. It was with this motive that the philosophers, in order to wean men from sensible pleasures to virtue, took care to show that there are other goods of greater account than those which appeal to the senses, the taste of which things affords much greater delight to those who devote themselves to active or contemplative virtues.

Again it is necessary for this truth to be proposed to man as an object to faith in order that he may have truer knowledge of God. For then alone do we know God truly, when we believe that He is far above all that man can possibly think of God, because the divine essence surpasses man's natural knowledge, as stated above. Hence by the fact that certain things about God are proposed to man, which surpass his reason, he is strengthened in his opinion that God is far above what he is able to think.

There results also another advantage from this, namely, the checking of presumption which is the mother of error. For some there are who presume so far on their wits that they think themselves capable of measuring the whole nature of things by their intellect, in that they esteem all things true which they see, and false which they see not. Accordingly, in order that man's mind might be freed from this presumption, and seek the truth humbly, it was necessary that certain things far surpassing his intellect should be proposed to man by God.

Yet another advantage is made apparent by the words of the Philosopher (10 *Ethic.*). For when a certain Simonides maintained that man should neglect the knowledge of God, and apply his mind to human affairs, and declared that *a man ought to relish human things, and a mortal, mortal things:* the Philosopher contradicted him, saying that *a man ought to devote himself to immortal and divine things as much as he can.* Hence he says (11 *De Animal.*) that though it is but little that we perceive of higher substances, yet that little is more loved and desired than all the knowledge we have of lower substances. He says also (2 *De Coelo et Mundo*) that when questions about the heavenly bodies can be answered by a short and probable solution, it happens that the hearer is very much rejoiced. All this shows that however imperfect the knowledge of the highest things may be, it bestows very great perfection on the soul: and consequently, although human reason is unable to grasp fully things that are above reason, it nevertheless acquires much perfection, if at least it hold things, in any way whatever, by faith.

Wherefore it is written (Eccles. iii. 25): *Many things are shown to thee above the understanding of men,* and (I Cor. ii. 10, 11): *The things . . . that are of God no man knoweth, but the Spirit of God: but to us God hath revealed them by His Spirit.*

Chapter VI

THAT IT IS NOT A MARK OF LEVITY TO
ASSENT TO THE THINGS THAT ARE OF FAITH,
ALTHOUGH THEY ARE ABOVE REASON

Now those who believe this truth, of *which reason affords a proof*, believe not lightly, as though *following foolish fables* (2 Pet. i. 16). For divine Wisdom Himself, Who knows all things most fully, designed to reveal to man *the secrets of God's wisdom:* and by suitable arguments proves His presence, and the truth of His doctrine and inspiration, by performing works surpassing the capability of the whole of nature, namely, the wondrous healing of the sick, the raising of the dead to life, a marvellous control over the heavenly bodies, and what excites yet more wonder, the inspiration of human minds, so that unlettered and simple persons are filled with the Holy Ghost, and in one instant are endowed with the most sublime wisdom and eloquence. And after considering these arguments, convinced by the strength of the proof, and not by the force of arms, nor by the promise of delights, but—and this is the greatest marvel of all —amidst the tyranny of persecutions, a countless crowd of not only simple but also of the wisest men, embraced the Christian faith, which inculcates things surpassing all human understanding, curbs the pleasures of the flesh, and teaches contempt of all worldly things. That the minds of mortal beings should assent to such things, is both the greatest of miracles, and the evident work of divine inspiration, seeing that they despise visible things and desire only those that are invisible. And that this happened not suddenly nor by chance, but by the disposition of God, is shown by the fact that God foretold that He would do so by the manifold oracles of the prophets, whose books we hold in veneration as bearing witness to our faith. This particular kind of proof is alluded to in the words of

Heb. ii. 3, 4: *Which*, namely the salvation of mankind, *having begun to be declared by the Lord, was confirmed with us by them that heard Him, God also bearing witness by signs and wonders, and divers . . . distributions of the Holy Ghost.*

Now such a wondrous conversion of the world to the Christian faith is a most indubitable proof that such signs did take place, so that there is no need to repeat them, seeing that there is evidence of them in their result. For it would be the most wondrous sign of all if without any wondrous signs the world were persuaded by simple and lowly men to believe things so arduous, to accomplish things so difficult, and to hope for things so sublime. Although God ceases not even in our time to work miracles through His saints in confirmation of the faith.

On the other hand those who introduced the errors of the sects proceeded in contrary fashion, as instanced by Mohammed, who enticed peoples with the promise of carnal pleasures, to the desire of which the concupiscence of the flesh instigates. He also delivered commandments in keeping with his promises, by giving the reins to carnal pleasure, wherein it is easy for carnal men to obey: and the lessons of truth which he inculcated were only such as can be easily known to any man of average wisdom by his natural powers: yea rather the truths which he taught were mingled by him with many fables and most false doctrines. Nor did he add any signs of supernatural agency, which alone are a fitting witness to divine inspiration, since a visible work that can be from God alone, proves the teacher of truth to be invisibly inspired: but he asserted that he was sent in the power of arms, a sign that is not lacking even to robbers and tyrants. Again, those who believed in him from the outset were not wise men practised in things divine and human, but beastlike men who dwelt in the wilds, utterly ignorant of all divine teaching; and it was by a multitude of such men and the force of arms that he compelled others to submit to his law.

Lastly, no divine oracles or prophets in a previous age bore witness to him; rather did he corrupt almost all the teaching of the Old and New Testaments by a narrative replete with fables, as one may see by a perusal of his law. Hence by a cunning device, he did not commit the reading of the Old and New Testament Books to his followers, lest he should thereby be convicted of falsehood. Thus it is evident that those who believe his words believe lightly.

Chapter VII

THAT THE TRUTH OF REASON IS NOT IN OPPOSITION TO THE TRUTH OF THE CHRISTIAN FAITH

Now though the aforesaid truth of the Christian faith surpasses the ability of human reason, nevertheless those things which are naturally instilled in human reason cannot be opposed to this truth. For it is clear that those things which are implanted in reason by nature, are most true, so much so that it is impossible to think them to be false. Nor is it lawful to deem false that which is held by faith, since it is so evidently confirmed by God. Seeing then that the false alone is opposed to the true, as evidently appears if we examine their definitions, it is impossible for the aforesaid truth of faith to be contrary to those principles which reason knows naturally.

Again. The same thing which the disciple's mind receives from its teacher is contained in the knowledge of the teacher, unless he teach insincerely, which it were wicked to say of God. Now the knowledge

of naturally known principles is instilled into us by God, since God Himself is the author of our nature. Therefore the divine Wisdom also contains these principles. Consequently whatever is contrary to these principles, is contrary to the divine Wisdom; wherefore it cannot be from God. Therefore those things which are received by faith from divine revelation cannot be contrary to our natural knowledge.

Moreover. Our intellect is stayed by contrary arguments, so that it cannot advance to the knowledge of truth. Wherefore if conflicting knowledges were instilled into us by God, our intellect would thereby be hindered from knowing the truth. And this cannot be ascribed to God.

Furthermore. Things that are natural are unchangeable so long as nature remains. Now contrary opinions cannot be together in the same subject. Therefore God does not instil into man any opinion or belief contrary to natural knowledge.

Hence the Apostle says (Rom. x. 8): *The word is nigh thee even in thy heart and in thy mouth. This is the word of faith which we preach.* Yet because it surpasses reason some look upon it as though it were contrary thereto; which is impossible.

This is confirmed also by the authority of Augustine who says *That which truth shall make known can nowise be in opposition to the holy books whether of the Old or of the New Testament.*

From this we may evidently conclude that whatever arguments are alleged against the teachings of faith, they do not rightly proceed from the first self-evident principles instilled by nature. Wherefore they lack the force of demonstration, and are either probable or sophistical arguments, and consequently it is possible to solve them.

SUMMA THEOLOGICA

. . .

OF CHEATING WHICH IS COMMITTED IN
BUYING AND SELLING

*First Article: Whether it is lawful to sell a
thing for more than its worth?*

We proceed thus to the First Article:—

Objection 1. It would seem that it is lawful to sell a thing for more than its worth.
In the commutations of human life, civil
laws determine that which is just. Now according to these laws it is just for buyer
and seller to deceive one another: and this
occurs by the seller selling a thing for more
than its worth, and the buyer buying a
thing for less than its worth. Therefore it
is lawful to sell a thing for more than its
worth.

Obj. 2. Further, That which is common
to all would seem to be natural and not
sinful. Now Augustine relates that the saying of a certain jester was accepted by all,
*You wish to buy for a song and to sell at a
premium,* which agrees with the saying of
Prov. xx. 14, *It is naught, it is naught, saith
every buyer: and when he is gone away,
then he will boast.* Therefore it is lawful to
sell a thing for more than its worth.

Obj. 3. Further, It does not seem unlawful if that which honesty demands be done
by mutual agreement. Now, according to
the Philosopher, in the friendship which is
based on utility, the amount of the recompense for a favour received should depend
on the utility accruing to the receiver: and
this utility sometimes is worth more than
the thing given, for instance if the receiver
be in great need of that thing, whether for

THE "SUMMA THEOLOGICA" OF ST. THOMAS AQUINAS,
Part II (New York: Benziger Brothers, Inc.), X,
317-320, 326-333, 337-341. Courtesy of the publishers.

the purpose of avoiding a danger, or of
deriving some particular benefit. Therefore,
in contracts of buying and selling, it is lawful to give a thing in return for more than
its worth.

On the contrary, It is written: *All things
. . . whatsoever you would that men
should do to you, do you also to them.* But
no man wishes to buy a thing for more
than its worth. Therefore no man should
sell a thing to another man for more than
its worth.

I answer that, It is altogether sinful to
have recourse to deceit in order to sell a
thing for more than its just price, because
this is to deceive one's neighbour so as to
injure him. Hence Tully says: *Contracts
should be entirely free from double-dealing;
the seller must not impose upon the bidder,
nor the buyer upon one that bids against
him.*

But, apart from fraud, we may speak of
buying and selling in two ways. First, as
considered in themselves, and from this
point of view, buying and selling seem to
be established for the common advantage of
both parties, one of whom requires that
which belongs to the other, and vice versa,
as the Philosopher states. Now whatever is
established for the common advantage,
should not be more of a burden to one
party than to another, and consequently all
contracts between them should observe
equality of thing and thing. Again, the quality of a thing that comes into human use is
measured by the price given for it, for
which purpose money was invented, as
stated in *Ethic.* v.5. Therefore if either the
price exceed the quantity of the thing's
worth, or, conversely, the thing exceed the
price, there is no longer the equality of justice: and consequently, to sell a thing for
more than its worth, or to buy it for less

than its worth, is in itself unjust and unlaw-ful.

Secondly we may speak of buying and selling, considered as accidentally tending to the advantage of one party, and to the disadvantage of the other: for instance, when a man has great need of a certain thing, while another man will suffer if he be without it. In such a case the just price will depend not only on the thing sold, but on the loss which the sale brings on the seller. And thus it will be lawful to sell a thing for more than it is worth in itself, though the price paid be not more than it is worth to the owner. Yet if the one man derive a great advantage by becoming pos-sessed of the other man's property, and the seller be not at a loss through being with-out that thing, the latter ought not to raise the price, because the advantage accruing to the buyer, is not due to the seller, but to a circumstance affecting the buyer. Now no man should sell what is not his, though he may charge for the loss he suffers.

On the other hand if a man find that he derives great advantage from something he has bought, he may, of his own accord, pay the seller something over and above: and this pertains to his honesty.

Reply Obj. 1. As stated above human law is given to the people among whom there are many lacking virtue, and it is not given to the virtuous alone. Hence human law was unable to forbid all that is contrary to virtue; and it suffices for it to prohibit whatever is destructive of human inter-course, while it treats other matters as though they were lawful, not by approving of them, but by not punishing them. Ac-cordingly, if without employing deceit the seller disposes of his goods for more than their worth, or the buyer obtain them for less than their worth, the law looks upon this as licit, and provides no punishment for so doing, unless the excess be too great, because then even human law demands res-titution to be made, for instance if a man be deceived in regard of more than half the amount of the just price of a thing.

On the other hand the Divine law leaves nothing unpunished that is contrary to virtue. Hence, according to the Divine law, it is reckoned unlawful if the equality of justice be not observed in buying and sell-ing: and he who has received more than he ought must make compensation to him that has suffered loss, if the loss be considerable. I add this condition, because the just price of things is not fixed with mathematical precision, but depends on a kind of esti-mate, so that a slight addition or subtrac-tion would not seem to destroy the equality of justice.

Reply Obj. 2. As Augustine says *this jester, either by looking into himself or by his experience of others, thought that all men are inclined to wish to buy for a song and sell at a premium. But since in reality this is wicked, it is in every man's power to acquire that justice whereby he may resist and overcome this inclination.* And then he gives the example of a man who gave the just price for a book to a man who through ignorance asked a low price for it. Hence it is evident that this common desire is not from nature but from vice, wherefore it is common to many who walk along the broad road of sin.

Reply Obj. 3. In commutative justice we consider chiefly real equality. On the other hand, in friendship based on utility we con-sider equality of usefulness, so that the recompense should depend on the usefulness accruing, whereas in buying it should be equal to the thing bought.

· · ·

Fourth Article: Whether, in trading, it is lawful to sell a thing at a higher price than what was paid for it?

We proceed thus to the Fourth Article:—

Objection 1. It would seem that it is not lawful, in trading, to sell a thing for a higher price than we paid for it. For Chrysostom says on Matth. xxi. 12: *He that buys a thing in order that he may sell it, entire and unchanged, at a profit, is the trader who is cast out of God's temple.* Cassiodorus speaks in the same sense in his commentary on Ps. lxx. 15, *Because I have not known learning,* or *trading* according to another version: *What is trade*, says he, *but buying at a cheap price with the purpose of retailing at a higher price?* and he adds: *Such were the tradesmen whom Our Lord cast out of the temple.* Now no man is cast out of the temple except for a sin. Therefore suchlike trading is sinful.

Obj. 2. Further, It is contrary to justice to sell goods at a higher price than their worth, or to buy them for less than their value, as shown above. Now if you sell a thing for a higher price than you paid for it, you must either have bought it for less than its value, or sell it for more than its value. Therefore this cannot be done without sin.

Obj. 3. Further, Jerome says *Shun, as you would the plague, a cleric who from being poor has become wealthy, or who, from being a nobody has become a celebrity.* Now trading would not seem to be forbidden to clerics except on account of its sinfulness. Therefore it is a sin in trading, to buy at a low price and to sell at a higher price.

On the contrary, Augustine commenting on Ps. lxx. 15, *Because I have not known learning*, says: *The greedy tradesman blasphemes over his losses; he lies and perjures himself over the price of his wares. But these are vices of the man, not of the craft, which can be exercised without these vices.* Therefore trading is not in itself unlawful.

I answer that, A tradesman is one whose business consists in the exchange of things. According to the Philosopher exchange of things is twofold; one, natural as it were, and necessary, whereby one commodity is exchanged for another, or money taken in exchange for a commodity, in order to satisfy the needs of life. Suchlike trading, properly speaking, does not belong to tradesmen, but rather to housekeepers or civil servants who have to provide the household or the state with the necessaries of life. The other kind of exchange is either that of money for money, or of any commodity for money, not on account of the necessities of life, but for profit, and this kind of exchange, properly speaking, regards tradesmen, according to the Philosopher. The former kind of exchange is commendable because it supplies a natural need: but the latter is justly deserving of blame, because, considered in itself, it satisfies the greed for gain, which knows no limit and tends to infinity. Hence trading, considered in itself, has a certain debasement attaching thereto, in so far as, by its very nature, it does not imply a virtuous or necessary end. Nevertheless gain which is the end of trading, though not implying, by its nature, anything virtuous or necessary, does not, in itself, connote anything sinful or contrary to virtue: wherefore nothing prevents gain from being directed to some necessary or even virtuous end, and thus trading becomes lawful. Thus, for instance, a man may intend the moderate gain which he seeks to acquire by trading for the upkeep of his household, or for the assistance of the needy: or again, a man may take to trade for some public advantage, for instance, lest his country lack the necessaries of life, and seek gain, not as an end, but as payment for his labour.

Reply Obj. 1. The saying of Chrysostom refers to the trading which seeks gain as a last end. This is especially the case where a man sells something at a higher price without its undergoing any change. For if he sells at a higher price something that has changed for the better, he would seem to receive the reward of his labour. Nevertheless the gain itself may be lawfully intended, not as a last end, but for the sake of some other end which is necessary or virtuous, as stated above.

Reply Obj. 2. Not everyone that sells at a higher price than he bought is a tradesman, but only he who buys that he may sell at a profit. If, on the contrary, he buys not for sale but for possession, and afterwards, for some reason wishes to sell, it is not a trade transaction even if he sell at a profit. For he may lawfully do this, either because he has bettered the thing, or because the value of the thing has changed with the change of place or time, or on account of the danger he incurs in transferring the thing from one place to another, or again in having it carried by another. In this sense neither buying nor selling is unjust.

Reply Obj. 3. Clerics should abstain not only from things that are evil in themselves, but even from those that have an appearance of evil. This happens in trading, both because it is directed to worldly gain, which clerics should despise, and because trading is open to so many vices, since *a merchant is hardly free from sins of the lips.* There is also another reason, because trading engages the mind too much with worldly cares, and consequently withdraws it from spiritual cares; wherefore the Apostle says: *No man being a soldier to God entangleth himself with secular businesses.* Nevertheless it is lawful for clerics to engage in the first mentioned kind of exchange, which is directed to supply the necessaries of life, either by buying or by selling.

OF THE SIN OF USURY

First Article: Whether it is a sin to take usury for money lent?

We proceed thus to the First Article:—

Objection 1. It would seem that it is not a sin to take usury for money lent. For no man sins through following the example of Christ. But Our Lord said of Himself: *At My coming I might have exacted it,* i.e. the money lent, *with usury.* Therefore it is not a sin to take usury for lending money.

Obj. 2. Further, According to Ps. xviii. 8, *The law of the Lord is unspotted,* because, to wit, it forbids sin. Now usury of a kind is allowed in the Divine law, according to Deut. xxiii, 19, 20, *Thou shalt not fenerate to thy brother money, nor corn, nor any other thing, but to the stranger:* nay more, it is even promised as a reward for the observance of the Law, according to Deut. xxviii, 12: *Thou shalt fenerate to many nations, and shalt not borrow of any one.* Therefore it is not a sin to take usury.

Obj. 3. Further, In human affairs justice is determined by civil laws. Now civil law allows usury to be taken. Therefore it seems to be lawful.

Obj. 4. Further, The counsels are not binding under sin. But, among other counsels we find: *Lend, hoping for nothing thereby.* Therefore it is not a sin to take usury.

Obj. 5. Further, It does not seem to be in itself sinful to accept a price for doing what one is not bound to do. But one who has money is not bound in every case to lend it to his neighbour. Therefore it is lawful for him sometimes to accept a price for lending it.

Obj. 6. Further, Silver made into coins does not differ specifically from silver made into a vessel. But it is lawful to accept a price for the loan of a silver vessel. Therefore it is also lawful to accept a price for the loan of a silver coin. Therefore usury is not in itself a sin.

Obj. 7. Further, Anyone may lawfully accept a thing which its owner freely gives him. Now he who accepts the loan, freely gives the usury. Therefore he who lends may lawfully take the usury.

On the contrary, It is written: *If thou lend money to any of thy people that is poor, that dwelleth with thee, thou shalt not be hard upon them as an extortioner, nor oppress them with usuries.*

I answer that, To take usury for money lent is unjust in itself, because this is to sell what does not exist, and this evidently leads to inequality which is contrary to justice.

In order to make this evident, we must observe that there are certain things the use of which consists in their consumption: thus we consume wine when we use it for drink, and we consume wheat when we use it for food. Wherefore in suchlike things the use of the thing must not be reckoned apart from the thing itself, and whoever is granted the use of the thing, is granted the thing itself; and for this reason, to lend things of this kind is to transfer the ownership. Accordingly if a man wanted to sell wine separately from the use of the wine, he would be selling the same thing twice, or he would be selling what does not exist, wherefore he would evidently commit a sin of injustice. In like manner he commits an injustice who lends wine or wheat, and asks for double payment, viz. one, the return of the thing in equal measure, the other, the price of the use, which is called usury.

On the other hand there are things the use of which does not consist in their consumption: thus to use a house is to dwell in it, not to destroy it. Wherefore in such things both may be granted: for instance, one man may hand over to another the ownership of his house while reserving to himself the use of it for a time, or vice versa, he may grant the use of the house, while retaining the ownership. For this reason a man may lawfully make a charge for the use of his house, and, besides this, revendicate the house from the person to whom he has granted its use, as happens in renting and letting a house.

Now money, according to the Philosopher, was invented chiefly for the purpose of exchange: and consequently the proper and principal use of money is its consumption or alienation whereby it is sunk in exchange. Hence it is by its very nature unlawful to take payment for the use of money lent, which payment is known as usury: and just as a man is bound to restore other ill-gotten goods, so is he bound to restore the money which he has taken in usury.

Reply Obj. 1. In this passage usury must be taken figuratively for the increase of spiritual goods which God exacts from us, for He wishes us ever to advance in the goods which we receive from Him: and this is for our own profit not for His.

Reply Obj. 2. The Jews were forbidden to take usury from their brethren, i.e. from other Jews. By this we are given to understand that to take usury from any man is evil simply, because we ought to treat every man as our neighbour and brother, especially in the state of the Gospel, whereto all are called. Hence it is said without any distinction in Ps. xiv. 5: *He that hath not put out his money to usury,* and: *Who hath not taken usury.* They were permitted, however, to take usury from foreigners, not as though it were lawful, but in order to avoid a greater evil, lest, to wit, through avarice to which they were prone according to Is. lvi. II, they should take usury from the Jews who were worshippers of God.

Where we find it promised to them as a reward, *Thou shalt fenerate to many nations,* etc., fenerating is to be taken in a broad sense for lending, as in Ecclus. xxix. 10, where we read, *Many have refused to fenerate, not out of wickedness,* i.e. they would not lend. Accordingly the Jews are promised in reward an abundance of wealth, so that they would be able to lend to others.

Reply Obj. 3. Human laws leave certain things unpunished, on account of the condition of those who are imperfect, and who would be deprived of many advantages, if all sins were strictly forbidden and punishments appointed for them. Wherefore human law has permitted usury, not that it looks upon usury as harmonizing with justice, but lest the advantage of many should be hindered. Hence it is that in civil law it is stated that *those things according to natural reason and civil law which are consumed by being used, do not admit of usufruct*, and that *the senate did not (nor could it) appoint a usufruct to such things, but established a quasi-usufruct*, namely by permitting usury. Moreover the Philosopher, led by natural reason, says that *to make money by usury is exceedingly unnatural.*

Reply Obj. 4. A man is not always bound to lend, and for this reason it is placed among the counsels. Yet it is a matter of precept not to seek profit by lending: although it may be called a matter of counsel in comparison with the maxims of the Pharisees, who deemed some kinds of usury to be lawful, just as love of one's enemies is a matter of counsel. Or again, He speaks here not of the hope of usurious gain, but of the hope which is put in man. For we ought not to lend or do any good deed through hope in man, but only through hope in God.

Reply Obj. 5. He that is not bound to lend, may accept repayment for what he has done, but he must not exact more. Now he is repaid according to equality of justice if he is repaid as much as he lent. Wherefore if he exacts more for the usufruct of a thing which has no other use but the consumption of its substance, he exacts a price of something non-existent: and so his exaction is unjust.

Reply Obj. 6. The principal use of a silver vessel is not its consumption, and so one may lawfully sell its use while retaining one's ownership of it. On the other hand the principal use of silver money is sinking it in exchange, so that it is not lawful to sell its use and at the same time expect the restitution of the amount lent. It must be observed, however, that the secondary use of silver vessels may be an exchange, and such use may not be lawfully sold. In like manner there may be some secondary use

of silver money; for instance, a man might lend coins for show, or to be used as security.

Reply Obj. 7. He who gives usury does not give it voluntarily simply, but under a certain necessity, in so far as he needs to borrow money which the owner is unwilling to lend without usury.

.　.　.

Third Article: Whether a man is bound to restore whatever profits he has made out of money gotten by usury?

We proceed thus to the Third Article:—

Objection 1. It would seem that a man is bound to restore whatever profits he has made out of money gotten by usury. For the Apostle says: *If the root be holy, so are the branches.* Therefore likewise if the root be rotten so are the branches. But the root was infected with usury. Therefore whatever profit is made therefrom is infected with usury. Therefore he is bound to restore it.

Obj. 2. Further, It is laid down: *Property accruing from usury must be sold, and the price repaid to the persons from whom the usury was extorted.* Therefore, likewise, whatever else is acquired from usurious money must be restored.

Obj. 3. Further, That which a man buys with the proceeds of usury is due to him by reason of the money he paid for it. Therefore he has no more right to the thing purchased than to the money he paid. But he was bound to restore the money gained through usury. Therefore he is also bound to restore what he acquired with it.

On the contrary, A man may lawfully hold what he has lawfully acquired. Now that which is acquired by the proceeds of usury is sometimes lawfully acquired. Therefore it may be lawfully retained.

I answer that, As stated above there are certain things whose use is their consumption, and which do not admit of usufruct, according to law. Wherefore if suchlike things be extorted by means of usury, for instance money, wheat, wine and so forth, the lender is not bound to restore more than he received (since what is acquired by such things is the fruit not of the thing but of human industry), unless indeed the other party by losing some of his own goods be injured through the lender retaining them: for then he is bound to make good the loss.

On the other hand there are certain things whose use is not their consumption: such things admit of usufruct, for instance house or land property and so forth. Wherefore if a man has by usury extorted from another his house or land, he is bound to restore not only the house or land but also the fruits accruing to him therefrom, since they are the fruits of things owned by another man and consequently are due him.

Reply Obj. 1. The root has not only the character of matter, as money made by usury has; but has also somewhat the character of an active cause, in so far as it administers nourishment. Hence the comparison fails.

Reply Obj. 2. Further, Property acquired from usury does not belong to the person who paid usury, but to the person who bought it. Yet he that paid usury has a certain claim on that property just as he has on the other goods of the usurer. Hence it is not prescribed that such property should be assigned to the persons who paid usury, since the property is perhaps worth more than what they paid in usury, but it is commanded that the property be sold, and the price be restored, of course according to the amount taken in usury.

Reply Obj. 3. The proceeds of money taken in usury are due to the person who acquired them not by reason of the usurious money as instrumental cause, but on account of his own industry as principal cause. Wherefore he has more right to the goods acquired with usurious money than to the usurious money itself.

Fourth Article: Whether it is lawful to borrow money under a condition of usury?

We proceed thus to the Fourth Article:—

Objection 1. It would seem that it is not lawful to borrow money under a condition of usury. For the Apostle says that they *are worthy of death . . . not only they that do* these sins, *but they also that consent to them that do them.* Now he that borrows money under a condition of usury consents in the sin of the usurer, and gives him an occasion of sin. Therefore he sins also.

Obj. 2. Further, For no temporal advantage ought one to give another an occasion of committing a sin: for this pertains to active scandal, which is always sinful, as stated above. Now he that seeks to borrow from a usurer gives him an occasion of sin. Therefore he is not to be excused on account of any temporal advantage.

Obj. 3. Further, It seems no less necessary sometimes to deposit one's money with a usurer than to borrow from him. Now it seems altogether unlawful to deposit one's money with a usurer, even as it would be unlawful to deposit one's sword with a madman, a maiden with a libertine, or food with a glutton. Neither therefore is it lawful to borrow from a usurer.

On the contrary, He that suffers injury does not sin, according to the Philosopher (*Ethic,* v.11), wherefore justice is not a mean between two vices, as stated in the same book (ch. 5). Now a usurer sins by doing an injury to the person who borrows from him under a condition of usury. Therefore he that accepts a loan under a condition of usury does not sin.

I answer that, It is by no means lawful to induce a man to sin, yet it is lawful to make use of another's sin for a good end, since even God uses all sin for some good, since He draws some good from every evil as stated in the *Enchiridion* (xi.). Hence when Publicola asked whether it were lawful to make use of an oath taken by a man swearing by false gods (which is a manifest sin, for he gives Divine honour to them) Augustine answered that he who uses, not for a bad but for a good purpose, the oath of a man that swears by false gods, is a party, not to his sin of swearing by demons, but to his good compact whereby he kept his word. If however he were to induce him to swear by false gods, he would sin.

Accordingly we must also answer to the question in point that it is by no means lawful to induce a man to lend under a condition of usury: yet it is lawful to borrow for usury from a man who is ready to do so and is a usurer by profession; provided the borrower have a good end in view, such as the relief of his own or another's need. Thus too it is lawful for a man who has fallen among thieves to point out his property to them (which they sin in taking) in order to save his life, after the example of the ten men who said to Ismahel: *Kill us not: for we have stores in the field.*

Reply Obj. 1. He who borrows for usury does not consent to the usurer's sin but makes use of it. Nor is it the usurer's acceptance of usury that pleases him, but his lending, which is good.

Reply Obj. 2. He who borrows for usury gives the usurer an occasion, not for taking usury, but for lending; it is the usurer who finds an occasion of sin in the malice of his heart. Hence there is passive scandal on his part, while there is no active scandal on the part of the person who seeks to borrow. Nor is this passive scandal a reason why the other person should desist from borrowing if he is in need, since this passive scandal arises not from weakness or ignorance but from malice.

Reply Obj. 3. If one were to entrust one's money to a usurer lacking other means of practising usury; or with the intention of making a greater profit from his money by reason of the usury, one would be giving a sinner matter for sin, so that one would be a participator in his guilt. If, on the other hand, the usurer to whom one entrusts one's money has other means of practising usury, there is no sin in entrusting it to him that it may be in safer keeping, since this is to use a sinner for a good purpose.

Sir John Froissart

Tales of high adventure, tales of glorious deeds, and tales of knightly virtue— these are the chronicles of Sir John Froissart (1338-*c.*1410). But these *Chronicles of England, France, Spain, and the Adjoining Countries from the Latter Part of the Reign of Edward II to the Coronation of Henry IV* are also a major source of information on the history of the fourteenth century. They are shaped by the prejudices of the author, and they are derived in part from other writings; but still they are the best summary account of the times. Froissart is not analytical, nor even particularly descriptive, but he is brilliantly narrative; and his story reflects his admiration for the pageantry and chivalry of the later Middle Ages. That the romance and daring of the society he so admired were fast disappearing was an idea utterly beyond the conception of this knighted raconteur.

CHRONICLES

. . .

Chap. CLXII

THE PRINCE OF WALES MAKES A HANDSOME
PRESENT TO THE LORD JAMES AUDLEY,
AFTER THE BATTLE OF POITIERS

Soon after the earl of Warwick and the lord Reginald Cobham had
left the prince, as has been above related,
he inquired from those knights who were
about him of lord James Audley, and asked
if any one knew what was become of him:
'Yes, sir,' replied some of the company,
'he is very badly wounded, and is lying in a
litter hard by.' 'By my troth,' replied the
prince, 'I am sore vexed that he is so
wounded. See, I beg of you, if he be able
to bear being carried hither: otherwise I
will come and visit him.' Two knights directly left the prince, and, coming to lord
James, told him how desirous the prince
was of seeing him. 'A thousand thanks to
the prince,' answered lord James, 'for con-
descending to remember so poor a knight
as myself.' He then called eight of his servants, and had himself borne in his litter to
where the prince was. When he was come
into his presence, the prince bent down
over him, and embraced him, saying; 'My
lord James, I am bound to honour you very
much; for, by your valour this day, you
have acquired glory and renown above us
all, and your prowess has proved you
the bravest knight.' Lord James replied;
'My lord, you have a right to say whatever
you please, but I wish it were as you have
said. If I have this day been forward to
serve you, it has been to accomplish a vow

CHRONICLES *of England, France, Spain, and the*
Adjoining Countries from the Latter Part of the
Reign of Edward II to the Coronation of Henry
IV, Sir John Froissart, trans. T. Johnes (London,
1808), II, 340-356.

that I had made, and it ought not to be
thought so much of.' 'Sir James,' answered
the prince, 'I and all the rest of us deem
you the bravest knight on our side in this
battle; and to increase your renown, and
furnish you withal to pursue your career
of glory in war, I retain you henceforward,
for ever, as my knight, with five hundred
marcs of yearly revenue, which I will secure to you from my estates in England.'
'Sir,' said lord James, 'God make me deserving of the good fortune you bestow upon
me.' At these words he took leave of the
prince, as he was very weak, and his servants carried him back to his tent: he could
not have been at a great distance, when
the earl of Warwick and lord Reginald
Cobham entered the pavilion of the
prince, and presented the king of France to
him.

The prince made a very low obeisance to
the king, and gave him as much comfort as
he was able, which he knew well how to
administer. He ordered wine and spices to
be brought, which he presented to the king
himself, as a mark of his great affection.

Chap. CLXIII

THE ENGLISH GAIN VERY CONSIDERABLY AT
THE BATTLE OF POITIERS

Thus was this battle won, as
you have heard related, in the plains of
Maupertuis, two leagues from the city of
Poitiers, on the 19th day of September
1356. It commenced about nine o'clock,
and was ended by noon; but the English
were not all returned from the pursuit,
and it was to recall his people that the
prince had placed his banner upon a high
bush. They did not return till late after
vespers from pursuing the enemy.

It was reported that all the flower of

French knighthood were slain; and that, with the king and his son the lord Philip, seventeen earls, without counting barons, knights or squires, were made prisoners, and from five to six thousand of all sorts left dead in the field.

When they were all collected, they found they had twice as many prisoners as themselves: they therefore consulted, if, considering the risk they might run, it would not be more advisable to ransom them on the spot. This was done: and the prisoners found the English and Gascons very civil, for there were many set at liberty that day on their promise of coming to Bourdeaux before Christmas to pay their ransom.

When all were returned to their banners, they retired to their camp, which was adjoining to the field of battle. Some disarmed themselves, and did the same to their prisoners, to whom they shewed every kindness; for whoever made any prisoners, they were solely at his disposal, to ransom or not, as he pleased. It may be easily supposed that all those who accompanied the prince were very rich in glory and wealth, as well by the ransoms of their prisoners, as by the quantities of gold and silver plate, rich jewels, and trunks stuffed full of belts that were weighty from their gold and silver ornaments, and furred mantles. They set no value on armour, tents or other things; for the French had come there as magnificently and richly dressed as if they had been sure of gaining the victory.

Chap. CLXIV

THE LORD JAMES AUDLEY GIVES TO HIS SQUIRES THE PENSION OF FIVE HUNDRED MARCS HE HAD RECEIVED FROM THE PRINCE

When the lord James Audley was brought back to his tent, after having most respectfully thanked the prince for his gift, he did not remain long before he sent for his brother sir Peter Audley, the lord Bartholomew Burghersh, sir Stephen Coffington, lord Willoughby of Ereshby and lord William Ferrers of Groby: they were all his relations. He then sent for his four squires that had attended upon him that day, and, addressing himself to the knights, said: 'Gentlemen, it has pleased my lord the prince to give me five hundred marcs as a yearly inheritance; for which gift I have done him very trifling bodily service. You see here these four squires, who have always served me most loyally, and especially in this day's engagement. What glory I may have gained has been through their means, and by their valour: on which account I wish to reward them. I therefore give and resign into their hands the gift of five hundred marcs, which my lord the prince has been pleased to bestow me, in the same form and manner that it has been presented to me. I disinherit myself of it, and give it to them simply, and without a possibility of revoking it.'

The knights present looked on each other, and said, 'It is becoming the noble mind of lord James to make such a gift,' and then unanimously added; 'May the Lord God remember you for it! We will bear witness of this gift to them wheresoever and whensoever they may call on us.'

They then took leave of him; when some went to the prince of Wales, who that night was to give a supper to the king of France from his own provisions; for the French had brought vast quantities with them, which were now fallen into the hands of the English, many of whom had not tasted bread for the last three days.

Chap. CLXV

THE PRINCE OF WALES ENTERTAINS THE KING OF FRANCE AT SUPPER, THE EVENING AFTER THE BATTLE

When evening was come, the prince of Wales gave a supper in his pavilion to the king of France, and to the greater part of the princes and barons who were prisoners. The prince seated the king of France and his son the lord Philip at an elevated and well covered table: with them were sir James de Bourbon, the lord John d'Artois, the earls of Tancarville, of Estampes, of Dammartin, of Graville, and the lord of Partenay. The other knights and squires were placed at different tables.

The prince himself served the king's table, as well as the others, with every mark of humility, and would not sit down at it, in spite of all his intreaties for him so to do, saying, that 'he was not worthy of such an honor, nor did it appertain to him to seat himself at the table of so great a king, or of so valiant a man as he had shewn himself by his actions that day.' He added also with a noble air; 'Dear sir, do not make a poor meal because the Almighty God has not gratified your wishes in the event of this day; for be assured that my lord and father will shew you every honor and friendship in his power, and will arrange your ransom so reasonably, that you will henceforward always remain friends. In my opinion, you have cause to be glad that the success of this battle did not turn out as you desired; for you have this day acquired such high renown for prowess, that you have surpassed all the best knights on your side. I do not, dear sir, say this to flatter you, for all those of our side who have seen and observed the actions of each party, have unanimously allowed this to be your due, and decree you the prize and garland for it.'

At the end of this speech there were murmurs of praise heard from every one; and the French said, the prince had spoken nobly and truly, and that he would be one of the most gallant princes in Christendom, if God should grant him life to pursue his career of glory.

Chap. CLXVI

THE PRINCE OF WALES RETURNS TO BOURDEAUX, AFTER THE BATTLE OF POITIERS

When they had supped and sufficiently regaled themselves, each departed to his lodging with the knights and squires they had captured. Those that had taken them asked, what they could pay for their ransoms, without much hurting their fortunes; and willingly believed whatever they told them; for they had declared publicly, that they did not wish to deal harshly with any knight or squire that his ransom should be so burdensome as to prevent his following the profession of arms, or advancing his fortune.

Towards morning, when these lords had heard mass, and had eaten and drank a little, whilst the servants were packing up or loading the baggage, they decamped and advanced toward Poitiers.

That same night, the lord of Roye had entered the city of Poitiers with a hundred lances, that had not been engaged in the battle, for, having met the duke of Normandy near Chauvigny, he had commanded him to march for Poitiers, and to guard it until he should receive other orders.

When the lord of Roye had entered Poitiers, he ordered the gates, towers, and walls to be well watched that night, on account of the English being so near; and on the morning he armed all sorts of people, and posted them wherever he judged most convenient for the defense of the town.

The English, however, passed by, without making any attempt upon it; for they were so laden with gold, silver, jewels, and great prisoners, that they did not attack any fortress in their march, but thought they should do great things if they were able to convey the king of France and his son, with all their booty, in safety to the city of Bourdeaux. They returned, therefore, by easy marches, on account of their prisoners and heavy baggage, never advancing more than four or five leagues a-day: they encamped early, and marched in one compact body, without quitting the road, except the division of the marshals, who advanced in front, with about five hundred men at arms, to clear the country. They met with no resistance any where; for the whole country was in a state of consternation, and all the men at arms had retreated into the strong fortresses.

During this march, the prince of Wales was informed how lord James Audley had made a present of his pension of five hundred marcs to his four squires. He sent for him: lord James was carried in his litter to the presence of the prince, who received him very graciously, and said to him; 'Sir James, I have been informed, that after you had taken leave of me, and were returned to your tent, you made a present to your four squires of the gift I presented to you. I should like to know if this be true, why you did so, and if the gift were not agreeable to you?'

'Yes, my lord,' answered lord James, 'it was most agreeable to me, and I will tell you the reasons which induced me to bestow it on my squires. These four squires, who are here, have long and loyally served me, on many great and dangerous occasions; and until the day that I made them this present, I had not any way rewarded them for all their services; and never in this life were they of such help to me as on that day. I hold myself much bound to them for what they did at the battle of Poitiers; for, dear sir, I am but a single man, and can do no more than my powers admit, but, through their aid and assistance, I have accomplished my vow, which for a long time I had made, and by their means was the first combatant, and should have paid for it with my life, if they had not been near to me. When, therefore,

I consider their courage, and the love they bear to me, I should not have been courteous nor grateful, if I had not rewarded them. Thank God, my lord, I have a sufficiency for my life, to maintain my state; and wealth has never yet failed me, nor do I believe it ever will. If, therefore, I have in this acted contrary to your wishes, I beseech you, dear sir, to pardon me; for you will be ever as loyally served by me and my squires, to whom I gave your present, as heretofore.' The prince answered; 'Sir James, I do not in the least blame you for what you have done, but, on the contrary, acknowledge your bounty to your squires whom you praise so much. I readily confirm your gift to them; but I shall insist upon your accepting of six hundred marcs, upon the same terms and conditions as the former gift.'

The prince of Wales and his army kept advancing, without meeting any obstacle, and, having passed through Poitou and Saintonge, came to Blaye, where he crossed the Garonne, and arrived in the good city of Bourdeaux.

It is not possible to relate all the feasts and entertainments which the citizens and clergy of Bourdeaux made for the prince, and with what joy they received him and the king of France.

The prince conducted the king to the monastery of St. Andrew, where they were both lodged; the king on one side, and the prince on the other. The prince purchased from the barons, knights and squires of Gascony, the ransoms of the greater part of the French earls who were there, and paid ready money for them.

There were many meetings and disputes among the knights and squires of Gascony, and others, relative to the capture of the king of France. On this account, Denys de Morbeque truly and by right of arms claimed him. He challenged another squire of Gascony, named Bernard de Trouttes, who had declared that he had an equal right to him. There was much disputing between them before the prince and the barons present: and as they had engaged to fight each other, the prince put them under an arrest, until they should be arrived in England, and forbade any thing more being said on the subject till they were in the presence of the king his father.

However, as the king of France gave every assistance to sir Denys in support of his claim, and leaned more to him than to any of the other claimants, the prince ordered two thousand nobles to be given privately to sir Denys, in order to enable him the better to support his rank.

Soon after the prince's arrival at Bourdeaux, the cardinal de Perigord came thither as, it was said, ambassador from the pope. It was upwards of a fortnight before the prince would speak to him, on account of the castellan of Amposta and his people having been engaged against him at the battle of Poitiers. The prince believed that the cardinal had sent them thither; but the cardinal, through the means of his relations, the lord of Chaumont, the lord of Montserrant and the captal of Buch, gave

such good reasons for his conduct to the prince, that he admitted him to an audience. Having obtained this, he exculpated himself so clearly that the prince and his council were satisfied; and he regained the place he before held in the prince's affection. All his people were set at liberty at moderate ransoms: the castellan's amounted to ten thousand franks, which he paid.

The cardinal, soon after, began to touch upon the deliverance of king John: but I shall say little on that head, as nothing was done in the business.

The prince, with his Gascons and English, remained all that winter at Bourdeaux, where was much feasting and merriment; and they foolishly expended the gold and silver they had gained.

In England also, there were great rejoicings, when the news arrived of the affair at Poitiers, and of the defeat of the French. Solemn thanksgivings were offered up in all churches, and bonfires made in every town and village. Those knights and squires who returned to England, after having been in this battle, were honoured in preference to any others.

RENAISSANCE AND REFORMATION

THE RENAISSANCE was a cultural and intellectual revival that had its beginnings in the city-states of northern Italy during the fourteenth and fifteenth centuries. The gradual change from the medieval outlook was probably caused by several factors—the great economic prosperity of these city-states, their contacts through trade with other cultures, the reduction of the papacy to the role of an Italian principality, and the Church's loss of emotional prestige. These elements combined to produce the highly secular outlook that is the essence of the Renaissance.

This secular outlook is commonly referred to as "humanism," a term that may be defined in two ways. According to the narrower definition, humanism was a rebirth, or renaissance, of interest in classical antiquity. Men turned to a re-reading of the great (and not so great) works of Greek and Roman literature, a re-examination and preservation of classical architecture and sculpture, and a re-study of the classical languages themselves. This very interest in the glories of Greece and Rome, however, exacted its price, for Renaissance literature and some of its art tended to be imitative, to rely too heavily on the models of a by-gone day. The conviction that it was impossible to surpass or even to equal the achievements of the ancients tended to inhibit the mind and imagination of the men of the Renaissance.

The broader definition of humanism states the typically Renaissance notion that man and his activities are the most important and interesting elements of the universe. Thus, man himself, rather than God, is the proper subject of contemplation and examination. This secular, humanistic outlook posed many interesting problems. If man and his life on this earth are the most important concern of man, how may the "good" man or the "good" life be determined? Castiglione, in his manual on conduct, *The Book of the Courtier,* claimed that virtue is its own reward, that one does not do good or bad out of hope for reward or fear of punishment in an afterlife, but only because it is good to be good. Some of the same secular ethic is implied in the political theories of Machiavelli, whose ideal prince was not concerned with or troubled by an angry or beneficent God but only with the problems of acquiring and maintaining power to ensure a stable political order in which the citizenry could live in peace and plenty.

During the fifteenth and sixteenth centuries the Renaissance spread from Italy to France, England, Spain, the Lowlands, and throughout Germany and Poland. Italian manners and customs were widely adopted and it became fashionable to build "in the Italian fashion" and to dress "in the Italian mode." More important, however, than the adoption of these cultural superficialities was the ready acceptance by scholars in northern Europe of the critical methods developed by Pico, Valla, and others, of reading and analyzing documents, literature, and writings of all kinds. Moreover, the scientific attitude and the widespread curiosity about the physical world led many Europeans to inquire, to study, to dissect, to experiment, and to seek a fuller understanding of the nature of the universe and man's place in it.

Among the leaders of the New Learning in the North was Sir Thomas More of England, who looked closely at his society and found it mean and corrupt. This conclusion he elaborated in his brilliant and immensely popular satire, *Utopia*, which was published in 1516 in Latin and subsequently translated into English, French, Spanish, German, and Italian. More's close friend, Erasmus of Rotterdam, was also deeply influenced by the skeptical, critical thought of the Renaissance. Erasmus translated the New Testament from Greek into Latin, wrote various *Colloquies* containing observations and commentaries on the contemporary world, and, more lasting perhaps, published his penetrating analysis of people and affairs under the title *In Praise of Folly*.

Not everyone, however, received the New Learning with the same enthusiasm. A German monk, Martin Luther, though he accepted the typically humanistic ideas regarding the critical examination of texts, could not accept the Renaissance notion that this world and its affairs were of primary importance. For he was unwilling to divorce himself from the crucial problem of the salvation of man's soul. Most of the men of the Renaissance simply shelved the problem of salvation—for them, life was for the living, to be enjoyed and possibly to be remembered without remorse or regret. Benvenuto Cellini, an Italian goldsmith, was a perfect exemplar of this attitude. But for Luther (a contemporary of Cellini) life on this earth was but a transient aspect of the eternal life of the soul. In this one sense, Luther represented a reversion to the medieval outlook. But at the same time he shared in the new intellectual movements, being convinced that everyone was competent to read and understand the holy writings and to find his own salvation through faith.

Justification by faith lay at the heart of the Lutheran break with the Catholic Church. Originally, Luther sought only the reform of church practice, not doctrine. But the indifference of the church leaders, together with what seemed to him an almost institutionalized acceptance of abuses, made Luther's outcries go unheard. The Church finally became seriously enough concerned over Luther's protests to excommunicate him, thereby laying the ground for the Protestant movement.

For centuries, the Catholic Church had been flexible enough in its thinking and its practices to adjust to reform movements from within— for example, the Cluniac movement of the eleventh century, the Cistercian of the twelfth, and the Franciscan of the thirteenth. But by the end of the fifteenth century the Church was no longer able to provide the spiritual comfort required to sustain a great number of loyal and devoted followers. During the fifteenth century a group of mystics, who dedicated their lives to poverty and the education of the young, had appeared in Germany—the Brotherhood of the Common Life. This relatively obscure group felt that the conventional Catholic Church was somehow failing in its purposes, and sought to restore a measure of fervor to the traditional faith. Even Erasmus was concerned about the abuses in church practice and the indifference of church leadership to the needs of the people. He presented his solutions to these problems in what he called "the philosophy of Christ."

One of the outcomes of the conflict between the Protestant movement and the Catholic Church was a revitalization of the Catholic faith. Led mostly by the militant order of the Society of Jesus, founded in 1540 by Saint Ignatius of Loyola, the Catholics re-converted Poland, Bohemia, and large areas of France and Germany. Of course, this revitalization was not accomplished without bitterness, heroism, and conflict from both Protestant and Catholic. The Peasants Revolt in Germany in the early sixteenth century, the religious wars in France in the late sixteenth century, and the Thirty Years' War in the early seventeenth century were only outstanding examples of the hatred, fear, and bloodshed provoked by conflicting religious opinions.

During the Renaissance, then, Europe was expanding intellectually and culturally through scientific investigation and literary and artistic innovation, and was attempting to find some solution to religious controversy. Europe was expanding geographically as well. For the time of the Renaissance and Reformation was also the age of exploration and commercial revolution. To the west new continents were discovered, new colonies were planted, and new empires were created. The discovery of a sea route around Africa immensely stimulated traffic between western Europe and the Orient, leading finally to a relative decline in the economic status of the great Italian cities and the emergence of Portugal, Spain, the Dutch Republic, and finally France and England as world powers with great fleets and vast overseas holdings. The influx of wealth (both in goods and precious metals) from East and West created severe economic dislocations and upheavals in Europe, thus adding another source of strife and discontent to a culture already troubled by the ferment of Renaissance skepticism and Reformation religious enthusiasm. It was from this matrix that the modern world emerged; many of the problems posed then remain today.

Pico della Mirandola

Giovanni Pico, the Count of Mirandola (1463-1494), epitomized both in his life and in his writings the Renaissance ideal of manhood. Wealthy, nobly born, handsome, and brilliant, he was well embarked on a distinguished intellectual career which would certainly have made him the undisputed leader of the humanistic movement when he fell victim to fever at the age of thirty. Unwilling to limit himself, as many other humanists did, to translating and imitating the literature of classical Greece and Rome, he undertook the task of assimilating all the great writings of the past, searching out the elements of truth contained in each of them, and assembling these truths into a new philosophical synthesis of his own.

The *Oration on the Dignity of Man* is a part of this ambitious project. After seven years of study in various European universities, Pico arrived in Rome at the age of twenty-three and announced that he was prepared to defend in public debate against anyone in Europe a list of nine hundred theses representing the conclusions that he had derived from his studies. (He even offered to pay the travel expenses of scholars coming long distances.) The debate, scheduled for January, 1487, never took place. Pope Innocent VIII, suspicious that Pico was straying from orthodoxy, appointed a commission to examine the list of theses. When the commission confirmed the pope's suspicions by labeling a number of them heretical, Innocent forced the debate to be canceled.

The nature of the *Oration*, which Pico had intended as an introductory address for the debate. is evident from its title. Apart from the intrinsic interest of the discussion itself, including the many references which Pico makes to the most diverse literary sources, the significance of the *Oration* lies in its eloquent summation of the Renaissance interest in man and the belief in the dignity of human life. The selection that follows includes the first seven sections of the *Oration*.

ON THE DIGNITY OF MAN

Most reverend fathers: I have read in the writings of the Arabs that Abdallah the Saracen, when asked what thing on this worldly stage appeared most marvelous to him, replied that he perceived nothing more wonderful than Man. This

DE HOMINIS DIGNITATE, *Giovanni Pico della Mirandola,* trans. Douglass S. Parker of the University of California at Riverside.

opinion is concurred in by that famous statement of Hermes Trismegistus:

"Man, Asclepius, is a great miracle."

As I pondered the sense of these sayings, I became dissatisfied with those arguments which are brought forth in profusion by many people to establish the excellence of Humanity: namely, that Man is the intermediary of all created beings, slave to those above him, king to those below; that Man is the interpreter of nature, by virtue of the sharpness of his senses, the searching of his reason, and the light of his understanding; that Man is the interval between time and eternity, the copula of the universe (as the Persians say), or even its wedding, a little lower, on David's authority, than the angels. These are great things, certainly, but not of prime importance; not so great that they lay just claim to the highest admiration. For, under these conditions, why should we not give even greater admiration to the angels themselves, and to the blessed choir of Heaven?

At length, I felt that I had come to understand both why Man is the most fortunate of creatures, and thus worthy of all admiration, and what, finally, this situation is which he has received in the scheme of the universe—a position to be envied, not only by the beasts, but by the stars, by the spirits beyond the world. The answer is marvelous and incredible. How could it be otherwise? For it is on this account that Man is rightly said and believed to be a great miracle, truly a being to be admired.

Hear now, Fathers, what this solution is, and, in your courtesy, grant my discourse a friendly audience.

The Supreme Father, God the Creator, had already fashioned this worldly residence which we see about us, the majestic temple of His Godhood, after the laws of His secret wisdom. He had adorned the zone beyond the heavens with intellects; He had quickened the ethereal spheres into life with eternal souls; He had filled the foul and filthy regions of the lower world with a multitude of animals of every sort. But, His work completed, the Demiurge desired that there be someone to contemplate the reason of such a great work, to love its beauty, to wonder at its vastness. Thus, when everything had been finished (as Moses and Timaeus bear witness), He

turned His thoughts last of all to bringing forth Man. But there remained no archetype on which to pattern the new creature, no treasure to bestow on the new son as an inheritance, no place in all the world where that contemplator of the universe might sit. By this time, all things were full; all things had been distributed in the highest, middle, and lowest orders. But it was not the nature of the Father's power to fail, as though exhausted, in the last act of creation; nor of His wisdom, to waver in a necessary deed through lack of a plan; nor of His beneficent love, to compel the very being who was to praise the divine generosity in other things to impugn that generosity in himself. At length the Greatest Craftsman decided that this being, to whom He could give nothing of its own, should share in everything which he had assigned to each of the other beings. Thus he received Man as a work of undefined pattern, and, placing him in the center of the world, addressed him as follows:

I have given you, O Adam, neither a fixed location, nor an especial appearance, nor any gift peculiarly your own; therefore, you may attain and possess, as you wish and as you will, whatever location, whatever appearance, whatever gifts you yourself desire. The nature of all other things is limited and confined within laws which I have laid down. You, confined by no limits, will determine your nature for yourself by your judgment, into whose power I have consigned you. I have placed you in the middle of the world, whence you may survey the more conveniently everything which is in the world. I have made you neither heavenly nor earthly, neither mortal nor immortal; thus, as a free and sovereign craftsman, you may mold yourself whatever form you choose. You will be able to degenerate into those lower creatures, which are brutes; you will be able, by the determination of your mind, to be reborn into those higher creatures, which are divine.

How great is the generosity of God the Father! How great and admirable is the happiness of Man, whose gift it is to have that which he wishes! Upon their birth, beasts bring with them from their mother's bag (as Lucilius says) all that they will ever possess. From the beginning of time, or soon after, the supreme spirits have been that which they will be throughout all eternity. But as Man is born, the Father has planted in him seeds of every sort, shoots of every life; those which each man cultivates will grow, and bear their fruits in him. If these are vegetable, he will become a plant; if sensual, a brute; if rational, a heavenly being; if intellectual, an angel and son of God. But if Man, not contented with any creature's lot, betakes himself into the center of his oneness, then, made one with God, in the solitary darkness of the Father he who was created above all things will excell all things.

Who would not admire this chameleon of ours? Or, rather, who would admire anything else more greatly? Asclepius of Athens does no wrong when he says of man that, in accordance with his changing aspect and his self-transforming nature, he was symbolized in the mysteries by Proteus. Hence those metamorphoses celebrated among the Hebrews and the Pythagoreans: indeed, the most secret Hebrew theology makes transformations, now of holy Enoch into an angel of the divinity, now of other men into other divine spirits; the Pythagoreans transform evildoers into beasts, and even (if we may believe Empedocles) into plants. Imitating this, Mohammed would often say, "He who departs from the divine law becomes a beast," and rightly so. For not the bark, but the dull and insensible nature makes the plant; not the hide, but the brutish and sensual soul the beast; not the circular body, but correct reason the heavens; not separation from the body, but spiritual intelligence the angel. For should you see a man given up to his belly and creeping on the ground, you see a plant, not a man; should you see someone blinded by the empty illusions of an apparition like Calypso, enticed by titil-lating allurements, a slave to his senses, you see a beast, not a man; should you see a philosopher perceiving all by his correct reasoning, you would revere him—he is a being of heaven, not of earth; should you see a pure contemplator, unconscious of his body, completely withdrawn into the sanctuary of his mind, this is no earthly, no celestial being:—this is a most majestic spirit dressed in human flesh.

Is there anyone, then, who would not admire man? Not wrongly, in both the Mosaic and the Christian scriptures, is he called now by the name of "all flesh," now by the name of "every creature," since he molds, fashions, and transforms himself after the appearance of all flesh and after the nature of every creature. Therefore Evanthes the Persian, in his account of the Chaldean theology, writes that Man possesses no innate form of his own, but many extraneous and foreign ones, whence that saying of the Chaldeans that man is an animal of varied and manifold and unstable nature.

But to what end do I record this? So that, after we have been born in this condition—that of being what we wish—we shall understand that we must take especial care that it not be said against us, that we were in honor and knew it not, and became as brutes and foolish beasts. Rather, may the words of the prophet Asaph apply—"Ye are gods, and all of you are children of the most High,"—lest we, abusing the Father's most indulgent generosity, render that unfettered choice which He gave us harmful rather than beneficial. May some holy aspiration enter our hearts, so that we are not content with middling things, but pant for the highest and strain to achieve them, since we can if we will.

Let us scorn the earthly, despise the heavenly, and thus, disdaining everything which is of the world, fly to that assembly beyond the world which is nearest God, who towers over all. There, as the holy mysteries tell, Seraphim, Cherubim, and Thrones occupy the first place; let us strive to equal their dignity and glory. And, if we wish it, we shall be in no wise lower than they.

Niccolò Machiavelli

A reading of *The Prince* by Machiavelli (1469-1527) makes it easy to understand the evil connotations that have come to surround the term "Machiavellian." Written as a handbook for political leaders, *The Prince* is most famous as the source of the doctrine that, in politics, the end always justifies the means. With Machiavelli, this doctrine was no theoretical assumption; it was a conclusion derived from acute observation and analysis of the political practices of the day. As a diplomat in the service of his native city of Florence, Machiavelli was able to observe the tactics of the men who were struggling for control of the Italian peninsula in the early sixteenth century. The most colorful of these power-hungry men was the notorious Caesar Borgia, son of Pope Alexander VI, whom Machiavelli met on numerous occasions during his diplomatic career. For Borgia, power clearly was an end in itself.

Although, in *The Prince*, Machiavelli praises Borgia and advocates the pursuit of power without regard to the methods employed, to be fair we must realize that Machiavelli himself was not an unqualified Machiavellian. In the final chapter of *The Prince*, he urges Lorenzo de' Medici to exert his princely power to unify Italy and drive out foreign oppressors, an end that Machiavelli valued more highly than the mere pursuit of power for its own sake. And in his *Discourses* he concludes that the best-governed state is a state ruled, not by a Machiavellian prince, but by the people themselves. In spite of these qualifications, however, Machiavelli is commonly regarded as the champion of power politics and of the doctrine that the end justifies the means.

To capture something of the flavor and diversity of the Italian Renaissance, we have only to realize that Machiavelli and Pico della Mirandola were contemporaries living in the city of Florence. Yet while Pico was writing on the dignity of man, Machiavelli was observing, "For it may be truly affirmed of mankind in general, that they are ungrateful, fickle, timid, dissembling, and self-interested. . . ."

THE PRINCE

NICCOLÒ MACHIAVELLI, CITIZEN AND
SECRETARY OF FLORENCE, TO THE MOST
MAGNIFICENT LORENZO DE MEDICI:

Those who court the favour of princes generally present them with whatever they possess that is most rare, curious, or valuable; as horses, armour, embroidered cloths, precious stones, &c., according to the dignity of the personage they seek to propitiate. For my part, my anxiety to present myself to the notice of your highness, with the best proof of my devotion, has not enabled me to discover, amongst all I possess, anything that I esteem more, or account so valuable, as a knowledge of the actions of celebrated men; a knowledge acquired by a long experience of modern times, and a diligent perusal of the ancients. The observations which I have made with all the accuracy, reflection, and care of which I am capable, are contained in the small volume now addressed to you. And although I have not the vanity to deem it worthy of your acceptance, yet I am persuaded that your goodness will not refuse the offering, since it is impossible to present you with anything more valuable than a work which will place before you, in a small compass, all the experience I have acquired during many years of continual meditation and suffering in the school of adversity.

You will find in this fragment neither a glowing and lofty style, nor any of those meretricious ornaments with which authors seek to embellish their works. Its interest must depend upon the importance of the subject, the solidity of the reflections, and the truth of the facts recorded.

"THE PRINCE," Niccolò Machiavelli, from *The History of Florence and the Affairs of Italy* (London, 1854), pp. 405-406, 450-461, 481-487.

It will, perhaps, appear presumptuous in me, a man of humble birth, to propose rules of conduct to those who govern; but as the painter when about to sketch a mountainous country places himself in the plain, and in order to draw the scenery of a vale, ascends an eminence, even so, I conceive, that a person must be a prince to discover the nature and character of a people, and one of the people to judge properly of a prince.

I am therefore bold enough to hope that you will accept this feeble tribute in reference to the intention with which it is offered; and if you condescend to read it with attention, you will have evidence of my ardent desire to see you fill with glory those high destinies, to which fortune and your splendid talents have called you.

If from your elevated position you should condescend to look down on a person in my lowly station, you will see how long and how unworthily I have been persecuted by the extreme and unrelenting malevolence of fortune.

Niccolò Machiavelli

. . .

Chapter XIV

OF THE DUTIES OF A PRINCE RELATIVE TO
HIS MILITARY FORCE

Princes ought . . . to make the art of war their sole study and occupation, for it is peculiarly the science of those who govern. War, and the several sorts of discipline and institutions relative to it, should be his only study, the only profession he should follow, and the object he ought always to have in view. By this means princes can maintain possession of their dominions; and private individuals are sometimes raised thereby to supreme authority; whilst, on the other hand, we frequently see princes shamefully reduced to nothing, by suffering themselves to be enfeebled by slothful inactivity. I repeat, therefore, that by a neglect of this art it is that states are lost, and by cultivating it they are acquired.

Francis Sforza, from a private station, attained the rank of duke of Milan, by having an army always at his disposal; and by a deviation from this rule his children, who succeeded to the dukedom, were reduced to the station of private individuals. And this is not surprising: for, in the first place, nothing is so likely to impair our esteem for the character of a prince as to see him destitute of a military force; and, as I shall endeavour to prove hereafter, that a prince should most particularly beware of falling into general contempt.

We cannot establish a comparison between men who are armed, and those who are not so; and it would be equally absurd to suppose that the disarmed should command, and the others obey. A prince who is ignorant of the art of war can never enjoy repose or safety amongst armed subjects; he will always be to them an object of contempt, as they to him will justly be subjects of suspicion; how is it possible then that they should act in concert? In short, a prince who does not understand the art of war can never be esteemed by his troops, nor can he ever confide in them.

It is necessary therefore that princes should pay their whole attention to the art of war, which includes mental labour and study as well as the military exercise. To begin with the latter, the prince should take the utmost care that his troops be well disciplined and regularly exercised. The chase is well adapted to inure the body to fatigue, and to all the intemperances of weather. This exercise will also teach him to observe the sources and situations, as well as the nature of rivers and marshes; to measure the extent of plains, and the

declivity of mountains. By these means he will acquire a knowledge of the topography of a country which he has to defend, and will easily habituate himself to select the places where war may be best carried on. For the plain and valleys of Tuscany resemble more or less those of other countries; so that a perfect knowledge of one will enable them to form a tolerably accurate judgment of the other.

This study is particularly useful to commanders. A general who neglects it will never know where to look for an enemy, nor how to conduct his troops, nor to encamp, nor the proper time to attack. The Greek and Roman historians deservedly praised Philopomenes, prince of Achaia, for his application to the study of war in time of peace. He was accustomed in his travels to stop and ask his friends, which of two armies would have the advantage, if one posted on such or such a hill, and the other in such a particular place? In what manner this, if commanded by himself, should join and give battle to the other? What steps he ought to take in order to secure a retreat, or pursue the enemy, in case he should retire? He thus proposed to them every case which might happen in war, listened attentively to their opinion, and then gave his own, together with the reasons on which it was founded. By these means he was always prepared to meet unforeseen events.

As to that part of military science which is learned in the closet, a prince ought to read history, and to pay particular attention to the achievements of great generals, and the cause of their victories and defeats; but above all he should follow the example of those great men who, when they select a model, resolve to follow in his steps. It was thus that Alexander the Great immortalized himself by following the example of Achilles, Caesar by imitating Alexander, and Scipio by copying Cyrus. If we take the trouble to compare the life of the latter Roman with that of Cyrus, we shall see how nearly Scipio copied the modesty, affability, humanity, liberality, and the other virtues with which Xenophon adorns his hero.

It is thus a wise prince should conduct himself, and so employ his time during peace, that if fortune should change, he may be prepared equally for her frowns or her favours.

Chapter XV

WHAT DESERVES PRAISE OR BLAME IN MEN, AND ABOVE ALL IN PRINCES

It now remains to show in what manner a prince should behave to his subjects and friends. This matter having been already discussed by others, it may seem arrogant in me to pursue it farther, especially if I should differ in opinion from them; but as I write only for those who possess sound judgment, I thought it better to treat this subject as it really is, in fact, than to amuse the imagination with visionary models of republics and governments which have never existed. For the manner in which men now live is so different from the manner in which they ought to live, that he who deviates from the common course of practice, and endeavours to act as duty dictates, necessarily ensures his own destruction. Thus, a good man, and one who wishes to prove himself so in all respects, must be undone in a contest with so many who are evilly disposed. A prince who wishes to maintain his power ought therefore to learn that he should not be always good, and must use that knowledge as circumstances and the exigencies of his own affairs may seem to require.

Laying aside, then, the false ideas which have been formed as to princes, and adhering only to those which are true, I say, that all men, and especially princes, are marked and distinguished by some quality or other which entails either reputation or dishonour. For instance, men are liberal or parsimonious, honourable or dishonourable, effeminate or pusillanimous, courageous or enterprising, humane or cruel, affable or haughty, wise or debauched, honest or dishonest, good tempered or surly, sedate or inconsiderate, religious or impious, and so forth.

It would, doubtless, be happy for a prince to unite in himself every species of good quality; but as our nature does not allow so great a perfection, a prince should have prudence enough to avoid those defects and vices which may occasion his ruin; and as to those which can only compromise his safety and the possession of his dominions, he ought, if possible, to guard against them; but if he cannot succeed in this, he need not embarrass himself in escaping the scandal of those vices, but should devote his whole energies to avoid those which may cause his ruin. He should not shrink from encountering some blame on account of vices which are important to the support of his states; for everything well considered, there are some things having the appearance of virtues, which would prove the ruin of a prince, should he put them in practice, and others, upon which, though seemingly bad and vicious, his actual welfare and security entirely depend.

Chapter XVI

OF LIBERALITY AND ECONOMY

To begin with the first qualities of the above-mentioned, I must observe that it is for the interest of a prince to be accounted liberal, but dangerous so to exercise his liberality, that he is thereby neither feared nor respected. I will explain myself. If a prince be only liberal, as far as it suits his purposes, that is to say, within certain bounds, he will please but few, and will be called selfish. A prince who wishes to gain the reputation of being liberal, should be regardless of expense; but then to support this reputation, he will often be reduced to the necessity of levying taxes on his subjects, and adopting every species of fiscal resource which cannot fail to make him odious. Besides exhausting the public treasure by his prodigality, his credit will be destroyed, and he will run the risk of losing his dominions on the first reverse of fortune, his liberality, as it always happens, having ensured him more enemies than friends. And which is worse, he cannot retrace his steps and replenish his finances, without being charged with avarice.

A prince, therefore, who cannot be liberal without prejudicing his state, should not trouble himself much about the imputation of being covetous; for he will be esteemed liberal in time, when people see that by parsimony he has improved his revenue, become able to defend his dominions, and even to undertake useful enterprises without the aid of new taxes; then the many from whom he takes nothing will deem him sufficiently liberal, and the few only, whose expectations he has failed to realize, will accuse him of avarice. In our own times we have seen no great exploits performed, except by those who have been accounted avaricious; all the others have failed. Julius II attained the pontifical chair by means of his bounty; but he judged rightly in supposing, that in order to enable him to prosecute the war against France, it would do him injury to preserve his reputation for liberality. By his parsimony he was able to support the expense of all his wars without the imposition of new taxes. The present king of Spain could never have accomplished all his great enterprises, if he had felt any ambition to be thought liberal.

A prince, then, who would avoid poverty, and always be in a condition to defend his dominions without imposing new taxes on his subjects, should care little for being charged with avarice, since the imputed vice may be the very means of securing the prosperity and stability of his government.

It may however be alleged that Caesar would never have attained the empire but by his liberality, and that many others have arrived at the highest honours by the same means. I answer, you are either in possession of dominion already, or you are not. In the first place, liberality would be prejudicial; in the second, the reputation of it is serviceable and necessary. Caesar endeavoured to appear liberal whilst he aspired to the empire of Rome. But if he had lived longer, he would have lost that reputation for liberality which had paved him the way to empire, or he would have lost himself in the attempt to preserve it.

There have been, however, some princes who have performed splendid actions, and who have distinguished themselves by their liberality; but then their prodigality did not come from the public purse. Such were Cyrus, Alexander, and Caesar. A prince ought to be very sparing of his own and his subjects' property; but he should be equally lavish of that which he takes from the enemy, if he desires to be popular with his troops; for that will not diminish his reputation, but rather add to it. He who is too liberal cannot long continue so; he will become poor and contemptible unless he grinds his subjects with new taxes—which cannot fail to render him odious to them. Now there is nothing a prince ought to dread so much as his subjects' hatred; unless, indeed, it be their contempt. And both these evils may be occasioned by over liberality. If he must choose between extremes, it is better to submit to the imputation of parsimony than to make a show of liberality; since the first, though it may not be productive of honour, never gives birth to hatred and contempt.

Chapter XVII

OF CRUELTY AND CLEMENCY, AND
WHETHER IT IS BETTER TO BE LOVED
THAN FEARED

To proceed to other qualities which are requisite in those who govern. A prince ought unquestionably to be merciful, but should take care how he executes his clemency. Caesar Borgia was accounted cruel; but it was to that cruelty that he was indebted for the advantage of uniting Romagna to his other dominions, and of establishing in that province peace and tranquillity, of which it had been so long deprived. And, every thing well considered, it must be allowed that this prince showed greater clemency than the people of Florence, who, to avoid the reproach of cruelty, suffered Pistoia to be destroyed. When it is necessary for a prince to restrain his subjects within the bounds of duty, he should not regard the imputation of cruelty, because by making a few examples, he will find that he really showed more humanity in the end, than he, who by too great indulgence, suffers disorders to arise, which commonly terminate in rapine and murder. For such disorders disturb a whole community, whilst punishments inflicted by the prince affect only a few individuals.

This is particularly true with respect to a new prince, who can scarcely avoid the reproach of cruelty, every new government being replete with dangers. Thus Virgil makes Dido excuse her severity, by the necessity to which she was reduced of maintaining the interests of a throne which she did not inherit from her ancestors:—

Res dura et regni novitas me talia cogunt
Moliri, et late fines custode tueri.

A prince, however, should not be afraid of phantoms of his own raising; neither should he lend too ready an ear to terrifying tales which may be told him, but should temper his mercy with prudence, in such a manner, that too much confidence may not put him off his guard, nor causeless jealousies make him insupportable. There is a medium between a foolish security and an unreasonable distrust.

It has been sometimes asked, whether it is better to be loved than feared; to which I answer, that one should wish to be both. But as that is a hard matter to accomplish, I think, if it is necessary to make a selection, that it is safer to be feared than be loved. For it may be truly affirmed of mankind in general, that they are ungrateful, fickle, timid, dissembling, and self-interested; so long as you can serve them, they are entirely devoted to you; their wealth, their blood, their lives, and even their offspring are at your disposal, when you have no occasion for them; but in the day of need, they turn their back upon you. The prince who relies on professions, courts his own destruction, because the friends whom he acquires by means of money alone, and whose attachment does not spring from a regard for personal merit, are seldom proof against reverse of fortune, but abandon their benefactor when he most requires their services. Men are generally more inclined to submit to him who makes himself dreaded, than to one who merely strives to be beloved; and the reason is obvious, for friendship of this kind, being a mere moral tie, a species of duty resulting from a benefit, cannot endure against the calculations of interest: whereas fear carries with it the dread of punishment, which never loses its influence. A prince, however, ought to make himself feared, in such a manner, that if he cannot gain the love, he may at least avoid the hatred, of his subjects; and he may attain this object by respecting his subjects' property and the honour of their wives. If he finds it absolutely necessary to inflict the punishment of death, he should avow the reason for it, and above all things, he should abstain from touching the property of the condemned party. For certain it is that men sooner forget the death of their relations than the loss of their patrimony. Besides, when he once begins to live by means of rapine, many occasions offer for seizing the wealth of his subjects; but there will be little or no necessity for shedding blood.

But when a prince is at the head of his army, and has under his command a multitude of soldiers, he should make little account of being esteemed cruel; such a character will be useful to him, by keeping his troops in obedience, and preventing every species of faction.

Hannibal, among many other admirable talents, possessed in a high degree that of making himself feared by his troops; insomuch, that having led a very large army, composed of all kinds of people, into a foreign country, he never had occasion, either in prosperity or adversity, to punish the least disorder or the slightest want of discipline: and this can only be attributed to his extreme severity, and such other qualities as caused him to be feared and respected by his soldiers, and without which his extraordinary talents and courage would have been unavailing.

There have been writers notwithstanding, but, in my opinion, very injudicious ones who, whilst they render every degree of justice to his talents and his splendid achievements, still condemn the principle on which he acted. But nothing can in this respect more fully justify him than the example of Scipio, one of the greatest generals mentioned in history. His extreme indulgence towards the troops he commanded in Spain occasioned disorders, and at length a revolt, which drew on him from Fabius Maximus, in full senate, the reproach of having destroyed the Roman soldiery. This general having suffered the barbarous conduct of one of his lieutenants towards the Locrians to go unpunished, a senator, in his justification, observed that there were some men who knew better how to avoid doing ill themselves than to punish it in others. This excess of indulgence would in time have tarnished the glory and reputation of Scipio, if he had been a prince; but as he lived under a republican government, it was not only connived at, but redounded to his glory.

I conclude, then, with regard to the question, whether it is better to be loved than feared,—that it depends on the inclinations of the subjects themselves, whether they will love their prince or not; but the prince has it in his own power to make them fear him, and if he is wise, he will rather rely on his own resources than on the caprice of others, remembering that he should at the same time so conduct himself as to avoid being hated.

Chapter XVIII

WHETHER PRINCES OUGHT TO BE FAITHFUL TO THEIR ENGAGEMENTS

It is unquestionably very praiseworthy in princes to be faithful to their engagements; but among those of the present day, who have been distinguished for great exploits, few indeed have been remarkable for this virtue, or have scrupled to deceive others who may have relied on their good faith.

It should therefore be known, that there are two ways of deciding any contest: the one by laws, the other by force. The first is peculiar to men, the second to beasts; but when laws are not sufficiently powerful, it is necessary to recur to force: a prince ought therefore to understand how to use both these descriptions of arms. This doctrine is admirably illustrated to us by the ancient poets in the allegorical history of the education of Achilles, and many other princes of antiquity, by the centaur Chiron, who, under the double form of man and beast, taught those who were destined to govern, that it was their duty to use by turns the arms adapted to both these natures, seeing that one without the other cannot be of any durable advantage. Now, as a prince must learn how to act the part of a beast sometimes, he should make the fox and the lion his patterns. The first can but feebly defend himself against the wolf, and the latter readily falls into such snares as are laid for him. From the fox, therefore, a prince will learn dexterity in avoiding snares; and from the lion, how to employ his strength to keep the wolves in awe. But they who entirely rely upon the lion's strength, will not always meet with success: in other words, a prudent prince cannot and ought not to keep his word, except when he can do it without injury to himself, or when the circumstances under which he contracted the engagement still exist.

I should be cautious in inculcating such a precept if all men were good; but as the generality of mankind are wicked, and ever ready to break their words, a prince should not pique himself in keeping his more scrupulously, especially as it is always easy to justify a breach of faith on his part. I could give numerous proofs of this, and show numberless engagements and treaties which have been violated by the treachery of princes, and that those who enacted the part of the fox, have always succeeded best in their affairs. It is necessary, however, to disguise the appearance of craft, and thoroughly to understand the art of feigning and dissembling; for men are generally so simple and so weak, that he who wishes to deceive easily finds dupes.

One example, taken from the history of our own times, will be sufficient. Pope Alexander VI played during his whole life a game of deception; and notwithstanding his faithless conduct was extremely well known, his artifices always proved successful. Oaths and protestations cost him

nothing; never did a prince so often break his word or pay less regard to his engagements. This was because he so well understood this chapter in the art of government.

It is not necessary, however, for a prince to possess all the good qualities I have enumerated, but it is indispensable that he should appear to have them. I will even venture to affirm, that it is sometimes dangerous to use, though it is always useful to seem to possess them. A prince should earnestly endeavour to gain the reputation of kindness, clemency, piety, justice, and fidelity to his engagements. He ought to possess all these good qualities, but still retain such power over himself as to display their opposites whenever it may be expedient. I maintain, that a prince, and especially a new prince, cannot with impunity exercise all the virtues, because his own self-preservation will often compel him to violate the laws of charity, religion, and humanity. He should habituate himself to bend easily to the various circumstances which may from time to time surround him. In a word, it will be as useful to him to persevere in the path of rectitude, while he feels no inconvenience in doing so, as to know how to deviate from it when circumstances dictate such a course. He should make it a rule above all things, never to utter anything which does not breathe of kindness, justice, good faith, and piety: this last quality it is most important for him to appear to possess, as men in general judge more from appearances than from reality. All men have eyes, but few have the gift of penetration. Every one sees your exterior, but few can discern what you have in your heart; and those few dare not oppose the voice of the multitude, who have the majesty of their prince on their side. Now, in forming a judgment of the minds of men, and more especially of princes, as we cannot recur to any tribunal, we must attend only to results. Let it then be the prince's chief care to maintain his authority; the means he employs, be what they may, will, for this purpose, always appear honourable and meet applause; for the vulgar are ever caught by appearances, and judge only by the event. And as the world is chiefly composed of such as are called the vulgar, the voice of the few is seldom or never heard or regarded.

There is a prince now alive (whose name it may not be proper to mention) who ever preaches the doctrines of peace and good faith; but if he had observed either the one or the other, he would long ago have lost both his reputation and dominions [*Ferdinand of Spain*].

· · ·

Chapter XXV

HOW FAR FORTUNE INFLUENCES THE
THINGS OF THIS WORLD, AND HOW
FAR SHE MAY BE RESISTED

I know that several have thought, and many still are of opinion, that all sublunary events are governed either by Divine Providence or by chance, in such a manner that human wisdom has no share in their direction; and hence they infer that man should abstain from interfering with their course, and leave everything to its natural tendency.

The revolutions which in our times are of such frequent recurrence, seem to support this doctrine, and I own, that I, myself, am almost inclined to favour such opinions, particularly when I consider how far those events surpass all human conjecture; yet, as we confessedly possess a free will, it must, I think, be allowed, that chance does not so far govern the world as to leave no province for the exercise of human prudence.

For my own part, I cannot help comparing the blind power of chance to a rapid river, which, having overflowed its banks, inundates the plain, uproots trees, carries away houses and lands, and sweeps all before it in its destructive progress; everybody flies possessing neither resolution nor power to oppose its fury. But this should not discourage us, when the river has returned within its natural limits, from constructing dykes and banks to prevent a recurrence of similar disasters. It is the same with fortune; she exercises her power when we oppose no barrier to her progress.

If we cast our eyes on Italy, which has been the theatre of these revolutions, and consider the causes by which they have been provoked, we shall find it to be a defenceless country. If she had been properly fortified like Germany, Spain, or France, such inundations of foreigners would never have happened, or at least their irruptions would have been attended with less devastation.

Let this suffice in general concerning the necessity of opposing fortune. But to descend to particulars. It is no uncommon thing to see a prince fall from prosperity to adversity, without our being able to attribute his fate to any change in conduct or character; for, as I have already shown at large, he who relies solely on fortune must be ruined inevitably whenever she abandons him.

Those princes who adapt their conduct to circumstances are rarely unfortunate. Fortune is only changeable to those who cannot conform themselves to the varying exigencies of the times; for we see different men take different courses to obtain the end they have in view; for instance, in pursuit of riches or glory, one prosecutes his object at random, the other with caution and prudence: one employs art, the other force; one is impetuosity itself, the other all patience; means by which each may severally succeed. It also happens that of two who follow the same route, one may arrive at his destination, and the other fail; and that if two other persons, whose dispositions are diametrically opposite, pursue the same object by wholly different means, yet both shall equally prosper; which is entirely owing to the temper of the times, which always prove favourable or adverse, according as men conform to them.

Circumstances also frequently decide whether a prince conducts himself well or ill on any particular occasion. There are times when an extraordinary degree of prudence is necessary; there are others when the prince should know how to trust some things to chance; but there is nothing more difficult than suddenly to change his conduct and character; sometimes from inability to resist his old habits and inclinations, at others, from want of resolution to quit a course in which he had always been successful.

Julius II, who was of a fiery and violent disposition, succeeded in all his enterprises; doubtless, because a prince of such a character was best adapted to the circumstances under which the church was then governed by this pontiff. Witness his first invasion of the territory of Bologna, in the life of John Bentivoglio, which gave great umbrage to the Venetians and the kings of France and Spain, but none of them dared to interfere. The first, because they did not feel themselves strong enough to cope with a pontiff of his character; Spain, because she was engaged in the conquest of Naples; and France, besides having an interest in keeping fair with Julius, wished still to humble the Venetians; so that she, without hesitation, granted the pope all the assistance he required.

Julius II, therefore, by a precipitate mode of proceeding, succeeded in an enterprise which could not have been accomplished by cool and deliberate measures. He would unquestionably have failed had he given Spain and the Venetians time to reflect on his designs, and if he had allowed France the opportunity of amusing him by excuses and delays.

Julius II displayed in all his enterprises the same character of violence; and his successes have in that respect fully justified him; but he did not perhaps live long enough to experience the inconstancy of fortune; for had an occasion unexpectedly occurred in which it would have been necessary to act with prudence and circumspection, he would infallibly have been ruined, in consequence of that impetuosity and inflexibility of character which wholly governed him.

From all these circumstances we may conclude, that those who cannot change their system when occasion requires it, will no doubt continue prosperous as long as they glide with the stream of fortune; but when that turns against them, they are ruined, from not being able to follow that blind goddess through all her variations.

Besides, I think that it is better to be bold than too circumspect; because fortune is of a sex that likes not a tardy wooer, and repulses all who are not ardent; she declares also, more frequently, in favour of those who are young, because they are bold and enterprising.

Chapter XXVI

EXHORTATION TO DELIVER ITALY FROM FOREIGN POWERS

When I take a review of the subject matter treated of in this book, and examine whether the circumstances in which we are now placed would be favourable to the establishment of a new government, honourable alike to its founder and advantageous to Italy, it appears to me that there never was, nor ever will be, a period more appropriate for the execution of so glorious an undertaking.

If it was necessary that the people of Israel should be slaves to Egypt, in order to elicit the rare talents of Moses; that the Persians should groan under the oppression of the Medes, in order to prove the courage and magnanimity of Cyrus; and that the Athenians should be scattered and dispersed, in order to make manifest the rare virtues of Theseus, it will be likewise necessary, for the glory of some Italian hero, that his country should be reduced to its present miserable condition, that they should be greater slaves than the Israelites, more oppressed than the Persians, and still more dispersed than the Athenians; in a word, that they should be without laws and without chiefs, pillaged, torn to pieces, and enslaved by foreign powers.

And though it has sometimes unquestionably happened that men have arisen, who appeared to be sent by Heaven to achieve our deliverance; yet jealous fortune has ever abandoned them in the midst of their career; so that our unfortunate country still groans and pines away in the expectation of a deliverer, who may put an end to the devastations in Lombardy, Tuscany, and the kingdom of Naples. She supplicates Heaven to raise up a prince who may free her from the odious and humiliating yoke of foreigners, who may close the numberless wounds with which she has been so long afflicted, and under whose standard she may march against her cruel oppressors.

But on whom can Italy cast her eyes except upon your illustrious house, which, visibly favoured by Heaven and the church, the government of which is confided to its care, possesses also the wisdom and the power necessary to undertake so glorious an enterprise? and I cannot think that the execution of this project will seem difficult if you reflect on the actions and conduct of the heroes whose examples I have above adduced. Though their exploits were indeed wonderful, they were still but men; and although their merit raised them above others, yet none of them certainly were placed in a situation so favourable as that in which you now stand. You have justice on your side; their cause was not

more lawful than yours, and the blessing of God will attend you no less than them. Every war that is necessary is just; and it is humanity to take up arms for the defence of a people to whom no other resource is left.

All circumstances concur to facilitate the execution of so noble a project, for the accomplishment of which it will only be necessary to tread in the steps of those great men whom I have had an opportunity of mentioning in the course of this work. For though some of them, it is true, were conducted by the hand of God in a wonderful manner, though the sea divided to let them pass, a cloud directed their course, a rock streamed with water to assuage their thirst, and manna fell from heaven to appease their hunger, yet there is no occasion for such miracles at present, as you possess in yourself sufficient power to execute a plan you ought by no means to neglect. God will not do everything for us; much is left to ourselves, and the free exercise of our will, that so our own actions may not be wholly destitute of merit.

If none of our princes have hitherto been able to effect what is now expected from your illustrious house, and if Italy has continually been unfortunate in her wars, the evil has arisen from the defects in military discipline, which no person has possessed the ability to reform.

Nothing reflects so much honour on a new prince as the new laws and institutions established under his direction, especially when they are good, and bear the character of grandeur. Now it must be acknowledged that Italy soon accommodates herself to new forms. Her inhabitants are by no means deficient in courage, but they are destitute of proper chiefs; the proof of this is in the duels and other individual combats in which the Italians have always evinced consummate ability, whilst their valour in battles has appeared well-nigh extinguished. This can only be attributed to the weakness of the officers, who are unable to ensure obedience from those who know, or think they know, the art of war. Thus we have seen the greatest generals of the present day, whose orders were never executed with exactness and celerity. These are the reasons why, in the wars in which we have been for the last twenty years engaged, the armies raised in Italy have been almost always beaten. Witness Tarus, Alexandria, Capua, Genoa, Vaila, Bologna, and Mestri.

If therefore your illustrious house is willing to regulate its conduct by the example of our ancestors, who have delivered their country from the rule of foreigners, it is necessary, above all things, as the only true foundation of every enterprise, to set on foot a national army; you cannot have better or more faithful soldiers, and though every one of them may be a good man, yet they will become still better when they are all united, and see themselves honoured, caressed, and rewarded by a prince of their own.

It is therefore absolutely necessary to have troops raised in our own country, if we wish to protect it from the invasion of foreign powers. The Swiss as well as the Spanish infantry are highly esteemed, but both have defects which may be avoided in the formation of our troops, which would render them superior to both of those powers. The Spaniards cannot support the shock of cavalry, and the Swiss cannot maintain their ground against infantry that is equally resolute with themselves.

Experience has fully shown that the Spanish battalions cannot resist the French cavalry, and that the Swiss have been beaten by the infantry of Spain. And though there has not been any thorough trial with regard to the Swiss on this point, yet there was a sort of specimen at the battle of Ravenna, where the Spanish infantry came in contact with the German troops, who fought in the same order as the Swiss. Upon that occasion, the Spaniards, having with their accustomed vivacity, and under the protection of their bucklers, thrown themselves across the pikes of the Germans, the latter were obliged to give way, and would have been entirely defeated, if their cavalry had not come to their relief.

It is necessary therefore to institute a military force possessing neither the defects of the Swiss or the Spanish infantry, and that may be able to maintain its ground against the French cavalry, and this is to be effected, not by changing their arms, but by altering their discipline. Nothing is more likely to make a new prince esteemed, and to render his reign illustrious.

Such an opportunity ought eagerly to be embraced, that Italy, after her long sufferings, may at last behold her deliverer appear. With what demonstrations of joy and gratitude, with what affection, with what impatience for revenge, would he not be received by those unfortunate provinces, who have so long groaned under such odious oppression. What city would shut her gates against him, and what people would be so blind as to refuse him obedience? What rivals would he have to dread? Is there one Italian who would not hasten to pay him homage? All are weary of the tyranny of these barbarians. May your illustrious house, strong in all the hopes which justice gives our cause, deign to undertake this noble enterprise, that so, under your banners, our nation may resume its ancient splendour, and, under your auspices, behold the prophecy of Petrarch at last fulfilled.

When virtue takes the field,
  Short will the conflict be,
  Barbarian rage shall yield
  The palm to Italy:
For patriot blood still warms Italian veins,
Though low the fire, a spark at least remains.

Benvenuto Cellini

The term "Renaissance man" has come to suggest one who has an almost universal genius, an ability to do all things well. It also implies a confidence in the human potential, a conviction that a man with reason and taste can do anything if he merely applies his human resources to the task at hand. Leonardo da Vinci once wrote a letter to Lodovico Sforza, who afterward became the Duke of Milan, applying for a job. In cataloguing his abilities, Leonardo exudes self-confidence. He claims that he can ". . . construct very light bridges, easy to transport from one place to another . . . [in case of siege] remove the water from the ditches, and make an infinite variety of scaling-ladders . . . [make] a kind of cannon that is easy and convenient to carry, and that will throw out inflammable matters, causing great affright and damage to the enemy . . . make cannon, mortars, and field pieces of beautiful and useful shape, and different from those in common use . . . equal all others in architecture, in designing both public and private edifices, and in conducting water from one place to another . . . undertake in sculpture works in marble, bronze, or terra-cotta; likewise in painting can do what can be done equal to any other, whoever he may be. . . ." The letter closes with this assurance: "And if any of the above-mentioned things seem to any impossible and impracticable, I offer to make trial of them in your park, or in any other place that may please your Excellency, to whom I commend myself with all possible humility." And the remarkable thing is that Leonardo could actually do what he said he could.

Another Renaissance figure with the same kind of brash assurance was Benvenuto Cellini (1500-1571), who, though a lesser artist than Leonardo, was his equal in confidence and probably his superior in the ability to live life to its fullest. Actually, Cellini was a semi-frustrated sculptor who is best known for his work as a goldsmith. Although little of his work has survived, Cellini's great masterpiece, the gold salt-cellar made for Francis I of France, is preserved at the Kunsthistorisches Museum in Vienna.

Cellini's *Autobiography*, from which the following selections are taken, was written between 1558 and 1562, but it was not published until the early eighteenth century. It enjoyed enormous popularity as a highly revealing personal document and as an intimate portrait of the sixteenth century—nor has it lost its fascination for modern readers.

THE LIFE OF BENVENUTO CELLINI

Book First

I

All men of whatsoever quality they be, who have done anything of ex-

THE LIFE OF BENVENUTO CELLINI [autobiography], trans. J. A. Symonds, 4th. ed. (New York, 1896), pp. 1-3, 11, 18-25, 30-41.

cellence, or which may properly resemble excellence, ought, if they are persons of truth and honesty, to describe their life with their own hand; but they ought not to attempt so fine an enterprise till they have passed the age of forty. This duty occurs to my own mind, now that I am travelling beyond the term of fifty-eight years, and am in Florence, the city of my birth. Many untoward things can I remember, such as happen to all who live upon our earth; and from those adversities I am now more free than at any previous period of my career—nay, it seems to me that I enjoy greater content of soul and health of body than ever I did in bygone years. I can also bring to mind some pleasant goods and some inestimable evils, which, when I turn my thoughts backward, strike terror in me, and astonishment that I should have reached this age of fifty-eight, wherein, thanks be to God, I am still travelling prosperously forward.

II

It is true that men who have laboured with some show of excellence, have already given knowledge of themselves to the world; and this alone ought to suffice them; I mean the fact that they have proved their manhood and achieved renown. Yet one must needs live like others; and so in a work like this there will always be found occasion for natural bragging, which is of divers kinds, and the first is that a man should let others know he draws his lineage from persons of worth and most ancient origin.

I am called Benvenuto Cellini, son of Maestro Giovanni, son of Andrea, son of Cristofano Cellini; my mother was Madonna Elisabetta, daughter to Stefano Granacci; both parents citizens of Florence. It is found written in chronicles made by our ancestors of Florence, men of old time and of credibility, even as Giovanni Villani writes, that the city of Florence was evidently built in imitation of the fair city of Rome; and certain remnants of the Colosseum and the Baths can yet be traced. These things are near Santa Croce. The Capitol was where is now the Old Market. The Rotonda is entire, which was made for the temple of Mars, and is now dedicated

to our Saint John. That thus it was, can very well be seen, and cannot be denied; but the said buildings are much smaller than those of Rome. He who caused them to be built, they say, was Julius Caesar, in concert with some noble Romans, who, when Fiesole had been stormed and taken, raised a city in this place, and each of them took in hand to erect one of these notable edifices.

Julius Caesar had among his captains a man of highest rank and valour, who was called Fiorino of Cellino, which is a village about two miles distant from Monte Fiascone. Now this Fiorino took up his quarters under the hill of Fiesole, on the ground where Florence now stands, in order to be near the river Arno, and for the convenience of the troops. All those soldiers and others who had to do with the said captain, used then to say: "Let us go to Fiorenze;" as well because the said captain was called Fiorino, as also because the place he had chosen for his quarters was by nature very rich in flowers. Upon the foundation of the city, therefore, since this name struck Julius Caesar as being fair and apt, and given by circumstance, and seeing furthermore that flowers themselves bring good augury, he appointed the name of Florence for the town. He wished besides to pay his valiant captain this compliment; and he loved him all the more for having drawn him from a very humble place, and for the reason that so excellent a man was a creature of his own. The name that learned inventors and investigators of such etymologies adduce, as that Florence is flowing at the Arno, cannot hold; seeing that Rome is flowing at the Tiber, Ferrara is flowing at the Po, Lyons is flowing at the Saône, Paris is flowing at the Seine, and yet the names of all these towns are different, and have come to them by other ways.

Thus then we find; and thus we believe that we are descended from a man of worth. Furthermore, we find that there are

Cellinis of our stock in Ravenna, that most ancient town of Italy, where too are plenty of gentle folk. In Pisa also there are some, and I have discovered them in many parts of Christendom; and in this state also the breed exists, men devoted to the profession of arms; for not many years ago a young man, called Luca Cellini, a beardless youth, fought with a soldier of experience and a most valorous man, named Francesco da Vicorati, who had frequently fought before in single combat. This Luca, by his own valour, with sword in hand, overcame and slew him, with such bravery and stoutness that he moved the folk to wonder, who were expecting quite the contrary issue; so that I glory in tracing my descent from men of valour.

As for the trifling honours which I have gained for my house, under the well-known conditions of our present ways of living, and by means of my art, albeit the same are matters of no great moment, I will relate these in their proper time and place, taking much more pride in having been born humble and having laid some honourable foundation for my family, than if I had been born of great lineage and had stained or overclouded that by my base qualities. So then I will make a beginning by saying how it pleased God I should be born.

·   ·   ·

When I reached the age of fifteen, I put myself, against my father's will, to the goldsmith's trade with a man called Antonio, son of Sandro, known commonly as Marcone the goldsmith. He was a most excellent craftsman and a very good fellow to boot, high-spirited and frank in all his ways. My father would not let him give me wages like the other apprentices; for having taken up the study of this art to please myself, he wished me to indulge my whim for drawing to the full. I did so willingly enough; and that honest master of mine took marvellous delight in my per-

formances. He had an only son, a bastard, to whom he often gave his orders, in order to spare me. My liking for the art was so great, or, I may truly say, my natural bias, both one and the other, that in a few months I caught up the good, nay, the best young craftsmen in our business, and began to reap the fruits of my labours. I did not, however, neglect to gratify my good father from time to time by playing on the flute or cornet. Each time he heard me, I used to make his tears fall accompanied with deep-drawn sighs of satisfaction. My filial piety often made me give him that contentment, and induced me to pretend that I enjoyed the music too.

·   ·   ·

XII

When I had recovered my health, I returned to my old friend Marcone, the worthy goldsmith, who put me in the way of earning money, with which I helped my father and our household. About that time there came to Florence a sculptor named Piero Torrigiani; he arrived from England, where he had resided many years; and being intimate with my master, he daily visited his house; and when he saw my drawings and the things which I was making, he said: "I have come to Florence to enlist as many young men as I can; for I have undertaken to execute a great work for my king, and want some of my own Florentines to help me. Now your method of working and your designs are worthy rather of a sculptor than a goldsmith; and since I have to turn out a great piece of bronze, I will at the same time turn you into a rich and able artist." This man had a splendid person and a most arrogant spirit, with the air of a great soldier more than of a sculptor, especially in regard to his vehement gestures and his resonant voice, together with a habit he had of knitting his brows, enough to frighten any man of courage. He kept talking every day about his gallant feats among those beasts of Englishmen.

In course of conversation he happened to mention Michel Agnolo Buonarroti, led thereto by a drawing I had made from a cartoon of that divinest painter. This cartoon was the first masterpiece which Michel Agnolo exhibited, in proof of his stupendous talents. He produced it in competition with another painter, Lionardo da Vinci, who also made a cartoon; and both were intended for the council-hall in the palace of the Signory. They represented the taking of Pisa by the Florentines; and our admirable Lionardo had chosen to depict a battle of horses, with the capture of some standards, in as divine a style as could possibly be imagined. Michel Agnolo in his cartoon portrayed a number of foot-soldiers, who, the season being summer, had gone to bathe in Arno. He drew them at the very moment the alarm is sounded, and the men all naked run to arms; so splendid in their action that nothing survives of ancient or of modern art which touches the same lofty point of excellence; and as I have already said, the design of the great Lionardo was itself most admirably beautiful. These two cartoons stood, one in the palace of the Medici, the other in the hall of the Pope. So long as they remained intact, they were the school of the world. Though the divine Michel Agnolo in later life finished that great chapel of Pope Julius, he never rose halfway to the same pitch of power; his genius never afterwards attained to the force of those first studies.

XIII

Now let us return to Piero Torrigiani, who, with my drawing in his hand, spoke as follows: "This Buonarroti and I used, when we were boys, to go into the Church of the Carmine, to learn drawing from the chapel of Masaccio. It was Buonarroti's habit to banter all who were drawing there; and one day, among others, when he was annoying me, I got more angry than usual, and clenching my fist, gave him such a blow on the nose, that I felt bone and cartilage go down like biscuit beneath my knuckles; and this mark of mine he will carry with him to the grave." These words begat in me such hatred of the man, since I was always gazing at the masterpieces of the divine Michel Agnolo, that although I felt a wish to go with him to England, I now could never bear the sight of him.

All the while I was at Florence, I studied the noble manner of Michel Agnolo, and from this I have never deviated. About that time I contracted a close and familiar friendship with an amiable lad of my own age, who was also in the goldsmith's trade. He was called Francesco, son of Filippo, and grandson of Fra Lippo Lippi, that most excellent painter. Through intercourse together, such love grew up between us that, day or night, we never stayed apart. The house where he lived was still full of the fine studies which his father had made, bound up in several books of drawings by his hand, and taken from the best antiquities of Rome. The sight of these things filled me with passionate enthusiasm; and for two years or thereabouts we lived in intimacy. At that time I fashioned a silver bas-relief of the size of a little child's hand. It was intended for the clasp to a man's belt; for they were then worn as large as that. I carved on it a knot of leaves in the antique style, with figures of children and other masks of great beauty. This piece I made in the workshop of one Francesco Salimbene; and on its being exhibited to the trade, the goldsmiths praised me as the best young craftsman of their art.

There was one Giovan Battista, surnamed Il Tasso, a woodcarver, precisely of my own age, who one day said to me that if I was willing to go to Rome, he should be glad to join me. Now we had this conversation together immediately after dinner; and I being angry with my father for the same old reason of the music, said to Tasso: "You are a fellow of words, not deeds." He answered: "I too have come to anger with my mother; and if I had cash enough to take me to Rome, I would not turn back to lock the door of that wretched little workshop I call mine." To these words I replied that if that was all that kept him in Florence I had money enough in my pockets to bring us both to Rome. Talking thus and walking onwards, we found ourselves at the gate San Piero Gattolini without noticing that we had got there; whereupon I said: "Friend Tasso, this is God's doing that we have reached this gate without either you or me noticing that we were there; and now that I am here, it seems to me that I have finished half the journey." And so, being of one accord, we pursued our way together, saying, "Oh, what will our old folks say this evening?" We then made an agreement not to think more about them till we reached Rome. So we tied our aprons behind our backs, and trudged almost in silence to Siena. When we arrived at Siena, Tasso said (for he had hurt his feet) that he would not go farther, and asked me to lend him money to get back. I made answer: "I should not have enough left to go forward; you ought indeed to have thought of this on leaving Florence; and if it is because of your feet that you shirk the journey, we will find a return horse for Rome, which will deprive you of the excuse." Accordingly I hired a horse; and seeing that he did not answer, I took my way toward the gate of Rome. When he knew that I was firmly resolved to go, muttering between his teeth, and limping as well as he could, he came on behind me very slowly and at a great distance. On reaching the gate, I felt pity for my comrade, and waited for him, and took him on the crupper, saying: "What would our friends speak of us to-morrow, if, having left for Rome, we had not pluck to get beyond Siena?" Then the good Tasso said I spoke the truth; and as he was a pleasant fellow, he began to laugh and sing; and in this way, always singing and laughing, we travelled the whole way to Rome. I had just nineteen years then, and so had the century.

When we reached Rome, I put myself under a master who was known as Il Firenzuola. His name was Giovanni, and he came from Firenzuola in Lombardy, a most able craftsman in large vases and big plate of that kind. I showed him part of the model for the clasp which I had made in Florence at Salimbene's. It pleased him exceedingly; and turning to one of his journeymen, a Florentine called Giannotto Giannotti, who had been several years with him, he spoke as follows: "This fellow is one of the Florentines who know something, and you are one of those who know nothing." Then I recognised the man, and turned to speak with him; for before he went to Rome, we often went to draw together, and had been very intimate comrades. He was so put out by the words his master flung at him, that he said he did not recognise me or know who I was; whereupon I got angry, and cried out: "O Giannotto, you who were once my friend—for have we not been together in such and such places, and drawn, and ate, and drunk, and slept in company at your house in the country? I don't want you to bear witness on my behalf to this worthy man, your master, because I hope my hands are such that without aid from you they will declare what sort of a fellow I am."

XIV

When I had thus spoken, Firenzuola, who was a man of hot spirit and brave, turned to Giannotto, and said to him: "You vile rascal, aren't you ashamed to treat a man who has been so intimate a comrade with you in this way?" And with the same movement of quick feeling, he faced round and said to me: "Welcome to my workshop; and do as you have promised; let your hands declare what man you are."

He gave me a very fine piece of silver plate to work on for a cardinal. It was a little oblong box, copied from the porphyry sarcophagus before the door of the Rotonda. Beside what I copied, I enriched it with so many elegant masks of my invention, that my master went about showing it through the art, and boasting that so good a piece of work had been turned out from his shop. It was about half a cubit in size, and was so constructed as to serve for a salt-cellar at table. This was the first earning that I touched at Rome, and part of it I sent to assist my good father; the rest I kept for my own use, living upon it while I went about studying the antiquities of Rome, until my money failed, and I had to return to the shop for work. Battista del Tasso, my comrade, did not stay long in Rome, but went back to Florence.

After undertaking some new commissions, I took it into my head, as soon as I had finished them, to change my master; I had indeed been worried into doing so by a certain Milanese, called Pagolo Arsago. My first master, Firenzuola, had a great quarrel about this with Arsago, and abused him in my presence; whereupon I took up speech in defence of my new master. I said that I was born free, and free I meant to live, and that there was no reason to complain of him, far less of me, since some few crowns of wages were still due to me; also that I chose to go, like a free journeyman, where it pleased me, knowing I did wrong to no man. My new master then put in with his excuses, saying that he had not asked me to come, and that I should gratify him by returning with Firenzuola. To this I replied that I was not aware of wronging the latter in any way, and as I had completed his commissions, I chose to

be my own master and not the man of others, and that he who wanted me must beg me of myself. Firenzuola cried: "I don't intend to beg you of yourself; I have done with you; don't show yourself again upon my premises." I reminded him of the money he owed me. He laughed me in the face; on which I said that if I knew how to use my tools in handicraft as well as he had seen, I could be quite as clever with my sword in claiming the just payment of my labour. While we were exchanging these words, an old man happened to come up, called Maestro Antonio, of San Marino. He was the chief among the Roman goldsmiths, and had been Firenzuola's master. Hearing what I had to say, which I took good care that he should understand, he immediately espoused my cause, and bade Firenzuola pay me. The dispute waxed warm, because Firenzuola was an admirable swordsman, far better than he was a goldsmith. Yet reason made itself heard; and I backed my cause with the same spirit, till I got myself paid. In course of time Firenzuola and I became friends, and at his request I stood godfather to one of his children.

XV

I went on working with Pagolo Arsago, and earned a good deal of money, the greater part of which I always sent to my good father. At the end of two years, upon my father's entreaty, I returned to Florence, and put myself once more under Francesco Salimbene, with whom I earned a great deal, and took continual pains to improve in my art. I renewed my intimacy with Francesco di Filippo; and though I was too much given to pleasure, owing to that accursed music, I never neglected to devote some hours of the day or night to study. At that time I fashioned a silver heart's-key (*chiavacuore*), as it was then called. This was a girdle three inches broad, which used to be made for brides, and was executed in half relief with some small figures in the round. It was a commission from a man called Raffaello Lapaccini. I was very badly paid; but the honour which it brought me was worth far more than the gain I might have justly made by it. Having at this time worked with many different persons in Florence, I had come to know some worthy men among the goldsmiths, as, for instance, Marcone, my first master; but I also met with others reputed honest, who did all they could to ruin me, and robbed me grossly. When I perceived this, I left their company, and held them for thieves and blackguards. One of the goldsmiths, called Giovanbattista Sogliani, kindly accommodated me with part of his shop, which stood at the side of the New Market near the Landi's bank. There I finished several pretty pieces, and made good gains, and was able to give my family much help. This roused the jealousy of the bad men among my former masters, who were called Salvadore and Michele Guasconti. In the guild of the goldsmiths they had three big shops, and drove a thriving trade. On becoming aware of their evil will against me, I complained to certain worthy fellows, and remarked that they ought to have been satisfied with the thieveries they practised on me under the cloak of hypocritical kindness. This coming to their ears, they threatened to make me sorely repent of such words; but I, who knew not what the colour of fear was, paid them little or no heed.

·   ·   ·

XIX

At Siena I waited for the mail to Rome, which I afterwards joined; and when we passed the Paglia, we met a courier carrying news of the new Pope Clement VII. Upon my arrival in Rome, I went to work in the shop of the master-goldsmith Santi. He was dead; but a son of his carried on the business. He did not work himself,

but entrusted all his commissions to a young man named Lucagnolo from Iesi, a country fellow, who while yet a child had come into Santi's service. This man was short but well proportioned, and was a more skilful craftsman than any one whom I had met with up to that time; remarkable for facility and excellent in design. He executed large plate only; that is to say, vases of the utmost beauty, basons, and such pieces. Having put myself to work there, I began to make some candelabra for the Bishop of Salamanca, a Spaniard. They were richly chased, so far as that sort of work admits. A pupil of Raffaello da Urbino called Gian Francesco, and commonly known as Il Fattore, was a painter of great ability; and being on terms of friendship with the Bishop, he introduced me to his favour, so that I obtained many commissions from that prelate, and earned considerable sums of money.

During that time I went to draw, sometimes in Michel Agnolo's chapel, and sometimes in the house of Agostino Chigi of Siena, which contained many incomparable paintings by the hand of that great master Raffaello. This I did on feast-days, because the house was then inhabited by Messer Gismondo, Agostino's brother. They plumed themselves exceedingly when they saw young men of my sort coming to study in their palaces. Gismondo's wife, noticing my frequent presence in that house—she was a lady as courteous as could be, and of surpassing beauty—came up to me one day, looked at my drawings, and asked me if I was a sculptor or a painter; to whom I said I was a goldsmith. She remarked that I drew too well for a goldsmith; and having made one of her waiting-maids bring a lily of the finest diamonds set in gold, she showed it to me, and bade me value it. I valued it at 800 crowns. Then she said that I had very nearly hit the mark, and asked me whether I felt capable of setting the stones really well. I said that I should much like to do so, and began before her eyes to make a little sketch for it, working all the better because of the pleasure I took in conversing with so lovely and agreeable a gentlewoman. When the sketch was finished, another Roman lady of great beauty joined us; she had been above, and now descending to the ground-floor, asked Madonna Porzia what she was doing there. She answered with a smile: "I am amusing myself by watching this worthy young man at his drawing; he is as good as he is handsome." I had by this time acquired a trifle of assurance, mixed, however, with some honest bashfulness; so I blushed and said: "Such as I am, lady, I shall ever be most ready to serve you." The gentlewoman, also slightly blushing, said: "You know well that I want you to serve me;" and reaching me the lily, told me to take it away; and gave me besides twenty golden crowns which she had in her bag, and added: "Set me the jewel after the fashion you have sketched, and keep for me the old gold in which it is now set." On this the Roman lady observed: "If I were in that young man's body, I should go off without asking leave." Madonna Porzia replied that virtues rarely are at home with vices, and that if I did such a thing, I should strongly belie my good looks of an honest man. Then turning round, she took the Roman lady's hand, and with a pleasant smile said: "Farewell, Benvenuto." I stayed on a short while at the drawing I was making, which was a copy of a Jove by Raffaello. When I had finished it and left the house, I set myself to making a little model of wax, in order to show how the jewel would look when it was completed. This I took to Madonna Porzia, whom I found with the same Roman lady. Both of them were highly satisfied with my work, and treated me so kindly that, being somewhat emboldened, I promised the jewel should be twice as good as the model. Accordingly I set hand to it, and in twelve days I finished it in the form of a fleur-de-lys, as I have said above, ornamenting it with little masks, children, and animals, exquisitely enamelled, whereby the diamonds which formed the lily were more than doubled in effect.

XX

While I was working at this piece, Lucagnolo, of whose ability I have before spoken, showed considerable discontent, telling me over and over again that I might acquire far more profit and honour by helping him to execute large plate, as I had done at first. I made him answer that, whenever I chose, I should always be capable of working at great silver pieces; but that things like that on which I was now engaged were not commissioned every day; and beside their bringing no less honour than large silver plate, there was also more profit to be made by them. He laughed me in the face, and said: "Wait and see Benvenuto; for by the time that you have finished that work of yours, I will make haste to have finished this vase, which I took in hand when you did the jewel; and then experience shall teach you what profit I shall get from my vase, and what you will get from your ornament." I answered that I was very glad indeed to enter into such a competition with so good a craftsman as he was, because the end would show which of us was mistaken. Accordingly both the one and the other of us, with a scornful smile upon our lips, bent our heads in grim earnest to the work, which both were now desirous of accomplishing; so that after about ten days, each had finished his undertaking with great delicacy and artistic skill.

Lucagnolo's was a huge silver piece, used at the table of Pope Clement, into which he flung away bits of bone and the rind of divers fruits, while eating; an object of ostentation rather than necessity. The vase was adorned with two fine handles, together with many masks, both small and great, and masses of lovely foliage, in as exquisite a style of elegance as could be imagined; on seeing which I said it was the most beautiful vase that ever I set eyes on. Thinking he had convinced me, Lucagnolo replied: "Your work seems to me no less beautiful, but we shall soon perceive the difference between the two." So he took his vase and carried it to the Pope, who was very well pleased with it, and ordered at once that he should be paid at the ordinary rate of such large plate. Meanwhile I carried mine to Madonna Porzia, who looked at it with astonishment, and told me I had far surpassed my promise. Then she bade me ask for my reward whatever I liked; for it seemed to her my desert was so great that if I craved a castle she could hardly recompense me; but since that was not in her hands to bestow, she added laughing that I must beg what lay within her power. I answered that the greatest reward I could desire for my labour was to have satisfied her ladyship. Then, smiling in my turn, and bowing to her, I took my leave, saying I wanted no reward but that. She turned to the Roman lady and said: "You see that the qualities we discerned in him are companied by virtues, and not vices." They both expressed their admiration, and then Madonna Porzia continued: "Friend Benvenuto, have you never heard it said that when the poor give to the rich, the devil laughs?" I replied: "Quite true! and yet, in the midst of all his troubles, I should like this time to see him laugh;" and as I took my leave, she said that this time she had no will to bestow on him that favour.

When I came back to the shop, Lucagnolo had the money for his vase in a paper packet; and on my arrival he cried out: "Come and compare the price of your jewel with the price of my plate." I said that he must leave things as they were till the next day, because I hoped that even as

my work in its kind was not less excellent than his, so I should be able to show him quite an equal price for it.

XXI

On the day following, Madonna Porzia sent a major-domo of hers to my shop, who called me out, and putting into my hands a paper packet full of money from his lady, told me that she did not choose the devil should have his whole laugh out: by which she hinted that the money sent me was not the entire payment merited by my industry, and other messages were added worthy of so courteous a lady. Lucagnolo, who was burning to compare his packet with mine, burst into the shop; then in the presence of twelve journeymen and some neighbours, eager to behold the result of this competition, he seized his packet, scornfully exclaiming "Ou! ou!" three or four times, while he poured his money on the counter with a great noise. They were twenty-five crowns in giulios; and he fancied that mine would be four or five crowns *di moneta*. I for my part, stunned and stifled by his cries, and by the looks and smiles of the bystanders, first peeped into my packet; then, after seeing that it contained nothing but gold, I retired to one end of the counter, and, keeping my eyes lowered and making no noise at all, I lifted it with both hands suddenly above my head, and emptied it like a mill hopper. My coin was twice as much as his; which caused the onlookers, who had fixed their eyes on me with some derision, to turn round suddenly to him and say: "Lucagnolo, Benvenuto's pieces, being all of gold and twice as many as yours, make a far finer effect." I thought for certain that, what with jealousy and what with shame, Lucagnolo would have fallen dead upon the spot; and though he took the third part of my gain, since I was a journeyman (for such is the custom of the trade, two-thirds fall to the workman and one-third to the masters of the shop), yet inconsiderate envy had more power in him than avarice: it ought indeed to have worked quite the other way, he being a peasant's son from Iesi. He cursed his art and those who taught it him, vowing that thenceforth he would never work at large plate, but give his whole attention to those whoreson gewgaws, since they were so well paid. Equally enraged on my side, I answered that every bird sang its own note; that he talked after the fashion of the hovels he came from; but that I dared swear that I should succeed with ease in making his lubberly lumber, while he would never be successful in my whoreson gewgaws. Thus I flung off in a passion, telling him that I would soon show him that I spoke truth. The bystanders openly declared against him, holding him for a lout, as indeed he was, and me for a man, as I had proved myself.

XXII

Next day, I went to thank Madonna Porzia, and told her that her ladyship had done the opposite of what she said she would; for that while I wanted to make the devil laugh, she had made him once more deny God. We both laughed pleasantly at this, and she gave me other commissions for fine and substantial work.

Meanwhile, I contrived, by means of a pupil of Raffaello da Urbino, to get an order from the Bishop of Salamanca for one of those great water-vessels called *acquereccia*, which are used for ornaments to place on sideboards. He wanted a pair made of equal size; and one of them he intrusted to Lucagnolo, the other to me. Giovan Francesco, the painter I have mentioned, gave us the design. Accordingly I set hand with marvellous good-will to this piece of plate, and was accommodated with a part of his workshop by a Milanese named Maestro Giovan Piero della Tacca. Having made my preparations, I calculated how much

money I should need for certain affairs of my own, and sent all the rest to assist my poor father.

It so happened that just when this was being paid to him in Florence, he stumbled upon one of those Radicals who were in the Eight at the time when I got into that little trouble there. It was the very man who had abused him so rudely, and who swore that I should certainly be sent into the country with the lances. Now this fellow had some sons of very bad morals and repute; wherefore my father said to him: "Misfortunes can happen to anybody, especially to men of choleric humour when they are in the right, even as it happened to my son; but let the rest of his life bear witness how virtuously I have brought him up. Would God, for your wellbeing, that your sons may act neither worse nor better towards you than mine do to me. God rendered me able to bring them up as I have done; and where my own power could not reach, 'twas He who rescued them, against your expectation, out of your violent hands." On leaving the man, he wrote me all this story, begging me for God's sake to practise music at times, in order that I might not lose the fine accomplishment which he had taught me with such trouble. The letter so overflowed with expressions of the tenderest fatherly affection, that I was moved to tears of filial piety, resolving, before he died, to gratify him amply with regard to music. Thus God grants us those lawful blessings which we ask in prayer, nothing doubting.

XXIII

While I was pushing forward Salamanca's vase, I had only one little boy as help, whom I had taken at the entreaty of friends, and half against my own will, to be my workman. He was about fourteen years of age, bore the name of Paulino, and was son to a Roman burgess, who lived upon the income of his property. Paulino was the best-mannered, the most honest, and the most beautiful boy I ever saw in my whole life. His modest ways and actions, together with his superlative beauty and his devotion to myself, bred in me as great an affection for him as a man's breast can hold. This passionate love led me oftentimes to delight the lad with music; for I observed that his marvellous features, which by complexion wore a tone of modest melancholy, brightened up, and when I took my cornet, broke into a smile so lovely and so sweet, that I do not marvel at the silly stories which the Greeks have written about the deities of heaven. Indeed, if my boy had lived in those times, he would probably have turned their heads still more. He had a sister, named Faustina, more beautiful, I verily believe, than that Faustina about whom the old books gossip so. Sometimes he took me to their vineyard, and, so far as I could judge, it struck me that Paulino's good father would have welcomed me as a son-in-law. This affair led me to play more than I was used to do.

It happened at that time that one Giangiacomo of Cesena, a musician in the Pope's band, and a very excellent performer, sent word through Lorenzo, the trumpeter of Lucca, who is now in our Duke's service, to inquire whether I was inclined to help them at the Pope's Ferragosto, playing soprano with my cornet in some motets of great beauty selected by them for that occasion. Although I had the greatest desire to finish the vase I had begun, yet, since music has a wondrous charm of its own, and also because I wished to please my old father, I consented to join them. During eight days before the festival we practised two hours a day together; then on the first of August we went to the Belvedere, and while Pope Clement was at table, we played those carefully studied motets so well that his Holiness protested he had never heard music more sweetly

executed or with better harmony of parts. He sent for Giangiacomo, and asked him where and how he had procured so excellent a cornet for soprano, and inquired particularly who I was. Giangiacomo told him my name in full. Whereupon the Pope said: "So, then, he is the son of Maestro Giovanni?" On being assured I was, the Pope expressed his wish to have me in his service with the other bandsmen. Giangiacomo replied: "Most blessed Father, I cannot pretend for certain that you will get him, for his profession, to which he devotes himself assiduously, is that of a goldsmith, and he works in it miraculously well, and earns by it far more than he could do by playing." To this the Pope added: "I am the better inclined to him now that I find him possessor of a talent more than I expected. See that he obtains the same salary as the rest of you; and tell him from me to join my service, and that I will find work enough by the day for him to do in his other trade." Then stretching out his hand, he gave him a hundred golden crowns of the Camera in a handkerchief, and said: "Divide these so that he may take his share."

When Giangiacomo left the Pope, he came to us, and related in detail all that the Pope had said; and after dividing the money between the eight of us, and giving me my share, he said to me: "Now I am going to have you inscribed among our company." I replied: "Let the day pass; to-morrow I will give my answer." When I left them, I went meditating whether I ought to accept the invitation, inasmuch as I could not but suffer if I abandoned the noble studies of my art. The following night my father appeared to me in dream, and begged me with tears of tenderest affection, for God's love and his, to enter upon this engagement. Methought I answered that nothing would induce me to do so. In an instant he assumed so horrible an aspect as to frighten me out of my wits, and cried: "If you do not, you will have a father's curse; but if you do, may you be ever blessed by me!" When I woke, I ran, for very fright, to have myself inscribed. Then I wrote to my old father, telling him the news, which so affected him with extreme joy that a sudden fit of illness took him, and well-nigh brought him to death's door. In his answer to my letter, he told me that he too had dreamed nearly the same as I had.

XXIV

Knowing now that I had gratified my father's honest wish, I began to think that everything would prosper with me to a glorious and honourable end. Accordingly, I set myself with indefatigable industry to the completion of the vase I had begun for Salamanca. That prelate was a very extraordinary man, extremely rich, but difficult to please. He sent daily to learn what I was doing; and when his messenger did not find me at home, he broke into fury, saying that he would take the work out of my hands and give it to others to finish. This came of my slavery to that accursed music. Still I laboured diligently night and day, until, when I had brought my work to a point when it could be exhibited, I submitted it to the inspection of the Bishop. This so increased his desire to see it finished, that I was sorry I had shown it. At the end of three months I had it ready, with little animals and foliage and masks, as beautiful as one could hope to see. No sooner was it done than I sent it by the hand of my workman, Paulino, to show that able artist Lucagnolo, of whom I have spoken above. Paulino, with the grace and beauty which belonged to him, spoke as follows: "Messer Lucagnolo, Benvenuto bids me say that he has sent to show you his promises and your lumber, expecting in return to see from you his gewgaws." This message given, Lucagnolo took up the vase, and carefully examined it; then he

said to Paulino: "Fair boy, tell your master that he is a great and able artist, and that I beg him to be willing to have me for a friend, and not to engage in aught else." The mission of that virtuous and marvellous lad caused me the greatest joy; and then the vase was carried to Salamanca, who ordered it to be valued. Lucagnolo took part in the valuation, estimating and praising it far above my own opinion. Salamanca, lifting up the vase, cried like a true Spaniard: "I swear by God that I will take as long in paying him as he has lagged in making it." When I heard this, I was exceedingly put out, and fell to cursing all Spain and every one who wished well to it.

Amongst other beautiful ornaments, this vase had a handle, made all of one piece, with most delicate mechanism, which, when a spring was touched, stood upright above the mouth of it. While the prelate was one day ostentatiously exhibiting my vase to certain Spanish gentlemen of his suite, it chanced that one of them, upon Monsignor's quitting the room, began roughly to work the handle, and as the gentle spring which moved it could not bear his loutish violence, it broke in his hand. Aware what mischief he had done, he begged the butler who had charge of the Bishop's plate to take it to the master who had made it, for him to mend, and promised to pay what price he asked, provided it was set to rights at once. So the vase came once more into my hands, and I promised to put it forthwith in order, which indeed I did. It was brought to me before dinner; and at twenty-two o'clock the man who brought it returned, all in a sweat, for he had run the whole way, Monsignor having again asked for it to show to certain other gentlemen. The butler, then, without giving me time to utter a word, cried: "Quick, quick, bring the vase." I, who wanted to act at leisure and not to give it up to him, said that I did not mean to be so quick. The serving-man got into such a rage that he made as though he would put one hand to his sword, while with the other he threatened to break the shop open. To this I put a stop at once with my own weapon, using therewith spirited language, and saying: "I am not going to give it to you! Go and tell Monsignor, your master, that I want the money for my work before I let it leave this shop." When the fellow saw he could not obtain it by swaggering, he fell to praying me, as one prays to the Cross, declaring that if I would only give it up, he would take care I should be paid. These words did not make me swerve from my purpose; but I kept on saying the same thing. At last, despairing of success, he swore to come with Spaniards enough to cut me in pieces. Then he took to his heels; while I, who inclined to believe partly in their murderous attack, resolved that I would defend myself with courage. So I got an admirable little gun ready, which I used for shooting game, and muttered to myself: "He who robs me of my property and labour may take my life too, and welcome." While I was carrying on this debate in my own mind, a crowd of Spaniards arrived, led by their major-domo, who, with the headstrong rashness of his race, bade them go in and take the vase and give me a good beating. Hearing these words, I showed them the muzzle of my gun, and prepared to fire, and cried in a loud voice: "Renegade Jews, traitors, is it thus that one breaks into houses and shops in our city of Rome? Come as many of you thieves as like, an inch nearer to this wicket, and I'll blow all their brains out with my gun." Then I turned the muzzle toward their major-domo, and making as though I would discharge it, called out: "And you big thief, who are egging them on, I mean to kill you first." He clapped spurs to the jennet he was riding, and took flight headlong. The commotion we were making stirred up all the neighbours, who came crowding round, together with some Roman gentlemen who chanced to pass, and cried: "Do but kill the renegades, and we will stand by you." These words had the effect of frightening the Spaniards in good earnest. They withdrew, and were compelled by the circumstances to relate the whole affair to Monsignor. Being a man of inordinate haughtiness, he rated the members of his household, both because they had engaged in such an act of violence, and also because, having begun, they had not gone through with it. At this juncture the painter, who had been concerned in the whole matter, came in, and the Bishop bade him go and tell me that if I did not bring the vase at once, he would make mincemeat of me; but if I brought it, he would pay its price down. These threats were so far from terrifying me, that I sent him word I was going immediately to lay my case before the Pope.

In the meantime, his anger and my fear subsided; whereupon, being guaranteed by some Roman noblemen of high degree that the prelate would not harm me, and having assurance that I should be paid, I armed myself with a large poniard and my good coat of mail, and betook myself to his palace, where he had drawn up all his household. I entered, and Paulino followed with the silver vase. It was just like passing through the Zodiac, neither more nor less; for one of them had the face of the lion, another of the scorpion, a third of the crab. However, we passed onward to the presence of the rascally priest, who spouted out a torrent of such language as only priests and Spaniards have at their command. In return I never raised my eyes to look at him, nor answered word for word. That seemed to augment the fury of his anger; and causing paper to be put before me, he commanded me to write an acknowledgment to the effect that I had been amply satisfied and paid in full. Then I raised my head and said I should be very glad to do so when I had received the money. The Bishop's rage continued to rise; threats and recriminations were flung about; but at last the money was paid, and I wrote the receipt. Then I departed, glad at heart and in high spirits.

Desiderius Erasmus

In contrast to the Italian Renaissance, which became quite secular and pagan in temper, the Renaissance in northern Europe retained more of the medieval Christian outlook. The combination of Renaissance humanism with Christianity, characteristic of the northern Renaissance, is exemplified most clearly in the writings of Erasmus of Rotterdam (1466-1536). Intensely aware of the shortcomings of the Catholic Church of his day, Erasmus was nevertheless convinced that the elimination of these evils lay not in a rejection of Christianity but rather in a return to it. Believing that the Church had departed from the true teachings of its founder, he urged a reform of religious beliefs and practices based on a return to the gospel of the New Testament or, as he called it, the "philosophy of Christ." Erasmus felt that such a reform should be inaugurated and carried forward by the Church itself through a program of widespread education. He broke off a long-standing friendship with Martin Luther because he was unwilling to go along with Luther's insistence that, since gradual reform from within based on an appeal to reason was futile, the only solution lay in violent revolt against the Church. Although Erasmus refused to join the Protestant movement, he contributed significantly to the Reformation by appealing for a return to the original teachings of Christ and by directing pointed satires against abuses within the Church.

The following selection is from the most famous work of Erasmus, *In Praise of Folly* (1509). In it are most of the major Erasmian theses, in language that reveals the literary genius of its author.

IN PRAISE OF FOLLY

How slightly soever I am esteemed in the common vogue of the world, for I well know how disingenuously Folly

IN PRAISE OF FOLLY, *Desiderius Erasmus*, (London, 1887), pp. 9-10, 23-28, 34-37, 112-117, 126-133, 143-150, 158-170, 215-216.

is decried, even by those who are themselves the greatest fools, yet it is from my influence alone that the whole universe receives her ferment of mirth and jollity. Of which this may be urged as a convincing argument, in that as soon as I appeared to speak before this numerous assembly all their countenances were gilded over with a lively sparkling pleasantness. You soon welcomed me with so encouraging a look, you spurred me on with so cheerful a hum, that truly in all appearance, you seemed now flushed with a good dose of reviving nectar, when as just before, you sate drowsy and melancholy, as if you were lately come out of some hermit's cell. But as it is usual, that as soon as the sun peeps from her eastern bed, and draws back the curtains of the darksome night; or as when, after a hard winter, the restorative spring breathes a more enlivening air, nature forthwith changes her apparel, and all things seem to renew their age; so at the first sight of me you all unmask, and appear in more lively colours.

.   .   .

Can any one be said properly to live to whom pleasure is denied? You will give me your assent; for there is none I know among you so wise shall I say, or so silly, as to be of a contrary opinion. The Stoics indeed contemn, and pretend to banish pleasure; but this is only a dissembling trick, and a putting the vulgar out of conceit with it, that they may more quietly engross it to themselves; but I dare them now to confess what one stage of life is not melancholy, dull, tiresome, tedious, and uneasy, unless we spice it with pleasure, that hautgoust of Folly. Of the truth whereof, the never enough to be commended Sophocles is sufficient authority, who gives me the highest character in that sentence of his,

To know nothing is the sweetest life.

Yet abating from this, let us examine the case more narrowly. Who knows not that the first scene of infancy is far the most pleasant and delightsome? What, then, is it in children that makes us so kiss, hug, and play with them, and that the bloodiest enemy can scarce have the heart to hurt

them; but their ingredients of innocence and Folly? Of which nature out of providence did purposely compound and blend their tender infancy that by a frank return of pleasure they might make some sort of amends for their parents' trouble, and give in caution as it were for the discharge of a future education; the next advance from childhood is youth, and how favourably is this dealt with; how kind, courteous, and respectful are all to it? and how ready to become serviceable upon all occasions?

And whence reaps it this happiness? Whence indeed, but from me only, by whose procurement it is furnished with little of wisdom, and so with the less of disquiet? And when once lads begin to grow up, and attempt to write man, their prettiness does then soon decay, their briskness flags, their humours stagnate, their jollity ceases, and their blood grows cold; and the further they proceed in years, the more they grow backward in the enjoyment of themselves, till waspish old age comes on, a burden to itself as well as others, and that so heavy and oppressive, as none would bear the weight of, unless out of pity to their sufferings.

I again intervene, and lend a helping hand, assisting them at a dead lift, in the same method the poets feign their gods to succour dying men, by transforming them into new creatures, which I do by bringing them back, after they have one foot in the grave, to their infancy again; so as there is a great deal of truth couched in that old proverb, "Once an old man, and twice a child." Now if any one be curious to understand what course I take to effect this alteration, my method is this. I bring them to my well of forgetfulness, the fountain whereof is in the Fortunate Islands, and the river Lethe in hell but a small stream of it, and when they have there filled their bellies full, and washed down care, by the virtue and operation whereof they become young again. Ay, but, say you, they merely dote, and play the fool. Why yes, this is what I mean by growing young again. For what else is it to be a child than to be a fool and an idiot? It is the being such that makes that age so acceptable: for who does not esteem it somewhat ominous to see a boy endowed with the discretion of a man, and therefore for the curbing of too forward parts we have a disparaging proverb, "Soon ripe, soon rotten?"

And farther, who would keep company or have any thing to do with such an old blade, as, after the wear and harrowing of so many years should yet continue of as clear a head and sound a judgment as he had at any time been in his middle-age. And therefore it is great kindness of me that old men grow fools, since it is hereby only that they are freed from such vexations as would torment them if they were more wise: they can drink briskly, bear up stoutly, and lightly pass over such infirmities, as a far stronger constitution could scarce master. Sometime, with the old fellow in Plautus, they are brought back to their horn-book again, to learn to spell their fortune in love. Most wretched would they needs be if they had but wit enough to be sensible of their hard condition; but by my assistance, they carry off all well, and to their respective friends approve themselves good, sociable, jolly companions. Thus Homer makes aged Nestor famed for a smooth oily-tongued orator, while the delivery of Achilles was but rough, harsh, and hesitant; and the same poet elsewhere tells us of old men that sate on the walls, and spake with a great deal of flourish and elegance.

And in this point indeed they surpass and outdo children, who are pretty forward in a softly, innocent prattle, but otherwise are too much tongue-tied, and want the other's most acceptable embellishment of a perpetual talkativeness. Add to this, that old men love to be playing with children, and children delight as much in them, to verify the proverb, that "Birds of a feather flock together." And indeed what difference can be discerned between them, but that the one is more furrowed with wrinkles, and has seen a little more of the world than the other? For otherwise their whitish hair, their want of teeth, their smallness of stature, their milk diet, their bald crowns, their prattling, their playing, their short memory, their heedlessness, and all their other endowments, exactly agree. And the more they advance in years the nearer they come back to their cradle, till like children indeed, at last they depart the world, without any remorse at the loss of life, or sense of the pangs of death.

And now let any one compare the excellency of my metamorphosing power to that which Ovid attributes to the gods; their strange feats in some drunken passions we will omit for their credit sake, and instance only in such persons as they pretend great kindness for; these they transformed into trees, birds, insects, and sometimes serpents. But alas, their very change into somewhat else argues the destruction of what they were before. Whereas I can restore the same numerical man to his pristine state of youth, health and strength; yea, what is more, if men would but so far consult their own interest, as to discard all thoughts of wisdom, and entirely resign themselves to my guidance and conduct, old age should be a paradox, and each man's years a perpetual spring.

・ ・ ・

Now therefore, like Homer's wandering muse, I will take my leave of heaven, and come down again here below, where we shall find nothing happy, nay, nothing tolerable, without my presence and assistance. And in the first place consider how providently nature has took care that in all her works there should be some piquant smack and relish of Folly, for since the

Stoics define wisdom to be conducted by reason, and folly nothing else but the being hurried by passion, lest our life should otherwise have been too dull and inactive, that creator, who out of clay first tempered and made us up, put into the composition of our humanity more than a pound of passions to an ounce of reason; and reason he confined within the narrow cells of the brain, whereas he left passions the whole body to range in.

Farther, he set up two sturdy champions to stand perpetually on the guard, that reason might make no assault, surprise, nor in-road. Anger, which keeps its station in the fortress of the heart, and lust, which like the signs Virgo and Scorpio, rules the belly and secret members. Against the forces of these two warriors how unable is reason to bear up and withstand, every day's experience does abundantly witness. While let reason be never so importunate in urging and reinforcing her admonitions to virtue, yet the passions bear all before them, and by the least offer of curb or restraint grow but more imperious, till reason itself, for quietness' sake, is forced to desist from all further remonstrance.

But because it seemed expedient that man, who was born for the transaction of business, should have so much wisdom as should fit and capacitate him for the discharge of his duty herein, and yet lest such a measure as is requisite for this purpose might prove too dangerous and fatal, I was advised with for an antidote, who prescribed this infallible recipe of taking a wife, a creature so harmless and silly, and yet so useful and convenient, as might mollify and make pliable the stiffness and morose humour of man. Now that which made Plato doubt under which genus to rank woman, whether among brutes or rational creatures, was only meant to denote the extreme stupidness and folly of that sex. A sex so unalterably simple, that for any of

them to thrust forward, and reach at the name of wise, is but to make themselves the more remarkable fools, such an endeavour, being but a swimming against the stream, nay, the turning the course of nature, the bare attempting whereof is as extravagant as the effecting of it is impossible. For as it is a trite proverb, "That an ape will be an ape, though clad in purple;" so a woman will be a woman, *i.e.*, a fool, whatever disguise she takes up.

And yet there is no reason women should take it amiss to be thus charged; for if they do but rightly consider they will find it is to Folly they are beholden for those endowments, wherein they so far surpass and excel man. As first, for their unparalleled beauty, by the charm whereof they tyrannize over the greatest tyrants. For what is it but too great a smatch of wisdom that makes men so tawny and thin-skinned, so rough and prickly-bearded, like an emblem of winter or old age, while women have such dainty smooth cheeks, such a low gentle voice, and so pure a complexion, as if nature had drawn them for a standing pattern of all symmetry and comeliness? Beside, what greater or juster aim and ambition have they than to please their husbands? In order whereunto they garnish themselves with paint, washes, curls, perfumes, and all other mysteries of ornament; yet after all they become acceptable to them only for their Folly. Wives are always allowed their humour, yet it is only in exchange for gratification and pleasure, which indeed are but other names for Folly.

. . . .

It is indeed almost incredible to relate what mirth, what sport, what diversion, the grovelling inhabitants here on earth give to the above-seated gods in heaven. For these exalted deities spend their fasting sober hours in listening to those petitions that are offered up, and in succouring such as they are appealed to for redress. But when they are a little entered at a glass of nectar, they then throw off all serious concerns, and go and place themselves on the ascent of some promontory in heaven, and from thence survey the little molehill of earth. And trust me, there cannot be a more delightsome prospect than to view such a theatre so stuffed and crammed with swarms of fools.

One falls desperately in love, and the more he is slighted the more does his spaniel-like passion increase; another is wedded to wealth rather than to a wife; a third pimps for his own spouse, and is content to be a cuckold so he may wear his horns gilt; a fourth is haunted with a jealousy of his visiting neighbours; another sobs and roars, and plays the child, for the death of a friend or relation; and lest his own tears should not rise high enough to express the torrent of his grief, he hires other mourners to accompany the corpse to the grave, and sing its *requiem* in sighs and lamentations; another hypocritically weeps at the funeral of one whose death at heart he rejoices for; here a gluttonous cormorant, whatever he can scrape up, thrusts all into his guts to pacify the cryings of a hungry stomach; there a lazy wretch sits yawning and stretching, and thinks nothing so desirable as sleep and idleness.

Some are extremely industrious in other men's business, and sottishly neglectful of their own; some think themselves rich because their credit is great, though they can never pay, till they break, and compound for their debts; one is so covetous that he lives poor to die rich; one for a little uncertain gain will venture to cross the roughest seas, and expose his life for the purchase of a livelihood; another will depend on the plunders of war, rather than on the honest gains of peace; some will close with and humour such warm old blades as have a good estate, and no children of their own to bestow it upon; others practice the same art of wheedling upon

good old women, that have hoarded and coffered up more bags than they know how to dispose of; both of these sly flatteries make fine sport for the gods, when they are beat at their own weapons, and as oft happens are gulled by those very persons they intended to make a prey of.

There is another sort of base scoundrels in gentility, such scraping merchants, who although, for the better vent of their commodities they lie, swear, cheat, and practice all the intrigues of dishonesty, yet think themselves no way inferior to persons of the highest quality, only because they have raked together a plentiful estate. And there are not wanting such insinuating hangers on, as shall caress and compliment them with the greatest respect, in hopes to go snacks in some of their dishonest gains. There are others so infected with the philosophical paradox of banishing property, and having all things in common, that they make no conscience of fastening on, and purloining whatever they can get, and converting it to their own use and possession. There are some who are rich only in wishes, and yet while they barely dream of vast mountains of wealth, they are as happy as if their imaginary fancies commenced real truths.

Some put on the best side outermost, and starve themselves at home to appear gay and splendid abroad. One with an open-handed freedom spends all he lays his fingers on; another with a logic-fisted gripingness catches at and grasps all he can come within the reach of; one apes it about in the streets to court popularity; another consults his ease, and sticks to the confinement of a chimney-corner; many others are tugging hard at law for a trifle, and drive on an endless suit, only to enrich a deferring judge, or a knavish advocate; one is for new-modelling a settled government; another is for some notable heroical attempt; and a third by all means must travel a pilgrim to Rome, Jerusalem, or some shrine of a saint elsewhere, though he have no other business than the paying of a formal impertinent visit, leaving his wife and children to fast, while he himself forsooth is gone to pray.

In short, if, as Lucian fancies Menippus to have done heretofore, any man could now again look down from the orb of the moon, he would see thick swarms as it were of flies and gnats, that were quarrelling with each other, justling, fighting, fluttering, skipping, playing, just new produced, soon after decaying, and then immediately vanishing; and it can scarce be thought how many tumults and tragedies so inconsiderate a creature as man does give occasion to, and that in so short a space as the small span of life; subject to so many casualties, that the sword, pestilence, and other epidemic accidents, shall many times sweep away whole thousands at a brush.

But hold. I should but expose myself too far, and incur the guilt of being roundly laughed at, if I proceed to enumerate the several kinds of the folly of the vulgar. I shall confine therefore my following discourse only to such as challenge the repute of wisdom, and seemingly pass for men of the soundest intellectuals.

.   .   .

Nay, even the learned and more judicious, that have wit enough to laugh at the other's folly, are very much beholden to my goodness; which, except ingratitude have drowned their ingenuity, they must be ready upon all occasions to confess. Among these I suppose the lawyers will shuffle in for precedence, and they of all men have the greatest conceit of their own abilities. They will argue as confidentially as if they spoke gospel instead of law; they will cite you six hundred several precedents, though not one of them come near to the case in hand. They will muster up the authority of judgments, deeds, glosses, and reports, and tumble over so many musty

records, that they make their employ, though in itself easy, the greatest slavery imaginable; always accounting that the best plea which they have took most pains for.

To these, as bearing great resemblance to them, may be added Logicians and Sophisters, fellows that talk as much by rote as a parrot; who shall run down a whole gossiping of old women, nay, silence the very noise of a belfry, with louder clappers than those of the steeple. And if their unappeasable clamorousness were their only fault it would admit of some excuse; but they are at the same time so fierce and quarrelsome, that they will wrangle bloodily for the least trifle, and be so over intent and eager, that they many times lose their game in the chase and fright away that truth they are hunting for. Yet self-conceit makes these nimble disputants such doughty champions, that armed with three or four close-linked syllogisms, they shall enter the lists with the greatest masters of reason, and not question the foiling of them in an irresistible baffle. Nay, their obstinacy makes them so confident of their being in the right, that all the arguments in the world shall never convince them to the contrary.

Next to these come the Philosophers in their long beards and short cloaks, who esteem themselves the only favourites of wisdom, and look upon the rest of mankind as the dirt and rubbish of the creation. Yet these men's happiness is only a frantic craziness of brain; they build castles in the air, and infinite worlds in a vacuum. They will give you to a hair's breadth the dimensions of the sun, moon, and stars, as easily as they would do that of a flaggon or pipkin. They will give a punctual account of the rise of thunder, of the origin of winds, of the nature of eclipses, and of all the other obstrusest difficulties in physics, without the least demur or hesitation, as if they had been admitted into the cabinet council of nature, or had been eye-witnesses to all the accurate methods of creation; though alas nature does but laugh at all their puny conjectures. For they never yet made one considerable discovery, as appears in that they are unanimously agreed in no one point of the smallest moment; nothing so plain or evident but what by some or other is opposed and contradicted.

But though they are ignorant of the artificial contexture of the least insect, they vaunt however, and brag that they know all things, when indeed they are unable to construe the mechanism of their own body. Nay, when they are so purblind as not to be able to see a stone's cast before them, yet they shall be as sharp-sighted as possible in spying-out ideas, universals, separate forms, first matters, quiddities, formalities, and a hundred such like niceties, so diminutively small, that were not their eyes extremely magnifying, all the art of optics could never make them discernible.

But they then most despise the low grovelling vulgar when they bring out their parallels, triangles, circles, and other mathematical figures, drawn up in battalia, like so many spells and charms of conjuration in muster, with letters to refer to the explication of the several problems; hereby raising devils as it were, only to have the credit of laying them, and amusing the ordinary spectators into wonder, because they have not wit enough to understand the juggle. Of these some undertake to profess themselves judicial astrologers, pretending to keep correspondence with the stars, and so from their information can resolve any query. And though it is all but a presumptuous imposture, yet some to be sure will be so great fools as to believe them.

The divines present themselves next. But it may perhaps be most safe to pass them by, and not to touch upon so harsh a string as this subject would afford. Be-

side, the undertaking may be very hazardous; for they are a sort of men generally very hot and passionate; and should I provoke them, I doubt not would set upon me with a full cry, and force me with shame to recant, which if I stubbornly refuse to do, they will presently brand me for a heretic, and thunder out an excommunication, which is their spiritual weapon to wound such as lift up a hand against them.

It is true, no men own a less dependence on me, yet have they reason to confess themselves indebted for no small obligations. For it is by one of my properties, self-love, that they fancy themselves, with their elder brother Paul, caught up into the third heaven, from whence, like shepherds indeed, they look down upon their flock, the laity, grazing as it were, in the vales of the world below. They fence themselves in with so many surrounders of magisterial definitions, conclusions, corollaries, propositions explicit and implicit, that there is no falling in with them. Or if they do chance to be urged to a seeming non-plus, yet they find out so many evasions, that all the art of man can never bind them so fast, but that an easy distinction shall give them a starting-hold to escape the scandal of being baffled.

They will cut asunder the toughest argument with as much ease as Alexander did the gordian knot; they will thunder out so many rattling terms as shall fright an adversary into conviction. They are exquisitely dexterous in unfolding the most intricate mysteries; they will tell you to a tittle all the successive proceedings of Omnipotence in the creation of the universe; they will explain the precise manner of original sin being derived from our first parents. They will satisfy you in what manner, by what degrees, and in how long a time, our Saviour was conceived in the Virgin's womb, and demonstrate in the consecrated wafer how accidents may subsist without a subject. Nay, these are accounted trivial, easy questions; they have yet far greater difficulties behind, which notwithstanding they solve with as much expedition as the former.

As namely, whether supernatural generation requires any instant of time for its acting? Whether Christ, as a son, bears a double specifically distinct relation to God the Father, and his virgin mother? Whether this proposition is possible to be true, the first person of the Trinity hated the second? Whether God, who took our nature upon him in the form of a man, could as well have become a woman, a devil, a beast, an herb, or a stone? And were it so possible that the Godhead had appeared in any shape of an inanimate substance, how he should then have preached his gospel? Or how have been nailed to the cross? Whether if St. Peter had celebrated the eucharist at the same time our Saviour was hanging on the cross, the consecrated bread would have been transubstantiated into the same body that remained on the tree? Whether in Christ's corporal presence in the sacramental wafer, his humanity be not abstracted from his Godhead? Whether after the resurrection we shall carnally eat and drink as we do in this life?

.   .   .

The next to these are another sort of brainsick fools, who style themselves monks and of religious orders, though they assume both titles very unjustly. For as to the last, they have very little religion in them; and as to the former, the etymology of the word monk implies a solitariness, or being alone; whereas they are so thick abroad that we cannot pass any street or alley without meeting them. Now I cannot imagine what one degree of men would be more hopelessly wretched, if I did not stand their friend, and buoy them up in that lake of misery, which by the engagements of a holy vow they have voluntarily immerged themselves in.

But when these sort of men are so unwelcome to others, as that the very sight of them is thought ominous, I yet make them highly in love with themselves, and fond admirers of their own happiness. The first step whereunto they esteem a profound ignorance, thinking carnal knowledge a great enemy to their spiritual welfare, and seem confident of becoming greater proficients in divine mysteries the less they are poisoned with any human learning. They imagine that they bear a sweet consort with the heavenly choir, when they tone out their daily tally of psalms, which they rehearse only by rote, without permitting their understanding or affections to go along with their voice.

Among these, some make a good profitable trade of beggary, going about from house to house, not like the apostles, to break, but to beg, their bread. Nay, thrust into all public-houses, come aboard the passage-boats, get into the travelling waggons, and omit no opportunity of time or place for the craving people's charity; doing a great deal of injury to common highway beggars by interloping in their traffic of alms. And when they are thus voluntarily poor, destitute, not provided with two coats, nor with any money in their purse, they have the impudence to pretend that they imitate the first disciples, whom their master expressly sent out in such an equipage.

It is pretty to observe how they regulate all their actions as it were by weight and measure to so exact a proportion, as if the whole loss of their religion depended upon the omission of the least punctilio. Thus they must be very critical in the precise number of knots to the tying on of their sandals; what distinct colours their respective habits, and what stuff made of; how broad and long their girdles; how big, and in what fashion, their hoods; whether their bald crowns be to a hair's-breadth of the right cut; how many hours they must sleep, at what minute rise to prayers, etc.

And these several customs are altered according to the humours of different persons and places. While they are sworn to the superstitious observance of these trifles, they do not only despise all others, but are very inclinable to fall out among themselves; for though they make profession of an apostolic charity, yet they will pick a quarrel, and be implacably passionate for such poor provocations, as the girting on a coat the wrong way, for the wearing of clothes a little too darkish coloured, or any such nicety not worth the speaking of. Some are so obstinately superstitious that they will wear their upper garment of some coarse dog's hair stuff, and that next their skin as soft as silk. But others, on the contrary, will have linen frocks outermost, and their shirts of wool or hair. Some, again, will not touch a piece of money, though they make no scruple of the sin of drunkenness and the lust of the flesh.

All their several orders are mindful of nothing more than of their being distinguished from each other by their different customs and habits. They seem, indeed, not so careful of becoming like Christ, and of being known to be his disciples, as the being unlike to one another, and distinguishable for followers of their several founders. A great part of their religion consists in their title. Some will be called cordeliers, and these subdivided into capuchines, minors, minims, and mendicants; some, again, are styled Benedictines, others of the order of St. Bernard, others of that of St. Bridget; some are Augustin monks, some Willielmites, and others Jacobists, as if the common name of Christian were too mean and vulgar.

Most of them place their greatest stress for salvation on a strict conformity to their foppish ceremonies, and a belief of their legendary traditions. Wherein they fancy to have acquitted themselves with so much

of supererogation, that one heaven can never be a condign reward for their meritorious life; little thinking that the Judge of all the earth at the last day shall put them off, with a "Who hath required these things at your hands?" and call them to account only for the stewardship of his legacy, which was the precept of love and charity.

It will be pretty to hear their pleas before the great tribunal. One will brag how he mortified his carnal appetite by feeding only upon fish. Another will urge that he spent most of his time on earth in the divine exercise of singing psalms. A third will tell how many days he fasted, and what severe penance he imposed on himself for the bringing his body into subjection. Another shall produce in his own behalf as many ceremonies as would load a fleet of merchantmen. A fifth shall plead that in threescore years he never so much as touched a piece of money, except he fingered it through a thick pair of gloves. A sixth, to testify his former humility, shall bring along with him his sacred hood, so old and nasty, that any seaman had rather stand bare headed on the deck, than put it on to defend his ears in the sharpest storms. The next that comes to answer for himself shall plead, that for fifty years together, he had lived like a sponge upon the same place, and was content never to change his homely habitation. Another shall whisper softly, and tell the judge he has lost his voice by a continual singing of holy hymns and anthems. The next shall confess how he fell into a lethargy by a strict, reserved, and sedentary life. And the last shall intimate that he has forgot to speak, by having always kept silence, in obedience to the injunction of taking heed lest he should have offended with his tongue.

But amidst all their fine excuses our Saviour shall interrupt them with this answer, Woe unto you, scribes and pharisees, hypocrites, verily I know you not; I left you but one precept, of loving one another, which I do not hear any one plead he has faithfully discharged; I told you plainly in my gospel, without any parable, that my father's kingdom was prepared not for such as should lay claim to it by austerities, prayers, or fastings, but for those who should render themselves worthy of it by the exercise of faith, and the offices of charity; I cannot own such as depend on their own merits without a reliance on my mercy; as many of you therefore as trust to the broken reeds of your own deserts may even go search out a new heaven, for you shall never enter into that, which from the foundations of the world was prepared only for such as are true of heart.

When these monks and friars shall meet with such a shameful repulse, and see that ploughmen and mechanics are admitted into that kingdom, from which they themselves are shut out, how sneakingly will they look, and how pitifully slink away?

· · ·

But these stage-divines, not less ungrateful disowners of their obligations to folly, than they are impudent pretenders to the profession of piety, I willingly take my leave of, and pass now to kings, princes, and courtiers, who, paying me a devout acknowledgment, may justly challenge back the respect of being mentioned and taken notice of by me. And first, had they wisdom enough to make a true judgment of things, they would find their own condition to be more despicable and slavish than that of the most menial subjects. For certainly none can esteem perjury or parricide a cheap purchase for a crown, if he does but seriously reflect on that weight of cares a princely diadem is loaded with. He that sits at the helm of government acts in a public capacity, and so must sacrifice all private interest to the attainment of the common good. He must himself be conformable to those laws his prerogative ex-

acts, or else he can expect no obedience paid them from others; he must have a strict eye over all his inferior magistrates and officers, or otherwise it is to be doubted they will but carelessly discharge their respective duties.

Every king, within his own territories, is placed for a shining example as it were in the firmament of his wide-spread dominions, to prove either a glorious star of benign influence, if his behaviour be remarkably just and innocent; or else to impend as a threatening comet, if his blazing power be pestilent and hurtful. Subjects move in a darker sphere, and so their wanderings and failings are less discernible. Whereas princes, being fixed in a more exalted orb, and encompassed with a brighter dazzling lustre, their spots are more apparently visible, and their eclipses, or other defects, influential on all that is inferior to them. Kings are baited with so many temptations and opportunities to vice and immorality, such as are high feeding, liberty, flattery, luxury, and the like, that they must stand perpetually on their guard, to fence off those assaults that are always ready to be made upon them.

In fine, abating from treachery, hatred, dangers, fear, and a thousand other mischiefs impending on crowned heads, however uncontrollable they are this side heaven; yet after their reign here they must appear before a supremer judge, and there be called to an exact account for the discharge of that great stewardship which was committed to their trust. If princes did but seriously consider, and consider they would if they were but wise, these many hardships of a royal life, they would be so perplexed in the result of their thoughts thereupon, as scarce to eat or sleep in quiet.

But now by my assistance they leave all these cares to the gods, and mind only their own ease and pleasure, and therefore will admit none to their attendance but who will divert them with sport and mirth, lest they should otherwise be seized and damp-ed with the surprisal of sober thoughts. They think they have sufficiently acquitted themselves in the duty of governing, if they do but ride constantly a-hunting, breed up good race-horses, sell places and offices to those of the courtiers that will give most for them, and find out new ways for invading of their people's prop-erty, and hooking in a larger revenue to their own exchequer. For the procure-ment whereof they will always have some pretended claim and title; that though it be manifest extortion, yet it may bear the show of law and justice. And then they daub over their oppression with a submis-sive, flattering carriage, that they may so far insinuate into the affections of the vul-gar, as they may not tumult nor rebel, but patiently crouch to burdens and exactions.

Let us feign now a person ignorant of the laws and constitutions of that realm he lives in, an enemy to the public good, studious only for his own private interest, addicted wholly to pleasures and delights, a hater of learning, a professed enemy to liberty and truth, careless and unmindful of the common concerns, taking all the measures of justice and honesty from the false beam of self-interest and advantage, after this hang about his neck a gold chain, for an intimation that he ought to have all virtues linked together. Then set a crown of gold and jewels on his head, for a token that he ought to overtop and outshine others in all commendable quali-fications; next, put into his hand a royal sceptre for a symbol of justice and integ-rity; lastly clothe him with purple, for an hieroglyphic of a tender love and affec-tion to the commonwealth. If a prince should look upon this portraiture, and draw a comparison between that and himself, certainly he would be ashamed of his en-signs of majesty, and be afraid of being laughed out of them.

Next to kings themselves may come their courtiers, who, though they are for the most part a base, servile, cringing, low-spirited sort of flatterers, yet they look big, swell great, and have high thoughts of their honour and grandeur. Their con-fidence appears upon all occasions; yet in this one thing they are very modest, in that they are content to adorn their bodies with gold, jewels, purple, and other glori-ous ensigns of virtue and wisdom, but leave their minds empty and unfraught; and tak-ing the resemblance of goodness to them-selves, turn over the truth and reality of it to others.

They think themselves mighty happy in that they can call the king master, and be allowed the familiarity of talking with him. That they can volubly rehearse his several titles of august highness, superemi-nent excellence, and most serene majesty, that they can boldly usher in any discourse, and that they have the complete knack of insinuation and flattery; for these are the arts that make them truly genteel and no-ble. If you make a stricter enquiry after their other endowments, you shall find them mere sots and dolts. They will sleep generally till noon, and then their mer-cenary chaplains shall come to their bed-side, and entertain them perhaps with a short morning prayer. As soon as they are dressed they must go to breakfast, and when that is done, immediately to dinner. When the cloth is taken away, then to cards, dice, tables, or some such like diver-sion. After this they must have one or two afternoon banquets, and so in the evening to supper. When they have supped then begins the game of drinking; the bottles are marshalled, the glasses ranked, and round go the healths and bumpers till they are carried to bed.

And this is the constant method of pass-ing away their hours, days, months, years, and ages. I have many times took great satisfaction by standing in the court, and seeing how the tawdry butterflies vie upon one another. The ladies shall measure the height of their humours by the length of their trails, which must be borne up by a page behind. The nobles jostle one another to get nearest to the king's elbow, and wear gold chains of that weight and bigness as require no less strength to carry than they do wealth to purchase.

And now for some reflections upon popes, cardinals, and bishops, who in pomp and splendour have almost equalled if not outdone secular princes. Now if any one consider that their upper crotchet of white linen is to signify their unspotted purity and innocence; that their forked mitres, with both divisions tied together by the same knot, are to denote the joint knowledge of the Old and New Testament. That their always wearing gloves, represents their keeping their hands clean and undefiled from lucre and covetousness; that the pastoral staff implies the care of a flock committed to their charge; that the cross carried before them expresses their victory over all carnal affections. He that considers this, and much more of the like nature, must needs conclude they are entrusted with a very weighty and difficult office. But alas, they think it sufficient if they can but feed themselves; and as to their flock, either commend them to the care of Christ himself, or commit them to the guidance of some inferior vicars and curates. Not so much as remembering what their name of bishop imports, to wit, labour, pains, and diligence, but by base simoniacal contracts, they are in a profane sense *Episcopi, i.e.,* overseers of their own gain and income.

So cardinals, in like manner, if they did but consider that the church supposes them to succeed in the room of the apostles; that therefore they must behave themselves as their predecessors, and so not be lords, but dispensers of spiritual gifts, of the disposal whereof they must one day render a strict account. Or if they

would but reflect a little on their habit, and thus reason with themselves, what means this white upper garment, but only an unspotted innocence? What signifies my inner purple, but only an ardent love and zeal to God? What imports my outermost pall, so wide and long that it covers the whole mule when I ride, nay, should be big enough to cover a camel, but only a diffusive charity, that should spread itself for a succour and protection to all, by teaching, exhorting, comforting, reproving, admonishing, composing of differences, courageously withstanding wicked princes, and sacrificing for the safety of our flock our life and blood, as well as our wealth and riches. Though indeed riches ought not to be at all possessed by such as boast themselves successors to the apostles, who were poor, needy, and destitute. I say, if they did but lay these considerations to heart they would never be so ambitious of being created to this honour, they would willingly resign it when conferred upon them, or at least would be as industrious, watchful and laborious, as the primitive apostles were.

Now as to the popes of Rome, who pretend themselves Christ's vicars, if they would but imitate his exemplary life, in the being employed in an unintermitted course of preaching. In the being attended with poverty, nakedness, hunger, and a contempt of this world; if they did but consider the import of the word pope, which signifies a father; or if they did but practice their surname of most holy, what order or degrees of men would be in a worse condition? There would be then no such vigorous making of parties, and buying of votes, in the conclave upon a vacancy of that see.

And those who, by bribery or other indirect courses, should get themselves elected, would never secure their sitting firm in the chair by pistol, poison, force, and violence. How much of their pleasure would be abated if they were but endowed with one dram of wisdom? Wisdom, did I say? Nay, with one grain of that salt which our Saviour bid them not lose the savour of. All their riches, all their honour, their jurisdictions, their Peter's patrimony, their offices, their dispensations, their licences, their indulgences, their long train and attendants, see in how short a compass I have abbreviated all their marketing of religion; in a word, all their perquisites would be forfeited and lost; and in their room would succeed watchings, fastings, tears, prayers, sermons, hard studies, repenting sighs, and a thousand such like severe penalties. Nay, what's yet more deplorable, it would then follow, that all their clerks, amanuenses, notaries, advocates, proctors, secretaries, the offices of grooms, ostlers, serving-men, pimps, and somewhat else which for modesty's sake I shall not mention; in short, all these troops of attendants, which depends on his holiness, would all lose their several employments. This indeed would be hard, but what yet remains would be more dreadful. The very Head of the Church, the spiritual prince, would then be brought from all his splendour to the poor equipage of a scrip and staff.

But all this is upon the supposition only that they understood what circumstances they are placed in; whereas now, by a wholesome neglect of thinking, they live as well as heart can wish. Whatever of toil and drudgery belongs to their office that they assign over to St. Peter, or St. Paul, who have time enough to mind it; but if there be any thing of pleasure and grandeur, that they assume to themselves, as being hereunto called. So that by my influence no sort of people live more to their own ease and content. They think to satisfy that Master they pretend to serve, our Lord and Saviour, with their great state and magnificence, with the ceremonies of instalments, with the titles of reverence and holiness, and with exercising their epis-

copal function only in blessing and cursing.

The working of miracles is old and outdated; to teach the people is too laborious; to interpret scripture is to invade the prerogative of the schoolmen; to pray is too idle; to shed tears is cowardly and unmanly; to fast is too mean and sordid; to be easy and familiar is beneath the grandeur of him who, without being sued to and entreated, will scarce give princes the honour of kissing his toe; finally, to die for religion is too self-denying; and to be crucified as their Lord of life, is base and ignominious. Their only weapons ought to be those of the Spirit; and of these indeed they are mighty liberal, as of their interdicts, their suspensions, their denunciations, their aggravations, their greater and lesser excommunications, and their roaring bulls, that fright whomever they are thundered against. And these most holy fathers never issue them out more frequently than against those who, at the instigation of the devil, and not having the fear of God before their eyes, do feloniously and maliciously attempt to lessen and impair St. Peter's patrimony.

And though that apostle tells our Saviour in the gospel, in the name of all the other disciples, we have left all and followed you, yet they challenge as his inheritance, fields, towns, treasures, and large dominions. For the defending whereof, inflamed with a holy zeal, they fight with fire and sword, to the great loss and effusion of Christian blood, thinking they are apostolical maintainers of Christ's spouse, the church, when they have murdered all such as they call her enemies. Though, indeed, the church has no enemies more bloody and tyrannical than such impious popes, who give dispensations for the not preaching of Christ; evacuate the main effect and design of our redemption by their pecuniary bribes and sales; adulterate the gospel by their forced interpretations, and undermining traditions; and lastly, by their lusts and wickedness grieve the Holy Spirit, and make their Saviour's wounds to bleed anew.

. . .

But I doubt I have forgot myself, and have already transgressed the bounds of modesty. However, if I have said anything too confidently or impertinently, be pleased to consider that it was spoke by Folly, and that under the person of a woman; yet at the same time remember the applicableness of that Greek proverb:—

A fool oft speaks a seasonable truth:

Unless you will be so witty as to object that this makes no apology for me, be-cause the word ἀνήρ signifies a man, not a woman, and consequently my sex debars me from the benefit of that observation.

I perceive now, that, for a concluding treat, you expect a formal epilogue, and the summing up of all in a brief recitation; but I will assure you, you are grossly mistaken if you suppose that after such a hodge-podge medley of speech I should be able to recollect anything I have delivered. Beside, as it is an old proverb, "I hate a pot-companion with a good memory;" so indeed I may as truly say, "I hate a hearer that will carry any thing away with him." Wherefore, in short:—

Farewell! live long, drink deep, be jolly,
Ye most illustrious votaries of folly!

Martin Luther

The theory that all events are interrelated receives dramatic confirmation in the relationship between the Renaissance and the Reformation. In order to raise money to build St. Peter's Cathedral in Rome, the greatest monument of Renaissance art, Pope Leo X authorized the granting of papal indulgences in return for suitable donations to the Church. In 1517, one of the papal agents, a Dominican friar named John Tetzel, appeared in Central Germany, to grant these indulgences. Martin Luther (1483-1546), a professor at the University of Wittenberg, re-sponded by posting a list of Ninety-Five Theses, in which he attacked the entire theory and practice of indulgences, on the door of the Castle Church. Luther's act, in turn, set in motion a series of events that resulted finally in the Protestant Reformation.

Although it was Tetzel's activities that set him off, Luther based his opposition to the Church on grounds far deeper than the problem of indulgences. Basically, the question centered on the salvation of man's soul. From his studies of St. Paul and St. Augustine, Luther became convinced that, since all men are utterly con-demned and lost as a result of original sin, it is impossible for them to achieve salvation by any works of their own. Rather, salvation is the free gift of God's grace through faith. This doctrine of justification by faith rather than works undercut the position of the Catholic Church, which maintained that, since the works necessary to salvation (*e.g.*, the sacraments) could be performed only with the aid of the priesthood, the Church provided the only means to salvation. In place of the priestly hierarchy, Luther substituted the notion of "the priesthood of all believers."

AN OPEN LETTER TO THE CHRISTIAN NOBILITY OF THE GERMAN NATION CONCERNING THE REFORM OF THE CHRISTIAN ESTATE, 1520

TO HIS MOST ILLUSTRIOUS AND MIGHTY IMPERIAL MAJESTY, AND TO THE CHRISTIAN NOBILITY OF THE GERMAN NATION,

DOCTOR MARTIN LUTHER

Grace and power from God, Most Illustrious Majesty, and most gracious and dear Lords.

It is not out of sheer forwardness or rashness that I, a single, poor man, have undertaken to address your worships. The distress and oppression which weigh down all the Estates of Christendom, especially of Germany, and which move not me alone, but everyone to cry out time and again, and to pray for help, have forced me even now to cry aloud that God may inspire some one with His Spirit to lend this suffering nation a helping hand. Ofttimes the councils have made some pretence at reformation, but their attempts have been cleverly hindered by the guile of certain men and things have gone from bad to worse. I now intend, by the help of God, to throw some light upon the wiles and wickedness of these men, to the end that when they are known, they may not henceforth be so hurtful and so great a hindrance. God has given us a noble youth to be our head and thereby has awakened great hopes of good in many hearts; wherefore it is meet that we should do our part and profitably use this time of grace. In this whole matter the first and most important thing is that we take earnest heed not to enter on it trusting in great

might or in human reason, even though all power in the world were ours; for God cannot and will not suffer a good work to be begun with trust in our own power or reason. Such works He crushes ruthlessly to earth, as it is written in the xxxiii Psalm, "There is no king saved by the multitude of an host: a mighty man is not delivered by much strength." On this account, I fear, it came to pass of old that the good Emperors Frederick I and II, and many other German emperors were shamefully oppressed and trodden under foot by the popes, although all the world feared them. It may be that they relied on their own might more than on God, and therefore they had to fall. In our own times, too, what was it that raised the bloodthirsty Julius II to such heights? Nothing else, I fear, except that France, the Germans and Venice relied upon themselves. The children of Benjamin slew 42,000 Israelites because the latter relied on their own strength.

That it may not so fare with us and our noble young Emperor Charles, we must be sure that in this matter we are dealing not with men, but with the princes of hell, who can fill the world with war and bloodshed, but whom war and bloodshed do not overcome. We must go at this work despairing of physical force and humbly trusting God; we must seek God's help with earnest prayer, and fix our minds on nothing else than the misery and distress of suffering Christendom, without regard to the deserts of evil men. Otherwise we may start the game with great prospect of success, but when we get well into it the evil spirits will stir up such confusion that the whole world will swim in blood, and

"AN OPEN LETTER *to the Christian Nobility of the German Nation Concerning the Reform of the Christian Estate*," trans. C. M. Jacobs, in *Works of Martin Luther* (Philadelphia: Muhlenberg Press, 1915), II, 63-84. Courtesy of Muhlenberg Press.

yet nothing will come of it. Let us act wisely, therefore, and in the fear of God. The more force we use, the greater our disaster if we do not act humbly and in God's fear. The popes and the Romans have hitherto been able, by the devil's help, to set kings at odds with one another, and they may well be able to do it again, if we proceed by our own might and cunning, without God's help.

I. THE THREE WALLS OF THE ROMANISTS

The Romanists, with great adroitness, have built three walls about them, behind which they have hitherto defended themselves in such wise that no one has been able to reform them; and this has been the cause of terrible corruption throughout all Christendom.

First, when pressed by the temporal power, they have made decrees and said that the temporal power has no jurisdiction over them, but, on the other hand, that the spiritual is above the temporal power. Second, when the attempt is made to reprove them out of the Scriptures, they raise the objection that the interpretation of the Scriptures belongs to no one except the pope. Third, if threatened with a council, they answer with the fable that no one can call a council but the pope.

In this wise they have slyly stolen from us our three rods, that they may go unpunished, and have ensconced themselves within the safe stronghold of these three walls, that they may practise all the knavery and wickedness which we now see. Even when they have been compelled to hold a council they have weakened its power in advance by previously binding the princes with an oath to let them remain as they are. Moreover, they have given the pope full authority over all the decisions of the council, so that it is all one whether there are many councils or no councils,—except that they deceive us

with puppet-shows and sham-battles. So terribly do they fear for their skin in a really free council! And they have intimidated kings and princes by making them believe it would be an offence against God not to obey them in all these knavish, crafty deceptions.

Now God help us, and give us one of the trumpets with which the walls of Jericho were overthrown, that we may blow down these walls of straw and paper, and may set free the Christian rods for the punishment of sin, bringing to light the craft and deceit of the devil, to the end that through punishment we may reform ourselves, and once more attain God's favor.

Against the first wall we will direct our first attack.

It is pure invention that pope, bishops, priests and monks are to be called the "spiritual estate"; princes, lords, artisans, and farmers the "temporal estate." That is indeed a fine bit of lying and hypocrisy. Yet no one should be frightened by it; and for this reason—*viz.*, that all Christians are truly of the "spiritual estate," and there is among them no difference at all but that of office, as Paul says in I Corinthians xii, We are all one body, yet every member has its own work, whereby it serves every other, all because we have one baptism, one Gospel, one faith, and are all alike Christians; for baptism, Gospel and faith alone make us "spiritual" and a Christian people.

But that a pope or a bishop anoints, confers tonsures, ordains, consecrates, or prescribes dress unlike that of the laity, —this may make hypocrites and graven images, but it never makes a Christian or "spiritual" man. Through baptism all of us are consecrated to the priesthood, as St. Peter says in I Peter ii, "Ye are a royal priesthood, a priestly kingdom," and the book of Revelation says, "Thou hast made us by Thy blood to be priests and kings."

For if we had no higher consecration than pope or bishop gives, the consecration by pope or bishop would never make a priest, nor might anyone either say mass or preach a sermon or give absolution. Therefore when the bishop consecrates it is the same thing as if he, in the place and stead of the whole congregation, all of whom have like power, were to take one out of their number and charge him to use this power for the others; just as though ten brothers, all king's sons and equal heirs, were to choose one of themselves to rule the inheritance for them all,—they would all be kings and equal in power, though one of them would be charged with the duty of ruling.

To make it still clearer. If a little group of pious Christian laymen were taken captive and set down in a wilderness, and had among them no priest consecrated by a bishop, and if there in the wilderness they were to agree in choosing one of themselves, married or unmarried, and were to charge him with the office of baptising, saying mass, absolving and preaching, such a man would be as truly a priest as though all bishops and popes had consecrated him. That is why in cases of necessity any one can baptise and give absolution, which would be impossible unless we were all priests. This great grace and power of baptism and of the Christian Estate they have well-nigh destroyed and caused us to forget through the canon law. It was in the manner aforesaid that Christians in olden days chose from their number bishops and priests, who were afterwards confirmed by other bishops, without all the show which now obtains. It was thus that Sts. Augustine, Ambrose and Cyprian became bishops.

Since, then, the temporal authorities are baptised with the same baptism and have the same faith and Gospel as we, we must grant that they are priests and bishops, and count their office one which has a proper and a useful place in the Christian community. For whoever comes out of the water of baptism can boast that he is already consecrated priest, bishop and pope, though it is not seemly that every one should exercise the office. Nay, just because we are all in like manner priests, no one must put himself forward and undertake, without our consent and election, to do what is in the power of all of us. For what is common to all, no one dare take upon himself without the will and the command of the community; and should it happen that one chosen for such an office were deposed for malfeasance, he would then be just what he was before he held office. Therefore a priest in Christendom is nothing else than an office-holder. While he is in office, he has precedence; when deposed, he is a peasant or a townsman like the rest. Beyond all doubt, then, a priest is no longer a priest when he is deposed. But now they have invented *characteres indelebiles*, and prate that a deposed priest is nevertheless something different from a mere layman. They even dream that a priest can never become a layman, or be anything else than a priest. All this is mere talk and man-made law.

From all this it follows that there is really no difference between laymen and priests, princes and bishops, "spirituals" and "temporals," as they call them, except that of office and work, but not of "estate"; for they are all of the same estate,—true priests, bishops and popes,—though they are not all engaged in the same work, just as all priests and monks have not the same work. This is the teaching of St. Paul in Romans xii and I Corinthians xii, and of St. Peter in I Peter ii, as I have said above, *viz.*, that we are all one body of Christ, the Head, all members one of another. Christ has not two different bodies, one "temporal," the other "spiritual." He is one Head, and He has one body.

Therefore, just as those who are now

called "spiritual"—priests, bishops or popes —are neither different from other Christians nor superior to them, except that they are charged with the administration of the Word of God and the sacraments, which is their work and office, so it is with the temporal authorities,—they bear sword and rod with which to punish the evil and to protect the good. A cobbler, a smith, a farmer, each has the work and office of his trade, and yet they are all alike consecrated priests and bishops, and every one by means of his own work or office must benefit and serve every other, that in this way many kinds of work may be done for the bodily and spiritual welfare of the community, even as all the members of the body serve one another.

See, now, how Christian is the decree which says that the temporal power is not above the "spiritual estate" and may not punish it. That is as much as to say that the hand shall lend no aid when the eye is suffering. Is it not unnatural, not to say unchristian, that one member should not help another and prevent its destruction? Verily, the more honorable the member, the more should the others help. I say then, since the temporal power is ordained of God to punish evil-doers and to protect them that do well, it should therefore be left free to perform its office without hindrance through the whole body of Christendom without respect of persons, whether it affect pope, bishops, priests, monks, nuns or anybody else. For if the mere fact that the temporal power has a smaller place among the Christian offices than has the office of preachers or confessors, or of the clergy, then the tailors, cobblers, masons, carpenters, pot-boys, tapsters, farmers, and all the secular tradesmen, should also be prevented from providing pope, bishops, priests and monks with shoes, clothing, houses, meat and drink, and from paying them tribute. But if these laymen are allowed to do their work unhindered, what

do the Roman scribes mean by their laws, with which they withdraw themselves from the jurisdiction of the temporal Christian power, only so that they may be free to do evil and to fulfil what St. Peter has said: "There shall be false teachers among you, and through covetousness shall they with feigned words make merchandise of you."

On this account the Christian temporal power should exercise its office without let or hindrance, regardless whether it be pope, bishop or priest whom it affects; whoever is guilty, let him suffer. All that the canon law has said to the contrary is sheer invention of Roman presumption. For thus saith St. Paul to all Christians: "Let every soul (I take that to mean the pope's soul also) be subject unto the higher powers; for they bear not the sword in vain, but are the ministers of God for the punishment of evil-doers, and for the praise of them that do well." St. Peter also says: "Submit yourselves unto every ordinance of man for the Lord's sake, for so is the will of God." He has also prophesied that such men shall come as will despise the temporal authorities, and this has come to pass through the canon law.

So then, I think this first paper-wall is overthrown, since the temporal power has become a member of the body of Christendom, and is of the "spiritual estate," though its work is of a temporal nature. Therefore its work should extend freely and without hindrance to all the members of the whole body; it should punish and use force whenever guilt deserves or necessity demands, without regard to pope, bishops and priests, —let them hurl threats and bans as much as they will.

This is why guilty priests, if they are surrendered to the temporal law, are first deprived of their priestly dignities, which would not be right unless the temporal sword had previously had authority over them by divine right.

Again, it is intolerable that in the canon

law so much importance is attached to the freedom, life and property of the clergy, as though the laity were not also as spiritual and as good Christians as they, or did not belong to the Church. Why are your life and limb, your property and honor so free, and mine not? We are all alike Christians, and have baptism, faith, Spirit and all things alike. If a priest is killed, the land is laid under interdict,— why not when a peasant is killed? Whence comes this great distinction between those who are equally Christians? Only from human laws and inventions!

Moreover, it can be no good spirit who has invented such exceptions and granted to sin such license and impunity. For if we are bound to strive against the works and words of the evil spirit, and to drive him out in whatever way we can, as Christ commands and His Apostles, ought we, then, to suffer it in silence when the pope or his satellites are bent on devilish words and works? Ought we for the sake of men to allow the suppression of divine commandments and truths which we have sworn in baptism to support with life and limb? Of a truth we should then have to answer for all the souls that would thereby be abandoned and led astray.

It must therefore have been the very prince of devils who said what is written in the canon law: "If the pope were so scandalously bad as to lead souls in crowds to the devil, yet he could not be deposed." On this accursed and devilish foundation they build at Rome, and think that we should let all the world go to the devil, rather than resist their knavery. If the fact that one man is set over others were sufficient reason why he should escape punishment, then no Christian could punish another, since Christ commands that every man shall esteem himself the lowliest and the least.

Where sin is, there is no escape from punishment; as St. Gregory also writes

that we are indeed all equal, but guilt puts us in subjection one to another. Now we see how they whom God and the Apostles have made subject to the temporal sword deal with Christendom, depriving it of its liberty by their own wickedness, without warrant of Scripture. It is to be feared that this is a game of Anti-christ or a sign that he is close at hand.

The second wall is still more flimsy and worthless. They wish to be the only Masters of the Holy Scriptures, even though in all their lives they learn nothing from them. They assume for themselves sole authority, and with insolent juggling of words they would persuade us that the pope, whether he be a bad man or a good man, cannot err in matters of faith; and yet they cannot prove a single letter of it. Hence it comes that so many heretical and unchristian, nay, even unnatural ordinances have a place in the canon law, of which, however, there is no present need to speak. For since they think that the Holy Spirit never leaves them, be they never so unlearned and wicked, they make bold to decree whatever they will. And if it were true, where would be the need or use of the Holy Scriptures? Let us burn them, and be satisfied with the unlearned lords at Rome, who are possessed of the Holy Spirit,—although He can possess only pious hearts! Unless I had read it myself, I could not have believed that the devil would make such clumsy pretensions at Rome, and find a following.

But not to fight them with mere words, we will quote the Scriptures. St. Paul says in I Corinthians xiv: "If to anyone something better is revealed, though he be sitting and listening to another in God's Word, then the first, who is speaking, shall hold his peace and give place." What would be the use of this commandment, if we were only to believe him who does the talking or who has the highest seat? Christ also says in John vi, that all Christians shall be taught of God. Thus it may well happen that the pope and his followers are wicked men, and no true Christians, not taught of God, not having true understanding. On the other hand, an ordinary man may have true understanding; why then should we not follow him? Has not the pope erred many times? Who would help Christendom when the pope errs, if we were not to believe another, who had the Scriptures on his side, more than the pope?

Therefore it is a wickedly invented fable, and they cannot produce a letter in defence of it, that the interpretation of Scripture or the confirmation of its interpretation belongs to the pope alone. They have themselves usurped this power; and although they allege that this power was given to Peter when the keys were given to him, it is plain enough that the keys were not given to Peter alone, but to the whole community. Moreover, the keys were not ordained for doctrine or government, but only for the binding and loosing of sin, and whatever further power of the keys they arrogate to themselves is mere invention. But Christ's word to Peter, "I have prayed for thee that thy faith fail not," cannot be applied to the pope, since the majority of the popes have been without faith, as they must themselves confess. Besides, it is not only for Peter that Christ prayed, but also for all Apostles and Christians, as he says in John xvii: "Father, I pray for those whom Thou hast given Me, and not for these only, but for all who believe on Me through their word." Is not this clear enough?

Only think of it yourself! They must confess that there are pious Christians among us, who have the true faith, Spirit, understanding, word and mind of Christ. Why, then, should we reject their word and understanding and follow the pope, who has neither faith nor Spirit? That would be to deny the whole faith and the Christian Church. Moreover, it is not the pope alone who is always in the right, if the article of the Creed is correct: "I believe in one holy Christian Church"; otherwise the prayer must run: "I believe in the pope at Rome," and so reduce the Christian Church to one man,—which would be nothing else than a devilish and hellish error.

Besides, if we are all priests, as was said above, and all have one faith, one Gospel, one sacrament, why should we not also have the power to test and judge what is correct or incorrect in matters of faith? What becomes of the words of Paul in I Corinthians ii: "He that is spiritual judgeth all things, yet he himself is judged of no man," and II Corinthians iv: "We have all the same Spirit of faith"? Why, then, should not we perceive what squares with faith and what does not, as well as does an unbelieving pope?

All these and many other texts should make us bold and free, and we should not allow the Spirit of liberty, as Paul calls Him, to be frightened off by the fabrications of the popes, but we ought to go boldly forward to test all that they do or leave undone, according to our interpretation of the Scriptures, which rests on faith, and compel them to follow not their own interpretation, but the one that is better. In the olden days Abraham had to listen to his Sarah, although she was in more complete subjection to him than we are to anyone on earth. Balaam's ass, also, was wiser than the prophet himself. If God then spoke by an ass against a prophet, why should He not be able even now to speak by a righteous man against the pope? In like manner St. Paul rebukes St. Peter as a man in error. Therefore it behooves every Christian to espouse the cause of the faith, to understand and defend it, and to rebuke all errors.

The third wall falls of itself when the first two are down. For when the pope acts contrary to the Scriptures, it is our duty to stand by the Scriptures, to reprove him, and to constrain him, according to the word of Christ in Matthew xviii: "If thy brother sin against thee, go and tell it him between thee and him alone; if he hear thee not, then take with thee one or two more; if he hear them not, tell it to the Church; if he hear not the Church, consider him a heathen." Here every member is commanded to care for every other. How much rather should we do this when the member that does evil is a ruling member, and by his evil-doing is the cause of much harm and offence to the rest! But if I am to accuse him before the Church, I must bring the Church together.

They have no basis in Scripture for their contention that it belongs to the pope alone to call a council or confirm its actions; for this is based merely upon their own laws, which are valid only in so far as they are not injurious to Christendom or contrary to the laws of God. When the pope deserves punishment, such laws go out of force, since it is injurious to Christendom not to punish him by means of a council.

Thus we read in Acts xv that it was not St. Peter who called the Apostolic Council, but the Apostles and elders. If, then, that right had belonged to St. Peter alone, the council would not have been a Christian council, but an heretical *conciliabulum*. Even the Council of Nicaea— the most famous of all—was neither called nor confirmed by the Bishop of Rome, but by the Emperor Constantine, and many other emperors after him did the like, yet these councils were the most Christian of all. But if the pope alone had the right to call councils, then all these councils must have been heretical. Moreover, if I consider the councils which the pope has created, I find that they have done nothing of special importance.

Therefore, when necessity demands, and the pope is an offence to Christendom, the first man who is able should, as a faithful member of the whole body, do what he can to bring about a truly free council. No one can do this so well as the temporal authorities, especially since now they also are fellow-Christians, fellow-priests, "fellow-spirituals," fellow-lords over all things, and whenever it is needful or profitable, they should give free course to the office and work in which God has put them above every man. Would it not be an unnatural thing, if a fire broke out in a city, and every body were to stand by and let it burn on and on and consume everything that could burn, for the sole reason that nobody had the authority of the burgomaster, or because, perhaps, the fire broke out in the burgomaster's house? In such case is it not the duty of every citizen to arouse and call the rest? How much more should this be done in the spiritual city of Christ, if a fire of offence breaks out, whether in the papal government, or anywhere else? In the same way, if the enemy attacks a city, he who first rouses the others deserves honor and thanks; why then should he not deserve honor who makes known the presence of the enemy from hell, and awakens the Christians, and calls them together?

But all their boasts of an authority which dare not be opposed amount to nothing after all. No one in Christendom has authority to do injury, or to forbid the resisting of injury. There is no authority in the Church save for edification. Therefore, if the pope were to use his authority to prevent the calling of a free council, and thus became a hindrance to the edification of the Church, we should have regard neither for him nor for his authority; and if he were to hurl his bans and thunderbolts, we should despise his conduct as that of a madman, and relying on God, hurl back the ban on him, and coerce him as best we could. For this presumptuous authority of his is nothing; he has no such authority, and he is quickly overthrown by a text of Scripture; for Paul says to the Corinthians, "God has given us authority not for the destruction, but for the edification of Christendom." Who is ready to overleap this text? It is only the power of the devil and of Antichrist which resists the things that serve for the edification of Christendom; it is, therefore, in no wise to be obeyed, but is to be opposed with life and goods and all our strength.

Even though a miracle were to be done in the pope's behalf against the temporal powers, or though someone were to be stricken with a plague—which they boast has sometimes happened—it should be considered only the work of the devil, because of the weakness of our faith in God. Christ Himself prophesied in Matthew xxiv: "There shall come in My Name false Christs and false prophets, and do signs and wonders, so as to deceive even the elect," and Paul says in II Thessalonians ii, that Antichrist shall, through the power of Satan, be mighty in lying wonders.

Let us, therefore, hold fast to this: No Christian authority can do anything against Christ; as St. Paul says, "We can do nothing against Christ, but for Christ." Whatever does aught against Christ is the power of Antichrist and of the devil, even though it were to rain and hail wonders and plagues. Wonders and plagues prove nothing, especially in these last evil times, for which all the Scriptures prophesy false wonders. Therefore we must cling with firm faith to the words of God, and then the devil will cease from wonders.

Thus I hope that the false, lying terror with which the Romans have this long time made our conscience timid and stupid, has been allayed. They, like all of us, are subject to the temporal sword; they have no power to interpret the Scriptures by mere authority, without learning; they have no authority to prevent a council or, in sheer wantonness, to pledge it, bind it,

or take away its liberty; but if they do this, they are in truth in the communion of Antichrist and of the devil, and have nothing at all of Christ except the name.

II. ABUSES TO BE DISCUSSED IN COUNCILS

We shall now look at the matters which should be discussed in the councils, and with which popes, cardinals, bishops and all the scholars ought properly to be occupied day and night if they loved Christ and His Church. But if they neglect this duty, then let the laity and the temporal authorities see to it, regardless of bans and thunders; for an unjust ban is better than ten just releases, and an unjust release worse than ten just bans. Let us, therefore, awake, dear Germans, and fear God rather than men, that we may not share the fate of all the poor souls who are so lamentably lost through the shameful and devilish rule of the Romans, in which the devil daily takes a larger and larger place,—if, indeed, it were possible that such a hellish rule could grow worse, a thing I can neither conceive nor believe.

1. It is a horrible and frightful thing that the ruler of Christendom, who boasts himself vicar of Christ and successor of St. Peter, lives in such worldly splendor that in this regard no king nor emperor can equal or approach him, and that he who claims the title of "most holy" and "most spiritual" is more worldly than the world itself. He wears a triple crown, when the greatest kings wear but a single crown; if that is like the poverty of Christ and of St. Peter, then it is a new kind of likeness. When a word is said against it, they cry out "Heresy!" but that is because they do not wish to hear how unchristian and ungodly such a practice is. I think, however, that if the pope were with tears to pray to God, he would have to lay aside these crowns, for our God can suffer no pride; and his office is nothing else than this,—daily to

weep and pray for Christendom, and to set an example of all humility.

However that may be, this splendor of his is an offence, and the pope is bound on his soul's salvation to lay it aside, because St. Paul says, "Abstain from all outward shows, which give offence," and in Rom. xii, "We should provide good, not only in the sight of God, but also in the sight of all men." An ordinary bishop's crown would be enough for the pope; he should be greater than others in wisdom and holiness, and leave the crown of pride to Antichrist, as did his predecessors several centuries ago. They say he is a lord of the world; that is a lie; for Christ, Whose vicar and officer he boasts himself to be, said before Pilate, "My kingdom is not of this world," and no vicar's rule can go beyond his lord's. Moreover he is not the vicar of the glorified, but of the crucified Christ, as Paul says, "I was willing to know nothing among you save Christ, and Him only as the Crucified"; and in Philippians ii, "So think of yourselves as ye see in Christ, Who emptied Himself and took upon Him the appearance of a servant"; and again in I Corinthians i, "We preach Christ, the Crucified." Now they make the pope a vicar of the glorified Christ in heaven, and some of them have allowed the devil to rule them so completely that they have maintained that the pope is above the angels in heaven and has authority over them. These are indeed the very works of the very Antichrist.

2. What is the use in Christendom of those people who are called the cardinals? I shall tell you. Italy and Germany have many rich monasteries, foundations, benefices, and livings. No better way has been discovered to bring all these to Rome than by creating cardinals and giving them the bishoprics, monasteries and prelacies, and so overthrowing the worship of God. For this reason we now see Italy a very wilderness—monasteries in ruins, bishoprics devoured, the prelacies and the revenues of all the churches drawn to Rome, cities decayed, land and people laid waste, because there is no more worship or preaching. Why? The cardinals must have the income. No Turk could have so devastated Italy and suppressed the worship of God.

Now that Italy is sucked dry, they come into Germany, and begin oh, so gently. But let us beware, or Germany will soon become like Italy. Already we have some cardinals; what the Romans seek by that the "drunken Germans" are not to understand until we have not a bishopric, a monastery, a living, a benefice, a *heller* or a *pfennig* left. Antichrist must take the treasures of the earth, as it was prophesied. So it goes on. They skim the cream off the bishoprics, monasteries and benefices, and because they do not yet venture to turn them all to shameful use, as they have done in Italy, they only practise for the present the sacred trickery of coupling together ten or twenty prelacies and taking a yearly portion from each of them, so as to make a tidy sum after all. The priory of Würzburg yields a thousand *gulden;* that of Bamberg, something; Mainz, Trier and the others, something more; and so from one to ten thousand *gulden* might be got together, in order that a cardinal might live at Rome like a rich king.

"After they are used to this, we will create thirty or forty cardinals in a day, and give to one Mount St. Michael at Bamberg and the bishopric of Würzburg to boot, hang on to these a few rich livings, until churches and cities are waste, and after that we will say, 'We are Christ's vicars and shepherds of Christ's sheep; the mad, drunken Germans must put up with it.'"

I advise, however, that the number of the cardinals be reduced, or that the pope be made to keep them at his own expense. Twelve of them would be more than enough, and each of them might have an income of a thousand *gulden* a year. How comes it that we Germans must put up with such robbery and such extortion of our property, at the hands of the pope? If the Kingdom of France has prevented it, why do we Germans let them make such fools and apes of us? It would all be more bearable if in this way they only stole our property; but they lay waste the churches and rob Christ's sheep of their pious shepherds, and destroy the worship and the Word of God. Even if there were not a single cardinal, the Church would not go under. As it is they do nothing for the good of Christendom; they only wrangle about the incomes of bishoprics and prelacies, and that any robber could do.

3. If ninety-nine parts of the papal court were done away and only the hundredth part allowed to remain, it would still be large enough to give decisions in matters of faith. Now, however, there is such a swarm of vermin yonder in Rome, all boasting that they are "papal," that there was nothing like it in Babylon. There are more than three thousand papal secretaries alone; who will count the other offices, when they are so many that they scarcely can be counted? And they all lie in wait for the prebends and benefices of Germany as wolves lie in wait for the sheep. I believe that Germany now gives much more to the pope at Rome than it gave in former times to the emperors. Indeed, some estimate that every year more than three hundred thousand *gulden* find their way from Germany to Rome, quite uselessly and fruitlessly; we get nothing for it but scorn and contempt. And yet we wonder that princes, nobles, cities, endowments, land and people are impoverished! We should rather wonder that we still have anything to eat!

The Counter Reformation

The Counter Reformation of the Catholic Church expressed itself in three major institutions: the Council of Trent, the Society of Jesus (usually called the Jesuits), and the Inquisition. The Council of Trent, called originally by Pope Paul III in 1545, met at irregular intervals over a period of nearly twenty years under three different popes in the capital of the Italian Tyrol. The Council responded to the Protestant movement by reaffirming the basic doctrines of the Catholic Church while at the same time calling for a reform of abuses within the Church. The first of the selections that follow includes some of the more important decrees, concerning both doctrine and practice, adopted by the Council.

The Company or Society of Jesus was founded by St. Ignatius of Loyola (1491- 1556), an unlettered Spanish soldier who, as the result of a religious experience he underwent after being wounded in battle, resolved to become a "soldier of Christ." Once he had recovered, he set about educating himself, starting with elementary school and continuing through the University of Paris. While he was attending the university he organized a religious fraternity that later became the Society of Jesus. Loyola's new order was established along military lines; an iron discipline demanded that each member show complete obedience to his immediate superiors and ultimately to his supreme commander, the pope. During the religious conflicts of the sixteenth and seventeenth centuries, the Jesuits were always to be found on the side of the papal forces, in opposition primarily to the Protestants but to Catholic liberals as well. Later, the Jesuits acted in the capacity of confessors to kings, a position that often involved them in political intrigue and, for a time, gained them a reputation as religious Machiavellians. They were also active as missionaries in areas of Europe that had accepted Protestantism, and among the pagans of Asia and the New World.

The second selection that follows is the final section of Loyola's *Spiritual Exercises*, a training manual designed for members of the Society of Jesus.

THE CANONS AND DECREES OF THE COUNCIL OF TRENT

DECREE TOUCHING THE OPENING OF THE COUNCIL.

Doth it please you,—unto the praise and glory of the holy and undivided Trinity, Father, and Son, and Holy Ghost; for the increase and exaltation of the Christian faith and religion; for the extirpation of heresies; for the peace and union of the Church; for the reformation of the Clergy and Christian people; for the depression and extinction of the enemies of the Christian name,—to decree and declare that the sacred and general council of Trent do begin, and hath begun?

They answered: It pleaseth us.

DECREE CONCERNING THE CANONICAL SCRIPTURES.

The sacred and holy, oecumenical, and general Synod of Trent,—lawfully assembled in the Holy Ghost, the same three legates of the Apostolic See presiding therein,—keeping this always in view, that,

THE CANONS AND DECREES OF THE SACRED AND OECU-MENICAL COUNCIL OF TRENT, trans. J. Waterworth (London, 1848), pp. 12, 17-23, 39-40, 54-56, 76, 82-84, 172-173, 194-195, 233-235, 253-254, 277-278.

errors being removed, the purity itself of the Gospel be preserved in the Church; which (Gospel), before promised through the prophets in the holy Scriptures, our Lord Jesus Christ, the Son of God, first promulgated with His own mouth, and then commanded to be preached by His Apostles to every creature, as the fountain of all, both saving truth, and moral discipline; and seeing clearly that this truth and books, and the unwritten traditions which, received by the Apostles from the mouth of Christ himself, or from the Apostles themselves, the Holy Ghost dictating, have come down even unto us, transmitted as it were from hand to hand; (the Synod) following the examples of the orthodox Fathers, receives and venerates with an equal affection of piety, and reverence, all the books both of the Old and of the New Testament—seeing that one God is the author of both—as also the said traditions, as well those appertaining to faith as to morals, as having been dictated, either by Christ's own word of mouth, or by the Holy Ghost, and preserved in the Catholic Church by a continuous succession.

. . .

DECREE CONCERNING THE EDITION, AND
THE USE, OF THE SACRED BOOKS.

Moreover, the same sacred and holy
Synod,—considering that no small utility
may accrue to the Church of God, if it be
made known which out of all the Latin
editions, now in circulation, of the sacred
books, is to be held as authentic,—ordains
and declares, that the said old and vulgate
edition, which, by the lengthened usage of
so many ages, has been approved of in the
Church, be, in public lectures, disputations,
sermons and expositions, held as authentic; and that no one is to dare, or presume
to reject it under any pretext whatever.

Furthermore, in order to restrain petu-
lant spirits, It decrees, that no one, relying
on his own skill, shall,—in matters of faith,
and of morals pertaining to the edification
of Christian doctrine,—wresting the sacred
Scripture to his own senses, presume to interpret the said sacred Scripture contrary
to that sense which holy mother Church,
—whose it is to judge of the true sense and
interpretation of the holy Scriptures,—
hath held and doth hold; or even contrary
to the unanimous consent of the Fathers;
even though such interpretations were
never (intended) to be at any time published. . . .

DECREE CONCERNING ORIGINAL SIN.

That our Catholic *faith, without which it
is impossible to please God*, may, errors being purged away, continue in its own perfect and spotless integrity, and that the
Christian people may not *be carried about
with every wind of doctrine;* whereas that
old serpent, the perpetual enemy of mankind, amongst the very many evils with
which the Church of God is in these our
times troubled, has also stirred up not
only new, but even old, dissensions touching original sin, and the remedy thereof;
the sacred and holy, oecumenical and general Synod of Trent,—lawfully assembled

in the Holy See presiding therein,—wishing
now to come to the reclaiming of the erring, and the confirming of the wavering,
—following the testimonies of the sacred
Scriptures, of the holy Fathers, of the most
approved councils, and the judgment and
consent of the Church itself, ordains, con-
fesses, and declares these things touching
the said original sin:

1. If any one does not confess that
the first man, Adam, when he had transgressed the commandment of God in Paradise, immediately lost the holiness and justice wherein he had been constituted; and
that he incurred, through the offence of
that prevarication, the wrath and indignation of God, and consequently death, with
which God had previously threatened him,
and, together with death, captivity under
his power who thenceforth *had the empire
of death, that is to say, the devil*, and that
the entire Adam, through that offence of
prevarication, was changed, in body and
soul, for the worse; let him be anathema.

2. If any one asserts, that the prevarication of Adam injured himself alone, and not
his posterity; and that the holiness and justice, received of God, which he lost, he lost
for himself alone, and not for us also; or
that he, being defiled by the sin of disobedience, has only transfused death, and
pains of the body, into the whole human
race, but not sin also, which is the death
of the soul; let him be anathema:—whereas
he contradicts the apostle who says; *By
one man sin entered into the world, and by
sin death, and so death passed upon all
men, in whom all have sinned.*

3. If any one asserts, that this sin of
Adam,—which in its origin is one, and being transfused into all by propagation, not
by imitation, is in each one as his own,—
is taken away either by the powers of human nature, or by any other remedy than
the merit of the *one mediator, our Lord
Jesus Christ, who hath reconciled us to God
in his own blood, made unto us justice,*

sanctification, and redemption; or if he denies that the said merit of Jesus Christ is applied, both to adults and to infants, by the sacrament of baptism rightly administered in the form of the Church; let him be anathema: *For there is no other name under heaven given to men, whereby we must be saved.* Whence that voice; *Behold the lamb of God, behold him who taketh away the sins of the world; and that other; As many as have been baptized, have put on Christ.*

· · ·

THAT A RASH PRESUMPTUOUSNESS IN THE
MATTER OF PREDESTINATION IS
TO BE AVOIDED.

No one, moreover, so long as he is in this mortal life, ought so far to presume as regards the secret mystery of divine predestination, as to determine for certain that he is assuredly in the number of the predestinate; as if it were true, that he that is justified, either cannot sin any more, or, if he do sin, that he ought to promise himself an assured repentance; for except by special revelation, it cannot be known whom God hath chosen unto Himself.

· · ·

ON THE SACRAMENTS IN GENERAL.

Canon I.—If any one saith, that the sacraments of the New Law were not all instituted by Jesus Christ, our Lord; or, that they are more, or less, than seven, to wit, Baptism, Confirmation, the Eucharist, Penance, Extreme Unction, Order, and Matrimony; or even that any one of these seven is not truly and properly a sacrament; let him be anathema.

Canon II.—If any one saith, that these said sacraments of the New Law do not differ from the sacraments of the Old Law, save that the ceremonies are different, and different the outward rites; let him be anathema.

Canon III.—If any one saith, that these seven sacraments are in such wise equal to each other, as that one is not in any way more worthy than another; let him be anathema.

Canon IV.—If any one saith, that the sacraments of the New Law are not necessary unto salvation, but superfluous; and that, without them, or without the desire thereof, men obtain of God, through faith alone, the grace of justification;—though all (the sacraments) are not indeed necessary for every individual; let him be anathema.

Canon V.—If any one saith, that these sacraments were instituted for the sake of nourishing faith alone; let him be anathema.

Canon VI.—If any one saith, that the sacraments of the New Law do not contain the grace which they signify; or, that they do not confer that grace on those who do not place an obstacle thereunto; as though they were merely outward signs of grace or justice received through faith, and certain marks of the Christian profession, whereby believers are distinguished amongst men from unbelievers; let him be anathema.

Canon VII.—If any one saith, that grace, as far as God's part is concerned, is not given through the said sacraments, always, and to all men, even though they receive them rightly, but (only) sometimes, and to some persons; let him be anathema.

Canon VIII.—If any one saith, that by the said sacraments of the New Law grace is not conferred through the act performed, but that faith alone in the divine promise suffices for the obtaining of grace; let him be anathema.

Canon IX.—If any one saith, that, in the three sacraments, Baptism, to wit, Confirmation, and Order, there is not imprinted in the soul a character, that is, a certain spiritual and indelible sign, on account of which they cannot be repeated; let him be anathema.

Canon X.—If any one saith, that all Christians have power to administer the word, and all the sacraments; let him be anathema.

Canon XI.—If any one saith, that, in ministers, when they effect, and confer the sacraments, there is not required the intention at least of doing what the Church does; let him be anathema.

Canon XII.—If any one saith, that a minister, being in mortal sin,—if so be that he observe all the essentials which belong to the effecting, or conferring of, the sacrament,—neither effects, nor confers the sacrament; let him be anathema.

Canon XIII.—If any one saith, that the received and approved rites of the Catholic Church, wont to be used in the solemn administration of the sacraments, may be contemned, or without sin be omitted at pleasure by the ministers, or be changed, by every pastor of the churches, into other new ones; let him be anathema.

.   .   .

ON THE REAL PRESENCE OF OUR LORD JESUS CHRIST IN THE MOST HOLY SACRAMENT OF THE EUCHARIST.

In the first place, the holy Synod teaches, and openly and simply professes, that, in the august sacrament of the holy Eucharist, after the consecration of the bread and wine, our Lord Jesus Christ, true God and man, is truly, really, and substantially contained under the species of those sensible things. For neither are these things mutually repugnant,—that our Saviour Himself always sitteth at the right hand of the Father in heaven, according to the natural mode of existing, and that, nevertheless, He be, in many other places, sacramentally present to us in his own substance, by a manner of existing, which, though we can scarcely express it in words, yet can we, by the understanding illuminated by faith, conceive, and we ought most firmly to believe, to be possible unto God:

for thus all our forefathers, as many as were in the true Church of Christ, who have treated of this most holy Sacrament, have most openly professed, that our Redeemer instituted this so admirable a sacrament at the last supper, when, after the blessing of the bread and wine, He testified, in express and clear words, that He gave them His own very Body, and His own Blood; words which,—recorded by the holy Evangelists, and afterwards repeated by Saint Paul, whereas they carry with them that proper and most manifest meaning in which they were understood by the Fathers,—it is indeed a crime the most unworthy that they should be wrested, by certain contentious and wicked men, to fictitious and imaginary tropes, whereby the verity of the flesh and blood of Christ is denied, contrary to the universal sense of the Church, which, as *the pillar and ground of truth,* has detested, as satanical, these inventions devised by impious men; she recognising, with a mind ever grateful and unforgetting, this most excellent benefit of Christ.

.   .   .

ON THE MOST HOLY SACRAMENT OF THE EUCHARIST.

Canon I.—If any one denieth, that, in the sacrament of the most holy Eucharist, are contained truly, really, and substantially, the body and blood together with the soul and divinity of our Lord Jesus Christ, and consequently the whole Christ; but saith that He is only therein as in a sign, or in figure, or virtue; let him be anathema.

Canon II.—If any one saith, that, in the sacred and holy sacrament of the Eucharist, the substance of the bread and wine remains conjointly with the body and blood of our Lord Jesus Christ, and denieth that wonderful and singular conversion of the whole substance of the bread into the Body, and of the whole substance of the wine into the Blood—the species only of the bread and wine remaining—which conversion indeed the Catholic Church most aptly calls Transubstantiation; let him be anathema.

. . .

Canon IX.—If any one denieth, that all and each of Christ's faithful of both sexes are bound, when they have attained to years of discretion, to communicate every year, at least at Easter, in accordance with the precept of the holy Mother Church; let him be anathema.

. . .

Canon XI.—If any one saith, that faith alone is a sufficient preparation for receiving the sacrament of the most holy Eucharist; let him be anathema. And for fear lest so great a sacrament may be received unworthily, and so unto death and condemnation, this holy Synod ordains and declares, that sacramental confession, when a confessor may be had, is of necessity to be made beforehand, by those whose conscience is burthened with mortal sin, how contrite even soever they may think themselves. But if any one shall presume to teach, preach, or obstinately to assert, or even in public disputation to defend the contrary, he shall be thereupon excommunicated.

. . .

ON THE ECCLESIASTICAL HIERARCHY, AND ON ORDINATION.

But, forasmuch as in the sacrament of Order, as also in Baptism and Confirmation, a character is imprinted, which can neither be effaced nor taken away; the holy Synod with reason condemns the opinion of those, who assert that the priests of the New Testament have only a temporary power; and that those who have once been rightly ordained, can again become laymen, if they do not exercise the ministry of the word of God. And if any one affirm, that all Christians indiscriminately are priests of the New Testament, or that they are

all mutually endowed with an equal spiritual power, he clearly does nothing but confound the ecclesiastical hierarchy, which is *as an army set in array;* as if, contrary to the doctrine of blessed Paul, *all* were *apostles, all prophets, all evangelists, all pastors, all doctors.* Wherefore, the holy Synod declares that, besides the other ecclesiastical degrees, bishops, who have succeeded to the place of the apostles, principally belong to this hierarchical order; that they are *placed,* as the same apostle says, *by the Holy Ghost, to rule the Church of God;* that they are superior to priests; administer the sacrament of Confirmation; ordain the ministers of the Church; and that they can perform very many other things; over which functions others of an inferior order have no power. Furthermore, the sacred and holy Synod teaches, that, in the ordination of bishops, priests, and of the other orders, neither the consent, nor vocation, nor authority, whether of the people, or of any civil power or magistrate whatsoever, is required in such wise as that, without this, the ordination is invalid: yea rather doth It decree, that all those who, being only called and instituted by the people, or by the civil power and magistrate, ascend to the exercise of these ministrations, and those who of their own rashness assume them to themselves, are not ministers of the Church, but are to be looked upon as *thieves and robbers, who have not entered by the door.* These are the things which it hath seemed good to the sacred Synod to teach the faithful of Christ, in general terms, touching the sacrament of Order.

. . .

ON THE SACRAMENT OF MATRIMONY.

. . .

Canon IX.—If any one saith, that clerics constituted in sacred orders or Regulars, who have solemnly professed chastity, are able to contract marriage, and that being contracted it is valid, notwithstanding the ecclesiastical law, or vow; and that the contrary is nothing else than to condemn marriage; and, that all who do not feel that they have the gift of chastity, even though they have made a vow thereof, may contract marriage; let him be anathema: seeing that God refuses not that gift to those who ask for it rightly, neither does *He suffer us to be tempted above that which we are able.*

Canon X.—If any one saith, that the marriage state is to be placed above the state of virginity, or of celibacy, and that it is not better and more blessed to remain in virginity, or in celibacy, than to be united in matrimony; let him be anathema.

· · ·

ON THE INVOCATION, VENERATION, AND RELICS, OF SAINTS, AND ON SACRED IMAGES.

The holy Synod enjoins on all bishops, and others who sustain the office and charge of teaching, that, agreeably to the usage of the Catholic and Apostolic Church, received from the primitive times of the Christian religion, and agreeably to the consent of the holy Fathers, and to the decrees of sacred Councils, they especially instruct the faithful diligently concerning the intercession and invocation of saints; the honour (paid) to relics; and the legitimate use of images: teaching them, that the saints, who reign together with Christ, offer up their own prayers to God for men; that it is good and useful suppliantly to invoke them, and to have recourse to their prayers, aid, (and) help for obtaining benefits from God, through His Son, Jesus Christ our Lord, who is our alone Redeemer and Saviour; but that they think impiously, who deny that the saints, who enjoy eternal happiness in heaven, are to be invocated; or who assert either that they do not pray for men; or, that the invocation of them to pray for each of us even in par-

ticular, is idolatry; or, that it is repugnant to the word of God; and is opposed to the honour of the *one mediator of God and men, Christ Jesus;* or, that it is foolish to supplicate, vocally, or mentally, those who reign in heaven. Also, that the holy bodies of holy martyrs, and of others now living with Christ,—which bodies were the living members of Christ, and *the temple of the Holy Ghost,* and which are by Him to be raised unto eternal life, and to be glorified,—are to be venerated by the faithful; through which (bodies) many benefits are bestowed by God on men; so that they who affirm that veneration and honour are not due to the relics of saints; or, that these, and other sacred monuments, are uselessly honoured by the faithful; and that the places dedicated to the memories of the saints are in vain visited with the view of obtaining their aid; are wholly to be condemned, as the Church has already long since condemned, and now also condemns them.

Moreover, that the images of Christ, of the Virgin Mother of God, and of the other saints, are to be had and retained particularly in temples, and that due honour and veneration are to be given them; not that any divinity, or virtue, is believed to be in them, on account of which they are to be worshipped; or that anything is to be asked of them; or, that trust is to be reposed in images, as was of old done by the Gentiles who placed their hope in idols; but because the honour which is shown them is referred to the prototypes which those images represent; in such wise that by the images which we kiss, and before which we uncover the head, and prostrate ourselves, we adore Christ; and we venerate the saints, whose similitude they bear: as by the decrees of Councils, and especially of the second Synod of Nicaea, has been defined against the opponents of images.

· · ·

CARDINALS AND ALL PRELATES OF THE
CHURCHES SHALL BE CONTENT WITH
MODEST FURNITURE AND A FRUGAL TABLE:
THEY SHALL NOT ENRICH THEIR RELATIVES
OR DOMESTICS OUT OF THE PROPERTY
OF THE CHURCH.

It is to be wished, that those who undertake the office of a bishop should understand what their portion is; and comprehend that they are called, not to their own convenience, not to riches or luxury, but to labours and cares for the glory of God. For it is not to be doubted, that the rest of the faithful also will be more easily excited to religion and innocence, if they shall see those who are set over them, not fixing their thoughts on the things of this world, but on the salvation of souls, and on their heavenly country. Wherefore the holy Synod, being minded that these things are of the greatest importance towards restoring ecclesiastical discipline, admonishes all bishops, that, often meditating thereon, they show themselves conformable to their office, by their actual deeds, and the actions of their lives; which is a kind of perpetual sermon; but above all that they so order their whole conversation, as that others may thence be able to derive examples of frugality, modesty, continency, and of that holy humility which so much recommends us to God.

Wherefore, after the example of our fathers in the Council of Carthage, It not only orders that bishops be content with modest furniture, and a frugal table and diet, but that they also give heed that in the rest of their manner of living, and in their whole house, there be nothing seen that is alien from this holy institution, and which does not manifest simplicity, zeal towards God, and a contempt of vanities. Also, it wholly forbids them to strive to enrich their own kindred or domestics out of the revenues of the Church: seeing that even the canons of the Apostles forbid

them to give to their kindred the property of the church, which belongs to God; but if their kindred be poor, let them distribute to them thereof as poor, but not misapply, or waste, it for their sakes: yea, the holy Synod with the utmost earnestness, admonishes them completely to lay aside all this human and carnal affection towards brothers, nephews and kindred, which is the seed-plot of many evils in the Church. And what has been said of bishops, the same is not only to be observed by all who hold ecclesiastical benefices, whether Secular or Regular, each according to the nature of his rank, but the Synod decrees that it also regards the cardinals of the holy Roman Church; for whereas, upon their advice to the most holy Roman Pontiff, the administration of the universal Church depends, it would seem to be a shame, if they did not at the same time shine so preeminent in virtue and in the discipline of their lives, as deservedly to draw upon themselves the eyes of all men.

. . . .

DECREE CONCERNING INDULGENCES.

Whereas the power of conferring Indulgences was granted by Christ to the Church; and she has, even in the most ancient times, used the said power, delivered unto her of God; the sacred holy Synod teaches, and enjoins, that the use of Indulgences, for the Christian people most salutary, and approved of by the authority of sacred Councils, is to be retained in the Church; and It condemns with anathema those who either assert, that they are useless; or who deny that there is in the Church the power of granting them. In granting them, however, It desires that, in accordance with the ancient and approved custom in the Church, moderation be observed; lest, by excessive facility, ecclesiastical discipline be enervated. And being desirous that the abuses which have crept therein, and by occasion of which this honourable name of Indulgences is blasphemed by heretics, be amended and corrected, It ordains generally by this decree, that all evil gains for the obtaining thereof, —whence a most prolific cause of abuses amongst the Christian people has been derived,—be wholly abolished. But as regards the other abuses which have proceeded from superstition, ignorance, irreverance, or from whatsoever other source, since, by reason of the manifold corruptions in the places and provinces where the said abuses are committed, they cannot conveniently be specially prohibited; It commands all bishops, diligently to collect, each in his own church, all abuses of this nature, and to report them in the first provincial Synod; that, after having been reviewed by the opinions of the other bishops also, they may forthwith be referred to the Sovereign Roman Pontiff, by whose authority and prudence that which may be expedient for the universal Church will be ordained; that thus the gift of holy Indulgences may be dispensed to all the faithful, piously, holily, and incorruptly.

SPIRITUAL EXERCISES

. . .

RULES FOR THINKING WITH THE CHURCH

For the true understanding which we ought to have in the Militant Church, let the following rules be observed.

The first: having put aside all judgment, we ought to have our mind prepared and ready to obey in all things the true Spouse of Christ our Lord, which is our Holy Mother Hierarchical Church.

The second: to praise confessing to a priest, and taking the Holy Sacrament once a year, and much more once a month, and much better once a week, with the requisite and just conditions.

The third: to praise hearing Mass frequently; likewise chants, psalms, and prolonged prayers in and out of church. Likewise the hours set apart at a designated time for all Divine Office and for all prayer and all canonical Hours.

The fourth: to praise at length Religious

EJERCICIOS ESPIRITUALES, Ignatius of Loyola, trans. Terrence L. Hansen of the University of California at Riverside.

Orders, virginity and continence; and marriage not as much as any of the above.

The fifth: to praise vows of religion, of obedience, of poverty, of chastity, and of other perfections of supererogation; and it is to be observed that inasmuch as a vow concerns things which approach Evangelical perfection, in things that are not a part of it, vows should not be made; for example, of being a merchant, or of being married.

The sixth: to praise relics of Saints, venerating some and praying to others; praising stations, pilgrimages, indulgences, jubilees, crusades, and lighted candles in the churches.

The seventh: to praise Constitutions regarding fasts and abstinences, as of Lent, Ember Days, Vigils, Friday and Saturday: likewise penances, not only internal, but even external.

The eighth: to praise adornments and buildings of churches, likewise images, and to venerate them according to what they represent.

The ninth: to praise, finally, all precepts

of the Church, keeping the mind ready to seek reasons in her defense and in no way in her offense.

The tenth: we ought to be more prompt to indorse and praise the Constitutions and Ordinances as well as the ways of our Superiors: because, assuming that some are not or were not such as to merit praise, to speak against them, whether preaching in public, or conversing in the presence of the common people, would engender more murmuring and scandal than benefit; and thus the people would become indignant against their leaders, whether temporal or spiritual. So that as it is harmful to the common people to speak ill of the Superiors in their absence, so it may be advantageous to speak of the evil customs to the same persons who can remedy them.

The eleventh: to praise Positive and Scholastic doctrine; because as it is more characteristic of the Positive Doctors, like St. Jerome, St. Augustine, and St. Gregory, etc., to move the emotions to love and serve God our Lord in all things, so it is more characteristic of the Scholastics like St. Thomas, St. Bonaventure, and the Master of the Sentences, etc., to define or manifest for our times the things necessary for eternal salvation; and, in addition, to oppose and declare all errors, and all fallacies; because the Scholastic Doctors, since they are more modern, not only benefit from the true understanding of the Holy Scripture, and of the Positive and Holy Doctors; but also, being illuminated and enlightened by the divine virtue, they are aided by the Councils, Canons and Constitutions of our Holy Mother Church.

The twelfth: we ought to guard against making comparisons between those of us who are still living and the Blessed of the past; because no little error is committed in this respect; namely, by saying 'He knows more than St. Augustine'; 'He is another St. Francis, or greater'; 'He is another St. Paul in goodness, holiness, etc.'

The thirteenth: to be right in all things we ought to adhere always to the principle that the white which I see I will believe to be black if the Hierarchical Church so rules, believing that between Christ our Lord the Bridegroom and the Church His Bride, there is the same Spirit that governs and guides us for the salvation of our souls; because by the same Spirit and our Lord who gave us the ten commandments our Holy Mother Church is guided and governed.

The fourteenth: assuming that it is very true that no one can be saved without being predestined, and without having faith and grace; there is much to take into account in the manner of speaking and conversing on all these subjects.

The fifteenth: we ought not to speak much about predestination by way of habit; but if in any manner or at any times it is discussed, let it be so discussed that the common people may not come into any error as it sometimes happens, by saying: 'If I am bound to be saved or damned, it is already decided; and as for my doing good or evil, it cannot now be otherwise'; and with this obstructing they neglect the works that lead to the salvation and spiritual benefit of their souls.

The sixteenth: in the same manner it should be taken into account that by speaking of faith at length and with much intensity without any distinction and explanation, that occasion be not given to the people to become negligent and slothful in works, whether before faith based on charity or after it.

The seventeenth: likewise we ought not to speak at such length insisting so much upon grace, because poison may be engendered to take away liberty. Thus we may speak about faith and grace as much as possible by means of the divine aid for the greater praise of His Divine Majesty; but not in such a way nor by such means, especially in our time so perilous, that works and free will may receive any detriment or be held for nought.

The eighteenth: provided that above all else we are to esteem serving continuously God our Lord out of pure love, we ought to praise in the full extent the fear of His Divine Majesty; because not only is filial fear a pious and most holy thing, but even servile fear, where man does not attain to anything better or more beneficial, is very helpful toward getting out of mortal sins, and having gotten out, he comes easily to filial fear, which is fully acceptable and pleasing to God our Lord, because it is at one with divine love.

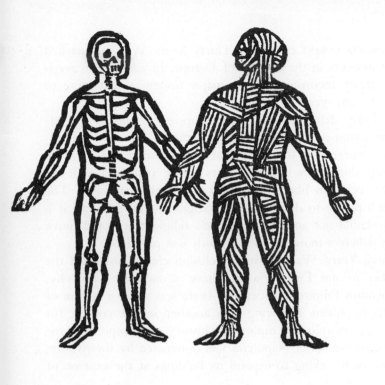

EARLY MODERN EUROPE

THE PEACE OF WESTPHALIA (1648) ended the Thirty Years' War and marked the beginning of a new era in the history of Europe. In addition to territorial changes, the treaty incorporated two major principles that were to influence events for many years to come.

First, the Peace fairly definitely ended the wars over religion and effectively ended the notion of Protestant versus Catholic. The idea that religious beliefs were matters for the individual's own conscience to settle had grown up slowly during the hundred years before 1648, and with the Peace of Westphalia religious liberty became rather well established. The treaty left it to each prince to determine the religion of his subjects; if a subject felt that he could not accept his prince's religion, he could move to another country where a more acceptable faith was practiced.

Second, the Thirty Years' War and its conclusion clearly answered the question of whether or not Europe would have a universal monarchy, such as the Holy Roman Empire. Henceforth, there was to be a system of independent sovereign powers balancing one another in the contest for power. The political, economic, and diplomatic history of Europe from the Peace of Westphalia to the fall of Napoleon was dominated by the rivalries of dynastic families, each seeking to expand its holdings at the expense of the others.

To implement this rivalry—some prefer to describe the situation as anarchy, but that depends on how you look at it—the entire machinery of international politics was either created or refined. Diplomatic services were called into being and sanctioned, international law was developed to regulate affairs between states, the law of war was formulated (a curious contradiction in itself), elaborate alliance systems were negotiated, and numerous wars were fought. There were even visionary projects for seventeenth- and eighteenth-century versions of a United Nations organization.

All these developments provide us with clues to an understanding of early modern European history, for they reflect a self-conscious attempt to regularize and limit the effects of competition among states. Thus, even the wars were fought for very limited objectives, such as the conquest of a particular bit of land. The idea of limited warfare with limited objectives differs radically from the twentieth-century notion of unlimited, total war fought to destroy an entire people or a government or a philosophy. In the seventeenth and eighteenth centuries, war tended to be an honorable game between princes who could accept defeat gracefully, knowing their thrones were secure even if a war were lost.

Another reason for limiting warfare was to protect the domestic scene from serious disruption. Whenever possible, the general population was not disturbed or its daily routines changed. The armies themselves were recruited from among those who were least essential to the functioning of the economy —the beggar, the ne'er-do-well, and the unskilled worker constituted the raw material that was molded into highly trained, severely disciplined armies by a corps of officers drawn mostly from the hereditary nobility. Thus, there was a deliberate attempt to isolate and confine both warfare and the military organizations that carried it on.

The purpose of even limited war, of course, was to increase the power and territory of the prince. But war was not the sole means of accomplishing these ends. Since agriculture, industry, and commerce could also contribute to the strength of the ruler, these activities were carefully fostered and protected from the effects of war. Stimulation and protection, however, meant control and regulation. In industry, for example, the quality of manufactures was maintained at a high level, costs were kept low, and the most advantageous commodities were produced. This system of regulation, called *mercantilism*, was adopted in one form or another in all the countries of Western Europe.

The mercantilists started from two basic principles: One, that the wealth of a state was determined by the quantity of gold and silver it possessed; two, that the total amount of trade in the world was fixed. It was from these two assumptions that most of the mercantilist practices were deduced. Wealth— that is, bullion—was necessary to support the prince in his wars and other activities; and if his country lacked adequate gold and silver mines, the only way it could obtain this wealth was to export more goods than it imported. Furthermore, since wealth was power, it followed that the power of one's rivals could be reduced by cutting down their supplies of gold and silver— that is, by selling them goods and by taking gold and silver in payment. Also, since the mercantilists thought that the total amount of trade was fixed, if one country could increase its share, the shares of all the others would be smaller and, consequently, they would be less able to accumulate wealth.

This same logic operated in the creation and administration of overseas empires. Colonies were intended to produce raw materials that could be shipped to the mother country for fabrication and then exported, either back to the colonies or, better, to the political and economic rivals of the mother country. The colonies were prohibited from trading with any state other than the parent.

By the end of the eighteenth century, however, mercantilism was falling under heavy criticism. The most telling attack on the system was published in 1776 by Adam Smith, who argued that the wealth of nations lay not so much in bullion as in productive capacity.

Smith's work was an expression of the major intellectual movement of the eighteenth century, which is often called the Age of Reason or the Enlightenment. The writers and thinkers of this century were convinced that the universe was regulated by natural laws, and that these laws could be discovered through the use of man's power to think and reason. This conviction was bolstered by the discoveries of Sir Isaac Newton, who in the late seventeenth century had worked out the laws of the physical universe by means of experimentation, observation, and deduction. The task the men of the Enlightenment set for themselves was to find the equivalent laws that governed human relationships, politics, and economics. Their search for the natural laws of society led them to examine and to criticize existing ideas and institutions. The theory of divine-right monarchy, for example, presented by Bishop Bossuet the century before, was held up to ridicule by both John Locke and Jean Jacques Rousseau; mercantilism was attacked as an interference with the natural laws of supply and demand; the Catholic Church was severely criticized (particularly by Voltaire) on the grounds that it rested on superstition rather than on reason, and that it undertook to censor and condemn books and articles.

We find one insistent emphasis throughout the Age of Reason. The mind must be free to inquire, to learn, and to communicate. Any social institution or tradition that interfered with this freedom had to be either recast according to the dictates of reason or else discarded. Remnants from the past that were no longer useful or that had survived only because of tradition were to be abolished. Dramatic evidence of this insistence appears in the lists of grievances (*Cahiers de Doléances*) that were drawn up in France on the eve of the French Revolution.

If the desire for liberty was strong in the eighteenth century, so too was the desire for equality. In a sense, the idea of social and political equality stemmed from the idea of liberty, for, if a man was free to do and think as he pleased, he should be judged on the basis of his thoughts and actions, rather than on the basis of hereditary rights, ranks, and privileges. Nor should his freedom be limited by arbitrary prohibitions on what he could or could not do. It was felt, for example, that a man should be able to rise to the highest ranks in the army if he had the necessary talent and ability, and that to require noble birth for high rank was unreasonable and senseless. "Equality of opportunity" and "the career open to talent" were later pointed to by Napoleon as the very essence of the French Revolution.

The eighteenth century ended in violence, revolution, terror, and tumult. Western civilization had come to the end of one era and the beginning of another. The gracious aristocrat was rapidly becoming an anachronism, and his political and economic power was being taken over by a middle class whose position rested on commercial and industrial wealth, not on patents of rank and the titles of ennobled ancestors. This new middle class found the doctrines of the Enlightenment acceptable also—liberty and equality were very appealing to men who chose to rely on themselves for prestige and social status. But they faced one major problem: If these high ideals were accepted, how could they be practiced? It is around attempts to answer this question that much of the history of the next century centers.

Francis Bacon

rancis Bacon (1561–1626) was a prophet of the scientific revolution of the seventeenth century—a revolution that transformed the foundations of European thought and ushered in the new Age of Science. Like the prophets of the Old Testament, Bacon concentrated his attention first on the evils he found around him. Although for him these evils were intellectual rather than moral or religious, he couched his criticism of contemporary science in Biblical terms. The leading thinkers of his age, following in the wake of the medieval schoolmen, he argued, had wandered from the path of truth into the worship of Idols. In the selection that follows he lists four such Idols, to which he gives the picturesque titles of Idols of the Tribe, the Cave, the Market-place, and the Theatre. To avoid falling prey to these Idols, Bacon held that men must turn their backs on scholastic philosophy and develop a new science based on a true knowledge, derived from careful and continued observation, of the workings of nature. This observational method, which Bacon called induction, is explained and illustrated in his major work, the *Instauratio Magna* (or Great Renewal), which, in his opinion, represented a "total reconstruction of the sciences, arts, and all human knowledge."

Although he was a prophet of the new science, Bacon himself did not fully grasp the nature of the method that men like Galileo and Newton were to employ in their work. His concept of induction, or the careful examination of particular occurrences in nature, fails to take adequate account of two other elements that are basic to modern scientific method: the formulation of hypotheses, and the deduction and verification of the consequences of these. Living at the height of the English Renaissance (which followed a hundred years behind that of Italy), Bacon exemplifies many of the attitudes found in previous Renaissance writers—the rejection of the medieval world-view as pernicious error, the somewhat naive optimism about his ability to take the whole of human knowledge as his sphere of activity, and the faith that he stood on the threshold of a new intellectual era. Finally, in his assertion that "knowledge is power" Bacon repeated a central concept of Machiavelli. But with a significant difference. For, although both men were interested in power, Machiavelli was concerned with the power that a prince could wield over his subjects, while Bacon was concerned with the power, derived from scientific understanding, that all men could wield over nature.

The following is from *Novum Organum*, which forms a part of *Instauratio Magna*.

NOVUM ORGANUM

I

Man, being the servant and interpreter of Nature, can do and understand so much and so much only as he has observed in fact or in thought of the course of nature: beyond this he neither knows anything nor can do anything.

II

Neither the naked hand nor the understanding left to itself can effect much. It is by instruments and helps that the work is done, which are as much wanted for the understanding as for the hand. And as the instruments of the hand either give motion or guide it, so the instruments of the mind supply either suggestions for the understanding or cautions.

III

Human knowledge and human power meet in one; for where the cause is not known the effect cannot be produced. Nature to be commanded must be obeyed; and that which in contemplation is as the cause is in operation as the rule.

IV

Towards the effecting of works, all that man can do is to put together or put asunder natural bodies. The rest is done by nature working within.

VI

It would be an unsound fancy and self-contradictory to expect that things which

have never yet been done can be done except by means which have never yet been tried.

XI

As the sciences which we now have do not help us in finding out new works, so neither does the logic which we now have help us in finding out new sciences.

XII

The logic now in use serves rather to fix and give stability to the errors which have their foundation in commonly received notions than to help the search after truth. So it does more harm than good.

XVIII

The discoveries which have hitherto been made in the sciences are such as lie close to vulgar notions, scarcely beneath the surface. In order to penetrate into the inner and further recesses of nature, it is necessary that both notions and axioms be derived from things by a more sure and guarded way; and that a method of intellectual operation be introduced altogether better and more certain.

XIX

There are and can be only two ways of searching into and discovering truth. The one flies from the senses and particulars to the most general axioms, and from these principles, the truth of which it takes for settled and immoveable, proceeds to judgment and to the discovery of middle axioms. And this way is now in fashion. The other derives axioms from the senses and particulars, rising by a gradual and unbroken ascent, so that it arrives at the most general axioms last of all. This is the true way, but as yet untried.

NOVUM ORGANUM, "The New Organon," in *The Works of Francis Bacon*, trans. J. Spedding. New ed. (London, 1875), IV, 47-50, 52-66, 69.

XXII

Both ways set out from the senses and particulars, and rest in the highest generalities; but the difference between them is infinite. For the one just glances at experiment and particulars in passing, the other dwells duly and orderly among them. The one, again, begins at once by establishing certain abstract and useless generalities, the other rises by gradual steps to that which is prior and better known in the order of nature.

XXXI

It is idle to expect any great advancement in science from the superinducing and engrafting of new things upon old. We must begin anew from the very foundations, unless we would revolve for ever in a circle with mean and contemptible progress.

XXXV

It was said by Borgia of the expedition of the French into Italy, that they came with chalk in their hands to mark out their lodgings, not with arms to force their way in. I in like manner would have my doctrine enter quietly into the minds that are fit and capable of receiving it; for confutations cannot be employed, when the difference is upon first principles and very notions and even upon forms of demonstration.

XXXVI

One method of delivery alone remains to us; which is simply this: we must lead men to the particulars themselves, and their series and order; while men on their side must force themselves for awhile to lay their notions by and begin to familiarise themselves with facts.

XXXVII

The doctrine of those who have denied that certainty could be attained at all, has some agreement with my way of proceeding at the first setting out; but they end in being infinitely separated and opposed. For the holders of that doctrine assert simply that nothing can be known; I also assert that not much can be known in nature by the way which is now in use. But then they go on to destroy the authority of the senses and understanding; whereas I proceed to devise and supply helps for the same.

XXXVIII

The idols and false notions which are now in possession of the human understanding, and have taken deep root therein, not only so beset men's minds that truth can hardly find entrance, but even after entrance is obtained, they will again in the very instauration of the sciences meet and trouble us, unless men being forewarned of the danger fortify themselves as far as may be against their assaults.

XXXIX

There are four classes of Idols which beset men's minds. To these for distinction's sake I have assigned names,—calling the first class *Idols of the Tribe;* the second, *Idols of the Cave;* the third, *Idols of the Market-place;* the fourth, *Idols of the Theatre.*

XL

The formation of ideas and axioms by true induction is no doubt the proper remedy to be applied for the keeping off and clearing away of idols. To point them out, however, is of great use; for the doctrine of Idols is to the Interpretation of Nature what the doctrine of the refutation of Sophisms is to common Logic.

XLI

The Idols of the Tribe have their foundation in human nature itself, and in the tribe or race of men. For it is a false assertion that the sense of man is the measure of things. On the contrary, all perceptions as well of the sense as of the mind are according to the measure of the individual and not according to the measure of the universe. And the human understanding is like a false mirror, which, receiving rays irregularly, distorts and discolours the nature of things by mingling its own nature with it.

XLII

The Idols of the Cave are the idols of the individual man. For every one (besides the errors common to human nature in general) has a cave or den of his own, which refracts and discolours the light of nature; owing either to his own proper and peculiar nature; or to his education and conversation with others; or to the reading of books, and the authority of those whom he esteems and admires; or to the differences of impressions, accordingly as they take place in a mind preoccupied and predisposed or in a mind indifferent and settled; or the like. So that the spirit of man (according as it is meted out to different individuals) is in fact a thing variable and full of perturbation, and governed as it were by chance. Whence it was well observed by Heraclitus that men look for sciences in their own lesser worlds, and not in the greater or common world.

XLIII

There are also Idols formed by the intercourse and association of men with each other, which I call Idols of the Marketplace, on account of the commerce and consort of men there. For it is by discourse that men associate; and words are imposed according to the apprehension of the vulgar. And therefore the ill and unfit choice of words wonderfully obstructs the understanding. Nor do the definitions or explanations wherewith in some things learned men are wont to guard and defend themselves, by any means set the matter right.

But words plainly force and overrule the understanding, and throw all into confusion, and lead men away into numberless empty controversies and idle fancies.

XLIV

Lastly, there are Idols which have immigrated into men's minds from the various dogmas of philosophies, and also from wrong laws of demonstration. These I call Idols of the Theatre; because in my judgment all the received systems are but so many stage-plays, representing worlds of their own creation after an unreal and scenic fashion. Nor is it only of the systems now in vogue, or only of the ancient sects and philosophies, that I speak; for many more plays of the same kind may yet be composed and in like artificial manner set forth; seeing that errors the most widely different have nevertheless causes for the most part alike. Neither again do I mean this only of entire systems, but also of many principles and axioms in science, which by tradition, credulity, and negligence have come to be received. But of these several kinds of Idols I must speak more largely and exactly, that the understanding may be duly cautioned.

XLV

The human understanding is of its own nature prone to suppose the existence of more order and regularity in the world than it finds. And though there be many things in nature which are singular and unmatched, yet it devises for them parallels and conjugates and relatives which do not exist. Hence the fiction that all celestial bodies move in perfect circles; spirals and dragons being (except in name) utterly rejected. Hence too the element of Fire with its orb is brought in, to make up the square with the other three which the sense perceives. Hence also the ratio of density of the so-called elements is arbitrarily fixed at ten to one. And so on of other dreams. And these fancies affect not dogmas only, but simple notions also.

XLVI

The human understanding when it has once adopted an opinion (either as being the received opinion or as being agreeable to itself) draws all things else to support and agree with it. And though there be a greater number and weight of instances to be found on the other side, yet these it either neglects and despises, or else by some distinction sets aside and rejects; in order that by this great and pernicious predetermination the authority of its former conclusions may remain inviolate. And therefore it was a good answer that was made by one who when they showed him hanging in a temple a picture of those who had paid their vows as having escaped shipwreck, and would have him say whether he did not now acknowledge the power of the gods,—"Aye," asked he again, "but where are they painted that were drowned after their vows?" And such is the way of all superstition, whether in astrology, dreams, omens, divine judgments, or the like; wherein men, having a delight in such vanities, mark the events where they are fulfilled, but where they fail, though this happens much oftener, neglect and pass them by. But with far more subtlety does this mischief insinuate itself into philosophy and the sciences; in which the first conclusion colours and brings into conformity with itself all that come after, though far sounder and better. Besides, independently of that delight and vanity which I have described, it is the peculiar and perpetual error of the human intellect to be more moved and excited by affirmatives than by negatives; whereas it ought properly to hold itself indifferently disposed towards both alike. Indeed in the establishment of any true axiom, the negative instance is the more forcible of the two.

XLVII

The human understanding is moved by those things most which strike and enter the mind simultaneously and suddenly, and so fill the imagination; and then it feigns and supposes all other things to be somehow, though it cannot see how, similar to those few things by which it is surrounded. But for that going to and fro to remote and heterogeneous instances, by which axioms are tried as in the fire, the intellect is altogether slow and unfit, unless it be forced thereto by severe laws and overruling authority.

XLVIII

The human understanding is unquiet; it cannot stop or rest, and still presses onward, but in vain. Therefore it is that we cannot conceive of any end or limit to the world; but always as of necessity it occurs to us that there is something beyond. Neither again can it be conceived how eternity has flowed down to the present day; for that distinction which is commonly received of infinity in time past and in time to come can by no means hold; for it would thence follow that one infinity is greater than another, and that infinity is wasting away and tending to become finite. The like subtlety arises touching the infinite divisibility of lines, from the same inability of thought to stop. But this inability interferes more mischievously in the discovery of causes: for although the most general principles in nature ought to be held merely positive, as they are discovered, and cannot with truth be referred to a cause; nevertheless the human understanding being unable to rest still seeks something prior in the order of nature. And then it is that in struggling towards that which is further off it falls back upon that which is more nigh at hand; namely, on final causes: which have relation clearly to the nature of man rather than to the nature of the universe; and from this source have strangely defiled philosophy. But he is no less an unskilled and shallow philosopher who seeks causes of that which is most general, than he who in things subordinate and subaltern omits to do so.

XLIX

The human understanding is no dry light, but receives an infusion from the will and affections; whence proceed sciences which may be called "sciences as one would." For what a man had rather were true he more readily believes. Therefore he rejects difficult things from impatience of research; sober things, because they narrow hope; the deeper things of nature, from superstition; the light of experience, from arrogance and pride, lest his mind should seem to be occupied with things mean and transitory; things not commonly believed, out of deference to the opinion of the vulgar. Numberless in short are the ways, and sometimes imperceptible, in which the affections colour and infect the understanding.

L

But by far the greatest hindrance and aberration of the human understanding proceeds from the dulness, incompetency, and deceptions of the senses; in that things which strike the sense outweigh things which do not immediately strike it, though they be more important. Hence it is that speculation commonly ceases where sight ceases; insomuch that of things invisible there is little or no observation. Hence all the working of the spirits inclosed in tangible bodies lies hid and unobserved of men. So also all the more subtle changes of form in the parts of coarser substances (which they commonly call alteration, though it is in truth local motion through exceedingly small spaces) is in like manner unobserved. And yet unless these two things just mentioned be searched out and brought to light, nothing

great can be achieved in nature, as far as the production of works is concerned. So again the essential nature of our common air, and of all bodies less dense than air (which are very many), is almost unknown. For the sense by itself is a thing infirm and erring; neither can instruments for enlarging or sharpening the senses do much; but all the truer kind of interpretation of nature is effected by instances and experiments fit and apposite; wherein the sense decides touching the experiment only, and the experiment touching the point in nature and the thing itself.

LI

The human understanding is of its own nature prone to abstractions and gives a substance and reality to things which are fleeting. But to resolve nature into abstractions is less to our purpose than to dissect her into parts; as did the school of Democritus, which went further into nature than the rest. Matter rather than forms should be the object of our attention, its configurations and changes of configuration, and simple action, and law of action or motion; for forms are figments of the human mind, unless you will call those laws of action forms.

LII

Such then are the idols which I call *Idols of the Tribe*; and which take their rise either from the homogeneity of the substance of the human spirit, or from its preoccupation, or from its narrowness, or from its restless motion, or from an infusion of the affections, or from the incompetency of the senses, or from the mode of impression.

LIII

The *Idols of the Cave* take their rise in the peculiar constitution, mental or bodily, of each individual; and also in education, habit, and accident. Of this kind there is a great number and variety; but I will instance those the pointing out of which contains the most important caution, and which have most effect in disturbing the clearness of the understanding.

LIV

Men become attached to certain particular sciences and speculations, either because they fancy themselves the authors and inventors thereof, or because they have bestowed the greatest pains upon them and become most habituated to them. But men of this kind, if they betake themselves to philosophy and contemplations of a general character, distort and colour them in obedience to their former fancies; a thing especially to be noticed in Aristotle, who made his natural philosophy a mere bond-servant to his logic, thereby rendering it contentious and well nigh useless. The race of chemists again out of a few experiments of the furnace have built up a fantastic philosophy, framed with reference to a few things; and Gilbert also, after he had employed himself most laboriously in the study and observation of the loadstone, proceeded at once to construct an entire system in accordance with his favourite subject.

LV

There is one principal and as it were radical distinction between different minds, in respect of philosophy and the sciences; which is this: that some minds are stronger and apter to mark the differences of things, others to mark their resemblances. The steady and acute mind can fix its contemplations and dwell and fasten on the subtlest distinctions: the lofty and discursive mind recognises and puts together the finest and most general resemblances. Both kinds however easily err in excess, by catching the one at gradations, the other at shadows.

LVI

There are found some minds given to an extreme admiration of antiquity, others to an extreme love and appetite for novelty: but few so duly tempered that they can hold the mean, neither carping at what has been well laid down by the ancients, nor despising what is well introduced by the moderns. This however turns to the great injury of the sciences and philosophy; since these affectations of antiquity and novelty are the humours of partisans rather than judgments; and truth is to be sought for not in the felicity of any age, which is an unstable thing, but in the light of nature and experience, which is eternal. These factions therefore must be adjured, and care must be taken that the intellect be not hurried by them into assent.

LVII

Contemplations of nature and of bodies in their simple form break up and distract the understanding, while contemplations of nature and bodies in their composition and configuration overpower and dissolve the understanding: a distinction well seen in the school of Leucippus and Democritus as compared with the other philosophies. For that school is so busied with the particles that it hardly attends to the structure; while the others are so lost in admiration of the structure that they do not penetrate to the simplicity of nature. These kinds of contemplation should therefore be alternated and taken by turns; that so the understanding may be rendered at once penetrating and comprehensive, and the inconveniences above mentioned, with the idols which proceed from them, may be avoided.

LVIII

Let such then be our provision and contemplative prudence for keeping off and dislodging the *Idols of the Cave*, which grow for the most part either out of the predominance of a favourite subject, or out of an excessive tendency to compare or to distinguish, or out of partiality for particular ages, or out of the largeness or minuteness of the objects contemplated. And generally let every student of nature take this as a rule,—that whatever his mind seizes and dwells upon with peculiar satisfaction is to be held in suspicion, and that so much the more care is to be taken in dealing with such questions to keep the understanding even and clear.

LIX

But the *Idols of the Market-place* are the most troublesome of all: idols which have crept into the understanding through the alliances of words and names. For men believe that their reason governs words; but it is also true that words react on the understanding; and this it is that has rendered philosophy and the sciences sophistical and inactive. Now words, being commonly framed and applied according to the capacity of the vulgar, follow those lines of division which are most obvious to the vulgar understanding. And whenever an understanding of greater acuteness or a more diligent observation would alter those lines to suit the true divisions of nature, words stand in the way and resist the change. Whence it comes to pass that the high and formal discussions of learned men end oftentimes in disputes about words and names; with which (according to the use and wisdom of the mathematicians) it would be more prudent to begin, and so by means of definitions reduce them to order. Yet even definitions cannot cure this evil in dealing with natural and material things; since the definitions themselves consist of words, and those words beget others: so that it is necessary to recur to individual instances, and those in due series and order; as I shall say presently when I come to the method and scheme for the formation of notions and axioms.

LX

The idols imposed by words on the understanding are of two kinds. They are either names of things which do not exist (for as there are things left unnamed through lack of observation, so likewise are there names which result from fantastic suppositions and to which nothing in reality corresponds), or they are names of things which exist, but yet confused and ill-defined, and hastily and irregularly derived from realities. Of the former kind are Fortune, the Prime Mover, Planetary Orbits, Element of Fire, and like fictions which owe their origin to false and idle theories. And this class of idols is more easily expelled, because to get rid of them it is only necessary that all theories should be steadily rejected and dismissed as obsolete.

But the other class, which springs out of a faulty and unskilful abstraction, is intricate and deeply rooted. Let us take for example such a word as *humid;* and see how far the several things which the word is used to signify agree with each other; and we shall find the word *humid* to be nothing else than a mark loosely and confusedly applied to denote a variety of actions which will not bear to be reduced to any constant meaning. For it both signifies that which easily spreads itself round any other body; and that which in itself is indeterminate and cannot solidise; and that which readily yields in every direction; and that which easily divides and scatters itself; and that which easily unites and collects itself; and that which readily flows and is put in motion; and that which readily clings to another body and wets it; and that which is easily reduced to a liquid, or being solid easily melts. Accordingly when you come to apply the word,—if you take it in one sense, flame is humid; if in another, air is not humid; if in another, fine dust is humid; if in another, glass is humid. So that it is easy to see that the notion is taken by abstraction only from water and common and ordinary liquids, without any due verification.

There are however in words certain degrees of distortion and error. One of the least faulty kinds is that of names of substances, especially of lowest species and well-deduced (for the notion of *chalk* and of *mud* is good, of *earth* bad); a more faulty kind is that of actions, as *to generate, to corrupt, to alter;* the most faulty is of qualities (except such as are the immediate objects of the sense) as *heavy, light, rare, dense,* and the like. Yet in all these cases some notions are of necessity a little better than others, in proportion to the greater variety of subjects that fall within the range of the human sense.

LXI

But the *Idols of the Theatre* are not innate, nor do they steal into the understanding secretly, but are plainly impressed and received into the mind from the play-books of philosophical systems and the perverted rules of demonstration. To attempt refutations in this case would be merely inconsistent with what I have already said: for since we agree neither upon principles nor upon demonstrations there is no place for argument. And this is so far well, inasmuch as it leaves the honour of the ancients untouched. For they are no wise disparaged—the question between them and me being only as to the way. For as the saying is, the lame man who keeps the right road outstrips the runner who takes a wrong one. Nay it is obvious that when a man runs the wrong way, the more active and swift he is the further he will go astray.

But the course I propose for the discovery of sciences is such as leaves but little to the acuteness and strength of wits, but places all wits and understandings nearly on a level. For as in the drawing of a straight line or a perfect circle, much depends on the steadiness and practice of the hand, if it be done by aim of hand only, but if with the aid of rule or compass, little or nothing; so is it exactly with my plan. But though particular confutations would be of no avail, yet touching the sects and general divisions of such systems I must say something; something also touching the external signs which show that they are unsound; and finally something touching the causes of such great infelicity and of such lasting and general agreement in error; that so the access to truth may be made less difficult, and the human understanding may the more willingly submit to its purgation and dismiss its idols.

LXII

Idols of the Theatre, or of *Systems,* are many, and there can be and perhaps will be yet many more. For were it not that now for many ages men's minds have been busied with religion and theology; and were it not that civil governments, especially monarchies, have been averse to such novelties, even in matters speculative; so that men labour therein to the peril and harming of their fortunes,—not only unrewarded, but exposed also to contempt and envy; doubtless there would have arisen many other philosophical sects like to those which in great variety flourished once among the Greeks. For as on the phenomena of the heavens many hypotheses may be constructed, so likewise (and more also) many various dogmas may be set up and established on the phenomena of philosophy. And in the plays of this philosophical theatre you may observe the same thing which is found in the theatre of the poets, that stories invented for the stage are more compact and elegant, and more as one would wish them to be, than true stories out of history.

In general however there is taken for the material of philosophy either a great deal out of a few things, or a very little out of many things; so that on both sides philosophy is based on too narrow a foundation of experiment and natural history, and decides on the authority of too few cases. For the Rational School of philosophers snatches from experience a variety of common instances, neither duly ascertained nor diligently examined and weighed, and leaves all the rest to meditation and agitation of wit.

There is also another class of philosophers, who having bestowed much diligent and careful labour on a few experiments, have thence made bold to educe and construct systems; wresting all other facts in a strange fashion to conformity therewith.

And there is yet a third class, consisting of those who out of faith and veneration mix their philosophy with theology and traditions; among whom the vanity of some has gone so far aside as to seek the origin of sciences among spirits and genii. So that this parent stock of errors—this false philosophy—is of three kinds; the Sophistical, the Empirical, and the Superstitious.

LXIII

The most conspicuous example of the first class was Aristotle, who corrupted natural philosophy by his logic: fashioning the world out of categories; assigning to the human soul, the noblest of substances, a genus from words of the second intention; doing the business of density and rarity (which is to make bodies of greater or less dimensions, that is, occupy greater or less spaces), by the frigid distinction of act and power; asserting that single bodies have each a single and proper motion, and that if they participate in any other, then this results from an external cause;

and imposing countless other arbitrary restrictions on the nature of things; being always more solicitous to provide an answer to the question and affirm something positive in words, than about the inner truth of things; a failing best shown when his philosophy is compared with other systems of note among the Greeks. For the Homoeomera of Anaxagoras; the Atoms of Leucippus and Democritus; the Heaven and Earth of Parmenides; the Strife and Friendship of Empedocles; Heraclitus's doctrine how bodies are resolved into the indifferent nature of fire, and remoulded into solids; have all of them some taste of the natural philosopher,—some savour of the nature of things, and experience, and bodies; whereas in the physics of Aristotle you hear hardly anything but the words of logic; which in his metaphysics also, under a more imposing name, and more forsooth as a realist than a nominalist, he has handled over again. Nor let any weight be given to the fact, that in his books on animals and his problems, and other of his treatises, there is frequent dealing with experiments. For he had come to his conclusion before; he did not consult experience, as he should have done, in order to the framing of his decisions and axioms; but having first determined the question according to his will, he then resorts to experience, and bending her into conformity with his placets leads her about like a captive in a procession; so that even on this count he is more guilty than his modern followers, the schoolmen, who have abandoned experience altogether.

LXIV

But the Empirical school of philosophy gives birth to dogmas more deformed and monstrous than the Sophistical or Rational school. For it has its foundations not in the light of common notions, (which though it be a faint and superficial light, is yet in a manner universal, and has reference to many things), but in the narrowness and darkness of a few experiments. To those therefore who are daily busied with these experiments, and have infected their imagination with them, such a philosophy seems probable and all but certain; to all men else incredible and vain. Of this there is a notable instance in the alchemists and their dogmas; though it is hardly to be found elsewhere in these times, except perhaps in the philosophy of Gilbert. Nevertheless with regard to philosophies of this kind there is one caution not to be omitted; for I foresee that if ever men are roused by my admonitions to betake themselves seriously to experiment and bid farewell to sophistical doctrines, then indeed through the premature hurry of the understanding to leap or fly to universals and principles of things, great danger may be apprehended from philosophies of this kind; against which evil we ought even now to prepare.

LXV

But the corruption of philosophy by superstition and an admixture of theology is far more widely spread, and does the greatest harm, whether to entire systems or to their parts. For the human understanding is obnoxious to the influence of the imagination no less than to the influence of common notions. For the contentious and sophistical kind of philosophy ensnares the understanding; but this kind, being fanciful and tumid and half poetical, misleads it more by flattery. For there is in man an ambition of the understanding, no less than of the will, especially in high and lofty spirits.

Of this kind we have among the Greeks a striking example in Pythagoras, though he united with it a coarser and more cumbrous superstition; another in Plato and his school, more dangerous and subtle. It shows itself likewise in parts of other philosophies, in the introduction of abstract forms and final causes and first causes, with the omission in most cases of causes intermediate, and the like. Upon this point the greatest caution should be used. For nothing is so mischievous as the apotheosis of error; and it is a very plague of the understanding for vanity to become the object of veneration. Yet in this vanity some of the moderns have with extreme levity indulged so far as to attempt to found a system of natural philosophy on the first chapter of Genesis, on the book of Job, and other parts of the sacred writings; seeking for the dead among the living: which also makes the inhibition and repression of it the more important, because from this unwholesome mixture of things human and divine there arises not only a fantastic philosophy but also an heretical religion. Very meet it is therefore that we be sober-minded, and give to faith that only which is faith's.

LXVIII

So much concerning the several classes of Idols, and their equipage: all of which must be renounced and put away with a fixed and solemn determination, and the understanding thoroughly freed and cleansed; the entrance into the kingdom of man, founded on the sciences, being not much other than the entrance into the kingdom of heaven, whereinto none may enter except as a little child.

René Descartes

Unlike his contemporary, Francis Bacon, who tried to break completely with the medieval scholastic intellectual tradition, René Descartes (1596-1650) thought it possible to find a basis for traditional beliefs by using the methods of scientific inquiry. His attempt to combine the old with the new is clearly shown in the selection that follows. In it, after severely criticizing his own scholastic education, he gives a list of rules for the discovery of scientific truth. Through the application of these rules he is then able, by means of deductive reasoning, to prove the existence of God. Descartes was, thus, a transitional figure, living partly in the old intellectual world of the scholastics and partly in the new world of seventeenth-century science.

Despite his unwillingness to break completely with the past, Descartes was one of the most important of early modern scientists. In mathematics he was the founder of analytic geometry. And in physics he developed an explanation of the universe which for a century rivaled Newton's theory of universal gravitation. Although Descartes engaged in experimentation, he did not, like Bacon, believe that induction was the most fruitful scientific method. Instead, he was an advocate of the deductive method, his preference being undoubtedly a result of his successful use of deduction in mathematics.

DISCOURSE ON METHOD

Part One

Good Sense is, of all things among men, the most equally distributed; for every one thinks himself so abundantly provided with it, that those even who are the most difficult to satisfy in everything else, do not usually desire a larger measure of this quality than they already possess. And in this it is not likely that all are mistaken: the conviction is rather to be held as testifying that the power of judging aright and of distinguishing Truth from Error, which is properly what is called Good Sense or Reason, is by nature equal in all men; and that the diversity of our opinions, consequently, does not arise from some being endowed with a larger share of Reason than others, but solely from this, that we conduct our thoughts along different ways, and do not fix our attention on the same objects. For to be possessed of a vigorous mind is not enough; the prime requisite is rightly to apply it. The greatest minds, as they are capable of the highest excellencies, are open likewise to the greatest aberrations; and those who travel

DISCOURSE ON METHOD *of Rightly Conducting the Reason and Seeking Truth in the Sciences*, René Descartes, trans. J. Veitch. 4th ed. (Edinburgh, 1870), pp. 45-64, 74-82.

very slowly may yet make far greater progress, provided they keep always to the straight road, than those who, while they run, forsake it.

For myself, I have never fancied my mind to be in any respect more perfect than those of the generality; on the contrary, I have often wished that I were equal to some others in promptitude of thought, or in clearness and distinctness of imagination, or in fulness and readiness of memory. And besides these, I know of no other qualities that contribute to the perfection of the mind; for as to the Reason or Sense, inasmuch as it is that alone which constitutes us men, and distinguishes us from the brutes, I am disposed to believe that it is to be found complete in each individual; and on this point to adopt the common opinion of philosophers, who say that the difference of greater and less holds only among the *accidents*, and not among the *forms* or *natures* of *individuals* of the same *species*.

I will not hesitate, however, to avow my belief that it has been my singular good fortune to have very early in life fallen in with certain tracks which have conducted me to considerations and maxims, of which I have formed a Method that gives me the means, as I think, of gradually augmenting my knowledge, and of raising it by little and little to the highest point which the mediocrity of my talents and the brief duration of my life will permit me to reach. For I have already reaped from it such fruits that, although I have been accustomed to think lowly enough of myself, and although when I look with the eye of a philosopher at the varied courses and pursuits of mankind at large, I find scarcely one which does not appear vain and useless, I nevertheless derive the highest satisfaction from the progress I conceive myself to have already made in the search after truth, and cannot help entertaining such expectations of the future as

to believe that if, among the occupations of men as men, there is any one really excellent and important, it is that which I have chosen.

After all, it is possible I may be mistaken; and it is but a little copper and glass, perhaps, that I take for gold and diamonds. I know how very liable we are to delusion in what relates to ourselves, and also how much the judgements of our friends are to be suspected when given in our favour. But I shall endeavour in this Discourse to describe the paths I have followed, and to delineate my life as in a picture, in order that each one may be able to judge of them for himself, and that in the general opinion entertained of them, as gathered from current report, I myself may have a new help towards instruction to be added to those I have been in the habit of employing.

My present design, then, is not to teach the Method which each ought to follow for the right conduct of his Reason, but solely to describe the way in which I have endeavoured to conduct my own. They who set themselves to give precepts must of course regard themselves as possessed of greater skill than those to whom they prescribe; and if they err in the slightest particular, they subject themselves to censure. But as this Tract is put forth merely as a history, or, if you will, as a tale, in which, amid some examples worthy of imitation, there will be found, perhaps, as many more which it were advisable not to follow, I hope it will prove useful to some without being hurtful to any, and that my openness will find some favour with all.

From my childhood, I have been familiar with letters; and as I was given to believe that by their help a clear and certain knowledge of all that is useful in life might be acquired, I was ardently desirous of instruction. But as soon as I had finished the entire course of study, at the close of which it is customary to be admitted into the order of the learned, I completely changed my opinion. For I found myself involved in so many doubts and errors, that I was convinced that I had advanced no farther in all my attempts at learning, than the discovery at every turn of my own ignorance. And yet I was studying at one of the most celebrated Schools in Europe, in which I thought there must be learned men, if such were anywhere to be found. I had been taught all that others learned there; and not contented with the sciences actually taught us, I had, in addition, read all the books that had fallen into my hands, treating of such branches as are esteemed the most curious and rare. I knew the judgement which others had formed of me; and I did not find that I was considered inferior to my fellows, although there were among them some who were already marked out to fill the places of our instructors. And, in fine, our age appeared to me as flourishing, and as fertile in powerful minds as any preceding one. I was thus led to take the liberty of judging of all other men by myself, and of concluding that there was no science in existence that was of such a nature as I had previously been given to believe.

I still continued, however, to hold in esteem the studies of the Schools. I was aware that the Languages taught in them are necessary to the understanding of the writings of the ancients; that the grace of Fable stirs the mind; that the memorable deeds of History elevate it; and, if read with discretion, aid in forming the judgement; that the perusal of all excellent books is, as it were, to interview with the noblest men of past ages, who have written them, and even a studied interview, in which are discovered to us only their choicest thoughts; that Eloquence has incomparable force and beauty; that Poesy has its ravishing graces and delights; that in the Mathematics there are many refined discoveries eminently suited to gratify

the inquisitive, as well as further all the arts and lessen the labour of man; that numerous highly useful precepts and exhortations to virtue are contained in treatises on Morals; that Theology points out the path to heaven; that Philosophy affords the means of discoursing with an appearance of truth on all matters, and commands the admiration of the more simple; that Jurisprudence, Medicine, and the other Sciences, secure for their cultivators honours and riches; and, in fine, that it is useful to bestow some attention upon all, even upon those abounding the most in superstition and error, that we may be in a position to determine their real value, and guard against being deceived.

But I believed that I had already given sufficient time to Languages, and likewise to the reading of the writings of the ancients, to their Histories and Fables. For to hold converse with those of other ages and to travel, are almost the same thing. It is useful to know something of the manners of different nations, that we may be enabled to form a more correct judgment regarding our own, and be prevented from thinking that everything contrary to our customs is ridiculous and irrational,—a conclusion usually come to by those whose experience has been limited to their own country. On the other hand, when too much time is occupied in travelling, we become strangers to our native country; and the over curious in the customs of the past are generally ignorant of those of the present. Besides, fictitious narratives lead us to imagine the possibility of many events that are impossible; and even the most faithful histories, if they do not wholly misrepresent matters, or exaggerate their importance to render the account of them more worthy of perusal, omit, at least, almost always the meanest and least striking of the attendant circumstances; hence it happens that the remainder does not represent the truth, and that such as regulate their conduct by examples drawn from this source, are apt to fall into the extravagances of the knight-errants of Romance, and to entertain projects that exceed their powers.

I esteemed Eloquence highly, and was in raptures with Poesy; but I thought that both were gifts of nature rather than fruits of study. Those in whom the faculty of Reason is predominant, and who most skillfully dispose their thoughts with a view to render them clear and intelligible, are always the best able to persuade others of the truth of what they lay down, though they should speak only in the language of Lower Brittany, and be wholly ignorant of the rules of Rhetoric; and those whose minds are stored with the most agreeable fancies, and who can give expression to them with the greatest embellishment and harmony, are still the best poets, though unacquainted with the Art of Poetry.

I was especially delighted with the Mathematics, on account of the certitude and evidence of their reasonings: but I had not as yet a precise knowledge of their true use; and thinking that they but contributed to the advancement of the mechanical arts, I was astonished that foundations, so strong and solid, should have had no loftier superstructure reared on them. On the other hand, I compared the disquisitions of the ancient Moralists to very towering and magnificent palaces with no better foundation than sand and mud: they laud the virtues very highly, and exhibit them as estimable far above anything on earth; but they give us no adequate criterion of virtue, and frequently that which they designate with so fine a name is but apathy, or pride, or despair, or parricide.

I revered our Theology, and aspired as much as any one to reach heaven: but being given assuredly to understand that the way is not less open to the most ignorant than to the most learned, and that the revealed truths which lead to heaven are above our comprehension, I did not presume to subject them to the impotency of my Reason; and I thought that in order competently to undertake their examination, there was need of some special help from heaven, and of being more than man.

Of Philosophy I will say nothing, except that when I saw that it had been cultivated for many ages by the most distinguished men, and that yet there is not a single matter within its sphere which is not still in dispute, and nothing, therefore, which is above doubt, I did not presume to anticipate that my success would be greater in it than that of others; and further, when I considered the number of conflicting opinions touching a single matter that may be upheld by learned men, while there can be but one true, I reckoned as wellnigh false all that was only probable.

As to the other Sciences, inasmuch as these borrow their principles from Philosophy, I judged that no solid superstructures could be reared on foundations so infirm; and neither the honour nor the gain held out by them was sufficient to determine me to their cultivation: for I was not, thank heaven, in a condition which compelled me to make merchandise of Science for the bettering of my fortune; and though I might not profess to scorn glory as a Cynic, I yet made very slight account of that honour which I hoped to acquire only through fictitious titles. And, in fine, of false Sciences I thought I knew the worth sufficiently to escape being deceived by the professions of an alchemist, the predictions of an astrologer, the impostures of a magician, or by the artifices and boasting of any of those who profess to know things of which they are ignorant.

For these reasons, as soon as my age permitted me to pass from under the control of my instructors, I entirely abandoned the study of letters, and resolved no longer to seek any other science than the knowledge of myself, or of the great book of the world. I spent the remainder of my youth in travelling, in visiting courts and armies, in holding intercourse with men of different dispositions and ranks, in collecting varied experience, in proving myself in the different situations into which fortune threw me, and, above all, in making such reflection on the matter of my experience as to secure my improvement. For it occurred to me that I should find much more truth in the reasonings of each individual with reference to the affairs in which he is personally interested, and the issue of which must presently punish him if he has judged amiss, than in those conducted by a man of letters in his study, regarding speculative matters that are of no practical moment, and followed by no consequences to himself, farther, perhaps, than that they foster his vanity the better the more remote they are from common sense; requiring, as they must in this case, the exercise of greater ingenuity and art to render them probable. In addition, I had always a most earnest desire to know how to distinguish the true from the false, in order that I might be able clearly to discriminate the right path in life, and proceed in it with confidence.

It is true that, while busied only in considering the manners of other men, I found here, too, scarce any ground for settled conviction, and remarked hardly less contradiction among them than in the opinions of the philosophers. So that the greatest advantage I derived from the study consisted in this, that, observing many things which, however extravagant and ridiculous to our apprehension, are yet by common consent received and approved by other great nations, I learned to entertain too decided a belief in regard to nothing of the truth of which I had been persuaded merely by example and custom: and thus I

gradually extricated myself from many errors powerful enough to darken our Natural Intelligence, and incapacitate us in great measure from listening to Reason. But after I had been occupied several years in thus studying the book of the world, and in essaying to gather some experience, I at length resolved to make myself an object of study, and to employ all the powers of my mind in choosing the paths I ought to follow; an undertaking which was accompanied with greater success than it would have been had I never quitted my country or my books.

Part Two

I was then in Germany, attracted thither by the wars in that country, which have not yet been brought to a termination; and as I was returning to the army from the coronation of the Emperor, the setting in of winter arrested me in a locality where, as I found no society to interest me, and was besides fortunately undisturbed by any cares or passions, I remained the whole day in seclusion, with full opportunity to occupy my attention with my own thoughts. Of these one of the very first that occurred to me was, that there is seldom so much perfection in works composed of many separate parts, upon which different hands have been employed, as in those completed by a single master. Thus it is observable that the buildings which a single architect has planned and executed, are generally more elegant and commodious than those which several have attempted to improve, by making old walls serve for purposes for which they were not originally built. Thus also, those ancient cities which, from being at first only villages, have become, in course of time, large towns, are usually but ill laid out compared with the regularly constructed towns which a professional architect has freely planned on an open plain; so that although the several buildings of the former may often equal or surpass in beauty those of the latter, yet when one observes their indiscriminate juxtaposition, there a large one and here a small, and the consequent crookedness and irregularity of the streets, one is disposed to allege that chance rather than any human will guided by reason, must have led to such an arrangement. And if we consider that nevertheless there have been at all times certain officers whose duty it was to see that private buildings contributed to public ornament, the difficulty of reaching high perfection with but the materials of others to operate on, will be readily acknowledged. In the same way I fancied that those nations which, starting from a semi-barbarous state and advancing to civilisation by slow degrees, have had their laws successively determined, and, as it were, forced upon them simply by experience of the hurtfulness of particular crimes and disputes, would by this process come to be possessed of less perfect institutions than those which, from the commencement of their association as communities, have followed the appointments of some wise legislator. It is thus quite certain that the constitution of the true religion, the ordinances of which are derived from God, must be incomparably superior to that of every other. And, to speak of human affairs, I believe that the past pre-eminence of Sparta was due not to the goodness of each of its laws in particular, for many of these were very strange, and even opposed to good morals, but to the circumstance that, originated by a single individual, they all tended to a single end. In the same way I thought that the sciences contained in books, (such of them at least as are made up of probable reasonings, without demonstrations), composed as they are of the opinions of many different individuals massed together, are farther removed from truth than the simple inferences which a man of good sense using his natural and unprejudiced judgment draws respecting the matters of his experience. And because we have all to pass through a state of infancy to manhood, and have been of necessity, for a length of time, governed by our desires and preceptors, (whose dictates were frequently conflicting, while neither perhaps always counselled us for the best), I farther concluded that it is almost impossible that our judgments can be so correct or solid as they would have been, had our Reason been mature from the moment of our birth, and had we always been guided by it alone.

It is true, however, that it is not customary to pull down all the houses of a town with the single design of rebuilding them differently, and thereby rendering the streets more handsome; but it often happens that a private individual takes down his own with the view of erecting it anew, and that people are even sometimes constrained to this when their houses are in danger of falling from age, or when the foundations are insecure. With this before me by way of example, I was persuaded that it would indeed be preposterous for a private individual to think of reforming a state by fundamentally changing it throughout, and overturning it in order to set it up amended; and the same I thought was true of any similar project for reforming the body of the Sciences, or the order of teaching them established in the Schools: but as for the opinions which up to that time I had embraced, I thought that I could not do better than resolve at once to sweep them wholly away, that I might afterwards be in a position to admit either others more correct, or even perhaps the same when they had undergone the scrutiny of Reason. I firmly believed that in this way I should much better succeed in the conduct of my life, than if I built only upon old foundations, and leant upon principles which, in my youth, I had taken upon trust. For although I recognised various difficulties in this undertaking, these were not, however, without remedy, nor once to be compared with such as attend the slightest reformation in public affairs. Large bodies, if once overthrown, are with great difficulty set up again, or even kept erect when once seriously shaken, and the fall of such is always disastrous. Then if there are any imperfections in the constitutions of states, (and that many such exist the diversity of constitutions is alone sufficient to assure us), custom has without doubt materially smoothed their inconveniencies, and has even managed to steer altogether clear of, or insensibly corrected a number which sagacity could not have provided against with equal effect; and, in fine, the defects are almost always more tolerable than the change necessary for their removal; in the same manner that highways which wind among mountains, by being much frequented, become gradually so smooth and commodious, that it is much better to follow them than to seek a straighter path by climbing over the tops of rocks and descending to the bottoms of precipices.

Hence it is that I cannot in any degree approve of those restless and busy meddlers who, called neither by birth nor fortune to take part in the management of public affairs, are yet always projecting reforms; and if I thought that this Tract contained aught which might justify the suspicion that I was a victim of such folly, I would by no means permit its publication. I have never contemplated anything higher than the reformation of my own opinions, and basing them on a foundation wholly my own. And although my own satisfaction with my work has led me to present here a draft of it, I do not by any means therefore recommend to every one else to make a similar attempt. Those whom God has endowed with a larger measure of genius will entertain, perhaps, designs still more exalted; but for the many I am much afraid lest even the present undertaking be more

than they can safely venture to imitate. The single design to strip one's self of all past beliefs is one that ought not to be taken by every one. The majority of men is composed of two classes, for neither of which would this be at all a befitting resolution: in the *first* place, of those who with more than a due confidence in their own powers, are precipitate in their judgments and want the patience requisite for orderly and circumspect thinking; whence it happens, that if men of this class once take the liberty to doubt of their accustomed opinions, and quit the beaten highway, they will never be able to thread the byeway that would lead them by a shorter course, and will lose themselves and continue to wander for life; in the *second* place, of those who, possessed of sufficient sense or modesty to determine that there are others who excel them in the power of discriminating between truth and error, and by whom they may be instructed, ought rather to content themselves with the opinions of such than trust for more correct to their own Reason.

For my own part, I should doubtless have belonged to the latter class, had I received instruction from but one master, or had I never known the diversities of opinion that from time immemorial have prevailed among men of the greatest learning. But I had become aware, even so early as during my college life, that no opinion, however absurd and incredible, can be imagined, which has not been maintained by some one of the philosophers; and afterwards in the course of my travels I remarked that all those whose opinions are decidedly repugnant to ours are not on that account barbarians and savages, but on the contrary that many of these nations make an equally good, if not a better, use of their Reason than we do. I took into account also the very different character which a person brought up from infancy in France or Germany exhibits, from that which, with the same mind originally, this individual would have possessed had he lived always among the Chinese or with savages, and the circumstance that in dress itself the fashion which had pleased us ten years ago, and which may again, perhaps, be received into favour before ten years have gone, appears to us at this moment extravagant and ridiculous. I was thus led to infer that the ground of our opinions is far more custom and example than any certain knowledge. And, finally, although such be the ground of our opinions, I remarked that a plurality of suffrages is no guarantee of truth where it is at all of difficult discovery, as in such cases it is much more likely that it will be found by one than by many. I could, however, select from the crowd no one whose opinions seemed worthy of preference, and thus I found myself constrained, as it were, to use my own Reason in the conduct of my life.

But like one walking alone and in the dark, I resolved to proceed so slowly and with such circumspection, that if I did not advance far, I would at least guard against falling. I did not even choose to dismiss summarily any of the opinions that had crept into my belief without having been introduced by Reason, but first of all took sufficient time carefully to satisfy myself of the general nature of the task I was setting myself, and ascertain the true Method by which to arrive at the knowledge of whatever lay within the compass of my powers.

Among the branches of Philosophy, I had, at an earlier period, given some attention to Logic, and among those of the Mathematics to Geometrical Analysis and Algebra,—three Arts or Sciences which ought, as I conceived, to contribute something to my design. But, on examination, I found that, as for Logic, its syllogisms and the majority of its other precepts are of avail rather in the communication of what we already know, or even as the Art of Lully,

in speaking without judgment of things of which we are ignorant, than in the investigation of the unknown; and although this Science contains indeed a number of correct and very excellent precepts, there are, nevertheless, so many others, and these either injurious or superfluous, mingled with the former, that it is almost quite as difficult to effect a severance of the true from the false as it is to extract a Diana or a Minerva from a rough block of marble. Then as to the Analysis of the ancients and the Algebra of the moderns, besides that they embrace only matters highly abstract, and, to appearance, of no use, the former is so exclusively restricted to the consideration of figures, that it can exercise the Understanding only on condition of greatly fatiguing the Imagination; and, in the latter, there is so complete a subjection to certain rules and formulas, that there results an art full of confusion and obscurity calculated to embarrass, instead of a science fitted to cultivate the mind. By these considerations I was induced to seek some other Method which would comprise the advantages of the three and be exempt from their defects. And as a multitude of laws often only hampers justice, so that a state is best governed when, with few laws, these are rigidly administered; in like manner, instead of the great number of precepts of which Logic is composed, I believed that the four following would prove perfectly sufficient for me, provided I took the firm and unwavering resolution never in a single instance to fail in observing them.

The *first* was never to accept anything for true which I did not clearly know to be such; that is to say, carefully to avoid precipitancy and prejudice, and to comprise nothing more in my judgment than what was presented to my mind so clearly and distinctly as to exclude all ground of doubt.

The *second*, to divide each of the difficulties under examination into as many parts as possible, and as might be necessary for its adequate solution.

The *third*, to conduct my thoughts in such order that, by commencing with objects the simplest and easiest to know, I might ascend by little and little, and, as it were, step by step, to the knowledge of the more complex; assigning in thought a certain order even to those objects which in their own nature do not stand in a relation of antecedence and sequence.

And the *last*, in every case to make enumerations so complete, and reviews so general, that I might be assured that nothing was omitted.

The long chains of simple and easy reasonings by means of which geometers are accustomed to reach the conclusions of their most difficult demonstrations, had led me to imagine that all things, to the knowledge of which man is competent, are mutually connected in the same way, and that there is nothing so far removed from us as to be beyond our reach, or so hidden that we cannot discover it, provided only we abstain from accepting the false for the true, and always preserve in our thoughts the order necessary for the deduction of one truth from another. And I had little difficulty in determining the objects with which it was necessary to commence, for I was already persuaded that it must be with the simplest and easiest to know, and, considering that of all those who have hitherto sought truth in the Sciences, the mathematicians alone have been able to find any demonstrations, that is, any certain and evident reasons, I did not doubt but that such must have been the rule of their investigations. I resolved to commence, therefore, with the examination of the simplest objects, not anticipating, however, from this any other advantage than that to be found in accustoming my mind to the love and nourishment of truth, and to a distaste for all

such reasonings as were unsound. But I had no intention on that account of attempting to master all the particular Sciences commonly denominated Mathematics: but observing that, however different their objects, they all agree in considering only the various relations or proportions subsisting among those objects, I thought it best for my purpose to consider these proportions in the most general form possible, without referring them to any objects in particular, except such as would most facilitate the knowledge of them, and without by any means restricting them to these, that afterwards I might thus be the better able to apply them to every other class of objects to which they are legitimately applicable. Perceiving further, that in order to understand these relations I should sometimes have to consider them one by one, and sometimes only to bear them in mind, or embrace them in the aggregate, I thought that, in order the better to consider them individually, I should view them as subsisting between straight lines, than which I could find no objects more simple, or capable of being more distinctly represented to my imagination and senses; and on the other hand, that in order to retain them in the memory, or embrace an aggregate of many, I should express them by certain characters the briefest possible. In this way I believed that I could borrow all that was best both in Geometrical Analysis and in Algebra, and correct all the defects of the one by help of the other.

And, in point of fact, the accurate observance of these few precepts gave me, I take the liberty of saying, such ease in unravelling all the questions embraced in these two sciences, that in the two or three months I devoted to their examination, not only did I reach solutions of questions I had formerly deemed exceedingly difficult, but even as regards questions of the solution of which I continued ignorant, I was enabled, as it appeared to me, to determine the means whereby, and the extent to which, a solution was possible; results attributable to the circumstance that I commenced with the simplest and most general truths, and that thus each truth discovered was a rule available in the discovery of subsequent ones. Nor in this perhaps shall I appear too vain, if it be considered that, as the truth on any particular point is one, whoever apprehends the truth, knows all that on that point can be known. The child, for example, who has been instructed in the elements of Arithmetic, and has made a particular addition, according to rule, may be assured that he has found, with respect to the sum of the numbers before him, all that in this instance is within the reach of human genius. Now, in conclusion, the Method which teaches adherence to the true order, and an exact enumeration of all the conditions of the thing sought includes all that gives certitude to the rules of Arithmetic.

But the chief ground of my satisfaction with this Method, was the assurance I had of thereby exercising my reason in all matters, if not with absolute perfection, at least with the greatest attainable by me: besides, I was conscious that by its use my mind was becoming gradually habituated to clearer and more distinct conceptions of its objects; and I hoped also, from not having restricted this Method to any particular matter, to apply it to the difficulties of the other Sciences, with not less success than to those of Algebra. I should not, however, on this account have ventured at once on the examination of all the difficulties of the Sciences which presented themselves to me, for this would have been contrary to the order prescribed in the Method, but observing that the knowledge of such is dependent on principles borrowed from Philosophy, in which I found nothing certain, I thought it necessary first of all to endeavour to establish its principles. And because I observed, besides, that an inquiry of this kind was of all others of the greatest moment, and one in which precipitancy and anticipation in judgment were most to be dreaded, I thought that I ought not to approach it till I had reached a more mature age, (being at that time but twenty-three), and had first of all employed much of my time in preparation for the work, as well by eradicating from my mind all the erroneous opinions I had up to that moment accepted, as by amassing variety of experience to afford materials for my reasonings, and by continually exercising myself in my chosen Method with a view to increased skill in its application.

. . .

Part Four

I am in doubt as to the propriety of making my first meditations in the place above mentioned matter of discourse; for these are so metaphysical, and so uncommon, as not, perhaps, to be acceptable to every one. And yet, that it may be determined whether the foundations that I have laid are sufficiently secure, I find myself in a measure constrained to advert to them. I had long before remarked that, in relation to practice, it is sometimes necessary to adopt, as if above doubt, opinions which we discern to be highly uncertain, as has been already said; but as I then desired to give my attention solely to the search after truth, I thought that a procedure exactly the opposite was called for, and that I ought to reject as absolutely false all opinions in regard to which I could suppose the least ground for doubt, in order to ascertain whether after that there remained aught in my belief that was wholly indubitable. Accordingly, seeing that our senses sometimes deceive us, I was willing to suppose that there existed nothing really such as they presented to us; and because some men err in reasoning, and fall into paralogisms, even on the simplest matters of Geometry, I, convinced that I was as open to error as any other, rejected as false all the reasonings I had hitherto taken for demonstrations; and finally, when I considered that the very same thoughts (presentations) which we experience when awake may also be experienced when we are asleep, while there is at that time not one of them true, I supposed that all the objects (presentations) that had ever entered into my mind when awake, had in them no more truth than the illusions of my dreams. But immediately upon this I observed that, whilst I thus wished to think that all was false, it was absolutely necessary that I, who thus thought, should be somewhat; and as I observed that this truth, *I think, hence I am,* was so certain and of such evidence, that no ground of doubt, however extravagant, could be alleged by the Sceptics capable of shaking it, I concluded that I might, without scruple, accept it as the first principle of the Philosophy of which I was in search.

In the next place, I attentively examined what I was, and as I observed that I could suppose that I had no body, and that there was no world nor any place in which I might be; but that I could not therefore suppose that I was not; and that, on the contrary, from the very circumstance that I thought to doubt of the truth of other things, it most clearly and certainly followed that I was; while, on the other hand, if I had only ceased to think, although all the other objects which I had ever imagined had been in reality existent, I would have had no reason to believe that I existed; I thence concluded that I was a substance whose whole essence or nature consists only in thinking, and which, that it may exist, has need of no place, nor is dependent on any material thing; so that "I," that is to say, the mind by which I am what I am, is wholly distinct from the body, and is even

more easily known than the latter, and is such, that although the latter were not, it would still continue to be all that it is.

After this I inquired in general into what is essential to the truth and certainty of a proposition; for since I had discovered one which I knew to be true, I thought that I must likewise be able to discover the ground of this certitude. And as I observed that in the words *I think, hence I am,* there is nothing at all which gives me assurance of their truth beyond this, that I see very clearly that in order to think it is necessary to exist, I concluded that I might take, as a general rule, the principle, that all the things which we very clearly and distinctly conceive are true, only observing, however, that there is some difficulty in rightly determining the objects which we distinctly conceive.

In the next place, from reflecting on the circumstance that I doubted, and that consequently my being was not wholly perfect, (for I clearly saw that it was a greater perfection to know than to doubt), I was led to inquire whence I had learned to think of something more perfect than myself; and I clearly recognised that I must hold this notion from some Nature which in reality was more perfect. As for the thoughts of many other objects external to me, as of the sky, the earth, light, heat, and a thousand more, I was less at a loss to know whence these came; for since I remarked in them nothing which seemed to render them superior to myself, I could believe that, if these were true, they were dependencies on my own nature, in so far as it possessed a certain perfection, and, if they were false, that I held them from nothing, that is to say, that they were in me because of a certain imperfection of my nature. But this could not be the case with the idea of a Nature more perfect than myself; for to receive it from nothing was a thing manifestly impossible; and, because it is not less repugnant that the more perfect should be an effect of, and dependent on the less perfect, than that something should proceed from nothing, it was equally impossible that I could hold it from myself: accordingly, it but remained that it had been placed in me by a Nature which was in reality more perfect than mine, and which even possessed within itself all the perfections of which I could form any idea; that is to say, in a single word, which was God. And to this I added that, since I knew some perfections which I did not possess, I was not the only being in existence, (I will here, with your permission, freely use the terms of the schools); but, on the contrary, that there was of necessity some other more perfect Being upon whom I was dependent, and from whom I had received all that I possessed; for if I had existed alone, and independently of every other being, so as to have had from myself all the perfection, however little, which I actually possessed, I should have been able, for the same reason, to have had from myself the whole remainder of perfection, of the want of which I was conscious, and thus could of myself have become infinite, eternal, immutable, omniscient, all-powerful, and, in fine, have possessed all the perfections which I could recognise in God. For in order to know the nature of God, (whose existence has been established by the preceding reasonings), as far as my own nature permitted, I had only to consider in reference to all the properties of which I found in my mind some idea, whether their possession was a mark of perfection; and I was assured that no one which indicated any imperfection was in him, and that none of the rest was awanting. Thus I perceived that doubt, inconstancy, sadness, and such like, could not be found in God, since I myself would have been happy to be free from them. Besides, I had ideas of many sensible and corporeal things; for although I might suppose that I was dreaming, and that all

which I saw or imagined was false, I could not, nevertheless, deny that the ideas were in reality in my thoughts. But, because I had already very clearly recognised in myself that the intelligent nature is distinct from the corporeal, and as I observed that all composition is an evidence of dependency, and that a state of dependency is manifestly a state of imperfection, I therefore determined that it could not be a perfection in God to be compounded of these two natures, and that consequently he was not so compounded; but that if there were any bodies in the world, or even any intelligences, or other natures that were not wholly perfect, their existence depended on his power in such a way that they could not subsist without him for a single moment.

I was disposed straightway to search for other truths; and when I had represented to myself the object of the geometers, which I conceived to be a continuous body, or a space indefinitely extended in length, breadth, and height or depth, divisible into divers parts which admit of different figures and sizes, and of being moved or transposed in all manner of ways, (for all this the geometers suppose to be in the object they contemplate), I went over some of their simplest demonstrations. And, in the first place, I observed, that the great certitude which by common consent is accorded to these demonstrations, is founded solely upon this, that they are clearly conceived in accordance with the rules I have already laid down. In the next place, I perceived that there was nothing at all in these demonstrations which could assure me of the existence of their object: thus, for example, supposing a triangle to be given, I distinctly perceived that its three angles were necessarily equal to two right angles, but I did not on that account perceive anything which could assure me that any triangle existed: while, on the contrary, recurring to the examination of the idea of a Perfect Being, I found that the existence of the Being was comprised in the idea in the same way that the equality of its three angles to two right angles is comprised in the idea of a triangle, or as in the idea of a sphere, the equidistance of all points on its surface from the centre, or even still more clearly; and that consequently it is at least as certain that God, who is this Perfect Being, is, or exists, as any demonstration of Geometry can be.

But the reason which leads many to persuade themselves that there is a difficulty in knowing this truth, and even also in knowing what their mind really is, is that they never raise their thoughts above sensible objects, and are so accustomed to consider nothing except by way of imagination, which is a mode of thinking limited to material objects, that all that is not imaginable seems to them not intelligible. The truth of this is sufficiently manifest from the single circumstance, that the philosophers of the Schools accept as a maxim that there is nothing in the Understanding which was not previously in the Senses, in which however it is certain that the ideas of God and of the soul have never been; and it appears to me that they who make use of their imagination to comprehend these ideas do exactly the same thing as if, in order to hear sounds or smell odours, they strove to avail themselves of their eyes; unless indeed that there is this difference, that the sense of sight does not afford us an inferior assurance to those of smell or hearing; in place of which, neither our imagination nor our senses can give us assurance of anything unless our Understanding intervene.

Finally, if there be still persons who are not sufficiently persuaded of the existence of God and of the soul, by the reasons I have adduced, I am desirous that they should know that all the other propositions, of the truth of which they deem themselves perhaps more assured, as that we have a body, and that there exist stars and an earth, and such like, are less certain; for, although we have a moral assurance of these things, which is so strong that there is an appearance of extravagance in doubting of their existence, yet at the same time no one, unless his intellect is impaired, can deny, when the question relates to a metaphysical certitude, that there is sufficient reason to exclude entire assurance, in the observation that when asleep we can in the same way imagine ourselves possessed of another body and that we see other stars and another earth, when there is nothing of the kind. For how do we know that the thoughts which occur in dreaming are false rather than those other which we experience when awake, since the former are often not less vivid and distinct than the latter? And though men of the highest genius study this question as long as they please, I do not believe that they will be able to give any reason which can be sufficient to remove this doubt, unless they presuppose the existence of God.

Thomas Hobbes

The great revolutions in seventeenth-century England produced two major political philosophers, Thomas Hobbes (1588-1679) and John Locke (1632-1704). Their writings, which coincided respectively with the Puritan Revolution and the Glorious Revolution, reflect the ways in which these political upheavals compared with one another. Hobbes's *Leviathan*, published in 1651, is filled with overtones of the insecurity, fear, and violence of the civil war just finished. Hobbes himself, because of his associations with the English aristocracy, had been forced to flee during the revolution to France, where he tutored the future King Charles II, also a refugee, in mathematics. The *Levia-*

than, beyond mirroring its own troubled times, is a carefully argued defense of the theory of political absolutism. Hobbes found a philosophical justification for absolutism in the ancient theory of materialism, which had been revived during the seventeenth century in the scientific writings of men like Galileo and Descartes. Applying the assumptions of these scientists to human nature, Hobbes then deduced his absolutistic position in politics from them.

Hobbes's theory of absolutism is sometimes confused with the theory of the divine right of kings, as elaborated, for example, by his contemporary, Bishop Bossuet. Although both theories provide defenses of political absolut-

ism, the defenses given are very different. While Bossuet's is based on an interpretation of Christianity, Hobbes's rests on philosophical materialism, which logically cannot admit the existence of God. Also, for Bossuet the sovereign is justified in his rule by reason of his hereditary right of succession to the throne, but for Hobbes the right to rule rests on the sovereign's ability to maintain himself in power and to keep the peace.

In his emphasis on power, Hobbes picks up a theme from Machiavelli, but he transforms it into one element in a complete philosophy of society and government—something that the Florentine, for all his insight into practical politics, had not succeeded in doing.

LEVIATHAN

THE INTRODUCTION

Nature, the art whereby God hath made and governs the world, is by the *art* of man, as in many other things,

THE ENGLISH WORKS OF THOMAS HOBBES, ed. W. Molesworth (London, 1839), III, ix-x, 110-120, 124-125, 128-131, 153-158.

so in this also imitated, that it can make an artificial animal. For seeing life is but a motion of limbs, the beginning whereof is in some principal part within; why may we not say, that all *automata* (engines that move themselves by springs and wheels as doth a watch) have an artificial life? For what is the *heart*, but a *spring;* and the *nerves,* but so many *strings;* and the *joints,* but so many *wheels,* giving motion to the whole body, such as was intended by the artificer? *Art* goes yet further, imitating that rational and most excellent work of nature, *man.* For by art is created that great LEVIATHAN called a COMMONWEALTH, or STATE, in Latin CIVITAS, which is but an artificial man; though of greater stature and strength than the natural, for whose protection and defence it was intended; and in which the *sovereignty* is an artificial *soul,* as giving life and motion to the whole body; the *magistrates,* and other *officers* of judicature and execution, artificial *joints; reward* and *punishment,* by which fastened to the seat of the sovereignty every joint and member is moved to perform his duty, are the *nerves,* that do the same in the body natural; the *wealth* and *riches* of all the particular members, are the *strength; salus populi,* the *people's safety,* its *business; counsellors,* by whom all things needful for it to know are suggested unto it, are the *memory; equity,* and *laws,* an artificial *reason* and *will; concord, health; sedition, sickness;* and *civil war, death.* Lastly, the *pacts* and *covenants,* by which the parts of this body politic were at first made, set together, and united, resemble that *fiat,* or the *let us make man,* pronounced by God in the creation.

.   .   .

Chapter XIII

OF THE NATURAL CONDITION OF MANKIND
AS CONCERNING THEIR FELICITY, AND
MISERY

Nature hath made men so equal, in the faculties of the body, and mind; as that though there be found one man sometimes manifestly stronger in body, or of quicker mind than another; yet when all is reckoned together, the difference between man, and man, is not so considerable, as that one man can thereupon claim to him-

self any benefit, to which another may not pretend, as well as he. For as to the strength of body, the weakest has strength enough to kill the strongest, either by secret machination, or by confederacy with others, that are in the same danger with himself.

And as to the faculties of the mind, setting aside the arts grounded upon words, and especially that skill of proceeding upon general, and infallible rules, called science; which very few have, and but in few things; as being not a native faculty, born with us; nor attained, as prudence, while we look after somewhat else, I find yet a greater equality amongst men, than that of strength. For prudence, is but experience; which equal time, equally bestows on all men, in those things they equally apply themselves unto. That which may perhaps make such equality incredible, is but a vain conceit of one's own wisdom, which almost all men think they have in a greater degree, than the vulgar; that is, than all men but themselves, and a few others, whom by fame, or for concurring with themselves, they approve. For such is the nature of men, that howsoever they may acknowledge many others to be more witty, or more eloquent, or more learned; yet they will hardly believe there be many so wise as themselves; for they see their own wit at hand, and other men's at a distance. But this proveth rather that men are in that point equal, than unequal. For there is not ordinarily a greater sign of the equal distribution of any thing, than that every man is contented with his share.

From this equality of ability, ariseth equality of hope in the attaining of our ends. And therefore if any two men desire the same thing, which nevertheless they cannot both enjoy, they become enemies; and in the way to their end, which is principally their own conservation, and sometimes their delectation only, endeavour to destroy, or subdue one another. And from hence it comes to pass, that where an invader hath no more to fear, than another man's single power; if one plant, sow, build, or possess a convenient seat, others may probably be expected to come prepared with forces united, to dispossess, and deprive him, not only of the fruit of his labour, but also of his life, or liberty. And the invader again is in the like danger of another.

And from this diffidence of one another, there is no way for any man to secure himself, so reasonable, as anticipation; that is, by force, or wiles, to master the persons of all men he can, so long, till he see no other power great enough to endanger him: and this is no more than his own conservation requireth, and is generally allowed. Also because there be some, that taking pleasure in contemplating their own power in the acts of conquest, which they pursue farther than their security requires; if others, that otherwise would be glad to be at ease within modest bounds, should not by invasion increase their power, they would not be able, long time, by standing only on their defence, to subsist. And by consequence, such augmentation of dominion over men being necessary to a man's conservation, it ought to be allowed him.

Again, men have no pleasure, but on the contrary a great deal of grief, in keeping company, where there is no power able to over-awe them all. For every man looketh that his companion should value him, at the same rate he sets upon himself: and upon all signs of contempt, or undervaluing, naturally endeavours, as far as he dares, (which amongst them that have no common power to keep them in quiet, is far enough to make them destroy each other), to extort a greater value from his contemners, by damage; and from others, by the example.

So that in the nature of man, we find three principal causes of quarrel. First, competition; secondly, diffidence; thirdly, glory.

The first, maketh men invade for gain; the second, for safety; and the third, for reputation. The first use violence, to make themselves masters of other men's persons, wives, children, and cattle; the second, to defend them; the third, for trifles, as a word, a smile, a different opinion, and any other sign of undervalue, either direct in their persons, or by reflection in their kindred, their friends, their nation, their profession, or their name.

Hereby it is manifest, that during the time men live without a common power to keep them all in awe, they are in that condition which is called war; and such a war, as is of every man, against every man. For WAR, consisteth not in battle only, or the act of fighting; but in a tract of time, wherein the will to contend by battle is sufficiently known: and therefore the notion of *time*, is to be considered in the nature of war; as it is in the nature of weather. For as the nature of foul weather, lieth not in a shower or two of rain; but in an inclination thereto of many days together: so the nature of war, consisteth not in actual fighting; but in the known disposition thereto, during all the time there is no assurance to the contrary. All other time is PEACE.

Whatsoever therefore is consequent to a time of war, where every man is enemy to every man; the same is consequent to the time, wherein men live without other security, than what their own strength, and their own invention shall furnish them withal. In such condition, there is no place for industry; because the fruit thereof is uncertain: and consequently no culture of the earth; no navigation, nor use of the commodities that may be imported by sea; no commodious building; no instruments of moving, and removing, such things as require much force; no knowledge of the face of the earth; no account of time; no arts; no letters; no society; and which is worst of all, continual fear, and danger of violent death; and the life of man, solitary, poor, nasty, brutish, and short.

It may seem strange to some man, that

has not well weighed these things; that nature should thus dissociate, and render men apt to invade, and destroy one another: and he may therefore, not trusting to this inference, made from the passions, desire perhaps to have the same confirmed by experience. Let him therefore consider with himself, when taking a journey, he arms himself, and seeks to go well accompanied; when going to sleep, he locks his doors; when even in his house he locks his chests; and this when he knows there be laws, and public officers, armed, to revenge all injuries shall be done him; what opinion he has of his fellow-subjects, when he rides armed; of his fellow citizens, when he locks his doors; and of his children, and servants, when he locks his chests. Does he not there as much accuse mankind by his actions, as I do by my words? But neither of us accuse man's nature in it. The desires, and other passions of man, are in themselves no sin. No more are the actions, that proceed from those passions, till they know a law that forbids them: which till laws be made they cannot know: nor can any law be made, till they have agreed upon the person that shall make it.

It may peradventure be thought, there was never such a time, nor condition of war as this; and I believe it was never generally so, over all the world: but there are many places, where they live so now. For the savage people in many places of America, except the government of small families, the concord whereof dependeth on natural lust, have no government at all; and live at this day in that brutish manner, as I said before. Howsoever, it may be perceived what manner of life there would be, where there were no common power to fear, by the manner of life, which men that have formerly lived under a peaceful government, use to degenerate into, in a civil war.

But though there had never been any time, wherein particular men were in a con-

dition of war one against another; yet in all times, kings, and persons of sovereign authority, because of their independency, are in continual jealousies, and in the state and posture of gladiators; having their weapons pointing, and their eyes fixed on one another; that is, their forts, garrisons, and guns upon the frontiers of their kingdoms; and continual spies upon their neighbours; which is a posture of war. But because they uphold thereby, the industry of their subjects; there does not follow from it, that misery, which accompanies the liberty of particular men.

To this war of every man, against every man, this also is consequent; that nothing can be unjust. The notions of right and wrong, justice and injustice have there no place. Where there is no common power, there is no law: where no law, no injustice. Force, and fraud, are in war the two cardinal virtues. Justice, and injustice are none of the faculties neither of the body, nor mind. If they were, they might be in a man that were alone in the world, as well as his senses, and passions. They are qualities, that relate to men in society, not in solitude. It is consequent also to the same condition, that there be no propriety, no dominion, no *mine* and *thine* distinct; but only that to be every man's, that he can get; and for so long, as he can keep it. And thus much for the ill condition, which man by mere nature is actually placed in; though with a possibility to come out of it, consisting partly in the passions, partly in his reason.

The passions that incline men to peace, are fear of death; desire of such things as are necessary to commodious living; and a hope by their industry to obtain them. And reason suggesteth convenient articles of peace, upon which men may be drawn to agreement. These articles, are they, which otherwise are called the Laws of Nature: whereof I shall speak more particularly, in the two following chapters.

Chapter XIV

OF THE FIRST AND SECOND NATURAL LAWS,
AND OF CONTRACTS

The RIGHT OF NATURE, which writers commonly call *jus naturale*, is the liberty each man hath, to use his own power, as he will himself, for the preservation of his own nature; that is to say, of his own life; and consequently, of doing any thing, which in his own judgment, and reason, he shall conceive to be the aptest means thereunto.

By LIBERTY, is understood, according to the proper signification of the word, the absence of external impediments: which impediments, may oft take away part of a man's power to do what he would; but cannot hinder him from using the power left him, according as his judgment, and reason shall dictate to him.

A LAW OF NATURE, *lex naturalis*, is a precept or general rule, found out by reason, by which a man is forbidden to do that, which is destructive of his life, or taketh away the means of preserving the same; and to omit that, by which he thinketh it may be best preserved. For though they that speak of this subject, use to confound *jus*, and *lex*, *right* and *law*: yet they ought to be distinguished; because RIGHT, consisteth in liberty to do, or to forbear; whereas LAW, determineth, and bindeth to one of them: so that law, and right, differ as much, as obligation, and liberty; which in one and the same matter are inconsistent.

And because the condition of man, as hath been declared in the precedent chapter, is a condition of war of every one against every one: in which case every one is governed by his own reason; and there is nothing he can make use of, that may not be a help unto him, in preserving his life against his enemies; it followeth, that in such a condition, every man has a right to every thing; even to one another's body. And therefore, as long as this natural right

of every man to every thing endureth, there can be no security to any man, how strong or wise soever he be, of living out the time, which nature ordinarily alloweth men to live. And consequently it is a precept, or general rule of reason, *that every man, ought to endeavour peace, as far as he has hope of obtaining it; and when he cannot obtain it, that he may seek, and use, all helps, and advantages of war*. The first branch of which rule, containeth the first, and fundamental law of nature; which is, *to seek peace, and follow it*. The second, the sum of the right of nature; which is, *by all means we can, to defend ourselves*.

From this fundamental law of nature, by which men are commanded to endeavour peace, is derived this second law; *that a man be willing, when others are so too, as far-forth, as for peace, and defence of himself he shall think it necessary, to lay down this right to all things; and be contented with so much liberty against other men, as he would allow other men against himself*. For as long as every man holdeth this right, of doing any thing he liketh; so long are all men in the condition of war. But if other men will not lay down their right, as well as he; then there is no reason for any one, to divest himself of his: for that were to expose himself to prey, which no man is bound to, rather than to dispose himself to peace. This is that law of the Gospel; *whatsoever you require that others should do to you, that do ye to them*. And that law of all men, *quod tibi fieri non vis, alteri ne feceris*.

To *lay down* a man's *right* to any thing, is to *divest* himself of the *liberty*, of hindering another of the benefit of his own right to the same. For he that renounceth, or passeth away his right, giveth not to any other man a right which he had not before; because there is nothing to which every man had not right by nature: but only standeth out of his way, that he may enjoy his own original right, without hindrance from him; not without hindrance from another. So that the effect which redoundeth to one man, by another man's defect of right, is but so much diminution of impediments to the use of his own right original.

Right is laid aside, either by simply renouncing it; or by transferring it to another. By *simply* RENOUNCING; when he cares not to whom the benefit thereof redoundeth. By TRANSFERRING; when he intendeth the benefit thereof to some certain person, or persons. And when a man hath in either manner abandoned, or granted away his right, then is he said to be OBLIGED, or BOUND, not to hinder those, to whom such right is granted, or abandoned, from the benefit of it: and that he *ought,* and it is his DUTY, not to make void that voluntary act of his own: and that such hindrance is INJUSTICE, and INJURY, as being *sine jure;* the right being before renounced, or transferred. So that *injury,* or *injustice,* in the controversies of the world, is somewhat like to that, which in the disputations of scholars is called *absurdity.* For as it is there called an absurdity, to contradict what one maintained in the beginning: so in the world, it is called injustice, and injury, voluntarily to undo that, which from the beginning he had voluntarily done. The way by which a man either simply renounceth, or transferreth his right, is a declaration, or signification, by some voluntary and sufficient sign, or signs, that he doth so renounce, or transfer; or hath so renounced, or transferred the same, to him that accepteth it. And these signs are either words only, or actions only; or, as it happeneth most often, both words, and actions. And the same are the BONDS, by which men are bound, and obliged: bonds, that have their strength, not from their own nature, for nothing is more easily broken than a man's word, but from fear of some evil consequence upon the rupture.

Whensoever a man transferreth his right, or renounceth it; it is either in consideration of some right reciprocally transferred to himself; or for some other good he hopeth for thereby. For it is a voluntary act: and of the voluntary acts of every man, the object is some *good to himself.* And therefore there be some rights, which no man can be understood by any words, or other signs, to have abandoned, or transferred. As first a man cannot lay down the right of resisting them, that assault him by force, to take away his life; because he cannot be understood to aim thereby, at any good to himself. The same may be said of wounds, and chains, and imprisonment; both because there is no benefit consequent to such patience; as there is to the patience of suffering another to be wounded, or imprisoned: as also because a man cannot tell, when he seeth men proceed against him by violence, whether they intend his death or not. And lastly the motive, and end for which this renouncing, and transferring of right is introduced, is nothing else but the security of a man's person, in his life, and in the means of so preserving life, as not to be weary of it. And therefore if a man by words, or other signs, seem to despoil himself of the end, for which those signs were intended; he is not to be understood as if he meant it, or that it was his will; but that he was ignorant of how such words and actions were to be interpreted.

The mutual transferring of right, is that which men call CONTRACT.

•   •   •

If a covenant be made, wherein neither of the parties perform presently, but trust one another; in the condition of mere nature, which is a condition of war of every man against every man, upon any reasonable suspicion, it is void: but if there be a common power set over them both, with right and force sufficient to compel performance, it is not void. For he that performeth first, has no assurance the other will perform after; because the bonds of words are too weak to bridle men's ambition, avarice, anger, and other passions, without the fear of some coercive power; which in the condition of mere nature, where all men are equal, and judges of the justness of their own fears, cannot possibly be supposed. And therefore he which performeth first, does but betray himself to his enemy; contrary to the right, he can never abandon, of defending his life, and means of living.

But in a civil estate, where there is a power set up to constrain those that would otherwise violate their faith, that fear is no more reasonable; and for that cause, he which by the covenant is to perform first, is obliged so to do.

· · ·

The force of words, being, as I have formerly noted, too weak to hold men to the performance of their covenants; there are in man's nature, but two imaginable helps to strengthen it. And those are either a fear of the consequence of breaking their word; or a glory, or pride in appearing not to need to break it. This latter is a generosity too rarely found to be presumed on, especially in the pursuers of wealth, command, or sensual pleasure; which are the greatest part of mankind. The passion to be reckoned upon, is fear.

· · ·

Chapter XV

OF OTHER LAWS OF NATURE

From that law of nature, by which we are obliged to transfer to another, such rights, as being retained, hinder the peace of mankind, there followeth a third; which is this, *that men perform their covenants made:* without which, covenants are in vain, and but empty words; and the right of all men to all things remaining, we are still in the condition of war.

And in this law of nature, consisteth the fountain and original of JUSTICE. For where no covenant hath preceded, there hath no right been transferred, and every man has right to every thing; and consequently, no action can be unjust. But when a covenant is made, then to break it is *unjust:* and the definition of INJUSTICE, is no other than *the*

not performance of covenant. And whatsoever is not unjust, is *just.*

But because covenants of mutual trust, where there is a fear of not performance on either part, as hath been said in the former chapter, are invalid; though the original of justice be the making of covenants; yet injustice actually there can be none, till the cause of such fear be taken away; which while men are in the natural condition of war, cannot be done. Therefore before the names of just, and unjust can have place, there must be some coercive power, to compel men equally to the performance of their covenants, by the terror of some punishment, greater than the benefit they expect by the breach of their covenant; and to make good that propriety, which by mutual contract men acquire, in recompense of the universal right they abandon: and such power there is none before the erection of a commonwealth. And this is also to be gathered out of the ordinary definition of justice in the Schools: for they say, that *justice is the constant will of giving to every man his own.* And therefore where there is no *own,* that is no propriety, there is no injustice; and where there is no coercive power erected, that is, where there is no commonwealth, there is no propriety; all men having right to all things: therefore where there is no commonwealth, there nothing is unjust. So that the nature of justice, consisteth in keeping of valid covenants: but the validity of covenants begins not but with the constitution of a civil power, sufficient to compel men to keep them: and then it is also that propriety begins.

· · ·

Chapter XVII

OF THE CAUSES, GENERATION, AND DEFINITION OF A COMMONWEALTH

The final cause, end, or design of men, who naturally love liberty, and dominion over others, in the introduction of that restraint upon themselves, in which we see them live in commonwealths, is the foresight of their own preservation, and of a more contented life thereby; that is to say, of getting themselves out from that miserable condition of war, which is necessarily consequent, as hath been shown in chapter XIII, to the natural passions of men, when there is no visible power to keep them in awe, and tie them by fear of punishment to the performance of their covenants, and observation of those laws of nature set down in the fourteenth and fifteenth chapters.

For the laws of nature, as *justice, equity, modesty, mercy,* and, in sum, *doing to others, as we would be done to,* of themselves, without the terror of some power, to cause them to be observed, are contrary to our natural passions, that carry us to partiality, pride, revenge, and the like. And covenants, without the sword, are but words, and of no strength to secure a man at all. Therefore notwithstanding the laws of nature, which every one hath then kept, when he has the will to keep them, when he can do it safely, if there be no power erected, or not great enough for our security; every man will, and may lawfully rely on his own strength and art, for caution against all other men. And in all places, where men have lived by small families, to rob and spoil one another, has been a trade, and so far from being reputed against the law of nature, that the greater spoils they gained, the greater was their honour; and men observed no other laws therein, but the laws of honour; that is, to abstain from cruelty, leaving to men their lives, and instruments of husbandry. And as small families did then; so now do cities and kingdoms which are but greater families, for their own security, enlarge their dominions, upon all pretences of danger, and fear of invasion, or assistance that may be given to invaders, and endeavour as much as they can, to subdue, or weaken their neighbours, by open force, and secret arts, for want of other caution, justly; and are remembered for it in after ages with honour.

Nor is it the joining together of a small number of men, that gives them this security; because in small numbers, small additions on the one side or the other, make the advantage of strength so great, as is sufficient to carry the victory; and therefore gives encouragement to an invasion. The multitude sufficient to confide in for our security, is not determined by any certain number, but by comparison with the enemy we fear; and is then sufficient, when the odds of the enemy is not of so visible and conspicuous moment, to determine the event of war, as to move him to attempt.

And be there never so great a multitude; yet if their actions be directed according to their particular judgments, and particular appetites, they can expect thereby no defence, nor protection, neither against a common enemy, nor against the injuries of one another. For being distracted in opinions concerning the best use and application of their strength, they do not help but hinder one another; and reduce their strength by mutual opposition to nothing: whereby they are easily, not only subdued by a very few that agree together; but also when there is no common enemy, they make war upon each other, for their particular interests. For if we could suppose a great multitude of men to consent in the observation of justice, and other laws of nature, without a common power to keep them all in awe; we might as well suppose all mankind to do the same; and then there neither would be, nor need to be any civil government, or commonwealth at all; because there would be peace without subjection.

Nor is it enough for the security, which men desire should last all the time of their life, that they be governed, and directed by one judgment, for a limited time; as in one battle, or one war. For though they obtain a victory by their unanimous endeavour against a foreign enemy; yet afterwards, when either they have no common enemy, or he that by one part is held for an enemy, is by another part held for a friend, they must needs by the difference of their interests dissolve, and fall again into a war amongst themselves.

It is true, that certain living creatures, as bees, and ants, live sociably one with another, which are therefore by Aristotle numbered amongst political creatures; and yet have no other direction, than their particular judgments and appetites; nor speech, whereby one of them can signify to another, what he thinks expedient for the common benefit: and therefore some man may perhaps desire to know, why mankind cannot do the same. To which I answer,

First, that men are continually in competition for honour and dignity, which these creatures are not; and consequently amongst men there ariseth on that ground, envy and hatred, and finally war; but amongst these not so.

Secondly, that amongst these creatures, the common good differeth not from the private; and being by nature inclined to their private, they procure thereby the common benefit. But man, whose joy consisteth in comparing himself with other men, can relish nothing but what is eminent.

Thirdly, that these creatures, having not, as man, the use of reason, do not see, nor think they see any fault, in the administration of their common business; whereas amongst men, there are very many, that think themselves wiser, and abler to govern the public, better than the rest; and these strive to reform and innovate, one this way, another that way; and thereby bring it into distraction and civil war.

Fourthly, that these creatures, though they have some use of voice, in making known to one another their desires, and other affections; yet they want that art of words, by which some men can represent to others, that which is good, in the likeness of evil; and evil, in the likeness of good; and augment, or diminish the apparent greatness of good and evil; discontenting men, and troubling their peace at their pleasure.

Fifthly, irrational creatures cannot distinguish between *injury*, and *damage;* and therefore as long as they be at ease, they are not offended with their fellows: whereas man is then most troublesome, when he is most at ease: for then it is that he loves to shew his wisdom, and control the actions of them that govern the commonwealth.

Lastly, the agreement of these creatures is natural; that of men, is by covenant only, which is artificial: and therefore it is no wonder if there be somewhat else required, besides covenant, to make their agreement constant and lasting; which is a common power, to keep them in awe, and to direct their actions to the common benefit.

The only way to erect such a common power, as may be able to defend them from the invasion of foreigners, and the injuries of one another, and thereby to secure them in such sort, as that by their own industry, and by the fruits of the earth, they may nourish themselves and live contentedly; is, to confer all their power and strength upon one man, or upon one assembly of men, that may reduce all their wills, by plurality of voices, unto one will: which is as much as to say, to appoint one man, or assembly of men, to bear their person; and every one to own, and acknowledge himself to be author of whatsoever he that so beareth their person, shall act, or cause to be acted, in those things which concern the common peace and safety; and therein to submit their wills, every one to his will, and their judgments, to his judgment. This is more than consent, or concord; it is a real unity of them all, in one and the same person, made by covenant of every man with every man, in such manner, as if every man should say to every man, *I authorise and give up my right of governing myself, to this man, or to this assembly of men, on this condition, that thou give up thy right to him, and authorise all his actions in like manner.* This done, the multitude so united in one person, is called a COMMONWEALTH, in Latin CIVITAS. This is the generation of that great LEVIATHAN, or rather, to speak more reverently, of that *mortal god,* to which we owe under the *immortal God,* our peace and defence. For by this authority, given him by every particular man in the commonwealth, he hath the use of so much power and strength conferred on him, that by terror thereof, he is enabled to perform the wills of them all, to peace at home, and mutual aid against their enemies abroad. And in him consisteth the essence of the commonwealth; which, to define it, is *one person, of whose acts a great multitude, by mutual covenants one with another, have made themselves every one the author, to the end he may use the strength and means of them all, as he shall think expedient, for their peace and common defence.*

And he that carrieth this person, is called SOVEREIGN, and said to have *sovereign power;* and every one besides, his SUBJECT.

Bishop Bossuet

Bishop Bossuet's *Politics Drawn from the Very Words of Holy Scripture* presents a doctrine that was popular in the royal courts of Europe during the seventeenth century—the doctrine of the divine right of kings. Written for the instruction of the Dauphin (the heir to the throne of Louis XIV), over whose education Bossuet had charge, the text amply justifies its title; for every conclusion which the author reaches is reinforced with copious references from scripture.

To Bossuet (1627-1704), living amidst the splendor of the court of Louis XIV, the theory of divine right undoubtedly provided a seemingly rational justification of the social order. Other political theorists of the time, however, were beginning to view the situation in another light. Among these was the Englishman, John Locke. In his *First Treatise of Civil Government,* written within a few years of Bossuet's *Politics,* Locke turned to the scriptures to find arguments with which to refute the divine-right theory defended by Bishop Bossuet.

POLITICS DRAWN FROM THE VERY WORDS OF HOLY SCRIPTURE

Third Book

IN WHICH WE BEGIN TO EXPLAIN THE
NATURE AND PROPERTIES OF ROYAL
AUTHORITY

Article I. Essential characteristics are noted.

SINGLE PROPOSITION: *there are four characteristics or qualities essential to royal authority:* Firstly, royal authority is sacred; Secondly, it is paternal; Thirdly, it is absolute; Fourthly, it is subject to reason. This is what must be established systematically in the following articles.

Article II. Royal authority is sacred.

FIRST PROPOSITION: *God establishes kings as his ministers and reigns through them over the peoples of the world.*—We have already seen that all power comes from God.

"The ruler," adds St. Paul, "is God's minister for good. But if you do evil, be afraid, for he does not wield the sword in vain. He is a minister of God, an avenger of evil deeds."

Rulers thus act as God's ministers and as His lieutenants on earth. It is through them that He exercises his dominion. "Do you believe yourselves capable of resisting the kingdom of the Lord, that He possesses through the children of David?"

It is for this reason that we have seen that the royal throne is not the throne of a man, but the throne of God himself. "God has chosen my son Solomon in order to place him on the throne where the Lord reigns over Israel." And furthermore: "Solomon sits on the throne of the Lord."

And in order that we should not believe that to have kings established by God is

POLITIQUE TIRÉE DE L'ECRITURE SAINTE, Jacques Bénigne Bossuet, trans. Owen Ulph of Scripps College.

characteristic only of the Israelites, here is what *Ecclesiastes* says: "God gives to each people their governor; and Israel is manifestly reserved for Himself."

He thus governs all peoples, and gives to all of them their kings. However He governs Israel in a more particular and more direct fashion.

SECOND PROPOSITION: *The person of the king is sacred.*—It follows from the above that the person of the king is sacred, and any attempt upon the lives of kings is a sacrilege.

God has had them anointed by His prophets with a sacred ointment, as He has had His pontiffs and His altars anointed.

But even without the application of this ointment to their bodies, they are sacred by virtue of their charge, as the representatives of the divine majesty, delegated by His providence to the execution of His designs. It is thus that God, Himself, calls Cyrus His anointed. "Here is what the Lord said to Cyrus, my anointed, whom I have taken by the hand to subject all peoples to him."

The title of christ is given to kings, and everywhere they are seen to be called christs, or the anointed of the Lord.

Under this venerable name, even the prophets revere them, and regard them as associated with the sovereign power of God, whose authority they exercise over the people. "Speak of me boldly before the Lord, and before His christ. Speak out if I have taken someone's bull or someone's ass, if I have taken bribes from someone, if I have oppressed someone. And they replied: Never. And Samuel said: the Lord and His christ are thus witnesses that you have no complaint against me."

It is thus that Samuel, after having judged the people for God with absolute power for twenty-one years, gives an account of his conduct before God and before Saul, to whom he appeals as witnesses to the testimony establishing his innocence.

Kings must be protected as sacred objects; and whoever neglects to protect them is worthy of death. "Long live the Lord," said David to Saul's captains, "all of you who do not safeguard your master, the anointed of the Lord, are the children of death."

. . .

THIRD PROPOSITION: *The ruler must be obeyed out of the principle of religion and conscience.*—St. Paul, after having stated that the ruler is the minister of God, concluded as follows: "It is thus necessary that you subject yourself to him not only through fear of his wrath, but through the obligation of your conscience."

This is why "it is necessary to serve him not merely in a way to meet the eye as if to please men, but with pure intent, with fear, with respect, and with a heart as sincere as that of Jesus Christ."

And furthermore: "Servants, obey your temporal masters in all things, never serving only in a way to meet the eye as if to please men, but in simplicity of heart and in the fear of God. Do all that you do with a good heart as though serving God and not men, assured of receiving from God Himself the reward for your services. Look upon Jesus Christ as your master."

If the apostle speaks thus of servitude, a state contrary to nature, what ought we to think of legitimate subjection to rulers and magistrates, protectors of public liberty!

That is why St. Peter said: "For the love of God, be thus subjected to the order which is established among men. Be subjected to the king as to God, possessor of the supreme power. Be subjected to those to whom He gives His authority and who are sent by him to praise good deeds and punish evil ones."

Even though they may not acquit themselves of this duty, their charge and their ministry must be respected. "Obey your masters, not only those who are good and moderate, but even those who are vexatious and unjust."

There is thus something religious in the respect one renders to the ruler. Service to God and respect for kings are one and St. Peter links these two duties together: "Fear God, honor the king."

Thus has God put into rulers something divine. "I have said: You are gods, and you are all children of the Almighty." It is God Himself whom David causes to speak thus.

From this it ensues that the servants of God swear by the safety and life of the king, as by a divine and sacred thing. Uriah speaking to David: "By your safety and by the conservation of your life, I will never do that thing."

Even though the king should prove unfaithful, according to the view we must hold of the order of God: "By the safety of Pharoah, I will not let you leave here."

It is necessary to listen to the first Christians, and to Tertullian who speaks for all of them as follows: "We swear not by the ghosts of the caesars; but by their life and safety, which is more august than all their ghosts. Don't you know that spirits are demons? But we, who see in the emperors the choice and judgment of God who has given them command over all peoples, respect in them what God has placed there and we hold these things at great oath."

He adds: "What more shall I say for our religion and our piety towards the emperor than that we should respect the one whom our God has chosen. In a manner I can say that Caesar is more ours than yours because it is our God who has established him."

It is therefore the spirit of Christianity to cause kings to be respected religiously. So much so that the same Tertullian appropriately calls our faith, "the religion of the second majesty."

This second majesty is but a derivative of

the first, that is to say, of the divine being, Who, for the good of human things, has wished to cause some portion of His splendor to shine forth upon kings.

FOURTH PROPOSITION: *Kings must respect their own power and use it only for the public good.*—Since their power, as it has thus been said, comes from on high, they must not believe that they are the masters to use it as they please. They must use it with fear and moderation as a thing which comes to them from God, and for which God will demand an accounting. "Listen, O kings, and understand! Learn, judges of the earth! Lend an ear, O you who hold the peoples under your power, and be pleased to see the multitudes that surround you. It is God who has given you power. Your strength comes from the Almighty who will examine your work and sound the depths of your thoughts. Because, being ministers of His kingdom, you have not judged well and you have not proceeded according to His will, He will soon appear to you in a terrible manner. Because to those who command is reserved the most harsh punishment, the small and the weak will be pitied but the powerful will be severely tormented. God fears the power of no one, because He has made both the great and the small and He is equally concerned for one and the other. And the strongest will be tormented most strongly. I speak unto you, O kings! so that you may be wise, and so that you fall not from grace."

Kings must, therefore, tremble as they use the power that God gives them, and reflect how horrible is the sacrilege of using a power that comes from God for evil.

We have seen the kings seated on the throne of the Lord, holding the sword that He has placed in their hands. How profane and audacious are those unjust kings who sit on the throne of God and use the sword, which He puts into their hands, to commit violent deeds, and to cut the throats of His children!

Thus they respect their power because it is not their power, but the power of God which it is necessary to employ in a holy and religious manner. St. Gregory of Nazianzus speaks thus to the emperors: "Respect your purple. Recognize within your persons the mystery of God. He governs celestial things alone, He shares those of the earth with you. Be thus gods to your subjects." That is to say, govern them as God governs, in a noble, impartial, beneficial, and, in a word, in a manner divine.

Article III. Royal authority is paternal, and its fundamental quality is benevolence. After what has been said, this truth needs no further proofs.

We have seen that kings hold rank from God, who is the true father of the human race. We have also seen that the first concept of power that existed among men is that of paternal power and that kings have been molded in the image of fathers. Also, everyone is in agreement that the obedience which is due to public power is found in the *Decalogue* only in the precept that obliges us to honor our fathers. From all this it seems that the appellation *king* is synonymous with the appellation *father*, and that benevolence is the most natural characteristic of kings.

Book IV

CONTINUATION OF THE CHARACTERISTICS OF ROYALTY

First Article. Royal authority is absolute.

In order to render this term odious and insufferable, many persons attempt to confuse absolute government with arbitrary government. But there are no terms more distinguished by their difference as we shall see when we speak of justice.

FIRST PROPOSITION: *The prince need render account to no one for what he orders.*— "Observe the commandments that come from the mouth of the king, and keep the oath that you have made to him. Do not seek to escape his view, and do not indulge in evil undertakings, because he will do what he wishes. The word of the king is powerful. And no one can say to him: Why do you act thus? He who obeys will come to no harm."

Without this absolute authority he can neither do good nor suppress evil. His power must be such that no one may hope to escape from it. And finally, the only defense of individuals against public power must be their innocence.

This doctrine conforms to the words of St. Paul: "If you do not want to fear power, do good."

SECOND PROPOSITION: *Once the prince has judged there is no other judgment.*—Sovereign judgments are attributed to God Himself. When Joseph established the judges to judge the people, he said: "It is not in the name of men that you judge, but in the name of God."

That is what causes Ecclesiastes to say: "Do not judge against the judge." This is even more important when the sovereign judge is the king. And the reason that supports this, "is that he is judging according to justice." It is not that he is always so judging, but that he is assumed to be so judging and no one has the right to judge or to review after him.

It is thus necessary to obey rulers as though they were identical with justice, without which there is neither order nor justice in affairs.

They are gods, and in a manner they share divine independence. "I have said: You are gods and you are all children of the Almighty."

Only God is able to judge their judgments and their persons. "God has taken his seat in the assembly of the gods and, seated in the center, He judges the gods."

It is for that reason that St. Gregory, bishop of Tours, said to King Chilperic in a council: "We speak to you, but you listen to us only if you want to. If you don't want to, who will condemn you other than He who has said that He was justice itself?"

It follows that he who does not want to obey the ruler is not referred to another tribunal, but is condemned irremissably to death as an enemy of the public peace and of human society. "Whoever will be proud and will not obey the command of the pontiff and the ordinance of the judge will die and you will thus eradicate the evil from among you." And furthermore: "Whoever shall refuse to obey all your orders, may he die." It is the people who speak thus to Joshua.

The ruler can correct himself when he knows that he has done badly, but against his authority there can be no remedy except his authority.

That is why he must certainly be careful what he orders. "Be careful of what you order. All that you judge will fall back upon you. Fear God. Do everything with great care."

It is thus that Joseph instructed the judges to whom he was entrusting his authority. How much of this he recollected when he himself had to judge.

THIRD PROPOSITION: *There is no co-active force against the ruler.*—A co-active force is a power to constrain and to execute what is legitimately ordained. Legitimate power belongs to the ruler alone. To him alone belongs the co-active force.

It is for that reason also that St. Paul gives the sword to him alone. "If you do not do well, be afraid, because it is not in vain that he wields the sword."

In the state only the ruler should be armed, otherwise everything is in confusion and the state falls back into anarchy.

He who creates a sovereign ruler puts everything together into his hands, all the sovereign authority to judge and all the forces of the state. "Our king will judge and he will march before us and he will conduct our wars." This is what the Jewish people said when they asked for a king. Samuel declares to them upon this basis that the power of their ruler will be absolute, incapable of being restrained by any other power. Here is the right of the king who will reign over you, sayeth the Lord: "He will take your children and place them into his service. He will seize some of your lands and the best of that which you have in order to give it to his servants," and so forth.

Will they have the right to do all that legally? God forbid! Because God does not grant such powers. But they will have the right to do it with impunity and without regard for human justice. That is why David said: "I have sinned against you alone. O Lord, have pity on me!" Commenting on this passage, St. Jerome said: "Because he was king, he had only God to fear."

.   .   .

To the ruler alone belongs the general care of the people. That is the first article and the foundation of all others. To him the public works; to him the squares and arms; to him the decrees and ordinances; to him the marks of distinction; no power but that which is dependent on his; no assembly except by his authority.

It is thus that for the good of a state all the power is united in one. To put the power somewhere else is to divide the state. It is to destroy the public peace. It is to create two masters against which the oracle of the *Scriptures* states: "No man can serve two masters."

The ruler is by his charge the father of the people. He is by his grandeur above petty interests. Even more, all his grandeur and all his natural interest is that the people be conserved, since lacking the people he is no longer ruler. There is nothing better than to leave all the power of the state to the one who has the greatest interest in the conservation and the glory of the state itself.

.   .   .

SIXTH PROPOSITION: *The people must fear the ruler; but the ruler must only fear doing evil.*—"Whoever will be proud and will not obey the commandment of the pontiff and the ordinance of the judge will die and you shall remove the evil from within Israel. And all who shall hear his torment will be afraid so that no one shall allow himself to succumb to pride."

Fear is a restraint necessary to men because of their pride and their natural indocility.

The people must thus fear the ruler, but if the ruler fears the people all is lost. The weakness of Aaron, to whom Moses had left the command while he was on the mountain, was the cause of the adoration of the golden calf. "What have these people done to you?" Moses said to him, "And why have you led them to so great an evil." He blames the crime of the people on Aaron who had not repressed it even though it was within his power to do so.

Note closely the following terms: "What have these people done to you for you to lead them to so great an evil?" One is the enemy of the people by not resisting them on such occasions.

Aaron answered him: "May my Lord not be angry with me. You know that these people are inclined toward evil. They came to tell me: Create gods to lead us because we do not know what has happened to Moses who has rescued us from Egypt."

What an excuse for a sovereign magistrate to fear angering the people. God does not receive it, "and irritated to the last degree against Aaron, He wanted to crush him, but Moses prayed for him."

Saul attempts to place the blame on the people for not having executed the orders of God. It is a vain excuse that God rejects for he was established on the throne to resist the people whenever they drifted into evil. Samuel said to him: "Listen to what the Lord has pronounced against you. You have rejected his word. Also he has rejected you and you shall not be king." Saul replied to Samuel, "By fearing the people and ceding to their harangues, I have sinned in having disobeyed the Lord and you."

The ruler must firmly repulse importunate persons who ask him for unjust things.

The fear of angering, pushed too far, degenerates into a criminal weakness. "There are people who lose their souls through misguided humility. The impudent one that they dare not refuse causes them to perish."

Fifth Book

FOURTH AND FINAL CHARACTERISTIC OF
ROYAL AUTHORITY

First Article. Royal authority is subject to reason.

FIRST PROPOSITION: *Government is a work of reason and intelligence.*—"Now, listen, O kings, and be instructed, judges of the earth."

All men are created capable of understanding. But principally you upon whom reposes an entire nation, you who should be the soul and intelligence of a State, in whom must be found the first reason for all its movements, the less it is necessary for you to justify yourself to others, the more you must have justification and intelligence within yourself.

The contrary of acting out of reason is to act out of passion or anger. To act out of anger as Saul acted against David, driven by his jealousy or possessed by his black melancholy, entails all kinds of irregularities, inconsistencies, inequalities, anomalies, injustices, and confusion in one's conduct.

Though one has only a horse to lead and a flock to guide, one cannot do it without reason. How much more is needed for the leadership of men and a rational flock!

"The Lord took David from the care of his sheep to have him conduct Jacob, his servant, and Israel, his inheritance. And he led them in the innocence of his heart with an able and intelligent hand."

Everything among men is accomplished through intelligence and through counsel. "Houses are built out of wisdom and become solid through prudence. Ability fills the granaries and amasses riches. The wise man is courageous. The able man is robust and strong because war is waged by strategy and by industry, and salvation is found where there is much counsel."

Wisdom herself says: "It is through me that kings rule and through me legislators prescribe what is just."

She is so born to command that she gives the empire even to those born in servitude. "The wise servant will command the children of the house who lack wisdom, and he will apportion their lots." And furthermore: "Free people will subject themselves to a judicious servant."

God, upon installing Joshua, orders him to study the law of Moses which was the law of the kingdom, "in order," he says, "that you should understand all that you do." And furthermore: "And then you will carry out your designs and you will understand what you do."

David said as much to Solomon in the last instructions he gave to him upon dying. "Take care to observe the laws of God so that you may understand all that you do and to which side you are to turn.

"So that you may not be turned, turn yourself knowingly. Let reason direct all your movements. Know what you do and why you are doing it."

. . .

Article IV. Consequences of the Preceding Doctrine of Majesty and its Attendant Features.

FIRST PROPOSITION: *What majesty is.*—I do not call majesty that pomp which surrounds kings, or that external brilliance which dazzles the vulgar. That is the reflection of majesty and not majesty itself.

Majesty is the image of the grandeur of God in the ruler.

God is infinite. God is all. The ruler in

his capacity as ruler is not looked upon as a private individual. He is a public figure. The entire state is in him. The will of all the people is contained in his. As all perfection and all virtue is united in God, thus all the power of individuals is reunited in the person of the ruler. What grandeur that a single man should contain so much of it!

The power of God makes itself felt in an instant from one end of the world to the other. Royal power acts simultaneously throughout the entire kingdom. It holds the whole kingdom in a state of polity as God holds the whole world.

Should God withdraw his hand, the world will fall back into nothingness. Should authority cease in the kingdom, all will be in confusion.

Consider the ruler in his cabinet. From there all orders emanate which make the magistrates and the captains, the citizens and the soldiers, the provinces and the armies on land and sea, act in concert. It is the image of God who seated on His throne in the highest part of the heavens directs all of nature.

"What movement is caused," said St. Augustine, "simply by the command of the emperor! He only moves his lips—there is no slighter movement—and the whole empire moves. It is the image of God who does all by His word. He has spoken and things have been done. He has commanded and they have been created."

We admire his works. Nature is a matter to expound upon for the curious. "God gives them the world to meditate upon, but they will never discover the secret of His work from the beginning to the end." We see some portion of it, but the depth is impenetrable. Thus is the secret of the ruler.

The designs of the ruler are only known through their execution. Thus are the counsels of God likewise manifested, and no one shares them save those whom God admits.

If the power of God extends everywhere, magnificence accompanies it. There is no corner of the universe where shining examples of his goodness do not appear. Behold the order, behold the justice, behold the tranquility in all the kingdom! It is the natural effect of the authority of the ruler.

There is nothing more majestic than kindness widely displayed, and there is no greater vilification of majesty than the misery of the people caused by the ruler.

The evil hide in vain. God's light follows them everywhere. His arm reaches them from the highest heavens to the depths of the abyss. "Where shall I go before your spirit and where shall I flee before your face? If I climb to heaven you are there. If I throw myself into the depths of hell, I find you there. If I rise in the morning and retreat to the most distant seas it is your hand that leads me there and your right hand holds me there. And I have said that perhaps the shadows will cover me, but night has been as day around me. Before you, darkness is not dark. The night is lighted as the day. Darkness and light are one and the same." The evil find God everywhere, high and low, night and day. Whatever morning they get up, he warns them. However far they should travel, his hand is on them.

Thus God gives the ruler the power of discovering the most secret conspiracies. He has eyes and hands everywhere. We have seen that the birds of the sky report to him what is going on. He has even received from God through practiced experience a certain insight which makes one suspect him of powers of divination. Once he has penetrated intrigue, his long arms reach out to seize his enemies from the extremities of the world. He ferrets them out from the depths of the abyss. There is no asylum secure against such power.

Finally, let yourself gather before your eyes those things so great and so august that we have said concerning royal authority. Behold an immense people united in a single person. Behold the sacred power, paternal and absolute. Behold the secret reason which governs the entire body of the state enclosed in a single head. See the image of God in the king and you have the concept of royal majesty.

God is holiness itself, goodness itself, power itself, reason itself. In these things resides the majesty of God. In the image of these things is the majesty of the ruler.

This majesty is so great that it cannot be the same in the ruler as it is in the source. It is borrowed from God who gives it to him for the good of the people for whom it is good to be constrained by a superior force.

I do not know what divine attribute attaches itself to the ruler and inspires fear in the people. May the king not forget himself for that reason. "I have said that it is God who speaks. I have said: You are gods and you are all children of the Almighty, but you will die like men and you will fall like the great." I have said, you are gods. That is to say, you have authority in you. You carry on your forehead a divine character. You are the children of the Almighty. It is He who has established your power for the welfare of mankind. But, O gods of flesh and blood, O gods of mud and dust, you will die like men, you will fall like the great. Greatness separates men for a time. A common fall at the end makes them all equal.

O kings, exercise your power thus boldly because it is divine and beneficial to mankind! But exercise it with humility. It is applied to you from without. In the end it leaves you feeble, it leaves you mortal, it leaves you sinners and makes you all the more responsible before God.

Jean-Baptiste Colbert

The leading minister of France during many of the years of Louis XIV's reign was Jean-Baptiste Colbert. Born in 1619 into a thoroughly middle-class family, Colbert did not rise to power particularly rapidly, nor did his early career show signs of great distinction. He first attracted the attention of Le Tellier, the Secretary of State for War, by his devotion to duty, his tirelessness, and his administrative talents. In 1647, Colbert was elevated to the post of personal secretary to the Minister, Le Tellier. Two years later (after a financially judicious marriage), he left Le Tellier's service and entered the household of Cardinal Mazarin, who was in effect the ruler of France.

Again Colbert's talents and perseverance brought him advancement. When Mazarin died in 1661 and Louis XIV took over control of the government, Colbert moved easily into the top rank of ministers and advisers to the king. In 1665 he was made Comptroller-General, and later he became Secretary of State for Naval Affairs as well as Superintendent of Buildings—a highly significant post, for he was responsible for all government construction, including the great palace of Versailles.

One of the results of this first minister's tireless industry was that he stamped his name upon that brand of state activity which attempts to regulate everything for the sake of the political power and prestige of the country and its monarch. In fact, the term "Colbertism" came to stand for state interest and activity in all sorts of enterprises—encouraging new commerce and industry, fostering agriculture, establishing price and wage levels, fixing standards of quality for goods, forbidding certain imports and exports, supporting the arts and crafts, developing a large, well-trained army and navy, simplifying the legal system and procedures for tax assessment and collection, and abolishing accretions of custom and practice that infringed on the power of the state.

The three selections that follow give a good picture of the busy Frenchman's activities. In the first he tells of some of the measures taken by the king to stimulate commerce and industry; in the second—this was ostensibly a letter from Louis XIV, but it was actually written by Colbert—he exhorts the commercial class to ever-greater effort; and in the third, he reveals the lengths to which he is willing to go in order to acquire a greater share of the world's wealth. The translation has been left awkward, involved, and rough, because that was Colbert's own style.

MEMOIRS ON THE FINANCIAL AFFAIRS OF FRANCE TO SERVE AS A HISTORY, 1663

. . . Not being content to seek means of obtaining relief for his people, the King again wanted to act with the same application to procure some benefits for them; and, thinking that the means of re-establishing abundance and wealth among his subjects could not help but follow the restoration of manufacturing within the Kingdom and of domestic and foreign commerce, after being carefully informed on all details, he found:

The internal commerce, which consists of nothing but the communication of one city with the others and the easy transportation of merchandise, entirely ruined. . . .

The transportation of merchandise almost ruined by the number of tolls which have been established upon many pretexts.

All manufacturing, which was once so great within the Kingdom, entirely gone, the Dutch and the English having taken nearly all by various evil means outside their State, except the lone manufacture of silk which still exists at Lyons and Tours, although muchly diminished.

As for external commerce, it is not known, so to speak, in the kingdom except by the Dutch who come to take all the excess merchandise in our ports, and who bring us all those of which we could have need; in sort that he does not find, according to the research that His Majesty has made, that on the three hundred leagues of coastline on the Ocean sea and on the more than one hundred leagues on the Mediterranean sea, there were two hundred vessels of all burden belonging to his subjects, and he finds more than six thousand sailors who serve the foreigners. This deplorable state of commerce which no other prince before this one thought of recognizing, being clearly known every-

LETTRES, INSTRUCTIONS ET MÉMOIRES, Jean-Baptiste Colbert, trans. by the editor, John Louis Beatty.

where else, His Majesty, well realizing that, not having ships in his realm, which was the only way to attract wealth, resolved to give that all his protection and made it a customary affair of his councils.

To begin, he named some councillors to his councils; and by some decrees which he gave them, he ordered the masters of requests in the provinces to work at the verification of all the debts of the towns, of all the tolls and of all the titles by which these were established. . . .

He willed that all the records on the liquidation (of the debts) be reported before him, in order that he himself with the advice of his council might rule on the validity or invalidity of these debts.

He determined to observe the same thing in regard to the tolls established on the rivers; and after a report long and boring to all others, he suppressed by means of decrees issued over a period of five or six months, all the tolls on the rivers of Garonne, Dordogne, Charente, Loire, Seine, Somme, Marne, Oise, Saône and Rhone, for the titles were vicious, in such a way he made the great rivers navigable and by these means settled the transportation of merchandise within the kingdom. . . .

With regard to manufacturing, since it is a difficult matter and one which takes much time to resolve, His Majesty gives all the necessary care to raise the spirits of his people and to give them the means (of improving manufacturing).

As to foreign trade, having recognized that, his power at sea being entirely withered away, he must of necessity begin by re-establishing his maritime forces, in order to give courage to his peoples and to the principal merchants of his kingdom to buy and have built some vessels and to give themselves up in earnest to the sea service.

To this end His Majesty, having had the condition of his ships and galleys inspected, found that for ten years one could see no more than two or three French warships at sea, that the ship-yards were denuded entirely of all stores, that the number of vessels was reduced to twenty or twenty-two, many of which in an unfit condition to serve having almost been destroyed in port without serving for lack of repairs; that the captains were inexperienced because of the long cessation of activity; that the better sailors and an infinity of others had passed into the service of foreigners because they could find no employment in France.

In regard to the galleys: all the rowers reduced to eight or nine hundred galley slaves, most of them sick and enfeebled by the misery they have suffered in the years past; six miserable hulls of galleys, all the others sunk in the port of Toulon; finally, this state of affairs, on which rests the larger part of the glory of the prince and the respect and veneration of his name in foreign countries, reduced to the most pitiable condition one can imagine.

This, having been clearly recognized by the King, he gave both his orders and the necessary funds for the re-establishment of both of these two powers. To achieve this, he ordered a general refitting of all his vessels. He got from Holland and sent to Sweden in order to buy not only all the needed supplies to refit and build ships, but also two hundred thousands of copper for the casting of large cannon and set about madly to put a powerful force to sea.

At the same time he cut timber in the forests of Bourgogne and Brittany and began to have some vessels built at Toulon and Brest.

In regard to the galleys he gave orders to buy all the slaves to be found at Malta and wrote vigorously to the grand master of that religion there (*i.e.*, the Grand Master of the Order of St. John of Malta). He gave orders to his procurers-general in the sovereign companies that they take the opportunity to sentence to the galleys guilty persons who could be executed. . . .

For the liberal arts His Majesty has established, formed and given the necessary funds for the Academy of Painting and Sculpture, in which all the young people are taught by the most excellent masters of these two arts. And not only has he given salaries for this purpose to the directors and teachers, but also he has given divers prizes now and then to stimulate the young people, and every year he has taken one or two of the best prepared in each art to send to Rome, where he gives them a pension on which to live for two or three years until their art is perfected, and then to return to France and be employed in the buildings of the royal house.

He has established the royal manufacture of tapestry at the house of Gobelins, and he put people to work at the designs by Monsieur Le Brun, his premier painter, who is certainly recognized as the first painter in Europe. At the same time he put people to work at an infinity of new kinds of goldsmithing, embroidery and all sorts of furniture, having already furnished two of his country houses more superbly than the Louvre had ever been furnished.

LOUIS XIV TO THE MUNICIPAL MAGISTRATES AND INHABITANTS OF MARSEILLES

August 26, 1664

Very dear and well-loved, having considered that it would be useful to this kingdom to re-establish the commerce inside and outside of this place . . . we have resolved to hold, for this purpose, every fifteenth day in our presence, a special Council of commerce, in which all the interests of merchants and the means of achieving this re-establishment will be examined and resolved, as also all that which relates to manufacturing. We say to you also that we assign, in the expenses of our State, one million livres each year for the rehabilitation of manufacturing and the improvement of navigation, exclusive of the other larger amounts which we have caused to be raised to supply the companies of the East and West Indies;

That we also work constantly to abolish all the tolls which are asked on the navigable rivers;

That already more than one million livres have been spent on the restoration of the public roads, a project at which we will also work without ceasing;

That we will with the funds of our royal treasury assist all those who want to undertake the restoration of old manufactures or who will propose new;

That we give orders to all our ambassadors, or residents among the princes our allies, to take in our name all convenient steps to render judgments on all complaints of merchants and to conserve the complete freedom of trade;

That we will house comfortably, at our court and household, all and each of the merchants who have business there, for all the time they will be obliged to stay, having ordered the grand Sergeant of our House to set aside a proper house for this purpose which will be called the *Maison du Commerce;*

That if the said merchants wish to depute someone among those at our court and household to take care of their affairs, we will lodge him at the said *Maison* and will grant him audience at all times;

That if they have trouble finding someone who can or will leave his family and his business for this position, we will appoint an intelligent and able person to whom we will give the means to live in the said *Maison,* there to receive all the merchants who have some business at our court and household, and to take their appeals and to forward them immediately with all the speed necessary, all without a single cost or expense;

That all the overseas merchants and traders who will purchase some vessels or who will build some new ones for their trade or commerce will receive from us some gratuities to help them with the said purchases or in the construction of the said (ships);

And that all those who will undertake long term voyages, in reporting for authentication in the form which will be prescribed by us, will also receive some gratuities for each ton of merchandise they will have carried or borne on the said voyages:

In all these matters we have asked you to give advice by this letter and say to you that, as soon as you have received it, you call together all the merchants and traders of our city of Marseilles, that you explain to them very carefully our intentions in regard to all the above, in order that, being informed of the favorable treatment which we desire to extend to them, they will be more especially invited to apply themselves to commerce. . . .

PROPOSAL AND USEFUL ADVICE CONCERNING THE COMMERCE OF HOLLAND, 1668

All the world knows that the city of Amsterdam is beyond comparison the most rich and most flourishing city of Europe, and that it did not reach this degree of grandeur and wealth until, by means of the revolt of the United Provinces of the Low Country and with the aid of France, the Estates-General, after a long time of war, having been superior to the House of Spain, closed the passage to the sea at the city of Antwerp by the means of Zeeland[1] and of the naval forces which the said Estates have always had at sea in much greater strength than those of Spain. As a result the city of Amsterdam has found itself the best fitted to gather the entire commerce of the said city of Antwerp, not only has she profited, but more she has attracted

to herself that which all the Dutch have established in the Indies, in the Baltic Sea, and all over the world. These are the means by which she has arrived at this degree of grandeur and of power so that she directs all the deliberations of the Estates and contributes only a seventh or an eighth of all costs.

All these reasons, and an infinity of others which are useless for the subject of this discourse, will require the said Estates to demand from the Spanish, (in accord with) the treaty of peace made with them in 1648, article 14, which follows:

"The Scheldt River, and the canals of the Sas, Zwyn and other such waterways debouching there shall be kept closed by the Lords of the Estates-General."

By this article they thought to secure forever the commerce of the city of Am-

[1] [*Islands off the mouth of the Scheldt River on which Antwerp is located.*]

sterdam to the exclusion of that of Antwerp.

Now that peace is established between France and Spain,[2] and that the Estates-General are also at peace with these two crowns, it is undoubted that the Dutch, as a result of the above article, have the power to prevent the passage into Antwerp, either by the Scheldt or by the other canals, to all vessels of the King of Spain or of his subjects; but they do not have the same power in regard to French vessels which can enter without difficulty, and, by this method, the King is able to

[2] [*Treaty of Aix-la-Chapelle, May 2, 1668.*]

re-establish the commerce of Antwerp, since the subjects of His Majesty can carry all kinds of merchandise there.

If the King announces this plan and has it executed, since the city of Antwerp is, beyond comparison, more ample than that of Amsterdam, either for the berthing of ships or for the distribution of merchandise, it follows of necessity either the Dutch run the risk of seeing the commerce leave their hands and pass into those of the French and the Flemish or they come to an agreement with France on terms advantageous to the service of the king and proportionate to the importance of these advantages.

Isaac Newton

Isaac Newton (1642–1727) had formulated his theory of universal gravitation by the time he was twenty-four. Several years later, at the insistence of friends, he published it under the title, *The Mathematical Principles of Natural Philosophy*. This triumph of scientific genius, which has been called "the greatest single monument of human learning," seems almost miraculous and its author somehow superhuman. And yet, without detracting from Newton's greatness, we must recognize that his theory of gravitation was the culmination of a scientific revival which had been in progress for well over a hundred years and had included such names as Copernicus, Kepler, and Galileo. But in an even broader sense Newton is the heir of the thinkers who had gone before. The selection from his *Optics* begins with a reaffirmation of the atomic theory of matter, which was first developed by the ancient Greek, Democritus; Newton, as a Christian, however, instead of regarding the atoms as eternal, argues that they were created by God. And in the second selection, from his *Mathematical Principles*, Rule I is Newton's restatement of a rule that was formulated at least as early as the fourteenth century, and Rule III clearly reveals the influence of Francis Bacon.

During his long lifetime, Newton was widely honored, both in his own country and abroad. Yet toward the end of his life, he was able to make this modest assessment of his career: "I know not what the world will think of my labors, but to myself it seems that I have been but as a child playing on the sea-shore; now finding some pebble rather more polished, and now some shell rather more agreeably variegated than another, while the immense ocean of truth extended itself unexplored before me."

OPTICS

. . .

All these things being considered, it seems probable to me, that God in the beginning formed matter in solid, massy, hard, impenetrable, moveable particles, of such sizes and figures, and with such other properties, and in such proportion to space, as most conduced to the end for which he formed them; and that these primitive particles, being solids, are incomparably harder than any porous bodies compounded of them; even so very hard, as never to wear or break in pieces; no ordinary power being able to divide what God himself made one in the first creation. While the particles continue entire, they may compose bodies of one and the same nature and texture in all ages: But should they wear away, or break in pieces, the nature of things depending on them, would be changed. Water and earth, composed of old worn particles and fragments of particles, would not be of the same nature and texture now, with water and earth composed of entire particles in the beginning. And therefore, that nature may be lasting, the changes of corporeal things are to be placed only in the various separations and new associations and motions of these permanent particles; compound bodies being apt to break, not in the midst of solid particles, but where those particles are laid together, and only touch in a few points.

It seems to me farther, that these particles have not only a force of inertia accompanied with such passive laws of motion as naturally result from that force, but also that they are moved by certain active principles, such as is that of gravity, and that

which causes fermentation, and the cohesion of bodies. These principles I consider, not as occult qualities, supposed to result from the specific forms of things, but as general laws of nature, by which the things themselves are formed; their truth appearing to us by phenomena, though their causes be not yet discovered. For these are manifest qualities, and their causes only are occult. And the *Aristotelians* gave the name of occult qualities, not to manifest qualities, but to such qualities only as they supposed to lie hid in bodies, and to be the unknown causes of manifest effects: Such as would be the causes of gravity, and of magnetic and electric attractions, and of fermentations, if we should suppose that these forces or actions arose from qualities unknown to us, and uncapable of being discovered and made manifest. Such occult qualities put a stop to the improvement of natural philosophy, and therefore of late years have been rejected. To tell us that every species of things is endowed with an occult specific quality by which it acts and produces manifest effects, is to tell us nothing: But to derive two or three general principles of motion from phenomena, and afterwards to tell us how the properties and actions of all corporeal things follow from those manifest principles, would be a very great step in philosophy, though the causes of those principles were not yet discovered: And therefore I scruple not to propose the principles of motion above-mentioned, they being of very general extent, and leave their causes to be found out.

Now by the help of these principles, all material things seem to have been composed of the hard and solid particles above-mentioned, variously associated in the first creation by the counsel of an in-

OPTICS, *or, A Treatise of the Reflections, Refractions, Inflections and Colours of Light,* Isaac Newton, 4th ed. (London, 1730), pp. 400-405. Capitalization and spelling have been modernized.

telligent agent. For it became him who created them to set them in order. And if he did so, it's unphilosophical to seek for any other origin of the world, or to pretend that it might arise out of a chaos by the mere laws of nature; though being once formed, it may continue by those laws for many ages. For while comets move in very eccentric orbs in all manner of positions, blind fate could never make all the planets move one and the same way in orbs concentric, some inconsiderable irregularities excepted, which may have risen from the mutual actions of comets and planets upon one another, and which will be apt to increase, till this system wants a reformation. Such a wonderful uniformity in the planetary system must be allowed the effect of choice. And so must the uniformity in the bodies of animals, they having generally a right and a left side shaped alike, and on either side of their bodies two legs behind, and either two arms, or two legs, or two wings before upon their shoulders, and between their shoulders a neck running down into a back-bone, and a head upon it; and in the head two ears, two eyes, a nose, a mouth, and a tongue, alike situated. Also the first contrivance of those very artificial parts of animals, the eyes, ears, brain, muscles, heart, lungs, midriff, glands, larynx, hands, wings, swimming bladders, natural spectacles, and other organs of sense and motion; and the instinct of brutes and insects, can be the effect of nothing else than the wisdom and skill of a powerful ever-living agent, who being in all places, is more able by his will to move the bodies within his boundless uniform sensorium, and thereby to form and reform the parts of the universe, than we are by our will to move the parts of our own bodies. And yet we are not to consider the world as the body of God, or the several parts thereof, as the parts of God. He is a uniform being, void of organs, members or parts, and they are his creatures subordinate to him, and subservient to his will; and he is no more the soul of them, than the soul of man is the soul of the species of things carried through the organs of sense into the place of its sensation, where it perceives them by means of its immediate presence, without the intervention of any third thing. The organs of sense are not for enabling the soul to perceive the species of things in its sensorium, but only for conveying them thither; and God has no need of such organs, he being everywhere present to the things themselves. And since space is divisible *in infinitum*, and matter is not necessarily in all places, it may be also allowed that God is able to create particles of matter of several sizes and figures, and in several proportions to space, and perhaps of different densities and forces, and thereby to vary the laws of nature, and make worlds of several sorts in several parts of the universe. At least, I see nothing of contradiction in all this.

As in mathematics, so in natural philosophy, the investigation of difficult things by the method of analysis, ought ever to precede the method of composition. This analysis consists in making experiments and observations, and in drawing general conclusions from them by induction, and admitting of no objections against the conclusions, but such as are taken from experiments, or other certain truths. For hypotheses are not to be regarded in experimental philosophy. And although the arguing from experiments and observations by induction be no demonstration of general conclusions; yet it is the best way of arguing which the nature of things admits of, and may be looked upon as so much the stronger, by how much the induction is more general. And if no exception occur from phenomena, the conclusion may be pronounced generally. But if at any time afterwards any exception shall occur from experiments, it may then begin to be pronounced with such exceptions as occur. By this way of analysis we may proceed from compounds to ingredients, and from motions to the forces producing them; and in general, from effects to their causes, and from particular causes to more general ones, till the argument ends in the most general. This is the method of analysis: And the synthesis consists in assuming the causes discovered, and established as principles, and by them explaining the phenomena proceeding from them, and proving the explanations.

THE MATHEMATICAL PRINCIPLES OF NATURAL PHILOSOPHY

THE RULES OF REASONING IN PHILOSOPHY

Rule I

We are to admit no more causes of natural things, than such as are both true and sufficient to explain their appearances.

To this purpose the philosophers say, that Nature does nothing in vain, and more is in vain, when less will serve; for Nature is pleased with simplicity, and affects not the pomp of superfluous causes.

Rule II

Therefore to the same natural effects we must, as far as possible, assign the same causes.

As to respiration in a man, and in a beast; the descent of stones in Europe and in America; the light of our culinary fire and of the sun; the reflection of light in the earth, and in the planets.

Rule III

The qualities of bodies, which admit neither intension nor remission of degrees, and which are found to belong to all bodies within the reach of our experiments, are to be esteemed the universal qualities of all bodies whatsoever.

THE MATHEMATICAL PRINCIPLES OF NATURAL PHILOSOPHY, Isaac Newton, trans. A. Motte (London, 1729), II, 202-205. Capitalization and spelling have been modernized.

For since the qualities of bodies are only known to us by experiments, we are to hold for universal, all such as universally agree with experiments; and such as are not liable to diminution, can never be quite taken away. We are certainly not to relinquish the evidence of experiments for the sake of dreams and vain fictions of our own devising; nor are we to recede from the analogy of Nature, which uses to be simple, and always consonant to itself. We no otherways know the extension of bodies, than by our senses, nor do these reach it in all bodies; but because we perceive extension in all that are sensible, therefore we ascribe it universally to all others also. That abundance of bodies are hard we learn by experience. And because the hardness of the whole arises from the hardness of the parts, we therefore justly infer the hardness of the undivided particles not only of the bodies we feel but of all others. That all bodies are impenetrable, we gather not from reason, but from sensation. The bodies which we handle we find impenetrable, and thence conclude impenetrability to be an universal property of all bodies whatsoever. That all bodies are moveable, and endowed with certain powers (which we call the forces of inertia) of persevering in their motion or in their rest, we only infer from the like properties observed in the bodies which we have seen. The extension, hardness, impenetrability, mobility, and force of inertia of the whole, result from the extension, hardness, impenetrability, mobility, and forces of inertia of the parts: and thence we conclude the least particles of all bodies to be also all extended, and hard, and impenetrable, and moveable, and endowed with their proper forces of inertia. And this is the foundation of all philosophy. Moreover, that the divided but contiguous particles of bodies may be separated from one another, is matter of observation; and, in the particles that remain undivided, our minds are able to distinguish yet lesser parts, as is mathematically demonstrated. But whether the parts so distinguished, and not yet divided, may, by the powers of nature, be actually divided and separated from one another, we cannot certainly determine. Yet had we the proof of but one experiment, that any undivided particle, in breaking a hard and solid body, suffered a division, we might by virtue of this rule, conclude, that the undivided as well as the divided particles, may be divided and actually separated to infinity.

Lastly, if it universally appears, by experiments and astronomical observations, that all bodies about the earth, gravitate towards the earth; and that in proportion to the quantity of matter which they severally contain; that the moon likewise, according

to the quantity of its matter, gravitates towards the earth; that on the other hand our sea gravitates towards the moon; and all the planets mutually one towards another; and the comets in like manner towards the sun; we must, in consequence of this rule, universally allow, that all bodies whatsoever are endowed with a principle of mutual gravitation. For the argument from the appearances concludes with more force for the universal gravitation of all bodies, than for their impenetrability; of which among those in the celestial regions, we have no experiments, nor any manner of observation. Not that I affirm gravity to be essential to bodies. By their inherent force I mean nothing but their force of inertia. This is immutable. Their gravity is diminished as they recede from the earth.

Rule IV

In experimental philosophy we are to look upon propositions collected by general induction from phenomena as accurately or very nearly true, notwithstanding any contrary hypotheses that may be imagined, till such time as other phenomena occur, by which they may either be made more accurate, or liable to exceptions.

This rule we must follow that the argument of induction may not be evaded by hypotheses.

John Locke

As the political philosophy of Thomas Hobbes was in part a reaction against the anarchy of the 1640's in England, so that of John Locke (1632-1704) represents a response to the Glorious Revolution of 1688. As Locke stated in the preface to his *Of Civil Government*, he hoped "to establish the throne of our great restorer, our present King William; to make good his title, in the consent of the people . . . and to justify to the world the people of England, whose love of their just and natural rights, with their resolution to preserve them, saved the nation when it was on the very birth of slavery and ruin."

Locke was personally involved in the crises that led up to the Revolution. As physician and secretary to the Earl of Shaftesbury, a prominent Whig politician and leader of the opposition against Charles II, he shared the political fortunes of his employer. When Shaftesbury, implicated in a plot to prevent the accession of James II, fled to Holland, Locke was forced to flee with him. It was during his exile in Holland that Locke wrote *Of Civil Government*, which is divided into two treatises. The first treatise is a refutation of the doctrine of divine right, and the second (from which the first selection is taken) is a statement of his own political theory. Although Locke's second treatise, like Hobbes's *Leviathan*, grew out of the author's reaction to a particular political situation, both in its content and its influence it far transcended the local scene. It was the first philosophical statement of the modern position known as liberalism, a position that was to be reformulated by Jeremy Bentham in the eighteenth century, John Stuart Mill in the nineteenth, and John Dewey in the twentieth. The second treatise had its greatest practical effects during the eighteenth century when the leaders of the American and French revolutions found in it an intellectual justification for their cause. Many of the passages in the Declaration of Independence, for example, paraphrase the language of the second treatise.

The second selection is from Locke's most important work, *An Essay Concerning Human Understanding*. This book, a detailed analysis of the source, nature, and scope of human knowledge, exerted a subtle but profound influence on subsequent Western thought, particularly that of the Enlightenment. The eighteenth-century intellectuals hailed Locke for having accomplished, in the realm of human understanding, what Newton had achieved in the realm of physical nature. Just as Newton's law of universal gravitation, they felt, had eliminated the necessity for an appeal to divine Providence in explaining the operations of the physical world, so, they argued, Locke's denial of innate ideas undermined the whole doctrine of the absolute, revealed truths of religion. Hence both Newton and Locke were used as intellectual weapons in the battle that the leaders of the Enlightenment were waging on behalf of reason against what they conceived to be the obscurantism of the Church. Unfortunately, neither Locke nor his admirers were aware that the Lockian assumptions, when pushed to their ultimate conclusions, would undermine the very reason they were meant to support. It remained for his successor, David Hume, to demonstrate this point.

OF CIVIL GOVERNMENT

BOOK II

Chapter I

. . .

I think it may not be amiss to set down what I take to be political power; that the power of a magistrate over a subject may be distinguished from that of a father over his children, a master over his servants, a husband over his wife, and a lord over his slave. All which distinct powers happening sometimes together in the same man, if he be considered under these different relations, it may help us to distinguish these powers one from another, and show the difference betwixt a ruler of a commonwealth, a father of a family, and a captain of a galley.

Political power, then, I take to be a right of making laws with penalties of death, and consequently all less penalties, for the regulating and preserving of property, and of employing the force of the community, in the execution of such laws, and in the defence of the commonwealth from foreign injury; and all this only for the public good.

Chapter II

OF THE STATE OF NATURE

To understand political power right, and derive it from its original, we must consider what state all men are naturally in, and that is, a state of perfect freedom to order their actions and dispose of their possessions and persons, as they think fit, within the bounds of the law of nature; without asking leave, or depending upon the will of any other man.

OF CIVIL GOVERNMENT, in *The Works of John Locke*, 12th ed. (London, 1824), IV, 339-342, 347-349, 351-356, 361, 389-391, 394-395, 411-415, 426-427, 469-474, 476.

A state also of equality, wherein all the power and jurisdiction is reciprocal, no one having more than another; there being nothing more evident, than that creatures of the same species and rank, promiscuously born to all the same advantages of nature, and the use of the same faculties, should also be equal one amongst another without subordination or subjection; unless the lord and master of them all should, by any manifest declaration of his will, set one above another, and confer on him, by an evident and clear appointment, an undoubted right to dominion and sovereignty. . . .

But though this be a state of liberty, yet it is not a state of licence: though man in that state have an uncontrollable liberty to dispose of his person or possessions, yet he has not liberty to destroy himself, or so much as any creature in his possession, but where some nobler use than its bare preservation calls for it. The state of nature has a law of nature to govern it, which obliges every one: and reason, which is that law, teaches all mankind, who will but consult it, that being all equal and independent, no one ought to harm another in his life, health, liberty, or possessions: for men being all the workmanship of one omnipotent and infinitely wise Maker; all the servants of one sovereign master, sent into the world by his order, and about his business; they are his property, whose workmanship they are, made to last during his, not another's pleasure: and being furnished with like faculties, sharing all in one community of nature, there cannot be supposed any such subordination among us, that may authorize us to destroy another, as if we were made for one another's uses, as the inferior ranks of creatures are for ours. Every one, as he is bound to preserve himself, and not to quit his station wilfully, so by the like reason, when his own preservation comes not in competition, ought he, as much as he can, to preserve the rest of mankind, and may not, unless it be to do justice to an offender, take away or impair the life, or what tends to the preservation of life, the liberty, health, limb, or goods of another.

And that all men may be restrained from invading others' rights, and from doing hurt to one another, and the law of nature be observed, which willeth the peace and preservation of all mankind, the execution of the law of nature is, in that state, put into every man's hands, whereby every one has a right to punish the transgressors of that law to such a degree as may hinder its violation: for the law of nature would, as all other laws that concern men in this world, be in vain, if there were nobody that in the state of nature had a power to execute that law, and thereby preserve the innocent and restrain offenders. And if any one in the state of nature may punish another for any evil he has done, every one may do so: for in that state of perfect equality, where naturally there is no superiority or jurisdiction of one over another, what any may do in prosecution of that law, every one must needs have a right to do.

And thus, in the state of nature, "one man comes by a power over another;" but yet no absolute or arbitrary power, to use a criminal, when he has got him in his hands, according to the passionate heats, or boundless extravagancy of his own will; but only to retribute to him, so far as calm reason and conscience dictate, what is proportionate to his transgression; which is so much as may serve for reparation and restraint: for these two are the only reasons, why one man may lawfully do harm to another, which is that we call punishment. In transgressing the law of nature, the offender declares himself to live by

another rule than that of reason and common equity, which is that measure God has set to the actions of men, for their mutual security; and so he becomes dangerous to mankind, the tie, which is to secure them from injury and violence, being slighted and broken by him. Which being a trespass against the whole species, and the peace and safety of it, provided for by the law of nature; every man upon this score, by the right he hath to preserve mankind in general, may restrain, or, where it is necessary, destroy things noxious to them, and so may bring such evil on any one, who hath transgressed that law, as may make him repent the doing of it, and thereby deter him, and by his example others, from doing the like mischief. And in this case, and upon this ground, "every man hath a right to punish the offender, and be executioner of the law of nature."

.   .   .

Chapter III

OF THE STATE OF WAR

The state of war is a state of enmity and destruction: and therefore declaring by word or action, not a passionate and hasty, but a sedate settled design upon another man's life, puts him in a state of war with him against whom he has declared such an intention, and so has exposed his life to the other's power to be taken away by him, or any one that joins with him in his defence, and espouses his quarrel; it being reasonable and just, I should have a right to destroy that which threatens me with destruction; for, by the fundamental law of nature, man being to be preserved as much as possible, when all cannot be preserved, the safety of the innocent is to be preferred: and one may destroy a man who makes war upon him, or has discovered an enmity to his being, for the same reason that he may kill a wolf or a lion; because such men are not under the ties of the common law of reason, have no other rule, but that of force and violence, and so may be treated as beasts of prey, those dangerous and noxious creatures, that will be sure to destroy him whenever he falls into their power.

And hence it is, that he who attempts to get another man into his absolute power, does thereby put himself into a state of war with him; it being to be understood as a declaration of a design upon his life: for I have reason to conclude, that he who would get me into his power without my consent, would use me as he pleased when he got me there, and destroy me too when he had a fancy to it; for nobody can desire to have me in his absolute power, unless it be to compel me by force to that which is against the right of my freedom, *i.e.*, make me a slave. To be free from such force is the only security of my preservation; and reason bids me look on him, as an enemy to my preservation, who would take away that freedom which is the fence to it; so that he who makes an attempt to enslave me, thereby puts himself into a state of war with me. He that, in the state of nature, would take away the freedom that belongs to any one in that state, must necessarily be supposed to have a design to take away every thing else, that freedom being the foundation of all the rest; as he that, in the state of society, would take away the freedom belonging to those of that society or commonwealth, must be supposed to design to take away from them every thing else, and so be looked on as in a state of war.

This makes it lawful for a man to kill a thief, who has not in the least hurt him, nor declared any design upon his life, any farther than, by the use of force, so to get him in his power, as to take away his money, or what he pleases, from him; because using force, where he has no right, to get me into his power, let his pretence be what it will, I have no reason to suppose, that he,

who would take away my liberty, would not, when he had me in his power, take away every thing else. And therefore it is lawful for me to treat him as one who has put himself into a state of war with me, *i.e.*, kill him if I can; for to that hazard does he justly expose himself, whoever introduces a state of war, and is aggressor in it.

And here we have the plain "difference between the state of nature and the state of war," which however some men have confounded, are as far distant, as a state of peace, good-will, mutual assistance and preservation, and a state of enmity, malice, violence and mutual destruction, are one from another. Men living together according to reason, without a common superiour on earth, with authority to judge between them, is properly the state of nature. But force, or a declared design of force, upon the person of another, where there is no common superiour on earth to appeal to for relief, is the state of war: and it is the want of such an appeal gives a man the right of war even against an aggressor, though he be in society and a fellow-subject.

.   .   .   .

Chapter IV

OF SLAVERY

The natural liberty of man is to be free from any superior power on earth, and not to be under the will or legislative authority of man, but to have only the law of nature for his rule. The liberty of man, in society, is to be under no other legislative power, but that established, by consent, in the commonwealth; nor under the dominion of any will, or restraint of any law, but what that legislative shall enact, according to the trust put in it. Freedom then is not what Sir Robert Filmer tells us, "a liberty for every one to do what he lists, to live as he pleases, and not to be tied by any laws:" but freedom of men under government is, to have a standing rule to live by, common to every one of that society, and made by the legislative power erected in it; a liberty to follow my own will in all things, where the rule prescribes not; and not to be subject to the inconstant, uncertain, unknown, arbitrary will of another man: as freedom of nature is, to be under no other restraint but the law of nature.

This freedom from absolute, arbitrary power, is so necessary to, and closely joined with a man's preservation, that he cannot part with it, but by what forfeits his preservation and life together.

. . .

Chapter V

OF PROPERTY

. . .

God, who hath given the world to men in common, hath also given them reason to make use of it to the best advantage of life, and convenience. The earth, and all that is therein, is given to men for the support and comfort of their being. And though all the fruits it naturally produces, and beasts it feeds, belong to mankind in common, as they are produced by the spontaneous hand of nature; and nobody has originally a private dominion, exclusive of the rest of mankind, in any of them, as they are thus in their natural state; yet being given for the use of men, there must of necessity be a means to appropriate them some way or other, before they can be of any use, or at all beneficial to any particular man. The fruit, or venison, which nourishes the wild Indian, who knows no enclosure, and is still a tenant in common, must be his, and so his, *i.e.*, a part of him, that another can no longer have any right to it, before it can do him any good for the support of his life.

Though the earth, and all inferior creatures, be common to all men, yet every man has a property in his own person: this nobody has any right to but himself. The labour of his body, and the work of his hands, we may say, are properly his. Whatsoever then he removes out of the state that nature hath provided, and left it in, he hath mixed his labour with, and joined to it something that is his own, and thereby makes it his property. It being by him removed from the common state nature hath placed it in, it hath by this labour something annexed to it, that excludes the common right of other men. For this labour being the unquestionable property of the labourer, no man but he can have a right to what that is once joined to, at least where there is enough, and as good, left in common for others.

He that is nourished by the acorns he picked up under an oak, or the apples he gathered from the trees in the wood, has certainly appropriated them to himself. Nobody can deny but the nourishment is his. I ask then, when did they begin to be his? when he digested? or when he eat? or when he boiled? or when he brought them home? or when he picked them up? and it is plain, if the first gathering made them not his, nothing else could. That labour put a distinction between them and common: that added something to them more than nature, the common mother of all, had done; and so they became his private right. And will any one say he had no right to those acorns or apples he thus appropriated, because he had not the consent of all mankind to make them his? was it a robbery thus to assume to himself what belonged to all in common? If such a consent as that was necessary, man had starved, notwithstanding the plenty God had given him. We see in commons, which remain so by compact, that it is the taking any part of what is common, and removing it out of the state nature leaves it in, which begins the property; without which the common is of no use. And the taking of this or that part does not depend on the express consent of all the commoners. Thus the grass my horse has bit; the turfs my servant has cut; and the ore I have digged in any place, where I have a right to them in common with others, become my property, without the assignation or consent of any body. The labour that was mine, removing them out of that common state they were in, hath fixed my property in them.

• • •

It will perhaps be objected to this, that "if gathering the acorns, or other fruits of the earth, &c. makes a right to them, then any one may engross as much as he will." To which I answer, Not so. The same law of nature, that does by this means give us property, does also bound that property too. "God has given us all things richly," 1 Tim. vi. 17, is the voice of reason confirmed by inspiration. But how far has he given it us? To enjoy. As much as any one can make use of to any advantage of life before it spoils, so much he may by his labour fix a property in: whatever is beyond this, is more than his share, and belongs to others. Nothing was made by God for man to spoil or destroy. And thus, considering the plenty of natural provisions there was a long time in the world, and the few spenders; and to how small a part of that provision the industry of one man could extend itself, and engross it to the prejudice of others; especially keeping within the bounds, set by reason, of what might serve for his use; there could be then little room for quarrels or contentions about property so established.

But the chief matter of property being now not the fruits of the earth, and the beasts that subsist on it, but the earth itself; as that which takes in, and carries with it all the rest; I think it is plain, that property in that too is acquired as the former. As much land as a man tills, plants, improves, cultivates, and can use the product of, so much is his property. He by his labour does, as it were, enclose it from the common. Nor will it invalidate his right, to say every body else has an equal title to it, and

therefore he cannot appropriate, he cannot enclose, without the consent of all his fellow commoners, all mankind. God, when he gave the world in common to all mankind, commanded man also to labour, and the penury of his condition required it of him. God and his reason commanded him to subdue the earth, *i.e.*, improve it for the benefit of life, and therein lay out something upon it that was his own, his labour. He that, in obedience to this command of God, subdued, tilled, and sowed any part of it, thereby annexed to it something that was his property, which another had no title to, nor could without injury take from him.

• • •

Nor is it so strange, as perhaps before consideration it may appear, that the property of labour should be able to over-balance the community of land: for it is labour indeed that put the difference of value on every thing; and let any one consider what the difference is between an acre of land planted with tobacco or sugar, sown with wheat or barley, and an acre of the same land lying in common, without any husbandry upon it, and he will find, that the improvement of labour makes the far greater part of the value. I think it will be but a very modest computation to say, that of the products of the earth useful to the life of man, nine-tenths are the effects of labour: nay, if we will rightly estimate things as they come to our use, and cast up the several expences about them, what in them is purely owing to nature, and what to labour, we shall find, that in most of them ninety-nine hundredths are wholly to be put on the account of labour.

• • •

Chapter VII

OF POLITICAL OR CIVIL SOCIETY

• • •

Whenever . . . any number of men are so united into one society, as to quit every one his executive power of the law of nature, and to resign it to the public, there and there only is a political, or civil society. And this is done, wherever any number of men, in the state of nature, enter into society to make one people, one body politic, under one supreme government; or else when any one joins himself to, and incorporates with any government already made: for hereby he authorizes the society, or, which is all one, the legislative thereof, to make laws for him, as the public good of the society shall require; to the execution whereof, his own assistance (as to his own degrees) is due. And this puts men out of a state of nature into that of a commonwealth, by setting up a judge on earth, with authority to determine all the controversies, and redress the injuries that may happen to any member of the commonwealth: which judge is the legislative, or magistrate appointed by it. And wherever there are any number of men, however associated, that have no such decisive power to appeal to, there they are still in the state of nature.

Hence it is evident, that absolute monarchy, which by some men is counted the only government in the world, is indeed inconsistent with civil society, and so can be no form of civil government at all; for the end of civil society being to avoid and remedy these inconveniencies of the state of nature, which necessarily follow from every man being judge in his own case, by setting up a known authority, to which every one of that society may appeal upon any injury received, or controversy that may arise, and which every one of the society ought to obey; wherever any persons are, who have not such an authority to appeal to for the decision of any difference between them, there those persons are still in the state of nature; and so is every absolute prince, in respect of those who are under his dominion.

For he being supposed to have all, both legislative and executive power in himself alone, there is no judge to be found, no appeal lies open to any one, who may fairly, and indifferently, and with authority decide, and from whose decision relief and redress may be expected of any injury or inconveniency that may be suffered from the prince, or by his order: so that such a man, however intitled, czar, or grand seignior, or how you please, is as much in the state of nature, with all under his dominion, as he is with the rest of mankind: for wherever any two men are, who have no standing rule, and common judge to appeal to on earth, for the determination of controversies of right betwixt them, there they are still in the state of nature, and under all the inconveniencies of it, with only this woeful difference to the subject, or rather slave of an absolute prince; that whereas in the ordinary state of nature he has a liberty to judge of his right, and, according to the best of his power, to maintain it; now, whenever his property is invaded by the will and order of his monarch, he has not only no appeal, as those in society ought to have, but, as if he were degraded from the common state of rational creatures, is denied a liberty to judge of, or to defend his right; and so is exposed to all the misery and inconveniencies, that a man can fear from one, who being in the unrestrained state of nature, is yet corrupted with flattery, and armed with power.

For he that thinks absolute power purifies men's blood, and corrects the baseness of human nature, need read but the history of this or any other age, to be convinced of the contrary.

·   ·   ·

Chapter VIII

OF THE BEGINNING OF POLITICAL SOCIETIES

Men being, as has been said, by nature, all free, equal, and independent, no one can be put out of this estate, and subjected to the political power of another, without his own consent. The only way, whereby any one divests himself of his natural liberty, and puts on the bonds of civil society, is by agreeing with other men to join and unite into a community, for their comfortable, safe, and peaceable living one amongst another, in a secure enjoyment of their properties, and a greater security against any, that are not of it. This any number of men may do, because it injures not the freedom of the rest; they are left as they were in the liberty of the state of nature. When any number of men have so consented to make one community or government, they are thereby presently incorporated, and make one body politic, wherein the majority have a right to act and conclude the rest.

For when any number of men have, by the consent of every individual, made a community, they have thereby made that community one body, with a power to act as one body, which is only by the will and determination of the majority: for that which acts any community, being only the consent of the individuals of it, and it being necessary to that which is one body to move one way; it is necessary the body should move that way whither the greater force carries it, which is the consent of the majority: or else it is impossible it should act or continue one body, one community, which the consent of every individual that united into it, agreed that it should; and so every one is bound by that consent to be concluded by the majority. And therefore we see, that in assemblies, impowered to act by positive laws, where no number is set by that positive law which impowers them, the act of the majority passes for the act of the whole, and of course determines; as having, by the law of nature and reason, the power of the whole.

And thus every man, by consenting with others to make one body politic under one government, puts himself under an obliga-tion, to every one of that society, to submit to the determination of the majority, and to be concluded by it; or else this original compact, whereby he with others incorporate into one society, would signify nothing, and be no compact, if he be left free, and under no other ties than he was in before in the state of nature.

. . . .

Chapter IX

OF THE ENDS OF POLITICAL SOCIETY AND GOVERNMENT

If man in the state of nature be so free, as has been said; if he be absolute lord of his own person and possessions, equal to the greatest, and subject to nobody, why will he part with his freedom? why will he give up his empire, and subject himself to the dominion and control of any other power? To which it is obvious to answer, that though in the state of nature he hath such a right, yet the enjoyment of it is very uncertain, and constantly exposed to the invasion of others; for all being kings as much as he, every man his equal, and the greater part no strict observers of equity and justice, the enjoyment of the property he has in this state is very unsafe, very unsecure. This makes him willing to quit a condition, which, however free, is full of fears and continual dangers: and it is not without reason, that he seeks out, and is willing to join in society with others, who are already united, or have a mind to unite, for the mutual preservation of their lives, liberties, and estates, which I call by the general name, property.

The great and chief end, therefore, of men's uniting into commonwealths, and putting themselves under government, is the preservation of their property. To which in the state of nature there are many things wanting.

First, There wants an established, settled, known law, received and allowed by common consent to be the standard of right and wrong, and the common measure to decide all controversies between them: for though the law of nature be plain and intelligible to all rational creatures; yet men being biassed by their interest, as well as ignorant for want of studying it, are not apt to allow of it as a law binding to them in the application of it to their particular cases.

Secondly, In the state of nature there wants a known and indifferent judge, with authority to determine all differences according to the established law: for every one in that state being both judge and executioner of the law of nature, men being partial to themselves, passion and revenge is very apt to carry them too far, and with too much heat, in their own cases; as well as negligence, and unconcernedness, to make them too remiss in other men's.

Thirdly, In the state of nature, there often wants power to back and support the sentence when right, and to give it due execution. They who by any injustice offend, will seldom fail, where they are able, by force to make good their injustice; such resistance many times makes the punishment dangerous, and frequently destructive, to those who attempt it.

Thus mankind, notwithstanding all the privileges of the state of nature, being but in an ill condition, while they remain in it, are quickly driven into society. Hence it comes to pass that we seldom find any number of men live any time together in this state. The inconveniencies that they are therein exposed to, by the irregular and uncertain exercise of the power every man has of punishing the transgressions of others, make them take sanctuary under the established laws of government, and therein seek the preservation of their property. It is this makes them so willingly give up every one his single power of punishing, to be exercised by such alone, as shall be appointed to it amongst them; and by such

rules as the community, or those authorized by them to that purpose, shall agree on. And in this we have the original right of both the legislative and executive power, as well as of the governments and societies themselves.

.   .   .

But though men, when they enter into society, give up the equality, liberty, and executive power they had in the state of nature, into the hands of the society, to be so far disposed of by the legislative, as the good of the society shall require; yet it being only with an intention in every one the better to preserve himself, his liberty and property; (for no rational creature can be supposed to change his condition with an intention to be worse) the power of the society, or legislative constituted by them, can never be supposed to extend farther, than the common good; but is obliged to secure every one's property, by providing against those three defects above mentioned, that made the state of nature so unsafe and uneasy. And so whoever has the legislative or supreme power of any commonwealth, is bound to govern by established standing laws, promulgated and known to the people, and not by extemporary decrees; by indifferent and upright judges, who are to decide controversies by those laws; and to employ the force of the community at home, only in the execution of such laws; or abroad to prevent or redress foreign injuries, and secure the community from inroads and invasion. And all this to be directed to no other end, but the peace, safety, and public good of the people.

.   .   .

Chapter XIII

OF THE SUBORDINATION OF THE POWERS OF THE COMMONWEALTH

Though in a constituted commonwealth, standing upon its own basis, and acting according to its own nature, that is, acting for the preservation of the community, there can be but one supreme power, which is the legislative, to which all the rest are and must be subordinate; yet the legislative being only a fiduciary power to act for certain ends, there remains still "in the people a supreme power to remove or alter the legislative," when they find the legislative act contrary to the trust reposed in them: for all power given with trust for the attaining an end, being limited by that end; whenever that end is manifestly neglected or opposed, the trust must necessarily be forfeited, and the power devolve into the hands of those that gave it, who may place it anew where they shall think best for their safety and security. And thus the community perpetually retains a supreme power of saving themselves from the attempts and designs of any body, even of their legislators, whenever they shall be so foolish, or so wicked, as to lay and carry on designs against the liberties and properties of the subject: for no man, or society of men, having a power to deliver up their preservation, or consequently the means of it, to the absolute will and arbitrary dominion of another; whenever any one shall go about to bring them into such a slavish condition, they will always have a right to preserve what they have not a power to part with; and to rid themselves of those who invade this fundamental, sacred, and unalterable law of self-preservation, for which they entered into society. And thus the community may be said in this respect to be always the supreme power.

· · ·

Chapter XIX

OF THE DISSOLUTION OF GOVERNMENT

· · ·

The reason why men enter into society, is the preservation of their property; and the end why they choose and authorize a legislative, is, that there may be laws made, and rules set, as guards and fences to the properties of all the members of the society: to limit the power, and moderate the dominion, of every part and member of the society: for since it can never be supposed to be the will of the society, that the legislative should have a power to destroy that which every one designs to secure by entering into society, and for which the people submitted themselves to legislators of their own making; whenever the legislators endeavour to take away and destroy the property of the people, or to reduce them to slavery under arbitrary power, they put themselves into a state of war with the people, who are thereupon absolved from any farther obedience, and are left to the common refuge, which God hath provided for all men, against force and violence. Whensoever therefore the legislative shall transgress this fundamental rule of society; and either by ambition, fear, folly or corruption, endeavour to grasp themselves, or put into the hands of any other, an absolute power over the lives, liberties, and estates of the people; by this breach of trust they forfeit the power the people had put into their hands for quite contrary ends, and it devolves to the people, who have a right to resume their original liberty, and, by the establishment of a new legislative, (such as they shall think fit) provide for their own safety and security, which is the end for which they are in society. What I have said here, concerning the legislative in general, holds true also concerning the supreme executor, who having a double trust put in him, both to have a part in the legislative, and the supreme execution of the law, acts against both, when he goes about to set up his own arbitrary will as the law of the society. He acts also contrary to his trust, when he either employs the force, treasure, and offices of the society to corrupt the representatives, and gain them to his purposes; or openly pre-engages the electors, and prescribes to their choice, such, whom he has, by solicitations, threats, promises, or otherwise, won to his designs: and employs them to bring in such, who have promised beforehand what to vote, and what to enact. Thus to regulate candidates and electors, and new-model the ways of election, what is it but to cut up the government by the roots, and poison the very fountain of public security?

. . .

But it will be said, this hypothesis lays a ferment for frequent rebellion. To which I answer,

First, no more than any other hypothesis: for when the people are made miserable, and find themselves exposed to the ill-usage of arbitrary power, cry up their governors as much as you will, for sons of Jupiter; let them be sacred or divine, descended, or authorized from heaven; give them out for whom or what you please, the same will happen. The people generally ill-treated, and contrary to right, will be ready upon any occasion to ease themselves of a burden that sits heavy upon them. They will wish, and seek for the opportunity, which in the change, weakness, and accidents of human affairs, seldom delays long to offer itself. He must have lived but a little while in the world, who has not seen examples of this in his time; and he must have read very little, who cannot produce examples of it in all sorts of governments in the world.

Secondly, I answer, such revolutions happen not upon every little mismanagement in public affairs. Great mistakes in the ruling part, many wrong and inconvenient laws, and all the slips of human frailty, will be borne by the people without mutiny or murmur. But if a long train of abuses, prevarications and artifices, all tending the same way, make the design visible to the people, and they cannot but feel what they

lie under, and see whither they are going; it is not to be wondered, that they should then rouse themselves, and endeavour to put the rule into such hands which may secure to them the ends for which government was at first erected; and without which, ancient names, and specious forms, are so far from being better, that they are much worse, than the state of nature, or pure anarchy; the inconveniencies being all as great and as near, but the remedy farther off and more difficult.

Thirdly, I answer, that this doctrine of a power in the people of providing for their safety anew, by a new legislative, when their legislators have acted contrary to their trust, by invading their property, is the best fence against rebellion, and the probablest means to hinder it: for rebellion being an opposition, not to persons, but authority, which is founded only in the constitutions and laws of the government; those, whoever they be, who by force break through, and by force justify their violation of them, are truly and properly rebels: for when men, by entering into society and civil government, have excluded force, and introduced laws for the preservation of property, peace, and unity amongst themselves; those who set up force again in opposition to the laws, do *rebellare*, that is, bring back again the state of war, and are properly rebels; which they who are in power, (by the pretence they have to authority, the temptation of force they have in their hands, and the flattery of those about them) being likeliest to do; the properest way to prevent the evil, is to show them the danger and injustice of it, who are under the greatest temptation to run into it.

In both the forementioned cases, when either the legislative is changed, or the legislators act contrary to the end for which they were constituted, those who are guilty are guilty of rebellion; for if any one by force takes away the established legislative of any society, and the laws by them made pursuant to their trust, he thereby takes away the umpirage, which every one had consented to, for a peaceable decision of all their controversies, and a bar to the state of war amongst them. They who remove, or change the legislative, take away this decisive power, which nobody can have but by the appointment and consent of the people; and so destroying the authority which the people did, and nobody else can set up, and introducing a power which the people hath not authorized, they actually introduce a state of war, which is that of force without authority; and thus by removing the legislative established by the society, (in whose decisions the people acquiesced and united, as to that of their own will) they untie the knot, and expose the people anew to the state of war. And if those, who by force take away the legislative, are rebels, the legislators themselves, as has been shown, can be no less esteemed so; when they, who were set up for the protection and preservation of the people, their liberties and properties, shall by force invade and endeavour to take them away; and so they putting themselves into a state of war with those who made them the protectors and guardians of their peace, are properly, and with the greatest aggravation, *rebellantes*, rebels.

But if they, who say, "it lays a foundation for rebellion," mean that it may occasion civil wars, or intestine broils, to tell the people they are absolved from obedience when illegal attempts are made upon their liberties or properties, and may oppose the unlawful violence of those who were their magistrates, when they invade their properties contrary to the trust put in them; and that therefore this doctrine is not to be allowed, being so destructive to the peace of the world: they may as well say, upon the same ground, that honest men may not oppose robbers or pirates, because this may occasion disorder or bloodshed. If any mischief come in such cases, it is not to be charged upon him who defends his own right, but on him that invades his neighbour's. If the innocent honest man must quietly quit all he has, for peace sake, to him who will lay violent hands upon it, I desire it may be considered, what a kind of peace there will be in the world, which consists only in violence and rapine; and which is to be maintained only for the benefit of robbers and oppressors.

.　　.　　.

Whosoever uses force without right, as every one does in society, who does it without law, puts himself into a state of war with those against whom he so used it; and in that state all former ties are cancelled, all other rights cease, and every one has a right to defend himself, and to resist the aggressor.

AN ESSAY CONCERNING HUMAN UNDERSTANDING

. . .

NO INNATE PRINCIPLES IN THE MIND

It is an established opinion amongst some men, that there are in the understanding certain innate principles; some primary notions, characters, as it were, stamped upon the mind of man, which the soul receives in its very first being; and brings into the world with it. It would be sufficient to convince unprejudiced readers of the falseness of this supposition, if I should only shew (as I hope I shall in the following parts of this discourse) how men, barely by the use of their natural faculties, may attain to all the knowledge they have, without the help of any innate impressions; and may arrive at certainty, without any such original notions or principles. For I imagine any one will easily grant, that it would be impertinent to suppose, the ideas of colours innate in a creature, to whom God hath given sight, and a power to receive them by the eyes, from external objects: and no less unreasonable would it be to attribute several truths to the impressions of nature, and innate characters, when we may observe in ourselves faculties, fit to attain as easy and certain knowledge of them, as if they were originally imprinted on the mind.

But because a man is not permitted without censure to follow his own thoughts in the search of truth, when they lead him ever so little out of the common road; I shall set down the reasons, that made me doubt of the truth of that opinion, as an excuse for my mistake, if I be in one; which I leave to be considered by those, who, with me, dispose themselves

AN ESSAY CONCERNING HUMAN UNDERSTANDING, John Locke, 21st ed. (London, 1805), I, 13-17, 77-79, 282-290.

to embrace truth, wherever they find it.

There is nothing more commonly taken for granted, than that there are certain principles, both speculative and practical (for they speak of both) universally agreed upon by all mankind: which therefore, they argue, must needs be constant impressions, which the souls of men receive in their first beings, and which they bring into the world with them, as necessarily and really as they do any of their inherent faculties.

This argument, drawn from universal consent, has this misfortune in it, that if it were true in matter of fact, that there were certain truths, wherein all mankind agreed, it would not prove them innate, if there can be any other way shewn, how men may come to that universal agreement, in the things they do consent in; which I presume may be done.

But, which is worse, this argument of universal consent, which is made use of to prove innate principles, seems to me a demonstration that there are none such; because there are none to which all mankind give an universal assent. I shall begin with the speculative, and instance in those magnified principles of demonstration; "whatsoever is, is;" and, "it is impossible for the same thing to be, and not to be;" which, of all others, I think have the most allowed title to innate. These have so settled a reputation of maxims universally received, that it will, no doubt, be thought strange, if any one should seem to question it. But yet I take liberty to say, that these propositions are so far from having an universal assent, that there are great part of mankind to whom they are not so much as known.

For, first, it is evident, that all children and idiots have not the least apprehension or thought of them; and the want of that is enough to destroy that universal assent, which must needs be the necessary concomitant of all innate truths: it seeming to me near a contradiction, to say, that there are truths imprinted on the soul, which it perceives or understands not: imprinting, if it signify any thing, being nothing else, but the making certain truths to be perceived. For to imprint any thing on the mind, without the mind's perceiving it, seems to me hardly intelligible. If therefore children and idiots have souls, have minds, with those impressions upon them, they must unavoidably perceive them, and necessarily know and assent to these truths; which since they do not, it is evident that there are no such impressions. For if they are not notions naturally imprinted, how can they be innate? and if they are notions imprinted, how can they be unknown? To say a notion is imprinted on the mind, and yet at the same time to say, that the mind is ignorant of it, and never yet took notice of it, is to make this impression nothing. No proposition can be said to be in the mind, which it never yet knew, which it was never yet conscious of. For if any one may, then, by the same reason, all propositions that are true, and the mind is capable of ever assenting to, may be said to be in the mind, and to be imprinted: since, if any one can be said to be in the mind, which it never yet knew, it must be only, because it is capable of knowing it, and so the mind is of all truths it ever shall know. Nay, thus truths may be imprinted on the mind, which it never did, nor ever shall know: for a man may live long, and die at last in ignorance of many truths, which his mind was capable of knowing, and that with certainty. So that if the capacity of knowing, be the natural impression contended for, all the truths a man ever comes to know, will, by this account, be every one of them innate; and this great point will amount to no more, but only to a very

improper way of speaking; which, whilst it pretends to assert the contrary, says nothing different from those, who deny innate principles. For nobody, I think, ever denied that the mind was capable of knowing several truths. The capacity, they say, is innate, the knowledge acquired. But then to what end such contest for certain innate maxims? If truths can be imprinted on the understanding without being perceived, I can see no difference there can be, between any truths the mind is capable of knowing, in respect of their original: they must all be innate, or all adventitious: in vain shall a man go about to distinguish them. He therefore, that talks of innate notions in the understanding, cannot (if he intend thereby any distinct sort of truths) mean such truths to be in the understanding, as it never perceived, and is yet wholly ignorant of. For if these words (to be in the understanding) have any propriety, they signify to be understood: so that, to be in the understanding, and not to be understood; to be in the mind, and never to be perceived; is all one, as to say, any thing is, and is not, in the mind or understanding. If therefore these two propositions, "whatsoever is, is;" and "it is impossible for the same thing to be, and not to be," are by nature imprinted, children cannot be ignorant of them; infants, and all that have souls, must necessarily have them in their understandings, know the truth of them, and assent to it.

To avoid this, it is usually answered, That all men know and assent to them, when they come to the use of reason, and this is enough to prove them innate. I answer,

Doubtful expressions, that have scarce any signification, go for clear reasons, to those, who being prepossessed, take not the pains to examine, even what they themselves say. For to apply this answer with any tolerable sense to our present purpose, it must signify one of these two things; either, that, as soon as men come to the use of reason, these supposed native inscriptions come to be known, and observed by them: or else, that the use and exercise of men's reason assists them in the discovery of these principles, and certainly makes them known to them.

If they mean, that by the use of reason men may discover these principles; and that this is sufficient to prove them innate: their way of arguing will stand thus, *viz.,* that whatever truths reason can certainly discover to us, and make us firmly assent to, those are all naturally imprinted on the mind: since that universal assent, which is made the mark of them, amounts to no more but this; that by the use of reason, we are capable to come to a certain knowledge of, and assent to them; and, by this means, there will be no difference between the maxims of the mathematicians, and theorems they deduce from them. All must be equally allowed innate; they being all discoveries made by the use of reason, and truths that a rational creature may certainly come to know, if he apply his thoughts rightly that way.

But how can these men think the use of reason necessary, to discover principles that are supposed innate, when reason (if we may believe them) is nothing else but the faculty of deducing unknown truths from principles, or propositions, that are already known? That certainly can never be thought innate, which we have need of reason to discover; unless, as I have said, we will have all the certain truths, that reason ever teaches us, to be innate. We may as well think the use of reason necessary to make our eyes discover visible objects, as that there should be need of reason, or the exercise thereof, to make the understanding see what is originally engraven on it, and cannot be in the understanding before it be perceived by it. So that to make reason discover those truths thus imprinted, is to say, that the use of reason discovers to

a man what he knew before: and if men have those innate impressed truths originally, and before the use of reason, and yet are always ignorant of them, till they come to the use of reason; it is in effect to say, that men know, and know them not, at the same time.

· · ·

I

OF IDEAS IN GENERAL, AND THEIR ORIGIN

Every man being conscious to himself that he thinks, and that which his mind is applied about, whilst thinking, being the ideas that are there, it is past doubt, that men have in their minds several ideas, such as are those expressed by the words, Whiteness, Hardness, Sweetness, Thinking, Motion, Man, Elephant, Army, Drunkenness, and others. It is in the first place then to be inquired, how he comes by them. I know it is a received doctrine, that men have native ideas, and original characters, stamped upon their minds, in their very first being. This opinion I have, at large, examined already; and, I suppose, what I have said, in the foregoing book, will be much more easily admitted, when I have shown, whence the understanding may get all the ideas it has, and by what ways and degrees they may come into the mind; for which I shall appeal to every one's own observation and experience.

Let us then suppose the mind to be, as we say, white paper, void of all characters, without any ideas; how comes it to be furnished? Whence comes it by that vast store which the busy and boundless fancy of man has painted on it, with an almost endless variety? Whence has it all the materials of reason and knowledge? To this I answer, in one word, from experience; in that all our knowledge is founded, and from that it ultimately derives itself. Our observation employed either about external sensible objects, or about the internal operations of our minds, perceived and reflected on by ourselves, is that which supplies our understandings with all the materials of thinking. These two are the fountains of knowledge, from whence all the ideas we have, or can naturally have, do spring.

First, Our senses, conversant about particular sensible objects, do convey into the mind several distinct perceptions of things, according to those various ways wherein those objects do affect them: and thus we come by those ideas we have, of Yellow, White, Heat, Cold, Soft, Hard, Bitter, Sweet, and all those which we call sensible qualities; which when I say the senses convey into the mind, I mean, they from external objects convey into the mind what produces there those perceptions. This great source of most of the ideas we have, depending wholly upon our senses, and derived by them to the understanding, I call *sensation.*

Secondly, The other fountain, from which experience furnisheth the understanding with ideas, is the perception of the operations of our own mind within us, as it is employed about the ideas it has got; which operations when the soul comes to reflect on and consider, do furnish the understanding with another set of ideas, which could not be had from things without; and such are Perception, Thinking, Doubting, Believing, Reasoning, Knowing, Willing, and all the different actings of our own minds; which we being conscious of and observing in ourselves, do from these receive into our understandings as distinct ideas, as we do from bodies affecting our senses. This source of ideas every man has wholly in himself; and though it be not sense, as having nothing to do with external objects, yet it is very like it, and might properly enough be called internal sense. But as I call the other sensation, so I call this *reflection*, the ideas it affords being such only as the mind gets by reflecting on its own operations within itself. By reflection then,

in the following part of this discourse, I would be understood to mean that notice which the mind takes of its own operations, and the manner of them; by reason whereof there come to be ideas of these operations in the understanding. These two, I say, *viz.*, external material things, as the objects of sensation; and the operations of our own minds within, as the objects of reflection; are to me the only originals from whence all our ideas take their beginnings. The term operations here I use in a large sense, as comprehending not barely the actions of the mind about its ideas, but some sort of passions arising sometimes from them, such as is the satisfaction or uneasiness arising from any thought.

The understanding seems to me not to have the least glimmering of any ideas, which it doth not receive from one of these two. External objects furnish the mind with the ideas of sensible qualities, which are all those different perceptions they produce in us: and the mind furnishes the understanding with ideas of its own operations.

These, when we have taken a full survey of them and their several modes, combinations, and relations, we shall find to contain all our whole stock of ideas; and that we have nothing in our minds which did not come in one of these two ways. Let any on examine his own thoughts, and thoroughl search into his understanding; and then le him tell me, whether all the original ideas he has there, are any other than of the objects of his senses, or of the operations of his mind, considered as objects of his reflection: and how great a mass of knowledge soever he imagines to be lodged there, he will, upon taking a strict view, see that he has not any idea in his mind, but what one of these two have imprinted; though perhaps, with infinite variety compounded and enlarged by the understanding, as we shall see hereafter.

•   •   •   •

OF OUR COMPLEX IDEAS OF SUBSTANCES

The mind being, as I have declared, furnished with a great number of the simple ideas, conveyed in by the senses, as they are found in exterior things, or by reflection on its own operations, takes notice also, that a certain number of these simple ideas go constantly together; which being presumed to belong to one thing, and words being suited to common apprehensions, and made use of for quick dispatch, are called, so united in one subject, by one name: which, by inadvertency, we are apt afterward to talk of, and consider as one simple idea, which indeed is a complication of many ideas together: because, as I have said, not imagining how these simple ideas can subsist by themselves, we accustom ourselves to suppose some substratum wherein they do subsist, and from which they do result; which therefore we call substance.

So that if any one will examine himself concerning his notion of pure substance in general, he will find he has no other idea of it at all, but only a supposition of he knows not what support of such qualities, which are capable of producing simple ideas in us; which qualities are commonly called accidents. If any one should be asked, what is the subject wherein colour or weight inheres, he would have nothing to say, but the solid extended parts: and if he were demanded, what is it that solidity and extension adhere in, he would not be in a much better case than the Indian before-mentioned, who, saying that the world was supported by a great elephant, was asked what the elephant rested on; to which his answer was, a great tortoise. But being again pressed to know what gave support to the broad-backed tortoise, replied, something, he knew not what. And thus here, as in all other cases where we use words without having clear and distinct ideas, we talk like children; who being questioned what such a thing is, which they know not, readily give

this satisfactory answer, that it is something; which in truth signifies no more, when so used either by children or men, but that they know not what; and that the thing they pretend to know and talk of, is what they have no distinct idea of at all, and so are perfectly ignorant of it, and in the dark. The idea then we have, to which we give the general name substance, being nothing but the supposed, but unknown support of those qualities we find existing, which we imagine cannot subsist, "sine re substante," without something to support them, we call that support substantia; which, according to the true import of the word, is in plain English, standing under or upholding.

An obscure and relative idea of substance in general being thus made, we come to have the ideas of particular sorts of substances, by collecting such combinations of simple ideas, as are by experience and observation of men's senses taken notice of to exist together, and are therefore supposed to flow from the particular internal constitution, or unknown essence of that substance. Thus we come to have the ideas of a man, horse, gold, water, etc., of which substances, whether any one has any other clear idea, farther than of certain simple ideas co-existent together, I appeal to every man's own experience. It is the ordinary qualities observable in iron, or a diamond, put together, that make the true complex idea of those substances, which a smith or a jeweller commonly knows better than a philosopher; who, whatever substantial forms he may talk of, has no other idea of those substances, than what is framed by a collection of those simple ideas which are to be found in them; only we must take notice, that our complex ideas of substances, besides all those simple ideas they are made up of, have always the confused idea of something to which they belong, and in which they subsist. And therefore when we speak of any sort of substance, we say it is a thing having such or such qualities; as body is a thing that is extended, figured, and capable of motion; spirit, a thing capable of thinking; and so hardness, friability, and power to draw iron, we say, are qualities to be found in a loadstone. These, and the like fashions of speaking, intimate, that the substance is supposed always something besides the extension, figure, solidity, motion, thinking, or other observable ideas, though we know not what it is.

Hence, when we talk or think of any particular sort of corporeal substances, as horse, stone, etc., though the idea we have of either of them be but the complication or collection of those several simple ideas of sensible qualities, which we used to find united in the thing called horse or stone; yet because we cannot conceive how they should subsist alone, or one in another, we suppose them existing in and supported by some common subject; which support we denote by the name substance, though it be certain we have no clear or distinct idea of that thing we suppose a support.

Voltaire

"Écrasez l'infâme," insisted Voltaire, in his ceaseless efforts to "crush the infamous thing" (the Church), which he felt was obstructing man's progress to a better world. Only when his pen was stilled by his death in 1778 at the age of eighty-three did he rest from his attack. An indefatigable and sparkling letter-writer, an inexhaustible but poor playwright, an indifferent but ardent poet, a devoted but unhistorical historian, and, above all, a superb and tireless propagandist, Voltaire used every method at his command to point up his conviction that the Church (or any organized religious body) had destroyed or was preventing the progress of mankind by hampering, through censorship and superstition, the activities of human reason. If left free to roam and investigate at will, human reason, Voltaire believed, could discover the natural laws of society, just as it had discerned the natural laws of the physical universe through the intellect and endeavors of Isaac Newton.

The first of the following selections is a rather random sampling from Voltaire's *Philosophical Dictionary*, first published in 1764 and later expanded. The second is an excerpt from *Candide*, a sparkling, witty satire on the manners and mores of the Western world in the eighteenth century.

PHILOSOPHICAL DICTIONARY

Atheism

. . .

MODERN ATHEISTS. ARGUMENTS OF THE
WORSHIPPERS OF GOD

We are intelligent beings, and
intelligent beings cannot have been formed
by a blind, brute, insensible being; there is
certainly some difference between a clod
and the ideas of Newton. Newton's intelligence, then, came from some other intelligence.

When we see a fine machine, we say there
is a good machinist, and that he has an excellent understanding. The world is assuredly an admirable machine; therefore there is
in the world, somewhere or other, an admirable intelligence. This argument is old,
but is not therefore the worse.

All animated bodies are composed of
levers and pulleys, which act according to
the laws of mechanics; of liquors, which are
kept in perpetual circulation by the laws of
hydrostatics; and the reflection that all
these beings have sentiment which has no
relation to their organization, fills us with
wonder.

The motions of the stars, that of our little earth round the sun—all are operated
according to the laws of the profoundest
mathematics. How could it be that Plato,
who knew not one of these laws—the eloquent but chimerical Plato, who said
that the foundation of the earth was an
equilateral triangle—the strange Plato, who
said there could be but five worlds, because there were but five regular bodies—
how, I say, was it that Plato, who was not
even acquainted with spherical trigonome-
try, had nevertheless so fine a genius, so

THE WORKS OF VOLTAIRE, trans. T. Smollett (Paris,
1901), VI, 109-115; VII, 58-61; XII, 289-293.

happy an instinct, as to call God the Eternal
Geometrician—to feel that there exists a
forming Intelligence? Spinoza himself con-
fesses it. It is impossible to controvert this
truth, which surrounds us and presses us on
all sides.

ARGUMENT OF THE ATHEISTS

I have, however, known refractory individuals, who have said that there is no
forming intelligence, and that motion alone
has formed all that we see and all that we
are. They say boldly that the combination
of this universe was possible because it exists; therefore it was possible for motion of
itself to arrange it. Take four planets
only—Mars, Venus, Mercury, and the
Earth; let us consider them solely in the
situations in which they now are; and let
us see how many probabilities we have that
motion will bring them again to those respective places. There are but twenty-four
chances in this combination; that is, it is
only twenty-four to one that these planets
will not be found in the same situations
with respect to one another. To these four
globes add that of Jupiter; and it is then
only a hundred and twenty to one that
Jupiter, Mars, Venus, Mercury, and our
globe will not be placed in the same positions in which we now see them.

Lastly, add Saturn; and there will then
be only seven hundred and twenty chances
to one against putting these planets in
their present arrangement, according to
their given distances. It is, then, demonstrated that once, at least, in seven hundred and twenty cases, chance might place
these planets in their present order.

Then take all the secondary planets, all
their motions, all the beings that vegetate,
live, feel, think, act, on all these globes; you
have only to increase the number of

chances; multiply this number to all eternity—to what our weakness calls *infinity*—there will still be a unit in favor of the formation of the world, such as it is, by motion alone; therefore it is possible that, in all eternity, the motion of matter alone has produced the universe as it exists. Nay, this combination must, in eternity, of necessity happen. Thus, say they, not only it is possible that the world is as it is by motion alone, but it was impossible that it should not be so after infinite combinations.

Answer. All this supposition seems to me to be prodigiously chimerical, for two reasons: the first is, that in this universe there are intelligent beings, and you cannot prove it possible for motion alone to produce understanding. The second is, that, by your own confession, the chances are infinity to unity, that an intelligent forming cause produced the universe. Standing alone against infinity, a unit makes but a poor figure.

Again Spinoza himself admits this intelligence; it is the basis of his system. You have not read him, but you must read him. Why would you go further than he, and, through a foolish pride, plunge into the abyss where Spinoza dared not to descend? Are you not aware of the extreme folly of saying that it is owing to a blind cause that the square of the revolution of one planet is always to the squares of the others as the cube of its distance is to the cubes of the distances of the others from the common centre? Either the planets are great geometricians, or the Eternal Geometrician has arranged the planets.

But where is the Eternal Geometrician? Is He in one place, or in all places, without occupying space? I know not. Has He arranged all things of His own substance? I know not. Is He immense, without quantity and without quality? I know not. All I know is, that we must adore Him and be just.

NEW OBJECTION OF A MODERN ATHEIST

Can it be said that the conformation of animals is according to their necessities? What are those necessities? Self-preservation and propagation. Now, is it astonishing that, of the infinite combinations produced by chance, those only have survived which had organs adapted for their nourishment and the continuation of their species? Must not all others necessarily have perished?

Answer. This argument, taken from Lucretius, is sufficiently refuted by the sensation given to animals and the intelligence given to man. How, as has just been said in the preceding paragraph, should combinations produced by chance produce this sensation and this intelligence? Yes, doubtless, the members of animals are made for all their necessities with an incomprehensible art, and you have not the boldness to deny it. You do not mention it. You feel that you can say nothing in answer to this great argument which Nature brings against you. The disposition of the wing of a fly, or of the feelers of a snail, is sufficient to confound you.

AN OBJECTION OF MAUPERTUIS

The natural philosophers of modern times have done nothing more than extend these pretended arguments; this they have sometimes done even to minuteness and indecency. They have found God in the folds of a rhinoceros's hide; they might, with equal reason, have denied His existence on account of the tortoise's shell.

Answer. What reasoning! The tortoise and the rhinoceros, and all the different species, prove alike in their infinite varieties the same cause, the same design, the same end, which are preservation, generation, and death. Unity is found in this immense variety; the hide and the shell bear equal testimony. What! deny God, because a shell is not like a skin! And journalists have lavished upon this coxcombry praises which they have withheld from Newton and Locke, both worshippers of the Divinity from thorough examination and conviction!

ANOTHER OF MAUPERTUIS'S OBJECTIONS

Of what service are beauty and fitness in the construction of a serpent? Perhaps, you say, it has uses of which we are ignorant. Let us then, at least, be silent, and not admire an animal which we know only by the mischief it does.

Answer. Be you silent, also, since you know no more of its utility than myself; or acknowledge that, in reptiles, everything is admirably proportioned. Some of them are venomous; you have been so too. The only subject at present under consideration is the prodigious art which has formed serpents, quadrupeds, birds, fishes, and bipeds. This art is evident enough. You ask, Why is not the serpent harmless? And why have you not been harmless? Why have you been a persecutor? which, in a philosopher, is the greatest of crimes. This is quite another question; it is that of physical and moral evil. It has long been asked, Why are there so many serpents, and so many wicked men worse than serpents? If flies could reason, they would complain to God of the existence of spiders; but they would, at the same time, acknowledge what Minerva confessed to Arachne in the fable, that they arrange their webs in a wonderful manner.

We cannot, then, do otherwise than acknowledge an ineffable Intelligence, which Spinoza himself admitted. We must own that it is displayed as much in the meanest insect as in the planets. And with regard to moral and physical evil, what can be done or said? Let us console ourselves by the enjoyment of physical and moral good, and adore the Eternal Being, who has ordained the one and permitted the other.

One word more on this topic. Atheism is the vice of some intelligent men, and superstition is the vice of fools. And what is the vice of knaves?—Hypocrisy.

.   .   .

Chain or Generation of Events

The present, we say, is pregnant with the future; events are linked one with another by an invincible fatality. This is the fate which, in Homer, is superior to Jupiter himself. The master of gods and men expressly declares that he cannot prevent his son Sarpedon from dying at the time appointed. Sarpedon was born at the moment when it was necessary that he should be born, and could not be born at any other; he could not die elsewhere than before Troy; he could not be buried elsewhere than in Lycia; his body must, in the appointed time, produce vegetables, which must change into the substance of some of the Lycians; his heirs must establish a new order of things in his states; that new order must influence neighboring kingdoms; thence must result a new arrangement in war and in peace with the neighbors of Lycia. So that, from link to link, the destiny of the whole earth depended on the elopement of Helen, which had a necessary connection with the marriage of Hecuba, which, ascending to higher events, was connected with the origin of things.

Had any one of these occurrences been ordered otherwise, the result would have been a different universe. Now, it was not possible for the actual universe not to exist; therefore it was not possible for Jupiter, Jove as he was, to save the life of his son. We are told that this doctrine of necessity and fatality has been invented in our own times by Leibnitz, under the name of sufficing reason. It is, however, of great antiquity. It is no recent discovery that there is no effect without a cause and that often the smallest cause produces the greatest effects.

Lord Bolingbroke acknowledges that he

was indebted to the petty quarrels between the duchess of Marlborough and Mrs. Masham for an opportunity of concluding the private treaty between Queen Anne and Louis XIV. This treaty led to the peace of Utrecht; the peace of Utrecht secured the throne of Spain to Philip V; Philip took Naples and Sicily from the house of Austria. Thus the Spanish prince, who is now king of Naples, evidently owes his kingdom to Mrs. Masham; he would not have had it, nor even have been born, if the duchess of Marlborough had been more complaisant towards the queen of England; his existence at Naples depended on one folly more or less at the court of London.

Examine the situations of every people upon earth; they are in like manner founded on a train of occurrences seemingly without connection, but all connected. In this immense machine all is wheel, pulley, cord, or spring. It is the same in physical order. A wind blowing from the southern seas and the remotest parts of Africa brings with it a portion of the African atmosphere, which, falling in showers in the valleys of the Alps, fertilizes our lands; on the other hand our north wind carries our vapors among the negroes; we do good to Guinea, and Guinea to us. The chain extends from one end of the universe to the other.

But the truth of this principle seems to me to be strangely abused; for it is thence concluded that there is no atom, however small, the movement of which has not influenced the actual arrangement of the whole world; that the most trivial accident, whether among men or animals, is an essential link in the great chain of destiny.

Let us understand one another. Every effect evidently has its cause, ascending from cause to cause, into the abyss of eternity; but every cause has not its effect, going down to the end of ages. I grant that all events are produced one by another; if the past was pregnant with the present, the present is pregnant with the future;

everything is begotten, but everything does not beget. It is a genealogical tree; every house, we know, ascends to Adam, but many of the family have died without issue.

The events of this world form a genealogical tree. It is indisputable that the inhabitants of Spain and Gaul are descended from Gomer, and the Russians from his younger brother Magog, for in how many great books is this genealogy to be found! It cannot then be denied that the grand Turk, who is also descended from Magog, is obliged to him for the good beating given him in 1769 by the Empress Catherine II. This occurrence is evidently linked with other great events; but whether Magog spat to the right or to the left near Mount Caucasus—made two or three circles in a well—or whether he lay on his right side or his left, I do not see that it could have much influence on present affairs.

It must be remembered, because it is proved by Newton, that nature is not a plenum, and that motion is not communicated by collision until it has made the tour of the universe. Throw a body of a certain density into water, you easily calculate that at the end of such a time the movement of this body, and that which it has given to the water, will cease; the motion will be lost and rest will be restored. So the motion produced by Magog in spitting into a well cannot have influenced what is now passing in Moldavia and Wallachia. Present events, then, are not the offspring of all past events, they have their direct lines, but with a thousand small collateral lines they have nothing to do. Once more be it observed that every being has a parent but every one has not an offspring.

*   *   *

Prejudice

Prejudice is an opinion without judgment. Thus, throughout the world, children are inspired with opinions before they can judge. There are universal and necessary prejudices, and these even constitute virtue. In all countries, children are taught to acknowledge a rewarding and punishing God; to respect and love their fathers and mothers; to regard theft as a crime, and interested lying as a vice, before they can tell what is a virtue or a vice. Prejudice may, therefore, be very useful, and such as judgment will ratify when we reason.

Sentiment is not simply prejudice, it is something much stronger. A mother loves not her son because she is told that she must love him; she fortunately cherishes him in spite of herself. It is not through prejudice that you run to the aid of an unknown child nearly falling down a precipice, or being devoured by a beast.

But it is through prejudice that you will respect a man dressed in certain clothes, walking gravely, and talking at the same time. Your parents have told you that you must bend to this man; you respect him before you know whether he merits your respect; you grow in age and knowledge; you perceive that this man is a quack, made up of pride, interest, and artifice; you despise that which you revered, and prejudice yields to judgment. Through prejudice, you have believed the fables with which your infancy was lulled: you are told that the Titans made war against the gods, that Venus was amorous of Adonis; at twelve years of age you take these fables for truth; at twenty, you regard them as ingenious allegories.

Let us examine, in a few words, the different kinds of prejudices, in order to arrange our ideas. We shall perhaps be like those who, in the time of the scheme of Law, perceived that they had calculated upon imaginary riches.

PREJUDICES OF THE SENSES

Is it not an amusing thing, that our eyes always deceive us, even when we see very well, and that on the contrary our ears do not? When your properly-formed ear hears: "You are beautiful; I love you," it is very certain that the words are not: "I hate you; you are ugly;" but you see a smooth mirror—it is demonstrated that you are deceived; it is a very rough surface. You see the sun about two feet in diameter; it is demonstrated that it is a million times larger than the earth.

It seems that God has put truth into your ears, and error into your eyes; but study optics, and you will perceive that God has not deceived you, and that it was impossible for objects to appear to you otherwise than you see them in the present state of things.

PHYSICAL PREJUDICES

The sun rises, the moon also, the earth is immovable; these are natural physical prejudices. But that crabs are good for the blood, because when boiled they are of the same color; that eels cure paralysis, because they frisk about; that the moon influences our diseases, because an invalid was one day observed to have an increase of fever during the wane of the moon: these ideas and a thousand others were the errors of ancient charlatans, who judged without reason, and who, being themselves deceived, deceived others.

HISTORICAL PREJUDICES

The greater part of historians have believed without examining, and this confidence is a prejudice. Fabius Pictor relates, that, several ages before him, a vestal of the town of Alba, going to draw water in her pitcher, was violated, that she was delivered of Romulus and Remus, that they were nourished by a she-wolf. The Roman people believed this fable; they examined not whether at that time there were vestals in Latium; whether it was likely that the daughter of a king should go out of her convent with a pitcher, or whether it was probable that a she-wolf should suckle two children, instead of eating them: prejudice established it.

A monk writes that Clovis, being in great danger at the battle of Tolbiac, made a vow to become a Christian if he escaped; but is it natural that he should address a strange god on such an occasion? Would not the religion in which he was born have acted the most powerfully? Where is the Christian who, in a battle against the Turks, would not rather address himself to the holy Virgin Mary, than to Mahomet? He adds, that a pigeon brought the vial in his beak to anoint Clovis, and that an angel brought the oriflamme to conduct him: the prejudiced believed all the stories of this kind. Those who are acquainted with human nature well know, that the usurper Clovis, and the usurper Rollo, or Rol, became Christians to govern the Christians more securely; as the Turkish usurpers became Mussulmans to govern the Mussulmans more securely.

RELIGIOUS PREJUDICES

If your nurse has told you, that Ceres presides over corn, or that Vishnu and Xac became men several times, or that Sammonocodom cut down a forest, or that Odin expects you in his hall near Jutland, or that Mahomet, or some other, made a journey to heaven; finally, if your preceptor afterwards thrusts into your brain what your nurse has engraven on it, you will possess it for life. If your judgment would rise above these prejudices, your neighbors, and above all, the ladies, exclaim "impiety!" and frighten you; your dervish, fearing to see his revenue diminished, accuses you before the cadi; and this cadi, if he can, causes you to be impaled, because he would command fools, and he believes that fools obey better than others; which state of things will last until your neighbors and the dervish and cadi begin to comprehend that folly is good for nothing, and that persecution is abominable.

CANDIDE: OR, THE OPTIMIST

Chapter I

HOW CANDIDE WAS BROUGHT UP IN A MAGNIFICENT CASTLE AND HOW HE WAS DRIVEN THENCE

In the country of Westphalia, in the castle of the most noble baron of Thunder-ten-tronckh, lived a youth whom nature had endowed with a most sweet disposition. His face was the true index of his mind. He had a solid judgment joined to the most unaffected simplicity; and hence, I presume, he had his name of Candide. The

THE WORKS OF VOLTAIRE, trans. T. Smollett (Paris, 1901), I, chaps. I-IV, XVII-XIX.

old servants of the house suspected him to have been the son of the baron's sister, by a very good sort of a gentleman of the neighborhood, whom that young lady refused to marry, because he could produce no more than threescore and eleven quarterings in his arms; the rest of the genealogical tree belonging to the family having been lost through the injuries of time.

The baron was one of the most powerful lords in Westphalia; for his castle had not only a gate, but even windows; and his great hall was hung with tapestry. He used to hunt with his mastiffs and spaniels instead of greyhounds; his groom served him for huntsman; and the parson of the parish officiated as his grand almoner. He was called My Lord by all his people, and he never told a story but every one laughed at it.

My lady baroness weighed three hundred and fifty pounds, consequently was a person of no small consideration; and then she did the honors of the house with a dignity that commanded universal respect. Her daughter was about seventeen years of age, fresh colored, comely, plump, and desirable. The baron's son seemed to be a youth in every respect worthy of the father he sprung from. Pangloss, the preceptor, was the oracle of the family, and little Candide listened to his instructions with all the simplicity natural to his age and disposition.

Master Pangloss taught the metaphysico-theologo-cosmolo-nigology. He could prove to admiration that there is no effect without a cause; and, that in this best of all possible worlds, the baron's castle was the most magnificent of all castles, and my lady the best of all possible baronesses.

It is demonstrable, said he, that things cannot be otherwise than as they are; for as all things have been created for some end, they must necessarily be created for the best end. Observe, for instance, the nose is formed for spectacles, therefore we wear spectacles. The legs are visibly designed for stockings, accordingly we wear stockings. Stones were made to be hewn, and to construct castles, therefore My Lord has a magnificent castle; for the greatest baron in the province ought to be the best lodged. Swine were intended to be eaten, therefore we eat pork all the year round: and they, who assert that everything is *right*, do not express themselves correctly; they should say that everything is *best*.

Candide listened attentively, and believed implicitly; for he thought Miss Cunegund excessively handsome, though he never had the courage to tell her so. He concluded that next to the happiness of be-

ing baron of Thunder-ten-tronckh, the next was that of being Miss Cunegund, the next that of seeing her every day, and the last that of hearing the doctrine of Master Pangloss, the greatest philosopher of the whole province, and consequently of the whole world.

One day when Miss Cunegund went to take a walk in a little neighboring wood which was called a park, she saw, through the bushes, the sage Doctor Pangloss giving a lecture in experimental philosophy to her mother's chambermaid, a little brown wench, very pretty, and very tractable. As Miss Cunegund had a great disposition for the sciences, she observed with the utmost attention the experiments, which were repeated before her eyes; she perfectly well understood the force of the doctor's reasoning upon causes and effects. She retired greatly flurried, quite pensive and filled with the desire of knowledge, imagining that she might be a *sufficing reason* for young Candide, and he for her.

On her way back she happened to meet the young man; she blushed, he blushed also; she wished him a good morning in a flattering tone, he returned the salute, without knowing what he said. The next day, as they were rising from dinner, Cunegund and Candide slipped behind the screen. The miss dropped her handkerchief, the young man picked it up. She innocently took hold of his hand, and he as innocently kissed hers with a warmth, a sensibility, a grace—all very particular; their lips met; their eyes sparkled; their knees trembled; their hands strayed. The baron chanced to come by; he beheld the cause and effect, and without hesitation, saluted Candide with some notable kicks on the breech, and drove him out of doors. The lovely Miss Cunegund fainted away, and, as soon as she came to herself, the baroness boxed her ears. Thus a general consternation was spread over this most magnificent and most agreeable of all possible castles.

Chapter II

WHAT BEFELL CANDIDE AMONG
THE BULGARIANS

Candide, thus driven out of this terrestrial paradise, rambled a long time without knowing where he went; sometimes he raised his eyes, all bedewed with tears, towards heaven, and sometimes he cast a melancholy look towards the magnificent castle, where dwelt the fairest of young baronesses. He laid himself down to sleep in a furrow, heartbroken, and supperless. The snow fell in great flakes, and, in the morning when he awoke, he was almost frozen to death; however, he made shift to crawl to the next town, which was called Waldberghoff-trarbk-dikdorff, without a penny in his pocket, and half dead with hunger and fatigue. He took up his stand at the door of an inn. He had not been long there, before two men dressed in blue, fixed their eyes steadfastly upon him. "Faith, comrade," said one of them to the other, "yonder is a well-made young fellow, and of the right size." Upon which they made up to Candide, and with the greatest civility and politeness invited him to dine with them. "Gentlemen," replied Candide, with a most engaging modesty, "you do me much honor, but upon my word I have no money." "Money, sir!" said one of the blues to him, "young persons of your appearance and merit never pay anything; why, are not you five feet five inches high?" "Yes, gentlemen, that is really my size," replied he, with a low bow. "Come then, sir, sit down along with us; we will not only pay your reckoning, but will never suffer such a clever young fellow as you to want money. Men were born to assist one another." "You are perfectly right, gentlemen," said Candide, "this is precisely the doctrine of Master Pangloss; and I am convinced that everything is for the best." His generous companions next entreated him to accept of a few crowns, which he readily complied with, at the same time offering them his note for the payment, which they refused, and sat down to table. "Have you not a great affection for—" "Oh yes! I have a great affection for the lovely Miss Cunegund." "May be so," replied one of the blues, "but that is not the question! We ask you whether you have not a great affection for the king of the Bulgarians?" "For the king of the Bulgarians?" said Candide, "Oh Lord! not at all, why I never saw him in my life." "Is it possible! oh, he is a most charming king! Come, we must drink his health." "With all my heart, gentlemen," says Candide, and off he tossed his glass. "Bravo!" cried the blues; "you are now the support, the defender, the hero of the Bulgarians; your fortune is made; you are in the high road to glory." So saying, they handcuffed him, and carried him away to the regiment. There he was made to wheel about to the right, to the left, to draw his rammer, to return his rammer, to present, to fire, to march, and they gave him thirty blows with a cane; the next day he performed his exercise a little better, and they gave him but twenty; the day following he came off with ten, and was looked upon as a young fellow of surprising genius by all his comrades.

Candide was struck with amazement, and could not for the soul of him conceive how he came to be a hero. One fine spring morning, he took it into his head to take a walk, and he marched straight forward, conceiving it to be a privilege of the human species, as well as of the brute creation, to make use of their legs how and when they pleased. He had not gone above two leagues when he was overtaken by four other heroes, six feet high, who bound him neck and heels, and carried him to a dungeon. A court-martial sat upon him, and he was asked which he liked better, to run the gauntlet six and thirty times through the whole regiment, or to have his brains blown out with a dozen musket-balls? In vain did he remonstrate to them that the human will is free, and that he chose neither; they obliged him to make a choice, and he determined, in virtue of that divine gift called free will, to run the gauntlet six and thirty times. He had gone through his discipline twice, and the regiment being composed of 2,000 men, they composed for him exactly 4,000 strokes, which laid bare all his muscles and nerves from the nape of his neck to his rump. As they were preparing to make him set out the third time our young hero, unable to support it any longer, begged as a favor that they would be so obliging as to shoot him through the head; the favor being granted, a bandage was tied over his eyes, and he was made to kneel down. At that very instant, his Bulgarian majesty happening to pass by made a stop, and inquired into the delinquent's crime, and being a prince of great penetration, he found, from what he heard of Candide, that he was a young metaphysician, entirely ignorant of the world; and therefore, out of his great clemency, he condescended to pardon him, for which his name will be celebrated in every journal, and in every age. A skilful surgeon made a cure of the flagellated Candide in three weeks by means of emollient unguents prescribed by Dioscorides. His sores were now skinned over and he was able to march, when the king of the Bulgarians gave battle to the king of the Abares.

Chapter III

HOW CANDIDE ESCAPED FROM THE
BULGARIANS, AND WHAT BEFELL
HIM AFTERWARDS

Never was anything so gallant, so well accoutred, so brilliant, and so finely disposed as the two armies. The trumpets, fifes, hautboys, drums, and cannon made such harmony as never was heard in hell itself. The entertainment began by a discharge of cannon, which, in the twinkling of an eye, laid flat about 6,000 men on each side. The musket bullets swept away, out of the best of all possible worlds, nine or ten thousand scoundrels that infested its surface. The bayonet was next the sufficient reason of the deaths of several thousands. The whole might amount to thirty thousand souls. Candide trembled like a philosopher, and concealed himself as well as he could during this heroic butchery.

At length, while the two kings were causing *Te Deums* to be sung in their camps, Candide took a resolution to go and reason somewhere else upon causes and effects. After passing over heaps of dead or dying men, the first place he came to was a neighboring village, in the Abarian territories, which had been burned to the ground by the Bulgarians, agreeably to the laws of war. Here lay a number of old men covered with wounds, who beheld their wives dying with their throats cut, and hugging their children to their breasts, all stained with blood. There several young virgins, whose bellies had been ripped open, after they had satisfied the natural necessities of the Bulgarian heroes, breathed their last; while others, half burned in the flames, begged to be despatched out of the world. The ground about them was covered with the brains, arms, and legs of dead men.

Candide made all the haste he could to another village, which belonged to the Bulgarians, and there he found the heroic Abares had enacted the same tragedy. Thence continuing to walk over palpitating limbs, or through ruined buildings, at length he arrived beyond the theatre of war, with a little provision in his budget, and Miss Cunegund's image in his heart. When he arrived in Holland his provision failed him; but having heard that the inhabitants of that country were all rich and Christians, he made himself sure of being treated by them in the same manner as at the baron's castle, before he had been driven thence through the power of Miss Cunegund's bright eyes.

He asked charity of several grave-looking

people, who one and all answered him, that if he continued to follow this trade they would have him sent to the house of correction, where he should be taught to get his bread.

He next addressed himself to a person who had just come from haranguing a numerous assembly for a whole hour on the subject of charity. The orator, squinting at him under his broad-brimmed hat, asked him sternly, what brought him thither and whether he was for the good old cause? "Sir," said Candide, in a submissive manner, "I conceive there can be no effect without a cause; everything is necessarily concatenated and arranged for the best. It was necessary that I should be banished from the presence of Miss Cunegund; that I should afterwards run the gauntlet; and it is necessary I should beg my bread, till I am able to get it: all this could not have been otherwise." "Hark ye, friend," said the orator, "do you hold the pope to be Antichrist?" "Truly, I never heard anything about it," said Candide, "but whether he is or not, I am in want of something to eat." "Thou deservest not to eat or to drink," replied the orator, "wretch, monster, that thou art! hence! avoid my sight, nor ever come near me again while thou livest." The orator's wife happened to put her head out of the window at that instant, when, seeing a man who doubted whether the pope was Antichrist, she discharged upon his head a chamberpot full of ——. Good heavens, to what excess does religious zeal transport womankind!

A man who had never been christened, an honest anabaptist named James, was witness to the cruel and ignominious treatment showed to one of his brethren, to a rational, two-footed unfledged being. Moved with pity he carried him to his own house, caused him to be cleaned, gave him meat and drink, and made him a present of two florins, at the same time proposing to instruct him in his own trade of weaving Persian silks, which are fabricated in Holland. Candide, penetrated with so much goodness, threw himself at his feet, crying, "Now I am convinced that my Master Pangloss told me truth when he said that everything was for the best in this world; for I am infinitely more affected with your extraordinary generosity than with the inhumanity of that gentleman in the black cloak, and his wife." The next day, as Candide was walking out, he met a beggar all covered with scabs, his eyes sunk in his head, the end of his nose eaten off, his mouth drawn on one side, his teeth as black as a cloak, snuffling and coughing most violently, and every time he attempted to spit out dropped a tooth.

Chapter IV

HOW CANDIDE FOUND HIS OLD MASTER PANGLOSS AGAIN AND WHAT HAPPENED TO HIM

Candide, divided between compassion and horror, but giving way to the former, bestowed on this shocking figure the two florins which the honest anabaptist, James, had just before given to him. The spectre looked at him very earnestly, shed tears and threw his arms about his neck. Candide started back aghast. "Alas!" said the one wretch to the other, "don't you know your dear Pangloss?" "What do I hear? Is it you, my dear master! you I behold in this piteous plight? What dreadful misfortune has befallen you? What has made you leave the most magnificent and delightful of all castles? What has become of Miss Cunegund, the mirror of young ladies, and nature's masterpiece?" "Oh Lord!" cried Pangloss, "I am so weak I cannot stand," upon which Candide instantly led him to the anabaptist's stable, and procured him something to eat. As soon as Pangloss had a little refreshed himself, Candide began to repeat his inquiries concerning Miss Cunegund. "She is dead," replied the other.

"Dead!" cried Candide, and immediately fainted away; his friend restored him by the help of a little bad vinegar, which he found by chance in the stable. Candide opened his eyes, and again repeated: "Dead! is Miss Cunegund dead? Ah, where is the best of worlds now? But of what illness did she die? Was it of grief on seeing her father kick me out of his magnificent castle?" "No," replied Pangloss, "her belly was ripped open by the Bulgarian soldiers, after they had ravished her as much as it was possible for damsel to be ravished; they knocked the baron, her father, on the head for attempting to defend her; my lady, her mother, was cut in pieces; my poor pupil was served just in the same manner as his sister, and as for the castle, they have not left one stone upon another; they have destroyed all the ducks, and the sheep, the barns, and the trees; but we have had our revenge, for the Abares have done the very same thing in a neighboring barony, which belonged to a Bulgarian lord."

At hearing this, Candide fainted away a second time, but, having come to himself again, he said all that it became him to say; he inquired into the cause and effect, as well as into the sufficing reason that had reduced Pangloss to so miserable a condition. "Alas," replied the preceptor, "it was love; love, the comfort of the human species; love, the preserver of the universe; the soul of all sensible beings; love! tender love!" "Alas," cried Candide, "I have had some knowledge of love myself, this sovereign of hearts, this soul of souls; yet it never cost me more than a kiss and twenty kicks on the backside. But how could this beautiful cause produce in you so hideous an effect?"

Pangloss made answer in these terms: "O my dear Candide, you must remember Pacquette, that pretty wench, who waited on our noble baroness; in her arms I tasted the pleasures of paradise, which produced these hell-torments with which you see me devoured. She was infected with the disease, and perhaps has since died of it; she received this present of a learned cordelier, who derived it from the fountain head; he was indebted for it to an old countess, who had it of a captain of horse, who had it of a marchioness, who had it of a page, the page had it of a Jesuit, who, during his novitiate, had it in a direct line from one of the fellow-adventurers of Christopher Columbus; for my part I shall give it to nobody, I am a dying man."

"O sage Pangloss," cried Candide, "what a strange genealogy is this! Is not the devil the root of it?" "Not at all," replied the great man, "it was a thing unavoidable, a necessary ingredient in the best of worlds; for if Columbus had not caught in an island in America this disease, which contaminates the source of generation, and frequently impedes propagation itself, and is evidently opposed to the great end of nature, we should have had neither chocolate nor cochineal. It is also to be observed, that, even to the present time, in this continent of ours, this malady, like our religious controversies, is peculiar to ourselves. The Turks, the Indians, the Persians, the Chinese, the Siamese, and the Japanese are entirely unacquainted with it; but there is a sufficing reason for them to know it in a few centuries. In the meantime, it is making prodigious havoc among us, especially in those armies composed of well-disciplined hirelings, who determine the fate of nations; for we may safely affirm, that, when an army of thirty thousand men engages another equal in size, there are about twenty thousand infected with syphilis on each side."

"Very surprising, indeed," said Candide, "but you must get cured." "Lord help me, how can I?" said Pangloss; "my dear friend, I have not a penny in the world; and you know one cannot be bled or have a clyster without money."

This last speech had its effect on Candide; he flew to the charitable anabaptist, James; he flung himself at his feet, and gave him so striking a picture of the miserable condition of his friend that the good man without any further hesitation agreed to take Doctor Pangloss into his house, and to pay for his cure. The cure was effected with only the loss of one eye and an ear. As he wrote a good hand, and understood accounts tolerably well, the anabaptist made him his bookkeeper. At the expiration of two months, being obliged by some mercantile affairs to go to Lisbon he took the two philosophers with him in the same ship; Pangloss, during the course of the voyage, explained to him how everything was so constituted that it could not be better. James did not quite agree with him on this point: "Men," said he "must, in some things, have deviated from their original innocence; for they were not born wolves, and yet they worry one another like those beasts of prey. God never gave them twenty-four pounders nor bayonets, and yet they have made cannon and bayonets to destroy one another. To this account I might add not only bankruptcies, but the law which seizes on the effects of bankrupts, only to cheat the creditors." "All this was indispensably necessary," replied the one-eyed doctor, "for private misfortunes are public benefits; so that the more private misfortunes there are, the greater is the general good." While he was arguing in this manner, the sky was overcast, the winds blew from the four quarters of the compass, and the ship was assailed by a most terrible tempest, within sight of the port of Lisbon.

[*After a remarkable series of experiences and adventures, including two murders, an earthquake, and a touching reunion with Cunegund, Candide and his valet Cacambo are forced to flee from the Jesuit state of Paraguay into the wilds of South America. There they are seized by the Oreillon Indians, who release them when it is discovered they have been telling the truth. Ed.*]

Chapter XVII

CANDIDE AND HIS VALET ARRIVE IN THE COUNTRY OF EL DORADO—WHAT THEY SAW THERE

When they got to the frontiers of the Oreillons, "You see," said Cacambo to Candide, "this hemisphere is not better than the other; now take my advice and let us return to Europe by the shortest way possible."

"But how can we get back?" said Candide; "and whither shall we go? To my own country? The Bulgarians and the Abares are laying that waste with fire and sword; or shall we go to Portugal? There I shall be burned; and if we abide here we are every moment in danger of being spitted. But how can I bring myself to quit that part of the world where my dear Miss Cunegund has her residence?"

"Let us return towards Cayenne," said Cacambo; "there we shall meet with some Frenchmen; for you know those gentry ramble all over the world; perhaps they will assist us, and God will look with pity on our distress."

It was not so easy to get to Cayenne. They knew pretty nearly whereabouts it lay; but the mountains, rivers, precipices, robbers, savages, were dreadful obstacles in the way. Their horses died with fatigue and their provisions were at an end. They subsisted a whole month on wild fruit, till at length they came to a little river bordered with cocoa trees; the sight of which at once revived their drooping spirits and furnished nourishment for their enfeebled bodies.

Cacambo, who was always giving as good advice as the old woman herself, said to

Candide: "You see there is no holding out any longer; we have travelled enough on foot. I spy an empty canoe near the river side; let us fill it with cocoanuts, get into it, and go down with the stream; a river always leads to some inhabited place. If we do not meet with agreeable things, we shall at least meet with something new."

"Agreed," replied Candide; "let us recommend ourselves to Providence."

They rowed a few leagues down the river, the banks of which were in some places covered with flowers; in others barren; in some parts smooth and level, and in others steep and rugged. The stream widened as they went further on, till at length it passed under one of the frightful rocks, whose summits seemed to reach the clouds. Here our two travellers had the courage to commit themselves to the stream, which, contracting in this part, hurried them along with a dreadful noise and rapidity. At the end of four-and-twenty hours they saw daylight again; but their canoe was dashed to pieces against the rocks. They were obliged to creep along, from rock to rock, for the space of a league, till at length a spacious plain presented itself to their sight. This place was bounded by a chain of inaccessible mountains. The country appeared cultivated equally for pleasure and to produce the necessaries of life. The useful and agreeable were here equally blended. The roads were covered, or rather adorned, with carriages formed of glittering materials, in which were men and women of a surprising beauty, drawn with great rapidity by red sheep of a very large size; which far surpassed the finest coursers of Andalusia, Tetuan, or Mecquinez.

"Here is a country, however," said Candide, "preferable to Westphalia."

He and Cacambo landed near the first village they saw, at the entrance of which they perceived some children covered with tattered garments of the richest brocade, playing at quoits. Our two inhabitants of the other hemisphere amused themselves greatly with what they saw. The quoits were large, round pieces, yellow, red, and green, which cast a most glorious lustre. Our travellers picked some of them up, and they proved to be gold, emeralds, rubies, and diamonds; the least of which would have been the greatest ornament to the superb throne of the Great Mogul.

"Without doubt," said Cacambo, "those children must be the king's sons that are playing at quoits." As he was uttering these words the schoolmaster of the village appeared, who came to call the children to school.

"There," said Candide, "is the preceptor of the royal family."

The little ragamuffins immediately quitted their diversion, leaving the quoits on the ground with all their other playthings. Candide gathered them up, ran to the schoolmaster, and, with a most respectful bow, presented them to him, giving him to understand by signs that their royal highnesses had forgot their gold and precious stones. The schoolmaster, with a smile, flung them upon the ground, then examining Candide from head to foot with an air of admiration, he turned his back and went on his way.

Our travellers took care, however, to gather up the gold, the rubies, and the emeralds.

"Where are we?" cried Candide. "The king's children in this country must have an excellent education, since they are taught to show such a contempt for gold and precious stones."

Cacambo was as much surprised as his master. They then drew near the first house in the village, which was built after the manner of a European palace. There was a crowd of people about the door, and a still greater number in the house. The sound of the most delightful instruments of music was heard, and the most agreeable smell came from the kitchen. Cacambo went up to the door and heard those within talking in the Peruvian language, which was his mother tongue; for every one knows that Cacambo was born in a village of Tucuman, where no other language is spoken.

"I will be your interpreter here," said he to Candide. "Let us go in; this is an eating-house."

Immediately two waiters and two servant-girls, dressed in cloth of gold, and their hair braided with ribbons of tissue, accosted the strangers and invited them to sit down to the ordinary. Their dinner consisted of four dishes of different soups, each garnished with two young paroquets, a large dish of bouille that weighed two hundred weight, two roasted monkeys of a delicious flavor, three hundred humming-birds in one dish, and six hundred fly-birds in another; some excellent ragouts, delicate tarts, and the whole served up in dishes of rock-crystal. Several sorts of liquors, extracted from the sugar-cane, were handed about by the servants who attended.

Most of the company were chapmen and wagoners, all extremely polite; they asked Cacambo a few questions with the utmost discretion and circumspection; and replied to his in a most obliging and satisfactory manner.

As soon as dinner was over, both Candide and Cacambo thought they should pay very handsomely for their entertainment by laying down two of those large gold pieces which they had picked off the ground; but the landlord and landlady burst into a fit of laughing and held their sides for some time. When the fit was over, "Gentlemen," said the landlord, "I plainly perceive you are strangers, and such we are not accustomed to charge; pardon us, therefore, for laughing when you offered us the common pebbles of our highways for payment of your reckoning. To be sure, you have none of the coin of this kingdom; but there is no necessity of having any money at all to dine in this house. All the inns, which are established for the convenience of those who carry on the trade of this nation, are maintained by the government. You have found but very indifferent entertainment here, because this is only a poor village; but in almost every other of these public houses you will meet with a reception worthy of persons of your merit." Cacambo explained the whole of this speech of the landlord to Candide, who listened to it with the same astonishment with which his friend communicated it.

"What sort of a country is this," said the one to the other, "that is unknown to all the world; and in which Nature has everywhere so different an appearance to what she has in ours? Possibly this is that part of the globe where everything is right, for there must certainly be some such place. And, for all that Master Pangloss could say, I often perceived that things went very ill in Westphalia."

Chapter XVIII

WHAT THEY SAW IN THE COUNTRY OF EL DORADO

Cacambo vented all his curiosity upon his landlord by a thousand different questions; the honest man answered him thus: "I am very ignorant, sir, but I am contented with my ignorance; however, we have in this neighborhood an old man retired from court, who is the most learned and communicative person in the whole kingdom." He then conducted Cacambo to the old man; Candide acted now only a second character, and attended his valet. They entered a very plain house, for the door was nothing but silver, and the ceiling was only of beaten gold, but wrought in such elegant taste as to vie with the richest. The antechamber, indeed, was only incrusted with rubies and emeralds; but the order in which everything was disposed made amends for this great simplicity.

The old man received the strangers on his

sofa, which was stuffed with humming-birds' feathers; and ordered his servants to present them with liquors in golden goblets, after which he satisfied their curiosity in the following terms:

"I am now one hundred and seventy-two years old, and I learned of my late father, who was equerry to the king, the amazing revolutions of Peru, to which he had been an eye-witness. This kingdom is the ancient patrimony of the Incas, who very imprudently quitted it to conquer another part of the world, and were at length conquered and destroyed themselves by the Spaniards.

"Those princes of their family who remained in their native country acted more wisely. They ordained, with the consent of their whole nation, that none of the inhabitants of our little kingdom should ever quit it; and to this wise ordinance we owe the preservation of our innocence and happiness. The Spaniards had some confused notion of this country, to which they gave the name of *El Dorado;* and Sir Walter Raleigh, an Englishman, actually came very near it about three hundred years ago; but the inaccessible rocks and precipices with which our country is surrounded on all sides, has hitherto secured us from the rapacious fury of the people of Europe, who have an unaccountable fondness for the pebbles and dirt of our land, for the sake of which they would murder us all to the very last man."

The conversation lasted some time and turned chiefly on the form of government, their manners, their women, their public diversions, and the arts. At length, Candide, who had always had a taste for metaphysics, asked whether the people of that country had any religion.

The old man reddened a little at this question.

"Can you doubt it?" said he; "do you take us for wretches lost to all sense of gratitude?"

Cacambo asked in a respectful manner what was the established religion of El Dorado. The old man blushed again, and said: "Can there be two religions then? Ours, I apprehend, is the religion of the whole world; we worship God from morning till night."

"Do you worship but one God?" said Cacambo, who still acted as the interpreter of Candide's doubts.

"Certainly," said the old man; "there are not two, nor three, nor four Gods. I must confess the people of your world ask very extraordinary questions."

However Candide could not refrain from making many more inquiries of the old man; he wanted to know in what manner they prayed to God in El Dorado.

"We do not pray to him at all," said the reverend sage; "we have nothing to ask of Him, He has given us all we want, and we give Him thanks incessantly." Candide had a curiosity to see some of their priests, and desired Cacambo to ask the old man where they were. At which he smiling said:

"My friends, we are all of us priests; the king and all the heads of families sing solemn hymns of thanksgiving every morning, accompanied by five or six thousand musicians."

"What!" said Cacambo, "have you no monks among you to dispute, to govern, to intrigue, and to burn people who are not of the same opinion with themselves?"

"Do you take us for fools?" said the old man. "Here we are all of one opinion, and know not what you mean by your monks."

During the whole of this discourse Candide was in raptures, and he said to himself, "What a prodigious difference is there between this place and Westphalia; and this house and the baron's castle. Ah, Master Pangloss! had you ever seen El Dorado, you would no longer have maintained that the castle of Thunder-ten-tronckh was the finest of all possible edifices; there is nothing like seeing the world, that's certain."

This long conversation being ended, the

old man ordered six sheep to be harnessed and put to the coach, and sent twelve of his servants to escort the travellers to court.

"Excuse me," said he, "for not waiting on you in person, my age deprives me of that honor. The king will receive you in such a manner that you will have no reason to complain; and doubtless you will make a proper allowance for the customs of the country if they should not happen altogether to please you."

Candide and Cacambo got into the coach, the six sheep flew, and, in less than a quarter of an hour, they arrived at the king's palace, which was situated at the further end of the capital. At the entrance was a portal two hundred and twenty feet high and one hundred wide; but it is impossible for words to express the materials of which it was built. The reader, however, will readily conceive that they must have a prodigious superiority over the pebbles and sand, which we call gold and precious stones.

Twenty beautiful young virgins in waiting received Candide and Cacambo on their alighting from the coach, conducted them to the bath and clad them in robes woven of the down of humming-birds; after which they were introduced by the great officers of the crown of both sexes to the king's apartment, between two files of musicians, each file consisting of a thousand, agreeable to the custom of the country. When they drew near to the presence-chamber, Cacambo asked one of the officers in what manner they were to pay their obeisance to his majesty; whether it was the custom to fall upon their knees, or to prostrate themselves upon the ground; whether they were to put their hands upon their heads, or behind their backs; whether they were to lick the dust off the floor; in short, what was the ceremony usual on such occasions.

"The custom," said the great officer, "is to embrace the king and kiss him on each cheek."

Candide and Cacambo accordingly threw their arms round his majesty's neck, who received them in the most gracious manner imaginable, and very politely asked them to sup with him.

While supper was preparing orders were given to show them the city, where they saw public structures that reared their lofty heads to the clouds; the market-places decorated with a thousand columns; fountains of spring water, besides others of rose water, and of liquors drawn from the sugar-cane, incessantly flowing in the great squares; which were paved with a kind of precious stones that emitted an odor like that of cloves and cinnamon. Candide asked to see the high court of justice, the parliament; but was answered that they had none in that country, being utter strangers to lawsuits. He then inquired if they had any prisons; they replied none. But what gave him at once the greatest surprise and pleasure was the palace of sciences, where he saw a gallery two thousand feet long, filled with the various apparatus in mathematics and natural philosophy.

After having spent the whole afternoon in seeing only about the thousandth part of the city, they were brought back to the king's palace. Candide sat down at the table with his majesty, his valet Cacambo, and several ladies of the court. Never was entertainment more elegant, nor could any one possibly show more wit than his majesty displayed while they were at supper. Cacambo explained all the king's *bons mots* to Candide, and, although they were translated, they still appeared to be *bons mots*. Of all the things that surprised Candide, this was not the least. They spent a whole month in this hospitable place, during which time Candide was continually saying to Cacambo:

"I own, my friend, once more, that the castle where I was born is a mere nothing in comparison to the place where we now are; but still Miss Cunegund is not here, and you yourself have doubtless some fair one in Europe for whom you sigh. If we remain here we shall only be as others are; whereas, if we return to our own world with only a dozen of El Dorado sheep, loaded with the pebbles of this country, we shall be richer than all the kings in Europe; we shall no longer need to stand in awe of the inquisitors; and we may easily recover Miss Cunegund."

This speech was perfectly agreeable to Cacambo. A fondness for roving, for making a figure in their own country, and for boasting of what they had seen in their travels, was so powerful in our two wanderers that they resolved to be no longer happy; and demanded permission of the king to quit the country.

"You are about to do a rash and silly action," said the king. "I am sensible my kingdom is an inconsiderable spot; but when people are tolerably at their ease in any place, I should think it would be to their interest to remain there. Most assuredly, I have no right to detain you, or any strangers, against your wills; this is an act of tyranny to which our manners and our laws are equally repugnant; all men are by nature free; you have therefore an undoubted liberty to depart whenever you please, but you will have many and great difficulties to encounter in passing the frontiers. It is impossible to ascend that rapid river which runs under high and vaulted rocks, and by which you were conveyed hither by a kind of miracle. The mountains by which my kingdom are hemmed in on all sides, are ten thousand feet high, and perfectly perpendicular; they are above ten leagues across, and the descent from them is one continued precipice. However, since you are determined to leave us, I will immediately give orders to the superintendent of my carriages to cause one to be made that will convey you very safely. When they have conducted you to the back of the mountains,

nobody can attend you farther; for my subjects have made a vow never to quit the kingdom, and they are too prudent to break it. Ask me whatever else you please."

"All we shall ask of your majesty," said Cacambo, "is only a few sheep laden with provisions, pebbles, and the clay of your country."

The king smiled at the request; and said: "I cannot imagine what pleasure you Europeans find in our yellow clay; but take away as much of it as you will, and much good may it do you."

He immediately gave orders to his engineers to make a machine to hoist these two extraordinary men out of the kingdom. Three thousand good machinists went to work and finished it in about fifteen days, and it did not cost more than twenty millions sterling of that country's money. Candide and Cacambo were placed on this machine, and they took with them two large red sheep, bridled and saddled, to ride upon, when they got on the other side of the mountains; twenty others to serve as sumpters for carrying provisions; thirty laden with presents of whatever was most curious in the country, and fifty with gold, diamonds, and other precious stones. The king, at parting with our two adventurers, embraced them with the greatest cordiality.

It was a curious sight to behold the manner of their setting off, and the ingenious method by which they and their sheep were hoisted to the top of the mountains. The machinists and engineers took leave of them as soon as they had conveyed them to a place of safety, and Candide was wholly occupied with the thoughts of presenting his sheep to Miss Cunegund.

"Now," cried he, "thanks to heaven, we have more than sufficient to pay the governor of Buenos Ayres for Miss Cunegund, if she is redeemable. Let us make the best of our way to Cayenne, where we will take shipping and then we may at leisure think of what kingdom we shall purchase with our riches.

Chapter XIX

WHAT HAPPENED TO THEM AT SURINAM, AND HOW CANDIDE BECAME ACQUAINTED WITH MARTIN

Our travellers' first day's journey was very pleasant; they were elated with the prospect of possessing more riches than were to be found in Europe, Asia, and Africa together. Candide, in amorous transports, cut the name of Miss Cunegund on almost every tree he came to. The second day two of their sheep sunk in a morass, and were swallowed up with their lading; two more died of fatigue; some few days afterwards seven or eight perished with hunger in a desert, and others, at different times, tumbled down precipices, or were otherwise lost, so that, after travelling about a hundred days they had only two sheep left of the hundred and two they brought with them from El Dorado. Said Candide to Cacambo:

"You see, my dear friend, how perishable the riches of this world are; there is nothing solid but virtue."

"Very true," said Cacambo, "but we have still two sheep remaining, with more treasure than ever the king of Spain will be possessed of; and I espy a town at a distance, which I take to be Surinam, a town belonging to the Dutch. We are now at the end of our troubles, and at the beginning of happiness."

As they drew near the town they saw a negro stretched on the ground with only one half of his habit, which was a kind of linen frock; for the poor man had lost his left leg and his right hand.

"Good God," said Candide in Dutch, "what dost thou here, friend, in this deplorable condition?"

"I am waiting for my master, Mynheer Vanderdendur, the famous trader," answered the negro.

"Was it Mynheer Vanderdendur that used you in this cruel manner?"

"Yes sir," said the negro; "it is the custom here. They give a linen garment twice a year, and that is all our covering. When we labor in the sugar works, and the mill happens to snatch hold of a finger, they instantly chop off our hand; and when we attempt to run away, they cut off a leg. Both these cases have happened to me, and it is at this expense that you eat sugar in Europe; and yet when my mother sold me for ten patacoons on the coast of Guinea, she said to me, 'My dear child, bless our fetiches; adore them forever; they will make thee live happy; thou hast the honor to be a slave to our lords the whites, by which thou wilt make the fortune of us thy parents.' Alas! I know not whether I have made their fortunes; but they have not made mine: dogs, monkeys, and parrots are a thousand times less wretched than I. The Dutch fetiches who converted me tell me every Sunday that the blacks and whites are all children of one father, whom they call Adam. As for me, I do not understand anything of genealogies; but if what these preachers say is true we are all second cousins; and you must allow that it is impossible to be worse treated by our relations than we are."

"O Pangloss!" cried out Candide, "such horrid doings never entered thy imagination. Here is an end of the matter; I find myself, after all, obliged to renounce thy Optimism."

"Optimism," said Cacambo, "what is that?"

"Alas!" replied Candide, "it is the obstinacy of maintaining that everything is best when it is worst." And so saying he turned his eyes towards the poor negro, and shed a flood of tears; and in this weeping mood he entered the town of Surinam.

Immediately upon their arrival our travellers inquired if there was any vessel in the harbor which they might send to Buenos Ayres. The person they addressed themselves to happened to be the master of a Spanish bark, who offered to agree with them on moderate terms, and appointed them a meeting at a public house. Thither Candide and his faithful Cacambo went to wait for him, taking with them their two sheep.

Candide, who was all frankness and sincerity, made an ingenuous recital of his adventures to the Spaniard, declaring to him at the same time his resolution of carrying off Miss Cunegund from the governor of Buenos Ayres.

"O ho!" said the shipmaster, "if that is the case, get whom you please to carry you to Buenos Ayres; for my part, I wash my hands of the affair. It would prove a hanging matter to us all. The fair Cunegund is the governor's favorite mistress." These words were like a clap of thunder to Candide; he wept bitterly for a long time, and, taking Cacambo aside, he said to him, "I'll tell you, my dear friend, what you must do. We have each of us in our pockets to the value of five or six millions in diamonds; you are cleverer at these matters than I; you must go to Buenos Ayres and bring off Miss Cunegund. If the governor makes any difficulty give him a million; if he holds out, give him two; as you have not killed an inquisitor, they will have no suspicion of you. I'll find out another ship and go to Venice, where I will wait for you. Venice is a free country, where we shall have nothing to fear from Bulgarians, Abares, Jews, or Inquisitors."

Cacambo greatly applauded this wise resolution. He was inconsolable at the thought of parting with so good a master, who treated him more like an intimate friend than a servant; but the pleasure of being able to do him a service soon got the better of his sorrow. They embraced each other with a flood of tears. Candide charged him not to forget the old woman. Cacambo set out the same day. This Cacambo was a very honest fellow.

Candide continued some days longer at Surinam, waiting for any captain to carry him and his two remaining sheep to Italy. He hired domestics, and purchased many things necessary for a long voyage; at length Mynheer Vanderdendur, skipper of a large Dutch vessel, came and offered his service.

"What will you have," said Candide, "to carry me, my servants, my baggage, and these two sheep you see here, directly to Venice?"

The skipper asked ten thousand piastres, and Candide agreed to his demand without hesitation.

"Ho, ho!" said the cunning Vanderdendur to himself, "this stranger must be very rich; he agrees to give me ten thousand piastres without hesitation." Returning a little while after he tells Candide that upon second consideration he could not undertake the voyage for less than twenty thousand. "Very well; you shall have them," said Candide.

"Zounds!" said the skipper to himself, "this man agrees to pay twenty thousand piastres with as much ease as ten." Accordingly he goes back again, and tells him roundly that he will not carry him to Venice for less than thirty thousand piastres.

"Then you shall have thirty thousand," said Candide.

"Odso!" said the Dutchman once more to himself, "thirty thousand piastres seem a trifle to this man. Those sheep must certainly be laden with an immense treasure. I'll e'en stop here and ask no more; but make him pay down the thirty thousand piastres, and then we may see what is to be done farther." Candide sold two small diamonds, the least of which was worth more than all the skipper asked. He paid him beforehand, the two sheep were put on board, and Candide followed in a small boat to join the vessel in the road. The skipper took advantage of his opportunity, hoisted sail, and put out to sea with a favorable wind. Candide, confounded and amazed, soon lost sight of the ship. "Alas!" said he, "this is a trick like those in our old world!"

He returned back to the shore overwhelmed with grief; and, indeed, he had lost what would have made the fortune of twenty monarchs.

Straightway upon his landing he applied to the Dutch magistrate; being transported with passion he thundered at the door, which being opened, he went in, told his case, and talked a little louder than was necessary. The magistrate began with fining him ten thousand piastres for his petulance, and then listened very patiently to what he had to say, promised to examine into the affair on the skipper's return, and ordered him to pay ten thousand piastres more for the fees of the court.

This treatment put Candide out of all patience; it is true, he had suffered misfortunes a thousand times more grievous, but the cool insolence of the judge, and the villainy of the skipper raised his choler and threw him into a deep melancholy. The villainy of mankind presented itself to his mind in all its deformity, and his soul was a prey to the most gloomy ideas. After some time, hearing that the captain of a French ship was ready to set sail for Bordeaux, as he had no more sheep loaded with diamonds to put on board, he hired the cabin at the usual price; and made it known in the town that he would pay the passage and board of any honest man who would give him his company during the voyage; besides making him a present of ten thousand piastres, on condition that such person was the most dissatisfied with his condition, and the most unfortunate in the whole province.

Upon this there appeared such a crowd of candidates that a large fleet could not have contained them. Candide, willing to choose from among those who appeared most likely to answer his intention, selected twenty, who seemed to him the most sociable, and who all pretended to merit the preference. He invited them to his inn, and promised to treat them with a supper, on condition that every man should bind himself by an oath to relate his own history; declaring at the same time, that he would make choice of that person who should appear to him the most deserving of compassion, and the most justly dissatisfied with his condition in life; and that he would make a present to the rest.

This extraordinary assembly continued sitting till four in the morning. Candide, while he was listening to their adventures, called to mind what the old woman had said to him in their voyage to Buenos Ayres, and the wager she had laid that there was not a person on board the ship but had met with great misfortunes. Every story he heard put him in mind of Pangloss.

"My old master," said he, "would be confoundedly put to it to demonstrate his favorite system. Would he were here! Certainly if everything is for the best, it is in El Dorado, and not in the other parts of the world."

At length he determined in favor of a poor scholar, who had labored ten years for the book-sellers at Amsterdam: being of opinion that no employment could be more detestable.

This scholar, who was in fact a very honest man, had been robbed by his wife, beaten by his son, and forsaken by his daughter, who had run away with a Portuguese. He had been likewise deprived of a small employment on which he subsisted, and he was persecuted by the clergy of Surinam, who took him for a Socinian. It must be acknowledged that the other competitors were, at least, as wretched as he; but Candide was in hopes that the company of a man of letters would relieve the tediousness of the voyage. All the other candidates complained that Candide had done them great injustice, but he stopped their mouths by a present of a hundred piastres to each.

Adam Smith

Although there had been many attacks on mercantilism both in England and on the Continent in the hundred years before Adam Smith, none was so sharply focused, so systematic, or so penetrating as *An Inquiry into the Nature and Causes of the Wealth of Nations*. It is interesting to note (and is probably suggestive of the motives and orientation of the author) that this work, which became a *magnum opus*, was originally designed as simply an appendix to a larger study on moral philosophy. In any event, *The Wealth of Nations*, the first volume of which appeared in 1776 (the same year in which the first volume of Edward Gibbon's *The Decline and Fall of the Roman Empire* appeared), has taken its place among the truly significant and influential works of modern times.

In analyzing the sources of the economic well-being of a nation, Smith concludes that specialization of labor and free enterprise are the most important. Here he reveals his acceptance of the intellectual movements of the eighteenth century. Although he refused to agree with the French physiocrats that agriculture alone was the source of a nation's wealth, Smith shared with the physiocrats the notion that each individual could best determine what was his own best interest. From this it followed logically that no one should be entitled to tell other people what sort of economic activity they should pursue. Thus, the government had no right to grant sole control over a market or an industry by patent or license, since such a grant violated the natural laws of political economy. That the free operation of the laws of supply and demand and the operations of the market economy should ever result in monopoly or monopsony Smith believed to be an impossibility, feeling instead that "enlightened self-interest" would always prevent such abuses.

Smith (1723-1790), a philosopher and a professor at the University of Edinburgh, would probably have been horrified at the crimes that were later committed under the sanction of his doctrines of *laissez-faire*, free enterprise, economic individualism, and the pursuit of self-interest. For while he did argue for a minimum of governmental interference and a maximum of individual enterprise, he also, and most importantly, felt that each person should govern his actions by *enlightened* self-interest. If one's self-interest is enlightened, Smith believed, he will realize that his own greatest good will be gained, not through the exploitation of his fellows, but through a recognition of his duties and obligations to the rest of society. Thus, to Smith, enlightened self-interest was a pursuit of what is best and most acceptable to the individual after, and only after, the concerns and interests of others have been satisfied.

AN INQUIRY INTO THE NATURE AND CAUSES OF THE WEALTH OF NATIONS

Introduction and Plan of the Work

The annual labour of every nation is the fund which originally supplies it with all the necessaries and conveniencies of life which it annually consumes, and which consist always either in the immediate produce of that labour, or in what is purchased with that produce from other nations.

According therefore, as this produce, or what is purchased with it, bears a greater or smaller proportion to the number of those who are to consume it, the nation will be better or worse supplied with all the necessaries and conveniencies for which it has occasion.

But this proportion must in every nation be regulated by two different circumstances; first, by the skill, dexterity, and judgment with which its labour is generally applied; and, secondly, by the proportion between the number of those who are employed in useful labour, and that of those who are not so employed. Whatever be the soil, climate, or extent of territory of any particular nation, the abundance or scantiness of its annual supply must, in that particular situation, depend upon those two circumstances.

The abundance or scantiness of this supply too seems to depend more upon the former of those two circumstances than upon the latter. Among the savage nations of hunters and fishers, every individual who is able to work, is more or less employed in useful labour, and endeavours to provide, as well as he can, the necessaries and conveniencies of life, for himself, or such of his family

AN INQUIRY INTO THE NATURE AND CAUSES OF THE WEALTH OF NATIONS, Adam Smith. 8th ed. (London, 1796), I, 1-5; II, 176-208.

or tribe as are either too old, or too young, or too infirm to go a hunting and fishing. Such nations, however, are so miserably poor, that from mere want, they are frequently reduced, or at least think themselves reduced, to the necessity sometimes of directly destroying, and sometimes of abandoning their infants, their old people, and those afflicted with lingering diseases, to perish with hunger, or to be devoured by wild beasts. Among civilized and thriving nations, on the contrary, though a great number of people do not labour at all, many of whom consume the produce of ten times, frequently of a hundred times more labour than the greater part of those who work; yet the produce of the whole labour of the society is so great, that all are often abundantly supplied, and a workman, even of the lowest and poorest order, if he is frugal and industrious, may enjoy a greater share of the necessaries and conveniencies of life than it is possible for any savage to acquire.

The causes of this improvement in the productive powers of labour, and the order, according to which its produce is naturally distributed among the different ranks and conditions of men in the society, make the subject of the First Book of this Inquiry.

Whatever be the actual state of the skill, dexterity, and judgment with which labour is applied in any nation, the abundance or scantiness of its annual supply must depend, during the continuance of that state, upon the proportion between the number of those who are annually employed in useful labour, and that of those who are not so employed. The number of useful and productive labourers, it will hereafter appear, is every where in proportion to the quantity of capital stock which is employed in setting them to work, and to the particular way in which it is so employed. The Second Book, therefore, treats of the nature of capital stock, of the manner in which it is gradually accumulated, and of the different quantities of labour which it puts into motion, according to the different ways in which it is employed.

Nations tolerably well advanced as to skill, dexterity, and judgment, in the application of labour, have followed very different plans in the general conduct or direction of it; and those plans have not all been equally favourable to the greatness of its produce. The policy of some nations has given extraordinary encouragement to the industry of the country; that of others to the industry of towns. Scarce any nation has dealt equally and impartially with every sort of industry. Since the downfall of the Roman empire, the policy of Europe has been more favourable to arts, manufactures, and commerce, the industry of towns; than to agriculture, the industry of the country. The circumstances which seem to have introduced and established this policy are explained in the Third Book.

Though those different plans were, perhaps, first introduced by the private interests and prejudices of particular orders of men, without any regard to, or foresight of, their consequences upon the general welfare of the society; yet they have given occasion to very different theories of political economy; of which some magnify the importance of that industry which is carried on in towns, others of that which is carried on in the country. Those theories have had a considerable influence, not only upon the opinions of men of learning, but upon the public conduct of princes and sovereign states. I have endeavoured in the Fourth Book, to explain, as fully and distinctly as I can, those different theories, and the principal effects which they have produced in different ages and nations.

To explain in what has consisted the revenue of the great body of the people, or what has been the nature of those funds, which, in different ages and nations, have supplied their annual consumption, is the object of these Four first Books. The Fifth and last Book treats of the revenue of the sovereignship, or commonwealth. In this Book I have endeavoured to show; first, what are the necessary expenses of the sovereign, or commonwealth; which of those expenses ought to be defrayed by the general contribution of the whole society; and which of them, by that of some particular part only, or of some particular members of it: secondly, what are the different methods in which the whole society may be made to contribute towards defraying the expenses incumbent on the whole society, and what are the principal advantages and inconveniencies of each of those methods: and, thirdly and lastly, what are the reasons and causes which have induced almost all modern governments to mortgage some part of this revenue, or to contract debts, and what have been the effects of those debts upon the real wealth, the annual produce of the land and labour of the society.

.   .   .

Book IV

CHAP. II.   OF RESTRAINTS UPON THE IMPORTATION FROM FOREIGN COUNTRIES OF SUCH GOODS AS CAN BE PRODUCED AT HOME

By restraining, either by high duties, or by absolute prohibitions, the importation of such goods from foreign countries as can be produced at home, the monopoly of the home-market is more or less secured to the domestic industry employed in producing them. Thus the prohibition of importing either live cattle or salt provisions from foreign countries secures to the graziers of Great Britain the monopoly of the home-market for butchers'-meat. The high duties upon the importation of corn, which in times of moderate plenty amount to a prohibition, give a like advantage to the growers of that commodity. The prohibition of the importation of foreign woolens is equally favourable to the woolen manufactures. The silk manufacture, though altogether employed upon foreign materials, has lately obtained the same advantage. The linen manufacture has not yet obtained it, but is making great strides towards it. Many other sorts of manufactures have, in the same manner, obtained in Great Britain, either altogether, or very nearly a monopoly against their countrymen. The variety of goods of which the importation into Great Britain is prohibited, either absolutely, or under certain circumstances, greatly exceeds what can easily be suspected by those who are not well acquainted with the laws of the customs.

That this monopoly of the home-market frequently gives great encouragement to that particular species of industry which enjoys it, and frequently turns towards that employment a greater share of both the labour and stock of the society than would otherwise have gone to it, cannot be doubted. But whether it tends either to increase the general industry of the society, or to give it the most advantageous direction, is not, perhaps, altogether so evident.

The general industry of the society never can exceed what the capital of the society can employ. As the number of workmen that can be kept in employment by any particular person must bear a certain proportion to his capital, so the number of those that can be continually employed by all the members of a great society, must bear a certain proportion to the whole capital of that society, and never can exceed that proportion. No regulation of commerce can increase the quantity of industry in any society beyond what its capital can maintain. It can only divert a part of it into a direction into which it might not otherwise have gone; and it is by no means certain that this artificial direction is likely to be more advantageous to the society than that into which it would have gone of its own accord.

Every individual is continually exerting himself to find out the most advantageous employment for whatever capital he can command. It is his own advantage, indeed, and not that of the society, which he has in view. But the study of his own advantage naturally, or rather necessarily leads him to prefer that employment which is most advantageous to the society.

First, every individual endeavours to employ his capital as near home as he can, and consequently as much as he can in the support of domestic industry; provided always that he can thereby obtain the ordinary, or not a great deal less than the ordinary profits of stock.

Thus, upon equal or nearly equal profits, every wholesale merchant naturally prefers the home-trade to the foreign trade of consumption, and the foreign trade of consumption to the carrying trade. In the home-trade his capital is never so long out of his sight as it frequently is in the foreign trade of consumption. He can know better the character and situation of the persons whom he trusts, and if he should happen to be deceived, he knows better the laws of the country from which he must seek redress. In the carrying trade, the capital of the merchant is, as it were, divided between two foreign countries, and no part of it is ever necessarily brought home, or placed under his own immediate view and command. The capital which an Amsterdam merchant employs in carrying corn from Königsberg to Lisbon, and fruit and wine from Lisbon to Königsberg, must generally be the one-half of it at Königsberg and the other half at Lisbon. No part of it need ever come to Amsterdam. The natural residence of such a merchant should either be at Königsberg or Lisbon, and it can only be some very particular circumstances which can make him prefer the residence of Amsterdam. The uneasiness, however, which he feels at being separated so far from his capital, generally determines him to bring part both of Königsberg goods which he destines for the market of Lisbon, and of the Lisbon goods which he destines for that of Königsberg, to Amsterdam: and though this necessarily subjects him to a double charge of loading and unloading, as well as to the payment of some duties and customs, yet for the sake of having some part of his capital always under his own view and command, he willingly submits to this extraordinary charge; and it is in this manner that every country which has any considerable share of the carrying trade, becomes always the emporium, or general market, for the goods of all the different countries whose trade it carries on. The merchant, in order to save a second loading and unloading, endeavours always to sell in the home-market as much of the goods of all those different countries as he can, and thus, so far as he can, to convert his carrying trade into a foreign trade of consumption. A merchant, in the same manner, who is engaged in the foreign trade of consumption, when he collects goods for foreign markets, will always be glad, upon equal or nearly equal profits, to sell as great a part of them at home as he can. He saves himself the risk and trouble of exportation, when, so far as he can, he thus converts his foreign trade of consumption into a home-trade. Home is in this manner the center, if I may say so, round which the capitals of the inhabitants of every country are continually circulating, and towards which they are always tending, though by particular causes they may sometimes be driven off and repelled from it towards more distant employments. But a capital employed in the home-trade, it has already been shown, necessarily puts into motion a greater quantity of domestic industry, and gives revenue and employment to a greater number of the inhabitants of

the country, than an equal capital employed in the foreign trade of consumption: and one employed in the foreign trade of consumption has the same advantage over an equal capital employed in the carrying trade. Upon equal, or only nearly equal profits, therefore, every individual naturally inclines to employ his capital in the manner in which it is likely to afford the greatest support to domestic industry, and to give revenue and employment to the greatest number of people of his own country.

Secondly, every individual who employs his capital in the support of domestic industry, necessarily endeavours so to direct that industry, that its produce may be of the greatest possible value.

The produce of industry is what it adds to the subject or materials upon which it is employed. In proportion as the value of this produce is great or small, so will likewise be the profits of the employer. But it is only for the sake of profit that any man employs a capital in the support of industry; and he will always, therefore, endeavour to employ it in the support of that industry of which the produce is likely to be of the greatest value, or to exchange for the greatest quantity either of money or of other goods.

But the annual revenue of every society is always precisely equal to the exchangeable value of the whole annual produce of its industry, or rather is precisely the same thing with that exchangeable value. As every individual, therefore, endeavours as much as he can both to employ his capital in the support of domestic industry, and so to direct that industry that its produce may be of the greatest value; every individual necessarily labours to render the annual revenue of the society as great as he can. He generally, indeed, neither intends to promote the public interest, nor knows how much he is promoting it. By preferring the support of domestic to that of foreign industry, he intends only his own security; and by directing that industry in such a manner as its produce may be of the greatest value, he intends only his own gain, and he is in this, as in many other cases, led by an invisible hand to promote an end which was no part of his intention. Nor is it always the worse for the society that it was no part of it. By pursuing his own interest he frequently promotes that of the society more effectually than when he really intends to promote it. I have never known much good done by those who affected to trade for the public good. It is an affectation, indeed, not very common among merchants, and very few words need be employed in dissuading them from it.

What is the species of domestic industry which his capital can employ, and of which the produce is likely to be of the greatest value, every individual, it is evident, can, in his local situation, judge much better than any statesman or lawgiver can do for him. The statesman, who should attempt to direct private people in what manner they ought to employ their capitals, would not only load himself with a most unnecessary attention, but assume an authority which could safely be trusted, not only to no single person, but to no council or senate whatever, and which would nowhere be so dangerous as in the hands of a man who had folly and presumption enough to fancy himself fit to exercise it.

To give the monopoly of the home-market to the produce of domestic industry, in any particular art or manufacture, is in some measure to direct private people in what manner they ought to employ their capitals, and must, in almost all cases, be either a useless or a hurtful regulation. If the produce of domestic can be brought there as cheap as that of foreign industry, the regulation is evidently useless. If it cannot, it must generally be hurtful. It is the maxim of every prudent master of a family, never to attempt to make at home what it will cost him more to make than to buy. The

taylor does not attempt to make his own shoes, but buys them of the shoemaker. The shoemaker does not attempt to make his own clothes, but employs a taylor. The farmer attempts to make neither the one nor the other, but employs those different artificers. All of them find it for their interest to employ their whole industry in a way in which they have some advantage over their neighbors, and to purchase with a part of its produce, or what is the same thing, with the price of a part of it, whatever else they have occasion for.

What is prudence in the conduct of every private family, can scarce be folly in that of a great kingdom. If a foreign country can supply us with a commodity cheaper than we ourselves can make it, better buy it of them with some part of the produce of our own industry, employed in a way in which we have some advantage. The general industry of the country, being always in proportion to the capital which employs it, will not thereby be diminished, no more than that of the above-mentioned artificers; but only left to find out the way in which it can be employed with the greatest advantage. It is certainly not employed to the greatest advantage, when it is thus directed towards an object which it can buy cheaper than it can make. The value of its annual produce is certainly more or less diminished, when it is thus turned away from producing commodities evidently of more value than the commodity which it is directed to produce. According to the supposition, that commodity could be purchased from foreign countries cheaper than it can be made at home. It could, therefore, have been purchased with a part only of the commodities, or, what is the same thing, with a part only of the price of the commodities, which the industry employed by an equal capital would have produced at home, had it been left to follow its natural course. The industry of the country, therefore, is thus turned away from a more to a less advantageous employment, and the exchangeable value of its annual produce, instead of being increased, according to the intention of the lawgiver, must necessarily be diminished by every such regulation.

By means of such regulations, indeed, a particular manufacture may sometimes be acquired sooner than it could have been otherwise, and after a certain time may be made at home as cheap or cheaper than in the foreign country. But though the industry of the society may be thus carried with advantage into a particular channel sooner than it could have been otherwise, it will by no means follow that the sum total, either of its industry, or of its revenue, can ever be augmented by any such regulation. The industry of the society can augment only in proportion as its capital augments, and its capital can augment only in proportion to what can be gradually saved out of its revenue. But the immediate effect of every such regulation is to diminish its revenue, and what diminishes its revenue is certainly not very likely to augment its capital faster than it would have augmented of its own accord, had both capital and industry been left to find out their natural employments.

Though for want of such regulations the society should never acquire the proposed manufacture, it would not, upon that account, necessarily be the poorer in any one period of its duration. In every period of its duration its whole capital and industry might still have been employed, though upon different objects, in the manner that was most advantageous at the time. In every period its revenue might have been the greatest which its capital could afford, and both capital and revenue might have been augmented with the greatest possible rapidity.

The natural advantages which one country has over another in producing particular commodities are sometimes so great, that it is acknowledged by all the world to

be in vain to struggle with them. By means of glasses, hotbeds, and hotwalls, very good grapes can be raised in Scotland, and very good wine too can be made of them at about thirty times the expense for which at least equally good can be brought from foreign countries. Would it be a reasonable law to prohibit the importation of all foreign wines, merely to encourage the making of claret and burgundy in Scotland? But if there would be a manifest absurdity in turning towards any employment, thirty times more of the capital and industry of the country, than would be necessary to purchase from foreign countries an equal quantity of the commodities wanted, there must be an absurdity, though not altogether so glaring, yet exactly of the same kind, in turning towards any such employment a thirtieth, or even a three hundreth part more of either. Whether the advantages which one country has over another, be natural or acquired, is in this respect of no consequence. As long as the one country has those advantages, and the other wants them, it will always be more advantageous for the latter, rather to buy of the former than to make. It is an acquired advantage only, which one artificer has over his neighbour, who exercises another trade; and yet they both find it more advantageous to buy of one another, than to make what does not belong to their particular trades.

Merchants and manufacturers are the people who derive the greatest advantage from this monopoly of the home-market. The prohibition of the importation of foreign cattle, and of salt provisions, together with the high duties upon foreign corn, which in times of moderate plenty amount to a prohibition, are not near so advantageous to the graziers and farmers of Great Britain, as other regulations of the same kind are to its merchants and manufacturers. Manufactures, those of the finer kind especially, are more easily transported from one country to another than corn or cattle. It is in the fetching and carrying manufactures, accordingly, that foreign trade is chiefly employed. In manufactures, a very small advantage will enable foreigners to undersell our own workmen, even in the home-market. It will require a very great one to enable them to do so in the rude produce of the soil. If the free importation of foreign manufactures were permitted, several of the home manufactures would probably suffer, and some of them, perhaps, go to ruin altogether, and a considerable part of the stock and industry at present employed in them would be forced to find out some other employment. But the freest importation of the rude produce of the soil could have no such effect upon the agriculture of the country.

If the importation of foreign cattle, for example, were made ever so free, so few could be imported, that the grazing trade of Great Britain could be little affected by it. Live cattle are, perhaps, the only commodity of which the transportation is more expensive by sea than by land. By land they carry themselves to market. By sea, not only the cattle, but their food and their water too, must be carried at no small expence and inconveniency. The short sea between Ireland and Great Britain, indeed, renders the importation of Irish cattle more easy. But though the free importation of them, which was lately permitted only for a limited time, were rendered perpetual, it could have no considerable effect upon the interest of the graziers of Great Britain. Those parts of Great Britain which border upon the Irish sea are all grazing countries. Irish cattle could never be imported for their use, but must be drove through those very extensive countries, at no small expense and inconvenience, before they could arrive at their proper market. Fat cattle could not be drove so far. Lean cattle, therefore, only could be imported, and such importation could interfere, not with the interest of the feeding or fattening countries, to which, by reducing the price of lean cattle, it would rather be advantageous, but with that of the breeding countries only. The small number of Irish cattle imported since their importation was permitted, together with the good price at which lean cattle still continue to sell, seem to demonstrate that even the breeding countries of Great Britain are never likely to be much affected by the free importation of Irish cattle. The common people of Ireland, indeed, are said to have sometimes opposed with violence the exportation of their cattle. But if the exporters had found any great advantage in continuing the trade, they could easily, when the law was on their side, have conquered this mobbish opposition.

Feeding and fattening countries, besides, must always be highly improved, whereas breeding countries are generally uncultivated. The high price of lean cattle, by augmenting the value of uncultivated land, is like a bounty against improvement. To any country which was highly improved throughout, it would be more advantageous to import its lean cattle than to breed them. The province of Holland, accordingly is said to follow this maxim at present. The mountains of Scotland, Wales and Northumberland, indeed, are countries not capable of much improvement, and seem destined by nature to be the breeding countries of Great Britain. The freest importation of foreign cattle could have no other effect than to hinder those breeding countries from taking advantage of the increasing population and improvement of the rest of the kingdom, from raising their price to an exorbitant height, and from laying a real tax upon all the more improved and cultivated parts of the country.

The freest importation of salt provisions, in the same manner, could have as little effect upon the interest of the graziers of Great Britain as that of live cattle. Salt

provisions are not only a very bulky commodity, but when compared with fresh
meat, they are a commodity both of worse
quality, and as they cost more labour and
expense of higher price. They could never,
therefore, come into competition with the
fresh meat, though they might with the
salt provisions of the country. They might
be used for victualling ships for distant
voyages, and such like uses, but could never
make any considerable part of the food of
the people. The small quantity of salt provisions imported from Ireland since their
importation was rendered free, is an experimental proof that our graziers have
nothing to apprehend from it. It does not
appear that the price of butchers'-meat
has ever been sensibly affected by it.

Even the free importation of foreign corn
could very little affect the interest of the
farmers of Great Britain. Corn is a much
more bulky commodity than butchers'-
meat. A pound of wheat at a penny is as
dear as a pound of butchers'-meat at four-
pence. The small quantity of foreign corn
imported even in times of the greatest
scarcity, may satisfy our farmers that they
can have nothing to fear from the freest
importation. The average quantity imported one year with another, amounts
only, according to the very well informed
author of the tracts upon the corn trade,
to twenty-three thousand seven hundred and
twenty-eight quarters of all sorts of grain,
and does not exceed the five hundredth
and seventy-one part of the annual consumption. But as the bounty upon corn occasions a greater exportation in years of
plenty, so it must of consequence occasion
a greater importation in years of scarcity,
than in the actual state of tillage would
otherwise take place. By means of it, the
plenty of one year does not compensate
the scarcity of another, and as the average quantity exported is necessarily augmented by it, so must likewise, in the actual state of tillage, the average quantity

imported. If there were no bounty, as less
corn would be exported, so it is probable
that, one year with another, less would be
imported than at present. The corn merchant, the fetchers and carriers of corn between Great Britain and foreign countries,
would have much less employment, and
might suffer considerably; but the country
gentlemen and farmers could suffer very little. It is in the corn merchants accordingly,
rather than in the country gentlemen and
farmers, that I have observed the greatest
anxiety for the renewal and continuation
of the bounty.

Country gentlemen and farmers are, to
their great honour, of all people, the least
subject to the wretched spirit of monopoly. The undertaker of a great manufac-
tory is sometimes alarmed if another work
of the same kind is established within
twenty miles of him. The Dutch undertaker of the woollen manufacture at Ab-
beville stipulated, that no work of the
same kind should be established within
thirty leagues of that city. Farmers and
country gentlemen, on the contrary, are
generally disposed rather to promote than
to obstruct the cultivation and improvement of their neighbours' farms and estates.
They have no secrets, such as those of the
greater part of manufacturers, but are generally rather fond of communicating to
their neighbours, and of extending as far
as possible any new practice which they
have found to be advantageous. . . . Country gentlemen and farmers, dispersed in different parts of the country, cannot so easily combine as merchants and manufacturers, who being collected into towns, and
accustomed to that exclusive corporation
spirit which prevails in them, naturally endeavour to obtain against all their countrymen, the same exclusive privilege which they
generally possess against the inhabitants of
their respective towns. They accordingly
seem to have been the original inventors of
those restraints upon the importation of

foreign goods, which secure to them the monopoly of the home-market. It was probably in imitation of them, and to put themselves upon a level with those who, they found, were disposed to oppress them, that the country gentlemen and farmers of Great Britain so far forgot the generosity which is natural to their station, as to demand the exclusive privilege of supplying their countrymen with corn and butchers'-meat. They did not perhaps take time to consider, how much less their interest could be affected by the freedom of trade than that of the people whose example they followed.

To prohibit by a perpetual law the importation of foreign corn and cattle, is in reality to enact, that the population and industry of the country shall at no time exceed what the rude produce of its own soil can maintain.

There seem, however, to be two cases in which it will generally be advantageous to lay some burden upon foreign, for the encouragement of domestic industry.

The first is, when some particular sort of industry is necessary for the defense of the country. The defense of Great Britain, for example, depends very much upon the number of its sailors and shipping. The act of navigation, therefore, very properly endeavours to give the sailors and shipping of Great Britain the monopoly of the trade of their own country, in some cases, by absolute prohibitions, and in others by heavy burdens upon the shipping of foreign countries. The following are the principal dispositions of this act.

First, all ships, of which the owners, masters, and three-fourths of the mariners are not British subjects, are prohibited, upon pain of forfeiting ship and cargo, from trading to the British settlements and plantations, or from being employed in the coasting trade of Great Britain.

Secondly, a great variety of the most bulky articles of importation can be brought into Great Britain only, either in such ships as are above described, or in ships of the country where those goods are produced, and of which the owners, masters, and three-fourths of the mariners, are of that particular country; and when imported even in ships of this latter kind, they are subject to double aliens duty. If imported in ships of any other country, the penalty is forfeiture of ship and goods. When this act was made, the Dutch were, what they still are, the great carriers of Europe, and by this regulation they were entirely excluded from being carriers to Great Britain, or from importing to us the goods of any other European country.

Thirdly, a great variety of the most bulky articles of importation are prohibited from being imported, even in British ships, from any country but that in which they are produced; under pain of forfeiting ship and cargo. This regulation too was probably intended against the Dutch. Holland was then, as now, the great emporium for all European goods, and by this regulation, British ships were hindered from loading in Holland the goods of any other European country.

Fourthly, salt fish of all kinds, whale fins, whale-bone, oil, and blubber, not caught by and cured on board British vessels, when imported into Great Britain, are subjected to double aliens duty. The Dutch, as they are still the principal, were then the only fishers in Europe that attempted to supply foreign nations with fish. By this regulation, a very heavy burden was laid upon their supplying Great Britain.

When the act of navigation was made, though England and Holland were not actually at war, the most violent animosity subsisted between the two nations. It had begun during the government of the long parliament, which first framed this act, and it broke out soon after in the Dutch wars during that of the Protector and of Charles the second. It is not impossible, therefore, that some of the regulations of this famous act may have proceeded from national animosity. They are as wise, however, as if they had all been dictated by the most deliberate wisdom. National animosity at that particular time aimed at the very same object which the most deliberate wisdom would have recommended, the diminution of the naval power of Holland, the only naval power which could endanger the security of England.

The act of navigation is not favourable to foreign commerce or to the growth of that opulence which can arise from it. The interest of a nation in its commercial relations to foreign nations is, like that of a merchant with regard to the different people with whom he deals, to buy as cheap and to sell as dear as possible. But it will be most likely to buy cheap, when by the most perfect freedom of trade it encourages all nations to bring to it the goods which it has occasion to purchase; and, for the same reason, it will be most likely to sell dear, when its markets are thus filled with the greatest number of buyers. The act of navigation, it is true, lays no burden upon foreign ships that come to export the produce of British industry. Even the ancient aliens duty, which used to be paid upon all goods exported as well as imported, has, by several subsequent acts, been taken off from the greater part of the articles of exportation. But if foreigners, either by prohibitions or high duties, are hindered from coming to sell, they cannot always afford to come to buy; because coming without a cargo, they must lose the freight from their own country to Great Britain. By diminishing the number of sellers, therefore, we necessarily diminish that of buyers, and are thus likely not only to buy foreign goods dearer, but to sell our own cheaper, than if there was a more perfect freedom of trade. As defense, however, is of much more importance than opulence, the act of navigation is, perhaps, the wisest of all

the commercial regulations of England.

The second case, in which it will generally be advantageous to lay some burden upon foreign for the encouragement of domestic industry, is, when some tax is imposed at home upon the produce of the latter. In this case, it seems reasonable that an equal tax should be imposed upon the like produce of the former. This would not give the monopoly of the home-market to domestic industry, nor turn towards a particular employment a greater share of the stock and labour of the country, than what would naturally go to it. It would only hinder any part of what would naturally go to it from being turned away by the tax, into a less natural direction, and would leave the competition between foreign and domestic industry, after the tax, as nearly as possible upon the same footing as before it. In Great Britain, when any such tax is laid upon the produce of domestic industry, it is usual at the same time, in order to stop the clamorous complaints of our merchants and manufacturers, that they will be undersold at home, to lay a much heavier duty upon the importation of all foreign goods of the same kind.

This second limitation of the freedom of trade according to some people should, upon some occasions, be extended much farther than to the precise foreign commodities which could come into competition with those which had been taxed at home. When the necessaries of life have been taxed in any country, it becomes proper, they pretend, to tax not only the like necessaries of life imported from other countries, but all sorts of foreign goods which can come into competition with any thing that is the produce of domestic industry. Subsistence, they say, becomes necessarily dearer in consequence of such taxes; and the price of labour must always rise with the price of the labourers subsistence. Every commodity, therefore, which is the produce of domestic industry, though not immediately taxed itself, becomes dearer in consequence of such taxes, because the labour which produces it becomes so. Such taxes, therefore, are really equivalent, they say, to a tax upon every particular commodity produced at home. In order to put domestic upon the same footing with foreign industry, therefore, it becomes necessary, they think, to lay some duty upon every foreign commodity, equal to this enhancement of the price of the home commodities with which it can come into competition.

Whether taxes upon the necessaries of life, such as those in Great Britain upon soap, salt, leather, candles, &c. necessarily raise the price of labour, and consequently that of all other commodities, I shall consider hereafter, when I come to treat of taxes. Supposing, however, in the mean time, that they have this effect, and they have it undoubtedly, this general enhancement of the price of all commodities, in consequence of that of labour, is a case which differs in the two following respects from that of a particular commodity, of which the price was enhanced by a particular tax immediately imposed upon it.

First, it might always be known with great exactness how far the price of such a commodity could be enhanced by such a tax: but how far the general enhancement of the price of labour might affect that of every different commodity about which labour was employed, could never be known with any tolerable exactness. It would be impossible, therefore, to proportion with any tolerable exactness the tax upon every foreign, to this enhancement of the price of every home commodity.

Secondly, taxes upon the necessaries of life have nearly the same effect upon the circumstances of the people as a poor soil and a bad climate. Provisions are thereby rendered dearer in the same manner as if it required extraordinary labour and expense to raise them. As in the natural scarcity arising from soil and climate, it would be absurd to direct the people in what manner they ought to employ their capitals and industry, so is it likewise in the artificial scarcity arising from such taxes. To be left to accommodate, as well as they could, their industry to their situation, and to find out those employments in which, notwithstanding their unfavourable circumstances, they might have some advantage either in the home or in the foreign market, is what in both cases would evidently be most for their advantage. To lay a new tax upon them, because they are already overburdened with taxes, and because they already pay too dear for the necessaries of life, to make them likewise pay too dear for the greater part of other commodities, is certainly a most absurd way of making amends.

Such taxes, when they have grown up to a certain height, are a curse equal to the barrenness of the earth and the inclemency of the heavens; and yet it is in the richest and most industrious countries that they have been most generally imposed. No other countries could support so great a disorder. As the strongest bodies only can live and enjoy health, under an unwholesome regimen; so the nations only, that in every sort of industry have the greatest natural and acquired advantages, can subsist and prosper under such taxes. Holland is the country in Europe in which they abound most, and which from peculiar circumstances continues to prosper, not by means of them, as has been most absurdly supposed, but in spite of them.

As there are two cases in which it will generally be advantageous to lay some burden upon foreign, for the encouragement of domestic industry; so there are two others in which it may sometimes be a matter of deliberation; in the one, how far it is proper to continue the free importation of certain foreign goods; and in the other, how far, or in what manner, it may be proper to restore that free importation after it has been for some time interrupted.

The case in which it may sometimes be a matter of deliberation how far it is proper to continue the free importation of certain foreign goods, is, when some foreign nation restrains by high duties or prohibitions the importation of some of our manufactures into their country. Revenge in this case naturally dictates retaliation, and that we should impose the like duties and prohibitions upon the importation of some or all of their manufactures into ours. Nations accordingly seldom fail to retaliate in this manner. The French have been particularly forward to favour their own manufactures by restraining the importation of such foreign goods as could come into competition with them. In this consisted a great part of the policy of Mr. Colbert, who, notwithstanding his great abilities, seems in this case to have been imposed upon by the sophistry of merchants and manufacturers, who are always demanding a monopoly against their countrymen. It is at present the opinion of the most intelligent men in France that his operations of this kind have not been beneficial to his country. That minister, by the tariff of 1667, imposed very high duties upon a great number of foreign manufactures. Upon his refusing to moderate them in favour of the Dutch, they in 1671 prohibited the importation of the wines, brandies, and manufactures of France. The war of 1672 seems to have been in part occasioned by this commercial dispute. The peace of Nimeguen put an end to it in 1678, by moderating some of those duties in favour of the Dutch, who in consequence took off their prohibition. It was about the same time that the French and English began mutually to oppress each other's industry, by the like duties and prohibitions, of which the French, however, seem to have set the first example. The spirit of hostility which has subsisted between the two nations ever since, has hitherto hindered them from being moderated on either side. In 1697 the English prohibited the importation of bonelace, the manufacture of Flanders. The government of that country, at that time under the dominion of Spain, prohibited in return the importation of English woollens. In 1700, the prohibition of importing bonelace into England was taken off upon condition that the importation of English woollens into Flanders should be put on the same footing as before.

There may be good policy in retaliations of this kind, when there is a probability that they will procure the repeal of the high duties or prohibitions complained of. The recovery of a great foreign market will generally more than compensate the transitory inconvenience of paying dearer during a short time for some sorts of goods. To judge whether such retaliations are likely to produce such an effect, does not, perhaps, belong so much to the science of a legislator, whose deliberations ought to be governed by general principles which are always the same, as to the skill of that insidious and crafty animal, vulgarly called a statesman or politician, whose councils are directed by the momentary fluctuations of affairs. When there is no probability that any such repeal can be procured, it seems a bad method of compensating the injury done to certain classes of our people, to do another injury ourselves, not only to those classes, but to almost all the other classes of them. When our neighbours prohibit some manufacture of ours, we generally prohibit, not only the same, for that alone would seldom affect them considerably, but some other manufacture of theirs. This may no doubt give encouragement to some particular class of workmen among ourselves, and by excluding some of their rivals, may enable them to raise their price in the home-market. Those workmen, however, who suffered by our neighbours' prohibition will not be benefited by ours.

On the contrary, they and almost all the other classes of our citizens will thereby be obliged to pay dearer than before for certain goods. Every such law, therefore, imposes a real tax upon the whole country, not in favour of that particular class of workmen who were injured by our neighbours' prohibition, but of some other class.

The case in which it may sometimes be a matter of deliberation, how far, or in what manner, it is proper to restore the free importation of foreign goods, after it has been for some time interrupted, is, when particular manufactures, by means of high duties or prohibitions upon all foreign goods which can come into competition with them, have been so far extended as to employ a great multitude of hands. Humanity may in this case require that the freedom of trade should be restored only by slow gradations, and with a good deal of reserve and circumspection. Were those high duties and prohibitions taken away all at once, cheaper foreign goods of the same kind might be poured so fast into the home market, as to deprive all at once many thousands of our people of their ordinary employment and means of subsistence. The disorder which this would occasion might no doubt be very considerable. It would in all probability, however, be much less than is commonly imagined, for the two following reasons:

First, all those manufactures, of which any part is commonly exported to other European countries without a bounty, could be very little affected by the freest importation of foreign goods. Such manufactures must be sold as cheap abroad as any other foreign goods of the same quality and kind, and consequently must be sold cheaper at home. They would still, therefore, keep possession of the home market, and though a capricious man of fashion might sometimes prefer foreign wares, merely because they were foreign, to cheaper and better goods of the same kind that were made at home, this folly could, from the nature of things, extend to so few, that it could make no sensible impression upon the general employment of the people. But a great part of all the different branches of our woollen manufacture, of our tanned leather, and of our hard-ware, are annually exported to other European countries without any bounty, and these are the manufactures which employ the greatest number of hands. The silk, perhaps, is the manufacture which would suffer the most by this freedom of trade, and after it the linen, though the latter much less than the former.

Secondly, though a great number of people should, by thus restoring the freedom of trade, be thrown all at once out of their ordinary employment and common method of subsistence, it would by no means follow that they would thereby be deprived either of employment or subsistence. By the reduction of the army and navy at the end of the late war, more than a hundred thousand soldiers and seamen, a number equal to what is employed in the greatest manufactures, were all at once thrown out of their ordinary employment; but, though they no doubt suffered some inconvenience, they were not thereby deprived of all employment and subsistence. The greater part of the seamen, it is probable, gradually betook themselves to the merchant-service as they could find occasion, and in the mean time both they and the soldiers were absorbed in the great mass of the people, and employed in a great variety of occupations. Not only no great convulsion, but no sensible disorder arose from so great a change in the situation of more than a hundred thousand men, all accustomed to the use of arms, and many of them to rapine and plunder. The number of vagrants was scarce anywhere sensibly increased by it, even the wages of labour were not reduced by it in any occupation, so far as I have been able to learn, except in that of seamen in the merchant-service. But if we compare together the habits of a soldier and of any sort of manufacturer, we shall find that those of the latter do not tend so much to disqualify him from being employed in a new trade, as those of the former from being employed in any. The manufacturer has always been accustomed to look for his subsistence from his labour only: the soldier to expect it from his pay. Application and industry have been familiar to the one; idleness and dissipation to the other. But it is surely much easier to change the direction of industry from one sort of labour to another, than to turn idleness and dissipation to any. To the greater part of manufactures besides, it has already been observed, there are other collateral manufactures of so similar a nature, that a workman can easily transfer his industry from one of them to another. The greater part of such workmen too are occasionally employed in country labour. The stock which employed them in a particular manufacture before, will still remain in the country to employ an equal number of people in some other way. The capital of the country remaining the same, the demand for labour will likewise be the same, or very nearly the same, though it may be exerted in different places and for different occupations. Soldiers and seamen, indeed, when discharged from the king's service, are at liberty to exercise any trade within any town or place of Great Britain or Ireland. Let the same natural liberty of exercising what species of industry they please, be restored to all his majesty's subjects, in the same manner as to soldiers and seamen; that is, break down the exclusive privileges of corporations, and repeal the statute of apprenticeship, both which are real encroachments upon natural liberty, and add to these the repeal of the law of settlements, so that a poor workman, when thrown out of employment either in one trade or in one place, may seek for it in another trade or in another place, without the fear either of a prosecution or of a removal, and neither the public nor the individuals will suffer much more from the occasional disbanding some particular classes of manufacturers, than from that of soldiers. Our manufacturers have no doubt great merit with their country, but they cannot have more than those who defend it with their blood, nor deserve to be treated with more delicacy.

To expect, indeed, that the freedom of trade should ever be entirely restored in Great Britain, is as absurd as to expect that an Oceana or Utopia should ever be established in it. Not only the prejudices of the public, but what is much more unconquerable, the private interests of many individuals, irresistibly oppose it. Were the officers of the army to oppose with the same zeal and unanimity any reduction in the number of forces, with which master manufacturers set themselves against every law that is likely to increase the number of their rivals in the home market; were the former to animate their soldiers, in the same manner as the latter inflame their workmen, to attack with violence and outrage the proposers of any such regulation; to attempt to reduce the army would be as dangerous as it has now become to attempt to diminish in any respect the monopoly which our manufacturers have obtained against us. This monopoly has so much increased the number of some particular tribes of them, that, like an overgrown standing army, they have become formidable to the government, and upon many occasions intimidate the legislature. The member of parliament who supports every proposal for strengthening this monopoly, is sure to acquire not only the reputation of understanding trade, but great popularity and influence with an order of men whose numbers and wealth render them of great importance. If he opposes them, on the contrary, and still more if he has authority enough to be able to thwart them, neither the most acknowledged probity, nor the highest rank, nor the greatest public services, can protect him from the most infamous abuse and detraction, from personal insults, nor sometimes from real danger, arising from the insolent outrage of furious and disappointed monopolists.

The undertaker of a great manufacture, who, by the home markets being suddenly laid open to the competition of foreigners, should be obliged to abandon his trade, would no doubt suffer very considerably. That part of his capital which had usually been employed in purchasing materials and in paying his workmen, might, without much difficulty, perhaps, find another employment. But that part of it which was fixed in workhouses, and in the instruments of trade, could scarce be disposed of without considerable loss. The equitable regard, therefore, to his interest requires that changes of this kind should never be introduced suddenly, but slowly, gradually, and after a very long warning. The legislature,

were it possible that its deliberations could be always directed, not by the clamorous importunity of partial interests, but by an extensive view of the general good, ought upon this very account, perhaps, to be particularly careful neither to establish any new monopolies of this kind, nor to extend further those which are already established. Every such regulation introduces some degree of real disorder into the constitution of the state, which it will be difficult afterwards to cure without occasioning another disorder.

How far it may be proper to impose taxes upon the importation of foreign goods, in order, not to prevent their importation, but to raise a revenue for government, I shall consider hereafter when I come to treat of taxes. Taxes imposed with a view to prevent or even to diminish importation, are evidently as destructive of the revenue of the customs as of the freedom of trade.

Jean Jacques Rousseau

In Jean Jacques Rousseau (1712-1778), eighteenth-century society found its severest critic. Born in Geneva, Rousseau spent much of his career in intimate contact with the leaders of the French Enlightenment. But rather than sharing their ideals, he rejected them, vehemently and violently. To Rousseau, the major evils of contemporary society were political absolutism, over-intellectualism, and general artificiality. Nor were these evils separable; on the contrary, each fed on the others. Hence Rousseau could not agree with reformers who looked to reason to lead the way to liberty and equality. Society was rotten to the core, he contended, hence no solution short of total regeneration could cure its ills.

In *The Social Contract* (1762), his most famous work, Rousseau attacked the problem of political despotism. Beginning with the provocative charge, "Man is born free; and everywhere he is in chains," he proposes a new social order in which freedom and equality will be the possession of all. How such a social order can be achieved in practice is the basic problem that he tries to solve in this book. How can we live under a government that, of necessity, exercises authority over us, and yet remain free men? This issue, with which Rousseau wrestled so earnestly in *The Social Contract*, still remains one of the fundamental political prob- lems facing the Western world.

In his other works Rous- seau attacked with vigor and eloquence almost every facet of his society. Perhaps his most sweeping condemnation of the Enlightenment is his early work, the *Discourse on the Arts and Sciences*, in which he offered up this prayer: "Al- mighty God! Thou who hold- est in Thy hand the minds of men, deliver us from the fatal arts and sciences of our forefathers; give us back igno- rance, innocence, and poverty, which alone can make us hap- py and are precious in Thy sight." The opposition be- tween this prayer and the ideals of the Enlightenment is obvious. To appreciate the ex- tent of Rousseau's influence, we have only to realize that within about fifty years roman- ticism, a movement of which he was the chief prophet, was to sweep over Europe.

THE SOCIAL CONTRACT

BOOK I

. . .

Chapter I

SUBJECT OF THE FIRST BOOK. Man is born free; and everywhere he is in chains. One thinks himself the master of others, and still remains a greater slave than they. How did this change come about? I do not know. What can make it legitimate? That ques- tion I think I can answer.

If I took into account only force, and the effects derived from it, I should say: "As long as a people is compelled to obey, and obeys, it does well; as soon as it can shake off the yoke, and shakes it off, it does still better; for, regaining its liberty by the same right as took it away, either it is justified in resuming it, or there was no justification for those who took it away." But the social order is a sacred right which

THE SOCIAL CONTRACT AND DISCOURSES by Jean Jacques Rousseau, translated by G. D. H. Cole. Everyman's Library Edition. Reprinted by permis- sion of the publishers, E. P. Dutton & Co., Inc.

is the basis of all rights. Nevertheless, this right does not come from nature, and must therefore be founded on conventions. Before coming to that, I have to prove what I have just asserted.

. . .

Chapter III

THE RIGHT OF THE STRONGEST. The strongest is never strong enough to be always the master, unless he transforms strength into right, and obedience into duty. Hence the right of the strongest, which, though to all seeming meant ironically, is really laid down as a fundamental principle. But are we never to have an explanation of this phrase? Force is a physical power, and I fail to see what moral effect it can have. To yield to force is an act of necessity, not of will—at the most, an act of prudence. In what sense can it be a duty?

Suppose for a moment that this so-called "right" exists. I maintain that the sole re- sult is a mass of inexplicable nonsense. For, if force creates right, the effect changes with the cause: every force that is greater than the first succeeds to its right. As soon as it is possible to disobey with impunity, disobedience is legitimate; and, the strongest being always in the right, the only thing that matters is to act so as to become the strongest. But what kind of right is that which perishes when force fails? If we must obey perforce, there is no need to obey because we ought; and if we are not forced to obey, we are under no obligation to do so. Clearly, the word "right" adds nothing to force: in this connection, it means absolutely nothing.

Obey the powers that be. If this means yield to force, it is a good precept, but superfluous: I can answer for its never being violated. All power comes from God, I admit; but so does all sickness: does that mean that we are forbidden to call in the doctor? A brigand surprises me at the edge of a wood: must I not merely surrender my purse on compulsion; but, even if I could withhold it, am I in conscience bound to give it up? For certainly the pistol he holds is also a power.

Let us then admit that force does not create right, and that we are obliged to obey only legitimate powers. In that case, my original question recurs.

. . .

Chapter IV

SLAVERY. To renounce liberty is to renounce being a man, to surrender the rights of humanity and even its duties. For him who renounces everything no indemnity is possible. Such a renunciation is incompatible with man's nature; to remove all liberty from his will is to remove all morality from his acts. Finally, it is an empty and contradictory convention that sets up, on the one side, absolute authority, and, on the other, unlimited obedience. Is it not clear that we can be under no obligation to a person from whom we have the right to exact everything? Does not this condition alone, in the absence of equivalence or exchange, in itself involve the nullity of the act? For what right can my slave have against me, when all that he has belongs to me, and, his right being mine, this right of mine against myself is a phrase devoid of meaning?

. . .

So, from whatever aspect we regard the question, the right of slavery is null and void, not only as being illegitimate, but also because it is absurd and meaningless. The words *slave* and *right* contradict each other, and are mutually exclusive. It will always be equally foolish for a man to say to a man or to a people: "I make with you a convention wholly at your expense and wholly to my advantage; I shall keep it as long as I like, and you will keep it as long as I like."

Chapter V

THAT WE MUST ALWAYS GO BACK TO A FIRST CONVENTION. Even if I granted all that I have been refuting, the friends of despotism would be no better off. There will always be a great difference between subduing a multitude and ruling a society. Even if scattered individuals were successively enslaved by one man, however numerous they might be, I still see no more than a master and his slaves, and certainly not a people and its ruler; I see what may be termed an aggregation, but not an association; there is as yet neither public good nor body politic. The man in question, even if he has enslaved half the world, is still only an individual; his interest, apart from that of others, is still a purely private interest. If this same man comes to die, his empire, after him, remains scattered and without unity, as an oak falls and dissolves into a heap of ashes when the fire has consumed it.

A people, says Grotius, can give itself to a king. Then according to Grotius, a people is a people before it gives itself. The gift is itself a civil act, and implies public deliberation. It would be better, before examining the act by which a people gives itself to a king, to examine that by which it has become a people; for this act, being necessarily prior to the other, is the true foundation of society.

Indeed, if there were no prior convention, where, unless the election were unanimous, would be the obligation on the minority to submit to the choice of the majority? How have a hundred men who wish for a master the right to vote on behalf of ten who do not? The law of majority voting is itself something established by convention, and presupposes unanimity, on one occasion at least.

Chapter VI

THE SOCIAL COMPACT. I suppose men to have reached the point at which the obstacles in the way of their preservation in the state of nature show their power of resistance to be greater than the resources at the disposal of each individual for his maintenance in that state. That primitive condition can then subsist no longer; and the human race would perish unless it change its manner of existence.

But, as men cannot engender new forces, but only unite and direct existing ones, they have no other means of preserving themselves than the formation, by aggregation, of a sum of forces great enough to overcome the resistance. These they have to bring into play by means of a single motive power, and cause to act in concert.

This sum of forces can arise only where several persons come together: but, as the force and liberty of each man are the chief instruments of his self-preservation, how can he pledge them without harming his own interests, and neglecting the care he owes to himself? This difficulty, in its bearing on my present subject, may be stated in the following terms:

"The problem is to find a form of association which will defend and protect with the whole common force the person and goods of each associate, and in which each, while uniting himself with all, may still obey himself alone, and remain as free as before." This is the fundamental problem of which the *Social Contract* provides the solution.

The clauses of this contract are so determined by the nature of the act that the slightest modification would make them vain and ineffective; so that, although they have perhaps never been formally set forth, they are everywhere the same and everywhere tacitly admitted and recognized, until, on the violation of the social compact, each regains his original rights and resumes his natural liberty, while losing the conventional liberty in favour of which he renounced it.

These clauses, properly understood, may be reduced to one—the total alienation of each associate, together with all his rights, to the whole community; for, in the first place, as each gives himself absolutely, the conditions are the same for all; and, this being so, no one has any interest in making them burdensome to others.

Moreover, the alienation being without reserve, the union is as perfect as it can be, and no associate has anything more to demand: for, if the individuals retained certain rights, as there would be no common superior to decide between them and the public, each, being on one point his own judge, would ask to be so on all; the state of nature would thus continue, and the association would necessarily become inoperative or tyrannical.

Finally, each man, in giving himself to all, gives himself to nobody; and as there is no associate over which he does not acquire the same right as he yields others over himself, he gains an equivalent for everything he loses, and an increase of force for the preservation of what he has.

If then we discard from the social compact what is not of its essence, we shall find that it reduces itself to the following terms:

"Each of us puts his person and all his power in common under the supreme direction of the general will, and, in our corporate capacity, we receive each member as an indivisible part of the whole."

At once, in place of the individual personality of each contracting party, this act of association creates a moral and collective body, composed of as many members as the assembly contains voters, and receiving from this act its unity, its common identity, its life, and its will. This public person, so formed by the union of all other persons, formerly took the name of *city*, and now takes that of *Republic* or *body politic;* it is called by its members *State* when passive, *Sovereign* when active, and *Power* when compared with others like itself. Those who are associated in it take collectively the name of *people*, and severally are called *citizens*, as sharing in the sovereign power, and *subjects*, as being under the laws of the State. But these terms are often confused and taken one for another: it is enough to know how to distinguish them when they are being used with precision.

Chapter VII

THE SOVEREIGN. This formula shows us that the act of association comprises a mutual undertaking between the public and the individuals, and that each individual, in making a contract, as we may say, with himself, is bound in a double capacity; as a member of the Sovereign he is bound to the individuals, and as a member of the State to the Sovereign. But the maxim of civil right, that no one is bound by undertakings made to himself, does not apply in this case; for there is a great difference between incurring an obligation to yourself and incurring one to a whole of which you form a part.

Attention must further be called to the fact that public deliberation, while competent to bind all the subjects to the Sovereign, because of the two different capacities in which each of them may be regarded, cannot, for the opposite reason, bind the Sovereign to itself; and that it is consequently against the nature of the body politic for the Sovereign to impose on itself a law which it cannot infringe. Being able to regard itself in only one capacity, it is in the position of an individual who makes a contract with himself; and this makes it clear that there neither is nor can be any kind of fundamental law binding on the body of the people—not even the social contract itself. This does not mean that the body politic cannot enter into undertakings with others, provided the contract is not infringed by them; for in relation to what is external to it, it becomes a simple being, an individual.

But the body politic or the Sovereign, drawing its being wholly from the sanctity of the contract, can never bind itself, even to an outsider, to do anything derogatory to the original act, for instance, to alienate any part of itself, or to submit to another Sovereign. Violation of the act by which it exists would be self-annihilation; and that which is itself nothing can create nothing.

As soon as this multitude is so united in one body, it is impossible to offend against one of the members without attacking the body, and still more to offend against the body without the members resenting it. Duty and interest therefore equally oblige the two contracting parties to give each other help; and the same men should seek to combine, in their double capacity, all the advantages dependent upon that capacity.

Again, the Sovereign, being formed wholly of the individuals who compose it, neither has nor can have any interest contrary to theirs; and consequently the sovereign power need give no guarantee to its subjects, because it is impossible for the body to wish to hurt all its members. We shall also see later on that it cannot hurt any in particular. The Sovereign, merely by virtue of what it is, is always what it should be.

This, however, is not the case with the relation of the subjects to the Sovereign, which, despite the common interest, would have no security that they would fulfil their undertakings, unless it found means to assure itself of their fidelity.

In fact, each individual, as a man, may have a particular will contrary or dissimilar to the general will which he has as a citizen. His particular interest may speak to him quite differently from the common interest: his absolute and naturally independent existence may make him look upon what he owes to the common cause as a gratuitous contribution, the loss of which will do less harm to others than the payment of it is burdensome to himself; and, regarding the moral person which constitutes the State as a *persona ficta,* because not a man, he may wish to enjoy the rights of citizenship without being ready to fulfil the duties of a subject. The continuance of such an injustice could not but prove the undoing of the body politic.

In order then that the social compact may not be an empty formula, it tacitly includes the undertaking, which alone can give force to the rest, that whoever refuses to obey the general will shall be compelled to do so by the whole body. This means nothing less than that he will be forced to be free; for this is the condition which, by giving each citizen to his country, secures him against all personal dependence. In this lies the key to the working of the political machine; this alone legitimizes civil undertakings, which, without it, would be absurd, tyrannical, and liable to the most frightful abuses.

Chapter VIII

THE CIVIL STATE. The passage from the state

of nature to the civil state produces a very remarkable change in man, by substituting justice for instinct in his conduct, and giving his actions the morality they had formerly lacked. Then only, when the voice of duty takes the place of physical impulses and right of appetite, does man, who so far had considered only himself, find that he is forced to act on different principles, and to consult his reason before listening to his inclinations. Although, in this state, he deprives himself of some advantages which he got from nature, he gains in return others so great, his faculties are so stimulated and developed, his ideas so extended, his feelings so ennobled, and his whole soul so uplifted, that, did not the abuses of this new condition often degrade him below that which he left, he would be bound to bless continually the happy moment which took him from it for ever, and, instead of a stupid and unimaginative animal, made him an intelligent being and a man.

Let us draw up the whole account in terms easily commensurable. What man loses by the social contract is his natural liberty and an unlimited right to everything he tries to get and succeeds in getting; what he gains is civil liberty and the proprietorship of all he possesses. If we are to avoid mistake in weighing one against the other, we must clearly distinguish natural liberty, which is bounded only by the strength of the individual, from civil liberty, which is limited by the general will; and possession, which is merely the effect of force or the right of the first occupier, from property, which can be founded only on a positive title.

We might, over and above all this, add, to what man acquires in the civil state, moral liberty, which alone makes him truly master of himself; for the mere impulse of appetite is slavery, while obedience to a law which we prescribe to ourselves is liberty. But I have already said too much on this head, and the philosophical meaning of the word liberty does not now concern us.

.   .   .

BOOK II

Chapter I

THAT SOVEREIGNTY IS INALIENABLE. The first and most important deduction from the principles we have so far laid down is that the general will alone can direct the State according to the object for which it was instituted, *i.e.* the common good: for if the clashing of particular interests made the establishment of societies necessary, the agreement of these very interests made it possible. The common element in these different interests is what forms the social tie; and, were there no point of agreement between them all, no society could exist. It is solely on the basis of this common interest that every society should be governed.

I hold then that Sovereignty, being nothing less than the exercise of the general will, can never be alienated, and that the Sovereign, who is no less than a collective being, cannot be represented except by himself: the power indeed may be transmitted, but not the will.

In reality, if it is not impossible for a particular will to agree on some point with the general will, it is at least impossible for the agreement to be lasting and constant; for the particular will tends, by its very nature, to partiality, while the general will tends to equality. It is even more impossible to have any guarantee of this agreement; for even if it should always exist, it would be the effect not of art, but of chance. The Sovereign may indeed say: "I now will actually what this man wills, or at least what he says he wills"; but it cannot say: "What he wills to-morrow, I too shall will" because it is absurd for the will to bind itself for the future, nor is it in-cumbent on any will to consent to anything that is not for the good of the being who wills. If then the people promises simply to obey, by that very act it dissolves itself and loses what makes it a people; the moment a master exists, there is no longer a Sovereign, and from that moment the body politic has ceased to exist.

This does not mean that the commands of the rulers cannot pass for general wills, so long as the Sovereign, being free to oppose them, offers no opposition. In such a case, universal silence is taken to imply the consent of the people. This will be explained later on.

.   .   .

Chapter III

WHETHER THE GENERAL WILL IS FALLIBLE. It follows from what has gone before that the general will is always right and tends to the public advantage; but it does not follow that the deliberations of the people are always equally correct. Our will is always for our own good, but we do not always see what that is; the people is never corrupted, but it is often deceived, and on such occasions only does it seem to will what is bad.

There is often a great deal of difference between the will of all and the general will; the latter considers only the common interest, while the former takes private interest into account, and is no more than a sum of particular wills: but take away from these same wills the pluses and minuses that cancel one another, and the general will remains as the sum of the differences.

If, when the people, being furnished with adequate information, held its deliberations, the citizens had no communication one with another, the grand total of the small differences would always give the general will, and the decision would always be good. But when factions arise, and partial associations are formed at the expense of the great association, the will of each of these associations becomes general in relation to its members, while it remains particular in relation to the State: it may then be said that there are no longer as many votes as there are men, but only as many as there are associations. The differences become less numerous and give a less general result. Lastly, when one of these associations is so great as to prevail over all the rest, the result is no longer a sum of small differences, but a single difference; in this case there is no longer a general will, and the opinion which prevails is purely particular.

It is therefore essential, if the general will is to be able to express itself, that there should be no partial society within the State, and that each citizen should think only his own thoughts: which was indeed the sublime and unique system established by the great Lycurgus. But if there are partial societies, it is best to have as many as possible and to prevent them from being unequal, as was done by Solon, Numa, and Servius. These precautions are the only ones that can guarantee that the general will shall be always enlightened, and that the people shall in no way deceive itself.

Chapter IV

THE LIMITS OF THE SOVEREIGN POWER. If the State is a moral person whose life is in the union of its members, and if the most important of its cares is the care for its own preservation, it must have a universal and compelling force, in order to move and dispose each part as may be most advantageous to the whole. As nature gives each man absolute power over all his members, the social compact gives the body politic absolute power over all its members also; and it is this power which, under the direction of the general will, bears, as I have said, the name of Sovereignty.

But, besides the public person, we have to consider the private persons composing it, whose life and liberty are naturally independent of it. We are bound then to distinguish clearly between the respective rights of the citizens and the Sovereign,[1] and between the duties the former have to fulfil as subjects, and the natural rights they should enjoy as men.

Each man alienates, I admit, by the social compact, only such part of his powers, goods, and liberty as it is important for the community to control; but it must also be granted that the Sovereign is sole judge of what is important.

Every service a citizen can render the State he ought to render as soon as the Sovereign demands it; but the Sovereign, for its part, cannot impose upon its subjects any fetters that are useless to the community, nor can it even wish to do so; for no more by the law of reason than by the law of nature can anything occur without a cause.

The undertakings which bind us to the social body are obligatory only because they are mutual; and their nature is such that in fulfilling them we cannot work for others without working for ourselves. Why is it that the general will is always in the right, and that all continually will the happiness of each one, unless it is because there is not a man who does not think of "each" as meaning him, and consider himself in voting for all? This proves that equality of rights and the idea of justice which such equality creates originate in the preference each man gives to himself, and accordingly in the very nature of man. It proves that the general will, to be really such, must be general in its object as well as its essence; that it must both come from all and apply to all; and that it loses its

[1] Attentive readers, do not, I pray, be in a hurry to charge me with contradicting myself. The terminology made it unavoidable, considering the poverty of the language; but wait and see.

natural rectitude when it is directed to some particular and determinate object, because in such a case we are judging of something foreign to us, and have no true principle of equity to guide us.

Indeed, as soon as a question of a particular fact or right arises on a point not previously regulated by a general convention, the matter becomes contentious. It is a case in which the individuals concerned are one party, and the public the other, but in which I can see neither the law that ought to be followed nor the judge who ought to give the decision. In such a case, it would be absurd to propose to refer the question to an express decision of the general will, which can be only the conclusion reached by one of the parties and in consequence will be, for the other party, merely an external and particular will, inclined on this occasion to injustice and subject to error. Thus, just as a particular will cannot stand for the general will, the general will, in turn, changes its nature, when its object is particular, and, as general, cannot pronounce on a man or a fact. When, for instance, the people of Athens nominated or displaced its rulers, decreed honours to one, and imposed penalties on another, and, by a multitude of particular decrees, exercised all the functions of government indiscriminately, it had in such cases no longer a general will in the strict sense; it was acting no longer as Sovereign, but as magistrate. This will seem contrary to current views; but I must be given time to expound my own.

It should be seen from the foregoing that what makes the will general is less the number of voters than the common interest uniting them; for, under this system, each necessarily submits to the conditions he imposes on others: and this admirable agreement between interest and justice gives to the common deliberations an equitable character which at once vanishes when any particular question is discussed, in the absence of a common interest to unite and identify the ruling of the judge with that of the party.

From whatever side we approach our principle, we reach the same conclusion, that the social compact sets up among the citizens an equality of such a kind, that they all bind themselves to observe the same conditions and should therefore all enjoy the same rights. Thus, from the very nature of the compact, every act of Sovereignty, *i.e.* every authentic act of the general will, binds or favours all the citizens equally; so that the Sovereign recognizes only the body of the nation, and draws no distinctions between those of whom it is made up. What, then, strictly speaking, is an act of Sovereignty? It is not a convention between a superior and an inferior, but a convention between the body and each of its members. It is legitimate, because based on the social contract, and equitable, because common to all; useful, because it can have no other object than the general good, and stable, because guaranteed by the public force and the supreme power. So long as the subjects have to submit only to conventions of this sort, they obey no one but their own will; and to ask how far the respective rights of the Sovereign and the citizens extend, is to ask up to what point the latter can enter into undertakings with themselves, each with all, and all with each.

We can see from this that the sovereign power, absolute, sacred, and inviolable as it is, does not and cannot exceed the limits of general conventions, and that every man may dispose at will of such goods and liberty as these conventions leave him; so that the Sovereign never has a right to lay more charges on one subject than on another, because, in that case, the question becomes particular, and ceases to be within its competency.

When these distinctions have once been admitted, it is seen to be so untrue that there is, in the social contract, any real renunciation on the part of the individuals, that the position in which they find themselves as a result of the contract is really preferable to that in which they were before. Instead of a renunciation, they have made an advantageous exchange: instead of an uncertain and precarious way of living they have got one that is better and more secure; instead of natural independence they have got liberty, instead of the power to harm others security for themselves, and instead of their strength, which others might overcome, a right which social union makes invincible. Their very life, which they have devoted to the State, is by it constantly protected; and when they risk it in the State's defence, what more are they doing than giving back what they have received from it? What are they doing that they would not do more often and with greater danger in the state of nature, in which they would inevitably have to fight battles at the peril of their lives in defence of that which is the means of their preservation? All have indeed to fight when their country needs them; but then no one has ever to fight for himself. Do we not gain something by running, on behalf of what gives us our security, only some of the risks we should have to run for ourselves, as soon as we lost it?

.   .   .

BOOK III

Before speaking of the different forms of government, let us try to fix the exact sense of the word, which has not yet been very clearly explained.

Chapter I

GOVERNMENT IN GENERAL. I warn the reader that this chapter requires careful reading, and that I am unable to make myself clear to those who refuse to be attentive.

Every free action is produced by the concurrence of two causes; one moral, *i.e.* the will which determines the act; the other physical, *i.e.* the power which executes it. When I walk towards an object, it is necessary first that I should will to go there, and, in the second place, that my feet should carry me. If a paralytic wills to run and an active man wills not to, they will both stay where they are. The body politic has the same motive powers; here too force and will are distinguished, will under the name of legislative power and force under that of executive power. Without their concurrence, nothing is, or should be, done.

We have seen that the legislative power belongs to the people, and can belong to it alone. It may, on the other hand, readily be seen, from the principles laid down above, that the executive power cannot belong to the generality as legislature or Sovereign, because it consists wholly of particular acts which fall outside the competency of the law, and consequently of the Sovereign, whose acts must always be laws.

The public force therefore needs an agent of its own to bind it together and set it to work under the direction of the general will, to serve as a means of communication between the State and the Sovereign, and to do for the collective person more or less what the union of soul and body does for man. Here we have what is, in the State, the basis of government, often wrongly confused with the Sovereign, whose minister it is.

What then is government? An intermediate body set up between the subjects and the Sovereign, to secure their mutual correspondence, charged with the execution of the laws and the maintenance of liberty, both civil and political.

The members of this body are called

magistrates or *kings*, that is to say *governors*, and the whole body bears the name *prince*. Thus those who hold that the act, by which a people puts itself under a prince, is not a contract, are certainly right. It is simply and solely a commission, an employment, in which the rulers, mere officials of the Sovereign, exercise in their own name the power of which it makes them depositaries. This power it can limit, modify, or recover at pleasure; for the alienation of such a right is incompatible with the nature of the social body, and contrary to the end of association.

I call then *government*, or supreme administration, the legitimate exercise of the executive power, and prince or magistrate the man or the body entrusted with that administration.

In government reside the intermediate forces whose relations make up that of the whole to the whole, or of the Sovereign to the State. This last relation may be represented as that between the extreme terms of a continuous proportion, which has government as its mean proportional. The government gets from the Sovereign the orders it gives the people, and, for the State to be properly balanced, there must, when everything is reckoned in, be equality between the product or power of the government taken in itself, and the product or power of the citizens, who are on the one hand sovereign and on the other subject.

Furthermore, none of these three terms can be altered without the equality being instantly destroyed. If the Sovereign desires to govern, or the magistrate to give laws, or if the subjects refuse to obey, disorder takes the place of regularity, force and will no longer act together, and the State is dissolved and falls into despotism or anarchy. Lastly, as there is also only one mean proportional between each relation, there is also only one good government possible for a State. But, as

countless events may change the relations of a people, not only may different governments be good for different peoples, but also for the same people at different times.

. . .

Chapter X

THE ABUSE OF GOVERNMENT AND ITS TENDENCY TO DEGENERATE. As the particular will acts constantly in opposition to the general will, the government continually exerts itself against the Sovereignty. The greater this exertion becomes, the more the constitution changes; and, as there is in this case no other corporate will to create an equilibrium by resisting the will of the prince, sooner or later the prince must inevitably suppress the Sovereign and break the social treaty. This is the unavoidable and inherent defect which, from the very birth of the body politic, tends ceaselessly to destroy it, as age and death end by destroying the human body. . . .

The dissolution of the State may come about in either of two ways.

First, when the prince ceases to administer the State in accordance with the laws, and usurps the Sovereign power. A remarkable change then occurs: not the government, but the State, undergoes contraction; I mean that the great State is dissolved, and another is formed within it, composed solely of the members of the government, which becomes for the rest of the people merely master and tyrant. So that the moment the government usurps the Sovereignty, the social compact is broken, and all private citizens recover by right their natural liberty, and are forced, but not bound, to obey.

The same thing happens when the members of the government severally usurp the power they should exercise only as a body; this is as great an infraction of the laws, and results in even greater disorders. There are then, so to speak, as many princes as there are magistrates, and the State, no less divided than the government, either perishes or changes its form.

When the State is dissolved, the abuse of government, whatever it is, bears the common name of *anarchy*. To distinguish, democracy degenerates into *ochlocracy*, and aristocracy into *oligarchy*; and I would add that royalty degenerates into *tyranny*; but this last word is ambiguous and needs explanation.

In vulgar usage, a tyrant is a king who governs violently and without regard for justice and law. In the exact sense, a tyrant is an individual who arrogates to himself the royal authority without having a right to it. This is how the Greeks understood the word "tyrant": they applied it indifferently to good and bad princes whose authority was not legitimate. *Tyrant* and *usurper* are thus perfectly synonymous terms.

In order that I may give different things different names, I call him who usurps the royal authority a *tyrant*, and him who usurps the sovereign power a *despot*. The tyrant is he who thrusts himself in contrary to the laws to govern in accordance with the laws; the despot is he who sets himself above the laws themselves. Thus the tyrant cannot be a despot, but the despot is always a tyrant.

.   .   .

Chapter XV

DEPUTIES OR REPRESENTATIVES. As soon as public service ceases to be the chief business of the citizens and they would rather serve with their money than with their persons, the State is not far from its fall. When it is necessary to march out to war, they pay troops and stay at home: when it is necessary to meet in council, they name deputies and stay at home. By reason of idleness and money, they end by having soldiers to enslave their country and representatives to sell it.

It is through the hustle of commerce and the arts, through the greedy self-interest of profit, and through softness and love of amenities that personal services are replaced by money payments. Men surrender a part of their profits in order to have time to increase them at leisure. Make gifts of money, and you will not be long without chains. The word "finance" is a slavish word, unknown in the city-state. In a country that is truly free, the citizens do everything with their own arms and nothing by means of money; so far from paying to be exempted from their duties, they would even pay for the privilege of fulfilling them themselves. I am far from taking the common view: I hold enforced labour to be less opposed to liberty than taxes.

The better the constitution of a State is, the more do public affairs encroach on private in the minds of the citizens. Private affairs are even of much less importance, because the aggregate of the common happiness furnishes a greater proportion of that of each individual, so that there is less for him to seek in particular cares. In a well-ordered city every man flies to the assemblies: under a bad government no one cares to stir a step to get to them, because no one is interested in what happens there, because it is foreseen that the general will will not prevail, and lastly because domestic cares are all-absorbing. Good laws lead to the making of better ones; bad ones bring about worse. As soon as any man says of the affairs of the State *What does it matter to me?* the State may be given up for lost.

General Cahiers

The *cahiers* were lists of grievances that each estate in each electoral division of France drew up for presentation to the king at the meeting of the Estates-General in 1789. Actually, there are two distinct types of *cahier:* the preliminary and the general. The preliminary *cahiers* were compiled at the first and second levels of election, and were submitted to the electoral body that actually chose the representatives sent to the Estates-General. The electoral body then compiled the general *cahiers* from the preliminary lists. This rather obscure method was followed by the first estate (the clergy) and the third estate (the commoners). The second estate (the nobility) developed only general *cahiers* which were sent directly to Versailles.

This method of recording the grievances of the people and classes of France in 1789 is a great help to the modern historian. For instance, the general *cahiers* tend to cite broad areas of needed reform, rather than specific abuses or corruptions within the system; moreover, they tend more clearly to reflect the political and economic philosophies that were occupying men's minds than any schedule of particulars would have.

The following selections consist of three general *cahiers,* one from each of the three estates of the *bailliage* of Dourdan in the *généralité* of Orléans. Although these *cahiers* are somewhat lengthy and repetitious, they give us a good picture of the contrasting aims, hopes, and desires of the major social and political groups of one community; and they indicate the degree to which current ideas on liberty and equality had penetrated each estate.

The "August 4th Decrees" (which make up the last of the following selections) reflect both the grievances appearing in the *cahiers* and the efforts of the National Assembly to remedy them.

CAHIER OF THE CLERGY OF DOURDAN

27 March, 1789

. . .

When the King summons his subjects about him to consult them concerning the needs of the State, the ministers of religion are among the most eager to give him proof of their respectful gratitude. Their

A DOCUMENTARY SURVEY OF THE FRENCH REVOLUTION, John Hall Stewart, ed. (New York: The Macmillan Co., 1951), pp. 57-59, 61-67, 70-79, 81-84. Courtesy of The Macmillan Company.

dual *rôle* as citizens and ecclesiastics entitles them to bring to the foot of the throne the most comprehensive wishes for the welfare of the monarchy and the maintenance of a religion that assures its tranquillity. Accordingly, His Majesty shall be humbly supplicated:

Chapter I: Religion

1. To preserve in its integrity the precious depository of the Catholic, Apostolic,

and Roman religion, the most stable support of the fundamental laws of the State, to effect the enforcement of ordinances concerning the respect which is due churches, sanctification of feast days and Sundays, and, in general, whatever affects public worship.

2. To give consideration to the representations made by the last assembly of the clergy concerning the edict on non-Catholics, and not to permit any religion other than the Catholic to hold worship or give public instruction.

3. To permit the Church of France to hold provincial or national councils with a view to re-establishing and maintaining ecclesiastical discipline in all its vigor, so that convocation of the said councils may be effected, without great delay, upon the request and according to the needs of every metropolitan see.

4. To maintain the execution of all laws and ordinances recognized in the kingdom as constituting the public, ecclesiastical, and canonical law thereof, and which the kings, his august predecessors, have stamped with the seal of their authority.

5. Imbued with profound grief at the sight of the appalling deterioration of religion and the depravation of morals in the kingdom, we direct to His Majesty the most ardent and humble representations concerning the disastrous and widely acknowledged cause of this deplorable subversion of all principles. It obviously derives from the disgraceful excess of writings in which the spirit of libertinage, incredulity, and independence prevails, in which faith, modesty, reason, the throne, and the altar are attacked with equal audacity—impious and corrupting books circulated on all sides with the most revolting profusion and licence, to which the strongest resistance could not be too promptly opposed.

6. Since diversity of religious opinions in the schools for French youth is the greatest

danger in the world, His Majesty shall be humbly supplicated also to order all necessary precautions lest there be admitted into any of the universities and academic societies of the kingdom any teacher or member who has not previously given proofs of the greatest ability and of his respectful devotion to the Catholic religion.

7. Since national education is degenerating daily, the King will be willing to take into consideration a matter so pertinent to morals and to the glory of the kingdom and in his wisdom to provide resources for the talents of indigence by the endowment of the provincial *collèges*, almost all of which are insufficiently endowed, because a good education is the only means of assuring the State of good citizens, and religion of virtuous ministers.

8. Since the education of the rural population is valuable to the State, it is highly desirable that in every parish schoolteachers be established, whose stipends, added to the payments of those pupils who can afford to pay, would provide an income sufficient for them and their families; which teachers would be under the guidance and inspection of the *curé*, who would ascertain their religion and talents in advance, and would have the right to dismiss them if they did not fulfill expectations, reserving their right of appeal to the lord bishop.

9. We dare to solicit from the goodness and piety of the King a special protection for religious orders of either sex throughout the kingdom, under the happy auspices of his favor and authority; we hope that such holy institutions, useful to religion, to the good of the State, to needy families, and above all to the support of the poor in the rural districts, will flourish and vivify increasingly.

10. In provincial cities, and especially in this *bailliage*, there are numerous communities devoted to the education of in-

digent young girls for religion and for work; we supplicate His Majesty to regard such useful establishments with benevolence, and to facilitate access thereto in the bureaux established for the relief of religious houses.

Chapter II: Constitution

1. Since monarchical government is the steadfast constitution of the nation, the most conducive to its internal tranquillity and external security, the most suitable for the extent of its provinces, and the most consistent with the character of its people, who always have distinguished themselves by their love for and devotion to their sovereigns, we will never countenance anything that would tend to alter this form of government. We are inviolably attached to it by the most sacred duties of obedience, by ties of oath and fidelity, by love and respect for our masters, and by the happiness of being subject thereto.

2. We desire that in matters brought under deliberation in the Estates General relative to all orders, voting be by head; but in those concerning more especially one of the three orders, we request that voting be by order.

. . .

Chapter IV: Civil Administration

1. Disposed to second the wishes of the nation, we are inclined zealously to share with all citizens the burden of taxation which we agree to pay as they do, reserving our estates, titles, and honorary rights.

2. The nation shall be supplicated most humbly to assume the present debt of the clergy and, since it was contracted for the service of the State, to consolidate it as a national debt.

3. The King having restored to the nation its former right to vote its own subsidies, a right which the clergy alone had preserved, the general assembly, at its very first meeting, shall decree the continuation of existing taxes until the end of its session, and shall rule definitively on that important matter before its adjournment.

4. His Majesty will be willing to make, in all branches of expenditure, whatever retrenchments his sense of economy and the needs of his people dictate. One part of the taxation should be designated for necessary expenditures, the remainder applied to the payment of interest and liquidation of the national debt.

5. Since every public loan implies a tax, because it must have security, and since the tax must be voted by the nation, every loan would be irregular if not authorized by the national assembly.

6. We request that the provincial assemblies or estates, if they are established, be charged with assessing, equalizing, and collecting the taxes; that such taxes be used, as far as possible, to discharge the obligations of the State in the province where they are collected; that, without distinction, all agents employed in the collection, receipt, custody, and payment thereof be entirely subordinate to the several assemblies.

7. That all brevets of pension be revised, in order to moderate those that are exorbitant and to suppress those not founded on real services rendered to the State.

8. That the Estates General publish an exact and detailed account of the debts which the nation is to assume; that they establish the tax quota to be set aside for the liquidation of same; and that they determine the happy time when the nation, finally liberated, will see its taxes decrease.

9. We further supplicate His Majesty that he be willing to adjust the royal courts in order to avoid frequent appeals, and likewise the different courts through which it is necessary to pass to be judged

in the last resort; also, that he reduce the formalities which cause so much delay in justice.

.   .   .

13. That nobility no longer be acquired by purchase, but that it be the reward for real and important services rendered the *Patrie*.

14. That, in order to encourage population, the King be willing to grant compensation to families with more than ten children.

15. That since the merger of several farms into one is as contrary to the profit of agriculture as to the interests of the rural inhabitants, a matter so pertinent to the public welfare be taken into consideration by the Estates General.

.   .   .

18. That the abuses which have gradually developed in the practice of gamekeepers and forest wardens, who ought not to be permitted to carry firearms or to have offenders convicted on their testimony alone, be reformed.

19. That every cultivator be permitted to defend his property against the intrusion of game, pigeons, etc.; that in estimating the damages and the compensation to be obtained, the testimony of the municipality be accepted, and that the decree of regulation rendered thereon be regarded as void.

20. That selection of the militia by lot be suppressed, as even more burdensome to the people than the tax of the *taille*.

21. That all beggars be most expressly forbidden to leave their parishes; that the provincial assemblies consult with the municipalities to provide for their sustenance, either by work or by alms.

22. That since salt is one of the commodities of prime necessity for the most needy class, and of the greatest benefit to cattle, the Estates General be requested to fix the price thereof at the best possible rate.

23. That the King be most humbly supplicated to have breaches of confidence reformed, such as the intermittent violation of the privacy of letters, the arbitrary tax on letters in the post, etc.

24. That the King be supplicated to reform also the abuses and tyranny of *lettres de cachet*.

25. That the ordinances on duels and suicide be renewed and put into effect; also, that all persons not qualified to sell medicines be forbidden to participate in the sale thereof.

26. That deputies be not liable for what they have said or written concerning public affairs, either during or after the assembly; that the assembly itself punish those whom it believes guilty, to the extent of excluding them from its midst if such action be deemed advisable.

27. That if any member of the two orders of the clergy or nobility be elected to represent the third estate, he may not vote in the assembly of the Estates General until he has formally renounced the privileges of his order.

28. That if privileges place the orders at variance and threaten the assembly with disunion, every order should sacrifice its own in a spirit of concord and through zeal for the public welfare.

29. That laws directed against fraudulent bankrupts be put into effect, and that every protection be forbidden them.

CAHIER OF THE NOBLES OF DOURDAN

29 March, 1789

. . .

Constitution

The citizens comprising the order of the nobility of the *bailliage* of Dourdan consider that, as soon as the Estates General is convened and the assembly constituted, an address should be voted to the King to thank him for the magnanimous act of justice he has just accorded the nation in restoring its rights, and to pledge to him, in the name of all Frenchmen, unlimited gratitude and love, inviolable submission and fidelity to his sacred person, his legitimate authority, and his august royal house. They would doubtless wish to use this liberty first in paying him new homage of their blood and fortune; but they wish more, they wish to contribute with all their power to the personal happiness of His Majesty, as well as to the general welfare of his people, by working in concert with him to bolster the tottering edifice of the French Constitution, by rendering his faithful commons happier through a just distribution of the taxes necessary to the State, by freeing him of the troubles and anxieties which extensive and absolute legislation necessarily entails; finally, by leaving to him only favors to grant and benefits to dispense throughout the free nation that he governs; thus the subjects of all orders, encompassing the Monarch with their liberty, their happiness, and their unlimited devotion, will render him, if possible, still more beloved throughout his realm, and assuredly more respected abroad.

Accordingly, the noble citizens of the *bailliage* of Dourdan request:

That the legislative power reside collectively in the hands of the King and the united nation.

That a formula for the drafting and publication of laws be established, and that it express both the right of the nation and that of the King, in these words, or similar ones:

The free and general Estates of France declare that the general will is ———. Accordingly, the said Estates most respectfully supplicate His Majesty to sanction the said articles by royal approbation ——— WE, KING OF FRANCE, upon the request of the Estates General, assembled at ———, have published and do publish ———, have ordered and do order ———. Thus, we inform all those whom it may concern that they are to take in hand and put into effect all articles above stated, according to their form, and tenor; FOR SUCH IS THE OUTCOME OF THE NATIONAL WILL, WHICH HAS RECEIVED THE SEAL OF OUR ROYAL AUTHORITY.

Since the constitutional laws assure each and every one of his liberty, fortune, position, and property, the nobility requests:

That every arbitrary order prejudicial to the liberty of citizens be abolished entirely;

That individual liberty be assured and guaranteed, so that every citizen arrested may be placed in the prisons of the courts which are to take cognizance of his offence within twenty-four hours of the time of his arrest; that, immediately upon his detention, he be permitted to choose a counsel or advocate.

Liberty shall be understood to include the right to come, go, live, and reside wheresoever one pleases, inside or outside the kingdom, without need of permission; referring to the Estates General the determination of cases in which it is necessary to restrict such liberty with regard to leaving the kingdom.

That liberty of the press be granted, upon condition that author and printer are responsible; and the Estates General shall determine the most severe restrictions in order to prevent such liberty from degenerating into licence.

The nobility of the *bailliage* of Dourdan requests, likewise, that, according to the formal wish of His Majesty, no tax be established and no loan be made without the concurrence of the legislative power.

That the administrator of finances be not permitted to make any anticipation or assignment other than on the annual income, under penalty for *lèse-patrie*, the lenders to forfeit all claim.

That any individual convicted of having collected any sum whatsoever in excess of that established by law be declared guilty of embezzlement and sentenced accordingly.

That no citizen be deprived of his rank, employment, or position, except according to a legal judgment.

That all property, whoever be the owner, be inviolable and sacred, property being whatever one owns on public faith and on the affirmation of the law; that no one be deprived thereof except for public interest, and that he then be compensated therefor without delay, and at the highest possible price.

Finally, that ministers henceforth be responsible and accountable to the Estates General.

But if it is magnanimous of the French Monarch to share the legislative power with free subjects, it is at the same time just and necessary that he be invested with all executive power, and that his person be ever sacred.

He must have command of the troops on land and sea, assign military positions, appoint generals and ministers, make peace or war, negotiate treaties of alliance or commerce with foreign powers, convoke, prorogue, and dissolve the Estates General, under the express condition, in case of dissolution, of effecting a new convocation immediately in the form and number approved by the assembled nation.

Finally, the King alone must preserve that right, so kind, so consoling, so worthy of a great monarch, that right to dispense benefits, to encourage virtue by dignities and marks of distinction, and, above all, the right to grant pardon.

The order of nobility desires further that the distinction of three orders in the Estates General be strengthened and regarded as inherent in the Constitution of the French monarchy, and that opinions be given therein only by order.

That in the event, however, that vote by order be absolutely rejected by the Estates General, and the deputy of the *bailliage* of Dourdan see that further resistance to vote by head is useless, he then request that vote by head be taken in the separate chamber of every order and not in the assembly of the three orders united.

That vote by head never take place on matters of particular interest to one of the three orders alone.

That the opposition of one order alone may not delay projects of the other two and result in *veto*, except by at least two-thirds of the votes.

That the Estates General be periodic; that it determine the time of its recurrence and the form of its convocation and composition; that it approve taxation only until its next assembly; and that if it be not convoked by the King at the established time, all taxes immediately cease to be valid throughout the entire extent of the kingdom.

That the Estates General may not concern itself with any deliberation until, in conjunction with the King, it has passed an act enunciating the Constitution and the rights above mentioned, and constituting, henceforth, the fundamental law of the kingdom.

That, in the event of a new reign or a regency, the Estates General be convoked within two months by the King, or, in his name, by a warrant of the Great Seal drawn up by the Chancellor of France.

That there be no intermediate commission during the interval between Estates General.

That the powers of deputies be limited to a term of two years, dating from the opening of the next Estates General, and that the persons of the deputies be inviolable during the session of the Estates.

That since the custom of giving proxies to deputies of the *bailliages* is most disadvantageous, the Estates be requested to suppress them, or to place thereon whatever restrictions they deem advisable.

That provincial administrations, the form and power of which shall be determined by the Estates General, be established in all provinces of the kingdom.

Finally, that, in order to render these laws of Frenchmen more impressive, a uniform and invariable formula be drafted for the oath which kings must take at their coronation; by which oath they shall swear, in the presence of the Estates General, to observe the declaratory act, a duplicate of which shall be deposited in the treasury of the Church of Saint-Remi at Rheims, and shall be presented to them with as much pomp as the Holy Ampulla. By such oath the monarch shall be formally bound to protect the Christian, Catholic, Apostolic and Roman religion, and likewise to use all his power and every means to maintain it in all its purity. Lastly, by said oath the constitution is to be fully guaranteed.

. . .

Morals

That no citizen occupy civil or military positions before the age of twenty, because his life up to that time ought to be devoted to education.

That religion always be the basis of scholastic and moral education.

That in the cities there be public schools, presided over by citizens of distinguished personal attainments and of recognized enlightenment. That only the following subjects be taught therein: 1st, the principles of natural law, which illumine the rights and duties of man; 2nd, the principles of civil law, which illumine the rights and duties of the citizen; 3rd, the principles of public law, which illumine the rights and duties of the nation.

That only those fifteen years or over be admitted to the schools.

That since scholastic education is to prepare for moral education, the headmasters of the scholastic schools be required to render account of their conduct and their pupils to the headmasters of the schools of morality, and to receive their certificates in that essential subject.

That in rural parishes there be vicars or officiating ministers of religion to aid the *curés* in the work of their ministry, to increase the opportunities for attending divine worship, and to supervise and conduct free schools for youth on behalf of the needy; and that this be made possible through pensions for the benefices.

That, in order that no citizen be lost to the *Patrie*, religious orders be divided into two classes, one devoted to the education of youth, the other to visiting the sick to administer spiritual and temporal aid.

That parents or natural guardians have absolute authority over their children until the age of twenty; that in the event that parents or guardians need the aid of the law against their children or wards, in order to avoid abuse of authority, a guardian *ad hoc* be named, who, in conjunction with the said parents or natural guardians, shall appeal to the courts of justice, where hearings shall always be held *in camera* to receive complaints brought in such cases.

Commerce

That, since all exclusive privileges whatsoever granted to individuals or companies are prejudicial to general liberty, they never be renewed, and new ones never be granted.

That essentially useful manufactures be encouraged and increased in preference to those for luxury purposes only; and that the primary ones be relieved of part of their tax, which should be transferred to those of secondary utility.

That the excessive number of *douanes* and barriers which impede the internal commerce of the kingdom be withdrawn to the frontiers.

That the excessive urban population, which results in the pernicious depopulation of rural districts, continue to be restricted by the collection of entrance fees at the gates of large cities.

Justice

That venality of offices be generally abolished, and that the Estates General consider the wisest means of reimbursing officeholders, at the same time undertaking to fill the vacant offices by election.

. . .

That criminal proceedings be public; that they take the form of an inquiry through the concurrence of the ordinary judges of the accused and twelve of his peers under oath, so that these latter pronounce solely and exclusively upon the fact, and the courts of justice pronounce solely upon the law and apply the penalty, textually enunciated by law, on the offence textually defined by said same law.

That the accused have the aid of counsel at all times, and that all supporting evidence be admitted throughout the entire proceeding.

That the deed or deeds with which the accused is charged be explicitly enumerated and defined in the complaint which constitutes the basis of the suit; that they be expressed in the sentence of condemnation, and that no other be included therein.

That the peers under oath pronounce, with hand on the Gospel, these words: *guilty* or *not guilty;* that they then retire, and the courts of justice pronounce acquittal or penalty.

That unanimity of the peers under oath be necessary to effect a conviction which is to subject an accused to the death penalty.

That like offences be punished with like penalties, whatever the rank or status of the offender.

That the death penalty be applied much less frequently; that it be effected in one manner only, and that the least painful; and that all those uselessly barbarous punishments, repugnant to the manners of a gentle nation, and offensive to both religion and humanity because they consign the condemned person's last moments to excessive suffering, be outlawed forever.

That any judge who, after a decree of condemnation has been pronounced, dares extend the penalty arbitrarily and subject the accused to a kind of punishment and disgrace to which the decree has not condemned him, be declared guilty of *lèse-humanité*, degraded, deprived of his position, and thenceforth disqualified.

. . .

Police

. . .

That ordinary hunting rights likewise be maintained as property; but that an estimate be made, according to the statement of appraisers, of the damage caused by the excessive amount of game, and that compensation be strictly exacted.

That the damage resulting from the excessive number of pigeons be reduced by reviving the regulations with regard thereto.

That poorhouses, always costly, useless, and ruinous, be abolished and replaced by public works, which may offer resources to the destitute and at the same time be of public usefulness; and that vagabonds and vagrants be employed in works regulated by the provincial administrations, to which such wise measures are to be entrusted.

That the Estates General which, on several occasions, has considered uniformity of weights and measures for the entire kingdom, but always in vain, undertake the settlement of said matter which is so important for the facility and activity of commerce.

That the regulations made for the maintenance of religion and morals be re-established in all their vigor; that some of them be revised in order to effect, if possible, their most desirable restoration.

That the magistrates responsible for the inspection of prisons be required to make frequent visits thereto, to supervise the wholesomeness of the air, the cleanliness and the health of the prisoners, and to suggest, and even provide them with, books of morality.

Finances

The nobles regard as decidedly advantageous and even necessary that the first declaration of the Estates General be that, since the nation has the right to consent to taxes, and since all existing taxes are of illegal origin and extension, the Estates General declares them all suppressed by law; that, nevertheless, because of the time required to reorganize this branch of national affairs, and also to avoid possible ill effects on future taxation from an absolute discontinuation of all relations between the taxpayers and the public treasury, the Estates General, desiring that there be no taxes other than those established by the present assembly before its first adjournment, enact provisionally that the present taxes, temporarily authorized, continue to be paid, but only during the present session.

.   .   .

Finally, the nobility declares that, in order to evince its sentiments of esteem, natural equity, and affection for its fellow citizens of the third estate, it wishes to share with them, in proportion to the property and possessions of all orders, whatever imposts and taxes are approved by the nation; claiming to reserve only the sacred rights of property, the prerogatives of rank, honor, and dignity which must appertain to it according to the constitutional principles of the French monarchy.

Clergy

His Majesty is further supplicated to order that all bishops and beneficiaries reside in their benefices.

That plurality of benefices and charges be proscribed.

.   .   .

Nobility

The nobility of the *bailliage* of Dourdan declares that it recognizes only one order of nobility enjoying the same rights.

It requests that nobility no longer be the concomitant of offices which are purely venal and without functions.

That nobility be the reward for distinguished services only.

That neither commerce nor any civil position henceforth be discreditable, provided that such position be not servile.

CAHIER OF THE THIRD ESTATE OF DOURDAN

29 March, 1789

. . .

The order of the third estate of the City, *Bailliage,* and County of Dourdan, imbued with gratitude prompted by the paternal kindness of the King, who deigns to restore its former rights and its former constitution, forgets at this moment its misfortunes and impotence, to harken only to its foremost sentiment and its foremost duty, that of sacrificing everything to the glory of the *Patrie* and the service of His Majesty. It supplicates him to accept the grievances, complaints, and remonstrances which it is permitted to bring to the foot of the throne, and to see therein only the expression of its zeal and the homage of its obedience.

It wishes:

1. That his subjects of the third estate, equal by such status to all other citizens, present themselves before the common father without other distinction which might degrade them.

2. That all the orders, already united by duty and a common desire to contribute equally to the needs of the State, also deliberate in common concerning its needs.

3. That no citizen lose his liberty except according to law; that, consequently, no one be arrested by virtue of special orders, or, if imperative circumstances necessitate such orders, that the prisoner be handed over to the regular courts of justice within forty-eight hours at the latest.

4. That no letters or writings intercepted in the post be the cause of the detention of any citizen, or be produced in court against him, except in case of conspiracy or undertaking against the State.

5. That the property of all citizens be inviolable, and that no one be required to make sacrifice thereof for the public welfare, except upon assurance of indemnification based upon the statement of freely selected appraisers.

6. That, since the maintenance of the commonwealth necessitates an effective revenue, all taxes established since 1614, the year of the last meeting of the Estates General, be confirmed provisionally by His Majesty on the request of the Estates General, and the collection thereof ordered during a limited period of time, not to exceed one year, despite the fact that, owing to lack of consent of the nation, such taxes may be regarded as illegal.

7. That the customary and ordinary charges of the State be regulated; that the expenditure of every department [of the Government], the appointment of all who are employed therein, and the retirement pensions of same be established invariably.

8. That the taxes on land and on all real or nominal property, the domains of the Crown, and other branches of revenue deriving from establishments useful to the public, such as postal and messenger service, etc., be preferably assigned to the aforementioned primarily necessary charges.

9. That the national debt be verified; that the payment of arrears of said debt be assured by such indirect taxes as may not be injurious to the husbandry, industry, commerce, liberty, or tranquillity of the citizens.

10. That an annual reimbursement fund be established to liquidate the capital of the debt.

11. That as one part of the debt is liquidated, a corresponding part of the indirect tax also be liquidated.

12. That every tax, direct or indirect, be granted only for a limited time, and

that every collection beyond such term be regarded as peculation, and punished as such.

13. That no loan be contracted, under any pretext or any security whatsoever, without the consent of the Estates General.

14. That every anticipation and every issuance of treasurer's notes or others on the account of the State, without public sanction, be regarded as a violation of public faith, and that the administrators ordering or authorizing them be punished.

15. That every personal tax be abolished; that thus the *capitation* and the *taille* and its accessories be merged with the *vingtièmes* in a tax on land and real or nominal property.

16. That such tax be borne equally, without distinction, by all classes of citizens and by all kinds of property, even feudal and contingent rights.

17. That the tax substituted for the *corvée* be borne by all classes of citizens equally and without distinction. That said tax, at present beyond the capacity of those who pay it and the needs to which it is destined, be reduced by at least one-half.

18. That provincial Estates, subordinate to the Estates General, be established and charged with the assessment and levying of subsidies, with their deposit in the national treasury, with the administration of all public works, and with the examination of all projects conducive to the prosperity of lands situated within the limits of their jurisdiction.

19. That such Estates be composed of freely elected deputies of the three orders from the cities, boroughs, and parishes subject to their administration, and in the proportion established for the next session of the Estates General.

20. That district bureaux under said Estates be established in the chief towns of the *bailliages;* and that such jurisdictions be created for said bureaux that there may be prompt and convenient correspondence between the chief town and all points accountable thereto.

21. That in case of the death or retirement of deputies of the order of the third estate in the Estates General, or of any one among them, during the course of the next session, the present electors be authorized to reassemble to elect others in their place.

Justice

1. That the administration of justice be reformed, either by restoring strict execution of ordinances, or by reforming the sections thereof that are contrary to the dispatch and welfare of justice.

2. That every royal *bailliage* have such jurisdiction that persons be not more than three or four leagues distant from their judges, and that these pass judgment in the last resort up to the value of 300 *livres.*

3. That seigneurial courts of justice created by purely gratuitous right be suppressed.

. . .

7. That venality of offices be suppressed by successive reimbursement in proportion to their disestablishment; that, accordingly, a fund be constituted forthwith to effect such reimbursement.

8. That the excessive number of offices in the necessary courts be reduced in just measure, and that no one be given an office of magistracy if he is not at least twenty-five years of age, and until after a substantial public examination has verified his morality, integrity, and ability.

. . .

12. That deliberations of courts and companies of magistracy which tend to prevent entry of the third estate thereto be rescinded and annulled as injurious to the citizens of that order, in contempt of the authority of the King, whose choice they limit, and contrary to the welfare of jus-

tice, the administration of which would become the patrimony of those of noble birth instead of being entrusted to merit, enlightenment, and virtue.

13. That military ordinances which restrict entrance to the service to those possessing nobility be reformed.

That naval ordinances establishing a degrading distinction between officers born into the order of nobility and those born into that of the third estate be revoked, as thoroughly injurious to an order of citizens and destructive to the competition so necessary to the glory and prosperity of the State.

•   •   •

Agriculture

•   •   •

3. That the privilege of hunting be restricted within its just limits; that the decrees of the *parlement* of the years 1778 and 1779, which tend rather to obstruct the claims of the cultivator than to effect his indemnification, be rescinded and annulled; that after having declared the excessive amount of game and summoned the seignieur to provide therefor, the landowner and the cultivator be authorized to destroy said game on their own lands and in their own woods—without permission, however, to use firearms, the carrying of which is forbidden by ordinances; that, moreover, a simple and easy method be established whereby every cultivator may have the damage verified and obtain compensation therefor.

•   •   •

5. That, in conformity with former ordinances, gamekeepers be forbidden to carry arms, even in the retinue of their masters.

6. That hunting offences be punished only by pecuniary fines.

7. That His Majesty be supplicated to have enclosed the parks and forests which are reserved for his enjoyment; also to authorize elsewhere the destruction of wild beasts which ruin the rural districts, and particularly that bordering on this forest of Dourdan.

8. That every individual who, without title or valid occupancy, has dovecotes or aviaries, be required to destroy them; that those who have title or valid occupancy be required to confine their pigeons at seedtime and harvest.

•   •   •

16. That individuals and communities be permitted to free themselves from the *rentes* which they owe to persons in *mainmorte,* by paying the principal at a rate to be established, upon condition that the persons in *mainmorte* invest such principal in loans authorized and guaranteed by the King and the nation.

17. That the ordinance and regulation concerning woods and forests be reformed so as to preserve property rights, encourage plantings, and prevent deforestation.

That the administration of forests and woods belonging to persons in *mainmorte* be subject to the provincial Estates and subordinate to the district bureaux, and that new laws be established to assure the preservation thereof and to punish offences pertaining thereto.

•   •   •

19. That seigneurs who are inspectors of highways may not plant or appropriate trees planted on property bordering the highways; that, on the contrary, such trees be designated as the property of the owners of the estates, who shall be reimbursed for the cost of the planting.

20. That the width of highways and connecting and rural roads be established uniformly and unalterably.

21. That penalties be imposed upon whomsoever cultivate connecting and rural roads.

Commerce

1. That every regulation which tends to impede the business of citizens be revoked.

2. That the exportation and circulation of grain be directed by the provincial Estates, which shall correspond among themselves in order to prevent sudden and artificial increases in the price of provisions.

3. That when wheat reaches the price of twenty-five *livres* per *septier* in the markets, all day laborers be forbidden to buy any, unless it be for their sustenance.

4. That if circumstances necessitate the revenue from certificates and letters of mastership in the arts and crafts, no member be admitted into corporations except upon condition of residing in the place of his establishment; that widows may carry on the profession of their husbands without new letters; that their children be admitted thereto at a moderate price; that all persons without an established and recognized domicile be forbidden to peddle.

5. That fraudulent bankruptcy be considered a public crime; that the public prosecutor be enjoined to prosecute it as such, and that privileged positions no longer serve as a refuge for bankrupts.

6. That all toll rights and other similar ones be suppressed throughout the interior of the Kingdom, that customhouses be moved back to the frontiers, and that rights of *traite* be entirely abolished.

7. That, within a given time, weights and measures be rendered uniform throughout the entire kingdom.

Morals

1. That in the chief town of every *bailliage* a public school be established, where young citizens may be brought up in the principles of religion and provided with the necessary education by methods authorized by His Majesty on the request of the nation.

2. That in cities and villages schools be established where the poor will be admitted without cost, and instructed in whatever is necessary for them concerning either morals or their individual interests.

3. That livings and benefices for the care of souls henceforth be granted only by competitive examination.

4. That prelates and *curés* be subject to perpetual residence, under penalty of loss of the fruits of their benefices.

5. That, under the same penalty, beneficiaries without a charge be bound to residence during most of the year in the chief town of their benefice, if they have an annual income of 1,000 *livres* or more.

6. That no ecclesiastic hold more than one benefice if such benefice is worth 3,000 *livres* revenue or over; that those in excess of such revenue be declared vacant.

7. That every lottery, the effect of which is to corrupt public morals, every loan involving the element of chance, the effect of which is to encourage speculation and divert funds destined for agriculture and commerce, be proscribed forever.

8. That every community be required to provide for the maintenance of its invalid poor; that, accordingly, all private alms be strictly forbidden; that in every district a charity workshop be established, the funds for which shall be composed of voluntary contributions of individuals and sums which the provincial Estates shall designate therefor, in order to assure constant work for the able-bodied poor.

9. That within the limits of every principal administration a house of correction be established for the confinement of beggars and vagabonds.

10. That all charlatans, and those who have not completed the necessary studies and passed the required examinations, be forbidden to sell drugs or medicines or to practise medicine or surgery, and that the granting of any certificate, permission, or exemption for such purpose be forbidden.

11. That no woman may practise the art of midwifery until she has taken a course in it, has obtained a certificate of competence from a college of surgery, and has been received into the *bailliage*.

12. That the *maréchaussées* be enjoined to obey the orders of the officials of the *bailliages* for the maintenance of public order; and that the municipalities of the several parishes be authorized to have internal police power therein, except in special cases which are to be reported to the public prosecutor of the *bailliage*.

13. That the sacraments be administered gratuitously, and contingent fees suppressed.

THE AUGUST 4TH DECREES

4-11 August, 1789

. . .

1. The National Assembly abolishes the feudal regime entirely, and decrees that both feudal and *censuel* rights and dues deriving from real or personal *mainmorte* and personal servitude, and those representative thereof, are abolished without indemnity, and all others declared redeemable; and that the price and manner of redemption shall be established by the National Assembly. Those of the said dues which are not suppressed by the present decree, however, shall continue to be collected until reimbursement has been made.

2. The exclusive right to *fuies* and *colombiers* is abolished; pigeons shall be confined at times determined by the communities; and during such periods they shall be regarded as game, and everyone shall have the right to kill them on his own land.

3. The exclusive right of hunting and open warrens is likewise abolished; and every proprietor has the right to destroy and to have destroyed, on his own property only, every kind of game, conditional upon conformity with police regulations relative to public security.

A DOCUMENTARY SURVEY OF THE FRENCH REVOLUTION, John Hall Stewart, ed. (New York: The Macmillan Company, 1951), pp. 107-110. Courtesy of The Macmillan Company.

All *capitaineries*, even royal ones, and all hunting preserves, under whatever denomination, are likewise abolished; and provision shall be made, by means compatible with the respect due property and liberty, for the preservation of the personal diversions of the King.

The President shall be charged with requesting the King for the recall of persons exiled and consigned to the galleys simply for hunting, the release of prisoners now detained, and the cancellation of existing proceedings in that connection.

4. All seigneurial courts of justice are suppressed without any indemnity; nevertheless, the officials of such courts shall continue in office until the National Assembly has provided for the establishment of a new judicial organization.

5. Tithes of every kind and dues which take the place thereof, under whatever denomination they are known and collected, even by subscription, *possessed by secular and regular bodies*, by beneficed clergymen, *fabriques* and all persons in *mainmorte*, even by the Order of Malta and other religious and military orders, even those abandoned to laity in substitution for and option of *portion congruë*, are abolished, subject to the devising of means for providing in some other manner for the expenses of divine worship, the maintenance of ministers of religion, relief of the poor, repairs and re-

building of churches and parsonages, and for all establishments, seminaries, schools, colleges, hospitals, communities and others, to the maintenance of which they are now assigned. Meanwhile, until such provision is made and the former possessors are furnished with their equivalent, the National Assembly orders that collection of the said tithes shall continue according to law and in the usual manner. Other tithes, of whatever nature, shall be redeemable according to the regulations of the Assembly; and until such regulations are made, the National Assembly orders that the collection thereof also be continued.

6. All perpetual ground rents, either in kind or in money, of whatever species, whatever their origin, to whatever persons they are due . . . shall be redeemable; *champarts* of every kind and denomination likewise shall be redeemable at a rate established by the Assembly. No nonredeemable due may be created henceforth.

7. Venality of judicial and municipal offices is suppressed henceforth. Justice shall be rendered gratuitously; nevertheless, the incumbents of said offices shall continue to perform their duties and to collect the emoluments thereof until the Assembly has provided means of procuring their reimbursement.

8. The contingent fees of country *curés* are suppressed, and shall cease to be paid as soon as provision has been made for the increase of the *portions congruës* and for the payment of vicars; and a regulation determining the lot of the town *curés* shall be made.

9. Pecuniary privileges, personal or real, in matters of taxation are abolished forever. Collection shall be made from all citizens and on all property, in the same manner and in the same form; and means of effecting proportional payment of all taxes, even for the last six months of the current year, shall be considered.

10. Since a national constitution and public liberty are more advantageous to the provinces than the privileges which some of them enjoy, and the sacrifice of which is necessary for the close union of all parts of the realm, all special privileges of provinces, principalities, *pays*, cantons, cities, and communities of inhabitants, whether pecuniary or of any other kind, are declared abolished forever, and shall be absorbed into the law common to all Frenchmen.

11. All citizens may be admitted, without distinction of birth, to all ecclesiastical, civil, and military employments and offices, and no useful profession shall entail forfeiture.

12. In future no *deniers* for annates or for any other cause whatsoever shall be dispatched to the court of Rome, the vicelegation at Avignon, or the nunciature at Lucerne; diocesans shall address themselves to their bishops for all provisions of benefices and dispensations, which shall be granted gratuitously . . .

13. The *déports*, rights of *côte-morte*, *dépouilles*, *vacat*, *censuel* dues, Peter's pence, and others of the same kind established in favor of bishops, archdeacons, archpriests, chapters, *curés primitifs*, and all others, under any name whatsoever, are abolished, subject to suitable provision for the endowment of insufficiently endowed archdeacons and archpriests.

14. Plurality of benefices shall no longer exist when the revenues of the benefice or benefices of an incumbent exceed the sum of 3,000 *livres*. Possession of several pensions on a benefice, or a pension and a benefice, shall no longer be permitted if the revenue from those already held exceeds the said sum of 3,000 *livres*.

15. On the basis of the account to be rendered concerning the state of pensions, favors, and stipends, the National Assembly, in concert with the King, shall undertake the suppression of those which are not merited, and the reduction of those which

are excessive, subject to determining for the future a sum which the King may use for such purpose.

16. The National Assembly decrees that, in memory of the impressive and momentous deliberations just held for the welfare of France, a medal shall be struck, and that, as an expression of gratitude, a *Te Deum* shall be sung in all parishes and churches of the kingdom.

17. The National Assembly solemnly proclaims King Louis XVI *Restorer of French Liberty*.

18. The National Assembly shall repair *en masse* to the King to present to His Majesty the decree just pronounced, to bear him the homage of its most respectful gratitude, and to supplicate him to permit the *Te Deum* to be sung in his chapel, and to be present there himself.

19. Immediately after the Constitution, the National Assembly shall undertake the drafting of laws necessary for the development of the principles established by the present decree, which, with the decree of the tenth of this month, shall be dispatched immediately by the deputies into all the provinces, there to be printed, proclaimed also at the parish sermons, and posted wherever necessary.

THE NINETEENTH CENTURY

THE HISTORY of the nineteenth century was molded in great part by two quite different but related events, the French Revolution and the Industrial Revolution. We can speak without ambiguity of the French Revolution as an event, for it can be dated with precision, from the spring of 1789 to the Battle of Waterloo in 1815. But the Industrial Revolution had neither a precise beginning nor an ending. The best we can say is that it had got underway, certainly in England, by the last quarter of the eighteenth century, that it transformed Europe's economy and society during the nineteenth, and that it has continued into the twentieth.

Although one of these revolutions was primarily political and the other economic, they were not without influence on each other. For it is now generally agreed, as Karl Marx first clearly pointed out, that the French Revolution was a bourgeois or middle-class upheaval. It was the rising capitalist class in France that led the revolution, profited most from it, and then assumed the initiative in the industrial expansion that followed. In England, too, the French Revolution had important economic consequences. For the difficulties caused by the Napoleonic Wars, including the effects on England of the Continental System and the necessity for a vast increase in military and naval power to defeat the French, led to a rapid expansion of English industrial production.

The nineteenth-century reaction to these two great revolutions can best be seen in the host of new doctrines and movements that appeared on the European scene, particularly in the years following 1815. Although most of these doctrines differed widely from one another, they all had one feature in common: the suffix "ism." That most of the major nineteenth-century "isms," particularly those that were primarily political or economic in emphasis, were responses to the revolutions can be seen by an examination of some of them. Both conservatism and nationalism, for example, were directly inspired by the events of the French Revolution and the Napoleonic era.

Conservatism rejected the French Revolution, not only for its effects but also for its methods. Revolution, conservatives like the Englishman Burke argued, necessarily destroys its ideals in its very attempt to achieve them. Social and political progress cannot be brought about through violence and destruction, but only through the conservation and enrichment of the traditions of the past. Although conservatism, in the able diplomatic hands of the Austrian foreign minister Metternich, exerted a considerable influence on European politics until mid-century, it rapidly lost ground after that. Its emphasis was on the past, but Europe's eyes in the nineteenth century were on the future.

Considerably more influential in the long term was nationalism. This doctrine, first espoused by the French during the Revolution, later spread across Europe in the reaction to the Napoleonic Empire. Across the Continent, peoples who had been conquered by the armies of Napoleon came to equate French culture with French imperialism. To assert their cultural independence from France, they searched their history and traditions for the foundations of a national culture which would equal or even surpass that of France. This cultural nationalism almost always had political implications. And political nationalism expressed itself in a variety of ways. With the German philosopher, Hegel, it led to a worship of the state; with the Italian patriot, Mazzini, it became the basis for a humanitarian crusade against political oppression. In practical politics, nationalism led to movements for independence in many areas of Europe, resulting, for example, in the liberation of Greece from the Turks, and of Belgium from the Dutch. Perhaps the most important result of nineteenth-century nationalism was the unification of Italy and Germany.

Three other nineteenth-century "isms," all of them both political and economic in nature, merit attention. The first of these was liberalism. Although liberalism eventually spread over most of Europe, its homeland was England and its greatest spokesman was John Stuart Mill. The liberals tried to adapt the ideals of the Enlightenment to the era of industrialism. Believing firmly in the rationality of man, they held that each individual must be given a maximum of freedom to develop his highest potentialities. The liberals were defenders of constitutional government and of lawful rather than violent political change. They believed, also, that government interference in the activities of citizens should be held to a minimum. In economics, this meant that they generally advocated *laissez-faire*. The history of liberalism in the past hundred years has centered around a growing conflict between the humanitarian ideals of the liberals, on the one hand, and their belief in government non-interference, on the other.

A second movement, more radical than liberalism, was republicanism. The republicans considered themselves the heirs of the French Revolution and the Republic of 1793. Republicanism, which spread from France over the entire Continent, was suppressed by the police of reactionary governments everywhere. But the republicans fought back by forming secret societies and by agitating for the revival of the revolutionary spirit in Europe. They were leaders in the many revolutions that rocked Europe during the century, particularly in 1848.

Most radical of the major "isms" was socialism, particularly as developed by Karl Marx. The socialists differed from the liberals and the republicans in one important respect. Both the liberals and the republicans rejected the pre-revolutionary social structure of Europe, but they accepted the new bourgeois society that grew out of industrialism. The socialists, however, rejected bourgeois society as well, and championed the cause of a new class, the industrial proletariat, also a product of the Industrial Revolution. Although Marx was the most important of the socialists, he had been preceded by several other socialist writers, mainly in France, and he was followed by a variety of socialistic groups that showed his influence. Among these groups were the British Fabian socialists, who helped found the Labor Party in Britain. The Fabian socialists differed from Marx mainly in their belief that the social goals of the laboring class could be attained through constitutional means without recourse either to class warfare or to the elimination of the bourgeoisie.

Perhaps the most pervasive "ism" of nineteenth-century society was optimism. With few exceptions the intellectual leaders of the period were firm believers in progress. For Hegel, progress was a metaphysical necessity; for Marx, it was a historical necessity; and even Darwin seemed to accept it as a biological necessity. The general optimism of nineteenth-century thought found a firm basis in the undeniable fact that progress was actually being made. For it was clear, even to the casual observer, that through industrialization man was rapidly conquering nature and bending her to serve his every material need. The prophets of progress looked forward to an era in which the economic, political, and social advances achieved by Europeans might be shared by all the world.

Such hopes plus, unfortunately, others less lofty, led to still another characteristic nineteenth-century "ism": imperialism. Even the United States, for a brief period at the end of the century, joined the imperialistic movement. As President Theodore Roosevelt proclaimed, "Nations that expand and nations that do not may both ultimately go down, but the one leaves heirs and a glorious memory, and the other leaves neither."

Another source for the optimism of the nineteenth century lay in the freedom from general warfare that lasted for an entire century, from Waterloo to 1914. No such era of peace had been known in the West since the *Pax Romana*. This is not to imply, though, that the period was without violence. For, in addition to several limited wars, the century witnessed a series of revolutions that were symptomatic of the underlying flaws in European society. The most serious flaw was the failure of society to keep pace with the rapid progress that was being made in politics and economics. The political developments leading to democracy, and the economic developments leading to industrial urbanization, combined to produce the modern "mass man," a man who could not be assimilated into the pattern of traditional European civilization. With the tremendous growth of population which almost all countries have experienced since the Industrial Revolution, this new type of man has become an increasingly influential force in society. The consequences of the appearance of this new social force on the European scene, though partially revealed in certain of the "isms" as well as in the revolutions of the nineteenth century, did not become fully apparent until our own century, on whose turbulent history they have had a profound effect.

In summary, the nineteenth century marked the climax of European civilization. By the end of the century, developments that had been in progress for hundreds of years came to final fruition, to make Western Europe—and, to a lesser extent, the United States—the leader and very nearly the master of the entire world. The supremacy of Western Europe exhibited itself in a variety of ways. In the first place, the nations of Western Europe were supreme in military power. Their armies could defeat any non-European foe. Secondly, these nations served as the center of the world's economy. Capital poured out from the great banking institutions of London and Paris to finance the economic exploitation of the most remote areas of the globe. Economic supremacy, in turn, contributed to a high standard of living. The people of Western Europe were able to enjoy the material comforts of life on a scale never before equaled. Politically, the West European nations were highly progressive. Although none of these nations was yet a full democracy, all seemed to be moving in that direction. At the least, all had governments based on constitutions and governed by law. In this respect alone, they were far in advance of much of the rest of mankind. Finally, Western Europe was generally acknowledged to be the cultural center of the world. Here were to be found the greatest universities, libraries, art galleries, and museums. No one who contemplated an intellectual or artistic career could count his education complete until he had made a pilgrimage to the shrines of European culture.

Edmund Burke

The French Revolution was greeted in many different ways, but most people felt that a new and better society would quickly emerge from the reform of the French monarchy. Conservatives had their moments of doubt and hesitation, of course, but the majority of people were more inclined to agree with Samuel Coleridge:

Shall France alone a Despot spurn?
  Shall she alone, O Freedom, boast thy care?
Lo, round thy standard Belgia's heroes burn,
  Tho' Power's blood-stain'd streamers fire the air,
    And wider yet thy influence spread,

Nor e'er recline thy weary head,
Till every land from pole to pole
Shall boast one independent soul!
And still, as erst, let favour'd Britain be
First ever of the first and freest of the free! [1]

William Wordsworth, in later years, was to recall his own

[1] Samuel Coleridge, "Destruction of the Bastille," stanza VI.

reaction to the stirring events of 1789:

But Europe at that time was thrilled with joy,
France standing on the top of golden hours,
And human nature seeming born again.[2]

These flowerings of hope rapidly faded, however, to be replaced by fear, distrust, and contempt when it was discovered that the Golden Age had not arrived. A leading spirit in the rejection of the French Revolution was Edmund Burke (1729-1797), whose influence in Britain and elsewhere be-

[2] William Wordsworth, "The Prelude," Book VI, lines 339-341.

came greater as the Revolution ran its violent course. In 1790, Burke published his *Reflections on the Revolution in France*, in which he insisted that men cannot create a totally new government and code of laws through the use of reason alone. Such reforms can come about only through the workings of history, through the gradual adaptation of the old and the traditional to serve the best interests of the new. Violence and revolution bring only more violence to a society and finally lead to the destruction of the society itself. Burke's *Reflections* were very widely read (the tenth edition was

exhausted less than a year after the original publication) and aroused in England and on the Continent a deep suspicion of anyone who seemed to advocate reform or who argued for the application of rational principles to political questions.

Burke wrote the *Reflections* ostensibly as a letter to a young Frenchman, but in reality he was replying to a sermon delivered before the Revolution Society (which was dedicated to the commemoration of the "Glorious Revolution" of 1688) in which the Reverend Richard Price had hailed the events in France and had exhorted England to follow along.

REFLECTIONS ON THE REVOLUTION IN FRANCE

.   .   .

Kings, in one sense, are undoubtedly the servants of the people, because their power has no other rational end than that of the general advantage; but it is not true that they are, in the ordinary sense, (by our constitution at least), anything like servants; the essence of whose situation is to obey the commands of some other, and to be removable at pleasure. But the king of Great Britain obeys no other person; all other persons are individually, and collectively too, under him, and owe to him a legal obedience. The law, which knows neither to flatter nor to insult, calls this high magistrate, not our servant, as this humble divine calls him, but *"our sovereign Lord the king;"* and we, on

works, Edmund Burke (London, 1867), II, 302-320.

our parts, have learned to speak only the primitive language of the law, and not the confused jargon of their Babylonian pulpits.

As he is not to obey us, but as we are to obey the law in him, our constitution has made no sort of provision towards rendering him, as a servant, in any degree responsible. Our constitution knows nothing of a magistrate like the *Justicia* of Arragon; nor of any court legally appointed, nor of any process legally settled, for submitting the king to the responsibility belonging to all servants. In this he is not distinguished from the Commons and the Lords; who, in their several public capacities, can never be called to an account for their conduct; although the Revolution Society chooses to assert, in direct opposition to one of the wisest and most beautiful parts of our constitution, that "a king is no more than the first servant of the public, created by it, *and responsible to it.*"

Ill would our ancestors at the Revolution have deserved their fame for wisdom, if they had found no security for their freedom, but in rendering their government feeble in its operations and precarious in its tenure; if they had been able to contrive no better remedy against arbitrary power than civil confusion. Let these gentlemen state who that *representative* public is to whom they will affirm the king, as a servant, to be responsible. It will be then time enough for me to produce to them the positive statute law which affirms that he is not.

The ceremony of cashiering kings, of which these gentlemen talk so much at their ease, can rarely, if ever, be performed without force. It then becomes a case of war, and not of constitution. Laws are commanded to hold their tongues amongst arms; and tribunals fall to the ground with the peace they are no longer able to uphold. The Revolution of 1688 was obtained by a just war, in the only case in which any war, and much more a civil war, can be just. "Justa bella quibus *necessaria.*" [1] The question of dethroning, or, if these gentlemen like the phrase better, "cashiering kings," will always be, as it has always been an extraordinary question of state, and wholly out of the law; a question (like all other questions of state) of dispositions, and of means, and of probable consequences, rather than of positive rights. As it was not made for common abuses, so it is not to be agitated by common minds. The speculative line of demarcation, where obedience ought to end, and resistance must begin, is faint, obscure, and not easily definable. It is not a single act, or a single event, which determines it. Governments must be abused and deranged indeed, before it can be thought of; and the prospect of the future must be

as bad as the experience of the past. When things are in that lamentable condition, the nature of the disease is to indicate the remedy to those whom nature has qualified to administer in extremities this critical, ambiguous, bitter potion to a distempered state. Times, and occasions, and provocations, will teach their own lessons. The wise will determine from the gravity of the case; the irritable, from sensibility to oppression; the high-minded, from disdain and indignation at abusive power in unworthy hands; the brave and bold, from the love of honourable danger in a generous cause: but, with or without right, a revolution will be the very last resource of the thinking and the good.

The third head of right, asserted by the pulpit of the Old Jewry, namely, the "right to form a government for ourselves," has, at least, as little countenance from anything done at the Revolution [*of 1688*], either in precedent or principle, as the two first of their claims. The Revolution was made to preserve our *ancient*, indisputable laws and liberties, and that *ancient* constitution of government which is our only security for law and liberty. If you are desirous of knowing the spirit of our constitution, and the policy which predominated in that great period which has secured it to this hour, pray look for both in our histories, in our records, in our acts of parliament, and journals of parliament, and not in the sermons of the Old Jewry, and the after-dinner toasts of the Revolution Society. In the former you will find other ideas and another language. Such a claim is as ill-suited to our temper and wishes as it is unsupported by any appearance of authority. The very idea of the fabrication of a new government is enough to fill us with disgust and horror. We wished at the period of the Revolution, and do now wish, to derive all we possess as *an inheritance from our forefathers.* Upon that body and stock of inheritance we have taken care not to in-

[1] ["*Wars are just to those to whom they are necessary.*"]

oculate any scion alien to the nature of the original plant. All the reformations we have hitherto made have proceeded upon the principle of reverence to antiquity: and I hope, nay I am persuaded, that all those which possibly may be made hereafter, will be carefully formed upon analogical precedent, authority, and example.

Our oldest reformation is that of Magna Charta. You will see that Sir Edward Coke, that great oracle of our law, and indeed all the great men who follow him, to Blackstone, are industrious to prove the pedigree of our liberties. They endeavour to prove, that the ancient charter, the Magna Charta of King John, was connected with another positive charter from Henry I, and that both the one and the other were nothing more than a re-affirmance of the still more ancient standing law of the kingdom. In the matter of fact, for the greater part, these authors appear to be in the right; perhaps not always; but if the lawyers mistake in some particulars, it proves my position still the more strongly; because it demonstrates the powerful prepossession towards antiquity, with which the minds of all our lawyers and legislators, and of all the people whom they wish to influence, have been always filled; and the stationary policy of this kingdom in considering their most sacred rights and franchises as an *inheritance*.

In the famous law of the 3rd of Charles I, called the *Petition of Right*, the parliament says to the king, "Your subjects have *inherited* this freedom," claiming their franchises not on abstract principles "as the rights of men," but as the rights of Englishmen, and as a patrimony derived from their forefathers. Selden, and the other profoundly learned men, who drew this Petition of Right, were as well acquainted, at least, with all the general theories concerning the "rights of men," as any of the discoursers in our pulpits, or on your tribune; full as well as Dr. Price, or as the Abbé Siéyès. But, for reasons worthy of that practical wisdom which superseded their theoretic science, they preferred this positive, recorded, *hereditary* title to all which can be dear to the man and the citizen, to that vague speculative right, which exposed their sure inheritance to be scrambled for and torn to pieces by every wild, litigious spirit.

The same policy pervades all the laws which have since been made for the preservation of our liberties. In the 1st of William and Mary, in the famous statute, called the Declaration of Right, the two Houses utter not a syllable of "a right to frame a government for themselves." You will see, that their whole care was to secure the religion, laws, and liberties, that had been long possessed, and had been lately endangered. "Taking into their most serious consideration the *best* means for making such an establishment, that their religion, laws, and liberties might not be in danger of being again subverted," they auspicate all their proceedings, by stating as some of those *best* means, "in the *first place*" to do "as their *ancestors in like cases have usually* done for vindicating their *ancient* rights and liberties, to *declare;*"—and then they pray the king and queen, "that it may be *declared* and enacted, that *all and singular* the rights and liberties *asserted and declared*, are the true *ancient* and indubitable rights and liberties of the people of this kingdom."

You will observe that from Magna Charta to the Declaration of Right, it has been the uniform policy of our constitution to claim and assert our liberties, as an *entailed inheritance* derived to us from our forefathers, and to be transmitted to our posterity; as an estate specially belonging to the people of this kingdom, without any reference whatever to any other more general or prior right. By this means our constitution preserves a unity in so great a diversity of its parts. We have an inheritable crown; an inheritable peerage; and a House of Commons and a people inheriting privileges, franchises, and liberties, from a long line of ancestors.

This policy appears to me to be the result of profound reflection; or rather the happy effect of following nature, which is wisdom without reflection, and above it. A spirit of innovation is generally the result of a selfish temper, and confined views. People will not look forward to posterity, who never look backward to their ancestors. Besides, the people of England well know, that the idea of inheritance furnishes a sure principle of conservation, and a sure principle of transmission; without at all excluding a principle of improvement. It leaves acquisition free; but it secures what it acquires. Whatever advantages are obtained by a state proceeding on these maxims, are locked fast as in a sort of family settlement; grasped as in a kind of mortmain for ever. By a constitutional policy, working after the pattern of nature, we receive, we hold, we transmit our government and our privileges, in the same manner in which we enjoy and transmit our property and our lives. The institutions of policy, the goods of fortune, the gifts of providence, are handed down to us, and from us, in the same course and order. Our political system is placed in a just correspondence and symmetry with the order of the world, and with the mode of existence decreed to a permanent body composed of transitory parts; wherein, by the disposition of a stupendous wisdom, moulding together the great mysterious incorporation of the human race, the whole, at one time, is never old, or middleaged, or young, but, in a condition of unchangeable constancy, moves on through the varied tenor of perpetual decay, fall, renovation, and progression. Thus, by preserving the method of nature in the conduct of the state, in what we improve, we are never wholly new; in what we retain, we are never wholly obsolete. By

adhering in this manner and on those principles to our forefathers, we are guided not by the superstition of antiquarians, but by the spirit of philosophic analogy. In this choice of inheritance we have given to our frame of polity the image of a relation in blood; binding up the constitution of our country with our dearest domestic ties; adopting our fundamental laws into the bosom of our family affections; keeping inseparable, and cherishing with the warmth of all their combined and mutually reflected charities, our state, our hearths, our sepulchres, and our altars.

Through the same plan of a conformity to nature in our artificial institutions, and by calling in the aid of her unerring and powerful instincts, to fortify the fallible and feeble contrivances of our reason, we have derived several other, and those no small benefits, from considering our liberties in the light of an inheritance. Always acting as if in the presence of canonized forefathers, the spirit of freedom, leading in itself to misrule and excess, is tempered with an awful gravity. This idea of a liberal descent inspires us with a sense of habitual native dignity, which prevents that upstart insolence almost inevitably adhering to and disgracing those who are the first acquirers of any distinction. By this means our liberty becomes a noble freedom. It carries an imposing and majestic aspect. It has a pedigree and illustrating ancestors. It has its bearings and its ensigns armorial. It has its gallery of portraits; its monumental inscriptions; its records, evidences, and titles. We procure reverence to our civil institutions on the principle upon which nature teaches us to revere individual men; on account of their age, and on account of those from whom they are descended. All your sophisters cannot produce anything better adapted to preserve a rational and manly freedom than the course that we have pursued, who have chosen our nature rather than our speculations, our breasts rather than our inventions, for the great conservatories and magazines of our rights and privileges.

You [*in France*] might, if you pleased, have profited of our example, and have given to your recovered freedom a correspondent dignity. Your privileges, though discontinued, were not lost to memory. Your constitution, it is true, whilst you were out of possession, suffered waste and dilapidation; but you possessed in some parts the walls, and, in all, the foundations, of a noble and venerable castle. You might have repaired those walls; you might have built on those old foundations. Your constitution was suspended before it was perfected; but you had the elements of a constitution very nearly as good as could be wished. In your old states you possessed that variety of parts corresponding with the various descriptions of which your community was happily composed; you had all that combination, and all that opposition of interests, you had that action and counteraction, which, in the natural and in the political world, from the reciprocal struggle of discordant powers, draws out the harmony of the universe. These opposed and conflicting interests, which you considered as so great a blemish in your old and in our present constitution, interpose a salutary check to all precipitate resolutions. They render deliberation a matter not of choice, but of necessity: they make all change a subject of *compromise*, which naturally begets moderation; they produce *temperaments* preventing the sore evil of harsh, crude, unqualified reformations; and rendering all the headlong exertions of arbitrary power, in the few or in the many, for ever impracticable. Through that diversity of members and interests, general liberty had as many securities as there were separate views in the several orders; whilst by pressing down the whole by the weight of a real monarchy, the separate parts would have been pre-

vented from warping, and starting from their allotted places.

You had all these advantages in your ancient states; but you chose to act as if you had never been moulded into civil society, and had everything to begin anew. You began ill, because you began by despising everything that belonged to you. You set up your trade without a capital. If the last generations of your country appeared without much lustre in your eyes, you might have passed them by, and derived your claims from a more early race of ancestors. Under a pious predilection for those ancestors, your imaginations would have realized in them a standard of virtue and wisdom, beyond the vulgar practice of the hour: and you would have risen with the example to whose imitation you aspired. Respecting your forefathers, you would have been taught to respect yourselves. You would not have chosen to consider the French as a people of yesterday, as a nation of low-born servile wretches until the emancipating year of 1789. In order to furnish, at the expense of your honour, an excuse to your apologists here for several enormities of yours, you would not have been content to be represented as a gang of Maroon slaves, suddenly broke loose from the house of bondage, and therefore to be pardoned for your abuse of the liberty to which you were not accustomed, and ill fitted. Would it not, my worthy friend, have been wiser to have you thought, what I, for one, always thought you, a generous and gallant nation, long misled to your disadvantage by your high and romantic sentiments of fidelity, honour, and loyalty; that events had been unfavourable to you, but that you were not enslaved through any illiberal or servile disposition; that in your most devoted submission, you were actuated by a principle of public spirit, and that it was your country you worshipped, in the person of your king? Had you made it to be understood, that in the delusion of this amiable error you had gone further than your wise ancestors; that you were resolved to resume your ancient privileges, whilst you preserved the spirit of your ancient and your recent loyalty and honour; or if, diffident of yourselves, and not clearly discerning the almost obliterated constitution of your ancestors, you had looked to your neighbours in this land, who had kept alive the ancient principles and models of the old common law of Europe meliorated and adapted to its present state—by following wise examples you would have given new examples of wisdom to the world. You would have rendered the cause of liberty venerable in the eyes of every worthy mind in every nation. You would have shamed despotism from the earth, by showing that freedom was not only reconcilable, but, as when well disciplined it is, auxiliary to law. You would have had an unoppressive but a productive revenue. You would have had a flourishing commerce to feed it. You would have had a free constitution; a potent monarchy; a disciplined army; a reformed and venerated clergy; a mitigated but spirited nobility, to lead your virtue, not to overlay it; you would have had a liberal order of commons, to emulate and to recruit that nobility; you would have had a protected, satisfied, laborious, and obedient people, taught to seek and to recognise the happiness that is to be found by virtue in all conditions; in which consists the true moral equality of mankind, and not in that monstrous fiction, which, by inspiring false ideas and vain expectations into men destined to travel in the obscure walk of laborious life, serves only to aggravate and embitter that real inequality, which it never can remove; and which the order of civil life establishes as much for the benefit of those whom it must leave in an humble state, as those whom it is able to exalt to a condition more splendid, but not more happy. You had a

smooth and easy career of felicity and glory laid open to you, beyond anything recorded in the history of the world; but you have shown that difficulty is good for men.

Compute your gains: see what is got by those extravagant and presumptuous speculations which have taught your leaders to despise all their predecessors, and all their contemporaries, and even to despise themselves, until the moment in which they became truly despicable. By following those false lights, France has bought undisguised calamities at a higher price than any nation has purchased the most unequivocal blessings! France has bought poverty by crime! France has not sacrificed her virtue to her interest, but she has abandoned her interest, that she might prostitute her virtue. All other nations have begun the fabric of a new government, or the reformation of an old, by establishing originally, or by enforcing with greater exactness, some rites or other of religion. All other people have laid the foundations of civil freedom in severer manners, and a system of a more austere and masculine morality. France, when she let loose the reins of regal authority, doubled the licence of a ferocious dissoluteness in manners, and of an insolent irreligion in opinions and practices; and has extended through all ranks of life, as if she were communicating some privilege, or laying open some secluded benefit, all the unhappy corruptions that usually were the disease of wealth and power. This is one of the new principles of equality in France.

France, by the perfidy of her leaders, has utterly disgraced the tone of lenient council in the cabinets of princes, and disarmed it of its most potent topics. She has sanctified the dark, suspicious maxims of tyrannous distrust; and taught kings to tremble at (what will hereafter be called) the delusive plausibilities of moral politicians. Sovereigns will consider those, who advise them to place an unlimited confidence in their people, as subverters of their thrones; as traitors who aim at their destruction, by leading their easy good-nature, under specious pretences, to admit combinations of bold and faithless men into a participation of their power. This alone (if there were nothing else) is an irreparable calamity to you and to mankind. Remember that your parliament of Paris told your king, that, in calling the states together, he had nothing to fear but the prodigal excess of their zeal in providing for the support of the throne. It is right that these men should hide their heads. It is right that they should bear their part in the ruin which their counsel has brought on their sovereign and their country. Such sanguine declarations tend to lull authority asleep; to encourage it rashly to engage in perilous adventures of untried policy; to neglect those provisions, preparations, and precautions, which distinguish benevolence from imbecility; and without which no man can answer for the salutary effect of any abstract plan of government or of freedom. For want of these, they have seen the medicine of the state corrupted into its poison. They have seen the French rebel against a mild and lawful monarch, with more fury, outrage, and insult, than ever any people has been known to rise against the most illegal usurper, or the most sanguinary tyrant. Their resistance was made to concession; their revolt was from protection; their blow was aimed at a hand holding out graces, favours, and immunities.

This was unnatural. The rest is in order. They have found their punishment in their success. Laws overturned; tribunals subverted; industry without vigour; commerce expiring; the revenue unpaid, yet the people impoverished; a church pillaged, and a state not relieved; civil and military anarchy made the constitution of the kingdom; everything human and divine sacrificed to the idol of public credit, and national bankruptcy the consequence; and, to crown all, the paper securities of new, precarious, tottering power, the discredited paper securities of impoverished fraud and beggared rapine, held out as a currency for the support of an empire, in lieu of the two great recognised species that represent the lasting, conventional credit of mankind, which disappeared and hid themselves in the earth from whence they came, when the principle of property, whose creatures and representatives they are, was systematically subverted.

Were all these dreadful things necessary? Were they the inevitable results of the desperate struggle of determined patriots, compelled to wade through blood and tumult, to the quiet shore of a tranquil and prosperous liberty? No! nothing like it. The fresh ruins of France, which shock our feelings wherever we can turn our eyes, are not the devastation of civil war; they are the sad but instructive monuments of rash and ignorant counsel in time of profound peace. They are the display of inconsiderate and presumptuous, because unresisted and irresistible, authority. The persons who have thus squandered away the precious treasure of their crimes, the persons who have made this prodigal and wild waste of public evils, (the last stake reserved for the ultimate ransom of the state), have met in their progress with little, or rather with no opposition at all. Their whole march was more like a triumphal procession, than the progress of a war. Their pioneers have gone before them, and demolished and laid everything level at their feet. Not one drop of *their* blood have they shed in the cause of the country they have ruined. They have made no sacrifices to their projects of greater consequence than their shoe-buckles, whilst they were imprisoning their king, murdering their fellow-citizens, and bathing in tears, and plunging in poverty and distress, thousands of worthy men and worthy families. Their cruelty has not even been the base result of fear. It has been the effect of their sense of perfect safety, in authorizing treasons, robberies, rapes, assassinations, slaughters, and burnings, throughout their harassed land. But the cause of all was plain from the beginning.

This unforced choice, this fond election of evil, would appear perfectly unaccountable, if we did not consider the composition of the National Assembly: I do not mean its formal constitution, which, as it now stands, is exceptional enough, but the materials of which, in a great measure, it is composed, which is of ten thousand times greater consequence than all the formalities in the world. If we were to know nothing of this assembly but by its title and function, no colours could paint to the imagination anything more venerable. In that light the mind of an inquirer, subdued by such an awful image as that of the virtue and wisdom of a whole people collected into a focus, would pause and hesitate in condemning things even of the very worst aspect. Instead of blameable, they would appear only mysterious. But no name, no power, no function, no artificial institution whatsoever, can make the men of whom any system of authority is composed, any other than God, and nature, and education, and their habits of life have made them. Capacities beyond these the people have not to give. Virtue and wisdom may be the objects of their choice; but their choice confers neither the one nor the other on those upon whom they lay their ordaining hands. They have not the engagement of nature, they have not the promise of revelation, for any such powers.

After I had read over the list of the persons and descriptions elected into the *Tiers Etat*, nothing which they afterwards did could appear astonishing. Among them, indeed, I saw some of known rank; some of shining talents; but of any practical experience in the state, not one man was to be found. The best were only men of theory. But whatever the distinguished few may have been, it is the substance the mass of the body which constitutes its character, and must finally determine its direction. In all bodies, those who will lead, must also, in a considerable degree, follow. They must conform their propositions to the taste, talent, and disposition, of those whom they wish to conduct: therefore, if an assembly is viciously or feebly composed in a very great part of it, nothing but such a supreme degree of virtue as very rarely appears in the world, and for that reason cannot enter into calculation, will prevent the men of talent disseminated through it from becoming only the expert instruments of absurd projects! If, what is the more likely event, instead of that unusual degree of virtue, they should be actuated by sinister ambition, and a lust of meretricious glory, then the feeble part of the assembly, to whom at first they conform, becomes in its turn the dupe and instrument of their designs. In this political traffic, the leaders will be obliged to bow to the ignorance of their followers, and the followers to become subservient to the worst designs of their leaders.

To secure any degree of sobriety in the propositions made by the leaders in any public assembly, they ought to respect, in some degree perhaps to fear, those whom they conduct. To be led any otherwise than blindly, the followers must be qualified, if not for actors, at least for judges; they must also be judges of natural weight and authority. Nothing can secure a steady and moderate conduct in such assemblies, but that the body of them should be respectably composed, in point of condition in life, of permanent property, of education, and of such habits as enlarge and liberalize the understanding.

In the calling of the States-General of France, the first thing that struck me, was a great departure from the ancient course. I found the representation for the third estate composed of six hundred persons. They were equal in number to the representatives of both the other orders. If the orders were to act separately, the number would not, beyond the consideration of the expense, be of much moment. But when it became apparent that the three orders were to be melted down into one, the policy and necessary effect of this numerous representation became obvious. A very small desertion from either of the other two orders must throw the power of both into the hands of the third. In fact, the whole power of the state was soon resolved into that body. Its due composition became therefore of infinitely the greater importance.

Judge, Sir, of my surprise, when I found that a very great proportion of the assembly (a majority, I believe, of the members who attended) was composed of practitioners in the law. It was composed, not of distinguished magistrates, who had given pledges to their country of their science, prudence, and integrity; not of leading advocates, the glory of the bar; not of renowned professors in universities;—but for the far greater part, as it must in such a number, of the inferior, unlearned, mechanical, merely instrumental members of the profession. There were distinguished exceptions; but the general composition was of obscure provincial advocates, of stewards of petty local jurisdictions, country attorneys, notaries, and the whole train of the ministers of municipal litigation, the fomenters and conductors of the petty war of village vexation. From the moment I read the list, I saw distinctly, and very nearly as it has happened, all that was to follow.

The degree of estimation in which any profession is held becomes the standard of the estimation in which the professors hold themselves. Whatever the personal merits of many individual lawyers might have been, and in many it was undoubtedly very considerable, in that military kingdom no part of the profession had been much regarded, except the highest of all, who often united to their professional offices great family splendour, and were invested with great power and authority. These certainly were highly respected, and even with no small degree of awe. The next rank was not much esteemed; the mechanical part was in a very low degree of repute.

Whenever the supreme authority is vested in a body so composed, it must evidently produce the consequences of supreme authority placed in the hands of men not taught habitually to respect themselves; who had no previous fortune in character at stake; who could not be expected to bear with moderation, or to conduct with discretion, a power, which they themselves, more than any others, must be surprised to find in their hands. Who could flatter himself that these men, suddenly, and, as it were, by enchantment, snatched from the humblest rank of subordination, would not be intoxicated with their unprepared greatness? Who could conceive that men, who are habitually meddling, daring, subtle, active, of litigious dispositions and unquiet minds would easily fall back into their old condition of obscure contention, and laborious, low, and unprofitable chicane? Who could doubt but that, at any expense to the state, of which they understood nothing, they must pursue their private interests which they understood but too well? It was not an event depending on chance, or contingency. It was inevitable; it was necessary; it was planted in the nature of things. They must *join* (if their capacity did not permit them to *lead*) in any project which could procure them those innumerable lucrative jobs, which follow in the train of all great convulsions and revolutions in the state, and particularly in all great and violent permutations of property. Was it to be expected that they would attend to the stability of property, whose existence had always depended upon whatever rendered property questionable, ambiguous, and insecure? Their objects would be enlarged with their elevation, but their disposition and habits, and mode of accomplishing their designs, must remain the same.

Well! but these men were to be tempered and restrained by other descriptions, of more sober and more enlarged understandings. Were they then to be awed by the supereminent authority and awful dignity of a handful of country clowns, who have seats in that assembly, some of whom are said not to be able to read and write? and by not a greater number of traders, who, though somewhat more instructed, and more conspicuous in the order of society, had never known anything beyond their counting-house. No! both these descriptions were more formed to be overborne and swayed by the intrigues and artifices of lawyers, than to become their counterpoise. With such a dangerous disproportion, the whole must needs be governed by them. To the faculty of law was joined a pretty considerable proportion of the faculty of medicine. This faculty had not, any more than that of the law, possessed in France its just estimation. Its professors, therefore, must have the qualities of men not habituated to sentiments of dignity. But supposing they had ranked as they ought to do, and as with us they do actually, the sides of sick beds are not the academies for forming statesmen and legislators. Then came the dealers in stocks and funds, who must be eager, at any expense to change their ideal paper wealth for the more solid substance of land. To these were joined men of other descriptions, from whom as little knowledge of, or attention to, the interests of a great state was to be expected, and as little regard to the stability of any institution; men formed to be instruments, not controls. Such in general was the composition of the *Tiers État* in the National Assembly; in which was

scarcely to be perceived the slightest traces of what we call the natural landed interest of the country.

We know that the British House of Commons, without shutting its doors to any merit in any class, is, by the sure operation of adequate causes, filled with everything illustrious in rank, in descent, in hereditary and in acquired opulence, in cultivated talents, in military, civil, naval, and politic distinction, that the country can afford. But supposing, what hardly can be supposed, as a case, that the House of Commons should be composed in the same manner with the *Tiers État* in France, would this dominion of chicane be borne with patience, or even conceived without horror? God forbid I should insinuate anything derogatory to that profession, which is another priesthood, administrating the rights of sacred justice. But whilst I revere men in the functions which belong to them, and would do as much as one man can do to prevent their exclusion from any, I cannot, to flatter them, give the lie to nature. They are good and useful in the composition; they must be mischievous if they preponderate so as virtually to become the whole. Their very excellence in their peculiar functions may be far from a qualification for others. It cannot escape observation, that when men are too much confined to professional and faculty habits, and as it were inveterate in the recurrent employment of that narrow circle, they are rather disabled than qualified for whatever depends on the knowledge of mankind, on experience in mixed affairs, on a comprehensive, connected view of the various, complicated, external and internal interests, which go to the formation of that multifarious thing called a state.

After all, if the House of Commons were to have a wholly professional and faculty composition, what is the power of the House of Commons, circumscribed and shut in by the immoveable barriers of laws, us-ages, positive rules of doctrine and practice, counterpoised by the House of Lords, and every moment of its existence at the discretion of the crown to continue, prorogue, or dissolve us? The power of the House of Commons, direct or indirect, is indeed great; and long may it be able to preserve its greatness, and the spirit belonging to true greatness, at the full; and it will do so, as long as it can keep the breakers of law in India from becoming the makers of law for England. The power, however, of the House of Commons, when least diminished, is as a drop of water in the ocean, compared to that residing in a settled majority of your National Assembly. That assembly, since the destruction of the orders, has no fundamental law, no strict convention, no respected usage to restrain it. Instead of finding themselves obliged to conform to a fixed constitution, they have a power to make a constitution which shall conform to their designs. Nothing in heaven or upon earth can serve as a control on them. What ought to be the heads, the hearts, the dispositions, that are qualified, or that dare, not only to make laws under a fixed constitution, but at one heat to strike out a totally new constitution for a great kingdom, and in every part of it, from the monarch on the throne to the vestry of a parish? But—"fools rush in where angels fear to tread." In such a state of unbounded power for undefined and undefinable purposes, the evil of a moral and almost physical inaptitude of the man to the function must be the greatest we can conceive to happen in the management of human affairs.

Having considered the composition of the third estate as it stood in its original frame, I took a view of the representatives of the clergy. There too it appeared, that full as little regard was had to the general security of property, or to the aptitude of the deputies for their public purposes, in the principles of their election. That election was so contrived, as to send a very large proportion of mere country curates to the great and arduous work of new-modelling a state; men who never had seen the state so much as in a picture; men who knew nothing of the world beyond the bounds of an obscure village; who, immersed in hopeless poverty, could regard all property, whether secular or ecclesiastical, with no other eye than that of envy; among whom must be many who, for the smallest hope of the meanest dividend in plunder, would readily join in any attempts upon a body of wealth, in which they could hardly look to have any share, except in a general scramble. Instead of balancing the power of the active chicaners in the other assembly, these curates must necessarily become the active coadjutors, or at best the passive instruments, of those by whom they had been habitually guided in their petty village concerns. They too could hardly be the most conscientious of their kind, who presuming upon their incompetent understanding, could intrigue for a trust which led them from their natural relation to their flocks, and their natural spheres of action, to undertake the regeneration of kingdoms. This preponderating weight, being added to the force of the body of chicane in the *Tiers Etat*, completed that momentum of ignorance, rashness, presumption, and lust of plunder, which nothing has been able to resist.

To observing men it must have appeared from the beginning, that the majority of the Third Estate, in conjunction with such a deputation from the clergy as I have described, whilst it pursued the destruction of the nobility, would inevitably become subservient to the worst designs of individuals in that class. In the spoil and humiliation of their own order these individuals would possess a sure fund for the pay of their new followers. To squander away the objects which made the happiness of their fellows, would be to them no sacrifice at all. Turbulent, discontented men of quality, in proportion as they are puffed up with personal pride and arrogance, generally despise their own order. One of the first symptoms they discover of a selfish and mischievous ambition, is a profligate disregard of a dignity which they partake with others. To be attached to the subdivision, to love the little platoon we belong to in society is the first principle (the germ as it were) of public affections. It is the first link in the series by which we proceed towards a love to our country, and to mankind. The interest of that portion of social arrangement is a trust in the hands of all those who compose it; and as none but bad men would justify it in abuse, none but traitors would barter it away for their own personal advantage.

Romanticism in Literature

It is often said that Romanticism was a reaction against the rationalism of the Enlightenment. And yet this interpretation does not provide a complete explanation of the movement. For Romanticism was more than an anti-intellectual outburst; it was a general rebellion against the whole civilization of late eighteenth-century Europe. Although the positive views of the Romantics were often quite divergent and sometimes even contradictory, almost without exception the Romantics shared a desire to escape from the immediate historical situation in which they found themselves. The escape routes varied. Some Romantics, like the novelists Hugo and Scott, immersed themselves in the medieval past; some, like the philosopher Hegel, identified themselves with a supernatural Reality transcending the vicissitudes of time and space; some, like the political theorist De Maistre, found refuge in the traditions and authority of the Church; some, like the poet Wordsworth, sought communion with an idyllic Nature, itself soon to be despoiled by the mills and factories of the Industrial Revolution.

The poems that follow illustrate respectively two major Romantic themes: the rebellion of the individual against the gods and the worship of Nature. The first, *Prometheus* (1774), is by the German writer, Johann Wolfgang von Goethe (1749-1832). Goethe was too broad in his interests and attitudes to be classified simply as a Romantic; indeed he has been called the last *uomo universale* in Western civilization. The second poem, *Tintern Abbey* (1798), is by the English Romantic poet, William Wordsworth (1770-1850).

PROMETHEUS

Cover your heavens
In cloud-mists, Zeus,
And like a boy
Beheading thistles, go practice
On oaks and mountain tops!
Still you'll have to
Leave me my earth,
The hut you did not build,
And the hearth,
Whose fire
You envy me.

I know nothing under the sun
Less enviable than you gods!
Your majesty,
Wretchedly nourished
On exacted sacrifice
And breath of prayer,
Would famish were not
Children and beggars
Hopeful fools.

While yet a child,
Knowing no other way,
Lost, I turned my face
To the sun, as if up there
Some ear might hear my lamentation,
Some heart like mine
Pity my affliction.

PROMETHEUS, Johann Wolfgang von Goethe,
trans. Milton Miller of the University of California at Riverside.

Who helped me
Resist Titanic arrogance?
Who rescued me from death,
From slavery?
Didn't you accomplish it yourself,
High impassioned heart?
And yet, youthfully passionate and good,
You gave deluded thanks for rescue
To the slumberer above.

Why should I honor you?
Did you ever soothe the pain
Of the oppressed?
Or still the tears
Of anguish, ever?
Wasn't I forged a man
By everlasting fate
And time omnipotent,
My lords and yours?

Did you suppose
I'd come to hate life,
Escape to deserts,
Because not all
Dreams blossomed?

Here I sit and create men
After my own image,
A race like myself,
To suffer, to weep,
To relish, to rejoice,
And to ignore you,
As do I!

TINTERN ABBEY

LINES COMPOSED A FEW MILES ABOVE
TINTERN ABBEY, ON REVISITING THE
BANKS OF THE WYE DURING A TOUR.

July 13, 1798

Five years have past; five summers, with the
    length
Of five long winters! and again I hear
These waters, rolling from their mountain-
    springs
With a soft inland murmur. —Once again
Do I behold these steep and lofty cliffs,
That on a wild secluded scene impress
Thoughts of more deep seclusion; and connect
The landscape with the quiet of the sky.
The day is come when I again repose
Here, under this dark sycamore, and view
These plots of cottage-ground, these orchard-
    tufts,
Which at this season, with their unripe fruits,
Are clad in one green hue, and lose them-
    selves
'Mid groves and copses. Once again I see
These hedge-rows, hardly hedge-rows, little
    lines
Of sportive wood run wild: these pastoral
    farms,
Green to the very door; and wreaths of smoke
Sent up, in silence, from among the trees!
With some uncertain notice, as might seem
Of vagrant dwellers in the houseless woods,
Or of some Hermit's cave, where by his fire
The Hermit sits alone.

                    These beauteous forms,
Through a long absence, have not been to me
As is a landscape to blind man's eye:
But oft, in lonely rooms, and 'mid the din
Of towns and cities, I have owed to them
In hours of weariness, sensations sweet,
Felt in the blood, and felt along the heart;
And passing even into my purer mind,
With tranquil restoration: —feelings too

Of unremembered pleasure: such, perhaps,
As have no slight or trivial influence
On that best portion of a good man's life,
His little, nameless, unremembered, acts
Of kindness and of love. Nor less, I trust,
To them I may have owed another gift,
Of aspect more sublime; that blessed mood,
In which the burthen of the mystery,
In which the heavy and the weary weight
Of all this unintelligible world,
Is lightened: —that serene and blessed mood,
In which the affections gently lead us on,—
Until, the breath of this corporeal frame
And even the motion of our human blood
Almost suspended, we are laid asleep
In body, and become a living soul:
While with an eye made quiet by the power
Of harmony, and the deep power of joy,
We see into the life of things.

                                    If this
Be but a vain belief, yet, oh! how oft—
In darkness and amid the many shapes
Of joyless daylight; when the fretful stir
Unprofitable, and the fever of the world,
Have hung upon the beatings of my heart—
How oft, in spirit, have I turned to thee,
O sylvan Wye! thou wanderer thro' the
    woods,
How often has my spirit turned to thee!
And now, with gleams of half-extinguished
    thought,
With many recognitions dim and faint,
And somewhat of a sad perplexity,
The picture of the mind revives again:
While here I stand, not only with the sense
Of present pleasure, but with pleasing thoughts
That in this moment there is life and food
For future years. And so I dare to hope,
Though changed, no doubt, from what I was
    when first
I came among these hills; when like a roe
I bounded o'er the mountains, by the sides
Of the deep rivers, and the lonely streams,
Wherever nature led: more like a man
Flying from something that he dreads, than
    one

"LINES COMPOSED A FEW MILES ABOVE TINTERN AB-
BEY," in *The Poetical Works of Wordsworth*
(London, 1889), pp. 115-117.

Who sought the thing he loved. For nature
  then
(The coarser pleasures of my boyish days,
And their glad animal movements all gone by)
To me was all in all. —I cannot paint
What then I was. The sounding cataract
Haunted me like a passion: the tall rock,
The mountain, and the deep and gloomy
  wood,
Their colours and their forms, were then to
  me
An appetite; a feeling and a love,
That had no need of a remoter charm,
By thought supplied, nor any interest
Unborrowed from the eye. —That time is past,
And all its aching joys are now no more,
And all its dizzy raptures. Not for this
Faint I, nor mourn nor murmur; other gifts
Have followed; for such loss, I would believe,
Abundant recompense. For I have learned
To look on nature, not as in the hour
Of thoughtless youth; but hearing oftentimes
The still, sad music of humanity,
Nor harsh nor grating, though of ample power
To chasten and subdue. And I have felt
A presence that disturbs me with the joy
Of elevated thoughts; a sense sublime
Of something far more deeply interfused,
Whose dwelling is the light of setting suns,
And the round ocean and the living air,
And the blue sky, and in the mind of man;
A motion and a spirit, that impels
All thinking things, all objects of all thought,
And rolls through all things. Therefore am I
  still
A lover of the meadows and the woods,
And mountains; and of all that we behold
From this green earth; of all the mighty world
Of eye, and ear, —both what they half create,
And what perceive; well pleased to recognise
In nature and the language of the sense,
The anchor of my purest thoughts, the nurse,
The guide, the guardian of my heart, and
  soul
Of all my moral being.

                              Nor perchance,
If I were not thus taught, should I the more
Suffer my genial spirits to decay:
For thou art with me here upon the banks
Of this fair river; thou my dearest Friend,

My dear, dear Friend;[1] and in thy voice I
  catch
The language of my former heart, and read
My former pleasures in the shooting lights
Of thy wild eyes. Oh! yet a little while
May I behold in thee what I was once,
My dear, dear Sister! and this prayer I make,
Knowing that Nature never did betray
The heart that loved her; 'tis her privilege,
Through all the years of this our life, to lead
From joy to joy: for she can so inform
The mind that is within us, so impress
With quietness and beauty, and so feed
With lofty thoughts, that neither evil tongues,
Rash judgments, nor the sneers of selfish men,
Nor greetings where no kindness is, nor all
The dreary intercourse of daily life,
Shall e'er prevail against us, or disturb
Our cheerful faith, that all which we be-
  hold
Is full of blessings. Therefore let the moon
Shine on thee in thy solitary walk;
And let the misty mountain-winds be free
To blow against thee: and, in after years,
When these wild ecstasies shall be matured
Into a sober pleasure; when thy mind
Shall be a mansion for all lovely forms,
Thy memory be as a dwelling-place
For all sweet sounds and harmonies; oh! then,
If solitude, or fear, or pain, or grief,
Should be thy portion, with what healing
  thoughts
Of tender joy wilt thou remember me,
And these my exhortations! Nor, perchance —
If I should be where I no more can hear
Thy voice, nor catch from thy wild eyes these
  gleams
Of past existence — wilt thou then forget
That on the banks of this delightful stream
We stood together; and that I, so long
A worshipper of Nature, hither came
Unwearied in that service; rather say
With warmer love — oh! with far deeper zeal
Of holier love. Nor wilt thou then forget,
That after many wanderings, many years
Of absence, these steep woods and lofty cliffs,
And this green pastoral landscape, were to me
More dear, both for themselves and for thy
  sake!

[1] [*Wordsworth is here addressing his sister Dor-
othy.*]

Thomas Malthus

After a tranquil youth, Thomas Malthus (1766-1834) entered Cambridge University and received his Master of Arts degree in 1797. The same year, he took orders in the Church of England. Most of his intellectual interests were centered on the problems of history and political economy, subjects that he taught at both Cambridge and Haileybury College (which trained candidates for service with the East India Company). His life in general was quiet and scholarly, though it was enlivened by a circle of distinguished friends, such as James Mill and David Ricardo, and spiced by the periodic outbursts of abuse and vilification that he suffered after his great study on population had been published. This work was denounced as unholy, atheistic, and subversive, but it was admired by such men as William Pitt and Archdeacon William Paley, and by such distinguished periodicals as the *Edinburgh Review* and the *Quarterly Review*.

The book that caused all this furor was *An Essay on the Principle of Population*, which first appeared in 1798. The first edition, however, was premature, for Malthus lacked sufficient evidence to support his thesis strongly, and he chose to write in an excessively rhetorical style. But as the years passed, he assembled more and more factual support, eliminated errors in interpretation, and excised some of the more polemical passages. At last, in 1826, he released the sixth and final edition. It is from this edition that the following selection has been taken. Some of the flavor—and the dogmatism—of the Malthusian argument is suggested by the full title of the work: *An Essay on the Principle of Population, or a View of its Past and Present Effects on Human Happiness with an Inquiry into Our Prospects Respecting the Future Removal or Mitigation of the Evils which it Occasions.*

AN ESSAY ON THE PRINCIPLE OF POPULATION

BOOK I

Of the Checks to Population in the Less Civilized Parts of the World and in Past Times

Chapter I

STATEMENT OF THE SUBJECT. RATIOS OF THE INCREASE OF POPULATION AND FOOD

In an inquiry concerning the improvement of society, the mode of conducting the subject which naturally presents itself, is,

1. To investigate the causes that have hitherto impeded the progress of mankind towards happiness; and,
2. To examine the probability of the total or partial removal of these causes in future.

To enter fully into this question, and to enumerate all the causes that have hitherto influenced human improvement, would be much beyond the power of an individual. The principal object of the present essay is

AN ESSAY ON THE PRINCIPLE OF POPULATION, Thomas Robert Malthus (London, 1890), pp. 2-14.

to examine the effects of the one great cause intimately united with the very nature of man; which, though it has been constantly and powerfully operating since the commencement of society, has been little noticed by the writers who have treated this subject. The facts which establish the existence of this cause have, indeed, been repeatedly stated and acknowledged; but its natural and necessary effects have been almost totally overlooked; though probably among these effects may be reckoned a very considerable portion of that vice and misery, and of that unequal distribution of the bounties of nature, which it has been the unceasing object of the enlightened philanthropist in all ages to correct.

The cause to which I allude, is the constant tendency in all animated life to increase beyond the nourishment prepared for it.

It is observed by Dr. Franklin that there is no bound to the prolific nature of plants or animals, but what is made by their crowding or interfering with each other's means of subsistence. Were the face of the earth, he says, vacant of other plants, it might gradually be sowed and overspread with one kind only, as for instance with fennel: and were it empty of other inhabitants, it might in a few ages be replenished from one nation only, as for instance with Englishmen.

This is incontrovertibly true. Through the animal and vegetable kingdoms Nature has scattered the seeds of life abroad with the most profuse and liberal hand; but has been comparatively sparing in the room and the nourishment necessary to rear them. The germs of existence contained in this earth, if they could freely develop themselves, would fill millions of worlds in the course of a few thousand years. Necessity, that imperious, all-pervading law of nature, restrains them within the prescribed bounds. The race of plants and the race of animals shrink under this great restrictive

law; and man cannot by any efforts of reason escape from it.

In plants and irrational animals, the view of the subject is simple. They are all impelled by a powerful instinct to the increase of their species; and this instinct is interrupted by no doubts about providing for their offspring. Wherever, therefore there is liberty, the power of increase is exerted; and the super-abundant effects are repressed afterwards by want of room and nourishment.

The effects of this check on man are more complicated. Impelled to the increase of his species by an equally powerful instinct, reason interrupts his career, and asks him whether he may not bring beings into the world, for whom he cannot provide the means of support. If he attend to this natural suggestion, the restriction too frequently produces vice. If he hear it not, the human race will be constantly endeavouring to increase beyond the means of subsistence. But as, by that law of our nature which makes food necessary to the life of man, population can never actually increase beyond the lowest nourishment capable of supporting it, a strong check on population, from the difficulty of acquiring food, must be constantly in operation. This difficulty must fall somewhere, and must necessarily be severely felt in some or other of the various forms of misery, or the fear of misery, by a large portion of mankind.

That population has this constant tendency to increase beyond the means of subsistence, and that it is kept to its necessary level by these causes, will sufficiently appear from a review of the different states of society in which man has existed. But, before we proceed to this review, the subject will, perhaps, be seen in a clearer light, if we endeavour to ascertain what would be the natural increase of population, if left to exert itself with perfect freedom; and what might be expected to be the rate of increase in the productions of the earth, under the most favourable circumstances of human industry.

It will be allowed that no country has hitherto been known, where the manners were so pure and simple, and the means of subsistence so abundant, that no check whatever has existed to early marriages from the difficulty of providing for a family, and that no waste of the human species has been occasioned by vicious customs, by towns, by unhealthy occupations, or too severe labour. Consequently in no state that we have yet known, has the power of population been left to exert itself with perfect freedom.

Whether the law of marriage be instituted, or not, the dictate of nature and virtue seems to be an early attachment to one woman; and where there were no impediments of any kind in the way of a union to which such an attachment would lead, and no causes of depopulation afterwards, the increase of the human species would be evidently much greater than any increase which has been hitherto known.

In the northern states of America, where the means of subsistence have been more ample, the manners of the people more pure, and the checks to early marriages fewer, than in any of the modern states of Europe, the population has been found to double itself, for above a century and a half successively, in less than twenty-five years. Yet, even during these periods, in some of the towns, the deaths exceed the births, a circumstance which clearly proves that, in those parts of the country which supplied this deficiency, the increase must have been much more rapid than the general average.

In the back settlements, where the sole employment is agriculture, and vicious customs and unwholesome occupations are little known, the population has been found to double itself in fifteen years. Even this extraordinary rate of increase is probably short of the utmost power of population. Very severe labour is requisite to clear a fresh country; such situations are not in general considered as particularly healthy; and the inhabitants, probably, are occasionally subject to the incursions of the Indians, which may destroy some lives, or at any rate diminish the fruits of industry.

According to a table of Euler, calculated on a mortality of 1 in 36, if the births be to the deaths in the proportion of 3 to 1, the period of doubling will be only 12 years and 4/5ths. And this proportion is not only a possible supposition, but has actually occurred for short periods in more countries than one.

Sir William Petty supposes a doubling possible in so short a time as ten years.

But, to be perfectly sure that we are far within the truth, we will take the slowest of these rates of increase, a rate in which all concurring testimonies agree, and which has been repeatedly ascertained to be from procreation only.

It may safely be pronounced, therefore, that population, when unchecked, goes on doubling itself every twenty-five years, or increases in a geometrical ratio.

The rate according to which the productions of the earth may be supposed to increase, it will not be so easy to determine. Of this, however, we may be perfectly certain, that the ratio of their increase in a limited territory must be of a totally different nature from the ratio of the increase of population. A thousand millions are just as easily doubled every twenty-five years by the power of population as a thousand. But the food to support the increase from the greater number will by no means be obtained with the same facility. Man is necessarily confined in room. When acre has been added to acre till all the fertile land is occupied, the yearly increase of food must depend upon the melioration of the land already in possession. This is a fund, which, from the nature of all soils, instead of increasing, must be gradually diminishing. But population, could it be supplied with food, would go on with unexhausted vigour; and the increase of one period would furnish the power of a greater increase the next, and this without any limit.

From the accounts we have of China and Japan, it may be fairly doubted, whether the best-directed efforts of human industry could double the produce of these countries even once in any number of years. There are many parts of the globe, indeed, hitherto uncultivated, and almost unoccupied; but the right of exterminating, or driving into a corner where they must starve, even the inhabitants of these thinly-peopled regions, will be questioned in a moral view. The process of improving their minds and directing their industry would necessarily be slow; and during this time, as population would regularly keep pace with the increasing produce, it would rarely happen that a great degree of knowledge and industry would have to operate at once upon rich unappropriated soil. Even where this might take place, as it does sometimes in new colonies, a geometrical ratio increases with such extraordinary rapidity, that the advantage could not last long. If the United States of America continue increasing, which they certainly will do, though not with the same rapidity as formerly, the Indians will be driven further and further back into the country, till the whole race is ultimately exterminated, and the territory is incapable of further extension.

These observations are, in a degree, applicable to all the parts of the earth, where the soil is imperfectly cultivated. To exterminate the inhabitants of the greatest part of Asia and Africa, is a thought that could not be admitted for a moment. To civilise and direct the industry of the various tribes of Tartars and Negroes, would certainly be a work of considerable time, and of variable and uncertain success.

Europe is by no means so fully peopled as it might be. In Europe there is the fairest chance that human industry may receive its best direction. The science of agriculture has been much studied in England and Scotland; and there is still a great portion of uncultivated land in these countries. Let us consider at what rate the produce of this island might be supposed to increase under circumstances the most favourable to improvement.

If it be allowed that by the best possible policy, and great encouragements to agriculture, the average produce of the island could be doubled in the first twenty-five years, it will be allowing, probably, a greater increase than could with reason be expected.

In the next twenty-five years, it is impossible to suppose that the produce could be quadrupled. It would be contrary to all our knowledge of the properties of land. The improvement of the barren parts would be a work of time and labour; and it must be evident to those who have the slightest acquaintance with agricultural subjects, that in proportion as cultivation extended, the additions that could yearly be made to the former average produce must be gradually and regularly diminishing. That we may be the better able to compare the increase of population and food, let us make a supposition, which, without pretending to accuracy, is clearly more favourable to the power of production in the earth, than any experience we have had of its qualities will warrant.

Let us suppose that the yearly additions which might be made to the former average produce, instead of decreasing, which they certainly would do, were to remain the same; and that the produce of this island might be increased every twenty-five years, by a quantity equal to what it at present produces. The most enthusiastic speculator cannot suppose a greater increase than this. In a few centuries it would make every acre of land in the island like a garden.

If this supposition be applied to the

whole earth, and if it be allowed that the subsistence for man which the earth affords might be increased every twenty-five years by a quantity equal to what it at present produces, this will be supposing a rate of increase much greater than we can imagine that any possible exertions of mankind could make it.

It may be fairly pronounced, therefore, that, considering the present average state of the earth, the means of subsistence, under circumstances the most favourable to human industry, could not possibly be made to increase faster than in an arithmetical ratio.

The necessary effects of these two different rates of increase, when brought together, will be very striking. Let us call the population of this island eleven millions; and suppose the present produce equal to the easy support of such a number. In the first twenty-five years the population would be twenty-two millions, and the food also being doubled, the means of subsistence would be equal to this increase. In the next twenty-five years, the population would be forty-four millions, and the means of subsistence only equal to the support of thirty-three millions. In the next period the population would be eighty-eight millions, and the means of subsistence just equal to the support of half that number. And, at the conclusion of the first century, the population would be a hundred and seventy-six millions, and the means of subsistence only equal to the support of fifty-five millions, leaving a population of a hundred and twenty-one millions totally unprovided for.

Taking the whole earth, instead of this island, emigration would of course be excluded; and, supposing the present population equal to a thousand millions, the human species would increase as the numbers 1, 2, 4, 8, 16, 32, 64, 128, 256, and subsistence as 1, 2, 3, 4, 5, 6, 7, 8, 9. In two centuries the population would be to the

means of subsistence as 256 to 9; in three centuries as 4096 to 13, and in two thousand years the difference would be almost incalculable.

In this supposition no limits whatever are placed to the produce of the earth. It may increase for ever and be greater than any assignable quantity; yet still the power of population being in every period so much superior, the increase of the human species can only be kept down to the level of the means of subsistence by the constant operation of the strong law of necessity, acting as a check upon the greater power.

Chapter II

OF THE GENERAL CHECKS TO POPULATION, AND THE MODE OF THEIR OPERATION

The ultimate check to population appears then to be a want of food, arising necessarily from the different ratios according to which population and food increase. But this ultimate check is never the immediate check, except in cases of actual famine.

The immediate check may be stated to consist in all those customs, and all those diseases, which seem to be generated by a scarcity of the means of subsistence; and all those causes, independent of this scarcity, whether of a moral or physical nature, which tend prematurely to weaken and destroy the human frame.

These checks to population, which are constantly operating with more or less force in every society, and keep down the number to the level of the means of subsistence, may be classed under two general heads—the preventive, and the positive checks.

The preventive check, as far as it is voluntary, is peculiar to man, and arises from that distinctive superiority in his reasoning faculties, which enables him to calculate distant consequences. The checks to the indefinite increase of plants and irrational animals are all either positive, or, if preventive, involuntary. But man cannot look around him, and see the distress which frequently presses upon those who have large families; he cannot contemplate his present possessions or earnings, which he now nearly consumes himself, and calculate the amount of each share, when with very little addition they must be divided, perhaps, among seven or eight, without feeling a doubt whether, if he follow the bent of his inclinations, he may be able to support the offspring which he will probably bring into the world. In a state of equality, if such can exist, this would be the simple question. In the present state of society other considerations occur. Will he not lower his rank in life, and be obliged to give up in great measure his former habits? Does any mode of employment present itself by which he may reasonably hope to maintain a family? Will he not at any rate subject himself to greater difficulties, and more severe labour, than in his single state? Will he not be unable to transmit to his children the same advantages of education and improvement that he had himself possessed? Does he even feel secure that, should he have a large family, his utmost exertions can save them from rags and squalid poverty, and their consequent degradation from the community? And may he not be reduced to the grating necessity of forfeiting his independence, and of being obliged to the sparing hand of Charity for support?

These considerations are calculated to prevent, and certainly do prevent, a great number of persons in all civilised nations from pursuing the dictate of nature in an early attachment to one woman.

If this restraint do not produce vice, it is undoubtedly the least evil that can arise from the principle of population. Considered as a restraint on a strong natural inclination, it must be allowed to produce a certain degree of temporary unhappiness; but evidently slight, compared with the evils which result from any of the other checks to population; and merely of the same nature as many other sacrifices of temporary to permanent gratification, which it is the business of a moral agent continually to make.

When this restraint produces vice, the evils which follow are but too conspicuous. A promiscuous intercourse to such a degree as to prevent the birth of children, seems to lower, in the most marked manner, the dignity of human nature. It cannot be without its effect on men, and nothing can be more obvious than its tendency to degrade the female character, and to destroy all its most amiable and distinguishing characteristics. Add to which, that among those unfortunate females, with which all great towns abound, more real distress and aggravated misery are, perhaps, to be found, than in any other department of human life.

When a general corruption of morals, with regard to the sex, pervades all the classes of society, its effects must necessarily be, to poison the springs of domestic happiness, to weaken conjugal and parental affection, and to lessen the united exertions and ardour of parents in the care and education of their children:—effects which cannot take place without a decided diminution of the general happiness and virtue of the society; particularly as the necessity of art in the accomplishment and conduct of intrigues, and in the concealment of their consequences necessarily leads to many other vices.

The positive checks to population are extremely various, and include every cause, whether arising from vice or misery, which in any degree contributes to shorten the natural duration of human life. Under this head, therefore, may be enumerated all unwholesome occupations, severe labour and exposure to the seasons, extreme poverty, bad nursing of children, great towns, excesses of all kinds, the whole train of common diseases and epidemics, wars, plagues, and famine.

On examining these obstacles to the increase of population which I have classed under the heads of preventive and positive checks, it will appear that they are all resolvable into moral restraint, vice, and misery.

Of the preventive checks, the restraint from marriage which is not followed by irregular gratifications may properly be termed moral restraint.[1]

Promiscuous intercourse, unnatural passions, violations of the marriage bed, and improper arts to conceal the consequences of irregular connexions, are preventive checks that clearly come under the head of vice.

Of the positive checks, those which appear to arise unavoidably from the laws of nature, may be called exclusively misery; and those which we obviously bring upon ourselves, such as wars, excesses, and many others which it would be in our power to avoid, are of a mixed nature. They are brought upon us by vice, and their consequences are misery.[2]

The sum of all these preventive and positive checks, taken together, forms the immediate check to population; and it is evident that, in every country where the whole of the procreative power cannot be called into action, the preventive and the positive checks must vary inversely as each other; that is, in countries either naturally unhealthy, or subject to a great mortality, from whatever cause it may arise, the preventive check will prevail very little. In those countries, on the contrary, which are naturally healthy, and where the preventive check is found to prevail with considerable force, the positive check will prevail very little, or the mortality be very small.

In every country some of these checks are, with more or less force, in constant operation; yet, notwithstanding their general prevalence, there are few states in which there is not a constant effort in the population to increase beyond the means of subsistence. This constant effort as constantly tends to subject the lower classes of society to distress, and to prevent any great permanent melioration of their condition.

These effects, in the present state of so-

---

[1] It will be observed, that I here use the term *moral* in its most confined sense. By moral restraint I would be understood to mean a restraint from marriage, from prudential motives, with a conduct strictly moral during the period of this restraint; and I have never intentionally deviated from this sense. When I have wished to consider the restraint from marriage connected with its consequences, I have either called it prudential restraint, or a part of the preventive check, of which indeed it forms the principal branch.

In my review of the different stages of society, I have been accused of not allowing sufficient weight in the prevention of population to moral restraint; but when the confined sense of the term, which I have here explained, is adverted to, I am fearful that I shall not be found to have erred much in this respect. I should be very glad to believe myself mistaken.

[2] As the general consequence of vice is misery, and as this consequence is the precise reason why an action is termed vicious, it may appear that the term misery alone would be here sufficient, and that it is superfluous to use both. But the rejection of the term vice would introduce a considerable

confusion into our language and ideas. We want it particularly to distinguish those actions, the general tendency of which is to produce misery, and which are therefore prohibited by the commands of the Creator, and the precepts of the moralist, although, in their immediate or individual effects, they may produce perhaps exactly the contrary. The gratification of all our passions in its immediate effect is happiness, not misery; and, in individual instances, even the remote consequences (at least in this life) may possibly come under the same denomination. There may have been some irregular connexions with women, which have added to the happiness of both parties, and have injured no one. These individual actions, therefore, cannot come under the head of misery. But they are still evidently vicious, because an action is so denominated, which violates an express precept, founded upon its general tendency to produce misery, whatever may be its individual effect; and no person can doubt the general tendency of an illicit intercourse between the sexes, to injure the **happiness** of society.

ciety, seem to be produced in the following manner. We will suppose the means of subsistence in any country just equal to the easy support of the inhabitants. The constant effort towards population, which is found to act even in the most vicious societies, increases the number of people before the means of subsistence are increased. The food, therefore, which before supported eleven millions, must now be divided among eleven millions and a half. The poor consequently must live much worse, and many of them be reduced to severe distress. The number of labourers also being above the proportion of work in the market, the price of labour must tend to fall, while the price of provisions would at the same time tend to rise. The labourer therefore must do more work, to earn the same as he did before. During this season of distress, the discouragements to marriage and the difficulty of rearing a family are so great, that the progress of population is retarded. In the mean time, the cheapness of labour, the plenty of labourers, and the necessity of an increased industry among them, encourage cultivators to employ more labour upon their land, to turn up fresh soil, and to manure and improve more completely what is already in tillage, till ultimately the means of subsistence may become in the same proportion to the population, as at the period from which we set out. The situation of the labourer being then again tolerably comfortable, the restraints to population are in some degree loosened; and, after a short period, the same retrograde and progressive movements, with respect to happiness, are repeated.

This sort of oscillation will not probably be obvious to common view; and it may be difficult even for the most attentive observer to calculate its periods. Yet that, in the generality of old states, some alternation of this kind does exist though in a much less marked, and in a much more irregular manner, than I have described it,

no reflecting man, who considers the subject deeply, can well doubt.

One principal reason why this oscillation has been less remarked, and less decidedly confirmed by experience than might naturally be expected, is, that the histories of mankind which we possess are, in general, histories only of the higher classes. We have not many accounts that can be depended upon, of the manners and customs of that part of mankind, where these retrograde and progressive movements chiefly take place. A satisfactory history of this kind, of one people and of one period, would require the constant and minute attention of many observing minds in local and general remarks on the state of the lower classes of society, and the causes that influenced it; and to draw accurate inferences upon this subject, a succession of such historians for some centuries would be necessary. This branch of statistical knowledge has, of late years, been attended to in some countries, and we may promise ourselves a clearer insight into the internal structure of human society from the progress of these inquiries. But the science may be said yet to be in its infancy, and many of the objects, on which it would be desirable to have information, have been either omitted or not stated with sufficient accuracy. Among these, perhaps, may be reckoned the proportion of the number of adults to the number of marriages; the extent to which vicious customs have prevailed in consequence of the restraints upon matrimony; the comparative mortality among the children of the most distressed part of the community, and of those who live rather more at their ease; the variations in the real price of labour; the observable differences in the state of the lower classes of society, with respect to ease and happiness, at different times during a certain period; and very accurate registers of births, deaths, and marriages, which are of the utmost importance in this subject.

A faithful history, including such particulars, would tend greatly to elucidate the manner in which the constant check upon population acts; and would probably prove that existence of the retrograde and progressive movements that have been mentioned; though the times of their vibration must necessarily be rendered irregular from the operation of many interrupting causes; such as, the introduction or failure of certain manufactures; a greater or less prevalent spirit of agricultural enterprise; years of plenty, or years of scarcity; wars, sickly seasons, poor-laws, emigrations and other causes of a similar nature.

A circumstance which has, perhaps, more than any other, contributed to conceal this oscillation from common view, is the difference between the nominal and real price of labour. It very rarely happens that the nominal price of labour universally falls; but we well know that it frequently remains the same, while the nominal price of provisions has been gradually rising. This, indeed, will generally be the case, if the increase of manufactures and commerce be sufficient to employ the new labourers that are thrown into the market, and to prevent the increased supply from lowering the money-price. But an increased number of labourers receiving the same money-wages will necessarily, by their competition, increase the money-price of corn. This is, in fact, a real fall in the price of labour; and, during this period, the condition of the lower classes of the community must be gradually growing worse. But the farmers and capitalists are growing rich from the real cheapness of labour. Their increasing capitals enable them to employ a greater number of men; and, as the population had probably suffered some check from the greater difficulty of supporting a family, the demand for labour, after a certain period, would be great in proportion to the supply, and its price would of course rise, if left to find its natural level; and thus the wages of labour, and consequently the condition of the lower classes of society, might have progressive and retrograde movements, though the price of labour might never nominally fall.

In savage life, where there is no regular price of labour, it is little to be doubted that similar oscillations took place. When population has increased nearly to the utmost limits of the food, all the preventive and the positive checks will naturally operate with increased force. Vicious habits with respect to the sex will be more general, the exposing of children more frequent, and both the probability and fatality of wars and epidemics will be considerably greater; and these causes will probably continue their operation till the population is sunk below the level of the food; and then the return to comparative plenty will again produce an increase, and, after a certain period, its further progress will again be checked by the same causes.

But without attempting to establish these progressive and retrograde movements in different countries, which would evidently require more minute histories than we possess, and which the progress of civilisation naturally tends to counteract, the following propositions are intended to be proved:—

1. Population is necessarily limited by the means of subsistence.
2. Population invariably increases when the means of subsistence increase, unless prevented by some very powerful and obvious checks.
3. These checks, and the checks which repress the superior power of population, and keep its effects on a level with the means of subsistence, are all resolvable into moral restraint, vice, and misery.

The first of these propositions scarcely needs illustration. The second and third will be sufficiently established by a review of the immediate checks to population in the past and present state of society.

Georg Wilhelm Friedrich Hegel

Georg Wilhelm Friedrich Hegel (1770-1831) was perhaps the most esoteric and obscure of all the great philosophers. And yet two social movements which have had the most intimate and far-reaching effects on the modern world—Marxian communism and fascism—both have their theoretical roots in the Hegelian philosophy.

Hegel's basic assumption was that the universe is rational. By this he meant not simply that it is ruled by a rational Being (God), but that it is itself the embodiment of that Being, which Hegel called the World-Spirit. To Hegel, the history of the world is the progressive revelation of the World-Spirit in time. This spirit has embodied itself in successive national cultures— *e.g.*, Greek, Roman, Germanic —and in each embodiment it has become what Hegel calls the *Volksgeist* (the spirit of a people). It is the *Volksgeist* that determines the distinctive character of a national culture and the form of its institutions, intellectual life, art, and religion. The state, as the rational organization of a national spirit, is the highest expression of the World-Spirit. Consequently, the individual can find realization, freedom, and value only by identifying himself with the state.

The successive embodiments of the World-Spirit in national cultures follow a rational plan, which Hegel terms the *dialec-tic* of history. History is dynamic and progressive, and its progress is the result of conflict. When any nation rises to the position where it dominates its age, it inevitably generates opposition from some other nation. This opposition leads finally to a conflict in which both contestants (called by Hegel *thesis* and *antithesis*) are destroyed. But out of their ashes rises a new and higher national culture (the *synthesis*). The synthesis in turn becomes a thesis itself, and generates its own antithesis. This dialectical pattern is repeated over and over, and history moves onward and upward.

The selection that follows is a statement of Hegel's conception of the state.

THE PHILOSOPHY OF RIGHT

. . .

THE STATE

The state is the realized ethical idea or ethical spirit. It is the will which

THE PHILOSOPHY OF RIGHT, G. W. F. Hegel, trans. S. W. Dyde (London: George Bell and Sons, 1896), pp. 240, 244-247, 270-271, 276, 330-333. Courtesy of G. Bell & Sons, Ltd.

manifests itself, makes itself clear and visible, substantiates itself. It is the will which thinks and knows itself, and carries out what it knows, and in so far as it knows. The state finds in ethical custom its direct and unreflected existence, and its indirect and reflected existence in the self-consciousness of the individual and in his knowledge and activity. Self-consciousness in the form of social disposition has its substantive freedom in the state, as the essence, purpose, and product of its activity.

. . .

The state as a completed reality is the ethical whole and the actualization of freedom. It is the absolute purpose of reason that freedom should be actualized. The state is the spirit, which abides in the world and there realizes itself consciously; while in nature it is realized only as the other of itself or the sleeping spirit. Only when it is present in consciousness, knowing itself as an existing object, is it the state. In thinking of freedom we must not take our departure from individuality or the individual's self-consciousness, but from the essence of self-consciousness. Let man be aware of it or not, this essence realizes itself as an independent power, in which particular persons are only phases. The state is the march of God in the world; its ground or cause is the power of reason realizing itself as will. When thinking of the idea of the state, we must not have in our mind any particular state, or particular institution, but must rather contemplate the idea, this actual God, by itself. Although a state may be declared to violate right principles and to be defective in various ways, it always contains the essential moments of its existence, if, that is to say, it belongs to the full formed states of our own time. But as it is more easy to detect short-comings than to grasp the positive meaning, one easily falls into the mistake of dwelling so much upon special aspects of the state as to overlook its inner organic being. The state is not a work of art. It is in the world, in the sphere of caprice, accident, and error. Evil behaviour can doubtless disfigure it in many ways, but the ugliest man, the criminal, the invalid, the cripple, are living men. The positive thing, the life, is present in spite of defects, and it is with this affirmative that we have here to deal.

. . .

The state is real. Its reality consists in its realizing the interest of the whole in particular ends. Actuality is always the unity of universality and particularity. Universality exists piecemeal in particularity. Each side appears as if self-sufficient, although it is upheld and sustained only in the whole. In so far as this unity is absent, the thing is unrealized, even though existence may be predicated of it. A bad state is one which merely exists. A sick body also exists, but it has no true reality. A hand, which is cut off, still looks like a hand and exists, though it is not real. True reality is necessity. What is real is in itself necessary. Necessity consists in this, that the whole is broken up into the differences contained in the conception. Then, as so broken up, it furnishes a fast and enduring character, not that of the fossil, but of that which in giving itself up always begets itself anew.

To the complete state essentially belong consciousness and thought. Hence the state knows what it wills, and knows it as something thought.

. . .

In the state we must have nothing which is not an expression of rationality. The state is the world, which the spirit has made for itself. Hence it has a definite self-begun and self-related course. Often we speak of the wisdom of God in nature, but we must not therefore believe that the physical world of nature is higher than the world of spirit. Just so high as the spirit stands above nature, the state stands above the physical life. We must hence honour the state as the divine on earth.

. . .

It is a very distorted account of the matter when the state, in demanding sacrifices from the citizens, is taken to be simply the civic community, whose object is merely the security of life and property. Security cannot possibly be obtained by the sacrifice of what is to be secured.

Herein is to be found the ethical element in war. War is not to be regarded as an absolute evil. It is not a merely external accident, having its accidental ground in the passions of powerful individuals or nations, in acts of injustice, or in anything which ought not to be. Accident befalls that which is by nature accidental, and this fate is a necessity. So from the standpoint of the conception and in philosophy the merely accidental vanishes, because in it, as it is a mere appearance, is recognized its essence, namely, necessity. It is necessary that what is finite, such as life and property, should have its contingent nature exposed, since contingency is inherent in the conception of the finite. This necessity has in one phase of it the form of a force of nature, since all that is finite is mortal and transient. But in the ethical life, that is to say, the state, this force and nature are separated. Necessity becomes in this way exalted to the work of freedom, and becomes a force which is ethical. What from the standpoint of nature is transient, is now transient because it is willed to be so; and that, which is fundamentally negative, becomes substantive and distinctive individuality in the ethical order.

It is often said, for the sake of edification, that war makes short work of the vanity of temporal things. It is the element by which the idealization of what is particular receives its right and becomes an actuality. Moreover, by it, as I have elsewhere expressed it, "finite pursuits are rendered unstable, and the ethical health of peoples is preserved. Just as the movement of the ocean prevents the corruption which would be the result of perpetual calm, so by war people escape the corruption which would be occasioned by a continuous or eternal peace. . . ." The idealization, which comes to the surface in war, viewed as an accidental foreign relation, is the same as the ideality by virtue of which the internal state functions are organic elements of the whole.

This principle is found in history in such a fact as that successful wars have prevented civil broils and strengthened the internal power of the state. So, too, peoples, who have been unwilling or afraid to endure internal sovereignty, have been subjugated by others, and in their struggles for independence have had honour and success small in proportion to their failure to establish within themselves a central political power; their freedom died through their fear of its dying. Moreover, states, which have no guarantee of independence in the strength of their army, states, *e.g.*, that are very small in comparison with their neighbours, have continued to subsist because of their internal constitution, which merely of itself would seem to promise them neither internal repose nor external security. These phenomena are illustrations of our principle drawn from history.

In peace the civic life becomes more and more extended. Each separate sphere walls itself in and becomes exclusive, and at last there is a stagnation of mankind. Their particularity becomes more and more fixed and ossified. Unity of the body is essential to health, and where the organs become hard death ensues. Everlasting peace is frequently demanded as the ideal towards which mankind must move. Hence, Kant proposed an alliance of princes, which should settle the controversies of states, and the Holy Alliance was probably intended to be an institution of this kind. But the state is individual, and in individuality negation is essentially implied. Although a number of states may make themselves into a family, the union, because it is an individuality, must create an opposition, and so beget an enemy. As a result of war peoples are strengthened, nations, which are involved in civil quarrels, winning repose at home by means of war abroad. It is true that war occasions insecurity of possessions, but this real insecurity is simply a necessary commotion. From the pulpit we hear much regarding the uncertainty, vanity, and instability of temporal things. At the very same time every one, no matter how much he is impressed by these utterances, thinks that he will manage to retain his own stock and store. But if the uncertainty comes in the form of hussars with glistening sabres, and begins to work in downright earnest, this touching edification turns right about face, and hurls curses at the invader. In spite of this, wars arise, when they lie in the nature of the matter. The seeds spring up afresh, and words are silenced before the earnest repetitions of history.

The Sadler Report

In the early nineteenth century, the Industrial Revolution had spread from England and was beginning to transform Europe from a rural to an urbanized society. In England, this transformation often depressed the living standards of workers to depths even lower than those that had characterized life under the cottage manufacturing system. In doing so, however, it paved the way for its own reform. For it laid bare to the public eye in an aggravated form conditions that had long existed but that had passed relatively unnoticed. Poverty and misery could be overlooked so long as the workers remained scattered about the countryside, but once they were congregated in the hideous slums of the Midlands industrial centers their plight became too obvious to remain unheeded. Consequently, social reform became the order of the day.

Among the most prominent of the English reformers was the seventh Earl of Shaftesbury (1801-1885), who concentrated his attention on working conditions in the factories. At Shaftesbury's instigation, another reformer, Michael Sadler, introduced a bill into Parliament in 1831 that would regulate the working conditions of children in textile mills. The bill was referred to a committee, with Sadler as chairman. The selection that follows is an excerpt from the evidence presented before that committee. The committee's investigations resulted in the enactment of the Factory Act of 1833, which limited the working hours of children and set up a system of inspection which would insure that its regulations were being carried out.

The Sadler Report requires no comment; it speaks for itself. The selection included here was picked almost at random from a bulky volume of testimony provided by literally hundreds of witnesses, each one presenting, with slight variations, the same picture of factory life in early nineteenth-century England.

THE SADLER REPORT

Veneris, 18° die Maii, 1832

MICHAEL THOMAS SADLER, ESQUIRE,
IN THE CHAIR.

. . .

MR. MATTHEW CRABTREE, *called in; and Examined.*

What age are you? —Twenty-two.

What is your occupation? —A blanket manufacturer.

Have you ever been employed in a factory? —Yes.

At what age did you first go to work in one? —Eight.

How long did you continue in that occupation? —Four years.

Will you state the hours of labour at the period when you first went to the factory, in ordinary times? —From 6 in the morning to 8 at night.

Fourteen hours? —Yes.

With what intervals for refreshment and rest? — An hour at noon.

Then you had no resting time allowed in which to take your breakfast, or what is in Yorkshire called your "drinking"? —No.

When trade was brisk what were your hours? —From 5 in the morning to 9 in the evening.

Sixteen hours? —Yes.

With what intervals at dinner? —An hour.

How far did you live from the mill? — About two miles.

Was there any time allowed for you to get your breakfast in the mill? —No.

Did you take it before you left your home? —Generally.

THE SADLER REPORT, Report from the Committee on the *Bill to Regulate the Labour of Children in the Mills and Factories of the United Kingdom* (London: The House of Commons, 1832), pp. 95-104.

During those long hours of labour could you be punctual; how did you awake? —I seldom did awake spontaneously; I was most generally awoke or lifted out of bed, sometimes asleep, by my parents.

Were you always in time? —No.

What was the consequence if you had been too late? —I was most commonly beaten.

Severely? —Very severely, I thought.

In whose factory was this? —Messrs. Hague & Cook's, of Dewsbury.

Will you state the effect that those long hours had upon the state of your health and feelings? —I was, when working those long hours, commonly very much fatigued at night, when I left my work; so much so that I sometimes should have slept as I walked if I had not stumbled and started awake again; and so sick often that I could not eat, and what I did eat I vomited.

Did this labour destroy your appetite? — It did.

In what situation were you in that mill? —I was a piecener.

Will you state to this Committee whether pieceening is a very laborious employment for children, or not? —It is a very laborious employment. Pieceeners are continually running to and fro, and on their feet the whole day.

The duty of the piecener is to take the cardings from one part of the machinery, and to place them on another? —Yes.

So that the labour is not only continual, but it is unabated to the last? —It is unabated to the last.

Do you not think, from your own experience, that the speed of the machinery is so calculated as to demand the utmost exertions of a child, supposing the hours were moderate? —It is as much as they could do at the best; they are always upon the stretch, and it is commonly very difficult to keep up with their work.

State the condition of the children towards the latter part of the day, who have thus to keep up with the machinery? —It is as much as they can do when they are not very much fatigued to keep up with their work, and towards the close of the day, when they come to be more fatigued, they cannot keep up with it very well, and the consequence is that they are beaten to spur them on.

Were you beaten under those circumstances? —Yes.

Frequently? —Very frequently.

And principally at the latter end of the day? —Yes.

And is it your belief that if you had not been so beaten, you should not have got through the work? —I should not if I had not been kept up to it by some means.

Does beating then principally occur at the latter end of the day, when the children are exceedingly fatigued? —It does at the latter end of the day, and in the morning sometimes, when they are very drowsy, and have not got rid of the fatigue of the day before.

What were you beaten with principally? —A strap.

Any thing else? —Yes, a stick sometimes; and there is a kind of roller which runs on the top of the machine called a billy, perhaps two or three yards in length, and perhaps an inch and a half, or more, in diameter; the circumference would be four or five inches; I cannot speak exactly.

Were you beaten with that instrument? —Yes.

Have you yourself been beaten, and have you seen other children struck severely with that roller? —I have been struck very severely with it myself, so much so as to knock me down, and I have seen other children have their heads broken with it.

You think that it is a general practice to beat the children with the roller? —It is.

You do not think then that you were worse treated than other children in the mill? —No, I was not, perhaps not so bad as some were.

In those mills is chastisement towards the latter part of the day going on perpetually? —Perpetually.

So that you can hardly be in a mill without hearing constant crying? —Never an hour, I believe.

Do you think that if the overlooker were naturally a humane person it would be still found necessary for him to beat the children, in order to keep up their attention and vigilance at the termination of those extraordinary days of labour? —Yes; the machine turns off a regular quantity of cardings, and of course they must keep as regularly to their work the whole of the day; they must keep with the machine, and therefore however humane the slubber may be, as he must keep up with the machine or be found fault with, he spurs the children to keep up also by various means but that which he commonly resorts to is to strap them when they become drowsy.

At the time when you were beaten for not keeping up with your work, were you anxious to have done it if you possibly could? —Yes; the dread of being beaten if we could not keep up with our work was a sufficient impulse to keep us to it if we could.

When you got home at night after this labour, did you feel much fatigued? —Very much so.

Had you any time to be with your parents, and to receive instruction from them? —No.

What did you do? —All that we did when we got home was to get the little bit of supper that was provided for us and go to bed immediately. If the supper had not been ready directly, we should have gone to sleep while it was preparing.

Did you not, as a child, feel it a very

grievous hardship to be roused so soon in the morning? —I did.

Were the rest of the children similarly circumstanced? —Yes, all of them; but they were not all of them so far from their work as I was.

And if you had been too late you were under the apprehension of being cruelly beaten? —I generally was beaten when I happened to be too late; and when I got up in the morning the apprehension of that was so great, that I used to run, and cry all the way as I went to the mill.

That was the way by which your punctual attendance was secured? —Yes.

And you do not think it could have been secured by any other means? —No.

Then it is your impression from what you have seen, and from your own experience, that those long hours of labour have the effect of rendering young persons who are subject to them exceedingly unhappy? —Yes.

You have already said it had a considerable effect upon your health? —Yes.

Do you conceive that it diminished your growth? —I did not pay much attention to that; but I have been examined by some persons who said they thought I was rather stunted, and that I should have been taller if I had not worked at the mill.

What were your wages at that time? —Three shillings [per week].

And how much a day had you for overwork when you were worked so exceedingly long? —A halfpenny a day.

Did you frequently forfeit that if you were not always there to a moment? —Yes; I most frequently forfeited what was allowed for those long hours.

You took your food to the mill; was it in your mill, as is the case in cotton mills, much spoiled by being laid aside? —It was very frequently covered by flues from the wool; and in that case they had to be blown off with the mouth, and picked off with the fingers before it could be eaten.

So that not giving you a little leisure for eating your food, but obliging you to take it at the mill, spoiled your food when you did get it? —Yes, very commonly.

And that at the same time that this over-labour injured your appetite? —Yes.

Could you eat when you got home? —Not always.

What is the effect of this piecening upon the hands? —It makes them bleed; the skin is completely rubbed off, and in that case they bleed in perhaps a dozen parts.

The prominent parts of the hand? —Yes, all the prominent parts of the hand are rubbed down till they bleed; every day they are rubbed in that way.

All the time you continue at work? —All the time we are working. The hands never can be hardened in that work, for the grease keeps them soft in the first instance, and long and continual rubbing is always wearing them down, so that if they were hard they would be sure to bleed.

Is it attended with much pain? —Very much.

Do they allow you to make use of the back of the hand? —No; the work cannot be so well done with the back of the hand, or I should have made use of that.

Is the work done as well when you are so many hours engaged in it, as it would be if you were at it a less time? —I believe it is not done so well in those long hours; towards the latter end of the day the children become completely bewildered, and know not what they are doing, so that they spoil their work without knowing.

Then you do not think that the masters gain much by the continuance of the work to so great a length of time? —I believe not.

Were there girls as well as boys employed in this manner? —Yes.

Were they more tenderly treated by the overlookers, or were they worked and beaten in the same manner? —There was no difference in their treatment.

Were they beaten by the overlookers, or by the slubber? —By the slubber.

But the overlooker must have been perfectly aware of the treatment that the children endured at the mill? —Yes; and sometimes the overlooker beat them himself; but the man that they wrought under had generally the management of them.

Did he pay them their wages? —No; their wages were paid by the master.

But the overlooker of the mill was perfectly well aware that they could not have performed the duty exacted from them in the mill without being thus beaten? —I believe he was.

You seem to say that this beating is absolutely necessary, in order to keep the children up to their work; is it universal throughout all factories? —I have been in several other factories, and I have witnessed the same cruelty in them all.

Did you say that you were beaten for being too late? —Yes.

Is it not the custom in many of the factories to impose fines upon children for being too late, instead of beating them? —It was not in that factory.

What then were the fines by which you lost the money you gained by your long hours? —The spinner could not get on so fast with his work when we happened to be too late; he could not begin his work so soon, and therefore it was taken by him.

Did the slubber pay you your wages? —No, the master paid our wages.

And the slubber took your fines from you? —Yes.

Then you were fined as well as beaten? —There was nothing deducted from the ordinary scale of wages, but only from that received for over-hours, and I had only that taken when I was too late, so that the fine was not regular.

When you were not working over-hours, were you so often late as when you were working over-hours? —Yes.

You were not very often late whilst you were not working over-hours? —Yes, I was often late when I was not working over-hours; I had to go at six o'clock in the morning, and consequently had to get up at five to eat my breakfast and go to the mill, and if I failed to get up by five I was too late; and it was nine o'clock before we could get home, and then we went to bed; in the best times I could not be much above eight hours at home, reckoning dressing and eating my meals, and every thing.

Was it a blanket-mill in which you worked? —Yes.

Did you ever know that the beatings to which you allude inflicted a serious injury upon the children? —I do not recollect any very serious injury, more than that they had their heads broken, if that may be called a serious injury; that has often happened; I, myself, had no more serious injury than that.

You say that the girls as well as the boys were employed as you have described, and you observed no difference in their treatment? —No difference.

The girls were beat in this unmerciful manner? —They were.

They were subject, of course, to the same bad effects from this over-working? —Yes.

Could you attend an evening-school during the time you were employed in the mill? —No, that was completely impossible.

Did you attend the Sunday-school? —Not very frequently when I work at the mill.

How then were you engaged during the Sunday? —I very often slept till it was too late for school time or for divine worship, and the rest of the day I spent in walking out and taking a little fresh air.

Did your parents think that it was necessary for you to enjoy a little fresh air? —I believe they did; they never said anything against it; before I went to the mill I used to go to the Sunday-school.

Did you frequently sleep nearly the

whole of the day on Sunday? —Very often.

At what age did you leave that employment? —I was about 12 years old.

Why did you leave that place? —I went very late one morning, about seven o'clock, and I got severely beaten by the spinner, and he turned me out of the mill, and I went home, and never went any more.

Was your attendance as good as the other children? —Being at rather a greater distance than some of them, I was generally one of the latest.

Where was your next work? —I worked as bobbin-winder in another part of the works of the same firm.

How long were you a bobbin-winder? —About two years, I believe.

What did you become after that? —A weaver.

How long were you a weaver? —I was a weaver till March in last year.

A weaver of what? —A blanket-weaver.

With the same firm? —With the same firm.

Did you leave them? —No; I was dismissed from my work for a reason which I am willing and anxious to explain.

Have you had opportunities of observing the way in which the children are treated in factories up to a late period? —Yes.

You conceive that their treatment still remains as you first found it, and that the system is in great want of regulation? —It does.

Children you still observe to be very much fatigued and injured by the hours of labour? —Yes.

From your own experience, what is your opinion as to the utmost labour that a child in piecening could safely undergo? —If I were appealed to from my own feelings to fix a limit, I should fix it at ten hours, or less.

And you attribute to longer hours all the cruelties that you describe? —A good deal of them.

Are the children sleepy in mills? —Very.

Are they more liable to accidents in the latter part of the day than in the other part? —I believe they are; I believe a greater number of accidents happen in the latter part of the day than in any other. I have known them so sleepy that in the short interval while the others have been going out, some of them have fallen asleep, and have been left there.

Is it an uncommon case for children to fall asleep in the mill, and remain there all night? —Not to remain there all night; but I have known a case the other day, of a child whom the overlooker found when he went to lock the door, that had been left there.

So that you think there has been no change for the better in the treatment of those children; is it your opinion that there will be none, except Parliament interfere in their behalf? —It is my decided conviction.

Have you recently seen any cruelties in mills? —Yes; not long since I was in a mill, and I saw a girl severely beaten; at a mill called Hick-lane Mill, in Batley; I happened to be in at the other end of the room, talking; and I heard the blows, and I looked that way, and saw the spinner beating one of the girls severely with a large stick. Hearing the sound, led me to look round, and to ask what was the matter, and they said it was "Nothing but —— paying [beating] 'his ligger-on.' "

What age was the girl? —About 12 years.

Was she very violently beaten? —She was.

Was this when she was over-fatigued? —It was in the afternoon.

Can you speak as to the effect of this labour in the mills and factories on the morals of the children, as far as you have observed? —As far as I have observed with regard to morals in the mills, there is every thing about them that is disgusting to every one conscious of correct morality.

Do you find that the children, the females especially, are very early demoralized in them? —They are.

Is their language indecent? —Very indecent; and both sexes take great familiarities with each other in the mills, without at all being ashamed of their conduct.

Do you connect their immorality of language and conduct with their excessive labour? —It may be somewhat connected with it, for it is to be observed that most of that goes on towards night, when they begin to be drowsy; it is a kind of stimulus which they use to keep them awake; they say some pert thing or other to keep themselves from drowsiness, and it generally happens to be some obscene language.

Have not a considerable number of the females employed in mills illegitimate children very early in life? —I believe there are; I have known some of them have illegitimate children when they were between 16 and 17 years of age.

How many grown-up females had you in the mill? —I cannot speak to the exact number that were grown up; perhaps there might be thirty-four or so that worked in the mill at that time.

How many of those had illegitimate children? —A great many of them; eighteen or nineteen of them, I think.

Did they generally marry the men by whom they had the children? —No; it sometimes happens that young women have children by married men, and I have known an instance, a few weeks since, where one of the young women had a child by a married man.

Is it your opinion that those who have the charge of mills very often avail themselves of the opportunity they have to debauch the young women? —No, not generally; most of the improper conduct takes place among the younger part of those that work in the mill.

Do you find that the children and young persons in those mills are moral in other respects, or does their want of education tend to encourage them in a breach of the law? —I believe it does, for there are very few of them that can know anything about it; few of them can either read or write.

Are criminal offences then very frequent? —Yes, theft is very common; it is practised a great deal in the mills, stealing their bits of dinner, or something of that sort. Some of them have not so much to eat as they ought to have, and if they can fall in with the dinner of some of their partners they steal it. The first day my brother and I went to the mill we had our dinner stolen, because we were not up to the tricks; we were more careful in future, but still we did not always escape.

Was there any correction going on at the mills for indecent language or improper conduct? —No, I never knew of any.

From what you have seen and known of those mills, would you prefer that the hours of labour should be so long with larger wages, or that they should be shortened with a diminution of wages? —If I were working at the mill now, I would rather have less labour and receive a trifle less, than so much labour and receive a trifle more.

Is that the general impression of individuals engaged in mills with whom you are acquainted? —I believe it is.

What is the impression in the country from which you come with respect to the effect of this Bill upon wages? —They do not anticipate that it will affect wages at all.

They think it will not lower wages? —They do.

Do you mean that it will not lower wages by the hour, or that you will receive the same wages per day? —They anticipate that it may perhaps lower their wages at a certain time of the year when they are working hard, but not at other times, so that they will have their wages more regular.

Does not their wish for this Bill mainly rest upon their anxiety to protect their children from the consequences of this excessive labour, and to have some opportunity of affording them a decent education? —Yes; such are the wishes of every humane father that I have heard speak about the thing.

Have they not some feeling of having the labour equalized? —That is the feeling of some that I have heard speak of it.

Did your parents work in the same factories? —No.

Were any of the slubbers' children working there? —Yes.

Under what slubber did you work in that mill? —Under a person of the name of Thomas Bennett, in the first place; and I was changed from him to another of the name of James Webster.

Did the treatment depend very much upon the slubber under whom you were? —No, it did not depend directly upon him, for he was obliged to do a certain quantity of work, and therefore to make us keep up with that.

Were the children of the slubbers strapped in the same way? —Yes, except that it is very natural for a father to spare his own child.

Did it depend upon the feelings of a slubber towards his children? —Very little.

Did the slubbers find their own spinners? —I believe not.

You said that the piecening was very hard labour; what labour is there besides moving about; have you anything heavy to carry or to lift? —We have nothing heavy to carry, but we are kept upon our feet in brisk times from 5 o'clock in the morning to 9 at night.

How soon does the hand get sore in piecening? —How soon mine became sore I cannot speak to exactly; but they get a little hard on the Sunday, when we are not working, and they will get sore again very soon on the Monday.

Is it always the case in piecening that the hand bleeds, whether you work short or long hours? —They bleed more when we work more.

Do they always bleed when you are working? —Yes.

Do you think that the children would not be more competent to this task, and their hands far less hurt, if the hours were fewer every day, especially when their hands had become seasoned to the labour? —I believe it would have an effect, for the longer they are worked the more their hands are worn, and the longer it takes to heal them, and they do not get hard enough after a day's rest to be long without bleeding again; if they were not so much worn down, they might heal sooner, and not bleed so often or so soon.

After a short day's work, have you found your hands hard the next morning? —They do not bleed much after we have ceased work; they then get hard; they will bleed soon in the morning when in regular work.

Do you think if the work of the children were confined to about ten hours a day, that after they were accustomed to it, they would not be able to perform this piecening without making their hands bleed? —I believe they would.

So that it is your opinion, from your experience, that if the hours were mitigated, their hands would not be so much worn, and would not bleed by the business of piecening? —Yes.

Do you mean to say that their hands would not bleed at all? —I cannot say exactly, for I always wrought long hours, and therefore my hands always did bleed.

Have you any experience of mills where they only work ten hours? —I have never wrought at such mills, and in most of the mills I have seen their hands bleed.

At a slack time, when you were working only a few hours, did your hands bleed? —No, they did not for three or four days, after we had been standing still for a week; the mill stood still sometimes for a week together, but when we did work we worked the common number of hours.

Were all the mills in the neighbourhood working the same number of hours in brisk times? —Yes.

So that if any parent found it necessary to send his children to the mill for the sake of being able to maintain them, and wished to take them from any mill where they were excessively worked, he could not have found any other place where they would have been less worked? —No, he could not; for myself, I had no desire to change, because I thought I was as well off as I could be at any other mill.

And if the parent, to save his child, had taken him from the mill, and had applied to the parish for relief, would the parish, knowing that he had withdrawn his child from its work, have relieved him? —No.

So that the long labour which you have described, or actual starvation, was, practically, the only alternative that was presented to the parent under such circumstances? —It was; they must either work at the mill they were at or some other, and there was no choice in the mills in that respect.

What, in your opinion, would be the effect of limiting the hours of labour upon the happiness, and the health, and the intelligence of the rising generation? —If the hours are shortened, the children may, perhaps, have a chance of attending some evening-school, and learning to read and write; and those that I know who have been to school and learned to read and write, have much more comfort than those who have not. For myself, I went to a school when I was 6 years old, and I learned to read and write a little then.

At a free-school? —Yes, at a free-school in Dewsbury; but I left school when I was 6 years old. The fact is, that my father was a small manufacturer, and in comfortable circumstances; and he got into debt with Mr. Cook for a wool bill, and as he had

no other means of paying him, he came and agreed with my father, that my brother and I should go to work at his mill till that debt was paid; so that the whole of the time that we wrought at the mill we had no wages.

THOMAS BENNETT, *called in; and Examined.*

Where do you reside? —At Dewsbury.

What is your business? —A slubber.

What age are you? —About 48.

Have you had much experience regarding the working of children in factories? —Yes, about twenty-seven years.

Have you a family? —Yes, eight children.

Have any of them gone to factories? —All.

At what age? —The first went at 6 years of age.

To whose mill? —To Mr. Halliley's, to piece for myself.

What hours did you work at that mill? —We have wrought from 4 to 9, from 4 to 10, and from 5 to 9, and from 5 to 10.

What sort of a mill was it? —It was a blanket-mill; we sometimes altered the time, according as the days increased and decreased.

What were your regular hours? —Our regular hours, when we were not so throng, was from 6 to 7.

And when you were the throngest, what were your hours then? —From 5 to 9, and from 5 to 10, and from 4 to 9.

Seventeen hours? —Yes.

What intervals for meals had the children at that period? —Two hours; an hour for breakfast, and an hour for dinner.

Did they always allow two hours for meals at Mr. Halliley's? —Yes, it was allowed, but the children did not get it, for they had business to do at that time, such as fettling and cleaning the machinery.

But they did not all stop in at that time, did they? —They all had their share of the cleaning and other work to do.

That is, they were cleaning the machinery? —Cleaning the machinery at the time of dinner.

How long a time together have you known those excessive hours to continue? —I have wrought so myself very nearly two years together.

Were your children working under you then? —Yes, two of them.

State the effect upon your children? —Of a morning when they had to get up, they have been so fast asleep that I have had to go up stairs and lift them out of bed, and have heard their crying with the feelings of a parent; I have been much affected by it.

Were not they much fatigued at the termination of such a day's labour as that? —Yes; many a time I have seen their hands moving while they have been nodding, almost asleep; they have been doing their business almost mechanically.

While they have been almost asleep, they have attempted to work? —Yes; and they have missed the carding and spoiled the thread, when we have had to beat them for it.

Could they have done their work towards the termination of such a long day's labour, if they had not been chastised to it? —No.

You do not think that they could have kept awake or up to their work till the seventeenth hour, without being chastised? —No.

Will you state what effect it had upon your children at the end of their day's work? —At the end of their day's work, when they have come home, instead of taking their victuals, they have dropped asleep with the victuals in their hands; and sometimes when we have sent them to bed with a little bread or something to eat in their hand, I have found it in their bed the next morning.

Has it affected their health? —I cannot say much of that; they were very hearty children.

Do you live at a distance from the mill? —Half a mile.

Did your children feel a difficulty in getting home? —Yes, I have had to carry the lesser child on my back, and it has been asleep when I got home.

Did these hours of labour fatigue you? —Yes; they fatigued me to that excess, that in divine worship I have not been able to stand according to order; I have sat to worship.

So that even during the Sunday you have felt fatigue from your labour in the week? —Yes, we felt it, and always took as much rest as we could.

Were you compelled to beat your own children, in order to make them keep up with the machine? —Yes, that was forced upon us, or we could not have done the work; I have struck them often, though I felt as a parent.

If the children had not been your own, you would have chastised them still more severely? —Yes.

What did you beat them with? —A strap sometimes; and when I have seen my work spoiled, with the roller.

Was the work always worst done at the end of the day? —That was the greatest danger.

Do you conceive it possible that the children could do their work well at the end of such a day's labour as that? —No.

Matthew Crabtree, the last Witness examined by this Committee, I think mentioned you as one of the slubbers under whom he worked? —Yes.

He states that he was chastised and beaten at the mill? —Yes, I have had to chastise him.

You can confirm then what he has stated as to the length of time he had to work as a child, and the cruel treatment that he received? —Yes, I have had to chastise him in the evening, and often in the morning, for being too late; when I had one out of the three wanting I could not keep up with the machine, and I was getting behind-hand compared with what another man was doing; and therefore I should have been called to account on Saturday night if the work was not done.

Was he worse than others? —No.

Was it the constant practice to chastise the children? —Yes.

It was necessary in order to keep up your work? —Yes.

And you would have lost your place if you had not done so? —Yes; when I was working at Mr. Wood's mill, at Dewsbury, which at present is burnt down, but where I slubbed for him until it was, while we were taking our meals he used to come up and put the machine agoing; and I used to say, "You do not give us time to eat;" he used to reply, "Chew it at your work;" and I often replied to him, "I have not yet become debased like a brute, I do not chew my cud." Often has that man done that, and then gone below to see if a strap were off, which would have shown the machinery was not working, and then he would come up again.

Was this at the drinking time? —Yes, at breakfast and at drinking.

Was this where the children were working? —Yes, my own children and others.

Were your own children obliged to employ most of their time at breakfast and at the drinking in cleansing the machine, and in fettling the spindles? —I have seen at that mill, and I have experienced and mentioned it with grief, that the English children were enslaved worse than the Africans. Once when Mr. Wood was saying to the carrier who brought his work in and out, "How long has that horse of mine been at work?" and the carrier told him the time, and he said, "Loose him directly, he has been in too long," I made this reply to him, "You have more mercy and pity for your horse than you have for your men."

Did not this beating go on principally at the latter part of the day? —Yes.

Was it not also dangerous for the children to move about those mills when they became so drowsy and fatigued? —Yes, especially by lamp-light.

Do the accidents principally occur at the latter end of those long days of labour? —Yes, I believe mostly so.

Do you know of any that have happened? —I know of one; it was at Mr. Wood's mill; part of the machine caught a lass who had been drowsy and asleep, and the strap which ran close by her catched her at about her middle, and bore her to the ceiling, and down she came, and her neck appeared broken, and the slubber ran up to her and pulled her neck, and I carried her to the doctor myself.

Did she get well? —Yes, she came about again.

What time was that? —In the evening.

You say that you have eight children who have gone to the factories? —Yes.

There has been no opportunity for you to send them to a day-school? —No; one boy had about twelve months' schooling.

Have they gone to Sunday-schools? —Yes.

Can any of them write? —Not one.

They do not teach writing at Sunday-schools? —No; it is objected to, I believe.

So that none of your children can write? —No.

What would be the effect of a proper limitation of the hours of labour upon the conduct of the rising generation? —I believe it would have a very happy effect in regard to correcting their morals; for I believe there is a deal of evil that takes place in one way or other in consequence of those long hours.

Is it your opinion that they would then have an opportunity of attending night-schools? —Yes; I have often regretted, while working those long hours, that I could not get my children there.

Is it your belief that if they were better instructed, they would be happier and better members of society? —Yes, I believe so.

Karl Marx and Friedrich Engels

According to Lenin, Marxism was derived from three sources: German philosophy, English political economy, and French socialism. The German philosophy was the Idealism of Hegel, which Marx had imbibed while a student at the University of Berlin. Central to this philosophy was the notion of *dialectic*, the theory that history is a series of struggles between opposing forces, with each successive struggle occurring on a higher level than the one that preceded it. For Hegel, the struggles took place between opposing ideas embodied in distinct national cultures. But Marx shifted the struggles from the ideational plane to the economic or material plane, and transformed the antagonists from nations to classes. In other words, he replaced Hegel's dialectical idealism with his own dialectical materialism; or, as he put it, he turned the dialectic, which Hegel had stood on its head, back on its feet again.

The English political economy that Lenin referred to consisted of the writings of the classical economists, Smith and Ricardo, whose labor theory of value provided Marx with the basic assumption underlying his greatest work, *Capital*. But Marx reversed the argument of the classical economists; where they found in the labor theory of value a defense of capitalism, he found a weapon to attack it.

Finally, in his reference to French socialism Lenin had in mind the works of a group of writers, including Saint-Simon, Fourier, Proudhon, and Blanc, whose views on the elimination of capitalism and the establishment of the ideal society greatly influenced Marx—even though later he scornfully brushed their theories aside as "utopian" socialism, while claiming that his own were "scientific."

Although Lenin and most other orthodox Marxists would vehemently deny it, Marxism owes a debt to a fourth source. This is the moral tradition of Western thought, stretching back all the way to Socrates and the Old Testament prophets. For Marx, the philosopher, historian, and economist, was above all else a moral reformer. Though he clothed his critique of capitalism in an elaborate intellectual framework, at heart it was a moral protest against the human misery and degradation resulting from early nineteenth-century industrialism. And though he assiduously repeated that his socialism was scientific, the new era of human happiness that he envisioned in the classless society following the revolution was an ideal as utopian as that of Plato's *Republic*.

The Communist Manifesto, the joint production of Marx (1818-1883) and his life-long friend and collaborator, Friedrich Engels (1820-1895), contains in capsule form most of the major Marxist doctrines. It was composed in 1848 as a platform for the Communist League, a small organization of radical workmen. The *Manifesto* is here reproduced complete except for Part III, in which the authors criticize other forms of socialism.

MANIFESTO OF THE COMMUNIST PARTY

A specter is haunting Europe —the specter of Communism. All the powers of Old Europe have entered into a holy alliance to exorcise this specter; Pope and Czar, Metternich and Guizot, French Radicals and German police-spies.

Where is the party in opposition that has not been decried as communistic by its opponents in power? Where the opposition that has not hurled back the branding reproach of Communism, against the more advanced opposition parties, as well as against its reactionary adversaries?

Two things result from this fact.

I. Communism is already acknowledged by all European powers to be in itself a power.

II. It is high time that Communists should openly, in the face of the whole world, publish their views, their aims, their tendencies, and meet this nursery tale of the specter of Communism with a Manifesto of the party itself.

To this end Communists of various nationalities have assembled in London, and sketched the following Manifesto to be published in the English, French, German, Italian, Flemish and Danish languages.

I

BOURGEOIS AND PROLETARIANS[1]

The history of all hitherto existing society is the history of class struggles.

Freeman and slave, patrician and plebeian,

lord and serf, guild-master and journeyman, in a word, oppressor and oppressed, stood in constant opposition to one another, carried on an uninterrupted, now hidden, now open fight, that each time ended, either in a revolutionary reconstitution of society at large, or in the common ruin of the contending classes.

In the earlier epochs of history we find almost everywhere a complicated arrangement of society into various orders, a manifold gradation of social rank. In ancient Rome we have patricians, knights, plebeians, slaves; in the middle ages, feudal lords, vassals, guild-masters, journeymen, apprentices, serfs; in almost all of these classes, again, subordinate gradations.

The modern bourgeois society that has sprouted from the ruins of feudal society, has not done away with class antagonisms. It has but established new classes, new conditions of oppression, new forms of struggle in place of the old ones.

Our epoch, the epoch of the bourgeoisie, possesses, however, this distinctive feature; it has simplified the class antagonisms. Society as a whole is more and more splitting up into two great hostile camps, into two great classes directly facing each other: Bourgeoisie and Proletariat.

From the serfs of the middle ages sprang the chartered burghers of the earliest towns. From these burgesses the first elements of the bourgeoisie were developed.

The discovery of America, the rounding of the Cape, opened up fresh ground for the rising bourgeoisie. The East-Indian and Chinese markets, the colonization of America, trade with the colonies, the increase in the means of exchange and in commodities generally, gave to commerce, to navigation, to industry, an impulse never before known, and thereby, to the revolutionary

MANIFESTO OF THE COMMUNIST PARTY, Karl Marx and Friedrich Engels, trans. S. Moore (New York, 1888), pp. 7-21, 28.

[1] By bourgeoisie is meant the class of modern Capitalists, owners of the means of social production and employers of wage-labor. By proletariat the class of modern wage-laborers who, having no means of production of their own, are reduced to selling their labor-power in order to live.

element in the tottering feudal society, a rapid development.

The feudal system of industry, under which industrial production was monopolized by closed guilds, now no longer sufficed for the growing wants of the new market. The manufacturing system took its place. The guild-masters were pushed on one side by the manufacturing middle class; division of labor between the different corporate guilds vanished in the face of division of labor in each single workshop.

Meantime the markets kept ever growing, the demand ever rising. Even manufacture no longer sufficed. Thereupon steam and machinery revolutionized industrial production. The place of manufacture was taken by the giant, Modern Industry, the place of the industrial middle class, by industrial millionaires, the leaders of whole industrial armies, the modern bourgeois.

Modern Industry has established the world's market, for which the discovery of America paved the way. This market has given an immense development to commerce, to navigation, to communication by land. This development has, in its turn, reacted on the extension of industry; and in proportion as industry, commerce, navigation, railways extended, in the same proportion, the bourgeoisie developed, increased its capital, and pushed into the background every class handed down from the Middle Ages.

We see, therefore, how the modern bourgeoisie is itself the product of a long course of development, of a series of revolutions in the modes of production and of exchange.

Each step in the development of the bourgeoisie was accompanied by a corresponding political advance of that class. An oppressed class under the sway of the feudal nobility, an armed and self-governing association in the mediaeval commune, here independent urban republic (as in Italy and Germany), there taxable "third estate" of the monarchy (as in France), afterwards, in

the period of manufacture proper, serving either the semi-feudal or the absolute monarchy as a counterpoise against the nobility, and, in fact, corner-stone of the great monarchies in general, the bourgeoisie has at last, since the establishment of Modern Industry and of the world's market, conquered for itself, in the modern representative State, exclusive political sway. The executive of the modern State is but a committee for managing the common affairs of the whole bourgeoisie.

The bourgeoisie, historically, has played a most revolutionary part.

The bourgeoisie, wherever it has got the upper hand, has put an end to all feudal, patriarchal, idyllic relations. It has pitilessly torn asunder the motley feudal ties that bound man to his "natural superiors," and has left remaining no other nexus between man and man than naked self-interest, than callous "cash payment." It has drowned the most heavenly ecstasies of religious fervor, of chivalrous enthusiasm, of Philistine sentimentalism, in the icy water of egotistical calculation. It has resolved personal worth into exchange value, and in place of the numberless indefeasible chartered freedoms, has set up that single, unconscionable freedom—Free Trade. In one word, for exploitation, veiled by religious and political illusions, it has substituted naked, shameless, direct, brutal exploitation.

The bourgeoisie has stripped of its halo every occupation hitherto honored and looked up to with reverent awe. It has converted the physician, the lawyer, the priest, the poet, the man of science, into its paid wage-laborers.

The bourgeoisie has torn away from the family its sentimental veil, and has reduced the family relation to a mere money relation.

The bourgeoisie has disclosed how it came to pass that the brutal display of vigor in the Middle Ages, which reactionists so much admire, found its fitting complement in the most slothful indolence. It has been the first to show what man's activity can bring about. It has accomplished wonders far surpassing Egyptian pyramids, Roman aqueducts, and Gothic cathedrals; it has conducted expeditions that put in the shade all former Exoduses of nations and crusades.

The bourgeoisie cannot exist without constantly revolutionizing the instruments of production, and thereby the relations of production, and with them the whole relations of society. Conservation of the old modes of production in unaltered form, was, on the contrary, the first condition of existence for all earlier industrial classes. Constant revolutionizing of production, uninterrupted disturbance of all social conditions, everlasting uncertainty and agitation, distinguish the bourgeois epoch from all earlier ones. All fixed, fast-frozen relations, with their train of ancient and venerable prejudices and opinions, are swept away; all new-formed ones become antiquated before they can ossify. All that is solid melts into air, all that is holy is profaned, and man is at last compelled to face with sober senses his real conditions of life, and his relations with his kind.

The need of a constantly expanding market for its products chases the bourgeoisie over the whole surface of the globe. It must nestle everywhere, settle everywhere, establish connections everywhere.

The bourgeoisie has through its exploitation of the world's market given a cosmopolitan character to production and consumption in every country. To the great chagrin of reactionists, it has drawn from under the feet of industry the national ground on which it stood. All old established national industries have been destroyed or are daily being destroyed. They are dislodged by new industries, whose introduction becomes a life and death question for all civilized nations, by industries that no longer work up indigenous raw material, but raw material drawn from the remotest zones, industries whose products are consumed, not only at home, but in every quarter of the globe. In place of the old wants, satisfied by the productions of the country, we find new wants, requiring for their satisfaction the products of distant lands and climes. In place of the old local and national seclusion and self-sufficiency we have had intercourse in every direction, universal interdependence of nations. And as in material, so also in intellectual production. The intellectual creations of individual nations become common property. National onesidedness and narrowmindedness become more and more impossible, and from the numerous national and local literatures, there arises a world-literature.

The bourgeoisie, by the rapid improvement of all instruments of production, by the immensely facilitated means of communication, draws all, even the most barbarian, nations into civilization. The cheap prices of its commodities are the heavy artillery with which it batters down all Chinese walls, with which it forces the barbarians' intensely obstinate hatred of foreigners to capitulate. It compels all nations, on pain of extinction, to adopt the bourgeois mode of production; it compels them to introduce what it calls civilization into their midst, *i.e.*, to become bourgeois themselves. In one word, it creates a world after its own image.

The bourgeoisie has subjected the country to the rule of the towns. It has created enormous cities, has greatly increased the urban population as compared with the rural, and has thus rescued a considerable part of the population from the idiocy of rural life. Just as it has made the country dependent on the towns, so it has made barbarian and semi-barbarian countries dependent on the civilized ones, nations of peasants on nations of bourgeois, the East on the West.

The bourgeoisie keeps more and more doing away with the scattered state of the population, of the means of production, and of property. It has agglomerated population, centralized means of production, and has concentrated property in a few hands. The necessary consequence of this was political centralization. Independent, or but loosely connected provinces, with separate interests, laws, governments, and systems of taxation, became lumped together into one nation, with one government, one code of laws, one national class interest, one frontier, and one customs tariff.

The bourgeoisie, during its rule of scarce one hundred years, has created more massive and more colossal productive forces than have all preceding generations together. Subjection of Nature's forces to man, machinery, application of chemistry to industry and agriculture, steam-navigation, railways, electric telegraphs, clearing of whole continents for cultivation, canalization of rivers, whole populations conjured out of the ground—what earlier century had even a presentiment that such productive forces slumbered in the lap of social labor?

We see then: the means of production and of exchange on whose foundation the bourgeoisie built itself up, were generated in feudal society. At a certain stage in the development of these means of production and of exchange, the conditions under which feudal society produced and exchanged, the feudal organization of agriculture and manufacturing industry, in one word, the feudal relations of property, became no longer compatible with the already developed productive forces; they became so many fetters. They had to burst asunder; they were burst asunder.

Into their places stepped free competition, accompanied by a social and political constitution adapted to it, and by the economical and political sway of the bourgeois class.

A similar movement is going on before our own eyes. Modern bourgeois society with its relations of production, of exchange, and of property, a society that has conjured up such gigantic means of production and of exchange, is like the sorcerer, who is no longer able to control the powers of the nether world whom he has called up by his spells. For many a decade past the history of industry and commerce is but the history of the revolt of modern productive forces against modern conditions of production, against the property relations that are the conditions for the existence of the bourgeoisie and of its rule. It is enough to mention the commercial crises that by their periodical return put on its trial, each time more threateningly, the existence of the bourgeois society. In these crises a great part not only of the existing products, but also of the previously created productive forces, is periodically destroyed. In these crises there breaks out an epidemic that, in all earlier epochs, would have seemed an absurdity—the epidemic of overproduction. Society suddenly finds itself put back into a state of momentary barbarism; it appears as if a famine, a universal war of devastation, had cut off the supply of every means of subsistence; industry and commerce seem to be destroyed; and why? because there is too much civilization, too much means of subsistence, too much industry, too much commerce. The productive forces at the disposal of society no longer tend to further the development of the conditions of bourgeois property; on the contrary, they have become too powerful for these conditions, by which they are fettered, and as soon as they overcome these fetters, they bring disorder into the whole of bourgeois society, endanger the existence of bourgeois property. The conditions of bourgeois society are too narrow to comprise the wealth created by them. And how does the bourgeoisie get over these crises? On the one hand by enforced destruction of a mass of productive forces;

on the other, by the conquest of new markets, and by the more thorough exploitation of the old ones. That is to say, by paving the way for more extensive and more destructive crises, and by diminishing the means whereby crises are prevented.

The weapons with which the bourgeoisie felled feudalism to the ground are now turned against the bourgeoisie itself.

But not only has the bourgeoisie forged the weapons that bring death to itself; it has also called into existence the men who are to wield those weapons—the modern working class—the proletarians.

In proportion as the bourgeoisie, *i.e.*, capital, is developed, in the same proportion is the proletariat, the modern working class, developed; a class of laborers, who live only so long as they find work, and who find work only so long as their labor increases capital. These laborers, who must sell themselves piecemeal, are a commodity, like every other article of commerce, and are consequently exposed to all the vicissitudes of competition, to all the fluctuations of the market.

Owing to the extensive use of machinery and to division of labor, the work of the proletarians has lost all individual character, and, consequently, all charm for the workman. He becomes an appendage of the machine, and it is only the most simple, most monotonous, and most easily acquired knack, that is required of him. Hence, the cost of production of a workman is restricted almost entirely to the means of subsistence that he requires for his maintenance, and for the propagation of his race. But the price of a commodity, and therefore also of labor, is equal to its cost of production. In proportion, therefore, as the repulsiveness of the work increases, the wage decreases. Nay, more, in proportion as the use of machinery and division of labor increases, in the same proportion the burden of toil also increases, whether by prolongation of the working hours, by increase of the work enacted in a given time, or by increased speed of the machinery, etc.

Modern industry has converted the little workshop of the patriarchal master into the great factory of the industrial capitalist. Masses of laborers, crowded into factories, are organized like soldiers. As privates of the industrial army they are placed under the command of a perfect hierarchy of officers and sergeants. Not only are they the slaves of the bourgeois class, and of the bourgeois State, they are daily and hourly enslaved by the machine, by the overlooker, and, above all, by the individual bourgeois manufacturer himself. The more openly this despotism proclaims gain to be its end and aim, the more petty, the more hateful and the more embittering it is.

The less skill and exertion of strength implied in manual labor, in other words, the more modern industry becomes developed, the more is the labor of men superseded by that of women. Differences of age and sex have no longer any distinctive social validity for the working class. All are instruments of labor, more or less expensive to use, according to age and sex.

No sooner is the exploitation of the laborer by the manufacturer, so far at an end, that he receives his wages in cash, than he is set upon by the other portions of the bourgeoisie, the landlord, the shopkeeper, the pawnbroker, etc.

The lower strata of the Middle class—the small tradespeople, shopkeepers, and retired tradesmen generally, the handicraftsmen and peasant—all these sink gradually into the proletariat, partly because their diminutive capital does not suffice for the scale on which modern industry is carried on, and is swamped in the competition with the large capitalists, partly because their specialized skill is rendered worthless by new methods of production. Thus the proletariat is recruited from all classes of the population.

The proletariat goes through various

stages of development. With its birth begins its struggle with the bourgeoisie. At first the contest is carried on by individual laborers, then by the workpeople of a factory, then by the operatives of one trade, in one locality, against the individual bourgeois who directly exploits them. They direct their attacks not against the bourgeois conditions of production, but against the instruments of production themselves; they destroy imported wares that compete with their labor, they smash to pieces machinery, they set factories ablaze, they seek to restore by force the vanished status of the workman of the Middle Ages.

At this stage the laborers still form an incoherent mass scattered over the whole country, and broken up by their mutual competition. If anywhere they unite to form more compact bodies, this is not yet the consequence of their own active union, but of the union of the bourgeoisie, which class, in order to attain its own political ends, is compelled to set the whole proletariat in motion, and is moreover yet, for a time, able to do so. At this stage, therefore, the proletarians do not fight their enemies, but the enemies of their enemies, the remnants of absolute monarchy, the landowners, the non-industrial bourgeois, the petty bourgeoisie. Thus the whole historical movement is concentrated in the hands of the bourgeoisie; every victory so obtained is a victory for the bourgeoisie.

But with the development of industry the proletariat not only increases in number; it becomes concentrated in greater masses, its strength grows and it feels that strength more. The various interests and conditions of life within the ranks of the proletariat are more and more equalized, in proportion as machinery obliterates all distinctions of labor, and nearly everywhere reduces wages to the same low level. The growing competition among the bourgeois, and the resulting commercial crises, make the wages of the workers even more fluctuating. The unceasing improvement of machinery, ever more rapidly developing, makes their livelihood more and more precarious; the collisions between individual workmen and individual bourgeois take more and more the character of collisions between two classes. Thereupon the workers begin to form combinations (Trades' Unions) against the bourgeois; they club together in order to keep up the rate of wages; they found permanent associations in order to make provision beforehand for these occasional revolts. Here and there the contest breaks out into riots.

Now and then the workers are victorious, but only for a time. The real fruit of their battles lies not in the immediate result but in the ever-improved means of communication that are created by modern industry, and that place the workers of different localities in contact with one another. It was just this contact that was needed to centralize the numerous local struggles, all of the same character, into one national struggle between classes. But every class struggle is a political struggle. And that union, to attain which the burghers of the Middle Ages, with their miserable highways, required centuries, the modern proletarians, thanks to railways, achieve in a few years.

This organization of the proletarians into a class, and consequently into a political party, is continually being upset again by the competition between the workers themselves. But it ever rises up again; stronger, firmer, mightier. It compels legislative recognition of particular interests of the workers, by taking advantage of the divisions among the bourgeoisie itself. Thus the ten-hours' bill in England was carried.

Altogether collisions between the classes of the old society further, in many ways, the course of development of the proletariat. The bourgeoisie finds itself involved in a constant battle. At first with the aristocracy; later on, with those portions of the bourgeoisie itself, whose interests have become antagonistic to the progress of industry; at all times with the bourgeoisie of foreign countries. In all these countries it sees itself compelled to appeal to the proletariat, to ask for its help, and thus to drag it into the political arena. The bourgeoisie itself, therefore, supplies the proletariat with weapons for fighting the bourgeoisie.

Further, as we have already seen, entire sections of the ruling classes are, by the advance of industry, precipitated into the proletariat, or are at least threatened in their conditions of existence. These also supply the proletariat with fresh elements of enlightenment and progress.

Finally, in times when the class struggle nears the decisive hour, the process of dissolution going on within the ruling class, in fact, within the whole range of an old society, assumes such a violent, glaring character, that a small section of the ruling class cuts itself adrift, and joins the revolutionary class, the class that holds the future in its hands. Just as, therefore, at an earlier period, a section of the nobility went over to the bourgeoisie, so now a portion of the bourgeoisie goes over to the proletariat, and in particular, a portion of the bourgeois ideologists, who have raised themselves to the level of comprehending theoretically the historical movement as a whole.

Of all the classes that stand face to face with the bourgeoisie today the proletariat alone is a really revolutionary class. The other classes decay and finally disappear in the face of modern industry; the proletariat is its special and essential product.

The lower middle class, the small manufacturer, the shopkeeper, the artisan, the peasant, all these fight against the bourgeoisie to save from extinction their existence as fractions of the middle class. They are therefore not revolutionary, but conservative. Nay, more, they are reactionary, for they try to roll back the wheel of history. If by chance they are revolutionary, they are so only in view of their impending transfer into the proletariat; they thus defend not their present, but their future interests, they desert their own standpoint to place themselves at that of the proletariat.

The "dangerous class," the social scum, that passively rotting class thrown off by the lowest layers of old society, may, here and there, be swept into the movement by a proletarian revolution; its conditions of life, however, prepare it far more for the part of a bribed tool of reactionary intrigue.

In the conditions of the proletariat, those of the old society at large are already virtually swamped. The proletarian is without property; his relation to his wife and children has no longer anything in common with the bourgeois family relations; modern industrial labor, modern subjection to capital, the same in England as in France, in America as in Germany, has stripped him of every trace of national character. Law, morality, religion, are to him so many bourgeois prejudices, behind which lurk in ambush just as many bourgeois interests.

All the preceding classes that got the upper hand sought to fortify their already acquired status by subjecting society at large to their conditions of appropriation. The proletarians cannot become masters of the productive forces of society, except by abolishing their own previous mode of appropriation, and thereby also every other previous mode of appropriation. They have nothing of their own to secure and to fortify; their mission is to destroy all previous securities for, and insurances of, individual property.

All previous historical movements were movements of minorities, or in the interest of minorities. The proletarian movement is the self-conscious, independent movement of the immense majority, in the immense majority. The proletariat, the lowest stratum of our present society, cannot stir, cannot raise itself up, without the whole super-incumbent strata of official society being sprung into the air.

Though not in substance, yet in form, the struggle of the proletariat with the bourgeoisie is at first a national struggle. The proletariat of each country must, of course, first of all settle matters with its own bourgeoisie.

In depicting the most general phases of the development of the proletariat, we traced the more or less veiled civil war, raging within existing society, up to the point where that war breaks out into open revolution, and where the violent overthrow of the bourgeoisie lays the foundation for the sway of the proletariat.

Hitherto every form of society has been based, as we have already seen, on the antagonism of oppressing and oppressed classes. But in order to oppress a class certain conditions must be assured to it under which it can, at least, continue its slavish existence. The serf, in the period of serfdom, raised himself to membership in the commune, just as the petty bourgeois, under the yoke of feudal absolutism, managed to develop into a bourgeois. The modern laborer, on the contrary, instead of rising with the progress of industry, sinks deeper and deeper below the conditions of existence of his own class. He becomes a pauper, and pauperism develops more rapidly than population and wealth. And here it becomes evident that the bourgeoisie is unfit any longer to be the ruling class in society and to impose its conditions of existence upon society as an over-riding law. It is unfit to rule because it is incompetent to assure an existence to its slave within his slavery, because it cannot help letting him sink into such a state that it has to feed him instead of being fed by him. Society can no longer live under this bourgeoisie, in other words its existence is no longer compatible with society.

The essential condition for the existence, and for the sway of the bourgeois class, is the formation and augmentation of capital; the condition for capital is wage-labor. Wage-labor rests exclusively on competition between the laborers. The advance of industry, whose involuntary promoter is the bourgeoisie, replaces the isolation of the laborers, due to competition, by their revolutionary combination, due to association. The development of modern industry, therefore, cuts from under its feet the very foundation on which the bourgeoisie produces and appropriates products. What the bourgeoisie therefore produces, above all, are its own grave-diggers. Its fall and the victory of the proletariat are equally inevitable.

II

PROLETARIANS AND COMMUNISTS

In what relation do the Communists stand to the proletarians as a whole?

The Communists do not form a separate party opposed to other working class parties.

They have no interests separate and apart from those of the proletariat as a whole.

They do not set up any sectarian principles of their own by which to shape and mould the proletarian movement.

The Communists are distinguished from the other working class parties by this only: 1. In the national struggles of the proletarians of the different countries, they point out and bring to the front the common interests of the entire proletariat, independently of all nationality. 2. In the various stages of development which the struggle of the working class against the bourgeoisie has to pass through, they always and everywhere represent the interests of the movement as a whole.

The Communists, therefore, are on the one hand, practically, the most advanced and resolute section of the working class parties of every country, that section which pushes forward all others; on the other hand, theoretically, they have over the great mass of the proletariat the advantage of clearly understanding the line of march, the conditions, and the ultimate general results of the proletarian movement.

The immediate aim of the Communists is the same as that of all the other proletarian parties: formation of the proletariat into a class, overthrow of the bourgeois supremacy, conquest of political power by the proletariat.

The theoretical conclusions of the Communists are in no way based on ideas or principles that have been invented, or discovered, by this or that would-be universal reformer.

They merely express, in general terms, actual relations springing from an existing class struggle, from a historical movement going on under our very eyes. The abolition of existing property relations is not at all a distinctive feature of Communism.

All property relations in the past have continually been subject to historical change, consequent upon the change in historical conditions.

The French Revolution, for example, abolished feudal property in favor of bourgeois property.

The distinguishing feature of Communism is not the abolition of property generally, but the abolition of bourgeois property. But modern bourgeois private property is the final and most complete expression of the system of producing and appropriating products, that is based on class antagonisms, on the exploitation of the many by the few.

In this sense the theory of the Communists may be summed up in the single sentence: Abolition of private property.

We Communists have been reproached with the desire of abolishing the right of personally acquiring property as the fruit of a man's own labor, which property is alleged to be the groundwork of all personal freedom, activity, and independence.

Hard-won, self-acquired, self-earned property! Do you mean the property of the petty artisan and of the small peasant, a form of property that preceded the bourgeois form? There is no need to abolish that; the development of industry has to a great extent already destroyed it, and is still destroying it daily.

Or do you mean modern bourgeois private property?

But does wage labor create any property for the laborer? Not a bit. It creates capital, *i.e.*, that kind of property which exploits wage-labor, and which cannot increase except upon condition of begetting a new supply of wage-labor for fresh exploitation. Property, in its present form, is based on the antagonism of capital and wage-labor. Let us examine both sides of this antagonism.

To be a capitalist, is to have not only a purely personal, but a social *status* in production. Capital is a collective product, and only by the united action of many members, nay, in the last resort, only by the united action of all members of society, can it be set in motion.

Capital is therefore not a personal, it is a social power.

When, therefore, capital is converted into common property, into the property of all members of society, personal property is not thereby transformed into social property. It is only the social character of the property that is changed. It loses its class character.

Let us now take wage-labor.

The average price of wage-labor is the minimum wage, *i.e.*, that quantum of the means of subsistence, which is absolutely requisite to keep the laborer in bare existence as a laborer. What, therefore, the wage-laborer appropriates by means of his labor, merely suffices to prolong and reproduce a bare existence. We by no means intend to abolish this personal appropriation of the products of labor, an appropriation that is made for the maintenance and reproduction of human life, and that leaves no surplus wherewith to command the labor of others. All that we want to do away with, is the miserable character of this appropriation, under which the laborer lives merely to increase capital, and is allowed to live only in so far as the interest of the ruling class requires it.

In bourgeois society living labor is but a means to increase accumulated labor. In Communist society accumulated labor is but a means to widen, to enrich, to promote the existence of the laborer.

In bourgeois society, therefore, the past dominates the present; in Communist society, the present dominates the past. In bourgeois society capital is independent and has individuality, while the living person is dependent and has no individuality.

And the abolition of this state of things is called by the bourgeois: abolition of individuality and freedom! And rightly so. The abolition of bourgeois individuality, bourgeois independence, and bourgeois freedom is undoubtedly aimed at.

By freedom is meant, under the present bourgeois conditions of production, free trade, free selling, and buying.

But if selling and buying disappears, free selling and buying disappears also. This talk about free selling and buying, and all the other "brave words" of our bourgeoisie about freedom in general, have a meaning, if any, only in contrast with restricted selling and buying, with the fettered traders of the Middle Ages, but have no meaning when opposed to the Communistic abolition of buying and selling, of the bourgeois conditions of production, and of the bourgeoisie itself.

You are horrified at our intending to do away with private property. But in your existing society private property is already done away with for nine-tenths of the population; its existence for the few is solely due to its non-existence in the hands of those nine-tenths. You reproach us, therefore, with intending to do away with a form of property, the necessary condition for whose existence is, the non-existence of any property for the immense majority of society.

In one word, you reproach us with intending to do away with your property. Precisely so: that is just what we intend.

From the moment when labor can no longer be converted into capital, money, or rent, into a social power capable of being monopolized, *i.e.*, from the moment when individual property can no longer be transformed into bourgeois property, into capital, from that moment, you say, individuality vanishes!

You must, therefore, confess that by "individual" you mean no other person than the bourgeois, than the middle-class owner of property. This person must, indeed, be swept out of the way, and made impossible. Communism deprives no man of the power to appropriate the products of society: all that it does is to deprive him of the power to subjugate the labor of others by means of such appropriation.

It has been objected, that upon the abolition of private property all work will cease, and universal laziness will overtake us.

According to this, bourgeois society ought long ago to have gone to the dogs through sheer idleness; for those of its members who work, acquire nothing, and those who acquire anything, do not work. The whole of this objection is but another expression of the tautology: that there can no longer be any wage-labor when there is no longer any capital.

All objections against the communistic mode of producing and appropriating material products, have, in the same way, been urged against the communistic modes of producing and appropriating intellectual products. Just as, to the bourgeois, the disappearance of class property is the disappearance of production itself, so the disappearance of class culture is to him identical with the disappearance of all culture.

That culture, the loss of which he laments, is, for the enormous majority, a mere training to act as a machine.

But don't wrangle with us so long as you apply to our intended abolition of bourgeois property, the standard of your bourgeois notions of freedom, culture, law, etc. Your very ideas are but the outgrowth of the conditions of your bourgeois production and bourgeois property, just as your jurisprudence is but the will of your class made into a law for all, a will, whose essential character and direction are determined by the economical conditions of existence of your class.

The selfish misconception that induces you to transform into eternal laws of nature and of reason, the social forms springing from your present mode of production and form of property—historical relations that rise and disappear in the progress of production—this misconception you share with every ruling class that has preceded you. What you see clearly in the case of ancient property, what you admit in the case of feudal property, you are of course forbidden to admit in the case of your own bourgeois form of property.

Abolition of the family! Even the most radical flare up at this infamous proposal of the Communists.

On what foundation is the present family, the bourgeois family, based? On capital, on private gain. In its completely developed form this family exists only among the bourgeoisie. But this state of things finds its complement in the practical absence of the family among the proletarians, and in public prostitution.

The bourgeois family will vanish as a matter of course when its complement vanishes, and both will vanish with the vanishing of capital.

Do you charge us with wanting to stop the exploitation of children by their parents? To this crime we plead guilty.

But, you will say, we destroy the most hallowed of relations, when we replace home education by social.

And your education! Is not that also social, and determined by the social conditions under which you educate, by the intervention, direct or indirect, of society by means of schools, etc.? The Communists have not invented the intervention of society in education; they do but seek to alter the character of that intervention, and to rescue education from the influence of the ruling class.

The bourgeois clap-trap about the family and education, about the hallowed co-relation of parent and child becomes all the more disgusting, as, by the action of modern industry, all family ties among the proletarians are torn asunder and their children transformed into simple articles of commerce and instruments of labor.

But you Communists would introduce community of women, screams the whole bourgeoisie in chorus.

The bourgeois sees in his wife a mere instrument of production. He hears that the instruments of production are to be exploited in common, and, naturally, can come to no other conclusion then that the lot of being common to all will likewise fall to the women.

He has not even a suspicion that the real point aimed at is to do away with the status of women as mere instruments of production.

For the rest nothing is more ridiculous than the virtuous indignation of our bourgeois at the community of women which, they pretend, is to be openly and officially established by the Communists. The Communists have no need to introduce community of women; it has existed almost from time immemorial.

Our bourgeois, not content with having the wives and daughters of their proletarians at their disposal, not to speak of common prostitutes, take the greatest pleasure in seducing each others' wives.

Bourgeois marriage is in reality a system of wives in common and thus, at the most, what the Communists might possibly be reproached with, is that they desire to introduce, in substitution for a hypocritically concealed, an openly legalized community of women. For the rest it is self-evident that the abolition of the present system of production must bring with it the abolition of the comminity of women springing from that system, *i.e.*, of prostitution both public and private.

The Communists are further reproached with desiring to abolish countries and nationality.

The workingmen have no country. We cannot take from them what they have not got. Since the proletariat must first of all acquire political supremacy, must rise to be the leading class of the nation, must constitute itself *the* nation, it is, so far, itself national, though not in the bourgeois sense of the word.

National differences and antagonisms between peoples are daily more and more vanishing, owing to the development of the bourgeoisie, to freedom of commerce, to the world's market, to uniformity in the mode of production and in the conditions of life corresponding thereto.

The supremacy of the proletariat will cause them to vanish still faster. United action, of the leading civilized countries at least, is one of the first conditions for the emancipation of the proletariat.

In proportion as the exploitation of one individual by another is put an end to, the exploitation of one nation by another will also be put an end to. In proportion as the antagonism between classes within the nation vanishes, the hostility of one nation to another will come to an end.

The charges against Communism made from a religious, a philosophical, and, generally, from an ideological standpoint, are not deserving of serious examination.

Does it require deep intuition to comprehend that man's ideas, views, and conceptions, in one word, man's consciousness changes with every change in the conditions of his material existence, in his social relations and in his social life?

What else does the history of ideas prove than that intellectual production changes its character in proportion as material production is changed? The ruling ideas of each age have ever been the ideas of its ruling class.

When people speak of ideas that revolutionize society they do but express the fact that within the old society the elements of a new one have been created, and that the dissolution of the old ideas keeps even pace with the dissolution of the old conditions of existence.

When the ancient world was in its last throes the ancient religions were overcome by Christianity. When Christian ideas succumbed in the 18th century to rationalist ideas, feudal society fought its death-battle with the then revolutionary bourgeoisie. The ideas of religious liberty and freedom of conscience merely gave expression to the sway of free competition within the domain of knowledge.

"Undoubtedly," it will be said, "religious, moral, philosophical and juridical ideas have been modified in the course of historical development. But religion, morality, philosophy, political science, and law, constantly survived this change.

"There are besides, eternal truths, such as Freedom, Justice, etc., that are common to all states of society. But Communism abolishes eternal truths, it abolishes all religion and all morality, instead of constituting them on a new basis; it therefore acts in contradiction to all past historical experience."

What does this accusation reduce itself to? The history of all past society has consisted in the development of class antagonisms, antagonisms that assumed different forms at different epochs.

But whatever form they may have taken, one fact is common to all past ages, *viz.,* the exploitation of one part of society by the other. No wonder, then, that the social consciousness of past ages, despite all the multiplicity and variety it displays, moves within certain common forms, or general ideas, which cannot completely vanish except with the total disappearance of class antagonisms.

The Communist revolution is the most radical rupture with traditional property relations; no wonder that its development involves the most radical rupture with traditional ideas.

But let us have done with the bourgeois objections to Communism.

We have seen above that the first step in the revolution by the working class is to raise the proletariat to the position of the ruling class, to win the battle of democracy.

The proletariat will use its political supremacy to wrest, by degrees, all capital from the bourgeoisie; to centralize all instruments of production in the hands of the State, *i.e.,* of the proletariat organized as the ruling class; and to increase the total of productive forces as rapidly as possible.

Of course, in the beginning this cannot be effected except by means of despotic inroads on the rights of property and on the conditions of bourgeois production; by means of measures, therefore, which appear economically insufficient and untenable, but which, in the course of the movement, outstrip themselves, necessitate further inroads upon the old social order and are unavoidable as a means of entirely

revolutionizing the mode of production.

These measures will of course be different in different countries.

Nevertheless in the most advanced countries the following will be pretty generally applicable:

1. Abolition of property in land and application of all rents of land to public purposes.

2. A heavy progressive or graduated income tax.

3. Abolition of all rights of inheritance.

4. Confiscation of the property of all emigrants and rebels.

5. Centralization of credit in the hands of the State, by means of a national bank with State capital and an exclusive monopoly.

6. Centralization of the means of communication and transport in the hands of the State.

7. Extension of factories and instruments of production owned by the State; the bringing into cultivation of waste lands, and the improvement of the soil generally in accordance with a common plan.

8. Equal liability of all to labor. Establishment of industrial armies, especially for agriculture.

9. Combination of agriculture with manufacturing industries: gradual abolition of the distinction between town and country, by a more equable distribution of the population over the country.

10. Free education for all children in public schools. Abolition of children's factory labor in its present form. Combination of education with industrial production, etc., etc.

When, in the course of development, class distinctions have disappeared and all production has been concentrated in the hands of a vast association of the whole nation, the public power will lose its political character. Political power, properly so called, is merely the organized power of one class for oppressing another. If the proletariat during its contest with the bourgeoisie is compelled, by the force of circumstances, to organize itself as a class, if, by means of a revolution, it makes itself the ruling class, and, as such, sweeps away by force the old conditions of production, then it will, along with these conditions, have swept away the conditions for the existence of class antagonism, and of classes generally, and will thereby have abolished its own supremacy as a class.

In place of the old bourgeois society with its classes and class antagonisms we shall have an association in which the free development of each is the condition for the free development of all.

.   .   .

IV

POSITION OF THE COMMUNISTS IN RELATION
TO THE VARIOUS EXISTING OPPOSITION
PARTIES

Section II has made clear the relations of the Communist to the existing working class parties, such as the Chartists in England and the Agrarian Reformers in America.

The Communists fight for the attainment of the immediate aims, for the enforcement of the momentary interests of the working class; but in the movement of the present they also represent and take care of the future of that movement. In France the Communists ally themselves with the Social-Democrats, against the conservative and radical bourgeoisie, reserving, however, the right to take up a critical position in regard to phrases and illusions traditionally handed down from the great Revolution.

In Switzerland they support the Radicals, without losing sight of the fact that this party consists of antagonistic elements, partly of Democratic Socialists, in the French sense, partly of radical bourgeois.

In Poland they support the party that insists on an agrarian revolution, as the prime condition for national emancipation, that party which fomented the insurrection of Cracow in 1846.

In Germany they fight with the bourgeoisie whenever it acts in a revolutionary way against the absolute monarchy, the feudal squirearchy, and the petty bourgeoisie.

But they never cease, for a single instant, to instill into the working class the clearest possible recognition of the hostile antagonism between bourgeoisie and proletariat, in order that the German workers may straightway use, as so many weapons against the bourgeoisie the social and political conditions that the bourgeoisie must necessarily introduce along with its supremacy, and in order that, after the fall of the reactionary classes in Germany, the fight against the bourgeoisie itself may immediately begin.

The Communists turn their attention chiefly to Germany, because that country is on the eve of a bourgeois revolution that is bound to be carried out under more advanced conditions of European civilization, and with a much more developed proletariat, than that of England was in the seventeenth, and of France in the eighteenth century, and because the bourgeois revolution in Germany will be but the prelude to an immediately following proletarian revolution.

In short, the Communists everywhere support every revolutionary movement against the existing social and political order of things.

In all these movements they bring to the front, as the leading question in each, the property question, no matter what its degree of development at the time.

Finally, they labor everywhere for the union and agreement of the democratic parties of all countries.

The Communists disdain to conceal their views and aims. They openly declare that their ends can be attained only by the forcible overthrow of all existing social conditions. Let the ruling classes tremble at a Communistic revolution. The proletarians have nothing to lose but their chains. They have a world to win.

Working men of all countries, unite!

John Stuart Mill

If John Stuart Mill (1806-1873) had been able to look ahead from his childhood to the years that followed, he would have found the entire course of his life laid out for him in advance. Educated at home by his father and by Jeremy Bentham, both of whom were leaders in an influential group of English intellectuals known as the "Philosophical Radicals," he was carefully groomed by his tutors to take over the leadership of the movement. The social program of the Radicals (later called Liberals) was based on Bentham's dictum that the goal of society must be to promote "the greatest happiness [pleasure] of the greatest number." Assuming with Hobbes that all men are innately selfish, Bentham argued that this very selfishness would produce the desired goal. For, if each person is free to seek his own happiness, the end result is bound to be the greatest happiness of all. Hence, all restraints upon the action of individuals, especially restraints exercised by government, must be eliminated. This freedom was regarded as particularly important in the economic realm, where the liberals, following Smith and Ricardo, advocated a policy of strict *laissez-faire*.

Young Mill seems to have learned his lessons well, for almost all his writings (including his essay *On Liberty*) commence with a reaffirmation of the principles of his elders. Yet the more we study his works the more apparent it becomes that he is often paying little more than lip-service to the doctrines instilled in him, while the real tenor of his views often represents a significant departure from the original Liberal position.

There were at least two reasons for Mill's defection. The first was personal. A man of great perceptiveness, warm sympathies, and intellectual breadth, he could no more contain himself within the doctrinaire limitations of the Benthamite position than he could accept its assumption of universal selfishness or its identi-fication of happiness with pleasure. The second reason was theoretical. While still a youth Mill had become acquainted, through reading the English poet-philosopher Coleridge, with the philosophy of the German idealists, Kant and Hegel, a philosophy that ran counter to the views of the Liberals. Man, the idealists argued, is not an atom, who can separate himself from the rest of society to pursue his own selfish ends. When anyone attempts to live this way, rather than attaining freedom and happiness, he destroys himself as a human being. On the contrary, man is, as Aristotle said, made for society; the true realization of his own selfhood, hence his freedom and happiness, can be achieved only through identifying his interests with those of his social group. Such a view, translated into practice, leads to some form of collectivism, the exact antithesis of the individualism of the Liberals.

The tension between these contrasting views of man's relationship to society is apparent throughout Mill's writings; in fact, it created a problem that he never succeeded in solving. And since his time it has occupied the attention of all social thinkers who have called themselves liberals, including, in our own century, the great American philosopher, John Dewey.

The selection that follows, from Mill's essay *On Liberty*, reveals not only the author's basic liberal position but also some of his qualifications of that position. But more than this, the essay stands as one of the most inspired defenses of human freedom to be found in Western literature.

ON LIBERTY

Chapter I

INTRODUCTORY

The subject of this Essay is not the so-called Liberty of the Will, so unfortunately opposed to the misnamed doctrine of Philosophical Necessity; but Civil, or Social Liberty: the nature and limits of the power which can be legitimately exercised by society over the individual. A question seldom stated, and hardly ever discussed, in general terms but which profoundly influences the practical controversies of the age by its latent presence, and is likely soon to make itself recognized as the vital question of the future. It is so far from being new, that, in a certain sense, it has divided mankind, almost from the remotest ages; but in the stage of progress into which the more civilized portions of the species have now entered, it presents itself under new conditions, and requires a different and more fundamental treatment.

The struggle between Liberty and Authority is the most conspicuous feature in the portions of history with which we are earliest familiar, particularly in that of Greece, Rome, and England. But in old times this contest was between subjects, or some classes of subjects, and the Government. By liberty, was meant protection

ON LIBERTY, John Stuart Mill (New York, 1885), pp. 7-12, 20-26, 29-32, 43-45, 90-107.

against the tyranny of the political rulers. The rulers were conceived (except in some of the popular governments of Greece) as in a necessarily antagonistic position to the people whom they ruled. They consisted of a governing One, or a governing tribe or caste, who derived their authority from inheritance or conquest, who, at all events, did not hold it at the pleasure of the governed, and whose supremacy men did not venture, perhaps did not desire, to contest, whatever precautions might be taken against its oppressive exercise. Their power was regarded as necessary, but also as highly dangerous; as a weapon which they would attempt to use against their subjects, no less than against external enemies. To prevent the weaker members of the community from being preyed upon by innumerable vultures, it was needful that there should be an animal of prey stronger than the rest, commissioned to keep them down. But as the king of the vultures would be no less bent upon preying on the flock than any of the minor harpies, it was indispensable to be in a perpetual attitude of defence against his beak and claws. The aim, therefore, of patriots was to set limits to the power which the ruler should be suffered to exercise over the community; and this limitation was what they meant by liberty. It was attempted in two ways. First, by obtaining a recognition of certain immunities, called political liberties or rights, which it was to be regarded as a breach of duty in the ruler to infringe, and which if he did infringe, specific resistance, or general rebellion, was held to be justifiable. A second, and generally a later expedient, was the establishment of constitutional checks, by which the consent of the community, or of a body of some sort, supposed to represent its interests, was made a necessary condition to some of the more important acts of the governing power. To the first of these modes of limitation, the ruling power, in most European countries, was compelled, more or less, to submit. It was not so with the second; and, to attain this, or when already in some degree possessed, to attain it more completely, became everywhere the principal object of the lovers of liberty. And so long as mankind were content to combat one enemy by another, and to be ruled by a master, on condition of being guaranteed more or less efficaciously against his tyranny, they did not carry their aspirations beyond this point.

A time, however, came, in the progress of human affairs, when men ceased to think it a necessity of nature that their governors should be an independent power, opposed in interest to themselves. It appeared to them much better that the various magistrates of the State should be their tenants or delegates, revocable at their pleasure. In that way alone, it seemed, they could have complete security that the powers of government would never be abused to their disadvantage. By degrees this new demand for elective and temporary rulers became the prominent object of the exertions of the popular party, wherever any such party existed; and superseded, to a considerable extent, the previous efforts to limit the power of rulers. As the struggle proceeded for making the ruling power emanate from the periodical choice of the ruled, some persons began to think that too much importance had been attached to the limitation of the power itself. *That* (it might seem) was a resource against rulers whose interests were habitually opposed to those of the people. What was now wanted was, that the rulers should be identified with the people; that their interest and will should be the interest and will of the nation. The nation did not need to be protected against its own will. There was no fear of its tyrannizing over itself. Let the rulers be effectually responsible to it, promptly removable by it, and it could afford to trust them with power of which it could itself dictate the use to be made. Their power was but the nation's own power, concentrated, and in a form convenient for exercise. This mode of thought, or rather perhaps of feeling, was common among the last generation of European liberalism, in the Continental section of which it still apparently predominates. Those who admit any limit to what a government may do, except in the case of such governments as they think ought not to exist, stand out as brilliant exceptions among the political thinkers of the Continent. A similar tone of sentiment might by this time have been prevalent in our own country, if the circumstances which for a time encouraged it, had continued unaltered.

But, in political and philosophical theories, as well as in persons, success discloses faults and infirmities which failure might have concealed from observation. The notion, that the people have no need to limit their power over themselves, might seem axiomatic, when popular government was a thing only dreamed about, or read of as having existed at some distant period of the past. Neither was that notion necessarily disturbed by such temporary aberrations as those of the French Revolution, the worst of which were the work of an usurping few, and which, in any case, belonged, not to the permanent working of popular institutions, but to a sudden and convulsive outbreak against monarchical and aristocratic despotism. In time, however, a democratic republic came to occupy a large portion of the earth's surface, and made itself felt as one of the most powerful members of the community of nations; and elective and responsible government became subject to the observations and criticisms which wait upon a great existing fact. It was now perceived that such phrases as 'self-government,' and 'the power of the people over themselves,' do not express the true state of the case. The 'people' who exercise the power are not always the same people with those over whom it is exercised; and the 'self-government' spoken of is not the government of each by himself, but of each by all the rest. The will of the people, moreover, practically means the will of the most numerous or the most active *part* of the people, the majority, or those who succeed in making themselves accepted as the majority; the people, consequently, *may* desire to oppress a part of their number; and precautions are as much needed against this as against any other abuse of power. The limitation, therefore, of the power of government over individuals loses none of its importance when the holders of power are regularly accountable to the community, that is, to the strongest party therein. This view of things, recommending itself equally to the intelligence of thinkers and to the inclination of those important classes in European society to whose real or supposed interests democracy is adverse, has had no difficulty in establishing itself; and in political speculations 'the tyranny of the majority' is now generally included among the evils against which society requires to be on its guard.

. . .

The object of this Essay is to assert one very simple principle, as entitled to govern absolutely the dealings of society with the individual in the way of compulsion and control, whether the means used be physical force in the form of legal penalties, or the moral coercion of public opinion. That principle is, that the sole end for which mankind are warranted, individually or collectively, in interfering with the liberty of action of any of their number, is self-protection. That the only purpose for which power can be rightfully exercised over any member of a civilized community, against his will, is to prevent harm to others. His own good, either physical or moral, is not a sufficient warrant. He cannot rightfully be compelled to do or forebear because it will be better for him to do so, because it will make him happier, because, in the opinions of others, to do so would be wise, or even right. These are good reasons for remonstrating with him, or reasoning with him, or persuading him, or entreating him, but not for compelling him, or visiting him with any evil in case he do otherwise. To justify that, the conduct from which it is desired to deter him, must be calculated to produce evil to some one else. The only part of the conduct of any one, for which he is amenable to society, is that which concerns others. In the part which merely concerns himself, his independence is, of right, absolute. Over himself, over his own body and mind, the individual is sovereign.

It is, perhaps, hardly necessary to say that this doctrine is meant to apply only to human beings in the maturity of their faculties. We are not speaking of children, or of young persons below the age which the law may fix as that of manhood or womanhood. Those who are still in a state to require being taken care of by others, must be protected against their own actions as well as against external injury. For the same reason, we may leave out of consideration those backward states of society in which the race itself may be considered as in its nonage. The early difficulties in the way of spontaneous progress are so great, that there is seldom any choice of means for overcoming them; and a ruler full of the spirit of improvement is warranted in the use of any expedients that will attain an end, perhaps otherwise unattainable. Despotism is a legitimate mode of government in dealing with barbarians, provided the end be their improvement, and the means justified by actually effecting that end. Liberty, as a principle, has no application to any state of things anterior to the time when mankind have become capable of being improved by free and equal discussion. Until then, there is nothing for them but implicit obedience to an Akbar or a Charlemagne, if they are so fortunate as to find one. But as soon as mankind have attained the capacity of being guided to their own improvement by conviction or persuasion (a period long since reached in all nations with whom we need here concern ourselves), compulsion, either in the direct form or in that of pains and penalties for non-compliance, is no longer admissible as a means to their own good, and justifiable only for the security of others.

It is proper to state that I forego any advantage which could be derived to my argument from the idea of abstract right, as a thing independent of utility. I regard utility as the ultimate appeal on all ethical questions: but it must be utility in the largest sense, grounded on the permanent interests of a man as a progressive being. Those interests, I contend, authorize the subjection of individual spontaneity to external control, only in respect to those actions of each, which concern the interest of other people. If any one does an act hurtful to others, there is a *prima facie* case for punishing him, by law, or, where legal penalties are not safely applicable, by general disapprobation. There are also many positive acts for the benefit of others, which he may rightfully be compelled to perform; such as to give evidence in a court of justice; to bear his fair share in the common defence, or in any other joint work necessary to the interest of the society of which he enjoys the protection; and to perform certain acts of individual beneficence, such as saving a fellow-creature's life, or interposing to protect the defenceless against ill-usage, things which whenever it is obviously a man's duty to do, he may rightfully be made responsible to society for not doing. A person may cause evil to others not only by his actions but by his inaction, and in either case he is justly accountable to them for the injury. The latter case, it is true, requires a much more cautious exercise of compulsion than the former. To make any one answerable for doing evil to others, is the rule; to make him answerable for not preventing evil, is, comparatively speaking, the exception. Yet there are many cases clear enough and grave enough to justify that exception. In all things which regard the external relations of the individual, he is *de jure* amenable to those whose interests are concerned, and if need be, to society as their protector. There are often good reasons for not holding him to the responsibility; but these reasons must arise from the special expediences of the case: either because it is a kind of case in which he is on the whole likely to act better, when left to his own discretion, than when controlled in any way in which society have it in their power to control him; or because the attempt to exercise control would produce other evils, greater than those which it would prevent. When such reasons as these preclude the enforcement of responsibility, the conscience of the agent himself should step into the vacant judgment seat, and protect those interests of others which have no external protection; judging himself all the more rigidly, because the case does not admit of his being made accountable to the judgment of his fellow-creatures.

But there is a sphere of action in which society, as distinguished from the individual, has, if any, only an indirect interest;

comprehending all that portion of a person's life and conduct which affects only himself, or if it also affects others, only with their free, voluntary, and undeceived consent and participation. When I say only himself, I mean directly and in the first instance; for whatever affects himself, may affect others through himself; and the objection which may be grounded on this contingency, will receive consideration in the sequel. This, then, is the appropriate region of human liberty. It comprises, first, the inward domain of consciousness; demanding liberty of conscience, in the most comprehensive sense; liberty of thought and feeling; absolute freedom of opinion and sentiment on all subjects, practical or speculative, scientific, moral or theological. The liberty of expressing and publishing opinions may seem to fall under a different principle, since it belongs to that part of the conduct of an individual which concerns other people; but, being almost of as much importance as the liberty of thought itself, and resting in great part on the same reasons, is practically inseparable from it. Secondly, the principle requires liberty of tastes and pursuits; of framing the plan of our life to suit our own character; of doing as we like, subject to such consequences as may follow: without impediment from our fellow-creatures, so long as what we do does not harm them, even though they should think our conduct foolish, perverse, or wrong. Thirdly, from this liberty of each individual, follows the liberty, within the same limits, of combination among individuals; freedom to unite, for any purpose not involving harm to others: the persons combining being supposed to be of full age, and not forced or deceived.

No society in which these liberties are not, on the whole, respected, is free, whatever may be its form of government; and none is completely free in which they do not exist absolutely and unqualified. The only freedom which deserves the name, is that of pursuing our own good in our own way, so long as we do not attempt to deprive others of theirs, or impede their efforts to obtain it. Each is the proper guardian of his own health, whether bodily, or mental and spiritual. Mankind are greater gainers by suffering each other to live as seems good to themselves, than by compelling each to live as seems good to the rest.

.   .   .

Chapter II

OF THE LIBERTY OF THOUGHT AND DISCUSSION

The time, it is to be hoped, is gone by, when any defence would be necessary of the 'liberty of the press' as one of the securities against corrupt or tyrannical government. No argument, we may suppose, can now be needed, against permitting a legislature or an executive, not identified in interest with the people, to prescribe opinions to them, and determine what doctrines or what arguments they shall be allowed to hear. This aspect of the question, besides, has been so often and so triumphantly enforced by preceding writers, that it needs not be specially insisted on in this place. Though the law of England on the subject of the press, is as servile to this day as it was in the time of the Tudors, there is little danger of its being actually put in force against political discussion, except during some temporary panic, when fear of insurrection drives ministers and judges from their propriety; and, speaking generally, it is not, in constitutional countries, to be apprehended, that the government, whether completely responsible to the people or not, will often attempt to control the expression of opinion, except when in doing so it makes itself the organ of the general intolerance of the public. Let us suppose, therefore, that the government is entirely at one with the people, and never thinks of exerting any power of coercion unless in agreement with what it conceives to be their voice. But I deny the right of the people to exercise such coercion, either by themselves, or by their government. The power itself is illegitimate. The best government has no more title to it than the worst. It is as noxious, or more noxious, when exerted in accordance with public opinion, than when in opposition to it. If all mankind minus one, were of one opinion, and only one person were of the contrary opinion, mankind would be no more justified in silencing that one person, than he, if he had the power, would be justified in silencing mankind. Were an opinion a personal possession of no value except to the owner; if to be obstructed in the enjoyment of it were simply a private injury, it would make some difference whether the injury was inflicted only on a few persons or on many. But the peculiar evil of silencing the expression of an opinion is, that it is robbing the human race, posterity as well as the existing generation; those who dissent from the opinion, still more than those who hold it. If the opinion is right, they are deprived of the opportunity of exchanging error for truth: if wrong, they lose, what is almost as great a benefit, the clearer perception and livelier impression of truth, produced by its collision with error.

It is necessary to consider separately these two hypotheses, each of which has a distinct branch of the argument corresponding to it. We can never be sure that the opinion we are endeavoring to stifle is a false opinion; and if we were sure, stifling it would be an evil still.

. . .

Mankind can hardly be too often reminded, that there was once a man named Socrates, between whom and the legal authorities and public opinion of his time, there took place a memorable collision. Born in an age and country abounding in individual greatness, this man has been handed down to us by those who best knew both him and the age, as the most virtuous man in it; while *we* know him as the head and prototype of all subsequent teachers of virtue, the source equally of the lofty inspiration of Plato and the judicious utilitarianism of Aristotle, '*i maestri di color che sanno,*' the two headsprings of ethical as of all other philosophy. This acknowledged master of all the eminent thinkers who have since lived—whose fame, still growing after more than two thousand years, all but outweighs the whole remainder of the names which make his native city illustrious—was put to death by his countrymen, after a judicial conviction, for impiety and immorality. Impiety, in denying the gods recognized by the State; indeed his accuser asserted (see the 'Apologia') that he believed in no gods at all. Immorality, in being, by his doctrines and instructions, a 'corrupter of youth.' Of these charges the tribunal, there is every ground for believing, honestly found him guilty, and condemned the man who probably of all then born had deserved best of mankind, to be put to death as a criminal.

To pass from this to the only other instance of judicial iniquity, the mention of which, after the condemnation of Socrates, would not be an anti-climax: the event which took place on Calvary rather more than eighteen hundred years ago. The man who left on the memory of those who witnessed his life and conversation, such an impression of his moral grandeur, that eighteen subsequent centuries have done homage to him as the Almighty in person, was ignominiously put to death, as what? As a blasphemer. Men did not merely mistake their benefactor; they mistook him for the exact contrary of what he was, and treated him as that prodigy of impiety, which they themselves are now held to be, for their treatment of him. The feelings with which mankind now regard these lamentable transactions, especially the later of the two, render them extremely unjust in their judgment of the unhappy actors. These were, to all appearance, not bad men —not worse than men commonly are, but rather the contrary; men who possessed in a full, or somewhat more than a full measure, the religious, moral, and patriotic feelings of their time and people: the very kind of men who, in all times, our own included, have every chance of passing through life blameless and respected. The high-priest who rent his garments when the words were pronounced, which according to all the ideas of his country, constituted the blackest guilt, was in all probability quite as sincere in his horror and indignation, as the generality of respectable and pious men now are in the religious and moral sentiments they profess; and most of those who now shudder at his conduct, if they had lived in his time, and been born Jews, would have acted precisely as he did. Orthodox Christians who are tempted to think that those who stoned to death the first martyrs must have been worse men than they themselves are, ought to remember that one of those persecutors was Saint Paul.

.   .   .

Before quitting the subject of freedom of opinion, it is fit to take some notice of those who say, that the free expression of all opinions should be permitted, on condition that the manner be temperate, and do not pass the bounds of fair discussion. Much might be said on the impossibility of fixing where these supposed bounds are to be placed; for if the test be offence to those whose opinions are attacked, I think experience testifies that this offence is given whenever the attack is telling and powerful, and that every opponent who pushes them hard, and whom they find it difficult to answer, appears to them, if he shows any strong feeling on the subject, an intemperate opponent. But this, though an

important consideration in a practical point of view, merges in a more fundamental objection. Undoubtedly the manner of asserting an opinion, even though it be a true one, may be very objectionable, and may justly incur severe censure. But the principal offences of the kind are such as it is mostly impossible, unless by accidental self-betrayal, to bring home to conviction. The gravest of them is, to argue sophistically, to suppress facts or arguments, to misstate the elements of the case, or misrepresent the opposite opinion. But all this, even to the most aggravated degree, is so continually done in perfect good faith, by persons who are not considered, and in many other respects may not deserve to be considered, ignorant or incompetent, that it is rarely possible, on adequate grounds, conscientiously to stamp the misrepresentation as morally culpable; and still less could law presume to interfere with this kind of controversial misconduct. With regard to what is commonly meant by intemperate discussion, namely, invective, sarcasm, personality, and the like, the denunciation of these weapons would deserve more sympathy if it were ever proposed to interdict them equally to both sides; but it is only desired to restrain the employment of them against the prevailing opinion: against the unprevailing they may not only be used without general disapproval, but will be likely to obtain for him who uses them the praise of honest zeal and righteous indignation. Yet whatever mischief arises from their use, is greatest when they are employed against the comparatively defenceless; and whatever unfair advantage can be derived by an opinion from this mode of asserting it, accrues almost exclusively to received opinions. The worst offence of this kind which can be committed by a polemic, is to stigmatize those who hold the contrary opinion as bad and immoral men. To calumny of this sort, those who hold any unpopular opinion are peculiarly exposed, because they are in general few and uninfluential, and nobody but themselves feels much interested in seeing justice done them; but this weapon is, from the nature of the case, denied to those who attack a prevailing opinion: they can neither use it with safety to themselves, nor, if they could, would it do anything but recoil on their own cause. In general, opinions contrary to those commonly received can only obtain a hearing by studied moderation of language, and the most cautious avoidance of unnecessary offence, from which they hardly ever deviate even in a slight degree without losing ground: while unmeasured vituperation employed on the side of the prevailing opinion, really does deter people from professing contrary opinions, and from listening to those who profess them. For the interest, therefore, of truth and justice, it is far more important to restrain this employment of vituperative language than the other; and, for example, if it were necessary to choose, there would be much more need to discourage offensive attacks on infidelity than on religion. It is, however, obvious that law and authority have no business with restraining either, while opinion ought, in every instance, to determine its verdict by the circumstances of the individual case; condemning every one, on whichever side of the argument he places himself, in whose mode of advocacy either want of candor, or malignity, bigotry, or intolerance of feeling manifest themselves; but not inferring these vices from the side which a person takes, though it be the contrary side of the question to our own: and giving merited honor to every one, whatever opinion he may hold, who has calmness to see and honesty to state what his opponents and their opinions really are, exaggerating nothing to their discredit, keeping nothing back which tells, or can be supposed to tell, in their favor. This is the real morality of public discussion: and if often violated, I

am happy to think that there are many controversialists who to a great extent observe it, and a still greater number who conscientiously strive towards it.

Chapter III

OF INDIVIDUALITY, AS ONE OF THE ELEMENTS OF WELL-BEING

Such being the reasons which make it imperative that human beings should be free to form opinions, and to express their opinions without reserve; and such the baneful consequences to the intellectual, and through that to the moral nature of man, unless this liberty is either conceded, or asserted in spite of prohibition; let us next examine whether the same reasons do not require that men should be free to act upon their opinions—to carry these out in their lives, without hindrance, either physical or moral, from their fellow-men, so long as it is at their own risk and peril. This last proviso is of course indispensable. No one pretends that actions should be as free as opinions. On the contrary, even opinions lose their immunity, when the circumstances in which they are expressed are such as to constitute their expression a positive instigation to some mischievous act. An opinion that corn-dealers are starvers of the poor, or that private property is robbery, ought to be unmolested when simply circulated through the press, but may justly incur punishment when delivered orally to an excited mob, assembled before the house of a corn-dealer, or when handed about among the same mob in the form of a placard. Acts, of whatever kind, which, without justifiable cause, do harm to others, may be, and in the more important cases absolutely require to be, controlled by the unfavorable sentiments, and, when needful, by the active interference of mankind. The liberty of the individual must be thus far limited; he must not make himself a nuisance to other people. But if he refrains from molesting others in what concerns them, and merely acts according to his own inclination and judgment in things which concern himself, the same reasons which show that opinion should be free, prove also that he should be allowed, without molestation, to carry his opinions into practice at his own cost. That mankind are not infallible; that their truths, for the most part, are only half-truths; that unity of opinion, unless resulting from the fullest and freest comparison of opposite opinions, is not desirable, and diversity not an evil, but a good, until mankind are much more capable than at present of recognizing all sides of the truth, are principles applicable to men's modes of action, not less than to their opinions. As it is useful that while mankind are imperfect there should be different opinions, so it is that there should be different experiments of living; that free scope should be given to varieties of character short of injury to others; and that the worth of different modes of life should be proved practically, when any one thinks fit to try them. It is desirable, in short, that in things which do not primarily concern others, individuality should assert itself. Where, not the person's own character, but the traditions or customs of other people are the rule of conduct, there is wanting one of the principal ingredients of human happiness, and quite the chief ingredient of individual and social progress.

In maintaining this principle, the greatest difficulty to be encountered does not lie in the appreciation of means towards an acknowledged end, but in the indifference of persons in general to the end itself. If it were felt that the free development of individuality is one of the leading essentials of well-being; that it is not only a co-ordinate element with all that is designated by the terms civilization, instruction, education, culture, but is itself a necessary part and condition of all those

things; there would be no danger that liberty should be under-valued, and the adjustment of the boundaries between it and social control would present no extraordinary difficulty. But the evil is, that individual spontaneity is hardly recognized by the common modes of thinking, as having any intrinsic worth, or deserving any regard on its own account. The majority, being satisfied with the ways of mankind as they now are (for it is they who make them what they are), cannot comprehend why those ways should not be good enough for everybody; and what is more, spontaneity forms no part of the ideal of the majority of moral and social reformers, but is rather looked on with jealousy, as a troublesome and perhaps rebellious obstruction to the general acceptance of what these reformers, in their own judgment, think would be best for mankind. Few persons, out of Germany, even comprehend the meaning of the doctrine which Wilhelm von Humboldt, so eminent both as a *savant* and as a politician, made the text of a treatise—that 'the end of man, or that which is prescribed by the eternal or immutable dictates of reason, and not suggested by vague and transient desires, is the highest and most harmonious development of his powers to a complete and consistent whole;' that, therefore, the object 'towards which every human being must ceaselessly direct his efforts, and on which especially those who design to influence their fellow-men must ever keep their eyes, is the individuality of power and development,' that for this there are two requisites, 'freedom, and variety of situations;' and that from the union of these arise 'individual vigor and manifold diversity,' which combine themselves in 'originality.'

Little, however, as people are accustomed to a doctrine like that of Von Humboldt, and surprising as it may be to them to find so high a value attached to individuality, the question one must nevertheless think, can only be one of degree. No one's idea of excellence in conduct is that people should do absolutely nothing but copy one another. No one would assert that people ought not to put into their mode of life, and into the conduct of their concerns, any impress whatever of their own judgment, or of their own individual character. On the other hand, it would be absurd to pretend that people ought to live as if nothing whatever had been known in the world before they came into it; as if experience had as yet done nothing towards showing that one mode of existence, or of conduct, is preferable to another. Nobody denies that people should be so taught and trained in youth, as to know and benefit by the ascertained results of human experience. But it is the privilege and proper condition of a human being, arrived at the maturity of his faculties, to use and interpret experience in his own way. It is for him to find out what part of recorded experience is properly applicable to his own circumstances and character. The traditions and customs of other people are, to a certain extent, evidence of what their experience has taught *them;* presumptive evidence, and as such, have a claim to his deference: but, in the first place, their experience may be too narrow; or they may not have interpreted it rightly. Secondly, their interpretation of experience may be correct, but unsuitable to him. Customs are made for customary circumstances, and customary characters; and his circumstances or his character may be uncustomary. Thirdly, though the customs be both good as customs, and suitable to him yet to conform to custom, merely *as* custom, does not educate or develop in him any of the qualities which are the distinctive endowment of a human being. The human faculties of perception, judgment, discriminative feeling, mental activity, and even moral preference, are exercised only in making a choice. He who does anything be-

cause it is the custom, makes no choice. He gains no practice either in discerning or in desiring what is best. The mental and moral, like the muscular powers, are improved only by being used. The faculties are called into no exercise by doing a thing merely because others do it, no more than by believing a thing only because others believe it. If the grounds of an opinion are not conclusive to the person's own reason, his reason cannot be strengthened, but is likely to be weakened, by his adopting it: and if the inducements to an act are not such as are consentaneous to his own feelings and character (where affection, or the rights of others, are not concerned) it is so much done towards rendering his feelings and character inert and torpid, instead of active and energetic.

He who lets the world, or his own portion of it, choose his plan of life for him, has no need of any other faculty than the ape-like one of imitation. He who chooses his plan for himself, employs all his faculties. He must use observation to see, reasoning and judgment to foresee, activity to gather materials for decision, discrimination to decide, and when he has decided, firmness and self-control to hold to his deliberate decision. And these qualities he requires and exercises exactly in proportion as the part of his conduct which he determines according to his own judgment and feelings is a large one. It is possible that he might be guided in some good path, and kept out of harm's way, without any of these things. But what will be his comparative worth as a human being? It really is of importance, not only what men do, but also what manner of men they are that do it. Among the works of man, which human life is rightly employed in perfecting and beautifying, the first in importance surely is man himself. Supposing it were possible to get houses built, corn grown, battles fought, causes tried, and even churches erected and prayers said, by machinery—by automatons in human form—it would be a considerable loss to exchange for these automatons even the men and women who at present inhabit the more civilized parts of the world, and who assuredly are but starved specimens of what nature can and will produce. Human nature is not a machine to be built after a model, and set to do exactly the work prescribed for it, but a tree, which requires to grow and develop itself on all sides, according to the tendency of the inward forces which make it a living thing.

It will probably be conceded that it is desirable people should exercise their understandings, and that an intelligent following of custom, or even occasionally an intelligent deviation from custom, is better than a blind and simply mechanical adhesion to it. To a certain extent it is admitted, that our understanding should be our own: but there is not the same willingness to admit that our desires and impulses should be our own likewise; or that to possess impulses of our own, and of any strength, is anything but a peril and a snare. Yet desires and impulses are as much a part of a perfect human being, as beliefs and restraints: and strong impulses are only perilous when not properly balanced; when one set of aims and inclinations is developed into strength, while others, which ought to co-exist with them, remain weak and inactive. It is not because men's desires are strong that they are ill; it is because their consciences are weak. There is no natural connection between strong impulses and a weak conscience. The natural connection is the other way. To say that one person's desires and feelings are stronger and more various than those of another, is merely to say that he has more of the raw material of human nature, and is therefore capable, perhaps of more evil, but certainly of more good. Strong impulses are but another name for energy. Energy may be turned to

bad uses; but more good may always be made of an energetic nature, than of an indolent and impassive one. Those who have most natural feeling, are always those whose cultivated feelings may be made the strongest. The same strong susceptibilities which make the personal impulses vivid and powerful, are also the source from whence are generated the most passionate love of virtue, and the sternest self-control. It is through the cultivation of these, that society both does its duty and protects its interests: not by rejecting the stuff of which heroes are made, because it knows not how to make them. A person whose desires and impulses are his own—are the expression of his own nature, as it has been developed and modified by his own culture—is said to have a character. One whose desires and impulses are not his own, has no character, no more than a steam-engine has a character. If, in addition to being his own, his impulses are strong, and are under the government of a strong will, he has an energetic character. Whoever thinks that individuality of desires and impulses should not be encouraged to unfold itself, must maintain that society has no need of strong natures—is not the better for containing many persons who have much character—and that a high general average of energy is not desirable.

In some early states of society, these forces might be, and were, too much ahead of the power which society then possessed of disciplining and controlling them. There has been a time when the element of spontaneity and individuality was in excess and the social principle had a hard struggle with it. The difficulty then was, to induce men of strong bodies or minds to pay obedience to any rules which required them to control their impulses. To overcome this difficulty, law and discipline, like the Popes struggling against the Emperors, asserted a power over the whole man, claiming to control all his life in order to control his character—which society had not found any other sufficient means of binding. But society has now fairly got the better of individuality; and the danger which threatens human nature is not the excess, but the deficiency, of personal impulses and preferences. Things are vastly changed, since the passions of those who were strong by station or by personal endowment were in a state of habitual rebellion against laws and ordinances, and required to be rigorously chained up to enable the persons within their reach to enjoy any particle of security. In our times, from the highest class of society down to the lowest, every one lives as under the eye of a hostile and dreaded censorship. Not only in what concerns others, but in what concerns only themselves, the individual or the family do not ask themselves—what do I prefer? or, what would suit my character and disposition? or, what would allow the best and highest in me to have fair play, and enable it to grow and thrive? They ask themselves, what is suitable to my position? what is usually done by persons of my station and pecuniary circumstances? or (worse still) what is usually done by persons of a station and circumstances superior to mine? I do not mean that they choose what is customary, in preference to what suits their own inclination. It does not occur to them to have any inclination, except for what is customary. Thus the mind itself is bowed to the yoke: even in what people do for pleasure, conformity is the first thing thought of; they like in crowds; they exercise choice only among things commonly done: peculiarity of taste, eccentricity of conduct, are shunned equally with crimes: until by dint of not following their own nature, they have no nature to follow: their human capacities are withered and starved: they become incapable of any strong wishes or native pleasures, and are generally without either opinions or feelings of home growth, or properly their own. Now is this, or is it not, the desirable condition of human nature?

It is so, on the Calvinistic theory. According to that, the one great offence of man is self-will. All the good of which humanity is capable, is comprised in obedience. You have no choice; thus you must do, and no otherwise: 'whatever is not a duty, is a sin.' Human nature being radically corrupt, there is no redemption for any one until human nature is killed within him. To one holding this theory of life, crushing out any of the human faculties, capacities, and susceptibilities, is no evil: man needs no capacity, but that of surrendering himself to the will of God: and if he uses any of his faculties for any other purpose but to do that supposed will more effectually, he is better without them. This is the theory of Calvinism; and it is held, in a mitigated form by many who do not consider themselves Calvinists; the mitigation consisting in giving a less ascetic interpretation to the alleged will of God; asserting it to be his will that mankind should gratify some of their inclinations; of course not in the manner they themselves prefer, but in the way of obedience, that is, in a way prescribed to them by authority; and, therefore, by the necessary condition of the case, the same for all.

In some such insidious form, there is at present a strong tendency to this narrow theory of life, and to the pinched and hidebound type of human character which it patronizes. Many persons, no doubt, sincerely think that human beings thus cramped and dwarfed, are as their Maker designed them to be; just as many have thought that trees are a much finer thing when clipped into pollards, or cut out into figures of animals, than as nature made them. But if it be any part of religion to believe that man was made by a good Being, it is more consistent with that faith to believe, that this Being gave all human faculties that they might be cultivated and unfolded, not rooted out and consumed, and that he takes delight in every nearer approach made by his creatures to the ideal conception embodied in them, every increase in any of their capabilities of comprehension, of action, or of enjoyment. There is a different type of human excellence from the Calvinistic: a conception of humanity as having its nature bestowed on it for other purposes than merely to be abnegated. 'Pagan self-assertion' is one of the elements of human worth, as well as 'Christian self-denial.' There is a Greek ideal of self-development, which the Platonic and Christian ideal of self-government blends with, but does not supersede. It may be better to be a John Knox than an Alcibiades, but it is better to be a Pericles than either; nor would a Pericles, if we had one in these days, be without anything good which belonged to John Knox.

It is not by wearing down into uniformity all that is individual in themselves, but by cultivating it, and calling it forth, within the limits imposed by the rights and interests of others, that human beings become a noble and beautiful object of contemplation; and as the works partake the character of those who do them, by the same process human life also becomes rich, diversified, and animating, furnishing more abundant aliment to high thoughts and elevating feelings, and strengthening the tie which binds every individual to the race, by making the race infinitely better worth belonging to. In proportion to the development of his individuality, each person becomes more valuable to himself, and is therefore capable of being more valuable to others. There is a greater fulness of life about his own existence, and when there is more life in the units there is more in the mass which is composed of them. As much compression as is necessary to prevent the stronger specimens of human nature from encroaching on the rights of others, cannot be dispensed with; but for this there is ample compensation even in the point of view of human development. The means of development which the individual loses by being prevented from gratifying his inclinations to the injury of others, are chiefly obtained at the expense of the development of other people. And even to himself there is a full equivalent in the better development of the social part of his nature, rendered possible by the restraint put upon the selfish part. To be held to rigid rules of justice for the sake of others, develops the feelings and capacities which have the good of others for their object. But to be restrained in things not affecting their good, by their mere displeasure, develops nothing valuable, except such force of character as may unfold itself in resisting the restraint. If acquiesced in, it dulls and blunts the whole nature. To give any fair play to the nature of each, it is essential that different persons should be allowed to lead different lives. In proportion as this latitude has been exercised in any age, has that age been noteworthy to posterity. Even despotism does not produce its worst effects, so long as individuality exists under it; and whatever crushes individuality is despotism, by whatever name it may be called, and whether it professes to be enforcing the will of God or the injunctions of men.

Charles Darwin

In 1831, having graduated from Cambridge University where he had been a theology student, Charles Darwin (1809-1882) accepted the position of naturalist aboard the ship *Beagle*, which was setting sail on an extended surveying expedition to South America and the Pacific. During the voyage, which lasted five years, Darwin observed plant and animal life in widely scattered areas of the earth, gathering the evidence on which he was later to base his theory of biological evolution. To render the theory of evolution plausible, however, Darwin had to overcome two obstacles: First, he had to find evidence that the earth was old enough to provide time for the evolutionary process to have taken place, and, second, he had to provide an explanation of this process.

His first problem was solved by the geologist, Sir Charles Lyell, whose *Principles of Geology* (published in 1830) established the fact that the earth had existed through vast periods of geological time. The clue to the solution of his second problem came from Malthus's *Essay on Population*, with its view that organic beings multiply faster than their food supply. Starting from Malthus's assumption, Darwin undertook in *The Origin of Species* to deduce the process by which biological evolution is accomplished and to provide empirical evidence to support his deduction. Darwin's theory of evolution, in its assumption that new species evolve from older ones, repudiated the doctrine, which had stemmed from Aristotle and had been defended on theological grounds from the time of the Middle Ages, of the immutability of species. Thus it marked a major revolution in the history of thought.

The selections that follow are taken from Darwin's two great works, *The Origin of Species* and *The Descent of Man*. The first book, which was published in 1859, contains Darwin's statement of the theory of biological evolution, along with the evidence on which it rests. In the second, published in 1871, Darwin completes his theory by including man within the evolutionary process.

THE ORIGIN OF SPECIES

Nothing is easier than to admit in words the truth of the universal struggle for life, or more difficult—at least

THE ORIGIN OF SPECIES, BY MEANS OF NATURAL SELECTION OR THE PRESERVATION OF FAVOURED RACES IN THE STRUGGLE FOR LIFE, Charles Darwin, 6th ed. (London, 1900), pp. 77-78, 79-84, 87, 90-91, 159-163, 657-670.

I have found it so—than constantly to bear this conclusion in mind. Yet unless it be thoroughly engrained in the mind, the whole economy of nature, with every fact on distribution, rarity, abundance, extinction, and variation, will be dimly seen or quite misunderstood. We behold the face of nature bright with gladness, we often see superabundance of food; we do not see or we forget, that the birds which are idly singing round us mostly live on insects or seeds, and are thus constantly destroying life; or we forget how largely these songsters, or their eggs, or their nestlings, are destroyed by birds and beasts of prey; we do not always bear in mind, that, though food may be now superabundant, it is not so at all seasons of each recurring year.

·   ·   ·

A struggle for existence inevitably follows from the high rate at which all organic beings tend to increase. Every being, which during its natural lifetime produces several eggs or seeds, must suffer destruction during some period of its life, and during some season or occasional year, otherwise, on the principle of geometrical increase, its numbers would quickly become so inordinately great that no country could support the product. Hence, as more individuals are produced than can possibly survive, there must in every case be a struggle for existence, either one individual with another of the same species, or with the individuals of distinct species, or with the physical conditions of life. It is the doctrine of Malthus applied with manifold force to the whole animal and vegetable kingdoms; for in this case there can be no artificial increase of food, and no prudential restraint from marriage. Although some species may be now increasing, more or less rapidly, in numbers, all cannot do so, for the world would not hold them.

There is no exception to the rule that every organic being naturally increases at so high a rate, that, if not destroyed, the earth would soon be covered by the progeny of a single pair. Even slow-breeding man has doubled in twenty-five years, and at this rate, in less than a thousand years, there would literally not be standing-room for his progeny. Linnaeus has calculated that if an annual plant produced only two seeds—and there is no plant so unproductive

as this—and their seedlings next year produced two, and so on, then in twenty years there would be a million plants. The elephant is reckoned the slowest breeder of all known animals, and I have taken some pains to estimate its probable minimum rate of natural increase; it will be safest to assume that it begins breeding when thirty years old, and goes on breeding till ninety years old, bringing forth six young in the interval, and surviving till one hundred years old; if this be so, after a period of from 740 to 750 years there would be nearly nineteen million elephants alive, descended from the first pair.

But we have better evidence on this subject than mere theoretical calculations, namely, the numerous recorded cases of the astonishingly rapid increase of various animals in a state of nature, when circumstances have been favourable to them during two or three following seasons. Still more striking is the evidence from our domestic animals of many kinds which have run wild in several parts of the world; if the statements of the rate of increase of slow-breeding cattle and horses in South America, and latterly in Australia, had not been well authenticated, they would have been incredible. So it is with plants; cases could be given of introduced plants which have become common throughout whole islands in a period of less than ten years. Several of the plants, such as the cardoon and a tall thistle, which are now the commonest over the wide plains of La Plata, clothing square leagues of surface almost to the exclusion of every other plant, have been introduced from Europe; and there are plants which now range in India, as I hear from Dr. Falconer, from Cape Comorin to the Himalaya, which have been imported from America since its discovery. In such cases, and endless others could be given, no one supposes, that the fertility of the animals or plants has been suddenly and temporarily increased in any sensible degree. The obvious explanation is that the conditions of life have been highly favourable, and that there has consequently been less destruction of the old and young, and that nearly all the young have been enabled to breed. Their geometrical ratio of increase, the result of which never fails to be surprising, simply explains their extraordinarily rapid increase and wide diffusion in their new homes.

In a state of nature almost every full-grown plant annually produces seed, and amongst animals there are very few which do not annually pair. Hence we may confidently assert, that all plants and animals are tending to increase at a geometrical ratio,—that all would rapidly stock every station in which they could anyhow exist, —and that this geometrical tendency to increase must be checked by destruction at some period of life. Our familiarity with the larger domestic animals tends, I think, to mislead us: we see no great destruction falling on them, but we do not keep in mind that thousands are annually slaughtered for food, and that in a state of nature an equal number would have somehow to be disposed of.

The only difference between organisms which annually produce eggs or seeds by the thousand, and those which produce extremely few, is, that the slow-breeders would require a few more years to people, under favourable conditions, a whole district, let it be ever so large. The condor lays a couple of eggs and the ostrich a score, and yet in the same country the condor may be the more numerous of the two; the Fulmar petrel lays but one egg, yet it is believed to be the most numerous bird in the world. One fly deposits hundreds of eggs, and another, like the hippobosca, a single one; but this difference does not determine how many individuals of the two species can be supported in a district. A large number of eggs is of some importance to those species which depend on a fluctuat-

ing amount of food, for it allows them rapidly to increase in number. But the real importance of a large number of eggs or seeds is to make up for much destruction at some period of life; and this period in the great majority of cases is an early one. If an animal can in any way protect its own eggs or young, a small number may be produced, and yet the average stock be fully kept up; but if many eggs or young are destroyed, many must be produced, or the species will become extinct. It would suffice to keep up the full number of a tree, which lived on an average for a thousand years, if a single seed were produced once in a thousand years, supposing that this seed were never destroyed, and could be ensured to germinate in a fitting place. So that, in all cases, the average number of any animal or plant depends only indirectly on the number of its eggs or seeds.

In looking at Nature, it is most necessary to keep the foregoing considerations always in mind—never to forget that every single organic being may be said to be striving to the utmost to increase in numbers; that each lives by a struggle at some period of its life; that heavy destruction inevitably falls either on the young or old, during each generation or at recurrent intervals. Lighten any check, mitigate the destruction ever so little, and the number of the species will almost instantaneously increase to any amount.

The causes which check the natural tendency of each species to increase are most obscure. Look at the most vigorous species; by as much as it swarms in numbers, by so much will it tend to increase still further. We know not exactly what the checks are even in a single instance. Nor will this surprise any one who reflects how ignorant we are on this head, even in regard to mankind, although so incomparably better known than any other animal. This subject of the checks to increase has been ably treated by several authors, and I hope in a future work to discuss it at considerable length, more especially in regard to the feral animals of South America. Here I will make only a few remarks, just to recall to the reader's mind some of the chief points. Eggs or very young animals seem generally to suffer most, but this is not invariably the case. With plants there is a vast destruction of seeds, but, from some observations which I have made it appears that the seedlings suffer most from germinating in ground already thickly stocked with other plants. Seedlings, also, are destroyed in vast numbers by various enemies; for instance, on a piece of ground three feet long and two wide, dug and cleared, and where there could be no choking from other plants, I marked all the seedlings of our native weeds as they came up, and out of 357 no less than 295 were destroyed, chiefly by slugs and insects. If turf which has long been mown, and the case would be the same with turf closely browsed by quadrupeds, be let to grow, the more vigorous plants gradually kill the less vigorous, though fully grown plants; thus out of twenty species growing on a little plot of mown turf (three feet by four) nine species perished, from the other species being allowed to grow up freely.

The amount of food for each species of course gives the extreme limit to which each can increase; but very frequently it is not the obtaining food, but the serving as prey to other animals, which determines the average numbers of a species. Thus, there seems to be little doubt that the stock of partridges, grouse, and hares on any large estate depends chiefly on the destruction of vermin. If not one head of game were shot during the next twenty years in England, and, at the same time, if no vermin were destroyed, there would, in all probability, be less game than at present, although hundreds of thousands of game animals are now annually shot. On the other hand, in some cases, as with the ele-

phant, none are destroyed by beasts of prey; for even the tiger in India most rarely dares to attack a young elephant protected by its dam.

. . .

Many cases are on record showing how complex and unexpected are the checks and relations between organic beings, which have to struggle together in the same country.

. . .

[*I give an*] instance showing how plants and animals, remote in the scale of nature, are bound together by a web of complex relations. I shall hereafter have occasion to show that the exotic Lobelia fulgens is never visited in my garden by insects, and consequently, from its peculiar structure, never sets a seed. Nearly all our orchidaceous plants absolutely require the visits of insects to remove their pollen-masses and thus to fertilise them. I find from experiments that humble-bees are almost indispensable to the fertilisation of the heartsease (Violo tricolor), for other bees do not visit this flower. I have also found that the visits of bees are necessary for the fertilisation of some kinds of clover; for instance, 20 heads of Dutch clover (Trifolium repens) yielded 2,290 seeds, but 20 other heads protected from bees produced not one. Again, 100 heads of red clover (T. pratense) produced 2,700 seeds, but the same number of protected heads produced not a single seed. Humble-bees alone visit red clover, as other bees cannot reach the nectar. It has been suggested that moths may fertilise the clovers; but I doubt whether they could do so in the case of the red clover, from their weight not being sufficient to depress the wing petals. Hence we may infer as highly probable that, if the whole genus of humble-bees became extinct or very rare in England, the heartsease and red clover would become very rare, or wholly disappear. The number of humble-bees in any district depends in a great measure upon the number of field-mice, which destroy their combs and nests; and Col. Newman, who has long attended to the habits of humble-bees, believes that "more than two-thirds of them are thus destroyed all over England." Now the number of mice is largely dependent, as every one knows, on the number of cats; and Col. Newman says, "Near villages and small towns I have found the nests of humble-bees more numerous than elsewhere, which I attribute to the number of cats that destroy the mice." Hence it is quite credible that the presence of a feline animal in large numbers in a district might determine, through the intervention first of mice and then of bees, the frequency of certain flowers in that district!

. . . .

If under changing conditions of life organic beings present individual differences in almost every part of their structure, and this cannot be disputed; if there be, owing to their geometrical rate of increase, a severe struggle for life at some age, season, or year, and this certainly cannot be disputed; then, considering the infinite complexity of the relations of all organic beings to each other and to their conditions of life, causing an infinite diversity in structure, constitution, and habits, to be advantageous to them, it would be a most extraordinary fact if no variations had ever occurred useful to each being's own welfare, in the same manner as so many variations have occurred useful to man. But if variations useful to any organic being ever do occur, assuredly individuals thus characterised will have the best chance of being preserved in the struggle for life; and from the strong principle of inheritance, these will tend to produce offspring similarly characterised. This principle of preservation, or the survival of the fittest, I have called Natural Selection. It leads to the improvement of each creature in relation to its organic and inorganic conditions of life; and consequently, in most cases, to what must be regarded as an advance in organisation. Nevertheless, low and simple forms will long endure if well fitted for their simple conditions of life.

Natural selection, on the principle of qualities being inherited at corresponding ages, can modify the egg, seed, or young, as easily as the adult. Amongst many animals, sexual selection will have given its aid to ordinary selection, by assuring to the most vigorous and best adapted males the greatest number of offspring. Sexual selection will also give characters useful to the males alone, in their struggles or rivalry with other males; and these characters will be transmitted to one sex or to both sexes, according to the form of inheritance which prevails.

Whether natural selection has really thus acted in adapting the various forms of life to their several conditions and stations, must be judged by the general tenor and balance of evidence given in the following chapters. But we have already seen how it entails extinction; and how largely extinction has acted in the world's history, geology plainly declares. Natural selection, also, leads to divergence of character; for the more organic beings diverge in structure, habits, and constitution, by so much the more can a large number be supported on the area,—of which we see proof by looking to the inhabitants of any small spot, and to the productions naturalised in foreign lands. Therefore, during the modification of the descendants of any one species, and during the incessant struggle of all species to increase in numbers, the more diversified the descendants become, the better will be their chance of success in the battle for life. Thus the small differences distinguishing varieties of the same species, steadily tend to increase, till they equal the greater differences between species of the same genus, or even of distinct genera.

We have seen that it is the common, the widely-diffused and widely-ranging species, belonging to the larger genera within each class, which vary most; and these tend to transmit to their modified offspring that superiority which now makes them dominant in their own countries. Natural selection, as has just been remarked, leads to divergence of character and to much extinction of the less improved and intermediate forms of life. On these principles, the nature of the affinities, and the generally well-defined distinctions between the innumerable organic beings in each class throughout the world, may be explained. It is a truly wonderful fact—the wonder of which we are apt to overlook from familiarity—that all animals and all plants throughout all time and space should be related to each other in groups, subordinate to groups, in the manner which we everywhere behold—namely, varieties of the same species most closely related, species of the same genus less closely and unequally related, forming sections and sub-genera, species of distinct genera much less closely related, and genera related in different degrees, forming sub-families, families, orders, sub-classes and classes. The several subordinate groups in any class cannot be ranked in a single file, but seem clustered round points, and these round other points, and so on in almost endless cycles. If species had been independently created, no explanation would have been possible of this kind of classification; but it is explained through inheritance and the complex action of natural selection, entailing extinction and divergence of character, as we have seen illustrated in the diagram.

The affinities of all the beings of the same class have sometimes been represented by a great tree. I believe this simile largely speaks the truth. The green and budding twigs may represent existing species; and those produced during former years may represent the long succession of extinct species. At each period of growth all the growing twigs have tried to branch out on all sides, and to overtop and kill the surrounding twigs and branches, in the same manner as species and groups of species have at all times overmastered other species in the great battle for life. The limbs divided into great branches, and these into lesser and lesser branches, were themselves once, when the tree was young, budding twigs; and this connection of the former and present buds by ramifying branches may well represent the classification of all extinct and living species in groups subordinate to groups. Of the many twigs which flourished when the tree was a mere bush, only two or three, now grown into great branches, yet survive and bear the other branches; so with the species which lived during long-past geological periods, very few have left living and modified descendants. From the first growth of the tree, many a limb and branch has decayed and dropped off; and these fallen branches of various sizes may represent those whole orders, families, and genera which have now no living representatives, and which are known to us only in a fossil state. As we here and there see a thin straggling branch springing from a fork low down in a tree, and which by some chance has been favoured and is still alive on its summit, so we occasionally see an animal like the Ornithorhynchus or Lepidosiren, which in some small degree connects by its affinities two large branches of life, and which has apparently been saved from fatal competition by having inhabited a protected station. As buds give rise by growth to fresh buds, and these, if vigorous, branch out and overtop on all sides many a feebler branch, so by generation I believe it has been with the great Tree of Life, which fills with its dead and broken branches the crust of the earth, and covers the surface with its ever-branching and beautiful ramifications.

• • • •

I have now recapitulated the facts and considerations which have thoroughly convinced me that species have been modified, during a long course of descent. This has been effected chiefly through the natural selection of numerous successive, slight, favourable variations; aided in an important manner by the inherited effects of the use and disuse of parts; and in an unimportant manner, that is in relation to adaptive structures, whether past or present, by the direct action of external conditions, and by variations which seem to us in our ignorance to arise spontaneously. It appears that I formerly underrated the frequency and value of these latter forms of variation, as leading to permanent modifications of structure independently of natural selection. But as my conclusions have lately been much misrepresented, and it has been stated that I attribute the modification of species exclusively to natural selection, I may be permitted to remark that in the first edition of this work, and subsequently, I placed in a most conspicuous position— namely, at the close of the Introduction— the following words: "I am convinced that natural selection has been the main but not the exclusive means of modification." This has been of no avail. Great is the power of steady misrepresentation; but the history of science shows that fortunately this power does not long endure.

It can hardly be supposed that a false theory would explain, in so satisfactory a manner as does the theory of natural selection, the several large classes of facts above specified. It has recently been objected that this is an unsafe method of arguing; but it is a method used in judging of the common events of life, and has often been used by the greatest natural philosophers. The undulatory theory of light has thus been arrived at; and the belief in the revolution of the earth on its own axis was until lately supported by hardly any direct evidence. It is no valid objection that science as yet throws no light on the far higher problem of the essence or origin of life. Who can explain what is the essence of the attraction of gravity? No one now objects to following out the results consequent on this unknown element of attraction; notwithstanding that Leibnitz formerly accused Newton of introducing "occult qualities and miracles into philosophy."

I see no good reason why the views given in this volume should shock the religious feelings of any one. It is satisfactory, as showing how transient such impressions are, to remember that the greatest discovery ever made by man, namely, the law of the attraction of gravity, was also attacked by Leibnitz, "as subversive of natural, and inferentially of revealed, religion." A celebrated author and divine has written to me that "he has gradually learnt to see that it is just as noble a conception of the Deity to believe that He created a few original forms capable of self-development into other and needful forms, as to believe that He required a fresh act of creation to supply the voids caused by the action of His laws."

Why, it may be asked, until recently did nearly all the most eminent living naturalists and geologists disbelieve in the mutability of species. It cannot be asserted that organic beings in a state of nature are subject to no variation; it cannot be proved that the amount of variation in the course of long ages is a limited quantity; no clear distinction has been, or can be, drawn between species and well-marked varieties. It cannot be maintained that species when intercrossed are invariably sterile, and varieties invariably fertile; or that sterility is a special endowment and sign of creation. The belief that species were immutable productions was almost unavoidable as long as the history of the world was thought to be of short duration; and now that we have acquired some idea of the lapse of time, we are too apt to assume, without proof, that the geological record is so perfect that it would have afforded us plain evidence of the mutation of species, if they had undergone mutation.

But the chief cause of our natural unwillingness to admit that one species has given birth to other and distinct species, is that we are always slow in admitting great changes of which we do not see the steps. The difficulty is the same as that felt by so many geologists, when Lyell first insisted that long lines of inland cliffs had been formed, and great valleys excavated, by the agencies which we see still at work. The mind cannot possibly grasp the full meaning of the term of even a million years; it cannot add up and perceive the full effects of many slight variations, accumulated during an almost infinite number of generations.

Although I am fully convinced of the truth of the views given in this volume under the form of an abstract, I by no means expect to convince experienced naturalists whose minds are stocked with a multitude of facts all viewed, during a long course of years, from a point of view directly opposite to mine. It is so easy to hide our ignorance under such expressions as the "plan of creation," "unity of design," &c., and to think that we give an explanation when we only re-state a fact. Any one whose disposition leads him to attach more weight to unexplained difficulties than to the explanation of a certain number of facts will certainly reject the theory. A few naturalists, endowed with much flexibility of mind, and who have already begun to doubt the immutability of species, may be influenced by this volume; but I look with confidence to the future,—to young and rising naturalists, who will be able to view both sides of the question with impartiality. Whoever is led to believe that species are mutable will do good service by conscientiously expressing his conviction; for thus only can the load of prejudice by which this subject is overwhelmed be removed.

Several eminent naturalists have of late published their belief that a multitude of reputed species in each genus are not real species; but that other species are real, that is, have been independently created. This seems to me a strange conclusion to arrive at. They admit that a multitude of forms, which till lately they themselves thought were special creations, and which are still thus looked at by the majority of naturalists, and which consequently have all the external characteristic features of true species,—they admit that these have been produced by variation, but they refuse to extend the same view to other and slightly different forms. Nevertheless they do not pretend that they can define, or even conjecture, which are the created forms of life, and which are those produced by secondary laws. They admit variation as a *vera causa* in one case, they arbitrarily reject it in another, without assigning any distinction in the two cases. The day will come when this will be given as a curious illustration of the blindness of preconceived opinion. These authors seem no more startled at a miraculous act of creation than at an ordinary birth. But do they really believe that at innumerable periods in the earth's history certain elemental atoms have been commanded suddenly to flash into living tissues? Do they believe that at each supposed act of creation one individual or many were produced? Were all the infinitely numerous kinds of animals and plants created as eggs or seed, or as full grown? and in the case of mammals, were they created bearing the false marks of nourishment from the mother's womb? Undoubtedly some of these same questions cannot be answered by those who believe in the appearance or creation of only a few forms of life, or of some one form alone. It has been maintained by several authors that it is as easy to believe in the creation of a million beings as of one; but Maupertuis' philosophical axiom "of least action" leads the mind more willingly to admit the smaller number; and certainly we ought not to believe that innumerable beings within each great class have been created with plain, but deceptive, marks of descent from a single parent.

As a record of a former state of things, I have retained in the foregoing paragraphs, and elsewhere, several sentences which imply that naturalists believe in the separate creation of each species; and I have been much censured for having thus expressed myself. But undoubtedly this was the general belief when the first edition of the present work appeared. I formerly spoke to very many naturalists on the subject of evolution, and never once met with any sympathetic agreement. It is probable that some did then believe in evolution, but they were either silent, or expressed themselves so ambiguously that it was not easy to understand their meaning. Now things are wholly changed, and almost every naturalist admits the great principle of evolution. There are, however, some who still think that species have suddenly given birth, through quite unexplained means, to new and totally different forms: but, as I have attempted to show, weighty evidence can be opposed to the admission of great and abrupt modifications. Under a scientific point of view, and as leading to further investigation, but little advantage is gained by believing that new forms are suddenly developed in an inexplicable manner from old and widely different forms, over the old belief in the creation of species from the dust of the earth.

It may be asked how far I extend the doctrine of the modification of species. The question is difficult to answer, because the more distinct the forms are which we consider, by so much the arguments in favour of community of descent become fewer in number and less in force. But some

arguments of the greatest weight extend very far. All the members of whole classes are connected together by a chain of affinities, and all can be classed on the same principle, in groups subordinate to groups. Fossil remains sometimes tend to fill up very wide intervals between existing orders.

Organs in a rudimentary condition plainly show that an early progenitor had the organ in a fully developed condition; and this in some cases implies an enormous amount of modification in the descendants. Throughout whole classes various structures are formed on the same pattern, and at a very early age the embryos closely resemble each other. Therefore I cannot doubt that the theory of descent with modification embraces all the members of the same great class or kingdom. I believe that animals are descended from at most only four or five progenitors, and plants from an equal or lesser number.

Analogy would lead me one step farther, namely, to the belief that all animals and plants are descended from some one prototype. But analogy may be a deceitful guide. Nevertheless all living things have much in common, in their chemical composition, their cellular structure, their laws of growth, and their liability to injurious influences. We see this even in so trifling a fact as that the same poison often similarly affects plants and animals; or that the poison secreted by the gall-fly produces monstrous growths on the wild rose or oak-tree. With all organic beings, excepting perhaps some of the very lowest, sexual reproduction seems to be essentially similar. With all, as far as is at present known, the germinal vesicle is the same; so that all organisms start from a common origin. If we look even to the two main divisions —namely, to the animal and vegetable kingdoms—certain low forms are so far intermediate in character that naturalists have disputed to which kingdom they should be referred. As Professor Asa Gray has remarked, "the spores and other reproductive bodies of many of the lower algae may claim to have first a characteristically animal, and then an unequivocally vegetable existence." Therefore, on the principle of natural selection with divergence of character, it does not seem incredible that, from such low and intermediate form, both animals and plants may have been developed; and, if we admit this, we must likewise admit that all the organic beings which have ever lived on this earth may be descended from some one primordial form. But this inference is chiefly grounded on analogy, and it is immaterial whether or not it be accepted. No doubt it is possible, as Mr. G.H. Lewes has urged, that at the first commencement of life many different forms were evolved; but if so, we may conclude that only a very few have left modified descendants. For, as I have recently remarked in regard to the members of each great kingdom, such as the Vertebrata, Articulata, &c., we have distinct evidence in their embryological, homologous, and rudimentary structures, that within each kingdom all the members are descended from a single progenitor.

When the views advanced by me in this volume, and by Mr. Wallace, or when analogous views on the origin of species are generally admitted, we can dimly foresee that there will be a considerable revolution in natural history. Systematists will be able to pursue their labours as at present; but they will not be incessantly haunted by the shadowy doubt whether this or that form be a true species. This, I feel sure and I speak after experience, will be no slight relief. The endless disputes whether or not some fifty species of British brambles are good species will cease. Systematists will have only to decide (not that this will be easy) whether any form be sufficiently constant and distinct from other forms, to be capable of definition; and if definable,

whether the differences be sufficiently important to deserve a specific name. This latter point will become a far more essential consideration than it is at present; for differences, however slight, between any two forms, if not blended by intermediate gradations, are looked at by most naturalists as sufficient to raise both forms to the rank of species.

Hereafter we shall be compelled to acknowledge that the only distinction between species and well-marked varieties is, that the latter are known, or believed, to be connected at the present day by intermediate gradations whereas species were formerly thus connected. Hence, without rejecting the consideration of the present existence of intermediate gradations between any two forms, we shall be led to weigh more carefully and to value higher the actual amount of difference between them. It is quite possible that forms now generally acknowledged to be merely varieties may hereafter be thought worthy of specific names; and in this case scientific and common language will come into accordance. In short, we shall have to treat species in the same manner as those naturalists treat genera, who admit that genera are merely artificial combinations made for convenience. This may not be a cheering prospect; but we shall at least be freed from the vain search for the undiscovered and undiscoverable essence of the term species.

The other and more general departments of natural history will rise greatly in interest. The terms used by naturalists, of affinity, relationship, community of type, paternity, morphology, adaptive characters, rudimentary and aborted organs, &c., will cease to be metaphorical, and will have a plain signification. When we no longer look at an organic being as a savage looks at a ship, as something wholly beyond his comprehension; when we regard every production of nature as one which has had a long history; when we contemplate every complex structure and instinct as the summing up of many contrivances, each useful to the possessor, in the same way as any great mechanical invention is the summing up of the labour, the experience, the reason, and even the blunders of numerous workmen; when we thus view each organic being, how far more interesting—I speak from experience —does the study of natural history become!

A grand and almost untrodden field of inquiry will be opened, on the causes and laws of variation, on correlation, on the effects of use and disuse, on the direct action of external conditions, and so forth. The study of domestic productions will rise immensely in value. A new variety raised by man will be a more important and interesting subject for study than one more species added to the infinitude of already recorded species. Our classifications will come to be, as far as they can be so made, genealogies; and will then truly give what may be called the plan of creation. The rules for classifying will no doubt become simpler when we have a definite object in view. We possess no pedigrees or armorial bearings; and we have to discover and trace the many diverging lines of descent in our natural genealogies, by characters of any kind which have long been inherited. Rudimentary organs will speak infallibly with respect to the nature of long-lost structures. Species and groups of species which are called aberrant, and which may fancifully be called living fossils, will aid us in forming a picture of the ancient forms of life. Embryology will often reveal to us the structure, in some degree obscured, of the prototypes of each great class.

When we can feel assured that all the individuals of the same species, and all the closely allied species of most genera, have within a not very remote period descended from one parent, and have migrated from some one birth-place; and when we better know the many means of migration, then, by the light which geology now throws, and will continue to throw, on former changes of climate and of the level of the land, we shall surely be enabled to trace in an admirable manner the former migrations of the inhabitants of the whole world. Even at present, by comparing the differences between the inhabitants of the sea on the opposite sides of a continent, and the nature of the various inhabitants on that continent in relation to their apparent means of immigration, some light can be thrown on ancient geography.

The noble science of Geology loses glory from the extreme imperfection of the record. The crust of the earth with its imbedded remains must not be looked at as a well-filled museum, but as a poor collection made at hazard and at rare intervals. The accumulation of each great fossiliferous formation will be recognised as having depended on an unusual concurrence of favourable circumstances, and the blank intervals between the successive stages as having been of vast duration. But we shall be able to gauge with some security the duration of these intervals by a comparison of the preceding and succeeding organic forms. We must be cautious in attempting to correlate as strictly contemporaneous two formations, which do not include many identical species, by the general succession of the forms of life. As species are produced and exterminated by slowly acting and still existing causes, and not by miraculous acts of creation; and as the most important of all causes of organic change is one which is almost independent of altered and perhaps suddenly altered physical conditions, namely, the mutual relation of organism to organism,—the improvement of one organism entailing the improvement or the extermination of others; it follows, that the amount of organic change in the fossils of consecutive formations probably serves as a fair measure of the relative, though not actual lapse of time. A number of species, however, keeping in a body might remain for a long period unchanged, whilst within the same period several of these species by migrating into new countries and coming into competition with foreign associates, might become modified; so that we must not overrate the accuracy of organic change as a measure of time.

In the future I see open fields for far more important researches. Psychology will be securely based on the foundation already well laid by Mr. Herbert Spencer, that of the necessary acquirement of each mental power and capacity by gradation. Much light will be thrown on the origin of man and his history.

Authors of the highest eminence seem to be fully satisfied with the view that each species has been independently created. To my mind it accords better with what we know of the laws impressed on matter by the Creator, that the production and extinction of the past and present inhabitants of the world should have been due to secondary causes, like those determining the birth and death of the individual. When I view all beings not as special creations, but as the lineal descendants of some few beings which lived long before the first bed of the Cambrian system was deposited, they seem to me to become ennobled. Judging from the past, we may safely infer that not one living species will transmit its unaltered likeness to a distant futurity. And of the species now living very few will transmit progeny of any kind to a far distant futurity; for the manner in which all organic beings are grouped, shows that the greater number of species in each genus, and all the species in many genera, have left no descendants, but have become utterly extinct. We can so far take a prophetic glance into futurity as to foretell that it will be the common and widely-spread species, belonging to the larger and dominant groups within each class, which will ultimately prevail and procreate new and dominant species. As all the living forms of life are the lineal descendants of those which lived long before the Cambrian epoch, we may feel certain that the ordinary succession by generation has never once been broken, and that no cataclysm has desolated the whole world. Hence we may look with some confidence to a secure future of great length. And as natural selection works solely by and for the good of each being, all corporeal and mental endowments will tend to progress towards perfection.

It is interesting to contemplate a tangled bank, clothed with many plants of many kinds, with birds singing on the bushes, with various insects flitting about, and with worms crawling through the damp earth, and to reflect that these elaborately constructed forms, so different from each other, and dependent upon each other in so complex a manner, have all been produced by laws acting around us. These laws, taken in the largest sense, being Growth with Reproduction; Inheritance which is almost implied by reproduction; Variability from the indirect and direct action of the conditions of life, and from use and disuse: a Ratio of Increase so high as to lead to a Struggle for Life, and as a consequence to Natural Selection, entailing Divergence of Character and the Extinction of less-improved forms. Thus, from the war of nature, from famine and death, the most exalted object which we are capable of conceiving, namely, the production of the higher animals, directly follows. There is grandeur in this view of life, with its several powers, having been originally breathed by the Creator into a few forms or into one; and that, whilst this planet has gone cycling on according to the fixed law of gravity, from so simple a beginning endless forms most beautiful and most wonderful have been, and are being evolved.

THE DESCENT OF MAN

Chapter XXI

GENERAL SUMMARY AND CONCLUSION

. . .

The main conclusion arrived at in this work, and now held by many naturalists who are well competent to form a sound judgment, is that man is descended from some less highly-organized form. The grounds upon which this conclusion rests will never be shaken, for the close similarity between man and the lower animals in embryonic development, as well as in innumerable points of structure and constitution, both of high and of the most trifling importance—the rudiments which he retains, and the abnormal reversions to which he is occasionally liable—are facts which cannot be disputed. They have long been known, but until recently they told us nothing with respect to the origin of man. Now, when viewed by the light of our knowledge of the whole organic world, their meaning is unmistakable. The great principle of evolution stands up clear and firm, when these groups of facts are considered in connection with others, such as the mutual affinities of the members of the same group, their geographical distribution in past and present times, and their geological succession. It is incredible that all these facts should speak falsely. He who is not content to look, like a savage, at the phenomena of Nature as disconnected, cannot any longer believe that man is the work of a separate act of creation. He will be forced to admit that the close resemblance of the embryo of man to that, for instance, of a dog—the construction of his

THE DESCENT OF MAN, AND SELECTION IN RELATION TO SEX, Charles Darwin (New York, 1872), II, 368-369, 386-387.

skull, limbs, and whole frame, independently of the uses to which the parts may be put, on the same plan with that of other mammals—the occasional reappearance of various structures, for instance, of several distinct muscles, which man does not normally possess, but which are common to the Quadrumana—and a crowd of analogous facts—all point in the plainest manner to the conclusion that man is the co-descendant with other mammals of a common progenitor.

[*This*] conclusion . . . that man is descended from some lowly-organized form, will, I regret to think, be highly distasteful to many persons. But there can hardly be a doubt that we are descended from barbarians. The astonishment which I felt on first seeing a party of Fuegians on a wild and broken shore will never be forgotten by me, for the reflection at once rushed into my mind—such were our ancestors. These men were absolutely naked and bedaubed with paint, their long hair was tangled, their mouths frothed with excitement, and their expression was wild, startled, and distrustful. They possessed hardly any arts, and, like wild animals, lived on what they could catch; they had no government, and were merciless to every one not of their own small tribe. He who has seen a savage in his native land will not feel much shame, if forced to acknowledge that the blood of some more humble creature flows in his veins. For my own part, I would as soon be descended from that heroic little monkey, who braved his dreaded enemy in order to save the life of his keeper; or from that old baboon, who, descending from the mountains, carried away in triumph his young comrade from a crowd of astonished dogs—as from a savage who delights to torture his enemies, offers up bloody sacrifices, practises infanticide without remorse, treats his wives like slaves, knows no decency, and is haunted by the grossest superstitions.

Man may be excused for feeling some pride at having risen, though not through his own exertions, to the very summit of the organic scale; and the fact of his having thus risen, instead of having been aboriginally placed there, may give him hopes for a still higher destiny in the distant future. But we are not here concerned with hopes or fears, only with the truth as far as our reason allows us to discover it. I have given the evidence to the best of my ability; and we must acknowledge, as it seems to me, that man with all his noble qualities, with sympathy which feels for the most debased, with benevolence which extends not only to other men but to the humblest living creature, with his godlike intellect which has penetrated into the movements and constitution of the solar system—with all these exalted powers—Man still bears in his bodily frame the indelible stamp of his lowly origin.

William Graham Sumner

For Darwin, the biologist, the theory of evolution was never anything more than a scientific explanation of the origin of biological species. But for many of Darwin's contemporaries it became the basis for an entirely new way of looking at the universe and everything that has happened in it, particularly since the arrival on the scene of *Homo sapiens*. Seizing upon the key ideas of the struggle for existence and the survival of the fittest, these writers (who are generally called Social Darwinists) found in them concepts capable of explaining the data of morals, politics, economics, sociology, history, and philosophy, as well as those of biology. Although the details of the explanations varied from field to field, in their general outline they were pretty much the same.

In economics—and it was here that Social Darwinism had perhaps its strongest immediate impact—the theory usually ran as follows: Having been victorious in the struggle for existence against other species, men are now engaged in the same struggle among themselves. The fruits of this struggle lie in social status, which is generally conceived in monetary terms. In other words, the fit become rich and the unfit poor; hence the standard by which the fitness of any individual must be judged is the size of his bankroll. Finally, since economic success is the mark of fitness, and since, the argument ran, fitness can be equated with goodness, the rich are not only the highest products of the evolutionary process, but morally they are the best members of society as well. The opposite, of course, holds true for the poor.

Among the most prominent Social Darwinists was the American scholar and teacher, William Graham Sumner (1840-1910). After a brief career in the ministry, Sumner joined the faculty of Yale University, where he remained for the rest of his life. He is a figure of the first rank in the intellectual history of our country and a world pioneer in the study of anthropology and sociology, in which his major work, *Folkways*, is considered a classic. In the essay that follows, he applies the concepts of evolution to the field of economics.

THE CHALLENGE OF FACTS

Socialism is no new thing. In one form or another it is to be found throughout all history. It arises from an observation of certain harsh facts in the lot of man on earth, the concrete expression of which is poverty and misery. These facts challenge us. It is folly to try to shut our eyes to them. We have first to notice what they are, and then to face them squarely.

Man is born under the necessity of sustaining the existence he has received by an onerous struggle against nature, both to win what is essential to his life and to ward off what is prejudicial to it. He is born under a burden and a necessity. Nature holds what is essential to him, but she offers nothing gratuitously. He may win for his use what she holds, if he can. Only the most meager and inadequate supply for human needs can be obtained directly from nature. There are trees which may be used for fuel and for dwellings, but labor is required to fit them for this use. There are ores in the ground, but labor is necessary to get out the metals and make tools or weapons. For any real satisfaction, labor is necessary to fit the products of nature for human use. In this struggle every individual is under the pressure of the necessities for food, clothing, shelter, fuel, and every individual brings with him more or less energy for the conflict necessary to supply his needs. The relation, therefore, between each man's needs and each man's energy, or "individualism," is the first fact of human life.

It is not without reason, however, that we speak of a "man" as the individual in

question, for women (mothers) and children have special disabilities for the struggle with nature, and these disabilities grow greater and last longer as civilization advances. The perpetuation of the race in health and vigor, and its success as a whole in its struggle to expand and develop human life on earth, therefore, require that the head of the family shall, by his energy, be able to supply not only his own needs, but those of the organisms which are dependent upon him. The history of the human race shows a great variety of experiments in the relation of the sexes and in the organization of the family. These experiments have been controlled by economic circumstances, but, as man has gained more and more control over economic circumstances, monogamy and the family education of children have been more and more sharply developed. If there is one thing in regard to which the student of history and sociology can affirm with confidence that social institutions have made "progress" or grown "better," it is in this arrangement of marriage and the family. All experience proves that monogamy, pure and strict, is the sex relation which conduces most to the vigor and intelligence of the race, and that the family education of children is the institution by which the race as a whole advances most rapidly, from generation to generation, in the struggle with nature. Love of man and wife, as we understand it, is a modern sentiment. The devotion and sacrifice of parents for children is a sentiment which has been developed steadily and is now more intense and far more widely practiced throughout society than in earlier times. The relation is also coming to be regarded in a light quite different from that in which it was formerly viewed. It used to be believed that

"THE CHALLENGE OF FACTS," in *The Challenge of Facts and Other Essays*, W. G. Sumner, ed. A. G. Keller (New Haven: Yale University Press, 1914), pp. 17-52. Courtesy of Yale University Press.

the parent had unlimited claims on the child and rights over him. In a truer view of the matter, we are coming to see that the rights are on the side of the child and the duties on the side of the parent. Existence is not a boon for which the child owes all subjection to the parent. It is a responsibility assumed by the parent towards the child without the child's consent, and the consequence of it is that the parent owes all possible devotion to the child to enable him to make his existence happy and successful.

The value and importance of the family sentiments, from a social point of view, cannot be exaggerated. They impose self-control and prudence in their most important social bearings, and tend more than any other forces to hold the individual up to the virtues which make the sound man and the valuable member of society. The race is bound, from generation to generation, in an unbroken chain of vice and penalty, virtue and reward. The sins of the fathers are visited upon the children, while, on the other hand, health, vigor, talent, genius, and skill are, so far as we can discover, the results of high physical vigor and wise early training. The popular language bears witness to the universal observation of these facts, although general social and political dogmas have come into fashion which contradict or ignore them. There is no other such punishment for a life of vice and self-indulgence as to see children grow up cursed with the penalties of it, and no such reward for self-denial and virtue as to see children born and grow up vigorous in mind and body. It is time that the true import of these observations for moral and educational purposes was developed, and it may well be questioned whether we do not go too far in our reticence in regard to all these matters when we leave it to romances and poems to do almost all the educational work that is done in the way of spreading ideas about them. The defense of marriage and the family, if their sociologi-

cal value were better understood, would be not only instinctive but rational. The struggle for existence with which we have to deal must be understood, then, to be that of a man for himself, his wife, and his children.

The next great fact we have to notice in regard to the struggle of human life is that labor which is spent in a direct struggle with nature is severe in the extreme and is but slightly productive. To subjugate nature, man needs weapons and tools. These, however, cannot be won unless the food and clothing and other prime and direct necessities are supplied in such amount that they can be consumed while tools and weapons are being made, for the tools and weapons themselves satisfy no needs directly. A man who tills the ground with his fingers or with a pointed stick picked up without labor will get a small crop. To fashion even the rudest spade or hoe will cost time, during which the laborer must still eat and drink and wear, but the tool, when obtained, will multiply immensely the power to produce. Such products of labor, used to assist production, have a function so peculiar in the nature of things that we need to distinguish them. We call them capital. A lever is capital, and the advantage of lifting a weight with a lever over lifting it by direct exertion is only a feeble illustration of the power of capital in production. The origin of capital lies in the darkness before history, and it is probably impossible for us to imagine the slow and painful steps by which the race began the formation of it. Since then it has gone on rising to higher and higher powers by a ceaseless involution, if I may use a mathematical expression. Capital is labor raised to a higher power by being constantly multiplied into itself. Nature has been more and more subjugated by the human race through the power of capital, and every human being now living shares the improved status of the race to a degree which neither he nor any one else can measure, and for which he pays nothing.

Let us understand this point, because our subject will require future reference to it. It is the most shortsighted ignorance not to see that, in a civilized community, all the advantage of capital except a small fraction is gratuitously enjoyed by the community. For instance, suppose the case of a man utterly destitute of tools, who is trying to till the ground with a pointed stick. He could get something out of it. If now he should obtain a spade with which to till the ground, let us suppose, for illustration, that he could get twenty times as great a product. Could, then, the owner of a spade in a civilized state demand, as its price, from the man who had no spade, nineteen-twentieths of the product which could be produced by the use of it? Certainly not. The price of a spade is fixed by the supply and demand of products in the community. A spade is bought for a dollar and the gain from the use of it is an inheritance of knowledge, experience, and skill which every man who lives in a civilized state gets for nothing. What we pay for steam transportation is no trifle, but imagine, if you can, eastern Massachusetts cut off from steam connection with the rest of the world, turnpikes and sailing vessels remaining. The cost of food would rise so high that a quarter of the population would starve to death and another quarter would have to emigrate. To-day every man here gets an enormous advantage from the status of a society on a level of steam transportation, telegraph, and machinery, for which he pays nothing.

So far as I have yet spoken, we have before us the struggle of man with nature, but the social problems, strictly speaking, arise at the next step. Each man carries on the struggle to win his support for himself, but there are others by his side engaged in the same struggle. If the stores of nature were unlimited, or if the last unit of the supply she offers could be won as easily as the first, there would be no social problem. If a square mile of land could support an indefinite number of human beings, or if it cost only twice as much labor to get forty bushels of wheat from an acre as to get twenty, we should have no social problem. If a square mile of land could support millions, no one would ever emigrate and there would be no trade or commerce. If it cost only twice as much labor to get forty bushels as twenty, there would be no advance in the arts. The fact is far otherwise. So long as the population is low in proportion to the amount of land, on a given stage of the arts, life is easy and the competition of man with man is weak. When more persons are trying to live on a square mile than it can support, on the existing stage of the arts, life is hard and the competition of man with man is intense. In the former case, industry and prudence may be on a low grade; the penalties are not severe, or certain, or speedy. In the latter case, each individual needs to exert on his own behalf every force, original or acquired, which he can command. In the former case, the average condition will be one of comfort and the population will be all nearly on the average. In the latter case, the average condition will not be one of comfort, but the population will cover wide extremes of comfort and misery. Each will find his place according to his ability and his effort. The former society will be democratic; the latter will be aristocratic.

The constant tendency of population to outstrip the means of subsistence is the force which has distributed population over the world, and produced all advance in civilization. To this day the two means of escape for an overpopulated country are emigration and an advance in the arts. The former wins more land for the same people; the latter makes the same land support more persons. If, however, either of these means opens a chance for an increase of population, it is evident that the advantage so won may be speedily exhausted if the increase takes place. The social difficulty has only undergone a temporary amelioration, and when the conditions of pressure and competition are renewed, misery and poverty reappear. The victims of them are those who have inherited disease and depraved appetites, or have been brought up in vice and ignorance, or have themselves yielded to vice, extravagance, idleness, and imprudence. In the last analysis, therefore, we come back to vice, in its original and hereditary forms, as the correlative of misery and poverty.

The condition for the complete and regular action of the force of competition is liberty. Liberty means the security given to each man that, if he employs his energies to sustain the struggle on behalf of himself and those he cares for, he shall dispose of the product exclusively as he chooses. It is impossible to know whence any definition or criterion of justice can be derived, if it is not deduced from this view of things; or if it is not the definition of justice that each shall enjoy the fruit of his own labor and self-denial, and of injustice that the idle and the industrious, the self-indulgent and the self-denying, shall share equally in the product. Aside from the *a priori* speculations of philosophers who have tried to make equality an essential element in justice, the human race has recognized, from the earliest times, the above conception of justice as the true one, and has founded upon it the right of property. The right of property, with marriage and the family, gives the right of bequest.

Monogamic marriage, however, is the most exclusive of social institutions. It contains, as essential principles, preference, superiority, selection, devotion. It would not be at all what it is if it were not for these characteristic traits, and it always degenerates when these traits are not present. For instance, if a man should not have a distinct preference for the woman he married, and if he did not select her as superior to others, the marriage would be an imperfect one according to the standard of true monogamic marriage. The family under monogamy, also, is a closed group, having special interests and estimating privacy and reserve as valuable advantages for family development. We grant high prerogatives, in our society, to parents, although our observation teaches us that thousands of human beings are unfit to be parents or to be entrusted with the care of children. It follows, therefore, from the organization of marriage and the family, under monogamy, that great inequalities must exist in a society based on those institutions. The son of wise parents cannot start on a level with the son of foolish ones, and the man who has had no home discipline cannot be equal to the man who has had home discipline. If the contrary were true, we could rid ourselves at once of the wearing labor of inculcating sound morals and manners in our children.

Private property, also, which we have seen to be a feature of society organized in accordance with the natural conditions of the struggle for existence produces inequalities between men. The struggle for existence is aimed against nature. It is from her niggardly hand that we have to wrest the satisfaction for our needs, but our fellow-men are our competitors for the meager supply. Competition, therefore, is a law of nature. Nature is entirely neutral; she submits to him who most energetically and resolutely assails her. She grants her rewards to the fittest, therefore, without regard to other considerations of any kind. If, then, there be liberty, men get from her just in proportion to their works, and their having and enjoying are just in proportion to their being and their doing. Such is the system of nature. If we do not like it, and if we try to amend it, there is only one way in which we can do it. We can take from the better and give to the worse. We can deflect the penalties of those who have done ill and throw them on those who have done better. We can take the rewards from those who have done better and give them to those who have done worse. We shall thus lessen the inequalities. We shall favor the survival of the unfittest, and we shall accomplish this by destroying liberty. Let it be understood that we cannot go outside of this alternative: liberty, inequality, survival of the fittest; not-liberty, equality, survival of the unfittest. The former carries society forward and favors all its best members; the latter carries society downwards and favors all its worst members.

For three hundred years now men have been trying to understand and realize liberty. Liberty is not the right or chance to do what we choose; there is no such liberty as that on earth. No man can do as he chooses: the autocrat of Russia or the King of Dahomey has limits to his arbitrary will; the savage in the wilderness, whom some people think free, is the slave of routine, tradition, and superstitious fears; the civilized man must earn his living, or take care of his property, or concede his own will to the rights and claims of his parents, his wife, his children, and all the persons with whom he is connected by the ties and contracts of civilized life.

What we mean by liberty is civil liberty, or liberty under law; and this means the guarantees of law that a man shall not be interfered with while using his own powers for his own welfare. It is, therefore, a civil and political status; and that nation has the freest institutions in which the guarantees of peace for the laborer and security for the capitalist are the highest. Liberty, therefore, does not by any means do away with the struggle for existence. We might as well try to do away with the need of eating, for that would, in effect, be the same thing. What civil liberty does is to turn the competition of man with man from violence and brute force into an industrial competition under which men vie with one another for the acquisition of material goods by industry, energy, skill, frugality, prudence, temperance, and other industrial virtues. Under this changed order of things the inequalities are not done away with. Nature still grants her rewards of having and enjoying, according to our being and doing, but it is now the man of the highest training and not the man of the heaviest fist who gains the highest reward. It is impossible that the man with capital and the man without capital should be equal. To affirm that they are equal would be to say that a man who has no tool can get as much food out of the ground as the man who has a spade or a plough; or that the man who has no weapon can defend himself as well against hostile beasts or hostile men as the man who has a weapon. If that were so, none of us would work any more. We work and deny ourselves to get capital just because, other things being equal, the man who has it is superior, for attaining all the ends of life, to the man who has it not. Considering the eagerness with which we all seek capital and the estimate we put upon it, either in cherishing it if we have it, or envying others who have it while we have it not, it is very strange what platitudes pass current about it in our society so soon as we begin to generalize about it. If our young people really believed some of the teachings they hear, it would not be amiss to preach them a sermon once in a while to reassure them, setting forth that it is not wicked to be rich, nay even, that it is not wicked to be richer than your neighbor.

It follows from what we have observed that it is the utmost folly to denounce capital. To do so is to undermine civilization, for capital is the first requisite of every social gain, educational, ecclesiastical, political, aesthetic, or other.

It must also be noticed that the popular antithesis between persons and capital is very fallacious. Every law or institution which protects persons at the expense of capital makes it easier for persons to live and to increase the number of consumers of capital while lowering all the motives to prudence and frugality by which capital is created. Hence every such law or institution tends to produce a large population, sunk in misery. All poor laws and all eleemosynary institutions and expenditures have this tendency. On the contrary, all laws and institutions which give security to capital against the interests of other persons than its owners, restrict numbers while preserving the means of subsistence. Hence every such law or institution tends to produce a small society on a high stage of comfort and well-being. It follows that the antithesis commonly thought to exist between the protection of persons and the protection of property is in reality only an antithesis between numbers and quality.

I must stop to notice, in passing, one other fallacy which is rather scientific than popular. The notion is attributed to certain economists that economic forces are self-correcting. I do not know of any economists who hold this view, but what is intended probably is that many economists, of whom I venture to be one, hold that economic forces act compensatingly, and that whenever economic forces have so acted as to produce an unfavorable situation, other economic forces are brought into action which correct the evil and restore the equilibrium. For instance, in Ireland overpopulation and exclusive devotion to agriculture, both of which are plainly traceable to unwise statesmanship in the past, have produced a situation of distress. Steam navigation on the ocean has introduced the competition of cheaper land with Irish agriculture. The result is a social and industrial crisis. There are, however, millions of acres of fertile land on earth which are un-

occupied and which are open to the Irish, and the economic forces are compelling the direct corrective of the old evils, in the way of emigration or recourse to urban occupations by unskilled labor. Any number of economic and legal nostrums have been proposed for this situation, all of which propose to leave the original causes untouched. We are told that economic causes do not correct themselves. That is true. We are told that when an economic situation becomes very grave it goes on from worse to worse and that there is no cycle through which it returns. That is not true, without further limitation. We are told that moral forces alone can elevate any such people again. But it is plain that a people which has sunk below the reach of the economic forces of self-interest has certainly sunk below the reach of moral forces, and that this objection is superficial and short-sighted. What is true is that economic forces always go before moral forces. Men feel self-interest long before they feel prudence, self-control, and temperance. They lose the moral forces long before they lose the economic forces. If they can be regenerated at all, it must be first by distress appealing to self-interest and forcing recourse to some expedient for relief. Emigration is certainly an economic force for the relief of Irish distress. It is a palliative only, when considered in itself, but the virtue of it is that it gives the non-emigrating population a chance to rise to a level on which the moral forces can act upon them. Now it is terribly true that only the better ones emigrate, and only the better ones among those who remain are capable of having their ambition and energy awakened, but for the rest the solution is famine and death, with a social regeneration through decay and the elimination of that part of the society which is not capable of being restored to health and life. As Mr. Huxley once said, the method of nature is not even a word and a blow, with the blow first. No explanation is vouchsafed. We are left to find out for ourselves why our ears are boxed. If we do not find out, and find out correctly, what the error is for which we are being punished, the blow is repeated and poverty, distress, disease, and death finally remove the incorrigible ones. It behooves us men to study these terrible illustrations of the penalties which follow on bad statesmanship, and of the sanctions by which social laws are enforced. The economic cycle does complete itself; it must do so, unless the social group is to sink in permanent barbarism. A law may be passed which shall force somebody to support the hopelessly degenerate members of a society, but such a law can only perpetuate the evil and entail it on future generations with new accumulations of distress.

The economic forces work with moral forces and are their handmaidens, but the economic forces are far more primitive, original, and universal. The glib generalities in which we sometimes hear people talk, as if you could set moral and economic forces separate from and in antithesis to each other, and discard the one to accept and work by the other, gravely misconstrue the realities of the social order.

We have now before us the facts of human life out of which the social problem springs. These facts are in many respects hard and stern. It is by strenuous exertion only that each one of us can sustain himself against the destructive forces and the ever recurring needs of life; and the higher the degree to which we seek to carry our development the greater is the proportionate cost of every step. For help in the struggle we can only look back to those in the previous generation who are responsible for our existence. In the competition of life the son of wise and prudent ancestors has immense advantages over the son of vicious and imprudent ones. The man who has capital possesses immeasurable advantages for the struggle of life over him who has none.

The more we break down privileges of class, or industry, and establish liberty, the greater will be the inequalities and the more exclusively will the vicious bear the penalties. Poverty and misery will exist in society just so long as vice exists in human nature.

I now go on to notice some modes of trying to deal with this problem. There is a modern philosophy which has never been taught systematically, but which has won the faith of vast masses of people in the modern civilized world. For want of a better name it may be called the sentimental philosophy. It has colored all modern ideas and institutions in politics, religion, education, charity, and industry, and is widely taught in popular literature, novels, and poetry, and in the pulpit. The first proposition of this sentimental philosophy is that nothing is true which is disagreeable. If, therefore, any facts of observation show that life is grim or hard, the sentimental philosophy steps over such facts with a genial platitude, a consoling commonplace, or a gratifying dogma. The effect is to spread an easy optimism, under the influence of which people spare themselves labor and trouble, reflection and forethought, pains and caution—all of which are hard things, and to admit the necessity for which would be to admit that the world is not all made smooth and easy, for us to pass through it surrounded by love, music, and flowers.

Under this philosophy, "progress" has been represented as a steadily increasing and unmixed good; as if the good steadily encroached on the evil without involving any new and other forms of evil; and as if we could plan great steps in progress in our academies and lyceums, and then realize them by resolution. To minds trained to this way of looking at things, any evil which exists is a reproach. We have only to consider it, hold some discussions about it, pass resolutions, and have done with it.

Every moment of delay is, therefore, a social crime. It is monstrous to say that misery and poverty are as constant as vice and evil passions of men! People suffer so under misery and poverty! Assuming, therefore, that we can solve all these problems and eradicate all these evils by expending our ingenuity upon them, of course we cannot hasten too soon to do it.

A social philosophy, consonant with this, has also been taught for a century. It could not fail to be popular, for it teaches that ignorance is as good as knowledge, vulgarity as good as refinement, shiftlessness as good as painstaking, shirking as good as faithful striving, poverty as good as wealth, filth as good as cleanliness—in short, that quality goes for nothing in the measurement of men, but only numbers. Culture, knowledge, refinement, skill, and taste cost labor, but we have been taught that they have only individual, not social value, and that socially they are rather drawbacks than otherwise. In public life we are taught to admire roughness, illiteracy, and rowdyism. The ignorant, idle, and shiftless have been taught that they are "the people," that the generalities inculcated at the same time about the dignity, wisdom, and virtue of "the people" are true of them, that they have nothing to learn to be wise, but that, as they stand, they possess a kind of infallibility, and that to their "opinion" the wise must bow. It is not cause for wonder if whole sections of these classes have begun to use the powers and wisdom attributed to them for their interests, as they construe them, and to trample on all the excellence which marks civilization as an obsolete superstition.

Another development of the same philosophy is the doctrine that men come into the world endowed with "natural rights," or as joint inheritors of the "rights of man," which have been "declared" times without number during the last century. The divine rights of man have succeeded to the obsolete divine right of kings. If it is true, then, that a man is born with rights, he comes into the world with claims on somebody besides his parents. Against whom does he hold such rights? There can be no rights against nature or against God. A man may curse his fate because he is born of an inferior race, or with an hereditary disease, or blind, or, as some members of the race seem to do, because they are born females; but they get no answer to their imprecations. But, now, if men have rights by birth, these rights must hold against their fellow-men and must mean that somebody else is to spend his energy to sustain the existence of the persons so born. What then becomes of the natural rights of the one whose energies are to be diverted from his own interests? If it be said that we should all help each other, that means simply that the race as a whole should advance and expand as much and as fast as it can in its career on earth; and the experience on which we are now acting has shown that we shall do this best under liberty and under the organization which we are now developing, by leaving each to exert his energies for his own success. The notion of natural rights is destitute of sense, but it is captivating, and it is the more available on account of its vagueness. It lends itself to the most vicious kind of social dogmatism, for if a man has natural rights, then the reasoning is clear up to the finished socialistic doctrine that a man has a natural right to whatever he needs, and that the measure of his claims is the wishes which he wants fulfilled. If, then, he has a need, who is bound to satisfy it for him? Who holds the obligation corresponding to his right? It must be the one who possesses what will satisfy that need, or else the state which can take the possession from those who have earned and saved it, and give it to him who needs it and who, by the hypothesis, has not earned and saved it.

It is with the next step, however, that

we come to the complete and ruinous absurdity of this view. If a man may demand from those who have a share of what he needs and has not, may he demand the same also for his wife and for his children, and for how many children? The industrious and prudent man who takes the course of labor and self-denial to secure capital, finds that he must defer marriage, both in order to save and to devote his life to the education of fewer children. The man who can claim a share in another's product has no such restraint. The consequence would be that the industrious and prudent would labor and save, without families, to support the idle and improvident who would increase and multiply, until universal destitution forced a return to the principles of liberty and property; and the man who started with the notion that the world owed him a living would once more find, as he does now, that the world pays him its debt in the state prison.

The most specious application of the dogma of rights is to labor. It is said that every man has a right to work. The world is full of work to be done. Those who are willing to work find that they have three days' work to do in every day that comes. Work is the necessity to which we are born. It is not a right, but an irksome necessity, and men escape it whenever they can get the fruits of labor without it. What they want is the fruits, or wages, not work. But wages are capital which some one has earned and saved. If he and the workman can agree on the terms on which he will part with his capital, there is no more to be said. If not, then the right must be set up in a new form. It is now not a right to work, nor even a right to wages, but a right to a certain rate of wages, and we have simply returned to the old doctrine of spoliation again. It is immaterial whether the demand for wages be addressed to an individual capitalist or to a civil body, for the latter can give no wages which it does not collect by taxes out of the capital of those who have labored and saved.

Another application is in the attempt to fix the hours of labor *per diem* by law. If a man is forbidden to labor over eight hours per day (and the law has no sense or utility for the purposes of those who want it until it takes this form), he is forbidden to exercise so much industry as he may be willing to expend in order to accumulate capital for the improvement of his circumstances.

A century ago there were very few wealthy men except owners of land. The extension of commerce, manufactures, and mining, the introduction of the factory system and machinery, the opening of new countries, and the great discoveries and inventions have created a new middle class, based on wealth, and developed out of the peasants, artisans, unskilled laborers, and small shopkeepers of a century ago. The consequence has been that the chance of acquiring capital and all which depends on capital has opened before classes which formerly passed their lives in a dull round of ignorance and drudgery. This chance has brought with it the same alternative which accompanies every other opportunity offered to mortals. Those who were wise and able to profit by the chance succeeded grandly; those who were negligent or unable to profit by it suffered proportionately. The result has been wide inequalities of wealth within the industrial classes. The net result, however, for all, has been the cheapening of luxuries and a vast extension of physical enjoyment. The appetite for enjoyment has been awakened and nourished in classes which formerly never missed what they never thought of, and it has produced eagerness for material good, discontent, and impatient ambition. This is the reverse side of that eager uprising of the industrial classes which is such a great force in modern life. The chance is opened to advance, by industry, prudence, economy, and emigration, to the possession of capital; but the way is long and tedious. The impatience for enjoyment and the thirst for luxury which we have mentioned are the greatest foes to the accumulation of capital; and there is a still darker side of the picture when we come to notice that those who yield to the impatience to enjoy, but who see others outstrip them, are led to malice and envy. Mobs arise which manifest the most savage and senseless disposition to burn and destroy what they cannot enjoy. We have already had evidence, in more than one country, that such a wild disposition exists and needs only opportunity to burst into activity.

The origin of socialism, which is the extreme development of the sentimental philosophy, lies in the undisputed facts which I described at the outset. The socialist regards this misery as the fault of society. He thinks that we can organize society as we like and that an organization can be devised in which poverty and misery shall disappear. He goes further even than this. He assumes that men have artificially organized society as it now exists. Hence if anything is disagreeable or hard in the present state of society it follows, on that view, that the task of organizing society has been imperfectly and badly performed, and that it needs to be done over again. These are the assumptions with which the socialist starts, and many socialists seem also to believe that if they can destroy belief in an Almighty God who is supposed to have made the world such as it is, they will then have overthrown the belief that there is a fixed order in human nature and human life which man can scarcely alter at all, and, if at all, only infinitesimally.

The truth is that the social order is fixed by laws of nature precisely analogous to those of the physical order. The most that man can do is by ignorance and self-conceit to mar the operation of social laws. The evils of society are to a great extent the result of the dogmatism and self-interest of statesmen, philosophers, and ecclesiastics who in past time have done just what the socialists now want to do. Instead of studying the natural laws of the social order, they assumed that they could organize society as they chose, they made up their minds what kind of a society they wanted to make, and they planned their little measures for the ends they had resolved upon. It will take centuries of scientific study of the facts of nature to eliminate from human society the mischievous institutions and traditions which the said statesmen, philosophers, and ecclesiastics have introduced into it. Let us not, however, even then delude ourselves with any impossible hopes. The hardships of life would not be eliminated if the laws of nature acted directly and without interference. The task of right living forever changes its form, but let us not imagine that that task will ever reach a final solution or that any race of men on this earth can ever be emancipated from the necessity of industry, prudence, continence, and temperance if they are to pass their lives prosperously. If you believe the contrary you must suppose that some men can come to exist who shall know nothing of old age, disease, and death.

The socialist enterprise of reorganizing society in order to change what is harsh and sad in it at present is therefore as impossible, from the outset, as a plan for changing the physical order. I read the other day a story in which a man dreamt that somebody had invented an application of electricity for eradicating certain facts from the memory. Just think of it! What an emancipation to the human race, if a man could so emancipate himself from all those incidents in his past life which he regrets! Let there no longer be such a thing as remorse or vain regret! It would be half as good as finding a fountain of eternal youth. Or invent us a world in which two and two could make five. Two two-dollar notes could then pay five dollars of debts.

They say that political economy is a dismal science and that its doctrines are dark and cruel. I think the hardest fact in human life is that two and two cannot make five; but in sociology while people will agree that two and two cannot make five, yet they think that it might somehow be possible by adjusting two and two to one another in some way or other to make two and two equal to four and one-tenth.

I have shown how men emerge from barbarism only by the use of capital and why it is that, as soon as they begin to use capital, if there is liberty, there will be inequality. The socialist looking at these facts says that it is capital which produces the inequality. It is the inequality of men in what they get out of life which shocks the socialist. He finds enough to criticize in the products of past dogmatism and bad statesmanship to which I have alluded, and the program of reforms to be accomplished and abuses to be rectified which the socialists have set up have often been admirable. It is their analysis of the situation which is at fault. Their diagnosis of the social disease is founded on sectarian assumptions, not on the scientific study of the structure and functions of the social body. In attacking capital they are simply attacking the foundations of civilization, and every socialistic scheme which has ever been proposed, so far as it has lessened the motives to saving or the security of capital, is anti-social and anti-civilizing.

Rousseau, who is the great father of the modern socialism, laid accusation for the inequalities existing amongst men upon wheat and iron. What he meant was that wheat is a symbol of agriculture, and when men took to agriculture and wheat diet they broke up their old tribal relations, which were partly communistic, and developed individualism and private property. At the same time agriculture called for tools and machines, of which iron is a symbol; but these tools and machines are capi-

tal. Agriculture, individualism, tools, capital were, according to Rousseau's ideas, the causes of inequality. He was, in a certain way, correct, as we have already seen by our own analysis of the facts of the social order. When human society reached the agricultural stage machinery became necessary. Capital was far more important than on the hunting or pastoral stage, and the inequalities of men were developed with great rapidity, so that we have a Humboldt, a Newton, or a Shakespeare at one end of the scale and a Digger Indian at the other. The Humboldt or Newton is one of the highest products produced by the constant selection and advance of the best part of the human race, *viz.*, those who have seized every chance of advancing; and the Digger Indian is a specimen of that part of the race which withdrew from the competition clear back at the beginning and has consequently never made any advance beyond the first superiority of man to beasts. Rousseau, following the logic of his own explanation of the facts, offered distinctly as the cure for inequality a return to the hunting stage of life as practiced by the American Indians. In this he was plainly and distinctly right. If you want equality you must not look forward for it on the path of advancing civilization. You may go back to the mode of life of the American Indian, and, although you will not then reach equality, you will escape those glaring inequalities of wealth and poverty by coming down to a comparative equality, that is, to a status in which all are equally miserable. Even this, however, you cannot do without submitting to other conditions which are far more appalling than any sad facts in the existing order of society. The population of Massachusetts is about two hundred to the square mile; on the hunting stage Massachusetts could not probably support, at the utmost, five to the square mile; hence to get back to the hunting stage would cost the reduction of the population to two and a half where there are now one hundred. In Rousseau's day people did not even know that this question of the power of land to support population was to be taken into account.

Socialists find it necessary to alter the definition of capital in order to maintain their attacks upon it. Karl Marx, for instance, regards capital as an accumulation of the differences which a merchant makes between his buying price and his selling price. It is, according to him, an accumulation of the differences which the employer gains between what he pays to the employees for making the thing and what he obtains for it from the consumer. In this view of the matter the capitalist employer is a pure parasite, who has fastened on the wage-receiving employee without need or reason and is levying toll on industry. All socialistic writers follow, in different degrees, this conception of capital. If it is true, why do not I levy on some workers somewhere and steal this difference in the product of their labor? Is it because I am more honest or magnanimous than those who are capitalist-employers? I should not trust myself to resist the chance if I had it. Or again, let us ask why, if this conception of the origin of capital is correct, the workmen submit to a pure and unnecessary imposition. If this notion were true, co-operation in production would not need any effort to bring it about; it would take an army to keep it down. The reason why it is not possible for the first comer to start out as an employer of labor is that capital is a prerequisite to all industry. So soon as men pass beyond the stage of life in which they live, like beasts, on the spontaneous fruits of the earth, capital must precede every productive enterprise. It would lead me too far away from my present subject to elaborate this statement as it deserves and perhaps as it needs, but I may say that there is no sound political economy and es-

pecially no correct conception of wages which is not based on a complete recognition of the character of capital as necessarily going before every industrial operation. The reason why co-operation in production is exceedingly difficult, and indeed is not possible except in the highest and rarest conditions of education and culture amongst artisans, is that workmen cannot undertake an enterprise without capital, and that capital always means the fruits of prudence and self-denial already accomplished. The capitalist's profits, therefore, are only the reward for the contribution he has made to a joint enterprise which could not go on without him, and his share is as legitimate as that of the hand-worker.

The socialist assails particularly the institution of bequest or hereditary property, by which some men come into life with special protection and advantage. The right of bequest rests on no other grounds than those of expediency. The love of children is the strongest motive to frugality and to the accumulation of capital. The state guarantees the power of bequest only because it thereby encourages the accumulation of capital on which the welfare of society depends. It is true enough that inherited capital often proves a curse. Wealth is like health, physical strength, education, or anything else which enhances the power of the individual; it is only a chance; its moral character depends entirely upon the use which is made of it. Any force which, when well used, is capable of elevating a man, will, if abused, debase him in the same proportion. This is true of education, which is often and incorrectly vaunted as a positive and purely beneficent instrumentality. An education ill used makes a man only a more mischievous scoundrel, just as an education well used makes him a more efficient, good citizen and producer. So it is with wealth; it is a means to all the higher developments of intellectual and moral culture. A man of inherited wealth can gain in youth all the advantages which are essential to high culture, and which a man who must first earn the capital cannot attain until he is almost past the time of life for profiting by them. If one should believe the newspapers, one would be driven to a philosophy something like this: it is extremely praiseworthy for a man born in poverty to accumulate a fortune; the reason why he wants to secure a fortune is that he wants to secure the position of his children and start them with better advantages than he enjoyed himself; this is a noble desire on his part, but he really ought to doubt and hesitate about so doing because the chances are that he would do far better for his children to leave them poor. The children who inherit his wealth are put under suspicion by it; it creates a presumption against them in all the activities of citizenship.

Now it is no doubt true that the struggle to win a fortune gives strength of character and a practical judgment and efficiency which a man who inherits wealth rarely gets, but hereditary wealth transmitted from generation to generation is the strongest instrument by which we keep up a steadily advancing civilization. In the absence of laws of entail and perpetuity it is inevitable that capital should speedily slip from the hold of the man who is not fit to possess it, back into the great stream of capital, and so find its way into the hands of those who can use it for the benefit of society.

The love of children is an instinct which, as I have said before, grows stronger with advancing civilization. All attacks on capital have, up to this time, been shipwrecked on this instinct. Consequently the most rigorous and logical socialists have always been led sooner or later to attack the family. For, if bequest should be abolished, parents would give their property to their children in their own life-time; and so it be-comes a logical necessity to substitute some sort of communistic or socialistic life for family life, and to educate children in masses without the tie of parentage. Every socialistic theory which has been pursued energetically has led out to this consequence. I will not follow up this topic, but it is plain to see that the only equality which could be reached on this course would be that men should be all equal to each other when they were all equal to swine.

Socialists are filled with the enthusiasm of equality. Every scheme of theirs for securing equality has destroyed liberty. The student of political philosophy has the antagonism of equality and liberty constantly forced upon him. Equality of possession or of rights and equality before the law are diametrically opposed to each other. The object of equality before the law is to make the state entirely neutral. The state, under that theory, takes no cognizance of persons. It surrounds all, without distinctions, with the same conditions and guarantees. If it educates one, it educates all—black, white, red, or yellow; Jew or Gentile; native or alien. If it taxes one, it taxes all, by the same system and under the same conditions. If it exempts one from police regulations in home, church, and occupation, it exempts all. From this statement it is at once evident that pure equality before the law is impossible. Some occupations must be subjected to police regulation. Not all can be made subject to militia duty even for the same limited period. The exceptions and special cases furnish the chance for abuse. Equality before the law, however, is one of the cardinal principles of civil liberty, because it leaves each man to run the race of life for himself as best he can. The state stands neutral but benevolent. It does not undertake to aid some and handicap others at the outset in order to offset hereditary advantages and disadvantages, or to make them start equally. Such a notion would belong to the false and spurious theory of equality which is socialistic. If the state should attempt this it would make itself the servant of envy. I am entitled to make the most I can of myself without hindrance from anybody, but I am not entitled to any guarantee that I shall make as much of myself as somebody else makes of himself.

The modern thirst for equality of rights is explained by its historical origin. The mediaeval notion of rights was that rights were special privileges, exemptions, franchises, and powers given to individuals by the king; hence each man had just so many as he and his ancestors had been able to buy or beg by force or favor, and if a man had obtained no grants he had no rights. Hence no two persons were equal in rights and the mass of the population had none. The theory of natural rights and of equal rights was a revolt against the mediaeval theory. It was asserted that men did not have to wait for a king to grant them rights; they have them by nature, or in the nature of things, because they are men and members of civil society. If rights come from nature, it is inferred that they fall like air and light on all equally. It was an immense step in advance for the human race when this new doctrine was promulgated. Its own limitations and errors need not now be pointed out. Its significance is plain, and its limits are to some extent defined when we note its historical origin.

I have already shown that where these guarantees exist and where there is liberty, the results cannot be equal, but with all liberty there must go responsibility. If I take my own way I must take my own consequences; if it proves that I have made a mistake, I cannot be allowed to throw the consequences on my neighbor. If my neighbor is a free man and resents interference from me he must not call on me to bear the consequences of his mistakes. Hence it

is plain that liberty, equality before the law, responsibility, individualism, monogamy, and private property all hold together as consistent parts of the same structure of society, and that an assault on one part must sooner or later involve an assault on all the others.

To all this must be added the political element in socialism. The acquisition of some capital—the amount is of very subordinate importance—is the first and simplest proof that an individual possesses the industrial and civil virtues which make a good citizen and a useful member of society. Political power, a century ago, was associated more or less, even in the United States, with the possession of land. It has been gradually extended until the suffrage is to all intents and purposes universal in North and South America, in Australia, and in all Europe except Russia and Turkey. On this system political control belongs to the numerical majority, limited only by institutions. It may be doubted, if the terms are taken strictly and correctly, whether the non-capitalists outnumber the capitalists in any civilized country, but in many cities where capital is most collected they certainly do. The powers of government have been abused for ages by the classes who possessed them to enable kings, courtiers, nobles, politicians, demagogues, and their friends to live in exemption from labor and self-denial, that is, from the universal lot of man. It is only a continuation of the same abuse if the new possessors of power attempt to employ it to secure for themselves the selfish advantages which all possessors of power have taken. Such a course would, however, overthrow all that we think has been won in the way of making government an organ of justice, peace, order, and security, without respect of persons; and if those gains are not to be lost they will have to be defended, before this century closes, against popular majorities, especially in cities, just as they had to be won in a struggle with kings and nobles in the centuries past.

The newest socialism is, in its method, political. The essential feature of its latest phases is the attempt to use the power of the state to realize its plans and to secure its objects. These objects are to do away with poverty and misery, and there are no socialistic schemes yet proposed, of any sort, which do not, upon analysis, turn out to be projects for curing poverty and misery by making those who have share with those who have not. Whether they are paper-money schemes, tariff schemes, subsidy schemes, internal improvement schemes, or usury laws, they all have this in common with the most vulgar of the communistic projects, and the errors of this sort in the past which have been committed in the interest of the capitalist class now furnish precedents, illustration, and encouragement for the new category of demands. The latest socialism divides into two phases: one which aims at centralization and despotism—believing that political form more available for its purposes; the other, the anarchical, which prefers to split up the state into townships, or "communes," to the same end. The latter furnishes the true etymology and meaning of "communism" in its present use, but all socialism, in its second stage, merges into a division of property according to the old sense of communism.

It is impossible to notice socialism as it presents itself at the present moment without pointing out the immense mischief which has been done by sentimental economists and social philosophers who have thought it their professional duty, not to investigate and teach the truth, but to dabble in philanthropy. It is in Germany that this development has been most marked, and as a consequence of it the judgment and sense of the whole people in regard to political and social questions have been corrupted. It is remarkable that the country whose learned men have wrought so much for every other science, especially by virtue of their scientific method and rigorous critical processes, should have furnished a body of social philosophers without method, discipline, or severity of scholarship, who have led the nation in pursuit of whims and dreams and impossible desires. Amongst us there has been less of it, for our people still possess enough sterling sense to reject sentimental rubbish in its grosser forms, but we have had and still have abundance of the more subtle forms of socialistic doctrine, and these open the way to the others. We may already see the two developments forming a congenial alliance. We have also our writers and teachers who seem to think that "the weak" and "the poor" are terms of exact definition; that government exists, in some especial sense, for the sake of the classes so designated; and that the same classes (whoever they are) have some especial claim on the interest and attention of the economist and social philosopher. It may be believed that, in the opinion of these persons, the training of men is the only branch of human effort in which the labor and care should be spent, not on the best specimens but on the poorest.

It is a matter of course that a reactionary party should arise to declare that universal suffrage, popular education, machinery, free trade, and all the other innovations of the last hundred years are all a mistake. If any one ever believed that these innovations were so many clear strides towards the millennium, that they involve no evils or abuses of their own, that they tend to emancipate mankind from the need for prudence, caution, forethought, vigilance —in short, from the eternal struggle against evil—it is not strange that he should be disappointed. If any one ever believed that some "form of government" could be found which would run itself and turn out the pure results of abstract peace, justice, and righteousness without any trouble to anybody, he may well be dissatisfied. To talk of turning back, however, is only to enhance still further the confusion and danger of our position. The world cannot go back. Its destiny is to go forward and to meet the new problems which are continually arising. Under our so-called progress evil only alters its forms, and we must esteem it a grand advance if we can believe that, on the whole, and over a wide view of human affairs, good has gained a hair's breadth over evil in a century. Popular institutions have their own abuses and dangers just as much as monarchical or aristocratic institutions. We are only just finding out what they are. All the institutions which we have inherited were invented to guard liberty against the encroachments of a powerful monarch or aristocracy, when these classes possessed land and the possession of land was the greatest social power. Institutions must now be devised to guard civil liberty against popular majorities, and this necessity arises first in regard to the protection of property, the first and greatest function of government and element in civil liberty. There is no escape from any dangers involved in this or any other social struggle save in going forward and working out the development. It will cost a struggle and will demand the highest wisdom of this and the next generation. It is very probable that some nations—those, namely, which come up to this problem with the least preparation, with the least intelligent comprehension of the problem, and under the most inefficient leadership—will suffer a severe check in their development and prosperity; it is very probable that in some nations the development may lead through revolution and bloodshed; it is very probable that in some nations the consequence may be a reaction towards arbitrary power.

In every view we take of it, it is clear that the general abolition of slavery has only cleared the way for a new social problem of far wider scope and far greater difficulty. It seems to me, in fact, that this must always be the case. The conquest of one difficulty will only open the way to another; the solution of one problem will only bring man face to face with another. Man wins by the fight, not by the victory, and therefore the possibilities of growth are unlimited, for the fight has no end.

The progress which men have made in developing the possibilities of human existence has never been made by jumps and strides. It has never resulted from the schemes of philosophers and reformers. It has never been guided through a set program by the wisdom of any sages, statesmen, or philanthropists. The progress which has been made has been won in minute stages by men who had a definite task before them, and who have dealt with it in detail, as it presented itself, without referring to general principles, or attempting to bring it into logical relations to an *a priori* system. In most cases the agents are unknown and cannot be found. New and better arrangements have grown up imperceptibly by the natural effort of all to make the best of actual circumstances. In this way, no doubt, the new problems arising in our modern society must be solved or must solve themselves. The chief safeguard and hope of such a development is in the sound instincts and strong sense of the people, which, although it may not reason closely, can reject instinctively. If there are laws—and there certainly are such—which permit the acquisition of property without industry, by cunning, force, gambling, swindling, favoritism, or corruption, such laws transfer property from those who have earned it to those who have not. Such laws contain the radical vice of socialism. They demand correction and offer an open field for reform because reform would lie in the direction of greater purity and security of the right of property. Whatever assails that right, or goes in the direction of making it still more uncertain whether the industrious man can dispose of the fruits of his industry for his own interests exclusively, tends directly towards violence, bloodshed, poverty, and misery. If any large section of modern society should rise against the rest for the purpose of attempting any such spoliation, either by violence or through the forms of law, it would destroy civilization as it was destroyed by the irruption of the barbarians into the Roman Empire.

The sound student of sociology can hold out to mankind, as individuals or as a race, only one hope of better and happier living. That hope lies in an enhancement of the industrial virtues and of the moral forces which thence arise. Industry, self-denial, and temperance are the laws of prosperity for men and states; without them advance in the arts and in wealth means only corruption and decay through luxury and vice. With them progress in the arts and increasing wealth are the prime conditions of an advancing civilization which is sound enough to endure. The power of the human race to-day over the conditions of prosperous and happy living are sufficient to banish poverty and misery if it were not for folly and vice. The earth does not begin to be populated up to its power to support population on the present stage of the arts; if the United States were as densely populated as the British Islands, we should have 1,000,000,000 people here. If, therefore, men were willing to set to work with energy and courage to subdue the outlying parts of the earth, all might live in plenty and prosperity. But if they insist on remaining in the slums of great cities or on the borders of an old society, and on a comparatively exhausted soil, there is no device of economist or statesman which can prevent them from falling victims to poverty and misery or from succumbing in the competition of life to those who have greater command of capital. The socialist or philanthropist who nourishes them in their situation and saves them from the distress of it is only cultivating the distress which he pretends to cure.

Friedrich Nietzsche

To most readers, Friedrich Nietzsche is a profoundly shocking writer. He meant to be. To read him with profit, therefore, requires both imagination and sympathy. If the reader is willing to make the necessary effort, he may be surprised (and somewhat disconcerted) to find himself agreeing with the author from time to time. Like Marx, Nietzsche (1844-1900) rejected wholesale the economic, political, social, and intellectual ideals of the nineteenth century. But unlike Marx, he did so in the interest, not of an ideal classless society, but of a society in which class distinctions would be hardened into caste barriers. To most of us, who are committed to the ideals of democratic society, such an ideal is repugnant, both politically and morally. It is a simple task, too, to draw a line from Nietzsche to Hitler, especially when we remember Nietzsche's use of such terms as "Supermen" and "the great blonde beasts." Nevertheless, whatever the similarities between them—and there can be no doubt that Hitler borrowed from Nietzsche—to reduce Nietzsche to nothing more than a proto-Nazi would be to miss the complexities and subtleties of his thinking that make him worth our consideration. In fact, a good case could be made for the thesis that, had he been living under the Nazis, he would have turned his back with contempt and disgust on Hitler and all his works. Rather than dismiss Nietzsche without a hearing, then, we may be able to discern in his writings the reaction of a highly sensitive and intelligent, though arrogant, personality to the far-from-ideal realities of nineteenth-century industrial civilization.

The following is from Nietzsche's unfinished *The Will to Power*. The order of sections has been altered slightly.

THE WILL TO POWER

854. In this age of universal suffrage, in which everybody is allowed to sit in judgment upon everything and everybody, I feel compelled to re-establish the order of rank.

855. Quanta of power alone determine rank and distinguish rank: nothing else does.

. . .

857. I distinguish between the type which represents ascending life and that which represents decay, decomposition and weakness. Ought one to suppose that the question of rank between these two types can be at all doubtful?

. . .

859. The advantages of standing detached from one's age.—Detached from the two movements, that of individualism and that of collectivist morality; for even the first

THE WILL TO POWER, Friedrich Nietzsche, trans. Anthony M. Ludovici (Edinburgh: T. N. Foulis, 1910), I: 295-298, 382-384; II: 188-189, 206-207, 295-298, 305-307, 310-314, 316-317, 327-328, 344-345, 361-364, 386-387. Courtesy of George Allen & Unwin Ltd.

does not recognize the order of rank, and would give one individual the same freedom as another. My thoughts are not concerned with the degree of freedom which should be granted to the one or to the other or to all, but with the degree of power which the one or the other should exercise over his neighbour or over all; and more especially with the question to what extent a sacrifice of freedom, or even enslavement, may afford the basis for the cultivation of a *superior* type. In plain words: *how could one sacrifice the development of mankind* in order to assist a higher species than man to come into being.

. . .

861. It is necessary for *higher* men to declare war upon the masses! In all directions mediocre people are joining hands in order to make themselves masters. Everything that pampers, that softens, and that brings the "people" or "woman" to the front, operates in favour of universal suffrage—that is to say, the dominion of *inferior* men. But we must make reprisals, and draw the whole state of affairs (which commenced in

Europe with Christianity) to the light of day and to judgment.

862. A teaching is needed which is strong enough to work in a *disciplinary* manner; it should operate in such a way as to strengthen the strong and to paralyse and smash up the world-weary.

The annihilation of declining races. The decay of Europe. The annihilation of slave-tainted valuations. The dominion of the world as a means to the rearing of a higher type. The annihilation of the humbug which is called morality (Christianity as a hysterical kind of honesty in this regard: Augustine, Bunyan). The annihilation of universal suffrage—that is to say, that system by means of which the lowest natures prescribe themselves as a law for higher natures. The annihilation of mediocrity and its prevalence.

.   .   .

866. It is *necessary* to show *that a counter-movement is inevitably associated* with any increasingly economical consumption of men and mankind, and with an ever more closely involved "machinery" of interests and services. I call this counter-movement the *separation of the luxurious surplus of mankind:* by means of it a stronger kind, a higher type, must come to light, which has other conditions for its origin and for its maintenance than the average man. My concept, my metaphor for this type is, as you know, the word "Superman." Along the first road, which can now be completely surveyed, arose adaptation, stultification, higher Chinese culture, modesty in the instincts, and satisfaction at the sight of the belittlement of man—a kind of *stationary level of mankind*. If ever we get that inevitable and imminent, general control of the economy of the earth, then mankind *can* be used as machinery and find its best purpose in the service of this economy—as an enormous piece of clock-work consisting of ever smaller and ever more subtly adapted wheels; then all the domi-

nating and commanding elements will become ever more superfluous; and the whole gains enormous energy, while the individual factors which compose it represent but small modicums of strength and of *value*. To oppose this dwarfing and adaptation of man to a specialised kind of utility, a reverse movement is needed—the procreation of the *synthetic* man who *embodies* everything and *justifies* it; that man for whom the turning of mankind into a machine is a first condition of existence, for whom the rest of mankind is but soil on which he can devise his *higher mode* of existence.

He is in need of the *opposition* of the masses, of those who are "levelled down"; he requires that feeling of distance from them; he stands upon them, he lives on them. This higher form of *aristocracy* is the form of the future. From the moral point of view, the collective machinery above described, that solidarity of all wheels, represents the most extreme example in the *exploitation of mankind:* but it presupposes the existence of those for whom such an exploitation would have some *meaning*. Otherwise it would signify, as a matter of fact, merely the general depreciation of the type man,—a *retrograde phenomenon* on a grand scale.

Readers are beginning to see what I am combating—namely, *economic* optimism: as if the general welfare of everybody must necessarily increase with the growing self-sacrifice of everybody. The very reverse seems to me to be the case, *the self-sacrifice of everybody amounts to a collective loss;* man becomes *inferior*—so that nobody knows what end this monstrous purpose has served. A wherefore? a *new* wherefore? —this is what mankind requires.

.   .   .

881. *Concerning the order of rank*.—What is it that constitutes the *mediocrity* of the typical man? That he does not understand that things necessarily have *their other side;* that he combats evil conditions as if

they could be dispensed with; that he will not take the one with the other; that he would fain obliterate and erase the *specific character of a thing*, of a circumstance, of an age, and of a person, by calling only a portion of their qualities good, and suppressing the remainder. The "desirability" of the mediocre is that which we others combat: their *ideal* is something which shall no longer contain anything harmful, evil, dangerous, questionable, and destructive. We recognise the reverse of this: that with every growth of man his other side must grow as well; that the highest man, if such a concept be allowed, would be that man who would represent *the antagonistic character of existence* most strikingly, and would be its glory and its only justification. . . . Ordinary men may only represent a small corner and nook of this natural character; they perish the moment the multifariousness of the elements composing them, and the tension between their antagonistic traits, increases: but this is the prerequisite for *greatness in man*. That man should become better and at the same time more evil, is my formula for this inevitable fact.

The majority of people are only piecemeal and fragmentary examples of man: only when all these creatures are jumbled together does one whole man arise. Whole ages and whole peoples in this sense, have a fragmentary character about them; it may perhaps be part of the economy of human development that man should develop himself only piecemeal. But, for this reason, one should not forget that the only important consideration is the rise of the synthetic man; that inferior men, and by far the great majority of people, are but rehearsals and exercises out of which here and there *a whole man* may arise; a man who is a human milestone, and who indicates how far mankind has advanced up to a certain point. Mankind does not advance in a straight line; often a type is attained which is again lost (for instance, with all the efforts of three hundred years, we have not reached the *men of the Renaissance* again, and in addition to this we must not forget that the man of the Renaissance was already behind his brother of classical antiquity).

      .   .   .

874. *The degeneration of the ruler and of the ruling classes* has been the cause of all the great disorders in history! Without the Roman Caesars and Roman society, Christianity would never have prevailed.

When it occurs to inferior men to doubt whether higher men exist, then the danger is great! It is then that men finally discover that there are virtues even among inferior, suppressed, and poor-spirited men, and that everybody is equal before God: which is the *non plus ultra* of all confounded nonsense that has ever appeared on earth! For in the end higher men begin to measure themselves according to the standard of virtues upheld by the slaves— and discover that they are "proud," etc., and that all their higher qualities should be condemned.

When Nero and Caracalla stood at the helm, it was then that the paradox arose: "The lowest man is of more value than that one on the throne!" And thus the path was prepared for an *image of God* which was as remote as possible from the image of the mightiest,—God on the Cross!

      .   .   .

871. . . . It was the appalling barbarity of morality which was principally responsible in the Middle Ages for the compulsory recourse to a veritable "league of virtue"— and this was coupled with an equally appalling exaggeration of all that which constitutes the value of man. Militant "civilisation" (taming) is in need of all kinds of irons and tortures in order to maintain itself against terrible and beast-of-prey natures.

In this case, confusion, although it may

have the most nefarious influences, is quite natural: that which *men of power and will are able to demand of themselves* gives them the standard for what they may also allow themselves. Such natures are the very opposite of the *vicious* and the *unbridled;* although under certain circumstances they may perpetrate deeds for which an inferior man would be convicted of vice and intemperance.

In this respect the concept, *"all men are equal before God,"* does an extraordinary amount of harm; actions and attitudes of mind were forbidden which belonged to the prerogative of the strong alone, just as if they were in themselves unworthy of man. All the tendencies of strong men were brought into disrepute by the fact that the defensive weapons of the most weak (even of those who were weakest towards themselves) were established as a standard of valuation.

The confusion went so far that precisely the great *virtuosos* of life (whose self-control presents the sharpest contrast to the vicious and the unbridled) were branded with the most opprobrious names. Even to this day people feel themselves compelled to disparage a Caesar Borgia: it is simply ludicrous. The Church has anathematised German Kaisers owing to their vices: as if a monk or a priest had the right to say a word as to what a Frederick II. should allow himself. Don Juan is sent to hell: this is very *naïf.* Has anybody ever noticed that all interesting men are lacking in heaven? . . . This is only a hint to the girls, as to where they may best find salvation. If one think at all logically, and also have a profound insight into that which makes a great man, there can be no doubt at all that the Church has dispatched all "great men" to Hades—its fight is *against* all "greatness in man."

.   .   .

877. The Revolution made Napoleon possible: that is its justification. We ought to desire the anarchical collapse of the whole of our civilisation if such a reward were to be its result. Napoleon made nationalism possible: that is the latter's excuse.

The value of a man (apart, of course, from morality and immorality: because with these concepts a man's *worth* is not even skimmed) does not lie in his utility; because he would continue to exist even if there were nobody to whom he could be useful. And why could not that man be the very pinnacle of manhood who was the source of the worst possible effects for his race: so high and so superior, that in his presence everything would go to rack and ruin from envy?

.   .   .

373. *The origin of moral values.*—Selfishness has as much value as the physiological value of him who possesses it. Each individual represents the whole course of Evolution, and he is not, as morals teach, something that begins at his birth. If he represent the *ascent* of the line of mankind, his value is, in fact, very great; and the concern about his maintenance and the promoting of his growth may even be extreme. (It is the concern about the promise of the future in him which gives the well-constituted individual such an extraordinary right to egoism.) If he represent *descending* development, decay, chronic sickening, he has little worth: and the greatest fairness would have him take as little room, strength, and sunshine as possible from the well-constituted. In this case society's duty is to *suppress egoism* (for the latter may sometimes manifest itself in an absurd, morbid, and seditious manner): whether it be a question of the decline and pining away of single individuals or of whole classes of mankind. A morality and a religion of "love," the *curbing* of the self-affirming spirit, and a doctrine encouraging patience, resignation, helpfulness, and co-operation in word and deed may be of the highest value within the confines of such classes, even in the eyes of

their rulers: for it restrains the feelings of rivalry, of resentment, and of envy,—feelings which are only too natural in the bungled and the botched,—and it even deifies them under the ideal of humility, of obedience, of slave-life, of being ruled, of poverty, of illness, and of lowliness. This explains why the ruling classes (or races) and individuals of all ages have always upheld the cult of unselfishness, the gospel of the lowly and of "God on the Cross."

The preponderance of an altruistic way of valuing is the result of a consciousness of the fact that one is botched and bungled. Upon examination, this point of view turns out to be: "I am not worth much," simply a psychological valuation; more plainly still: it is the feeling of impotence, of the lack of the great self-asserting impulses of power (in muscles, nerves, and ganglia). This valuation gets translated, according to the particular culture of these classes, into a moral or religious principle (the pre-eminence of religious or moral precepts is always a sign of low culture): it tries to justify itself in spheres whence, as far as it is concerned, the notion "value" hails. The interpretation by means of which the Christian sinner tries to understand himself, is an attempt at justifying his lack of power and of self-confidence: he prefers to feel himself a sinner rather than feel bad for nothing: it is in itself a symptom of decay when interpretations of this sort are used at all. In some cases the bungled and the botched do not look for the reason of their unfortunate condition in their own guilt (as the Christian does), but in society: when, however, the Socialist, the Anarchist, and the Nihilist are conscious that their existence is something for which some one must be *guilty*, they are very closely related to the Christian, who also believes that he can more easily endure his ill ease and his wretched constitution when he has found some one whom he can hold *responsible* for it. The instinct of *revenge* and *resentment*

appears in both cases here as a means of enduring life, as a self-preservative measure, as is also the favour shown to *altruistic* theory and practice. The *hatred of egoism*, whether it be one's own (as in the case of the Christian), or another's (as in the case of the Socialists), thus appears as a valuation reached under the predominance of revenge; and also as an act of prudence on the part of the preservative instinct of the suffering, in the form of an increase in their feelings of co-operation and unity. . . . At bottom, as I have already suggested, the discharge of resentment which takes place in the act of judging, rejecting, and punishing egoism (one's own or that of others) is still a self-preservative measure on the part of the bungled and the botched. In short; the cult of altruism is merely a particular form of egoism, which regularly appears under certain definite physiological circumstances.

When the Socialist, with righteous indignation, cries for "justice," "rights," "equal rights," it only shows that he is oppressed by his inadequate culture, and is unable to understand why he suffers: he also finds pleasure in crying;—if he were more at ease he would take jolly good care not to cry in that way: in that case he would seek his pleasure elsewhere. The same holds good of the Christian: he curses, condemns, and slanders the "world"—and does not even except himself. But that is no reason for taking him seriously. In both cases we are in the presence of invalids who feel better for crying, and who find relief in slander.

· · ·

753. I am opposed to Socialism because it dreams ingenuously of "goodness, truth, beauty, and equal rights" (anarchy pursues the same ideal, but in a more brutal fashion).

I am opposed to parliamentary government and the power of the press, because they are the means whereby cattle become masters.

• • •

755. Socialists are particularly ridiculous in my eyes, because of their absurd optimism concerning the "good man" who is supposed to be waiting in their cupboard, and who will come into being when the present order of society has been overturned and has made way for natural instincts. But the opposing party is quite as ludicrous, because it will not see the act of violence which lies beneath every law, the severity and egoism inherent in every kind of authority. "I and my kind will rule and prevail. Whoever degenerates will be either expelled or annihilated."— This was the fundamental feeling of all ancient legislation. The idea of a higher order of man is hated much more profoundly than monarchs themselves. Hatred of aristocracy always uses hatred of monarchy as a mask.

• • •

926. *Against John Stuart Mill.*— I abhor the man's vulgarity when he says: "What is right for one man is right for another"; "Do not to others that which you would not that they should do unto you." Such principles would fain establish the whole of human traffic *upon mutual services*, so that every action would appear to be a cash payment for something done to us. The hypothesis here is ignoble to the last degree: it is taken for granted that there is some sort of *equivalence in value between my actions and thine;* the most personal value of an action is simply cancelled in this manner (that part of an action which has no equivalent and which cannot be remunerated). "Reciprocity" is a piece of egregious vulgarity; the mere fact that what I do *cannot* and *may* not be done by another, that there is *no such thing* as *equivalence* (except in those *very select circles* where one actually has one's equal, *inter-pares*), that in a really profound sense a man never requites because he is something *unique* in himself and can only do *unique* things,—this fundamental conviction contains the cause of

aristocratic aloofness from the mob, because the latter believes in equality, and *consequently* in the feasibility of equivalence and "reciprocity."

• • •

728. The very notion, "living organism," implies that there must be growth,—that there must be a striving after an extension of power, and therefore a process of absorption of other forces. Under the drowsiness brought on by moral narcotics, people speak of the right of the individual to *defend* himself; on the same principle one might speak of his right to *attack:* for *both*—and the latter more than the former—are necessities where all living organisms are concerned: aggressive and defensive egoism are not questions of choice or even of "free will," but they are fatalities of life itself.

In this respect it is immaterial whether one have an individual, a living body, or "an advancing society" in view. The right to punish (or society's means of defence) has been arrived at only through a misuse of the word "right": a right is acquired only by contract,—but self-defence and self-preservation do not stand upon the basis of a contract. A people ought at least, with quite as much justification, to be able to regard its lust of power, either in arms, commerce, trade, or colonisation, as a right— the right of growth, perhaps. . . . When the instincts of a society ultimately make it give up war and renounce conquest, it is decadent: it is ripe for democracy and the rule of shopkeepers. In the majority of cases, it is true, assurances of peace are merely stupefying draughts.

• • •

898. *The strong of the future.*— To what extent necessity on the one hand and accident on the other have attained to conditions from which a *stronger species* may be reared: this we are now able to understand and to bring about consciously; we

can now create those conditions under which such an elevation is possible.

Hitherto education has always aimed at the utility of society: *not* the greatest possible utility for the future, but the utility of the society actually extant. What people required were "instruments" for this purpose. Provided the *wealth of forces were greater*, it would be possible to think of a draft being made upon them, the aim of which would not be the utility of society, but some future utility.

The more people grasped to what extent the present form of society was in such a state of transition as sooner or later to be *no longer able to exist for its own sake*, but only as a means in the hands of a stronger race, the more *this task would have to be brought forward*.

The increasing belittlement of man is precisely the impelling power which leads one to think of the cultivation of a *stronger race:* a race which would have a surplus precisely there where the dwarfed species was weak and growing weaker (will, responsibility, self-reliance, the ability to postulate aims for one's self).

The means would be those which history teaches: *isolation* by means of preservative interests which would be the reverse of those generally accepted; exercise in transvalued valuations; distance as pathos; a clean conscience in what to-day is most despised and most prohibited.

The *levelling* of the mankind of Europe is the great process which should not be arrested; it should even be accelerated. The necessity of *cleaving gulfs*, of *distance*, of the *order of rank*, is therefore imperative; but not the necessity of retarding the process above mentioned.

This *levelled-down* species requires justification as soon as it is attained: its justification is that it exists for the service of a higher and sovereign race which stands upon it and can only be elevated upon its shoulders to the task which it is destined to perform. Not only a ruling race whose task would be consummated in ruling alone; but a race with *vital spheres* of its own, with an overflow of energy for beauty, bravery, culture, and manners, even for the most abstract thought; a yea-saying race which would be able to allow itself every kind of great luxury—strong enough to be able to dispense with the tyranny of the imperatives of virtue, rich enough to be in no need of economy or pedantry; beyond good and evil; a forcing-house for rare and exceptional plants.

. . .

957. The question, and at the same time the task, is approaching with hesitation, terrible as Fate, but nevertheless inevitable: how shall the earth as a whole be ruled? And to what end shall man as a whole—no longer as a people or as a race—be reared and trained?

Legislative moralities are the principal means by which one can form mankind, according to the fancy of a creative and profound will: provided, of course, that such an artistic will of the first order gets the power into its own hands, and can make its creative will prevail over long periods in the form of legislation, religions, and morals. At present, and probably for some time to come, one will seek such colossally creative men, such really great men, as I understand them, in vain: they will be lacking, until, after many disappointments, we are forced to begin to understand why it is they are lacking, and that nothing bars with greater hostility their rise and development, at present and for some time to come, than that which is now called *the* morality in Europe. Just as if there were no other kind of morality, and could be no other kind, than the one we have already characterised as herd-morality. It is this morality which is now striving with all its power to attain to that green-meadow happiness on earth, which consists in security, absence of danger, ease, facilities for livelihood, and, last but not least, "if all goes well," even hopes to dispense with all kinds of shepherds and bell-wethers. The two doctrines which it preaches most universally are "equality of rights" and "pity for all sufferers"—and it even regards suffering itself as something which must be got rid of absolutely. That such ideas may be modern leads one to think very poorly of modernity. He, however, who has reflected deeply concerning the question, how and where the plant man has hitherto grown most vigorously, is forced to believe that this has always taken place under the opposite conditions; that to this end the danger of the situation has to increase enormously, his inventive faculty and dissembling powers have to fight their way up under long oppression and compulsion, and his will to life has to be increased to the unconditioned will to power, to overpower: he believes that danger, severity, violence, peril in the street and in the heart, inequality of rights, secrecy, stoicism, seductive art, and devilry of every kind—in short, the opposite of all gregarious desiderata—are necessary for the elevation of man. Such a morality with opposite designs, which would rear man upwards instead of to comfort and mediocrity; such a morality, with the intention of producing a ruling caste—the future lords of the earth—must, in order to be taught at all, introduce itself as if it were in some way correlated to the prevailing moral law, and must come forward under the cover of the latter's words and forms. But seeing that, to this end, a host of transitionary and deceptive measures must be discovered, and that the life of a single individual stands for almost nothing in view of the accomplishment of such lengthy tasks and aims, the first thing that must be done is to rear *a new kind* of man in whom the duration of the necessary will and the necessary instincts is guaranteed for many generations. This must be a new kind of ruling species and caste—this ought to be quite as clear as the somewhat lengthy and not easily expressed consequences of this thought. The aim should be to prepare a *transvaluation of values* for a particularly strong kind of man, most highly gifted in intellect and will, and, to this end, slowly and cautiously to liberate in him a whole host of slandered instincts hitherto held in check: whoever meditates about this problem belongs to us, the free spirits.

. . . .

464. . . . But in what direction may I turn with any hope of finding my particular kind of philosophers themselves, or at least *my yearning for new philosophers?* In that direction, alone, where a *noble* attitude of mind prevails, an attitude of mind which believes in slavery and in manifold orders or rank, as the prerequisites of any high degree of culture. In that direction, alone, where a *creative* attitude of mind prevails, an attitude of mind which does not regard the world of happiness and repose, the "Sabbath of Sabbaths" as an end to be desired, and which, even in peace, honours the means which lead to new wars; an attitude of mind which would prescribe laws for the future, which for the sake of the future would treat everything that exists to-day with harshness and even tyranny; a daring and "immoral" attitude of mind, which would wish to see both the good and the evil qualities in man developed to their fullest extent, because it would feel itself able to put each in its right place—that is to say, in that place in which each would need the other. But what prospect has he of finding what he seeks, who goes in search of philosophers to-day? Is it not probable that, even with the best Diogenes-lantern in his hand, he will wander about by night and day in vain? This age is possessed of the *opposite* instincts. What it wants, above all, is comfort; secondly, it wants publicity and the deafening din of actors' voices, the big drum which appeals to its Bank-Holiday

tastes; thirdly, that every one should lie on his belly in utter subjection before the greatest of all lies—which is "the equality of men"—and should honour only those virtues which *make men equal and place them in equal positions*. But in this way, the rise of the philosopher, as I understand him, is made completely impossible—despite the fact that many may regard the present tendencies as rather favourable to his advent. As a matter of fact, the whole world mourns, to-day, the hard times that philosophers *used* to have, hemmed in between the fear of the stake, a guilty conscience, and the presumptuous wisdom of the Fathers of the Church: but the truth is, that precisely these conditions were *ever so much more favourable* to the education of a mighty, extensive, subtle, rash, and daring intellect than the conditions prevailing to-day. At present another kind of intellect, the intellect of the demagogue, of the actor, and perhaps of the beaver- and ant-like scholar too, finds the best possible conditions for its development. But even for artists of a superior calibre the conditions are already far from favourable: for does not every one of them, almost, perish owing to his want of discipline? They are no longer tyrannised over by an outside power—by the tables of absolute values enforced by a Church or by a monarch: and thus they no longer learn to develop their "inner tyrant," their *will*. And what holds good of artists also holds good, to a greater and more fatal degree, of philosophers. Where, then, are free spirits to be found to-day? Let any one show me a free spirit to-day!

.   .   .

997. I teach that there are higher and lower men, and that a single individual may under certain circumstances justify whole millenniums of existence—that is to say, a wealthier, more gifted, greater, and more complete man, as compared with innumerable imperfect and fragmentary men.

998. Away from rulers and rid of all bonds, live the highest men: and in the rulers they have their instruments.

999. *The order of rank:* he who *determines* values and leads the will of millenniums, and does this by leading the highest natures—he *is the highest man*.

1000. I fancy I have divined some of the things that lie hidden in the soul of the highest man; perhaps every man who has divined so much must go to ruin: but he who has seen the highest man must do all he can to make him *possible*.

Fundamental thought: we must make the future the standard of all our valuations—and not seek the laws for our conduct behind us.

1001. Not "mankind," but *Superman* is the goal!

Theodore Roosevelt

At the Mount Rushmore National Memorial in South Dakota the chief attraction for sightseers is the mountainside converted into portraits of four American presidents. Presumably these four were the greatest chief executives of the United States —at least if this was not the criterion, one can wonder what the standards might have been. Certainly cragginess of physiognomy could hardly have swayed the final decision, else it would have been impossible to ignore Andrew Jackson. In any event, there at Rushmore are the four gigantic heads—Washington, Jefferson, Lincoln, and Theodore Roosevelt.

At the time the following essay was first published (1899), Theodore Roosevelt (1858-1919) was Governor of the state of New York, and was soon to become Vicepresident of the United States and then, with the assassination of William McKinley (1901), President. At other points in his career he was a successful Police Commissioner of New York City and Assistant Secretary of the Navy. He resigned the latter post to head the cavalry unit known as the Roosevelt Roughriders (even though they left their horses in the United States when they sailed to Cuba during the Spanish-American War). During World War I, he bedeviled Woodrow Wilson for permission to raise and command his own division of troops. At one point, he even recommended himself for the Congressional Medal of Honor.

A prolific writer, Theodore Roosevelt published many volumes of history, travel, big-game hunting, memoirs, and general reflections, of which the essay, "Expansion and Peace," is one. While the views that Roosevelt expresses in the essay may seem naive as well as distasteful to the reader of today, we must remember that he was far from alone in his advocacy of a righteous war, a morally justified conquest of "primitive" people. The latter part of the nineteenth century is replete with discussions of the "white man's burden," to use Rudyard Kipling's phrase, in defense of imperialism. Kipling and Joseph Chamberlain in England, Jules Ferry in France, Leopold II in Belgium, and many others were all convinced that it was their duty to carry their civilization to the backward peoples of the world.

In the essay that follows, Roosevelt reveals a belligerency of character that is perhaps expressed best in his famous "big-stick" policy. Nevertheless, it should not be forgotten that, for his efforts in bringing to an end the Russo-Japanese War of 1904-1905, Roosevelt was awarded the Nobel Peace Prize in 1906.

EXPANSION AND PEACE

It was the gentlest of our poets who wrote:

"Be bolde! Be bolde! and everywhere, Be
  bolde";
Be not too bold! Yet better the excess
Than the defect; better the more than less.

Longfellow's love of peace was profound;
but he was a man, and a wise man, and he
knew that cowardice does not promote
peace, and that even the great evil of war
may be a less evil than cringing to iniquity.

Captain Mahan, than whom there is not
in the country a man whom we can more
appropriately designate by the fine and
high phrase, "a Christian gentleman," and
who is incapable of advocating wrongdoing
of any kind, national or individual, gives
utterance to the feeling of the great majority of manly and thoughtful men
when he denounces the great danger of
indiscriminate advocacy of peace at any
price, because "it may lead men to tam-
per with iniquity, to compromise with
unrighteousness, soothing their conscience
with the belief that war is so entirely wrong
that beside it no other tolerated evil is
wrong. Witness Armenia and witness Crete.
War has been avoided; but what of the national consciences that beheld such iniquity
and withheld the hand?"

Peace is a great good; and doubly harmful, therefore, is the attitude of those who
advocate it in terms that would make it
synonymous with selfish and cowardly
shrinking from warring against the existence
of evil. The wisest and most far-seeing champions of peace will ever remember that,
in the first place, to be good it must be
righteous, for unrighteous and cowardly
peace may be worse than any war; and, in
the second place, that it can often be ob-

THE WORKS OF THEODORE ROOSEVELT (New York,
1900), XII, 23-36.

tained only at the cost of war. Let me take
two illustrations:

The great blot upon European international morality in the closing decade of
this century has been not a war, but the
infamous peace kept by the joint action
of the great powers, while Turkey inflicted
the last horrors of butchery, torture, and
outrage upon the men, women, and children of despairing Armenia. War was
avoided; peace was kept; but what a peace!
Infinitely greater human misery was inflicted
during this peace than in the late wars of
Germany with France, of Russia with Turkey; and this misery fell, not on armed men,
but upon defenceless women and children,
upon the gray-beard and the stripling no
less than upon the head of the family; and
it came, not in the mere form of death or
imprisonment, but of tortures upon men,
and, above all, upon women, too horrible to
relate—tortures of which it is too terrible
even to think. Moreover, no good resulted
from the bloodshed and misery. Often this
is the case in a war, but often it is not the
case. The result of the last Turko-Russian
war was an immense and permanent increase
of happiness for Bulgaria, Servia, Bosnia, and
Herzegovina. These provinces became independent or passed under the dominion of
Austria, and the advantage that accrued
to them because of this expansion of the
domain of civilization at the expense of
barbarism has been simply incalculable. This
expansion produced peace, and put a stop
to the ceaseless, grinding, bloody tyranny
that had desolated the Balkans for so many
centuries. There are many excellent people who have praised Tolstoi's fantastic religious doctrines, his fantastic advocacy of
peace. The same quality that makes the
debauchee and the devotee alternate in
certain decadent families, the hysterical

development which leads to violent emotional reaction in a morbid nature from vice to virtue, also leads to the creation of Tolstoi's "Kreutzer Sonata" on the one hand, and of his unhealthy peace-mysticism on the other. A sane and healthy mind would be as incapable of the moral degradation of the novel as of the decadent morality of the philosophy. If Tolstoi's countrymen had acted according to his moral theories they would now be extinct, and savages would have taken their place. Unjust war is a terrible sin. It does not nowadays in the aggregate cause anything like the misery that is caused in the aggregate by unjust dealing toward one's neighbors in the commercial and social world; and to condemn all war is just as logical as to condemn all business and all social relations, as to condemn love and marriage because of the frightful misery caused by brutal and unregulated passion. If Russia had acted upon Tolstoi's philosophy, all its people would long ago have disappeared from the face of the earth, and the country would now be occupied by wandering tribes of Tartar barbarians. The Armenian massacres are simply illustrations on a small scale of what would take place on the very largest scale if Tolstoi's principles became universal among civilized people. It is not necessary to point out that the teaching which would produce such a condition of things is fundamentally immoral.

Again, peace may come only through war. There are men in our country who seemingly forget that at the outbreak of the Civil War the great cry raised by the opponents of the war was the cry for peace. One of the most amusing and most biting satires written by the friends of union and liberty during the Civil War was called the "New Gospel of Peace," in derision of this attitude. The men in our own country who, in the name of peace, have been encouraging Aguinaldo and his people to shoot down our soldiers in the Philippines might profit not a little if they would look back to the days of the bloody draft riots, which were deliberately incited in the name of peace and free speech, when the mob killed men and women in the streets and burned orphan children in the asylums as a protest against the war. Four years of bloody struggle with an armed foe, who was helped at every turn by the self-styled advocates of peace, were needed in order to restore the Union; but the result has been that the peace of this continent has been effectually assured. Had the shortsighted advocates of peace for the moment had their way, and secession become an actual fact, nothing could have prevented a repetition in North America of the devastating anarchic warfare that obtained for three quarters of a century in South America after the yoke of Spain was thrown off. We escaped generations of anarchy and bloodshed, because our fathers who upheld Lincoln and followed Grant were men in every sense of the term, with too much common sense to be misled by those who preached that war was always wrong, and with a fund of stern virtue deep in their souls which enabled them to do deeds from which men of oversoft natures would have shrunk appalled.

Wars between civilized communities are very dreadful, and as nations grow more and more civilized we have every reason, not merely to hope, but to believe that they will grow rarer and rarer. Even with civilized peoples, as was shown by our own experience in 1861, it may be necessary at last to draw the sword rather than to submit to wrong-doing. But a very marked feature in the world-history of the present century has been the growing infrequency of wars between great civilized nations. The Peace Conference at the Hague is but one of the signs of this growth. I am among those who believe that much was accomplished at that conference, and I am proud of the leading position taken in the conference by our delegates. Incidentally I may mention that the testimony is unanimous that they were able to take this leading position chiefly because we had just emerged victorious from our most righteous war with Spain. Scant attention is paid to the weakling or the coward who babbles of peace; but due heed is given to the strong man with the sword girt on thigh who preaches peace, not from ignoble motives, not from fear or distrust of his own powers, but from a deep sense of moral obligation.

The growth of peacefulness between nations, however, has been confined strictly to those that are civilized. It can only come when both parties to a possible quarrel feel the same spirit. With a barbarous nation peace is the exceptional condition. On the border between civilization and barbarism war is generally normal because it must be under the conditions of barbarism. Whether the barbarian be the Red Indian on the frontier of the United States, the Afghan on the border of British India, or the Turkoman who confronts the Siberian Cossack, the result is the same. In the long run civilized man finds he can keep the peace only by subduing his barbarian neighbor; for the barbarian will yield only to force, save in instances so exceptional that they may be disregarded. Back of the force must come fair dealing, if the peace is to be permanent. But without force fair dealing usually amounts to nothing. In our history we have had more trouble from the Indian tribes whom we pampered and petted than from those we wronged; and this has been true in Siberia, Hindustan, and Africa.

Every expansion of civilization makes for peace. In other words, every expansion of a great civilized power means a victory for law, order, and righteousness. This has been the case in every instance of expansion during the present century, whether the expanding power were France or England, Russia or America. In every instance the expansion has been of benefit, not so much to the power nominally benefited, as to the whole world. In every instance the result proved that the expanding power was doing a duty to civilization far greater and more important than could have been done by any stationary power. Take the case of France and Algiers. During the early decades of the present century piracy of the most dreadful description was rife on the Mediterranean, and thousands of civilized men were yearly dragged into slavery by the Moorish pirates. A degrading peace was purchased by the civilized powers by the payment of tribute. Our own country was one among the tributary nations which thus paid blood-money to the Moslem bandits of the sea. We fought occasional battles with them; and so, on a larger scale, did the English. But peace did not follow, because the country was not occupied. Our last payment was made in 1830, and the reason it was the last was because in that year the French conquest of Algiers began. Foolish sentimentalists, like those who wrote little poems in favor of the Mahdists against the English, and who now write little essays in favor of Aguinaldo against the Americans, celebrated the Algerian freebooters as heroes who were striving for liberty against the invading French. But the French continued to do their work; France expanded over Algiers, and the result was that piracy on the Mediterranean came to an end, and Algiers has thriven as never before in its history. On an even larger scale the same thing is true of England and the Soudan. The expansion of England throughout the Nile valley has been an incalculable gain for civilization. Any one who reads the writings of the Austrian priests and laymen who were prisoners in the Soudan under the Mahdi will realize that when England crushed him and conquered the Soudan she conferred a priceless boon upon humanity and made the civilized world her debtor. Again, the same thing is true of the Russian advance in Asia. As in the Soudan the English conquest is followed by peace, and the endless massacres of the Mahdi are stopped forever, so the Russian conquest of the khanates of central Asia meant the cessation of the barbarous warfare under which Asian civilization had steadily withered away since the days of Genghis Khan, and the substitution in its place of the reign of peace and order. All civilization has been the gainer by the advance of France in North Africa; as it has been the gainer by the advance of England in both Asia and Africa, both Canada and Australia. Above all, there has been the greatest possible gain in peace. The rule of law and of order has succeeded to the rule of barbarous and bloody violence. Until the great civilized nations stepped in there was no chance for anything but such bloody violence.

So it has been in the history of our own country. Of course our whole national history has been one of expansion. Under Washington and Adams we expanded westward to the Mississippi; under Jefferson we expanded across the continent to the mouth of the Columbia; under Monroe we expanded into Florida; and then into Texas and California; and finally, largely through the instrumentality of Seward, into Alaska; while under every administration the process of expansion in the great plains and the Rockies has continued with growing rapidity. While we had a frontier the chief feature of frontier life was the endless war between the settlers and the red men. Sometimes the immediate occasion for the war was to be found in the conduct of the whites and sometimes in that of the reds, but the ultimate cause was simply that we were in contact with a country held by savages or half-savages.

Where we abut on Canada there is no danger of war, nor is there any danger where we abut on the well-settled regions of Mexico. But elsewhere war had to continue until we expanded over the country. Then it was succeeded at once by a peace which has remained unbroken to the present day. In North America, as elsewhere throughout the entire world, the expansion of a civilized nation has invariably meant the growth of the area in which peace is normal throughout the world.

The same will be true of the Philippines. If the men who have counseled national degradation, national dishonor, by urging us to leave the Philippines and put the Aguinaldan oligarchy in control of those islands, could have their way, we should merely turn them over to rapine and bloodshed until some stronger, manlier power stepped in to do the task we had shown ourselves fearful of performing. But, as it is, this country will keep the islands and will establish therein a stable and orderly government, so that one more fair spot of the world's surface shall have been snatched from the forces of darkness. Fundamentally the cause of expansion is the cause of peace.

With civilized powers there is but little danger of our getting into war. In the Pacific, for instance, the great progressive, colonizing nations are England and Germany. With England we have recently begun to feel ties of kindness as well as of kinship, and with her our relations are better than ever before; and so they ought to be with Germany. Recently affairs in Samoa have been straightened out, although there we suffered from the worst of all types of government, one in which three powers had a joint responsibility (the type, by the way, which some of the anti-imperialists actually advocated our introducing in the Philippines, under the pretence of rendering them neutral). This was accomplished very largely because the three nations set good-humoredly to work to come to an agreement which would do justice to all. In the preliminary negotiations the agents of America and Germany were Mr. Tripp and Baron Sternburg. No difficulty can ever arise between Germany and the United States which will not be settled with satisfaction to both, if the negotiations are conducted by such representatives of the two powers as these two men. What is necessary is to approach the subject, not with a desire to get ahead of one another, but to do even and exact justice, and to put into operation a scheme which will work, while scrupulously conserving the honor and interest of all concerned.

Nations that expand and nations that do not expand may both ultimately go down, but the one leaves heirs and a glorious memory, and the other leaves neither. The Roman expanded, and he has left a memory which has profoundly influenced the history of mankind, and he has further left as the heirs of his body, and, above all, of his tongue and culture, the so-called Latin peoples of Europe and America. Similarly to-day it is the great expanding peoples who bequeath to the future ages the great memories and material results of their achievements, and the nations which shall have sprung from their loins, England standing as the archetype and best exemplar of all such mighty nations. But the peoples that do not expand leave, and can leave, nothing behind them.

It is only the warlike power of a civilized people that can give peace to the world.

The Arab wrecked the civilization of the Mediterranean coasts, the Turk wrecked the civilization of southeastern Europe, and the Tartar desolated from China to Russia and to Persia, setting back the progress of the world for centuries, solely because the civilized nations opposed to them had lost the great fighting qualities, and, in becoming overpeaceful, had lost the power of keeping peace with a strong hand. Their passing away marked the beginning of a period of chaotic barbarian warfare. Those whose memories are not so short as to have forgotten the defeat of the Greeks by the Turks, of the Italians by the Abyssinians, and the feeble campaigns waged by Spain against feeble Morocco, must realize that at the present moment the Mediterranean coasts would be overrun either by the Turks or by the Soudan Mahdists if these warlike barbarians had only to fear those southern European powers which have lost the fighting edge. Such a barbarian conquest would mean endless war; and the fact that nowadays the reverse takes place, and that the barbarians recede or are conquered, with the attendant fact that peace follows their retrogression or conquest, is due solely to the power of the mighty civilized races which have not lost the fighting instinct, and which by their expansion are gradually bringing peace into the red wastes where the barbarian peoples of the world hold sway.

Sidney Webb

Throughout the nineteenth century there were many voices of discontent and protest. Men sensed that something had gone wrong with the economic and industrial system in which Adam Smith had foreseen the wealth of nations. A few, like William Morris, inventor and social reformer, and Thomas Carlyle, novelist, historian, and biographer, advocated a return to a bygone age when craftsmen had produced useful goods that were aesthetically appealing to the consumer and psychologically satisfying to the workman. Karl Marx protested against "bourgeois capitalism," insisting that workers should (and ultimately would) reap the full rewards of their efforts by displacing those who had exploited them. But many thinkers felt that Marxian economics was inadequate, largely because of its philosophical anarchism. Georges Sorel, for example, turned to syndicalism, which provided an organizational principle and a system of production and distribution that were more acceptable to the logical mind. Various forms of socialism—democratic, fascist, utopian, national, Christian—were also suggested.

The form of socialism most acceptable to the democratic tradition was developed in England by a group of young intellectuals. They named their association the Fabian Society, after the Roman general, Fabius, who frustrated Hannibal by avoiding battle until Hannibal's resources were virtually exhausted. These young social reformers dedicated themselves to the cause of evolutionary social control over the means of production. They rejected the need for force and violence in achieving this goal, insisting that it could be attained by gradual means, by operating *within* the framework of contemporary legal institutions.

George Bernard Shaw, playwright, H. G. Wells, novelist, and Sidney and Beatrice Webb, historians, were among the most persistent and persuasive of the Fabians. The Webbs (who later became Lord and Lady Passfield) were particularly tireless in their efforts to sway people to their beliefs. The following selection is from one of many socialist tracts written by Sidney Webb (1859-1947). Here he expresses the Fabians' objections to revolution and their conviction that a new and better world can be achieved naturally, without recourse to violence.

SOCIALISM: TRUE AND FALSE

I do not know whether many of those here present are aware that we celebrate to-night what may be regarded as the tenth anniversary of the foundation of this Society. It was on the 4th of January, 1884, that the little group which had been for some months discussing the Regen-

SOCIALISM: TRUE AND FALSE, Sidney Webb, Fabian Tract #51 (London: The Fabian Society, 1894), pp. 3-10. Courtesy of the Fabian Society.

eration of the World and a Fellowship of the New Life, formally adopted the title of the Fabian Society—thereby indicating, as I take it, an underlying suspicion that the Devil of Individualism was not to be driven out by any short and sharp encounter, but that it behoved all true believers to watch and wait and diligently equip themselves for a warfare which must necessarily be harassing and protracted. But though we took the title of the Fabian Society in January, 1884, it was two or three years before we had quite found out what our instinctive choice of a title really portended. In 1884 the Fabian Society, like the other Socialist organizations, had its enthusiastic young members—aye, and old ones, too—who placed all their hopes on a sudden tumultuous uprising of a united proletariat, before whose mighty onrush, kings, landlords and capitalists would go down like ninepins, leaving society quietly to re-sort itself into Utopia. The date for this Social Revolution was sometimes actually fixed for 1889, the centenary of the opening of the French Revolution. I remember myself that one of our friends, in his zeal that the rural districts might not be forgotten, printed and circulated a proposal that a few Socialist missionaries should buy a gipsy caravan and live in it "until the Revolution," an event evidently to be expected before the ensuing winter!

It was against all thinking and teaching of this catastrophic kind that the Society gradually came to set its face—not, as I believe, because we were any less in earnest in our warfare against existing evils, or less extreme in our remedies, but because we were sadly and sorrowfully driven to the conclusion that no sudden or simultaneous transformation of society from an Individualist to a Collectivist basis was possible, or even thinkable.

On the other hand we had but little sympathy with schemes for the regeneration of mankind by the establishment of local Utopias, whether in Cumberland or in Chili. To turn our back on the Unearned Increment and the Machine Industry seemed a poor way of conquering them. We had no faith in the recuperative qualities of spade husbandry or in any devices for dodging the Law of Rent. In short, we repudiated the common assumption that Socialism was necessarily bound up with Insurrectionism on the one hand or Utopianism on the other, and we set to work to discover for ourselves and to teach to others how practically to transform England into a Social Democratic Commonwealth.

Well, we have I hope, all learnt a great deal since 1884, but everything that has happened during these ten years has strengthened our faith in the fundamental principles of our association. If I might speak in the name of our members, I should say that we are more than ever convinced of the utter impossibility of what may be called Catastrophic Socialism, and all its attendant heresies. Nor have we seen reason to alter our distrust of separate Socialist communities, in whatever specious new form the old idea may clothe itself. For ten years we have held on our course, turning neither to Insurrectionism on the one hand nor to Utopianism on the other.

If now I briefly recall to your mind some instances of the progress of Collectivist ideas during these years, I trust that no one will imagine that I am attempting to claim that progress as the work of the Fabian Society, or indeed of any society whatever. Nothing is more futile than to endeavor to ascribe the exact cause and origin of a general intellectual movement, of which we are, indeed, ourselves a product. The seeds of the Socialist harvest of the last few years were sown by the great thinkers and teachers of the last two generations; and it would be idle to attempt to measure the exact influence of any one of them in the transformation of ideas amid which we are now living.

I take as a starting point, not 1884, but the year 1880, which as I conceive, approximately marks the turning of thought.

Fourteen years ago we may almost say that an unsystematic and empirical Individualism reigned supreme. Not in one political party alone, or in one class of society, but in all alike, we find the assumption that the functions of government ought to be reduced to the barest minimum; that free competition, leading as it was supposed to the survival of the fittest, was the only sure foundation of a prosperous State; and that the incessant private "war which leads each man to strive to place himself on another's shoulders and to remain there," was, on the whole, a benevolent dispensation of Providence, and part of the "Laws of Nature," not impiously to be interfered with.

The Liberal Party, at that time almost exclusively dominated by the manufacturers and the Whig families, was living on the remnants of the political reputation of the Manchester School. A vague belief in the saving grace of non-intervention abroad and *laisser faire* at home, was vitalised only by a practical programme of the extension of household franchise to the counties. To the rising desire for social reform it presented no more hopeful solution than the economic negations of Nassau Senior and Fawcett. The object of all social reforms, authorised or unauthorised, was to enable the artisan to become a small capitalist, and the laborer a small landowner. "Three acres and a cow" in the country had its analogue in schemes of leasehold enfranchisement in the towns. As an alternative to the existing order of squires and captains of industry, we had offered to us a millennium of peasant proprietors and small masters. It is needless to enlarge upon the self-complacency with which both Liberal and Conservative capitalists delighted in reminding the working-men of all the future possibilities of self-advancement, when land

should be "free," food cheap, and industrial competition unrestricted. The epics of this faith have been written by that unconscious corrupter of youth, Mr. Samuel Smiles, and are still fresh in the memories of most of us.

In 1880, Mr. Gladstone came into power on a wave of popular indignation against atrocities in Bulgaria, which dispensed with the necessity for any programme of social reforms in England. The political Radicals, swept along by the same wave, were too busy denouncing international aggression to be effective even on fiscal reform and political democracy, beyond which they had practically no vision. The Conservatives, less traditionally bound to Administrative Nihilism, had just consolidated the Factory Acts, but their leaders had been so far perverted as deliberately to leave the whole range of sweated trades outside the effective scope of the law and to give up all attempts to shorten the hours of labor. Even the working-men had been permeated by the same policy. The Trade Union leaders could think of only four trivial amendments to propose to the Factory Bill of 1878. The Trade Union Congress of those years asked for practically nothing but an Employers' Liability Bill. In 1879 there were a great many more unemployed than there have ever been since, but no responsible authority thought of anything but charity or poor relief for them. Free Education, Extension of the Factory Acts, Limitation of the Hours of Labor, Expansion of Municipal Activity, though all proposed long before, seem, in 1880, scarcely to have entered the heads of any of those who were leading either the Conservative, the Liberal, the Radical, or the Trade Union forces. But more striking even than this barrenness of programme was the total absence of any systematic view of politics as a whole. In this respect the most advanced statesmen of fourteen years ago stood in marked contrast with the Philosophic

Radicals of the first half of the century. I will quote the significant comment of a shrewd critic of Mr. Gladstone's Cabinet:

James Mill and his school had two characteristics which have not always marked energetic types of Liberalism, and perhaps do not mark them in our own day. The advanced Liberals of his time were systematic, and they were constructive. They surveyed society and institutions as a whole; they connected their advocacy of political and legal changes with theories of human nature; they considered the great art of government in connection with the character of man, his proper education, his potential capacities. They could explain in the large dialect of a definite scheme what were their aims and whither they were going. . . . Is there any such approach to a body of systematic political thought in our own day? We cannot say that there is.[1]

Now, in estimating the progress of Collectivism between 1880 and 1894, I do not propose to make any parade of the membership and influence of the various Socialist societies, which seem to me to be, at the present time, far greater than at any previous period. Nor will I recite a long list of bills which have been passed during the last fourteen years, and claim these as more or less triumphs of Collectivism. It would be easy to argue that the multiplication of municipal gasworks is an unconscious adoption of the principle of Socialism, just as the freeing of schools and the building of gratuitous libraries is of that of Communism. But what we Socialists are aiming at is not to secure this or that reform, still less to put this or that party into power, but to convert the great mass of the English people to our own views. We are trying to satisfy the ordinary man, not merely that most of the existing arrangements of society are fundamentally defective—for on that point the great majority have always been most painfully convinced—but also that the main principle of reform must be the substitution of Collective Ownership and Control for Individual Private Property in the means of production. In short, the Socialist task is to contribute to this generation the "body of systematic political thought," of which Mr. John Morley was in 1882 deploring the lack. Though we cannot count among our ranks any men of the calibre of Bentham and James Mill, though we have neither the wealth nor the position of the Philosophic Radicals of the first part of the century, yet I take it that the work set before us is analogous to theirs. The Socialists are the Benthamites of this generation. And if I had to sum up the effect upon the public mind of the Socialist propaganda of the past fourteen years, I could find no better description than that given of the work of the Benthamites.

"They produced," says a very competent observer,

a much more serious effect on public opinion than superficial inquirers perceived, or interested ones would acknowledge. The important practical effect was not made evident by converting and bringing over large numbers of political partisans from one banner or class to another, or by making them renounce one appellation and adopt another; but it was shown by affecting the conclusions of all classes, and inducing them, while they retained their old distinctive names, to reason after a new fashion, and according to principles wholly different from those to which they had been previously accustomed.[2]

It is, of course, especially in the economic and industrial field that we find this reasoning "after a new fashion, and according to principles wholly different from those to which they had been previously accustomed." It has become more and more plain that the facts of industrial life are "dead against" the realization of the individualist ideal of each man becoming his

[1] Mr. John Morley, in a review of Bain's "Life of James Mill," *Fortnightly Review* vol. xxxi, p. 503 (April, 1882).

[2] J. A. Roebuck.

own master. The Industrial Revolution, with its aggregation of production into ever larger enterprises, has rendered it practically impossible for five-sixths of the population to be anything but hired servants, dependent on the owners of land and capital for leave to earn a living. At the same time the spread of economic knowledge has made it clear that even the most virtuous artizan cannot dodge the law of rent; and he is therefore left face to face with the grim fact of a colossal tribute levied by ownership upon industry without any obligation on the part of the receivers to render social service in return. It is especially the growing understanding of this Ricardian law of rent which has revolutionized London politics, and has caused the hostile indifference with which the artizan in other centres is coming to regard both the great political parties. The outcome of this new ferment is the formation of an incipient Collectivist body of opinion among the great bulk of the younger men, the rising London party, and the new-born Labor Movement.

The political effect of this change of opinion is seen in the gradual transformation of party programmes, especially on the Land question. In the Liberal party the new Collectivist section is in direct antagonism to the "old gang." Its aim is not the subdivision of property, whether capital or land, but the control and administration of it by the representatives of the community. It has no desire to see the Duke of Bedford replaced by five hundred little Dukes of Bedford under the guise of enfranchised leaseholders, but prefers to assert the claim of the whole community to the land, and especially to that "unearned increment" of value which the whole community creates. It has no vain dream of converting the agricultural laborer into a freeholder, farming his own land, but looks to the creation of parish councils empowered to acquire land for communal owner-

ship, and to build cottages for the laborers to rent. The path to its town Utopia is that of Mr. Chamberlain's early career, though not of his political programme—unlimited municipalization of local public services and a wide extension of corporate activity. London in particular has caught up the old Birmingham cry of "High rates and a healthy city," but with a significant difference. Our modern economists tell us that the first source of public revenue for a rising city is the growing rental value of its site, which at present falls into private hands. Hence the new demand for the gradual municipalization by taxation of urban land values—a demand still so little understood by most of our statesmen that they fondly imagine it to have something to do with a division of rates between house-owner and occupier. It is coming to be remembered, in short, that Bentham himself, the great father of Political Radicalism, urged that taxation need not be limited to the supply of funds for the bare administrative expenses of the State, but that, wisely handled, it also supplied a means of gradually securing the great end of equality of opportunity to every citizen.

The typical young politician, who twenty years ago was a convinced Individualist quoting Mr. Herbert Spencer, is nowadays an empirical Collectivist of a practical kind. His face is turned away from the Individualist ideal of his fathers towards a period of ever-increasing collective action. Happily, however, he is no Utopian, and realizes that it is impossible all at once to take over the administration of the land and capital of the community. Where direct public administration is still impracticable, the public interest can only be secured by collective regulation of the conditions of labor, in order to prevent the Standard of Life of the workers from being degraded by private greed. And hence it is that the extremely valuable mantle shared by Robert Owen and Lord Shaftesbury, and despised by the older Liberals, is now the joint heritage of the Labor party and the Collectivist Radicals; Eight Hours Bills, practicable and impracticable, are the order of the day, and drastic proposals for the annihilation of "Sweating" excite the undisguised horror of the older members of both Liberal and Conservative parties. And since all this regulation and supervision of private enterprises is burdensome and expensive, the presumption of the younger politicians is distinctly against individual profit-making where it is possible to dispense with it. The best Government is no longer "that which governs least," but "that which can safely and advantageously administer most."

All this is encouraging progress for so short a period as fourteen years. But it amounts, of course, to no more than the preliminary steps in the conversion of England. Public opinion, in fact, is in "a fine state to begin on." Adhesion to Socialism is no longer a disqualification for a candidate. Politicians lend a willing ear to Socialist proposals. Now is the time to bring to bear a body of systematic and constructive political thought such as that with which the Philosophic Radicals won their great triumphs. The greatest need of the English Socialist Party at this moment is men and women of brains who will deliberately set themselves, by serious study, to work out the detailed application of Collectivist principles to the actual problems of modern life. We need to do a great deal more hard thinking in almost every department of our Socialist programme. I am appalled when I realize how little attention we have yet been able to pay to what I may call the Unsettled Questions of Democratic Administration.

To take, for instance, the pressing problem of the Unemployed. In my humble judgment no plan has yet been devised by which the fluctuations of work could be entirely prevented, or safe and profitable employment found for those rendered idle by no fault of their own. It is easy enough to demand that something should be done; and I entirely agree with agitating the subject; but something more than agitation is required. It is of no use urging remedies which can be demonstrably proved to be worse for the patient than the disease itself. I fear that if we were given full power to-morrow to deal with the unemployed all over England we should find ourselves hard put to it how to solve the problem. Or to turn to another field, in which practically nothing has yet been done. Have we any clear and decided view as to the relation between central and local authorities? How far do we wish to increase the power of the national administration at the expense of local governing bodies—to what extent, that is, will our Social-Democracy be consistent with local Home Rule? The Glasgow Town Council, for instance, is at this moment quarrelling with the Postmaster-General as to whether the telephone shall fall within the sphere of municipal or of national Socialism. It is evident that some departments of public administration can be best managed from one central office. It is, I suppose, equally evident that others must be administered locally, under some kind of central control. But which subjects should be local and which should be central—upon what principle the division should be made, and in what form and to what extent there should be a central control—these are problems to which, as far as I know, no solution has been found and very little serious thought been given.

I do not suggest that we Socialists are more ignorant than other people: on the contrary, the two puzzles that I have chosen are at present puzzles to the whole world. But the whole world is not equally interested with ourselves in getting a solution of them. Those who believe that nothing ought to be done for the unemployed are not likely to succeed in finding anything; and we can hardly expect those who object to any extension of Democracy to help us to solve the problems which it presents. It is we who must discover the answers to our own conundrums; and I do most seriously suggest that there is no more valuable field of work for any group of Socialists, no more fruitful service to the Socialist cause, than for them earnestly and persistently to study, in the light of the ascertained facts, some one of the many social problems to which we have to apply our Socialist faith. Depend upon it, the first step to getting what we want is a very clear and precise knowledge of what it is that we want.

But this want of precision in our thinking may easily do worse than merely delay our progress; there is, as it seems to me, a good deal of danger of its leading us positively astray from the Socialist goal. The circumstances of modern life are so complicated, the problems to be dealt with are so difficult, the need for prompt action is often so great that we may easily be led to take up schemes of reform which promise some immediate improvement on the present state of things, but which are not really in the line of advance towards a genuine Collectivism.

Here I venture on dangerous ground. But if we are to clear up our ideas, and apply our Socialist principles to the practical problems of life, we must definitely make up our mind between contrary ideals. If our aim is the transformation of England into a Social-Democracy, we must frankly accept the changes brought about by the Industrial Revolution, the factory system, the massing of population in great cities, the elaborate differentiation and complication of modern civilization, the subordination of the worker to the citizen, and of the individual to the community. We must rid ourselves resolutely of those schemes and projects of byegone Socialisms which have now passed out of date, as well as from the specious devices of Individualism in a new dress. All these I class together as Spurious Collectivism, making, in my view, not for social progress, but for reaction.

THE CONTEMPORARY WORLD

ANY HISTORIAN who tries to generalize about twentieth-century civilization faces two serious obstacles: lack of perspective and complexity of detail. Inevitably caught up in the events that he wishes to analyze, he must somehow free himself from them, stand back, and view them objectively and dispassionately. To achieve such detachment is not an easy task. The second obstacle is the tremendous complexity of his subject matter. Both in scope and detail, the data on which the historian of contemporary civilization must base his generalizations vastly exceed those of any earlier time. And yet it is possible at least to indicate the most significant features of our twentieth-century world.

When we glance at the history of our century so far, the events which first strike our eye are probably the two world wars, a fact that may lead us to conclude that we live in a period of almost constant warfare. But this is not a peculiarity of our own time, for the Western world has seldom been without war. What sets our time apart is not the *fact* of war so much as the *nature* of war. Twentieth-century warfare has tended to become total both in scope and intensity. While earlier wars were usually limited in geographical extent, our two, particularly the second, have been conducted on virtually a world-wide scale. Nor, like earlier conflicts, have their effects been limited primarily to a professional military class. Rather, the brunt of the devastation has often fallen directly upon civilians.

Although these two great wars have undoubtedly been the most dramatic episodes of the twentieth century, they have not been the most significant ones. Less obvious, but of more lasting effect on our civilization, are certain basic changes that have been in process constantly throughout the century, and even before. The details of these changes are almost infinitely complex, but the changes themselves can be divided into three major types—political, economic, and scientific-technological.

The most important political change of the twentieth century has been a shift of the center of power away from Western Europe. After hundreds of years of supremacy, Western Europe is no longer the political center of the world. Political power has moved in three main directions: to the United States, to Russia, and to Asia. Of these shifts of power, that to the United States appears least likely to cause either abrupt or major changes in the future course of world history and civilization. For we are basically a cultural extension of Western Europe, the direct heirs of her civilization. Russia, though closer geographically to Western Europe, is separated by greater cultural barriers. In all its historical contacts with the West,

Russia has remained half-alien. Even in periods when their leaders have deliberately copied the ways of the West, the Russians have retained their own, non-European, point of view. The rapid growth of Russia's power is even now causing changes in the lives of people in Europe, America, and elsewhere. The future will undoubtedly witness an increase in these changes. The twentieth century, finally, has witnessed a remarkable increase in the political power of Asia, primarily in Japan, China, and India. Although these countries do not equal either the United States or Russia in power today, it would be hazardous to predict either the limit of their potential or the effects that their increasing power will have on the future of our civilization.

We are in the midst, then, of a period of fundamental political change. This is an exciting time in which to live, and it is a time of uncertainty. The shifts in power that have already taken place have aroused concern in many Europeans, as well as Americans, who fear that the political ascendancy of non-Western peoples may mean the destruction of our civilization.

In economics, as in politics, the world today is undergoing basic and sometimes violent change. The capitalist system, which was developed in the West over several hundred years, and which reached its climax only in the late nineteenth century, seems now to be on the decline. Although capitalism has been under attack by its opponents from before the time of Marx, the most serious blow it has yet suffered was self-inflicted —the great depression of the thirties. While it has not been wholly rejected by any of the Western countries, as it has been by some of the non-Western nations, still capitalism has, particularly since the depression, been compromised and supplemented by non-capitalistic forms of economic organization. The current decline of capitalism poses serious problems: Has capitalism had its day, or will it recover? If the former, what kind of economic organization will replace it, and can the transition be accomplished without social cataclysm?

Finally, we are in the midst of a scientific-technological revolution. Although this revolution began as far back as the time of Copernicus, its pace has been greatly accelerated in recent years. It holds forth great promise for man's future, but it poses great dangers as well. And it is the dangers, symbolized by the term "ultimate weapon"—whether this be an intercontinental ballistics missile with a nuclear warhead or some even more fantastic creation of modern science and technology—that occupy our attention. The fact that man's greatest achievements in science, which have done so much to enrich human life, may be used as a means for extinguishing human life is a clear indication of the grave problems facing us today. These problems have not been created by science and technology; rather, they have sprung from the underlying political, economic, and social dislocations that plague our world.

None of the three changes that are in process in today's world, taken in itself, *need* be a cause for great concern. The shifts in political power could well lead to the end of an old era of national rivalries and the effective development of a new world-wide political organization. As for the decline of capitalism, it is far from complete, and in nations like Britain and the Scandinavian countries, non-capitalistic economic systems have been developed without either revolution or war. Turning to the achievements in science and technology, it is not even necessary to list the benefits that we have received from them. Why, then, do men today fear for the future of the human race? The answer lies mainly in the relationships between the three changes we have been discussing. Starting with the fact that the shifts in political power have generally benefited the non-Western at the expense of the Western world, adding to this the fact that the most powerful of these non-Western nations are anti-capitalistic, and concluding with the fact that weapons of great destructive force have been perfected and are now in production, we can easily understand why men are apprehensive of the future.

Our century is often called "the age of anxiety." With the experience of two world wars behind us and the threat of a third hanging over our heads, there is just cause for anxiety. What is perhaps more important than our emotional reactions to world events, though, is the way in which we attempt to deal with the problems these events raise. On this score, the record of twentieth-century civilization has been far from encouraging. The growth of totalitarianism, in Germany, Italy, and elsewhere, revealed a serious breakdown in the morale of Western Europe. The peoples of these countries, finding themselves unable to cope with the problems facing them, proved willing to give up their freedom and responsibility and to accept the authority of a dictator, provided he would insure their security. The quest for security is not a phenomenon peculiar to the twentieth century. Neither is absolute government. What is most disturbing in the recent history of Europe is the fact that people, instead of proving more jealous of their freedom than did those of the past, have too often shown themselves to be just the opposite. Although earlier forms of absolute government exercised virtually complete control over limited areas of social life, modern totalitarianism implies total control over all. In theory at least, every act that an individual performs and even every thought that he thinks are prescribed by the political leaders. And, though fascistic totalitarianism was almost completely destroyed by World War II, the communistic variety today dominates an even greater proportion of the world and its inhabitants.

What, then, of the future? What chance does our civilization have to survive? In the opinion of many sober analysts, our prospects are dim. Even without considering the possibility of annihilation in a third world war, these men see little hope for the survival of those ideals and institutions we have developed in the West since the time of the Greeks. The novelist, George Orwell, for example, in his book *Nineteen Eighty-Four*, visualizes the world a generation from now divided into three totalitarian superstates, in which all human freedom and dignity have been obliterated.

On the other hand, there are those who believe that man can survive the crises he faces and at the same time preserve the basic values he has developed in his historical past. Among the optimists are two twentieth-century philosophers, John Dewey and A.N. Whitehead, both of whom insist that we can solve the problems that lie ahead through the active and practical employment of our intelligence or reason. To develop the individual's intellectual potentialities, however, both agree on the necessity for education. But what kind of education? To this question everyone seems to have a different answer. Without attempting to give the final answer here, we merely suggest that one area of education that can contribute to man's ability to preserve his civilization for future generations is a knowledge and appreciation of that civilization's past.

Sigmund Freud

It is tempting to describe Sigmund Freud (1856-1939) as one of the last of the great eighteenth-century rationalists, for there are striking similarities between his thought and that of the *philosophes*. First, there is the assumption common to both that "knowledge is power," that once man knows the *why* of an event or relationship he can exercise rational control over it. In his lectures on the origin and development of psychoanalysis, Freud often concluded his descriptions of case histories with remarks such as, "When the memory of this scene was revived in hypnosis, the paralysis of the right arm, which had existed since the beginning of the illness, was cured and the treatment ended"; or "She remembered it during the treatment, reproduced the pathogenic moment with every sign of intense emotional excitement, and was cured by this treatment. . . ." Second, both Freud and the eighteenth-century *philosophes* accept John Locke's *tabula rasa*, his denial that men are born with innate ideas, although Freud put heavier emphasis on the nature and function of instincts, particularly biological, than did the earlier writers.

But to suggest such parallels tends to minimize the extraordinary contributions made by this Viennese physician. Freud first became interested in the problems of mental health in Vienna and later pursued the study of hysteria and hysterical symptoms in Paris. In 1893 he persuaded Dr. Joseph Breuer to collaborate on a work that later appeared as *Studien über Hysterie* (1895). From then until 1906, Freud worked on alone, perfecting his psychoanalytic techniques and substituting for hypnosis the major element of the new psychology—the technique of free association of ideas. After 1906, Freud was joined by an enthusiastic band of followers and disciples, including A. A. Brill, Carl Jung, Alfred Adler, and Ernest Jones. To the end of his long life Freud contin-

ued his studies, although they occasionally were impaired by profound disagreements with some of his younger colleagues. Freud retained his conviction that the most basic instinct in man was the desire to achieve sensory (sexual) pleasure, an instinct that automatically brought the individual into conflict with society.

This particular emphasis was minimized by Jung and Adler, who, though disagreeing with each other, agreed that Freud had over-simplified and over-stated his case.

The two selections that follow are taken from the unfinished *An Outline of Psychoanalysis*, Freud's last major work.

AN OUTLINE OF PSYCHOANALYSIS

Chapter One

THE PSYCHICAL APPARATUS

Psychoanalysis makes a basic assumption,[1] the discussion of which falls within the sphere of philosophical thought, but the justification of which lies in its results. We know two things concerning what we call our psyche or mental life: firstly, its bodily organ and scene of action, the brain (or nervous system), and secondly, our acts of consciousness, which are immediate data and cannot be more fully explained by any kind of description. Everything that lies between these two terminal points is unknown to us and, so far as we are aware, there is no direct relation between them. If it existed, it would at the most afford an exact localization of the processes of consciousness and would give us no help toward understanding them.

Our two hypotheses start out from these ends or beginnings of our knowledge.

The first is concerned with localization. We assume that mental life is the function of an apparatus to which we ascribe the characteristics of being extended in space and of being made up of several portions—which we imagine, that is, as being like a telescope or microscope or something of the sort. The consistent carrying through of a conception of this kind is a scientific novelty, even though some attempts in that direction have been made previously.

We have arrived at our knowledge of this psychical apparatus by studying the individual development of human beings. To the oldest of these mental provinces or agencies we give the name of *id.* It contains everything that is inherited, that is present at birth, that is fixed in the constitution—above all, therefore, the instincts, which originate in the somatic organization and which find their first mental expression in the id in forms unknown to us.[2]

AN OUTLINE OF PSYCHOANALYSIS by Sigmund Freud. By permission of W. W. Norton & Company, Inc. Copyright 1949 by W. W. Norton & Company, Inc. Translated by James Strachey.

[1] [It will be seen that this basic assumption is a double-barrelled one and is sometimes referred to by the author as two separate hypotheses. *Trans.*]

[2] This oldest portion of the mental apparatus remains the most important throughout life, and it was the first subject of the investigations of psychoanalysis. [Throughout this book the English word "instinct" is, with some misgivings, used to render the German "*Trieb.*" The sense in which Freud uses the term is, in any case, made clear in the following pages. *Trans.*]

Under the influence of the real external world which surrounds us, one portion of the id has undergone a special development. From what was originally a cortical layer, provided with organs for receiving stimuli and with apparatus for protection against excessive stimulation, a special organization has arisen which henceforward acts as an intermediary between the id and the external world. This region of our mental life has been given the name of *ego.*

The principal characteristics of the ego are these. In consequence of the relation which was already established between sensory perception and muscular action, the ego is in control of voluntary movement. It has the task of self-preservation. As regards *external* events, it performs that task by becoming aware of the stimuli from without, by storing up experiences of them (in the memory), by avoiding excessive stimuli (through flight), by dealing with moderate stimuli (through adaptation) and, finally, by learning to bring about appropriate modifications in the external world to its own advantage (through activity). As regards *internal* events, in relation to the id, it performs that task by gaining control over the demands of the instincts, by deciding whether they shall be allowed to obtain satisfaction, by postponing that satisfaction to times and circumstances favorable in the external world or by suppressing their excitations completely. Its activities are governed by consideration of the tensions produced by stimuli present within it or introduced into it. The raising of these tensions is in general felt as *unpleasure* and their lowering as *pleasure.* It is probable, however, that what is felt as pleasure or unpleasure is not the *absolute* degree of the tensions but something in the rhythm of their changes. The ego pursues pleasure and seeks to avoid unpleasure. An increase in unpleasure which is expected and foreseen is met by a *signal of anxiety;* the occasion of this increase, whether it threatens from without or within, is called a *danger.* From time to time the ego gives up its connection with the external world and withdraws into the state of sleep, in which its organization undergoes far-reaching changes. It may be inferred from the state of sleep that that organization consists in a particular distribution of mental energy.

The long period of childhood, during which the growing human being lives in dependence upon his parents, leaves behind it a precipitate, which forms within his ego a special agency in which this parental influence is prolonged. It has received the name of *superego.* In so far as the superego is differentiated from the ego or opposed to it, it constitutes a third force which the ego must take into account.

Thus, an action by the ego is as it should be if it satisfies simultaneously the demands of the id, of the superego and of reality, that is to say if it is able to reconcile their demands with one another. The details of the relation between the ego and the superego become completely intelligible if they are carried back to the child's attitude toward his parents. The parents' influence naturally includes not merely the personalities of the parents themselves but also the racial, national, and family traditions handed on through them as well as the demands of the immediate social *milieu* which they represent. In the same way, an individual's superego in the course of his development takes over contributions from later successors and substitutes of his parents, such as teachers, admired figures in public life, or high social ideals. It will be seen that, in spite of their fundamental difference, the id and the superego have one thing in common: they both represent the influences of the past (the id the influence of heredity, the superego essentially the influence of what is taken over from other people), whereas the ego is principally determined by the individual's own experience, that is to say by accidental and current events.

This general pattern of a psychical apparatus may be supposed to apply equally to the higher animals which resemble man mentally. A superego must be presumed to be present wherever, as in the case of man, there is a long period of dependence in childhood. The assumption of a distinction between ego and id cannot be avoided.

Animal psychology has not yet taken in hand the interesting problem which is here presented.

Chapter Two

THE THEORY OF THE INSTINCTS

The power of the id expresses the true purpose of the individual organism's life. This consists in the satisfaction of its innate needs. No such purpose as that of keeping itself alive or of protecting itself from dangers by means of anxiety can be attributed to the id. That is the business of the ego, which is also concerned with discovering the most favorable and least perilous method of obtaining satisfaction, taking the external world into account. The superego may bring fresh needs to the fore, but its chief function remains the limitation of satisfactions.

The forces which we assume to exist behind the tensions caused by the needs of the id are called *instincts*. They represent the somatic demands upon mental life. Though they are the ultimate cause of all activity, they are by nature conservative; the state, whatever it may be, which a living thing has reached, gives rise to a tendency to reestablish that state so soon as it has been abandoned. It is possible to distinguish an indeterminate number of instincts and in common practice this is in fact done. For us, however, the important question arises whether we may not be able to derive all of these various instincts from a few fundamental ones. We have found that instincts can change their aim (by displacement) and also that they can replace one another —the energy of one instinct passing over to another. This latter process is still insufficiently understood. After long doubts and vacillations we have decided to assume the existence of only two basic instincts, *Eros* and *the destructive instinct.* (The contrast between the instincts of self-preservation and of the preservation of the species, as well as the contrast between ego-love and object-love, fall within the bounds of Eros.) The aim of the first of these basic instincts is to establish ever greater unities and to preserve them thus—in short, to bind together; the aim of the second, on the contrary, is to undo connections and so to destroy things. We may suppose that the final aim of the destructive instinct is to reduce living things to an inorganic state. For this reason we also call it the *death instinct*. If we suppose that living things appeared later than inanimate ones and arose out of them, then the death instinct agrees with the formula that we have stated, to the effect that instincts tend toward a return to an earlier state. We are unable to apply the formula to Eros (the love instinct). That would be to imply that living substance had once been a unity but had subsequently been torn apart and was now tending toward reunion.[3]

In biological functions the two basic instincts work against each other or combine with each other. Thus, the act of eating is a destruction of the object with the final aim of incorporating it, and the sexual act is an act of aggression having as its purpose the most intimate union. This interaction of the two basic instincts with and against each other gives rise to the whole variegation of the phenomena of life. The analogy of our two basic instincts ex-

[3] Something of the sort has been imagined by poets, but nothing like it is known to us from the actual history of living substance.

tends from the region of animate things to the pair of opposing forces—attraction and repulsion—which rule in the inorganic world.[4]

. . .

Chapter Six

THE TECHNIQUE OF PSYCHOANALYSIS

A dream, then, is a psychosis, with all the absurdities, delusions and illusions of a psychosis. No doubt it is a psychosis which has only a short duration, which is harmless and even performs a useful function, which is brought about with the subject's consent and is ended by an act of his will. Nevertheless it *is* a psychosis, and we learn from it that even so deep-going a modification of mental life as this can be undone and can give place to normal functioning. Is it too bold, then, to hope that it must also be possible to submit the dreaded spontaneous illnesses of the mind to our control and bring about their cure?

We already possess much knowledge preliminary to such an undertaking. We have postulated that it is the ego's task to meet the demands of the three forces upon which it is dependent—reality, the id and the superego—and meanwhile to preserve its own organization and maintain its own autonomy. The necessary condition for the pathological states we have mentioned can only be a relative or absolute weakening of the ego which prevents it from performing its tasks. The severest demand upon the ego is probably the keeping down of the instinctual claims of the id, and for this end the ego is obliged to maintain great expenditures of energy upon anti-cathexes. But the claims made by the superego, too, may become so powerful and so remorseless that the ego may be

crippled, as it were, for its other tasks. We may suspect that, in the economic conflicts which now arise, the id and the superego often make common cause against the hardpressed ego, which, in order to retain its normal state, clings on to reality. But if the other two are too strong, they may succeed in loosening the organization of the ego and altering it so that its proper relation to reality is disturbed or even abolished. We have seen it happen in dreams: when the ego is detached from the reality of the external world, then, under the influence of the internal world, it slips down into psychosis.

Our plan of cure is based upon these views. The ego has been weakened by the internal conflict; we must come to its aid. The position is like a civil war which can only be decided by the help of an ally from without. The analytical physician and the weakened ego of the patient, basing themselves upon the real external world, are to combine against the enemies, the instinctual demands of the id, and the moral demands of the superego. We form a pact with each other. The patient's sick ego promises us the most complete candor, promises, that is, to put at our disposal all of the material which his self-perception provides; we, on the other hand, assure him of the strictest discretion and put at his service our experience in interpreting material that has been influenced by the unconscious. Our knowledge shall compensate for his ignorance and shall give his ego once more mastery over the lost provinces of his mental life. This pact constitutes the analytic situation.

No sooner have we taken this step than we meet with a first disappointment, a first warning against complacency. If the patient's ego is to be a useful ally in our common work, it must, however hard it may be pressed by the hostile powers, have retained a certain degree of coherence, a fragment at least of understanding for the

[4] This picture of the basic forces or instincts, which still arouses much opposition among analysts, was already a familiar one to the philosopher Empedocles of Acragas.

demands of reality. But this is not to be expected from the ego of a psychotic; it cannot carry out a pact of this sort, indeed it can scarcely engage in it. It will very soon toss us away and the help we offer it, to join the portions of the external world that no longer mean anything to it. Thus we learn that we must renounce the idea of trying our plan of cure upon psychotics —renounce it forever, perhaps, or only for the moment, until we have discovered some other plan better suited for that purpose.

But there is another class of psychological patients who evidently resemble the psychotics very closely, the immense number of sufferers from severe neuroses. The causes as well as the pathogenic mechanisms of their illness must be the same or at least very similar. Their ego, however, has proved more resistant and has become less disorganized. Many of them, in spite of their troubles and of their consequent inadequacy, are none the less able to maintain their position in real life. It may be that these neurotics will show themselves ready to accept our help. We will confine our interest to them and see how far and by what means we can "cure" them.

We conclude our pact then with the neurotics: complete candor on one side, strict discretion on the other. This looks as though we were aiming at the post of a secular father confessor. But there is a great difference, for what we want to hear from our patient is not only what he knows and conceals from other people, but what he does *not* know. With this end in view we give him a more detailed definition of what we mean by candor. We impose upon him the *fundamental rule* of analysis, which is henceforward to govern his behavior to us. He must tell us not only what he can say intentionally and willingly, what will give him relief like a confession, but everything else besides that his self-observation presents him with—everything that comes into his head, even if it is *disagreeable* to say it, even if it seems *unimportant* or positively *meaningless*. If he can succeed after this injunction in putting his self-criticism out of action, he will provide us with a mass of material—thoughts, ideas, recollections —which already lie under the influence of the unconscious, which are often its direct derivatives, and which thus put us in a position to conjecture the nature of his repressed unconscious material and to extend, by the information we give him, his ego's knowledge of his unconscious.

Vladimir Ilyich Lenin

The history of communism presents one of the major anomalies of the modern world. In their writings, Marx and Engels always assumed that the revolution and the consequent ushering in of the classless society would occur first in the most advanced industrial countries of Europe—England, France, and Germany. Russia, still slumbering in a state of semi-barbaric feudalism, was almost the last place in the world in which they expected their ideas to bear fruit. Nevertheless, it has been Russia, rather than Western Europe, that has become communistic. The reasons for this unforeseen historical development obviously are numerous and highly complex. Yet, important among them is the personal career of Vladimir Ilyich Lenin* (1870-1924). For it was Lenin who revised the Marxist theory to fit conditions in Russia, and then led the bitter struggle, both against the existing regime and against rival revolutionaries and re-

*Born Vladimir Ilyich Ulyanov.

formers, that resulted in 1917 in the victory of his version of Marxism in Russia. As critics have often pointed out, however, Lenin so modified Marx's doctrines in the process that the result ought to be labeled, as one writer has put it, "inverted Marxism."

The first of the two following selections, taken from a pamphlet entitled *What Is To Be Done?*, written in 1902, contains Lenin's most complete and significant departure from Marx—namely, his views on the nature and function of the "Party." Leon Trotsky, Lenin's famous brother-revolutionary, made the following prophecy about Lenin's views on the

Party: "The organization of the Party takes the place of the Party itself; the Central Committee takes the place of the organization; and finally the dictator takes the place of the Central Committee." The subsequent history of Russia has amply justified this prophecy. The second selection is from Lenin's most important work, *State and Revolution*, written during the revolution of 1917 in Russia. Ostensibly a commentary on Marxist doctrine, it became a detailed statement of Lenin's own views, often quite un-Marxian, regarding the political and social organization that was to follow the revolution.

WHAT IS TO BE DONE?

. . .

The history of all countries shows that the working class, exclusively by its own effort, is able to develop only trade union consciousness, *i.e.*, it may itself realise the necessity for combining in unions, for fighting against the employers and for striving to compel the government to pass necessary labour legislation, etc. The theory of socialism, however, grew out of the philosophic, historical and economic theories that were elaborated by the educated representatives of the propertied classes, the intellectuals. According to their social status, the founders of modern scientific socialism, Marx and Engels, them-

WHAT IS TO BE DONE? V. I. Lenin. New ed. (London: Lawrence & Wishart Ltd., 1944), pp. 33, 98-99, 100-112. Courtesy of Lawrence & Wishart Ltd.

selves belonged to the bourgeois intelligentsia. Similarly, in Russia, the theoretical doctrine of Social-Democracy arose quite independently of the spontaneous growth of the labour movement; it arose as a natural and inevitable outcome of the development of ideas among the revolutionary socialist intelligentsia. At the time of which we are speaking, *i.e.*, the middle of the 'nineties, this doctrine not only represented the completely formulated programme of the Emancipation of Labour group, but had already won the adherence of the majority of the revolutionary youth in Russia.

. . .

It is only natural that a Social-Democrat, who conceives the political struggle as being identical with the "economic struggle against the employers and the government," should conceive of an "organisation of revolutionaries" as being more or less identical with an "organisation of workers." And this, in fact, is what actually happens; so that when we talk about organisation, we literally talk in different tongues. I recall a conversation I once had with a fairly consistent Economist, with whom I had not been previously acquainted. We were discussing the pamphlet *Who Will Make the Political Revolution?* and we were very soon agreed that the principal defect in that brochure was that it ignored the question of organisation. We were beginning to think that we were in complete agreement with each other—but as the conversation proceeded, it became clear that we were talking of different things. My interlocutor accused the author of the brochure just mentioned of ignoring strike funds, mutual aid societies, etc.; whereas I had in mind an organisation of revolutionaries as an essential factor in "making" the political revolution. After that became clear, I hardly remember a single question of importance upon which I was in agreement with that Economist!

What was the source of our disagreement? The fact that on questions of organisation and politics the Economists are forever lapsing from Social-Democracy into trade unionism. The political struggle carried on by the Social-Democrats is far more extensive and complex than the economic struggle the workers carry on against the employers and the government. Similarly (and indeed for that reason), the organisation of a revolutionary Social-Democratic Party must inevitably *differ* from the organisations of the workers designed for the latter struggle. A workers' organisation must in the first place be a trade organisation; secondly, it must be as wide as possible; and thirdly, it must be as public as conditions will allow (here, and further on, of course, I have only autocratic Russia in

mind). On the other hand, the organisations of revolutionaries must consist first and foremost of people whose profession is that of a revolutionary (that is why I speak of organisations of *revolutionaries*, meaning revolutionary Social-Democrats). In view of this common feature of the members of such an organisation, *all distinctions as between workers and intellectuals,* and certainly distinctions of trade and profession, must be obliterated. Such an organisation must of necessity be not too extensive and as secret as possible.

.   .   .

I assert: (1) that no movement can be durable without a stable organisation of leaders to maintain continuity; (2) that the more widely the masses are spontaneously drawn into the struggle and form the basis of the movement and participate in it, the more necessary is it to have such an organisation, and the more stable must it be (for it is much easier for demagogues to sidetrack the more backward sections of the masses); (3) that the organisation must consist chiefly of persons engaged in revolutionary activities as a profession; (4) that in a country with an autocratic government, the more we *restrict* the membership of this organisation to persons who are engaged in revolutionary activities as a profession and who have been professionally trained in the art of combating the political police, the more difficult will it be to catch the organisation, and (5) the *wider* will be the circle of men and women of the working class or of other classes of society able to join the movement and perform active work in it. . . .

The active and widespread participation of the masses will not suffer; on the contrary, it will benefit by the fact that a "dozen" experienced revolutionaries, no less professionally trained than the police, will centralise all the secret side of the work—prepare leaflets, work out approximate plans and appoint bodies of leaders for each urban district, for each factory district and for each educational institution, etc. (I know that exception will be taken to my "undemocratic" views, but I shall reply to this altogether unintelligent objection later on.) The centralisation of the more secret functions in an organisation of revolutionaries will not diminish, but rather increase the extent and the quality of the activity of a large number of other organisations intended for wide membership and which, therefore, can be as loose and as public as possible, for example, trade unions, workers' circles for self-education and the reading of illegal literature, and socialist and also democratic circles for *all other sections of the population*, etc., etc. We must have *as large a number as possible* of such organisations having the widest possible variety of functions, but it is absurd and dangerous to *confuse these with organisations of revolutionaries*, to erase the line of demarcation between them, to dim still more the masses' already incredibly hazy appreciation of the fact that in order to "serve" the mass movement we must have people who will devote themselves exclusively to Social-Democratic activities, and that such people must *train* themselves patiently and steadfastly to be professional revolutionaries.

Aye, this appreciation has become incredibly dim. The most grievous sin we have committed in regard to organisation is that *by our primitiveness we have lowered the prestige of revolutionaries in Russia*. A man who is weak and vacillating on theoretical questions, who has a narrow outlook, who makes excuses for his own slackness on the ground that the masses are awakening spontaneously, who resembles a trade union secretary more than a people's tribune, who is unable to conceive of a broad and bold plan, who is incapable of inspiring even his opponents with respect for himself, and who is inexperienced and clumsy in his own professional art—the art of combating the political police—such a man is not a revolutionary but a wretched amateur!

Let no active worker take offense at these frank remarks, for as far as insufficient training is concerned, I apply them first and foremost to myself. I used to work in a circle that set itself great and all-embracing tasks; and every member of that circle suffered to the point of torture from the realisation that we were proving ourselves to be amateurs at a moment in history when we might have been able to say, paraphrasing a well-known epigram: "Give us an organisation of revolutionaries, and we shall overturn the whole of Russia!"

STATE AND REVOLUTION

Chapter 1

CLASS SOCIETY AND THE STATE

.   .   .

4. The "Withering Away" of the State and Violent Revolution. Engels' words regarding the "withering away" of the state enjoy such popularity, they are so often quoted, and they show so clearly the essence of the usual adulteration by means of which Marxism is made to look like opportunism, that we must dwell on them in detail. Let us quote the whole passage from which they are taken.

The proletariat seizes state power, and then transforms the means of production into state property. But in doing this, it puts an end to itself as the proletariat, it puts an end to all class differences and class antagonisms, it puts an end also to the state as the state. Former society, moving in class antagonisms, had need of the state, that is, an organisation of the exploiting class at each period for the maintenance of its external conditions of production; therefore, in particular, for the forcible holding down of the exploited class in the conditions of oppression (slavery, bondage or serfdom, wage-labour) determined by the existing mode of production. The state was the official representative of society as a whole, its embodiment in a visible corporate body; but it was this only in so far as it was the state of that class which itself, in its epoch, represented society as a whole: in ancient times, the state of the slave-owning citizens; in the Middle Ages, of the feudal nobility; in our epoch, of the bourgeoisie. When ultimately it becomes really representative of society as a whole, it makes itself superfluous. As soon as there is no longer any class of society to be held in subjection; as soon as, along with class domination and the struggle for individual existence based on the former anarchy of production, the collisions and excesses arising from these have

STATE AND REVOLUTION, V. I. Lenin (New York: International Publishers, 1932), pp. 15-17, 20, 70-75, 78-85. Courtesy of International Publishers Co., Inc.

also been abolished, there is nothing more to be repressed, and a special repressive force, a state, is no longer necessary. The first act in which the state really comes forward as the representative of society as a whole—the seizure of the means of production in the name of society—is at the same time its last independent act as a state. The interference of a state power in social relations becomes superfluous in one sphere after another, and then becomes dormant of itself. Government over persons is replaced by the administration of things and the direction of the processes of production. The state is not "abolished," *it withers away*. It is from this standpoint that we must appraise the phrase "people's free state"—both its justification at times for agitational purposes, and its ultimate scientific inadequacy—and also the demand of the so-called Anarchists that the state should be abolished overnight.

Without fear of committing an error, it may be said that of this argument by Engels so singularly rich in ideas, only one point has become an integral part of Socialist thought among modern Socialist parties, namely, that, unlike the Anarchist doctrine of the "abolition" of the state, according to Marx the state "withers away." To emasculate Marxism in such a manner is to reduce it to opportunism, for such an "interpretation" only leaves the hazy conception of a slow, even, gradual change, free from leaps and storms, free from revolution. The current popular conception, if one may say so, of the "withering away" of the state undoubtedly means a slurring over, if not a negation, of revolution.

Yet, such an "interpretation" is the crudest distortion of Marxism, which is advantageous only to the bourgeoisie; in point of theory, it is based on a disregard for the most important circumstances and considerations pointed out in the very passage summarising Engels' ideas, which we have just quoted in full.

In the first place, Engels at the very outset of his argument says that, in assuming state power, the proletariat by that very act "puts an end to the state as the state." One is "not accustomed" to reflect on what this really means. Generally, it is either ignored altogether, or it is considered as a piece of "Hegelian weakness" on Engels' part. As a matter of fact, however, these words express succinctly the experience of one of the greatest proletarian revolutions—the Paris Commune of 1871, of which we shall speak in greater detail in its proper place. As a matter of fact, Engels speaks here of the destruction of the bourgeois state by the proletarian revolution, while the words about its withering away refer to the remains of *proletarian* statehood *after* the Socialist revolution. The bourgeois state does not "wither away," according to Engels, but is "put an end to" by the proletariat in the course of the revolution. What withers away after the revolution is the proletarian state or semi-state.

Secondly, the state is a "special repressive force." This splendid and extremely profound definition of Engels' is given by him here with complete lucidity. It follows from this that the "special repressive force" of the bourgeoisie for the suppression of the proletariat, of the millions of workers by a handful of the rich, must be replaced by a "special repressive force" of the proletariat for the suppression of the bourgeoisie (the dictatorship of the proletariat). It is just this that constitutes the destruction of "the state as the state." It is just this that constitutes the "act" of "the seizure of the means of production in the name of society." And it is obvious that such a substitution of one (proletarian) "special repressive force" for another (bourgeois) "special repressive force" can in no way take place in the form of a "withering away."

Thirdly, as to the "withering away" or, more expressively and colourfully, as to the state "becoming dormant," Engels refers quite clearly and definitely to the period *after* "the seizure of the means of production [by the state] in the name of society," that is, *after* the Socialist revolution. We all know that the political form of the "state" at that time is complete democracy. But it never enters the head of any of the opportunists who shamelessly distort Marx that when Engels speaks here of the state "withering away," or "becoming dormant," he speaks of *democracy*. At first sight this seems very strange. But it is "unintelligible" only to one who has not reflected on the fact that democracy is *also* a state and that, consequently, democracy will *also* disappear when the state disappears. The bourgeois state can only be "put an end to" by a revolution. The state in general, *i.e.*, most complete democracy, can only "wither away."

. . .

The replacement of the bourgeois by the proletarian state is impossible without a violent revolution. The abolition of the proletarian state, *i.e.*, of all states, is only possible through "withering away."

. . .

Chapter V

THE ECONOMIC BASE OF THE WITHERING AWAY OF THE STATE

1. Formulation of the Question by Marx.

. . .

The whole theory of Marx is an application of the theory of evolution—in its most consistent, complete, well considered and fruitful form—to modern capitalism. It was natural for Marx to raise the question of applying this theory both to the *coming* collapse of capitalism and to the *future* evolution of *future* Communism.

On the basis of what *data* can the future evolution of future Communism be considered?

On the basis of the fact that *it has its origin* in capitalism, that it develops historically from capitalism, that it is the result of the action of a social force to which capitalism *has given birth*. There is no shadow of an attempt on Marx's part to conjure up a Utopia, to make idle guesses about that which cannot be known. Marx treats the question of Communism in the same way as a naturalist would treat the question of the evolution of, say, a new biological species, if he knew that such and such was its origin, and such and such the direction in which it changed.

.   .   .

The first fact that has been established with complete exactness by the whole theory of evolution, by science as a whole—a fact which the Utopians forgot, and which is forgotten by the present-day opportunists who are afraid of the Socialist revolution—is that, historically, there must undoubtedly be a special stage or epoch of *transition* from capitalism to Communism.

2. Transition from Capitalism to Communism. Marx continues:

Between capitalist and Communist society lies the period of the revolutionary transformation of the former into the latter. To this also corresponds a political transition period, in which the state can be no other than the *revolutionary dictatorship of the proletariat.*

This conclusion Marx bases on an analysis of the role played by the proletariat in modern capitalist society, on the data concerning the evolution of this society, and on the irreconcilability of the opposing interests of the proletariat and the bourgeoisie.

Earlier the question was put thus: to attain its emancipation, the proletariat must overthrow the bourgeoisie, conquer political power and establish its own revolutionary dictatorship.

Now the question is put somewhat differently: the transition from capitalist society, developing towards Communism, towards a Communist society, is impossible without a "political transition period," and the state in this period can only be the revolutionary dictatorship of the proletariat.

What, then, is the relation of this dictatorship to democracy?

We have seen that the *Communist Manifesto* simply places side by side the two ideas: the "transformation of the proletariat into the ruling class" and the "establishment of democracy." On the basis of all that has been said above, one can define more exactly how democracy changes in the transition from capitalism to Communism.

In capitalist society, under the conditions most favourable to its development, we have more or less complete democracy in the democratic republic. But this democracy is always bound by the narrow framework of capitalist exploitation, and consequently always remains, in reality, a democracy for the minority, only for the possessing classes, only for the rich. Freedom in capitalist society always remains just about the same as it was in the ancient Greek republics: freedom for the slave-owners. The modern wage-slaves, owing to the conditions of capitalist exploitation, are so much crushed by want and poverty that "democracy is nothing to them," "politics is nothing to them"; that, in the ordinary peaceful course of events, the majority of the population is debarred from participating in social and political life.

The correctness of this statement is perhaps most clearly proved by Germany, just because in this state constitutional legality lasted and remained stable for a remarkably long time—for nearly half a century (1871-1914)—and because Social-Democracy in Germany during that time was able to achieve far more than in other countries in "utilising legality," and was able to organise into a political party a larger proportion of the working class than anywhere else in the world.

What, then, is this largest proportion of politically conscious and active wage-slaves that has so far been observed in capitalist society? One million members of the Social-Democratic party—out of fifteen million wage-workers! Three million organized in trade unions—out of fifteen million.

Democracy for an insignificant minority, democracy for the rich—that is the democracy of capitalist society. If we look more closely into the mechanism of capitalist democracy, everywhere, both in the "petty"—so-called petty—details of the suffrage (residential qualification, exclusion of women, etc.), and in the technique of the representative institutions, in the actual obstacles to the right of assembly (public buildings are not for "beggars"!), in the purely capitalist organisation of the daily press, etc., etc.—on all sides we see restriction after restriction upon democracy. These restrictions, exceptions, exclusions, obstacles for the poor, seem slight, especially in the eyes of one who has himself never known want and has never been in close contact with the oppressed classes in their mass life (and nine-tenths, if not ninety-nine hundredths, of the bourgeois publicists and politicians are of this class), but in their sum total these restrictions exclude and squeeze out the poor from politics and from an active share in democracy.

Marx splendidly grasped this *essence* of capitalist democracy, when, in analysing the experience of the Commune, he said that the oppressed were allowed, once every few years, to decide which particular representatives of the oppressing class should be in parliament to represent and repress them!

But from this capitalist democracy—inevitably narrow, subtly rejecting the poor, and therefore hypocritical and false to the core—progress does not march onward, simply, smoothly and directly, to "greater and greater democracy," as the liberal professors and petty-bourgeois opportunists would have us believe. No, progress marches onward, *i.e.,* towards Communism, through the dictatorship of the proletariat; it cannot do otherwise, for there is no one else and no other way to *break the resistance* of the capitalist exploiters.

But the dictatorship of the proletariat —*i.e.,* the organisation of the vanguard of the oppressed as the ruling class for the purpose of crushing the oppressors—cannot produce merely an expansion of democracy. *Together* with an immense expansion of democracy which *for the first time* becomes democracy for the poor, democracy for the people, and not democracy for the rich folk, the dictatorship of the proletariat produces a series of restrictions of liberty in the case of the oppressors, the exploiters, the capitalists. We must crush them in order to free humanity from wage-slavery; their resistance must be broken by force; it is clear that where there is suppression there is also violence, there is no liberty, no democracy.

Engels expressed this splendidly in his letter to Bebel when he said, as the reader will remember, that "as long as the proletariat still *needs* the state, it needs it not in the interests of freedom, but for the purpose of crushing its antagonists; and as soon as it becomes possible to speak of freedom, then the state, as such, ceases to exist."

Democracy for the vast majority of the people, and suppression by force, *i.e.,* exclusion from democracy, of the exploiters and oppressors of the people—this is the modification of democracy during the *transition* from capitalism to Communism.

Only in Communist society, when the resistance of the capitalists has been completely broken, when the capitalists have disappeared, when there are no classes (*i.e.,* there is no difference between the members of society in their relation to the social means of production), *only then* "the state ceases to exist," and "*it becomes possible to speak of freedom.*" Only then a really full democracy, a democracy without any exceptions, will be possible and will be realised. And only then will democracy itself begin to *wither away* due to the simple fact that, freed from capitalist slavery, from the untold horrors, savagery, absurdities and infamies of capitalist exploitation, people will gradually *become accustomed* to the observance of the elementary rules of social life that have been known for centuries and repeated for thousands of years in all school books; they will become accustomed to observing them without force, without compulsion, without subordination, without the *special apparatus* for compulsion which is called the state.

The expression "the state *withers away*," is very well chosen, for it indicates both the gradual and the elemental nature of the process. Only habit can, and undoubtedly will, have such an effect; for we see around us millions of times how readily people get accustomed to observe the necessary rules of life in common, if there is no exploitation, if there is nothing that causes indignation, that calls forth protest and revolt and has to be *suppressed*.

Thus, in capitalist society, we have a democracy that is curtailed, poor, false; a democracy only for the rich, for the minority. The dictatorship of the proletariat, the period of transition to Communism, will, for the first time, produce democracy for the people, for the majority, side by side with the necessary suppression of the minority—the exploiters. Communism alone is capable of giving a really complete democracy, and the more complete it is the more quickly will it become unnecessary and wither away of itself.

In other words: under capitalism we have a state in the proper sense of the word, that is, special machinery for the suppression of one class by another, and of the majority by the minority at that. Naturally, for the successful discharge of such a task as the systematic suppression by the exploiting minority of the exploited majority, the greatest ferocity and savagery of suppression are required, seas of blood are required, through which mankind is marching in slavery, serfdom, and wage-labor.

Again, during the *transition* from capitalism to Communism, suppression is *still* necessary; but it is the suppression of the minority of exploiters by the majority of exploited. A special apparatus, special machinery for suppression, the "state," is *still* necessary, but this is now a transitional state, no longer a state in the usual sense, for the suppression of the minority of exploiters, by the majority of the wage slaves of *yesterday*, is a matter comparatively so easy, simple and natural that it will cost far less bloodshed than the suppression of the risings of slaves, serfs or wage labourers, and will cost mankind far less. This is compatible with the diffusion of democracy among such an overwhelming majority of the population, that the need for *special machinery* of suppression will begin to disappear. The exploiters are, naturally, unable to suppress the people without a most complex machinery for performing this task; but *the people* can suppress the exploiters even with very simple "machinery," almost without any "machinery," without any special apparatus, by the simple *organisation of the armed masses* (such as the Soviets of Workers' and Soldiers' Deputies, we may remark, anticipating a little).

Finally, only Communism renders the state absolutely unnecessary, for there is *no one* to be suppressed—"no one" in the sense of a *class,* in the sense of a systematic struggle with a definite section of the population. We are not Utopians, and we do not in the least deny the possibility and inevitability of excesses on the part of *individual persons,* nor the need to suppress *such* excesses.

But, in the first place, no special machinery, no special apparatus of repression is needed for this; this will be done by the armed people itself, as simply and as readily as any crowd of civilised people, even in modern society, parts a pair of combatants or does not allow a woman to be outraged. And, secondly, we know that the fundamental social cause of excesses which consist in violating the rules of social life is the exploitation of the masses, their want and their poverty. With the removal of this chief cause, excesses will inevitably begin to *"wither away."* We do not know how quickly and in what succession, but we know that they will wither away. With their withering away, the state will also *wither away.*

Without going into Utopias, Marx defined more fully what can *now* be defined regarding this future, namely, the difference between the lower and higher phases (degrees, stages) of Communist society.

. . . .

4. Higher Phase of Communist Society. Marx continues:

In a higher phase of Communist society, when the enslaving subordination of individuals in the division of labour has disappeared, and with it also the antagonism between mental and physical labour; when labour has become not only a means of living, but itself the first necessity of life; when, along with the all-round development of individuals, the productive forces too have grown, and all the springs of social wealth are flowing more freely—it is only at that stage that it will be possible to pass completely beyond the narrow horizon of bourgeois rights, and for society to inscribe on its banners: from each according to his ability; to each according to his needs!

Only now can we appreciate the full correctness of Engels' remarks in which he mercilessly ridiculed all the absurdity of combining the words "freedom" and "state." While the state exists there is no freedom. When there is freedom, there will be no state.

The economic basis for the complete withering away of the state is that high stage of development of Communism when the antagonism between mental and physical labour disappears, that is to say, when one of the principal sources of modern *social* inequality disappears—a source, moreover, which it is impossible to remove immediately by the mere conversion of the means of production into public property, by the mere expropriation of the capitalists.

This expropriation will make a gigantic development of the productive forces *possible*. And seeing how incredibly, even now, capitalism *retards* this development, how much progress could be made even on the basis of modern technique at the level it has reached, we have a right to say, with the fullest confidence, that the expropriation of the capitalists will inevitably result in a gigantic development of the productive forces of human society. But how rapidly this development will go forward, how soon it will reach the point of breaking away from the division of labour, of removing the antagonism between mental and physical labour, of transforming work into the "first necessity of life"—this we do not and *cannot* know.

Consequently, we have a right to speak solely of the inevitable withering away of the state, emphasising the protracted nature of this process and its dependence upon the rapidity of development of the *higher phase* of Communism; leaving quite open the question of lengths of time, or the concrete forms of withering away, since material for the solution of such questions is *not available.*

The state will be able to wither away completely when society has realised the rule: "From each according to his ability; to each according to his needs," *i.e.*, when people have become accustomed to observe the fundamental rules of social life, and their labour is so productive, that they voluntarily work *according to their ability*.

"The narrow horizon of bourgeois rights," which compels one to calculate, with the hard-heartedness of a Shylock, whether he has not worked half an hour more than another, whether he is not getting less pay than another—this narrow horizon will then be left behind. There will then be no need for any exact calculation by society of the quantity of products to be distributed to each of its members; each will take freely "according to his needs."

· · · ·

What is generally called Socialism was termed by Marx the "first" or lower phase of Communist society. In so far as the means of production become *public* property, the word "Communism" is also applicable here, providing we do not forget that it is *not* full Communism. The great significance of Marx's elucidations consist in this: that here, too, he consistently applied materialist dialectics, the doctrine of evolution, looking upon Communism as something which evolves *out of* capitalism. Instead of artificial, "elaborate," scholastic definitions and profitless disquisitions on the meaning of words (what Socialism is, what Communism is), Marx gives an analysis of what may be called stages in the economic ripeness of Communism.

In its first phase or first stage Communism *cannot* as yet be economically ripe and entirely free of all tradition and of all taint of capitalism. Hence the interesting phenomenon of Communism retaining, in its first phase, "the narrow horizon of bourgeois rights." Bourgeois rights, with respect to distribution of articles of *consumption*, inevitably presupposes, of course, the existence of the *bourgeois state,* for rights are nothing without an apparatus capable of *enforcing* the observance of the rights.

Consequently, for a certain time not only bourgeois rights, but even the bourgeois state remains under Communism, without the bourgeoisie!

This may look like a paradox, or simply a dialectical puzzle for which Marxism is often blamed by people who would not make the least effort to study its extraordinarily profound content.

But, as a matter of fact, the old surviving in the new confronts us in life at every step, in nature as well as in society. Marx did not smuggle a scrap of "bourgeois" rights into Communism of his own accord; he indicated what is economically and politically inevitable in a society issuing *from the womb* of capitalism.

Democracy is of great importance for the working class in its struggle for freedom against the capitalists. But democracy is by no means a limit one may not overstep; it is only one of the stages in the course of development from feudalism to capitalism, and from capitalism to Communism.

Democracy means equality. The great significance of the struggle of the proletariat for equality, and the significance of equality as a slogan, are apparent, if we correctly interpret it as meaning the abolition of *classes*. But democracy means only *formal* equality. Immediately after the attainment of equality for all members of society *in respect of* the ownership of the means of production, that is, of equality of labour and equality of wages, there will inevitably arise before humanity the question of going further from formal equality to real equality, *i.e.,* to realising the rule, "From each according to his ability; to each according to his needs." By what stages, by means of what practical measures humanity will proceed to this higher aim—this we do not and cannot know. But it is important to realise how infinitely mendacious is the usual bourgeois presentation of Socialism as something lifeless, petrified, fixed once for all, whereas in reality, it is *only* with Socialism that there will commence a rapid, genuine, real mass advance, in which first the *majority* and then the whole of the population will take part—an advance in all domains of social and individual life.

Democracy is a form of the state—one of its varieties. Consequently, like every state, it consists in organised, systematic application of force against human beings. This on the one hand. On the other hand, however, it signifies the formal recognition of the equality of all citizens, the equal right of all to determine the structure and administration of the state. This, in turn, is connected with the fact that, at a certain stage in the development of democracy, it first rallies the proletariat as a revolutionary class against capitalism, and gives it an opportunity to crush, to smash to bits, to wipe off the face of the earth the bourgeois state machinery—even its republican variety: the standing army, the police, and bureaucracy; then it substitutes for all this a *more* democratic, but still a state machinery in the shape of armed masses of workers, which becomes transformed into universal participation of the people in the militia.

Here "quantity turns into quality": *such* a degree of democracy is bound up with the abandonment of the framework of bourgeois society, and the beginning of its Socialist reconstruction. If *every one* really takes part in the administration of the state, capitalism cannot retain its hold. In its turn, capitalism, as it develops, itself creates *prerequisites* for "every one" *to be able* really to take part in the administration of the state. Among such prerequisites are: universal literacy, already realised in most of the advanced capitalist countries, then the "training and disciplining" of millions of workers by the huge, complex, and socialised apparatus of the post-office, the railways, the big factories, large-scale commerce, banking, etc., etc.

With such *economic* prerequisites it is perfectly possible, immediately, within twenty-four hours after the overthrow of the capitalists and bureaucrats, to replace them, in the control of production and distribution, in the business of *control* of labour and products, by the armed workers, by the whole people in arms. (The question of control and accounting must not be confused with the question of the scientifically educated staff of engineers, agronomists and so on. These gentlemen work today, obeying the capitalists; they will work even better tomorrow, obeying the armed workers.)

Accounting and control—these are the *chief* things necessary for the organising and correct functioning of the *first phase* of Communist society. *All* citizens are here transformed into hired employees of the state, which is made up of the armed workers. *All* citizens become employees and workers of *one* national state "syndicate." All that is required is that they should work equally, should regularly do their share of work, and should receive equal pay. The accounting and control necessary for this have been *simplified* by capitalism to the utmost, till they have become the extraordinarily simple operations of watching, recording and issuing receipts, within the reach of anybody who can read and write and knows the first four rules of arithmetic.[1]

When the *majority* of the people begin everywhere to keep such accounts and maintain such control over the capitalists (now converted into employees) and over the intellectual gentry, who still retain capitalist habits, this control will really become universal, general, national; and there will be no way of getting away from it, there will be "nowhere to go."

The whole of society will have become one office and one factory, with equal work and equal pay.

[1] When most of the functions of the state are reduced to this accounting and control by the workers themselves, then it ceases to be a "political state," and the "public functions will lose their political character and be transformed into simple administrative functions."

But this "factory" discipline, which the proletariat will extend to the whole of society after the defeat of the capitalists and the overthrow of the exploiters, is by no means our ideal, or our final aim. It is but a *foothold* necessary for the radical cleansing of society of all the hideousness and foulness of capitalist exploitation, *in order to advance further.*

From the moment when all members of society, or even only the overwhelming majority, have learned how to govern the state *themselves*, have taken this business into their own hands, have "established" control over the insignificant minority of capitalists, over the gentry with capitalist leanings, and the workers thoroughly demoralised by capitalism—from this moment the need for any government begins to disappear. The more complete the democracy, the nearer the moment when it begins to be unnecessary. The more democratic the "state" consisting of armed workers, which is "no longer a state in the proper

sense of the word," the more rapidly does *every* state begin to wither away.

For when *all* have learned to manage, and independently are actually managing by themselves social production, keeping accounts, controlling the idlers, the gentlefolk, the swindlers and similar "guardians of capitalist traditions," then the escape from this national accounting and control will inevitably become so increasingly difficult, such a rare exception, and will probably be accompanied by such swift and severe punishment (for the armed workers are men of practical life, not sentimental intellectuals, and they will scarcely allow any one to trifle with them), that very soon the *necessity* of observing the simple, fundamental rules of every-day social life in common will have become a *habit.*

The door will then be wide open for the transition from the first phase of Communist society to its higher phase, and along with it to the complete withering away of the state.

Fascism

Strictly speaking, the term fascism applies to the party and the regime that Mussolini led in Italy during the years from World War I to World War II. In general usage, however, the term has come to designate any non-communistic authoritarian movement or government in the contemporary Western world. The most important of these was the National Socialist (or Nazi) government of Hitler in Germany. In addition to Germany and Italy, though, there have been lesser fascist regimes, some of which are still with us, in other countries. The tendency to identify modern fascism with earlier tyrannies, though it has some validity, overlooks features of the modern movement that are genuinely novel. Among the most important of these, as Mussolini points out, is the fascist conception of *totalitarianism,* the view that the state must dominate and, in fact, permeate the lives and activities of all its members. As the fascist motto puts it: "Everything for the state; nothing against the state; nothing outside the state."

The two selections that follow are from the main works of Adolf Hitler (1889-1945) and Benito Mussolini (1883-1945), respectively. The first comes from Chapter XI of the first volume of Hitler's *Mein Kampf* ("My Battle"), written while Hitler was in prison following his unsuccessful "beer hall" *putsch* in 1923. Because of copyright restrictions, it has been impossible to include a longer selec-

tion from this chapter. But even the short passage presented provides insight not only into the beliefs of Hitler on the vital topic of racism but also into the character of the man himself. For a more complete and revealing view, we recommend reading the chapter in its entirety.

The second selection, *The Doctrine of Fascism* (which is presented in its entirety) was written by Mussolini with the aid of the Italian philosopher, Giovanni Gentile, and first appeared in the *Enciclopedia Italiana* (1932). In it, Mussolini touches on most of the major strains in fascist philosophy and practice—the rejection of reason in favor of emotion and will, the subordi-

nation of the individual to the state, the conception of the state as an organic being that must either increase its power or perish, the acceptance of war as not only necessary but desirable, and the rejection of the ideals of freedom, equality, and individualism that form the foundations of liberal democracy. Although the historical sources of these fascist beliefs are very complex, at least two, both from the nineteenth century, can be identified: romanticism and the philosophical idealism of Hegel. A striking feature of the article, particularly when it is viewed from the perspective of subsequent history, is the lofty, idealistic tone in which most of it is written.

MEIN KAMPF

XI. NATION AND RACE

. . .

Everything we admire on this earth today—science and art, technology and inventions—is only the creative product of a few peoples and originally perhaps of *one* race. On them depends the existence of this whole culture. If they perish, the beauty of this earth will sink into the grave with them.

However much the soil, for example, can influence men, the result of the influence will always be different depending on the races in question. The low fertility of a liv-

MEIN KAMPF, Adolf Hitler, trans. Ralph Manheim (Boston: Houghton Mifflin Company, 1943), pp. 288-292, 300, 303. Courtesy of Houghton Mifflin Company.

ing space may spur the one race to the highest achievements; in others it will only be the cause of bitterest poverty and final undernourishment with all its consequences. The inner nature of peoples is always determining for the manner in which outward influences will be effective. What leads the one to starvation trains the other to hard work.

All great cultures of the past perished only because the originally creative race died out from blood poisoning.

The ultimate cause of such a decline was their forgetting that all culture depends on men and not conversely; hence that to preserve a certain culture the man who creates it must be preserved. This preservation is bound up with the rigid law of necessity and the right to victory of the best and stronger in this world.

Those who want to live, let them fight, and those who do not want to fight in this world of eternal struggle do not deserve to live.

Even if this were hard—that is how it is! Assuredly, however, by far the harder fate is that which strikes the man who thinks he can overcome Nature, but in the last analysis only mocks her. Distress, misfortune, and diseases are her answer.

The man who misjudges and disregards the racial laws actually forfeits the happiness that seems destined to be his. He thwarts the triumphal march of the best race and hence also the precondition for all human progress, and remains, in consequence, burdened with all the sensibility of man, in the animal realm of helpless misery.

It is idle to argue which race or races were the original representative of human culture and hence the real founders of all that we sum up under the word "humanity." It is simpler to raise this question with regard to the present, and here an easy, clear answer results. All the human culture, all the results of art, science, and technology that we see before us today, are almost exclusively the creative product of the Aryan. This very fact admits of the not unfounded inference that he alone was the founder of all higher humanity, therefore representing the prototype of all that we understand by the word "man." He is the Prometheus of mankind from whose bright forehead the divine spark of genius has sprung at all times, forever kindling anew that fire of knowledge which illumined the night of silent mysteries and thus caused man to climb the path to mastery over the other beings of this earth. Exclude him—and perhaps after a few thousand years darkness will again descend on the earth, human culture will pass, and the world turn to a desert.

If we were to divide mankind into three groups, the founders of culture, the bearers of culture, the destroyers of culture, only the Aryan could be considered as the representative of the first group. From him originate the foundations and walls of all human creation, and only the outward form and color are determined by the changing traits of character of the various peoples. He provides the mightiest building stones and plans for all human progress and only the execution corresponds to the nature of the varying men and races. . . .

But if it is established that a people receives the most essential basic materials of its culture from foreign races, that it assimilates and adapts them, and that then, if further external influence is lacking, it rigidifies again and again, such a race may be designated as "culture-bearing," but never as "culture-creating." An examination of the various peoples from this standpoint points to the fact that practically none of them were originally culture-founding, but almost always culture-bearing.

Approximately the following picture of their development always results:

Aryan races—often absurdly small numerically—subject foreign peoples, and then, stimulated by the special living conditions of the new territory (fertility, climatic conditions, etc.) and assisted by the multitude of lower-type beings standing at their disposal as helpers, develop the intellectual and organizational capacities dormant within them. Often in a few millenniums or even centuries they create cultures which originally bear all the inner characteristics of their nature, adapted to the above-indicated special qualities of the soil and subjected beings. In the end, however, the conquerors transgress against the principle of blood purity, to which they had first adhered; they begin to mix with the subjugated inhabitants and thus end their own existence; for the fall of man in paradise has always been followed by his expulsion.

.   .   .   .

The mightiest counterpart to the Aryan is represented by the Jew. In hardly any people in the world is the instinct of self-preservation developed more strongly than in the so-called "chosen." Of this, the mere fact of the survival of this race may be considered the best proof. Where is the people which in the last two thousand years has been exposed to so slight changes of inner disposition, character, etc., as the Jewish people? What people, finally, has gone through greater upheavals than this one—and nevertheless issued from the mightiest catastrophes of mankind unchanged? What an infinitely tough will to live and preserve the species speaks from these facts!

. . .

In judging the Jewish people's attitude on the question of human culture, the most essential characteristic we must always bear in mind is that there has never been a Jewish art and accordingly there is none today either; that above all the two queens of all the arts, architecture and music, owe nothing original to the Jews. What they do accomplish in the field of art is either patchwork or intellectual theft. Thus, the Jew lacks those qualities which distinguish the races that are creative and hence culturally blessed.

To what an extent the Jew takes over foreign culture, imitating or rather ruining it, can be seen from the fact that he is mostly found in the art which seems to require least original invention, the art of acting. But even here, in reality, he is only a "juggler," or rather an ape; for even here he lacks the last touch that is required for real greatness; even here he is not the creative genius, but a superficial imitator, and all the twists and tricks that he uses are powerless to conceal the inner lifelessness of his creative gift. Here the Jewish press most lovingly helps him along by raising such a roar of hosannahs about even the most mediocre bungler, just so long as he is a Jew, that the rest of the world actually ends up by thinking that they have an artist before them, while in truth it is only a pitiful comedian.

No, the Jew possesses no culture-creating force of any sort, since the idealism, without which there is no true higher development of man, is not present in him and never was present. Hence his intellect will never have a constructive effect, but will be destructive, and in very rare cases perhaps will at most be stimulating, but then as the prototype of the "force which always wants evil and nevertheless creates good." Not through him does any progress of mankind occur, but in spite of him.

THE DOCTRINE OF FASCISM

FUNDAMENTAL IDEAS

1. Like every sound political conception, Fascism is both practice and thought; action

"THE DOCTRINE OF FASCISM," Benito Mussolini, ed. and trans. M. Oakeshott, in *The Social and Political Doctrines of Contemporary Europe* (Cambridge University Press, 1953), pp. 164-79. Courtesy of Cambridge University Press.

in which a doctrine is immanent, and a doctrine which, arising out of a given system of historical forces, remains embedded in them and works there from within. Hence it has a form correlative to the contingencies of place and time, but it has also a content of thought which raises it to a formula of truth in the higher level of the history of thought. In the world one does not act spiritually as a human will dominating other wills without a conception of the transient and particular reality under which it is necessary to act, and of the permanent and universal reality in which the first has its being and its life. In order to know men it is necessary to know man; and in order to know man it is necessary to know reality and its laws. There is no concept of the State which is not fundamentally a concept of life: philosophy or intuition, a system of ideas which develops logically or is gathered up into a vision or into a faith, but which is always, at least virtually, an organic conception of the world.

2. Thus Fascism could not be understood in many of its practical manifestations as a party organization, as a system of education, as a discipline, if it were not always looked at in the light of its whole way of conceiving life, a spiritualized way. The world seen through Fascism is not this material world which appears on the surface, in which man is an individual separated from all others and standing by himself, and in which he is governed by a natural law that makes him instinctively live a life of selfish and momentary pleasure. The man of Fascism is an individual who is nation and fatherland, which is a moral law, binding together individuals and the generations into a tradition and a mission, suppressing the instinct for a life enclosed within the brief round of pleasure in order to restore within duty a higher life free from the limits of time and space: a life in which the individual, through the denial of himself, through the sacrifice of his own private interests, through death itself, realizes that completely spiritual existence in which his value as a man lies.

3. Therefore it is a spiritualized conception, itself the result of the general reaction of modern times against the flabby materialistic positivism of the nineteenth century. Anti-positivistic, but positive: not sceptical, nor agnostic, nor pessimistic, nor passively optimistic, as are, in general, the doctrines (all negative) that put the centre of life outside man, who with his free will can and must create his own world. Fascism desires an active man, one engaged in activity with all his energies: it desires a man virilely conscious of the difficulties that exist in action and ready to face them. It conceives of life as a struggle, considering that it behoves man to conquer for himself that life truly worthy of him, creating first of all in himself the instrument (physical, moral, intellectual) in order to construct it. Thus for the single individual, thus for the nation, thus for humanity. Hence the high value of culture in all its forms (art, religion, science), and the enormous importance of education. Hence also the essential value of work, with which man conquers nature and creates the human world (economic, political, moral, intellectual).

4. This positive conception of life is clearly an ethical conception. It covers the whole of reality, not merely the human activity which controls it. No action can be divorced from moral judgment; there is nothing in the world which can be deprived of the value which belongs to everything in its relation to moral ends. Life, therefore, as conceived by the Fascist, is serious, austere, religious: the whole of it is poised in a world supported by the moral and responsible forces of the spirit. The Fascist disdains the "comfortable" life.

5. Fascism is a religious conception in which man is seen in his immanent relationship with a superior law and with an objective Will that transcends the particular individual and raises him to conscious membership of a spiritual society. Whoever has seen in the religious politics of the Fascist regime nothing but mere opportunism has not understood that Fascism besides being a system of government is also, and above all, a system of thought.

6. Fascism is an historical conception, in which man is what he is only in so far as he

works with the spiritual process in which he finds himself, in the family or social group, in the nation and in the history in which all nations collaborate. From this follows the great value of tradition, in memories, in language, in customs, in the standards of social life. Outside history man is nothing. Consequently Fascism is opposed to all the individualistic abstractions of a materialistic nature like those of the eighteenth century; and it is opposed to all Jacobin utopias and innovations. It does not consider that "happiness" is possible upon earth, as it appeared to be in the desire of the economic literature of the eighteenth century, and hence it rejects all teleological theories according to which mankind would reach a definitive stabilized condition at a certain period in history. This implies putting oneself outside history and life, which is a continual change and coming to be. Politically, Fascism wishes to be a realistic doctrine; practically, it aspires to solve only the problems which arise historically of themselves and that of themselves find or suggest their own solution. To act among men, as to act in the natural world, it is necessary to enter into the process of reality and to master the already operating forces.

7. Against individualism, the Fascist conception is for the State; and it is for the individual in so far as he coincides with the State, which is the conscience and universal will of man in his historical existence. It is opposed to classical Liberalism, which arose from the necessity of reacting against absolutism, and which brought its historical purpose to an end when the State was transformed into the conscience and will of the people. Liberalism denied the State in the interests of the particular individual; Fascism reaffirms the State as the true reality of the individual. And if liberty is to be the attribute of the real man, and not of that abstract puppet envisaged by individualistic Liberalism, Fascism is for lib-

erty. And for the only liberty which can be a real thing, the liberty of the State and of the individual within the State. Therefore, for the Fascist, everything is in the State, and nothing human or spiritual exists, much less has value, outside the State. In this sense Fascism is totalitarian, and the Fascist State, the synthesis and unity of all values, interprets, develops and gives strength to the whole life of the people.

8. Outside the State there can be neither individuals nor groups (political parties, associations, syndicates, classes). Therefore Fascism is opposed to Socialism, which confines the movement of history within the class struggle and ignores the unity of classes established in one economic and moral reality in the State; and analogously it is opposed to class syndicalism. Fascism recognizes the real exigencies for which the socialist and syndicalist movement arose, but while recognizing them wishes to bring them under the control of the State and give them a purpose within the corporative system of interests reconciled within the unity of the State.

9. Individuals form classes according to the similarity of their interests, they form syndicates according to differentiated economic activities within these interests; but they form first, and above all, the State, which is not to be thought of numerically as the sum-total of individuals forming the majority of a nation. And consequently Fascism is opposed to Democracy, which equates the nation to the majority, lowering it to the level of that majority; nevertheless it is the purest form of democracy if the nation is conceived, as it should be, qualitatively and not quantitatively, as the most powerful idea (most powerful because most moral, most coherent, most true) which acts within the nation as the conscience and the will of a few, even of One, which ideal tends to become active within the conscience and the will of all those who rightly constitute a na-

tion by reason of nature, history or race, and have set out upon the same line of development and spiritual formation as one conscience and one sole will. Not a race, nor a geographically determined region, but as a community historically perpetuating itself, a multitude unified by a single idea, which is the will to existence and to power: consciousness of itself, personality.

10. This higher personality is truly the nation in so far as it is the State. It is not the nation that generates the State, as according to the old naturalistic concept which served as the basis of the political theories of the national States of the nineteenth century. Rather the nation is created by the State, which gives to the people, conscious of its own moral unity, a will and therefore an effective existence. The right of a nation to independence derives not from a literary and ideal consciousness of its own being, still less from a more or less unconscious and inert acceptance of a *de facto* situation, but from an active consciousness, from a political will in action and ready to demonstrate its own rights: that is to say, from a state already coming into being. The State, in fact, as the universal ethical will, is the creator of right.

11. The nation as the State is an ethical reality which exists and lives in so far as it develops. To arrest its development is to kill it. Therefore the State is not only the authority which governs and gives the form of laws and the value of spiritual life to the wills of individuals, but it is also a power that makes its will felt abroad, making it known and respected, in other words, demonstrating the fact of its universality in all the necessary directions of its development. It is consequently organization and expansion, at least virtually. Thus it can be likened to the human will which knows no limits to its development and realizes itself in testing its own limitlessness.

12. The Fascist State, the highest and most powerful form of personality, is a force, but a spiritual force, which takes over all the forms of the moral and intellectual life of man. It cannot therefore confine itself simply to the functions of order and supervision as Liberalism desired. It is not simply a mechanism which limits the sphere of the supposed liberties of the individual. It is the form, the inner standard and the discipline of the whole person; it saturates the will as well as the intelligence. Its principle, the central inspiration of the human personality living in the civil community, pierces into the depths and makes its home in the heart of the man of action as well as of the thinker, of the artist as well as of the scientist: it is the soul of the soul.

13. Fascism, in short, is not only the giver of laws and the founder of institutions, but the educator and promoter of spiritual life. It wants to remake, not the forms of human life, but its content, man, character, faith. And to this end it requires discipline and authority that can enter into the spirits of men and there govern unopposed. Its sign, therefore, is the Lictors' rods, the symbol of unity, of strength and justice.

POLITICAL AND SOCIAL DOCTRINE

1. When in the now distant March of 1919 I summoned to Milan, through the columns of the *Popolo d'Italia*, my surviving supporters who had followed me since the constitution of the Fasces of Revolutionary Action, founded in January 1915, there was no specific doctrinal plan in my mind. I had known and lived through only one doctrine, that of the Socialism of 1903-4 up to the winter of 1914, almost ten years. My experience in this had been that of a follower and of a leader, but not that of a theoretician. My doctrine, even in that period, had been a doctrine of action. An unequivocal Socialism, universally ac-

cepted, did not exist after 1905, when the Revisionist Movement began in Germany under Bernstein and there was formed in opposition to that, in the seesaw of tendencies, an extreme revolutionary movement, which in Italy never emerged from the condition of mere words, whilst in Russian Socialism it was the prelude to Bolshevism. Reform, Revolution, Centralization—even the echoes of the terminology are now spent; whilst in the great river of Fascism are to be found the streams which had their source in Sorel, Peguy, in the Lagardelle of the *Mouvement Socialiste* and the groups of Italian Syndicalists, who between 1904 and 1914 brought a note of novelty into Italian Socialism, which by that time had been devitalized and drugged by fornication with Giolitti, in *Pagine Libere* of Olivetti, *La Lupa* of Orano and *Divenire Sociale* of Enrico Leone.

In 1919, at the end of the War, Socialism as a doctrine was already dead: it existed only as hatred, it had still only one possibility, especially in Italy, that of revenge against those who had wished for the War and who should be made to expiate it. The *Popolo d'Italia* expressed it in its sub-title —"The Newspaper of Combatants and Producers." The word "producers" was already the expression of a tendency. Fascism was not given out to the wet nurse of a doctrine elaborated beforehand round a table: it was born of the need for action; it was not a party, but in its first two years it was a movement against all parties. The name which I gave to the organization defined its characteristics. Nevertheless, whoever rereads, in the now crumpled pages of the time, the account of the constituent assembly of the *Fasci italiani di Combattimento* will not find a doctrine, but a series of suggestions, of anticipations, of admonitions, which when freed from the inevitable vein of contingency, were destined later, after a few years, to develop into a series of doctrinal attitudes which made of

Fascism a self-sufficient political doctrine able to face all others, both past and present. "If the bourgeoisie," I said at that time, "thinks to find in us a lightning-conductor, it is mistaken. We must go forward in opposition to Labour. . . . We want to accustom the working classes to being under a leader, to convince them also that it is not easy to direct an industry or a commercial undertaking successfully. . . . We shall fight against technical and spiritual retrogression. . . . The successors of the present regime still being undecided, we must not be unwilling to fight for it. We must hasten; when the present regime is superseded, we must be the ones to take its place. The right of succession belongs to us because we pushed the country into the War and we lead it to victory. The present method of political representation cannot be sufficient for us, we wish for a direct representation of individual interests. . . . It might be said against this programme that it is return to the corporations. It doesn't matter! . . . I should like, nevertheless, the Assembly to accept the claims of national syndicalism from the point of view of economics. . . ."

Is it not surprising that from the first day in the Piazza San Sepolcro there should resound the word "Corporation" which was destined in the course of the revolution to signify one of the legislative and social creations at the base of the regime?

2. The years preceding the March on Rome were years during which the necessity of action did not tolerate enquiries or complete elaborations of doctrine. Battles were being fought in the cities and villages. There were discussions, but—and this is more sacred and important—there were deaths. People knew how to die. The doctrine—beautiful, well-formed, divided into chapters and paragraphs and surrounded by a commentary—might be missing; but there was present something more decisive to supplant it—Faith. Nevertheless, he who

recalls the past with the aid of books, articles, votes in Parliament, the major and the minor speeches, he who knows how to investigate and weigh evidence, will find that the foundations of the doctrine were laid while the battle was raging. It was precisely in these years that Fascist thought armed itself, refined itself, moving towards one organization of its own. The problems of the individual and the State; the problems of authority and liberty; political and social problems and those more specifically national; the struggle against liberal, democratic, socialist, Masonic, demagogic doctrines was carried on at the same time as the "punitive expeditions." But since the "system" was lacking, adversaries ingenuously denied that Fascism had any power to make a doctrine of its own, while the doctrine rose up, even though tumultuously, at first under the aspect of a violent and dogmatic negation, as happens to all ideas that break new ground, then under the positive aspect of a constructive policy which, during the years 1926, 1927, 1928, was realized in the laws and institutions of the regime.

Fascism is to-day clearly defined not only as a regime but as a doctrine. And I mean by this that Fascism to-day, self-critical as well as critical of other movements, has an unequivocal point of view of its own, a criterion, and hence an aim, in face of all the material and intellectual problems which oppress the people of the world.

3. Above all, Fascism, in so far as it considers and observes the future and the development of humanity quite apart from the political considerations of the moment, believes neither in the possibility nor in the utility of perpetual peace. It thus repudiates the doctrine of Pacifism—born of a renunciation of the struggle and an act of cowardice in the face of sacrifice. War alone brings up to their highest tension all human energies and puts the stamp of nobility upon the peoples who have the courage to meet it. All other trials are substitutes, which never really put a man in front of himself in the alternative of life and death. A doctrine, therefore, which begins with a prejudice in favour of peace is foreign to Fascism; as are foreign to the spirit of Fascism, even though acceptable by reason of the utility which they might have in given political situations, all internationalistic and socialistic systems which, as history proves, can be blown to the winds when emotional, idealistic and practical movements storm the hearts of peoples. Fascism carries over this antipacifist spirit even into the lives of individuals. The proud motto of the *Squadrista*, "Me ne frego," written on the bandages of a wound is an act of philosophy which is not only stoical, it is the epitome of a doctrine that is not only political: it is education for combat, the acceptance of the risks which it brings; it is a new way of life for Italy. Thus the Fascist accepts and loves life, he knows nothing of suicide and despises it; he looks on life as duty, ascent, conquest: life which must be noble and full: lived for oneself, but above all for those others near and far away, present and future.

4. The "demographic" policy of the regime follows from these premises. Even the Fascist does in fact love his neighbour, but this "neighbour" is not for him a vague and ill-defined concept; love for one's neighbour does not exclude necessary educational severities, and still less differentiations and distances. Fascism rejects universal concord, and, since it lives in the community of civilized peoples, it keeps them vigilantly and suspiciously before its eyes, it follows their states of mind and the changes in their interests and it does not let itself be deceived by temporary and fallacious appearances.

5. Such a conception of life makes Fascism the precise negation of that doctrine which formed the basis of the so-called Scientific or Marxian Socialism: the doc-

trine of historical Materialism, according to which the history of human civilizations can be explained only as the struggle of interest between the different social groups and as arising out of change in the means and instruments of production. That economic improvements—discoveries of raw materials, new methods of work, scientific inventions—should have an importance of their own, no one denies, but that they should suffice to explain human history to the exclusion of all other factors is absurd: Fascism believes, now and always, in holiness and in heroism, that is in acts in which no economic motive—remote or immediate—plays a part. With this negation of historical materialism, according to which men would be only by-products of history, who appear and disappear on the surface of the waves while in the depths the real directive forces are at work, there is also denied the immutable and irreparable "class struggle" which is the natural product of this economic conception of history, and above all it is denied that the class struggle can be the primary agent of social changes. Socialism, being thus wounded in these two primary tenets of its doctrine, nothing of it is left save the sentimental aspiration—old as humanity—towards a social order in which the sufferings and the pains of the humblest folk could be alleviated. But here Fascism rejects the concept of an economic "happiness" which would be realized socialistically and almost automatically at a given moment of economic evolution by assuring to all a maximum prosperity. Fascism denies the possibility of the materialistic conception of "happiness" and leaves it to the economists of the first half of the eighteenth century; it denies, that is, the equation of prosperity with happiness, which would transform men into animals with one sole preoccupation: that of being well-fed and fat, degraded in consequence to a merely physical existence.

6. After Socialism, Fascism attacks the whole complex of democratic ideologies and rejects them both in their theoretical premises and in their applications or practical manifestations. Fascism denies that the majority, through the mere fact of being a majority, can rule human societies; it denies that this majority can govern by means of a periodical consultation; it affirms the irremediable, fruitful and beneficent inequality of men, who cannot be levelled by such a mechanical and extrinsic fact as universal suffrage. By democratic regimes we mean those in which from time to time the people is given the illusion of being sovereign, while true effective sovereignty lies in other, perhaps irresponsible and secret, forces. Democracy is a regime without a king, but with very many kings, perhaps more exclusive, tyrannical and violent than one king even though a tyrant. This explains why Fascism, although before 1922 for reasons of expediency it made a gesture of republicanism, renounced it before the March on Rome, convinced that the question of the political forms of a State is not pre-eminent to-day, and that studying past and present monarchies, past and present Republics it becomes clear that monarchy and republic are not to be judged *sub specie aeternitatis*, but represent forms in which the political evolution, the history, the tradition, the psychology of a given country are manifested. Now Fascism overcomes the antithesis between monarchy and republic which retarded the movements of democracy, burdening the former with every defect and defending the latter as the regime of perfection. Now it has been seen that there are inherently reactionary and absolutistic republics, and monarchies that welcome the most daring political and social innovations.

7. "Reason, Science," said Renan (who was inspired before Fascism existed) in one of his philosophical Meditations, "are products of humanity, but to expect reason directly from the people and through

the people is a chimera. It is not necessary for the existence of reason that everybody should know it. In any case, if such an initiation should be made, it would not be made by means of base democracy, which apparently must lead to the extinction of every difficult culture, and every higher discipline. The principle that society exists only for the prosperity and the liberty of the individuals who compose it does not seem to conform with the plans of nature, plans in which the species alone is taken into consideration and the individual seems to be sacrificed. It is strongly to be feared lest the last word of democracy thus understood (I hasten to say that it can also be understood in other ways) would be a social state in which a degenerate mass would have no other care than to enjoy the ignoble pleasures of vulgar men."

Thus far Renan. Fascism rejects in democracy the absurd conventional lie of political equalitarianism clothed in the dress of collective irresponsibility and the myth of happiness and indefinite progress. But if democracy can be understood in other ways, that is, if democracy means not to relegate the people to the periphery of the State, then Fascism could be defined as an "organized, centralized, authoritarian democracy."

8. In face of Liberal doctrines, Fascism takes up an attitude of absolute opposition both in the field of politics and in that of economics. It is not necessary to exaggerate—merely for the purpose of present controversies—the importance of Liberalism in the past century, and to make of that which was one of the numerous doctrines sketched in that century a religion of humanity for all times, present and future. Liberalism flourished for no more than some fifteen years. It was born in 1830, as a reaction against the Holy Alliance that wished to drag Europe back to what it had been before 1789, and it had its year of splendour in 1848 when even Pius IX was a Liberal.

Immediately afterwards the decay set in. If 1848 was a year of light and of poetry, 1849 was a year of darkness and of tragedy. The Republic of Rome was destroyed by another Republic, that of France. In the same year Marx launched the gospel of the religion of Socialism with the famous *Communist Manifesto*. In 1851 Napoleon III carried out his unliberal *coup d'état* and ruled over France until 1870, when he was dethroned by a popular revolt, but as a consequence of a military defeat which ranks among the most resounding that history can relate. The victor was Bismarck, who never knew the home of the religion of liberty or who were its prophets. It is symptomatic that a people of high culture like the Germans should have been completely ignorant of the religion of liberty during the whole of the nineteenth century. It was, there, no more than a parenthesis, represented by what has been called the "ridiculous Parliament of Frankfort" which lasted only a season. Germany has achieved her national unity outside the doctrines of Liberalism, against Liberalism, a doctrine which seems foreign to the German soul, a soul essentially monarchical, whilst Liberalism is the historical and logical beginning of anarchism. The stages of German unity are the three wars of 1864, 1866 and 1870, conducted by "Liberals" like Moltke and Bismarck. As for Italian unity, Liberalism has had in it a part absolutely inferior to the share of Mazzini and of Garibaldi, who were not Liberals. Without the intervention of the unliberal Napoleon we should not have gained Lombardy, and without the help of the unliberal Bismarck at Sadowa and Sedan, very probably we should not have gained Venice in 1866; and in 1870 we should not have entered Rome. From 1870-1915 there occurs the period in which the very priests of the new creed had to confess the twilight of their religion: defeated as it was by decadence in literature, by activism in practice. Activism:

that is to say, Nationalism, Futurism, Fascism. The "Liberal" century, after having accumulated an infinity of Gordian knots, tried to untie them by the hecatomb of the World War. Never before has any religion imposed such a cruel sacrifice. Were the gods of Liberalism thirsty for blood? Now Liberalism is about to close the doors of its deserted temples because the peoples feel that its agnosticism in economics, its indifferentism in politics and in morals, would lead, as they have led, the States to certain ruin. In this way one can understand why all the political experiences of the contemporary world are anti-Liberal, and it is supremely ridiculous to wish on that account to class them outside of history; as if history were a hunting ground reserved to Liberalism and its professors, as if Liberalism were the definitive and no longer surpassable message of civilization.

9. But the Fascist repudiations of Socialism, Democracy, Liberalism must not make one think that Fascism wishes to make the world return to what it was before 1789, the year which has been indicated as the year of the beginning of the liberal-democratic age. One does not go backwards. The Fascist doctrine has not chosen De Maistre as its prophet. Monarchical absolutism is a thing of the past and so also is every theocracy. So also feudal privileges and division into impenetrable and isolated castes have had their day. The theory of Fascist authority has nothing to do with the police State. A party that governs a nation in a totalitarian way is a new fact in history. References and comparisons are not possible. Fascism takes over from the ruins of Liberal Socialistic democratic doctrines those elements which still have a living value. It preserves those that can be called the established facts of history, it rejects all the rest, that is to say the idea of a doctrine which holds good for all times and all peoples. If it is admitted that the nineteenth century has been the century of

Socialism, Liberalism and Democracy, it does not follow that the twentieth must also be the century of Liberalism, Socialism and Democracy. Political doctrines pass; peoples remain. It is to be expected that this century may be that of authority, a century of the "Right," a Fascist century. If the nineteenth was the century of the individual (Liberalism means individualism) it may be expected that this one may be the century of "collectivism" and therefore the century of the State. That a new doctrine should use the still vital elements of other doctrines is perfectly logical. No doctrine is born quite new, shining, never before seen. No doctrine can boast of an absolute "originality." It is bound, even if only historically, to other doctrines that have been, and to develop into other doctrines that will be. Thus the scientific socialism of Marx is bound to the Utopian Socialism of the Fouriers, the Owens and the Saint-Simons; thus the Liberalism of the nineteenth century is connected with the whole "Enlightenment" of the eighteenth century. Thus the doctrines of democracy are bound to the *Encyclopedie*. Every doctrine tends to direct the activity of men towards a determined objective; but the activity of man reacts upon the doctrine, transforms it, adapts it to new necessities or transcends it. The doctrine itself, therefore, must be, not words, but an act of life. Hence, the pragmatic veins in Fascism, its will to power, its will to be, its attitude in the face of the fact of "violence" and of its own courage.

10. The keystone of Fascist doctrine is the conception of the State, of its essence, of its tasks, of its ends. For Fascism the State is an absolute before which individuals and groups are relative. Individuals and groups are "thinkable" in so far as they are within the State. The Liberal State does not direct the interplay and the material and spiritual development of the groups, but limits itself to registering the results;

the Fascist State has a consciousness of its own, a will of its own, on this account it is called an "ethical" State. In 1929, at the first quinquennial assembly of the regime, I said: "For Fascism, the State is not the night-watchman who is concerned only with the personal security of the citizens; nor is it an organization for purely material ends, such as that of guaranteeing a certain degree of prosperity and a relatively peaceful social order, to achieve which a council of administration would be sufficient, nor is it a creation of mere politics with no contact with the material and complex reality of the lives of individuals and the life of peoples. The State, as conceived by Fascism and as it acts, is a spiritual and moral fact because it makes concrete the political, juridical, economic organization of the nation and such an organization is, in its origin and in its development, a manifestation of the spirit. The State is the guarantor of internal and external security, but it is also the guardian and the transmitter of the spirit of the people as it has been elaborated through the centuries in language, custom, faith. The State is not only present, it is also past, and above all future. It is the State which, transcending the brief limit of individual lives, represents the immanent conscience of the nation. The forms in which States express themselves change, but the necessity of the State remains. It is the State which educates citizens for civic virtue, makes them conscious of their mission, calls them to unity; harmonizes their interests in justice; hands on the achievements of thought in the sciences, the arts, in law, in human solidarity; it carries men from the elementary life of the tribe to the highest human expression of power which is Empire; it entrusts to the ages the names of those who died for its integrity or in obedience to its laws; it puts forward as an example and recommends to the generations that are to come the lead-ers who increased its territory and the men of genius who gave it glory. When the sense of the State declines and the disintegrating and centrifugal tendencies of individuals and groups prevail, national societies move to their decline."

11. From 1929 up to the present day these doctrinal positions have been strengthened by the whole economico-political evolution of the world. It is the State alone that grows in size, in power. It is the State alone that can solve the dramatic contradictions of capitalism. What is called the crisis cannot be overcome except by the State, within the State. Where are the shades of the Jules Simons who, at the dawn of liberalism, proclaimed that "the State must strive to render itself unnecessary and to prepare for its demise"; of the MacCullochs who, in the second half of the last century, affirmed that the State must abstain from too much governing? And faced with the continual, necessary and inevitable interventions of the State in economic affairs what would the Englishman Bentham now say, according to whom industry should have asked of the State only to be left in peace? Or the German Humboldt, according to whom the "idle" State must be considered the best? It is true that the second generation of liberal economists was less extremist than the first, and already Smith himself opened, even though cautiously, the door to State intervention in economics. But when one says liberalism, one says the individual; when one says Fascism, one says the State. But the Fascist State is unique; it is an original creation. It is not reactionary, but revolutionary in that it anticipates the solutions of certain universal problems. These problems are no longer seen in the same light: in the sphere of politics they are removed from party rivalries, from the supreme power of parliament, from the irresponsibility of assemblies; in the sphere of economics they are removed from the

sphere of the syndicates' activities—activities that were ever widening their scope and increasing their power both on the workers' side and on the employers'—removed from their struggles and their designs; in the moral sphere they are divorced from ideas of the need for order, discipline and obedience, and lifted into the plane of the moral commandments of the fatherland. Fascism desires the State to be strong, organic and at the same time founded on a wide popular basis. The Fascist State has also claimed for itself the field of economics and, through the corporative, social and educational institutions which it has created, the meaning of the State reaches out to and includes the farthest off-shoots; and within the State, ramed in their respective organizations, there revolve all the political, economic and spiritual forces of the nation. A State founded on millions of individuals who recognize it, feel it, are ready to serve it, is not the tyrannical State of the medieval lord. It has nothing in common with the absolutist States that existed either before or after 1789. In the Fascist State the individual is not suppressed, but rather multiplied, just as in a regiment a soldier is not weakened but multiplied by the number of his comrades. The Fascist State organizes the nation, but it leaves sufficient scope to individuals; it has limited useless or harmful liberties and has preserved those that are essential. It cannot be the individual who decides in this matter, but only the State.

12. The Fascist State does not remain indifferent to the fact of religion in general and to that particular positive religion which is Italian Catholicism. The State has no theology, but it has an ethic. In the Fascist State religion is looked upon as one of the deepest manifestations of the spirit; it is, therefore, not only respected, but defended and protected. The Fascist State does not create a "God" of its own, as Robespierre once, at the height of the Convention's foolishness, wished to do; nor does it vainly seek, like Bolshevism, to expel religion from the minds of men; Fascism respects the God of the ascetics, of the saints, of the heroes, and also God as seen and prayed to by the simple and primitive heart of the people.

13. The Fascist State is a will to power and to government. In it the tradition of Rome is an idea that has force. In the doctrine of Fascism Empire is not only a territorial, military or mercantile expression, but spiritual or moral. One can think of an empire, that is to say a nation that directly or indirectly leads other nations, without needing to conquer a single square kilometre of territory. For Fascism the tendency to Empire, that is to say, to the expansion of nations, is a manifestation of vitality; its opposite, staying at home, is a sign of decadence: peoples who rise or rerise are imperialist, peoples who die are renunciatory. Fascism is the doctrine that is most fitted to represent the aims, the states of mind, of a people, like the Italian people, rising again after many centuries of abandonment or slavery to foreigners. But Empire calls for discipline, co-ordination of forces, duty and sacrifice; this explains many aspects of the practical working of the regime and the direction of many of the forces of the State and the necessary severity shown to those who would wish to oppose this spontaneous and destined impulse of the Italy of the twentieth century, to oppose it in the name of the superseded ideologies of the nineteenth, repudiated wherever great experiments of political and social transformation have been courageously attempted: especially where, as now, peoples thirst for authority, for leadership, for order. If every age has its own doctrine, it is apparent from a thousand signs that the doctrine of the present age is Fascism. That it is a doctrine of life is shown by the fact that it has resuscitated a faith. That this faith has conquered

minds is proved by the fact that Fascism has had its dead and its martyrs.

Fascism henceforward has in the world the universality of all those doctrines which, by fulfilling themselves, have significance in the history of the human spirit.

John Dewey

For the first half of the twentieth century, the American intellectual scene was dominated by the figure of John Dewey (1859-1952). Born of a family whose roots reached back to the early colonial days of New England, Dewey became interested in philosophy while he was attending the University of Vermont. After finishing college he entered graduate school at Johns Hopkins University to study for his doctorate in philosophy. There, as almost everywhere else in late nineteenth-century America, the philosophy that was taught was the absolute idealism of Hegel. Though Dewey accepted Hegelian idealism for a time, he gave it up before long in favor of the pragmatic philosophy of the great American philosopher, William James (1842-1910).

Pragmatism, as developed first by James and later more fully by Dewey, was an at-tempt to find a basis for philosophy in the experimental methods employed by the empirical sciences. During the preceding three hundred years scientists had achieved phenomenal results through the method of experimentation. And Dewey believed that the use of this same method could lead to similar advances in every field of intellectual endeavor. This conviction became the basis for Dewey's pragmatic philosophy, which rested on two basic theses: (1) that the truth or validity of any hypothesis depended on the results it produced when it was put into practice, and, therefore, (2) that experimental verification was the ideal method for attaining truth and, hence, for solving man's problems in all areas of life and thought.

In the selection that follows, Dewey uses the pragmatic theory to solve one of the great problems of contemporary pol-itics. The problem with which he is concerned is evident from the title of the book from which the selection is taken, *Liberalism and Social Action.* Historically, the liberal movement (particularly with such writers as Locke and Bentham) had stood for a minimum of social action by government agencies. Even Mill, though he had begun to have doubts, still believed that the liberty of the individual must be preserved from the encroachments of government. But Dewey, writing in the middle of the great depression of the thirties, could see that the policy of *laissez-faire* could no longer be defended. So the problem, as he saw it, was this: How can one preserve the human liberty in which liberals believe, and yet admit the need for society to act in behalf of its members? His answer, which he gives in the final chapter of the book, is reproduced in the selection that follows.

LIBERALISM AND SOCIAL ACTION

.   .   .

RENASCENT LIBERALISM

Nothing is blinder than the supposition that we live in a society and world so static that either nothing new will happen or else it will happen because of the use of violence. Social change is here as a fact, a fact having multifarious forms and marked in intensity. Changes that are revolutionary in effect are in process in every phase of life. Transformations in the family, the church, the school, in science and art, in economic and political relations, are occurring so swiftly that imagination is baffled in attempt to lay hold of them. Flux does not have to be created. But it does have to be directed. It has to be so controlled that it will move to some end in accordance with the principles of life, since life itself is development. Liberalism is committed to an end that is at once enduring and flexible: the liberation of individuals so that realization of their capacities may be the law of their life. It is committed to the use of freed intelligence as the method of directing change. In any case, civilization is faced with the problem of uniting the changes that are going on into a coherent pattern of social organization. The liberal spirit is marked by its own picture of the pattern that is required: a social organization that will make possible effective liberty and opportunity for personal growth in mind and spirit in all individuals. Its present need is recognition that established material security is a prerequisite of the ends which it cherishes, so that, the basis of life being secure, individuals may actively share in the wealth of cultural resources that now exist and

may contribute, each in his own way, to their further enrichment.

The fact of change has been so continual and so intense that it overwhelms our minds. We are bewildered by the spectacle of its rapidity, scope and intensity. It is not surprising that men have protected themselves from the impact of such vast change by resorting to what psychoanalysis has taught us to call rationalizations, in other words, protective fantasies. The Victorian idea that change is a part of an evolution that necessarily leads through successive stages to some preordained divine far-off event is one rationalization. The conception of a sudden, complete, almost catastrophic, transformation, to be brought about by the victory of the proletariat over the class now dominant, is a similar rationalization. But men have met the impact of change in the realm of actuality, mostly by drift and by temporary, usually incoherent, improvisations. Liberalism, like every other theory of life, has suffered from the state of confused uncertainty that is the lot of a world suffering from rapid and varied change for which there is no intellectual and moral preparation.

Because of this lack of mental and moral preparation the impact of swiftly moving changes produced, as I have just said, confusion, uncertainty and drift. Change in patterns of belief, desire and purpose has lagged behind the modification of the external conditions under which men associate. Industrial habits have changed most rapidly; there has followed at considerable distance, change in political relations; alterations in legal relations and methods have lagged even more, while changes in the institutions that deal most directly with patterns of thought and belief have taken place to the least extent. This fact defines the primary, though not by any means the ultimate, responsibility of a liberalism that intends to be a vital force. Its work is first of all education, in the broadest sense of that term. Schooling is a part of the work of education, but education in its full meaning includes all the influences that go to form the attitudes and dispositions (of desire as well as of belief), which constitute dominant habits of mind and character.

Let me mention three changes that have taken place in one of the institutions in which immense shifts have occurred, but that are still relatively external—external in the sense that the pattern of intelligent purpose and emotion has not been correspondingly modified. Civilization existed for most of human history in a state of scarcity in the material basis for a humane life. Our ways of thinking, planning and working have been attuned to this fact. Thanks to science and technology we now live in an age of potential plenty. The immediate effect of the emergence of the new possibility was simply to stimulate, to a point of incredible exaggeration, the striving for the material resources, called wealth, opened to men in the new vista. It is a characteristic of all development, physiological and mental, that when a new force and factor appears, it is first pushed to an extreme. Only when its possibilities have been exhausted (at least relatively) does it take its place in the life perspective. The economic-material phase of life, which belongs in the basal ganglia of society, has usurped for more than a century the cortex of the social body. The habits of desire and effort that were bred in the age of scarcity do not readily subordinate themselves and take the place of the matter-of-course routine that becomes appropriate to them when machines and impersonal power have the capacity to liberate man from bondage to the strivings that were once needed to make secure his

physical basis. Even now when there is a vision of an age of abundance and when the vision is supported by hard fact, it is material security as an end that appeals to most rather than the way of living which this security makes possible. Men's minds are still pathetically held in the clutch of old habits and haunted by old memories.

For, in the second place, insecurity is the natural child and the foster child, too, of scarcity. Early liberalism emphasized the importance of insecurity as a fundamentally necessary economic motive, holding that without this goad men would not work, abstain or accumulate. Formulation of this conception was new. But the fact that was formulated was nothing new. It was deeply rooted in the habits that were formed in the long struggle against material scarcity. The system that goes by the name of capitalism is a systematic manifestation of desires and purposes built up in an age of ever threatening want and now carried over into a time of ever increasing potential plenty. The conditions that generate insecurity for the many no longer spring from nature. They are found in institutions and arrangements that are within deliberate human control. Surely this change marks one of the greatest revolutions that has taken place in all human history. Because of it, insecurity is not now the motive to work and sacrifice but to despair. It is not an instigation to put forth energy but to an impotency that can be converted from death into endurance only by charity. But the habits of mind and action that modify institutions to make potential abundance an actuality are still so inchoate that most of us discuss labels like individualism, socialism and communism instead of even perceiving the possibility, much less the necessity for realizing what can and should be.

In the third place, the patterns of belief and purpose that still dominate economic institutions were formed when individuals produced with their hands, alone or in small groups. The notion that society in general is served by the unplanned coincidence of the consequences of a vast multitude of efforts put forth by isolated individuals without reference to any social end, was also something new as a formulation. But it also formulated the working principle of an epoch which the advent of new forces of production was to bring to an end. It demands no great power of intelligence to see that under present conditions the isolated individual is well-nigh helpless. Concentration and corporate organization are the rule. But the concentration and corporate organization are still controlled in their operation by ideas that were institutionalized in eons of separate individual effort. The attempts at cooperation for mutual benefit that are put forth are precious as experimental moves. But that society itself should see to it that a cooperative industrial order be instituted, one that is consonant with the realities of production enforced by an era of machinery and power, is so novel an idea to the general mind that its mere suggestion is hailed with abusive epithets—sometimes with imprisonment.

When, then, I say that the first object of a renascent liberalism is education, I mean that its task is to aid in producing the habits of mind and character, the intellectual and moral patterns, that are somewhere near even with the actual movements of events. It is, I repeat, the split between the latter as they have externally occurred and the ways of desiring, thinking, and of putting emotion and purpose into execution that is the basic cause of present confusion in mind and paralysis in action. The educational task cannot be accomplished merely by working upon men's minds, without action that effects actual change in institutions. The idea that dispositions and attitudes can be altered by merely "moral" means conceived of as something that goes on wholly inside of persons is itself one of the old patterns that has to be changed. Thought, desire and purpose exist in a constant give and take of interaction with environing conditions. But resolute thought is the first step in that change of action that will itself carry further the needed change in patterns of mind and character.

In short, liberalism must now become radical, meaning by "radical" perception of the necessity of thoroughgoing changes in the set-up of institutions and corresponding activity to bring the changes to pass. For the gulf between what the actual situation makes possible and the actual state itself is so great that it cannot be bridged by piecemeal policies undertaken *ad hoc*. The process of producing the changes will be, in any case, a gradual one. But "reforms" that deal now with this abuse and now with that without having a social goal based upon an inclusive plan, differ entirely from effort at re-forming, in its literal sense, the institutional scheme of things. The liberals of more than a century ago were denounced in their time as subversive radicals, and only when the new economic order was established did they become apologists for the *status quo* or else content with social patchwork. If radicalism be defined as perception of need for radical change, then today any liberalism which is not also radicalism is irrelevant and doomed.

But radicalism also means, in the minds of many, both supporters and opponents, dependence upon use of violence as the main method of effecting drastic changes. Here the liberal parts company. For he is committed to the organization of intelligent action as the chief method. Any frank discussion of the issue must recognize the extent to which those who decry the use of any violence are themselves willing to resort to violence and are ready to put their will into operation. Their fundamental objection is to change in the economic institution that now exists, and for its maintenance they resort to the use of the force that is placed in their hands by this very institution. They do not need to advocate the use of force; their only need is to employ it. Force, rather than intelligence, is built into the procedures of the existing social system, regularly as coercion, in times of crisis as overt violence. The legal system, conspicuously in its penal aspect, more subtly in civil practice, rests upon coercion. Wars are the methods recurrently used in settlement of disputes between nations. One school of radicals dwells upon the fact that in the past the transfer of power in one society has either been accomplished by or attended with violence. But what we need to realize is that physical force is used, at least in the form of coercion, in the very set-up of our society. That the competitive system, which was thought of by early liberals as the means by which the latent abilities of individuals were to be evoked and directed into socially useful channels, is now in fact a state of scarcely disguised battle hardly needs to be dwelt upon. That the control of the means of production by the few in legal possession operates as a standing agency of coercion of the many, may need emphasis in statement, but is surely evident to one who is willing to observe and honestly report the existing scene. It is foolish to regard the political state as the only agency now endowed with coercive power. Its exercise of this power is pale in contrast with that exercised by concentrated and organized property interests.

It is not surprising in view of our standing dependence upon the use of coercive force that at every time of crisis coercion breaks out into open violence. In this country, with its tradition of violence fostered by frontier conditions and by the conditions under which immigration went

on during the greater part of our history, resort to violence is especially recurrent on the part of those who are in power. In times of imminent change, our verbal and sentimental worship of the Constitution, with its guarantees of civil liberties of expression, publication and assemblage, readily goes overboard. Often the officials of the law are the worst offenders, acting as agents of some power that rules the economic life of a community. What is said about the value of free speech as a safety valve is then forgotten with the utmost of ease: a comment, perhaps, upon the weakness of the defense of freedom of expression that values it simply as a means of blowing-off steam.

It is not pleasant to face the extent to which, as matter of fact, coercive and violent force is relied upon in the present social system as a means of social control. It is much more agreeable to evade the fact. But unless the fact is acknowledged as a fact in its full depth and breadth, the meaning of dependence upon intelligence as the alternative method of social direction will not be grasped. Failure in acknowledgment signifies, among other things, failure to realize that those who propagate the dogma of dependence upon force have the sanction of much that is already entrenched in the existing system. They would but turn the use of it to opposite ends. The assumption that the method of intelligence already rules and that those who urge the use of violence are introducing a new element into the social picture may not be hypocritical but it is unintelligently unaware of what is actually involved in intelligence as an alternative method of social action.

I begin with an example of what is really involved in the issue. Why is it, apart from our tradition of violence, that liberty of expression is tolerated and even lauded when social affairs seem to be going in a quiet fashion, and yet is so readily destroyed whenever matters grow critical? The general answer, of course, is that at bottom social institutions have habituated us to the use of force in some veiled form. But a part of the answer is found in our ingrained habit of regarding intelligence as an individual possession and its exercise as an individual right. It is false that freedom of inquiry and of expression are not modes of action. They are exceedingly potent modes of action. The reactionary grasps this fact, in practice if not in express idea, more quickly than the liberal, who is too much given to holding that this freedom is innocent of consequences, as well as being a merely individual right. The result is that this liberty is tolerated as long as it does not seem to menace in any way the *status quo* of society. When it does, every effort is put forth to identify the established order with the public good. When this identification is established, it follows that any merely individual right must yield to the general welfare. As long as freedom of thought and speech is claimed as a merely individual right, it will give way, as do other merely personal claims, when it is, or is successively represented to be, in opposition to the general welfare.

I would not in the least disparage the noble fight waged by early liberals in behalf of individual freedom of thought and expression. We owe more to them than it is possible to record in words. No more eloquent words have ever come from any one than those of Justice Brandeis in the case of a legislative act that in fact restrained freedom of political expression. He said: "Those who won our independence believed that the final end of the State was to make men free to develop their faculties, and that in its government the deliberative faculties should prevail over the arbitrary. They valued liberty both as an end and as a means. They believed liberty to be the secret of happiness and courage to be the secret of liberty. They believed that freedom to think as you will and to speak

as you think are means indispensable to the discovery and spread of political truth; that without free speech and assembly discussion would be futile; that with them, discussion affords ordinary adequate protection against the dissemination of noxious doctrines; that the greatest menace to freedom is an inert people; that public discussion is a political duty; and that this should be a fundamental principle of the American government." This is the creed of a fighting liberalism. But the issue I am raising is connected with the fact that these words are found in a dissenting, a minority opinion of the Supreme Court of the United States. The public function of free individual thought and speech is clearly recognized in the words quoted. But the reception of the truth of the words is met by an obstacle: the old habit of defending liberty of thought and expression as something inhering in individuals apart from and even in opposition to social claims.

Liberalism has to assume the responsibility for making it clear that intelligence is a social asset and is clothed with a function as public as is its origin, in the concrete, in social cooperation. It was Comte who, in reaction against the purely individualistic ideas that seemed to him to underlie the French Revolution, said that in mathematics, physics and astronomy there is no right of private conscience. If we remove the statement from the context of actual scientific procedure, it is dangerous because it is false. The individual inquirer has not only the right but the duty to criticize the ideas, theories and "laws" that are current in science. But if we take the statement in the context of scientific method, it indicates that he carries on this criticism in virtue of a socially generated body of knowledge and by means of methods that are not of private origin and possession. He uses a method that retains public validity even when innovations are introduced in its use and application.

Henry George, speaking of ships that ply the ocean with a velocity of five or six hundred miles a day, remarked, "There is nothing whatever to show that the men who today build and navigate and use such ships are one whit superior in any physical or mental quality to their ancestors, whose best vessel was a coracle of wicker and hide. The enormous improvement which these ships show is not an improvement of human nature; it is an improvement of society—it is due to a wider and fuller union of individual efforts in accomplishment of common ends." This single instance, duly pondered, gives a better idea of the nature of intelligence and its social office than would a volume of abstract dissertation. Consider merely two of the factors that enter in and their social consequences. Consider what is involved in the production of steel, from the first use of fire and then the crude smelting of ore, to the processes that now effect the mass production of steel. Consider also the development of the power of guiding ships across trackless wastes from the day when they hugged the shore, steering by visible sun and stars, to the appliances that now enable a sure course to be taken. It would require a heavy tome to describe the advances in science, in mathematics, astronomy, physics, chemistry, that have made these two things possible. The record would be an account of a vast multitude of cooperative efforts, in which one individual uses the results provided for him by a countless number of other individuals, and uses them so as to add to the common and public store. A survey of such facts brings home the actual social character of intelligence as it actually develops and makes its way. Survey of the consequences upon the ways of living of individuals and upon the terms on which men associate together, due to the new method of transportation would take us to the wheat farmer of the prairies, the cattle raiser of the plains, the cotton grower of the South; into a multitude of mills and factories, and to the counting-room of banks, and what would be seen in this country would be repeated in every country of the globe.

It is to such things as these, rather than to abstract and formal psychology that we must go if we would learn the nature of intelligence: in itself, in its origin and development, and its uses and consequences. At this point, I should like to recur to an idea put forward in the preceding chapter. I then referred to the contempt often expressed for reliance upon intelligence as a social method, and I said this scorn is due to the identification of intelligence with native endowments of individuals. In contrast to this notion, I spoke of the power of individuals to appropriate and respond to the intelligence, the knowledge, ideas and purposes that have been integrated in the medium in which individuals live. Each of us knows, for example, some mechanic of ordinary native capacity who is intelligent within the matters of his calling. He has lived in an environment in which the cumulative intelligence of a multitude of cooperating individuals is embodied, and by the use of his native capacities he makes some phase of this intelligence his own. Given a social medium in whose institutions the available knowledge, ideas and art of humanity were incarnate, and the average individual would rise to undreamed heights of social and political intelligence.

The rub, the problem is found in the proviso. Can the intelligence actually existent and potentially available be embodied in that institutional medium in which an individual thinks, desires and acts? Before dealing directly with this question, I wish to say something about the operation of intelligence in our present political institutions, as exemplified by current practices of democratic government. I would not minimize the advance scored in substitution of methods of discussion and conference for the method of arbitrary rule. But the better is too often the enemy of the still better. Discussion, as the manifestation of intelligence in political life, stimulates publicity; by its means sore spots are brought to light that would otherwise remain hidden. It affords opportunity for promulgation of new ideas. Compared with despotic rule, it is an invitation to individuals to concern themselves with public affairs. But discussion and dialectic, however indispensable they are to the elaboration of ideas and policies after ideas are once put forth, are weak reeds to depend upon for systematic origination of comprehensive plans, the plans that are required if the problem of social organization is to be met. There was a time when discussion, the comparison of ideas already current so as to purify and clarify them, was thought to be sufficient in discovery of the structure and laws of physical nature. In the latter field, the method was displaced by that of experimental observation guided by comprehensive working hypotheses, and using all the resources made available by mathematics.

But we still depend upon the method of discussion, with only incidental scientific control, in politics. Our system of popular suffrage, immensely valuable as it is in comparison with what preceded it, exhibits the idea that intelligence is an individualistic possession, at best enlarged by public discussion. Existing political practice, with its complete ignoring of occupational groups and the organized knowledge and purposes that are involved in the existence of such groups, manifests a dependence upon a summation of individuals quantitatively, similar to Bentham's purely quantitative formula of the greatest sum of pleasures of the greatest possible number. The formation of parties or, as the eighteenth-century writers called them, factions, and the system of party government is the practically nec-

essary counterweight to a numerical and atomistic individualism. The idea that the conflict of parties will, by means of public discussion, bring out necessary public truths is a kind of political watered-down version of the Hegelian dialectic, with its synthesis arrived at by a union of antithetical conceptions. The method has nothing in common with the procedure of organized cooperative inquiry which has won the triumphs of science in the field of physical nature.

Intelligence in politics when it is identified with discussion means reliance upon symbols. The invention of language is probably the greatest single invention achieved by humanity. The development of political forms that promote the use of symbols in place of arbitrary power was another great invention. The nineteenth-century establishment of parliamentary institutions, written constitutions and the suffrage as means of political rule, is a tribute to the power of symbols. But symbols are significant only in connection with realities behind them. No intelligent observer can deny, I think, that they are often used in party politics as a substitute for realities instead of as means of contact with them. Popular literacy, in connection with the telegraph, cheap postage and the printing press, has enormously multiplied the number of those influenced. That which we term education has done a good deal to generate habits that put symbols in the place of realities. The forms of popular government make necessary the elaborate use of words to influence political action. "Propaganda" is the inevitable consequence of the combination of these influences and it extends to every area of life. Words not only take the place of realities but are themselves debauched. Decline in the prestige of suffrage and of parliamentary government are intimately associated with the belief, manifest in practice even if not expressed in words, that intelligence is an individual possession to be reached by means of verbal persuasion.

This fact suggests, by way of contrast, the genuine meaning of intelligence in connection with public opinion, sentiment and action. The crisis in democracy demands the substitution of the intelligence that is exemplified in scientific procedure for the kind of intelligence that is now accepted. The need for this change is not exhausted in the demand for greater honesty and impartiality, even though these qualities be now corrupted by discussion carried on mainly for purposes of party supremacy and for imposition of some special but concealed interest. These qualities need to be restored. But the need goes further. The social use of intelligence would remain deficient even if these moral traits were exalted, and yet intelligence continued to be identified simply with discussion and persuasion, necessary as are these things. Approximation to use of scientific method in investigation and of the engineering mind in the invention and projection of far-reaching social plans is demanded. The habit of considering social realities in terms of cause and effect and social policies in terms of means and consequences is still inchoate. The contrast between the state of intelligence in politics and in the physical control of nature is to be taken literally. What has happened in this latter is the outstanding demonstration of the meaning of organized intelligence. The combined effect of science and technology has released more productive energies in a bare hundred years than stands to the credit of prior human history in its entirety. Productively it has multiplied nine million times in the last generation alone. The prophetic vision of Francis Bacon of subjugation of the energies of nature through change in methods of inquiry has well-nigh been realized. The stationary engine, the locomotive, the dynamo, the motor car, turbine, telegraph, telephone, radio and moving picture are not the products of either isolated individual minds nor of the particular economic regime called capitalism. They are the fruit of methods that first penetrated to the working causalities of nature and then utilized the resulting knowledge in bold imaginative ventures of invention and construction.

We hear a great deal in these days about class conflict. The past history of man is held up to us as almost exclusively a record of struggles between classes, ending in the victory of a class that had been oppressed and the transfer of power to it. It is difficult to avoid reading the past in terms of the contemporary scene. Indeed, fundamentally it is impossible to avoid this course. With a certain proviso, it is highly important that we are compelled to follow this path. For the past as past is gone, save for esthetic enjoyment and refreshment, while the present is with us. Knowledge of the past is significant only as it deepens and extends our understanding of the present. Yet there is a proviso. We must grasp the things that are most important in the present when we turn to the past and not allow ourselves to be misled by secondary phenomena no matter how intense and immediately urgent they are. Viewed from this standpoint, the rise of scientific method and of technology based upon it is the genuinely active force in producing the vast complex of changes the world is now undergoing, not the class struggle whose spirit and method are opposed to science. If we lay hold upon the causal force exercised by this embodiment of intelligence we shall know where to turn for the means of directing further change.

When I say that scientific method and technology have been the active force in producing the revolutionary transformations society is undergoing, I do not imply no other forces have been at work to arrest, deflect and corrupt their operation. Rather this fact is positively implied. At this point, indeed, is located the conflict that underlies the confusions and uncertainties of the present scene. The conflict is between institutions and habits originating in the pre-scientific and pre-technological age and the new forces generated by science and technology. The application of science, to a considerable degree, even its own growth, has been conditioned by the system to which the name of capitalism is given, a rough designation of a complex of political and legal arrangements centering about a particular mode of economic relations. Because of the conditioning of science and technology by this setting, the second and humanly most important part of Bacon's prediction has so far largely missed realization. The conquest of natural energies has not accrued to the betterment of the common human estate in anything like the degree he anticipated.

Because of conditions that were set by the legal institutions and the moral ideas existing when the scientific and industrial revolutions came into being, the chief usufruct of the latter has been appropriated by a relatively small class. Industrial entrepreneurs have reaped out of all proportion to what they sowed. By obtaining private ownership of the means of production and exchange they deflected a considerable share of the results of increased productivity to their private pockets. This appropriation was not the fruit of criminal conspiracy or of sinister intent. It was sanctioned not only by legal institutions of age-long standing but by the entire prevailing moral code. The institution of private property long antedated feudal times. It is the institution with which men have lived, with few exceptions, since the dawn of civilization. Its existence has deeply impressed itself upon mankind's moral conceptions. Moreover, the new industrial forces tended to break down many of the rigid class barriers that had been in force, and to give to millions a new outlook and inspire a new hope;—especially in this country with no feudal background and no fixed class system.

Since the legal institutions and the patterns of mind characteristic of ages of civilization still endure, there exists the conflict that brings confusion into every phase of present life. The problem of bringing into being a new social orientation and organization is, when reduced to its ultimates, the problem of using the new resources of production, made possible by the advance of physical science, for social ends, for what Bentham called the greatest good of the greatest number. Institutional relationships fixed in the pre-scientific age stand in the way of accomplishing this great transformation. Lag in mental and moral patterns provides the bulwark of the older institutions; in expressing the past they still express present beliefs, outlooks and purposes. Here is the place where the problem of liberalism centers today.

The argument drawn from past history that radical change must be effected by means of class struggle, culminating in open war, fails to discriminate between the two forces, one active, the other resistant and deflecting, that have produced the social scene in which we live. The active force is, as I have said, scientific method and technological application. The opposite force is that of older institutions and the habits that have grown up around them. Instead of discrimination between forces and distribution of their consequences, we find the two things lumped together. The compound is labeled the capitalistic or the bourgeois class, and to this class as a class is imputed all the important features of present industrialized society —much as the defenders of the regime of economic liberty exercised for private property are accustomed to attribute every improvement made in the last century and a half to the same capitalistic regime. Thus in orthodox communist literature, from the Communist Manifesto of 1848 to the present day, we are told that the bourgeoisie, the name for a distinctive class, has done this and that. It has, so it is said, given a cosmopolitan character to production and consumption; has destroyed the national basis of industry; has agglomerated population in urban centers; has transferred power from the country to the city, in the process of creating colossal productive force, its chief achievement. In addition, it has created crises of ever renewed intensity; has created imperialism of a new type in frantic effort to control raw materials and markets. Finally, it has created a new class, the proletariat, and has created it as a class having a common interest opposed to that of the bourgeoisie, and is giving an irresistible stimulus to its organization, first as a class and then as a political power. According to the economic version of the Hegelian dialectic, the bourgeois class is thus creating its own complete and polar opposite, and this in time will end the old power and rule. The class struggle of veiled civil war will finally burst into open revolution and the result will be either the common ruin of the contending parties or a revolutionary reconstitution of society at large through a transfer of power from one class to another.

The position thus sketched unites vast sweep with great simplicity. I am concerned with it here only as far as it emphasizes the idea of a struggle between classes, culminating in open and violent warfare as being the method for production of radical social change. For, be it noted, the issue is not whether some amount of violence will accompany the effectuation of radical change of institutions. The question is whether force or intelligence is to be the method upon which we consistently rely and to whose promotion we devote our energies. Insistence that the use of violent force is *inevitable* limits the use of available intelligence, for wherever the inevitable reigns intelligence cannot be used. Com-

mitment to inevitability is always the fruit of dogma; intelligence does not pretend to *know* save as a result of experimentation, the opposite of preconceived dogma. Moreover, acceptance in advance of the inevitability of violence tends to produce the use of violence in cases where peaceful methods might otherwise avail. The curious fact is that while it is generally admitted that this and that particular social problem, say of the family, or railroads or banking, must be solved, if at all, by the method of intelligence, yet there is supposed to be some one all-inclusive social problem which can be solved only by the use of violence. This fact would be inexplicable were it not a conclusion from dogma as its premise.

It is frequently asserted that the method of experimental intelligence can be applied to physical facts because physical nature does not present conflicts of class interests, while it is inapplicable to society because the latter is so deeply marked by incompatible interests. It is then assumed that the "experimentalist" is one who has chosen to ignore the uncomfortable fact of conflicting interests. Of course, there *are* conflicting interests; otherwise there would be no social problems. The problem under discussion is precisely *how* conflicting claims are to be settled in the interest of the widest possible contribution to the interests of all—or at least of the great majority. The method of democracy—inasfar as it is that of organized intelligence—is to bring these conflicts out into the open where their special claims can be seen and appraised, where they can be discussed and judged in the light of more inclusive interests than are represented by either of them separately. There is, for example, a clash of interests between munition manufacturers and most of the rest of the population. The more the respective claims of the two are publicly and scientifically weighed, the more likely it is that the public interest will be disclosed and be made effective. There is an undoubted objective clash of interests between finance-capitalism that controls the means of production and whose profit is served by maintaining relative scarcity, and idle workers and hungry consumers. But what generates violent strife is failure to bring the conflict into the light of intelligence where the conflicting interests can be adjudicated in behalf of the interest of the great majority. Those most committed to the dogma of inevitable force recognize the need for intelligently discovering and expressing the dominant social interest up to a certain point and then draw back. The "experimentalist" is one who would see to it that the method depended upon by all in some degree in every democratic community be followed through to completion.

In spite of the existence of class conflicts, amounting at times to veiled civil war, any one habituated to the use of the method of science will view with considerable suspicion the erection of actual human beings into fixed entities called classes, having no overlapping interests and so internally unified and externally separated that they are made the protagonists of history—itself hypothetical. Such an idea of classes is a survival of a rigid logic that once prevailed in the sciences of nature, but that no longer has any place there. This conversion of abstractions into entities smells more of a dialectic of concepts than of a realistic examination of facts, even though it makes more of an emotional appeal to many than do the results of the latter. To say that all past historic social progress has been the result of cooperation and not of conflict would be also an exaggeration. But exaggeration against exaggeration, it is the more reasonable of the two. And it is no exaggeration to say that the measure of civilization is the degree in which the method of cooperative intelligence replaces the method of brute conflict.

But the point I am especially concerned with just here is the indiscriminate lumping together as a single force of two different things—the results of scientific technology and of a legal system of property relations. It is science and technology that have had the revolutionary social effect while the legal system has been the relatively static element. According to the Marxians themselves, the economic foundations of society consist of two things, the forces of production on one side and, on the other side, the social relations of production, that is, the legal property system under which the former operates. The latter lags behind, and "revolutions" are produced by the power of the forces of production to change the system of institutional relations. But what are the modern forces of production save those of scientific technology? And what is scientific technology save a large-scale demonstration of organized intelligence in action?

It is quite true that what is happening socially is the result of the combination of the two factors, one dynamic, the other relatively static. If we choose to call the combination by the name of capitalism, then it is true, or a truism, that capitalism is the "cause" of all the important social changes that have occurred—an argument that the representatives of capitalism are eager to put forward whenever the increase of productivity is in question. But if we want to *understand*, and not just to paste labels, unfavorable or favorable as the case may be, we shall certainly begin and end with discrimination. Colossal increase in productivity, the bringing of men together in cities and large factories, the elimination of distance, the accumulation of capital, fixed and liquid—these things would have come about, at a certain stage, no matter what the established institutional system. They are the consequence of the new means of technological production. Certain other things have happened because of inherited institutions and the habits of belief and character that accompany and support them. If we begin at this point, we shall see that the release of productivity is the product of cooperatively organized intelligence, and shall also see that the institutional framework is precisely that which is not subjected as yet, in any considerable measure, to the impact of inventive and constructive intelligence. That coercion and oppression on a large scale exists, no honest person can deny. But these things are not the product of science and technology but of the perpetuation of old institutions and patterns untouched by scientific method. The inference to be drawn is clear.

The argument, drawn from history, that great social changes have been effected only by violent means, needs considerable qualification, in view of the vast scope of changes that are taking place without the use of violence. But even if it be admitted to hold of the past, the conclusion that violence is the method now to be depended upon does not follow—unless one is committed to a dogmatic philosophy of history. The radical who insists that the future method of change must be like that of the past has much in common with the hide-bound reactionary who holds to the past as an ultimate fact. Both overlook the *fact that history in being a process of change generates change not only in details but also in the method of directing social change*. I recur to what I said at the beginning of this chapter. It is true that the social order is largely conditioned by the use of coercive force, bursting at times into open violence. But what is also true is that mankind now has in its possession a new method, that of cooperative and experimental science which expresses the method of intelligence. I should be meeting dogmatism with dogmatism if I asserted that the existence of this historically new factor completely invalidates all arguments drawn from the effect of force in the past. But it is within the

bounds of reason to assert that the presence of this social factor demands that the present situation be analyzed on its own terms, and not be rigidly subsumed under fixed conceptions drawn from the past.

Any analysis made in terms of the present situation will not fail to note one fact that militates powerfully against arguments drawn from past use of violence. Modern warfare is destructive beyond anything known in older times. This increased destructiveness is due primarily, of course, to the fact that science has raised to a new pitch of destructive power all the agencies of armed hostility. But it is also due to the much greater interdependence of all the elements of society. The bonds that hold modern communities and states together are as delicate as they are numerous. The self-sufficiency and independence of a local community, characteristic of more primitive societies, have disappeared in every highly industrialized country. The gulf that once separated the civilian population from the military has virtually gone. War involves paralysis of all normal social activities, and not merely the meeting of armed forces in the field. The Communist Manifesto presented two alternatives: *either* the revolutionary change and transfer of power to the proletariat, *or* the common ruin of the contending parties. Today, the civil war that would be adequate to effect transfer of power and a reconstitution of society at large, as understood by official Communists, would seem to present but one possible consequence: the ruin of all parties and the destruction of civilized life. This fact alone is enough to lead us to consider the potentialities of the method of intelligence.

The argument for putting chief dependence upon violence as the method of effecting radical change is, moreover, usually put in a way that proves altogether too much for its own case. It is said that the dominant economic class has all the agencies of power in its hands, directly the army, militia and police; indirectly, the courts, schools, press and radio. I shall not stop to analyze this statement. But if one admits it to be valid, the conclusion to be drawn is surely the folly of resorting to a use of force against force that is so well intrenched. The positive conclusion that emerges is that conditions that would promise success in the case of use of force are such as to make possible great change without any great recourse to such a method.

Those who uphold the necessity of dependence upon violence usually much oversimplify the case by setting up a disjunction they regard as self-evident. They say that the sole alternative is putting our trust in parliamentary procedures as they now exist. This isolation of law-making from other social forces and agencies that are constantly operative is wholly unrealistic. Legislatures and congresses do not exist in a vacuum— not even the judges on the bench live in completely secluded sound-proof chambers. The assumption that it is possible for the constitution and activities of law-making bodies to persist unchanged while society itself is undergoing great change is an exercise in verbal formal logic.

It is true that in this country, because of the interpretations made by courts of a written constitution, our political institutions are unusually inflexible. It is also true, as well as even more important (because it is a factor in causing this rigidity) that our institutions, democratic in form, tend to favor in substance a privileged plutocracy. Nevertheless, it is sheer defeatism to assume in advance of actual trial that democratic political institutions are incapable either of further development or of constructive social application. Even as they now exist, the forms of representative government are potentially capable of expressing the public will when that assumes anything like unification. And there is nothing inherent in them that forbids

their supplementation by political agencies that represent definitely economic social interests, like those of producers and consumers.

The final argument in behalf of the use of intelligence is that as are the means used so are the actual ends achieved—that is, the consequences. I know of no greater fallacy than the claim of those who hold to the dogma of the necessity of brute force that this use will be the method of calling genuine democracy into existence—of which they profess themselves the simon-pure adherents. It requires an unusually credulous faith in the Hegelian dialectic of opposites to think that all of a sudden the use of force by a class will be transmuted into a democratic classless society. Force breeds counterforce; the Newtonian law of action and reaction still holds in physics, and violence is physical. To profess democracy as an ultimate ideal and the suppression of democracy as a means to the ideal may be possible in a country that has never known even rudimentary democracy, but when professed in a country that has anything of a genuine democratic spirit in its traditions, it signifies desire for possession and retention of power by a class, whether that class be called Fascist or Proletarian. In the light of what happens in non-democratic countries, it is pertinent to ask whether the rule of a class signifies the dictatorship of the majority, or dictatorship over the chosen class by a minority party; whether dissenters are allowed even within the class the party claims to represent; and whether the development of literature and the other arts proceeds according to a formula prescribed by a party in conformity with a doctrinaire dogma of history and of infallible leadership, or whether artists are free from regimentation? Until these questions are satisfactorily answered, it is permissible to look with considerable suspicion upon those who assert that suppression of democracy is the road to the adequate establishment of genuine democracy. The one exception—and that apparent rather than real—to dependence upon organized intelligence as the method for directing social change is found when society through an authorized majority has entered upon the path of social experimentation leading to great social change, and a minority refuses by force to permit the method of intelligent action to go into effect. Then force may be intelligently employed to subdue and disarm the recalcitrant minority.

There may be some who think I am unduly dignifying a position held by a comparatively small group by taking their arguments as seriously as I have done. But their position serves to bring into strong relief the alternatives before us. It makes clear the meaning of renascent liberalism. The alternatives are continuation of drift with attendant improvisations to meet special emergencies; dependence upon violence; dependence upon socially organized intelligence. The first two alternatives, however, are not mutually exclusive, for if things are allowed to drift the result may be some sort of social change effected by the use of force, whether so planned or not. Upon the whole, the recent policy of liberalism has been to further "social legislation"; that is, measures which add performance of social services to the older functions of government. The value of this addition is not to be despised. It marks a decided move away from *laissez faire* liberalism, and has considerable importance in educating the public mind to a realization of the possibilities of organized social control. It has helped to develop some of the techniques that in any case will be needed in a socialized economy. But the cause of liberalism will be lost for a considerable period if it is not prepared to go further and socialize the forces of production, now at hand, so that the liberty of individuals will be supported by the very structure of economic organization.

The ultimate place of economic organization in human life is to assure the secure basis for an ordered expression of individual capacity and for the satisfaction of the needs of man in non-economic directions. The effort of mankind in connection with material production belongs, as I said earlier, among interests and activities that are, relatively speaking, routine in character, "routine" being defined as that which, without absorbing attention and energy, provides a constant basis for liberation of the values of intellectual, esthetic and companionship life. Every significant religious and moral teacher and prophet has asserted that the material is instrumental to the good life. Nominally at least, this idea is accepted by every civilized community. The transfer of the burden of material production from human muscles and brain to steam, electricity and chemical processes now makes possible the effective actualization of this idea. Needs, wants and desires are always the moving force in generating creative action. When these wants are compelled by force of conditions to be directed for the most part, among the mass of mankind, into obtaining the means of subsistence, what should be a means becomes perforce an end in itself. Up to the present the new mechanical forces of production, which are the means of emancipation from this state of affairs, have been employed to intensify and exaggerate the reversal of the true relation between means and ends. Humanly speaking, I do not see how it would have been possible to avoid an epoch having this character. But its perpetuation is the cause of the continually growing social chaos and strife. Its termination cannot be effected by preaching to individuals that they should place spiritual ends above material means. It can be brought about by organized social reconstruction that puts the results of the mechanism of abundance at the free disposal of individuals. The actual corrosive "materialism" of our times does not proceed from science. It springs from the notion, sedulously cultivated by the class in power, that the creative capacities of individuals can be evoked and developed only in a struggle for material possessions and material gain. We either should surrender our professed belief in the supremacy of ideal and spiritual values and accommodate our beliefs to the predominant material orientation, or we should through organized endeavor institute the socialized economy of material security and plenty that will release human energy for pursuit of higher values.

Since liberation of the capacities of individuals for free, self-initiated expression is an essential part of the creed of liberalism, liberalism that is sincere must will the means that condition the achieving of its ends. Regimentation of material and mechanical forces is the only way by which the mass of individuals can be released from regimentation and consequent suppression of their cultural possibilities. The eclipse of liberalism is due to the fact that it has not faced the alternatives and adopted the means upon which realization of its professed aims depends. Liberalism can be true to its ideals only as it takes the course that leads to their attainment. The notion that organized social control of economic forces lies outside the historic path of liberalism shows that liberalism is still impeded by remnants of its earlier *laissez faire* phase, with its opposition of society and the individual. The thing which now dampens liberal ardor and paralyzes its efforts is the conception that liberty and development of individuality as ends exclude the use of organized social effort as means. Earlier liberalism regarded the separate and competing economic action of individuals as the means of social well-being as the end. We must reverse the perspective and see that socialized economy is the means of free individual development as the end.

That liberals are divided in outlook and endeavor while reactionaries are held together by community of interests and the ties of custom is well-nigh a commonplace. Organization of standpoint and belief among liberals can be achieved only in and by unity of endeavor. Organized unity of action attended by consensus of beliefs will come about in the degree in which social control of economic forces is made the goal of liberal action. The greatest educational power, the greatest force in shaping the dispositions and attitudes of individuals, is the social medium in which they live. The medium that now lies closest to us is that of unified action for the inclusive end of a socialized economy. The attainment of a state of society in which a basis of material security will release the powers of individuals for cultural expression is not the work of a day. But by concentrating upon the task of securing a socialized economy as the ground and medium for release of the impulses and capacities men agree to call ideal, the now scattered and often conflicting activities of liberals can be brought to effective unity.

It is no part of my task to outline in detail a program for renascent liberalism. But the question of "what is to be done" cannot be ignored. Ideas must be organized, and this organization implies an organization of individuals who hold these ideas and whose faith is ready to translate itself into action. Translation into action signifies that the general creed of liberalism be formulated as a concrete program of action. It is in organization for action that liberals are weak, and without this organization there is danger that democratic ideals may go by default. Democracy has been a fighting faith. When its ideals are reenforced by those of scientific method and experimental intelligence, it cannot be that it is incapable of evoking discipline, ardor and organization. To narrow the issue for the future to a struggle between Fascism and Communism is to invite a catastrophe that may carry civilization down in the struggle. Vital and courageous democratic liberalism is the one force that can surely avoid such a disastrous narrowing of the issue. I for one do not believe that Americans living in the tradition of Jefferson and Lincoln will weaken and give up without a whole-hearted effort to make democracy a living reality. This, I repeat, involves organization.

The question cannot be answered by argument. Experimental method means experiment, and the question can be answered only by trying, by organized effort. The reasons for making the trial are not abstract or recondite. They are found in the confusion, uncertainty and conflict that mark the modern world. The reasons for thinking that the effort if made will be successful are also not abstract and remote. They lie in what the method of experimental and cooperative intelligence has already accomplished in subduing to potential human use the energies of physical nature. In material production, the method of intelligence is now the established rule; to abandon it would be to revert to savagery. The task is to go on, and not backward, until the method of intelligence and experimental control is the rule in social relations and social direction. Either we take this road or we admit that the problem of social organization in behalf of human liberty and the flowering of human capacities is insoluble.

It would be fantastic folly to ignore or to belittle the obstacles that stand in the way. But what has taken place, also against great odds, in the scientific and industrial revolutions, is an accomplished fact; the way is marked out. It may be that the way will remain untrodden. If so, the future holds the menace of confusion moving into chaos, a chaos that will be externally masked for a time by an organization of force, coercive and violent, in which the liberties of men will all but disappear. Even so, the cause of the liberty of the human spirit, the cause of opportunity of human beings for full development of their powers, the cause for which liberalism enduringly stands, is too precious and too ingrained in the human constitution to be forever obscured. Intelligence after millions of years of errancy has found itself as a method, and it will not be lost forever in the blackness of night. The business of liberalism is to bend every energy and exhibit every courage so that these precious goods may not even be temporarily lost but be intensified and expanded here and now.

George Orwell

NINETEEN EIGHTY-FOUR is a prophetic novel in which the author, George Orwell (1903-1950), presents a picture of our society as he envisions it a generation from now. Orwell's main interest, though, is not with the future but with the present. For in his representation of society in 1984 he simply pushes to their logical culmination trends that he has found within our own society. Orwell's primary concern in the novel is to reveal the true nature of these trends as a warning to his contemporaries.

In the selection that follows, the protagonist, Winston Smith, is undergoing "brain-washing" in the Ministry of Love. He has been apprehended by the secret police for the crime of treason. Specifically, he was caught reading a book, allegedly written by the arch-traitor, Goldstein, which advocated a revolution against the Party. But this is not Smith's real crime. What condemns him is his unwillingness, or inability, to accept the Party's definition of truth. As an employee in the Ministry of Truth, where his job was to rewrite history, he had several years previously stumbled on evidence, in the form of a newspaper photograph, which proved that the Party was deliberately falsifying events. His faith in the Party had been undermined, and he had never been able fully to believe again. In the eyes of the Party, such doubt is the highest crime.

NINETEEN EIGHTY-FOUR is clearly a satire on the dictatorships, both fascist and communist, of our century. But what is even more important is that Orwell's attack is not directed merely against the totalitarians but at our own governments and society as well. For the book is set in London, now located in Oceania, a super-state composed mainly of the British Isles and the Americas. Notice, too, Orwell's analysis of the philosophical bases of the society of 1984. He finds these, as O'Brien explains to Smith, in the skepticism concerning the possibility of knowledge characteristic of the empiricist tradition of John Locke and his followers, particularly David Hume.

NINETEEN EIGHTY-FOUR

·   ·   ·

[*Winston*] was lying on something that felt like a camp bed, except that it was higher off the ground and that he was fixed down in some way so that he could not move. Light that seemed stronger than usual was falling on his face. O'Brien was standing at his side, looking down at him intently. At the other side of him stood a man in a white coat, holding a hypodermic syringe.

Even after his eyes were open he took in his surroundings only gradually. He had the impression of swimming up into this room from some quite different world, a sort of underwater world far beneath it. How long he had been down there he did not know. Since the moment when they arrested him he had not seen darkness or daylight. Besides, his memories were not continuous. There had been times when consciousness, even the sort of consciousness that one has in sleep, had stopped dead and started again after a blank interval. But whether the intervals were of days or weeks or only seconds, there was no way of knowing.

With that first blow on the elbow the nightmare had started. Later he was to realize that all that then happened was merely a preliminary, a routine interrogation to which nearly all prisoners were subjected. There was a long range of crimes—espionage, sabotage, and the like—to which everyone had to confess as a matter of course. The confession was a formality, though the torture was real. How many times he had been beaten, how long the beatings had continued, he could not remember. Always there were five or six men

NINETEEN EIGHTY-FOUR, George Orwell. Harcourt, Brace and Company, Inc. Copyright, 1949, by Harcourt, Brace and Company, Inc.

in black uniforms at him simultaneously. Sometimes it was fists, sometimes it was truncheons, sometimes it was steel rods, sometimes it was boots. There were times when he rolled about the floor, as shameless as an animal, writhing his body this way and that in an endless, hopeless effort to dodge the kicks and simply inviting more and yet more kicks, in his ribs, in his belly, on his elbows, on his shins, in his groin, in his testicles, on the bone at the base of his spine. There were times when it went on and on until the cruel, wicked, unforgivable thing seemed to him not that the guards continued to beat him but that he could not force himself into losing consciousness. There were times when his nerve so forsook him that he began shouting for mercy even before the beating began, when the mere sight of a fist drawn back for a blow was enough to make him pour forth a confession of real and imaginary crimes. There were other times when he started out with the resolve of confessing nothing, when every word had to be forced out of him between gasps of pain, and there were times when he feebly tried to compromise, when he said to himself: "I will confess, but not yet. I must hold out till the pain becomes unbearable. Three more kicks, two more kicks, and then I will tell them what they want." Sometimes he was beaten till he could hardly stand, then flung like a sack of potatoes onto the stone floor of a cell, left to recuperate for a few hours, and then taken out and beaten again. There were also longer periods of recovery. He remembered them dimly, because they were spent chiefly in sleep or stupor. He remembered a cell with a plank bed, a sort of shelf sticking out from the wall, and a tin washbasin, and meals of hot soup and bread and sometimes coffee. He remembered a surly barber arriving to scrape his chin and crop his hair, and businesslike, unsympathetic men in white coats feeling his pulse, tapping his reflexes, turning up his eyelids, running harsh fingers over him in search of broken bones, and shooting needles into his arm to make him sleep.

The beatings grew less frequent, and became mainly a threat, a horror to which he could be sent back at any moment when his answers were unsatisfactory. His questioners now were not ruffians in black uniforms but Party intellectuals, little rotund men with quick movements and flashing spectacles, who worked on him in relays over periods which lasted—he thought, he could not be sure—ten or twelve hours at a stretch. These other questioners saw to it that he was in constant slight pain, but it was not chiefly pain that they relied on. They slapped his face, wrung his ears, pulled his hair, made him stand on one leg, refused him leave to urinate, shone glaring lights in his face until his eyes ran with water; but the aim of this was simply to humiliate him and destroy his power of arguing and reasoning. Their real weapon was the merciless questioning that went on and on hour after hour, tripping him up, laying traps for him, twisting everything that he said, convicting him at every step of lies and self-contradiction, until he began weeping as much from shame as from nervous fatigue. Sometimes he would weep half a dozen times in a single session. Most of the time they screamed abuse at him and threatened at every hesitation to deliver him over to the guards again; but sometimes they would suddenly change their tune, call him comrade, appeal to him in the name of Ingsoc and Big Brother, and ask him sorrowfully whether even now he had not enough loyalty to the Party left to make him wish to undo the evil he had done. When his nerves were in rags after hours of questioning, even this appeal could reduce him to sniveling tears. In the end the nagging voices broke him down more completely than the boots and fists of the guards. He became simply a mouth that uttered, a hand that signed whatever was demanded of him. His sole concern was to find out what they wanted him to confess, and then confess it quickly, before the bullying started anew. He confessed to the assassination of eminent Party members, the distribution of seditious pamphlets, embezzlement of public funds, sale of military secrets, sabotage of every kind. He confessed that he had been a spy in the pay of the Eastasian government as far back as 1968. He confessed that he was a religious believer, and an admirer of capitalism, and a sexual pervert. He confessed that he had murdered his wife although he knew, and his questioners must have known, that his wife was still alive. He confessed that for years he had been in personal touch with Goldstein and had been a member of an underground organization which had included almost every human being he had ever known. It was easier to confess everything and implicate everybody. Besides, in a sense it was all true. It was true that he had been the enemy of the Party, and in the eyes of the Party there was no distinction between the thought and the deed.

There were also memories of another kind. They stood out in his mind disconnectedly, like pictures with blackness all round them.

He was in a cell which might have been either dark or light, because he could see nothing except a pair of eyes. Near at hand some kind of instrument was ticking slowly and regularly. The eyes grew larger and more luminous. Suddenly he floated out of his seat, dived into the eyes, and was swallowed up.

He was strapped into a chair surrounded by dials, under dazzling lights. A man in a white coat was reading the dials. There was a tramp of heavy boots outside. The door clanged open. The waxen-faced officer marched in, followed by two guards.

"Room 101," said the officer.

The man in the white coat did not turn round. He did not look at Winston either; he was looking only at the dials.

He was rolling down a mighty corridor, a kilometer wide, full of glorious, golden light, roaring with laughter and shouting out confessions at the top of his voice. He was confessing everything, even the things he had succeeded in holding back under the torture. He was relating the entire history of his life to an audience who knew it already. With him were the guards, the other questioners, the men in white coats, O'Brien, Julia, Mr. Charrington, all rolling down the corridor together and shouting with laughter. Some dreadful thing which had lain embedded in the future had somehow been skipped over and had not happened. Everything was all right, there was no more pain, the last detail of his life was laid bare, understood, forgiven.

He was starting up from the plank bed in the half-certainty that he had heard O'Brien's voice. All through his interrogation, although he had never seen him, he had had the feeling that O'Brien was at his elbow, just out of sight. It was O'Brien who was directing everything. It was he who set the guards onto Winston and who prevented them from killing him. It was he who decided when Winston should scream with pain, when he should have a respite, when he should be fed, when he should sleep, when the drugs should be pumped into his arm. It was he who asked the questions and suggested the answers. He was the tormentor, he was the protector, he was the inquisitor, he was the friend. And once—Winston could not remember whether it was in drugged sleep, or in normal sleep, or even in a moment of wakefulness—a voice murmured in his ear: "Don't worry, Winston; you are in my keeping. For seven years I have watched over you. Now the turning point has come. I shall save you, I shall make you perfect." He was not sure whether it was O'Brien's voice; but it was the same voice that had said to him, "We shall meet in the place where there is no darkness," in that other dream, seven years ago.

He did not remember any ending to his interrogation. There was a period of blackness and then the cell, or room, in which he now was had gradually materialized round him. He was almost flat on his back, and unable to move. His body was held down at every essential point. Even the back of his head was gripped in some manner. O'Brien was looking down at him gravely and rather sadly. His face, seen from below, looked coarse and worn, with pouches under the eyes and tired lines from nose to chin. He was older than Winston had thought him; he was perhaps forty-eight or fifty. Under his hand there was a dial with a lever on top and figures running round the face.

"I told you," said O'Brien, "that if we met again it would be here."

"Yes," said Winston.

Without any warning except a slight movement of O'Brien's hand, a wave of pain flooded his body. It was a frightening pain, because he could not see what was happening, and he had the feeling that some mortal injury was being done to him. He did not know whether the thing was really happening, or whether the effect was electrically produced; but his body was being wrenched out of shape, the joints were being slowly torn apart. Although the pain had brought the sweat out on his forehead, the worst of all was the fear that his backbone was about to snap. He set his teeth and breathed hard through his nose, trying to keep silent as long as possible.

"You are afraid," said O'Brien, watching his face, "that in another moment something is going to break. Your especial fear is that it will be your backbone. You have a vivid mental picture of the vertebrae snapping apart and the spinal fluid dripping out of them. That is what you are thinking, is it not, Winston?"

Winston did not answer. O'Brien drew back the lever on the dial. The wave of pain receded almost as quickly as it had come.

"That was forty," said O'Brien. "You can see that the numbers on this dial run up to a hundred. Will you please remember, throughout our conversation, that I have it in my power to inflict pain on you at any moment and to whatever degree I choose. If you tell me any lies, or attempt to prevaricate in any way, or even fall below your usual level of intelligence, you will cry out with pain, instantly. Do you understand that?"

"Yes," said Winston.

O'Brien's manner became less severe. He resettled his spectacles thoughtfully, and took a pace or two up and down. When he spoke his voice was gentle and patient. He had the air of a doctor, a teacher, even a priest, anxious to explain and persuade rather than to punish.

"I am taking trouble with you, Winston," he said, "because you are worth trouble. You know perfectly well what is the matter with you. You have known it for years, though you have fought against the knowledge. You are mentally deranged. You suffer from a defective memory. You are unable to remember real events, and you persuade yourself that you remember other events which never happened. Fortunately it is curable. You have never cured yourself of it, because you did not choose to. There was a small effort of the will that you were not ready to make. Even now, I am well aware, you are clinging to your disease under the impression that it is a virtue. Now we will take an example. At this moment, which power is Oceania at war with?"

"When I was arrested, Oceania was at war with Eastasia."

"With Eastasia. Good. And Oceania has always been at war with Eastasia, has it not?"

Winston drew in his breath. He opened his mouth to speak and then did not speak. He could not take his eyes away from the dial.

"The truth, please, Winston. *Your* truth. Tell me what you think you remember."

"I remember that until only a week before I was arrested, we were not at war with Eastasia at all. We were in alliance with them. The war was against Eurasia. That had lasted for four years. Before that—"

O'Brien stopped him with a movement of the hand.

"Another example," he said. "Some years ago you had a very serious delusion indeed. You believed that three men, three one-time Party members named Jones, Aaronson, and Rutherford—men who were executed for treachery and sabotage after making the fullest possible confession—were not guilty of the crimes they were charged with. You believed that you had seen unmistakable documentary evidence proving that their confessions were false. There was a certain photograph about which you had a hallucination. You believed that you had actually held it in your hands. It was a photograph something like this."

An oblong slip of newspaper had appeared between O'Brien's fingers. For perhaps five seconds it was within the angle of Winston's vision. It was a photograph, and there was no question of its identity. It was *the* photograph of Jones, Aaronson, and Rutherford at the Party function in New York, which he had chanced upon eleven years ago and promptly destroyed. For only an instant it was before his eyes, then it was out of sight again. But he had seen it, unquestionably he had seen it! He made a desperate, agonizing effort to wrench the top half of his body free. It was impossible to move so much as a centimeter in any direction. For the moment he had even forgotten the dial. All he wanted was to hold the photograph in his fingers again, or at least to see it.

"It exists!" he cried.

"No," said O'Brien.

He stepped across the room. There was a memory hole in the opposite wall. O'Brien lifted the grating. Unseen, the frail slip of paper was whirling away on the current of warm air; it was vanishing in a flash of flame. O'Brien turned away from the wall.

"Ashes," he said. "Not even identifiable ashes. Dust. It does not exist. It never existed."

"But it did exist! It does exist! It exists in memory. I remember it. You remember it."

"I do not remember it," said O'Brien.

Winston's heart sank. That was doublethink. He had a feeling of deadly helplessness. If he could have been certain that O'Brien was lying, it would not have seemed to matter. But it was perfectly possible that O'Brien had really forgotten the photograph. And if so, then already he would have forgotten his denial of remembering it, and forgotten the act of forgetting. How could one be sure that it was simply trickery? Perhaps that lunatic dislocation in the mind could really happen: that was the thought that defeated him.

O'Brien was looking down at him speculatively. More than ever he had the air of a teacher taking pains with a wayward but promising child.

"There is a Party slogan dealing with the control of the past," he said. "Repeat it, if you please."

" 'Who controls the past controls the future; who controls the present controls the past,' " repeated Winston obediently.

" 'Who controls the present controls the past,' " said O'Brien, nodding his head with slow approval. "Is it your opinion, Winston, that the past has real existence?"

Again the feeling of helplessness descended upon Winston. His eyes flitted toward the dial. He not only did not know whether "yes" or "no" was the answer that would save him from pain; he did not even know which answer he believed to be the true one.

O'Brien smiled faintly. "You are no metaphysician, Winston," he said. "Until this moment you had never considered what is meant by existence. I will put it more precisely. Does the past exist concretely, in space? Is there somewhere or other a place, a world of solid objects, where the past is still happening?"

"No."

"Then where does the past exist, if at all?"

"In records. It is written down."

"In records. And—?"

"In the mind. In human memories."

"In memory. Very well, then. We, the Party, control all records, and we control all memories. Then we control the past, do we not?"

"But how can you stop people remembering things?" cried Winston, again momentarily forgetting the dial. "It is involuntary. It is outside oneself. How can you control memory? You have not controlled mine!"

O'Brien's manner grew stern again. He laid his hand on the dial.

"On the contrary," he said, "*you* have not controlled it. That is what has brought you here. You are here because you have failed in humility, in self-discipline. You would not make the act of submission which is the price of sanity. You preferred to be a lunatic, a minority of one. Only the disciplined mind can see reality, Winston. You believe that reality is something objective, external, existing in its own right. You also believe that the nature of reality is self-evident. When you delude yourself into thinking that you see something, you assume that everyone else sees the same thing as you. But I tell you, Winston, that reality is not external. Reality exists in the human mind, and nowhere else. Not in the individual mind, which can make mistakes, and in any case soon perishes; only in the mind of the Party, which is collective and immortal. Whatever the Party holds to be truth *is* truth. It is impossible to see reality except by looking through the eyes of the Party. That is the fact that you have got to relearn, Winston. It needs an act of self-destruction, an effort of the will. You must humble yourself before you can become sane."

He paused for a few moments, as though to allow what he had been saying to sink in.

"Do you remember," he went on, "writing in your diary, 'Freedom is the freedom to say that two plus two make four'?"

"Yes," said Winston.

O'Brien held up his left hand, its back toward Winston, with the thumb hidden and the four fingers extended.

"How many fingers am I holding up, Winston?"

"Four."

"And if the Party says that it is not four but five—then how many?"

"Four."

The word ended in a gasp of pain. The needle of the dial had shot up to fifty-five. The sweat had sprung out all over Winston's body. The air tore into his lungs and issued again in deep groans which even by clenching his teeth he could not stop. O'Brien watched him, the four fingers still extended. He drew back the lever. This time the pain was only slightly eased.

"How many fingers, Winston?"

"Four."

The needle went up to sixty.

"How many fingers, Winston?"

"Four! Four! What else can I say? Four!"

The needle must have risen again, but he did not look at it. The heavy, stern face and the four fingers filled his vision. The fingers stood up before his eyes like pillars, enormous, blurry, and seeming to vibrate, but unmistakably four.

"How many fingers, Winston?"

"Four! Stop it, stop it! How can you go on? Four! Four!"

"How many fingers, Winston?"

"Five! Five! Five!"

"No, Winston, that is no use. You are lying. You still think there are four. How many fingers, please?"

"Four! Five! Four! Anything you like. Only stop it, stop the pain!"

Abruptly he was sitting up with O'Brien's arm round his shoulders. He had perhaps lost consciousness for a few seconds. The bonds that had held his body down were loosened. He felt very cold, he was shaking uncontrollably, his teeth were chattering, the tears were rolling down his cheeks. For a moment he clung to O'Brien like a baby, curiously comforted by the heavy arm round his shoulders. He had the feeling that O'Brien was his protector, that the pain was something that came from outside, from some other source, and that it was O'Brien who would save him from it.

"You are a slow learner, Winston," said O'Brien gently.

"How can I help it?" he blubbered. "How can I help seeing what is in front of my eyes? Two and two are four."

"Sometimes, Winston. Sometimes they are five. Sometimes they are three. Sometimes they are all of them at once. You must try harder. It is not easy to become sane."

He laid Winston down on the bed. The grip on his limbs tightened again, but the pain had ebbed away and the trembling had stopped, leaving him merely weak and cold. O'Brien motioned with his head to the man in the white coat, who had stood immobile throughout the proceedings. The man in the white coat bent down and looked closely into Winston's eyes, felt his pulse, laid an ear against his chest, tapped here and there; then he nodded to O'Brien.

"Again," said O'Brien.

The pain flowed into Winston's body. The needle must be at seventy, seventy-five. He had shut his eyes this time. He knew that the fingers were still there, and still four. All that mattered was somehow to stay alive until the spasm was over. He had ceased to notice whether he was crying out or not. The pain lessened again. He opened his eyes. O'Brien had drawn back the lever.

"How many fingers, Winston?"

"Four. I suppose there are four. I would see five if I could. I am trying to see five."

"Which do you wish: to persuade me that you see five, or really to see them?"

"Really to see them."

"Again," said O'Brien.

Perhaps the needle was at eighty—ninety. Winston could only intermittently remember why the pain was happening. Behind his screwed-up eyelids a forest of fingers seemed to be moving in a sort of dance, weaving in and out, disappearing behind one another and reappearing again. He was trying to count them, he could not remember why. He knew only that it was impossible to count them, and that this was somehow due to the mysterious identity between five and four. The pain died down again. When he opened his eyes it was to find that he was still seeing the same thing. Innumerable fingers, like moving trees, were still streaming past in either direction, crossing and recrossing. He shut his eyes again.

"How many fingers am I holding up, Winston?"

"I don't know. I don't know. You will kill me if you do that again. Four, five, six—in all honesty I don't know."

"Better," said O'Brien.

A needle slid into Winston's arm. Almost in the same instant a blissful, healing warmth spread all through his body. The pain was already half-forgotten. He opened his eyes and looked up gratefully at O'Brien. At sight of the heavy, lined face, so ugly and so intelligent, his heart seemed to turn over. If he could have moved he would have stretched out a hand and laid it on O'Brien's arm. He had never loved him so deeply as at this moment, and not merely because he had stopped the pain. The old feeling, that at bottom it did not matter whether O'Brien was a friend or an enemy, had come back. O'Brien was a person who could be talked to. Perhaps one did not want to be loved so much as to be understood. O'Brien had tortured him to the edge of lunacy, and in a little while, it was certain, he would send him to his death. It made no difference.

In some sense that went deeper than friendship, they were intimates; somewhere or other, although the actual words might never be spoken, there was a place where they could meet and talk. O'Brien was looking down at him with an expression which suggested that the same thought might be in his own mind. When he spoke it was in an easy, conversational tone.

"Do you know where you are, Winston?" he said.

"I don't know. I can guess. In the Ministry of Love."

"Do you know how long you have been here?"

"I don't know. Days, weeks, months—I think it is months."

"And why do you imagine that we bring people to this place?"

"To make them confess."

"No, that is not the reason. Try again."

"To punish them."

"No!" exclaimed O'Brien. His voice had changed extraordinarily, and his face had suddenly become both stern and animated. "No! Not merely to extract your confession, nor to punish you. Shall I tell you why we have brought you here? To cure you! To make you sane! Will you understand, Winston, that no one whom we bring to this place ever leaves our hands uncured? We are not interested in those stupid crimes that you have committed. The Party is not interested in the overt act; the thought is all we care about. We do not merely destroy our enemies; we change them. Do you understand what I mean by that?"

He was bending over Winston. His face looked enormous because of its nearness, and hideously ugly because it was seen from below. Moreover it was filled with a sort of exaltation, a lunatic intensity. Again Winston's heart shrank. If it had been possible he would have cowered deeper into the bed. He felt certain that O'Brien was about to twist the dial out of sheer wantonness. At this moment, however, O'Brien turned away. He took a pace or two up and down. Then he continued less vehemently:

"The first thing for you to understand is that in this place there are no martyrdoms. You have read of the religious persecutions of the past. In the Middle Ages there was the Inquisition. It was a failure. It set out to eradicate heresy, and ended by perpetuating it. For every heretic it burned at the stake, thousands of others rose up. Why was that? Because the Inquisition killed its enemies in the open, and killed them while they were still unrepentant; in fact, it killed them because they were unrepentant. Men were dying because they would not abandon their true beliefs. Naturally all the glory belonged to the victim and all the shame to the Inquisitor who burned him. Later, in the twentieth century, there were the totalitarians, as they were called. There were the German Nazis and the Russian Communists. The Russians persecuted heresy more cruelly than the Inquisition had done. And they imagined that they had learned from the mistakes of the past; they knew, at any rate, that one must not make martyrs. Before they exposed their victims to public trial, they deliberately set themselves to destroy their dignity. They wore them down by torture and solitude until they were despicable, cringing wretches, confessing whatever was put into their mouths, covering themselves with abuse, accusing and sheltering behind one another, whimpering for mercy. And yet after only a few years the same thing had happened over again. The dead men had become martyrs and their degradation was forgotten. Once again, why was it? In the first place, because the confessions that they had made were obviously extorted and untrue. We do not make mistakes of that kind. All the confessions that are uttered here are true. We make them true. And, above all, we do not allow the dead to rise up against us. You must stop imagining that posterity will vindicate you, Winston. Posterity will never hear of you. You will be lifted clean out from the stream of history. We shall turn you into gas and pour you into the stratosphere. Nothing will remain of you: not a name in a register, not a memory in a living brain. You will be annihilated in the past as well as in the future. You will never have existed."

Then why bother to torture me? thought Winston, with a momentary bitterness. O'Brien checked his step as though Winston had uttered the thought aloud. His large ugly face came nearer, with the eyes a little narrowed.

"You are thinking," he said, "that since we intend to destroy you utterly, so that nothing that you say or do can make the smallest difference—in that case, why do we go to the trouble of interrogating you first? That is what you were thinking, was it not?"

"Yes," said Winston.

O'Brien smiled slightly. "You are a flaw in the pattern, Winston. You are a stain that must be wiped out. Did I not tell you just now that we are different from the persecutors of the past? We are not content with negative obedience, nor even with the most abject submission. When finally you surrender to us, it must be of your own free will. We do not destroy the heretic because he resists us; so long as he resists us we never destroy him. We convert him, we capture his inner mind, we reshape him. We burn all evil and all illusion out of him; we bring him over to our side, not in appearance, but genuinely, heart and soul. We make him one of ourselves before we kill him. It is intolerable to us that an erroneous thought should exist anywhere in the world, however secret and powerless it may be. Even in the instant of death we cannot permit any deviation. In the old days the heretic walked to the stake still a heretic, proclaiming his heresy, exulting in it. Even the victim of the Russian purges could carry rebellion locked up in his skull as he walked down the passage waiting for the bullet. But we make

the brain perfect before we blow it out. The command of the old despotisms was 'Thou shalt not.' The command of the totalitarians was 'Thou shalt.' Our command is '*Thou art.*' No one whom we bring to this place ever stands out against us. Everyone is washed clean. Even those three miserable traitors in whose innocence you once believed—Jones, Aaronson, and Rutherford—in the end we broke them down. I took part in their interrogation myself. I saw them gradually worn down, whimpering, groveling, weeping—and in the end it was not with pain or fear, only with penitence. By the time we had finished with them they were only the shells of men. There was nothing left in them except sorrow for what they had done, and love of Big Brother. It was touching to see how they loved him. They begged to be shot quickly, so that they could die while their minds were still clean."

His voice had grown almost dreamy. The exaltation, the lunatic enthusiasm, was still in his face. He is not pretending, thought Winston; he is not a hypocrite; he believes every word he says. What most oppressed him was the consciousness of his own intellectual inferiority. He watched the heavy yet graceful form strolling to and fro, in and out of the range of his vision. O'Brien was a being in all ways larger than himself. There was no idea that he had ever had, or could have, that O'Brien had not long ago known, examined, and rejected. His mind *contained* Winston's mind. But in that case how could it be true that O'Brien was mad? It must be he, Winston, who was mad. O'Brien halted and looked down at him. His voice had grown stern again.

"Do not imagine that you will save yourself, Winston, however completely you surrender to us. No one who has once gone astray is ever spared. And even if we chose to let you live out the natural term of your life, still you would never escape from us. What happens to you here is forever. Understand that in advance. We shall crush you down to the point from which there is no coming back. Things will happen to you from which you could not recover, if you lived a thousand years. Never again will you be capable of ordinary human feeling. Everything will be dead inside you. Never again will you be capable of love, or friendship, or joy of living, or laughter, or curiosity, or courage, or integrity. You will be hollow. We shall squeeze you empty, and then we shall fill you with ourselves."

He paused and signed to the man in the white coat. Winston was aware of some heavy piece of apparatus being pushed into place behind his head. O'Brien had sat down beside the bed, so that his face was almost on a level with Winston's.

"Three thousand," he said, speaking over Winston's head to the man in the white coat.

Two soft pads, which felt slightly moist, clamped themselves against Winston's temples. He quailed. There was pain coming, a new kind of pain. O'Brien laid a hand reassuringly, almost kindly, on his.

"This time it will not hurt," he said. "Keep your eyes fixed on mine."

At this moment there was a devastating explosion, or what seemed like an explosion, though it was not certain whether there was any noise. There was undoubtedly a blinding flash of light. Winston was not hurt, only prostrated. Although he had already been lying on his back when the thing happened, he had a curious feeling that he had been knocked into that position. A terrific, painless blow had flattened him out. Also something had happened inside his head. As his eyes regained their focus he remembered who he was, and where he was, and recognized the face that was gazing into his own; but somewhere or other there was a large patch of emptiness, as though a piece had been taken out of his brain.

"It will not last," said O'Brien. "Look me in the eyes. What country is Oceania at war with?"

Winston thought. He knew what was meant by Oceania, and that he himself was a citizen of Oceania. He also remembered Eurasia and Eastasia; but who was at war with whom he did not know. In fact he had not been aware that there was any war.

"I don't remember."

"Oceania is at war with Eastasia. Do you remember that now?"

"Yes."

"Oceania has always been at war with Eastasia. Since the beginning of your life, since the beginning of the Party, since the beginning of history, the war has continued without a break, always the same war. Do you remember that?"

"Yes."

"Eleven years ago you created a legend about three men who had been condemned to death for treachery. You pretended that you had seen a piece of paper which proved them innocent. No such piece of paper ever existed. You invented it, and later you grew to believe in it. You remember now the very moment at which you first invented it. Do you remember that?"

"Yes."

"Just now I held up the fingers of my hand to you. You saw five fingers. Do you remember that?"

"Yes."

O'Brien held up the fingers of his left hand, with the thumb concealed.

"There are five fingers there. Do you see five fingers?"

"Yes."

And he did see them, for a fleeting instant, before the scenery of his mind changed. He saw five fingers, and there was no deformity. Then everything was normal again, and the old fear, the hatred, and the bewilderment came crowding back again. But there had been a moment—he did not know how long, thirty seconds, perhaps—of luminous certainty, when each new suggestion of O'Brien's had filled up a patch of emptiness and become absolute truth, and when two and two could have been three as easily as five, if that were what was needed. It had faded out before O'Brien had dropped his hand; but though he could not recapture it, he could remember it, as one remembers a vivid experience at some remote period of one's life when one was in effect a different person.

"You see now," said O'Brien, "that it is at any rate possible."

"Yes," said Winston.

O'Brien stood up with a satisfied air. Over to his left Winston saw the man in the white coat break an ampoule and draw back the plunger of a syringe. O'Brien turned to Winston with a smile. In almost the old manner he resettled his spectacles on his nose.

"Do you remember writing in your diary," he said, "that it did not matter whether I was a friend or an enemy, since I was at least a person who understood you and could be talked to? You were right. I enjoy talking to you. Your mind appeals to me. It resembles my own mind except that you happen to be insane. Before we bring the session to an end you can ask me a few questions, if you choose."

"Any question I like?"

"Anything." He saw that Winston's eyes were upon the dial. "It is switched off. What is your first question?"

"What have you done with Julia?" said Winston.

O'Brien smiled again. "She betrayed you Winston. Immediately—unreservedly. I have seldom seen anyone come over to us so promptly. You would hardly recognize her if you saw her. All her rebelliousness, her deceit, her folly, her dirty-mindedness—everything has been burned out of her. It was a perfect conversion, a textbook case."

"You tortured her."

O'Brien left this unanswered. "Next question," he said.

"Does Big Brother exist?"

"Of course he exists. The Party exists. Big Brother is the embodiment of the Party."

"Does he exist in the same way as I exist?"

"You do not exist," said O'Brien.

Once again the sense of helplessness assailed him. He knew, or he could imagine, the arguments which proved his own non-existence; but they were nonsense, they were only a play on words. Did not the statement, "You do not exist," contain a logical absurdity? But what use was it to say so? His mind shriveled as he thought of the unanswerable, mad arguments with which O'Brien would demolish him.

"I think I exist," he said wearily. "I am conscious of my own identity. I was born, and I shall die. I have arms and legs. I occupy a particular point in space. No other solid object can occupy the same point simultaneously. In that sense, does Big Brother exist?"

"It is of no importance. He exists."

"Will Big Brother ever die?"

"Of course not. How could he die? Next question."

"Does the Brotherhood exist?"

"That, Winston, you will never know. If we choose to set you free when we have finished with you, and if you live to be ninety years old, still you will never learn whether the answer to that question is Yes or No. As long as you live, it will be an unsolved riddle in your mind."

Winston lay silent. His breast rose and fell a little faster. He still had not asked the question that had come into his mind the first. He had got to ask it, and yet it was as though his tongue would not utter it. There was a trace of amusement in O'Brien's face. Even his spectacles seemed to wear an ironical gleam. He knows, thought Winston suddenly, he knows what I am going to ask! At the thought the words burst out of him:

"What is in Room 101?"

The expression on O'Brien's face did not change. He answered drily:

"You know what is in Room 101, Winston. Everyone knows what is in Room 101."

He raised a finger to the man in the white coat. Evidently the session was at an end. A needle jerked into Winston's arm. He sank almost instantly into deep sleep.

"There are three stages in your reintegration," said O'Brien. "There is learning, there is understanding, and there is acceptance. It is time for you to enter upon the second stage."

As always, Winston was lying flat on his back. But of late his bonds were looser. They still held him to the bed, but he could move his knees a little and could turn his head from side to side and raise his arms from the elbow. The dial, also, had grown to be less of a terror. He could evade its pangs if he was quick-witted enough; it was chiefly when he showed stupidity that O'Brien pulled the lever. Sometimes they got through a whole session without use of the dial. He could not remember how many sessions there had been. The whole process seemed to stretch out over a long, indefinite time—weeks, possibly—and the intervals between the sessions might sometimes have been days, sometimes only an hour or two.

"As you lie there," said O'Brien, "you have often wondered—you have even asked me—why the Ministry of Love should expend so much time and trouble on you. And when you were free you were puzzled by what was essentially the same question. You could grasp the mechanics of the society you lived in, but not its underlying motives. Do you remember writing in your diary, 'I understand *how*; I do not understand *why*'? It was when you thought about 'why' that you doubted your own sanity. You have read *the book*, Goldstein's book, or parts of it, at least. Did it tell you anything that you did not know already?"

"You have read it?" said Winston.

"I wrote it. That is to say, I collaborated in writing it. No book is produced individually, as you know."

"Is it true, what it says?"

"As description, yes. The program it sets forth is nonsense. The secret accumulation of knowledge—a gradual spread of enlightenment—ultimately a proletarian rebellion—the overthrow of the Party. You foresaw yourself that that was what it would say. It is all nonsense. The proletarians will never revolt, not in a thousand years or a million. They cannot. I do not have to tell you the reason; you know it already. If you have ever cherished any dreams of violent insurrection, you must abandon them. There is no way in which the Party can be overthrown. The rule of the Party is forever. Make that the starting point of your thoughts."

He came closer to the bed. "Forever!" he repeated. "And now let us get back to the question of 'how' and 'why.' You understand well enough *how* the Party maintains itself in power. Now tell me *why* we cling to power. What is our motive? Why should we want power? Go on, speak," he added as Winston remained silent.

Nevertheless Winston did not speak for another moment or two. A feeling of weariness had overwhelmed him. The faint, mad gleam of enthusiasm had come back into O'Brien's face. He knew in advance what O'Brien would say: that the Party did not seek power for its own ends, but only for the good of the majority. That it sought power because men in the mass were frail, cowardly creatures who could not endure liberty or face the truth, and must be ruled over and systematically deceived by others who were stronger than themselves. That the choice for mankind lay between freedom and happiness, and that, for the great bulk of mankind, happiness was better. That the Party was the eternal guardian of the weak, a dedicated sect doing evil that good might come, sacrificing its own happiness to that of others. The terrible thing, thought Winston, the terrible thing was that when O'Brien said this he would believe it. You could see it in his face. O'Brien knew everything. A thousand times better than Winston, he knew what the world was really like, in what degradation the mass of human beings lived and by what lies and barbarities the Party kept them there. He had understood it all, weighed it all, and it made no difference: all was justified by the ultimate purpose. What can you do, thought Winston, against the lunatic who is more intelligent than yourself, who gives your arguments a fair hearing and then simply persists in his lunacy?

"You are ruling over us for our own good," he said feebly. "You believe that human beings are not fit to govern themselves, and therefore—"

He started and almost cried out. A pang of pain had shot through his body. O'Brien had pushed the lever of the dial up to thirty-five.

"That was stupid, Winston, stupid!" he said. "You should know better than to say a thing like that."

He pulled the lever back and continued: "Now I will tell you the answer to my question. It is this. The Party seeks power entirely for its own sake. We are not interested in the good of others; we are interested solely in power. Not wealth or luxury or long life or happiness; only power, pure power. What pure power means you will understand presently. We are different from all the oligarchies of the past in that we know what we are doing. All the others, even those who resembled ourselves, were cowards and hypocrites. The German Nazis and the Russian Communists came very close to us in their methods, but they never had the courage to recognize their own motives. They pretended, perhaps they even believed, that they had seized power unwillingly and for a limited time, and that just around the corner there lay a paradise where human beings would be free and equal. We are not like that. We know that no one ever seizes power with the intention of relinquishing it. Power is not a means; it is an end. One does not establish a dictatorship in order to safeguard a revolution; one makes the revolution in order to establish the dictatorship. The object of persecution is persecution. The object of torture is torture. The object of power is power. Now do you begin to understand me?"

Winston was struck, as he had been struck before, by the tiredness of O'Brien's face. It was strong and fleshy and brutal, it was full of intelligence and a sort of controlled passion before which he felt himself helpless; but it was tired. There were pouches under the eyes, the skin sagged from the cheekbones. O'Brien leaned over him, deliberately bringing the worn face nearer.

"You are thinking," he said, "that my face is old and tired. You are thinking that I talk of power, and yet I am not even able to prevent the decay of my own body. Can you not understand, Winston, that the individual is only a cell? The weariness of the cell is the vigor of the organism. Do you die when you cut your fingernails?"

He turned away from the bed and began strolling up and down again, one hand in his pocket.

"We are the priests of power," he said. "God is power. But at present power is only a word so far as you are concerned. It is time for you to gather some idea of what power means. The first thing you must realize is that power is collective. The individual only has power in so far as he ceases to be an individual. You know the Party slogan: 'Freedom is Slavery.' Has it ever occurred to you that it is reversible? Slavery is freedom. Alone—free—the human being is always defeated. It must be so, because every human being is doomed to die, which is the greatest of all failures. But if he can make complete, utter submission, if he can escape from his identity, if he can merge himself in the Party so that he *is* the Party, then he is all-powerful and immortal. The second thing for you to realize is that power is power over human beings. Over the body—but, above all, over the mind. Power over matter—external reality, as you would call it—is not important. Already our control over matter is absolute."

For a moment Winston ignored the dial. He made a violent effort to raise himself into a sitting position, and merely succeeded in wrenching his body painfully.

"But how can you control matter?" he burst out. "You don't even control the climate or the law of gravity. And there are disease, pain, death—"

O'Brien silenced him by a movement of the hand. "We control matter because we control the mind. Reality is inside the skull. You will learn by degrees, Winston. There is nothing that we could not do. Invisibility, levitation—anything. I could float off this floor like a soap bubble if I wished to. I do not wish to, because the Party does not wish it. You must get rid of those nineteenth-century ideas about the laws of nature. We make the laws of nature."

"But you do not! You are not even masters of this planet. What about Eurasia and Eastasia? You have not conquered them yet."

"Unimportant. We shall conquer them when it suits us. And if we did not, what difference would it make? We can shut them out of existence. Oceania is the world."

"But the world itself is only a speck of dust. And man is tiny—helpless! How long has he been in existence? For millions of years the earth was uninhabited."

"Nonsense. The earth is as old as we are, no older. How could it be older? Nothing exists except through human consciousness."

"But the rocks are full of the bones of extinct animals—mammoths and mastodons and enormous reptiles which lived here long before man was ever heard of."

"Have you ever seen those bones, Winston? Of course not. Nineteenth-century biologists invented them. Before man there was nothing. After man, if he could come to an end, there would be nothing. Outside man there is nothing."

"But the whole universe is outside us. Look at the stars! Some of them are a million light-years away. They are out of our reach forever."

"What are the stars?" said O'Brien indifferently. "They are bits of fire a few kilometers away. We could reach them if we wanted to. Or we could blot them out. The earth is the center of the universe. The sun and the stars go round it."

Winston made another convulsive movement. This time he did not say anything. O'Brien continued as though answering a spoken objection:

"For certain purposes, of course, that is not true. When we navigate the ocean, or when we predict an eclipse, we often find it convenient to assume that the earth goes round the sun and that the stars are millions upon millions of kilometers away. But what of it? Do you suppose it is beyond us to produce a dual system of astronomy? The stars can be near or distant, according as we need them. Do you suppose our mathematicians are unequal to that? Have you forgotten doublethink?"

Winston shrank back upon the bed. Whatever he said, the swift answer crushed him like a bludgeon. And yet he knew, he *knew*, that he was in the right. The belief that nothing exists outside your own mind—surely there must be some way of demonstrating that it was false. Had it not been exposed long ago as a fallacy? There was even a name for it, which he had forgotten. A faint smile twitched the corners of O'Brien's mouth as he looked down at him.

"I told you, Winston," he said, "that metaphysics is not your strong point. The word you are trying to think of is solipsism. But you are mistaken. This is not solipsism. Collective solipsism, if you like. But that is a different thing; in fact, the opposite thing. All this is a digression," he added in a different tone. "The real power, the power we have to fight for night and day, is not power over things, but over men." He paused, and for a moment assumed again his air of a schoolmaster questioning a promising pupil: "How does one man assert his power over another, Winston?"

Winston thought. "By making him suffer," he said.

"Exactly. By making him suffer. Obedience is not enough. Unless he is suffering, how can you be sure that he is obeying your will and not his own? Power is in inflicting pain and humiliation. Power is in tearing human minds to pieces and putting them together again in new shapes of your own choosing. Do you begin to see, then, what kind of world we are creating? It is the exact opposite of the stupid hedonistic Utopias that the old reformers imagined. A world of fear and treachery and torment, a world of trampling and being trampled upon, a world which will grow not less but *more* merciless as it refines itself. Progress in our world will be progress toward more pain. The old civilizations claimed that they were founded on love or justice. Ours is founded upon hatred. In our world there will be no emotions except fear, rage, triumph, and self-abasement. Everything else we shall destroy—everything. Already we are breaking down the habits of thought which have survived from before the Revolution. We have cut the links between child and parent, and between man and man, and between man and woman. No one dares trust a wife or a child or a friend any longer. But in the future there will be no wives and no friends. Children will be taken from their mothers at birth, as one takes eggs from a hen. The sex instinct will be eradicated. Procreation will be an annual formality like the renewal of a ration card. We shall abolish the orgasm. Our neurologists are at work upon it now. There will be no loyalty, except loyalty toward the Party. There will be no love, except the love of Big Brother. There will be no laughter, except the laugh of triumph over a defeated enemy. There will be no art, no literature, no science. When we are omnipotent we shall have no more need of science. There will be no distinction between beauty and ugliness. There will be no curiosity, no enjoyment of the process of life. All competing pleasures will be destroyed. But always— do not forget this, Winston—always there will be the intoxication of power, constantly increasing and constantly growing subtler. Always, at every moment, there will be the thrill of victory, the sensation of trampling on an enemy who is helpless. If you want a picture of the future, imagine a boot stamping on a human face—forever."

Alfred North Whitehead

In his long and active life, Alfred North Whitehead (1861-1947) pursued two distinct, and highly distinguished, careers. The first was in mathematics, a subject that he taught for nearly forty years at Cambridge University and the University of London. This career was capped by the publication of *Principia Mathematica* (1910), a three-volume work written in collaboration with Bertrand Russell, in which logic and mathematics are combined into one theoretical discipline. *Principia Mathematica* is one of the intellectual landmarks of our century.

Toward the end of his career at the University of London, Whitehead became interested in philosophy. Upon his retirement, at the age of sixty-three, he accepted an offer to come to Harvard University as professor of philosophy. Thus began his second career, which lasted until his death at the age of eighty-six and which established him as one of the eminent philosophical thinkers of our era. *Science and the Modern World* (1926) was the first of ten books on philosophy that Whitehead wrote during these years. In it he analyzes modern science and its effects upon our civilization. Then, in the last chapter (which is given in the following selection), he states what he believes to be the requisites for the future progress of our society.

SCIENCE AND THE MODERN WORLD

. . .

REQUISITES FOR SOCIAL PROGRESS

It has been the purpose of these lectures to analyse the reactions of science in forming that background of instinctive ideas which control the activities of successive generations. Such a background takes the form of a certain vague philosophy as to the last word about things, when all is said. The three centuries, which form the epoch of modern science, have revolved round the ideas of *God, mind, mat-*

SCIENCE AND THE MODERN WORLD, A. N. Whitehead (New York: The Macmillan Company, 1926), pp. 277-300. Courtesy of The Macmillan Company.

ter, and also of *space* and *time* in their characters of expressing *simple location* for matter. Philosophy has on the whole emphasised *mind,* and has thus been out of touch with science during the two latter centuries. But it is creeping back into its old importance owing to the rise of psychology and its alliance with physiology. Also, this rehabilitation of philosophy has been facilitated by the recent breakdown of the seventeenth century settlement of the principles of physical science. But, until that collapse, science seated itself securely upon the concepts of matter, space, time, and latterly, of energy. Also there were arbitrary laws of nature determining locomotion. They were empirically observed, but for some obscure reason were known to be universal. Anyone who in practice or theory disregarded them was denounced with unsparing vigour. This position on the part of scientists was pure bluff, if one may credit them with believing their own statements. For their current philosophy completely failed to justify the assumption that the immediate knowledge inherent in any present occasion throws any light either on its past, or its future.

I have also sketched an alternative philosophy of science in which *organism* takes the place of *matter*. For this purpose, the mind involved in the materialist theory dissolves into a function of organism. The psychological field then exhibits what an event is in itself. Our bodily event is an unusually complex type of organism and consequently includes cognition. Further, space and time, in their most concrete signification, become the locus of events. An organism is the realisation of a definite shape of value. The emergence of some actual value depends on limitation which excludes neutralising cross-lights. Thus an event is a matter of fact which by reason of its limitation is a value for itself; but by reason of its very nature it also requires the whole universe in order to be itself.

Importance depends on endurance. Endurance is the retention through time of an achievement of value. What endures is identity of pattern, self-inherited. Endurance requires the favourable environment. The whole of science revolves round this question of enduring organisms.

The general influence of science at the present moment can be analysed under the headings: General Conceptions Respecting the Universe, Technological Applications, Professionalism in Knowledge, Influence of Biological Doctrines on the Motives of Conduct. I have endeavoured in the preceding lectures to give a glimpse of these points. It lies within the scope of this concluding lecture to consider the reaction of science upon some problems confronting civilised societies.

The general conceptions introduced by science into modern thought cannot be separated from the philosophical situation as expressed by Descartes. I mean the assumption of bodies and minds as independent individual substances, each existing in its own right apart from any necessary reference to each other. Such a conception was very concordant with the individualism which had issued from the moral discipline of the Middle Ages. But, though the easy reception of the idea is thus explained, the derivation in itself rests upon a confusion, very natural but none the less unfortunate. The moral discipline had emphasised the intrinsic value of the individual entity. This emphasis had put the notions of the individual and of its experiences into the foreground of thought. At this point the confusion commences. The emergent individual value of each entity is transformed into the independent substantial existence of each entity, which is a very different notion.

I do not mean to say that Descartes made this logical, or rather illogical transition, in the form of explicit reasoning. Far from it. What he did, was first to concentrate upon his own conscious experiences, as being facts within the independent world of his own mentality. He was led to speculate in this way by the current emphasis upon the individual value of his total self. He implicitly transformed this emergent individual value, inherent in the very fact of his own reality, into a private world of passions, or modes, of independent substance.

Also the independence ascribed to bodily substances carried them away from the realm of values altogether. They degenerated into a mechanism entirely valueless, except as suggestive of an external ingenuity. The heavens had lost the glory of God. This state of mind is illustrated in the recoil of Protestantism from aesthetic effects dependent upon a material medium. It was taken to lead to an ascription of value to what is in itself valueless. This recoil was already in full strength antecedently to Descartes. Accordingly, the Cartesian scientific doctrine of bits of matter, bare of intrinsic value, was merely a formulation, in explicit terms, of a doctrine which was current before its entrance into scientific thought or Cartesian philosophy. Probably this doctrine was latent in the scholastic philosophy, but it did not lead to its consequences till it met with the mentality of northern Europe in the sixteenth century. But science, as equipped by Descartes, gave stability and intellectual status to a point of view which has had very mixed effects upon the moral presuppositions of modern communities. Its good effects arose from its efficiency as a method for scientific researches within those limited regions which were then best suited for exploration. The result was a general clearing of the European mind away from the stains left upon it by the hysteria of remote barbaric ages. This was all to the good, and was most completely exemplified in the eighteenth century.

But in the nineteenth century, when society was undergoing transformation into the manufacturing system, the bad effects of these doctrines have been very fatal. The doctrine of minds, as independent substances, leads directly not merely to private worlds of experience, but also to private worlds of morals. The moral intuitions can be held to apply only to the strictly private world of psychological experience. Accordingly, self-respect, and the making the most of your own individual opportunities, together constituted the efficient morality of the leaders among the industrialists of that period. The western world is now suffering from the limited moral outlook of the three previous generations.

Also the assumption of the bare value-lessness of mere matter led to a lack of reverence in the treatment of natural or artistic beauty. Just when the urbanisation of the western world was entering upon its state of rapid development, and when the most delicate, anxious consideration of the aesthetic qualities of the new material environment was requisite, the doctrine of the irrelevance of such ideas was at its height. In the most advanced industrial countries, art was treated as a frivolity. A striking example of this state of mind in the middle of the nineteenth century is to be seen in London where the marvellous beauty of the estuary of the Thames, as it curves through the city, is wantonly defaced by the Charing Cross railway bridge, constructed apart from any reference to aesthetic values.

The two evils are: one, the ignoration of the true relation of each organism to its environment; and the other, the habit of ignoring the intrinsic worth of the environment which must be allowed its weight in any consideration of final ends.

Another great fact confronting the modern world is the discovery of the method of training professionals, who specialise in particular regions of thought and thereby progressively add to the sum of knowledge within their respective limitations of subject. In consequence of the success of this professionalising of knowledge, there are two points to be kept in mind, which differentiate our present age from the past. In the first place, the rate of progress is such that an individual human being, of ordinary length of life, will be called upon to face novel situations which find no parallel in his past. The fixed person for the fixed duties, who in older societies was such a godsend, in the future will be a public danger. In the second place, the modern professionalism in knowledge works in the opposite direction so far as the intellectual sphere is concerned. The modern chemist is likely to be weak in zoology, weaker still in his general knowledge of the Elizabethan drama, and completely ignorant of the principles of rhythm in English versification. It is probably safe to ignore his knowledge of ancient history. Of course I am speaking of general tendencies; for chemists are no worse than engineers, or mathematicians, or classical scholars. Effective knowledge is professionalised knowledge, supported by a restricted acquaintance with useful subjects subservient to it.

This situation has its dangers. It produces minds in a groove. Each profession makes progress, but it is progress in its own groove. Now to be mentally in a groove is to live in contemplating a given set of abstractions. The groove prevents straying across country, and the abstraction abstracts from something to which no further attention is paid. But there is no groove of abstractions which is adequate for the comprehension of human life. Thus in the modern world, the celibacy of the medieval learned class has been replaced by a celibacy of the intellect which is divorced from the concrete contemplation of the complete facts. Of course, no one is merely a mathematician, or merely a lawyer. People have lives outside their professions or their businesses. But the point is the restraint of serious thought within a groove. The remainder of life is treated superficially, with the imperfect categories of thought derived from one profession.

The dangers arising from this aspect of professionalism are great, particularly in our democratic societies. The directive force of reason is weakened. The leading intellects lack balance. They see this set of circumstances, or that set; but not both sets together. The task of coordination is left to those who lack either the force or the character to succeed in some definite career. In short, the specialised functions of the community are performed better and

more progressively, but the generalised direction lacks vision. The progressiveness in detail only adds to the danger produced by the feebleness of coordination.

This criticism of modern life applies throughout, in whatever sense you construe the meaning of a community. It holds if you apply it to a nation, a city, a district, an institution, a family, or even to an individual. There is a development of particular abstractions, and a contraction of concrete appreciation. The whole is lost in one of its aspects. It is not necessary for my point that I should maintain that our directive wisdom, either as individuals or as communities, is less now than in the past. Perhaps it has slightly improved. But the novel pace of progress requires a greater force of direction if disasters are to be avoided. The point is that the discoveries of the nineteenth century were in the direction of professionalism, so that we are left with no expansion of wisdom and with greater need of it.

Wisdom is the fruit of a balanced development. It is this balanced growth of individuality which it should be the aim of education to secure. The most useful discoveries for the immediate future would concern the furtherance of this aim without detriment to the necessary intellectual professionalism.

My own criticism of our traditional educational methods is that they are far too much occupied with intellectual analysis, and with the acquirement of formularised information. What I mean is, that we neglect to strengthen habits of concrete appreciation of the individual facts in their full interplay of emergent values, and that we merely emphasise abstract formulations which ignore this aspect of the interplay of diverse values.

In every country the problem of the balance of the general and specialist education is under consideration. I cannot speak with first-hand knowledge of any country but my own. I know that there, among practical educationalists, there is considerable dissatisfaction with the existing practice. Also, the adaptation of the whole system to the needs of a democratic community is very far from being solved. I do not think that the secret of the solution lies in terms of the antithesis between thoroughness in special knowledge and general knowledge of a slighter character. The make-weight which balances the thoroughness of the specialist intellectual training should be of a radically different kind from purely intellectual analytical knowledge. At present our education combines a thorough study of a few abstractions, with a slighter study of a larger number of abstractions. We are too exclusively bookish in our scholastic routine. The general training should aim at eliciting our concrete apprehensions, and should satisfy the itch of youth to be doing something. There should be some analysis even here, but only just enough to illustrate the ways of thinking in diverse spheres. In the Garden of Eden Adam saw the animals before he named them; in the traditional system, children named the animals before they saw them.

There is no easy single solution of the practical difficulties of education. We can, however, guide ourselves by a certain simplicity in its general theory. The student should concentrate within a limited field. Such concentration should include all practical and intellectual acquirements requisite for that concentration. This is the ordinary procedure; and, in respect to it, I should be inclined even to increase the facilities for concentration rather than to diminish them. With the concentration there are associated certain subsidiary studies, such as languages for science. Such a scheme of professional training should be directed to a clear end congenial to the student. It is not necessary to elaborate the

qualifications of these statements. Such a training must, of course, have the width requisite for its end. But its design should not be complicated by the consideration of other ends. This professional training can only touch one side of education. Its centre of gravity lies in the intellect, and its chief tool is the printed book. The centre of gravity of the other side of training should lie in intuition without an analytical divorce from the total environment. Its object is immediate apprehension with the minimum of eviscerating analysis. The type of generality, which above all is wanted, is the appreciation of variety of value. I mean an aesthetic growth. There is something between the gross specialised values of the mere practical man, and the thin specialised values of the mere scholar. Both types have missed something; and if you add together the two sets of values, you do not obtain the missing elements. What is wanted is an appreciation of the infinite variety of vivid values achieved by an organism in its proper environment. When you understand all about the sun and all about the atmosphere and all about the rotation of the earth, you may still miss the radiance of the sunset. There is no substitute for the direct perception of the concrete achievement of a thing in its actuality. We want concrete fact with a high light thrown on what is relevant to its preciousness.

What I mean is art and aesthetic education. It is, however, art in such a general sense of the term that I hardly like to call it by that name. Art is a special example. What we want is to draw out habits of aesthetic apprehension. According to the metaphysical doctrine which I have been developing, to do so is to increase the depth of individuality. The analysis of reality indicates the two factors, activity emerging into individualised aesthetic value. Also the emergent value is the measure of the individualisation of the activity. We must foster the creative initiative towards the maintenance of objective values. You will not obtain the apprehension without the initiative, or the initiative without the apprehension. As soon as you get towards the concrete, you cannot exclude action. Sensitiveness without impulse spells decadence, and impulse without sensitiveness spells brutality. I am using the word "sensitiveness" in its most general signification, so as to include apprehension of what lies beyond oneself; that is to say, sensitiveness to all the facts of the case. Thus "art" in the general sense which I require is any selection by which the concrete facts are so arranged as to elicit attention to particular values which are realisable by them. For example, the mere disposing of the human body and the eyesight so as to get a good view of a sunset is a simple form of artistic selection. The habit of art is the habit of enjoying vivid values.

But, in this sense, art concerns more than sunsets. A factory, with its machinery, its community of operatives, its social service to the general population, its dependence upon organising and designing genius, its potentialities as a source of wealth to the holders of its stock is an organism exhibiting a variety of vivid values. What we want to train is the habit of apprehending such an organism in its completeness. It is very arguable that the science of political economy, as studied in its first period after the death of Adam Smith (1790), did more harm than good. It destroyed many economic fallacies, and taught how to think about the economic revolution then in progress. But it riveted on men a certain set of abstractions which were disastrous in their influence on modern mentality. It de-humanised industry. This is only one example of a general danger inherent in modern science. Its methodological procedure is exclusive and intolerant, and rightly so. It fixes attention on a definite group of abstractions, neglects everything else, and elicits every

scrap of information and theory which is relevant to what it has retained. This method is triumphant, provided that the abstractions are judicious. But, however triumphant, the triumph is within limits. The neglect of these limits leads to disastrous oversights. The anti-rationalism of science is partly justified, as a preservation of its useful methodology; it is partly mere irrational prejudice. Modern professionalism is the training of minds to conform to the methodology. The historical revolt of the seventeenth century, and the earlier reaction towards naturalism, were examples of transcending the abstractions which fascinated educated society in the Middle Ages. These early ages had an ideal of rationalism, but they failed in its pursuit. For they neglected to note that the methodology of reasoning requires the limitations involved in the abstract. Accordingly, the true rationalism must always transcend itself by recurrence to the concrete in search of inspiration. A self-satisfied rationalism is in effect a form of anti-rationalism. It means an arbitrary halt at a particular set of abstractions. This was the case with science.

There are two principles inherent in the very nature of things, recurring in some particular embodiments whatever field we explore—the spirit of change, and the spirit of conservation. There can be nothing real without both. Mere change without conservation is a passage from nothing to nothing. Its final integration yields mere transient non-entity. Mere conservation without change cannot conserve. For after all, there is a flux of circumstance, and the freshness of being evaporates under mere repetition. The character of existent reality is composed of organisms enduring through the flux of things. The low type of organisms have achieved a self-identity dominating their whole physical life. Electrons, molecules, crystals, belong to this type. They exhibit a massive and complete sameness.

In the higher types, where life appears, there is greater complexity. Thus, though there is a complex, enduring pattern, it has retreated into deeper recesses of the total fact. In a sense, the self-identity of a human being is more abstract than that of a crystal. It is the life of the spirit. It relates rather to the individualisation of the creative activity; so that the changing circumstances received from the environment, are differentiated from the living personality, and are thought of as forming its perceived field. In truth, the field of perception and the perceiving mind are abstractions which, in the concrete, combine into the successive bodily events. The psychological field, as restricted to sense-objects and passing emotions, is the minor permanence, barely rescued from the nonentity of mere change; and the mind is the major permanence, permeating that complete field, whose endurance is the living soul. But the soul would wither without fertilisation from its transient experiences. The secret of the higher organisms lies in their two grades of permanences. By this means the freshness of the environment is absorbed into the permanence of the soul. The changing environment is no longer, by reason of its variety, an enemy to the endurance of the organism. The pattern of the higher organism has retreated into the recesses of the individualised activity. It has become a uniform way of dealing with circumstances; and this way is only strengthened by having a proper variety of circumstances to deal with.

This fertilisation of the soul is the reason for the necessity of art. A static value, however serious and important, becomes unendurable by its appalling monotony of endurance. The soul cries aloud for release into change. It suffers the agonies of claustrophobia. The transitions of humour, wit, irreverence, play, sleep, and—above all—of art are necessary for it. Great art is the arrangement of the environment so as to provide for the soul vivid, but transient, values. Human beings require something which absorbs them for a time, something out of the routine which they can stare at. But you cannot subdivide life, except in the abstract analysis of thought. Accordingly, the great art is more than a transient refreshment. It is something which adds to the permanent richness of the soul's self-attainment. It justifies itself both by its immediate enjoyment, and also by its discipline of the inmost being. Its discipline is not distinct from enjoyment, but by reason of it. It transforms the soul into the permanent realisation of values extending beyond its former self. This element of transition in art is shown by the restlessness exhibited in its history. An epoch gets saturated by the masterpieces of any one style. Something new must be discovered. The human being wanders on. Yet there is a balance in things. Mere change before the attainment of adequacy of achievement, either in quality or output, is destructive of greatness. But the importance of a living art, which moves on and yet leaves its permanent mark, can hardly be exaggerated.

In regard to the aesthetic needs of civilised society the reactions of science have so far been unfortunate. Its materialistic basis has directed attention to *things* as opposed to *values*. The antithesis is a false one, if taken in a concrete sense. But it is valid at the abstract level of ordinary thought. This misplaced emphasis coalesced with the abstractions of political economy, which are in fact the abstractions in terms of which commercial affairs are carried on. Thus all thought concerned with social organisation expressed itself in terms of material things and of capital. Ultimate values were excluded. They were politely bowed to, and then handed over to the clergy to be kept for Sundays. A creed of competitive business morality was evolved, in some respects curiously high; but entirely devoid of consideration for the value of human life. The workmen were conceived as mere hands, drawn from the pool of labour. To God's question, men gave the answer of Cain—"Am I my brother's keeper?"; and they incurred Cain's guilt. This was the atmosphere in which the industrial revolution was accomplished in England, and to a large extent elsewhere. The internal history of England during the last half century has been an endeavour slowly and painfully to undo the evils wrought in the first stage of the new epoch. It may be that civilisation will never recover from the bad climate which enveloped the introduction of machinery. This climate pervaded the whole commercial system of the progressive northern European races. It was partly the result of aesthetic errors of Protestantism and partly the result of scientific materialism, and partly the result of the natural greed of mankind, and partly the result of the abstractions of political economy. An illustration of my point is to be found in Macaulay's Essay criticising Southey's *Colloquies on Society*. It was written in 1830. Now Macaulay was a very favourable example of men living at that date, or at any date. He had genius; he was kind-hearted, honourable, and a reformer. This is the extract:—"We are told, that our age has invented atrocities beyond the imagination of our fathers; that society has been brought into a state compared with which extermination would be a blessing; and all because the dwellings of cotton-spinners are naked and rectangular. Mr. Southey has found out a way he tells us, in which the effects of manufactures and agriculture may be compared. And what is this way? To stand on a hill, to look at a cottage and a factory, and to see which is the prettier."

Southey seems to have said many silly things in his book; but, so far as this extract is concerned, he could make a good case for himself if he returned to earth after the lapse of nearly a century. The evils of the early industrial system are now a commonplace of knowledge. The point which I am insisting on is the stone-blind eye with which even the best men of that time regarded the importance of aesthetics in a nation's life. I do not believe that we have as yet nearly achieved the right estimate. A contributory cause, of substantial efficacy to produce this disastrous error, was the scientific creed that matter in motion is the one concrete reality in nature; so that aesthetic values form an adventitious, irrelevant addition.

There is another side to this picture of the possibilities of decadence. At the present moment a discussion is raging as to the future of civilisation in the novel circumstances of rapid scientific and technological advance. The evils of the future have been diagnosed in various ways, the loss of religious faith, the malignant use of material power, the degradation attending a differential birth rate favouring the lower types of humanity, the suppression of aesthetic creativeness. Without doubt, these are all evils, dangerous and threatening. But they are not new. From the dawn of history, mankind has always been losing its religious faith, has always suffered from the malignant use of material power, has always suffered from the infertility of its best intellectual types, has always witnessed the periodical decadence of art. In the reign of the Egyptian king, Tutankhamen, there was raging a desperate religious struggle between Modernists and Fundamentalists; the cave pictures exhibit a phase of delicate aesthetic achievement as superseded by a period of comparative vulgarity; the religious leaders, the great thinkers, the great poets and authors, the whole clerical caste in the Middle Ages, have been notably infertile; finally, if we attend to what actually has happened in the past, and disregard romantic visions of democracies, aristocracies, kings, generals, armies, and merchants, material power has generally been wielded with blindness, obstinacy and self-ishness, often with brutal malignancy. And yet, mankind has progressed. Even if you take a tiny oasis of peculiar excellence, the type of modern man who would have most chance of happiness in ancient Greece at its best period is probably (as now) an average professional heavy-weight boxer, and not an average Greek scholar from Oxford or Germany. Indeed, the main use of the Oxford scholar would have been his capability of writing an ode in glorification of the boxer. Nothing does more harm in unnerving men for their duties in the present, than the attention devoted to the points of excellence in the past as compared with the average failure of the present day.

But, after all, there have been real periods of decadence; and at the present time, as at other epochs, society is decaying, and there is need for preservative action. Professionals are not new to the world. But in the past, professionals have formed unprogressive castes. The point is that professionalism has now been mated with progress. The world is now faced with a self-evolving system, which it cannot stop. There are dangers and advantages in this situation. It is obvious that the gain in material power affords opportunity for social betterment. If mankind can rise to the occasion, there lies in front a golden age of beneficent creativeness. But material power in itself is ethically neutral. It can equally well work in the wrong direction. The problem is not how to produce great men, but how to produce great societies. The great society will put up the men for the occasions. The materialistic philosophy emphasised the given quantity of material, and thence derivatively the given nature of the environment. It thus operated most unfortunately upon the social conscience of mankind. For it directed almost exclusive attention to the aspect of struggle for existence in a fixed environment. To a large extent the environment is fixed, and to this extent there

is a struggle for existence. It is folly to look at the universe through rose-tinted spectacles. We must admit the struggle. The question is, who is to be eliminated. In so far as we are educators, we have to have clear ideas upon that point; for it settles the type to be produced and the practical ethics to be inculcated.

But during the last three generations, the exclusive direction of attention to this aspect of things has been a disaster of the first magnitude. The watchwords of the nineteenth century have been, struggle for existence, competition, class warfare, commercial antagonism between nations, military warfare. The struggle for existence has been construed into the gospel of hate. The full conclusion to be drawn from a philosophy of evolution is fortunately of a more balanced character. Successful organisms modify their environment. Those organisms are successful which modify their environments so as to assist each other. This law is exemplified in nature on a vast scale. For example, the North American Indians accepted their environment, with the result that a scanty population barely succeeded in maintaining themselves over the whole continent. The European races when they arrived in the same continent pursued an opposite policy. They at once cooperated in modifying their environment. The result is that a population more than twenty times that of the Indian population now occupies the same territory, and the continent is not yet full. Again, there are associations of different species which mutually cooperate. This differentiation of species is exhibited in the simplest physical entities, such as the associaton between electrons and positive nuclei, and in the whole realm of animate nature. The trees in a Brazilian forest depend upon the association of various species of organisms, each of which is mutually dependent on the other species. A single tree by itself is dependent upon all the adverse chances of shifting circumstances. The wind stunts it: the variations in temperature check its foliage: the rains denude its soil: its leaves are blown away and are lost for the purpose of fertilisation. You may obtain individual specimens of fine trees either in exceptional circumstances, or where human cultivation has intervened. But in nature the normal way in which trees flourish is by their association in a forest. Each tree may lose something of its individual perfection of growth, but they mutually assist each other in preserving the conditions for survival. The soil is preserved and shaded; and the microbes necessary for its fertility are neither scorched, nor frozen, nor washed away. A forest is the triumph of the organisation of mutually dependent species. Further a species of microbes which kills the forest, also exterminates itself. Again the two sexes exhibit the same advantage of differentiation. In the history of the world, the prize has not gone to those species which specialised in methods of violence, or even in defensive armour. In fact, nature began with producing animals encased in hard shells for defence against the ills of life. It also experimented in size. But smaller animals, without external armour, warm-blooded, sensitive, and alert, have cleared these monsters off the face of the earth. Also, the lions and tigers are not the successful species. There is something in the ready use of force which defeats its own object. Its main defect is that it bars cooperation. Every organism requires an environment of friends, partly to shield it from violent changes, and partly to supply it with its wants. The Gospel of Force is incompatible with a social life. By *force*, I mean *antagonism* in its most general sense.

Almost equally dangerous is the Gospel of Uniformity. The differences between the nations and races of mankind are required to preserve the conditions under which higher development is possible. One main factor in the upward trend of animal life

has been the power of wandering. Perhaps this is why the armour-plated monsters fared badly. They could not wander. Animals wander into new conditions. They have to adapt themselves or die. Mankind has wandered from the trees to the plains, from the plains to the seacoast, from climate to climate, from continent to continent, and from habit of life to habit of life. When man ceases to wander, he will cease to ascend in the scale of being. Physical wandering is still important, but greater still is the power of man's spiritual adventures—adventures of thought, adventures of passionate feeling, adventures of aesthetic experience. A diversification among human communities is essential for the provision of the incentive and material for the Odyssey of the human spirit. Other nations of different habits are not enemies: they are godsends. Men require of their neighbours something sufficiently akin to be understood, something sufficiently different to provoke attention, and something great enough to command admiration. We must not expect, however, all the virtues. We should even be satisfied if there is something odd enough to be interesting.

Modern science has imposed on humanity the necessity for wandering. Its progressive thought and its progressive technology make the transition through time, from generation to generation, a true migration into uncharted seas of adventure. The very benefit of wandering is that it is dangerous and needs skill to avert evils. We must expect, therefore, that the future will disclose dangers. It is the business of the future to be dangerous; and it is among the merits of science that it equips the future for its duties. The prosperous middle classes, who ruled the nineteenth century, placed an excessive value upon placidity of existence. They refused to face the necessities for social reform imposed by the new industrial system, and they are now refusing to face the necessities for intellectual reform imposed by the new knowledge. The middle class pessimism over the future of the world comes from a confusion between civilisation and security. In the immediate future there will be less security than in the immediate past, less stability. It must be admitted that there is a degree of instability which is inconsistent with civilisation. But, on the whole, the great ages have been unstable ages.

I have endeavoured in these lectures to give a record of a great adventure in the region of thought. It was shared in by all the races of western Europe. It developed with the slowness of a mass movement. Half a century is its unit of time. The tale is the epic of an episode in the manifestation of reason. It tells how a particular direction of reason emerges in a race by the long preparation of antecedent epochs, how after its birth its subject-matter gradually unfolds itself, how it attains its triumphs, how its influence moulds the very springs of action of mankind, and finally how at its moment of supreme success its limitations disclose themselves and call for a renewed exercise of the creative imagination. The moral of the tale is the power of reason, its decisive influence on the life of humanity. The great conquerors, from Alexander to Caesar, and from Caesar to Napoleon, influenced profoundly the lives of subsequent generations. But the total effect of this influence shrinks to insignificance, if compared to the entire transformation of human habits and human mentality produced by the long line of men of thought from Thales to the present day, men individually powerless, but ultimately the rulers of the world.